Professional
Visual Basic® 20

G000276344

Professional
Visual Basic® 2008

Bill Evjen
Billy Hollis
Bill Sheldon
Kent Sharkey

WILEY

Wiley Publishing, Inc.

Professional Visual Basic® 2008

Published by
Wiley Publishing, Inc.
10475 Crosspoint Boulevard
Indianapolis, IN 46256
www.wiley.com

About the Authors

Bill Evjen is an active proponent of .NET technologies and community-based learning initiatives for .NET. He has been actively involved with .NET since the first bits were released in 2000. In the same year, Bill founded the St. Louis .NET User Group (www.stlnet.org), one of the world's first such groups. Bill is also the founder and former executive director of the International .NET Association (www.ineta.org), which represents more than 500,000 members worldwide.

Based in St. Louis, Missouri, Bill is an acclaimed author and speaker on ASP.NET and XML Web Services. He has authored or co-authored more than 15 books, including *Professional ASP.NET 3.5*, *Professional C# 2008*, *ASP.NET Professional Secrets*, *XML Web Services for ASP.NET*, and *Web Services Enhancements: Understanding the WSE for Enterprise Applications* (all published by Wiley). In addition to writing, Bill is a speaker at numerous conferences, including DevConnections, VSLive, and TechEd. He also works closely with Microsoft as a Microsoft Regional Director and an MVP.

Bill is the technical architect for Lipper (www.lipperweb.com), a wholly owned subsidiary of Reuters, the international news and financial services company. He graduated from Western Washington University in Bellingham, Washington, with a Russian language degree. When he isn't tinkering on the computer, he can usually be found at his summer house in Toivakka, Finland. You can reach Bill at evjen@yahoo.com.

The .NET Framework 3.5 release came quickly for us writers, and it wouldn't have been possible to produce this book as fast as we did if it weren't for the dedication of the teams built for it. Tremendous thanks to Katie Mohr for being more than patient with me in getting this and some other .NET 3.5 books out the door. Also, big thanks go out to Kevin Kent for doing his best to helping me stay on schedule.

Finally, to the ones who paid the biggest price for this writing session — my wife, Tuija, and our three kids: Sofia, Henri, and Kalle — thanks for all you do!

Billy Hollis is an author and software consultant based in Nashville, Tennessee. Billy was co-author of the first book ever published on Visual Basic .NET, as well as many other books on software development. He is a member of the Microsoft Regional Director program and a Microsoft MVP. In 2002, Billy was selected as one of the original .NET "Software Legends." He is heavily involved with consulting, training, and development on the .NET platform, focusing on architecture, smart-client development, commercial packages, and user-interface technologies. He regularly speaks on software development at major conferences all over the world, including Microsoft's PDC and TechEd events, DevConnections, VSLive, and architecture events such as the Patterns and Practices Architect Summit.

I owe tremendous thanks to my family, who have somehow learned to put up with marathon writing sessions, and to my business partner, Gary Bailey, for keeping our clients happy while I'm writing.

Bill Sheldon is a software architect and engineer, originally from Baltimore, Maryland. Holding a degree in computer science from the Illinois Institute of Technology (IIT), Bill has been actively employed as a software engineer since resigning his commission with the United States Navy. He is a Microsoft MVP for Visual Basic employed as a principal engineer with InterKnowlogy in Carlsbad, California, and works as an instructor for Visual Basic–related courses at the University of California San Diego Extension.

In addition to writing books, Bill has published dozens of articles, including the Developer Update Newsletter, *SQL Server Magazine* feature articles, and other Penton publications. He is an established online presenter for MSDN and speaks at live events such as VSLive, DevConnections, Office

Developers Conference, and community events such as user groups and code camp. Bill is an avid cyclist and is active in the fight against diabetes.

To my wonderful wife, Tracie, who is forced to carry on while I isolate myself to concentrate on writing. And to the next generation of children who have joined our extended Sheldon family (my own and my brothers') in the past five years — Nick, Elena, Ben, Billy V, Abigail, and our next son (this spring's coming attraction) — each and every one of you is a valuable part of our lives.

Kent Sharkey is an independent consultant who lives and codes in Comox, British Columbia. Before going solo, Kent worked at Microsoft as a technical evangelist and content strategist, promoting the use of .NET technologies. He lives with his wife, Margaret, and three "children" — Squirrel, Cica, and Toffee.

To Babi, for keeping me alive and putting up with me — hopefully, for a long time to come.

About the Technical Editors

Mark Lavoie is the information system manager for a midsized insurance company located in Charlotte, North Carolina. Mark has worked with Microsoft products and technologies for nine years. He has worked as a consultant, managed IT projects, and designed and programmed custom applications. He is a native of Canada and, when not working, enjoys cooking and vacationing with his wonderful wife.

Todd Meister has been developing using Microsoft technologies for over ten years. He's been a technical editor for more than 40 titles, ranging from SQL Server to the .NET Framework. Besides technical editing, he is an assistant director for Computing Services at Ball State University in Muncie, Indiana. His latest development accomplishment was developing an e-commerce site from scratch, which included over 15,000 lines of .NET code, credit card integration, gift certificate functionality, and discount codes. He lives with his wife, Kimberly, and their four children in central Indiana. Contact Todd at tmeister@sycamoresolutions.com.

Andrew Moore is a graduate of Purdue University–Calumet in Hammond, Indiana, and has been developing software since 1998 for radar systems, air traffic management, discrete-event simulation, and business communications applications using C, C++, C#, and Java on the Windows, UNIX, and Linux platforms. Andrew is the author of two Wrox Blox titles: "Create Amazing Custom User Interfaces with WPF, C#, and XAML in .NET 3.0" (www.wrox.com/WileyCDA/WroxTitle/productCd-0470258713.html) and ".NET 3.5 CD Audio Player." He is currently working as a software engineer at Interactive Intelligence, Inc., in Indianapolis, Indiana, developing Microsoft-based applications for business communications. Andrew lives in Indiana with his wife, Barbara, and their two children, Sophia and Andrew.

Credits

Acquisitions Editor
Katie Mohr

Senior Development Editor
Kevin Kent

Technical Editors
Mark Lavoie
Todd Meister
Andrew Moore

Production Editor
William A. Barton

Copy Editor
Luann Rouff

Editorial Manager
Mary Beth Wakefield

Production Manager
Tim Tate

Vice President and Executive Group Publisher
Richard Swadley

Vice President and Executive Publisher
Joseph B. Wikert

Project Coordinator, Cover
Lynsey Stanford

Proofreaders
Edward Moyer, Paul Sagan, Word One

Indexer
Robert Swanson

Contents

Contents

Contents

Contents

Contents

Contents

Contents

Contents

Contents

Contents

Contents

Contents

Introduction

In 2002, Visual Basic took the biggest leap in innovation since it was released, with the introduction of Visual Basic .NET (as it was renamed). After more than a decade, Visual Basic was overdue for a major overhaul. Nevertheless, .NET goes beyond an overhaul. It changes almost every aspect of software development. From integrating Internet functionality to creating object-oriented frameworks, Visual Basic .NET challenged traditional VB developers to learn dramatic new concepts and techniques.

2008 brought forth an even more enhanced Visual Basic language. New features have been added that cement this language's position as a true object-oriented language and provide better access to underlying data. Visual Basic 2008 is still going to be a challenge for traditional VB6 developers to learn, but it's an easy road for those with any familiarity with previous versions, and this book is here to help you on your way.

This .NET Framework 3.5 version of this book provides details about not only the latest version of Visual Basic — version 2008 — but also the new framework that gives Visual Basic developers the capability to build new application types using Windows Presentation Foundation (WPF) and applications and libraries based upon the Windows Communication Foundation (WCF), the Windows Workflow Foundation (WF), and Windows CardSpace. It also covers one of the more important features: LINQ.

These additions are what constitute the .NET Framework 3.5, as this version of the framework installs and works from the previous .NET Framework 2.0 and 3.0. This book includes numerous chapters that focus on the new technologies brought forth by the .NET Framework 3.0 and 3.5.

First, it is necessary to learn the differences between Visual Basic 2008 and the older versions of the language. In some cases, the same functionality is implemented in a different way. This was not done arbitrarily — there are good reasons for the changes. However, you must be prepared to unlearn old habits and form new ones.

Next, you must be open to the new concepts. Full object orientation, new component techniques, new visual tools for both local and Internet interfaces — all of these and more must become part of your skill set to effectively develop applications in Visual Basic.

This book covers Visual Basic from start to finish. We begin by looking at the .NET Framework and end by looking at the best practices for deploying .NET applications. In between, you will learn everything from database access to integration with other technologies such as XML, along with investigating the new features in detail. You will see that Visual Basic 2008 has emerged as a powerful yet easy-to-use language that enables you to target the Internet just as easily as the desktop. This book covers the .NET Framework 2.0, the .NET Framework 3.0, and the newly released .NET Framework 3.5. If you are coding using version 1.0, 1.1, or just 2.0, some sections of the book will not work for you. Items that are new to the .NET Framework 3.5 are specifically noted as such.

The Importance of Visual Basic

Early in the adoption cycle of .NET, Microsoft's new language, C#, got the lion's share of attention. However, as .NET adoption has increased, Visual Basic's continuing importance has also been apparent. Microsoft has publicly stated that it considers Visual Basic to be the language of choice for applications where developer productivity is one of the highest priorities.

Future development of Visual Basic is emphasizing capabilities that enable access to the whole expanse of the .NET Framework in the most productive way, while C# development is emphasizing the experience of writing code. That fits the traditional role of Visual Basic as the language developers use in the real world to create business applications as quickly as possible.

This difference is more than academic. One of the most important advantages of the .NET Framework is that it enables applications to be written with dramatically less code. In the world of business applications, the goal is to concentrate on writing business logic and to eliminate routine coding tasks as much as possible. In other words, of greatest value in this new paradigm is writing robust, useful applications with as little code as possible, not churning out a lot of code.

Visual Basic is an excellent fit for this type of development, which makes up the bulk of software development in today's economy. Moreover, it will grow to be an even better fit as it is refined and evolves for exactly that purpose.

Who This Book Is For

This book was written to help experienced developers learn Visual Basic 2008. From those who are just starting the transition from earlier versions to those who have used Visual Basic for a while and need to gain a deeper understanding, this book provides information on the most common programming tasks and concepts you need.

Professional Visual Basic 2008 offers a wide-ranging presentation of Visual Basic concepts, but the .NET Framework is so large and comprehensive that no single book can cover it all. The main area in which this book does not attempt to be complete is Web development. While chapters discussing the basics of browser-based programming in Visual Basic are included, professional Web developers should instead refer to *Professional ASP.NET 3.5*.

What You Need to Use This Book

Although it is possible to create Visual Basic applications using the command-line tools contained in the .NET Framework SDK, you need Visual Studio 2008 (Professional or higher), which includes the .NET Framework SDK, to get the most out of this book. You may use Visual Studio 2005, Visual Studio .NET 2002, or Visual Studio 2003 instead, but in some cases the exercises won't work because functionalities and capabilities are not available in these older versions. In addition, note the following:

❑ You need the .NET Framework 3.5 (which will install the .NET Framework 2.0 by default if it isn't already present on the machine).

❑ Some chapters make use of SQL Server 2005 and SQL Server 2008, but you can also run the example code using Microsoft's SQL Express, which ships with Visual Studio 2008.

❑ Several chapters make use of l.
Windows Server 2008, Window
and Windows XP, although it i

❑ Chapter 30 makes use of MSMQ to wo.
Windows versions, but it is not installed by

What This Book Covers

Chapter 1, "Visual Basic 2008 Core Elements" — This chapter introduces many of the typ.
used in Visual Basic 2008. Topics discussed in this chapter include type coverage, type conversi... .ly
ence types, arrays, and other collections, parameter passing, and boxing. The full syntax basics of Visu.
Basic are provided in this chapter.

Chapter 2, "Object Syntax Introduction" — This is the first of three chapters that explore object-oriented
programming in Visual Basic. This chapter defines objects, classes, instances, encapsulation, abstraction,
polymorphism, and inheritance.

Chapter 3, "Object-Oriented Programming" — This chapter examines inheritance and how it can be
used within Visual Basic. You create simple and abstract base classes and learn how to create base classes
from which other classes can be derived. This chapter puts the theory for much of what has been discussed thus far into practice. The four defining object-oriented concepts (abstraction, encapsulation,
polymorphism, inheritance) are described, and we explain how these concepts can be applied in design
and development to create effective object-oriented applications.

Chapter 4, "The Common Language Runtime" — This chapter examines the core of the .NET platform: the common language runtime (CLR). The CLR is responsible for managing the execution of code
compiled for the .NET platform. You learn about versioning and deployment, memory management,
cross-language integration, metadata, and the IL Disassembler.

Chapter 5, "Localization" — Developers usually build applications in the English language. Then, as the
audience for the application expands, they realize the need to globalize the application. Of course, the
ideal is to build the application to handle an international audience right from the start — but in many
cases, this isn't possible because of the extra work it requires. The .NET Framework made a considerable
effort to address the internationalization of the applications you build. Changes to the API, the addition of capabilities to the server controls, and even Visual Studio itself equip you to do the extra work
required more easily to bring your application to an international audience. This chapter looks at some
of the important items to consider when building your applications for the world. It looks closely at the
System.Globalization namespace and everything it offers your applications.

Chapter 6, "Generics" — This chapter focuses on one of the biggest enhancements to Visual Basic in
this version — generics. Generics enables you to make a generic collection that is still strongly typed —
providing fewer chances for errors, increasing performance, and giving you IntelliSense features when
you are working with your collections.

Chapter 7, "Namespaces" — This chapter introduces namespaces and their hierarchical structure. An
explanation of namespaces and some common examples are provided. In addition, you learn how to
create new namespaces, and how to import and alias existing namespaces within projects. This chapter
also looks at the My namespace available in Visual Basic.

...gging" — This chapter covers how error handling and ...discussing the CLR exception handler and the `Try...Catch...` ...error and trace logging, and how you can use these methods to ...program is working.

Chapter 8, "Ex...debugging w...Finally str...obtain fee...

...with ADO.NET 3.5" — This chapter focuses on what you need to know about ...model in order to build flexible, fast, and scalable data-access objects and applica-...ion of ADO into ADO.NET is explored, and the main objects in ADO.NET that you need **Chapt**...the...in order to build data access into your .NET applications are explained. tio...

...ter 10, "Using XML in Visual Basic 2008" — This chapter presents the features of the .NET Frame-work that facilitate the generation and manipulation of XML. We describe the .NET Framework's XML-related namespaces, and a subset of the classes exposed by these namespaces is examined in detail. This chapter also touches on a set of technologies that utilize XML — specifically, ADO.NET and SQL Server. This chapter focuses on XML usage prior to LINQ.

Chapter 11, "LINQ" — This chapter presents one of the coolest and most anticipated features provided in the .NET Framework 3.5. LINQ offers the capability to easily access underlying data — basically a layer on top of ADO.NET. Microsoft has provided LINQ as a lightweight façade that provides a strongly typed interface to the underlying data stores. Using LINQ, you can query against objects, data sets, a SQL Server database, XML, and more.

Chapter 12, "Security in the .NET Framework" — This chapter examines additional tools and func-tionality with regard to the security provided by .NET. `Caspol.exe` and `Permview.exe`, which assist in establishing and maintaining security policies, are discussed. The `System.Security.Permissions` namespace is also covered, and we discuss how it relates to managing permissions. Finally, you look at the `System.Security.Cryptography` namespace and run through some code that demonstrates its capabilities.

Chapter 13, "Visual Studio 2008" — This chapter introduces the next generation of the major IDE for developing .NET applications: Visual Studio 2008. Previous releases of this IDE included Visual Studio .NET 2003, Visual Studio .NET 2002, and Visual Studio 2005. This chapter focuses on the Visual Studio 2008 release and how you can use it to build better applications more quickly.

Chapter 14, "Working with SQL Server" — This chapter describes how to work with the new SQL Server 2008 along with your .NET applications. SQL Server provides a strong connection to your appli-cations, and this chapter explains how to effectively utilize this powerful database.

Chapter 15, "Windows Forms" — This chapter looks at Windows Forms, concentrating primarily on forms and built-in controls. What is new and what has been changed from previous versions of Visual Basic are discussed, along with the `System.Windows.Forms` namespace.

Chapter 16, "Windows Forms Advanced Features" — This chapter looks at some of the more advanced features that are available to you in building your Windows Forms applications.

Chapter 17, "Windows Presentation Foundation" — A component that was introduced in the .NET 3.0 and enhanced in the .NET Framework 3.5, Windows Presentation Foundation offers a new vehicle for building applications. This chapter describes the new way in which Microsoft is promoting the presen-tation of a GUI, and WPF provides a presentation layer that you should find rather fluid and enriching. This chapter describes the basics of WPF and how to build simple XAML-based applications.

Chapter 18, "Integrating WPF with Windows Forms investments in Windows Forms, and they are not ready t̶ technology. For this reason, Microsoft has provided significar̶ dows Forms applications, as well as the capability to bring your application. This chapter focuses on these capabilities.

Chapter 19, "Working with ASP.NET 3.5" — This chapter explores the bas̶ It looks at building Web applications using Visual Studio 2008 and includes dis̶ application and page frameworks.

Chapter 20, "ASP.NET 3.5 Advanced Features" — This chapter looks at several of the adv̶ tures that are available to you with the latest release of ASP.NET 3.5. Examples of items covere̶ca̶ cross-page posting, master pages, site navigation, personalization, and more.

Chapter 21, "Silverlight Development" — This chapter looks at the new technology for the Web provided by Silverlight. This new capability provides the means of using XAML and brings a more fluid experience to the end user in the browser.

Chapter 22, "Visual Studio Tools for Office" — This chapter looks at using Visual Basic to work with your Microsoft Office–focused applications.

Chapter 23, "Assemblies" — This chapter examines assemblies and their use within the CLR. The structure of an assembly, what it contains, and the information it contains are described. In addition, you will look at the manifest of the assembly and its role in deployment.

Chapter 24, "Deployment" — This chapter takes a close look at the available deployment options for Windows Forms and Web Forms, including the ClickOnce deployment feature and creating .msi files.

Chapter 25, "Working with Classic COM and Interfaces" — This chapter discusses COM and .NET component interoperability, and what tools are provided to help link the two technologies.

Chapter 26, "Threading" — This chapter explores threading and explains how the various objects in the .NET Framework enable any of its consumers to develop multithreaded applications. You will learn how threads can be created, how they relate to processes, and the differences between multitasking and multithreading.

Chapter 27, "Windows Workflow Foundation" — This chapter takes a look at this relatively new capability to easily integrate workflow into your applications. Windows Workflow was introduced in the .NET Framework 3.0, but it is a big part of .NET 3.5 and Visual Studio 2008.

Chapter 28, "XML Web Services" — This chapter describes how to create and consume Web services using VB 2008. The abstract classes provided by the CLR to set up and work with Web services are discussed, as well as some of the technologies that support Web services. Also examined are some of the disadvantages to using any distributed architecture, and the future of Web services.

Chapter 29, "Remoting" — This chapter takes a detailed look at how to use remoting in classic three-tier application design. You examine the basic architecture of remoting and build a basic server and client that uses a singleton object for answering client requests in the business tier. You will also learn how to use serialization to return more complex objects from the server to the client, and how to use the call context for passing extra data from the client to the server along with each call, without having to change the object model.

— This chapter explores the .NET component services — in particular, ...ed components.

Chapter 30, "Ent.gramming" — This chapter covers working with some of the networking transaction pro ...able to you in your development and how to incorporate a wider network into the

Chapter 31, r applications. protocols r

function.**Windows Communication Foundation"** — This chapter looks at the newest way to build Char. .nted components that allow for standards-based communications over a number of protocols. ser. Microsoft's latest answer for component communications within and outside of the enterprise. V

..apter 33, "Windows Services"** — This chapter examines how Visual Basic is used in the production of Windows Services. The creation, installation, running, and debugging of Windows Services are covered.

Chapter 34, "Visual Basic and the Internet" — This chapter describes how to download resources from the Web, how to design your own communication protocols, and how to reuse the Web browser control in your applications.

Appendix A, "The Visual Basic Compiler" — This appendix covers the Visual Basic compiler vbc.exe and the functionality it provides.

Appendix B, "Visual Basic Power Packs Tools" — This appendix looks at the Visual Basic Power Packs Tools, a set of off-cycle release packages that focus on helping developers who are maintaining traditional Visual Basic 6.0 applications begin the process of transitioning to Visual Basic .NET.

Appendix C, "Visual Basic Resources" — This appendix provides a short list of VB resources available.

Conventions

To help you get the most from the text and keep track of what's happening, we've used a number of conventions throughout the book.

> **Boxes like this one hold important, not-to-be forgotten information that is directly relevant to the surrounding text.**

Tips, hints, tricks, and asides to the current discussion are offset and placed in italics like this.

As for styles in the text:

❏ We *italicize* new terms and important words when we introduce them.

❏ We show keyboard strokes like this: Ctrl+A.

❏ We show filenames, URLs, and code within the text like so: persistence.properties.

❏ We present code in two different ways:

```
We use a monofont type with no highlighting for most code examples.
We use gray highlighting to emphasize code that's particularly
important in the present context.
```

Source Code

As you work through the examples in this book, you may choose to either type in all the code manually or use the source code files that accompany the book. All of the source code used in this book is available for download at www.wrox.com. Once at the site, simply locate the book's title (either by using the Search box or by using one of the title lists) and click the Download Code link on the book's detail page to obtain all the source code for the book.

> Because many books have similar titles, you may find it easiest to search by ISBN; this book's ISBN is 978-0-470-19136-1.

Once you download the code, just decompress it with your favorite compression tool. Alternately, you can go to the main Wrox code download page at www.wrox.com/dynamic/books/download.aspx to see the code available for this book and all other Wrox books.

Errata

We make every effort to ensure that there are no errors in the text or in the code. However, no one is perfect, and mistakes do occur. If you find an error in one of our books, such as a spelling mistake or a faulty piece of code, we would be very grateful for your feedback. By sending in errata, you may save another reader hours of frustration, and at the same time you will be helping us provide even higher-quality information.

To find the errata page for this book, go to www.wrox.com and locate the title using the Search box or one of the title lists. Then, on the book details page, click the Book Errata link. On this page you can view all errata that has been submitted for this book and posted by Wrox editors. A complete book list including links to each book's errata is also available at www.wrox.com/misc-pages/booklist .shtml.

If you don't spot "your" error on the Book Errata page, go to www.wrox.com/contact/techsupport .shtml and complete the form there to send us the error you have found. We'll check the information and, if appropriate, post a message to the book's errata page and fix the problem in subsequent editions of the book.

p2p.wrox.com

For author and peer discussion, join the P2P forums at p2p.wrox.com. The forums are a Web-based system for you to post messages relating to Wrox books and related technologies and interact with other readers and technology users. The forums offer a subscription feature to e-mail you topics of interest of your choosing when new posts are made to the forums. Wrox authors, editors, other industry experts, and your fellow readers are present on these forums.

At http://p2p.wrox.com you will find a number of different forums that will help you not only as you read this book, but also as you develop your own applications. To join the forums, just follow these steps:

1. Go to p2p.wrox.com and click the Register link.
2. Read the terms of use and click Agree.

3. Complete the required information to join as well as any optional information you wish to provide and click Submit.

4. You will receive an e-mail with information describing how to verify your account and complete the joining process.

You can read messages in the forums without joining P2P, but in order to post your own messages, you must join.

Once you join, you can post new messages and respond to messages other users post. You can read messages at any time on the Web. If you would like to have new messages from a particular forum e-mailed to you, click the Subscribe to this Forum icon by the forum name in the forum listing.

For more information about how to use the Wrox P2P, be sure to read the P2P FAQs for answers to questions about how the forum software works as well as many common questions specific to P2P and Wrox books. To read the FAQs, click the FAQ link on any P2P page.

1

Visual Basic 2008 Core Elements

This chapter introduces the core elements that make up Visual Basic 2008. Every software development language has unique elements of syntax and behavior. Visual Basic 2008 has evolved significantly since Visual Basic was introduced in 1991. Although Visual Basic has its origins in traditional procedural-based programming languages, it began the transition to objects back in 1995 with Visual Basic 4.0.

With the release of Visual Basic .NET (that is, Version 7), Visual Basic became a fully object-oriented programming environment. Now with the release of Visual Basic 2008 (that is, Version 9), there are still more new features, but at the core are the same basic types and commands that have been with Visual Basic since its early stages. Object paradigms extend the *core elements* of the language. Therefore, while a very brief introduction to the existence of classes and objects within the language is presented in this chapter, the key concepts of object-oriented development are presented in detail in Chapters 2 and 3.

This chapter focuses on the core elements of the language, including questions about those language elements a new developer not familiar with Visual Basic might ask, such as where semicolons should be placed. The key topics of this chapter include the following:

- ❑ Initial syntax and keywords to understand the basic language elements
- ❑ Value versus reference types
- ❑ Primitive types
- ❑ Commands: `If Then Else`, `Select Case`
- ❑ Value types (structures)
- ❑ Reference types (classes)
- ❑ Commands: `For Each`, `For Next`, `Do While`

❑   Boxing

❑   Parameter passing `ByVal` and `ByRef`

❑   Variable scope

❑   Data type conversions, compiler options, and XML literals

The main goal of this chapter is to familiarize you with Visual Basic. The chapter begins by looking at some of the keywords and language syntax you need. Experienced developers will probably gloss over this information, as this is just a basic introduction to working with Visual Basic. After this, the chapter discusses primitive types and then introduces you to the key branching commands for Visual Basic. After you are able to handle simple conditions, the chapter introduces value and reference types. The code then looks at working with collections and introduces the primary looping control structure syntax for Visual Basic.

After this there is a brief discussion of boxing and value type conversions, conversions which often implicitly occur when values are passed as parameters. Following these topics is a discussion of *variable scope*, which defines the code that can see variables based on where they are defined in relationship to that block of code. Finally, the chapter introduces basic data type conversions, which includes looking at the compiler options for Visual Studio 2008. Visual Studio 2008 includes a new compiler option and a new data type, *XML literals*, which are also introduced in the context of conversions.

Initial Keywords and Syntax

While it would be possible to just add a giant glossary of keywords here, that isn't the focus of this chapter. Instead, a few basic elements of Visual Basic need to be spelled out, so that as you read, you can understand the examples. Chapter 7, for instance, covers working with namespaces, but some examples and other code are introduced in this chapter.

Let's begin with namespace. When .NET was being created, the developers realized that attempting to organize all of these classes required a system. A namespace is an arbitrary system that the .NET developers used to group classes containing common functionality. A namespace can have multiple levels of grouping, each separated by a period (.). Thus, the `System` namespace is the basis for classes that are used throughout .NET, while the `Microsoft.VisualBasic` namespace is used for classes in the underlying .NET Framework but specific to Visual Basic. At its most basic level, a namespace does not imply or indicate anything regarding the relationships between the class implementations in that namespace; it is just a way of managing the complexity of the .NET Framework's thousands of classes. As noted earlier, namespaces are covered in detail in Chapter 7.

Next is the `keyword` class. Chapters 2 and 3 provide details on object-oriented syntax and the related keywords for objects, but a basic definition of this keyword is needed here. The `Class` keyword designates a common set of data and behavior within your application. The class is the definition of an object, in the same way that your source code, when compiled, is the definition of an application. When someone runs your code, it is considered to be an instance of your application. Similarly, when your code creates or instantiates an object from your class definition, it is considered to be an instance of that class, or an instance of that object.

Creating an instance of an object has two parts. The first part is the `New` command, which tells the compiler to create an instance of that class. This command instructs code to call your object definition and instantiate it. In some cases you might need to run a method and get a return value, but in most cases you use the `New` command to assign that instance of an object to a variable.

To declare a variable in Visual Basic, you use the `Dim` statement. `Dim` is short for "dimension" and comes from the ancient past of Basic, which preceded Visual Basic as a language. The idea is that you are telling the system to allocate or dimension a section of memory to hold data. The `Dim` statement is used to declare a variable, to which the system can then assign a value. As discussed in subsequent chapters on objects, the `Dim` statement may be replaced by another keyword such as `Public` or `Private` that not only dimensions the new value but also limits accessibility of that value. Each variable declaration uses a `Dim` statement similar to the example that follows, which declares a new variable, `winForm`:

```
Dim winForm As System.Windows.Forms.Form = New System.Windows.Forms.Form()
```

As a best practice, always set a variable equal to something when it is declared. In the preceding example, the code declares a new variable (`winForm`) of the type `Form`. This variable is then set to an instance of a `Form` object. It might also be assigned to an existing instance of a `Form` object or alternatively to `Nothing`. The `Nothing` keyword is a way of telling the system that the variable does not currently have any value, and as such is not actually using any memory on the heap. Later in this chapter, in the discussion of value and reference types, keep in mind that only reference types can be set to `Nothing`.

What do we mean when we refer to a class consisting of data and behavior? For "data" this means that the class specifies certain variables that are within its scope. Embedded in the class definition are zero or more `Dim` statements that create variables used to store the properties of the class. When you create an instance of this class, you create these variables; and in most cases the class contains logic to populate them. The logic used for this, and to carry out other actions, is the *behavior*. This behavior is encapsulated in what, in the object-oriented world, are known as *methods*.

However, Visual Basic doesn't have a "method" keyword. Instead, it has two other keywords that are brought forward from VB's days as a procedural language. The first is `Sub`. `Sub` is short for "subroutine," and it defines a block of code that carries out some action. When this block of code completes, it returns control to the code that called it. To declare a function, you write code similar to the following:

```
Private Sub Load(ByVal object As System.Object)

End Sub
```

The preceding example shows the start of a method called `Load`. For now you can ignore the word `Private` at the start of this declaration; this is related to the object and is further explained in the next chapter. This method is implemented as a `Sub` because it doesn't return a value and accepts one parameter when it is called. Thus, in other languages this might be considered and written explicitly as a function that returns `Nothing`.

The preceding method declaration also includes a single parameter, which is declared as being of type `System.Object`. The meaning of the `ByVal` qualifier is explained later in this chapter, but is related to how that value is passed to this method. The code that actually loads the object would be written between the line declaring this method and the `End Sub` line.

In Visual Basic, the only difference between a `Sub` and the second method type, a `Function`, is the return type. Note that the `Function` declaration shown in the following sample code specifies the return type of the function. A function works just like a Sub with the exception that a Function returns a value, which can be Nothing. This is an important distinction, because when you declare a function you expect it to include a Return statement. The Return statement is used to indicate that even though additional lines of code may remain within a Function or Sub, those lines of code should not be executed. Instead, the Function or Sub should end processing at the current line.

```
Public Function Add(ByVal ParamArray values() As Integer) As Long
    Dim result As Long = 0

    Return result
    'TODO: Implement this function
    'What if user passes in only 1 value, what about 3 or more...
    result = values(0) + values(1)
    Return result
End Function
```

In the preceding example, note that after the function initializes the second line of code, there is a Return statement. Because the implementation of this function isn't currently shown (it is shown later in this chapter in the discussion of parameters), the developer wanted the code to exist with a safe value until the code was completed. Moreover, there are *two* Return statements in the code. However, as soon as the first Return statement is reached, none of the remaining code in this function is executed. The Return statement immediately halts execution of a method, even from within a loop.

As shown in the preceding example, the function's return value is assigned to a local variable until returned as part of the Return statement. For a Sub, there would be no value on the line with the Return statement, as a Sub does not return a value when it completes. When returned, the return value is usually assigned to something else. This is shown in the next example line of code, which calls a function to retrieve the currently active control on the executing Windows Form:

```
Dim ctrl As System.Windows.Forms.Control = Me.GetContainerControl().ActiveControl()
```

The preceding example demonstrates a call to a function. The value returned by the function ActiveControl is of type Control, and the code assigns this to the variable ctrl. It also demonstrates another keyword that you should be aware of: Me. The Me keyword is the way, within an object, that you can reference the current instance of that object. For example, in the preceding example, the object being referenced is the current window.

You may have noticed that in all the sample code presented thus far, each line is a complete command. If you're familiar with another programming language, then you may be used to seeing a specific character that indicates the end of a complete set of commands. Several popular languages use a semicolon to indicate the end of a command line. For those who are considering Visual Basic as their first programming language, consider the English language, in which we end each complete thought with a period.

Visual Basic doesn't use visible punctuation to end each line. Instead, it views its source files more like a list, whereby each item on the list is placed on its own line. The result is that Visual Basic ends each command line with the carriage-return linefeed. In some languages, a command such as X = Y can span several lines in the source file until a semicolon or other terminating character is reached. In Visual Basic, that entire statement would be found on a single line unless the user explicitly indicates that it is to continue onto another line.

When a line ends with the underscore character, this tells Visual Basic that the code on that line does not constitute a completed set of commands. The compiler will then continue onto the next line to find the continuation of the command, and will end as soon as a carriage-return linefeed is found without an accompanying underscore. In other words, Visual Basic enables you to use exceptionally long lines and indicate that the code has been spread across multiple lines to improve readability. The following line demonstrates the use of the underscore to extend a line of code:

```
MessageBox.Show("Hello World", "A First Look at VB.NET", _
            MessageBoxButtons.OK, MessageBoxIcon.Information)
```

In Visual Basic it is also possible to place multiple different statements on a single line, by separating the statements with colons. However, this is generally considered a poor coding practice because it reduces readability.

Console Applications

The simplest type of application is a *console application*. This application doesn't have much of a user interface; in fact, for those old enough to remember the MS-DOS operating system, a console application looks just like an MS-DOS application. It works in a command window without support for graphics or graphical devices such as a mouse. A console application is a text-based user interface that reads and writes characters from the screen.

The easiest way to create a console application is to use Visual Studio. However, for our purposes let's just look at a sample source file for a console application, as shown in the following example. Notice that the console application contains a single method, a Sub called Main. However, this Sub isn't contained in a class. Instead, the Sub is contained in a Module:

```
Module Module1
    Sub Main()
        Dim myObject As Object = New Object()
        Console.WriteLine("Hello World")
    End Sub
End Module
```

A module is another item dating to the procedural days of Visual Basic. It isn't a class, but rather a block of code that can contain methods, which are then referenced by classes — or, as in this case, it can represent the execution start for a program. The module in the preceding example contains a single method called Main. The Main method indicates the starting point for running this application. Once a local variable is declared, the only other action taken by this method is to output a line of text to the console.

Note that in this usage, the Console refers to the text-based window, which hosts a command prompt from which this program is run. The console window is best thought of as a window encapsulating the older nongraphical-style user interface whereby literally everything was driven from the command prompt. The Console class is automatically created when you start your application, and it supports a variety of Read and Write methods. In the preceding example, if you were to run the code from within Visual Studio's debugger, then the console window would open and close immediately. To prevent that, you include a final line in the Main Sub, which executes a Read statement so that the program continues to run while waiting for user input.

Because so many keywords have been covered, a glossary might be useful. The following table briefly summarizes most of the keywords discussed in the preceding section, and provides a short description of their meaning in Visual Basic:

Keyword	Description
Namespace	A collection of classes that provide related capabilities. For example, the System.Drawing namespace contains classes associated with graphics.
Class	A definition of an object. Includes properties (variables) and methods, which can be subs or functions.
Instance	When a class is created, the resulting object is an instance of the class's definition. Not a keyword in Visual Basic.
Method	A generic name for a named set of commands. In Visual Basic, both subs and functions are types of methods. Not a keyword in Visual Basic.
Sub	A method that contains a set of commands, allows data to be transferred as parameters, and provides scope around local variables and commands
Function	A method that contains a set of commands, returns a value, allows data to be transferred as parameters, and provides scope around local variables and commands
Return	Ends the currently executing sub or function. Combined with a return value for functions.
Dim	Declares and defines a new variable
New	Creates an instance of an object
Nothing	Used to indicate that a variable has no value. Equivalent to null in other languages and databases.
Me	A reference to the instance of the object within which a method is executing
Console	A type of application that relies on a command-line interface. Console applications are commonly used for simple test frames. Also refers to a command window to and from which applications can read and write text data.
Module	A code block that isn't a class but which can contain sub and function methods. Not frequently used for application development, but is part of a console application.

Finally, as an example of code in the sections ahead, we are going to use Visual Studio 2008 to create a simple console application. The sample code for this chapter uses a console application titled "ProVB_C01_Types." To create this, start Visual Studio 2008. From the File menu, select New. In some versions of Visual Studio, you then need to select the Project menu item from within the options for New; otherwise, the New option takes you to the window shown in Figure 1-1.

Select a new console application, name it ProVB_C01_Types, as shown in Figure 1-1, and click OK to continue. Visual Studio 2008 then goes to work for you, generating a series of files to support your new project. These files, which vary by project type, are explained in more detail in subsequent chapters. The only one that matters for this example is the one entitled Module1.vb. Fortunately, Visual Studio automatically opens this file for you for editing, as shown in Figure 1-2.

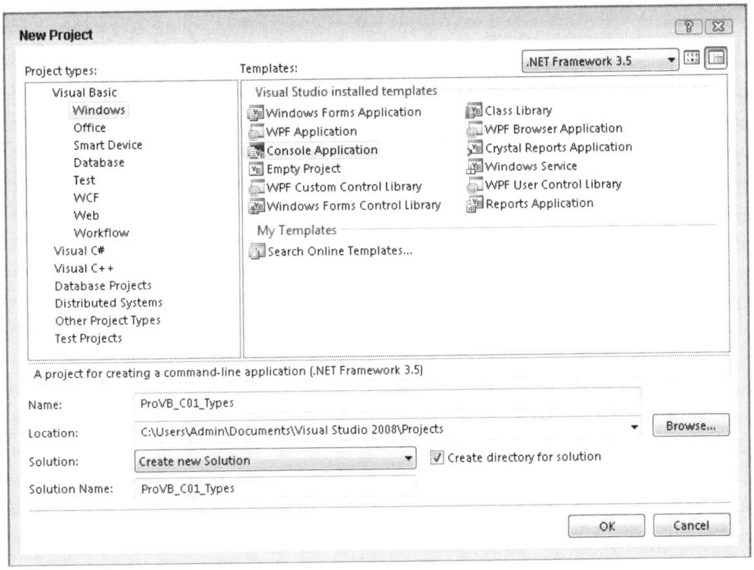

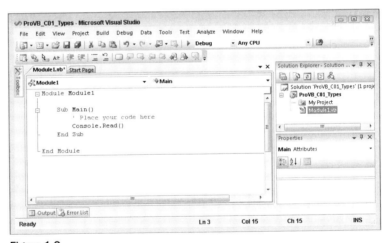

Figure 1-1

Figure 1-2

The sample shown in Figure 1-2 shows the default code with two lines of text added:

```
' Place your code here
Console.Read()
```

The first line of code represents a comment. A comment is text that is part of your source file but which the language compiler ignores. These lines enable you to describe what your code is doing, or describe what a given variable will contain. Placing a single quote on a line means that everything that follows on that line is considered to be a comment and should not be parsed as part of the Visual Basic language. This means you can have a line of code followed by a comment on the same line. Commenting code

7

is definitely considered a best practice, and, as discussed in Chapter 13, Visual Studio enables you to structure comments in XML so that they can be referenced for documentation purposes.

The second line of code tells the system to wait for the user to enter something in the Console window before continuing. Without this line of code, if you ran your project, you would see the project quickly run, but the window would immediately close before you could read anything. Adding this line ensures that your code entered prior to the line executes, after which the application waits until you press a key. Because this is the last line in this sample, once you press a key, the application reads what was typed and then closes, as there is no more code to execute.

To test this out, use the F5 key to compile and run your code, or use the play button shown in Figure 1-2 in the top toolbar to run your code. As you look at the sample code in this chapter, feel free to place code into this sample application and run it to see the results. More important, change it to see what happens when you introduce new conditions. As with examples in any book of this kind, the samples in this book are meant to help you get started; you can extend and modify these in any way you like.

With that in mind, now you can take a look at how data is stored and defined within your running application. While you might be thinking about permanent storage such as on your hard drive or within a database, the focus for this chapter is how data is stored in memory while your program is executing. To access data from within your program, you read and assign values to variables, and these variables take different forms or types.

Value and Reference Types

Experienced developers generally consider integers, characters, Booleans, and strings to be the basic building blocks of any language. In .NET, all objects share a logical inheritance from the base `Object` class. One of the advantages of this common heritage is the ability to rely on certain common methods of every variable. Another is that this allows all of .NET to build on a common type system. Visual Basic builds on the common type system shared across .NET languages.

Because all data types are based on the core `Object` class, every variable you dimension can be assured of having a set of common characteristics. However, this logical inheritance does not require a common physical implementation for all variables. This might seem like a conflicting set of statements, but .NET has a base type of `Object` and then allows simple structures to inherit from this base class. While everything in .NET is based on the `Object` class, under the covers .NET has two major variable types: value and reference.

For example, what most programmers see as some of the basic underlying types, such as `Integer`, `Long`, `Character`, and even `Byte`, are not implemented as classes. Thus, on the one hand, all types inherit from the `Object` class, and on the other hand, there are two core types. This is important, as you'll see when we discuss boxing and the cost of transitioning between value types and reference types. The key point is that every type, whether it is a built-in structure such as an integer or string, or a custom class such as `WroxEmployee`, does, in fact, inherit from the `Object` class. The difference between value and reference types is an underlying implementation difference:

❑ Value types represent simple data storage located on the stack. The stack is used for items of a known size, so items on the stack can be retrieved faster than those on the managed heap.

❑ Reference types are based on complex classes with implementation inheritance from their parent classes, and custom storage on the managed heap. The managed heap is optimized to support dynamic allocation of differently sized objects.

Note that the two implementations are stored in different portions of memory. As a result, value and reference types are treated differently within assignment statements, and their memory management is handled differently. It is important to understand how these differences affect the software you will write in Visual Basic. Understanding the foundations of how data is manipulated in the .NET Framework will enable you to build more reliable and better-performing applications.

Consider the difference between the stack and the heap. The stack is a comparatively small memory area in which processes and threads store data of fixed size. An integer or decimal value needs the same number of bytes to store data, regardless of the actual value. This means that the location of such variables on the stack can be efficiently determined. (When a process needs to retrieve a variable, it has to search the stack. If the stack contained variables that had dynamic memory sizes, then such a search could take a long time.)

Reference types do not have a fixed size — a string can vary in size from two bytes to nearly all the memory available on a system. The dynamic size of reference types means that the data they contain is stored on the heap, rather than the stack. However, the address of the reference type (that is, the location of the data on the heap) does have a fixed size, and thus can be (and, in fact, is) stored on the stack. By storing a reference only to a custom allocation on the stack, the program as a whole runs much more quickly, as the process can rapidly locate the data associated with a variable.

Storing the data contained in fixed and dynamically sized variables in different places results in differences in the way variables behave. Rather than limit this discussion to the most basic of types in .NET, this difference can be illustrated by comparing the behavior of the System.Drawing.Point structure (a value type) and the System.Text.StringBuilder class (a reference type).

The Point structure is used as part of the .NET graphics library, which is part of the System.Drawing namespace. The StringBuilder class is part of the System.Text namespace and is used to improve performance when you're editing strings.

First, here is an example of how the System.Drawing.Point structure is used:

```
Dim ptX As New System.Drawing.Point(10, 20)
Dim ptY As New System.Drawing.Point

ptY = ptX
ptX.X = 200

Console.WriteLine(ptY.ToString())
```

The output from this operation will be {X = 10, Y = 20}, which seems logical. When the code copies ptX into ptY, the data contained in ptX is copied into the location on the stack associated with ptY. Later, when the value of ptX changes, only the memory on the stack associated with ptX is altered. Altering the value of ptX has no effect on ptY. This is not the case with reference types. Consider the following code, which uses the System.Text.StringBuilder class:

```
Dim objX As New System.Text.StringBuilder("Hello World")
Dim objY As System.Text.StringBuilder

objY = objX
objX.Replace("World", "Test")

Console.WriteLine(objY.ToString())
```

The output from this operation will be "Hello Test," not "Hello World." The previous example using points demonstrated that when one value type is assigned to another, the data stored on the stack is copied. Similarly, this example demonstrates that when objY is assigned to objX, the data associated with objX on the stack is copied to the data associated with objY on the stack. However, what is copied in this case isn't the actual data, but rather the address on the managed heap where the data is actually located. This means that objY and objX now reference the same data. When the data on the heap is changed, the data associated with every variable that holds a reference to that memory is changed. This is the default behavior of reference types, and is known as a *shallow copy*. Later in this chapter, you'll see how this behavior has been overridden for strings (which perform a *deep copy*).

The differences between value types and reference types go beyond how they behave when copied, and later in this chapter you'll encounter some of the other features provided by objects. First, though, let's take a closer look at some of the most commonly used value types and learn how .NET works with them.

Primitive Types

Visual Basic, in common with other development languages, has a group of elements such as integers and strings that are termed *primitive types*. These primitive types are identified by keywords such as String, Long, and Integer, which are aliases for types defined by the .NET class library. This means that the line

```
Dim i As Long
```

is equivalent to the line

```
Dim i As System.Int64
```

The reason why these two different declarations are available has to do with long-term planning for your application. In most cases (such as when Visual Basic transitioned to .NET), you want to use the Short, Integer, and Long designations. When Visual Basic moved to .NET, the Integer type went from 16 bits to 32 bits. Code written with this Integer type would automatically use the larger value if you rewrote the code in .NET. Interestingly enough, however, the Visual Basic Migration Wizard actually recast Visual Basic 6 Integer values to Visual Basic .NET Short values.

This is the same reason why Int16, Int32, and Int64 exist. These types specify a physical implementation; therefore, if your code is someday migrated to a version of .NET that maps the Integer value to Int64, then those values defined as Integer will reflect the new larger capacity, while those declared as Int32 will not. This could be important if your code was manipulating part of an interface where changing the physical size of the value could break the interface.

The following table lists the primitive types that Visual Basic 2008 defines, and the structures or classes to which they map:

Primitive Type	.NET Class or Structure
Byte	System.Byte (structure)
Short	System.Int16 (structure)
Integer	System.Int32 (structure)

Primitive Type	.NET Class or Structure
Long	System.Int64 (structure)
Single	System.Single (structure)
Double	System.Double (structure)
Decimal	System.Decimal (structure)
Boolean	System.Boolean (structure)
Date	System.DateTime (structure)
Char	System.Char (structure)
String	System.String (class)

The String primitive type stands out from the other primitives. Strings are implemented as a class, not a structure. More important, strings are the one primitive type that is a reference type.

You can perform certain operations on primitive types that you can't on other types. For example, you can assign a value to a primitive type using a literal:

```
Dim i As Integer = 32
Dim str As String = "Hello"
```

It's also possible to declare a primitive type as a constant using the Const keyword, as shown here:

```
Dim Const str As String = "Hello"
```

The value of the variable str in the preceding line of code cannot be changed elsewhere in the application containing this code at runtime. These two simple examples illustrate the key properties of primitive types. As noted, most primitive types are, in fact, value types. The next step is to take a look at core language commands that enable you to operate on these variables.

Commands: Conditional

Unlike many programming languages, Visual Basic has been designed to focus on readability and clarity. Many languages are willing to sacrifice these attributes to enable developers to type as little as possible. Visual Basic, conversely, is designed under the paradigm that the readability of code matters more than saving a few keystrokes, so commands in Visual Basic tend to spell out the exact context of what is being done.

Literally dozens of commands make up the Visual Basic language, so there isn't nearly enough space here to address all of them. Moreover, many of the more specialized commands are covered later in this book. However, if you are not familiar with Visual Basic or are relatively new to programming, a few would be helpful to look at here. These fall into two basic areas: *conditional statements* and *looping statements*. This chapter addresses two statements within each of these categories, starting with the conditional statements and later, after collections and arrays have been introduced, covering looping statements.

Each of these statements has the ability not only to call another method, the preferred way to manage blocks of code, but also to literally encapsulate a block of code. Note that the variables declared within the context of a conditional statement (between the `If` and `End If` lines) are only visible up until the `End If` statement. After that these variables go out of scope. The concept of scoping is discussed in more detail later in this chapter.

If Then

The conditional is one of two primary programming constructs (the other being the loop) that is present in almost every programming language. After all, even in those rare cases where the computer is just repeatedly adding values or doing some other repetitive activity, at some point a decision is needed and a condition evaluated, even if the question is only "is it time to stop?" Visual Basic supports the `If-Then` statement as well as the `Else` statement; and unlike some languages, the concept of an `ElseIf` statement. The `ElseIf` and `Else` statements are totally optional, and it is not only acceptable but common to encounter conditionals that do not utilize either of these code blocks. The following example illustrates a simple pair of conditions that have been set up serially:

```
If i > 1 Then
    'Code A1
ElseIf i < 1 Then
    'Code B2
Else
    'Code C3
End If
```

If the first condition is true, then code placed at marker `A1` is executed. The flow would then proceed to the `End If`, and the program would not evaluate any of the other conditions. Note that for best performance, it makes the most sense to have your most common condition first in this structure, because if it is successful, none of the other conditions need to be tested.

If the initial comparison in the preceding example code were false, then control would move to the first `Else` statement, which in this case happens to be an `ElseIf` statement. The code would therefore test the next conditional to determine whether the value of `i` were less than 1. If this were the case, then the code associated with block `B2` would be executed.

However, if the second condition were also false, then the code would proceed to the `Else` statement, which isn't concerned with any remaining condition and just executes the code in block `C3`. Not only is the `Else` optional, but even if an `ElseIf` is used, the `Else` condition is still optional. It is acceptable for the `Else` and `C3` block to be omitted from the preceding example.

Comparison Operators

There are several ways to discuss what is evaluated in an `If` statement. Essentially, the code between the `If` and `Then` portion of the statement must eventually evaluate out to a Boolean. At the most basic level, this means you can write `If True Then`, which results in a valid statement, although the code would always execute the associated block of code with that `If` statement. The idea, however, is that for a basic comparison, you take two values and place between them a comparison operator. Comparison operators include the following symbols: =, >, <, >=, <=.

Additionally, certain keywords can be used with a comparison operator. For example, the keyword Not can be used to indicate that the statement should consider the failure of a given comparison as a reason to execute the code encapsulated by its condition. An example of this is shown in the next example:

```
If Not i = 1 Then
    'Code A1
End If
```

It is therefore possible to compare two values and then take the resulting Boolean from this comparison and reevaluate the result. In this case, the result is only reversed, but the If statement supports more complex comparisons using statements such as And and Or. These statements enable you to create a complex condition based on several comparisons, as shown here:

```
If Not i = 1 Or i < 0 And str = "Hello" Then
    'Code A1
Else
    'Code B2
End If
```

The And and Or conditions are applied to determine whether the first comparison's results are true or false along with the second value's results. The And conditional means that both comparisons must evaluate to true in order for the If statement to execute the code in block A1, and the Or statement means that if the condition on either side is true, then the If statement can evaluate code block A1. However, in looking at this statement, your first reaction should be to pause and attempt to determine in exactly what order all of the associated comparisons occur.

There is a precedence. First, any numeric style comparisons are applied, followed by any unary operators such as Not. Finally, proceeding from left to right, each Boolean comparison of And and Or is applied. However, a much better way to write the preceding statement is to use parentheses to identify in what order you want these comparisons to occur. The first If statement in the following example illustrates the default order, while the second and third use parentheses to force a different priority on the evaluation of the conditions:

```
If ((Not i = 1) Or i < 0) And (str = "Hello") Then
If (Not i = 1) Or (i < 0 And str = "Hello") Then
If Not ((i = 1 Or i < 0) And str = "Hello") Then
```

All three of the preceding If statements are evaluating the same set of criteria, yet their results are potentially very different. It is always best practice to enclose complex conditionals within parentheses to illustrate the desired order of evaluation. Of course, these comparisons have been rather simple; you could replace the variable value in the preceding examples with a function call that might include a call to a database. In such a situation, if the desired behavior were to execute this expensive call only when necessary, then you might want to use one of the shortcut comparison operators.

Since you know that for an And statement both sides of the If statement must be true, there are times when knowing that the first condition is false could save processing time; you would not bother executing the second condition. Similarly, if the comparison involves an Or statement, then once the first part of the condition is true, there is no reason to evaluate the second condition because you know that the net result is success. In this case, the AndAlso and OrElse statements allow for performance optimization.

```
If ((Not i = 1) Or i < 0) AndAlso (MyFunction() = "Success") Then
If Not i = 1 OrElse (i < 0 And MyFunction() = "Success") Then
```

The preceding code illustrates that instead of using a variable like str as used in the preceding samples, your condition might call a function you've written that returns a value. In this case, MyFunction would return a string that would then be used in the comparison. Each of these conditions has therefore been optimized so that there are situations where the code associated with MyFunction won't be executed.

This is potentially important, not only from a performance standpoint, but also in a scenario where given the first condition your code might throw an error. For example, it's not uncommon to first determine whether a variable has been assigned a value and then to test that value. This introduces yet another pair of conditional elements: the Is and IsNot conditionals.

Using Is enables you to determine whether a variable has been given a value, or to determine its type. In the past it was common to see nested If statements as a developer first determined whether the value was null, followed by a separate If statement to determine whether the value was valid. Starting with .NET 2.0, the short-circuit conditionals enable you to check for a value and then check whether that value meets the desired criteria. The short-circuit operator prevents the check for a value from occurring and causing an error if the variable is undefined, so both checks can be done with a single If statement:

```
Dim mystring as string = Nothing
If mystring IsNot Nothing AndAlso mystring.Length > 100 Then
    'Code A1
ElseIf mystring.GetType Is GetType(Integer) Then
    'Code B2
End If
```

The preceding code would fail on the first comparison because mystring has only been initialized to Nothing, meaning that by definition it doesn't have a length. Note also that the second condition will fail because you know that myString isn't of type Integer.

Select Case

The preceding section makes it clear that the If statement is the king of conditionals. However, in another scenario you may have a simple condition that needs to be tested repeatedly. For example, suppose a user selects a value from a drop-down list and different code executes depending on that value. This is a relatively simple comparison, but if you have 20 values, then you would potentially need to string together 20 different If Then and ElseIf statements to account for all of the possibilities.

A cleaner way of evaluating such a condition is to leverage a Select Case statement. This statement was designed to test a condition, but instead of returning a Boolean value, it returns a value that is then used to determine which block of code, each defined by a Case statement, should be executed:

```
Select Case i
    Case 1
        'Code A1
    Case 2
        'Code B2
    Case Else
        'Code C3
End Select
```

The preceding sample code shows how the Select portion of the statement determines the value represented by the variable i. Depending on the value of this variable, the Case statement executes the appropriate code block. For a value of 1, the code in block A1 is executed; similarly, a 2 results in code block B2 executing. For any other value, because this case statement includes an Else block, the case statement executes the code represented by C3. Finally, the next example illustrates that the cases do not need to be integer values and can, in fact, even be strings:

```
Dim mystring As String = "Intro"
Select Case mystring
    Case "Intro"
        'Code A1
    Case "Exit"
        'Code A2
    Case Else
        'Code A3
End Select
```

Now that you have been introduced to these two control elements that enable you to control what happens in your code, your next step is to review details of the different variable types that are available within Visual Basic 2008, starting with the value types.

Value Types (Structures)

Value types aren't as versatile as reference types, but they can provide better performance in many circumstances. The core value types (which include the majority of primitive types) are Boolean, Byte, Char, DateTime, Decimal, Double, Guid, Int16, Int32, Int64, SByte, Single, and TimeSpan. These are not the only value types, but rather the subset with which most Visual Basic developers consistently work. As you've seen, value types by definition store data on the stack.

Value types can also be referred to by their proper name: structures. The underlying principles and syntax of creating custom structures mirrors that of creating classes, covered in the next chapter. This section focuses on some of the built-in types provided by the .NET Framework — in particular, the built-in types known as *primitives*.

Boolean

The .NET Boolean type represents true or false. Variables of this type work well with the conditional statements that were just discussed. When you declare a variable of type Boolean, you can use it within a conditional statement directly:

```
Dim blnTrue As Boolean = True
Dim blnFalse As Boolean = False
If blnTrue Then
    Console.WriteLine(blnTrue)
    Console.WriteLine(blnFalse.ToString)
End If
```

Always use the True *and* False *constants when working with Boolean variables.*

Unfortunately, in the past developers had a tendency to tell the system to interpret a variable created as a `Boolean` as an `Integer`. This is referred to as *implicit conversion* and is discussed later in this chapter. It is not the best practice, and when .NET was introduced, it caused issues for Visual Basic because the underlying representation of `True` in other languages wasn't going to match those of Visual Basic. The result was that Visual Basic represents `True` differently for implicit conversions than other .NET languages.

`True` has been implemented in such a way that when converted to an integer, Visual Basic converts a value of `True` to -1 (negative one). This is one of the few (but not the only) legacy carryovers from older versions of Visual Basic and is different from other languages, which typically use the value integer value 1. Generically, all languages tend to implicitly convert `False` to 0 and `True` to a nonzero value.

However, Visual Basic works as part of a multilanguage environment, with metadata-defining interfaces, so the external value of `True` is as important as its internal value. Fortunately, Microsoft implemented Visual Basic in such a way that while -1 is supported, the .NET standard of 1 is exposed from Visual Basic methods to other languages.

To create reusable code, it is always better to avoid implicit conversions. In the case of `Boolean`s, if the code needs to check for an integer value, then you should explicitly evaluate the `Boolean` and create an appropriate integer. The code will be far more maintainable and prone to fewer unexpected results.

Integer Types

Now that `Boolean`s have been covered in depth, the next step is to examine the `Integer` types that are part of Visual Basic. Visual Basic 6.0 included two types of integer values: The `Integer` type was limited to a maximum value of 32767, and the `Long` type supported a maximum value of 2147483647. The .NET Framework added a new integer type, the `Short`. The `Short` is the equivalent of the `Integer` value from Visual Basic 6.0; the `Integer` has been promoted to support the range previously supported by the Visual Basic 6.0 `Long` type, and the Visual Basic .NET `Long` type is an eight-byte value. The new `Long` type provides support for 64-bit values, such as those used by current 64-bit processors. In addition, each of these types also has two alternative types. In all, Visual Basic supports nine `Integer` types:

Type	Allocated Memory	Minimum Value	Maximum Value
Short	2 bytes	−32768	32767
Int16	2 bytes	−32768	32767
UInt16	2 bytes	0	65535
Integer	4 bytes	−2147483648	2147483647
Int32	4 bytes	−2147483648	2147483647
UInt32	4 bytes	0	4294967295
Long	8 bytes	−9223372036854775808	9223372036854775807
Int64	8 bytes	−9223372036854775808	9223372036854775807
UInt64	8 bytes	0	18446744073709551615

Short

A `Short` value is limited to the maximum value that can be stored in two bytes. This means there are 16 bits and the value can range between −32768 and 32767. This limitation may or may not be based on the amount of memory physically associated with the value; it is a definition of what must occur in the .NET Framework. This is important, because there is no guarantee that the implementation will actually use less memory than when using an `Integer` value. It is possible that in order to optimize memory or processing, the operating system will allocate the same amount of physical memory used for an `Integer` type and then just limit the possible values.

The `Short` (or `Int16`) value type can be used to map SQL `smallint` values.

Integer

An `Integer` is defined as a value that can be safely stored and transported in four bytes (not as a four-byte implementation). This gives the `Integer` and `Int32` value types a range from −2147483648 to 2147483647. This range is more than adequate to handle most tasks.

The main reason to use an `Int32` in place of an integer value is to ensure future portability with interfaces. For example, the `Integer` value in Visual Basic 6.0 was limited to a two-byte value, but is now a four-byte value. In future 64-bit platforms, the `Integer` value might be an eight-byte value. Problems could occur if an interface used a 64-bit `Integer` with an interface that expected a 32-bit `Integer` value, or, conversely, if code using the `Integer` type is suddenly passed to a variable explicitly declared as `Int32`.

The solution is to be consistent. Use `Int32`, which would remain a 32-bit value, even on a 64-bit platform, if that is what you need. In addition, as a best practice, use `Integer` so your code can be unconcerned with the underlying implementation.

The Visual Basic .NET `Integer` value type matches the size of an integer value in SQL Server, which means that you can easily align the column type of a table with the variable type in your programs.

Long

The `Long` type is aligned with the `Int64` value. `Long`s have an eight-byte range, which means that their value can range from −9223372036854775808 to 9223372036854775807. This is a big range, but if you need to add or multiply `Integer` values, then you need a large value to contain the result. It's common while doing math operations on one type of integer to use a larger type to capture the result if there's a chance that the result could exceed the limit of the types being manipulated.

The `Long` value type matches the `bigint` type in SQL.

Unsigned Types

Another way to gain additional range on the positive side of an `Integer` type is to use one of the unsigned types. The unsigned types provide a useful buffer for holding a result that might exceed an operation by a small amount, but this isn't the main reason they exist. The `UInt16` type happens to have the same characteristics as the `Character` type, while the `UInt32` type has the same characteristics as a system memory pointer on a 32-byte system.

However, never write code that attempts to leverage this relationship. Such code isn't portable, as on a 64-bit system the system memory pointer changes and uses the `UInt64` type. However, when larger integers are needed and all values are known to be positive, these values are of use. As for the low-level uses of these types, certain low-level drivers use this type of knowledge to interface with software that expects these values and they are the underlying implementation for other value types. This is why, when you move from a 32-bit system to a 64-bit system, you need new drivers for your devices, and why applications shouldn't leverage this same type of logic.

Decimal Types

Just as there are several types to store integer values, there are three implementations of value types to store real number values. The `Single` and `Double` types work the same way in Visual Basic .NET as they did in Visual Basic 6.0. The difference is the Visual Basic 6.0 `Currency` type (which was a specialized version of a `Double` type), which is now obsolete; it was replaced by the `Decimal` value type for very large real numbers.

Type	Allocated Memory	Negative Range	Positive Range
`Single`	4 bytes	−3.402823E38 to −1.401298E-45	1.401298E-45 to 3.402823E38
`Double`	8 bytes	−1.79769313486231E308 to −4.94065645841247E-324	4.94065645841247E-324 to 1.79769313486232E308
`Currency`	Obsolete	—	—
`Decimal`	16 bytes	−79228162514264 337593543950335 to 0.00000000000000 00000000000001	0.00000000000000 00000000000001 to 792281625142643 37593543950335

Single

The `Single` type contains four bytes of data, and its precision can range anywhere from 1.401298E-45 to 3.402823E38 for positive values and from −3.402823E38 to −1.401298E-45 for negative values.

It can seem strange that a value stored using four bytes (the same as the `Integer` type) can store a number that is larger than even the `Long` type. This is possible because of the way in which numbers are stored; a real number can be stored with different levels of precision. Note that there are six digits after the decimal point in the definition of the `Single` type. When a real number gets very large or very small, the stored value is limited by its significant places.

Because real values contain fewer significant places than their maximum value, when working near the extremes it is possible to lose precision. For example, while it is possible to represent a `Long` with the value of 9223372036854775805, the `Single` type rounds this value to 9.223372E18. This seems like a reasonable action to take, but it isn't a reversible action. The following code demonstrates how this loss of precision and data can result in errors:

```
Dim l As Long
Dim s As Single

l = Long.MaxValue
Console.WriteLine(l)
```

```
s = Convert.ToSingle(l)
Console.WriteLine(s)
s -= 1000000000000
l = Convert.ToInt64(s)

Console.WriteLine(l)
Console.WriteLine(Long.MaxValue - l)
```

I placed this code into the simple console application created earlier in this chapter and ran it. The code creates a Long that has the maximum value possible, and outputs this value. Then it converts this value to a Single and outputs it in that format. Next, the value 1000000000000 is subtracted to the Single using the -= syntax, which is similar to writing s = s − 1000000000000. Finally, the code assigns the Single value back into the Long and then outputs both the Long and the difference between the original value and the new value. The results are shown in Figure 1-3. The results probably aren't consistent with what you might expect.

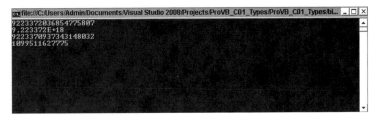

Figure 1-3

The first thing to notice is how the values are represented in the output based on type. The Single value actually uses an exponential display instead of displaying all of the significant digits. More important, as you can see, the result of what is stored in the Single after the math operation actually occurs is not accurate in relation to what is computed using the Long value. Therefore, both the Single and Double types have limitations in accuracy when you are doing math operations. These accuracy issues are because of limitations in what is stored and how binary numbers represent decimal numbers. To better address these issues for large numbers, .NET provides the decimal type.

Double

The behavior of the previous example changes if you replace the value type of Single with Double. A Double uses eight bytes to store values, and as a result has greater precision and range. The range for a Double is from 4.94065645841247E-324 to 1.79769313486232E308 for positive values and from −1.79769313486231E308 to −4.94065645841247E-324 for negative values. The precision has increased such that a number can contain 15 digits before the rounding begins. This greater level of precision makes the Double value type a much more reliable variable for use in math operations. It's possible to represent most operations with complete accuracy with this value. To test this, change the sample code from the previous section so that instead of declaring the variable s as a Single you declare it as a Double and rerun the code. Don't forget to also change the conversion line from ToSingle to ToDouble. Did you get an accurate difference? Or was yours like mine — the difference in value off by 1?

Decimal

The Decimal type is a hybrid that consists of a 12-byte integer value combined with two additional 16-bit values that control the location of the decimal point and the sign of the overall value. A Decimal value consumes 16 bytes in total and can store a maximum value of 79228162514264337593543950335.

19

This value can then be manipulated by adjusting where the decimal place is located. For example, the maximum value while accounting for four decimal places is 7922816251426433759354395.0335. This is because a `Decimal` isn't stored as a traditional number, but as a 12-byte integer value, with the location of the decimal in relation to the available 28 digits. This means that a `Decimal` does not inherently round numbers the way a `Double` does.

As a result of the way values are stored, the closest precision to zero that a `Decimal` supports is 0.0000000000000000000000000001. The location of the decimal point is stored separately; and the `Decimal` type stores a value that indicates whether its value is positive or negative separately from the actual value. This means that the positive and negative ranges are exactly the same, regardless of the number of decimal places.

Thus, the system makes a trade-off whereby the need to store a larger number of decimal places reduces the maximum value that can be kept at that level of precision. This trade-off makes a lot of sense. After all, it's not often that you need to store a number with 15 digits on both sides of the decimal point, and for those cases you can create a custom class that manages the logic and leverages one or more decimal values as its properties. You'll find that if you again modify and rerun the sample code you've been using in the last couple of sections that converts to and from `Long` values by using `Decimals` for the interim value and conversion, now your results are completely accurate.

Char and Byte

The default character set under Visual Basic is Unicode. Therefore, when a variable is declared as type `Char`, Visual Basic creates a two-byte value, since, by default, all characters in the Unicode character set require two bytes. Visual Basic supports the declaration of a character value in three ways. Placing a `$c$` following a literal string informs the compiler that the value should be treated as a character, or the `Chr` and `ChrW` methods can be used. The following code snippet shows that all three of these options work similarly, with the difference between the `Chr` and `ChrW` methods being the range of available valid input values. The `ChrW` method allows for a broader range of values based on wide character input.

```
Dim chrLtr_a As Char = "a"c
Dim chrAsc_a As Char = Chr(97)
Dim chrAsc_b as Char = ChrW(98)
```

To convert characters into a string suitable for an ASCII interface, the runtime library needs to validate each character's value to ensure that it is within a valid range. This could have a performance impact for certain serial arrays. Fortunately, Visual Basic supports the `Byte` value type. This type contains a value between 0 and 255 that exactly matches the range of the ASCII character set. When interfacing with a system that uses ASCII, it is best to use a `Byte` array. The runtime knows there is no need to perform a Unicode-to-ASCII conversion for a `Byte` array, so the interface between the systems operates significantly faster.

In Visual Basic, the `Byte` value type expects a numeric value. Thus, to assign the letter "a" to a `Byte`, you must use the appropriate character code. One option to get the numeric value of a letter is to use the `Asc` method, as shown here:

```
Dim bytLtrA as Byte = Asc("a")
```

DateTime

The Visual Basic Date keyword has always supported a structure of both date and time. You can, in fact, declare date values using both the DateTime and Date types. Note that internally Visual Basic no longer stores a date value as a Double; however, it provides key methods for converting the current internal date representation to the legacy Double type. The ToOADate and FromOADate methods support backward compatibility during migration from previous versions of Visual Basic.

Visual Basic also provides a set of shared methods that provides some common dates. The concept of shared methods is described in more detail in the next chapter, which covers object syntax, but, in short, shared methods are available even when you don't create an instance of a class. For the DateTime structure, the Now method returns a Date value with the local date and time. This method has not been changed from Visual Basic 6.0, but the Today and UtcNow methods have been added. These methods can be used to initialize a Date object with the current local date, or the date and time based on Universal Coordinated Time (also known as Greenwich Mean Time), respectively. You can use these shared methods to initialize your classes, as shown in the following code sample:

```
Dim dteNow as Date = Now()
Dim dteToday as Date = Today()
Dim dteGMT as DateTime = DateTime.UtcNow()
Dim dteString As Date = #4/16/1965#
Console.WriteLine(dteString.ToLongDateString)
```

The last two lines in the preceding example just demonstrate the use of Date as a primitive. As noted earlier, primitive values enable you to assign them directly within your code, but many developers seem unaware of the format for doing this with dates.

Reference Types (Classes)

A lot of the power of Visual Basic is harnessed in objects. An object is defined by its class, which describes what data, methods, and other attributes an instance of that class supports. Thousands of classes are provided in the .NET Framework class library.

When code instantiates an object from a class, the object created is a reference type. Recall that the data contained in value and reference types is stored in different locations, but this is not the only difference between them. A class (which is the typical way to refer to a reference type) has additional capabilities, such as support for protected methods and properties, enhanced event-handling capabilities, constructors, and finalizers, and can be extended with a custom base class via inheritance. Classes can also be used to define how operators such as "=" and "+" work on an instance of the class.

The intention of this chapter is to introduce you to some commonly used classes, and to complement your knowledge of the common value types already covered. Chapters 2 and 3 contain a detailed look at object orientation in Visual Basic. This chapter examines the features of the Object, String, DBNull, and Array classes, as well as the Collection classes found in the System.Collections namespace.

The Object Class

The Object class is the base class for every type in .NET, both value and reference types. At its core, every variable is an object and can be treated as such. You can think of the Object class (in some ways) as the replacement for the `Variant` type found in COM and COM-based versions of Visual Basic, but take care. COM, a `Variant` type, represents a variant memory location; in Visual Basic, an `Object` type represents a reference to an instance of the `Object` class. In COM, a `Variant` is implemented to provide a reference to a memory area on the heap, but its definition doesn't define any specific ways of accessing this data area. As you'll see during this look at objects, an instance of an "object" includes all the information needed to define the actual type of that object.

Because the `Object` class is the basis of all types, you can assign any variable to an object. Reference types maintain their current reference and implementation but are generically handled, whereas value types are packaged into a box and placed into the memory location associated with the `Object`. For example, there are instance methods that are available on `Object`, such as `ToString`. This method, if implemented, returns a string representation of an instance value. Because the `Object` class defines it, it can be called on any object:

```
Dim objMyClass as New MyClass("Hello World")

Console.WriteLine(objMyClass.ToString)
```

This brings up the question of how the `Object` class knows how to convert custom classes to `String` objects. The answer is that it doesn't. In order for this method to actually return the data in an instance of a `String`, a class must override this method. Otherwise, when this code is run, the default version of this method defined at the `Object` level returns the name of the current class (`MyClass`) as its string representation. This section will be clearer after you read Chapter 2. The key point is that if you create an implementation of `ToString` in your class definition, then even when an instance of your object is cast to the type `Object`, your custom method will still be called. The following snippet shows how to create a generic object under the `Option Strict` syntax:

```
Dim objVar as Object

objVar = Me

CType(objVar, Form).Text = "New Dialog Title Text"
```

That `Object` is then assigned a copy of the current instance of a Visual Basic form. In order to access the `Text` property of the original `Form` class, the `Object` must be cast from its declared type of `Object` to its actual type (`Form`), which supports the `Text` property. The `CType` command (covered later) accepts the object as its first parameter, and the class name (without quotes) as its second parameter. In this case, the current instance variable is of type `Form`; and by casting this variable, the code can reference the `Text` property of the current form.

The String Class

Another class that plays a large role in most development projects is the `String` class. Having `String`s defined as a class is more powerful than the Visual Basic 6.0 data type of `String` that you may be more familiar with. The `String` class is a special class within .NET because it is the one primitive type that is not a value type. To make `String` objects compatible with some of the underlying behavior in .NET, they have some interesting characteristics.

These methods are shared, which means that the methods are not specific to any instance of a `String`. The `String` class also contains several other methods that are called based on an instance of a specific

`String` object. The methods on the `String` class replace the functions that Visual Basic 6.0 had as part of the language for string manipulation, and they perform operations such as inserting strings, splitting strings, and searching strings.

String()

The `String` class has several different constructors for those situations in which you aren't simply assigning an existing value to a new string. The term *constructor* is expanded upon in Chapter 2. Constructors are methods that are used to construct an instance of a class. `String()` would be the default constructor for the `String` class, but the `String` class does not expose this constructor publicly. The following example shows the most common method of creating a `String`:

```
Dim strConstant as String = "ABC"
Dim strRepeat as New String("A"c, 20)
```

A variable is declared of type `String` and as a primitive is assigned the value `'ABC'`. The second declaration uses one of the parameterized versions of the `String` constructor. This constructor accepts two parameters: The first is a character and the second is the number of times that character should be repeated in the string.

In addition to creating an instance of a string and then calling methods on your variable, the `String` class has several shared methods. A shared method refers to a method on a class that does not require an instance of that class. Shared methods are covered in more detail in relation to objects in Chapter 2; for the purpose of this chapter, the point is that you can reference the class `String` followed by a "." and see a list of shared methods for that class. For strings, this list includes the following:

Shared Methods	Description
`Empty`	This is actually a property. It can be used when an empty `String` is required. It can be used for comparison or initialization of a `String`.
`Compare`	Compares two objects of type `String`
`CompareOrdinal`	Compares two `Strings`, without considering the local national language or culture
`Concat`	Concatenates one or more `Strings`
`Copy`	Creates a new `String` with the same value as an instance provided
`Equals`	Determines whether two `Strings` have the same value
`IsNullorEmpty`	This shared method is a very efficient way of determining whether a given variable has been set to the empty string or `Nothing`.

Not only have creation methods been encapsulated, but other string-specific methods, such as character and substring searching, and case changes, are now available from `String` objects instances.

The SubString Method

The .NET `String` class has a method called `SubString`. Thanks to overloading, covered in Chapter 2, there are two versions of this method: The first accepts a starting position and the number of characters to retrieve, while the second accepts simply the starting location. The following code shows examples of using both of these methods on an instance of a String:

```
Dim strMyString as String = "Hello World"

Console.WriteLine(strMystring.SubString(0,5))
Console.WriteLine(strMyString.SubString(6))
```

The PadLeft and PadRight Methods

These methods enable you to justify a String so that it is left- or right-justified. As with SubString, the PadLeft and PadRight methods are overloaded. The first version of these methods requires only a maximum length of the String, and then uses spaces to pad the String. The other version requires two parameters: the length of the returned String and the character that should be used to pad the original String. An example of working with the PadLeft method is as follows:

```
Dim strMyString as String = "Hello World"

Console.WriteLine(strMyString.PadLeft(30))
Console.WriteLine(strMyString.PadLeft(20,"."c))
```

The String.Split Method

This instance method on a string is designed to enable you to take a string and separate out that string into an array of components. For example, if you want to quickly find each of the different elements in a comma-delimited string, you could use the Split method to turn the string into an array of smaller strings, each of which contains one field of data. In the following example, the stringarray variable will contain an array of three elements:

```
Dim strMyString As String = "Column1, Col2, Col3"
Dim stringarray As String() = strMyString.Split(","c)
Console.WriteLine(stringarray.Count.ToString())
```

The String Class Is Immutable

The Visual Basic String class isn't entirely different from the String type that VB programmers have used for years. The majority of string behaviors remain unchanged, and the majority of methods are now available as classes. However, to support the default behavior that people associate with the String primitive type, the String class isn't declared in the same way as several other classes. Strings in .NET do not allow editing of their data. When a portion of a string is changed or copied, the operating system allocates a new memory location and copies the resulting string to this new location. This ensures that when a string is copied to a second variable, the new variable references its own copy.

To support this behavior in .NET, the String class is defined as an *immutable class*. This means that each time a change is made to the data associated with a string, a new instance is created, and the original referenced memory is released for garbage collection. This is an expensive operation, but the result is that the String class behaves as people expect a primitive type to behave. Additionally, when a copy of a string is made, the String class forces a new version of the data into the referenced memory. This ensures that each instance of a string references only its own memory. Consider the following code:

```
Dim strMyString as String
Dim intLoop as Integer
```

```
For intLoop = 1 to 1000
    strMyString = strMyString & "A very long string "
Next
Console.WriteLine(strMyString)
```

This code does not perform well. For each assignment operation on the `strMyString` variable, the system allocates a new memory buffer based on the size of the new string, and copies both the current value of `strMyString` and the new text that is to be appended. The system then frees the previous memory that must be reclaimed by the garbage collector. As this loop continues, the new memory allocation requires a larger chunk of memory. Therefore, operations such as this can take a long time. However, .NET offers an alternative in the `System.Text.StringBuilder` object, shown in the following example:

```
Dim objMyStrBldr as New System.Text.StringBuilder()
Dim intLoop as Integer

For intLoop = 1 to 1000
    ObjMyStrBldr.Append("A very long string ")
Next
Console.WriteLine(objMyStrBldr.ToString())
```

The preceding code works with strings but does not use the `String` class. The .NET class library contains a class called `System.Text.StringBuilder`, which performs better when strings will be edited repeatedly. This class does not store strings in the conventional manner; it stores them as individual characters, with code in place to manage the ordering of those characters. Thus, editing or appending more characters does not involve allocating new memory for the entire string. Because the preceding code snippet does not need to reallocate the memory used for the entire string, each time another set of characters is appended it performs significantly faster. Ultimately, an instance of the `String` class is never explicitly needed because the `StringBuilder` class implements the `ToString` method to roll up all of the characters into a string. While the concept of the `StringBuilder` class isn't new, because it is now available as part of the Visual Basic implementation, developers no longer need to create their own string memory managers.

String Constants

If you ever have to produce output based on a string you'll quickly find yourself needing to embed certain constant values. For example, it's always useful to be able to add a carriage-return linefeed combination to trigger a new line in a message box. One way to do this is to learn the underlying ASCII codes and then embed these control characters directly into your string or string-builder object.

Visual Basic provides an easier solution for working with these: the `Microsoft.VisualBasic.Constants` class. The `Constants` class, which you can tell by its namespace is specific to Visual Basic, contains definitions for several standard string values that you might want to embed. The most common, of course, is `Constants.VbCrLf`, which represents the carriage-return linefeed combination. Feel free to explore this class for additional constants that you might need to manipulate string output.

The DBNull Class and IsDBNull Function

When working with a database, a value for a given column may not be defined. For a reference type this isn't a problem, as it is possible to set reference types to `Nothing`. However, for value types, it is necessary to determine whether a given column from the database or other source has an actual value.

The first way to manage this task is to leverage the DBNull call and the IsDBNull function. The IsDBNull function accepts an object as its parameter and returns a Boolean that indicates whether the variable has been initialized.

In addition to this method, Visual Basic has access to the DBNull class. This class is part of the System namespace, and to use it you declare a local variable with the DBNull type. This variable is then used with an is comparison operator to determine whether a given variable has been initialized:

```
Dim sysNull As System.DBNull = System.DBNull.Value
Dim strMyString As String = Nothing

If strMyString Is sysNull Then
   strMyString = "Initialize my String"
End If
If Not IsDBNull(strMyString) Then
   Console.WriteLine(strMyString)
End If
```

In this code, the strMyString variable is declared and initialized to Nothing. The first conditional is evaluated to True, and as a result the string is initialized. The second conditional then ensures that the declared variable has been initialized. Because this was accomplished in the preceding code, this condition is also True. In both cases, the sysNull value is used not to verify the type of the object, but to verify that it has not yet been instantiated with a value.

Nullable Types

In addition to having the option to explicitly check for the DBNull value, Visual Basic 2005 introduced the capability to create a nullable value type. In the background, when this syntax is used, the system creates a reference type containing the same data that would be used by the value type. Your code can then check the value of the nullable type before attempting to set this into a value type variable. Nullable types are built using generics, discussed in Chapter 6.

For consistency, however, let's take a look at how nullable types work. The key, of course, is that value types can't be set to null. This is why nullable types aren't value types. The following statement shows how to declare a nullable integer:

```
Dim intValue as Nullable(Of Integer)
```

The intValue variable acts like an integer, but isn't actually an integer. As noted, the syntax is based on generics, but essentially you have just declared an object of type Nullable and declared that this object will, in fact, hold integer data. Thus, both of the following assignment statements are valid:

```
intValue = 123
intValue = Nothing
```

However, at some point you are going to need to pass intValue to a method as a parameter, or set some property on an object that is looking for an object of type Integer. Because intValue is actually of type Nullable, it has the properties of a nullable object. The nullable class has two properties of interest when you want to get the underlying value. The first is the property value. This represents the underlying value type associated with this object. In an ideal scenario, you would just use the value property of the nullable object in order to assign to your actual value a type of integer and everything would work. If the `intValue.value` wasn't assigned, you would get the same value as if you had just declared a new `Integer` without assigning it a value.

Unfortunately, that's not how the nullable type works. If the `intValue.value` property contains `Nothing` and you attempt to assign it, then it throws an exception. To avoid getting this exception, you always need to check the other property of the nullable type: `HasValue`. The `HasValue` property is a Boolean that indicates whether a value exists; if one does not, then you shouldn't reference the underlying value. The following code example shows how to safely use a nullable type:

```
Dim int as Integer
If intValue.HasValue Then
    int = intValue.Value
End If
```

Of course, you could add an `Else` statement to the preceding and use either `Integer.MinValue` or `Integer.MaxValue` as an indicator that the original value was `Nothing`. The key point here is that nullable types enable you to easily work with nullable columns in your database, but you must still verify whether an actual value or null was returned.

Arrays

It is possible to declare any type as an array of that type. Because an array is a modifier of another type, the basic `Array` class is never explicitly declared for a variable's type. The `System.Array` class that serves as the base for all arrays is defined such that it cannot be created, but must be inherited. As a result, to create an `Integer` array, a set of parentheses is added to the declaration of the variable. These parentheses indicate that the system should create an array of the type specified. The parentheses used in the declaration may be empty or may contain the size of the array. An array can be defined as having a single dimension using a single number, or as having multiple dimensions.

All .NET arrays at an index of zero have a defined number of elements. However, the way an array is declared in Visual Basic varies slightly from other .NET languages such as C#. Back when the first .NET version of Visual Basic was announced, it was also announced that arrays would always begin at 0 and that they would be defined based on the number of elements in the array. In other words, Visual Basic would work the same way as the other initial .NET languages. However, in older versions of Visual Basic, it is possible to specify that an array should start at 1 instead of 0. This meant that a lot of existing code didn't define arrays based on their upper limit. To resolve this issue, the engineers at Microsoft decided on a compromise: All arrays in .NET begin at 0, but when an array is declared in Visual Basic, the definition is based on the upper limit of the array, not the number of elements.

The main result of this upper-limit declaration is that arrays defined in Visual Basic have one more entry by definition than those defined with other .NET languages. Note that it's still possible to declare an array in Visual Basic and reference it in C# or another .NET language. The following code illustrates some simple examples that demonstrate five different ways to create arrays, using a simple integer array as the basis for the comparison:

```
Dim arrMyIntArray1(20) as Integer
Dim arrMyIntArray2() as Integer = {1, 2, 3, 4}
Dim arrMyIntArray3(4,2) as Integer
Dim arrMyIntArray4( , ) as Integer = _
    { {1, 2, 3},{4, 5, 6}, {7, 8, 9},{10, 11, 12},{13, 14 , 15} }
Dim arrMyIntArray5() as Integer
```

In the first case, the code defines an array of integers that spans from `arrMyIntArray1(0)` to `arrMyIntArray1(20)`. This is a 21-element array, because all arrays start at 0 and end with the value defined in the declaration as the upper bound. The second statement creates an array with four elements numbered 0 through 3, containing the values 1 to 4. The third statement creates a multidimensional array containing five elements at the first level, with each of those elements containing three child elements. The challenge is to remember that all subscripts go from 0 to the upper bound, meaning that each array contains one more element than its upper bound. The result is an array with 15 elements. The next line of code, the fourth, shows an alternative way of creating the same array, but in this case there are four elements, each containing four elements, with subscripts from 0 to 3 at each level. Finally, the last line demonstrates that it is possible to simply declare a variable and indicate that the variable is an array, without specifying the number of elements in the array.

Multidimensional Arrays

As shown earlier in the sample array declarations, the definition of `arrMyIntArray3` is a multi-dimensional array. This declaration creates an array with 15 elements (five in the first range, each containing three elements) ranging from `arrMyIntArray3(0,0)` through `arrMyIntArray3(2,1)` to `arrMyIntArray3(4,2)`. As with all elements of an array, when it is created without specific values, the value of each of these elements is created with the default value for that type. This case also demonstrates that the size of the different dimensions can vary. It is possible to nest deeper than two levels, but this should be done with care because such code is difficult to maintain.

The fourth declaration shown previously creates `arrMyIntArray4(, )` with predefined values. The values are mapped based on the outer set being the first dimension and the inner values being associated with the next inner dimension. For example, the value of `arrMyIntArray4(0,1)` is 2, while the value of `arrMyIntArray4(2,3)` is 12. The following code snippet illustrates this using a set of nested loops to traverse the array. It also provides an example of calling the `UBound` method with a second parameter to specify that you are interested in the upper bound for the second dimension of the array:

```
Dim intLoop1 as Integer
Dim intLoop2 as Integer
For intLoop1 = 0 to UBound(arrMyIntArray4)
  For intLoop2 = 0 to UBound(arrMyIntArray4, 2)
    Console.WriteLine arrMyIntArray4(intLoop1, intLoop2).ToString
  Next
Next
```

The UBound Function

Continuing to reference the arrays defined earlier, the declaration of `arrMyIntArray2` actually defined an array that spans from `arrMyIntArray2(0)` to `arrMyIntArray2(3)`. This is the case because when you declare an array by specifying the set of values, it still starts at 0. However, in this case you are not specifying the upper bound, but rather initializing the array with a set of values. If this set of values came from a database or other source, then it might not be clear what the upper limit on the array was. To verify the upper bound of an array, a call can be made to the `UBound` function:

```
Console.Writeline CStr(UBound(ArrMyIntArray2))
```

The preceding line of code retrieves the upper bound of the first dimension of the array. However, as noted in the preceding section, you can specify an array with several different dimensions. Thus, this old-style method of retrieving the upper bound carries the potential for an error of omission. The better way to retrieve the upper bound is to use the `GetUpperBound` method. In this case, you need to tell the array which upper-bound value you want, as shown here:

```
ArrMyIntArray2.GetUpperBound(0)
```

This is the preferred method of getting an array's upper bound because it explicitly indicates which upper bound is wanted when using multidimensional arrays.

The `UBound` function has a companion called `LBound`. The `LBound` function computes the lower bound for a given array. However, as all arrays and collections in Visual Basic are 0-based, it doesn't have much value anymore.

The ReDim Statement

The final declaration demonstrated previously is for `arrMyIntArray5()`. This is an example of an array that has not yet been instantiated. If an attempt were made to assign a value to this array, it would trigger an exception. The solution to this is to use the `ReDim` keyword. Although `ReDim` was part of Visual Basic 6.0, it has changed slightly. The first change is that code must first `Dim` an instance of the variable; it is not acceptable to declare an array using the `ReDim` statement. The second change is that code cannot change the number of dimensions in an array. For example, an array with three dimensions cannot grow to an array of four dimensions, nor can it be reduced to only two dimensions. To further extend the example code associated with arrays, consider the following, which manipulates some of the arrays previously declared. Note that the `arrMyIntArray5` declaration was repeated for this example because this variable isn't actually usable until after it is redimensioned in the following code:

```
Dim arrMyIntArray5() as Integer

' The commented statement below would compile but would cause a runtime exception.
'arrMyIntArray5(0) = 1

ReDim arrMyIntArray5(2)
ReDim arrMyIntArray3(5,4)
ReDim Preserve arrMyIntArray4(UBound(arrMyIntArray4),2)
```

The `ReDim` of `arrMyIntArray5` instantiates the elements of the array so that values can be assigned to each element. The second statement redimensions the `arrMyIntArray3` variable defined earlier. Note that it is changing the size of both the first dimension and the second dimension. While it is not possible to change the number of dimensions in an array, it is possible to resize any of an array's dimensions. This capability is required if declarations such as `Dim arrMyIntArray6( , , ,) As Integer` are to be legal.

By the way, while it is possible to repeatedly `ReDim` a variable, this type of action should ideally be done only rarely, and never within a loop. If you intend to loop through a set of entries and add entries to an array, try to determine the number of entries you'll need before entering the loop, or at a minimum `ReDim` the size of your array in chunks to improve performance.

The Preserve Keyword

The last item in the code snippet in the preceding section illustrates an additional keyword associated with redimensioning. The `Preserve` keyword indicates that the data stored in the array prior to redimensioning should be transferred to the newly created array. If this keyword is not used, then the data stored in an array is lost. Additionally, in the preceding example, the `ReDim` statement actually reduces the second dimension of the array. While this is a perfectly legal statement, this means that even though you have specified preserving the data, the data values 4, 8, 12, and 16 that were assigned in the original definition of this array will be discarded. These are lost because they were assigned in the highest index of the second array. Because arrMyIntArray4(1,3) is no longer valid, the value that resided at this location has been lost.

Arrays continue to be very powerful in Visual Basic, but the basic Array class is just that, basic. It provides a powerful framework, but it does not provide a lot of other features that would allow for more robust logic to be built into the array. To achieve more advanced features, such as sorting and dynamic allocation, the base Array class has been inherited by the classes that make up the Collections namespace.

Collections

The Collections namespace is part of the System namespace and provides a series of classes that implement advanced array features. While the capability to make an array of existing types is powerful, sometimes more power is needed in the array itself. The capability to inherently sort or dynamically add dissimilar objects in an array is provided by the classes of the Collections namespace. This namespace contains a specialized set of objects that can be instantiated for additional features when working with a collection of similar objects. The following table defines several of the objects that are available as part of the System.Collections namespace:

Class	Description
ArrayList	Implements an array whose size increases automatically as elements are added
BitArray	Manages an array of Booleans that are stored as bit values
Hashtable	Implements a collection of values organized by key. Sorting is done based on a hash of the key.
Queue	Implements a first in, first out collection
SortedList	Implements a collection of values with associated keys. The values are sorted by key and are accessible by key or index.
Stack	Implements a last in, first out collection

Each of the objects listed focuses on storing a collection of objects. This means that in addition to the special capabilities each provides, it also provides one additional capability not available to objects created based on the Array class. In short, because every variable in .NET is based on the Object class, it is possible to have a collection defined, because one of these objects contains elements that are defined with different types. This is true because each of these collection types stores an array of objects, and because all classes are of type Object, a string could be stored alongside an integer value. As a result, it's possible within the collection classes for the actual objects being stored to be different. Consider the following example code:

```
Dim objMyArrList As New System.Collections.ArrayList()
Dim objItem As Object
Dim intLine As Integer = 1
Dim strHello As String = "Hello"
```

```
Dim objWorld As New System.Text.StringBuilder("World")

' Add an integer value to the array list.
objMyArrList.Add(intLine)

' Add an instance of a string object
objMyArrList.Add(strHello)

' Add a single character cast as a character.
objMyArrList.Add(" "c)

' Add an object that isn't a primitive type.
objMyArrList.Add(objWorld)

' To balance the string, insert a break between the line
' and the string "Hello", by inserting a string constant.
objMyArrList.Insert(1, ". ")

For Each objItem In objMyArrList
  ' Output the values...
  Console.Write(objItem.ToString())
Next
Console.WriteLine()
For Each objItem In objMyArrList
  ' Output the types...
  Console.Write(objItem.GetType.ToString() + " : ")
Next
```

The preceding code is an example of implementing the `ArrayList` collection class. The collection classes, as this example shows, are versatile. The preceding code creates a new instance of an `ArrayList`, along with some related variables to support the demonstration. The code then shows four different types of variables being inserted into the same `ArrayList`. Next, the code inserts another value into the middle of the list. At no time has the size of the array been declared, nor has a redefinition of the array size been required.

Part of the reason for this is that the `Add` and `Insert` methods on the `ArrayList` class are defined to accept a parameter of type `Object`. This means that the `ArrayList` object can literally accept any value in .NET.

Specialized and Generic Collections

Visual Basic has additional classes available as part of the `System.Collections.Specialized` name-space. These classes tend to be oriented around a specific problem. For example, the `ListDictionary` class is designed to take advantage of the fact that while a hash table is very good at storing and retrieving a large number of items, it can be costly when there are only a few items. Similarly, the `StringCollection` and `StringDictionary` classes are defined so that when working with strings, the time spent interpreting the type of object is reduced and overall performance is improved. Each class defined in this namespace represents a specialized implementation that has been optimized for handling specific data types.

This specialization is different from the specialization provided by one of the features introduced with Visual Studio 2005 and .NET 2.0, generics. The `System.Collections.Generics` namespace contains versions of the collection classes that have been defined to support generics. The basic idea of generics is that because performance costs and reliability concerns are associated with casting to and from the object type, collections should allow you to specify what specific type they will contain. Generics not only prevent you from paying the cost of boxing for value types but, more important, add to the capability to create type-safe code at compile time. Generics are a powerful extension to the .NET environment and are covered in detail in Chapter 6.

Commands: Looping Statements

Just as with conditional statements, it is possible in Visual Basic to loop or cycle through all of the elements in an array. The preceding examples have relied on the use of the For statement, which has not yet been covered. Since you've now covered both arrays and collections, it's appropriate to introduce the primary commands for working with the elements contained in those variable types. Both the For loop and While loop share similar characteristics, and which to use is often a matter of preference.

For Each and For Next

The For structure in Visual Basic is the primary way of managing loops. It actually has two different formats. A standard For Next statement enables you to set a loop control variable that can be incremented by the For statement and custom exit criteria from your loop. Alternatively, if you are working with a collection in which the items in the array are not indexed numerically, then it is possible to use a For Each loop to automatically loop through all of the items in that collection. The following code shows a typical For Next statement that cycles through each of the items in an array:

```
For i As Integer = 0 To 10 Step 2
    arrMyIntArray1(i) = i
Next
```

The preceding example sets the value of every other array element to its index, starting with the first item, since like all .NET collections, the collection starts at 0. The result is that items 0, 2, 4, 6, 8, 10 are set, but items 1, 3, 5, 7, 9 may not be defined because the loop doesn't address that value.

The For Next structure is most commonly set up to traverse an array or similar construct (for example, a data set). The control variable i in the preceding example must be numeric. The value can be incremented from a starting value to an ending value, which are 0 and 10, respectively, in this example. Finally, it is possible to accept the default increment of 1; or, if desired, you can add a Step qualifier to your command and update the control value by a value other than 1. Note that setting the value of Step to 0 means that your loop will theoretically loop an infinite number of times. Best practices suggest your control value should be an integer greater than 0 and not a decimal or other floating-point number.

Visual Basic provides two additional commands that can be used within the For loop's block to enhance performance. The first is Exit For; and as you might expect, this statement causes the loop to end and not continue to the end of the processing. The other is Continue, which tells the loop that you are finished executing code with the current control value and that it should increment the value and reenter the loop for its next iteration:

```
For i = 1 To 100 Step 2
    If arrMyIntArray1.Count <= i Then Exit For
    If i = 5 Then Continue For
    arrMyIntArray1 (i) = i - 1
Next
```

Both the `Exit For` and `Continue` keywords were used in the preceding example. Note how each uses a format of the `If-Then` structure that places the command on the same line as the `If` statement so that no `End If` statement is required. This loop exits if the control value is larger than the number of rows defined for `arrMyIntArray1`.

Next, if the control variable `i` indicates you are looking at the sixth item in the array (index of five), then this row is to be ignored but processing should continue within the loop. Keep in mind that even though the loop control variable starts at 1, the first element of the array is still at zero. The `Continue` statement indicates that the loop should return to the `For` statement and increment the associated control variable. Thus, the code does not process the next line for item six, where `i` equals 5.

The preceding examples demonstrate that in most cases, because your loop is going to process a known collection, Visual Basic provides a command that encapsulates the management of the loop control variable. The `For Each` structure automates the counting process and enables you to quickly assign the current item from the collection so that you can act on it in your code. It is a common way to process all of the rows in a data set or most any other collection, and all of the loop control elements such as `Continue` and `Exit` are still available:

```
For Each item As Object In objMyArrList
    'Code A1
Next
```

While, Do While, and Do Until

In addition to the `For` loop, Visual Basic includes the `While` and `Do` loops, with two different versions of the `Do` loop. The first is the `Do While` loop. With a `Do While` loop, your code starts by checking for a condition; and as long as that condition is true, it executes the code contained in the `Do` loop. Optionally, instead of starting the loop by checking the `While` condition, the code can enter the loop and then check the condition at the end of the loop. The `Do Until` loop is similar to the `Do While` loop:

```
Do While blnTrue = True
    'Code A1
Loop
```

The `Do Until` differs from the `Do While` only in that, by convention, the condition for a `Do Until` is placed after the code block, thus requiring the code in the `Do` block to execute once before the condition is checked. It bears repeating, however, that a `Do Until` block can place the `Until` condition with the `Do` statement instead of with the `Loop` statement, and a `Do While` block can similarly have its condition at the end of the loop:

```
Do
    'Code A1
Loop Until (blnTrue = True)
```

In both cases, instead of basing the loop around an array of items or a fixed number of iterations, the loop is instead instructed to continue perpetually until a condition is met. A good use for these loops involves tasks that need to repeat for as long as your application is running. Similar to the `For` loop, there are `Exit Do` and `Continue` commands that end the loop or move to the next iteration, respectively. Note that parentheses are allowed but are not required for both the `While` and the `Until` conditional expression.

The other format for creating a loop is to omit the Do statement and just create a While loop. The While loop works similarly to the Do loop, with the following differences. First, the While loop's endpoint is an End While statement instead of a loop statement. Second, the condition must be at the start of the loop with the While statement, similar to the Do While. Finally, the While loop has an Exit While statement instead of Exit Do, although the behavior is the same. An example is shown here:

```
While blnTrue = True
    If blnFalse Then
        blnTrue = False
    End if
    If not blnTrue Then Exit While
    System.Threading.Thread.Sleep(500)
    blnFalse = True
End While
```

The While loop has more in common with the For loop, and in those situations where someone is familiar with another language such as C++ or C#, it is more likely to be used than the older Do-Loop syntax that is more specific to Visual Basic.

Finally, before leaving the discussion of looping, note the potential use of endless loops. Seemingly endless, or infinite, loops play a role in application development, so it's worthwhile to illustrate how you might use one. For example, if you were writing an e-mail program, you might want to check the user's mailbox on the server every 20 seconds. You could create a Do While or Do Until loop that contains the code to open a network connection and check the server for any new mail messages to download. You would continue this process until either the application was closed or you were unable to connect to the server. When the application was asked to close, the loop's Exit statement would execute, thus terminating the loop. Similarly, if the code were unable to connect to the server, it might exit the current loop, alert the user, and probably start a loop that would look for network connectivity on a regular basis.

One warning with endless loops: Always include a call to Thread.Sleep so that the loop only executes a single iteration within a given time frame to avoid consuming too much processor time.

Boxing

Normally, when a conversion (implicit or explicit) occurs, the original value is read from its current memory location, and then the new value is assigned. For example, to convert a Short to a Long, the system reads the two bytes of Short data and writes them to the appropriate bytes for the Long variable. However, under Visual Basic, if a value type needs to be managed as an object, then the system performs an intermediate step. This intermediate step involves taking the value on the stack and copying it to the heap, a process referred to as *boxing*. As noted earlier, the Object class is implemented as a reference type, so the system needs to convert value types into reference types for them to be objects. This doesn't cause any problems or require any special programming, because boxing isn't something you declare or directly control, but it does affect performance.

If you're copying the data for a single value type, this is not a significant cost, but if you're processing an array that contains thousands of values, the time spent moving between a value type and a temporary reference type can be significant.

Fortunately, there are ways to limit the amount of boxing that occurs. One method that works well is to create a class based on the value type you need to work with. This might seem counterintuitive at first because it costs more to create a class. The key is how often you reuse the data contained in the class. By repeatedly using the object to interact with other objects, you avoid creating a temporary boxed object.

Examples in two important areas will help illustrate boxing. The first involves the use of arrays. When an array is created, the portion of the class that tracks the element of the array is created as a reference object, but each element of the array is created directly. Thus, an array of integers consists of the array object and a set of integer value types. When you update one of these values with another integer value, no boxing is involved:

```
Dim arrInt(20) as Integer
Dim intMyValue as Integer = 1

arrInt(0) = 0
arrInt(1) = intMyValue
```

Neither of these assignments of an integer value into the integer array that was defined previously requires boxing. In each case, the array object identifies which value on the stack needs to be referenced, and the value is assigned to that value type. The point here is that just because you have referenced an object doesn't mean you are going to box a value. The boxing occurs only when the values being assigned are being transitioned from value types to reference types:

```
Dim strBldr as New System.Text.StringBuilder()
Dim mySortedList as New System.Collections.SortedList()
Dim count as Integer
For count = 1 to 100
  strBldr.Append(count)
  mySortedList.Add(count, count)
Next
```

The preceding snippet illustrates two separate calls to object interfaces. One call requires boxing of the value intCount, while the other does not. Nothing in the code indicates which call is which, but the Append method of StringBuilder has been overridden to include a version that accepts an integer, while the Add method of the SortedList collection expects two objects. Although the integer values can be recognized by the system as objects, doing so requires the runtime library to box these values so that they can be added to the sorted list.

The key to boxing isn't that you are working with objects as part of an action, but that you are passing a value to a parameter that expects an object, or you are taking an object and converting it to a value type. However, boxing does not occur when you call a method on a value type. There is no conversion to an object, so if you need to assign an integer to a string using the ToString method, there is no boxing of the integer value as part of the creation of the string. Conversely, you are explicitly creating a new string object, so the cost is similar.

Parameter Passing

When an object's methods or an assembly's procedures and methods are called, it's often appropriate to provide input for the data to be operated on by the code. The values are referred to as *parameters*, and any object can be passed as a parameter to a Function or Sub.

When passing parameters, be aware of whether the parameter is being passed "by value" (ByVal) or "by reference" (ByRef). Passing a parameter by value means that if the value of that variable is changed, then when the `Function`/`Sub` returns, the system automatically restores that variable to the value it had before the call. Passing a parameter by reference means that if changes are made to the value of a variable, then these changes affect the actual variable and, therefore, are still present when the variable returns.

This is where it gets a little challenging for new Visual Basic developers. Under .NET, passing a parameter by value indicates only how the top-level reference (the portion of the variable on the stack) for that object is passed. Sometimes referred to as a *shallow copy operation*, the system copies only the top-level reference value for an object passed by value. This is important to remember because it means that referenced memory is not protected. When you pass an integer by value, if the program changes the value of the integer, then your original value is restored. Conversely, if you pass a reference type, then only the location of your referenced memory is protected, not the data located within that memory location. Thus, while the reference passed as part of the parameter remains unchanged for the calling method, the actual values stored in referenced objects can be updated even when an object is passed by value.

In addition to mandatory parameters, which must be passed with a call to a given function, it is possible to declare optional parameters. Optional parameters can be omitted by the calling code. This way, it is possible to call a method such as `PadRight`, passing either a single parameter defining the length of the string and using a default of space for the padding character, or with two parameters, the first still defining the length of the string but the second now replacing the default of space with a dash.

```
Public Function PadRight(ByVal intSize as Integer, _
                    Optional ByVal chrPad as Char = " "c)
End Function
```

To use default parameters, it is necessary to make them the last parameters in the function declaration. Visual Basic also requires that every optional parameter have a default value. It is not acceptable to merely declare a parameter and assign it the `Optional` keyword. In Visual Basic, the `Optional` keyword must be accompanied by a value that is assigned if the parameter is not passed in.

ParamArray

In addition to passing explicit parameters, it is also possible to tell .NET that you would like to allow a user to pass any number of parameters of the same type. This is called a *parameter array*, and it enables a user to pass as many instances of a given parameter as are appropriate. For example, the following code creates a function `Add`, which allows a user to pass an array of integers and get the sum of these integers:

```
Public Function Add(ByVal ParamArray values() As Integer) As Long
    Dim result As Long = 0
    For Each value As Integer In values
        result += value
    Next
    Return result
End Function
```

The preceding code illustrates a function (first shown at the beginning of this chapter without its implementation) that accepts an array of integers. Notice that the `ParamArray` qualifier is preceded by a `ByVal` qualifier for this parameter. The `ParamArray` requires that the associated parameters be passed by value; they cannot be optional parameters.

You might think this looks like a standard parameter passed by value except that it's an array, but there is more to it than that. In fact, the power of the `ParamArray` derives from how it can be called, which also explains many of its limitations. The following code shows one way this method can be called:

```
Dim int1 as Integer = 2
Dim int2 as Integer = 3
Dim sum as Long = Add(1, int1, int2)
```

Notice that the preceding line, which calls this `Add` function, doesn't pass an array of integers; instead, it passes three distinct integer values. The `ParamArray` keyword tells Visual Basic to automatically join these three distinct values into an array for use within this method. However, the following lines also represent an acceptable way to call this method, by passing an actual array of values:

```
Dim myIntArray() as Integer = {1, 2, 3, 4}
Dim sum as Long = Add(myIntArray)
```

Finally, note one last limitation on the `ParamArray` keyword: It can only be used on the last parameter defined for a given method. Because Visual Basic is grabbing an unlimited number of input values to create the array, there is no way to indicate the end of this array, so it must be the final parameter.

Variable Scope

The concept of variable scope encapsulates two key elements. In all the discussion so far of variables, we have not focused on the allocation and deallocation of those variables from memory. The first allocation challenge is related to what happens when you declare two variables with the same name but at different locations in the code. For example, suppose a class declares a variable called `myObj` that holds a property for that class. Then, within one of that class's methods, you declare a different variable also named `myObj`. What will happen in that method? *Scope* defines the lifetime and precedence of every variable you declare, and it handles this question.

Similarly, there is question of the removal of variables that you are no longer using, so you can free up memory. Chapter 4 covers the collection of variables and memory once it is no longer needed by an application, so this discussion focuses on priority, with the understanding that when a variable is no longer "in scope," it is available to the garbage collector for cleanup.

.NET essentially defines four levels of variable scope. The outermost scope is *global*. Essentially, just as your source code defines classes, it can also declare variables that exist the entire time that your application runs. These variables have the longest lifetime because they exist as long as your application is executing. Conversely, these variables have the lowest precedence. Thus, if within a class or method you declare another variable with the same name, then the variable with the smaller, more local scope is used before the global version.

After global scope, the next scope is at the *class* or *module* level. When you add properties to a class, you are creating variables that will be created with each instance of that class. The methods of that class will then reference those member variables from the class, before looking for any global variables. Note that because these variables are defined within a class, they are only visible to methods within that class. The scope and lifetime of these variables is limited by the lifetime of that class, and when the class is removed from the system, so are those variables. More important, those variables declared in one instance of a class are not visible in other classes or in other instances of the same class (unless you actively expose them, in which case the object instance is used to fully qualify a reference to them; this concept is explored further in Chapter 2).

The next shorter lifetime and smaller scope is that of method variables. When you declare a new variable within a method, such variables, as well as those declared as parameters, are only visible to code that exists within that module. Thus, the method Add wouldn't see or use variables declared in the method Subtract in the same class.

Finally, within a given method are various commands that can encapsulate a block of code (mentioned earlier in this chapter). Commands such as If Then and For Each create blocks of code within a method, and it is possible within this block of code to declare new variables. These variables then have a scope of only that block of code. Thus, variables declared within an If Then block or a For loop only exist within the constraints of the If block or execution of the loop. Creating variables in a For loop is a known performance mistake and should be avoided.

Data Type Conversions

So far, this chapter has focused primarily on individual variables; but when developing software, it is often necessary to take a numeric value and convert it to a string to display in a text box. Similarly, it is often necessary to accept input from a text box and convert this input to a numeric value. These conversions, unlike some, can be done in one of two fashions: *implicitly* or *explicitly*.

Implicit conversions are those that rely on the system taking the data at runtime and adjusting it to the new type without any guidance. Often, Visual Basic's default settings enable developers to write code containing many implicit conversions that the developer may not even notice.

Explicit conversions, conversely, are those for which the developer recognizes the need to change a variable's type and assign it to a different variable. Unlike implicit conversions, explicit conversions are easily recognizable within the code. Some languages such as C# require that essentially all conversions that might be type unsafe be done through an explicit conversion; otherwise, an error is thrown.

It is therefore important to understand what a type-safe implicit conversion is. In short, it's a conversion that cannot fail because of the nature of the data involved. For example, if you assign the value of a smaller type, Short, into a larger type, Long, then there is no way this conversion can fail. As both values are integer-style numbers, and the maximum and minimum values of a Short variable are well within the range of a Long, this conversion will always succeed and can safely be handled as an implicit conversion:

```
Dim shortNumber As Short = 32767
Dim longNumber As Long = shortNumber
```

However, the reverse of this is not a type-safe conversion. In a system that demands explicit conversions, the assignment of a Long value to a Short variable results in a compilation error, as the compiler doesn't have any safe way to handle the assignment when the larger value is outside the range of the smaller value. It is still possible to explicitly cast a value from a larger type to a smaller type, but this is an explicit conversion. By default, Visual Basic supports certain unsafe implicit conversions. Thus, adding the following line will not, by default, cause an error under Visual Basic:

```
shortNumber = longNumber
```

This is possible for two reasons. One is based on Visual Basic's legacy support. Previous versions of Visual Basic supported the capability to implicitly cast across types that don't fit the traditional implicit casting boundaries. It has been maintained in the language because one of the goals of Visual Basic is to support rapid prototyping. In a rapid prototyping model, a developer is writing code that "works" for demonstration purposes but may not be ready for deployment. This distinction is important because in the discussion of implicit conversions, you should always keep in mind that they are not a best practice for production software.

Implicit Conversions and Compiler Options

As noted in the introduction to this section, Visual Basic supports certain unsafe implicit conversions. This capability is on by default but can be disabled in two ways. The first method is specific to each source file and involves adding a line to the top of the source file to indicate to the compiler the status of Option Strict.

The following line will override whatever the default project setting for Option Strict is for your project. However, while this can be done on a per-source listing basis, this is not the recommended way to manage Option Strict. For starters, consistently adding this line to each of your source files isn't a good practice:

```
Option Strict On
```

The preferred method to manage the Option Strict setting is to change the setting for your entire project. Without going into details about the XML associated with your project file, the easiest way to accomplish this is to use Visual Studio 2008. Visual Studio 2008 and the various versions of this tool are discussed in more detail in Chapter 13; however, for completeness, the compilation settings are discussed in this context.

Visual Studio 2008 includes a tab on the Project Settings page to edit the compiler settings for an entire project. You can access this screen by right-clicking the project in the Solution Explorer and selecting Properties from the context menu. When you select the Compile tab of the Project Properties dialog, you should see a window similar to the one shown in Figure 1-4.

Aside from your default project file output directory, this page contains several compiler options. These options are covered here because the Option Explicit and Option Strict settings directly affect your variable usage:

❑　**Option Explicit** — This option has not changed from previous versions of Visual Basic. When enabled, it ensures that every variable is explicitly declared. Of course, if you are using Option Strict, then this setting doesn't matter because the compiler won't recognize the type of an undeclared variable. To my knowledge, there's no good reason to ever turn this option off.

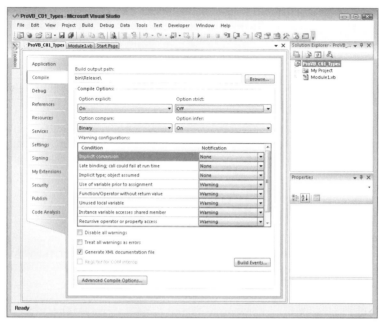

Figure 1-4

❑ **Option Strict** — When this option is enabled, the compiler must be able to determine the type of each variable, and if an assignment between two variables requires a type conversion — for example, from `Integer` to `Boolean` — then the conversion between the two types must be expressed explicitly. This setting can be edited by adding an Option Strict declaration to the top of your source code file. The statement within a source file applies to all of the code entered in that source file, but only to the code in that file.

❑ **Option Compare** — This option determines whether strings should be compared as binary strings or whether the array of characters should be compared as text. In most cases, leaving this as binary is appropriate. Doing a text comparison requires the system to convert the binary values that are stored internally prior to comparison. However, the advantage of a text-based comparison is that the character "A" is equal to "a" because the comparison is case-insensitive. This enables you to perform comparisons that don't require an explicit case conversion of the compared strings. In most cases, however, this conversion still occurs, so it's better to use binary comparison and explicitly convert the case as required.

❑ **Option Infer** — This option is new to Visual Studio 2008 and is brought to you by the require-ments of LINQ. When you execute a LINQ statement, you can have returned a data table that may or may not be completely typed in advance. As a result, the types need to be inferred when the command is executed. Thus, instead of a variable that is declared without an explicit type being defined as an object, the compiler and runtime attempt to infer the correct type for this object.

Existing code developed with Visual Studio 2005 is unaware of this concept, so this option will be off by default for any project that is migrated to Visual Studio 2008. New projects will have this option turned on, but this means that if you cut and paste code from a Visual Studio 2005 project into a Visual Studio 2008 project, or vice versa, you'll need to be prepared for an error in the pasted code because of changes in how types are inferred.

In addition to setting `Option Explicit`, `Option Strict`, `Option Compare`, and `Option Infer` to either `On` or `Off` for your project, Visual Studio 2008 allows you to customize specific compiler conditions that may occur in your source file. Thus, it is possible to leverage individual settings, such as requiring early binding as opposed to runtime binding, without limiting implicit conversions. These individual settings are included in the table of individual compiler settings listed below the `Option Strict` setting. Therefore, you can literally create a custom version of the `Option Strict` settings by turning on and off individual compiler settings for your project.

Notice that as you change your `Option Strict` setting, the notifications with the top few conditions are automatically updated to reflect the specific requirements of this new setting. In general, this table lists a set of conditions that relate to programming practices you might want to avoid or prevent, and which you should definitely be aware of. The use of warnings for the majority of these conditions is appropriate, as there are valid reasons why you might want to use or avoid each.

Basically, these conditions represent possible runtime error conditions that the compiler can't truly detect, except to identify that an increased possibility for error exists. Selecting Warning for a setting bypasses that behavior, as the compiler will warn you but allow the code to remain. Conversely, setting a behavior to `Error` prevents compilation.

An example of why these conditions are noteworthy is the warning on accessing shared member variables. If you are unfamiliar with shared member values, they are part of the discussion of classes in Chapter 2. At this point, it's just necessary to understand that these values are shared across all instances of a class. Thus, if a specific instance of a class is updating a shared member value, then it is appropriate to get a warning to that effect. The action is one that can lead to errors, as new developers sometimes fail to realize that a shared member value is common across all instances of a class, so if one instance updates the value, then the new value is seen by all other instances.

While many of these conditions are only addressed as individual settings, Visual Studio 2008 carries forward the `Option Strict` setting. Most experienced developers agree that using `Option Strict` and being forced to recognize when type conversions are occurring is a good thing. Certainly, when developing software that will be deployed in a production environment, anything that can be done to help prevent runtime errors is desirable. However, `Option Strict` can slow the development of a program because you are forced to explicitly define each conversion that needs to occur. If you are developing a prototype or demo component that has a limited life, you might find this option limiting.

If that were the end of the argument, then many developers would simply turn the option off and forget about it, but `Option Strict` has a runtime benefit. When type conversions are explicitly identified, the system performs them faster. Implicit conversions require the runtime system to first identify the types involved in a conversion and then obtain the correct handler.

Another advantage of `Option Strict` is that during implementation, developers are forced to consider every place a conversion might occur. Perhaps the development team didn't realize that some of the assignment operations resulted in a type conversion. Setting up projects that require explicit conversions means that the resulting code tends to have type consistency to avoid conversions, thus reducing the number of conversions in the final code. The result is not only conversions that run faster, but also, it is hoped, a smaller number of conversions.

As for `Option Infer`, well, it is a powerful new feature. On the one hand, it will be used as part of LINQ and the features that support LINQ, but it affects all code. In the past you needed to write the `AS <mytype>` portion of every variable definition in order to have a variable defined with an explicit type. However, now you can dimension a variable and assign it an integer or set it equal to another object, and the `AS`

Integer portion of your declaration isn't required. On the other hand, you can now dimension a variable and assign it to a specific type without declaration, which reduces the readability of your code. Be careful with Option Infer; it can make your code obscure.

In addition, note that Option Infer is directly affected by Option Strict. In an ideal world, Option Strict Off would require that Option Infer also be turned off or disabled in the user interface. That isn't the case, although it is the behavior that is seen; once Option Strict is off, Option Infer is essentially ignored.

> *How* Option Infer *is used in LINQ is covered in Chapter 11.*

XML Literals

One of the main new features in Visual Basic 2008 is the introduction of XML literals. With Visual Studio 2008, it is possible within Visual Basic to create a new variable and assign a block of well-formatted XML code to that string. This is being introduced here because it demonstrates a great example of a declaration that leverages Option Infer. Start by declaring a string variable called myString and setting this to a value such as "Hello World". In the code block that follows, notice that the first Dim statement used does not include the "As" clause that is typically used in such declarations:

```
            Dim myString = "Hello World"
            Dim myXMLElement = <MyXMLNode attribute1="1">This is formatted Text.
Print these lines separately.
    Ensure whitespace is also maintained.
<%= myString %>
                            </MyXMLNode>
```

Instead, the declaration of the myString variable relies on type inference. The compiler recognizes that this newly declared variable is being assigned a string, so the variable is automatically defined as a string. After the first variable is declared on the first line of the code block, the second line of code makes up the remainder of the code block, and you may notice that it spans multiple lines without any line continuation characters.

The second Dim statement declares another new variable, but in this case the variable is set equal to raw XML. Note that the "<" is not preceded by any quotes in the code. Instead, that angle bracket indicates that what follows will be a well-formed XML statement. At this point the Visual Basic compiler stops treating what you have typed as Visual Basic code and instead reads this text as XML. Thus, the top-level node can be named, attributes associated with that node can be defined, and text can be assigned to the value of the node. The only requirement is that the XML be well formed, which means you need to have a closing declaration, the last line in the preceding code block, to end that XML statement.

By default, because this is just an XML node and not a full document, Visual Basic infers that you are defining an XMLElement and will define the mXMLElement variable as an instance of that class. Beyond this, however, there is the behavior of your static XML. Note that the text itself contains comments about being formatted. That is because within your static XML, Visual Basic automatically recognizes and embeds literally everything.

Thus, the name *XML literal*. The text is captured as is, with any embedded white space or carriage returns/line feeds captured. The other interesting capability is shown on the line that reads as follows:

```
    <%= myString %>
```

This is a shorthand declaration that enables you to insert the value of the variable `myString` into your literal XML. In this case, `myString` is set on the preceding line, but it could easily be an input parameter to a method that returns an XML element. When you run this code, the current value of `myString` will be inserted into your XML declaration.

Figure 1-5 shows a bit more code than you saw in the preceding code block. It also includes a set of `Console.WriteLine` statements. These statements were added to display the data from your new XML element. Two different statements displaying the contents of the XML element as a string appear because each results in slightly different output:

```
Console.WriteLine("----------The XML-----------")
Console.WriteLine(myXMLElement.ToString())
Console.WriteLine()
Console.WriteLine("----------The Data----------")
Console.WriteLine(myXMLElement.Value.ToString())
```

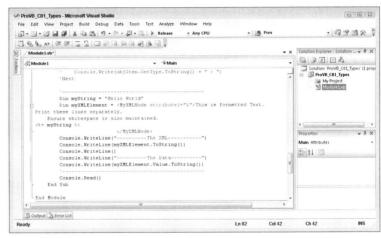

Figure 1-5

Of the five `Console.WriteLine` statements, only the second and fifth are important. The first statement on the second line instructs the XML element object to return a string representing itself. As such, the XML element will return all of the content of that object, including the raw XML itself. The writeline that ends the preceding code block has output the XML element to a string that only reflects the value of the data defined for that element. Note that if the basic XML element you defined in the previous code block had any nested XML elements, then these would be considered part of the contents of your XML element, and their definitions and attributes would be output as part of this statement.

As shown in Figure 1-6, the result of this output is that the first block of text outputted includes your custom XML node and its attribute. Not only do you see the text that identifies the value of the XML, you also see that actual XML structure. However, when you instead print only the value from the XML block, what you see is in fact just that text. Note that XML has embedded the carriage returns and left-hand white space that was part of your XML literal so that your text appears formatted. With the use of XML literals, you "literally" have the capability to replace the somewhat cryptic `String.Format` method call with a very explicit means of formatting an output string. Of course, not everything can rely on `Option Infer` and implicit conversions.

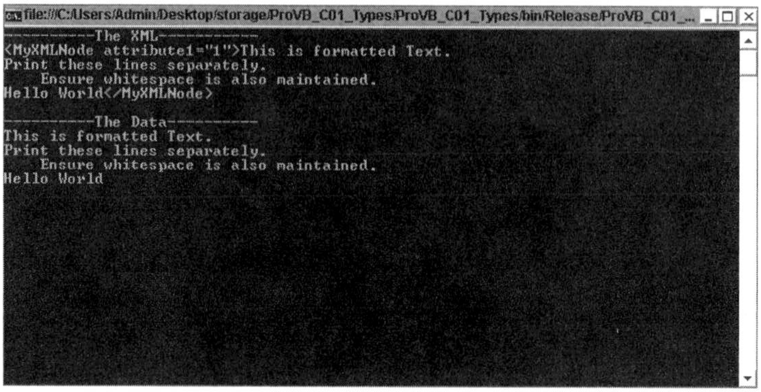

Figure 1-6

Performing Explicit Conversions

Keep in mind that even when you choose to allow implicit conversions, these are only allowed for a relatively small number of data types. At some point you'll need to carry out explicit conversions. The following code is an example of some typical conversions between different integer types when Option Strict is enabled:

```vb
Dim myShort As Short
Dim myUInt16 As UInt16
Dim myInt16 As Int16
Dim myInteger As Integer
Dim myUInt32 As UInt32
Dim myInt32 As Int32
Dim myLong As Long
Dim myInt64 As Int64

myShort = 0
myUInt16 = Convert.ToUInt16(myShort)
myInt16 = myShort
myInteger = myShort
myUInt32 = Convert.ToUInt32(myShort)
myInt32 = myShort
myInt64 = myShort

myLong = Long.MaxValue
If myLong < Short.MaxValue Then
  myShort = Convert.ToInt16(myLong)
End If
myInteger = CInt(myLong)
```

The preceding snippet provides some excellent examples of what might not be intuitive behavior. The first thing to note is that you can't implicitly cast from Short to UInt16, or any of the other unsigned types for that matter. That's because with Option Strict the compiler won't allow an implicit conversion that might result in a value out of range or loss of data. You may be thinking that an unsigned Short has a maximum that is twice the maximum of a signed Short, but in this case, if the variable myShort contained a -1, then the value wouldn't be in the allowable range for an unsigned type.

Just for clarity, even with the explicit conversion, if `myShort` were a negative number, then the `Convert.ToUInt32` method would throw a runtime exception. Managing failed conversions requires either an understanding of exceptions and exception handling, as covered in Chapter 8, or the use of a conversion utility such as `TryParse`, covered later in this section.

The second item illustrated in this code is the shared method `MaxValue`. All of the integer and decimal types have this property. As the name indicates, it returns the maximum value for the specified type. There is a matching `MinValue` method for getting the minimum value. As shared properties, the properties can be referenced from the class (`Long.MaxValue`) without requiring an instance.

Finally, although this code will compile, it won't always execute correctly. It illustrates a classic error, which in the real world is often intermittent. The error occurs because the final conversion statement does not check to ensure that the value being assigned to `myInteger` is within the maximum range for an integer type. On those occasions when `myLong` is larger than the maximum allowed, this code will throw an exception.

Visual Basic provides many ways to convert values. Some of them are updated versions of techniques that are supported from previous versions of Visual Basic. Others, such as the `ToString` method, are an inherent part of every class (although the .NET specification does not guarantee how a `ToString` class is implemented for each type).

The following set of conversion methods is based on the conversions supported by Visual Basic. They coincide with the primitive data types described earlier; however, continued use of these methods is not considered a best practice. That bears repeating: While you may find the following methods in existing code, you should strive to avoid and replace these calls:

CBool()	CByte()
CChar()	CDate()
CDbl()	CDec()
CInt()	CLng()
CObj()	CShort()
CSng()	CStr()

Each of these methods has been designed to accept the input of the other primitive data types (as appropriate) and to convert such items to the type indicated by the method name. Thus, the `CStr` class is used to convert a primitive type to a `String`. The disadvantage of these methods is that they have been designed to support any object. This means that if a primitive type is used, then the method automatically boxes the parameter prior to getting the new value. This results in a loss of performance. Finally, although these are available as methods within the VB language, they are actually implemented in a class (as with everything in the .NET Framework). Because the class uses a series of type-specific overloaded methods, the conversions run faster when the members of the `Convert` class are called explicitly:

```
Dim intMyShort As Integer = 200
Convert.ToInt32(intMyShort)
Convert.ToDateTime("9/9/2001")
```

The classes that are part of `System.Convert` implement not only the conversion methods listed earlier, but also other common conversions. These additional methods include standard conversions for things such as unsigned integers and pointers.

All the preceding type conversions are great for value types and the limited number of classes to which they apply, but these implementations are oriented toward a limited set of known types. It is not possible to convert a custom class to an `Integer` using these classes. More important, there should be no reason to have such a conversion. Instead, a particular class should provide a method that returns the appropriate type. That way, no type conversion is required. However, when `Option Strict` is enabled, the compiler requires you to cast an object to an appropriate type before triggering an implicit conversion. Note, however, that the `Convert` method isn't the only way to indicate that a given variable can be treated as another type.

Parse and TryParse

Most value types, at least those which are part of the .NET Framework, provide a pair of shared methods called `Parse` and `TryParse`. These methods accept a value of your choosing and then attempt to convert this variable into the selected value type. The `Parse` and `TryParse` methods are only available on value types. Reference types have related methods called `DirectCast` and `Cast`, which are optimized for reference variables.

The `Parse` method has a single parameter. This input parameter accepts a value that is the target for the object you are looking to create of a given type. This method then attempts to create a value based on the data passed in. However, be aware that if the data passed into the `Parse` method cannot be converted, then this method will throw an exception that your code needs to catch. The following line illustrates how the `Parse` function works:

```
result = Long.Parse("100")
```

Unfortunately, when you embed this call within a `Try-Catch` statement for exception handling, you create a more complex block of code. Because you always need to encapsulate such code within a `Try-Catch` block, the .NET development team decided that it would make more sense to provide a version of this method that encapsulated that exception-handling logic.

This is the origin of the `TryParse` method. The `TryParse` method works similarly to the `Parse` method except that it has two parameters and returns a Boolean, rather than a value. Instead of assigning the value of the `TryParse` method, you test it as part of an `If-Then` statement to determine whether the conversion of your data to the selected type was successful. If the conversion was successful, then the new value is stored in the second parameter passed to this method, which you can then assign to the variable you want to hold that value:

```
Dim converted As Long
If Long.TryParse("100", converted) Then
    result = converted
End If
```

CType

The `CType` method accepts two parameters: the first is the object that is having its type cast, and the second is the name of the object to which it is being cast. This system enables you to cast objects from parent to child types or from child to parent types. There is a limitation to the second parameter in that it can't be a variable containing the name of the casting target. Casting is defined at compile time, and any form of dynamic name selection would occur at runtime. An example of casting was shown as part of the discussion of working with the `Object` class earlier in this chapter.

Support for a runtime determination of object types is based on treating variables as objects and using the object metadata and the `TypeOf` operator to verify that an object supports various method and property calls. The `CType` method accepts both value and reference types. More detailed information regarding its use is presented in Chapter 2.

DirectCast and TryCast

The `DirectCast` method works similarly to the `CType` method, with a couple of minor differences. First, unlike `CType`, the `DirectCast` method accepts only reference types. This is because the `DirectCast` method is tied much more closely to objects and the use of inheritance and interfaces. Additionally, in order to make it perform faster, `DirectCast` does not include any logic to actually check for and convert an object to the requested type. The `DirectCast` method is meant to allow your code to take an object that has been cast as its base type of object and recast it in its original form. Similar to `CType`, these methods are covered in more detail in Chapter 2.

Summary

This chapter looked at many of the basic building blocks of Visual Basic that are used throughout project development. Understanding not only the basic components, but also how they work will help you to write more stable and better performing software. Note the following highlights of this chapter:

❑ Beware of array sizes; all arrays start at 0 and are defined not by size, but by the highest index.

❑ Remember to use the `StringBuilder` class for string manipulation.

❑ Pay attention to variable scope, and rely on it for cleaning up variables you no longer need.

❑ Use `Option Strict`; it's not about style, it's about reliability and performance.

❑ Try to avoid legacy methods for conversions.

❑ Attempt to leverage the `TryParse` and `TryCast` methods.

❑ Understand variable scope and when variables will go out of scope.

While this chapter covered many other items, including the `Decimal` type and how boxing works, these bullets highlight some of the more important items. Whether you are creating a new library of methods or a new user interface, these items consistently turn up in some form. You have seen that while .NET provides a tremendous amount of power, that power comes at a sometimes significant performance cost.

Object Syntax Introduction

Visual Basic supports the four major defining concepts required for a language to be fully object-oriented:

❏ **Abstraction** — Abstraction is merely the ability of a language to create "black box" code, to take a concept and create an abstract representation of that concept within a program. A `Customer` object, for instance, is an abstract representation of a real-world customer. A `DataTable` object is an abstract representation of a set of data.

❏ **Encapsulation** — This is the concept of a separation between interface and implementation. The idea is that you can create an interface (`Public` methods, properties, fields, and events in a class), and, as long as that interface remains consistent, the application can interact with your objects. This remains true even when you entirely rewrite the code within a given method — thus, the interface is independent of the implementation. Encapsulation enables you to hide the internal implementation details of a class. For example, the algorithm you use to compute pi might be proprietary. You can expose a simple API to the end user, but hide all the logic used by the algorithm by encapsulating it within your class.

❏ **Polymorphism** — Polymorphism is reflected in the ability to write one routine that can operate on objects from more than one class — treating different objects from different classes in exactly the same way. For instance, if both the `Customer` and the `Vendor` objects have a `Name` property and you can write a routine that calls the `Name` property regardless of whether you are using a `Customer` or `Vendor` object, then you have polymorphism.

Visual Basic supports polymorphism in two ways — through late binding (much like Smalltalk, a classic example of a true object-oriented language) and through the implementation of multiple interfaces. This flexibility is very powerful and is preserved within Visual Basic.

❏ **Inheritance** — Inheritance is the idea that a class can gain the interface and behaviors of a preexisting class. This is done by inheriting these behaviors from the existing class through a process known as *subclassing*.

The next chapter discusses these four concepts in detail; this chapter focuses on the syntax that enables you to utilize these concepts.

Visual Basic is also a component-based language. Component-based design is often viewed as a successor to object-oriented design, so component-based languages have some other capabilities. These are closely related to the traditional concepts of object orientation:

- **Multiple interfaces** — Each class in Visual Basic defines a *primary interface* (also called the *default* or *native interface*) through its `Public` methods, properties, and events. Classes can also implement other, secondary interfaces in addition to this primary interface. An object based on this class has multiple interfaces, and a client application can choose with which interface it will interact with the object.

- **Assembly (component) level scoping** — Not only can you define your classes and methods as `Public` (available to anyone), `Protected` (available through inheritance), and `Private` (available only locally), you can also define them as `Friend` — meaning they are available only within the current assembly or component. This is not a traditional object-oriented concept, but is very powerful when used with component-based applications.

This chapter explains how to create and use classes and objects in Visual Basic. We won't get too deeply into code, but it is important that you spend a little time familiarizing yourself with basic object-oriented terms and concepts.

Object-Oriented Terminology

To begin, let's take a look at the word *object* itself, along with the related *class* and *instance* terms. Then we will move on to discuss the four terms that define the major functionality in the object-oriented world: encapsulation, abstraction, polymorphism, and inheritance.

Objects, Classes, and Instances

An *object* is a code-based abstraction of a real-world entity or relationship. For instance, you might have a `Customer` object that represents a real-world customer, such as customer number 123, or you might have a `File` object that represents `C:\config.sys` on your computer's hard drive.

A closely related term is *class*. A class is the code that defines an object, and all objects are created based on a class. A class is an abstraction of a real-world concept, and it provides the basis from which you create instances of specific objects. For example, in order to have a `Customer` object representing customer number 123, you must first have a `Customer` class that contains all of the code (methods, properties, events, variables, and so on) necessary to create `Customer` objects. Based on that class, you can create any number of objects, each one an *instance* of the class. Each object is identical to the others, except that it may contain different data.

You can create many instances of `Customer` objects based on the same `Customer` class. All of the `Customer` objects are identical in terms of what they can do and the code they contain, but each one contains its own unique data. This means that each object represents a different physical customer.

Composition of an Object

You use an *interface* to get access to an object's data and behaviors. The object's data and behaviors are contained within the object, so a client application can treat the object like a black box, accessible only through its interface. This is a key object-oriented concept called *encapsulation*. The idea is that any program that makes use of this object will not have direct access to the behaviors or data; rather, those programs must make use of your object's interface.

Let's walk through each of the three elements in detail.

Interface

The interface is defined as a set of methods (Sub and Function routines), properties (Property routines), events, and fields (also known as variables) that are declared Public in scope.

You can also have Private methods and properties in your code. While these methods can be called by code within your object, they are not part of the interface and cannot be called by programs written to use your object. Another option is to use the Friend keyword, which defines the scope to be your current project, meaning that any code within your project can call the method, but no code outside your project (that is, from a different .NET assembly) can call the method. To complicate things a bit, you can also declare methods and properties as Protected, and these are available to classes that inherit from your class. You will look at Protected in Chapter 3, along with inheritance.

For example, you might have the following code in a class:

```
Public Function CalculateValue() As Integer

End Function
```

Because this method is declared with the Public keyword, it is part of the interface and can be called by client applications that are using the object. You might also have a method such as this:

```
Private Sub DoSomething()

End Sub
```

This method is declared as being Private, so it is not part of the interface. This method can only be called by code within the class — not by any code outside the class, such as code in a program that's using one of the objects.

Conversely, you can do something like this:

```
Public Sub CalculateValue()
  DoSomething()
End Sub
```

In this case, you're calling the Private method from within a Public method. While code using your objects can't directly call a Private method, you will frequently use Private methods to help structure the code in a class to make it more maintainable and easier to read.

Finally, you can use the Friend keyword:

```
Friend Sub DoSomething()

End Sub
```

In this case, the `DoSomething` method can be called by code within the class, or from other classes or modules within the current Visual Basic project. Code from outside the project will not have access to the method.

The `Friend` scope is very similar to the `Public` scope in that it makes methods available for use by code outside the object itself. Unlike `Public`, however, the `Friend` keyword restricts access to code within the current Visual Basic project, preventing code in other .NET assemblies from calling the method.

Implementation or Behavior

The code inside a method is called the *implementation*. Sometimes it is also called *behavior*, as it is this code that actually makes the object do useful work. For instance, you might have an `Age` property as part of the object's interface. Within that method, you might have code similar to the following:

```
Private _Age As Integer

Public ReadOnly Property Age() As Integer
  Get
    Return _Age
  End Get
End Property
```

In this case, the code is returning a value directly out of a variable, rather than doing something better such as calculate the value based on a birth date. However, this kind of code is often written in applications, and it seems to work fine for a while.

The key point is to understand that client applications can use the object even if you change the implementation, as long as you do not change the interface. If the method name and its parameter list and return data type remain unchanged, then you can change the implementation any way you want.

The code necessary to call the `Age` property would look something like this:

```
theAge = myObject.Age
```

The result of running this code is that you get the `Age` value returned for your use. While the client application will work fine, you will soon discover that hard-coding the age into the application is a problem, so at some point you'll want to improve this code. Fortunately, you can change the implementation without changing the client code:

```
Private _BirthDate As Date

Public ReadOnly Property Age() As Integer
  Get
    Return CInt(DateDiff(DateInterval.Year, _BirthDate, Now))
  End Get
End Property
```

You have changed the implementation behind the interface, effectively changing how it behaves, without changing the interface itself. Now, when you run the client application, the `Age` value returned is accurate over time, whereas in the previous implementation it was not.

Keep in mind that encapsulation is a *syntactic* tool — it enables the code to continue to run without change. However, it is not *semantic*, meaning that just because the code continues to run, that does not mean it continues to do what you actually want it to do.

In this example, the client code may have been written to overcome the initial limitations of the implementation in some way, and thus the client code might both rely on being able to retrieve the Age value, and count on the result of that call being a fixed value over time.

The update to the implementation won't stop the client program from running, but it may very well prevent it from running correctly.

Fields or Instance Variables

The third key part of an object is its data, or state. In fact, it might be argued that the only important part of an object is its data. After all, every instance of a class is absolutely identical in terms of its interface and its implementation; the only thing that can vary at all is the data contained within that particular object.

Fields are variables that are declared so that they are available to all code within the class. Typically, fields that are declared Private in scope are available only to the code in the class itself. They are also sometimes referred to as *instance variables* or *member variables*.

Don't confuse fields with properties. In Visual Basic, a Property is a type of method geared to retrieving and setting values, whereas a field is a variable within the class that may hold the value exposed by a Property. For instance, you might have a class that has these fields:

```
Public Class TheClass

    Private _Name As String
    Private _BirthDate As Date
End Class
```

Each instance of the class — each object — will have its own set of these fields in which to store data. Because these fields are declared with the Private keyword, they are only available to code within each specific object.

While fields can be declared as Public in scope, this makes them available to any code using the objects in a manner you cannot control. This directly breaks the concept of encapsulation, as code outside your object can directly change data values without following any rules that might otherwise be set in the object's code.

If you want to make the value of a field available to code outside of the object, you should instead use a property:

```
Public Class TheClass
    Private _Name As String
    Private _BirthDate As Date

    Public ReadOnly Property Name() As String
        Get
```

```
        Return _Name
      End Get
    End Property

  End Class
```

Because the `Name` property is a method, you are not directly exposing the internal variables to client code, so you preserve encapsulation of the data. At the same time, through this mechanism, you are able to safely provide access to your data as needed.

Fields can also be declared with the `Friend` scope, meaning they are available to all code in your project. Therefore, like declaring them as `Public`, this breaks encapsulation and is strongly discouraged.

Now that you have a grasp of some of the basic object-oriented terminology, you are ready to explore the creation of classes and objects. First you will see how Visual Basic enables you to interact with objects, and then you will dive into the actual process of authoring those objects.

Working with Objects

In the .NET environment in general and within Visual Basic in particular, you use objects all the time without even thinking about it. Every control on a form — in fact, every form — is an object. When you open a file or interact with a database, you are using objects to do that work.

Object Declaration and Instantiation

Objects are created using the `New` keyword, indicating that you want a new instance of a particular class. There are numerous variations on how or where you can use the `New` keyword in your code. Each one provides different advantages in terms of code readability or flexibility.

The most obvious way to create an object is to declare an object variable and then create an instance of the object:

```
Dim obj As TheClass
obj = New TheClass()
```

The result of this code is that you have a new instance of `TheClass` ready for use. To interact with this new object, you use the `obj` variable that you declared. The `obj` variable contains a reference to the object, a concept explored later.

You can shorten the preceding code by combining the declaration of the variable with the creation of the instance, as illustrated here:

```
Dim obj As New TheClass()
```

In previous versions of Visual Basic, this substitution was a bad idea because it had negative performance and maintainability effects. However, since Visual Basic 2005, there is no difference between the first example and this one, other than code length.

The preceding code both declares the variable `obj` as data type `TheClass` and creates an instance of the class, immediately creating an object that you can use. Another variation on this theme is as follows:

```
Dim obj As TheClass = New TheClass()
```

Again, this both declares a variable of data type `TheClass` and creates an instance of the class. It is up to you how you create these instances, as it is really a matter of style. This third syntax example provides a great deal of flexibility while remaining compact. Though it is a single line of code, it separates the declaration of the variable's data type from the creation of the object.

Such flexibility is very useful when working with inheritance or multiple interfaces. You might declare the variable to be of one type — say, an interface — and instantiate the object based on a class that implements that interface. You will revisit this syntax when interfaces are covered in detail in Chapter 3.

So far, you've been declaring a variable for new objects, but sometimes you simply need to pass an object as a parameter to a method, in which case you can create an instance of the object right in the call to that method:

```
DoSomething(New TheClass())
```

This calls the `DoSomething` method, passing a new instance of `TheClass` as a parameter. This can be even more complex. Perhaps, instead of needing an object reference, your method needs an `Integer`. You can provide that `Integer` value from a method on the object:

```
Public Class TheClass
   Public Function GetValue() As Integer
      Return 42
   End Function
End Class
```

You can then instantiate the object and call the method all in one shot, thus passing the value returned from the method as a parameter:

```
DoSomething(New TheClass().GetValue())
```

Obviously, you need to carefully weigh the readability of such code against its compactness. At some point, having code that is more compact can detract from readability, rather than enhance it.

Object References

Typically, when you work with an object, you are using a reference to that object. Conversely, when you are working with simple data types, such as `Integer`, you are working with the actual value, rather than a reference. Let's explore these concepts and see how they work and interact.

When you create a new object using the `New` keyword, you store a reference to that object in a variable, as shown here:

```
Dim obj As New TheClass()
```

This code creates a new instance of `TheClass`. You gain access to this new object via the `obj` variable. This variable holds a reference to the object. You might then do something like this:

```
Dim another As TheClass
another = obj
```

Now, you have a second variable, `another`, which also has a reference to the same object. You can use either variable interchangeably, as they both reference the exact same object. Remember that the variable you have is not the object itself but just a reference, or pointer, to the object.

Dereferencing Objects

When you are done working with an object, you can indicate that you are through with it by *dereferencing* the object. To dereference an object, simply set the object reference to `Nothing`:

```
Dim obj As TheClass

obj = New TheClass()
obj = Nothing
```

After any or all variables that reference an object are set to `Nothing`, the .NET runtime knows that you no longer need that object. At some point, the runtime destroys the object and reclaims the memory and resources it consumed. You can find more information on the garbage collector in Chapter 4.

Between the time when you dereference the object and the time when the .NET Framework gets around to actually destroying it, the object simply sits in the memory, unaware that it has been dereferenced. Right before .NET destroys the object, the `Finalize` method is called on the object (if it has one).

Early Binding versus Late Binding

One of the strengths of Visual Basic has long been that it provides access to both early and late binding when interacting with objects. Early binding means that code directly interacts with an object by directly calling its methods. Because the Visual Basic compiler knows the object's data type ahead of time, it can directly compile code to invoke the methods on the object. Early binding also enables the IDE to use IntelliSense to aid development efforts by enabling the compiler to ensure that you are referencing methods that exist and are providing the proper parameter values.

Late binding means that your code interacts with an object dynamically at runtime. This provides a great deal of flexibility because the code doesn't care what type of object it is interacting with as long as the object supports the methods you want to call. Because the type of the object is not known by the IDE or compiler, neither IntelliSense nor compile-time syntax checking is possible, but in exchange you get unprecedented flexibility.

If you enable strict type checking by using `Option Strict On` in the project's Properties dialog or at the top of the code modules, then the IDE and compiler enforce early binding behavior. By default, `Option Strict` is turned off, so you have easy access to the use of late binding within the code. Chapter 1 discusses `Option Strict`. You can change this default directly in Visual Studio 2008 by selecting Tools⇨Options from the VS menu. The Options dialog is shown in Figure 2-1. Expanding the Projects and Solutions node reveals the VB defaults. Feel free to change any of these default settings.

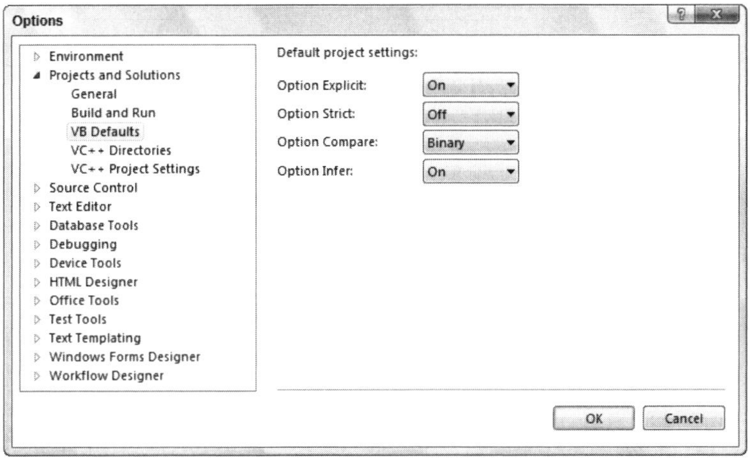

Figure 2-1

Implementing Late Binding

Late binding occurs when the compiler cannot determine the type of object that you'll be calling. This level of ambiguity is achieved using the Object data type. A variable of data type Object can hold virtually any value, including a reference to any type of object. Thus, code such as the following could be run against any object that implements a DoSomething method that accepts no parameters:

```
Option Strict Off

Module LateBind
   Public Sub DoWork(ByVal obj As Object)
     obj.DoSomething()
   End Sub
End Module
```

If the object passed into this routine does not have a DoSomething method that accepts no parameters, then an exception will be thrown. Thus, it is recommended that any code that uses late binding always provide exception handling:

```
Option Strict Off

Module LateBind
   Public Sub DoWork(ByVal obj As Object)
     Try
        obj.DoSomething()
     Catch ex As MissingMemberException
        ' do something appropriate given failure
        ' to call this method
     End Try
   End Sub
End Module
```

Here, the call to the DoSomething method has been put in a Try block. If it works, then the code in the Catch block is ignored; but in the case of a failure, the code in the Catch block is run. You need to write code in the `Catch` block to handle the case in which the object does not support the `DoSomething` method call. This `Catch` block only catches the `MissingMemberException`, which indicates that the method does not exist on the object.

While late binding is flexible, it can be error prone and is slower than early-bound code. To make a late-bound method call, the .NET runtime must dynamically determine whether the target object actually has a method that matches the one you are calling. It must then invoke that method on your behalf. This takes more time and effort than an early-bound call whereby the compiler knows ahead of time that the method exists and can compile the code to make the call directly. With a late-bound call, the compiler has to generate code to make the call dynamically at runtime.

Using the CType Function

Whether you are using late binding or not, it can be useful to pass object references around using the `Object` data type, converting them to an appropriate type when you need to interact with them. This is particularly useful when working with objects that use inheritance or implement multiple interfaces, concepts discussed in Chapter 3.

If `Option Strict` is turned off, which is the default, then you can write code using a variable of type `Object` to make an early-bound method call:

```
Module LateBind
  Public Sub DoWork(obj As Object)

      Dim local As TheClass
      local = obj
      local.DoSomething()

  End Sub
End Module
```

This code uses a strongly typed variable, `local`, to reference what was a generic object value. Behind the scenes, Visual Basic converts the generic type to a specific type so that it can be assigned to the strongly typed variable. If the conversion cannot be done, then you get a trappable runtime error.

The same thing can be done using the `CType` function. If `Option Strict` is enabled, then the previous approach will not compile, and the `CType` function must be used. Here is the same code making use of `CType`:

```
Module LateBind
  Public Sub DoWork(obj As Object)

      Dim local As TheClass
      local = CType(obj, TheClass)
      local.DoSomething()

  End Sub
End Module
```

This code declares a variable of type `TheClass`, which is an early-bound data type that you want to use. The parameter you're accepting is of the generic `Object` data type, though, so you use the `CType` method to gain an early-bound reference to the object. If the object isn't of type `TheClass`, then the call to `CType` fails with a trappable error.

Once you have a reference to the object, you can call methods by using the early-bound variable `local`. This code can be shortened to avoid the use of the intermediate variable. Instead, you can simply call methods directly from the data type:

```
Module LateBind
   Public Sub DoWork(obj As Object)
      CType(obj, TheClass).DoSomething()
   End Sub
End Module
```

Even though the variable you are working with is of type `Object` and therefore any calls to it will be late bound, you use the `CType` method to temporarily convert the variable into a specific type — in this case, the type `TheClass`.

If the object passed as a parameter is not of type `TheClass`, then you get a trappable error, so it is always wise to wrap this code in a `Try ... Catch` block.

As shown in Chapter 3, the `CType` function can also be very useful when working with objects that implement multiple interfaces. When an object has multiple interfaces, you can reference a single object variable through the appropriate interface as needed.

Using the DirectCast Function

Another function that is very similar to `CType` is the method `DirectCast`. The `DirectCast` call also converts values of one type into another type. It works in a more restrictive fashion than `CType`, but the trade-off is that it can be somewhat faster than `CType`:

```
Dim obj As TheClass

obj = New TheClass
DirectCast(obj, ITheInterface).DoSomething()
```

This is similar to the last example with `CType`, illustrating the parity between the two functions. There are differences, however. First, `DirectCast` works only with reference types, whereas `CType` accepts both reference and value types. For instance, `CType` can be used in the following code:

```
Dim int As Integer = CType(123.45, Integer)
```

Trying to do the same thing with `DirectCast` would result in a compiler error, as the value `123.45` is a value type, not a reference type.

Second, `DirectCast` is not as aggressive about converting types as `CType`. `CType` can be viewed as an intelligent combination of all the other conversion functions (such as `CInt`, `CStr`, and so on). `DirectCast`, conversely, assumes that the source data is directly convertible, and it won't take extra steps to convert the data.

As an example, consider the following code:

```
Dim obj As Object = 123.45

Dim int As Integer = DirectCast(obj, Integer)
```

59

If you were using CType this would work, as CType uses CInt-like behavior to convert the value to an Integer. DirectCast, however, will throw an exception because the value is not directly convertible to Integer.

Using the TryCast Function

A function similar to DirectCast is TryCast. TryCast converts values of one type into another type, but unlike DirectCast, if it can't do the conversion, then TryCast doesn't throw an exception. Instead, TryCast simply returns Nothing if the cast can't be performed. TryCast only works with reference values; it cannot be used with value types such as Integer or Boolean.

Using TryCast, you can write code like this:

```
Module LateBind

  Public Sub DoWork(obj As Object)
     Dim temp As TheClass = TryCast(obj, Object)
     If temp Is Nothing Then
       ' the cast couldn't be accomplished
       ' so do no work
     Else
       temp.DoSomething()
     End If
  End Sub

End Module
```

If you are not sure whether a type conversion is possible, then it is often best to use TryCast. This function avoids the overhead and complexity of catching possible exceptions from CType or DirectCast and still provides you with an easy way to convert an object to another type.

Creating Classes

Using objects is fairly straightforward and intuitive. It is the kind of thing that even the most novice programmers pick up and accept rapidly. Creating classes and objects is a bit more complex and interesting.

Basic Classes

As discussed earlier, objects are merely instances of a specific template (a class). The class contains the code that defines the behavior of its objects, and defines the instance variables that will contain the object's individual data.

Classes are created using the Class keyword, and include definitions (declaration) and implementations (code) for the variables, methods, properties, and events that make up the class. Each object created based on this class will have the same methods, properties, and events, and its own set of data defined by the fields in the class.

The Class Keyword

If you want to create a class that represents a person — a `Person` class — you could use the `Class` keyword:

```
Public Class Person

    ' Implementation code goes here

End Class
```

As you know, Visual Basic projects are composed of a set of files with the `.vb` extension. It is possible for each file to contain multiple classes, which means that within a single file you could have something like this:

```
Public Class Adult
    ' Implementation code goes here.
End Class

Public Class Senior
    ' Implementation code goes here.
End Class

Public Class Child
    ' Implementation code goes here.
End Class
```

The most common and preferred approach is to have a single class per file. This is because the Visual Studio 2008 Solution Explorer and the code-editing environment are tailored to make it easy to navigate from file to file to find code. For instance, if you create a single class file with all these classes, the Solution Explorer simply displays a single entry, as shown in Figure 2-2.

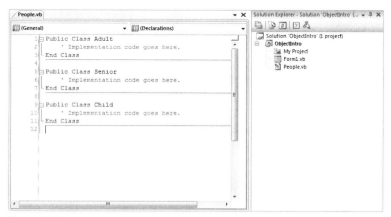

Figure 2-2

However, the Visual Studio IDE does provide the Class View window. If you do decide to put multiple classes in each physical .vb file, you can make use of the Class View window to quickly and efficiently navigate through the code, jumping from class to class without having to manually locate those classes in specific code files, as shown in Figure 2-3.

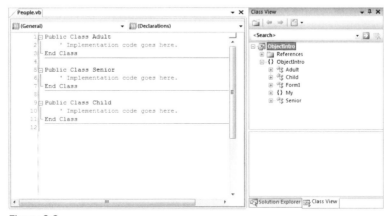

Figure 2-3

The Class View window is extremely useful even if you stick with one class per file, as it still provides you with a class-based view of the entire application.

This chapter uses one class per file in the examples, as this is the most common approach. To begin, open the Visual Studio IDE and create a new Windows Application project named "ObjectIntro." Choose the Project⇨Add Class menu option to add a new class module to the project. You'll be presented with the standard Add New Item dialog box. Change the name to Person.vb and click Open. The result will be the following code, which defines the Person class:

```
Public Class Person

End Class
```

With the Person class created, you are ready to start adding code to declare the interface, implement the behaviors, and declare the instance variables.

Fields

Fields are variables declared in the class. They will be available to each individual object when the application is run. Each object gets its own set of data — basically, each object gets its own copy of the fields.

Earlier, you learned that a class is simply a template from which you create specific objects. Variables that you define within the class are also simply templates — and each object gets its own copy of those variables in which to store its data.

Declaring member variables is as easy as declaring variables within the Class block structure. Add the following code to the Person class:

```
Public Class Person

    Private mName As String
    Private mBirthDate As Date
End Class
```

You can control the scope of the fields with the following keywords:

❑   Private — Available only to code within the class

❑   Friend — Available only to code within the project/component

❑   Protected — Available only to classes that inherit from the class (discussed in detail in Chapter 3)

❑   Protected Friend — Available to code within your project/component and classes that inherit from the class whether in the project or not (discussed in detail in Chapter 3)

❑   Public — Available to code outside the class and to any projects that reference the assembly

Typically, fields are declared using the Private keyword, making them available only to code within each instance of the class. Choosing any other option should be done with great care, because all the other options allow code outside the class to directly interact with the variable, meaning that the value could be changed and your code would never know that a change took place.

> *One common exception to making fields* Private *is to use the* Protected *keyword, as discussed in Chapter 3.*

Methods

Objects typically need to provide services (or functions) that can be called when working with the object. Using their own data or data passed as parameters to the method, they manipulate information to yield a result or perform an action.

Methods declared as Public, Friend, or Protected in scope define the interface of the class. Methods that are Private in scope are available to the code only within the class itself, and can be used to provide structure and organization to code. As discussed earlier, the actual code within each method is called an *implementation*, while the declaration of the method itself is what defines the interface.

Methods are simply routines that are coded within the class to implement the services you want to provide to the users of an object. Some methods return values or provide information to the calling code. These are called *interrogative methods*. Others, called *imperative methods*, just perform an action and return nothing to the calling code.

In Visual Basic, methods are implemented using Sub (for imperative methods) or Function (for interrogative methods) routines within the class module that defines the object. Sub routines may accept parameters, but they do not return any result value when they are complete. Function routines can also accept parameters, and they always generate a result value that can be used by the calling code.

A method declared with the `Sub` keyword is merely one that returns no value. Add the following code to the `Person` class:

```
Public Sub Walk()

    ' implementation code goes here

End Sub
```

The `Walk` method presumably contains some code that performs some useful work when called but has no result value to return when it is complete. To make use of this method, you might write code such as this:

```
Dim myPerson As New Person()
myPerson.Walk()
```

Once you've created an instance of the `Person` class, you can simply invoke the `Walk` method.

Methods That Return Values

If you have a method that does generate some value that should be returned, you need to use the `Function` keyword:

```
Public Function Age() As Integer
    Return CInt(DateDiff(DateInterval.Year, mBirthDate, Now()))
End Function
```

Note that you must indicate the data type of the return value when you declare a `Function`. This example returns the calculated age as a result of the method. You can return any value of the appropriate data type by using the `Return` keyword.

You can also return the value without using the `Return` keyword, by setting the value of the function name itself:

```
Public Function Age() As Integer
    Age = CInt(DateDiff(DateInterval.Year, mBirthDate, Now()))
End Function
```

This is functionally equivalent to the previous code. Either way, you can use this method with code similar to the following:

```
Dim myPerson As New Person()
Dim age As Integer

age = myPerson.Age()
```

The `Age` method returns an `Integer` data value that you can use in the program as required; in this case, you're just storing it in a variable.

Indicating Method Scope

Adding the appropriate keyword in front of the method declaration indicates the scope:

```
Public Sub Walk()
```

This indicates that Walk is a Public method and thus is available to code outside the class and even outside the current project. Any application that references the assembly can use this method. Being Public, this method becomes part of the object's interface.

Alternately, you might restrict access to the method somewhat:

```
Friend Sub Walk()
```

By declaring the method with the Friend keyword, you are indicating that it should be part of the object's interface only for code inside the project; any other applications or projects that make use of the assembly will not be able to call the Walk method.

The Private keyword indicates that a method is only available to the code within your particular class:

```
Private Function Age() As Integer
```

Private methods are very useful to help organize complex code within each class. Sometimes the methods contain very lengthy and complex code. In order to make this code more understandable, you may choose to break it up into several smaller routines, having the main method call these routines in the proper order. Moreover, you can use these routines from several places within the class, so by making them separate methods, you enable reuse of the code. These subroutines should never be called by code outside the object, so you make them Private.

Method Parameters

You will often want to pass information into a method as you call it. This information is provided via parameters to the method. For instance, in the Person class, you may want the Walk method to track the distance the person walks over time. In such a case, the Walk method would need to know how far the person is to walk each time the method is called. Add the following code to the Person class:

```
Public Class Person
   Private mName As String
   Private mBirthDate As Date
   Private mTotalDistance As Integer

   Public Sub Walk(ByVal distance As Integer)
      mTotalDistance += distance
   End Sub
   Public Function Age() As Integer
      Return CInt(DateDiff(DateInterval.Year, mBirthDate, Now()))
   End Function
End Class
```

With this implementation, a Person object sums all of the distances walked over time. Each time the Walk method is called, the calling code must pass an Integer value, indicating the distance to be walked. The code to call this method would be similar to the following:

```
Dim myPerson As New Person()
myPerson.Walk(12)
```

The parameter is accepted using the ByVal keyword, which indicates that the parameter value is a copy of the original value. This is the default way in which Visual Basic accepts all parameters. Typically, this is desirable because it means that you can work with the parameter inside the code, changing its value with no risk of accidentally changing the original value in the calling code.

If you do want to be able to change the value in the calling code, you can change the declaration to pass the parameter by reference by using the `ByRef` qualifier:

```
Public Sub Walk(ByRef distance As Integer)
```

In this case, you get a reference (or pointer) back to the original value, rather than a copy. This means that any change you make to the `distance` parameter is reflected back in the calling code, very similar to the way object references work, as discussed earlier in this chapter.

Using this technique can be dangerous, as it is not explicitly clear to the caller of the method that the value will change. Such unintended side effects can be hard to debug and should be avoided.

Properties

The .NET environment provides for a specialized type of method called a *property*. A property is a method specifically designed for setting and retrieving data values. For instance, you declared a variable in the `Person` class to contain a name, so the `Person` class may include code to allow that name to be set and retrieved. This can be done using regular methods:

```
Public Sub SetName(ByVal name As String)
   mName = name
End Sub

Public Function GetName() As String
   Return mName
End Function
```

Using methods like these, you write code to interact with the object:

```
Dim myPerson As New Person()

myPerson.SetName("Jones")
Messagebox.Show(myPerson.GetName())
```

While this is perfectly acceptable, it is not as nice as it could be with the use of a property. A `Property` style method consolidates the setting and retrieving of a value into a single structure, and makes the code within the class smoother overall. You can rewrite these two methods into a single property. Add the following code to the `Person` class:

```
Public Property Name() As String
   Get
       Return mName
   End Get
   Set(ByVal Value As String)
     mName = Value
   End Set
End Property
```

By using a property method instead, you can make the client code much more readable:

```
Dim myPerson As New Person()

myPerson.Name = "Jones"
Messagebox.Show(myPerson.Name)
```

The `Property` method is declared with both a scope and a data type:

```
Public Property Name() As String
```

In this example, you've declared the property as `Public` in scope, but it can be declared using the same scope options as any other method — `Public`, `Friend`, `Private`, or `Protected`.

The return data type of this property is `String`. A property can return virtually any data type appropriate for the nature of the value. In this regard, a property is very similar to a method declared using the `Function` keyword.

Though a `Property` method is a single structure, it is divided into two parts: a getter and a setter. The getter is contained within a `Get...End Get` block and is responsible for returning the value of the property on demand:

```
Get
    Return mName
End Get
```

Though the code in this example is very simple, it could be more complex, perhaps calculating the value to be returned, or applying other business logic to change the value as it is returned. Likewise, the code to change the value is contained within a `Set ... End Set` block:

```
Set(ByVal Value As String)
    mName = Value
End Set
```

The `Set` statement accepts a single parameter value that stores the new value. The code in the block can then use this value to set the property's value as appropriate. The data type of this parameter must match the data type of the property itself. Declaring the parameter in this manner enables you to change the name of the variable used for the parameter value if needed.

By default, the parameter is named `Value`, but you can change the parameter name to something else, as shown here:

```
Set(ByVal NewName As String)
    mName = NewName
End Set
```

In many cases, you can apply business rules or other logic within this routine to ensure that the new value is appropriate before you actually update the data within the object. It is also possible to restrict either the `Get` or `Set` block to be narrower in scope than the scope of the property itself. For instance, you may want to allow any code to retrieve the property value, but only allow other code in your project to alter the value. In this case, you can restrict the scope of the Set block to Friend, while the Property itself is scoped as Public:

```
Public Property Name() As String
  Get
    Return mName
  End Get
  Friend Set(ByVal Value As String)
    mName = Value
  End Set
End Property
```

The new scope must be more restrictive than the scope of the Property itself, and either the Get or Set block can be restricted, but not both. The one you do not restrict uses the scope of the Property method.

Parameterized Properties

The Name property you created is an example of a single-value property. You can also create property arrays or parameterized properties. These properties reflect a range, or array, of values. For example, people often have several phone numbers. You might implement a PhoneNumber property as a parameterized property, storing not only phone numbers, but also a description of each number. To retrieve a specific phone number you would write code such as the following:

```
Dim myPerson As New Person()
Dim homePhone As String

homePhone = myPerson.Phone("home")
```

Or, to add or change a specific phone number, you'd write the following code:

```
myPerson.Phone("work") = "555-9876"
```

Not only are you retrieving and updating a phone number property, you are also updating a specific phone number. This implies a couple of things. First, you can no longer use a simple variable to hold the phone number, as you are now storing a list of numbers and their associated names. Second, you have effectively added a parameter to your property. You are actually passing the name of the phone number as a parameter on each property call.

To store the list of phone numbers, you can use the Hashtable class. The Hashtable is very similar to the standard VB Collection object, but it is more powerful — allowing you to test for the existence of a specific element. Add the following declaration to the Person class:

```
Public Class Person
  Private mName As String
  Private mBirthDate As Date
  Private mTotalDistance As Integer
  Private mPhones As New Hashtable
```

You can implement the Phone property by adding the following code to the Person class:

```
Public Property Phone(ByVal location As String) As String
  Get
```

```
      Return CStr(mPhones.Item(Location))
    End Get
    Set(ByVal Value As String)
      If mPhones.ContainsKey(location) Then
        mPhones.Item(location) = Value
      Else
        mPhones.Add(location, Value)
      End If
    End Set
  End Property
```

The declaration of the `Property` method itself is a bit different from what you have seen:

```
Public Property Phone(ByVal location As String) As String
```

In particular, you have added a parameter, `location`, to the property itself. This parameter will act as the index into the list of phone numbers, and must be provided when either setting or retrieving phone number values.

Because the `location` parameter is declared at the `Property` level, it is available to all code within the property, including both the `Get` and `Set` blocks. Within your `Get` block, you use the `location` parameter to select the appropriate phone number to return from the `Hashtable`:

```
Get
  Return mPhones.Item(location)
End Get
```

With this code, if there is no value stored matching the `location`, then you get a trappable runtime error.

Similarly, in the `Set` block, you use the `location` to update or add the appropriate element in the `Hashtable`. In this case, you are using the `ContainsKey` method of `Hashtable` to determine whether the phone number already exists in the list. If it does, then you simply update the value in the list; otherwise, you add a new element to the list for the value:

```
Set(ByVal Value As String)
  If mPhones.ContainsKey(location) Then
    mPhones.Item(location) = Value
  Else
    mPhones.Add(location, Value)
  End If
End Set
```

This way, you are able to add or update a specific phone number entry based on the parameter passed by the calling code.

Read-Only Properties

Sometimes you may want a property to be read-only, so that it cannot be changed. In the `Person` class, for instance, you may have a read-write property for `BirthDate`, but only a read-only property for `Age`. If so, the `BirthDate` property is a normal property, as follows:

```
Public Property BirthDate() As Date
  Get
```

```
      Return mBirthDate
    End Get
    Set(ByVal Value As Date)
     mBirthDate = Value
    End Set
End Property
```

The `Age` value, conversely, is a derived value based on `BirthDate`. This is not a value that should ever be directly altered, so it is a perfect candidate for read-only status.

You already have an `Age` method implemented as a `Function`. Remove that code from the `Person` class because you will replace it with a `Property` routine instead. The difference between a `Function` routine and a `ReadOnly Property` is quite subtle. Both return a value to the calling code, and either way the object is running a subroutine defined by the class module to return the value.

The difference is less a programmatic one than a design choice. You could create all your objects without any `Property` routines at all, just using methods for all interactions with the objects. However, `Property` routines are obviously attributes of an object, whereas a `Function` might be an attribute or a method. By carefully implementing all attributes as `ReadOnly Property` routines, and any interrogative methods as `Function` routines, you create more readable and understandable code.

To make a property read-only, use the `ReadOnly` keyword and only implement the `Get` block:

```
Public ReadOnly Property Age() As Integer
  Get
    Return CInt(DateDiff(DateInterval.Year, mdtBirthDate, Now()))
  End Get
End Property
```

Because the property is read-only, you will get a syntax error if you attempt to implement a `Set` block.

Write-Only Properties

As with read-only properties, sometimes a property should be write-only, whereby the value can be changed but not retrieved.

Many people have allergies, so perhaps the `Person` object should have some understanding of the ambient allergens in the area. This is not a property that should be read from the `Person` object, as allergens come from the environment, rather than from the person, but it is data that the `Person` object needs in order to function properly. Add the following variable declaration to the class:

```
Public Class Person
  Private mstrName As String
  Private mdtBirthDate As Date
  Private mintTotalDistance As Integer
  Private colPhones As New Hashtable()
  Private mAllergens As Integer
```

You can implement an `AmbientAllergens` property as follows:

```
Public WriteOnly Property AmbientAllergens() As Integer
  Set(ByVal Value As Integer)
    mAllergens = Value
```

```
      End Set
   End Property
```

To create a write-only property, use the `WriteOnly` keyword and only implement a `Set` block in the code. The property is write-only, so you will get a syntax error if you try to implement a `Get` block.

The Default Property

Objects can implement a default property, which can be used to simplify the use of an object at times by making it appear as if the object has a native value. A good example of this behavior is the `Collection` object, which has a default property called `Item` that returns the value of a specific item, allowing you to write the following:

```
Dim mData As New HashTable()

Return mData(index)
```

Default properties must be parameterized properties. A property without a parameter cannot be marked as the default. This is a change from previous versions of Visual Basic, in which any property could be marked as the default.

Our `Person` class has a parameterized property — the `Phone` property you built earlier. You can make this the default property by using the `Default` keyword:

```
Default Public Property Phone(ByVal location As String) As String
   Get
      Return CStr(mPhones.Item(location))
   End Get
   Set(ByVal Value As String)
      If mPhones.ContainsKey(location) Then
         mPhones.Item(location) = Value
      Else
         mPhones.Add(location, Value)
      End If
   End Set
End Property
```

Prior to this change, you would have needed code such as the following to use the `Phone` property:

```
Dim myPerson As New Person()

MyPerson.Phone("home") = "555-1234"
```

Now, with the property marked as `Default`, you can simplify the code:

```
myPerson("home") = "555-1234"
```

By picking appropriate default properties, you can potentially make the use of objects more intuitive.

Events

Both methods and properties enable you to write code that interacts with your objects by invoking specific functionality as needed. It is often useful for objects to provide notification as certain activities occur during processing. You see examples of this all the time with controls, where a button indicates that it was clicked via a Click event, or a text box indicates that its contents have been changed via the TextChanged event.

Objects can raise events of their own, providing a powerful and easily implemented mechanism by which objects can notify client code of important activities or events. In Visual Basic, events are provided using the standard .NET mechanism of *delegates*, but before discussing delegates, let's explore how to work with events in Visual Basic.

Handling Events

We are all used to seeing code in a form to handle the Click event of a button, such as the following code:

```
Private Sub Button1_Click(ByVal sender As System.Object, _
  ByVal e As System.EventArgs) Handles Button1.Click

End Sub
```

Typically, we write our code in this type of routine without paying a lot of attention to the code created by the Visual Studio IDE. However, let's take a second look at that code, which contains some important things to note here.

First, notice the use of the Handles keyword. This keyword specifically indicates that this method will be handling the Click event from the Button1 control. Of course, a control is just an object, so what is indicated here is that this method will be handling the Click event from the Button1 object.

Second, notice that the method accepts two parameters. The Button control class defines these parameters. It turns out that any method that accepts two parameters with these data types can be used to handle the Click event. For instance, you could create a new method to handle the event:

```
Private Sub MyClickMethod(ByVal s As System.Object, _
    ByVal args As System.EventArgs) Handles Button1.Click

End Sub
```

Even though you have changed the method name and the names of the parameters, you are still accepting parameters of the same data types, and you still have the Handles clause to indicate that this method handles the event.

Handling Multiple Events

The Handles keyword offers even more flexibility. Not only can the method name be anything you choose, but a single method can handle multiple events if you desire. Again, the only requirement is that the method and all the events being raised must have the same parameter list.

This explains why all the standard events raised by the .NET system class library have exactly two parameters — the sender and an EventArgs object. Being so generic makes it possible to write very generic and powerful event handlers that can accept virtually any event raised by the class library.

One common scenario where this is useful is when you have multiple instances of an object that raises events, such as two buttons on a form:

```
Private Sub MyClickMethod(ByVal sender As System.Object, _
    ByVal e As System.EventArgs) _
    Handles Button1.Click, Button2.Click

End Sub
```

Notice that the `Handles` clause has been modified so that it has a comma-separated list of events to handle. Either event will cause the method to run, providing a central location for handling these events.

The WithEvents Keyword

The `WithEvents` keyword tells Visual Basic that you want to handle any events raised by the object within the code:

```
Friend WithEvents Button1 As System.Windows.Forms.Button
```

The `WithEvents` keyword makes any events from an object available for use, whereas the `Handles` keyword is used to link specific events to the methods so that you can receive and handle them. This is true not only for controls on forms, but also for any objects that you create.

The `WithEvents` keyword cannot be used to declare a variable of a type that does not raise events. In other words, if the `Button` class did not contain code to raise events, you would get a syntax error when you attempted to declare the variable using the `WithEvents` keyword.

The compiler can tell which classes will and will not raise events by examining their interface. Any class that will be raising an event has that event declared as part of its interface. In Visual Basic, this means that you will have used the `Event` keyword to declare at least one event as part of the interface for the class.

Raising Events

Your objects can raise events just like a control, and the code using the object can receive these events by using the `WithEvents` and `Handles` keywords. Before you can raise an event from your object, however, you need to declare the event within the class by using the `Event` keyword.

In the `Person` class, for instance, you may want to raise an event anytime the `Walk` method is called. If you call this event `Walked`, you can add the following declaration to the `Person` class:

```
Public Class Person
    Private mstrName As String
    Private mdtBirthDate As Date
    Private mintTotalDistance As Integer
    Private colPhones As New Hashtable()
    Private mintAllergens As Integer

    Public Event Walked()
```

Events can also have parameters, values that are provided to the code receiving the event. A typical button's `Click` event receives two parameters, for instance. In the `Walked` method, perhaps you want to also indicate the distance that was walked. You can do this by changing the event declaration:

```
Public Event Walked(ByVal distance As Integer)
```

Now that the event is declared, you can raise that event within the code where appropriate. In this case, you'll raise it within the `Walk` method, so anytime a `Person` object is instructed to walk, it fires an event indicating the distance walked. Make the following change to the `Walk` method:

```
Public Sub Walk(ByVal distance As Integer)
   mTotalDistance += distance

   RaiseEvent Walked(distance)
End Sub
```

The `RaiseEvent` keyword is used to raise the actual event. Because the event requires a parameter, that value is passed within parentheses and is delivered to any recipient that handles the event.

In fact, the `RaiseEvent` statement causes the event to be delivered to all code that has the object declared using the `WithEvents` keyword with a `Handles` clause for this event, or any code that has used the `AddHandler` method. The `AddHandler` method is discussed shortly.

If more than one method will be receiving the event, then the event is delivered to each recipient one at a time. By default, the order of delivery is not defined — meaning you can't predict the order in which the recipients receive the event — but the event is delivered to all handlers. Note that this is a serial, synchronous process. The event is delivered to one handler at a time, and it is not delivered to the next handler until the current handler is complete. Once you call the `RaiseEvent` method, the event is delivered to all listeners one after another until it is complete; there is no way for you to intervene and stop the process in the middle.

Declaring and Raising Custom Events

As just noted, by default you have no control over how events are raised. You can overcome this limitation by using a more explicit form of declaration for the event itself. Rather than use the simple `Event` keyword, you can declare a custom event. This is for more advanced scenarios, as it requires that you provide the implementation for the event itself.

The concept of delegates is covered in detail later in this chapter, but it is necessary to look at them briefly here in order to declare a custom event. A delegate is a definition of a method signature. When you declare an event, Visual Basic defines a delegate for the event behind the scenes based on the signature of the event. The `Walked` event, for instance, has a delegate like the following:

```
Public Delegate Sub WalkedEventHandler(ByVal distance As Integer)
```

Notice how this code declares a "method" that accepts an `Integer` and has no return value. This is exactly what you defined for the event. Normally, you do not write this bit of code, because Visual Basic does it automatically; but if you want to declare a custom event, then you need to manually declare the event delegate.

You also need to declare within the class a variable where you can keep track of any code that is listening for, or handling, the event. It turns out that you can tap into the prebuilt functionality of delegates for this purpose. By declaring the `WalkedEventHandler` delegate, you have defined a data type that automatically tracks event handlers, so you can declare the variable like this:

```
Private mWalkedHandlers As WalkedEventHandler
```

You can use the preceding variable to store and raise the event within the custom event declaration:

```
Public Custom Event Walked As WalkedEventHandler
  AddHandler(ByVal value As WalkedEventHandler)
    mWalkedHandlers = _
      CType([Delegate].Combine(mWalkedHandlers, value), WalkedEventHandler)
  End AddHandler

  RemoveHandler(ByVal value As WalkedEventHandler)
    mWalkedHandlers = _
      CType([Delegate].Remove(mWalkedHandlers, value), WalkedEventHandler)
  End RemoveHandler

  RaiseEvent(ByVal distance As Integer)
    If mWalkedHandlers IsNot Nothing Then
      mWalkedHandlers.Invoke(distance)
    End If
  End RaiseEvent
End Event
```

In this case, you have used the `Custom Event` key phrase, rather than just `Event` to declare the event. A `Custom Event` declaration is a block structure with three sub-blocks: AddHandler, RemoveHandler, and RaiseEvent.

The `AddHandler` block is called anytime a new handler wants to receive the event. The parameter passed to this block is a reference to the method that will be handling the event. It is up to you to store the reference to that method, which you can do however you choose. In this implementation, you are storing it within the delegate variable, just like the default implementation provided by Visual Basic.

The `RemoveHandler` block is called anytime a handler wants to stop receiving your event. The parameter passed to this block is a reference to the method that was handling the event. It is up to you to remove the reference to the method, which you can do however you choose. In this implementation, you are replicating the default behavior by having the delegate variable remove the element.

Finally, the `RaiseEvent` block is called anytime the event is raised. Typically, it is invoked when code within the class uses the `RaiseEvent` statement. The parameters passed to this block must match the parameters declared by the delegate for the event. It is up to you to go through the list of methods that are handling the event and call each of those methods. In the example shown here, you are allowing the delegate variable to do that for you, which is the same behavior you get by default with a normal event.

The value of this syntax is that you could opt to store the list of handler methods in a different type of data structure, such as a `Hashtable` or collection. You could then invoke them asynchronously, or in a specific order or based on some other behavior required by the application.

Receiving Events with WithEvents

Now that you have implemented an event within the Person class, you can write client code to declare an object using the WithEvents keyword. For instance, in the project's Form1 code module, you can write the following code:

```
Public Class Form1
    Inherits System.Windows.Forms.Form
    Private WithEvents mPerson As Person
```

By declaring the variable WithEvents, you are indicating that you want to receive any events raised by this object. You can also choose to declare the variable without the WithEvents keyword, although in that case you would not receive events from the object as described here. Instead, you would use the AddHandler method, which is discussed after WithEvents.

You can then create an instance of the object, as the form is created, by adding the following code:

```
Private Sub Form1_Load(ByVal sender As System.Object, _
    ByVal e As System.EventArgs) Handles MyBase.Load

  mPerson = New Person()

End Sub
```

At this point, you have declared the object variable using WithEvents and have created an instance of the Person class, so you actually have an object with which to work. You can now proceed to write a method to handle the Walked event from the object by adding the following code to the form. You can name this method anything you like; it is the Handles clause that is important because it links the event from the object directly to this method, so it is invoked when the event is raised:

```
Private Sub OnWalk(ByVal distance As Integer) Handles mPerson.Walked
    MsgBox("Person walked " & distance)
End Sub
```

You are using the Handles keyword to indicate which event should be handled by this method. You are also receiving an Integer parameter. If the parameter list of the method doesn't match the list for the event, then you'll get a compiler error indicating the mismatch.

Finally, you need to call the Walk method on the Person object. Add a button to the form and write the following code for its Click event:

```
Private Sub Button1_Click(ByVal sender As System.Object, _
    ByVal e As System.EventArgs) Handles button1.Click

  mPerson.Walk(42)

End Sub
```

When the button is clicked, you simply call the Walk method, passing an Integer value. This causes the code in your class to be run, including the RaiseEvent statement. The result is an event firing back into the form, because you declared the mPerson variable using the WithEvents keyword. The OnWalk method will be run to handle the event, as it has the Handles clause linking it to the event.

Figure 2-4 illustrates the flow of control, showing how the code in the button's Click event calls the Walk method, causing it to add to the total distance walked and then raise its event. The RaiseEvent causes the form's OnWalk method to be invoked; and once it is done, control returns to the Walk method in the object. Because you have no code in the Walk method after you call RaiseEvent, the control returns to the Click event back in the form, and then you are done.

Many people assume that events use multiple threads to do their work. This is not the case. Only one thread is involved in the process. Raising an event is like making a method call, as the existing thread is used to run the code in the event handler. Therefore, the application's processing is suspended until the event processing is complete.

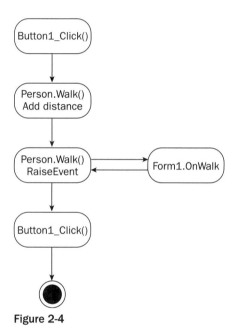

Figure 2-4

Receiving Events with AddHandler

Now that you have seen how to receive and handle events using the WithEvents and Handles keywords, consider an alternative approach. You can use the AddHandler method to dynamically add event handlers through your code, and RemoveHandler to dynamically remove them.

WithEvents and the Handles clause require that you declare both the object variable and event handler as you build the code, effectively creating a linkage that is compiled right into the code. AddHandler, conversely, creates this linkage at runtime, which can provide you with more flexibility. However, before getting too deeply into that, let's see how AddHandler works.

In Form1, you can change the way the code interacts with the Person object, first by eliminating the WithEvents keyword

```
Private mPerson As Person
```

and then by also eliminating the Handles clause:

```
Private Sub OnWalk(ByVal distance As Integer)
  MsgBox("Person walked " & distance)
End Sub
```

With these changes, you've eliminated all event handling for the object, and the form will no longer receive the event, even though the Person object raises it.

Now you can change the code to dynamically add an event handler at runtime by using the AddHandler method. This method simply links an object's event to a method that should be called to handle that event. Anytime after you have created the object, you can call AddHandler to set up the linkage:

```
Private Sub Form1_Load(ByVal sender As System.Object, _
    ByVal e As System.EventArgs) Handles MyBase.Load

  mPerson = New Person()

  AddHandler mPerson.Walked, AddressOf OnWalk
End Sub
```

This single line of code does the same thing as the earlier use of WithEvents and the Handles clause, causing the OnWalk method to be invoked when the Walked event is raised from the Person object.

However, this linkage is performed at runtime, so you have more control over the process than you would have otherwise. For instance, you could have extra code to determine which event handler to link up. Suppose that you have another possible method to handle the event for cases when a message box is not desirable. Add this code to Form1:

```
Private Sub LogOnWalk(ByVal distance As Integer)
  System.Diagnostics.Debug.WriteLine("Person walked " & distance)
End Sub
```

Rather than pop up a message box, this version of the handler logs the event to the output window in the IDE. Now you can enhance the AddHandler code to determine which handler should be used dynamically at runtime:

```
Private Sub Form1_Load(ByVal sender As System.Object, _
    ByVal e As System.EventArgs) Handles MyBase.Load

  mPerson = New Person()

  If Microsoft.VisualBasic.Command = "nodisplay" Then
    AddHandler mPerson.Walked, AddressOf LogOnWalk
  Else
    AddHandler mPerson.Walked, AddressOf OnWalk
  End If
End Sub
```

If the word nodisplay is on the command line when the application is run, then the new version of the event handler is used; otherwise, you continue to use the message-box handler.

The counterpart to AddHandler is RemoveHandler. RemoveHandler is used to detach an event handler from an event. One example of when this is useful is if you ever want to set the mPerson variable to Nothing or to a new Person object. The existing Person object has its events attached to handlers, and before you get rid of the reference to the object, you must release those references:

```
If Microsoft.VisualBasic.Command = "nodisplay" Then
  RemoveHandler mPerson.Walked, AddressOf LogOnWalk
Else
  RemoveHandler mPerson.Walked, AddressOf OnWalk
End If
mPerson = New Person
```

If you do not detach the event handlers, the old Person object remains in memory because each event handler still maintains a reference to the object even after mPerson no longer points to the object.

This illustrates one key reason why the WithEvents keyword and Handles clause are preferable in most cases. AddHandler and RemoveHandler must be used in pairs; failure to do so can cause memory leaks in the application, whereas the WithEvents keyword handles these details for you automatically.

Constructor Methods

In Visual Basic, classes can implement a special method that is always invoked as an object is being created. This method is called the *constructor*, and it is always named New.

The constructor method is an ideal location for such initialization code, as it is always run before any other methods are ever invoked, and it is only run once for an object. Of course, you can create many objects based on a class, and the constructor method will be run for each object that is created.

You can implement a constructor in your classes as well, using it to initialize objects as needed. This is as easy as implementing a Public method named New. Add the following code to the Person class:

```
Public Sub New()
  Phone("home") = "555-1234"
  Phone("work") = "555-5678"
End Sub
```

In this example, you are simply using the constructor method to initialize the home and work phone numbers for any new Person object that is created.

Parameterized Constructors

You can also use constructors to enable parameters to be passed to the object as it is being created. This is done by simply adding parameters to the New method. For example, you can change the Person class as follows:

```
Public Sub New(ByVal name As String, ByVal birthDate As Date)
  mName = name
  mBirthDate = birthDate
  Phone("home") = "555-1234"
  Phone("work") = "555-5678"
End Sub
```

With this change, anytime a `Person` object is created, you will be provided with values for both the name and birth date. However, this changes how you can create a new `Person` object. Whereas you used to have code such as

```
Dim myPerson As New Person()
```

now you will have code such as

```
Dim myPerson As New Person("Bill", "1/1/1970")
```

In fact, because the constructor expects these values, they are mandatory — any code that needs to create an instance of the `Person` class must provide these values. Fortunately, there are alternatives in the form of optional parameters and method overloading (which enables you to create multiple versions of the same method, each accepting a different parameter list). These topics are discussed later in the chapter.

Termination and Cleanup

In the .NET environment, an object is destroyed and the memory and resources it consumes are reclaimed when there are no references remaining for the object. As discussed earlier in the chapter, when you are using objects, the variables actually hold a reference or pointer to the object itself. If you have code such as

```
Dim myPerson As New Person()
```

you know that the `myPerson` variable is just a reference to the `Person` object you created. If you also have code like

```
Dim anotherPerson As Person
anotherPerson = myPerson
```

you know that the `anotherPerson` variable is also a reference to the same object. This means that this specific `Person` object is being referenced by two variables.

When there are no variables left to reference an object, it can be terminated by the .NET runtime environment. In particular, it is terminated and reclaimed by a mechanism called *garbage collection*, or the *garbage collector*, covered in detail in Chapter 4.

> *Unlike COM (and thus VB6), the .NET runtime does not use reference counting to determine when an object should be terminated. Instead, it uses garbage collection to terminate objects. This means that in Visual Basic you do not have deterministic finalization, so it is not possible to predict exactly when an object will be destroyed.*

Let's review how you can eliminate references to an object. You can explicitly remove a reference by setting the variable equal to `Nothing`, with the following code:

```
myPerson = Nothing
```

You can also remove a reference to an object by changing the variable to reference a different object. Because a variable can only point to one object at a time, it follows naturally that changing a variable to point at another object must cause it to no longer point to the first one. This means that you can have code such as the following:

```
myPerson = New Person()
```

This causes the variable to point to a brand-new object, thus releasing this reference to the prior object. These are examples of *explicit dereferencing*.

Visual Basic also provides facilities for *implicit dereferencing* of objects when a variable goes out of scope. For instance, if you have a variable declared within a method, then when that method completes, the variable is automatically destroyed, thus dereferencing any object to which it may have pointed. In fact, anytime a variable referencing an object goes out of scope, the reference to that object is automatically eliminated. This is illustrated by the following code:

```
Private Sub DoSomething()
  Dim myPerson As Person

  myPerson = New Person()
End Sub
```

Even though the preceding code does not explicitly set the value of myPerson to Nothing, you know that the myPerson variable will be destroyed when the method is complete because it will fall out of scope. This process implicitly removes the reference to the Person object created within the routine.

Of course, another scenario in which objects become dereferenced is when the application itself completes and is terminated. At that point, all variables are destroyed, so, by definition, all object references go away as well.

Advanced Concepts

So far, you have learned how to work with objects, how to create classes with methods, properties, and events, and how to use constructors. You have also learned how objects are destroyed within the .NET environment and how you can hook into that process to do any cleanup required by the objects.

Now you can move on to some more complex topics and variations on what has been discussed so far. First you'll look at some advanced variations of the methods you can implement in classes, including an exploration of the underlying technology behind events.

Overloading Methods

Methods often accept parameter values. The Person object's Walk method, for instance, accepts an Integer parameter:

```
Public Sub Walk(ByVal distance As Integer)
  mTotalDistance += distance
  RaiseEvent Walked(distance)
End Sub
```

Sometimes there is no need for the parameter. To address this, you can use the `Optional` keyword to make the parameter optional:

```
Public Sub Walk(Optional ByVal distance As Integer = 0)
   mTotalDistance += distance
   RaiseEvent Walked(distance)
End Sub
```

This does not provide you with a lot of flexibility, however, as the optional parameter or parameters must always be the last ones in the list. In addition, this merely enables you to pass or not pass the parameter. Suppose that you want to do something fancier, such as allow different data types or even entirely different lists of parameters.

Use of the `Optional` keyword makes the code harder to consume from C# or other .NET languages because they do not support optional parameters as VB does. If you are only working in Visual Basic, this may be a non-issue, but if you are working in a multilanguage environment, avoid using the `Optional` keyword. In addition, optional parameters require a default value.

Method overloading provides exactly those capabilities. By overloading methods, you can create several methods of the same name, with each one accepting a different set of parameters, or parameters of different data types.

As a simple example, instead of using the `Optional` keyword in the `Walk` method, you could use overloading. You keep the original `Walk` method, but you also add another `Walk` method that accepts a different parameter list. Change the code in the `Person` class back to the following:

```
Public Sub Walk(ByVal distance As Integer)
   mTotalDistance += distance
   RaiseEvent Walked(distance)
End Sub
```

Now create another method with the same name but with a different parameter list (in this case, no parameters). Add this code to the class, without removing or changing the existing `Walk` method:

```
Public Sub Walk()
   RaiseEvent Walked(0)
End Sub
```

At this point, you have two `Walk` methods. The only way to tell them apart is by the list of parameters each accepts: the first requiring a single `Integer` parameter, the second having no parameter.

There is an `Overloads` keyword as well. This keyword is not needed for the simple overloading of methods described here, but it is required when combining overloading and inheritance, which is discussed in Chapter 3.

You can call the `Walk` method either with or without a parameter, as shown in the following examples:

```
objPerson.Walk(42)
objPerson.Walk()
```

You can have any number of `Walk` methods in the class as long as each individual `Walk` method has a different method signature.

Method Signatures

All methods have a signature, which is defined by the method name and the data types of its parameters:

```
Public Function CalculateValue() As Integer

End Sub
```

In this example, the signature is f(). The letter *f* is often used to indicate a method or function. It is appropriate here because you do not care about the name of the function; only its parameter list is important.

If you add a parameter to the method, then the signature is considered changed. For instance, you could change the method to accept a `Double`:

```
Public Function CalculateValue(ByVal value As Double) As Integer
```

In that case, the signature of the method is f(Double).

Notice that in Visual Basic the return value is not part of the signature. You cannot overload a `Function` routine by just having its return value's data type vary. It is the data types in the parameter list that must vary to utilize overloading.

Also note that the name of the parameter is totally immaterial; only the data type is important. This means that the following methods have identical signatures:

```
Public Sub DoWork(ByVal x As Integer, ByVal y As Integer)

Public Sub DoWork(ByVal value1 As Integer, ByVal value2 As Integer)
```

In both cases, the signature is f(Integer, Integer).

The data types of the parameters define the method signature, but whether the parameters are passed `ByVal` or `ByRef` does not. Changing a parameter from `ByVal` to `ByRef` will not change the method signature.

Combining Overloading and Optional Parameters

Overloading is more flexible than using optional parameters, but optional parameters have the advantage that they can be used to provide default values, as well as make a parameter optional.

You can combine the two concepts: overloading a method and having one or more of those methods utilize optional parameters. Obviously, this sort of thing can become very confusing if overused, as you are employing two types of method "overloading" at the same time.

The `Optional` keyword causes a single method to effectively have two signatures. This means that a method declared as

```
Public Sub DoWork(ByVal x As Integer, Optional ByVal y As Integer = 0)
```

has two signatures at once: f(Integer, Integer) and f(Integer).

Because of this, when you use overloading along with optional parameters, the other overloaded methods cannot match either of these two signatures. However, as long as other methods do not match either signature, you can use overloading, as discussed earlier. For instance, you could implement methods with the signatures

```
Public Sub DoWork(ByVal x As Integer, Optional ByVal y As Integer = 0)
```

and

```
Public Sub DoWork(ByVal data As String)
```

because there are no conflicting method signatures. In fact, with these two methods, you have actually created three signatures:

❑   f(Integer, Integer)

❑   f(Integer)

❑   f(String)

The IntelliSense built into the Visual Studio IDE will indicate that you have two overloaded methods, one of which has an optional parameter. This is different from creating three different overloaded methods to match these three signatures, in which case the IntelliSense would list three variations on the method, from which you could choose.

Overloading Constructor Methods

In many cases, you may want the constructor to accept parameter values for initializing new objects, but also want to have the capability to create objects without providing those values. This is possible through method overloading, which is discussed later, or by using optional parameters.

Optional parameters on a constructor method follow the same rules as optional parameters for any other Sub routine: They must be the last parameters in the parameter list, and you must provide default values for the optional parameters.

For instance, you can change the Person class as shown here:

```
    Public Sub New(Optional ByVal name As String = "", _
        Optional ByVal birthDate As Date = #1/1/1900#)
      mName = name
      mBirthDate = birthDate

      Phone("home") = "555-1234"
      Phone("work") = "555-5678"
    End Sub
```

The preceding example changed both the Name and BirthDate parameters to be optional, and provides default values for both of them. Now you have the option to create a new Person object with or without the parameter values:

```
Dim myPerson As New Person("Bill", "1/1/1970")
```

or

```
Dim myPerson As New Person()
```

If you do not provide the parameter values, then the default values of an empty `String` and `1/1/1900` will be used and the code will work just fine.

Overloading the Constructor Method

You can combine the concept of a constructor method with method overloading to allow for different ways of creating instances of the class. This can be a very powerful combination because it allows a great deal of flexibility in object creation.

You have already explored how to use optional parameters in the constructor. Now let's change the implementation in the `Person` class to make use of overloading instead. Change the existing `New` method as follows:

```
Public Sub New(ByVal name As String, ByVal birthDate As Date)
     mName = name
     mBirthDate = birthDate
     Phone("home") = "555-1234"
     Phone("work") = "555-5678"
  End Sub
```

With this change, you require the two parameter values to be supplied. Now add that second implementation, as shown here:

```
Public Sub New()
   Phone("home") = "555-1234"
   Phone("work") = "555-5678"
End Sub
```

This second implementation accepts no parameters, meaning you can now create `Person` objects in two different ways — either with no parameters or by passing the name and birth date:

```
Dim myPerson As New Person()
```

or

```
Dim myPerson As New Person("Fred", "1/11/60")
```

This type of capability is very powerful because it enables you to define the various ways in which applications can create objects. In fact, the Visual Studio IDE considers this, so when you are typing the code to create an object, the IntelliSense tooltip displays the overloaded variations on the method, providing a level of automatic documentation for the class.

Shared Methods, Variables, and Events

So far, all of the methods you have built or used have been instance methods, methods that require you to have an actual instance of the class before they can be called. These methods have used instance variables or member variables to do their work, which means that they have been working with a set of data that is unique to each individual object.

With Visual Basic, you can create variables and methods that belong to the class, rather than to any specific object. In other words, these variables and methods belong to all objects of a given class and are shared across all the instances of the class.

You can use the Shared keyword to indicate which variables and methods belong to the class, rather than to specific objects. For instance, you may be interested in knowing the total number of Person objects created as the application is running — kind of a statistical counter.

Shared Variables

Because regular variables are unique to each individual Person object, they do not enable you to easily track the total number of Person objects ever created. However, if you had a variable that had a common value across all instances of the Person class, you could use that as a counter. Add the following variable declaration to the Person class:

```
Public Class Person
    Implements IDisposable

    Private Shared mCounter As Integer
```

By using the Shared keyword, you are indicating that this variable's value should be shared across all Person objects within your application. This means that if one Person object makes the value 42, then all other Person objects will see the value as 42: It is a shared piece of data.

You can now use this variable within the code. For instance, you can add code to the constructor method, New, to increment the variable so that it acts as a counter — adding 1 each time a new Person object is created. Change the New methods as shown here:

```
Public Sub New()
    Phone("home") = "555-1234"
    Phone("work") = "555-5678"

    mCounter += 1
End Sub

Public Sub New(ByVal name As String, ByVal birthDate As Date)
    mName = name
    mBirthDate = birthDate

    Phone("home") = "555-1234"
    Phone("work") = "555-5678"

    mCounter += 1
End Sub
```

The mCounter variable will now maintain a value indicating the total number of Person objects created during the life of the application. You may want to add a property routine to allow access to this value by writing the following code:

```
Public ReadOnly Property PersonCount() As Integer
    Get
        Return mCounter
    End Get
End Property
```

Note that you are creating a regular property that returns the value of a shared variable, which is perfectly acceptable. As shown shortly, you could also create a shared property to return the value.

Now you could write code to use the class as follows:

```
Dim myPerson As Person
myPerson = New Person()
myPerson = New Person()
myPerson = New Person()

Messagebox.Show(myPerson.PersonCount)
```

The resulting display would show 3, because you've created three instances of the Person class. You would also need to decrement the counter after the objects are destroyed.

Shared Methods

You can share not only variables across all instances of a class, but also methods. Whereas a regular method or property belongs to each specific object, a shared method or property is common across all instances of the class. There are a couple of ramifications to this approach.

First, because shared methods do not belong to any specific object, they can't access any instance variables from any objects. The only variables available for use within a shared method are shared variables, parameters passed into the method, or variables declared locally within the method itself. If you attempt to access an instance variable within a shared method, you'll get a compiler error.

In addition, because shared methods are actually part of the class, rather than any object, you can write code to call them directly from the class without having to create an instance of the class first.

For instance, a regular instance method is invoked from an object:

```
Dim myPerson As New Person()

myPerson.Walk(42)
```

However, a shared method can be invoked directly from the class itself:

```
Person.SharedMethod()
```

This saves the effort of creating an object just to invoke a method, and can be very appropriate for methods that act on shared variables, or methods that act only on values passed in via parameters. You can also invoke a shared method from an object, just like a regular method. Shared methods are flexible in that they can be called with or without creating an instance of the class first.

To create a shared method, you again use the Shared keyword. For instance, the PersonCount property created earlier could easily be changed to become a shared method instead:

```
Public Shared ReadOnly Property PersonCount() As Integer
  Get
    Return mCounter
  End Get
End Property
```

Because this property returns the value of a shared variable, it is perfectly acceptable for it to be implemented as a shared method. With this change, you can now determine how many `Person` objects have ever been created without having to actually create a `Person` object first:

```
Messagebox.Show(CStr(Person.PersonCount))
```

As another example, in the `Person` class, you could create a method that compares the ages of two people. Add a shared method with the following code:

```
Public Shared Function CompareAge(ByVal person1 As Person, _
    ByVal person2 As Person) As Boolean

  Return person1.Age > person2.Age
End Function
```

This method simply accepts two parameters — each a `Person` — and returns `True` if the first is older than the second. Use of the `Shared` keyword indicates that this method doesn't require a specific instance of the `Person` class in order for you to use it.

Within this code, you are invoking the `Age` property on two separate objects, the objects passed as parameters to the method. It is important to recognize that you're not directly using any instance variables within the method; rather, you are accepting two objects as parameters, and invoking methods on those objects. To use this method, you can call it directly from the class:

```
If Person.CompareAge(myPerson1, myPerson2) Then
```

Alternately, you can also invoke it from any `Person` object:

```
Dim myPerson As New Person()

If myPerson.CompareAge(myPerson, myPerson2) Then
```

Either way, you're invoking the same shared method, and you'll get the same behavior, whether you call it from the class or a specific instance of the class.

Shared Properties

As with other types of methods, you can also have shared property methods. Properties follow the same rules as regular methods. They can interact with shared variables but not member variables. They can also invoke other shared methods or properties, but cannot invoke instance methods without first creating an instance of the class. You can add a shared property to the `Person` class with the following code:

```
Public Shared ReadOnly Property RetirementAge() As Integer
  Get
    Return 62
  End Get
End Property
```

This simply adds a property to the class that indicates the global retirement age for all people. To use this value, you can simply access it directly from the class:

```
Messagebox.Show(Person.RetirementAge)
```

Alternately, you can access it from any `Person` object:

```
Dim myPerson As New Person()

Messagebox.Show(myPerson.RetirementAge)
```

Either way, you are invoking the same shared property.

Shared Events

As with other interface elements, events can also be marked as `Shared`. For instance, you could declare a shared event in the `Person` class:

```
Public Shared Event NewPerson()
```

Shared events can be raised from both instance methods and shared methods. Regular events cannot be raised by shared methods. Because shared events can be raised by regular methods, you can raise this one from the constructors in the `Person` class:

```
Public Sub New()
   Phone("home") = "555-1234"
   Phone("work") = "555-5678"
   mCounter += 1

   RaiseEvent NewPerson()
End Sub

Public Sub New(ByVal name As String, ByVal birthDate As Date)
   mName = Name
   mBirthDate = BirthDate

   Phone("home") = "555-1234"
   Phone("work") = "555-5678"
   mCounter += 1

   RaiseEvent NewPerson()
End Sub
```

The interesting thing about receiving shared events is that you can get them from either an object, such as a normal event, or from the class itself. For instance, you can use the `AddHandler` method in the form's code to catch this event directly from the `Person` class.

First, add a method to the form to handle the event:

```
Private Sub OnNewPerson()
   Messagebox.Show("new person " & Person.PersonCount)
End Sub
```

Then, in the form's `Load` event, add a statement to link the event to this method:

```
Private Sub Form1_Load(ByVal sender As System.Object, _
    ByVal e As System.EventArgs) Handles MyBase.Load

   AddHandler Person.NewPerson, AddressOf OnNewPerson
```

```
      mPerson = New Person()
      If Microsoft.VisualBasic.Command = "nodisplay" Then
        AddHandler mPerson.Walked, AddressOf LogOnWalk
      Else
        AddHandler mPerson.Walked, AddressOf OnWalk
      End If
  End Sub
```

Notice that you are using the class, rather than any specific object in the AddHandler statement. You could use an object as well, treating this like a normal event, but this illustrates how a class itself can raise an event. When you run the application now, anytime a Person object is created you will see this event raised.

Shared Constructor

A class can also have a Shared constructor:

```
Shared Sub New()

End Sub
```

Normal constructors are called when an instance of the class is created. The Shared constructor is called only once during the lifetime of an application, immediately before any use of the class.

This means that the Shared constructor is called before any other Shared methods, and before any instances of the class are created. The first time any code attempts to interact with any method on the class, or attempts to create an instance of the class, the Shared constructor is invoked.

Because you never directly call the Shared constructor, it cannot accept any parameters. Moreover, because it is a Shared method, it can only interact with Shared variables or other Shared methods in the class.

Typically, a Shared constructor is used to initialize Shared fields within an object. In the Person class, for instance, you can use it to initialize the mCount variable:

```
Shared Sub New()
  mCount = 0
End Sub
```

Because this method is called only once during the lifetime of the application, it is safe to do one-time initializations of values in this constructor.

Operator Overloading

Many basic data types, such as Integer and String, support the use of operators, including +, −, =, <>, and so forth. When you create a class, you are defining a new type, and sometimes it is appropriate for types to also support the use of operators.

In your class, you can write code to define how each of these operators works when applied to objects. What does it mean when two objects are added together? Or multiplied? Or compared? If you can define what these operations mean, you can write code to implement appropriate behaviors. This is called *operator overloading*, as you are overloading the meaning of specific operators.

Operator overloading is performed by using the Operator keyword, in much the same way that you create a Sub, Function, or Property method.

Most objects at least provide for some type of comparison, and so will often overload the comparison operators (=, <>, and maybe <, >, <=, and >=). You can do this in the Person class, for example, by adding the following code:

```
Public Shared Operator =(ByVal person1 As Person, _
  ByVal person2 As Person) As Boolean

  Return person1.Name = person2.Name
End Operator

Public Shared Operator <>(ByVal person1 As Person, _
  ByVal person2 As Person) As Boolean

  Return person1.Name <> person2.Name
End Operator
```

Note that you overload both the = and <> operators. Many operators come in pairs, including the equality operator. If you overload =, then you must overload <> or a compiler error will result. Now that you have overloaded these operators, you can write code in Form1 such as the following:

```
Dim p1 As New Person("Fred", #1/1/1960#)
Dim p2 As New Person("Mary", #1/1/1980#)
Dim p3 As Person = p1

Debug.WriteLine(CStr(p1 = p2))
Debug.WriteLine(CStr(p1 = p3))
```

Normally, it would be impossible to compare two objects using a simple comparison operator, but because you overloaded the operator, this becomes valid code. The result will display False and True.

Both the = and <> operators accept two parameters, so these are called *binary operators*. There are also *unary operators* that accept a single parameter. For instance, you might define the capability to convert a String value into a Person object by overloading the CType operator:

```
Public Shared Narrowing Operator CType(ByVal name As String) As Person
  Dim obj As New Person
  obj.Name = name
  Return obj
End Operator
```

To convert a String value to a Person, you assume that the value should be the Name property. You create a new object, set the Name property, and return the result. Because String is a broader, or less specific, type than Person, this is a Narrowing conversion. Were you to do the reverse, convert a Person to a String, that would be a Widening conversion:

```
Public Shared Widening Operator CType(ByVal person As Person) As String
  Return person.Name
End Operator
```

Few non-numeric objects will overload most operators. It is difficult to imagine the result of adding, subtracting, or dividing two Customer objects against each other. Likewise, it is difficult to imagine performing bitwise comparisons between two `Invoice` objects. The following chart lists the various operators that can be overloaded:

Operators	Description
=, <>	Equality and inequality. These are binary operators to support the a = b and a <> b syntax. If you implement one, then you must implement both.
>, <	Greater than and less than. These are binary operators to support the a > b and a < b syntax. If you implement one, then you must implement both.
>=, <=	Greater than or equal to and less than or equal to. These are binary operators to support the a >= b and a <= b syntax. If you implement one, then you must implement both.
IsFalse, IsTrue	Boolean conversion. These are unary operators to support the AndAlso and OrElse statements. The IsFalse operator accepts a single object and returns False if the object can be resolved to a False value. The IsTrue operator accepts a single value and returns True if the object can be resolved to a True value. If you implement one, then you must implement both.
CType	Type conversion. This is a unary operator to support the CType(a) statement. The CType operator accepts a single object of another type and converts that object to the type of your class. This operator must be marked as either Narrowing, to indicate that the type is more specific than the original type, or Widening, to indicate that the type is broader than the original type.
+, -	Addition and subtraction. These operators can be unary or binary. The unary form exists to support the a += b and a −= b syntax, while the binary form exists to support a + b and a − b.
*, /, \, ^, Mod	Multiplication, division, exponent, and Mod. These are binary operators to support the a * b, a / b, a \ b, a ^ b, and a Mod b syntax.
&	Concatenation. This binary operator supports the a & b syntax. While this operator is typically associated with String manipulation, the & operator is not required to accept or return String values, so it can be used for any concatenation operation that is meaningful for your object type.
<<, >>	Bit shifting. These binary operators support the a << b and a >> b syntax. The second parameter of these operators must be a value of type Integer, which will be the integer value to be bit-shifted based on your object value.
And, Or, Xor	Logical comparison or bitwise operation. These binary operators support the a And b, a Or b, and a Xor b syntax. If the operators return Boolean results, then they are performing logical comparisons. If they return results of other data types, then they are performing bitwise operations.
Like	Pattern comparison. This binary operator supports the a Like b syntax.

If an operator is meaningful for your data type, then you are strongly encouraged to overload that operator.

Defining AndAlso and OrElse

Notice that neither the `AndAlso` nor the `OrElse` operators can be directly overloaded. This is because these operators use other operators behind the scenes to do their work. To overload `AndAlso` and `OrElse`, you need to overload a set of other operators, as shown here:

AndAlso	OrElse
Overload the `And` operator to accept two parameters of your object's type and to return a result of your object's type.	Overload the `Or` operator to accept two parameters of your object's type and to return a result of your object's type.
Overload `IsFalse` for your object's type (meaning that you can return `True` or `False` by evaluating a single instance of your object).	Overload `IsTrue` for your object's type (meaning that you can return `True` or `False` by evaluating a single instance of your object).

If these operators are overloaded in your class, then you can use `AndAlso` and `OrElse` to evaluate statements that involve instances of your class.

Delegates

Sometimes it would be nice to be able to pass a procedure as a parameter to a method. The classic scenario is when building a generic sort routine, for which you need to provide not only the data to be sorted, but also a comparison routine appropriate for the specific data.

It is easy enough to write a sort routine that sorts `Person` objects by name, or to write a sort routine that sorts `SalesOrder` objects by sales date. However, if you want to write a sort routine that can sort any type of object based on arbitrary sort criteria, that gets pretty difficult. At the same time, because some sort routines can get very complex, it would be nice to reuse that code without having to copy and paste it for each different sort scenario.

By using *delegates*, you can create such a generic routine for sorting; and in so doing, you can see how delegates work and can be used to create many other types of generic routines. The concept of a delegate formalizes the process of declaring a routine to be called and calling that routine.

> *The underlying mechanism used by the .NET environment for callback methods is the delegate. Visual Basic uses delegates behind the scenes as it implements the* `Event`, `RaiseEvent`, `WithEvents`, *and* `Handles` *keywords.*

Declaring a Delegate

In your code, you can declare what a delegate procedure must look like from an interface standpoint. This is done using the `Delegate` keyword. To see how this works, let's create a routine to sort any kind of data.

To do this, you will declare a delegate that defines a method signature for a method that compares the value of two objects and returns a `Boolean` indicating whether the first object has a larger value than the second object. You will then create a sort algorithm that uses this generic comparison method to sort data. Finally, you will create an actual method that implements the comparison, and then you will pass the method's address to the sort routine.

Add a new module to the project by choosing Project⇨Add Module. Name the module Sort.vb, and then add the following code:

```
Module Sort

    Public Delegate Function Compare(ByVal v1 As Object, ByVal v2 As Object) _
        As Boolean
End Module
```

This line of code does something interesting. It actually defines a method signature as a data type. This new data type is named Compare, and it can be used within the code to declare variables or parameters that are accepted by your methods. A variable or parameter declared using this data type could actually hold the address of a method that matches the defined method signature, and you can then invoke that method by using the variable.

Any method with the following signature can be viewed as being of type Compare:

```
f(Object, Object)
```

Using the Delegate Data Type

You can write a routine that accepts this data type as a parameter, meaning that anyone calling your routine must pass the address of a method that conforms to this interface. Add the following sort routine to the code module:

```
Public Sub DoSort(ByVal theData() As Object, ByVal greaterThan As Compare)
    Dim outer As Integer
    Dim inner As Integer
    Dim temp As Object

    For outer = 0 To UBound(theData)
    For inner = outer + 1 To UBound(theData)
       If greaterThan.Invoke(theData(outer), theData(inner)) Then
         temp = theData(outer)
         theData(outer) = theData(inner)
         theData(inner) = temp
       End If
     Next
   Next
End Sub
```

The GreaterThan parameter is a variable that holds the address of a method matching the method signature defined by the Compare delegate. The address of any method with a matching signature can be passed as a parameter to your Sort routine.

Note the use of the Invoke method, which is how a delegate is called from the code. In addition, note that the routine deals entirely with the generic System.Object data type, rather than with any specific type of data. The specific comparison of one object to another is left to the delegate routine that is passed in as a parameter.

Implementing a Delegate Method

Now create the implementation of the delegate routine and call the sort method. On a very basic level, all you need to do is create a method that has a matching method signature, as shown in the following example:

```
Public Function PersonCompare(ByVal person1 As Object, _
  ByVal person2 As Object) As Boolean

End Function
```

The method signature of this method exactly matches what you defined by your delegate earlier:

```
Compare(Object, Object)
```

In both cases, you are defining two parameters of type `Object`.

Of course, there is more to it than simply creating the stub of a method. The method needs to return a value of `True` if its first parameter is greater than the second parameter. Otherwise, it should be written to deal with some specific type of data.

The `Delegate` statement defines a data type based on a specific method interface. To call a routine that expects a parameter of this new data type, it must pass the address of a method that conforms to the defined interface.

To conform to the interface, a method must have the same number of parameters with the same data types defined in your `Delegate` statement. In addition, the method must provide the same return type as defined. The actual name of the method does not matter; it is the number, order, and data type of the parameters and the return value that count.

To find the address of a specific method, you can use the `AddressOf` operator. This operator returns the address of any procedure or method, enabling you to pass that value as a parameter to any routine that expects a delegate as a parameter.

The `Person` class already has a shared method named `CompareAge` that generally does what you want. Unfortunately, it accepts parameters of type `Person`, rather than of type `Object` as required by the `Compare` delegate. You can use method overloading to solve this problem.

Create a second implementation of `CompareAge` that accepts parameters of type `Object` as required by the delegate, rather than of type `Person` as shown in the existing implementation:

```
Public Shared Function CompareAge(ByVal person1 As Object, _
    ByVal person2 As Object) As Boolean

  Return CType(person1, Person).Age > CType(person2, Person).Age

End Function
```

This method simply returns `True` if the first `Person` object's age is greater than the second. The routine accepts two `Object` parameters, rather than specific `Person` type parameters, so you have to use the

CType method to access those objects as type Person. You accept the parameters as type Object because that is what is defined by the Delegate statement. You are matching its method signature:

```
f(Object, Object)
```

Because this method's parameter data types and return value match the delegate, you can use it when calling the Sort routine. Place a button on the form and write the following code behind that button:

```
Private Sub Button2_Click(ByVal sender As System.Object, _
    ByVal e As System.EventArgs) Handles button2.Click

  Dim myPeople(4) As Person

  myPeople(0) = New Person("Fred", #7/9/1960#)
  myPeople(1) = New Person("Mary", #1/21/1955#)
  myPeople(2) = New Person("Sarah", #2/1/1960#)
  myPeople(3) = New Person("George", #5/13/1970#)
  myPeople(4) = New Person("Andre", #10/1/1965#)

  DoSort(myPeople, AddressOf Person.CompareAge)
End Sub
```

This code creates an array of Person objects and populates them. It then calls the DoSort routine from the module, passing the array as the first parameter, and the address of the shared CompareAge method as the second parameter. To display the contents of the sorted array in the IDE's output window, you can add the following code:

```
Private Sub button2_Click(ByVal sender As System.Object, _
    ByVal e As System.EventArgs) Handles button2.Click

  Dim myPeople(4) As Person

  myPeople(0) = New Person("Fred", #7/9/1960#)
  myPeople(1) = New Person("Mary", #1/21/1955#)
  myPeople(2) = New Person("Sarah", #2/1/1960#)
  myPeople(3) = New Person("George", #5/13/1970#)
  myPeople(4) = New Person("Andre", #10/1/1965#)

  DoSort(myPeople, AddressOf Person.CompareAge)
  Dim myPerson As Person
  For Each myPerson In myPeople
    System.Diagnostics.Debug.WriteLine(myPerson.Name & " " & myPerson.Age)
  Next
End Sub
```

When you run the application and click the button, the output window displays a list of the people sorted by age, as shown in Figure 2-5.

What makes this so powerful is that you can change the comparison routine without changing the sort mechanism. Simply add another comparison routine to the Person class:

```
Public Shared Function CompareName(ByVal person1 As Object, _
    ByVal person2 As Object) As Boolean
```

```
      Return CType(person1, Person).Name > CType(person2, Person).Name

End Function
```

Figure 2-5

Then, change the code behind the button on the form to use that alternate comparison routine:

```
Private Sub Button2_Click(ByVal sender As System.Object, _
    ByVal e As System.EventArgs) Handles Button2.Click

  Dim myPeople(4) As Person

  myPeople(0) = New Person("Fred", #7/9/1960#)
  myPeople(1) = New Person("Mary", #1/21/1955#)
  myPeople(2) = New Person("Sarah", #2/1/1960#)
  myPeople(3) = New Person("George", #5/13/1970#)
  myPeople(4) = New Person("Andre", #10/1/1965#)

  DoSort(myPeople, AddressOf Person.CompareName)

  Dim myPerson As Person

  For Each myPerson In myPeople
    System.Diagnostics.Debug.WriteLine(myPerson.Name & " " & myPerson.Age)
  Next
End Sub
```

When you run this updated code, you will find that the array contains a set of data sorted by name, rather than age, as shown in Figure 2-6.

Figure 2-6

Simply by creating a new compare routine and passing it as a parameter, you can entirely change the way that the data is sorted. Better still, this sort routine can operate on any type of object, as long as you provide an appropriate delegate method that knows how to compare that type of object.

Classes versus Components

Visual Basic has another concept that is very similar to a class: the *component*. In fact, you can pretty much use a component and a class interchangeably, though there are some differences.

A component is little more than a regular class, but one that supports a graphical designer within the Visual Studio IDE. This means you can use drag-and-drop to provide the code in the component with access to items from the Server Explorer or the Toolbox.

To add a component to a project, select Project⇨Add Component, give the component a name, and click Open in the Add New Item dialog box.

When you add a class to the project, you are presented with the code window. When you add a component, you are presented with a graphical designer surface, much like what you would see when adding a Web Form to the project.

If you switch to the code view (by right-clicking in the Design view and choosing View Code), you will see the code that is created automatically, just as it is with a Windows Form, Web Form, or regular class:

```
Public Class Component1

End Class
```

This is not a lot more code than you see with a regular class, though there are differences behind the scenes. A component uses the same partial class technology as Windows Forms or Web Forms. This means that the code here is only part of the total code in the class. The rest of the code is hidden behind the designer's surface and is automatically created and managed by Visual Studio.

In the designer code is an `Inherits` statement that makes every component inherit from `System.ComponentModel.Component`. Chapter 3 discusses the concept of inheritance, but note here that this `Inherits` line is what brings in all the support for the graphical designer in Visual Studio.

The designer also manages any controls or components that are dropped on it. Those controls or components are automatically made available to your code. For instance, if you drag and drop a `Timer` control from the Windows Forms tab of the Toolbox onto the component, it will be displayed in the designer.

From here, you can set its properties using the standard Properties window in the IDE, just as you would for a control on a form. Using the Properties window, set the `Name` property to `theTimer`. You now automatically have access to a `Timer` object named `theTimer`, simply by dragging and dropping and setting some properties.

This means that you can write code within the component, just as you might in a class, to use this object:

```
Public Sub Start()
   theTimer.Enabled = True
End Sub
```

```
Public Sub Stop()
  theTimer.Enabled = False
End Sub

Private Sub theTimer_Tick(ByVal sender As System.Object, _
  ByVal e As System.EventArgs) Handles theTimer.Tick

  ' do work
End Sub
```

For the most part, you can use a component interchangeably with a basic class, but using a component also provides some of the designer benefits of working with Windows Forms or Web Forms.

Summary

Visual Basic offers a fully object-oriented language with all the capabilities you would expect. This chapter described the basic concepts behind classes and objects, as well as the separation of interface from implementation and data. You have learned how to use the Class keyword to create classes, and how those classes can be instantiated into specific objects, each one an instance of the class. These objects have methods and properties that can be invoked by the client code, and can act on data within the object stored in member or instance variables.

You also explored some more advanced concepts, including method overloading, shared or static variables and methods, and the use of delegates. Finally, the chapter provided a brief overview of attributes and how you can use them to affect the interaction of classes or methods with the .NET environment.

The next chapter continues the discussion of object syntax as you explore the concept of inheritance and all the syntax that enables inheritance within Visual Basic. You will also walk through the creation, implementation, and use of multiple interfaces — a powerful concept that enables objects to be used in different ways, depending on the interface chosen by the client application.

Also covered in the next chapter is a discussion of objects and object-oriented programming, applying all of this syntax. It explains the key object-oriented concepts of abstraction, encapsulation, polymorphism, and inheritance, and shows how they work together to provide a powerful way to design and implement applications.

Chapter 4 explores the .NET common language runtime (CLR). Because the .NET platform and runtime are object-oriented at their very core, this chapter examines how objects interact with the runtime environment and covers topics such as using and disposing of objects and memory management.

3

Object-Oriented Programming

Visual Basic is a fully object-oriented language. Chapter 2 covered the basics of creating classes and objects, including the creation of methods, properties, events, operators, and instance variables. You have seen the basic building blocks for abstraction, encapsulation, and polymorphism — concepts discussed in more detail at the end of this chapter. The final major techniques you need to understand are *inheritance* and the use of *multiple interfaces*.

Inheritance is the idea that you can create a class that reuses methods, properties, events, and variables from another class. You can create a class with some basic functionality, and then use that class as a base from which to create other, more detailed, classes. All these derived classes will have the same common functionality as that base class, along with new, enhanced, or even completely changed functionality.

This chapter covers the syntax that supports inheritance within Visual Basic. This includes creating the base classes from which other classes can be derived, as well as creating those derived classes.

Visual Basic also supports a related concept: multiple interfaces. As shown in Chapter 2, all objects have a native or default interface, which is defined by the public methods, properties, and events declared in the class. In the .NET environment, an object can have other interfaces in addition to this native interface — in other words, .NET objects can have multiple interfaces.

These secondary interfaces define alternative ways in which your object can be accessed by providing clearly defined sets of methods, properties, and events. Like the native interface, these secondary interfaces define how the client code can interact with your object, essentially providing a "contract" that enables the client to know exactly what methods, properties, and events the object will provide. When you write code to interact with an object, you can choose which of the interfaces you want to use; basically, you are choosing how you want to view or interact with that object.

This chapter uses relatively basic code examples so that you can focus on the technical and syntactic issues surrounding inheritance and multiple interfaces. The last part of this chapter revisits these concepts using a more sophisticated set of code as you continue to explore object-oriented programming and how to apply inheritance and multiple interfaces in a practical manner.

Of course, just knowing the syntax and learning the tools is not enough to be successful. Successfully applying Visual Basic's object-oriented capabilities requires an understanding of object-oriented programming. This chapter also applies Visual Basic's object-oriented syntax, showing how it enables you to build object-oriented applications. It also describes the four major object-oriented concepts: abstraction, encapsulation, polymorphism, and inheritance. By the end of this chapter, you will understand how to apply these concepts in your design and development efforts to create effective object-oriented applications.

Inheritance

Inheritance is the concept that a new class can be based on an existing class, inheriting the interface and functionality from the original class. In Chapter 2, you explored the relationship between a class and an object, and saw that the class is essentially a template from which objects can be created.

While this is very powerful, it does not provide all the capabilities you might like. In particular, in many cases a class only partially describes what you need for your object. You may have a class called Person, for instance, which has all the properties and methods that apply to all types of people, such as first name, last name, and birth date. While useful, this class probably does not have everything you need to describe a specific type of person, such as an employee or a customer. An employee would have a hire date and a salary, which are not included in Person, while a customer would have a credit rating, something neither the Person nor the Employee classes would need.

Without inheritance, you would probably end up replicating the code from the Person class in both the Employee and Customer classes so that they would have that same functionality as well as the ability to add new functionality of their own.

Inheritance makes it very easy to create classes for Employee, Customer, and so forth. You do not have to re-create that code for an employee to be a person; it automatically inherits any properties, methods, and events from the original Person class.

You can think of it this way: When you create an Employee class, which inherits from a Person class, you are effectively merging these two classes. If you then create an object based on the Employee class, then it has not only the interface (properties, methods, and events) and implementation from the Employee class, but also those from the Person class.

While an Employee object represents the merger between the Employee and Person classes, understand that the variables and code contained in each of those classes remain independent. Two perspectives are involved.

From the outside, the client code that interacts with the Employee object sees a single, unified object that represents the merger of the Employee and Person classes.

From the inside, the code in the Employee class and the code in the Person class are not totally intermixed. Variables and methods that are Private are only available within the class they were written. Variables and methods that are Public in one class can be called from the other class. Variables and methods that are declared as Friend are only available between classes if both classes are in the same Visual Basic project. As discussed later in the chapter, there is also a Protected scope that is designed to work with inheritance, but, again, this provides a controlled way for one class to interact with the variables and methods in the other class.

Visual Studio 2008 includes a Class Designer tool that enables you to easily create diagrams of your classes and their relationships. The Class Designer diagrams are a derivative of a standard notation called the *Unified Modeling Language (UML)* that is typically used to diagram the relationships between classes, objects, and other object-oriented concepts. The Class Designer diagrams more accurately and completely model .NET classes, so that is the notation used in this chapter. The relationship between the Person, Employee, and Customer classes is illustrated in Figure 3-1.

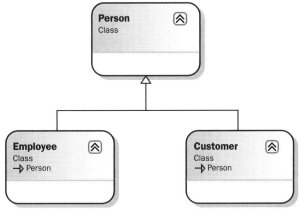

Figure 3-1

Each box in this diagram represents a class; in this case, you have Person, Employee, and Customer classes. The line from Employee back up to Person, terminating in a triangle, indicates that Employee is derived from, or inherits from, Person. The same is true for the Customer class.

Later in this chapter, you will learn when and how inheritance should be used in software design. The beginning part of this chapter covers the syntax and programming concepts necessary to implement inheritance. First you will create a base Person class. Then you will use that class to create both Employee and Customer classes that inherit behavior from Person.

Before getting into the implementation, however, it's necessary to understand some basic terms associated with inheritance — and there are a lot of terms, partly because there are often several ways to say the same thing. The various terms are all used quite frequently and interchangeably.

> *Though we attempt to use consistent terminology in this book, be aware that in other books and articles, and online, all these terms are used in various permutations.*

Inheritance, for instance, is also sometimes referred to as *generalization* because the class from which you are inheriting your behavior is virtually always a more general form of your new class. A person is more general than an employee, for instance.

The inheritance relationship is also referred to as an *is-a* relationship. When you create a Customer class that inherits from a Person class, that customer *is a* person. The employee is a person as well. Thus, you have the *is-a* relationship. As shown later in the chapter, multiple interfaces can be used to implement something similar to the *is-a* relationship, the *act-as* relationship.

When you create a class using inheritance, it inherits behaviors and data from an existing class. That existing class is called the *base class*. It is also often referred to as a *superclass* or a *parent class*.

The class you create using inheritance is based on the parent class. It is called a *subclass*. Sometimes it is also called a *child class* or a *derived class*. In fact, the process of inheriting from a base class by a subclass is referred to as *deriving*. You are deriving a new class from the base class. The process is also called *subclassing*.

Implementing Inheritance

When you set out to implement a class using inheritance, you must first start with an existing class from which you will derive your new subclass. This existing class, or base class, may be part of the .NET system class library framework, it may be part of some other application or .NET assembly, or you may create it as part of your existing application.

Once you have a base class, you can then implement one or more subclasses based on that base class. Each of your subclasses automatically inherits all of the methods, properties, and events of that base class — including the implementation behind each method, property, and event. Your subclass can also add new methods, properties, and events of its own, extending the original interface with new functionality. In addition, a subclass can replace the methods and properties of the base class with its own new implementation — effectively overriding the original behavior and replacing it with new behaviors.

Essentially, inheritance is a way of merging functionality from an existing class into your new subclass. Inheritance also defines rules for how these methods, properties, and events can be merged, including control over how they can be changed or replaced, and how the subclass can add new methods, properties, and events of its own. This is what you will learn in the following sections — what these rules are and what syntax you use in Visual Basic to make it all work.

Creating a Base Class

Virtually any class you create can act as a base class from which other classes can be derived. In fact, unless you specifically indicate in the code that your class cannot be a base class, you can derive from it (you will come back to this later).

Create a new Windows Application project in Visual Basic. Then add a class to the project using the Project ➪ Add Class menu option and name it `Person.vb`. Begin with the following code:

```
Public Class Person

End Class
```

At this point, you technically have a base class, as it is possible to inherit from this class even though it doesn't do or contain anything. You can now add methods, properties, and events to this class as you normally would. All of those interface elements would be inherited by any class you might create based on `Person`. For instance, add the following code:

```
Public Class Person

    Private mName As String
    Private mBirthDate As Date

    Public Property Name() As String
```

```
      Get
         Return mName
      End Get
      Set(ByVal value As String)
         mName = value
      End Set
   End Property

   Public Property BirthDate() As Date
      Get
         Return mBirthDate
      End Get
      Set(ByVal value As Date)
         mBirthDate = value
      End Set
   End Property
End Class
```

This provides a simple method that can be used to illustrate how basic inheritance works. This class can be represented by the class diagram in Visual Studio, as shown in Figure 3-2.

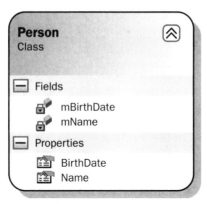

Figure 3-2

In this representation of the class as it is presented from Visual Studio, the overall box represents the Person class. In the top section of this box is the name of the class and a specification that it is a class. The section below it contains a list of the instance variables, or fields, of the class, with their scope marked as Private (note the lock icon). The bottom section lists the properties exposed by the class, both marked as Public. If the class had methods or events, then they would be displayed in their own sections in the diagram.

Creating a Subclass

To implement inheritance, you need to add a new class to your project. Use the Project ⇨ Add Class menu option and add a new class named Employee.vb. Begin with the following code:

```
Public Class Employee
   Private mHireDate As Date
```

```
      Private mSalary As Double

      Public Property HireDate() As Date
        Get
          Return mHireDate
        End Get
        Set(ByVal value As Date)
          mHireDate = value
        End Set
      End Property

      Public Property Salary() As Double
        Get
          Return mSalary
        End Get
        Set(ByVal value As Double)
          mSalary = value
        End Set
      End Property
    End Class
```

This is a regular standalone class with no explicit inheritance. It can be represented by the following class diagram (see Figure 3-3).

Figure 3-3

Again, you can see the class name, its list of instance variables, and the properties it includes as part of its interface. It turns out that, behind the scenes, this class inherits some capabilities from System.Object. In fact, every class in the entire .NET platform ultimately inherits from System.Object either implicitly or explicitly. This is why all .NET objects have a basic set of common functionality, including, most notably, the GetType method, which is discussed in detail later in the chapter.

While having an Employee object with a hire date and salary is useful, it should also have Name and BirthDate properties, just as you implemented in the Person class. Without inheritance, you would probably just copy and paste the code from Person directly into the new Employee class, but with inheritance, you can directly reuse the code from the Person class. Let's make the new class inherit from Person.

The Inherits Keyword

To make `Employee` a subclass of `Person`, add a single line of code:

```
Public Class Employee
    Inherits Person
```

The `Inherits` keyword indicates that a class should derive from an existing class, inheriting the interface and behavior from that class. You can inherit from almost any class in your project, or from the .NET system class library or from other assemblies. It is also possible to prevent inheritance, which is covered later in the chapter. When using the `Inherits` keyword to inherit from classes outside the current project, you need to either specify the namespace that contains that class or place an `Imports` statement at the top of the class to import that namespace for your use.

The diagram in Figure 3-4 illustrates the fact that the `Employee` class is now a subclass of `Person`.

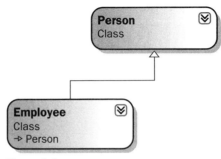

Figure 3-4

The line running from `Employee` back up to `Person` ends in an open triangle, which is the symbol for inheritance when using the Class Designer in Visual Studio. It is this line that indicates that the `Employee` class includes all the functionality, as well as the interface, of `Person`.

This means that an object created based on the `Employee` class has not only the methods `HireDate` and `Salary`, but also `Name` and `BirthDate`. To test this, bring up the designer for `Form1` (which is automatically part of your project, because you created a Windows Application project) and add the following `TextBox` controls, along with a button, to the form:

Control Type	Name	Text Value
TextBox	txtName	<blank>
TextBox	txtBirthDate	<blank>
TextBox	txtHireDate	<blank>
TextBox	txtSalary	<blank>
button	btnOK	OK

You can also add some labels to make the form more readable. The Form Designer should now look something like Figure 3-5.

Figure 3-5

Double-click the button to bring up the code window, and enter the following code:

```
Private Sub btnOK_Click(ByVal sender As System.Object, _
                        ByVal e As System.EventArgs) Handles btnOK.Click
    Dim emp As New Employee()

    With emp
      .Name = "Fred"
      .BirthDate = #1/1/1960#
      .HireDate = #1/1/1980#
      .Salary = 30000

      txtName.Text = .Name
      txtBirthDate.Text = Format(.BirthDate, "Short date")
      txtHireDate.Text = Format(.HireDate, "Short date")
      txtSalary.Text = Format(.Salary, "$0.00")
    End With
End Sub
```

The best Visual Basic practice is to use the With *keyword, but be aware that this might cause issues with portability and converting code to other languages.*

Even though Employee does not directly implement the Name or BirthDate methods, they are available for use through inheritance. When you run this application and click the button, your controls are populated with the values from the Employee object.

When the code in Form1 invokes the Name property on the Employee object, the code from the Person class is executed, as the Employee class has no such method built in. However, when the HireDate property is invoked on the Employee object, the code from the Employee class is executed, as it does have that method as part of its code.

From the form's perspective, it doesn't matter whether a method is implemented in the Employee class or the Person class; they are all simply methods of the Employee object. In addition, because the code in these classes is merged to create the Employee object, there is no performance difference between calling a method implemented by the Employee class or calling a method implemented by the Person class.

Overloading Methods

Although your `Employee` class automatically gains the `Name` and `BirthDate` methods through inheritance, it also has methods of its own — `HireDate` and `Salary`. This shows how you have extended the base `Person` interface by adding methods and properties to the `Employee` subclass.

You can add new properties, methods, and events to the `Employee` class, and they will be part of any object created based on `Employee`. This has no impact on the `Person` class whatsoever, only on the `Employee` class and `Employee` objects.

You can even extend the functionality of the base class by adding methods to the subclass that have the same name as methods or properties in the base class, as long as those methods or properties have different parameter lists. You are effectively overloading the existing methods from the base class. It is essentially the same thing as overloading regular methods, as discussed in Chapter 2.

For example, your `Person` class is currently providing your implementation for the `Name` property. Employees may have other names you also want to store, perhaps an informal name and a formal name in addition to their regular name. One way to accommodate this requirement is to change the `Person` class itself to include an overloaded `Name` property that supports this new functionality. However, you are really only trying to enhance the `Employee` class, not the more general `Person` class, so what you want is a way to add an overloaded method to the `Employee` class itself, even though you are overloading a method from its base class.

You can overload a method from a base class by using the `Overloads` keyword. The concept is the same as described in Chapter 2, but in this case an extra keyword is involved. To overload the `Name` property, for instance, you can add a new property to the `Employee` class. First, though, define an enumerated type using the `Enum` keyword. This `Enum` will list the different types of name you want to store. Add this `Enum` to the `Employee.vb` file, before the declaration of the class itself:

```
Public Enum NameTypes
  Informal = 1
  Formal = 2
End Enum


  Public Class Employee
```

You can then add an overloaded `Name` property to the `Employee` class itself:

```
Public Class Employee
  Inherits Person

  Private mHireDate As Date
  Private mSalary As Double

  Private mNames As New Generic.Dictionary(Of NameTypes, String)

  Public Overloads Property Name(ByVal type As NameTypes) As String
    Get
      Return mNames(type)
    End Get
    Set(ByVal value As String)
```

```
        If mNames.ContainsKey(type) Then
          mNames.Item(type) = value
        Else
          mNames.Add(type, value)
        End If
    End Set
  End Property
```

This `Name` property is actually a property array, which enables you to store multiple values via the same property. In this case, you are storing the values in a `Generic.Dictionary(Of K, V)` object, which is indexed by using the `Enum` value you just defined. Chapter 6 discusses generics in detail. For now, you can view this generic `Dictionary` just like any collection object that stores key/value data.

If you omit the `Overloads` keyword here, your new implementation of the `Name` method will shadow the original implementation. Shadowing is very different from overloading, and is covered later in the chapter.

Though this method has the same name as the method in the base class, the fact that it accepts a different parameter list enables you to use overloading to implement it here. The original `Name` property, as implemented in the `Person` class, remains intact and valid, but now you have added a new variation with this second `Name` property, as shown in Figure 3-6.

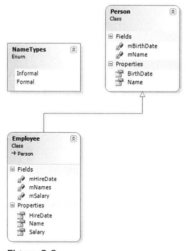

Figure 3-6

The diagram clearly indicates that the `Name` method in the `Person` class and the `Name` method in the `Employee` class both exist. If you hover over each `Name` property, you will see a tooltip showing the method signatures, making it clear that each one has a different signature.

You can now change `Form1` to make use of this new version of the `Name` property. First, add a couple of new `TextBox` controls and associated labels. The `TextBox` controls should be named `txtFormal` and txtInformal, and the form should now look like the one shown in Figure 3-7. Double-click the form's button to bring up the code window and add the code to work with the overloaded version of the Name property:

```
Private Sub btnOK_Click(ByVal sender As System.Object, _
    ByVal e As System.EventArgs) Handles btnOK.Click

    Dim emp As New Employee()

    With emp
      .Name = "Fred"
      .Name(NameTypes.Formal) = "Mr. Frederick R. Jones, Sr."
      .Name(NameTypes.Informal) = "Freddy"
      .BirthDate = #1/1/1960#
      .HireDate = #1/1/1980#
      .Salary = 30000

      txtName.Text = .Name
      txtFormal.Text = .Name(NameTypes.Formal)
      txtInformal.Text = .Name(NameTypes.Informal)
      txtBirthDate.Text = Format(.BirthDate, "Short date")
      txtHireDate.Text = Format(.HireDate, "Short date")
      txtSalary.Text = Format(.Salary, "$0.00")
    End With
End Sub
```

Figure 3-7

The code still interacts with the original Name property as implemented in the Person class, but you are now also invoking the overloaded version of the property implemented in the Employee class.

Overriding Methods

So far, you have seen how to implement a base class and then use it to create a subclass. You also extended the interface by adding methods, and you explored how to use overloading to add methods that have the same name as methods in the base class but with different parameters.

However, sometimes you may want to not only extend the original functionality, but also actually change or entirely replace the functionality of the base class. Instead of leaving the existing functionality and just adding new methods or overloaded versions of those methods, you might want to entirely override the existing functionality with your own.

You can do exactly that. If the base class allows it, then you can substitute your own implementation of a base class method — meaning your new implementation will be used instead of the original.

The Overridable Keyword

By default, you can't override the behavior of methods on a base class. The base class must be coded specifically to allow this to occur, by using the `Overridable` keyword. This is important, as you may not always want to allow a subclass to entirely change the behavior of the methods in your base class. However, if you do wish to allow the author of a subclass to replace your implementation, you can do so by adding the `Overridable` keyword to your method declaration.

Returning to the `Employee` example, you may not like the implementation of the `BirthDate` method as it stands in the `Person` class. Suppose, for instance, that you can't employ anyone younger than 16 years of age, so any birth-date value more recent than 16 years ago is invalid for an employee.

To implement this business rule, you need to change the way the `BirthDate` property is implemented. While you could make this change directly in the `Person` class, that would not be ideal. It is perfectly acceptable to have a person under age 16, just not an employee.

Open the code window for the `Person` class and change the `BirthDate` property to include the `Overridable` keyword:

```
Public Overridable Property BirthDate() As Date
   Get
     Return mBirthDate
   End Get
   Set(ByVal value As Date)
     mBirthDate = value
   End Set
End Property
```

This change allows any class that inherits from `Person` to entirely replace the implementation of the `BirthDate` property with a new implementation.

By adding the `Overridable` keyword to your method declaration, you are indicating that you allow any subclass to override the behavior provided by this method. This means you are permitting a subclass to totally ignore your prior implementation, or to extend your implementation by doing other work before or after your implementation is run.

If the subclass does not override this method, the method works just like a regular method and is automatically included as part of the subclass's interface. Putting the `Overridable` keyword on a method simply allows a subclass to override the method if you choose to let it do so.

The Overrides Keyword

In a subclass, you override a method by implementing a method of the same name, and with the same parameter list as the base class, and then you use the `Overrides` keyword to indicate that you are overriding that method.

This is different from overloading, because when you overload a method you are adding a new method with the same name but a different parameter list. When you override a method, you are actually replacing the original method with a new implementation.

Without the `Overrides` keyword, you will receive a compilation error when you implement a method with the same name as one from the base class. Open the code window for the `Employee` class and add a new `BirthDate` property:

```
Public Class Employee
  Inherits Person

    Private mHireDate As Date
    Private mSalary As Double
    Private mBirthDate As Date

    Private mNames As New Generic.Dictionary(Of NameTypes, String)

    Public Overrides Property BirthDate() As Date
      Get
        Return mBirthDate
      End Get
      Set(ByVal value As Date)
        If DateDiff(DateInterval.Year, Value, Now) >= 16 Then
          mBirthDate = value
        Else
          Throw New ArgumentException( _
            "An employee must be at least 16 years old.")
        End If
      End Set
    End Property
```

Because you are implementing your own version of the property, you have to declare a variable to store that value within the `Employee` class. This is not ideal, and there are a couple of ways around it, including the `MyBase` keyword and the `Protected` scope.

Notice also that you have enhanced the functionality in the `Set` block, so it now raises an error if the new birth-date value would cause the employee to be less than 16 years of age. With this code, you have now entirely replaced the original `BirthDate` implementation with a new one that enforces your business rule (see Figure 3-8).

The diagram now includes a `BirthDate` method in the `Employee` class. While perhaps not entirely intuitive, this is how the class diagram indicates that you have overridden the method. If you hover the mouse over the property in the `Employee` class, the tooltip will show the method signature, including the `Overrides` keyword.

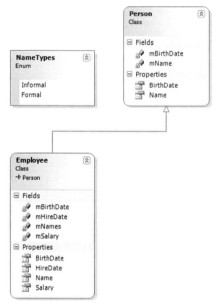

Figure 3-8

If you run your application and click the button on the form, then everything should work as it did before because the birth date you are supplying conforms to your new business rule. Now change the code in your form to use an invalid birth date:

```
With emp
   .Name = "Fred"
   .Name(NameTypes.Formal) = "Mr. Frederick R. Jones, Sr."
   .Name(NameTypes.Informal) = "Freddy"
   .BirthDate = #1/1/2000#
```

When you run the application (from within Visual Studio) and click the button, you receive an error indicating that the birth date is invalid. This proves that you are now using the implementation of the `BirthDate` method from the `Employee` class, rather than the one from the `Person` class. Change the date value in the form back to a valid value so that your application runs properly.

The MyBase Keyword

You have just seen how you can entirely replace the functionality of a method in the base class by over-riding it in your subclass. However, this can be somewhat extreme; sometimes it's preferable to override methods so that you extend the base functionality, rather than replace the functionality.

To do this, you need to override the method using the `Overrides` keyword as you just did, but within your new implementation you can still invoke the original implementation of the method. This enables you to add your own code before or after the original implementation is invoked — meaning you can extend the behavior while still leveraging the code in the base class.

To invoke methods directly from the base class, you can use the MyBase keyword. This keyword is available within any class, and it exposes all the methods of the base class for your use.

Even a base class such as Person *is an implicit subclass of* System.Object, *so it can use* MyBase *to interact with its base class as well.*

This means that within the BirthDate implementation in Employee, you can invoke the BirthDate implementation in the base Person class. This is ideal, as it means that you can leverage any existing functionality provided by Person while still enforcing your Employee-specific business rules.

To take advantage of this, you can enhance the code in the Employee implementation of BirthDate. First, remove the declaration of mBirthDate from the Employee class. You won't need this variable any longer because the Person implementation will keep track of the value on your behalf. Then, change the BirthDate implementation in the Employee class as follows:

```
Public Overrides Property BirthDate() As Date
  Get
    Return MyBase.BirthDate
  End Get

  Set(ByVal value As Date)
    If DateDiff(DateInterval.Year, Value, Now) >= 16 Then
      MyBase.BirthDate = value
    Else
      Throw New ArgumentException( _
        "An employee must be at least 16 years old.")
    End If
  End Set
End Property
```

Run your application and you will see that it works just fine even though the Employee class no longer contains any code to actually keep track of the birth-date value. You have effectively merged the BirthDate implementation from Person right into your enhanced implementation in Employee, creating a hybrid version of the property.

The MyBase keyword is covered in more detail later in the chapter. Here, you can see how it enables you to enhance or extend the functionality of the base class by adding your own code in the subclass but still invoking the base-class method when appropriate.

Virtual Methods

The BirthDate method is an example of a *virtual method*. Virtual methods are those that can be overridden and replaced by subclasses.

Virtual methods are more complex to understand than regular nonvirtual methods. With a nonvirtual method, only one implementation matches any given method signature, so there's no ambiguity about which specific method implementation will be invoked. With virtual methods, however, there may be several implementations of the same method, with the same method signature, so you need to understand the rules that govern which specific implementation of that method will be called.

When working with virtual methods, keep in mind that the data type of the object is used to determine the implementation of the method to call, rather than the type of the variable that refers to the object.

Looking at the code in your form, you can see that you are declaring an object variable of type `Employee`, and then creating an `Employee` object that you can reference via that object:

```
Dim emp As New Employee()
```

It is not surprising, then, that you are able to invoke any of the methods that are implemented as part of the `Employee` class, and through inheritance, any of the methods implemented as part of the `Person` class:

```
With emp
  .Name = "Fred"
  .Name(NameTypes.Formal) = "Mr. Frederick R. Jones, Sr."
  .Name(NameTypes.Informal) = "Freddy"
  .BirthDate = #1/1/1960#
  .HireDate = #1/1/1980#
  .Salary = 30000
```

When you call the `BirthDate` property, you know that you are invoking the implementation contained in the `Employee` class, which makes sense because you know that you are using a variable of type `Employee` to refer to an object of type `Employee`.

Because your methods are virtual methods, you can experiment with some much more interesting scenarios. For instance, suppose that you change the code in your form to interact directly with an object of type `Person` instead of one of type `Employee`:

```
Private Sub btnOK_Click(ByVal sender As System.Object, _
    ByVal e As System.EventArgs) Handles btnOK.Click

    Dim person As New Person()

    With person
      .Name = "Fred"
      .BirthDate = #1/1/1960#

      txtName.Text = .Name
      txtBirthDate.Text = Format(.BirthDate, "Short date")
    End With

End Sub
```

You can no longer call the methods implemented by the `Employee` class because they do not exist as part of a `Person` object, but only as part of an `Employee` object. However, you can see that both the `Name` and `BirthDate` properties continue to function as you would expect. When you run the application now, it

will work just fine. You can even change the birth-date value to something that would be invalid for
`Employee`:

```
.BirthDate = #1/1/2000#
```

The application will now accept it and work just fine, because the `BirthDate` method you are invoking is
the original version from the `Person` class.

These are the two simple scenarios, when you have a variable and object of type `Employee` or a variable
and object of type `Person`. However, because `Employee` is derived from `Person`, you can do something a
bit more interesting. You can use a variable of type `Person` to hold a reference to an `Employee` object. For
example, you can change the code in `Form1` as follows:

```
Private Sub btnOK_Click(ByVal sender As System.Object, _
    ByVal e As System.EventArgs) Handles btnOK.Click

  Dim person As Person
  person = New Employee()
  With person
    .Name = "Fred"
    .BirthDate = #1/1/1960#

    txtName.Text = .Name
    txtBirthDate.Text = Format(.BirthDate, "Short date")
  End With
End Sub
```

What you are doing now is declaring your variable to be of type `Person`, but the object itself is an instance
of the `Employee` class. You have done something a bit complex here, as the data type of the variable is not
the same as the data type of the object itself. Remember that a variable of a base-class type can always
hold a reference to an object of any subclass.

> This is why a variable of type `System.Object` can hold a reference to literally
> anything in the .NET Framework, because all classes are ultimately derived from
> `System.Object`.

This technique is very useful when creating generic routines. It makes use of an object-oriented concept
called *polymorphism*, which is discussed more thoroughly later in this chapter. This technique enables
you to create a more general routine that populates your form for any object of type `Person`. Add the
following code to the form:

```
Private Sub DisplayPerson(ByVal thePerson As Person)
  With thePerson
    txtName.Text = .Name
    txtBirthDate.Text = Format(.BirthDate, "Short date")
  End With
End Sub
```

Now you can change the code behind the button to make use of this generic routine:

```
Private Sub btnOK_Click(ByVal sender As System.Object, _
    ByVal e As System.EventArgs) Handles btnOK.Click

  Dim person As Person
  person = New Employee()

  With person
    .Name = "Fred"
    .BirthDate = #1/1/1960#
  End With

    DisplayPerson(person)
  End Sub
```

The benefit here is that you can pass a Person object or an Employee object to DisplayPerson and the routine will work the same either way.

When you run the application now, things get interesting. You will get an error when you attempt to set the BirthDate property because it breaks your 16-year-old business rule, which is implemented in the Employee class. How can this be when your person variable is of type Person?

This clearly demonstrates the concept of a virtual method. It is the data type of the object, in this case Employee, that is important. The data type of the variable is not the deciding factor when choosing which implementation of an overridden method is invoked.

The following table shows which method is actually invoked based on the variable and object data types when working with virtual methods:

Variable Type	Object Type	Method Invoked
Base	Base	Base
Base	Subclass	Subclass
Subclass	Subclass	Subclass

Virtual methods are very powerful and useful when you implement polymorphism using inheritance. A base-class data type can hold a reference to any subclass object, but it is the type of that specific object which determines the implementation of the method. Therefore, you can write generic routines that operate on many types of object as long as they derive from the same base class. You will learn how to make use of polymorphism and virtual methods in more detail later in this chapter.

Overriding Overloaded Methods

Earlier, you wrote code in your Employee class to overload the Name method in the base Person class. This enabled you to keep the original Name functionality but also extend it by adding another Name method that accepted a different parameter list.

You have also overridden the `BirthDate` method. The implementation in the `Employee` class replaced the implementation in the `Person` class. Overriding is a related but different concept from overloading. It is also possible to both overload and override a method at the same time.

In the earlier overloading example, you added a new `Name` property to the `Employee` class, while retaining the functionality present in the base `Person` class. You may decide that you not only want to have your second overloaded implementation of the `Name` method, but also want to replace the existing one by overriding the existing method provided by the `Person` class.

In particular, you may want to do this so that you can store the `Name` value in the `Hashtable` object along with your `Formal` and `Informal` names. Before you can override the `Name` method, you need to add the `Overridable` keyword to the base implementation in the `Person` class:

```
Public Overridable Property Name() As String
   Get
     Return mName
   End Get
   Set(ByVal value As String)
     mName = value
   End Set
End Property
```

With that done, the `Name` method can now be overridden by any derived classes. In the `Employee` class, you can now override the `Name` method, replacing the functionality provided by the `Person` class. First add a `Normal` option to the `Enum` that controls the types of `Name` value you can store:

```
Public Enum NameTypes
   Informal = 1
   Formal = 2
   Normal = 3
End Enum
```

Now you can add code to the `Employee` class to implement a new `Name` property. This is in addition to the existing `Name` property already implemented in the `Employee` class:

```
Public Overloads Overrides Property Name() As String
   Get
     Return Name(NameTypes.Normal)
   End Get
   Set(ByVal value As String)
     Name(NameTypes.Normal) = value
   End Set
End Property
```

Note that you are using both the `Overrides` keyword, to indicate that you are overriding the `Name` method from the base class, and the `Overloads` keyword, to indicate that you are overloading this method in the subclass.

This new `Name` property merely delegates the call to the existing version of the `Name` property that handles the parameter-based names. To complete the linkage between this implementation of the `Name`

119

property and the parameter-based version, you need to make one more change to that original over-loaded version:

```
Public Overloads Property Name(ByVal type As NameTypes) As String
  Get
    Return mNames(Type)
  End Get
  Set(ByVal value As String)
    If mNames.ContainsKey(type) Then
      mNames.Item(type) = value
    Else
      mNames.Add(type, value)
    End If

    If type = NameTypes.Normal Then
      MyBase.Name = value
    End If
  End Set
End Property
```

This way, if the client code sets the `Name` property by providing the `Normal` index, you are still updating the name in the base class as well as in the `Dictionary` object maintained by the `Employee` class.

Shadowing

Overloading enables you to add new versions of existing methods as long as their parameter lists are different. *Overriding* enables your subclass to entirely replace the implementation of a base-class method with a new method that has the same method signature. As you just saw, you can even combine these concepts not only to replace the implementation of a method from the base class, but also to simultaneously overload that method with other implementations that have different method signatures.

However, any time you override a method using the `Overrides` keyword, you are subject to the rules governing virtual methods — meaning that the base class must give you permission to override the method. If the base class does not use the `Overridable` keyword, then you can't override the method. Sometimes you may need to override a method that is not marked as `Overridable`, and shadowing enables you to do just that.

The `Shadows` keyword can also be used to entirely change the nature of a method or other interface element from the base class, although that is something which should be done with great care, as it can seriously reduce the maintainability of your code. Normally, when you create an `Employee` object, you expect that it can act not only as an `Employee`, but also as a `Person` because `Employee` is a subclass of `Person`. However, with the `Shadows` keyword, you can radically alter the behavior of an `Employee` class so that it does not act like a `Person`. This sort of radical deviation from what is normally expected invites bugs and makes code hard to understand and maintain.

Shadowing methods is very dangerous and should be used as a last resort. It is primarily useful in cases where you have a preexisting component such as a Windows Forms control that was not designed for inheritance. If you absolutely *must* inherit from such a component, you may need to use shadowing to "override" methods or properties. Despite the serious limits and dangers, it may be your only option. You will explore this in more detail later. First, let's see how `Shadows` can be used to override nonvirtual methods.

Overriding Nonvirtual Methods

Earlier in the chapter you learned about virtual methods and how they are automatically created in Visual Basic when the `Overrides` keyword is employed. You can also implement nonvirtual methods in Visual Basic. Nonvirtual methods are methods that cannot be overridden and replaced by subclasses, so most methods you implement are nonvirtual.

> **If you do not use the `Overridable` keyword when declaring a method, then it is nonvirtual.**

In the typical case, nonvirtual methods are easy to understand. They can't be overridden and replaced, so you know that there's only one method by that name, with that method signature. Therefore, when you invoke it, there is no ambiguity about which specific implementation will be called. The reverse is true with virtual methods, where there may be more than one method of the same name, and with the same method signature, so you should understand the rules governing which implementation will be invoked.

Of course, you knew it couldn't be that simple, and it turns out that you can override nonvirtual methods by using the `Shadows` keyword. In fact, you can use the `Shadows` keyword to override methods regardless of whether or not they have the `Overridable` keyword in the declaration.

> **The `Shadows` keyword enables you to replace methods on the base class that the base-class designer didn't intend to be replaced.**

Obviously, this can be very dangerous. The designer of a base class must be careful when marking a method as `Overridable`, ensuring that the base class continues to operate properly even when that method is replaced by another code in a subclass. Designers of base classes typically just assume that if they do not mark a method as `Overridable`, it will be called and not overridden. Thus, overriding a nonvirtual method by using the `Shadows` keyword can have unexpected and potentially dangerous side effects, as you are doing something that the base-class designer assumed would never happen.

If that isn't enough complexity, it turns out that shadowed methods follow different rules than virtual methods when they are invoked. That is, they do not act like regular overridden methods; instead, they follow a different set of rules to determine which specific implementation of the method will be invoked. In particular, when you call a nonvirtual method, the data type of the variable refers to the object that indicates which implementation of the method is called, not the data type of the object, as with virtual methods.

To override a nonvirtual method, you can use the `Shadows` keyword instead of the `Overrides` keyword. To see how this works, add a new property to the base `Person` class:

```
Public ReadOnly Property Age() As Integer
  Get
    Return CInt(DateDiff(DateInterval.Year, Now, BirthDate))
  End Get
End Property
```

Here you have added a new method called `Age` to the base class, and thus automatically to the subclass. This code has a bug, introduced intentionally for illustration. The `DateDiff` parameters are in the wrong order, so you will get negative age values from this routine. The bug was introduced to highlight the fact that sometimes you will find bugs in base classes that you didn't write (and which you can't fix because you don't have the source code).

The following example walks you through the use of the `Shadows` keyword to address a bug in your base class, acting under the assumption that for some reason you can't actually fix the code in the `Person` class.

Note that you are not using the `Overridable` keyword on this method, so any subclass is prevented from overriding the method by using the `Overrides` keyword. The obvious intent and expectation of this code is that all subclasses will use this implementation and not override it with their own.

However, the base class cannot prevent a subclass from shadowing a method, so it does not matter whether you use `Overridable` or not; either way works fine for shadowing.

Before you shadow the method, let's see how it works as a regular nonvirtual method. First, you need to change your form to use this new value. Add a text box named `txtAge` and a related label to the form. Next, change the code behind the button to use the `Age` property. You will include the code to display the data on the form right here to keep things simple and clear:

```
Private Sub btnOK_Click(ByVal sender As System.Object, _
    ByVal e As System.EventArgs) Handles btnOK.Click

    Dim person As Employee = New Employee()


    With person
      .Name = "Fred"
      .BirthDate = #1/1/1960#

      txtName.Text = .Name
      txtBirthDate.Text = Format(.BirthDate, "Short date")
      txtAge.Text = CStr(.Age)
    End With

End Sub
```

Remember to change the `Employee` birth-date value to something valid. At this point, you can run the application. The age field should appear in your display as expected, though with a negative value due to the bug we introduced. There's no magic or complexity here. This is basic programming with objects, and basic use of inheritance as described earlier in this chapter.

Of course, you don't want a bug in your code, but nor do you have access to the `Person` class, and the `Person` class does not allow you to override the `Age` method, so what can you do? The answer lies in the `Shadows` keyword, which allows you to override the method anyway.

Let's shadow the `Age` method within the `Employee` class, overriding and replacing the implementation in the `Person` class even though it is not marked as `Overridable`. Add the following code to the `Employee` class:

```
Public Shadows ReadOnly Property Age() As Integer
  Get
    Return CInt(DateDiff(DateInterval.Year, BirthDate, Now))
  End Get
End Property
```

In many ways, this looks very similar to what you have seen with the `Overrides` keyword, in that you are implementing a method in your subclass with the same name and parameter list as a method in the base class. In this case, however, you will see some different behavior when you interact with the object in different ways.

Technically, the `Shadows` keyword is not required here. Shadowing is the default behavior when a subclass implements a method that matches the name and method signature of a method in the base class. However, if you omit the `Shadows` keyword, then the compiler will issue a warning indicating that the method is being shadowed, so it is always better to include the keyword, both to avoid the warning and to make it perfectly clear that you chose to shadow the method intentionally.

Remember that your form's code is currently declaring a variable of type `Employee` and is creating an instance of an `Employee` object:

```
Dim person As Employee = New Employee()
```

This is a simple case, and, surprisingly, when you run the application now you will see that the value of the age field is correct, indicating that you just ran the implementation of the `Age` property from the `Employee` class. At this point, you are seeing the same behavior that you saw when overriding with the `Overrides` keyword.

Let's take a look at the other simple case, when you are working with a variable and object that are both of data type `Person`. Change the code in `Form1` as follows:

```
Private Sub btnOK_Click(ByVal sender As System.Object, _
    ByVal e As System.EventArgs) Handles btnOK.Click

  Dim person As Person = New Person()

  With person
    .Name = "Fred"
    .BirthDate = #1/1/1960#

    txtName.Text = .Name
    txtBirthDate.Text = Format(.BirthDate, "Short date")
    txtAge.Text = CStr(.Age)
  End With
End Sub
```

Now you have a variable of type `Person` and an object of that same type. You would expect that the implementation in the `Person` class would be invoked in this case, and that is exactly what happens: The age field displays the original negative value, indicating that you are invoking the buggy implementation of the method directly from the `Person` class. Again, this is exactly the behavior you would expect from a method overridden via the `Overrides` keyword.

This next example is where things get truly interesting. Change the code in `Form1` as follows:

```
Private Sub btnOK_Click(ByVal sender As System.Object, _
    ByVal e As System.EventArgs) Handles btnOK.Click

    Dim person As Person = New Employee()
  With person
    .Name = "Fred"
    .BirthDate = #1/1/1960#

    txtName.Text = .Name
    txtBirthDate.Text = Format(.BirthDate, "Short date")
    txtAge.Text = CStr(.Age)
  End With
End Sub
```

Now you are declaring the variable to be of type `Person`, but you are creating an object that is of data type `Employee`. You did this earlier in the chapter when exploring the `Overrides` keyword as well, and in that case you discovered that the version of the method that was invoked was based on the data type of the object. The `BirthDate` implementation in the `Employee` class was invoked.

If you run the application now, the rules are different when the `Shadows` keyword is used. In this case, the implementation in the `Person` class is invoked, giving you the buggy negative value. When the implementation in the `Employee` class is ignored, you get the exact opposite behavior of what you got with `Overrides`.

The following table summarizes which method implementation is invoked based on the variable and object data types when using shadowing:

Variable Type	Object Type	Method Invoked
Base	Base	Base
Base	Subclass	Base
Subclass	Subclass	Subclass

In most cases, the behavior you will want for your methods is accomplished by the `Overrides` keyword and virtual methods. However, in cases where the base-class designer does not allow you to override a method and you want to do it anyway, the `Shadows` keyword provides you with the needed functionality.

Shadowing Arbitrary Elements

The `Shadows` keyword can be used not only to override nonvirtual methods, but also to totally replace and change the nature of a base-class interface element. When you override a method, you are providing a replacement implementation of that method with the same name and method signature. Using the Shadows keyword, you can do more extreme things, such as change a method into an instance variable or change a property into a function.

However, this can be very dangerous, as any code written to use your objects will naturally assume that you implement all the same interface elements and behaviors as your base class, because that is the nature of inheritance. Any documentation or knowledge of the original interface is effectively invalidated because the original implementation is arbitrarily replaced.

> **By totally changing the nature of an interface element, you can cause a great deal of confusion for programmers who might interact with your class in the future.**

To see how you can replace an interface element from the base class, let's entirely change the nature of the Age property. In fact, let's change it from a read-only property to a read-write property. You could get even more extreme — change it to a Function or a Sub.

Remove the Age property from the Employee class and add the following code:

```
Public Shadows Property Age() As Integer
  Get
    Return CInt(DateDiff(DateInterval.Year, BirthDate, Now))
  End Get
  Set(ByVal value As Integer)
    BirthDate = DateAdd(DateInterval.Year, -value, Now)
  End Set
End Property
```

With this change, the very nature of the Age method has changed. It is no longer a simple read-only property; now it is a read-write property that includes code to calculate an approximate birth date based on the age value supplied.

As it stands, your application will continue to run just fine because you are only using the read-only functionality of the property in your form. You can change the form to make use of the new read-write functionality:

```
Private Sub btnOK_Click(ByVal sender As System.Object, _
    ByVal e As System.EventArgs) Handles btnOK.Click

  Dim person As Person = New Employee()

  With person
    .Name = "Fred"
    .BirthDate = #1/1/1960#
    .Age = 20

    txtName.Text = .Name
    txtBirthDate.Text = Format(.BirthDate, "Short date")
    txtAge.Text = CStr(.Age)
  End With
End Sub
```

However, this results in a syntax error. The variable you are working with, person, is of data type Person, and that data type doesn't provide a writeable version of the Age property. In order to use your enhanced functionality, you must use a variable and object of type Employee:

```
Dim person As Employee = New Employee()
```

If you now run the application and click the button, the Age is displayed as 20, and the birth date is now a value calculated based on that age value, indicating that you are now running the shadowed version of the Age method as implemented in the Employee class.

As if that weren't odd enough, you can do some even stranger and more dangerous things. You can change Age into a variable, and you can even change its scope. For instance, you can comment out the Age property code in the Employee class and replace it with the following code:

```
Private Shadows Age As String
```

At this point, you have changed everything. Age is now a String instead of an Integer. It is a variable instead of a property or function. It has Private scope instead of Public scope. Your Employee object is now totally incompatible with the Person data type, something that shouldn't occur normally when using inheritance.

This means that the code you wrote in Form1 will no longer work. The Age property is no longer accessible and can no longer be used, so your project will no longer compile. This directly illustrates the danger in shadowing a base-class element such that its very nature or scope is changed by the subclass.

Because this change prevents your application from compiling, remove the line in the Employee class that shadows Age as a String variable, and uncomment the shadowed Property routine:

```
Public Shadows Property Age() As Integer
  Get
    Return CInt(DateDiff(DateInterval.Year, BirthDate, Now))
  End Get
  Set(ByVal value As Integer)
    BirthDate = DateAdd(DateInterval.Year, -value, Now)
  End Set
End Property
```

This restores your application to a working state.

Levels of Inheritance

So far, you have created a single base class and a single subclass, thus demonstrating that you can implement inheritance that is a single level deep. You can also create inheritance relationships that are several levels deep. These are sometimes referred to as *chains of inheritance*.

In fact, you have been creating a two-level inheritance hierarchy so far, because you know that your base class actually derived from System.Object, *but for most purposes it is easiest to simply ignore that and treat only your classes as part of the inheritance hierarchy.*

Multiple Inheritance

Don't confuse multilevel inheritance with multiple inheritance, which is an entirely different concept that is not supported by either Visual Basic or the .NET platform itself. The idea behind multiple inheritance is that you can have a single subclass that inherits from two base classes at the same time.

For instance, an application might have a class for Customer and another class for Vendor. It is quite possible that some customers are also vendors, so you might want to combine the functionality of these two classes into a CustomerVendor class. This new class would be a combination of both Customer and Vendor, so it would be nice to inherit from both of them at once.

While this is a useful concept, multiple inheritance is complex and somewhat dangerous. Numerous problems are associated with multiple inheritance, but the most obvious is the possibility of collisions of properties or methods from the base classes. Suppose that both Customer and Vendor have a Name property. CustomerVendor would need two Name properties, one for each base class. Yet it only makes sense to have one Name property on CustomerVendor, so to which base class does it link, and how will the system operate if it does not link to the other one?

These are complex issues with no easy answers. Within the object-oriented community, there is ongoing debate as to whether the advantages of code reuse outweigh the complexity that comes along for the ride.

Multiple inheritance isn't supported by the .NET Framework, so it is likewise not supported by Visual Basic, but you can use multiple interfaces to achieve an effect similar to multiple inheritance, a topic discussed later in the chapter when we talk about implementing multiple interfaces.

Multilevel Inheritance

You have seen how a subclass derives from a base class with the Person and Employee classes, but nothing prevents the Employee subclass from being the base class for yet another class, a sub-subclass, so to speak. This is not at all uncommon. In the working example, you may have different kinds of employees, some who work in the office and others who travel.

To accommodate this, you may want OfficeEmployee and TravelingEmployee classes. Of course, these are both examples of an employee and should share the functionality already present in the Employee class. The Employee class already reuses the functionality from the Person class. Figure 3-9 illustrates how these classes are interrelated.

The Employee is a subclass of Person, and your two new classes are both subclasses of Employee. While both OfficeEmployee and TravelingEmployee are employees, and thus also people, they are each unique. An OfficeEmployee almost certainly has a cube or office number, while a TravelingEmployee will keep track of the number of miles traveled.

Add a new class to your project and name it OfficeEmployee. To make this class inherit from your existing Employee class, add the following code to the class:

```
Public Class OfficeEmployee
    Inherits Employee

End Class
```

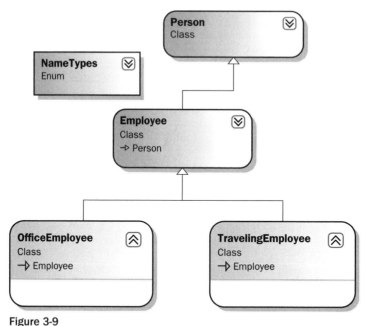

Figure 3-9

With this change, the new class now has Name, BirthDate, Age, HireDate, and Salary methods. Notice that methods from both Employee and Person are inherited. A subclass always gains all the methods, properties, and events of its base class.

You can now extend the interface and behavior of OfficeEmployee by adding a property to indicate which cube or office number the employee occupies:

```
Public Class OfficeEmployee
  Inherits Employee

  Private mOffice As String

  Public Property OfficeNumber() As String
    Get
      Return mOffice
    End Get
    Set(ByVal value As String)
      mOffice = value
    End Set
  End Property
End Class
```

To see how this works, let's enhance the form to display this value. Add a new TextBox control named txtOffice and an associated label so that your form looks like the one shown in Figure 3-10.

Figure 3-10

Now change the code behind the button to use the new property:

```
Private Sub btnOK_Click(ByVal sender As System.Object, _
    ByVal e As System.EventArgs) Handles btnOK.Click

    Dim person As OfficeEmployee = New OfficeEmployee()

    With person
      .Name = "Fred"
      .BirthDate = #1/1/1960#
      .Age = 20

      .OfficeNumber = "A42"

      txtName.Text = .Name
      txtBirthDate.Text = Format(.BirthDate, "Short date")
      txtAge.Text = CStr(.Age)

      txtOffice.Text = .OfficeNumber
    End With
End Sub
```

You have changed the routine to declare and create an object of type OfficeEmployee — thus enabling you to make use of the new property, as well as all existing properties and methods from Employee and Person, as they've been "merged" into the OfficeEmployee class via inheritance. If you now run the application, the name, birth date, age, and office values are displayed in the form.

Inheritance like this can go many levels deep, with each level extending and changing the behaviors of the previous levels. In fact, there is no specific technical limit to the number of levels of inheritance you can implement in Visual Basic, although very deep inheritance chains are typically not recommended and are often viewed as a design flaw, something discussed in more detail later in this chapter.

Interacting with the Base Class, Your Class, and Your Object

You have already seen how you can use the MyBase keyword to call methods on the base class from within a subclass. The MyBase keyword is one of three special keywords that enable you to interact with important object and class representations:

- ❑ Me
- ❑ MyBase
- ❑ MyClass

The Me Keyword

The Me keyword provides you with a reference to your current object instance. Typically, you do not need to use the Me keyword, because whenever you want to invoke a method within your current object, you can just call that method directly.

To see clearly how this works, let's add a new method to the Person class that returns the data of the Person class in the form of a String. This is interesting in and of itself, as the base System.Object class defines the ToString method for this exact purpose. Remember that all classes in the .NET Framework ultimately derive from System.Object, even if you do not explicitly indicate it with an Inherits statement. This means that you can simply override the ToString method from the Object class within your Person class by adding the following code:

```
Public Overrides Function ToString() As String
  Return Name
End Function
```

This implementation returns the person's Name property as a result when ToString is called.

> *By default,* ToString *returns the class name of the class. Until now, if you called the* ToString *method on a* Person *object, you would get a result of* InheritanceAndInterfaces.Person.

Notice that the ToString method is calling another method within your same class — in this case, the Name method.

You could also write this routine using the Me keyword:

```
Public Overrides Function ToString() As String
  Return Me.Name
End Function
```

This is redundant because Me is the default for all method calls in a class. These two implementations are identical, so typically the Me keyword is simply omitted to avoid the extra typing.

To see how the ToString method now works, you can change your code in Form1 to use this value instead of the Name property:

```
Private Sub btnOK_Click(ByVal sender As System.Object, _
    ByVal e As System.EventArgs) Handles btnOK.Click
```

```
Dim objPerson As OfficeEmployee = New OfficeEmployee()

With objPerson
  .Name = "Fred"
  .BirthDate = #1/1/1960#
  .Age = 20
  .OfficeNumber = "A42"

  txtName.Text = .ToString()
  txtBirthDate.Text = Format(.BirthDate, "Short date")
  txtAge.Text = CStr(.Age)
  txtOffice.Text = .OfficeNumber
End With
End Sub
```

When you run the application, the person's name is displayed appropriately, which makes sense, as the ToString method is simply returning the result from the Name property.

Earlier, you looked at virtual methods and how they work. Because either calling a method directly or calling it using the Me keyword invokes the method on the current object, the method calls conform to the same rules as an external method call. In other words, your ToString method may not actually end up calling the Name method in the Person class if that method was overridden by a class farther down the inheritance chain, such as the Employee or OfficeEmployee classes.

For example, you could override the Name property in your OfficeEmployee class such that it always returns the informal version of the person's name, rather than the regular name. You can override the Name property by adding this method to the OfficeEmployee class:

```
Public Overloads Overrides Property Name() As String
  Get
    Return MyBase.Name(NameTypes.Informal)
  End Get
  Set(ByVal value As String)
    MyBase.Name = value
  End Set
End Property
```

This new version of the Name method relies on the base class to actually store the value, but instead of returning the regular name on request, now you are always returning the informal name:

```
Return MyBase.Name(NameTypes.Informal)
```

Before you can test this, you need to enhance the code in your form to actually provide a value for the informal name. Make the following change to the code:

```
Private Sub btnOK_Click(ByVal sender As System.Object,
    ByVal e As System.EventArgs) Handles btnOK.Click

  Dim objPerson As OfficeEmployee = New OfficeEmployee()

  With objPerson
    .Name = "Fred"
```

```
        .Name(NameTypes.Informal) = "Freddy"
      .BirthDate = #1/1/1960#
      .Age = 20
      .OfficeNumber = "A42"

      txtName.Text = .ToString()
      txtBirthDate.Text = Format(.BirthDate, "Short date")
      txtAge.Text = CStr(.Age)
      txtOffice.Text = .OfficeNumber
    End With
  End Sub
```

When you run the application, the Name field displays the informal name. Even though the `ToString` method is implemented in the `Person` class, it is invoking the implementation of `Name` from the `OfficeEmployee` class. This is because method calls within a class follow the same rules for calling virtual methods as code outside a class, such as your code in the form. You will see this behavior with or without the `Me` keyword, as the default behavior for method calls is to implicitly call them via the current object.

While methods called from within a class follow the same rules for virtual methods, this is not the case for shadowed methods. Here, the rules for calling a shadowed method from within your class are different from those outside your class.

To see how this works, make the `Name` property in `OfficeEmployee` a shadowed method instead of an overridden method:

```
Public Shadows Property Name() As String
  Get
    Return MyBase.Name(NameTypes.Informal)
  End Get
  Set(ByVal value As String)
    MyBase.Name = value
  End Set
End Property
```

Before you can run your application, you must adjust some code in the form. Because you have shadowed the `Name` property in `OfficeEmployee`, the version of `Name` from `Employee` that acts as a property array is now invalid.

> **Shadowing a method replaces all implementations from higher in the inheritance chain, regardless of their method signature.**

To make your application operate, you need to change the variable declaration and object creation to declare a variable of type `Employee` so that you can access the property array while still creating an instance of `OfficeEmployee`:

```
Dim person As Employee = New OfficeEmployee()
```

Because your variable is now of type `Employee`, you also need to comment out the lines that refer to the `OfficeNumber` property, as it is no longer available:

```
With person
  .Name = "Fred"
  .Name(NameTypes.Informal) = "Freddy"
  .BirthDate = #1/1/1960#
  .Age = 20

  '.OfficeNumber = "A42"

  txtName.Text = .ToString()
  txtBirthDate.Text = Format(.BirthDate, "Short date")
  txtAge.Text = CStr(.Age)

  'txtOffice.Text = .OfficeNumber
End With
```

When you run the application now, it displays the name `Fred`, rather than `Freddy`, meaning it is not calling the `Name` method from `OfficeEmployee`; instead, it is calling the implementation provided by the `Employee` class. Remember that the code to make this call still resides in the `Person` class, but it now ignores the shadowed version of the `Name` method.

Shadowed implementations in subclasses are ignored when calling the method from within a class higher in the inheritance chain. You will get this same behavior with or without the `Me` keyword. The `Me` keyword, or calling methods directly, follows the same rules for overridden methods as any other method call. For shadowed methods, however, any shadowed implementations in subclasses are ignored, and the method is called from the current level in the inheritance chain.

The `Me` keyword exists primarily to enable you to pass a reference to the current object as a parameter to other objects or methods. As shown when you look at the `MyBase` and `MyClass` keywords, things can get very confusing, and there may be value in using the `Me` keyword when working with `MyBase` and `MyClass` to ensure that it is always clear which particular implementation of a method you intended to invoke.

The MyBase Keyword

While the `Me` keyword allows you to call methods on the current object instance, at times you might want to explicitly call into methods in your parent class. Earlier, you saw an example of this when you called back into the base class from an overridden method in the subclass.

The `MyBase` keyword references only the immediate parent class, and it works like an object reference. This means that you can call methods on `MyBase` knowing that they are being called just as if you had a reference to an object of your parent class's data type.

> There is no way to directly navigate up the inheritance chain beyond the immediate parent, so you can't directly access the implementation of a method in a base class if you are in a sub-subclass. Such behavior isn't a good idea anyway, which is why it isn't allowed.

The MyBase keyword can be used to invoke or use any Public, Friend, or Protected element from the parent class. This includes all elements directly on the base class, and any elements the base class inherited from other classes higher in the inheritance chain.

You already used MyBase to call back into the base Person class as you implemented the overridden Name property in the Employee class.

> **Any code within a subclass can call any method on the base class by using the MyBase keyword.**

You can also use MyBase to call back into the base class implementation even if you have shadowed a method. Though it wasn't noted at the time, you have already done this in your shadowed implementation of the Name property in the OfficeEmployee class. The highlighted lines indicate where you are calling into the base class from within a shadowed method:

```
Public Shadows Property Name() As String
   Get
      Return MyBase.Name(NameTypes.Informal)
   End Get
   Set(ByVal value As String)
      MyBase.Name = value
   End Set
End Property
```

The MyBase keyword enables you to merge the functionality of the base class into your subclass code as you deem fit.

The MyClass Keyword

As you have seen, when you use the Me keyword or call a method directly, your method call follows the rules for calling both virtual and nonvirtual methods. In other words, as shown earlier with the Name property, a call to Name from your code in the Person class actually invoked the overridden version of Name located in the OfficeEmployee class.

While this behavior is often useful, sometimes you will want to ensure that you truly are running the specific implementation from your class; even if a subclass overrode your method, you still want to ensure that you are calling the version of the method that is directly in your class.

Maybe you decide that your ToString implementation in Person should always call the Name implementation that you write in the Person class, totally ignoring any overridden versions of Name in any subclasses.

This is where the MyClass keyword shines. This keyword is much like MyBase, in that it provides you with access to methods as though it were an object reference — in this case, a reference to an instance of the class that contains the code you are writing when using the MyClass keyword. This is true even when the instantiated object is an instance of a class derived from your class.

You have seen that a call to ToString from within Person actually invokes the implementation in Employee or OfficeEmployee if your object is an instance of either of those types. Let's restore the Name property in OfficeEmployee so that it is an overridden method, rather than a shadowed method, to demonstrate how this works:

```
Public Overloads Overrides Property Name() As String
  Get
    Return MyBase.Name(NameTypes.Informal)
  End Get
  Set(ByVal value As String)
    MyBase.Name = value
  End Set
End Property
```

With this change, and based on your earlier testing, you know that the ToString implementation in Person will automatically call this overridden version of the Name property, as the call to the Name method follows the normal rules for virtual methods. In fact, if you run the application now, the Name field on the form displays Freddy, the informal name of the person.

You can force the use of the implementation in the current class through the use of MyClass. Change the ToString method in Person as follows:

```
Public Overrides Function ToString() As String
  Return MyClass.Name
End Function
```

You are now calling the Name method, but you are doing it using the MyClass keyword. When you run the application and click the button, the Name field in the form displays Fred rather than Freddy, proving that the implementation from Person was invoked even though the data type of the object itself is OfficeEmployee.

The ToString method is invoked from Person, as neither Employee nor OfficeEmployee provides an overridden implementation. Then, because you are using the MyClass keyword, the Name method is invoked directly from Person, explicitly defeating the default behavior you would normally expect.

Constructors

As discussed in Chapter 2, you can provide a special constructor method, named New, on a class and it will be the first code run when an object is instantiated. You can also receive parameters via the constructor method, enabling the code that creates your object to pass data into the object during the creation process.

Constructor methods are affected by inheritance differently than regular methods. A normal Public method, such as BirthDate on your Person class, is automatically inherited by any subclass. From there you can overload, override, or shadow that method, as discussed already.

Simple Constructors

Constructors do not quite follow the same rules. To explore the differences, let's implement a simple constructor method in the `Person` class:

```
Public Sub New()
  Debug.WriteLine("Person constructor")
End Sub
```

If you now run the application, you will see the text displayed in the output window in the IDE. This occurs even though the code in your form is creating an object of type `OfficeEmployee`:

```
Dim person As Employee = New OfficeEmployee()
```

As you might expect, the `New` method from your base `Person` class is invoked as part of the construction process of the `OfficeEmployee` object — simple inheritance at work. However, interesting things occur if you implement a `New` method in the `OfficeEmployee` class itself:

```
Public Sub New()
  Debug.WriteLine("OfficeEmployee constructor")
End Sub
```

Notice that you are not using the `Overrides` keyword, nor did you mark the method in `Person` as `Overridable`. These keywords have no use in this context, and, in fact, will cause syntax errors if you attempt to use them on constructor methods.

When you run the application now, you would probably expect that only the implementation of `New` in `OfficeEmployee` would be invoked. Certainly, that is what would occur with a normal overridden method. Of course, `New` isn't overridden, so when you run the application, both implementations are run, and both strings are output to the output window in the IDE.

Note that the implementation in the `Person` class ran first, followed by the implementation in the `OfficeEmployee` class. This occurs because when an object is created, all the constructors for the classes in the inheritance chain are invoked, starting with the base class and including all the subclasses one by one. In fact, if you implement a `New` method in the `Employee` class, you can see that it too is invoked:

```
Public Sub New()
  Debug.WriteLine("Employee constructor")
End Sub
```

When the application is run and the button is clicked, three strings appear in the output window. All three constructor methods were invoked, from the `Person` class to the `OfficeEmployee` class.

Constructors in More Depth

The rules governing constructors without parameters are pretty straightforward, but things get a bit more complex if you start requiring parameters on your constructors.

To understand why, you need to consider how even your simple constructors are invoked. While you may see them as being invoked from the base class down through all subclasses to your final subclass, what is really happening is a bit different.

In particular, it is the subclass New method that is invoked first. However, Visual Basic automatically inserts a line of code into your routine at compile time. For instance, in your OfficeEmployee class you have a constructor:

```
Public Sub New()
  Debug.WriteLine("OfficeEmployee constructor")
End Sub
```

Behind the scenes, Visual Basic inserts what is effectively a call to the constructor of your parent class on your behalf. You could do this manually by using the MyBase keyword with the following change:

```
Public Sub New()
  MyBase.New()
  Debug.WriteLine("OfficeEmployee constructor")
End Sub
```

This call must be the first line in your constructor. If you put any other code before this line, you will get a syntax error indicating that your code is invalid. Because the call is always required, and because it always must be the first line in any constructor, Visual Basic simply inserts it for you automatically.

Note that if you don't explicitly provide a constructor on a class by implementing a New method, Visual Basic creates one for you behind the scenes. The automatically created method simply has one line of code:

```
MyBase.New()
```

All classes have constructor methods, either created explicitly by you as you write a New method or created implicitly by Visual Basic as the class is compiled.

A constructor method is sometimes called a ctor, short for constructor. This term is often used by tools such as ILDASM or .NET Reflector.

By always calling MyBase.New as the first line in every constructor, you are guaranteed that it is the implementation of New in your top-level base class that actually runs first. Every subclass invokes the parent class implementation all the way up the inheritance chain until only the base class remains. Then its code runs, followed by each individual subclass, as shown earlier.

Constructors with Parameters

This works great when your constructors don't require parameters, but if your constructor does require a parameter, then it becomes impossible for Visual Basic to automatically make that call on your behalf. After all, how would Visual Basic know what values you want to pass as parameters?

To see how this works, change the New method in the Person class to require a name parameter. You can use that parameter to initialize the object's Name property:

```
Public Sub New(ByVal name As String)
  Me.Name = name
```

```
    Debug.WriteLine("Person constructor")
End Sub
```

Now your constructor requires a `String` parameter and uses it to initialize the `Name` property. You are using the `Me` keyword to make your code easier to read. Interestingly enough, the compiler actually understands and correctly compiles the following code:

```
Name = name
```

However, that is not at all clear to a developer reading the code. By prefixing the property name with the `Me` keyword, you make it clear that you are invoking a property on the object and providing it with the parameter value.

At this point, your application won't compile because there is an error in the `New` method of the `Employee` class. In particular, Visual Basic's attempt to automatically invoke the constructor on the `Person` class fails because it has no idea what data value to pass for this new `name` parameter. There are three ways you can address this error:

- ❑ Make the `name` parameter `Optional`.
- ❑ Overload the `New` method with another implementation that requires no parameter.
- ❑ Manually provide the `Name` parameter value from within the `Employee` class.

If you make the `Name` parameter `Optional`, then you are indicating that the `New` method can be called with or without a parameter. Therefore, one viable option is to call the method with no parameters, so Visual Basic's default of calling it with no parameters works just fine.

If you overload the `New` method, then you can implement a second `New` method that doesn't accept any parameters, again allowing Visual Basic's default behavior to work as you have seen. Keep in mind that this solution only invokes the overloaded version of `New` with no parameter; the version that requires a parameter would not be invoked.

The final way you can fix the error is by simply providing a parameter value yourself from within the `New` method of the `Employee` class. To do this, change the `Employee` class as shown:

```
Public Sub New()
    MyBase.New("George")
    Debug.WriteLine("Employee constructor")
End Sub
```

By explicitly calling the `New` method of the parent class, you are able to provide it with the required parameter value. At this point, your application will compile, but it won't run.

Constructors, Overloading, and Variable Initialization

What isn't clear from this code is that you have now introduced a very insidious bug. The constructor in the `Person` class is using the `Name` property to set the value:

```
Public Sub New(ByVal name As String)
    Me.Name = name
```

```
        Debug.WriteLine("Person constructor")
    End Sub
```

However, the `Name` property is overridden by the `Employee` class, so it is that implementation that will be run. Unfortunately, that implementation makes use of a `Dictionary` object, which isn't available yet! It turns out that any member variables declared in a class with the `New` statement, such as the `Dictionary` object in `Employee`, won't be initialized until after the constructor for that class has completed:

```
    Private mNames As New Generic.Dictionary(Of NameTypes, String)
```

Because you are still in the constructor for `Person`, there's no way the constructor for `Employee` can be complete. To resolve this, you need to change the `Employee` class a bit so that it does not rely on the `Dictionary` being created in this manner. Instead, you will add code to create it when needed.

First, change the declaration of the variable in the `Employee` class:

```
    Private mNames As Generic.Dictionary(Of NameTypes, String)
```

Then, update the `Name` property so that it creates the `Hashtable` object if needed:

```
    Public Overloads Property Name(ByVal type As NameTypes) As String
      Get
        If mNames Is Nothing Then mNames = New Generic.Dictionary(Of NameTypes, String)
          Return mNames(type)
      End Get
      Set(ByVal value As String)
        If mNames Is Nothing Then mNames = New Generic.Dictionary(Of NameTypes, String)
        If mNames.ContainsKey(type) Then
          mNames.Item(type) = value
        Else
          mNames.Add(type, value)
        End If
        If type = NameTypes.Normal Then
          MyBase.Name = value
        End If
      End Set
    End Property
```

This ensures that a `Dictionary` object is created in the `Employee` class code even though its constructor hasn't yet completed.

More Constructors with Parameters

Obviously, you probably do not want to hard-code a value in a constructor as you did in the `Employee` class, so you may choose instead to change this constructor to also accept a `name` parameter. Change the `Employee` class constructor as shown:

```
    Public Sub New(ByVal name As String)
      MyBase.New(name)
```

```
      Debug.WriteLine("Employee constructor")
   End Sub
```

Of course, this just pushed the issue deeper, and now the OfficeEmployee class has a compile error in its New method. Again, you can fix the problem by having that method accept a parameter so that it can provide it up the chain as required. Make the following change to OfficeEmployee:

```
Public Sub New(ByVal name As String)
  MyBase.New(name)
   Debug.WriteLine("OfficeEmployee constructor")
End Sub
```

Finally, the code in the form is no longer valid. You are attempting to create an instance of OfficeEmployee without passing a parameter value. Update that code as shown and then you can run the application:

```
Private Sub btnOK_Click(ByVal sender As System.Object, _
    ByVal e As System.EventArgs) Handles btnOK.Click

   Dim person As Employee = New OfficeEmployee("Mary")

   With person
     '.Name = "Fred"
```

Here, you are passing a name value to the constructor of OfficeEmployee. In addition, you have commented out the line of code that sets the Name property directly — meaning the value passed in the constructor will be displayed in the form.

Protected Scope

You have seen how a subclass automatically gains all the Public methods and properties that compose the interface of the base class. This is also true of Friend methods and properties; they are inherited as well and are available only to other code in the same project as the subclass.

Private methods and properties are not exposed as part of the interface of the subclass, meaning that the code in the subclass cannot call those methods, nor can any code using your objects. These methods are only available to the code within the base class itself. This can get confusing, as the implementations contained in the Private methods are inherited and are used by any code in the base class; it is just that they are not available to be called by any other code, including code in the subclass.

Sometimes you will want to create methods in your base class that can be called by a subclass as well as the base class but not by code outside of those classes. Basically, you want a hybrid between Public and Private — methods that are private to the classes in the inheritance chain but usable by any subclasses that might be created within the chain. This functionality is provided by the Protected scope.

Protected methods are very similar to Private methods in that they are not available to any code that calls your objects. Instead, these methods are available to code within the base class and to code within any subclass. The following table lists all the available scope options:

Scope	Description
Private	Available only to code within your class
Protected	Available only to classes that inherit from your class
Friend	Available only to code within your project/component
Protected Friend	Available to classes that inherit from your class (in any project) and to code within your project/component. This is a combination of Protected and Friend.
Public	Available to code outside your class

The Protected scope can be applied to Sub, Function, and Property methods. To see how the Protected scope works, let's add an Identity field to the Person class:

```
Public Class Person
    Private mName As String
    Private mBirthDate As String

    Private mID As String

    Protected Property Identity() As String
      Get
        Return mID
      End Get
      Set(ByVal value As String)
        mID = value
      End Set
    End Property
```

This data field represents some arbitrary identification number or value assigned to a person. This might be a social security number, an employee number, or whatever is appropriate.

The interesting thing about this value is that it is not currently accessible outside your inheritance chain. For instance, if you try to use it from your code in the form, then you will discover that there is no Identity property on your Person, Employee, or OfficeEmployee objects.

However, there is an Identity property now available inside your inheritance chain. The Identity property is available to the code in the Person class, just like any other method. Interestingly, even though Identity is not available to the code in your form, it is available to the code in the Employee and OfficeEmployee classes, because they are both subclasses of Person. Employee is directly a subclass, and OfficeEmployee is indirectly a subclass of Person because it is a subclass of Employee.

Thus, you can enhance your Employee class to implement an EmployeeNumber property by using the Identity property. To do this, add the following code to the Employee class:

```
Public Property EmployeeNumber() As Integer
  Get
    Return CInt(Identity)
```

```
      End Get
      Set(ByVal value As Integer)
        Identity = CStr(value)
      End Set
  End Property
```

This new property exposes a numeric identity value for the employee, but it uses the internal `Identity` property to manage that value. You can override and shadow `Protected` elements just as you do with elements of any other scope.

Protected Variables

Up to this point, we've focused on methods and properties and how they interact through inheritance. Inheritance, and, in particular, the `Protected` scope, also affects instance variables and how you work with them.

Though it is not recommended, you can declare variables in a class using `Public` scope. This makes the variable directly available to code both within and outside of your class, allowing any code that interacts with your objects to directly read or alter the value of that variable.

Variables can also have `Friend` scope, which likewise allows any code in your class or anywhere within your project to read or alter the value directly. This is also generally not recommended because it breaks encapsulation.

> Rather than declare variables with **Public** or **Friend** scope, it is better to expose the value using a **Property** method so that you can apply any of your business rules to control how the value is altered as appropriate.

Of course, you know that variables can be of `Private` scope, and this is typically the case. This makes the variables accessible only to the code within your class, and it is the most restrictive scope.

As with methods, however, you can also use the `Protected` scope when declaring variables. This makes the variable accessible to the code in your class and to the code in any class that derives from your class — all the way down the hierarchy chain.

Sometimes this is useful, because it enables you to provide and accept data to and from subclasses, but to act on that data from code in the base class. At the same time, exposing variables to subclasses is typically not ideal, and you should use `Property` methods with `Protected` scope for this instead, as they allow your base class to enforce any business rules that are appropriate for the value, rather than just hope that the author of the subclass only provides good values.

Events and Inheritance

So far, we've discussed methods, properties, and variables in terms of inheritance — how they can be added, overridden, extended, and shadowed. In Visual Basic, events are also part of the interface of an object, and they are affected by inheritance as well.

Inheriting Events

Chapter 2 discusses how to declare, raise, and receive events from objects. You can add such an event to the `Person` class by declaring it at the top of the class:

```
Public Class Person
   Private mName As String
   Private mBirthDate As String
   Private mID As String

   Public Event NameChanged(ByVal newName As String)
```

Then, you can raise this event within the class any time the person's name is changed:

```
Public Overridable Property Name() As String
   Get
      Return mName
   End Get
   Set(ByVal value As String)
      mName = value

      RaiseEvent NameChanged(mName)

   End Set
End Property
```

At this point, you can receive and handle this event within your form any time you are working with a `Person` object. The nice thing about this is that your events are inherited automatically by subclasses — meaning that your `Employee` and `OfficeEmployee` objects will also raise this event. Thus, you can change the code in your form to handle the event, even though you are working with an object of type `OfficeEmployee`.

First, you can add a method to handle the event to `Form1`:

```
Private Sub OnNameChanged(ByVal newName As String)
   MsgBox("New name: " & newName)
End Sub
```

Note that you are not using the `Handles` clause here. In this case, for simplicity, you use the `AddHandler` method to dynamically link the event to this method. However, you could have also chosen to use the `WithEvents` and `Handles` keywords, as described in Chapter 2 — either way works.

With the handler built, you can use the `AddHandler` method to link this method to the event on the object:

```
Private Sub btnOK_Click(ByVal sender As System.Object, _
    ByVal e As System.EventArgs) Handles btnOK.Click

   Dim person As Employee = New OfficeEmployee("Mary")

   AddHandler person.NameChanged, AddressOf OnNameChanged
```

```
With person
    .Name = "Fred"
```

Also note that you are uncommenting the line that changes the `Name` property. With this change, you know that the event should fire when the name is changed.

When you run the application now, you will see a message box, indicating that the name has changed and proving that the `NameChanged` event really is exposed and available even though your object is of type `OfficeEmployee`, rather than `Person`.

Raising Events from Subclasses

One caveat you should keep in mind is that while a subclass exposes the events of its base class, the code in the subclass cannot raise the event. In other words, you cannot use the `RaiseEvent` method in `Employee` or `OfficeEmployee` to raise the `NameChanged` event. Only code directly in the `Person` class can raise the event.

To see this in action, let's add another event to the `Person` class, an event that can indicate the change of other arbitrary data values:

```
Public Class Person
    Private mName As String
    Private mBirthDate As String
    Private mID As String

    Public Event NameChanged(ByVal newName As String)
    Public Event DataChanged(ByVal field As String, ByVal newValue As Object)
```

You can then raise this event when the `BirthDate` is changed:

```
Public Overridable Property BirthDate() As Date
  Get
    Return mBirthDate
  End Get
  Set(ByVal value As Date)
    mBirthDate = value
    RaiseEvent DataChanged("BirthDate", value)
  End Set
End Property
```

It would also be nice to raise this event from the `Employee` class when the `Salary` value is changed. Unfortunately, you can't use the `RaiseEvent` method to raise the event from a base class, so the following code won't work (do not enter this code):

```
Public Property Salary() As Double
  Get
    Return mSalary
  End Get
```

```
      Set(ByVal value As Double)
        mSalary = value
        RaiseEvent DataChanged("Salary", value)
      End Set
  End Property
```

Fortunately, there is a relatively easy way to get around this limitation. You can simply implement a `Protected` method in your base class that allows any derived class to raise the method. In the `Person` class, you can add such a method:

```
  Protected Sub OnDataChanged(ByVal field As String, _
      ByVal newValue As Object)

    RaiseEvent DataChanged(field, newValue)
  End Sub
```

You can use this method from within the `Employee` class to indicate that `Salary` has changed:

```
  Public Property Salary() As Double
    Get
      Return mSalary
    End Get
    Set(ByVal value As Double)
      mSalary = value
      OnDataChanged("Salary", value)
    End Set
  End Property
```

Note that the code in `Employee` is not raising the event, it is simply calling a `Protected` method in `Person`. The code in the `Person` class is actually raising the event, meaning everything will work as desired.

You can enhance the code in `Form1` to receive the event. First, create a method to handle the event:

```
  Private Sub OnDataChanged(ByVal field As String, ByVal newValue As Object)
    MsgBox("New " & field & ": " & CStr(newValue))
  End Sub
```

Then, link this handler to the event using the `AddHandler` method:

```
  Private Sub btnOK_Click(ByVal sender As System.Object, _
      ByVal e As System.EventArgs) Handles btnOK.Click

    Dim person As Employee = New OfficeEmployee("Mary")

    AddHandler person.NameChanged, AddressOf OnNameChanged
    AddHandler person.DataChanged, AddressOf OnDataChanged
```

Finally, ensure that you are changing and displaying the `Salary` property:

```
With person
    .Name = "Fred"
    .Name(NameTypes.Informal) = "Freddy"
    .BirthDate = #1/1/1960#
    .Age = 20
    .Salary = 30000


    txtName.Text = .ToString()
    txtBirthDate.Text = Format(.BirthDate, "Short date")
    txtAge.Text = CStr(.Age)

    txtSalary.Text = Format(.Salary, "0.00")
End With
```

When you run the application and click the button now, you will get message boxes displaying the changes to the `Name` property, the `BirthDate` property (twice, once for the `BirthDate` property and once for the `Age` property, which changes the birth date), and the `Salary` property.

Shared Methods

Chapter 2 explored shared methods and how they work: providing a set of methods that can be invoked directly from the class, rather than requiring that you create an actual object.

Shared methods are inherited just like instance methods and so are automatically available as methods on subclasses, just as they are on the base class. If you implement a shared method in `BaseClass`, you can call that method using any class derived from `BaseClass`.

Like regular methods, shared methods can be overloaded and shadowed. They cannot, however, be overridden. If you attempt to use the `Overridable` keyword when declaring a `Shared` method, you will get a syntax error. For instance, you can implement a method in your `Person` class to compare two `Person` objects:

```
Public Shared Function Compare(ByVal person1 As Person, _
    ByVal person2 As Person) As Boolean

  Return (person1.Name = person2.Name)

End Function
```

To test this method, let's add another button to the form, name it `btnCompare`, and set its `Text` value to `Compare`. Double-click the button to bring up the code window and enter the following:

```
Private Sub btnCompare_Click(ByVal sender As System.Object, _
    ByVal e As System.EventArgs) Handles btnCompare.Click

  Dim emp1 As New Employee("Fred")
```

```
        Dim emp2 As New Employee("Mary")

        MsgBox(Employee.Compare(emp1, emp2))

    End Sub
```

This code simply creates two Employee objects and compares them. Note, though, that the code uses the Employee class to invoke the Compare method, displaying the result in a message box. This establishes that the Compare method implemented in the Person class is inherited by the Employee class, as expected.

Overloading Shared Methods

Shared methods can be overloaded using the Overloads keyword in the same manner as you overload an instance method. This means that your subclass can add new implementations of the shared method as long as the parameter list differs from the original implementation.

For example, you can add a new implementation of the Compare method to Employee:

```
    Public Overloads Shared Function Compare(ByVal employee1 As Employee, _
        ByVal employee2 As Employee) As Boolean

        Return (employee1.EmployeeNumber = employee2.EmployeeNumber)

    End Function
```

This new implementation compares two Employee objects, rather than two Person objects, and, in fact, compares them by employee number, rather than name. You can enhance the code behind btnCompare in the form to set the EmployeeNumber properties:

```
    Private Sub btnCompare_Click(ByVal sender As System.Object, _
        ByVal e As System.EventArgs) Handles btnCompare.Click

        Dim emp1 As New Employee("Fred")
        Dim emp2 As New Employee("Mary")

        emp1.EmployeeNumber = 1
        emp2.EmployeeNumber = 1

        MsgBox(Employee.Compare(emp1, emp2))
    End Sub
```

While it might make little sense for these two objects to have the same EmployeeNumber value, it does prove a point. When you run the application now, even though the Name values of the objects are different, your Compare routine will return True, proving that you are invoking the overloaded version of the method that expects two Employee objects as parameters.

The overloaded implementation is available on the Employee class or any classes derived from Employee, such as OfficeEmployee. The overloaded implementation is not available if called directly from Person, as that class only contains the original implementation.

Shadowing Shared Methods

Shared methods can also be shadowed by a subclass. This allows you to do some very interesting things, including converting a shared method into an instance method or vice versa. You can even leave the method as shared but change the entire way it works and is declared. In short, just as with instance methods, you can use the Shadows keyword to entirely replace and change a shared method in a subclass.

To see how this works, use the Shadows keyword to change the nature of the Compare method in OfficeEmployee:

```
Public Shared Shadows Function Compare(ByVal person1 As Person, _
    ByVal person2 As Person) As Boolean

  Return (person1.Age = person2.Age)

End Function
```

Notice that this method has the same signature as the original Compare method you implemented in the Person class, but instead of comparing by name, here you are comparing by age. With a normal method you could have done this by overriding, but Shared methods can't be overridden, so the only thing you can do is shadow it.

Of course, the shadowed implementation is only available via the OfficeEmployee class. Neither the Person nor Employee classes, which are higher up the inheritance chain, are aware that this shadowed version of the method exists.

To use this from your Form1 code, you can change the code for btnCompare as follows:

```
Private Sub btnCompare_Click(ByVal sender As System.Object, _
    ByVal e As System.EventArgs) Handles btnCompare.Click

  Dim emp1 As New Employee("Fred")
  Dim emp2 As New Employee("Mary")

  emp1.Age = 20
  emp2.Age = 25

  MsgBox(OfficeEmployee.Compare(emp1, emp2))
End Sub
```

Instead of setting the EmployeeNumber values, you are now setting the Age values on your objects. More important, notice that you are now calling the Compare method via the OfficeEmployee class, rather than via Employee or Person. This causes the invocation of the new version of the method, and the ages of the objects are compared.

Shared Events

As discussed in Chapter 2, you can create shared events, events that can be raised by shared or instance methods in a class, whereas regular events can only be raised from within instance methods.

When you inherit from a class that defines a shared event, your new subclass automatically gains that event, just as it does with regular events. As with instance events, a shared event cannot be raised by code within the subclass; it can only be raised using the `RaiseEvent` keyword from code in the class where the event is declared. If you want to be able to raise the event from methods in your subclass, you need to implement a `Protected` method on the base class that actually makes the call to `RaiseEvent`.

This is no different from what you saw earlier in the chapter, other than that with a shared event you can use a method with `Protected` scope that is marked as shared to raise the event, rather than use an instance method.

Creating an Abstract Base Class

So far, you have seen how to inherit from a class, how to overload and override methods, and how virtual methods work. In all of the examples so far, the parent classes have been useful in their own right and could be instantiated and do some meaningful work. Sometimes, however, you want to create a class such that it can only be used as a base class for inheritance.

MustInherit Keyword

The current `Person` class is being used as a base class, but it can also be instantiated directly to create an object of type `Person`. Likewise, the `Employee` class is also being used as a base class for the `OfficeEmployee` class you created that derives from it.

If you want to make a class act only as a base class, you can use the `MustInherit` keyword, thereby preventing anyone from creating objects based directly on the class, and requiring them instead to create a subclass and then create objects based on that subclass.

This can be very useful when you are creating object models of real-world concepts and entities. You will look at ways to leverage this capability later in this chapter. Change `Person` to use the `MustInherit` keyword:

```
Public MustInherit Class Person
```

This has no effect on the code within `Person` or any of the classes that inherit from it, but it does mean that no code can instantiate objects directly from the `Person` class; instead, you can only create objects based on `Employee` or `OfficeEmployee`.

This does not prevent you from declaring variables of type `Person`; it merely prevents you from creating an object by using `New Person`. You can also continue to make use of `Shared` methods from the `Person` class without any difficulty.

MustOverride Keyword

Another option you have is to create a method (`Sub`, `Function`, or `Property`) that must be overridden by a subclass. You might want to do this when you are creating a base class that provides some behaviors but relies on subclasses to also provide other behaviors in order to function properly. This is accomplished by using the `MustOverride` keyword on a method declaration.

If a class contains any methods marked with `MustOverride`, the class itself must also be declared with the `MustInherit` keyword or you will get a syntax error:

```
Public MustInherit Class Person
```

This makes sense. If you are requiring that a method be overridden in a subclass, it stands to reason that your class can't be directly instantiated; it must be subclassed to be useful.

Let's see how this works by adding a `LifeExpectancy` method in `Person` that has no implementation and must be overridden by a subclass:

```
Public MustOverride Function LifeExpectancy() As Integer
```

Notice that there is no `End Function` or any other code associated with the method. When using `MustOverride`, you cannot provide any implementation for the method in your class. Such a method is called an *abstract method* or *pure virtual function*, as it only defines the interface, and no implementation.

Methods declared in this manner must be overridden in any subclass that inherits from your base class. If you do not override one of these methods, you will generate a syntax error in the subclass, and it won't compile. You need to alter the `Employee` class to provide an implementation for this method:

```
Public Overrides Function LifeExpectancy() As Integer
   Return 90
End Function
```

Your application will compile and run at this point because you are now overriding the `LifeExpectancy` method in `Employee`, so the required condition is met.

Abstract Base Classes

You can combine these two concepts, using both `MustInherit` and `MustOverride`, to create something called an *abstract base class*, sometimes referred to as a *virtual class*. This is a class that provides no implementation, only the interface definitions from which a subclass can be created, as shown in the following example:

```
Public MustInherit Class AbstractBaseClass
   Public MustOverride Sub DoSomething()
   Public MustOverride Sub DoOtherStuff()
End Class
```

This technique can be very useful when creating frameworks or the high-level conceptual elements of a system. Any class that inherits `AbstractBaseClass` must implement both `DoSomething` and `DoOtherStuff`; otherwise, a syntax error will result.

In some ways, an abstract base class is comparable to defining an interface using the `Interface` keyword. The `Interface` keyword is discussed in detail later in this chapter. You could define the same interface shown in this example with the following code:

```
Public Interface IAbstractBaseClass
   Sub DoSomething()
   Sub DoOtherStuff()
End Interface
```

Any class that implements the `IAbstractBaseClass` interface must implement both `DoSomething` and `DoOtherStuff` or a syntax error will result, and in that regard this technique is similar to an abstract base class.

Preventing Inheritance

If you want to prevent a class from being used as a base class, you can use the `NotInheritable` keyword. For instance, you can change your `OfficeEmployee` as follows:

```
Public NotInheritable Class OfficeEmployee
```

At this point, it is no longer possible to inherit from this class to create a new class. Your `OfficeEmployee` class is now sealed, meaning it cannot be used as a base from which to create other classes.

If you attempt to inherit from `OfficeEmployee`, you will get a compile error indicating that it cannot be used as a base class. This has no effect on `Person` or `Employee`; you can continue to derive other classes from them.

Typically, you want to design your classes so that they can be subclassed, because that provides the greatest long-term flexibility in the overall design. Sometimes, however, you want to ensure that your class cannot be used as a base class, and the `NotInheritable` keyword addresses that issue.

Multiple Interfaces

In Visual Basic, objects can have one or more interfaces. All objects have a *primary*, or *native*, interface, which is composed of any methods, properties, events, or member variables declared using the `Public` keyword. You can also have objects implement secondary interfaces in addition to their native interface by using the `Implements` keyword.

Object Interfaces

The native interface on any class is composed of all the methods, properties, events, and even variables that are declared as anything other than `Private`. Though this is nothing new, let's quickly review what is included in the native interface to set the stage for discussing secondary interfaces. To include a method as part of your interface, you can simply declare a `Public` routine:

```
Public Sub AMethod()

End Sub
```

Notice that there is no code in this routine. Any code would be implementation and is not part of the interface. Only the declaration of the method is important when discussing interfaces. This can seem confusing at first, but it is an important distinction, as the separation of the interface from its implementation is at the very core of object-oriented programming and design.

Because this method is declared as `Public`, it is available to any code outside the class, including other applications that may make use of the assembly. If the method has a property, then you can declare it as part of the interface by using the `Property` keyword:

```
Public Property AProperty() As String

End Property
```

You can also declare events as part of the interface by using the Event keyword:

```
Public Event AnEvent()
```

Finally, you can include actual variables, or attributes, as part of the interface:

```
Public AnInteger As Integer
```

This is strongly discouraged, because it directly exposes the internal variables for use by code outside the class. Because the variable is directly accessible from other code, you give up any and all control over the way the value may be changed or the code may be accessed.

Rather than make any variable Public, it is far preferable to make use of a Property method to expose the value. That way, you can implement code to ensure that your internal variable is only set to valid values and that only the appropriate code has access to the value based on your application's logic.

Using the Native Interface

Ultimately, the native (or primary) interface for any class is defined by looking at all the methods, properties, events, and variables that are declared as anything other than Private in scope. This includes any methods, properties, events, or variables that are inherited from a base class.

You are used to interacting with the default interface on most objects, so this should seem pretty straightforward. Consider this simple class:

```
Public Class TheClass
  Public Sub DoSomething()

  End Sub

  Public Sub DoSomethingElse()

  End Sub
End Class
```

This defines a class and, by extension, defines the native interface that is exposed by any objects you instantiate based on this class. The native interface defines two methods: DoSomething and DoSomethingElse. To make use of these methods, you simply call them:

```
Dim myObject As New TheClass()

myObject.DoSomething()

myObject.DoSomethingElse()
```

This is the same thing you did in Chapter 2 and so far in this chapter. However, let's take a look at creating and using secondary interfaces, because they are a bit different.

Secondary Interfaces

Sometimes it's helpful for an object to have more than one interface, thereby enabling you to interact with the object in different ways. Inheritance enables you to create subclasses that are specialized cases of the base class. For example, your Employee is a Person.

However, sometimes you have a group of objects that are not the same thing, but you want to be able to treat them as though they were the same. You want all these objects to act as the same thing, even though they are all different.

For instance, you may have a series of different objects in an application, product, customer, invoice, and so forth. Each of these would have default interfaces appropriate to each individual object — and each of them is a different class — so there's no natural inheritance relationship implied between these classes. At the same time, you may need to be able to generate a printed document for each type of object, so you would like to make them all act as a printable object.

> *This chapter discusses the is-a and act-as relationships in more detail later.*

To accomplish this, you can define a generic interface that enables generating such a printed document. You can call it `IPrintableObject`.

> *By convention, this type of interface is typically prefixed with a capital "I" to indicate that it is a formal interface.*

Each of your application objects can choose to implement the `IPrintableObject` interface. Every object that implements this interface must include code to provide actual implementation of the interface, which is unlike inheritance, whereby the code from a base class is automatically reused.

By implementing this common interface, you can write a routine that accepts any object that implements the `IPrintableObject` interface and then print it — while remaining totally oblivious to the "real" data type of the object or methods its native interface might expose. Before you learn how to use an interface in this manner, let's walk through the process of actually defining an interface.

Defining the Interface

You define a formal interface using the `Interface` keyword. This can be done in any code module in your project, but a good place to put this type of definition is in a standard module. An interface defines a set of methods (`Sub`, `Function`, or `Property`) and events that must be exposed by any class that chooses to implement the interface.

Add a module to the project using Project ⇨ Add Module and name it `Interfaces.vb`. Then, add the following code to the module, outside the `Module` code block itself:

```
Public Interface IPrintableObject

End Interface

Module Interfaces

End Module
```

A code module can contain a number of interface definitions, and these definitions must exist outside of any other code block. Thus, they do not go within a `Class` or `Module` block; they are at a peer level to those constructs.

Interfaces must be declared using either `Public` or `Friend` scope. Declaring a `Private` or `Protected` interface results in a syntax error. Within the `Interface` block of code, you can define the methods, properties, and events that make up your particular interface. Because the scope of the interface is defined by the `Interface` declaration itself, you can't specify scopes for individual methods and events; they are all scoped like the interface itself.

For instance, add the following code:

```
Public Interface IPrintableObject
    Function Label(ByVal index As Integer) As String
    Function Value(ByVal index As Integer) As String
    ReadOnly Property Count() As Integer
End Interface
```

This defines a new data type, somewhat like creating a class or structure, which you can use when declaring variables. For instance, you can now declare a variable of type `IPrintableObject`:

```
Private printable As IPrintableObject
```

You can also have your classes implement this interface, which requires each class to provide implementation code for each of the three methods defined on the interface.

Before you implement the interface in a class, let's see how you can use the interface to write a generic routine that can print any object that implements `IPrintableObject`.

Using the Interface

Interfaces define the methods and events (including parameters and data types) that an object is required to implement if you choose to support the interface. This means that, given just the interface definition, you can easily write code that can interact with any object that implements the interface, even though you do not know what the native data types of those objects will be.

To see how you can write such code, let's create a simple routine in your form that can display data to the output window in the IDE from any object that implements `IPrintableObject`. Bring up the code window for your form and add the following routine:

```
Public Sub PrintObject(obj As IPrintableObject)
  Dim index As Integer

  For index = 0 To obj.Count
    Debug.Write(obj.Label(index) & ": ")
    Debug.WriteLine(obj.Value(index))
  Next
End Sub
```

Notice that you are accepting a parameter of type `IPrintableObject`. This is how secondary interfaces are used, by treating an object of one type as though it were actually of the interface type. As long as the object passed to this routine implements the `IPrintableObject` interface, your code will work fine.

Within the `PrintObject` routine, you are assuming that the object will implement three elements — `Count`, `Label`, and `Value` — as part of the `IPrintableObject` interface. Secondary interfaces can include methods, properties, and events, much like a default interface, but the interface itself is defined and implemented using some special syntax.

Now that you have a generic printing routine, you need a way to call it. Bring up the designer for Form1, add a button, and name it btnPrint. Double-click the button and put this code behind it:

```
Private Sub btnPrint_Click(ByVal sender As System.Object, _
    ByVal e As System.EventArgs) Handles btnPrint.Click

    Dim obj As New Employee("Andy")

    obj.EmployeeNumber = 123
    obj.BirthDate = #1/1/1980#
    obj.HireDate = #1/1/1996#

    PrintObject(obj)
End Sub
```

This code simply initializes an Employee object and calls the PrintObject routine. Of course, this code produces runtime exceptions, because PrintObject is expecting a parameter that implements IPrintableObject, and Employee implements no such interface. Let's move on and implement that interface in Employee so that you can see how it works.

Implementing the Interface

Any class (other than an abstract base class) can implement an interface by using the Implements keyword. For instance, you can implement the IPrintableObject interface in Employee by adding the following line:

```
Public Class Employee
    Inherits Person
    Implements IPrintableObject
```

This causes the interface to be exposed by any object created as an instance of Employee. Adding this line of code and pressing Enter triggers the IDE to add skeleton methods for the interface to your class. All you need to do is provide implementations for the methods.

To implement an interface, you must implement all the methods and properties defined by that interface.

Before actually implementing the interface, however, let's create an array to contain the labels for the data fields so that you can return them via the IPrintableObject interface. Add the following code to the Employee class:

```
Public Class Employee
    Inherits Person
    Implements IPrintableObject
    Private mLabels() As String = {"ID", "Age", "HireDate"}
    Private mHireDate As Date
    Private mSalary As Double
```

To implement the interface, you need to create methods and properties with the same parameter and return data types as those defined in the interface. The actual name of each method or property does not matter because you are using the Implements keyword to link your internal method names to the external method names defined by the interface. As long as the method signatures match, you are all set.

This applies to scope as well. Although the interface and its methods and properties are publicly available, you do not have to declare your actual methods and properties as Public. In many cases, you can implement them as Private, so they do not become part of the native interface and are only exposed via the secondary interface.

However, if you do have a Public method with a method signature, you can use it to implement a method from the interface. This has the interesting side effect that this method provides implementation for both a method on the object's native interface and one on the secondary interface.

In this case, you will use a Private method, so it is only providing implementation for the IPrintableObject interface. Implement the Label method by adding the following code to Employee:

```
Private Function Label(ByVal index As Integer) As String _
    Implements IPrintableObject.Label

    Return mLabels(index)
End Function
```

This is just a regular Private method that returns a String value from the pre-initialized array. The interesting part is the Implements clause on the method declaration:

```
Private Function Label(ByVal index As Integer) As String _
    Implements IPrintableObject.Label
```

By using the Implements keyword in this fashion, you are indicating that this particular method is the implementation for the Label method on the IPrintableObject interface. The actual name of the private method could be anything. It is the use of the Implements clause that makes this work. The only requirement is that the parameter data types and the return value data type must match those defined by the IPrintableObject interface.

This is very similar to using the Handles clause to indicate which method should handle an event. In fact, like the Handles clause, the Implements clause allows you to have a comma-separated list of interface methods that should be implemented by this one function.

You can then move on to implement the other two elements defined by the IPrintableObject interface by adding this code to Employee:

```
Private Function Value(ByVal index As Integer) As String _
    Implements IPrintableObject.Value

    Select Case index
      Case 0
        Return CStr(EmployeeNumber)
      Case 1
        Return CStr(Age)
      Case Else
```

```
        Return Format(HireDate, "Short date")
    End Select
End Function

Private ReadOnly Property Count() As Integer _
    Implements IPrintableObject.Count
  Get
    Return UBound(mLabels)
  End Get
End Property
```

You can now run this application and click the button. The output window in the IDE will display your results, showing the ID, age, and hire-date values as appropriate.

Any object could create a similar implementation behind the IPrintableObject interface, and the PrintObject routine in your form would continue to work regardless of the native data type of the object itself.

Reusing Common Implementation

Secondary interfaces provide a guarantee that all objects implementing a given interface have exactly the same methods and events, including the same parameters.

The Implements clause links your actual implementation to a specific method on an interface. For instance, your Value method is linked to IPrintableObject.Value using the following clause:

```
Private Function Value(ByVal index As Integer) As String _
    Implements IPrintableObject.Value
```

Sometimes, your method might be able to serve as the implementation for more than one method, either on the same interface or on different interfaces.

Add the following interface definition to Interfaces.vb:

```
Public Interface IValues
  Function GetValue(ByVal index As Integer) As String
End Interface
```

This interface defines just one method, GetValue. Notice that it defines a single Integer parameter and a return type of String, the same as the Value method from IPrintableObject. Even though the method name and parameter variable name do not match, what counts here is that the parameter and return value data types do match.

Now bring up the code window for Employee. You will have it implement this new interface in addition to the IPrintableObject interface:

```
Public Class Employee
  Inherits Person
  Implements IPrintableObject

  Implements IValues
```

You already have a method that returns values. Rather than re-implement that method, it would be nice to just link this new `GetValues` method to your existing method. You can easily do this because the `Implements` clause allows you to provide a comma-separated list of method names:

```
Private Function Value(ByVal index As Integer) As String _
    Implements IPrintableObject.Value, IValues.GetValue
```

```
    Select Case Index
      Case 0
        Return CStr(EmployeeNumber)
      Case 1
        Return CStr(Age)
      Case Else
        Return Format(HireDate, "Short date")
    End Select
```

```
  End Function
```

This is very similar to the use of the `Handles` keyword, covered in Chapter 2. A single method within the class, regardless of scope or name, can be used to implement any number of methods as defined by other interfaces as long as the data types of the parameters and return values all match.

Combining Interfaces and Inheritance

You can combine implementation of secondary interfaces and inheritance at the same time. When you inherit from a class that implements an interface, your new subclass automatically gains the interface and implementation from the base class. If you specify that your base-class methods are overridable, then the subclass can override those methods. This not only overrides the base-class implementation for your native interface, but also overrides the implementation for the interface. For instance, you could declare the `Value` method in the interface as follows:

```
Public Overridable Function Value(ByVal index As Integer) As String _
    Implements IPrintableObject.Value, IValues.GetValue
```

Now it is `Public`, so it is available on your native interface, and it is part of both the `IPrintableObject` and `IValues` interfaces. This means that you can access the property three ways in client code:

```
Dim emp As New Employee()
Dim printable As IPrintableObject = emp
Dim values As IValues = emp

Debug.WriteLine(emp.Value(0))
Debug.WriteLine(printable.Value(0))
Debug.WriteLine(values.GetValue(0))
```

Note that you are also now using the `Overrides` keyword in the declaration. This means that a subclass of `Employee`, such as `OfficeEmployee`, can override the `Value` method. The overridden method will be the one invoked, regardless of whether you call the object directly or via an interface.

Combining the implementation of an interface in a base class along with overridable methods can provide a very flexible object design.

Abstraction

Abstraction is the process by which you can think about specific properties or behaviors without thinking about a particular object that has those properties or behaviors. Abstraction is merely the ability of a language to create "black box" code, to take a concept and create an abstract representation of that concept within a program.

A `Customer` object, for example, is an abstract representation of a real-world customer. A `DataSet` object is an abstract representation of a set of data.

Abstraction enables you to recognize how things are similar and to ignore differences, to think in general terms and not in specifics. A `TextBox` control is an abstraction because you can place it on a form and then tailor it to your needs by setting properties. Visual Basic enables you to define abstractions using classes.

Any language that enables a developer to create a class from which objects can be instantiated meets this criterion, and Visual Basic is no exception. You can easily create a class to represent a customer, essentially providing an abstraction. You can then create instances of that class, whereby each object can have its own attributes, representing a specific customer.

In Visual Basic, you implement abstraction by creating a class using the `Class` keyword. To see this in action, bring up Visual Studio and create a new Visual Basic Windows Application project named "OOExample." Once the project is open, add a new class to the project using the Project ⇨ Add Class menu option. Name the new class `Customer`, and add some code to make this class represent a real-world customer in an abstract sense:

```
Public Class Customer

    Private mID As Guid = Guid.NewGuid
    Private mName As String
    Private mPhone As String

    Public Property ID() As Guid
      Get
        Return mID
      End Get
      Set(ByVal value As Guid)
        mID = value
      End Set
    End Property

    Public Property Name() As String
      Get
        Return mName
      End Get
      Set(ByVal value As String)
        mName = value
      End Set
    End Property

    Public Property Phone() As String
      Get
```

```
        Return mPhone
      End Get
      Set(ByVal value As String)
        mPhone = value
      End Set
    End Property
  End Class
```

You know that a real customer is a lot more complex than an ID, name, and phone number; but at the same time, you know that in an abstract sense, your customers really do have names and phone numbers, and that you assign them unique ID numbers to keep track of them. In this case, you are using a globally unique identifier (GUID) as a unique ID. Thus, given an ID, name, and phone number, you know which customer you are dealing with, and so you have a perfectly valid abstraction of a customer within your application.

You can then use this abstract representation of a customer from within your code by using data binding to link the object to a form. First, build the project. Then click the Data ➪ Show Data Sources menu option to open the Data Sources window. Select the Add New Data Source link in the window to bring up the Data Source Configuration Wizard. Within the wizard, choose to add a new Object data source, click Next, and then select your Customer class, as shown in Figure 3-11.

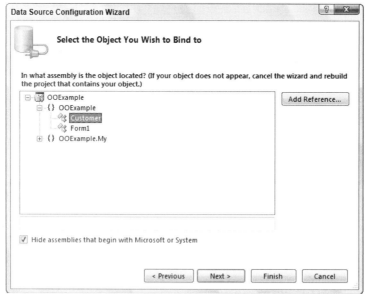

Figure 3-11

Finish the wizard. The Customer class will be displayed as an available data source, as shown in Figure 3-12, if you are working in Design view.

Click on Customer in the window. Customer should change its display to a combo box. Open the combo box and change the selection from DataGridView to Details. This way, you get a details view of the object on your form. Open the designer for Form1 and drag the Customer class from the Data Sources window onto the form. The result should look something like the dialog shown in Figure 3-13.

Figure 3-12

Figure 3-13

All you need to do now is add code to create an instance of the Customer class to act as a data source for the form. Double-click on the form to bring up its code window and add the following code:

```
Public Class Form1

    Private Sub Form1_Load(ByVal sender As System.Object, _
       ByVal e As System.EventArgs) Handles MyBase.Load

       Me.CustomerBindingSource.DataSource = New Customer()

    End Sub

End Class
```

You are using the ability of Windows Forms to data bind to a property on an object. You learn more about data binding later. For now, it is enough to know that the controls on the form are automatically tied to the properties on your object.

Now you have a simple user interface (UI) that both displays and updates the data in your `Customer` object, with that object providing the UI developer with an abstract representation of the customer. When you run the application, you will see a display like the one shown in Figure 3-14.

Figure 3-14

Here, you have displayed the pre-generated `ID` value, and have entered values for `Name` and `Phone` directly into the form.

Encapsulation

Perhaps the most important of the object-oriented concepts is that of *encapsulation*. Encapsulation is the idea that an object should totally separate its interface from its implementation. All the data and implementation code for an object should be entirely hidden behind its interface. This is the concept of an object as a black box.

The idea is that you can create an interface (by creating public methods in a class) and, as long as that interface remains consistent, the application can interact with your objects. This remains true even if you entirely rewrite the code within a given method. The interface is independent of the implementation.

Encapsulation enables you to hide the internal implementation details of a class. For example, the algorithm you use to find prime numbers might be proprietary. You can expose a simple API to the end user but hide all of the logic used in your algorithm by encapsulating it within your class.

This means that an object should completely contain any data it requires and should contain all the code required to manipulate that data. Programs should interact with an object through an interface, using the properties and methods of the object. Client code should never work directly with the data owned by the object.

> **Programs interact with objects by sending messages to the object indicating which method or property they want to have invoked. These messages are generated by other objects or external sources such as the user. The object reacts to these messages through methods or properties.**

Visual Basic classes entirely hide their internal data and code, providing a well-established interface of properties and methods with the outside world. Let's look at an example. Add the following class to your project; the code defines its native interface:

```
Public Class Encapsulation

   Public Function DistanceTo(ByVal x As Single, ByVal y As Single) As Single

   End Function

   Public Property CurrentX() As Single
     Get

     End Get
     Set(ByVal value As Single)

      End Set
   End Property

   Public Property CurrentY() As Single
     Get

     End Get
     Set(ByVal value As Single)

     End Set
   End Property

End Class
```

This creates an interface for the class. At this point, you can write client code to interact with the class, because from a client perspective, all you care about is the interface. Bring up the designer for Form1 and add a button to the form, and then write the following code behind the button:

```
Private Sub btnEncapsulation_Click(ByVal sender As System.Object, _
   ByVal e As System.EventArgs) Handles btnEncapsulation.Click

   Dim obj As New Encapsulation
   MsgBox(obj.DistanceTo(10, 10))

End Sub
```

Even though you have no actual code in the Encapsulation class, you can still write code to use that class because the interface is defined.

This is a powerful idea. It means you can rapidly create class interfaces against which other developers can create the UI or other parts of the application while you are still creating the implementation behind the interface.

From here, you could do virtually anything you like in terms of implementing the class. For example, you could use the values to calculate a direct distance:

```
Imports System.Math

Public Class Encapsulation
```

```
    Private mX As Single
    Private mY As Single

    Public Function DistanceTo(ByVal x As Single, ByVal y As Single) As Single
        Return CSng(Sqrt((x - mX) ^ 2 + (y - mY) ^ 2))
    End Function

    Public Property CurrentX() As Single
    Get
        Return mX
    End Get
    Set(ByVal value As Single)
        mX = value
    End Set
    End Property

    Public Property CurrentY() As Single
    Get
        Return mY

    End Get
    Set(ByVal value As Single)
        mY = value

    End Set
    End Property
End Class
```

Now when you run the application and click the button, you get a meaningful value as a result. Even better, encapsulation enables you to change the implementation without changing the interface. For example, you can change the distance calculation to find the distance between the points (assuming that no diagonal travel is allowed):

```
Public Function DistanceTo(ByVal x As Single, ByVal y As Single) As Single
    Return Abs(x - mX) + Abs(y - mY)
End Function
```

This results in a different value being displayed when the program is run. You have not changed the interface of the class, so your working client program has no idea that you have switched from one implementation to the other. You have achieved a total change of behavior without any change to the client code. This is the essence of encapsulation.

Of course, a user might have a problem if you make such a change to your object. If applications were developed expecting the first set of behaviors, and then you changed to the second, there could be some interesting side effects. The key point is that the client programs would continue to function, even if the results are quite different from when you began.

Polymorphism

Polymorphism is often considered to be directly tied to inheritance (discussed next). In reality, it is largely independent. Polymorphism means that you can have two classes with different implementations or code, but with a common set of methods, properties, or events. You can then write a program that operates upon that interface and does not care about which type of object it operates at runtime.

Method Signatures

To properly understand polymorphism, you need to explore the concept of a *method signature*, sometimes also called a *prototype*. All methods have a signature, which is defined by the method's name and the data types of its parameters. You might have code such as this:

```
Public Function CalculateValue() As Integer

End Sub
```

In this example, the signature is as follows:

```
f()
```

If you add a parameter to the method, the signature will change. For example, you could change the method to accept a `Double`:

```
Public Function CalculateValue(ByVal value As Double) As Integer
```

Then, the signature of the method is as follows:

```
f(Double)
```

Polymorphism merely says that you should be able to write client code that calls methods on an object, and as long as the object provides your methods with the method signatures you expect, it does not matter from which class the object was created. Let's look at some examples of polymorphism within Visual Basic.

Implementing Polymorphism

You can use several techniques to achieve polymorphic behavior:

❑ Late binding
❑ Multiple interfaces
❑ Reflection
❑ Inheritance

Late binding actually enables you to implement "pure" polymorphism, although at the cost of performance and ease of programming. Through multiple interfaces and inheritance, you can also achieve polymorphism with much better performance and ease of programming. Reflection enables you to use either late binding or multiple interfaces, but against objects created in a very dynamic way, even going so far as to dynamically load a DLL into your application at runtime so that you can use its classes. The following sections walk through each of these options to see how they are implemented and to explore their pros and cons.

Polymorphism through Late Binding

Typically, when you interact with objects in Visual Basic, you are interacting with them through strongly typed variables. For example, in Form1 you interacted with the Encapsulation object with the following code:

```
Private Sub btnEncapsulation_Click(ByVal sender As System.Object, _
   ByVal e As System.EventArgs) Handles btnEncapsulation.Click

   Dim obj As New Encapsulation
   MsgBox(obj.DistanceTo(10, 10))

End Sub
```

The obj variable is declared using a specific type (Encapsulation) — meaning that it is strongly typed or early bound.

You can also interact with objects that are late bound. Late binding means that your object variable has no specific data type, but rather is of type Object. To use late binding, you need to use the Option Strict Off directive at the top of your code file (or in the project's properties). This tells the Visual Basic compiler that you want to use late binding, so it will allow you to do this type of polymorphism. Add the following to the top of the Form1 code:

```
Option Strict Off
```

With Option Strict turned off, Visual Basic treats the Object data type in a special way, enabling you to attempt arbitrary method calls against the object even though the Object data type does not implement those methods. For example, you could change the code in Form1 to be late bound as follows:

```
Private Sub btnEncapsulation_Click(ByVal sender As System.Object, _
   ByVal e As System.EventArgs) Handles btnEncapsulation.Click

   Dim obj As Object = New Encapsulation
   MsgBox(obj.DistanceTo(10, 10))

End Sub
```

When this code is run, you get the same result as you did before, even though the Object data type has no DistanceTo method as part of its interface. The late-binding mechanism, behind the scenes, dynamically determines the real type of your object and invokes the appropriate method.

When you work with objects through late binding, neither the Visual Basic IDE nor the compiler can tell whether you are calling a valid method. Here, there is no way for the compiler to know that the object referenced by your `obj` variable actually has a `DistanceTo` method. It just assumes that you know what you are talking about and compiles the code.

At runtime, when the code is actually invoked, it attempts to dynamically call the `DistanceTo` method. If that is a valid method, then your code will work; otherwise, you will get an error.

Obviously, there is a level of danger when using late binding, as a simple typo can introduce errors that can only be discovered when the application is actually run. However, it also offers a lot of flexibility, as code that makes use of late binding can talk to any object from any class as long as those objects implement the methods you require.

There is a substantial performance penalty for using late binding. The existence of each method is discovered dynamically at runtime, and that discovery takes time. Moreover, the mechanism used to invoke a method through late binding is not nearly as efficient as the mechanism used to call a method that is known at compile time.

To make this more obvious, change the code in `Form1` by adding a generic routine that displays the distance:

```
Private Sub btnEncapsulation_Click(ByVal sender As System.Object, _
    ByVal e As System.EventArgs) Handles btnEncapsulation.Click

  Dim obj As New Encapsulation
  ShowDistance(obj)
End Sub

Private Sub ShowDistance(ByVal obj As Object)
   MsgBox(obj.DistanceTo(10, 10))
End Sub
```

Notice that the new `ShowDistance` routine accepts a parameter using the generic `Object` data type — so you can pass it literally any value — `String`, `Integer`, or one of your own custom objects. It will throw an exception at runtime, however, unless the object you pass into the routine has a `DistanceTo` method that matches the required method signature.

You know that your `Encapsulation` object has a method matching that signature, so your code works fine. Now let's add another simple class to demonstrate polymorphism. Add a new class to the project and name it `Poly.vb`:

```
Public Class Poly
   Public Function DistanceTo(ByVal x As Single, ByVal y As Single) As Single
      Return x + y
   End Function
End Class
```

This class is about as simple as you can get. It exposes a `DistanceTo` method as part of its interface and provides a very basic implementation of that interface.

You can use this new class in place of the Encapsulation class without changing the ShowDistance method by using polymorphism. Return to the code in Form1 and make the following change:

```
Private Sub btnEncapsulation_Click(ByVal sender As System.Object, _
  ByVal e As System.EventArgs) Handles btnEncapsulation.Click

    Dim obj As New Poly
    ShowDistance(obj)
End Sub
```

Even though you changed the class of object you are passing to ShowDistance to one with a different overall interface and different implementation, the method called within ShowDistance remains consistent, so your code will run.

Polymorphism with Multiple Interfaces

Late binding is flexible and easy, but it is not ideal because it defeats the IDE and compiler type checking that enables you to fix bugs due to typos during the development process. It also has a negative impact on performance.

Another way to implement polymorphism is to use multiple interfaces. This approach avoids late binding, meaning the IDE and compiler can check your code as you enter and compile it. Moreover, because the compiler has access to all the information about each method you call, your code runs much faster.

Remove the Option Strict directive from the code in Form1. This will cause some syntax errors to be highlighted in the code, but don't worry — you will fix those soon enough.

Visual Basic not only supports polymorphism through late binding, but also implements a stricter form of polymorphism through its support of multiple interfaces. (Earlier you learned about multiple interfaces, including the use of the Implements keyword and how to define interfaces.)

With late binding, you have learned how to treat all objects as equals by making them all appear using the Object data type. With multiple interfaces, you can treat all objects as equals by making them all implement a common data type or interface.

This approach has the benefit that it is strongly typed, meaning the IDE and compiler can help you find errors due to typos because the names and data types of all methods and parameters are known at design time. It is also fast in terms of performance: Because the compiler knows about the methods, it can use optimized mechanisms for calling them, especially compared to the dynamic mechanisms used in late binding.

Return to the project to implement polymorphism with multiple interfaces. First, add a module to the project using the Project ➪ Add Module menu option and name it Interfaces.vb. Replace the Module code block with an Interface declaration:

```
Public Interface IShared
  Function CalculateDistance(ByVal x As Single, ByVal y As Single) As Single
End Interface
```

Now you can make both the `Encapsulation` and `Poly` classes implement this interface. First, in the `Encapsulation` class, add the following code:

```
Public Class Encapsulation
  Implements IShared

  Private mX As Single
  Private mY As Single

  Public Function DistanceTo(ByVal x As Single, ByVal y As Single) _
      As Single Implements IShared.CalculateDistance

    Return CSng(Sqrt((x - mX) ^ 2 + (y - mY) ^ 2))
  End Function
```

Here you are implementing the `IShared` interface, and because the `CalculateDistance` method's signature matches that of your existing `DistanceTo` method, you are simply indicating that it should act as the implementation for `CalculateDistance`.

You can make a similar change in the `Poly` class:

```
Public Class Poly
  Implements IShared

  Public Function DistanceTo(ByVal x As Single, ByVal y As Single) As Single _
      Implements IShared.CalculateDistance

    Return x + y
  End Function
End Class
```

Now this class also implements the `IShared` interface, and you are ready to see polymorphism implemented in your code. Bring up the code window for `Form1` and change your `ShowDistance` method as follows:

```
Private Sub ShowDistance(ByVal obj As IShared)
  MsgBox(obj.CalculateDistance(10, 10))
End Sub
```

Note that this eliminates the compiler error you saw after removing the `Option Strict` directive from `Form1`.

Instead of accepting the parameter using the generic `Object` data type, you are now accepting an `IShared` parameter — a strong data type known by both the IDE and the compiler. Within the code itself, you are calling the `CalculateDistance` method as defined by that interface.

This routine can now accept any object that implements `IShared`, regardless of what class that object was created from, or what other interfaces that object may implement. All you care about here is that the object implements `IShared`.

Polymorphism through Reflection

You have learned how to use late binding to invoke a method on any arbitrary object as long as that object has a method matching the method signature you are trying to call. You have also walked through the use of multiple interfaces, which enables you to achieve polymorphism through a faster, early-bound technique. The challenge with these techniques is that late binding can be slow and hard to debug, and multiple interfaces can be somewhat rigid and inflexible.

Enter *reflection*. Reflection is a technology built into the .NET Framework that enables you to write code that interrogates an assembly to dynamically determine the classes and data types it contains. Using reflection, you can load the assembly into your process, create instances of those classes, and invoke their methods.

When you use late binding, Visual Basic makes use of the `System.Reflection` namespace behind the scenes on your behalf. You can choose to manually use reflection as well. This gives you even more flexibility in how you interact with objects.

For example, suppose that the class you want to call is located in some other assembly on disk — an assembly you did not specifically reference from within your project when you compiled it. How can you dynamically find, load, and invoke such an assembly? Reflection enables you to do this, assuming that the assembly is polymorphic. In other words, it has either an interface you expect or a set of methods you can invoke via late binding.

To see how reflection works with late binding, we'll create a new class in a separate assembly (project) and use it from within the existing application. Choose File ⇨ Add ⇨ New Project to add a new class library project to your solution. Name it `Objects`. It begins with a single class module that you can use as a starting point. Change the code in that class to the following:

```
Public Class External
  Public Function DistanceTo(ByVal x As Single, ByVal y As Single) As Single
    Return x * y
  End Function
End Class
```

Now compile the assembly by choosing Build ⇨ Build Objects. Next, bring up the code window for `Form1`. Add an `Imports` statement at the top, and add back the `Option Strict Off` statement:

```
Option Strict Off

Imports System.Reflection
```

Remember that because you are using late binding, `Form1` also must use `Option Strict Off`. Without this, late binding isn't available.

Add a button with the following code (you have to import the `System.Reflections` namespace for this to work):

```
Private Sub Button1_Click(ByVal sender As System.Object, _
      ByVal e As System.EventArgs) Handles button1.Click

    Dim obj As Object
```

```
        Dim dll As Assembly

        dll = Assembly.LoadFrom("..\..\..\Objects\bin\Release\Objects.dll")

        obj = dll.CreateInstance("Objects.External")
        MsgBox(obj.DistanceTo(10, 10))
    End Sub
```

There is a lot going on here, so let's walk through it. First, notice that you are reverting to late binding; your obj variable is declared as type Object. You will look at using reflection and multiple interfaces in a moment, but for now you will use late binding.

Next, you have declared a dll variable as type Reflection.Assembly. This variable will contain a reference to the Objects assembly that you will be dynamically loading through your code. Note that you are not adding a reference to this assembly via Project ⇨ Add References. You will dynamically access the assembly at runtime.

You then load the external assembly dynamically by using the Assembly.LoadFrom method:

```
    dll = Assembly.LoadFrom("..\..\Objects\bin\Objects.dll")
```

This causes the reflection library to load your assembly from a file on disk at the location you specify. Once the assembly is loaded into your process, you can use the myDll variable to interact with it, including interrogating it to get a list of the classes it contains or to create instances of those classes.

> You can also use the **[Assembly].Load** method, which scans the directory containing your application's .exe file (and the global assembly cache) for any EXE or DLL containing the **Objects** assembly. When it finds the assembly, it loads it into memory, making it available for your use.

You can then use the CreateInstance method on the assembly itself to create objects based on any class in that assembly. In this case, you are creating an object based on the External class:

```
    obj = dll.CreateInstance("Objects.External")
```

Now you have an actual object to work with, so you can use late binding to invoke its DistanceTo method. At this point, your code is really no different from that in the earlier late-binding example, except that the assembly and object were created dynamically at runtime, rather than being referenced directly by your project.

Now you should be able to run the application and have it dynamically invoke the assembly at runtime.

Polymorphism via Reflection and Multiple Interfaces

You can also use both reflection and multiple interfaces together. You have seen how multiple interfaces enable you to have objects from different classes implement the same interface and thus be treated identically. You have also seen how reflection enables you to load an assembly and class dynamically at runtime.

You can combine these concepts by using an interface shared in common between your main application and your external assembly, using reflection to load that external assembly dynamically at runtime.

First, create the interface that will be shared across both application and assembly. To do so, add a new Class Library project to your solution named `Interfaces`. Once it is created, drag and drop the `Interfaces.vb` module from your original application into the new project (hold down the Shift key as you move it). This makes the `IShared` interface part of that project and no longer part of your base application.

Of course, your base application still uses `IShared`, so you want to reference the `Interfaces` project from your application to gain access to the interface. Do this by right-clicking your OOExample project in the Solution Explorer window and selecting Add Reference. Then add the reference, as shown in Figure 3-15.

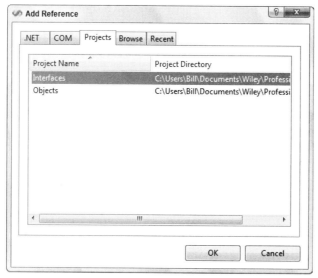

Figure 3-15

Because the `IShared` interface is now part of a separate assembly, add an `Imports` statement to `Form1`, `Encapsulation`, and `Poly` so that they are able to locate the `IShared` interface:

```
Imports Interfaces
```

Be sure to add this to the top of all three code modules.

You also need to have the `Objects` project reference `Interfaces`, so right-click `Objects` in the Solution Explorer and choose Add Reference there as well. Add the reference to `Interfaces` and click OK. At this point, both the original application and the external assembly have access to the `IShared` interface. You can now enhance the code in `Objects` by changing the `External` class:

```
Imports Interfaces

Public Class External
```

```
      Implements IShared
      Public Function DistanceTo(ByVal x As Single, ByVal y As Single) _
          As Single Implements IShared.CalculateDistance

        Return x * y
    End Function
  End Class
```

With both the main application and external assembly using the same data type, you are ready to implement the polymorphic behavior using reflection.

Remove the `Option Strict Off` code from `Form1`. Bring up the code window for `Form1` and change the code behind the button to take advantage of the `IShared` interface:

```
      Private Sub btnReflection_Click(ByVal sender As System.Object, _
        ByVal e As System.EventArgs) Handles Button1.Click

        Dim obj As IShared
        Dim dll As Assembly

        dll = Assembly.LoadFrom("..\..\..\Objects\bin\Release\Objects.dll")

        obj = CType(dll.CreateInstance("Objects.External"), IShared)
        ShowDistance(obj)
      End Sub
```

All you have done here is change the code so that you can pass your dynamically created object to the `ShowDistance` method, which you know requires a parameter of type `IShared`. Because your class implements the same `IShared` interface (from `Interfaces`) used by the main application, this will work perfectly. Rebuild and run the solution to see this in action.

This technique is very nice, as the code in `ShowDistance` is strongly typed, providing all the performance and coding benefits; but both the DLL and the object itself are loaded dynamically, providing a great deal of flexibility to your application.

Polymorphism with Inheritance

Inheritance, discussed earlier in this chapter, can also be used to enable polymorphism. The idea here is very similar to that of multiple interfaces, as a subclass can always be treated as though it were the data type of the parent class.

> **Many people consider the concepts of inheritance and polymorphism to be tightly intertwined. As you have seen, however, it is perfectly possible to use polymorphism without inheritance.**

At the moment, both your `Encapsulation` and `Poly` classes are implementing a common interface named `IShared`. You can use polymorphism to interact with objects of either class via that common interface.

The same is true if these are child classes based on the same base class through inheritance. To see how this works, in the OOExample project, add a new class named Parent and insert the following code:

```
Public MustInherit Class Parent
    Public MustOverride Function DistanceTo(ByVal x As Single, _
        ByVal y As Single) As Single
End Class
```

As described earlier, this is an abstract base class, a class with no implementation of its own. The purpose of an abstract base class is to provide a common base from which other classes can be derived.

To implement polymorphism using inheritance, you do not need to use an abstract base class. Any base class that provides overridable methods (using either the MustOverride or Overridable keywords) will work fine, as all its subclasses are guaranteed to have that same set of methods as part of their interface, and yet the subclasses can provide custom implementation for those methods.

In this example, you are simply defining the DistanceTo method as being a method that must be over-ridden and implemented by any subclass of Parent. Now you can bring up the Encapsulation class and change it to be a subclass of Parent:

```
Public Class Encapsulation
    Inherits Parent
    Implements IShared
```

You do not need to stop implementing the IShared interface just because you are inheriting from Parent; inheritance and multiple interfaces coexist nicely. You do, however, have to override the DistanceTo method from the Parent class.

The Encapsulation class already has a DistanceTo method with the proper method signature, so you can simply add the Overrides keyword to indicate that this method will override the declaration in the Parent class:

```
Public Overrides Function DistanceTo( _
    ByVal x As Single, _ByVal y As Single) _
    As Single Implements IShared.CalculateDistance
```

At this point, the Encapsulation class not only implements the common IShared interface and its own native interface, but also can be treated as though it were of type Parent, as it is a subclass of Parent. You can do the same thing to the Poly class:

```
Public Class Poly
    Inherits Parent
    Implements IShared

    Public Overrides Function DistanceTo( _
        ByVal x As Single, ByVal y As Single) _
        As Single Implements IShared.CalculateDistance

        Return x + y
```

```
      End Function
   End Class
```

Finally, you can see how polymorphism works by altering the code in Form1 to take advantage of the fact that both classes can be treated as though they were of type Parent. First, you can change the ShowDistance method to accept its parameter as type Parent and to call the DistanceTo method:

```
Private Sub ShowDistance(ByVal obj As Parent)
   MsgBox(obj.DistanceTo(10, 10))
End Sub
```

Then, you can add a new button to create an object of either type Encapsulation or Poly and pass it as a parameter to the method:

```
Private Sub btnInheritance_Click(ByVal sender As System.Object, _
   ByVal e As System.EventArgs) Handles btnInheritance.Click

      ShowDistance(New Poly)
      ShowDistance(New Encapsulation)

   End Sub
```

Polymorphism Summary

Polymorphism is a very important concept in object-oriented design and programming, and Visual Basic provides you with ample techniques through which it can be implemented.

The following table summarizes the different techniques and their pros and cons, and provides some high-level guidelines about when to use each:

Technique	Pros	Cons	Guidelines
Late binding	Flexible, "pure" polymorphism	Slow, hard to debug, no IntelliSense	Use to call arbitrary methods on literally any object, regardless of data type or interfaces
Multiple interfaces	Fast, easy to debug, full IntelliSense	Not totally dynamic or flexible, requires class author to implement formal interface	Use when you are creating code that interacts with clearly defined methods that can be grouped together into a formal interface
Reflection and late binding	Flexible, "pure" polymorphism, dynamically loads arbitrary assemblies from disk	Slow, hard to debug, no IntelliSense	Use to call arbitrary methods on objects when you do not know at design time which assemblies you will be using

Technique	Pros	Cons	Guidelines
Reflection and multiple interfaces	Fast, easy to debug, full IntelliSense, dynamically loads arbitrary assemblies from disk	Not totally dynamic or flexible, requires class author to implement formal interface	Use when you are creating code that interacts with clearly defined methods that can be grouped together into a formal interface, but when you do not know at design time which assemblies you will be using
Inheritance	Fast, easy to debug, full IntelliSense, inherits behaviors from base class	Not totally dynamic or flexible, requires class author to inherit from common base class	Use when you are creating objects that have an *is-a* relationship, i.e., when you have subclasses that are naturally of the same data type as a base class. Polymorphism through inheritance should occur because inheritance makes sense, not because you are attempting to merely achieve polymorphism.

Inheritance

Inheritance is the concept that a new class can be based on an existing class, inheriting its interface and functionality. The mechanics and syntax of inheritance are described earlier in this chapter, so we won't rehash them here. However, you have not yet looked at inheritance from a practical perspective, and that is the focus of this section.

When to Use Inheritance

Inheritance is one of the most powerful object-oriented features a language can support. At the same time, inheritance is one of the most dangerous and misused object-oriented features.

Properly used, inheritance enables you to increase the maintainability, readability, and reusability of your application by offering you a clear and concise way to reuse code, via both interface and implementation. Improperly used, inheritance creates applications that are very fragile, whereby a change to a class can cause the entire application to break or require changes.

Inheritance enables you to implement an *is-a* relationship. In other words, it enables you to implement a new class that "is a" more specific type of its base class. Properly used, inheritance enables you to create child classes that are actually the same as the base class.

For example, you know that a duck is a bird. However, a duck can also be food, though that is not its primary identity. Proper use of inheritance enables you to create a `Bird` base class from which you can derive a `Duck` class. You would not create a `Food` class and subclass `Duck` from `Food`, as a duck isn't primarily food — it merely acts as food sometimes.

This is the challenge. Inheritance is not just a mechanism for code reuse, but a mechanism to create classes that flow naturally from another class. If you use it anywhere you want code reuse, you will end up with a real mess on your hands. If you use it anywhere you just want a common interface but where the child class is not really the same as the base class, then you should use multiple interfaces — something we'll discuss shortly.

> **The question you must ask when using inheritance is whether the child class is a more specific version of the base class.**

For example, you might have different types of products in your organization. All of these products have some common data and behaviors — e.g., they all have a product number, a description, and a price. However, if you have an agricultural application, you might have chemical products, seed products, fertilizer products, and retail products. These are all different — each having its own data and behaviors — and yet each one of them really is a product. You can use inheritance to create this set of products, as illustrated by the class diagram in Figure 3-16.

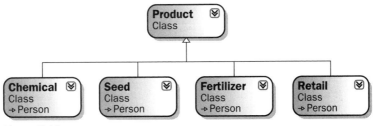

Figure 3-16

This diagram shows that you have an abstract base `Product` class, from which you derive the various types of product your system actually uses. This is an appropriate use of inheritance because each child class is obviously a more specific form of the general `Product` class.

Alternately, you might try to use inheritance just as a code-sharing mechanism. For example, you may look at your application, which has `Customer`, `Product`, and `SalesOrder` classes, and decide that all of them need to be designed so that they can be printed to a printer. The code to handle the printing will all be somewhat similar, so to reuse that printing code, you create a base `PrintableObject` class. This would result in the diagram shown in Figure 3-17.

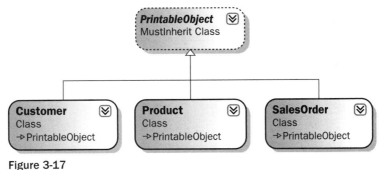

Figure 3-17

Intuitively, you know that this does not represent an *is-a* relationship. A `Customer` can be printed, and you are getting code reuse, but a customer is not a specific case of a printable object. Implementing a system such as this results in a fragile design and application. This is a case where multiple interfaces are a far more appropriate technology.

To illustrate this point, you might later discover that you have other entities in your organization that are similar to a customer but not quite the same. Upon further analysis, you may determine that `Employee` and `Customer` are related because they are specific cases of a `Contact` class. The `Contact` class provides commonality in terms of data and behavior across all these other classes (see Figure 3-18).

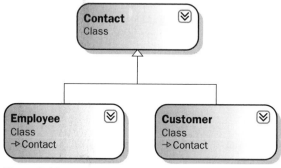

Figure 3-18

However, now your `Customer` is in trouble; you have said it is a `PrintableObject`, and you are now saying it is a `Contact`. You might be able to just derive `Contact` from `PrintableObject` (see Figure 3-19).

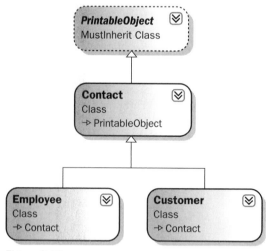

Figure 3-19

The problem with this is that now `Employee` is also of type `PrintableObject`, even if it shouldn't be, but you are stuck because, unfortunately, you decided early on to go against intuition and say that a `Customer` is a `PrintableObject`.

This problem could be solved by multiple inheritance, which would enable `Customer` to be a subclass of more than one base class — in this case, of both `Contact` and `PrintableObject`. However, the .NET platform and Visual Basic do not support multiple inheritance in this way. An alternative is to use inheritance for the *is-a* relationship with `Contact`, and use multiple interfaces to enable the `Customer` object to act as a `PrintableObject` by implementing an `IPrintableObject` interface.

Application versus Framework Inheritance

What you have just seen is how inheritance can accidentally cause reuse of code where no reuse was desired, but you can take a different view of this model by separating the concept of a framework from your actual application. The way you use inheritance in the design of a framework is somewhat different from how you use inheritance in the design of an actual application.

In this context, the word framework is being used to refer to a set of classes that provide base functionality that isn't specific to an application, but rather may be used across a number of applications within the organization, or perhaps even beyond the organization. The .NET Framework base class library is an example of a very broad framework you use when building your applications.

The `PrintableObject` class discussed earlier, for example, may have little to do with your specific application, but may be the type of thing that is used across many applications. If so, it is a natural candidate for use as part of a framework, rather than being considered part of your actual application.

Framework classes exist at a lower level than application classes. For example, the .NET base-class library is a framework on which all .NET applications are built. You can layer your own framework on top of the .NET Framework as well (see Figure 3-20).

Figure 3-20

If you take this view, then the `PrintableObject` class wouldn't be part of your application at all, but part of a framework on which your application is built. If so, then the fact that `Customer` is not a specific case of `PrintableObject` does not matter as much, as you are not saying that it is such a thing, but rather that it is leveraging that portion of the framework's functionality.

To make all this work requires a lot of planning and forethought in the design of the framework itself. To see the dangers you face, consider that you might want to not only print objects, but also store them in a file. In that case, you might have not only `PrintableObject`, but also `SavableObject` as a base class.

The question is, what do you do if `Customer` should be both printable and savable? If all printable objects are savable, you might have the result shown in Figure 3-21.

Alternately, if all savable objects are printable, you might have the result shown in Figure 3-22. However, neither of these truly provides a decent solution, as it is likely that the concept of being printable and the concept of being savable are different and not interrelated in either of these ways.

When faced with this sort of issue, it is best to avoid using inheritance and instead rely on multiple interfaces.

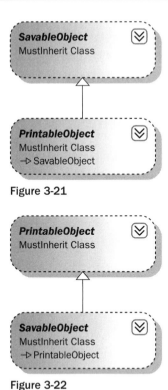

Figure 3-21

Figure 3-22

Inheritance and Multiple Interfaces

While inheritance is powerful, it is really geared around implementing the *is-a* relationship. Sometimes you will have objects that need a common interface, even though they are not really a specific case of some base class that provides that interface. We've just explored that issue in the discussion of the PrintableObject, SavableObject, and Customer classes.

Sometimes multiple interfaces are a better alternative than inheritance. The syntax for creating and using secondary and multiple interfaces was discussed.

Multiple interfaces can be viewed as another way to implement the *is-a* relationship, although it is often better to view inheritance as an *is-a* relationship and to view multiple interfaces as a way of implementing an *act-as* relationship.

Considering this further, we can say that the PrintableObject concept could perhaps be better expressed as an interface — IPrintableObject.

When the class implements a secondary interface such as IPrintableObject, you are not really saying that your class is a printable object, you are saying that it can "act as" a printable object. A Customer is a Contact, but at the same time it can act as a printable object. This is illustrated in Figure 3-23.

The drawback to this approach is that you have no inherited implementation when you implement IPrintableObject. Earlier you saw how to reuse common code as you implement an interface across multiple classes. While not as automatic or easy as inheritance, it is possible to reuse implementation code with a bit of extra work.

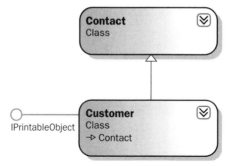

Figure 3-23

Applying Inheritance and Multiple Interfaces

Perhaps the best way to see how inheritance and multiple interfaces interact is to look at an example. Returning to the original OOExample project, the following example combines inheritance and multiple interfaces to create an object that has both an *is-a* and *act-as* relationship at the same time. As an additional benefit, you will be using the .NET Framework's capability to print to a printer or Print Preview dialog.

Creating the Contact Base Class

You already have a simple `Customer` class in the project, so now add a `Contact` base class. Choose Project ⇨ Add Class and add a class named `Contact`:

```
Public MustInherit Class Contact

  Private mID As Guid = Guid.NewGuid
  Private mName As String

  Public Property ID() As Guid
    Get
      Return mID
    End Get
    Set(ByVal value As Guid)
      mID = value
    End Set
  End Property

  Public Property Name() As String
    Get
      Return mName
    End Get
    Set(ByVal value As String)
      mName = value
    End Set
  End Property

End Class
```

Subclassing Contact

Now you can make the `Customer` class inherit from this base class because it is a `Contact`. In addition, because your base class now implements both the `ID` and `Name` properties, you can simplify the code in `Customer` by removing those properties and their related variables:

```
Public Class Customer
  Inherits Contact

  Private mPhone As String

  Public Property Phone() As String
    Get
      Return mPhone
    End Get
    Set(ByVal value As String)
      mPhone = value
    End Set
  End Property
End Class
```

This shows the benefit of subclassing `Customer` from `Contact`, as you are now sharing the `ID` and `Name` code across all other types of `Contact` as well.

Implementing IPrintableObject

You also know that a `Customer` should be able to act as a printable object. To do this in such a way that the implementation is reusable requires a bit of thought. First, though, you need to define the `IPrintableObject` interface.

You will use the standard printing mechanism provided by .NET from the `System.Drawing` namespace. As shown in Figure 3-24, add a reference to `System.Drawing.dll` to the `Interfaces` project.

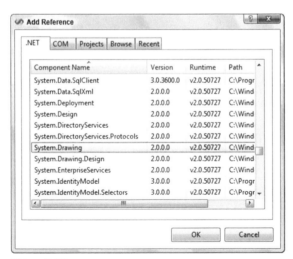

Figure 3-24

With that done, bring up the code window for `Interfaces.vb` in the `Interfaces` project and add the following code:

```
Imports System.Drawing

Public Interface IPrintableObject
  Sub Print()
  Sub PrintPreview()
  Sub RenderPage(ByVal sender As Object, _
      ByVal ev As System.Drawing.Printing.PrintPageEventArgs)
End Interface
```

This interface ensures that any object implementing `IPrintableObject` will have `Print` and `PrintPreview` methods, so you can invoke the appropriate type of printing. It also ensures that the object has a `RenderPage` method, which can be implemented by that object to render the object's data on the printed page.

At this point, you could simply implement all the code needed to handle printing directly within the `Customer` object. This isn't ideal, however, as some of the code will be common across any objects that want to implement `IPrintableObject`, and it would be nice to find a way to share that code.

To do this, you can create a new class, `ObjectPrinter`. This is a framework-style class, in that it has nothing to do with any particular application, but can be used across any application in which `IPrintableObject` will be used.

Add a new class named `ObjectPrinter` to the `ObjectAndComponents` project. This class will contain all the code common to printing any object. It makes use of the built-in printing support provided by the .NET Framework class library. To use this, you need to import a couple of namespaces, so add the following code to the new class:

```
Imports System.Drawing
Imports System.Drawing.Printing
Imports Interfaces
```

You can then define a `PrintDocument` variable, which will hold the reference to your printer output. You will also declare a variable to hold a reference to the actual object you will be printing. Notice that you are using the `IPrintableObject` interface data type for this variable:

```
Public Class ObjectPrinter
    Private WithEvents document As PrintDocument
    Private printObject As IPrintableObject
```

Now you can create a routine to kick off the printing process for any object implementing `IPrintableObject`. This code is totally generic; you will write it here so it can be reused across other classes:

```
Public Sub Print(ByVal obj As IPrintableObject)
  printObject = obj

  document = New PrintDocument()
```

```
            document.Print()
        End Sub
```

Likewise, you can implement a method to show a print preview of your object. This code is also totally generic, so add it here for reuse:

```
Public Sub PrintPreview(ByVal obj As IPrintableObject)
    Dim PPdlg As PrintPreviewDialog = New PrintPreviewDialog()

    printObject = obj

    document = New PrintDocument()
    PPdlg.Document = document
    PPdlg.ShowDialog()
End Sub
```

Finally, you need to catch the PrintPage event that is automatically raised by the .NET printing mechanism. This event is raised by the PrintDocument object whenever the document determines that it needs data rendered onto a page. Typically, it is in this routine that you would put the code to draw text or graphics onto the page surface. However, because this is a generic framework class, you won't do that here; instead, delegate the call back into the actual application object that you want to print:

```
Private Sub PrintPage(ByVal sender As Object, _
    ByVal ev As System.Drawing.Printing.PrintPageEventArgs) _
    Handles document.PrintPage

    printObject.RenderPage(sender, ev)
End Sub
```

```
End Class
```

This enables the application object itself to determine how its data should be rendered onto the output page. You can see how to do that by implementing the IPrintableObject interface on the Customer class:

```
Imports Interfaces

Public Class Customer
    Inherits Contact
    Implements IPrintableObject
```

By adding this code, you require that your Customer class implement the Print, PrintPreview, and RenderPage methods. To avoid wasting paper as you test the code, make both the Print and PrintPreview methods the same and have them just do a print preview display:

```
Public Sub Print() _
    Implements Interfaces.IPrintableObject.Print

    Dim printer As New ObjectPrinter()
    printer.PrintPreview(Me)

End Sub
```

Notice that you are using an `ObjectPrinter` object to handle the common details of doing a print preview. In fact, any class you ever create that implements `IPrintableObject` will have this exact same code to implement a print-preview function, relying on your common `ObjectPrinter` to take care of the details.

You also need to implement the `RenderPage` method, which is where you actually put your object's data onto the printed page:

```
Private Sub RenderPage(ByVal sender As Object, _
    ByVal ev As System.Drawing.Printing.PrintPageEventArgs) _
    Implements IPrintableObject.RenderPage

    Dim printFont As New Font("Arial", 10)
    Dim lineHeight As Single = printFont.GetHeight(ev.Graphics)
    Dim leftMargin As Single = ev.MarginBounds.Left
    Dim yPos As Single = ev.MarginBounds.Top

    ev.Graphics.DrawString("ID: " & ID.ToString, printFont, Brushes.Black, _
      leftMargin, yPos, New StringFormat())

    yPos += lineHeight
    ev.Graphics.DrawString("Name: " & Name, printFont, Brushes.Black, _
      leftMargin, yPos, New StringFormat())

    ev.HasMorePages = False

  End Sub
```

All of this code is unique to your object, which makes sense because you are rendering your specific data to be printed. However, you don't need to worry about the details of whether you are printing to paper or print preview; that is handled by your `ObjectPrinter` class, which in turn uses the .NET Framework. This enables you to focus on generating the output to the page within your application class.

By generalizing the printing code in `ObjectPrinter`, you have achieved a level of reuse that you can tap into via the `IPrintableObject` interface. Any time you want to print a `Customer` object's data, you can have it act as an `IPrintableObject` and call its `Print` or `PrintPreview` method. To see this work, add a new button control to `Form1` with the following code:

```
Private Sub btnPrint_Click(ByVal sender As System.Object, _
  ByVal e As System.EventArgs) Handles btnPrint.Click

  Dim obj As New Customer
  obj.Name = "Douglas Adams"
  CType(obj, IPrintableObject).PrintPreview()

  End Sub
```

This code creates a new `Customer` object and sets its `Name` property. You then use the `CType` method to access the object via its `IPrintableObject` interface to invoke the `PrintPreview` method.

When you run the application and click the button, you will get a print preview display showing the object's data (see Figure 3-25).

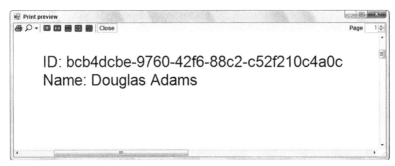

Figure 3-25

How Deep to Go?

Most of the examples discussed so far have illustrated how you can create a child class based on a single parent class. That is called *single-level inheritance*. In fact, inheritance can be many levels deep. For example, you might have a deep hierarchy such as the one shown in Figure 3-26.

From the root of System.Object down to NAFTACustomer you have four levels of inheritance. This can be described as a four-level inheritance chain.

There is no hard-and-fast rule about how deep inheritance chains should go, but conventional wisdom and general experience with inheritance in other languages such as Smalltalk and C++ indicate that the deeper an inheritance chain becomes, the harder it is to maintain an application.

This happens for two reasons. First is the fragile base class or fragile superclass issue, discussed shortly. The second reason is that a deep inheritance hierarchy tends to seriously reduce the readability of your code by scattering the code for an object across many different classes, all of which are combined by the compiler to create your object.

One of the reasons for adopting object-oriented design and programming is to avoid so-called *spaghetti code*, whereby any bit of code you might look at does almost nothing useful but instead calls various other procedures and routines in other parts of your application. To determine what is going on with spaghetti code, you must trace through many routines and mentally piece together what it all means.

Object-oriented programming can help you avoid this problem, but it is most definitely not a magic bullet. In fact, when you create deep inheritance hierarchies, you are often creating spaghetti code because each level in the hierarchy not only extends the previous level's interface, but almost always also adds functionality. Thus, when you look at the final NAFTACustomer class, it may have very little code. To figure out what it does or how it behaves, you have to trace through the code in the previous four levels of classes, and you might not even have the code for some of those classes, as they might come from other applications or class libraries you have purchased.

On the one hand, you have the benefit that you are reusing code, but on the other hand, you have the drawback that the code for one object is actually scattered through five different classes. Keep this in mind when designing systems with inheritance — use as few levels in the hierarchy as possible to provide the required functionality.

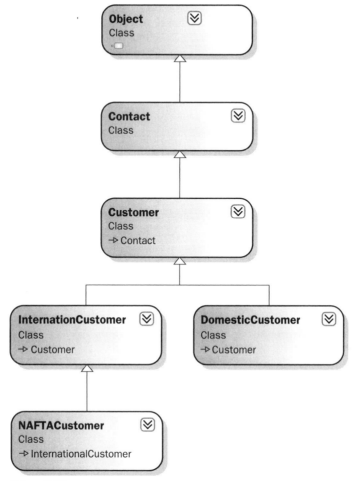

Figure 3-26

The Fragile-Base-Class Problem

You have explored where it is appropriate to use inheritance and where it is not. You have also explored how you can use inheritance and multiple interfaces in conjunction to implement both *is-a* and *act-as* relationships simultaneously within your classes.

Earlier, we noted that while inheritance is an incredibly powerful and useful concept, it can also be very dangerous if used improperly. You have seen some of this danger in the discussion of the misapplication of the *is-a* relationship, and how you can use multiple interfaces to avoid those issues.

One of the most classic and common problems with inheritance is the fragile-base-class problem. This problem is exacerbated when you have very deep inheritance hierarchies, but it exists even in a single-level inheritance chain.

The issue you face is that a change in the base class always affects all child classes derived from that base class. This is a double-edged sword. On the one hand, you get the benefit of being able to change code in one location and have that change automatically cascade through all derived classes. On the other hand, a change in behavior can have unintended or unexpected consequences farther down the inheritance chain, which can make your application very fragile and hard to change or maintain.

Interface Changes

There are obvious changes you might make, which require immediate attention. For example, you might change your `Contact` class to have `FirstName` and `LastName` instead of simply `Name` as a property. In the `Contact` class, replace the `mName` variable declaration with the following code:

```
Private mFirstName As String
Private mLastName As String
```

Now replace the `Name` property with the following code:

```
Public Property FirstName() As String
  Get
     Return mFirstName
  End Get
  Set(ByVal value As String)
    mFirstName = value
  End Set
End Property

Public Property LastName() As String
  Get
     Return mLastName
  End Get
  Set(ByVal value As String)
    mLastName = value
  End Set
End Property
```

At this point, the Error List window in the IDE will display a list of locations where you need to alter your code to compensate for the change. This is a graphic illustration of a base-class change that causes cascading changes throughout your application. In this case, you have changed the base-class interface, thus changing the interface of all subclasses in the inheritance chain.

To avoid having to fix code throughout your application, always strive to keep as much consistency in your base class interface as possible. In this case, you can implement a read-only `Name` property that returns the full name of the `Contact`:

```
Public ReadOnly Property Name() As String
  Get
     Return mFirstName & " " & mLastName
  End Get
End Property
```

This resolves most of the items in the Error List window. You can fix any remaining issues by using the `FirstName` and `LastName` properties. For example, in `Form1` you can change the code behind your button to the following:

```
Private Sub Button1_Click(ByVal sender As System.Object, _
    ByVal e As System.EventArgs) Handles button1.Click

  Dim obj As New Customer
  obj.FirstName = "Douglas"
  obj.LastName = "Adams"
  CType(obj, Interfaces.IPrintableObject).Print()
End Sub
```

Any change to a base class interface is likely to cause problems, so think carefully before making such a change.

Implementation Changes

Unfortunately, there is another, more subtle type of change that can wreak more havoc on your application: an implementation change. This is the core of the fragile-base-class problem.

Encapsulation provides you with a separation of interface from implementation. However, keeping your interface consistent is merely a syntactic concept. If you change the implementation, you are making a semantic change, a change that does not alter any of your syntax but can have serious ramifications on the real behavior of the application.

In theory, you can change the implementation of a class, and as long as you do not change its interface, any client applications using objects based on that class will continue to operate without change. Of course, reality is never as nice as theory, and more often than not a change to implementation will have some consequences on the behavior of a client application.

For example, you might use a SortedList to sort and display some Customer objects. To do this, add a new button to Form1 with the following code:

```
Private Sub btnSort_Click(ByVal sender As System.Object, _
  ByVal e As System.EventArgs) Handles btnSort.Click

  Dim col As New Generic.SortedDictionary(Of String, Customer)
  Dim obj As Customer

  obj = New Customer()
  obj.FirstName = "Douglas"
  obj.LastName = "Adams"
  col.Add(obj.Name, obj)

  obj = New Customer()
  obj.FirstName = "Andre"
  obj.LastName = "Norton"
  col.Add(obj.Name, obj)

  Dim item As Generic.KeyValuePair(Of String, Customer)
  Dim sb As New System.Text.StringBuilder

  For Each item In col
    sb.AppendLine(item.Value.Name)
```

189

```
    Next

    MsgBox(sb.ToString)
  End Sub
```

This code simply creates a couple of `Customer` objects, sets their `FirstName` and `LastName` properties, and inserts them into a generic `SortedDictionary` object from the `System.Collections.Generic` namespace.

Items in a `SortedDictionary` are sorted based on their key value, and you are using the `Name` property to provide that key, meaning that your entries will be sorted by name. Because your `Name` property is implemented to return first name first and last name second, your entries will be sorted by first name.

If you run the application, the dialog will display the following:

```
  Andre Norton
  Douglas Adams
```

However, you can change the implementation of your `Contact` class — not directly changing or affecting either the `Customer` class or your code in `Form1` — to return last name first and first name second, as shown here:

```
  Public ReadOnly Property Name() As String
    Get
      Return mLastName & ", " & mFirstName
    End Get
  End Property
```

While no other code requires changing, and no syntax errors are flagged, the behavior of the application is changed. When you run it, the output will now be as follows:

```
  Adams, Douglas
  Norton, Andre
```

Maybe this change is inconsequential. Maybe it totally breaks the required behavior of your form. The developer making the change in the `Contact` class might not even know that someone was using that property for sort criteria.

This illustrates how dangerous inheritance can be. Changes to implementation in a base class can cascade to countless other classes in countless applications, having unforeseen side effects and consequences of which the base-class developer is totally unaware.

Summary

This chapter demonstrated how Visual Basic enables you to create and work with classes and objects. Visual Basic provides the building blocks for abstraction, encapsulation, polymorphism, and inheritance.

You have learned how to create both simple base classes as well as abstract base classes. You have also explored how you can define formal interfaces, a concept quite similar to an abstract base class in many ways.

You also walked through the process of subclassing, creating a new class that derives both interface and implementation from a base class. The subclass can be extended by adding new methods or altering the behavior of existing methods on the base class.

By the end of this chapter, you have seen how object-oriented programming flows from the four basic concepts of abstraction, encapsulation, polymorphism, and inheritance. The chapter provided basic information about each concept and demonstrated how to implement them using Visual Basic.

By properly applying object-oriented design and programming, you can create very large and complex applications that remain maintainable and readable over time. Nonetheless, these technologies are not a magic bullet. Improperly applied, they can create the same hard-to-maintain code that you might create using procedural or modular design techniques.

It is not possible to fully cover all aspects of object-oriented programming in a single chapter. Before launching into a full-blown object-oriented project, we highly recommend looking at other books specifically geared toward object-oriented design and programming.

The Common Language

You've learned how to create simple applications and looked at how to create classes. Now it's time not only to start tying these elements together, but also to learn how to dispose of some of the classes that you have created. The architects of .NET realized that all procedural languages require certain base functionality. For example, many languages ship with their own runtime that provides features such as memory management, but what if, instead of each language shipping with its own runtime implementation, all languages used a common runtime? This would provide languages with a standard environment and access to all of the same features. This is exactly what the common language runtime (CLR) provides.

The CLR manages the execution of code on the .NET platform. .NET provided Visual Basic developers with better support for many advanced features, including operator overloading, implementation inheritance, threading, and the ability to marshal objects. Building such features into a language is not trivial. The CLR enabled Microsoft to concentrate on building this plumbing one time and then reuse it across different programming languages. Because the CLR supports these features and because Visual Basic is built on top of the CLR, Visual Basic can use these features. As a result, going forward, Visual Basic is the equal of every other .NET language, with the CLR eliminating many of the shortcomings of the previous versions of Visual Basic.

Visual Basic developers can view the CLR as a better Visual Basic runtime. However, this runtime, unlike the old standalone Visual Basic runtime, is common across all of .NET regardless of the underlying operating system. Thus, the functionality exposed by the CLR is available to all .NET languages; more important, all of the features available to other .NET languages via the CLR are available to Visual Basic developers. Additionally, as long as you develop using managed code — code that runs in the CLR — you'll find that it doesn't matter whether your application is installed on a Windows XP client or a Vista client; your application will run. The CLR provides an abstraction layer separate from the details of the operating system.

This chapter gets down into the belly of the application runtime environment, not to examine how .NET enables this abstraction from the operating system, but instead to look at some specific features related to how you build applications that run against the CLR. This includes an introduction to several basic elements of working with applications that run in the CLR, including the following:

❑ Elements of a .NET application

❑ Versioning and deployment

❑ Integration across .NET languages

❑ Microsoft Intermediate Language (MSIL)

❑ Memory management and the garbage collector (GC)

Elements of a .NET Application

A .NET application is composed of four primary entities:

❑ **Classes** — The basic units that encapsulate data and behavior

❑ **Modules** — The individual files that contain the intermediate language (IL) for an assembly

❑ **Assemblies** — The primary unit of deployment of a .NET application

❑ **Types** — The common unit of transmitting data between modules

Classes, covered in the preceding two chapters, are defined in the source files for your application or class library. Upon compilation of your source files, you produce a module. The code that makes up an assembly's modules may exist in a single executable (.exe) file or as a dynamic link library (.dll). A module is in fact a Microsoft Intermediate Language file, which is then used by the CLR when your application is run. However, compiling a .NET application doesn't produce only an MSIL file; it also produces a collection of files that make up a deployable application or assembly. Within an assembly are several different types of files, including not only the actual executable files, but also configuration files, signature keys, and, most important of all, the actual code modules.

Modules

A module contains Microsoft Intermediate Language (MSIL, often abbreviated to IL) code, associated metadata, and the assembly's manifest. By default, the Visual Basic compiler creates an assembly that is composed of a single module containing both the assembly code and the manifest.

IL is a platform-independent way of representing managed code within a module. Before IL can be executed, the CLR must compile it into the native machine code. The default method is for the CLR to use the JIT (just-in-time) compiler to compile the IL on a method-by-method basis. At runtime, as each method is called by an application for the first time, it is passed through the JIT compiler for compilation to machine code. Similarly, for an ASP.NET application, each page is passed through the JIT compiler the first time it is requested, to create an in-memory representation of the machine code that represents that page.

Additional information about the types declared in the IL is provided by the associated metadata. The metadata contained within the module is used extensively by the CLR. For example, if a client and an object reside within two different processes, then the CLR uses the type's metadata to marshal data between the client and the object. MSIL is important because every .NET language compiles down to IL.

The CLR doesn't care or need to know what the implementation language was; it knows only what the IL contains. Thus, any differences in .NET languages exist at the level where the IL is generated; but once generated, all .NET languages have the same runtime characteristics. Similarly, because the CLR doesn't care in which language a given module was originally written, it can leverage modules implemented in entirely different .NET languages.

A question that always arises when discussing the JIT compiler and the use of a runtime environment is "Wouldn't it be faster to compile the IL language down to native code before the user asks to run it?" Although the answer is not always yes, Microsoft has provided a utility to handle this compilation: Ngen.exe. Ngen (short for native image generator) enables you to essentially run the JIT compiler on a specific assembly, which is then installed into the user's application cache in its native format. The obvious advantage is that now when the user asks to execute something in that assembly, the JIT compiler is not invoked, saving a small amount of time. However, unlike the JIT compiler, which only compiles those portions of an assembly that are actually referenced, Ngen.exe needs to compile the entire codebase, so the time required for compilation is not the same as what a user actually experiences.

Ngen.exe is executed from the command line. The utility was updated as part of .NET 2.0 and now automatically detects and includes most of the dependent assemblies as part of the image-generation process. To use Ngen.exe, you simply reference this utility followed by an action; for example, **install** followed by your assembly reference. Several options are available as part of the generation process, but that subject is beyond the scope of this chapter, given that Ngen.exe itself is a topic that generates heated debate regarding its use and value.

Where does the debate begin about when to use Ngen.exe? Keep in mind that in a server application, where the same assembly will be referenced by multiple users between machine restarts, the difference in performance on the first request is essentially lost. This means that compilation to native code is more valuable to client-side applications. Unfortunately, using Ngen.exe requires running it on each client machine, which can become cost prohibitive in certain installation scenarios, particularly if you use any form of self-updating application logic.

Another issue relates to using *reflection*, which enables you to reference other assemblies at runtime. Of course, if you don't know what assemblies you will reference until runtime, then the native image generator has a problem, as it won't know what to reference either. You may have occasion to use Ngen.exe for an application you've created, but you should fully investigate this utility and its advantages and disadvantages beforehand, keeping in mind that even native images execute within the CLR. Native image generation only changes the compilation model, not the runtime environment.

Assemblies

An assembly is the primary unit of deployment for .NET applications. It is either a dynamic link library (.dll) or an executable (.exe). An assembly is composed of a manifest, one or more modules, and (optionally) other files, such as .config, .ASPX, .ASMX, images, and so on.

The manifest of an assembly contains the following:

❑ Information about the identity of the assembly, including its textual name and version number

❑ If the assembly is public, then the manifest will contain the assembly's public key. The public key is used to help ensure that types exposed by the assembly reside within a unique namespace. It may also be used to uniquely identify the source of an assembly.

❑ A declarative security request that describes the assembly's security requirements (the assembly is responsible for declaring the security it requires). Requests for permissions fall into three categories: required, optional, and denied. The identity information may be used as evidence by the CLR in determining whether or not to approve security requests.

❑ A list of other assemblies on which the assembly depends. The CLR uses this information to locate an appropriate version of the required assemblies at runtime. The list of dependencies also includes the exact version number of each assembly at the time the assembly was created.

❑ A list of all types and resources exposed by the assembly. If any of the resources exposed by the assembly are localized, the manifest will also contain the default culture (language, currency, date/time format, and so on) that the application will target. The CLR uses this information to locate specific resources and types within the assembly.

The manifest can be stored in a separate file or in one of the modules. By default, for most applications, it is part of the .dll or .exe file, which is compiled by Visual Studio. For Web applications, you will find that although there is a collection of ASPX pages, the actual assembly information is located in a DLL referenced by those ASPX pages.

Types

The type system provides a template that is used to describe the encapsulation of data and an associated set of behaviors. It is this common template for describing data that provides the basis for the metadata that .NET uses when applications interoperate. There are two kinds of types: reference and value. The differences between these two types are discussed in chapter 1.

Unlike COM, which is scoped at the machine level, types are scoped at either the global or the assembly level. All types are based on a common system that is used across all .NET languages. Similar to the MSIL code, which is interpreted by the CLR based upon the current runtime environment, the CLR uses a common metadata system to recognize the details of each type. The result is that all .NET languages are built around a common type system, unlike the different implementations of COM, which require special notation to allow translation of different data types between different .exe and .dll files.

A type has fields, properties, and methods:

❑ **Fields** — Variables that are scoped to the type. For example, a `Pet` class could declare a field called Name that holds the pet's name. In a well-engineered class, fields are often kept private and exposed only as properties or methods.

❑ **Properties** — These look like fields to clients of the type, but can have code behind them (which usually performs some sort of data validation). For example, a `Dog` data type could expose a property to set its gender. Code could then be placed behind the property so that it could be set only to "male" or "female," and then this property could be saved internally to one of the fields in the `dog` class.

❑ **Methods** — These define behaviors exhibited by the type. For example, the `Dog` data type could expose a method called `Sleep`, which would suspend the activity of the `Dog`.

The preceding elements make up each application. Note that some types are defined at the application level and others globally. Under COM, all components are registered globally, and certainly if you want to expose a .NET component to COM, you must register it globally. However, with .NET it is not only possible but often encouraged that the classes and types defined in your modules be visible only at the application level. The advantage of this is that you can run several different versions of an application side by side. Of course, once you have an application that can be versioned, the next challenge is knowing which version of that application you have.

Versioning and Deployment

Components and their clients are often installed at different times by different vendors. For example, a Visual Basic application might rely on a third-party grid control to display data. Runtime support for versioning is crucial for ensuring that an incompatible version of the grid control does not cause problems for the Visual Basic application.

In addition to this issue of compatibility, deploying applications written in previous versions of Visual Basic was problematic. Fortunately, .NET provides major improvements over the versioning and deployment offered by COM and the previous versions of Visual Basic.

Better Support for Versioning

Managing component versions was challenging in previous versions of Visual Basic. The version number of the component could be set, but this version number was not used by the runtime. COM components are often referenced by their ProgID, but Visual Basic does not provide any support for appending the version number on the end of the ProgID.

For those of you who are unfamiliar with the term ProgID, it's enough to know that ProgIDs are developer-friendly strings used to identify a component. For example, `Word.Application` describes Microsoft Word. ProgIDs can be fully qualified with the targeted version of the component — for example, `Word.Application.10` — but this is a limited capability and relies on both the application and whether the person using it chooses this optional addendum. As you'll see in chapter 7, a namespace is built on the basic elements of a ProgID, but provides a more robust naming system.

For many applications, .NET has removed the need to identify the version of each assembly in a central registry on a machine. However, some assemblies are installed once and used by multiple applications. .NET provides a global assembly cache (GAC), which is used to store assemblies that are intended for use by multiple applications. The CLR provides versioning support for all components loaded in the GAC.

The CLR provides two features for assemblies installed within the GAC:

❑ **Side-by-side versioning** — Multiple versions of the same component can be simultaneously stored in the GAC.

❑ **Automatic Quick Fix Engineering (QFE)** — Also known as hotfix support, if a new version of a component, which is still compatible with the old version, is available in the GAC, the CLR loads the updated component. The version number, which is maintained by the developer who created the referenced assembly, drives this behavior.

The assembly's manifest contains the version numbers of referenced assemblies. The CLR uses the assembly's manifest at runtime to locate a compatible version of each referenced assembly. The version number of an assembly takes the following form:

```
Major.Minor.Build.Revision
```

197

Changes to the major and minor version numbers of the assembly indicate that the assembly is no longer compatible with the previous versions. The CLR will not use versions of the assembly that have a different major or minor number unless it is explicitly told to do so. For example, if an assembly was originally compiled against a referenced assembly with a version number of 3.4.1.9, then the CLR will not load an assembly stored in the GAC unless it has a major and minor number of 3 and 4.

Incrementing the revision and build numbers indicates that the new version is still compatible with the previous version. If a new assembly that has an incremented revision or build number is loaded into the GAC, then the CLR can still load this assembly for applications that were compiled referencing a previous version. Versioning is discussed in greater detail in chapter 23.

Better Deployment

Applications written using previous versions of Visual Basic and COM were often complicated to deploy. Components referenced by the application needed to be installed and registered; and for Visual Basic components, the correct version of the Visual Basic runtime needed to be available. The Component Deployment tool helped in the creation of complex installation packages, but applications could be easily broken if the dependent components were inadvertently replaced by incompatible versions on the client's computer during the installation of an unrelated product.

In .NET, most components do not need to be registered. When an external assembly is referenced, the application decides between using a global copy (which must be in the GAC on the developer's system) or copying a component locally. For most references, the external assemblies are referenced locally, which means they are carried in the application's local directory structure. Using local copies of external assemblies enables the CLR to support the side-by-side execution of different versions of the same component. As noted earlier, to reference a globally registered assembly, that assembly must be located in the GAC. The GAC provides a versioning system that is robust enough to allow different versions of the same external assembly to exist side by side. For example, an application could use a newer version of ADO.NET without adversely affecting another application that relies on a previous version.

As long as the client has the .NET runtime installed (which only has to be done once), a .NET application can be distributed using a simple command like this:

```
xcopy \\server\appDirectory "C:\Program Files\appDirectory" /E /O /I
```

The preceding command would copy all of the files and subdirectories from \\server\appDirectory to C:\Program Files\appDirectory and would transfer the file's access control lists (ACLs).

Besides the capability to XCopy applications, Visual Studio provides a built-in tool for constructing simple .msi installations. The deployment settings can be customized for your project solution, enabling you to integrate the deployment project with your application output. Additionally, Visual Studio 2005 introduced the capability to create a ClickOnce deployment.

ClickOnce deployment provides an entirely new method of deployment, referred to as *smart-client deployment*. In the smart-client model, your application is placed on a central server from which the clients access the application files. Smart-client deployment builds on the XML Web Services architecture about which you are learning. It has the advantages of central application maintenance combined with a richer client interface and fewer server communication requirements, all of which you have become familiar with in Windows Forms applications. ClickOnce deployment is discussed in greater detail in chapter 24.

Cross-Language Integration

Prior to .NET, interoperating with code written in other languages was challenging. There were pretty much two options for reusing functionality developed in other languages: COM interfaces or DLLs with exported C functions. As for exposing functionality written in Visual Basic, the only option was to create COM interfaces.

Because Visual Basic is now built on top of the CLR, it's able to interoperate with the code written in other .NET languages. It's even able to derive from a class written in another language. To support this type of functionality, the CLR relies on a common way of representing types, as well as rich metadata that can describe these types.

The Common Type System

Each programming language seems to bring its own island of data types with it. For example, previous versions of Visual Basic represent strings using the BSTR structure, C++ offers char and wchar data types, and MFC offers the CString class. Moreover, the fact that the C++ int data type is a 32-bit value, whereas the Visual Basic 6 Integer data type is a 16-bit value, makes it difficult to pass parameters between applications written using different languages.

To help resolve this problem, C has become the lowest common denominator for interfacing between programs written in multiple languages. An exported function written in C that exposes simple C data types can be consumed by Visual Basic, Java, Delphi, and a variety of other programming languages. In fact, the Windows API is exposed as a set of C functions.

Unfortunately, to access a C interface, you must explicitly map C data types to a language's native data types. For example, a Visual Basic 6 developer would use the following statement to map the GetUserNameA Win32 function (GetUserNameA is the ANSI version of the GetUserName function):

```
' Map GetUserName to the GetUserNameA exported function
' exported by advapi32.dll.
'    BOOL GetUserName(
'        LPTSTR lpBuffer, // name buffer
'        LPDWORD nSize // size of name buffer
' );
Public Declare Function GetUserName Lib "advapi32.dll" _
Alias "GetUserNameA" (ByVal strBuffer As String, nSize As Long) As Long
```

This code explicitly maps the lpBuffer C character array data type to the Visual Basic 6 String parameter strBuffer. This is not only cumbersome, but also error prone. Accidentally mapping a variable declared as Long to lpBuffer wouldn't generate any compilation errors, but calling the function would more than likely result in a difficult-to-diagnose, intermittent-access violation at runtime.

COM provides a more refined method of interoperation between languages. Visual Basic 6 introduced a common type system (CTS) for all applications that supported COM — that is, variant-compatible data types. However, variant data types are as cumbersome to work with for non-Visual Basic 6 developers as the underlying C data structures that make up the variant data types (such as BSTR and SAFEARRAY) were for Visual Basic developers. The result is that interfacing between unmanaged languages is still more complicated than it needs to be.

The CTS provides a set of common data types for use across all programming languages. The CTS provides every language running on top of the .NET platform with a base set of types, as well as mechanisms for extending those types. These types may be implemented as classes or as structs, but in either case they are derived from a common System.Object class definition.

Because every type supported by the CTS is derived from System.Object, every type supports a common set of methods, as shown in the following table:

Method	Description
Boolean Equals(Object)	Used to test equality with another object. Reference types should return True if the Object parameter references the same object. Value types should return True if the Object parameter has the same value.
Int32 GetHashCode()	Generates a number corresponding to the value of an object. If two objects of the same type are equal, then they must return the same hash code.
Type GetType()	Gets a Type object that can be used to access metadata associated with the type. It also serves as a starting point for navigating the object hierarchy exposed by the Reflection API (discussed shortly).
String ToString()	The default implementation returns the fully qualified name of the object's class. This method is often overridden to output data that is more meaningful to the type. For example, all base types return their value as a string.

Metadata

Metadata is the information that enables components to be self-describing. Metadata is used to describe many aspects of a .NET component, including classes, methods, and fields, and the assembly itself. Metadata is used by the CLR to facilitate all sorts of behavior, such as validating an assembly before it is executed or performing garbage collection while managed code is being executed. Visual Basic developers have used metadata for years when developing and using components within their applications.

❑ Visual Basic developers use metadata to instruct the Visual Basic runtime how to behave. For example, you can set the Unattended Execution property to determine whether unhandled exceptions are shown on the screen in a message box or are written to the Event Log.

❑ COM components referenced within Visual Basic applications have accompanying type libraries that contain metadata about the components, their methods, and their properties. You can use the Object Browser to view this information. (The information contained within the type library is what is used to drive IntelliSense.)

❑ Additional metadata can be associated with a component by installing it within COM+. Metadata stored in COM+ is used to declare the support a component needs at runtime, including transactional support, serialization support, and object pooling.

Better Support for Metadata

Metadata associated with a Visual Basic 6 component was scattered in multiple locations and stored using multiple formats:

❑ Metadata instructing the Visual Basic runtime how to behave (such as the `Unattended Execution` property) is compiled into the Visual Basic–generated executable.

❑ Basic COM attributes (such as the required threading model) are stored in the registry.

❑ COM+ attributes (such as the transactional support required) are stored in the COM+ catalog.

.NET refines the use of metadata within applications in three significant ways:

❑ .NET consolidates the metadata associated with a component.

❑ Because a .NET component does not have to be registered, installing and upgrading the component is easier and less problematic.

❑ .NET makes a much clearer distinction between attributes that should only be set at compile time and those that can be modified at runtime.

All attributes associated with Visual Basic components are represented in a common format and consolidated within the files that make up the assembly.

Because much of a COM/COM+ component's metadata is stored separately from the executable, installing and upgrading components can be problematic. COM/COM+ components must be registered to update the registry/COM+ catalog before they can be used, and the COM/COM+ component executable can be upgraded without upgrading its associated metadata.

The process of installing and upgrading a .NET component is greatly simplified. Because all metadata associated with a .NET component must reside within the file that contains the component, no registration is required. After a new component is copied into an application's directory, it can be used immediately. Because the component and its associated metadata cannot become out of sync, upgrading the component becomes much less of a problem.

Another problem with COM+ is that attributes that should only be set at compile time may be reconfigured at runtime. For example, COM+ can provide serialization support for neutral components. A component that does not require serialization must be designed to accommodate multiple requests from multiple clients simultaneously. You should know at compile time whether or not a component requires support for serialization from the runtime. However, under COM+, the attribute describing whether or not client requests should be serialized can be altered at runtime.

.NET makes a much better distinction between attributes that should be set at compile time and those that should be set at runtime. For example, whether a .NET component is serializable is determined at compile time. This setting cannot be overridden at runtime.

Attributes

Attributes are used to decorate entities such as assemblies, classes, methods, and properties with additional information. Attributes can be used for a variety of purposes. They can provide information, request a certain behavior at runtime, or even invoke a particular behavior from another application. An example of this can be shown by using the Demo class defined in the following code block:

```
Module Module1

  <Serializable()> Public Class Demo

    <Obsolete("Use Method2 instead.")> Public Sub Method1()
      ' Old implementation ...
    End Sub

    Public Sub Method2()
      ' New implementation ...
    End Sub

  End Class

  Public Sub Main()
    Dim d As Demo = New Demo()
    d.Method1()
  End Sub
End Module
```

Create a new console application for Visual Basic and then add a new class into the sample file. A best practice is to place each class in its own source file, but in order to simplify this demonstration, the class Demo has been defined within the main module.

The first attribute on the Demo class marks the class with the Serializable attribute. The base class library will provide serialization support for instances of the Demo type. For example, the ResourceWriter type can be used to stream an instance of the Demo type to disk. The second attribute is associated with Method1. Method1 has been marked as obsolete, but it is still available. When a method is marked as obsolete, there are two options, one being that Visual Studio should prevent applications from compiling. However, a better strategy for large applications is to first mark a method or class as obsolete and then prevent its use in the next release. The preceding code causes Visual Studio to display an IntelliSense warning if Method1 is referenced within the application, as shown in Figure 4-1. Not only does the line with Method1 have a visual hint of the issue, but a task has also been automatically added to the task window.

If the developer leaves this code unchanged and then compiles it, the application will compile correctly. As shown in Figure 4-2, the compilation is complete, but the developer receives a warning with a meaningful message that the code should be changed to use the correct method.

Sometimes you might need to associate multiple attributes with an entity. The following code shows an example of using both of the attributes from the previous code at the class level. Note that in this case the Obsolete attribute has been modified to cause a compilation error by setting its second parameter to True:

```
<Serializable(), Obsolete("No longer used.", True)> Public Class Demo
  ' Implementation ...
End Class
```

Attributes play an important role in the development of .NET applications, particularly XML Web services. As you'll see in chapter 28, the declaration of a class as a Web service and of particular methods as Web methods are all handled through the use of attributes.

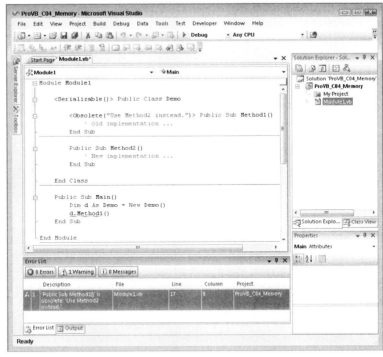

Figure 4-1

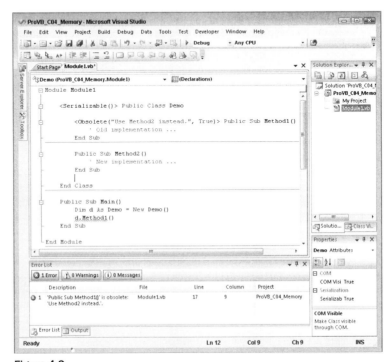

Figure 4-2

The Reflection API

The .NET Framework provides the Reflection API for accessing metadata associated with managed code. You can use the Reflection API to examine the metadata associated with an assembly and its types, and even to examine the currently executing assembly.

The `Assembly` class in the `System.Reflection` namespace can be used to access the metadata in an assembly. The `LoadFrom` method can be used to load an assembly, and the `GetExecutingAssembly` method can be used to access the currently executing assembly. The `GetTypes` method can then be used to obtain the collection of types defined in the assembly.

It's also possible to access the metadata of a type directly from an instance of that type. Because every object derives from `System.Object`, every object supports the `GetType` method, which returns a `Type` object that can be used to access the metadata associated with the type.

The `Type` object exposes many methods and properties for obtaining the metadata associated with a type. For example, you can obtain a collection of properties, methods, fields, and events exposed by the type by calling the `GetMembers` method. The `Type` object for the object's base type can also be obtained by calling the `DeclaringType` property.

A good tool that demonstrates the power of reflection is Lutz Roeder's Reflector for .NET (see `www.aisto .com/roeder/dotnet`). In addition to the core tool, you can find several add-ins related to the tool at `www.codeplex.com/reflectoraddins`.

IL Disassembler

One of the many handy tools that ships with Visual Studio is the IL Disassembler (ildasm.exe). It can be used to navigate the metadata within a module, including the types the module exposes, as well as their properties and methods. The IL Disassembler can also be used to display the IL contained within a module.

You can find the IL Disassembler under your installation directory for Visual Studio 2008; the default path is C:\Program Files\Microsoft SDKs\Windows\v6.0A\Bin\ILDasm.exe. Once the IL Disassembler has been started, select File ⇨ Open. Open mscorlib.dll, which is located in your system directory with a default path of C:\Windows\Microsoft.NET\Framework\V2.0.50727\mscorlib.dll. Once mscorlib.dll has been loaded, ILDasm will display a set of folders for each namespace in this assembly. Expand the `System` namespace, then the `ValueType` namespace, and finally double-click the `Equals` method. A window similar to the one shown in Figure 4-3 will be displayed.

Figure 4-3 shows the IL for the `Equals` method. Notice how the Reflection API is used to navigate through the instance of the value type's fields in order to determine whether the values of the two objects being compared are equal.

The IL Disassembler is a useful tool for learning how a particular module is implemented, but it could jeopardize your company's proprietary logic. After all, what's to prevent someone from using it to reverse engineer your code? Fortunately, Visual Studio 2008, like previous versions of Visual Studio, ships with a third-party tool called an *obfuscator*. The role of the obfuscator is to ensure that the IL Disassembler cannot build a meaningful representation of your application logic.

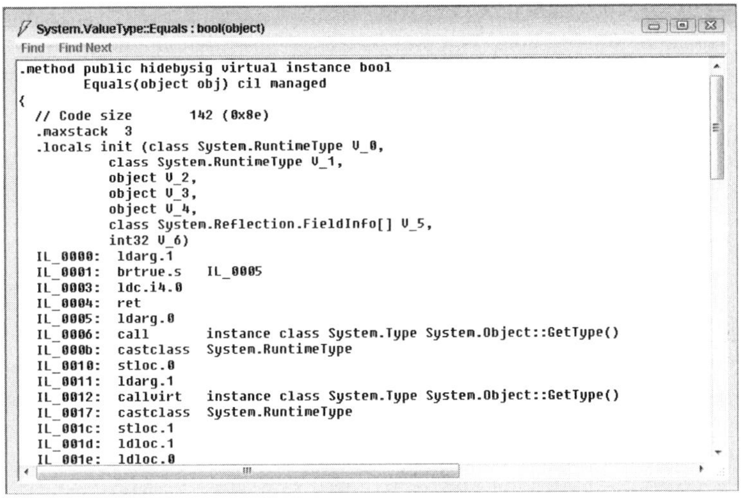

```
System.ValueType::Equals : bool(object)
Find   Find Next
.method public hidebysig virtual instance bool
        Equals(object obj) cil managed
{
  // Code size       142 (0x8e)
  .maxstack  3
  .locals init (class System.RuntimeType V_0,
           class System.RuntimeType V_1,
           object V_2,
           object V_3,
           object V_4,
           class System.Reflection.FieldInfo[] V_5,
           int32 V_6)
  IL_0000:  ldarg.1
  IL_0001:  brtrue.s    IL_0005
  IL_0003:  ldc.i4.0
  IL_0004:  ret
  IL_0005:  ldarg.0
  IL_0006:  call        instance class System.Type System.Object::GetType()
  IL_000b:  castclass   System.RuntimeType
  IL_0010:  stloc.0
  IL_0011:  ldarg.1
  IL_0012:  callvirt    instance class System.Type System.Object::GetType()
  IL_0017:  castclass   System.RuntimeType
  IL_001c:  stloc.1
  IL_001d:  ldloc.1
  IL_001e:  ldloc.0
```

Figure 4-3

A complete discussion of the obfuscator that ships with Visual Studio 2008 is beyond the scope of this chapter, but to access this tool, select the Tools menu and choose Dotfuscator Community Edition. The obfuscator runs against your compiled application, taking your IL file and stripping out many of the items that are embedded by default during the compilation process.

Memory Management

This section looks at one of the larger underlying elements of managed code. One of the reasons why .NET applications are referred to as "managed" is that memory deallocation is handled automatically by the system. The CLR's memory management fixes the shortcomings of the COM's memory management. Developers are accustomed to worrying about memory management only in an abstract sense. The basic rule has been that every object created and every section of memory allocated needs to be released (destroyed). The CLR introduces a garbage collector (GC), which simplifies this paradigm. Gone are the days when a misbehaving component — for example, one that failed to properly dispose of its object references or allocated and never released memory — could crash a web server.

However, the use of a GC introduces new questions about when and if objects need to be explicitly cleaned up. There are two elements in manually writing code to allocate and deallocate memory and system resources. The first is the release of any shared resources such as file handles and database connections. This type of activity needs to be managed explicitly and is discussed shortly. The second element of manual memory management involves letting the system know when memory is no longer in use by your application. Visual Basic COM developers, in particular, are accustomed to explicitly disposing of object references by setting variables to Nothing. While you can explicitly show your intent to destroy the object by setting it to Nothing manually, this doesn't actually free resources under .NET.

.NET uses a GC to automatically manage the cleanup of allocated memory, which means that you don't need to carry out memory management as an explicit action. Because the system is automatic, it's not up to you when resources are actually cleaned up; thus, a resource you previously used might sit in memory beyond the end of the method where you used it. Perhaps more important is the fact that the GC will at times reclaim objects in the middle of executing the code in a method. Fortunately, the system ensures that collection only happens as long as your code doesn't reference the object later in the method.

For example, you could actually end up extending the amount of time an object is kept in memory just by setting that object to Nothing. Thus, setting a variable to Nothing at the end of the method prevents the garbage collection mechanism from proactively reclaiming objects, and therefore is generally discouraged. After all, if the goal is simply to document a developer's intention, then a comment is more appropriate.

Given this change in paradigms, the next few sections look at the challenges of traditional memory management and peek under the covers to reveal how the garbage collector works, the basics of some of the challenges with COM-based memory management, and then a quick look at how the GC eliminates these challenges from your list of concerns. In particular, you should understand how you can interact with the garbage collector and why the Using command, for example, is recommended over a finalization method in .NET.

Traditional Garbage Collection

The unmanaged (COM/Visual Basic 6) runtime environment provides limited memory management by automatically releasing objects when they are no longer referenced by any application. Once all the references are released on an object, the runtime automatically releases the object from memory. For example, consider the following Visual Basic 6 code, which uses the Scripting.FileSystem object to write an entry to a log file:

```
' Requires a reference to Microsoft Scripting Runtime (scrrun.dll)
Sub WriteToLog(strLogEntry As String)
 Dim objFSO As Scripting.FileSystemObject
 Dim objTS As Scripting.TextStream

 objTS = objFSO.OpenTextFile("C:\temp\AppLog.log", ForAppending)
 Call objTS.WriteLine(Date & vbTab & strLogEntry)
End Sub
```

WriteToLog creates two objects, a FileSystemObject and a TextStream, which are used to create an entry in the log file. Because these are COM objects, they may live either within the current application process or in their own process. Once the routine exits, the Visual Basic runtime recognizes that they are no longer referenced by an active application and dereferences the objects. This results in both objects being deactivated. However, in some situations objects that are no longer referenced by an application are not properly cleaned up by the Visual Basic 6 runtime. One cause of this is the *circular reference*.

Circular References

One of the most common situations in which the unmanaged runtime is unable to ensure that objects are no longer referenced by the application is when these objects contain a circular reference. An example of a circular reference is when object *A* holds a reference to object *B* and object *B* holds a reference to object *A*.

Circular references are problematic because the unmanaged environment relies on the reference counting mechanism of COM to determine whether an object can be deactivated. Each COM object is responsible for maintaining its own reference count and for destroying itself once the reference count reaches zero. Clients of the object are responsible for updating the reference count appropriately, by calling the AddRef and Release methods on the object's IUnknown interface. However, in this scenario, object *A* continues to hold a reference to object *B*, and vice versa, so the internal cleanup logic of these components is not triggered.

In addition, problems can occur if the clients do not properly maintain the COM object's reference count. For example, an object will never be deactivated if a client forgets to call Release when the object is no longer referenced. To avoid this, the unmanaged environment may attempt to take care of updating the reference count for you, but the object's reference count can be an invalid indicator of whether or not the object is still being used by the application. For example, consider the references that objects *A* and *B* hold.

The application can invalidate its references to *A* and *B* by setting the associated variables equal to Nothing. However, even though objects *A* and *B* are no longer referenced by the application, the Visual Basic runtime cannot ensure that the objects are deactivated because *A* and *B* still reference each other. Consider the following (Visual Basic 6) code:

```
' Class:  CCircularRef

' Reference to another object.
Dim m_objRef As Object

Public Sub Initialize(objRef As Object)
   Set m_objRef = objRef
End Sub

Private Sub Class_Terminate()
   Call MsgBox("Terminating.")
   Set m_objRef = Nothing
End Sub
```

The CCircularRef class implements an Initialize method that accepts a reference to another object and saves it as a member variable. Notice that the class does not release any existing reference in the m_objRef variable before assigning a new value. The following code demonstrates how to use this CCircularRef class to create a circular reference:

```
Dim objA As New CCircularRef
Dim objB As New CCircularRef

Call objA.Initialize(objB)
Call objB.Initialize(objA)

Set objA = Nothing
Set objB = Nothing
```

After creating two instances (objA and objB) of CCircularRef, both of which have a reference count of one, the code then calls the Initialize method on each object by passing it a reference to the other. Now each of the object's reference counts is equal to two: one held by the application and one held by the other object. Next, explicitly setting objA and objB to Nothing decrements each object's reference count by one. However, because the reference count for both instances of CCircularRef is still greater than zero, the objects are not released from memory until the application is terminated. The CLR garbage collector solves the problem of circular references because it looks for a reference from the root application or thread to every class, and all classes that do not have such a reference are marked for deletion, regardless of any other references they might still maintain.

The CLR's Garbage Collector

The .NET garbage collection mechanism is complex, and the details of its inner workings are beyond the scope of this book, but it is important to understand the principles behind its operation. The GC is responsible for collecting objects that are no longer referenced. It takes a completely different approach from that of the Visual Basic runtime to accomplish this. At certain times, and based on internal rules, a task will run through all the objects looking for those that no longer have any references from the root application thread or one of the worker threads. Those objects may then be terminated; thus, the garbage is collected.

As long as all references to an object are either implicitly or explicitly released by the application, the GC will take care of freeing the memory allocated to it. Unlike COM objects, managed objects in .NET are not responsible for maintaining their reference count, and they are not responsible for destroying themselves. Instead, the GC is responsible for cleaning up objects that are no longer referenced by the application. The GC periodically determines which objects need to be cleaned up by leveraging the information the CLR maintains about the running application. The GC obtains a list of objects that are directly referenced by the application. Then, the GC discovers all the objects that are referenced (both directly and indirectly) by the "root" objects of the application. Once the GC has identified all the referenced objects, it is free to clean up any remaining objects.

The GC relies on references from an application to objects; thus, when it locates an object that is unreachable from any of the root objects, it can clean up that object. Any other references to that object will be from other objects that are also unreachable. Thus, the GC automatically cleans up objects that contain circular references.

In some environments, such as COM, objects are destroyed in a deterministic fashion. Once the reference count reaches zero, the object destroys itself, which means that you can tell exactly when the object will be terminated. However, with garbage collection, you can't tell exactly when an object will be destroyed. Just because you eliminate all references to an object doesn't mean that it will be terminated immediately. It just remains in memory until the garbage collection process gets around to locating and destroying it, a process called *nondeterministic finalization*.

This nondeterministic nature of CLR garbage collection provides a performance benefit. Rather than expend the effort to destroy objects as they are dereferenced, the destruction process can occur when the application is otherwise idle, often decreasing the impact on the user. Of course, if garbage collection must occur when the application is active, then the system may see a slight performance fluctuation as the collection is accomplished.

It is possible to explicitly invoke the GC by calling the `System.GC.Collect` method, but this process takes time, so it is not the sort of behavior to invoke in a typical application. For example, you could call this method each time you set an object variable to `Nothing`, so that the object would be destroyed almost immediately, but this forces the GC to scan all the objects in your application — a very expensive operation in terms of performance.

It's far better to design applications such that it is acceptable for unused objects to sit in the memory for some time before they are terminated. That way, the garbage collector can also run based on its optimal rules, collecting many dereferenced objects at the same time. This means you need to design objects that don't maintain expensive resources in instance variables. For example, database connections, open files on disk, and large chunks of memory (such as an image) are all examples of expensive resources. If you rely on the destruction of the object to release this type of resource, then the system might be keeping the resource tied up for a lot longer than you expect; in fact, on a lightly utilized web server, it could literally be days.

The first principle is working with object patterns that incorporate cleaning up such pending references before the object is released. Examples of this include calling the close method on an open database connection or file handle. In most cases, it's possible for applications to create classes that do not risk keeping these handles open. However, certain requirements, even with the best object design, can create a risk that a key resource will not be cleaned up correctly. In such an event, there are two occasions when the object could attempt to perform this cleanup: when the final reference to the object is released and immediately before the GC destroys the object.

One option is to implement the IDisposable interface. When implemented, this interface ensures that persistent resources are released. This is the preferred method for releasing resources. The second option is to add a method to your class that the system runs immediately before an object is destroyed. This option is not recommended for several reasons, including the fact that many developers fail to remember that the garbage collector is nondeterministic, meaning that you can't, for example, reference an SQLConnection object from your custom object's finalizer.

Finally, as part of .NET 2.0, Visual Basic introduced the Using command. The Using command is designed to change the way that you think about object cleanup. Instead of encapsulating your cleanup logic within your object, the Using command creates a window around the code that is referencing an instance of your object. When your application's execution reaches the end of this window, the system automatically calls the IDIsposable interface for your object to ensure that it is cleaned up correctly.

The Finalize Method

Conceptually, the GC calls an object's Finalize method immediately before it collects an object that is no longer referenced by the application. Classes can override the Finalize method to perform any necessary cleanup. The basic concept is to create a method that fills the same need as what in other object-oriented languages is referred to as a *destructor*. Similarly, the Class_Terminate event available in previous versions of Visual Basic does not have a functional equivalent in .NET. Instead, it is possible to create a Finalize method that is recognized by the GC and that prevents a class from being cleaned up until after the finalization method is completed, as shown in the following example:

```
Protected Overrides Sub Finalize()
  ' clean up code goes here
  MyBase.Finalize()
End Sub
```

This code uses both Protected scope and the Overrides keyword. Notice that not only does custom cleanup code go here (as indicated by the comment), but this method also calls MyBase.Finalize, which causes any finalization logic in the base class to be executed as well. Any class implementing a custom `Finalize` method should always call the base finalization class.

Be careful, however, not to treat the `Finalize` method as if it were a destructor. A destructor is based on a deterministic system, whereby the method is called when the object's last reference is removed. In the GC system, there are key differences in how a finalizer works:

❏ Because the GC is optimized to clean up memory only when necessary, there is a delay between the time when the object is no longer referenced by the application and when the GC collects it. Therefore, the same expensive resources that are released in the `Finalize` method may stay open longer than they need to be.

❏ The GC doesn't actually run `Finalize` methods. When the GC finds a `Finalize` method, it queues the object up for the finalizer to execute the object's method. This means that an object is not cleaned up during the current GC pass. Because of how the GC is optimized, this can result in the object remaining in memory for a much longer period.

❏ The GC is usually triggered when available memory is running low. As a result, execution of the object's `Finalize` method is likely to incur performance penalties. Therefore, the code in the `Finalize` method should be as short and quick as possible.

❏ There's no guarantee that a service you require is still available. For example, if the system is closing and you have a file open, then .NET may have already unloaded the object required to close the file, and thus a `Finalize` method can't reference an instance of any other .NET object.

All cleanup activities should be placed in the `Finalize` method, but objects that require timely cleanup should implement a `Dispose` method that can then be called by the client application just before setting the reference to `Nothing`:

```
Class DemoDispose
  Private m_disposed As Boolean = False

  Public Sub Dispose()
    If (Not m_disposed) Then
      ' Call cleanup code in Finalize.
      Finalize()

      ' Record that object has been disposed.
      m_disposed = True

      ' Finalize does not need to be called.
      GC.SuppressFinalize(Me)
    End If
  End Sub

  Protected Overrides Sub Finalize()
    ' Perform cleanup here \dots
    End Sub
End Class
```

The `DemoDispose` class overrides the `Finalize` method and implements the code to perform any necessary cleanup. This class places the actual cleanup code within the `Finalize` method. To ensure that the `Dispose` method only calls `Finalize` once, the value of the `private m_disposed` field is checked. Once

Finalize has been run, this value is set to True. The class then calls GC.SuppressFinalize to ensure that the GC does not call the Finalize method on this object when the object is collected. If you need to implement a Finalize method, this is the preferred implementation pattern.

This example implements all of the object's cleanup code in the Finalize method to ensure that the object is cleaned up properly before the GC collects it. The Finalize method still serves as a safety net in case the Dispose or Close methods were not called before the GC collects the object.

The IDisposable Interface

In some cases, the Finalize behavior is not acceptable. For an object that is using an expensive or limited resource, such as a database connection, a file handle, or a system lock, it is best to ensure that the resource is freed as soon as the object is no longer needed.

One way to accomplish this is to implement a method to be called by the client code to force the object to clean up and release its resources. This is not a perfect solution, but it is workable. This cleanup method must be called directly by the code using the object or via the use of the Using statement. The Using statement enables you to encapsulate an object's life span within a limited range, and automate the calling of the IDisposable interface.

The .NET Framework provides the IDisposable interface to formalize the declaration of cleanup logic. Be aware that implementing the IDisposable interface also implies that the object has overridden the Finalize method. Because there is no guarantee that the Dispose method will be called, it is critical that Finalize triggers your cleanup code if it was not already executed.

Having a custom finalizer ensures that, once released, the garbage collection mechanism will eventually find and terminate the object by running its Finalize method. However, when handled correctly, the IDisposable interface ensures that any cleanup is executed immediately, so resources are not consumed beyond the time they are needed.

Note that any class that derives from System.ComponentModel.Component automatically inherits the IDisposable interface. This includes all of the forms and controls used in a Windows Forms UI, as well as various other classes within the .NET Framework. Because this interface is inherited, let's review a custom implementation of the IDisposable interface based on the Person class defined in the preceding chapters. The first step involves adding a reference to the interface to the top of the class:

```
Public Class Person
  Implements IDisposable
```

This interface defines two methods, Dispose and Finalize, that need to be implemented in the class. Visual Studio automatically inserts both these methods into your code:

```
    Private disposed As Boolean = False

    ' IDisposable
    Private Overloads Sub Dispose(ByVal disposing As Boolean)
      If Not Me.disposed Then
        If disposing Then
          ' TODO: put code to dispose managed resources
        End If
```

```
      ' TODO: put code to free unmanaged resources here
    End If
    Me.disposed = True
  End Sub

#Region " IDisposable Support "
  ' This code added by Visual Basic to correctly implement the disposable pattern.
  Public Overloads Sub Dispose() Implements IDisposable.Dispose
    ' Do not change this code.
    ' Put cleanup code in Dispose(ByVal disposing As Boolean) above.
    Dispose(True)
    GC.SuppressFinalize(Me)
  End Sub

  Protected Overrides Sub Finalize()
    ' Do not change this code.
    ' Put cleanup code in Dispose(ByVal disposing As Boolean) above.
    Dispose(False)
    MyBase.Finalize()
  End Sub
#End Region
```

Notice the use of the `Overloads` and `Overrides` keywords. The automatically inserted code is following a best-practice design pattern for implementation of the `IDisposable` interface and the `Finalize` method. The idea is to centralize all cleanup code into a single method that is called by either the `Dispose` method or the `Finalize` method as appropriate.

Accordingly, you can add the cleanup code as noted by the `TODO:` comments in the inserted code. As mentioned in chapter 13, the `TODO:` keyword is recognized by Visual Studio's text parser, which triggers an entry in the task list to remind you to complete this code before the project is complete. Because this code frees a managed object (the `Hashtable`), it appears as shown here:

```
    Private Overloads Sub Dispose(ByVal disposing As Boolean)
      If Not Me.disposed Then
        If disposing Then
          ' TODO: put code to dispose managed resources
          mPhones = Nothing
        End If

        ' TODO: put code to free unmanaged resources here
      End If
      Me.disposed = True
    End Sub
```

In this case, we're using this method to release a reference to the object to which the `mPhones` variable points. While not strictly necessary, this illustrates how code can release other objects when the `Dispose` method is called. Generally, it is up to your client code to call this method at the appropriate time to ensure that cleanup occurs. Typically, this should be done as soon as the code is done using the object.

This is not always as easy as it might sound. In particular, an object may be referenced by more than one variable, and just because code in one class is dereferencing the object from one variable doesn't mean that it has been dereferenced by all the other variables. If the `Dispose` method is called while other references remain, then the object may become unusable and cause errors when invoked via those other references. There is no easy solution to this problem, so careful design is required if you choose to use the IDisposable interface.

Using IDisposable

One way to work with the IDisposable interface is to manually insert the calls to the interface implementation everywhere you reference the class. For example, in an application's Form1 code, you can override the OnLoad event for the form. You can use the custom implementation of this method to create an instance of the Person object. Then you create a custom handler for the form's OnClosed event, and make sure to clean up by disposing of the Person object. To do this, add the following code to the form:

```
Private Sub Form1_Closed(ByVal sender As Object, _
    ByVal e As System.EventArgs) Handles MyBase.Closed

  CType(mPerson, IDisposable).Dispose()


End Sub
```

The OnClosed method runs as the form is being closed, so it is an appropriate place to do cleanup work. Note that because the Dispose method is part of a secondary interface, use of the CType method to access that specific interface is needed in order to call the method.

This solution works fine for patterns where the object implementing IDisposable is used within a form, but it is less useful for other patterns, such as when the object is used as part of a Web service. In fact, even for forms, this pattern is somewhat limited in that it requires the form to define the object when the form is created, as opposed to either having the object created prior to the creation of the form or some other scenario that occurs only on other events within the form.

For these situations, .NET 2.0 introduced a new command keyword: Using. The Using keyword is a way to quickly encapsulate the life cycle of an object that implements IDisposable, and ensure that the Dispose method is called correctly:

```
Dim mPerson as New Person()
Using (mPerson)
    'insert custom method calls
End Using
```

The preceding statements allocate a new instance of the mPerson object. The Using command then instructs the compiler to automatically clean up this object's instance when the End Using command is executed. The result is a much cleaner way to ensure that the IDisposable interface is called.

Faster Memory Allocation for Objects

The CLR introduces the concept of a *managed heap*. Objects are allocated on the managed heap, and the CLR is responsible for controlling access to these objects in a type-safe manner. One of the advantages of the managed heap is that memory allocations on it are very efficient. When unmanaged code (such as Visual Basic 6 or C++) allocates memory on the unmanaged heap, it typically scans through some sort of data structure in search of a free chunk of memory that is large enough to accommodate the allocation. The managed heap maintains a reference to the end of the most recent heap allocation. When a new object needs to be created on the heap, the CLR allocates memory on top of memory that has previously been allocated and then increments the reference to the end of heap allocations accordingly. Figure 4-4 is a simplification of what takes place in the managed heap for .NET.

❑ **State 1** — A compressed memory heap with a reference to the endpoint on the heap

❑ **State 2** — Object B, although no longer referenced, remains in its current memory location. The memory has not been freed and does not alter the allocation of memory or of other objects on the heap.

❑ **State 3** — Even though there is now a gap between the memory allocated for object A and object C, the memory allocation for D still occurs on the top of the heap. The unused fragment of memory on the managed heap is ignored at allocation time.

❑ **State 4** — After one or more allocations, before there is an allocation failure, the garbage collector runs. It reclaims the memory that was allocated to B and repositions the remaining valid objects. This compresses the active objects to the bottom of the heap, creating more space for additional object allocations (refer to Figure 4-4).

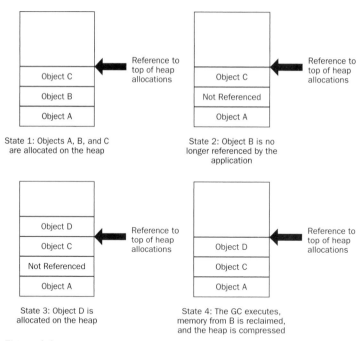

Figure 4-4

This is where the power of the GC really shines. Before the CLR is unable to allocate memory on the managed heap, the GC is invoked. The GC not only collects objects that are no longer referenced by the application, but also has a second task: compacting the heap. This is important because if all the GC did was clean up objects, then the heap would become progressively more fragmented. When heap memory becomes fragmented, you can wind up with the common problem of having a memory allocation fail, not because there isn't enough free memory, but because there isn't enough free memory in a contiguous section of memory. Thus, not only does the GC reclaim the memory associated with objects that are no longer referenced, it also compacts the remaining objects. The GC effectively squeezes out all of the spaces between the remaining objects, freeing up a large section of managed heap for new object allocations.

Garbage Collector Optimizations

The GC uses a concept known as *generations*, the primary purpose of which is to improve its performance. The theory behind generations is that objects that have been recently created tend to have a higher probability of being garbage-collected than objects that have existed on the system for a longer time.

To understand generations, consider the analogy of a mall parking lot where cars represent objects created by the CLR. People have different shopping patterns when they visit the mall. Some people spend a good portion of their day in the mall, and others stop only long enough to pick up an item or two. Applying the theory of generations to trying to find an empty parking space for a car yields a scenario in which the highest probability of finding a parking space is a place where other cars have recently parked. In other words, a space that was occupied recently is more likely to be held by someone who just needed to quickly pick up an item or two. The longer a car has been parked, the higher the probability that its owner is an all-day shopper and the lower the probability that the parking space will be freed up anytime soon.

Generations provide a means for the GC to identify recently created objects versus long-lived objects. An object's generation is basically a counter that indicates how many times it has successfully avoided garbage collection. An object's generation counter starts at zero and can have a maximum value of two, after which the object's generation remains at this value regardless of how many times it is checked for collection.

You can put this to the test with a simple Visual Basic application. From the File menu, select either File ⇨ New ⇨ Project or, if you have an open solution, File ⇨ Add ⇨ New Project. This opens the Add New Project dialog box. Select a console application, provide a name and directory for your new project, and click OK. After you create your new project, you will have a code module that looks similar to the code that follows. Within the `Main` module, add the highlighted code. Right-click your second project, and select the Set as Startup Project option so that when you run your solution, your new project is automatically started.

```
Module Module1

  Sub Main()
    Dim myObject As Object = New Object()
    Dim i As Integer

      For i = 0 To 3
        Console.WriteLine(String.Format("Generation = {0}", _
                     GC.GetGeneration(myObject)))
        GC.Collect()
        GC.WaitForPendingFinalizers()
      Next i
      Console.Read()
  End Sub

End Module
```

Regardless of the project you use, this code sends its output to the .NET console. For a Windows application, this console defaults to the Visual Studio Output window. When you run this code, it creates an instance of an object and then iterates through a loop four times. For each loop, it displays the current generation count of myObject and then calls the GC. The GC.WaitForPendingFinalizers method blocks execution until the garbage collection has been completed.

As shown in Figure 4-5, each time the GC was run, the generation counter was incremented for myObject, up to a maximum of 2.

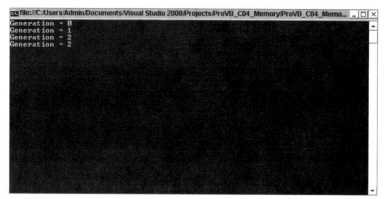

Figure 4-5

Each time the GC is run, the managed heap is compacted, and the reference to the end of the most recent memory allocation is updated. After compaction, objects of the same generation are grouped together. Generation-2 objects are grouped at the bottom of the managed heap, and generation-1 objects are grouped next. New generation-0 objects are placed on top of the existing allocations, so they are grouped together as well.

This is significant because recently allocated objects have a higher probability of having shorter lives. Because objects on the managed heap are ordered according to generations, the GC can opt to collect newer objects. Running the GC over a limited portion of the heap is quicker than running it over the entire managed heap.

It's also possible to invoke the GC with an overloaded version of the Collect method that accepts a generation number. The GC will then collect all objects no longer referenced by the application that belong to the specified (or younger) generation. The version of the Collect method that accepts no parameters collects objects that belong to all generations.

Another hidden GC optimization results from the fact that a reference to an object may implicitly go out of scope; therefore, it can be collected by the GC. It is difficult to illustrate how the optimization occurs only if there are no additional references to the object and the object does not have a finalizer. However, if an object is declared and used at the top of a module and not referenced again in a method, then in the release mode, the metadata will indicate that the variable is not referenced in the later portion of the code. Once the last reference to the object is made, its logical scope ends; and if the garbage collector runs, the memory for that object, which will no longer be referenced, can be reclaimed before it has gone out of its physical scope.

Summary

This chapter introduced the CLR. You looked at the memory management features of the CLR, including how the CLR eliminates the circular reference problem that has plagued COM developers. Next, the chapter examined the `Finalize` method and explained why it should not be treated like the `Class_Terminate` method. Chapter highlights include the following:

❑   Whenever possible, do not implement the `Finalize` method in a class.

❑   If the `Finalize` method is implemented, then also implement the `IDisposable` interface, which can be called by the client when the object is no longer needed.

❑   Code for the `Finalize` method should be as short and quick as possible.

❑   There is no way to accurately predict when the GC will collect an object that is no longer referenced by the application (unless the GC is invoked explicitly).

❑   The order in which the GC collects objects on the managed heap is nondeterministic. This means that the `Finalize` method cannot call methods on other objects referenced by the object being collected.

❑   Leverage the `Using` keyword to automatically trigger the execution of the `IDisposable` interface.

This chapter also examined the value of a common runtime and type system that can be targeted by multiple languages. You saw how the CLR offers better support for metadata. Metadata is used to make types self-describing and is used for language elements such as attributes. Included were examples of how metadata is used by the CLR and the .NET class library, and you saw how to extend metadata by creating your own attributes. Finally, the chapter presented a brief overview of the Reflection API and the IL Disassembler utility (`ildasm.exe`), which can display the IL contained within a module.

5

Localization

Developers usually build their applications in the English language. Then, as the audience for the application expands, they realize the need to globalize the application. Of course, the ideal is to build the application to handle an international audience right from the start, but in many cases this may not be possible because of the extra work it requires.

With the .NET Framework 3.5, a considerable effort has been made to address the internationalization of .NET applications. Changes to the API, the addition of capabilities to the server controls, and even Visual Studio itself equip you to do the extra work required to bring your application to an international audience. This chapter looks at some of the important items to consider when building your applications for the world.

Cultures and Regions

As an example, the ASP.NET page that is pulled up in an end user's browser runs under a specific culture and region setting. When building an ASP.NET application or page, the defined culture in which it runs is dependent upon a culture and region setting specified either in the server in which the application is run or in a setting applied by the client (the end user). By default, ASP.NET runs under a culture setting defined by the server.

The world is made up of a multitude of cultures, each of which has a language and a set of defined ways in which it views and consumes numbers, uses currencies, sorts alphabetically, and so on. The .NET Framework defines cultures and regions using the *Request for Comments 1766* standard definition (tags for identification of languages), which specifies a language and region using two-letter codes separated by a dash. The following table provides examples of some culture definitions:

Culture Code	Description
en-US	English language; United States
en-GB	English language; United Kingdom (Great Britain)
en-AU	English language; Australia
en-CA	English language; Canada

The examples in this table define four distinct cultures. These four cultures have some similarities and some differences. All four cultures speak the same language (English), so the language code of en is used in each culture setting. Following the language setting is the region setting. Even though these cultures speak the same language, it is important to distinguish them further by setting their region (such as US for the United States, GB for the United Kingdom, AU for Australia, and CA for Canada). These settings reflect the fact that the English used in the United States is slightly different from the English used in the United Kingdom, and so forth. Beyond language, differences exist in how dates and numerical values are represented. This is why a culture's language and region are presented together.

The differences do not break down by country only. Many countries contain more than a single language, and each area has its own preference for notation of dates and other items. For example, en-CA specifies English speakers in Canada. Because Canada is not only an English-speaking country, it also includes the culture setting of fr-CA for French-speaking Canadians.

Understanding Culture Types

The culture definition just given is called a *specific culture* definition. This definition is as detailed as you can possibly get, defining both the language and the region. The other type of culture definition is a *neutral culture* definition. Each specific culture has a specified neutral culture with which it is associated. For instance, the English language cultures shown in the previous table are separate, but they also belong to one neutral culture: EN (English). The diagram presented in Figure 5-1 illustrates how these culture types relate to one another.

From this diagram, you can see that many specific cultures belong to a neutral culture. Higher in the hierarchy than the neutral culture is an *invariant culture*, which is an agnostic culture setting that should be utilized when passing items (such as dates and numbers) around a network. When performing these kinds of operations, you should make your back-end data flows devoid of user-specific culture settings. Instead, apply these settings in the business and presentation layers of your applications.

In addition, pay attention to neutral culture when working with your applications. Invariably, you are going to build applications with views that are more dependent on a neutral culture than on a specific culture. For instance, if you have a Spanish version of your application, you'll probably make this version available to all Spanish speakers regardless of their regions. In many applications, it won't matter whether the Spanish speaker is from Spain, Mexico, or Argentina. In cases where it does make a difference, use the specific culture settings.

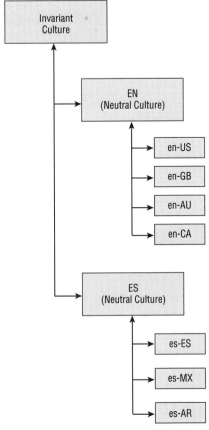

Figure 5-1

Looking at Your Thread

When the end user requests an ASP.NET page or runs a Windows Forms dialog, the item is executed on a thread from the thread pool. That thread has a culture associated with it. You can get information about the culture of the thread programmatically and then check for particular details about that culture.

To see an example of working with a thread and reading the culture information of that thread, create a Windows Forms application that is laid out as shown in Figure 5-2.

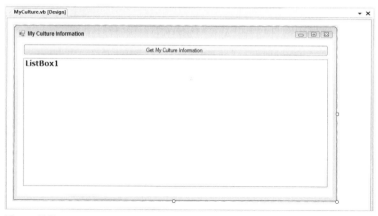

Figure 5-2

When the button on the form is pressed, the Button1_Click event is fired and the user's culture information is read and displayed in the ListBox control. The code for the form is presented here:

```
Imports System.Threading

Public Class MyCulture

    Private Sub Button1_Click(ByVal sender As System.Object, _
      ByVal e As System.EventArgs) Handles Button1.Click

        Dim ci As New _
          System.Globalization.CultureInfo( _
            Thread.CurrentThread.CurrentCulture.ToString())

        ListBox1.Items.Add("CURRENT CULTURE'S INFO")
        ListBox1.Items.Add("Culture's Name: " & ci.Name)
        ListBox1.Items.Add("Culture's Parent Name: " & ci.Parent.Name)
        ListBox1.Items.Add("Culture's Display Name: " & ci.DisplayName)
        ListBox1.Items.Add("Culture's English Name: " & ci.EnglishName)
        ListBox1.Items.Add("Culture's Native Name: " & ci.NativeName)
        ListBox1.Items.Add("Culture's Three Letter ISO Name: " & _
            ci.ThreeLetterISOLanguageName)
        ListBox1.Items.Add("Calendar Type: " & ci.Calendar.ToString())
    End Sub
End Class
```

Because this form is working with the Thread object, in order for this to work, you need to make a reference to the System.Threading namespace at the top of the form, as is done with the Imports statement. Threading is covered in Chapter 26.

This simple form creates a CultureInfo object from the System.Globalization namespace and assigns the culture from the current thread that is running using the Thread.CurrentThread .CurrentCulture.ToString call. Once the CultureInfo object is populated with the end user's culture, details about that culture can be called using a number of available properties that the CultureInfo object offers. Example results of running the form are shown in Figure 5-3.

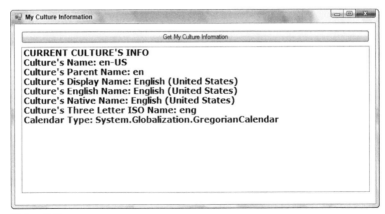

Figure 5-3

The `CultureInfo` object contains a number of properties that provide you with specific culture information. The items displayed are only a small sampling of what is available from the `CultureInfo` object. From this figure, you can see that the en-US culture is the default setting in which the thread executes. In addition to this, you can use the `CultureInfo` object to get at a lot of other descriptive information about the culture. You can always change a thread's culture on the overloads provided via a new instantiation of the `CultureInfo` object, as shown here:

```
Imports System.Globalization

Imports System.Threading

Public Class MyCulture

    Private Sub Button1_Click(ByVal sender As System.Object, _
        ByVal e As System.EventArgs) Handles Button1.Click

        Thread.CurrentThread.CurrentCulture = New CultureInfo("th-TH")
        Dim ci As CultureInfo = _
            System.Threading.Thread.CurrentThread.CurrentCulture

        ListBox1.Items.Add("CURRENT CULTURE'S INFO")
        ListBox1.Items.Add("Culture's Name: " & ci.Name)
        ListBox1.Items.Add("Culture's Parent Name: " & ci.Parent.Name)
        ListBox1.Items.Add("Culture's Display Name: " & ci.DisplayName)
        ListBox1.Items.Add("Culture's English Name: " & ci.EnglishName)
        ListBox1.Items.Add("Culture's Native Name: " & ci.NativeName)
        ListBox1.Items.Add("Culture's Three Letter ISO Name: " & _
            ci.ThreeLetterISOLanguageName)
        ListBox1.Items.Add("Calendar Type: " & ci.Calendar.ToString())
    End Sub
End Class
```

In this example, only a couple of lines of code are changed to assign a new instance of the `CultureInfo` object to the `CurrentCulture` property of the thread being executed by the application.

The culture setting enables the `CultureInfo` object to define the culture you want to utilize. In this case, the Thai language of Thailand is assigned. The results produced in the `ListBox` control are illustrated in Figure 5-4.

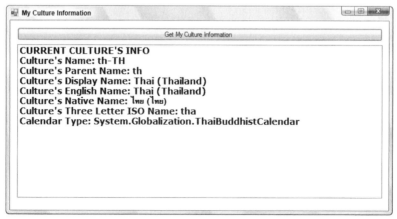

Figure 5-4

From this figure, you can see that the .NET Framework provides the native name of the language used even if it is not a Latin-based letter style. In this case, the results are presented for the Thai language in Thailand, including some of the properties associated with this culture (such as an entirely different calendar than the one used in Western Europe and the United States).

Declaring Culture Globally in ASP.NET

ASP.NET enables you to easily define the culture that is used either by your entire ASP.NET application or by a specific page within your Web application, using what are termed *server-side culture declarations*. You can specify the culture for any of your ASP.NET applications by means of the appropriate configuration files. In the default install of ASP.NET, no culture is specified, as is evident when you look at the global `web.config.comments` file found in the ASP.NET 2.0 `CONFIG` folder (`C:\WINDOWS \Microsoft.NET\Framework\v2.0.50727\CONFIG`). This file contains a `<globalization>` section of the configuration document, presented here:

```
<globalization requestEncoding="utf-8" responseEncoding="utf-8" fileEncoding=""
  culture="" uiCulture="" enableClientBasedCulture="false"
  responseHeaderEncoding="utf-8" resourceProviderFactoryType=""
  enableBestFitResponseEncoding="false" />
```

Note the two attributes represented in bold: **culture** and **uiCulture**. The `culture` attribute enables you to define the culture to use for processing incoming requests, whereas the `uiCulture` attribute enables you define the default culture needed to process any resource files in the application (use of these attributes is covered later in the chapter).

Looking at the configuration declaration in the preceding code block, you can see that nothing is specified for the culture settings. One option you have when specifying a culture on the server is to define this culture in the root `web.config` file. This causes every ASP.NET 3.5 application on that server to adopt this particular culture setting. The other option is to specify these settings in the web.config file of the application itself, as illustrated here:

```
<configuration>
    <system.web>

        <globalization culture="ru-RU" uiCulture="ru-RU" />

    </system.web>
</configuration>
```

In this case, the culture established for just this ASP.NET application is the Russian language in the country of Russia. In addition to setting the culture at either the server-wide or the application-wide level, another option is to set the culture at the page level, as shown here:

```
<%@ Page Language="VB" UICulture="ru-RU" Culture="ru-RU" %>
```

This example specifies that the Russian language and culture settings are used for everything on the page. You can see this in action by using this @Page directive and a simple calendar control on the page. Figure 5-5 shows the output.

Figure 5-5

Adopting Culture Settings in ASP.NET

In addition to using server-side settings to define the culture for your ASP.NET pages, you also have the option to define the culture according to what the client has set as his or her preference in a browser instance.

When end users install Microsoft's Internet Explorer and some of the other browsers, they have the option to select their preferred cultures in a particular order (if they have selected more than a single culture preference). To see this in action in IE, select Tools ⇨ Internet Options from the IE menu. On the first tab provided (General) is a Languages button at the bottom of the dialog. Select this button and you are provided with the Language Preference dialog shown in Figure 5-6.

Two cultures are selected from the list of available cultures. To add any additional cultures to the list, click the Add button and select the appropriate culture from the list. After you have selected any cultures present in the list, you can select the order in which you prefer to use them. In the case of Figure 5-6, the Finnish culture is selected as the most preferred culture, whereas the U.S. version of English is selected as the second preference. A user with this setting gets the Finnish language version of the application before anything else; if a Finnish version is not available, a U.S. English version is presented instead.

After making this selection, the end user can use the auto feature provided in ASP.NET 3.5. Instead of specifying a distinct culture in any of the configuration files or from the @Page directive, you can also state that ASP.NET should automatically select the culture provided by the end user requesting the page. This is done using the auto keyword, as illustrated here:

```
<%@ Page Language="VB" UICulture="auto" Culture="auto" %>
```

Figure 5-6

With this construction in your page, the dates, calendars, and numbers appear in the preferred culture of the requester. What happens if you have translated resources in resource files (shown later in the chapter) that depend on a culture specification? Or what if you have only specific translations and therefore can't handle every possible culture that might be returned to your ASP.NET page? In this case, you can specify the auto option with an additional fallback option if ASP.NET cannot find the culture settings of the user (such as culture-specific resource files). This usage is illustrated in the following code:

```
<%@ Page Language="VB" UICulture="auto:en-US" Culture="auto:en-US" %>
```

In this case, the automatic detection is utilized, but if the culture the end user prefers is not present, then en-US is used.

Translating Values and Behaviors

In the process of globalizing your .NET application, you may notice a number of aspects that are done differently compared to building an application that is devoid of globalization, including how dates are represented and how currencies are shown. This section looks at some of these issues.

Understanding Differences in Dates

Different cultures specify dates and time very differently. For instance, take the following date as an example:

```
08/11/2008
```

Is this date August 11, 2008 or is it November 8, 2008? Again, when storing values such as date/time stamps in a database or other type of back-end system, always use the same culture (or invariant culture) for these items to avoid any mistakes. It should be the job of the business logic layer or the presentation layer to convert these items for use by the end user.

Setting the culture at the server level in ASP.NET or within a Windows Forms application, as shown in the earlier samples, enables your .NET application to make these conversions for you. You can also simply assign a new culture to the thread in which the application is running. For instance, consider the following code:

```
Imports System.Globalization
Imports System.Threading

Public Class Differences

    Private Sub Button1_Click(ByVal sender As System.Object, _
      ByVal e As System.EventArgs) Handles Button1.Click

        Dim dt As DateTime = New DateTime(2008, 8, 11, 11, 12, 10, 10)

        Thread.CurrentThread.CurrentCulture = New CultureInfo("en-US")
        ListBox1.Items.Add( _
          Thread.CurrentThread.CurrentCulture.EnglishName & " : " & _
          dt.ToString())

        Thread.CurrentThread.CurrentCulture = New CultureInfo("ru-RU")
        ListBox1.Items.Add( _
          Thread.CurrentThread.CurrentCulture.EnglishName & " : " & _
          dt.ToString())

        Thread.CurrentThread.CurrentCulture = New CultureInfo("fi-FI")
        ListBox1.Items.Add( _
          Thread.CurrentThread.CurrentCulture.EnglishName & " : " & _
          dt.ToString())

        Thread.CurrentThread.CurrentCulture = New CultureInfo("th-TH")
        ListBox1.Items.Add( _
          Thread.CurrentThread.CurrentCulture.EnglishName & " : " & _
          dt.ToString())
    End Sub
End Class
```

In this case, a Windows Forms application is used again and four different cultures are utilized in the output. The date/time construction used by the defined culture is written to the ListBox control. The result from this code operation is presented in Figure 5-7.

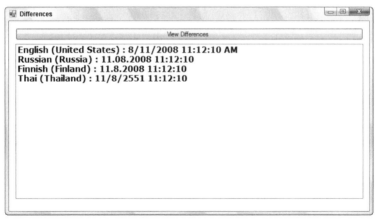

Figure 5-7

Clearly, the formats used to represent a date/time value are dramatically different from one another —
and the Thai culture (th-TH), even uses an entirely different calendar that labels 2008 as 2551.

Understanding Differences in Numbers and Currencies

In addition to date/time values, numbers are constructed quite differently from one culture to the next.
How can a number be represented differently in different cultures? Well, it has less to do with the actual
number (although certain cultures use different number symbols) and more to do with how the number
separators are used for decimals or for showing amounts such as thousands, millions, and more. For
instance, in the English culture of the United States (en-US), numbers are represented in the following
fashion:

```
5,123,456.00
```

From this example, you can see that the en-US culture uses a comma as a separator for thousands and a
period for signifying the start of any decimals that might appear after the number is presented. It is quite
different when working with other cultures. The following code block shows an example of representing
numbers in other cultures:

```
Imports System.Globalization
Imports System.Threading

Public Class Differences

    Private Sub Button1_Click(ByVal sender As System.Object, _
      ByVal e As System.EventArgs) Handles Button1.Click

        Dim myNumber As Double = 5123456.0

        Thread.CurrentThread.CurrentCulture = New CultureInfo("en-US")
        ListBox1.Items.Add(Thread.CurrentThread.CurrentCulture.EnglishName & _
            " : " & myNumber.ToString("n"))

        Thread.CurrentThread.CurrentCulture = New CultureInfo("vi-VN")
```

```
    ListBox1.Items.Add(Thread.CurrentThread.CurrentCulture.EnglishName & _
        " : " & myNumber.ToString("n"))

    Thread.CurrentThread.CurrentCulture = New CultureInfo("fi-FI")
    ListBox1.Items.Add(Thread.CurrentThread.CurrentCulture.EnglishName & _
        " : " & myNumber.ToString("n"))

    Thread.CurrentThread.CurrentCulture = New CultureInfo("fr-CH")
    ListBox1.Items.Add(Thread.CurrentThread.CurrentCulture.EnglishName & _
        " : " & myNumber.ToString("n"))
    End Sub
End Class
```

Running this example produces the results shown in Figure 5-8.

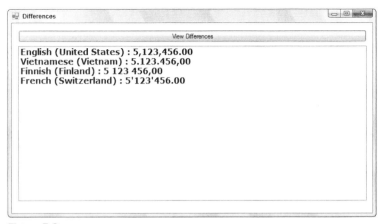

Figure 5-8

As you can see, cultures show numbers in numerous different formats. The second culture listed in the figure, vi-VN (Vietnamese in Vietnam), constructs a number exactly the opposite from the way it is constructed in en-US. The Vietnamese culture uses periods for the thousand separators and a comma for signifying decimals. Finnish uses spaces for the thousand separators and a comma for the decimal separator, whereas the French-speaking Swiss use an apostrophe for separating thousands and a period for the decimal separator. Therefore, it is important to "translate" numbers to the proper construction so that users of your application can properly understand the numbers represented.

Another scenario in which you represent numbers is when working with currencies. It is one thing to *convert* currencies so that end users understand the proper value of an item, but it is another to translate the construction of the currency just as you would a basic number.

Each culture has a distinct currency symbol used to signify that a number represented is an actual currency value. For instance, the en-US culture represents a currency in the following format:

```
$5,123,456.00
```

The en-US culture uses a U.S. dollar symbol ($), and the location of this symbol is just as important as the symbol itself. For en-US, the $ symbol directly precedes the currency value (with no space in between the symbol and the first character of the number). Other cultures use different symbols to represent currency and often place those currency symbols in different locations. Try changing the previous code block so that it now represents the number as a currency. The necessary changes are shown here:

```vb
Imports System.Globalization
Imports System.Threading

Public Class Differences

    Private Sub Button1_Click(ByVal sender As System.Object, _
        ByVal e As System.EventArgs) Handles Button1.Click

        Dim myNumber As Double = 5123456.0

        Thread.CurrentThread.CurrentCulture = New CultureInfo("en-US")
        ListBox1.Items.Add(Thread.CurrentThread.CurrentCulture.EnglishName & _
            " : " & myNumber.ToString("c"))
        Thread.CurrentThread.CurrentCulture = New CultureInfo("vi-VN")
        ListBox1.Items.Add(Thread.CurrentThread.CurrentCulture.EnglishName & _
            " : " & myNumber.ToString("c"))
        Thread.CurrentThread.CurrentCulture = New CultureInfo("fi-FI")
        ListBox1.Items.Add(Thread.CurrentThread.CurrentCulture.EnglishName & _
            " : " & myNumber.ToString("c"))
        Thread.CurrentThread.CurrentCulture = New CultureInfo("fr-CH")
        ListBox1.Items.Add(Thread.CurrentThread.CurrentCulture.EnglishName & _
            " : " & myNumber.ToString("c"))
    End Sub
End Class
```

Running this example shows how these cultures represent currency values (see Figure 5-9).

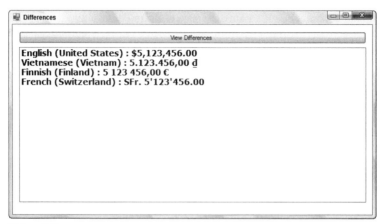

Figure 5-9

Not only are the numbers constructed quite differently from one another, but the currency symbol and the location of the symbol in regard to the number are quite different as well.

When working with currencies, note that when you are using currencies on an ASP.NET page, you have provided an automatic culture setting for the page as a whole (such as setting the culture in the @Page directive). You must specify a specific culture for the currency that is the same in all cases *unless* you are actually doing a currency conversion. For instance, if you are specifying a U.S. dollar currency value on your ASP.NET page, you do not want to specify that the culture of the currency is something else (for example, the euro).

An exception would be if you actually performed a currency conversion and showed the appropriate euro value along with the culture specification of the currency. Therefore, if you are using an automatic culture setting on your ASP.NET page and you are *not* converting the currency, then you perform something similar to what is illustrated in the following code for currency values:

```
Dim myNumber As Double = 5123456.00
Dim usCurr As CultureInfo = New CultureInfo("en-US")
Response.Write(myNumber.ToString("c", usCurr))
```

Understanding Differences in Sorting Strings

You have learned to translate textual values and alter the construction of the numbers, date/time values, currencies, and more when you are globalizing an application. You should also take care when applying culture settings to some of the programmatic behaviors that you establish for values in your applications. One operation that can change based upon the culture setting applied is how .NET sorts strings. You might think that all cultures sort strings in the same way (and generally they do), but sometimes differences exist. To give you an example, the following example shows a sorting operation occurring in the en-US culture:

```
Imports System.Globalization
Imports System.Threading

Public Class Differences

    Private Sub Button1_Click(ByVal sender As System.Object, _
      ByVal e As System.EventArgs) Handles Button1.Click

        Thread.CurrentThread.CurrentCulture = New CultureInfo("en-US")

        Dim myList As List(Of String) = New List(Of String)

        myList.Add("Washington D.C.")
        myList.Add("Helsinki")
        myList.Add("Moscow")
        myList.Add("Warsaw")
        myList.Add("Vienna")
        myList.Add("Tokyo")

        myList.Sort()
```

```
            For Each item As String In myList
                ListBox1.Items.Add(item.ToString())
            Next

        End Sub
End Class
```

For this example to work, you have to reference the `System.Collections` and the `System.Collections`
`.Generic` namespaces because this example makes use of the `List(Of String)` object.

In this example, a generic list of capitals from various countries of the world is created in random order.
Then the `Sort` method of the generic `List(Of String)` object is invoked. This sorting operation sorts the
strings based upon how sorting is done for the defined culture in which the application thread is running.
The preceding code shows the sorting as it is done for the en-US culture. The result of this operation is
shown in Figure 5-10.

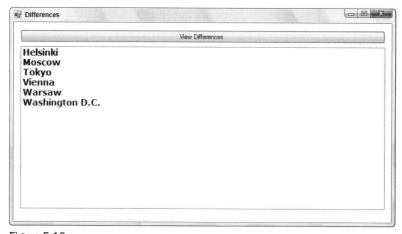

Figure 5-10

This is pretty much what you would expect. Now, however, change the previous example so that the
culture is set to the Finnish culture:

```
Imports System.Globalization
Imports System.Threading

Public Class Differences

    Private Sub Button1_Click(ByVal sender As System.Object, _
        ByVal e As System.EventArgs) Handles Button1.Click

        Thread.CurrentThread.CurrentCulture = New CultureInfo("fi-FI")

        Dim myList As List(Of String) = New List(Of String)
```

```
        myList.Add("Washington D.C.")
        myList.Add("Helsinki")
        myList.Add("Moscow")
        myList.Add("Warsaw")
        myList.Add("Vienna")
        myList.Add("Tokyo")

        myList.Sort()

        For Each item As String In myList
            ListBox1.Items.Add(item.ToString())
        Next

    End Sub
End Class
```

If you run the same bit of code under the Finnish culture setting, you get the results presented in Figure 5-11.

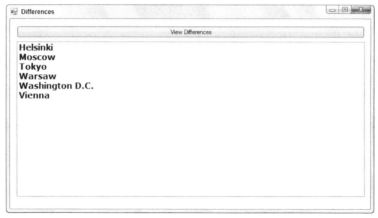

Figure 5-11

Comparing the Finnish culture sorting done in Figure 5-11 and the U.S. English culture sorting done in Figure 5-10, you can see that the city of Vienna is in a different place in the Finnish version. This is because in the Finnish language, there is no difference between the letter V and the letter W. Therefore, if you are sorting using the Finnish culture setting, then Vi comes after Wa, and thus Vienna comes last in the list of strings in the sorting operation.

Working with ASP.NET Resource Files

When you work with ASP.NET 3.5, all resources are handled by a resource file. A resource file is an XML-based file that has a .resx extension. You can have Visual Studio 2008 help you construct this file. Resource files provide a set of items that are utilized by a specified culture. In your ASP.NET 3.5

applications, you store resource files as either *local resources* or *global resources*. The following sections describe how to use each type of resource.

Making Use of Local Resources

You might be surprised how easily you can build an ASP.NET page so that it can be *localized* into other languages. In fact, the only thing you need to do is build the ASP.NET page as you normally would and then use some built-in capabilities from Visual Studio 2008 to convert the page to a format that enables you to plug in other languages easily.

To see this in action, build a simple ASP.NET page as presented here (referred to later in the chapter as the "ASP.NET page code block"):

```
<%@ Page Language="VB" %>

<script runat="server">

</script>

<html xmlns="http://www.w3.org/1999/xhtml">
<head runat="server">
    <title>Sample Page</title>
</head>
<body>
    <form id="form1" runat="server">
    <div>
        <asp:Label ID="Label1" runat="server"
         Text="What is your name?"></asp:Label><br />
        <br />
        <asp:TextBox ID="TextBox1" runat="server"></asp:TextBox> 
        <asp:Button ID="Button1" runat="server" Text="Submit Name" /><br />
        <br />
        <asp:Label ID="Label2" runat="server"></asp:Label>
    </div>
    </form>
</body>
</html>
```

As you can see, there is not much to this page. It is composed of a couple of `Label` controls, as well as `TextBox` and `Button` controls. The end user enters his or her name into the text box, and then the `Label2` server control is populated with the inputted name and a simple greeting.

The next step is what makes Visual Studio so great. To change the construction of this page so that it can be localized easily from resource files, open the page in Visual Studio and select Tools ➪ Generate Local Resource from the Visual Studio menu. Note that you can select this tool only when you are in the Design view of your page.

Selecting Generate Local Resource from the Tool menu causes Visual Studio to create an `App_Local Resources` folder in your project if you don't have one already. A .resx file based upon this ASP.NET page is then placed in the folder. For instance, if you are working with the `Default.aspx` page, then the resource file is named `Default.aspx.resx`. These changes are shown in Figure 5-12.

Figure 5-12

If you right-click on the .resx file and select View Code, notice that the .resx file is nothing more than an XML file with an associated schema at the beginning of the document. The resource file that is generated for you takes every possible property of every translatable control on the page and gives each item a key value that can be referenced in your ASP.NET page. Looking at the page's code, note that all the text values you placed in the page have been retained, but they have also been placed inside the resource file. Visual Studio changed the code of the Default.aspx page as shown in the following code block:

```
<%@ Page Language="C#" Culture="auto" meta:resourcekey="PageResource1"
    UICulture="auto" %>

<script runat="server">

</script>

<html xmlns="http://www.w3.org/1999/xhtml">
<head runat="server">
    <title>Sample Page</title>
</head>
<body>
    <form id="form1" runat="server">
    <div>
        <asp:Label ID="Label1" runat="server" Text="What is your name?"
         meta:resourcekey="Label1Resource1"></asp:Label><br />
        <asp:TextBox ID="TextBox1" runat="server"
         meta:resourcekey="TextBox1Resource1"></asp:TextBox> 
        <asp:Button ID="Button1"
         runat="server" Text="Submit Name"
         meta:resourcekey="Button1Resource1" /><br />
        <br />
        <asp:Label ID="Label2" runat="server"
```

```
            meta:resourcekey="Label2Resource1"></asp:Label>
        </div>
        </form>
    </body>
    </html>
```

From this bit of code, you can see that the `Culture` and `UICulture` attributes have been added to the `@Page` directive with a value of `auto`, thus enabling this application to be localized. In addition, the attribute `meta:resourcekey` has been added to each of the controls, along with an associated value. This is the key from the `.resx` file that was created on your behalf. Double-clicking on the `Default.aspx.resx` file opens the resource file in the Resource Editor, shown in Figure 5-13, built into Visual Studio.

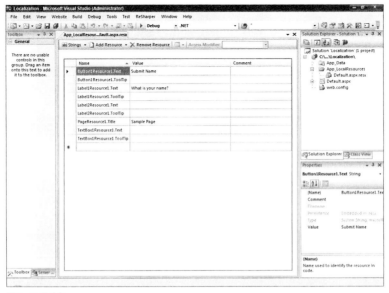

Figure 5-13

Note that a few properties from each of the server controls have been defined in the resource file. For instance, the `Button` server control has its `Text` and `ToolTip` properties exposed in this resource file, and the Visual Studio localization tool has pulled the default `Text` property value from the control based on what you placed there. Looking more closely at the `Button` server control constructions in this file, you can see that both the `Text` and `ToolTip` properties have a defining `Button1Resource1` value preceding the property name. This is the key that is used in the `Button` server control shown earlier.

```
<asp:Button ID="Button1"
 runat="server" Text="Submit Name"
 meta:resourcekey="Button1Resource1" />
```

Here, a `meta:resourcekey` attribute has been added; and in this case it references `Button1Resource1`. All the properties using this key in the resource file (for example, the `Text` and `ToolTip` properties) are applied to this `Button` server control at runtime.

Adding Another Language Resource File

Now that the `Default.aspx.resx` file is in place, this is a file for an invariant culture. No culture is assigned to this resource file. If no culture can be determined, then this is the resource file that is utilized. To add another resource file for the `Default.aspx` page that handles another language altogether, copy and paste the `Default.aspx.resx` file into the same `App_LocalResources` folder and rename the newly copied file. If you use `Default.aspx.fi-FI.resx`, give the following keys the values shown to make a Finnish-language resource file:

```
Button1Resource1.Text    Lähetä Nimi
Label1Resource1.Text     Mikä sinun nimi on?
PageResource1.Title      Näytesivu
```

You want to create a custom resource in both resource files using the key `Label2Answer`. The `Default.aspx.resx` file should have the following new key:

```
Label2Answer             Hello
```

Now you can add the key `Label2Answer` to the `Default.aspx.fi-FI.resx` file as shown here:

```
Label2Answer             Hei
```

You now have resources for specific controls, and a resource that you can access later programmatically.

Finalizing the Building of the Default.aspx Page

Finalizing the `Default.aspx` page, you want to add a `Button1_Click` event so that when the end user enters a name into the text box and clicks the Submit button, the `Label2` server control provides a greeting pulled from the local resource files. When all is said and done, you should have a `Default.aspx` page that looks like this:

```
<%@ Page Language="VB" Culture="auto" meta:resourcekey="PageResource1"
    UICulture="auto" %>

<script runat="server">
    Protected Sub Button1_Click(ByVal sender As Object, _
      ByVal e As System.EventArgs)

        Label2.Text = GetLocalResourceObject("Label2Answer").ToString() & _
           " " & TextBox1.Text
    End Sub
</script>

<html xmlns="http://www.w3.org/1999/xhtml" >
<head runat="server">
    <title>Sample Page</title>
</head>
<body>
    <form id="form1" runat="server">
    <div>
        <asp:Label ID="Label1" runat="server" Text="What is your name?"
```

```
        meta:resourcekey="Label1Resource1"></asp:Label><br />
        <br />
        <asp:TextBox ID="TextBox1" runat="server"
        meta:resourcekey="TextBox1Resource1"></asp:TextBox> 
        <asp:Button ID="Button1"
        runat="server" Text="Submit Name"

        meta:resourcekey="Button1Resource1" OnClick="Button1_Click" /><br />

        <br />
        <asp:Label ID="Label2" runat="server"
        meta:resourcekey="Label2Resource1"></asp:Label>
    </div>
    </form>
</body>
</html>
```

In addition to pulling local resources using the `meta:resourcekey` attribute in the server controls on the page to access the exposed attributes, you can also access any property value contained in the local resource file by using the `GetLocalResourceObject`. When using `GetLocalResourceObject`, you simply use the name of the key as a parameter, as shown here:

```
GetLocalResourceObject("Label2Answer")
```

You could just as easily get at any of the controls' property values from the resource file programmatically using the same construct:

```
GetLocalResourceObject("Button1Resource1.Text")
```

With the code from the `Default.aspx` page in place and the resource files completed, you can run the page, entering a name in the text box and then clicking the button to get a response, as shown in Figure 5-14.

Figure 5-14

What happened behind the scenes that caused this page to be constructed in this manner? First, only two resource files — `Default.aspx.resx` and `Default.aspx.fi-FI.resx` — are available. The `Default.aspx.resx` resource file is the invariant culture resource file, whereas the `Default.aspx.fi-FI.resx` resource file is for a specific culture (fi-FI). Because I requested the `Default.aspx` page and my browser is set to en-US as my preferred culture, ASP.NET found the local resources for the `Default.aspx` page. From there, ASP.NET checked for an en-US-specific version of the Default.aspx page. Because there isn't a specific page for the en-US culture, ASP.NET checked for an EN-(neutral culture)-specific page. Not finding a page for the EN neutral culture, ASP.NET was then forced to use the invariant culture resource file of Default.aspx.resx, producing the page shown in Figure 5-14.

If you now set your IE language preference as fi-FI and rerun the Default.aspx page, you see a Finnish version of the page (see Figure 5-15).

Figure 5-15

In this case, having set my IE language preference to fi-FI, I am presented with this culture's page instead of the invariant culture page presented earlier. ASP.NET found this specific culture through use of the Default.aspx.fi-FI.resx resource file.

You can see that all the control properties that were translated and placed within the resource file are utilized automatically by ASP.NET, including the page title presented in the title bar of IE.

Neutral Cultures Are Generally Preferred

When you are working with the resource files from this example, note that one of the resources is for a *specific culture*. The Default.aspx.fi-FI.resx file is for a specific culture — the Finnish language as spoken in Finland. Another option would be to make this file work not for a specific culture, but instead for a neutral culture. To do so, simply name the file Default.aspx.FI.resx. In this example, it doesn't make any difference because no other countries speak Finnish. It would make sense for languages such as German, Spanish, or French, which are spoken in multiple countries.

For instance, if you are going to have a Spanish version of the Default.aspx page, you could definitely build it for a specific culture, such as Default.aspx.es-MX.resx. This construction is for the Spanish language as spoken in Mexico. With this in place, if someone requests the Default.aspx page with the language setting of es-MX, that user is provided with the contents of this resource file. If the requester has a setting of es-ES, he or she will not get the Default.aspx.es-MX.resx resource file, but the invariant culture resource file of Default.aspx.resx. If you are going to make only a single translation for your site or any of your pages, construct the resource files to be for neutral cultures, not specific cultures.

If you have the resource file Default.aspx.ES.resx, then it won't matter if the end user's preferred setting is set to es-MX, es-ES, or even es-AR — that user gets the appropriate ES neutral-culture version of the page.

Making Use of Global Resources

Besides using only local resources that specifically deal with a particular page in your ASP.NET application, you also have the option to create *global* resources that can be used across multiple pages. To create a resource file that can be utilized across the entire application, right-click on the solution in the Solution Explorer of Visual Studio and select Add New Item. From the Add New Item dialog, select Resource file.

Selecting this option provides you with a Resource.resx file. Visual Studio places this file in a new folder called App_GlobalResources. Again, this first file is the invariant culture resource file. Add a single string resource, giving it the key of PrivacyStatement and a value of some kind (a long string).

After you have the invariant culture resource file completed, the next step is to add another resource file, but this time name it Resource.fi-FI.resx. Again, for this resource file, use a string key of PrivacyStatement and a different value altogether from the one you used in the other resource file.

The point of a global resource file is to have access to these resources across the entire application. You can access the values that you place in these files in several ways. One way is to work the value directly into any of your server control declarations. For instance, you can place the following privacy statement in a Label server control as shown here:

```
<asp:Label ID="Label1" runat="server"
 Text='<%$ Resources: Resource, PrivacyStatement %>'></asp:Label>
```

With this construction in place, you can now grab the appropriate value of the PrivacyStatement global resource, depending on the language preference of the end user requesting the page. To make this work, you use the keyword Resources followed by a colon. Next, you specify the name of the resource file. In this case, the name of the resource file is Resource, because this statement goes to the Resource.resx and Resource.fi-FI.resx files in order to find what it needs. After specifying the particular resource file to use, the next item in the statement is the key — in this case, PrivacyStatement.

Another way to achieve the same result is to use some built-in dialogs within Visual Studio. Highlight the server control you want in Visual Studio from Design view so that the control appears within the Properties window. For my example, I highlighted a Label server control. From the Properties window, click the button within the Expressions property. This launches the Expressions dialog, where you can bind the PrivacyStatement value to the Text property of the control (see Figure 5-16).

To make this work, highlight the Text property in the Bindable properties list. Then select an expression type from the drop-down list on the right-hand side of the dialog. Your options include AppSettings, ConnectionStrings, and Resources. Select Resources and you are then asked for the ClassKey and ResourceKey property values. The ClassKey is the name of the file that should be utilized. In this example, the name of the file is Resource.resx, so use the Resources keyword as a value. You are provided with a drop-down list in the ResourceKey property section, with all the keys available in this file. Because only a single key exists at this point, only the PrivacyStatement key appears in this list. Make this selection and click OK. The Label server control changes and now appears as it was presented earlier in the two-line code block.

One nice feature is that the resources provided via global resources are available in a strongly typed manner. For instance, you can programmatically get at a global resource value by using the construction presented in the following example:

```
Label1.Text = Resources.Resource.PrivacyStatement.ToString()
```

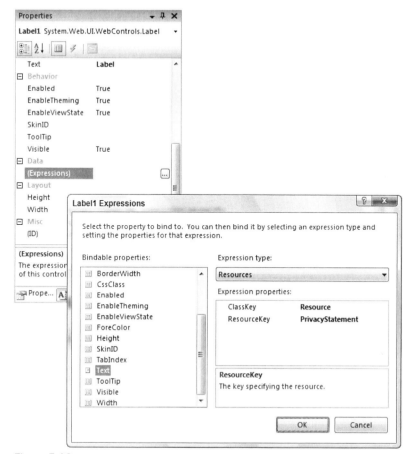

Figure 5-16

Figure 5-17 shows that you have full IntelliSense for these resource values.

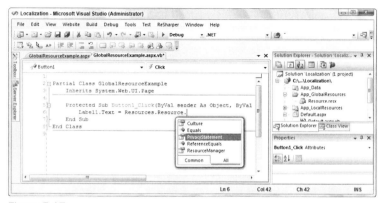

Figure 5-17

Resource Files in Windows Forms

Just as with ASP.NET, you can also work with resource files (.resx) right from Visual Studio. To see how to localize a Windows Forms application, create a new form in your Localization project called UsingResx.vb.

Like the ASP.NET form described earlier in this chapter (and identified as "ASP.NET page code block"), this Windows Form dialog contains a couple of Label controls, a Button, and a TextBox control. Ultimately, your form should look like the one shown in Figure 5-18.

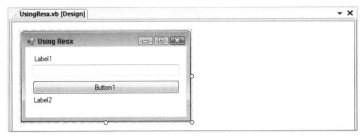

Figure 5-18

Note that the controls were just laid out on the form and no text was added yet. Before you get started, let's turn on localization features for the form. You can also do this to a form that is already completed if you are later converting a form to deal with more than one language.

Highlighting the form in the designer, change the Localizable property to True. This enables you to apply more than one language to a form and have the elements for a particular culture stored in a resource file. After you have set the Localizable property to True, you can then provide values to the Label and the Button controls on the form. The properties that you assign to the controls are done under the (Default) language setting. You will find this setting within the Language property of the form, as shown in Figure 5-19.

Figure 5-19

Setting the text values to the (Default) property setting means that if a culture is undetermined or a resource file is not available for this culture, then the default one will be utilized. From there, change the Language property of the form to Finnish. You can then change the values of the three controls as follows:

```
Button1.Text    Lähetä Nimi
Label1.Text     Mikä sinun nimi on?
Label2.Text     Hei
```

Double-clicking on the form's button will enable you to create a Button1_Click event. The code for this page is as follows:

```
Imports System.Globalization
Imports System.Threading

Public Class UsingResx

    Sub New()

        Thread.CurrentThread.CurrentCulture = New CultureInfo("en-US")
        Thread.CurrentThread.CurrentUICulture = New CultureInfo("en-US")

        ' This call is required by the Windows Form Designer.
        InitializeComponent()

    End Sub

    Private Sub Button1_Click(ByVal sender As System.Object, _
      ByVal e As System.EventArgs) Handles Button1.Click

        Label2.Visible = True
        Label2.Text += TextBox1.Text
    End Sub
End Class
```

This assigns the CurrentCulture and the CurrentUICulture properties to en-US; the form it produces is shown in Figure 5-20.

Figure 5-20

Now change the code so that it works with a Finnish culture setting:

```
Imports System.Globalization
Imports System.Threading

Public Class UsingResx

    Sub New()
```

243

```
        Thread.CurrentThread.CurrentCulture = New CultureInfo("fi-FI")
        Thread.CurrentThread.CurrentUICulture = New CultureInfo("fi-FI")


        ' This call is required by the Windows Form Designer.
        InitializeComponent()

    End Sub

    Private Sub Button1_Click(ByVal sender As System.Object, _
      ByVal e As System.EventArgs) Handles Button1.Click

        Label2.Visible = True
        Label2.Text += TextBox1.Text
    End Sub
End Class
```

Running the form with this change in place now produces the window shown in Figure 5-21.

Figure 5-21

So where are all the translations stored? Just like ASP.NET, they are stored in the resource file for this form. Looking in the Solution Explorer, you will now find a `UsingResx.resx` file and a `UsingResx .fi.resx` file, as shown in Figure 5-22.

Figure 5-22

Opening the `UsingResx.resx` file will cause Visual Studio to open the file in a manner that enables you to directly edit the values it stores. The default resource file stores some type references as well as other properties of the controls on the form, as shown in Figure 5-23.

Opening the `UsingResx.fi.resx` file instead shows only the three different properties that you changed. The rest of the properties are read from the default resource file. The contents of the Finnish resource file are presented in Figure 5-24.

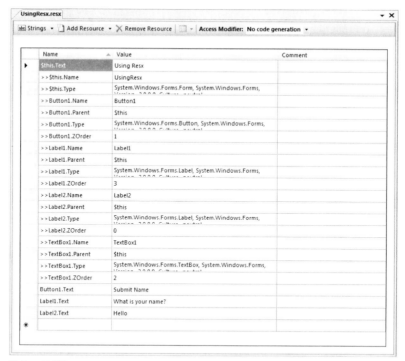

Figure 5-23

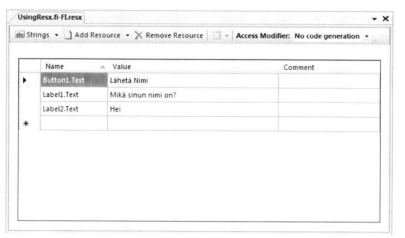

Figure 5-24

Visual Studio 2008 provides an editor for working with resource files. You have already seen some of the views available from the Resource Editor. Resources are categorized visually according to the data type of the resource. This chapter has covered only the handling of strings, but other categories exist (such as images, icons, audio files, miscellaneous files, and other items). These options are shown in Figure 5-25.

Figure 5-25

Summary

It is hoped that you see the value in localizing your .NET applications so that they can handle multiple cultures. This chapter described some of the issues you face when localizing your applications, and described some of the built-in tools provided via both Visual Studio and the .NET Framework to make this process easier for you.

6

Generics

One of the things developers often need to do is create new types for their programs. Early attempts at type creation led to user-defined types, or the use of the VB `Structure` statement. Another approach is to use classes and objects to create new types. Ever since the release of the .NET Framework 2.0, another approach is to use generics.

Generics refers to the technology built into the .NET Framework 3.5 (and the .NET Framework versions 2.0 and 3.0) that enables you to define a code template and then declare variables using that template. The template defines the operations that the new type can perform; and when you declare a variable based on the template, you are creating a new type. The benefit of generics over structures or objects is that a generic template makes it easier for your new types to be strongly typed. Generics also make it easier to reuse the template code in different scenarios.

The primary motivation for adding generics to .NET was to enable the creation of strongly typed collection types. Because generic collection types are strongly typed, they are significantly faster than the previous inheritance-based collection model. Anywhere you presently use collection classes in your code, you should consider revising that code to use generic collection types instead.

Visual Basic 2008 allows not only the use of preexisting generics, but also the creation of your own generic templates. Because the technology to support generics was created primarily to build collection classes, it naturally follows that you might create a generic collection anytime you would otherwise build a normal collection class. More specifically, anytime you find yourself using the `Object` data type, you should instead consider using generics.

This chapter begins with a brief discussion of the use of generics, followed by a walk-through of the syntax for defining your own generic templates.

Using Generics

There are many examples of generic templates in the .NET 3.5 Base Class Library (BCL). Many of them can be found in the `System.Collections.Generic` namespace, but others are scattered through the BCL as appropriate. Many of the examples focus on generic collection types, but this is only because it is here that the performance gains due to generics are most notable. In other cases, generics are used less for performance gains than for the strong typing benefits they provide. As noted earlier, anytime you use a collection data type, you should consider using the generic equivalent instead.

A generic is often written as something like List(Of T). The type (or class) name in this case is List. The letter T is a placeholder, much like a parameter. It indicates where you must provide a specific type value to customize the generic. For instance, you might declare a variable using the List(Of T) generic:

```
Dim data As New List(Of Date)
```

In this case, you are specifying that the type parameter, T, is a Date. By providing this type, you are specifying that the list will only contain values of type Date. To make this clearer, let's contrast the new List(Of T) collection with the older ArrayList type.

When you work with an ArrayList, you are working with a type of collection that can store many types of values at the same time:

```
Dim data As New ArrayList()
data.Add("Hello")
data.Add(5)
data.Add(New Customer())
```

This ArrayList is loosely typed, internally always storing the values as type Object. This is very flexible, but relatively slow because it is late bound. Of course, it offers the advantage of being able to store any data type, with the disadvantage that you have no control over what is actually stored in the collection.

The List(Of T) generic collection is quite different. It is not a type at all; it is just a template. A type is not created until you declare a variable using the template:

```
Dim data As New Generic.List(Of Integer)
data.Add(5)
data.Add(New Customer()) ' throws an exception
data.Add("Hello") ' throws an exception
```

When you declare a variable using the generic, you must provide the type of value that the new collection will hold. The result is that a new type is created — in this case, a collection that can only hold Integer values.

The important thing here is that this new collection type is strongly typed for Integer values. Not only does its external interface (its Item and Add methods, for instance) require Integer values, but its internal storage mechanism only works with type Integer. This means that it is not late bound like ArrayList, but rather is early bound. The net result is much higher performance, along with all the type-safety benefits of being strongly typed.

Generics are useful because they typically offer a higher performance option compared to traditional classes. In some cases, they can also save you from writing code, as generic templates can provide code reuse where traditional classes cannot. Finally, generics can sometimes provide better type safety compared to traditional classes, as a generic adapts to the specific type you require, whereas classes often must resort to working with a more general type such as Object.

Generics come in two forms: generic types and generic methods. For instance, List(Of T) is a generic type in that it is a template that defines a complete type or class. In contrast, some otherwise normal classes have single methods that are just method templates and that assume a specific type when they are called. We will look at both scenarios.

Generic Types

Now that you have a basic understanding of generics and how they compare to regular types, let's get into some more detail. To do this, you will make use of some other generic types provided in the .NET Framework. A generic type is a template that defines a complete class, structure, or interface. When you want to use such a generic, you declare a variable using the generic type, providing the real type (or types) to be used in creating the actual type of your variable.

Basic Usage

To begin, create a new Windows Application project named "Generics." On Form1 add a Button control (named btnDictionary) and a TextBox control (named txtDisplay). Set the TextBox control's Multiline property to True and anchor it to take up most of the form. You can also set the text of the button to Dictionary. The result should look something like what is shown in Figure 6-1.

Figure 6-1

First, consider the Dictionary(Of K, T) generic. This is much like the List(Of T) discussed earlier, but this generic requires that you define the types of both the key data and the values to be stored. When you declare a variable as Dictionary(Of K, T), the new Dictionary type that is created only accepts keys of the one type and values of the other.

Add the following code in the click event handler for btnDictionary:

```
Public Class Form1

    Private Sub btnDictionary_Click(ByVal sender As System.Object, _
      ByVal e As System.EventArgs) Handles btnDictionary.Click

        txtDisplay.Clear()
```

```
        Dim data As New Generic.Dictionary(Of Integer, String)
        data.Add(5, "Bill")
        data.Add(15, "George")

        For Each item As KeyValuePair(Of Integer, String) In data
            txtDisplay.AppendText("Data: " & item.Key & ", " & item.Value)
            txtDisplay.AppendText(Environment.NewLine)
        Next

        txtDisplay.AppendText(Environment.NewLine)
    End Sub

End Class
```

As you type, watch the IntelliSense information on the Add method. Notice how the key and value parameters are strongly typed based on the specific types provided in the declaration of the data variable. In the same code, you can create another type of Dictionary:

```
Public Class Form1

    Private Sub btnDictionary_Click(ByVal sender As System.Object, _
      ByVal e As System.EventArgs) Handles btnDictionary.Click

        txtDisplay.Clear()

        Dim data As New Generic.Dictionary(Of Integer, String)
        Dim info As New Generic.Dictionary(Of Guid, Date)

        data.Add(5, "Bill")
        data.Add(15, "George")

        For Each item As KeyValuePair(Of Integer, String) In data
            txtDisplay.AppendText("Data: " & item.Key & ", " & item.Value)
            txtDisplay.AppendText(Environment.NewLine)
        Next

        txtDisplay.AppendText(Environment.NewLine)

        info.Add(Guid.NewGuid, Now)

        For Each item As KeyValuePair(Of Guid, Date) In info
            txtDisplay.AppendText("Info: " & item.Key.ToString & _
                ", " & item.Value)
            txtDisplay.AppendText(Environment.NewLine)
        Next

        txtDisplay.AppendText(Environment.NewLine)
    End Sub

End Class
```

This code contains two completely different types. Both have the behaviors of a Dictionary, but they are not interchangeable because they have been created as different types.

Generic types may also be used as parameters and return types. For instance, add the following method to Form1:

```
Private Function LoadData() As Generic.Dictionary(Of Integer, String)
    Dim data As New Generic.Dictionary(Of Integer, String)
    data.Add(5, "Bill")
    data.Add(15, "George")

    Return data
End Function
```

To call this method from the btnDictionary_Click method, add this code:

```
Private Sub btnDictionary_Click(ByVal sender As System.Object, _
    ByVal e As System.EventArgs) Handles btnDictionary.Click

    txtDisplay.Clear()

    Dim data As New Generic.Dictionary(Of Integer, String)
    Dim info As New Generic.Dictionary(Of Guid, Date)

    data.Add(5, "Bill")
    data.Add(15, "George")

    For Each item As KeyValuePair(Of Integer, String) In data
        txtDisplay.AppendText("Data: " & item.Key & ", " & item.Value)
        txtDisplay.AppendText(Environment.NewLine)
    Next

    txtDisplay.AppendText(Environment.NewLine)

    info.Add(Guid.NewGuid, Now)

    For Each item As KeyValuePair(Of Guid, Date) In info
        txtDisplay.AppendText("Info: " & item.Key.ToString & _
            ", " & item.Value)
        txtDisplay.AppendText(Environment.NewLine)
    Next

    txtDisplay.AppendText(Environment.NewLine)

    Dim results As Generic.Dictionary(Of Integer, String)
    results = LoadData()

    For Each item As KeyValuePair(Of Integer, String) In results
        txtDisplay.AppendText("Results: " & item.Key & ", " & item.Value)
        txtDisplay.AppendText(Environment.NewLine)
    Next

    txtDisplay.AppendText(Environment.NewLine)
End Sub
```

The results of running this code are shown in Figure 6-2.

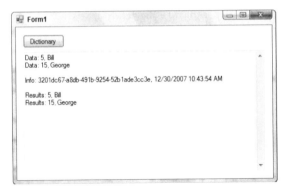

Figure 6-2

This works because both the return type of the function and the type of the data variable are exactly the same. Not only are they both `Generic.Dictionary` derivatives, they have exactly the same types in the declaration.

The same is true for parameters:

```
Private Sub DoWork(ByVal values As Generic.Dictionary(Of Integer, String))
   ' do work here
End Sub
```

Again, the parameter type is not only defined by the generic type, but also by the specific type values used to initialize the generic template.

Inheritance

It is possible to inherit from a generic type as you define a new class. For instance, the .NET BCL defines the `System.ComponentModel.BindingList(Of T)` generic type. This type is used to create collections that can support data binding. You can use this as a base class to create your own strongly typed, data-bindable collection. Add new classes named `Customer` and `CustomerList` to the project with the following code:

```
Public Class Customer
   Private mName As String

   Public Property Name() As String
     Get
       Return mName
     End Get
     Set(ByVal value As String)
       mName = value
     End Set
   End Property

End Class
```

```
Public Class CustomerList
  Inherits System.ComponentModel.BindingList(Of Customer)

  Private Sub CustomerList_AddingNew(ByVal sender As Object, _
    ByVal e As System.ComponentModel.AddingNewEventArgs) Handles Me.AddingNew

    Dim cust As New Customer()
    cust.Name = "<new>"
    e.NewObject = cust

  End Sub
End Class
```

When you inherit from `BindingList(Of T)`, you must provide a specific type — in this case, `Customer`. This means that your new `CustomerList` class extends and can customize `BindingList(Of Customer)`. Here you are providing a default value for the `Name` property of any new `Customer` object added to the collection.

When you inherit from a generic type, you can employ all the normal concepts of inheritance, including overloading and overriding methods, extending the class by adding new methods, handling events, and so forth.

To see this in action, add a new `Button` control named `btnCustomer` to `Form1` and add a new form named `CustomerForm` to the project. Add a `DataGridView` control to `CustomerForm` and dock it by selecting the Fill in the parent container option.

Behind the `btnCustomer` handler, add the following code:

```
CustomerForm.ShowDialog()
```

Then add the following code behind `CustomerForm`:

```
Dim list As New CustomerList()

Private Sub CustomerForm_Load(ByVal sender As Object, _
  ByVal e As System.EventArgs) Handles Me.Load

  DataGridView1.DataSource = list

End Sub
```

This code creates an instance of `CustomerList` and makes it the `DataSource` for the `DataGridView` control. When you run the program and click the button to open the `CustomerForm`, notice that the grid contains a newly added `Customer` object. As you interact with the grid, new `Customer` objects are automatically added, with a default name of <new>. An example is shown in Figure 6-3.

All this functionality of adding new objects and setting the default `Name` value occurs because `CustomerList` inherits from `BindingList(Of Customer)`.

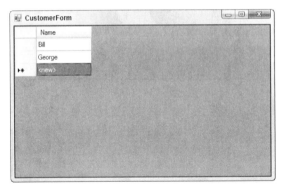

Figure 6-3

Generic Methods

A generic method is a single method that is called not only with conventional parameters, but also with type information that defines the method. Generic methods are far less common than generic types. Due to the extra syntax required to call a generic method, they are also less readable than a normal method.

A generic method may exist in any class or module; it does not need to be contained within a generic type. The primary benefit of a generic method is avoiding the use of CType or DirectCast to convert parameters or return values between different types.

It is important to realize that the type conversion still occurs; generics merely provide an alternative mechanism to use instead of CType or DirectCast.

Without generics, code often uses the Object type. Add the following method to Form1:

```
Public Function AreEqual(ByVal a As Object, ByVal b As Object) As Boolean
    Return a.Equals(b)
End Function
```

The problem with this code is that a and b could be anything. There is no restriction here, nothing to ensure that they are even the same type. An alternative is to use generics. Add the following method to Form1:

```
Public Function AreEqual(Of T)(ByVal a As T, ByVal b As T) As Boolean
    Return a.Equals(b)
End Function
```

Now a and b are forced to be the same type, and that type is specified when the method is invoked.

Add a new Button named btnEqual to Form1 with the following code in its click event:

```
Dim result As Boolean

' use normal method
result = AreEqual(1, 2)
result = AreEqual("one", "two")
```

```
result = AreEqual(1, "two")

' use generic method
result = AreEqual(Of Integer)(1, 2)
result = AreEqual(Of String)("one", "two")
'result = AreEqual(Of Integer)(1, "two")
```

However, why not just declare the method as a `Boolean`? This code will probably cause some confusion. The first three method calls are invoking the normal `AreEqual` method. Notice that there is no problem asking the method to compare an `Integer` and a `String`.

The second set of calls looks very odd. At first glance, they look like nonsense to many people. This is because invoking a generic method means providing two sets of parameters to the method, rather than the normal one set of parameters.

The first set of parameters defines the type or types required to define the method. This is much like the list of types you must provide when declaring a variable using a generic class. In this case, you're specifying that the `AreEqual` method will be operating on parameters of type `Integer`.

The second set of parameters are the conventional parameters that you'd normally supply to a method. What is special in this case is that the types of the parameters are being defined by the first set of parameters. In other words, in the first call, the type is specified to be `Integer`, so 1 and 2 are valid parameters. In the second call, the type is `String`, so `"one"` and `"two"` are valid. Notice that the third line is commented out. This is because 1 and `"two"` aren't the same type, so the compiler won't compile that line of code.

Creating Generics

Now that you have a good idea how to use preexisting generics in your code, let's take a look at how you can create generic templates. The primary reason to create a generic template instead of a class is to gain strong typing of your variables. Anytime you find yourself using the `Object` data type, or a base class from which multiple types inherit, you may want to consider using generics. By using generics, you can avoid the use of `CType` or `DirectCast`, thereby simplifying your code. If you can avoid using the `Object` data type, you will typically improve the performance of your code.

As discussed earlier, there are generic types and generic methods. A generic type is basically a class or structure that assumes specific type characteristics when a variable is declared using the generic. A generic method is a single method that assumes specific type characteristics, even though the method might be in an otherwise very conventional class, structure, or module.

Generic Types

Recall that a generic type is a class, structure, or interface template. You can create such templates yourself to provide better performance, strong typing, and code reuse to the consumers of your types.

Classes

A generic class template is created in the same way that you create a normal class, with the exception that you require the consumer of your class to provide you with one or more types for use in your code. In other words, as the author of a generic template, you have access to the type parameters provided by the user of your generic.

For example, add a new class to the project named `SingleLinkedList`:

```
Public Class SingleLinkedList(Of T)

End Class
```

In the declaration of the type, you specify the type parameters that will be required:

```
Public Class SingleLinkedList(Of T)
```

In this case, you are requiring just one type parameter. The name, T, can be any valid variable name. In other words, you could declare the type like this:

```
Public Class SingleLinkedList(Of ValueType)
```

Make this change to the code in your project.

By convention (carried over from C++ templates), the variable names for type parameters are single uppercase letters. This is somewhat cryptic, and you may want to use a more descriptive convention for variable naming.

Whether you use the cryptic standard convention or more readable parameter names, the parameter is defined on the class definition. Within the class itself, you then use the type parameter anywhere that you would normally use a type (such as String or Integer).

To create a linked list, you need to define a Node class. This will be a nested class:

```
Public Class SingleLinkedList(Of ValueType)

#Region " Node class "

  Private Class Node
     Private mValue As ValueType
     Private mNext As Node

     Public ReadOnly Property Value() As ValueType
       Get
          Return mValue
       End Get
     End Property

     Public Property NextNode() As Node
       Get
          Return mNext
       End Get
       Set(ByVal value As Node)
          mNext = value
       End Set
     End Property

     Public Sub New(ByVal value As ValueType, ByVal nextNode As Node)
       mValue = value
```

```
        mNext = nextNode
      End Sub
    End Class

  #End Region
  End Class
```

Notice how the `mValue` variable is declared as `ValueType`. This means that the actual type of `mValue` depends on the type supplied when an instance of `SingleLinkedList` is created.

Because `ValueType` is a type parameter on the class, you can use `ValueType` as a type anywhere in the code. As you write the class, you cannot tell what type `ValueType` will be. That information is provided by the user of your generic class. Later, when someone declares a variable using your generic type, that person will specify the type, like this:

```
Dim list As New SingleLinkedList(Of Double)
```

At this point, a specific instance of your generic class is created, and all cases of `ValueType` within your code are replaced by the VB compiler with `Double`. Essentially, this means that for this specific instance of `SingleLinkedList`, the `mValue` declaration ends up as follows:

```
    Private mValue As Double
```

Of course, you never get to see this code, as it is dynamically generated by the .NET Framework's JIT compiler at runtime based on your generic template code.

The same is true for methods within the template. Your example contains a constructor method, which accepts a parameter of type `ValueType`. Remember that `ValueType` will be replaced by a specific type when a variable is declared using your generic.

So, what type is `ValueType` when you are writing the template itself? Because it can conceivably be any type when the template is used, `ValueType` is treated like the `Object` type as you create the generic template. This severely restricts what you can do with variables or parameters of `ValueType` within your generic code.

The `mValue` variable is of `ValueType`, which means it is basically of type `Object` for the purposes of your template code. Therefore, you can do assignments (as you do in the constructor code), and you can call any methods that are on the `System.Object` type:

- ❏   `Equals()`
- ❏   `GetHashCode()`
- ❏   `GetType()`
- ❏   `ReferenceEquals()`
- ❏   `ToString()`

No operations beyond these basics are available by default. Later in the chapter, you will learn about the concept of *constraints*, which enables you to restrict the types that can be specified for a type parameter.

Constraints have the added benefit that they expand the operations you can perform on variables or parameters defined based on the type parameter.

However, this capability is enough to complete the `SingleLinkedList` class. Add the following code to the class after the `End Class` from the `Node` class:

```
Private mHead As Node

Default Public ReadOnly Property Item(ByVal index As Integer) As ValueType
  Get
    Dim current As Node = mHead

    For index = 1 To index
      current = current.NextNode
      If current Is Nothing Then
        Throw New Exception("Item not found in list")
      End If
    Next

    Return current.Value
  End Get
End Property

Public Sub Add(ByVal value As ValueType)
  mHead = New Node(value, mHead)
End Sub

Public Sub Remove(ByVal value As ValueType)

  Dim current As Node = mHead
  Dim previous As Node = Nothing

  While current IsNot Nothing
    If current.Value.Equals(value) Then
      If previous Is Nothing Then
        ' this was the head of the list
        mHead = current.NextNode
      Else
        previous.NextNode = current.NextNode
      End If
      Exit Sub
    End If
    previous = current
    current = current.NextNode
  End While

  ' You got to the end without finding the item.
  Throw New Exception("Item not found in list")

End Sub
```

```
Public ReadOnly Property Count() As Integer
  Get
    Dim result As Integer = 0
    Dim current As Node = mHead

    While current IsNot Nothing
      result += 1
      current = current.NextNode
    End While

    Return result
  End Get
End Property
```

Notice that the Item property and the Add and Remove methods all use ValueType as either return types or parameter types. More important, note the use of the Equals method in the Remove method:

```
If current.Value.Equals(value) Then
```

The reason why this compiles is that Equals is defined on System.Object and is therefore universally available. This code could not use the = operator because that is not universally available.

To try out the SingleLinkedList class, add a button to Form1 named btnList and add the following code to Form1:

```
Private Sub btnList_Click(ByVal sender As System.Object, _
  ByVal e As System.EventArgs) Handles btnList.Click

  Dim list As New SingleLinkedList(Of String)
  list.Add("Bill")
  list.Add("Tuija")
  list.Add("Sofia")
  list.Add("Henri")
  list.Add("Kalle")

  txtDisplay.Clear()
  txtDisplay.AppendText("Count: " & list.Count)
  txtDisplay.AppendText(Environment.NewLine)

  For index As Integer = 0 To list.Count - 1
    txtDisplay.AppendText("Item: " & list.Item(index))
    txtDisplay.AppendText(Environment.NewLine)
  Next

End Sub
```

When you run the code, you will see a display similar to Figure 6-4.

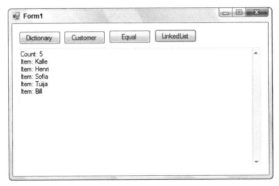

Figure 6-4

Other Generic Class Features

Earlier in the chapter, you used the `Dictionary` generic, which specifies multiple type parameters. To declare a class with multiple type parameters, you use syntax like the following:

```
Public Class MyCoolType(Of T, V)
  Private mValue As T
  Private mData As V

  Public Sub New(ByVal value As T, ByVal data As V)
    mValue = value
    mData = data
  End Sub
End Class
```

In addition, it is possible to use regular types in combination with type parameters, as shown here:

```
Public Class MyCoolType(Of T, V)
  Private mValue As T
  Private mData As V
  Private mActual As Double

  Public Sub New(ByVal value As T, ByVal data As V, ByVal actual As Double)
    mValue = value
    mData = data
    mActual = actual
  End Sub
End Class
```

Other than the fact that variables or parameters of types `T` or `V` must be treated as type `System.Object`, you can write virtually any code you choose. The code in a generic class is really no different from the code you'd write in a normal class.

This includes all the object-oriented capabilities of classes, including inheritance, overloading, overriding, events, methods, properties, and so forth. However, there are some limitations on overloading. In particular, when overloading methods with a type parameter, the compiler does not know what that specific type might be at runtime. Thus, you can only overload methods in ways in which the type parameter (which could be any type) does not lead to ambiguity.

For instance, adding these two methods to MyCoolType before the .NET Framework 3.5 would have resulted in a compiler error:

```
Public Sub DoWork(ByVal data As Integer)
   ' do work here
End Sub

Public Sub DoWork(ByVal data As V)
   ' do work here
End Sub
```

Now this is possible due to the support for implicitly typed variables. During compilation in .NET 3.5, the compiler figures out what the data type of V should be and makes the appropriate changes to compile V as what is utilized in your code. This was not the case prior to .NET 3.5. Before this version of the .NET Framework, this kind of code would have resulted in a compiler error. It wasn't legal because the compiler didn't know whether V would be an Integer at runtime. If V were to end up defined as an Integer, then you'd have two identical method signatures in the same class.

Classes and Inheritance

Not only can you create basic generic class templates, you can also combine the concept with inheritance. This can be as basic as having a generic template inherit from an existing class:

```
Public Class MyControls(Of T)
   Inherits Control

End Class
```

In this case, the MyControls generic class inherits from the Windows Forms Control class, thus gaining all the behaviors and interface elements of a Control.

Alternately, a conventional class can inherit from a generic template. Suppose that you have a simple generic template:

```
Public Class GenericBase(Of T)

End Class
```

It is quite practical to inherit from this generic class as you create other classes:

```
Public Class Subclass
   Inherits GenericBase(Of Integer)

End Class
```

Notice how the Inherits statement not only references GenericBase, but also provides a specific type for the type parameter of the generic type. Anytime you use a generic type, you must provide values for the type parameters, and this is no exception. This means that your new Subclass actually inherits from a specific instance of GenericBase, where T is of type Integer.

Finally, you can also have generic classes inherit from other generic classes. For instance, you can create a generic class that inherits from the GenericBase class:

```
Public Class GenericSubclass(Of T)
  Inherits GenericBase(Of Integer)

End Class
```

As with the previous example, this new class inherits from an instance of GenericBase, where T is of type Integer.

Things can get far more interesting. It turns out that you can use type parameters to specify the types for other type parameters. For instance, you could alter GenericSubclass like this:

```
Public Class GenericSubclass(Of V)
  Inherits GenericBase(Of V)

End Class
```

Notice that you're specifying that the type parameter for GenericBase is V — which is the type provided by the caller when it declares a variable using GenericSubclass. Therefore, if a caller does

```
Dim obj As GenericSubclass(Of String)
```

then V is of type String, meaning that GenericSubclass is inheriting from an instance of GenericBase, where its T parameter is also of type String. The type flows through from the subclass into the base class. If that is not complex enough, consider the following class definition:

```
Public Class GenericSubclass(Of V)
  Inherits GenericBase(Of GenericSubclass(Of V))

End Class
```

In this case, the GenericSubclass is inheriting from GenericBase, where the T type in GenericBase is actually a specific instance of the GenericSubclass type. A caller can create such an instance as follows:

```
Dim obj As GenericSubclass(Of Date)
```

In this case, the GenericSubclass type has a V of type Date. It also inherits from GenericBase, which has a T of type GenericSubclass(Of Date).

Such complex relationships are typically not useful, but it is important to recognize how types flow through generic templates, especially when inheritance is involved.

Structures

You can also define generic Structure types. Structures are discussed in Chapter 1. The basic rules and concepts are the same as for defining generic classes, as shown here:

```
Public Structure MyCoolStructure(Of T)
   Public Value As T
End Structure
```

As with generic classes, the type parameter or parameters represent real types that are provided by the user of the Structure in actual code. Thus, anywhere you see a T in the structure; it will be replaced by a real type such as String or Integer.

Code can use the structure in a manner similar to how a generic class is used:

```
Dim data As MyCoolStructure(Of Guid)
```

When the variable is declared, an instance of the Structure is created based on the type parameter provided. In this example, an instance of MyCoolStructure that holds Guid objects has been created.

Interfaces

Finally, you can define generic interface types. Generic interfaces are a bit different from generic classes or structures because they are implemented by other types when they are used. You can create a generic interface using the same syntax used for classes and structures:

```
Public Interface ICoolInterface(Of T)
   Sub DoWork(ByVal data As T)
   Function GetAnswer() As T
End Interface
```

Then the interface can be used within another type. For instance, you might implement the interface in a class:

```
Public Class ARegularClass
   Implements ICoolInterface(Of String)

   Public Sub DoWork(ByVal data As String) _
    Implements ICoolInterface(Of String).DoWork

   End Sub

   Public Function GetAnswer() As String _
    Implements ICoolInterface(Of String).GetAnswer

   End Function

End Class
```

Notice that you provide a real type for the type parameter in the Implements statement and Implements clauses on each method. In each case, you are specifying a specific instance of the ICoolInterface interface — one that deals with the String data type.

As with classes and structures, an interface can be declared with multiple type parameters. Those type parameter values can be used in place of any normal type (such as String or Date) in any Sub, Function, Property, or Event declaration.

Generic Methods

You have already seen examples of methods declared using type parameters such as T or V. While these are examples of generic methods, they have been contained within a broader generic type such as a class, structure, or interface.

It is also possible to create generic methods within otherwise normal classes, structures, interfaces, or modules. In this case, the type parameter is not specified on the class, structure, or interface, but rather is specified directly on the method itself.

For instance, you can declare a generic method to compare equality like this:

```
Public Module Comparisons

  Public Function AreEqual(Of T)(ByVal a As T, ByVal b As T) As Boolean
    Return a.Equals(b)
  End Function

End Module
```

In this case, the AreEqual method is contained within a module, though it could just as easily be contained in a class or structure. Notice that the method accepts two sets of parameters. The first set of parameters is the type parameter — in this example, just T. The second set of parameters consists of the normal parameters that a method would accept. In this example, the normal parameters have their types defined by the type parameter, T.

As with generic classes, it is important to remember that the type parameter is treated as a System.Object type as you write the code in your generic method. This severely restricts what you can do with parameters or variables declared using the type parameters. Specifically, you can perform assignment and call the various methods common to all System.Object variables.

In a moment you will look at constraints, which enable you to restrict the types that can be assigned to the type parameters and expand the operations that can be performed on parameters and variables of those types.

As with generic types, a generic method can accept multiple type parameters:

```
Public Class Comparisons

  Public Function AreEqual(Of T, R)(ByVal a As Integer, ByVal b As T) As R
    ' implement code here
  End Function

End Class
```

In this example, the method is contained within a class, rather than a module. Notice that it accepts two type parameters, T and R. The return type is set to type R, whereas the second parameter is of type T. Also, look at the first parameter, which is a conventional type. This illustrates how you can mix conventional types and generic type parameters in the method parameter list and return types, and by extension within the body of the method code.

Constraints

At this point, you have learned how to create and use generic types and methods, but there have been serious limitations on what you can do when creating generic type or method templates thus far. This is because the compiler treats any type parameters as the type System.Object within your template code. The result is that you can assign the values and call the various methods common to all System.Object instances, but you can do nothing else. In many cases, this is too restrictive to be useful.

Constraints offer a solution and at the same time provide a control mechanism. Constraints enable you to specify rules about the types that can be used at runtime to replace a type parameter. Using constraints, you can ensure that a type parameter is a Class or a Structure, or that it implements a certain interface or inherits from a certain base class.

Not only do constraints enable you to restrict the types available for use, but they also give the VB compiler valuable information. For example, if the compiler knows that a type parameter must always implement a given interface, then the compiler will allow you to call the methods on that interface within your template code.

Type Constraints

The most common type of constraint is a *type constraint*. A type constraint restricts a type parameter to be a subclass of a specific class or to implement a specific interface. This idea can be used to enhance the SingleLinkedList to sort items as they are added. First, change the declaration of the class itself to add the IComparable constraint:

```
Public Class SingleLinkedList(Of ValueType As IComparable)
```

With this change, ValueType is not only guaranteed to be equivalent to System.Object, it is also guaranteed to have all the methods defined on the IComparable interface.

This means that within the Add method you can make use of any methods in the IComparable interface (as well as those from System.Object). The result is that you can safely call the CompareTo method defined on the IComparable interface, because the compiler knows that any variable of type ValueType will implement IComparable:

```
Public Sub Add(ByVal value As ValueType)

  If mHead Is Nothing Then
    ' List was empty, just store the value.
    mHead = New Node(value, mHead)

  Else
    Dim current As Node = mHead
    Dim previous As Node = Nothing

    While current IsNot Nothing
      If current.Value.CompareTo(value) > 0 Then
        If previous Is Nothing Then
          ' this was the head of the list
          mHead = New Node(value, mHead)
        Else
          ' insert the node between previous and current
```

```
            previous.NextNode = New Node(value, current)
        End If
        Exit Sub
    End If
    previous = current
    current = current.NextNode
End While

' you're at the end of the list, so add to end
previous.NextNode = New Node(value, Nothing)
    End If
End Sub
```

Note the call to the CompareTo method:

```
If current.Value.CompareTo(value) > 0 Then
```

This is possible because of the IComparable constraint on ValueType. If you run the code now, the items should be displayed in sorted order, as shown in Figure 6-5.

Figure 6-5

Not only can you constrain a type parameter to implement an interface, but you can also constrain it to be a specific type (class) or subclass of that type. For example, you could implement a generic method that works on any Windows Forms control:

```
Public Shared Sub ChangeControl(Of C As Control)(ByVal control As C)

    control.Anchor = AnchorStyles.Top Or AnchorStyles.Left

End Sub
```

The type parameter, C, is constrained to be of type Control. This restricts calling code to only specify this parameter as Control or a subclass of Control such as TextBox.

Then the parameter to the method is specified to be of type C, which means that this method will work against any Control or subclass of Control. Because of the constraint, the compiler now knows that the variable will always be some type of `Control` object, so it allows you to use any methods, properties, or events exposed by the `Control` class as you write your code.

Finally, it is possible to constrain a type parameter to be of a specific generic type:

```
Public Class ListClass(Of T, V As Generic.List(Of T))

End Class
```

The preceding code specifies that the `V` type must be a `List(Of T)`, whatever type `T` might be. A caller can use your class like this:

```
Dim list As ListClass(Of Integer, Generic.List(Of Integer))
```

Earlier in the chapter, in the discussion of how inheritance and generics interact, you saw that things can get quite complex. The same is true when you constrain type parameters based on generic types.

Class and Structure Constraints

Another form of constraint enables you to be more general. Rather than enforce the requirement for a specific interface or class, you can specify that a type parameter must be either a reference type or a value type.

To specify that the type parameter must be a reference type, you use the `Class` constraint:

```
Public Class ReferenceOnly(Of T As Class)

End Class
```

This ensures that the type specified for `T` must be the type of an object. Any attempt to use a value type, such as `Integer` or `Structure`, results in a compiler error.

Likewise, you can specify that the type parameter must be a value type such as `Integer` or a `Structure` by using the `Structure` constraint:

```
Public Class ValueOnly(Of T As Structure)

End Class
```

In this case, the type specified for `T` must be a value type. Any attempt to use a reference type such as `String`, an interface, or a class results in a compiler error.

New Constraints

Sometimes you want to write generic code that creates instances of the type specified by a type parameter. In order to know that you can actually create instances of a type, you need to know that the type has a default public constructor. You can determine this using the `New` constraint:

```
Public Class Factories(Of T As New)

  Public Function CreateT() As T
```

```
            Return New T
    End Function

  End Class
```

The type parameter, T, is constrained so that it must have a public default constructor. Any attempt to specify a type for T that does not have such a constructor will result in a compile error.

Because you know that T will have a default constructor, you are able to create instances of the type, as shown in the CreateT method.

Multiple Constraints

In many cases, you will need to specify multiple constraints on the same type parameter. For instance, you might want to require that a type be a reference type and have a public default constructor.

Essentially, you are providing an array of constraints, so you use the same syntax you use to initialize elements of an array:

```
Public Class Factories(Of T As {New, Class})

  Public Function CreateT() As T
    Return New T
  End Function

  End Class
```

The constraint list can include two or more constraints, enabling you to specify a great deal of information about the types allowed for this type parameter.

Within your generic template code, the compiler is aware of all the constraints applied to your type parameters, so it allows you to use any methods, properties, and events specified by any of the constraints applied to the type.

Generics and Late Binding

One of the primary limitations of generics is that variables and parameters declared based on a type parameter are treated as type System.Object inside your generic template code. While constraints offer a partial solution, expanding the type of those variables based on the constraints, you are still very restricted in what you can do with the variables.

One key example is the use of common operators. There is no constraint you can apply that tells the compiler that a type supports the + or – operators. This means that you cannot write generic code like this:

```
Public Function Add(Of T)(ByVal val1 As T, ByVal val2 As T) As T
  Return val1 + val2
End Function
```

This will generate a compiler error because there is no way for the compiler to verify that variables of type T (whatever that is at runtime) support the + operator. Because there is no constraint that you can apply to T to ensure that the + operator will be valid, there is no direct way to use operators on variables of a generic type.

One alternative is to use Visual Basic's native support for late binding to overcome the limitations shown here. Recall that late binding incurs substantial performance penalties because a lot of work is done dynamically at runtime, rather than by the compiler when you build your project. It is also important to remember the risks that attend late binding — specifically, the fact that the code can fail at runtime in ways that early-bound code cannot. Nonetheless, given those caveats, late binding can be used to solve your immediate problem.

To enable late binding, be sure to put Option Strict Off at the top of the code file containing your generic template (or set the project property to change Option Strict project-wide from the project's properties). Then you can rewrite the Add function as follows:

```
Public Function Add(Of T)(ByVal value1 As T, ByVal value2 As T) As T
  Return CObj(value1) + CObj(value2)
End Function
```

By forcing the value1 and value2 variables to be explicitly treated as type Object, you are telling the compiler that it should use late binding semantics. Combined with the Option Strict Off setting, the compiler assumes that you know what you are doing and it allows the use of the + operator even though its validity can't be confirmed.

The compiled code uses dynamic late binding to invoke the + operator at runtime. If that operator does turn out to be valid for whatever type T is at runtime, then this code will work great. In contrast, if the operator is not valid, then a runtime exception will be thrown.

Summary

Generics enable you to create class, structure, interface, and method templates. These templates gain specific types based on how they are declared or called at runtime. Generics provide you with another code reuse mechanism, along with procedural and object-oriented concepts.

They also enable you to change code that uses parameters or variables of type Object (or other general types) to use specific data types. This often leads to much better performance and increases the readability of your code.

7

Namespaces

Even if you did not realize it, you have been using namespaces since the beginning of this book. For example, `System`, `System.Diagnostics`, and `System.Windows.Forms` are all namespaces contained within the .NET Framework. Namespaces are an easy concept to understand, but this chapter puts the ideas behind them on a firm footing — and clears up any misconceptions you might have about how they are used and organized.

If you are familiar with COM, you will find that the concept of namespaces is the logical extension of programmatic identifier (`ProgID`) values. For example, the functionality of Visual Basic 6's `FileSystemObject` is now mostly encompassed in .NET's `System.IO` namespace, though this is not a one-to-one mapping. However, namespaces reflect more than a change in name; they represent the logical extension of the COM naming structure, expanding its ease of use and extensibility.

In addition to the traditional `System` and `Microsoft` namespaces (for example, used in things such as Microsoft's Web Services Enhancements), the .NET Framework 3.5 includes a way to access some tough-to-find namespaces using the `My` namespace. The `My` namespace is a powerful way of "speed-dialing" specific functionalities in the base.

This chapter about namespaces covers the following:

❑ What namespaces are

❑ Which namespaces are used in Visual Studio 2008 projects by default

❑ How to reference namespaces and use the `Imports` statement

❑ How the compiler searches for class references

❑ How to alias namespaces and create your own namespaces

❑ How to use the `My` namespace

What Is a Namespace?

Namespaces are a way of organizing the vast number of classes, structures, enumerations, delegates, and interfaces that the .NET Framework class library provides. They are a hierarchically structured index into a class library, which is available to all of the .NET languages, not only the Visual Basic 2008 language (with the exception of the `My` namespace). The namespaces, or object references, are typically organized by function. For example, the `System.IO` namespace contains classes, structures, and interfaces for working with input/output streams and files. The classes in this namespace do not necessarily inherit from the same base classes (apart from `Object`, of course).

A namespace is a combination of a naming convention and an assembly, which organizes collections of objects and prevents ambiguity about object references. A namespace can be, and often is, implemented across several physical assemblies, but from the reference side, it is the namespace that ties these assemblies together. A namespace consists of not only classes, but also other (child) namespaces. For example, `IO` is a child namespace of the `System` namespace.

Namespaces provide identification beyond the component name. With a namespace, it is possible to use a more meaningful title (for example, `System`) followed by a grouping (for example, `Text`) to group together a collection of classes that contain similar functions. For example, the `System.Text` namespace contains a powerful class called `StringBuilder`. To reference this class, you can use the fully qualified namespace reference of `System.Text.StringBuilder`, as shown here:

```
Dim sb As New System.Text.StringBuilder()
```

The structure of a namespace is not a reflection of the physical inheritance of classes that make up the namespace. For example, the `System.Text` namespace contains another child namespace called `RegularExpressions`. This namespace contains several classes, but they do not inherit or otherwise reference the classes that make up the `System.Text` namespace.

Figure 7-1 shows how the `System` namespace contains the `Text` child namespace, which also has a child namespace, called `RegularExpressions`. Both of these child namespaces, `Text` and `RegularExpressions`, contain a number of objects in the inheritance model for these classes, as shown in the figure.

As shown in Figure 7-1, while some of the classes in each namespace do inherit from each other, and while all of the classes eventually inherit from the generic `Object`, the classes in `System.Text.RegularExpressions` do not inherit from the classes in `System.Text`.

To emphasize the usefulness of namespaces, we can draw another good example from Figure 7-1. If you make a reference to `System.Drawing.Imaging.Encoder` in your application, then you are making a reference to a completely different `Encoder` class than the namespace shown in Figure 7-1 — `System.Text.Encoder`. Being able to clearly identify classes that have the same name but very different functions, and disambiguate them, is yet another advantage of namespaces.

If you are an experienced COM developer, you may note that unlike a `ProgID`, which reflects a one-level relationship between the project assembly and the class, a single namespace can use child namespaces to extend the meaningful description of a class. The `System` namespace, imported by default as part of every project created with Visual Studio, contains not only the default `Object` class, but also many other classes that are used as the basis for every .NET language.

What if a class you need isn't available in your project? The problem may be with the references in your project. For example, by default, the `System.DirectoryServices` namespace, used to get programmatic access to the Active Directory objects, is not part of your project's assembly. Using it requires adding a reference to the project assembly. The concept of referencing a namespace is very similar to the capability to reference a COM object in VB6.

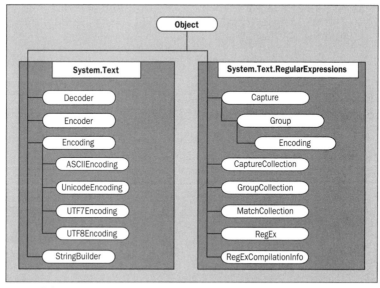

Figure 7-1

In fact, with all this talk about referencing, it is probably a good idea to look at an example of adding an additional namespace to a project. Before doing that, though, you should know a little bit about how a namespace is actually implemented.

Namespaces are implemented within .NET assemblies. The System namespace is implemented in an assembly called System.dll provided with Visual Studio. By referencing this assembly, the project is capable of referencing all the child namespaces of System that happen to be implemented in this assembly. Using the preceding table, the project can import and use the System.Text namespace because its implementation is in the System.dll assembly. However, although it is listed, the project cannot import or use the System.Data namespace unless it references the assembly that implements this child of the System namespace, System.Data.dll.

Let's create a sample project so you can examine the role that namespaces play within it. Using Visual Studio 2008, create a new Visual Basic Windows Application project called Namespace_Sampler.

The Microsoft.VisualBasic.Compatibility.VB6 library is not part of Visual Basic 2008 projects by default. To gain access to the classes that this namespace provides, you need to add it to your project. You can do this by using the Add Reference dialog box (available by right-clicking the Project Name node within the Visual Studio Solution Explorer). The Add Reference dialog box has five tabs, each containing elements that can be referenced from your project:

❑ **.NET** — This tab contains .NET assemblies that can be found in the GAC. In addition to providing the name of the assembly, you can also get the version of the assembly and the version of the framework to which the assembly is compiled. The final data point found in this tab is the location of the assembly on the machine.

273

❑ **COM** — This tab contains all the available COM components. It provides the name of the component, the TypeLib version, and the path of the component.

❑ **Projects** — This tab contains any custom .NET assemblies from any of the various projects contained within your solution.

❑ **Browse** — This tab enables you to look for any component files (`.dll`, `.tlb`, `.olb`, `.ocx`, `.exe`, or `.manifest`) on the network.

❑ **Recent** — This tab lists the most recently made references for quick referencing capabilities.

The Add Reference dialog is shown in Figure 7-2.

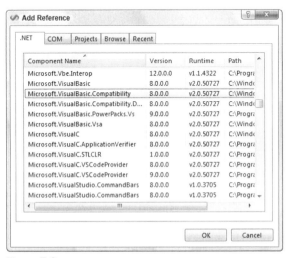

Figure 7-2

The available .NET namespaces are listed by *component name*. This is the same as the namespace name. Within the dialog, you can see a few columns that supply the namespace of the component, the version number of the component, the version of the .NET Framework for which the particular component is targeted, and the path location of the file. You can select a single namespace to make a reference to by clicking your mouse on the component that you are interested in. Holding down the Ctrl key and pressing the mouse button enables you to select multiple namespaces to reference.

To select a range of namespaces, first click on either the first or the last component in the dialog that is contained in the range, and then complete the range selection by holding down the Shift key and using the mouse to select the other component in the range. Once you have selected all the components that you are interested in referencing, click OK.

The example in Figure 7-2 is importing some namespaces from the `Microsoft.VisualBasic` namespace, even though only one selection has been made. This implementation, while a bit surprising at first, is very powerful. First, it shows the extensibility of namespaces. This is because the single `Microsoft.VisualBasic.Compatibility.VB6` namespace is actually implemented in two separate assemblies. If you also make a reference to the `Microsoft.VisualBasic.Compatibility` namespace as well as the `Microsoft.VisualBasic.Compatibility.Data` namespace, you will see (through the Object Browser found in Visual Studio) that the `Microsoft.VisualBasic.Compatibility.VB6` namespace is actually found in both locations, as shown in Figure 7-3.

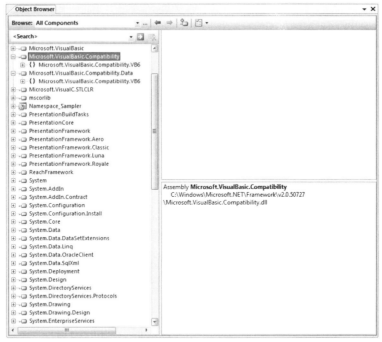

Figure 7-3

Second, this implementation enables you to include only the classes that you need — in this case, those related to the VB6 (Visual Basic 6) environment or to database tools, or both types.

Note some interesting points about the `Microsoft.VisualBasic` namespace. First, this namespace gives you access to all the functions that VB6 developers have had for years. Microsoft has implemented these in the .NET Framework and made them available for your use within your .NET projects. Because these functions have been implemented in the .NET Framework, there is absolutely no performance hit for using them, but you will most likely find the functionality that they provide available in newer .NET namespaces. Second, contrary to what the name of the namespace suggests, this namespace is available for use by all of the .NET languages, which means that even a C# developer could use the `Microsoft.VisualBasic` namespace if desired.

Namespaces and References

Highlighting their importance to every project, references (including namespaces) are no longer hidden from view, available only after opening a dialog box as they were in VB6. As shown in the Solution Explorer window in Figure 7-4, every new project includes a set of referenced namespaces. (If you do not see the references listed in the Solution Explorer, click the Show All Files button from the Solution Explorer menu.)

The list of default references varies depending on the type of project. The example in Figure 7-4 shows the default references for a Windows Forms project in Visual Studio 2008. If the project type were an ASP.NET Web Application, the list of references would change accordingly — the reference to the `System.Windows.Forms` namespace assembly would be replaced by a reference to `System.Web`. If the project type were an ASP.NET Web service (not shown), then the System.Windows.Forms namespace would be replaced by references to the System.Web and System.Web.Services namespaces.

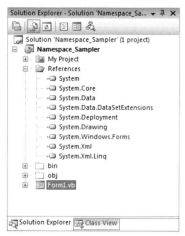

Figure 7-4

In addition to making the namespaces available, references play a second important role in your project. One of the advantages of .NET is using services and components built on the common language runtime (CLR), which enables you to avoid DLL conflicts. The various problems that can occur related to DLL versioning, commonly referred to as "DLL hell," involve two types of conflict.

The first situation occurs when you have a component that requires a minimum DLL version, and an older version of the same DLL causes your product to break. The alternative situation is when you require an older version of a DLL, and a new version is incompatible. In either case, the result is that a shared file, outside of your control, creates a systemwide dependency that affects your software. With .NET, it is possible, but not required, to indicate that a DLL should be shipped as part of your project to avoid an external dependency.

To indicate that a referenced component should be included locally, you can select the reference in the Solution Explorer and then examine the properties associated with that reference. One editable property is called Copy Local. You will see this property and its value in the Properties window within Visual Studio 2008. For those assemblies that are part of a Visual Studio 2008 installation, this value defaults to False, as shown in Figure 7-5. However, for custom references, this property defaults to True to indicate that the referenced DLL should be included as part of the assembly. Changing this property to True changes the path associated with the assembly. Instead of using the path to the referenced file's location on the system, the project creates a subdirectory based on the reference name and places the files required for the implementation of the reference in this subdirectory.

The benefit of this is that even when another version of the DLL is later placed on the system, your project's assembly will continue to function. However, this protection from a conflicting version comes at a price: Future updates to the namespace assembly to fix flaws will be in the system version but not in the private version that is part of your project's assembly.

To resolve this, Microsoft's solution is to place new versions in directories based on their version information. If you examine the path information for all of the Visual Studio 2008 references, you will see that it includes a version number. As new versions of these DLLs are released, they are installed in a separate directory. This method allows for an escape from DLL hell, by keeping new versions from stomping on old versions, and it enables old versions to be easily located for maintenance updates. Therefore, it is often better to leave alone the default behavior of Visual Studio 2008, which is set to copy only locally custom components, until your organization implements a directory structure with version information similar to that of Microsoft.

Figure 7-5

The Visual Basic 2008 compiler will not allow you to add a reference to your assembly if the targeted implementation includes a reference that is not also referenced in your assembly. The good news is that the compiler will help. If, after adding a reference, that reference does not appear in the IntelliSense list generated by Visual Studio 2008, then go ahead and type the reference to a class from that reference. The compiler will flag it with underlining, similar to the Microsoft Word spelling or grammar error underlines. When you click the underlined text, the compiler will tell you which other assemblies need to be referenced in the project in order to use the class in question.

Common Namespaces

The generated list of references shown in the Solution Explorer for the newly created `Namespace_Sampler` project includes most, but not all, of the namespaces that are part of your Windows Application project. For example, one namespace not displayed as a reference is `Microsoft.VisualBasic`, and the accompanying `Microsoft.VisualBasic.dll`. Every Visual Basic 2008 project includes the namespace `Microsoft.VisualBasic`. This namespace is part of the Visual Studio project templates for Visual Basic 2008 and is, in short, what makes Visual Basic 2008 different from C# or any other .NET language. The implicit inclusion of this namespace is the reason why you can call `IsDBNull` and other methods of Visual Basic 2008 directly. The only difference in the default namespaces included with Visual Basic 2008 and C# Windows Application projects is that the former use `Microsoft.VisualBasic` and the latter use `Microsoft.CSharp`.

To see all of the namespaces that are imported automatically, such as the `Microsoft.VisualBasic` namespace, right-click the project name in the Solution Explorer and select Properties from the context menu. This opens the project's Properties window in Visual Studio. Select the References tab from the left pane and you will see the reference `Microsoft.VisualBasic` at the top of the list (see Figure 7-6).

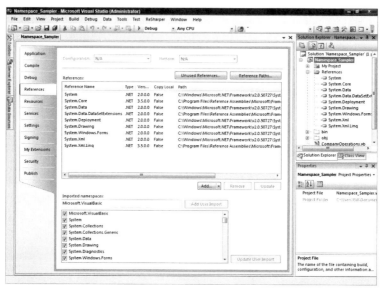

Figure 7-6

When looking at the project's global list of imports in the text area at the bottom of the page, you can see that in addition to the `Microsoft.VisualBasic` namespace, the `System.Collections` and `System.Diagnostics` namespaces are also imported into the project. This is signified by the check marks next to the namespace. Unlike the other namespaces in the list, these namespaces are not listed as references in the text area directly above this. That's because implementation of the `System.Collections` and `System.Diagnostics` namespaces is part of the referenced `System.dll`. Similarly to `Microsoft.VisualBasic`, importing these namespaces allows references to the associated classes, such that a fully qualified path is not required. Because these namespaces contain commonly used classes, it is worthwhile to always include them at the project level.

The following list briefly summarizes some of the namespaces commonly used in Visual Basic 2008 projects:

❑ **System.Collections** — Contains the classes that support various feature-rich object collections. Included automatically, it has classes for arrays, lists, dictionaries, queues, hash tables, and so on.

❑ **System.Collections.Generic** — Ever since .NET 2.0, this namespace has enabled working with the generics capabilities of the framework — a way to build type-safe collections as well as provide generic methods and classes.

❑ **System.Data** — This namespace contains the classes needed to support the core features of ADO.NET.

❑ **System.Diagnostics** — Included in all Visual Basic 2008 projects, this namespace includes the debugging classes. The `Trace` and `Debug` classes provide the primary capabilities, but the namespace contains dozens of classes to support debugging.

❑ **System.Drawing** — This namespace contains simple drawing classes to support Windows Application projects.

❑ **System.EnterpriseServices** — Not included automatically, the System.EnterpriseServices implementation must be referenced to make it available. This namespace contains the classes that interface .NET assemblies with COM+.

❑ **System.IO** — This namespace contains important classes that enable you to read and write to files as well as data streams.

❑ **System.Linq** — This namespace contains an object interface to work with disparate data sources in a new and easy manner. This is a new namespace in .NET 3.5.

❑ **System.Text** — This commonly used namespace enables you to work with text in a number of different ways, usually in regard to string manipulation. One of the more popular objects that this namespace offers is the StringBuilder object.

❑ **System.Threading** — This namespace contains the objects needed to work with and manipulate threads within your application.

❑ **System.Web** — This is the namespace that deals with one of the more exciting features of the .NET Framework: ASP.NET. This namespace provides the objects that deal with browser-server communications. Two main objects include HttpRequest, which deals with the request from the client to the server, and HttpResponse, which deals with the response from the server to the client.

❑ **System.Web.Services** — This is the main namespace you use when creating XML Web Services, one of the more powerful capabilities provided with the .NET Framework. This namespace offers the classes that deal with SOAP messages and the manipulation of these messages.

❑ **System.Windows.Forms** — This namespace provides classes to create Windows Forms in Windows Application projects. It contains the form elements.

Of course, to really make use of the classes and other objects in this list, you need more detailed information. In addition to resources such as Visual Studio 2008's help files, the best source of information is the Object Browser, available directly in the Visual Studio 2008 IDE. You can find it by selecting View➪Object Browser if you are using Visual Studio 2008, 2005, or 2003, or View➪Other Windows➪Object Browser if you are using Visual Studio 2002. The Visual Studio 2008 Object Browser is shown in Figure 7-7.

The Object Browser displays each of the referenced assemblies and enables you to drill down into the various namespaces. Figure 7-7 illustrates how the System.dll implements a number of namespaces, including some that are part of the System namespace. By drilling down into a namespace, you can see some of the classes available. By further selecting a class, the browser shows not only the methods and properties associated with the selected class, but also a brief outline of what that class does.

Using the Object Browser is an excellent way to gain insight into which classes and interfaces are available via the different assemblies included in your project, and how they work. Clearly, the ability to actually see which classes are available and know how to use them is fundamental to being able to work efficiently. Working effectively in the .NET CLR environment requires finding the right class for the task.

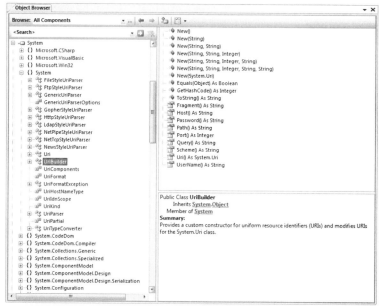

Figure 7-7

Importing and Aliasing Namespaces

Not all namespaces should be imported at the global level. Although you have looked at the namespaces included at this level, it is much better to import namespaces only in the module where they will be used. Importing a namespace at the module level does not change setting the reference, but you do not add it into the list of imports on the project's Properties page. As with variables used in a project, it is possible to define a namespace at the module level. The advantage of this is similar to using local variables in that it helps to prevent different namespaces from interfering with each other. As this section shows, it is possible for two different namespaces to contain classes or even child namespaces with the same name.

Importing Namespaces

The development environment and compiler need a way to prioritize the order in which namespaces should be checked when a class is referenced. It is always possible to unequivocally specify a class by stating its complete namespace path. This is referred to as *fully qualifying* your declaration. The following example fully qualifies a StringBuilder object:

```
Dim sb As New System.Text.StringBuilder
```

However, if every reference to every class needed its full namespace declaration, then Visual Basic 2008 and every other .NET language would be very difficult to program in. After all, who wants to type System.Collections.ArrayList each time an instance of the ArrayList class is wanted? If you review the global references, you will see the System.Collections namespace. Thus, you can just type `ArrayList` whenever you need an instance of this class, as the reference to the larger `System.Collections` namespace has already been made by the application.

In theory, another way to reference the `StringBuilder` class is to use `Text.StringBuilder`, but with all namespaces imported globally, there is a problem with this, caused by what is known as *namespace crowding*. Because there is a second namespace, `System.Drawing`, that has a child called `Text`, the compiler does not have a clear location for the `Text` namespace and, therefore, cannot resolve the `StringBuilder` class. The solution to this problem is to ensure that only a single version of the `Text` child namespace is found locally. That way, the compiler will use this namespace regardless of the global availability of the `System.Drawing.Text` namespace.

`Imports` statements specify to the compiler those namespaces that the code will use:

```
Imports Microsoft.Win32
Imports System
Imports SysDraw = System.Drawing
```

Once they are imported into the file, you are not required to fully qualify your object declarations in your code. For instance, if you imported the `System.Data.SqlClient` namespace into your file, then you would be able to create a `SqlConnection` object in the following manner:

```
Dim conn As New SqlConnection
```

Each of the preceding `Imports` statements illustrates a different facet of importing namespaces. The first namespace, `Imports Microsoft.Win32`, is not imported at the global level. Looking at the reference list, you may not see the Microsoft assembly referenced directly. However, opening the Object Browser reveals that this namespace is actually included as part of the `System.dll`.

As noted earlier, the `StringBuilder` references become ambiguous because both `System.Text` and `System.Drawing.Text` are valid namespaces at the global level. As a result, the compiler has no way to determine which `Text` child namespace is being referenced. Without any clear indication, the compiler flags `Text.StringBuilder` declarations in the command handler. However, using the `Imports System` declaration in the module tells the compiler that before checking namespaces imported at the global level, it should attempt to match incomplete references at the module level. Because the `System` namespace is declared at this level, if `System.Drawing` is not, then there is no ambiguity regarding which child namespace `Text.StringBuilder` belongs to.

This sequence demonstrates how the compiler looks at each possible declaration:

❑ It first determines whether the item is a complete reference, such as `System.Text.StringBuilder`.

❑ If the declaration does not match a complete reference, then the compiler tries to determine whether the declaration is from a child namespace of one of the module-level imports.

❑ Finally, if a match is not found, then the compiler looks at the global-level imports to determine whether the declaration can be associated with a namespace imported for the entire assembly.

While the preceding logical progression of moving from a full declaration through module- to global-level imports resolves the majority of issues, it does not handle all possibilities. Specifically, if you import

`System.Drawing` at the module level, the namespace collision would return. This is where the third import statement becomes important — this import statement uses an alias.

Aliasing Namespaces

Aliasing has two benefits in .NET. First, aliasing enables a long namespace such as `System.EnterpriseServices` to be replaced with a shorthand name such as `COMPlus`. Second, it adds a way to prevent ambiguity among child namespaces at the module level.

As noted earlier, the `System` and `System.Drawing` namespaces both contain a child namespace of `Text`. Because you will be using a number of classes from the `System.Drawing` namespace, it follows that this namespace should be imported into the form's module. However, were this namespace imported along with the `System` namespace, the compiler would again find references to the `Text` child namespace ambiguous. By aliasing the `System.Drawing` namespace to `SysDraw`, the compiler knows that it should only check the `System.Drawing` namespace when a declaration begins with that alias. The result is that although multiple namespaces with the same child namespace are now available at the module level, the compiler knows that one (or more) of them should only be checked at this level when they are explicitly referenced.

Aliasing as defined here is done in the following fashion:

```
Imports SysDraw = System.Drawing
```

Referencing Namespaces in ASP.NET

Making a reference to a namespace in ASP.NET is quite similar to working with Windows Forms, but you have to take some simple, additional steps. From your ASP.NET solution, first make a reference to the assemblies from the References folder, just as you do with Windows Forms. Once there, import these namespaces at the top of the page file in order to avoid having to fully qualify the reference every time on that particular page.

For example, instead of using `System.Collections.Generic` for each instance of use, use the `< %# Import % >` page directive at the top of the ASP.NET page (if the page is constructed using the inline coding style) or use the `Imports` keyword at the top of the ASP.NET page's code-behind file (just as you would with Windows Forms applications). The following example shows how to perform this task when using inline coding for ASP.NET pages:

```
<%# Import Namespace="System.Collections.Generic" %>
```

Now that this reference is in place on the page, you can access everything this namespace contains without having to fully qualify the object you are accessing. Note that the `Import` keyword in the inline example is not missing an "s" at the end. When importing in this manner, it is `Import` (without the "s") instead of `Imports` — as it is in the ASP.NET code-behind model and Windows Forms.

In ASP.NET 1.0/1.1, if you used a particular namespace on each page of your application, you need the `Import` statement on each and every page where that namespace was needed. ASP.NET 3.5 includes the capability to use the web.config file to make a global reference so that you don't need to make further references on the pages themselves, as shown in the following example:

```
<pages>
    <namespaces>
        <add namespace="System.Drawing" />
        <add namespace="Wrox.Books" />
    </namespaces>
</pages>
```

In this example, using the <namespaces> element in the web.config file, references are made to the System.Drawing namespace and the Wrox.Books namespace. Because these references are now contained within the web.config file, there is no need to again reference them on any of the ASP.NET pages contained within this solution.

Creating Your Own Namespaces

Every assembly created in .NET is part of some root namespace. By default, this logic actually mirrors COM, in that assemblies are assigned a namespace that matches the project name. However, unlike COM, in .NET it is possible to change this default behavior. Just as Microsoft has packaged the system-level and CLR classes using well-defined names, you can create your own namespaces. Of course, it is also possible to create projects that match existing namespaces and extend those namespaces, but that is very poor programming practice.

Creating an assembly in a custom namespace can be done at one of two levels, although unless you want the same name for each assembly that will be used in a large namespace, you would normally reset the root namespace for the assembly. This is done through the assembly's project pages, reached by right-clicking the solution name in the Solution Explorer window and working off the first tab (Application) within the Properties page that opens in the document window, as shown in Figure 7-8.

The next step is optional, but, depending on whether you want to create a class at the top level or at a child level, you can add a Namespace command to your code. There is a trick to being able to create top-level namespaces or multiple namespaces within the modules that make up an assembly. Instead of replacing the default namespace with another name, you can delete the default namespace and define the namespaces only in the modules, using the Namespace command.

The Namespace command is accompanied by an End Namespace command. This End Namespace command must be placed after the End Class tag for any classes that will be part of the namespace. The following code demonstrates the structure used to create a MyMetaNamespace namespace, which contains a single class:

```
Namespace MyMetaNamespace
    Class MyClass1
        ' Code
    End Class
End Namespace
```

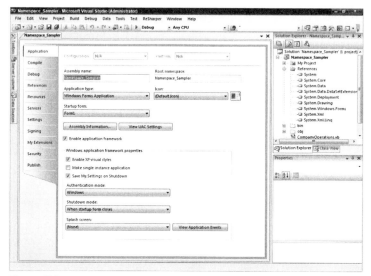

Figure 7-8

You can then utilize the MyClass1 object simply by referencing its namespace, MyMetaNamespace. MyClass1. It is also possible to have multiple namespaces in a single file, as shown here:

```
Namespace MyMetaNamespace1
    Class MyClass1
        ' Code
    End Class
End Namespace

Namespace MyMetaNamespace2
    Class MyClass2
        ' Code
    End Class
End Namespace
```

Using this kind of structure, if you want to utilize MyClass1, then you access it through the namespace MyMetaNamespace.MyClass1. This does not give you access to MyMetaNamespace2 and the objects that it offers; instead, you have to make a separate reference to MyMetaNamespace2.MyClass2.

The Namespace command can also be nested. Using nested Namespace commands is how child namespaces are defined. The same rules apply — each Namespace must be paired with an End Namespace and must fully encompass all of the classes that are part of that namespace. In the following example, the MyMetaNamespace has a child namespace called MyMetaNamespace.MyChildNamespace:

```
Namespace MyMetaNamespace
    Class MyClass1
        ' Code
    End Class

    Namespace MyChildNamespace
```

```
        Class MyClass2
            ' Code
        End Class
    End Namespace
End Namespace
```

This is another point to be aware of when you make references to other namespaces within your own custom namespaces. Consider the following example:

```
Imports System
Imports System.Data
Imports System.Data.SqlClient
Imports System.IO

Namespace MyMetaNamespace1
    Class MyClass1
        ' Code
    End Class
End Namespace
Namespace MyMetaNamespace2
    Class MyClass2
        ' Code
    End Class
End Namespace
```

In this example, a number of different namespaces are referenced in the file. The three namespaces referenced at the top of the code listing — the System, System.Data, and System.Data.SqlClient namespace references — are available to every namespace developed in the file. This is because these three references are sitting outside of any particular namespace declarations. However, the same is not true for the System.IO namespace reference. Because this reference is made within the MyMetaNamespace2 namespace, it is unavailable to any other namespace in the file.

> When you create your own namespaces, Microsoft recommends that you use a convention of CompanyName.TechnologyName — for example, Wrox.Books. This helps to ensure that all libraries are organized in a consistent way.

Sometimes when you are working with custom namespaces, you might find that you have locked yourself out of accessing a particular branch of a namespace, purely due to naming conflicts. Visual Basic includes the Global keyword, which can be used as the outermost root class available in the .NET Framework class library. Figure 7-9 shows a diagram of how the class structure looks with the Global keyword.

This means that you can make specifications such as

```
Global.System.String
```

or

```
Global.Wrox.System.Titles
```

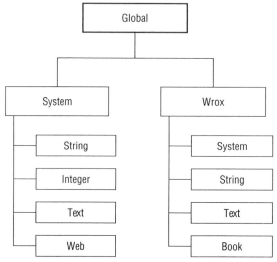

Figure 7-9

The My Keyword

The My keyword is a novel concept that was introduced in the .NET Framework 2.0 to quickly give you access to your application, your users, your resources, the computer, or the network on which the application resides. The My keyword has been referred to as a way of speed-dialing common but complicated resources to which you need access. Using the My keyword, you can quickly access a wide variety of items, such as user details or specific settings of the requestor's browser.

Though not really considered a true namespace, the My object declarations that you make work in the same way as the .NET namespace structure you are used to working with. To give you an example, let's first look at how you get the user's machine name using the traditional namespace structure:

```
Environment.MachineName.ToString()
```

For this example, you simply need to use the Environment class and use this namespace to get at the MachineName property. The following shows how you would accomplish this same task using the My keyword:

```
My.Computer.Info.MachineName.ToString()
```

Looking at this example, you may be wondering what the point is if the example that uses My is lengthier than the first example that just works off of the Environment namespace. Remember that the point is not the length of what you type to access specific classes, but a logical way to find frequently accessed resources without spending a lot of time hunting them down. Would you have known to look in the Environment class to get the machine name of the user's computer? Maybe, but maybe not. Using My.Computer.Info.MachineName.ToString is a tremendously more logical approach; and once compiled, this namespace declaration will be set to work with the same class as shown previously without a performance hit.

If you type the My keyword in your Windows Forms application, IntelliSense provides you with seven items to work with: Application, Computer, Forms, Resources, Settings, User, and WebServices. Though this keyword works best in the Windows Forms environment, there are still things that you can use in the Web Forms world. If you are working with a Web application, then you will have three items off the My keyword: Application, Computer, and User. Each of these is described further in the following sections.

My.Application

The My.Application namespace gives you quick access to specific settings and points that deal with your overall application. The following table details the properties and methods of the My.Application namespace:

Property/Method	Description
ApplicationContext	Returns contextual information about the thread of the Windows Forms application
ChangeCulture	A method that enables you to change the culture of the current application thread
ChangeUICulture	A method that enables you to change the culture that is being used by the Resource Manager
Culture	Returns the current culture being used by the current thread
Deployment	Returns an instance of the ApplicationDeployment object, which allows for programmatic access to the application's ClickOnce features
GetEnvironmentVariable	A method that enables you to access the value of an environment variable
Info	Provides quick access to the assembly of Windows Forms. You can get at assembly information such as version number, name, title, copyright information, and more.
IsNetworkDeployed	Returns a Boolean value that indicates whether the application was distributed via the network using the ClickOnce feature. If True, then the application was deployed using ClickOnce — otherwise False.
Log	Enables you to write to your application's Event Log listeners
MinimumSplashScreenDisplayTime	Enables you to set the time for the splash screen
OpenForms	Returns a FormCollection object, which allows access to the properties of the forms currently open
SaveMySettingsOnExit	Provides the capability to save the user's settings upon exiting the application. This method works only for Windows Forms and console applications.

Property/Method	Description
SplashScreen	Enables you to programmatically assign the splash screen for the application
UICulture	Returns the current culture being used by the Resource Manager

While much can be accomplished using the `My.Application` namespace, for an example of its use, let's focus on the `Info` property. This property provides access to the information stored in the application's `AssemblyInfo.vb` file, as well as other details about the class file. In one of your applications, you can create a message box that is displayed using the following code:

```
MessageBox.Show("Company Name: " & My.Application.Info.CompanyName & _
    vbCrLf & _
    "Description: " & My.Application.Info.Description & vbCrLf & _
    "Directory Path: " & My.Application.Info.DirectoryPath & vbCrLf & _
    "Copyright: " & My.Application.Info.Copyright & vbCrLf & _
    "Trademark: " & My.Application.Info.Trademark & vbCrLf & _
    "Name: " & My.Application.Info.AssemblyName & vbCrLf & _
    "Product Name: " & My.Application.Info.ProductName & vbCrLf & _
    "Title: " & My.Application.Info.Title & vbCrLf & _
    "Version: " & My.Application.Info.Version.ToString())
```

From this example, it is clear that you can get at quite a bit of information concerning the assembly of the running application. Running this code produces a message box similar to the one shown in Figure 7-10.

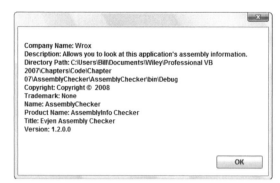

Figure 7-10

Another interesting property to look at from the `My.Application` namespace is the `Log` property. This property enables you to work with the log files for your application. For instance, you can easily write to the system's Application Event Log by first changing the application's `app.config` file to include the following:

```
<?xml version="1.0" encoding="utf-8" ?>
<configuration>
    <system.diagnostics>
        <sources>
            <source name="DefaultSource" switchName="DefaultSwitch">
```

```
                    <listeners>
                        <add name="EventLog"/>
                    </listeners>
                </source>
            </sources>
            <switches>
                <add name="DefaultSwitch" value="Information" />
            </switches>
            <sharedListeners>
                <add name="EventLog"
                  type="System.Diagnostics.EventLogTraceListener"
                  initializeData="EvjenEventWriter" />
            </sharedListeners>
        </system.diagnostics>
</configuration>
```

Once the configuration file is in place, you can record entries to the Application Event Log, as shown in the following simple example:

```
Private Sub Form1_Load(ByVal sender As System.Object, _
    ByVal e As System.EventArgs) Handles MyBase.Load

    My.Application.Log.WriteEntry("Entered Form1_Load", _
        TraceEventType.Information, 1)

End Sub
```

You could also just as easily use the `WriteExceptionEntry` method in addition to the `WriteEntry` method. After running this application and looking in the Event Viewer, you will see the event shown in Figure 7-11.

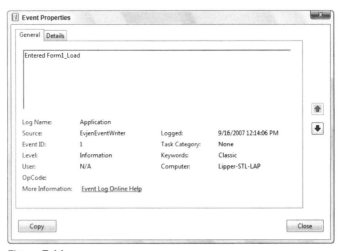

Figure 7-11

The previous example shows how to write to the Application Event Log when working with the objects that write to the event logs. In addition to the Application Event Log, there is also a Security Event Log and a System Event Log. Note that when using these objects, it is impossible to write to the Security

Event Log, and it is only possible to write to the System Event Log if the application does it under either the Local System or the Administrator accounts.

In addition to writing to the Application Event Log, you can just as easily write to a text file. As with writing to the Application Event Log, writing to a text file also means that you need to make changes to the `app.config` file:

```xml
<?xml version="1.0" encoding="utf-8" ?>
<configuration>
    <system.diagnostics>
        <sources>
            <source name="DefaultSource" switchName="DefaultSwitch">
                <listeners>
                    <add name="EventLog"/>
                    <add name="FileLog" />
                </listeners>
            </source>
        </sources>
        <switches>
            <add name="DefaultSwitch" value="Information" />
        </switches>
        <sharedListeners>
            <add name="EventLog"
              type="System.Diagnostics.EventLogTraceListener"
              initializeData="EvjenEventWriter" />
            <add name="FileLog"
              type="Microsoft.VisualBasic.Logging.FileLogTraceListener,
              Microsoft.VisualBasic, Version=8.0.0.0, Culture=neutral,
              PublicKeyToken=b03f5f7f11d50a3a, processorArchitecture=MSIL"
              initializeData="FileLogWriter"/>
        </sharedListeners>
    </system.diagnostics>
</configuration>
```

Now with this `app.config` file in place, you simply need to run the same `WriteEntry` method as before. This time, however, in addition to writing to the Application Event Log, the information is also written to a new text file. You can find the text file at `C:\Documents and Settings\[username]\Application Data\[AssemblyCompany]\[AssemblyProduct]\[Version]`. For instance, in my example, the log file was found at `C:\Documents and Settings\Administrator\Application Data\Wrox\Log Writer\1.2.0.0\`. In the `.log` file found, you will see a line such as the following:

```
DefaultSource    Information    1    Entered Form1_Load
```

By default, it is separated by tabs, but you can change the delimiter yourself by adding a delimiter attribute to the FileLog section in the `app.config` file:

```xml
<add name="FileLog"
  type="Microsoft.VisualBasic.Logging.FileLogTraceListener,
  Microsoft.VisualBasic, Version=8.0.0.0, Culture=neutral,
  PublicKeyToken=b03f5f7f11d50a3a, processorArchitecture=MSIL"
  initializeData="FileLogWriter" delimiter=";" />
```

In addition to writing to Event Logs and text files, you can also write to XML files, console applications, and more.

My.Computer

The `My.Computer` namespace can be used to work with the parameters and details of the computer in which the application is running. The following table details the objects contained in this namespace:

Property	Description
Audio	This object enables you to work with audio files from your application. This includes starting, stopping, and looping audio files.
Clipboard	This object enables you to read and write to the clipboard.
Clock	This enables access to the system clock to get at GMT and the local time of the computer running the application. You can also get at the tick count, which is the number of milliseconds that have elapsed since the computer was started.
FileSystem	This object provides a large collection of properties and methods that enable programmatic access to drives, folders, and files. This includes the ability to read, write, and delete items in the file system.
Info	This provides access to the computer's details, such as amount of memory, the operating system type, which assemblies are loaded, and the name of the computer itself.
Keyboard	This object provides information about which keyboard keys are pressed by the end user. Also included is a single method, `SendKeys`, which enables you to send the pressed keys to the active form.
Mouse	This provides a handful of properties that enable detection of the type of mouse installed, including details such as whether the left and right mouse buttons have been swapped, whether a mouse wheel exists, and how much to scroll when the user uses the wheel.
Name	This is a read-only property that provides access to the name of the computer.
Network	This object provides a single property and some methods that enable you to interact with the network to which the computer on which the application is running is connected. With this object, you can use the `IsAvailable` property to first verify that the computer is connected to a network. If so, then the `Network` object enables you to upload or download files, and ping the network.
Ports	This object can provide notification when ports are available, as well as allow access to the ports.
Registry	This object provides programmatic access to the registry and the registry settings. Using the `Registry` object, you can determine whether keys exist, determine values, change values, and delete keys.
Screen	This provides the capability to work with one or more screens that may be attached to the computer.

There is a lot to the `My.Computer` namespace, and it is impossible to cover all or even most of it. For an example that uses this namespace, we'll take a look at the `FileSystem` property. The `FileSystem` property enables you to easily and logically access drives, directories, and files on the computer.

To illustrate the use of this property, first create a Windows Form with a `DataGridView` with a single column and a `Button` control. It should appear as shown in Figure 7-12.

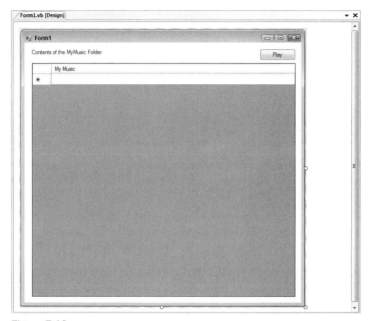

Figure 7-12

This little application will look in the user's My Music folder and list all of the .mp3 files found therein. Once listed, the user of the application will be able to select one of the listed files; and after pressing the Play button, the file will be launched and played inside Microsoft's Windows Media Player.

The first step after getting the controls on the form in place is to make a reference to the Windows Media Player DLL. You can find this on the COM tab, and the location of the DLL is `C:\WINDOWS\System32\wmp.dll`. This provides you with an object called WMPLib in the `References` folder of your solution.

You might be wondering why you would make a reference to a COM object in order to play a .wma file from your application, instead of using the `My.Computer.Audio` namespace that is provided to you. The `Audio` property only allows for the playing of .wav files, because to play .wma, .mp3, and similar files, users must have the proper codecs on their machine. These codecs are not part of the Windows OS, but are part of Windows Media Player.

Now that the reference to the `wmp.dll` is in place, let's put some code in the `Form1_Load` event:

```
Private Sub Form1_Load(ByVal sender As System.Object, _
    ByVal e As System.EventArgs) Handles MyBase.Load

        For Each MusicFile As String _
```

```
In My.Computer.FileSystem.GetFiles _
   (My.Computer.FileSystem.SpecialDirectories.MyMusic, _
    FileIO.SearchOption.SearchAllSubDirectories, "*.wma*")
      Dim MusicFileInfo As System.IO.FileInfo = _
         My.Computer.FileSystem.GetFileInfo(MusicFile.ToString())
      Me.DataGridView1.Rows.Add(MusicFileInfo.Directory.Parent.Name & _
         "\" & MusicFileInfo.Directory.Name & "\" & MusicFileInfo.Name)
   Next

End Sub
```

In this example, the `My.Computer.FileSystem.GetFiles` method points to the My Music folder through the use of the `SpecialDirectories` property. This property enables logical and easy access to folders such as Desktop, My Documents, My Pictures, Programs, and more. Though it is possible to use just this first parameter with the `GetFiles` method, this example makes further definitions. The second parameter defines the `recurse` value — which specifies whether the subfolders should be perused as well. In this case, the `SearchOption` enumeration is set to `SearchAllSubDirectories`. The last parameter defines the wildcard that should be used in searching for elements. In this case, the value of the `wildcard` is `*.wma`, which instructs the `GetFile` method to get only the files that are of type `.wma`. You could just as easily set it to `*.mp3` or even just `*.*` to get anything contained within the folders. After it is retrieved with the `GetFile` method, the file is then placed inside the `DataGridView` control, again using the `My.Computer.FileSystem` namespace to define the value of the item placed within the row.

After the `Form1_Load` event is in place, the last event to construct is the `Button1_Click` event:

```
Private Sub Button1_Click(ByVal sender As System.Object, _
   ByVal e As System.EventArgs) Handles Button1.Click
      Dim MediaPlayer As New WMPLib.WindowsMediaPlayer
      MediaPlayer.openPlayer(My.Computer.FileSystem.SpecialDirectories.MyMusic & _
         "\" & DataGridView1.SelectedCells.Item(0).Value)
End Sub
```

From this example, you can see that it is pretty simple to play one of the provided `.wma` files. It is as simple as creating an instance of the `WMPLib.WindowsMediaPlayer` object and using the `openPlayer` method, which takes as a parameter the location of the file to play. In this case, you are again using the `SpecialDirectories` property. The nice thing about using this property is that whereas it could be more difficult to find the user's My Music folder due to the username changing the actual location of the files that the application is looking for, using the `My` namespace enables it to figure out the exact location of the items. When built and run, the application provides a list of available music files, enabling you to easily select one for playing in the Media Player. This is illustrated in Figure 7-13.

Though it would be really cool if it were possible to play these types of files using the `Audio` property from the `My.Computer` namespace, it is still possible to use the `My.Computer.Audio` namespace for playing `.wav` files and system sounds.

To play a system sound, use the following construct:

```
My.Computer.Audio.PlaySystemSound(SystemSounds.Beep)
```

The system sounds in the `SystemSounds` enumeration include `Asterisk`, `Beep`, `Exclamation`, `Hand`, and `Question`.

Figure 7-13

My.Forms Namespace

The My.Forms namespace provides a quick and logical way to access the properties and methods of the forms contained within your solution. For instance, to get at the first form in your solution (assuming that it's named Form1), use the following namespace construct:

```
My.Form.Form1
```

To get at other forms, you simply change the namespace so that the name of the form you are trying to access follows the Form keyword in the namespace construction.

My.Resources

The My.Resources namespace is a very easy way to get at the resources stored in your application. If you open the MyResources.resx file from the My Projects folder in your solution, you can easily create as many resources as you wish. For example, you could create a single String resource titled MyResourceString and give it a value of St. Louis Rams.

To access the resources that you create, use the simple reference shown here:

```
My.Resources.MyResourceString.ToString()
```

Using IntelliSense, all of your created resources will appear after you type the period after the My. Resources string.

My.User

The `My.User` namespace enables you to work with the `IPrincipal` interface. You can use the `My.User` namespace to determine whether the user is authenticated or not, the user's name, and more. For instance, if you have a login form in your application, you could allow access to a particular form with code similar to the following:

```
If (Not My.User.IsInRole("Administrators")) Then
    ' Code here
End If
```

You can also just as easily get the user's name with the following:

```
My.User.Name
```

In addition, you can check whether the user is authenticated:

```
If My.User.IsAuthenticated Then
    ' Code here
End If
```

My.WebServices

When not using the `My.WebServices` namespace, you access your Web services references in a lengthier manner. The first step in either case is to make a Web reference to some remote XML Web Service in your solution. These references will then appear in the Web References folder in the Solution Explorer in Visual Studio 2008. Before the introduction of the `My` namespace, you would have accessed the values that the Web reference exposed in the following manner:

```
Dim ws As New ReutersStocks.GetStockDetails
Label1.Text = ws.GetLatestPrice.ToString()
```

This works, but now with the `My` namespace, you can use the following construct:

```
Label1.Text = My.WebServices.GetStockDetails.GetLatestPrice.ToString()
```

Extending the My Namespace

You are not limited to only what the `My` namespace provides. Just as you can with other namespaces, you can extend this namespace until your heart is content. To show an example of extending the `My` namespace so that it includes your own functions and properties, in your Windows Forms application, create a new module called `CompanyExtensions.vb`.

The code for the entire module and the associated class is presented here:

```
Namespace My
    <HideModuleName()> _
    Module CompanyOperations
```

```
        Private _CompanyExtensions As New CompanyExtensions

        Friend Property CompanyExtensions() As CompanyExtensions
            Get
                Return _CompanyExtensions
            End Get
            Set(ByVal value As CompanyExtensions)
                _CompanyExtensions = value
            End Set
        End Property
    End Module
End Namespace

Public Class CompanyExtensions
    Public ReadOnly Property CompanyDateTime() As DateTime
        Get
            Return DateTime.Now()
        End Get
    End Property
End Class
```

From this example, you can see that the module CompanyOperations is wrapped inside the My namespace. From there, a single property is exposed — CompanyExtensions. The class, CompanyExtensions, is a reference to the class found directly below in the same file. This class, CompanyExtensions, exposes a single ReadOnly Property called CompanyDateTime.

With this in place, build your application, and you are now ready to see the new expanded My namespace in action. From your Windows Form application's Page_Load event, add the following code snippet:

```
MessageBox.Show(My.CompanyExtensions.CompanyDateTime)
```

From the My namespace, you will now find the CompanyExtensions class directly in the IntelliSense, as presented in Figure 7-14.

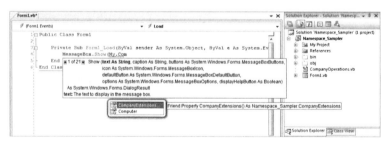

Figure 7-14

The name of the module CompanyOperations doesn't also appear in the list off My because the <Hide ModuleName()> attribute precedes the opening module statement. This attribute signifies that you don't want the module name exposed out to the My namespace.

The preceding example shows how to create your own sections within the `My` namespace, but you can also extend the sections that are already present (for example, `Computer`, `User`, etc.). Extending the `My` namespace is simply a matter of creating a partial class and extending it with the feature sets that you want to appear in the overall `My` namespace. An example of such an extension is presented in the following code sample:

```
Namespace My
    Partial Class MyComputer
        Public ReadOnly Property Hostname() As String
            Get
                Dim iphostentry As System.Net.IPHostEntry = _
                    System.Net.Dns.GetHostEntry(String.Empty)

                Return iphostentry.HostName.ToString()
            End Get
        End Property
    End Class
End Namespace
```

From this, you can see that this code is simply extending upon the already present `MyComputer` class:

```
Partial Class MyComputer

End Class
```

This extension exposes a single `ReadOnly Property` called `Hostname` that returns the local user's hostname. After compiling or utilizing this class in your project, you will find the `Hostname` property available to you within the `My.Computer` namespace, as shown in Figure 7-15.

Figure 7-15

Summary

The introduction of namespaces with the .NET Framework provides a powerful tool that helps to abstract logical capabilities from their physical implementation. While there are differences in the syntax of referencing objects from a namespace and referencing the same object from a COM-style component implementation, there are several similarities. After demonstrating the hierarchical structure of namespaces, this chapter covered the following:

❑   Why namespace hierarchies are not related to class hierarchies

❑   How to review and add references to a project

❑   How to import and alias namespaces at the module level

❑   How to create custom namespaces

❑   How to use the My namespace

Namespaces play an important role in enterprise software development. They enable you to separate the implementation of related functional objects while retaining the ability to group these objects, which improves the overall maintainability of your code. Anyone who has ever worked on a large project has experienced situations in which a fix to a component was delayed because of the potential impact on other components in the same project. Regardless of the logical separation of components in the same project, developers who take part in the development process worry about testing. With separate implementations for related components, it is not only possible to alleviate this concern, but also easier than ever before for a team of developers to work on different parts of the same project.

8

Exception Handling and Debugging

All professional-grade programs need to handle unexpected conditions. In programming languages before Microsoft .NET, this was often called *error handling*. Unexpected conditions generated error codes, which were trapped by programming logic that took appropriate action.

The common language runtime in .NET does not generate error codes. When an unexpected condition occurs, the CLR creates a special object called an *exception*. This object contains properties and methods that describe the unexpected condition in detail and provide various items of useful information about what went wrong.

Because the .NET Framework deals with exceptions instead of errors, the term *error handling* is seldom used in the .NET world. Instead, the term *exception handling* is preferred. This term refers to the techniques used in .NET to detect exceptions and take appropriate action.

This chapter covers how exception handling works in Visual Basic 2008. It discusses the common language runtime (CLR) exception handler in detail and the programming methods that are most efficient in catching errors. Specifically, it covers the following:

- ❑ A very brief overview of error handling in Visual Basic 6 (VB6), for those just moving to .NET

- ❑ The general principles behind exception handling

- ❑ The `Try ... Catch ... Finally` structure, the `Exit Try` statement, and nested `Try` structures

- ❑ The exception object's methods and properties

- ❑ Capabilities in Visual Studio for working with exceptions

- ❑ Error and trace logging and how you can use these methods to obtain feedback about how your program is working

A Brief Review of Error Handling in VB6

For compatibility, Visual Basic 2008 and other .NET versions of Visual Basic still support the old-style syntax for error handling that was used in Visual Basic 6 and earlier versions. That means you can still use the syntax presented in this review. However, it is strongly recommended that you avoid using this old-style syntax in favor of the exception handling features that are native to .NET. Using the more modern `Try ... Catch` syntax (presented after this review) will give you more flexibility and better code structure.

The old-style syntax in VB6 was handed down from DOS versions of BASIC. The `On Error` construct was created in an era when line labels and `GoTo` statements were commonly used. Such error handling is difficult to use and has limited functionality compared to more modern alternatives.

In VB6, a typical routine with error handling code looks like this:

```
Private Function OpenFile(sFileName As String) As Boolean

On Error GoTo ErrHandler:
Open sFileName For Random As #1
OpenFile = True
Exit Sub

ErrHandler:
Select Case Err.Number
    Case 53 ' File not found
        MessageBox.Show "File not found"
    Case Else
        MessageBox.Show "Other error"
End Select
OpenFile = False

End Function
```

The top of the routine points to a section of code called an *error handler*, which is usually placed at the bottom of the routine. The error handler takes control as soon as an error is detected in the routine, checking the error number to determine what action to take. The error number is available as a property of the `Err` object, which is a globally available object that holds error information in VB6.

There are several other error-handling syntax options not included in the preceding error-handling code. If the error handler can take care of the error without breaking execution, then it can resume execution with the line of code that generated the error (`Resume`), the one after that (`Resume Next`), or at a particular location (`Resume LineLabel`).

Error-handling code becomes more complex if the error handling needs to vary in the routine. Multiple `On Error GoTo` statements must be used to send errors to various error handlers, all of which are clustered at the bottom of the routine. With such a lack of organization of error-handling code, it is easy to become confused about what should happen under various conditions. There is also very little information available about the error during the process, except for the error number. You can't determine, for example, the line number on which the error was generated without single-stepping through the code.

Such logic can rapidly become convoluted and unmanageable. There's a much better way to manage errors in VB 2008: *structured exception handling*. The rest of this chapter explains this technique for working with code errors, and uses the term structured exception handling throughout, except for the small sections that discuss compatibility with older error-handling techniques.

Exceptions in .NET

.NET implements a systemwide, comprehensive approach to exception handling. As noted in the chapter introduction, instead of an *error number*, .NET uses an *exception object*. This object contains information relevant to the error, exposed as properties of the object. Later you'll see a table that summarizes the properties and information they expose.

Such an object is an instance of a class that derives from a class named `System.Exception`. As shown later, a variety of subclasses of `System.Exception` are used for different circumstances.

Important Properties and Methods of an Exception

The `Exception` class has properties that contain useful information about the exception, as shown in the following table:

Property	Description
HelpLink	A string indicating the link to help for this exception
InnerException	Returns the `exception` object reference to an inner (nested) exception
Message	A string that contains a description of the error, suitable for displaying to users
Source	A string containing the name of an object that generated the error
StackTrace	A read-only property that holds the stack trace as a text string. The stack trace is a list of the pending method calls at the point at which the exception was detected. That is, if `MethodA` called `MethodB`, and an exception occurred in `MethodB`, the stack trace would contain both `MethodA` and `MethodB`.
TargetSite	A read-only string property that holds the method that threw the exception

The two most important methods of the `Exception` class are as follows:

Method	Description
GetBaseException	Returns the first exception in the chain
ToString	Returns the error string, which might include as much information as the error message, the inner exceptions, and the stack trace, depending on the error

You will see these properties and methods used in the code examples shown later, after you have covered the syntax for detecting and handling exceptions.

How Exceptions Differ from the Err Object in VB6

Because an exception contains all of the information needed about an error, structured exception handling does not use error numbers and the `Err` object. The exception object contains all the relevant information about the error.

However, whereas there is only one global `Err` object in VB6, there are many types of exception objects in the .NET Framework. For example, if a divide by zero is done in code, then an `OverflowException` is generated. In addition to the dozens of exception types available in the .NET Framework, you can inherit from a class called `ApplicationException` and create your own exception classes (see Chapter 3 for a discussion of inheritance).

In .NET, all exceptions inherit from `System.Exception`. Special-purpose exception classes can be found in many namespaces. The following table lists four representative examples of the classes that extend `Exception`:

Namespace	Class	Description
System	InvalidOperationException	Generated when a call to an object method is inappropriate because of the object's state
System	OutOfMemoryException	Results when there is not enough memory to carry out an operation
System.XML	XmlException	Often caused by an attempt to read invalid XML
System.Data	DataException	Represents errors in ADO.NET components

There are literally dozens of exception classes scattered throughout the .NET Framework namespaces. It is common for an exception class to reside in a namespace with the classes that typically generate the exception. For example, the `DataException` class is in `System.Data`, with the ADO.NET components that often generate a `DataException` instance.

Having many types of exceptions in VB 2008 enables different types of conditions to be trapped with different exception handlers. This is a major advance over VB6. The syntax to accomplish that is discussed next.

Structured Exception-Handling Keywords

Structured exception handling depends on several keywords in VB 2008:

❑   `Try` — Begins a section of code in which an exception might be generated from a code error. This section of code is often called a `Try` block. A trapped exception is automatically routed to a `Catch` statement (discussed next).

❑   Catch — Begins an exception handler for a type of exception. One or more Catch code blocks follow a Try block, with each Catch block catching a different type of exception. When an exception is encountered in the Try block, the first Catch block that matches that type of exception receives control.

❑   Finally — Contains code that runs when the Try block finishes normally, or when a Catch block receives control and then finishes. That is, the code in the Finally block always runs, regardless of whether an exception was detected. Typically, the Finally block is used to close or dispose of any resources, such as database connections, that might have been left unresolved by the code that had a problem.

❑   Throw — Generates an exception. It's often done in a Catch block when the exception should be kicked back to a calling routine, or in a routine that has itself detected an error such as a bad argument passed in. Another common place to throw an exception is after a test on the arguments passed to a method or property, if it is discovered that the argument is not appropriate, such as when a negative number is passed in for a count that must be positive.

The Try, Catch, and Finally Keywords

Here is an example showing some typical, simple structured exception-handling code in VB 2008. In this case, the most likely source of an error is the iItems argument. If it has a value of zero, then this would lead to dividing by zero, which would generate an exception.

First, create a Windows Application in Visual Basic 2008 and place a button on the default Form1 created in the project. In the button's click event, place the following two lines of code:

```
Dim sngAvg As Single
sngAvg = GetAverage(0, 100)
```

Then put the following function in the form's code:

```
Private Function GetAverage(iItems As Integer, iTotal As Integer) as Single
    ' Code that might throw an exception is wrapped in a Try block
   Try
        Dim sngAverage As Single

        ' This will cause an exception to be thrown if iItems = 0
        sngAverage = CSng(iTotal \ iItems)

        ' This only executes if the line above generated no error
        MessageBox.Show("Calculation successful")
        Return sngAverage

    Catch excGeneric As Exception
        ' If the calculation failed, you get here
        MessageBox.Show("Calculation unsuccessful - exception caught")
        Return 0
    End Try

End Function
```

This code traps all the exceptions with a single generic exception type, and you don't have any `Finally` logic. Run the program and press the button. You will be able to follow the sequence better if you place a breakpoint at the top of the `GetAverage` function and step through the lines.

Here is a more complex example that traps the divide-by-zero exception explicitly. This second version of the `GetAverage` function (notice that the name is `GetAverage2`) also includes a `Finally` block:

```
Private Function GetAverage2(iItems As Integer, iTotal As Integer) as Single
    ' Code that might throw an exception is wrapped in a Try block
    Try
        Dim sngAverage As Single

        ' This will cause an exception to be thrown.
        sngAverage = CSng(iTotal \ iItems)

        ' This only executes if the line above generated no error.
        MessageBox.Show("Calculation successful")
        Return sngAverage

    Catch excDivideByZero As DivideByZeroException
        ' You'll get here with an DivideByZeroException in the Try block
        MessageBox.Show("Calculation generated DivideByZero Exception")
        Return 0

    Catch excGeneric As Exception
        ' You'll get here when any exception is thrown and not caught in
        ' a previous Catch block.
        MessageBox.Show("Calculation failed - generic exception caught")
        Return 0

    Finally
        ' Code in the Finally block will always run.
        MessageBox.Show("You always get here, with or without an error")
    End Try
End Function
```

This code contains two `Catch` blocks for different types of exceptions. If an exception is generated, then .NET will go down the `Catch` blocks looking for a matching exception type. That means the `Catch` blocks should be arranged with specific types first and more generic types after.

Place the code for `GetAverage2` in the form, and place another button on `Form1`. In the `Click` event for the second button, place the following code:

```
Dim sngAvg As Single
sngAvg = GetAverage2(0, 100)
```

Run the program again and press the second button. As before, it's easier to follow if you set a breakpoint early in the code and then step through the code line by line.

The Throw Keyword

Sometimes a Catch block is unable to handle an error. Some exceptions are so unexpected that they should be "sent back up the line" to the calling code, so that the problem can be promoted to code that can decide what to do with it. A Throw statement is used for that purpose.

A Throw statement ends execution of the exception handler — that is, no more code in the Catch block after the Throw statement is executed. However, Throw does not prevent code in the Finally block from running. That code still runs before the exception is kicked back to the calling routine.

You can see the Throw statement in action by changing the earlier code for GetAverage2 to look like this:

```
Private Function GetAverage3(iItems As Integer, iTotal as Integer) as Single
    ' Code that might throw an exception is wrapped in a Try block
    Try
        Dim sngAverage As Single

        ' This will cause an exception to be thrown.
        sngAverage = CSng(iTotal \ iItems)

        ' This only executes if the line above generated no error.
        MessageBox.Show("Calculation successful")
        Return sngAverage

    Catch excDivideByZero As DivideByZeroException
        ' You'll get here with an DivideByZeroException in the Try block.
        MessageBox.Show("Calculation generated DivideByZero Exception")

        Throw excDivideByZero

        MessageBox.Show("More logic after the throw - never executed")

    Catch excGeneric As Exception
        ' You'll get here when any exception is thrown and not caught in
        ' a previous Catch block.
        MessageBox.Show("Calculation failed - generic exception caught")

        Throw excGeneric

    Finally
        ' Code in the Finally block will always run, even if
        ' an exception was thrown in a Catch block.
        MessageBox.Show("You always get here, with or without an error")
    End Try
End Function
```

Here is some code to call GetAverage3. You can place this code in another button's click event to test it out:

```
Try
    Dim sngAvg As Single
    sngAvg = GetAverage3(0, 100)
```

```
Catch exc As Exception
    MessageBox.Show("Back in the click event after an error")
Finally
    MessageBox.Show("Finally block in click event")
End Try
```

Throwing a New Exception

Throw can also be used with exceptions that are created on-the-fly. For example, you might want your earlier function to generate an ArgumentException, as you can consider a value of iItems of zero to be an invalid value for that argument.

In such a case, a new exception must be instantiated. The constructor allows you to place your own custom message into the exception. To show how this is done, let's change the aforementioned example to throw your own exception instead of the one caught in the Catch block:

```
Private Function GetAverage4(iItems As Integer, iTotal as Integer) as Single

    If iItems = 0 Then
        Dim excOurOwnException As New _
            ArgumentException("Number of items cannot be zero")

        Throw excOurOwnException
    End If


    ' Code that might throw an exception is wrapped in a Try block.
    Try
        Dim sngAverage As Single

        ' This will cause an exception to be thrown.
        sngAverage = CSng(iTotal \ iItems)

        ' This only executes if the line above generated no error.
        MessageBox.Show("Calculation successful")
        Return sngAverage

    Catch excDivideByZero As DivideByZeroException
        ' You'll get here with an DivideByZeroException in the Try block.
        MessageBox.Show("Calculation generated DivideByZero Exception")
        Throw excDivideByZero
        MessageBox.Show("More logic after the thrown - never executed")
    Catch excGeneric As Exception
        ' You'll get here when any exception is thrown and not caught in
        ' a previous Catch block.
        MessageBox.Show("Calculation failed - generic exception caught")
        Throw excGeneric
    Finally
        ' Code in the Finally block will always run, even if
        ' an exception was thrown in a Catch block.
        MessageBox.Show("You always get here, with or without an error")
```

```
            End Try
    End Function
```

This code can be called from a button with similar code for calling `GetAverage3`. Just change the name of the function called to `GetAverage4`.

This technique is particularly well suited to dealing with problems detected in property procedures. Property `Set` procedures often do checking to ensure that the property is about to be assigned a valid value. If not, then throwing a new `ArgumentException` (instead of assigning the property value) is a good way to inform the calling code about the problem.

The Exit Try Statement

The `Exit Try` statement will, under a given circumstance, break out of the `Try` or `Catch` block and continue at the `Finally` block. In the following example, you exit a `Catch` block if the value of `iItems` is 0, because you know that your error was caused by that problem:

```
Private Function GetAverage5(iItems As Integer, iTotal as Integer) As Single
    ' Code that might throw an exception is wrapped in a Try block.
    Try
        Dim sngAverage As Single

        ' This will cause an exception to be thrown.
        sngAverage = CSng(iTotal \ iItems)

        ' This only executes if the line above generated no error.
        MessageBox.Show("Calculation successful")
        Return sngAverage

    Catch excDivideByZero As DivideByZeroException
        ' You'll get here with an DivideByZeroException in the Try block.
        If iItems = 0 Then
            Return 0
            Exit Try
        Else
            MessageBox.Show("Error not caused by iItems")
        End If
        Throw excDivideByZero
        MessageBox.Show("More logic after the thrown - never executed")

    Catch excGeneric As Exception
        ' You'll get here when any exception is thrown and not caught in
        ' a previous Catch block.
        MessageBox.Show("Calculation failed - generic exception caught")
        Throw excGeneric
    Finally
        ' Code in the Finally block will always run, even if
        ' an exception was thrown in a Catch block.
        MessageBox.Show("You always get here, with or without an error")
    End Try
End Sub
```

In your first `Catch` block, you have inserted an `If` block so that you can exit the block given a certain condition (in this case, if the overflow exception was caused because the value of `intY` was 0). The `Exit Try` goes immediately to the `Finally` block and completes the processing there:

```
If iItems = 0 Then
  Return 0
  Exit Try
Else
  MessageBox.Show("Error not caused by iItems")
End If
```

Now, if the overflow exception is caused by something other than division by zero, then you'll get a message box displaying "Error not caused by `iItems`."

Nested Try Structures

Sometimes particular lines in a `Try` block may need special exception processing. Moreover, errors can occur within the `Catch` portion of the `Try` structures and cause further exceptions to be thrown. For both of these scenarios, nested `Try` structures are available. You can alter the example under the section "The Throw Keyword" to demonstrate the following code:

```
Private Function GetAverage6(iItems As Integer, iTotal as Integer) As Single

    ' Code that might throw an exception is wrapped in a Try block.
    Try
        Dim sngAverage As Single


            ' Do something for performance testing ... .
            Try
                LogEvent("GetAverage")
            Catch exc As Exception
                MessageBox.Show("Logging function unavailable")
            End Try


        ' This will cause an exception to be thrown.
        sngAverage = CSng(iTotal \ iItems)

        ' This only executes if the line above generated no error.
        MessageBox.Show("Calculation successful")
        Return sngAverage

    Catch excDivideByZero As DivideByZeroException
        ' You'll get here with an DivideByZeroException in the Try block.
        MessageBox.Show("Error not divide by 0")
        Throw excDivideByZero
        MessageBox.Show("More logic after the thrown - never executed")
    Catch excGeneric As Exception
        ' You'll get here when any exception is thrown and not caught in
        ' a previous Catch block.
        MessageBox.Show("Calculation failed - generic exception caught")
        Throw excGeneric
```

```
        Finally
            ' Code in the Finally block will always run, even if
            ' an exception was thrown in a Catch block.
            MessageBox.Show("You always get here, with or without an error")
        End Try
    End Function
```

In the preceding example, you are assuming that a function exists to log an event. This function would typically be in a common library, and might log the event in various ways. You will look at logging exceptions in detail later in the chapter, but a simple `LogEvent` function might look like this:

```
    Public Sub LogEvent(ByVal sEvent As String)
        FileOpen(1, "logfile.txt", OpenMode.Append)
        Print(1, DateTime.Now & "-" & sEvent & vbCrLf)
        FileClose(1)

    End Sub
```

In this case, you don't want a problem logging an event, such as a "disk full" error, to crash the routine. The code for the `GetAverage` function triggers a message box to indicate trouble with the logging function.

A `Catch` block can be empty. In that case, it has a similar effect as `On Error Resume Next` in VB6: the exception is ignored. However, execution does not pick up with the line after the line that generated the error, but instead picks up with either the `Finally` block or the line after the `End Try` if no `Finally` block exists.

Using Exception Properties

The previous examples have displayed hard-coded messages in message boxes, which is obviously not a good technique for production applications. Instead, a message box or log entry describing an exception should provide as much information as possible concerning the problem. To do this, various properties of the exception can be used.

The most brutal way to get information about an exception is to use the `ToString` method of the exception. Suppose that you modify the earlier example of `GetAverage2` to change the displayed information about the exception like this:

```
    Private Function GetAverage2(ByVal iItems As Integer, ByVal iTotal As Integer) _
        As Single
        ' Code that might throw an exception is wrapped in a Try block.
        Try
            Dim sngAverage As Single

            ' This will cause an exception to be thrown.
            sngAverage = CSng(iTotal \ iItems)
            ' This only executes if the line above generated no error.
            MessageBox.Show("Calculation successful")
            Return sngAverage
```

```
    Catch excDivideByZero As DivideByZeroException
        ' You'll get here with an DivideByZeroException in the Try block.

        MessageBox.Show(excDivideByZero.ToString)

        Throw excDivideByZero
        MessageBox.Show("More logic after the thrown - never executed")

    Catch excGeneric As Exception
        ' You'll get here when any exception is thrown and not caught in
        ' a previous Catch block.
        MessageBox.Show("Calculation failed - generic exception caught")
        Throw excGeneric
    Finally
        ' Code in the Finally block will always run, even if
        ' an exception was thrown in a Catch block.
        MessageBox.Show("You always get here, with or without an error")
    End Try
End Function
```

When the function is accessed with iItems = 0, a message box similar to the one in Figure 8-1 will be displayed.

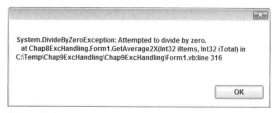

Figure 8-1

The Message Property

The message shown in Figure 8-1 is helpful to a developer because it contains a lot of information, but it's not something you would typically want users to see. Instead, a user normally needs to see a short description of the problem, and that is supplied by the Message property.

If the previous code is changed so that the Message property is used instead of ToString, then the message box will provide something like what is shown in Figure 8-2.

Figure 8-2

The InnerException and TargetSite Properties

The InnerException property is used to store an exception trail. This comes in handy when multiple exceptions occur. It's quite common for an exception to occur that sets up circumstances whereby further exceptions are raised. As exceptions occur in a sequence, you can choose to stack them for later reference by use of the InnerException property of your Exception object. As each exception joins the stack, the previous Exception object becomes the inner exception in the stack.

For simplicity, you'll start a new code sample, with just a subroutine that generates its own exception. You'll include code to add a reference to an InnerException object to the exception you are generating with the Throw method.

This example also includes a message box to show what's stored in the exception's TargetSite property. As shown in the results, TargetSite will contain the name of the routine generating the exception — in this case, HandlerExample. Here's the code:

```
Sub HandlerExample()
  Dim intX As Integer
  Dim intY As Integer
  Dim intZ As Integer
  intY = 0
  intX = 5
  ' First Required Error Statement.
  Try
     ' Cause a "Divide by Zero"
     intZ = CType((intX \ intY), Integer)
  ' Catch the error.
  Catch objA As System.DivideByZeroException
     Try
        Throw (New Exception("0 as divisor", objA))
     Catch objB As Exception
       Dim sError As String
       sError = "My Message: " & objB.Message & vbCrLf & vbCrLf
       sError &= "Inner Exception Message: " & _
           objB.InnerException.Message & vbCrLf & vbCrLf
       sError &= "Method Error Occurred: " & objB.TargetSite.Name
       MessageBox.Show(sError)
     End Try
  Catch
     Messagebox.Show("Caught any other errors")
  Finally
     Messagebox.Show(Str(intZ))
  End Try
End Sub
```

As before, you catch the divide-by-zero error in the first Catch block, and the exception is stored in objA so that you can reference its properties later.

You throw a new exception with a more general message ("0 as divisor") that is easier to interpret, and you build up your stack by appending objA as the InnerException object using an overloaded constructor for the Exception object:

```
Throw (New Exception("0 as divisor", objA))
```

You catch your newly thrown exception in another `Catch` statement. Note how it does not catch a specific type of error:

```
Catch objB As Exception
```

Then you construct an error message for the new exception and display it in a message box:

```
Dim sError As String
sError = "My Message: " & objB.Message & vbCrLf & vbCrLf
sError &= "Inner Exception Message: " & _
    objB.InnerException.Message & vbCrLf & vbCrLf
sError &= "Method Error Occurred: " & objB.TargetSite.Name
MessageBox.Show(sError)
```

The message box that is produced is shown in Figure 8-3.

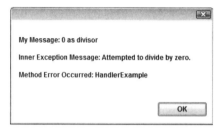

My Message: 0 as divisor

Inner Exception Message: Attempted to divide by zero.

Method Error Occurred: HandlerExample

OK

Figure 8-3

First your own message is included, based on the new exception thrown by your own code. Then the `InnerException` gets the next exception in the stack, which is the divide-by-zero exception, and its message is included. Finally, the `TargetSite` property gives you the name of the method that threw the exception. `TargetSite` is particularly helpful in logs or error reports from users that are used by developers to track down unexpected problems.

After this message box, the `Finally` clause displays another message box that just shows the current value of `intZ`, which is zero because the divide failed. This second box also occurs in other examples that follow.

Source and StackTrace

The `Source` and `StackTrace` properties provide the user with information regarding where the error occurred. This supplemental information can be invaluable, as the user can pass it on to the troubleshooter in order to help resolve errors more quickly. The following example uses these two properties and shows the feedback when the error occurs:

```
Sub HandlerExample2()
    Dim intX As Integer
    Dim intY As Integer
    Dim intZ As Integer
    intY = 0
    intX = 5
```

```
' First Required Error Statement.
Try
   ' Cause a "Divide by Zero"
   intZ = CType((intX \ intY), Integer)
' Catch the error.
Catch objA As System.DivideByZeroException
      objA.Source = "HandlerExample2"
      Messagebox.Show("Error Occurred at :" & _
         objA.Source & objA.StackTrace)
Finally
   Messagebox.Show(Str(intZ))
End Try
End Sub
```

The output from the Messagebox statement is very detailed, providing the entire path and line number where the error occurred, as shown in Figure 8-4.

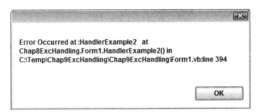

Error Occurred at :HandlerExample2   at
Chap8ExcHandling.Form1.HandlerExample2() in
C:\Temp\Chap9ExcHandling\Chap9ExcHandling\Form1.vb:line 394

OK

Figure 8-4

Notice that this information is also included in the ToString method examined earlier (refer to Figure 8-1).

GetBaseException

The GetBaseException method comes in very handy when you are deep in a set of thrown exceptions. This method returns the originating exception, which makes debugging easier and helps keep the troubleshooting process on track by sorting through information that can be misleading:

```
Sub HandlerExample3()
Dim intX As Integer
Dim intY As Integer
Dim intZ As Integer
intY = 0
intX = 5
' First Required Error Statement.
Try
   ' Cause a "Divide by Zero"
   intZ = CType((intX \ intY), Integer)
' Catch the error.
Catch objA As System.DivideByZeroException
```

```
      Try
        Throw (New Exception("0 as divisor", objA))
      Catch objB As Exception
        Try
          Throw (New Exception("New error", objB))
        Catch objC As Exception
          Messagebox.Show(objC.GetBaseException.Message)
        End Try
      End Try
    Finally
      Messagebox.Show(Str(intZ))
    End Try
  End Sub
```

The `InnerException` property provides the information that the `GetBaseException` method needs, so as your example executes the `Throw` statements, it sets up the `InnerException` property. The purpose of the `GetBaseException` method is to provide the properties of the initial exception in the chain that was produced. Hence, `objC.GetBaseException.Message` returns the `Message` property of the original `OverflowException` message even though you've thrown multiple errors since the original error occurred:

```
Messagebox.Show(objC.GetBaseException.Message)
```

To put it another way, the code traverses back to the exception caught as `objA` and displays the same message as the `objA.Message` property would, as shown in Figure 8-5.

Figure 8-5

HelpLink

The `HelpLink` property gets or sets the help link for a specific `Exception` object. It can be set to any string value, but is typically set to a URL. If you create your own exception in code, you might want to set `HelpLink` to some URL describing the error in more detail. Then the code that catches the exception can go to that link. You could create and throw your own custom application exception with code like the following:

```
Dim exc As New ApplicationException("A short description of the problem")
exc.HelpLink = "http://mysite.com/somehtmlfile.htm"
Throw exc
```

When trapping an exception, the `HelpLink` can be used to launch a viewer so the user can see details about the problem. The following example shows this in action, using the built-in Explorer in Windows:

```
Sub HandlerExample4()
Try

    Dim exc As New ApplicationException("A short description of the problem")
    exc.HelpLink = "http://mysite.com/somehtmlfile.htm"
    Throw exc


    ' Catch the error.
Catch objA As System.Exception
    Shell("explorer.exe " & objA.HelpLink)

End Try
End Sub
```

This results in launching Internet Explorer to show the page specified by the URL. Most exceptions thrown by the CLR or the .NET Framework's classes have a blank `HelpLink` property. You should only count on using `HelpLink` if you have previously set it to a URL (or some other type of link information) yourself.

Interoperability with VB6-Style Error Handling

Because VB 2008 still supports the older `On Error` statement from pre-.NET versions of VB, you may encounter code that handles errors with `On Error` instead of with structured exception handling. You can use both techniques in a single program, but it is not possible to use both in a single routine. If you attempt to use both `On Error` and `Try ... Catch` in a single routine, you will get a syntax error.

The VB compiler does allow the two techniques for handling errors to communicate with each other. For example, suppose you have a routine that uses `On Error` and then uses `Err.Raise` to promote the error to the calling code. Also suppose that the calling code makes the call in a `Try ... Catch` block. In that case, the error created by `Err.Raise` becomes an exception in the calling code and is trapped by a `Catch` block just as a normal exception would be. Here's a code example to illustrate. First, create a subroutine that creates an error with `Err.Raise`, like this:

```
Private Sub RaiseErrorWithErrRaise()
    Err.Raise(53)    ' indicates File Not Found
End Sub
```

Then call this routine from a button's `click` event, with the call inside a `Try ... Catch` block:

```
Private Sub Button2_Click(ByVal sender As System.Object, _
    ByVal e As System.EventArgs) Handles Button2.Click
    Try
        RaiseErrorWithErrRaise()
    Catch ex As Exception
        MessageBox.Show(ex.Message)
    End Try
End Sub
```

When the button is clicked, it will display a message box with `File Not Found`. Even though the `File Not Found` error is raised by `Err.Raise`, it is translated to a .NET exception automatically.

Similarly, exceptions that are generated by a `Throw` statement in a called routine can be trapped by `On Error` in a calling routine. The exception is then translated into an `Err` object that works like the VB6 `Err` object.

Error Logging

Error logging is important in many applications for thorough troubleshooting. It is common for end users of an application to forget exactly what the error said. Recording specific errors in a log enables you to get the specific error message without recreating the error.

While error logging is very important, you only want to use it to trap specific levels of errors because it carries overhead and can reduce the performance of your application. Specifically, log only errors that are critical to your application integrity — for instance, an error that would cause the data that the application is working with to become invalid.

There are three main approaches to error logging:

- ❏ Write error information in a text file or flat file located in a strategic location.
- ❏ Write error information to a central database.
- ❏ Write error information to the system Event Log, which is available on all versions of Windows supported by the .NET Framework 3.0. The .NET Framework includes a component that can be used to write to and read from the System, Application, and Security Logs on any given machine.

The type of logging you choose depends on the categories of errors you wish to trap and the types of machines on which you will run your application. If you choose to write to the Event Log, then you need to categorize the errors and write them in the appropriate log file. Resource-, hardware-, and system-level errors fit best into the System Event Log. Data access errors fit best into the Application Event Log. Permission errors fit best into the Security Event Log.

The Event Log

Three Event Logs are available: the System, Application, and Security Logs. Events in these logs can be viewed using the Event Viewer, which is accessed from the Control Panel. Access Administrative Tools and then select the Event Viewer subsection to view events. Typically, your applications would use the Application Event Log.

Event logging is available in your program through an `EventLog` component, which can both read and write to all of the available logs on a machine. The `EventLog` component is part of the `System .Diagnostics` namespace. This component allows adding and removing custom Event Logs, reading and writing to and from the standard Windows Event Logs, and creating customized Event Log entries.

Event Logs can become full, as they have a limited amount of space, so you only want to write critical information to your Event Logs. You can customize each of your system Event Log's properties by changing the log size and specifying how the system will handle events that occur when the log is full. You can configure the log to overwrite data when it is full or overwrite all events older than a given number of days. Remember that the Event Log that is written to is based on where the code is running from, so if there are many tiers, then you must locate the proper Event Log information to research the error further.

There are five types of Event Log entries you can make. These five types are divided into event type entries and audit type entries.

Event type entries are as follows:

❑ **Information** — Added when events such as a service starting or stopping occurs

❑ **Warning** — Occurs when a noncritical event happens that might cause future problems, such as disk space getting low

❑ **Error** — Should be logged when something occurs that prevents normal processing, such as a startup service not being able to start

Audit type entries usually go into the Security Log and can be either of the following:

❑ **Success audit** — For example, a success audit might be a successful login through an application to an SQL Server.

❑ **Failure audit** — A failure audit might come in handy if a user doesn't have access to create an output file on a certain file system.

If you don't specify the type of Event Log entry, an information type entry is generated.

Each entry in an Event Log has a `Source` property. This required property is a programmer-defined string that is assigned to an event to help categorize the events in a log. A new `Source` must be defined prior to being used in an entry in an Event Log. The `SourceExists` method is used to determine whether a particular source already exists on the given computer. Use a string that is relevant to where the error originated, such as the component's name. Packaged software often uses the software name as the `Source` in the Application Log. This helps group errors that occur by specific software package.

The `EventLog` component is in the `System.Diagnostics` namespace. To use it conveniently, include an `Imports System.Diagnostics` statement in the declarations section of your code.

> **Certain security rights must be obtained in order to manipulate Event Logs. Ordinary programs can read all of the Event Logs and write to the Application Event Log. Special privileges, on the administrator level, are required to perform tasks such as clearing and deleting Event Logs. Your application should not normally need to do these tasks, or write to any log besides the Application Event Log.**

The most common events, methods, and properties for the `EventLog` component are listed and described in the following tables.

Events, Methods, and Properties

The following table describes the relevant event:

Event	Description
EntryWritten	Generated when an event is written to a log

The following table describes the relevant methods:

Methods	Description
CreateEventSource	Creates an event source in the specified log
DeleteEventSource	Deletes an event source and associated entries
WriteEntry	Writes a string to a specified log
Exists	Used to determine whether a specific Event Log exists
SourceExists	Used to determine whether a specific source exists in a log
GetEventLogs	Retrieves a list of all Event Logs on a particular computer
Delete	Deletes an entire Event Log. Use this method with care.

The following table describes the relevant properties:

Properties	Description
Source	Specifies the source of the entry to be written
Log	Used to specify a log to write to. The three logs are System, Application, and Security. The System Log is the default if not specified.

The following example illustrates some of these methods and properties:

```
Sub LoggingExample1()
  Dim objLog As New EventLog()
  Dim objLogEntryType As EventLogEntryType
  Try
    Throw (New EntryPointNotFoundException())
  Catch objA As System.EntryPointNotFoundException
    If Not EventLog.SourceExists("Example") Then
      EventLog.CreateEventSource("Example", "System")
    End If
    objLog.Source = "Example"
```

```
        objLog.Log = "System"
        objLogEntryType = EventLogEntryType.Information
        objLog.WriteEntry("Error: " & objA.Message, objLogEntryType)
    End Try
End Sub
```

The preceding code declares two variables: one to instantiate your log and one to hold your entry's type information. Note that you need to check for the existence of a source prior to creating it. The following two lines of code accomplish that:

```
If Not EventLog.SourceExists("Example") Then
    EventLog.CreateEventSource("Example", "System")
```

After you have verified or created your source, you can set the `Source` property of the `EventLog` object, the `Log` property to specify which log you want to write to, and `EventLogEntryType` to `Information` (other options are `Warning`, `Error`, `SuccessAudit`, and `FailureAudit`). If you attempt to write to a source that does not exist in a specific log, then you get an error. After you have set these three properties of the `EventLog` object, you can then write your entry. In this example, you concatenated the word `Error` with the actual exception's `Message` property to form the string to write to the log:

```
objLog.Source = "Example"
objLog.Log = "System"
objLogEntryType = EventLogEntryType.Information
objLog.WriteEntry("Error: " & objA.Message, objLogEntryType)
```

Writing to Trace Files

As an alternative to the Event Log, you can write your debugging and error information to trace files. A *trace file* is a text-based file that you generate in your program to track detailed information about an error condition. Trace files are also a good way to supplement your event logging if you want to track detailed information that would potentially fill the Event Log.

A more detailed explanation of the variety of trace tools and their uses in debugging follows in the section "Analyzing Problems and Measuring Performance via the Trace Class." This section covers some of the techniques for using the `StreamWriter` interface in your development of a trace file.

The concepts involved in writing to text files include setting up streamwriters and debug listeners. The `StreamWriter` interface is handled through the `System.IO` namespace. It enables you to interface with the files in the file system on a given machine. The `Debug` class interfaces with these output objects through listener objects. The job of any listener object is to collect, store, and send the stored output to text files, logs, and the Output window. In the example, you will use the `TextWriterTraceListener` interface.

As you will see, the `StreamWriter` object opens an output path to a text file, and by binding the `StreamWriter` object to a listener object you can direct debug output to a text file.

Trace listeners are output targets and can be a `TextWriter` or an `EventLog`, or can send output to the default Output window (which is `DefaultTraceListener`). The `TextWriterTraceListener` accommodates the `WriteLine` method of a `Debug` interface by providing an output object that stores information to be flushed to the output stream, which you set up by the `StreamWriter` interface.

The following table lists some of the commonly used methods from the `StreamWriter` object:

Method	Description
Close	Closes the `StreamWriter`
Flush	Flushes all content of the `StreamWriter` to the output file designated upon creation of the `StreamWriter`
Write	Writes byte output to the stream. Optional parameters allow location designation in the stream (offset).
WriteLine	Writes characters followed by a line terminator to the current stream object

The following table lists some of the methods associated with the `Debug` object, which provides the output mechanism for the text file example to follow:

Method	Description
Assert	Checks a condition and displays a message if `False`
Close	Executes a flush on the output buffer and closes all listeners
Fail	Emits an error message in the form of an Abort/Retry/Ignore message box
Flush	Flushes the output buffer and writes it to the listeners
Write	Writes bytes to the output buffer
WriteLine	Writes characters followed by a line terminator to the output buffer
WriteIf	Writes bytes to the output buffer if a specific condition is `True`
WriteLineIf	Writes characters followed by a line terminator to the output buffer if a specific condition is `True`

The following example shows how you can open an existing file (called `mytext.txt`) for output and assign it to the `Listeners` object of the `Debug` object so that it can catch your `Debug.WriteLine` statements:

```
Sub LoggingExample2()
  Dim objWriter As New _
      IO.StreamWriter("C:\mytext.txt", True)
    Debug.Listeners.Add(New TextWriterTraceListener(objWriter))
  Try
    Throw (New EntryPointNotFoundException())
  Catch objA As System.EntryPointNotFoundException
    Debug.WriteLine(objA.Message)
```

```
        objWriter.Flush()
        objWriter.Close()
        objWriter = Nothing
    End Try
End Sub
```

Looking in detail at this code, you first create a `StreamWriter` that is assigned to a file in your local file system:

```
Dim objWriter As New _
    IO.StreamWriter("C:\mytext.txt", True)
```

You then assign your `StreamWriter` to a debug listener by using the `Add` method:

```
Debug.Listeners.Add(New TextWriterTraceListener (objWriter))
```

This example forces an exception and catches it, writing the `Message` property of the `Exception` object (which is `Entry point was not found`) to the debug buffer through the `WriteLine` method:

```
Debug.WriteLine(objA.Message)
```

Finally, you flush the listener buffer to the output file and free your resources:

```
objWriter.Flush()
objWriter.Close()
objWriter = Nothing
```

Analyzing Problems and Measuring Performance via the Trace Class

The trace tools in the .NET Framework make use of the `Trace` class, which provides properties and methods that help you trace the execution of your code. By default, tracing is enabled in VB 2008, so not unlike the previous debug discussion, all you have to do is set up the output and utilize its capabilities.

You can specify the detail level you want to perform for your tracing output by configuring trace switches. You will see an example of setting a trace switch shortly, but it is important to understand what a trace switch can do and what the settings for trace switches mean.

Trace switches can be either `BooleanSwitch` or `TraceSwitch`. `BooleanSwitch` has a value of either 0 or 1 and is used to determine whether tracing is off or on, respectively, whereas `TraceSwitch` enables you to specify a level of tracing based on five enumerated values. You can manage a `BooleanSwitch` or `TraceSwitch` as an environment variable. Once a switch is established, you can create and initialize it in code and use it with either trace or debug.

A `TraceSwitch` can have five enumerated levels, which can be read as 0–4 or checked with four properties provided in the switch class interface. The four properties return a Boolean value based on whether the switch is set to a certain level or higher. The five enumerated levels for `TraceSwitch` are as follows:

Level	Description
0	None
1	Only error messages
2	Warning and error messages
3	Information, warning, and error messages
4	Verbose, information, warning, and error messages

The four properties are `TraceError`, `TraceWarning`, `TraceInfo`, and `TraceVerbose`. For example, if your switch were set at number 2 and you asked for the `TraceError` or `TraceWarning` properties, they would return `True`, whereas the `TraceInformation` and `TraceVerbose` properties would return `False`.

An environment variable is managed either via the command line or under My computer ➪ Properties ➪ Advanced within the Environment Variables button. Within the Environment Variables button, you add a new `User` variable, giving it the `SwitchName` and `Value` for that switch.

From the command line, type **Set _Switch_MySwitch = 0**

The value on the left of the = symbol is the name of the switch; the value on its right is either 0 or 1 for a `BooleanSwitch` or 0–4 for a `TraceSwitch`. Note the space between the word `Set` and the leading underscore of `_Switch`. Once you have typed this line, if you follow that by the plain `SET` command at the command line, it will show your new switch as an environment variable, as shown in Figure 8-6.

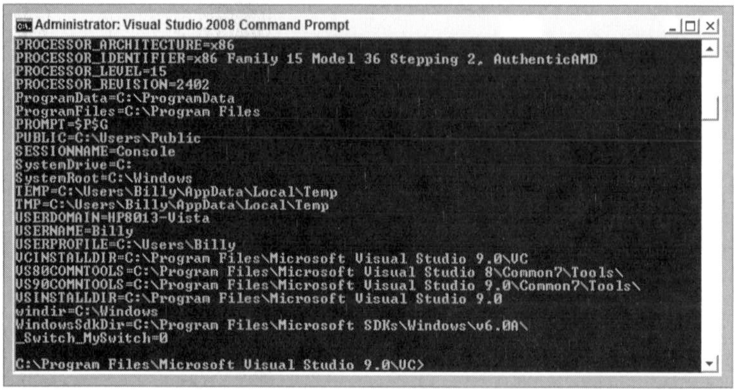

Figure 8-6

For the example that follows, the output is directed to the default Output window:

```
Sub TraceExample1()
  Dim objTraceSwitch As TraceSwitch
  objTraceSwitch = New TraceSwitch("ExampleSwitch", "Test Trace Switch")
  objTraceSwitch.Level = TraceLevel.Error
  Try
    Throw (New EntryPointNotFoundException())
  Catch objA As System.EntryPointNotFoundException
    Trace.WriteLineIf(objTraceSwitch.TraceVerbose, _
        "First Trace " & objA.Source)
    Trace.WriteLineIf(objTraceSwitch.TraceError, _
        "Second Trace " & objA.Message)
  End Try
End Sub
```

You begin by assigning your switch to an existing registry entry and setting its level:

```
objTraceSwitch = New TraceSwitch("ExampleSwitch", "Test Trace Switch")
objTraceSwitch.Level = TraceLevel.Error
```

After you throw your exception, you first cause your trace output listener to catch the Source property of your Exception object based on whether the value of your switch is TraceVerbose or better:

```
Trace.WriteLineIf(objTraceSwitch.TraceVerbose, _
    "First Trace " & objA.Source)
```

Because the tracing level is set to Error, this line is skipped; and you continue by writing a trace to the Output window to include the message information if the level is set to Error:

```
Trace.WriteLineIf(objTraceSwitch.TraceError, _
    "Second Trace " & objA.Message)
```

As indicated in your Output window, you successfully wrote only the second trace line, based on the level being Error on your trace switch (see Figure 8-7).

Figure 8-7

Tracing can also be helpful in determining the performance of your application. Overall, your application might appear to be working fine, but it is always good to be able to measure your application's performance so that environment changes or degradation over time can be counteracted. The basic concept here is to use conditional compilation so that you can toggle your performance-measuring code on and off:

```
Sub TraceExample2()
  Dim connInfo As New Connection()
  Dim rstInfo As New Recordset()
  #Const bTrace = 1
  Dim objWriter As New _
    IO.StreamWriter(IO.File.Open("c:\mytext.txt", IO.FileMode.OpenOrCreate))
  connInfo.ConnectionString = "Provider = sqloledb.1" & _
    ";Persist Security Info = False;" & "Initial Catalog = Northwind;" & _
    "DataSource = LocalServer"
  connInfo.Open(connInfo.ConnectionString, "sa")
  Trace.Listeners.Add(New TextWriterTraceListener(objWriter))
  #If bTrace Then
    Trace.WriteLine("Begun db query at " & now())
  #End If
  rstInfo.Open("SELECT CompanyName, OrderID, " & _
    "OrderDate FROM Orders AS a LEFT JOIN Customers" & _
    " AS b ON a.CustomerID = b.CustomerID WHERE " & _
    "a.CustomerID = 'Chops'", connInfo, _
    CursorTypeEnum.adOpenForwardOnly, _
    LockTypeEnum.adLockBatchOptimistic)
  #If bTrace Then
    Trace.WriteLine("Ended db query at " & now())
  #End If
  Trace.Listeners.Clear()
  objWriter.Close()
  rstInfo.Close()
  connInfo.Close()
  rstInfo = Nothing
  connInfo = Nothing
End Sub
```

> **This subroutine uses ADO, so be sure to add a reference to an ADO library and an `Imports ADODB` statement in the declarations section of the module.**

In this simple example, you are trying to measure the performance of a database query using a conditional constant defined as bTrace by the following code:

```
#Const bTrace = 1
```

You establish your database connection strings, and then right before you execute your query you write to a log file based on whether you are in tracing mode or not:

```
#If bTrace Then
  Trace.WriteLine("Begun db query at " & now())
#End If
```

Again, after your query returns you write to your log only if you are in tracing mode:

```
#If bTrace Then
  Trace.WriteLine("Ended db query at" & now())
#End If
```

Always remember that tracing can potentially slow the application down, so use this functionality only when troubleshooting, not all the time.

Summary

This chapter reviewed the exception object and the syntax available to work with exceptions. You have looked at the various properties of exceptions and learned how to use the exposed information. You have also seen how to promote exceptions to consuming code using the `Throw` statement, and how structured exception handling interoperates with the old-style `On Error`. As discussed, any new code you write should use structured exception handling. Avoid using the old-style `On Error` except for maintenance tasks in old code.

Also covered were other topics related to error handling:

❑ Error logging to Event Logs and trace files

❑ Instrumentation and measuring performance

❑ Tracing techniques

By using the full capabilities for error handling that are now available in VB 2008, you can make your applications more reliable and diagnose problems faster when they do occur. Proper use of tracing and instrumentation can also help you tune your application for better performance.

9

Data Access with
ADO.NET 3.5

ADO.NET 1.x was the successor to ActiveX Data Objects 2.6 (ADO). The main goal of ADO.NET 1.x was to enable developers to easily create distributed, data-sharing applications in the .NET Framework. The main goals of ADO.NET today are to improve the performance of existing features in ADO.NET 1.x, to provide easier use and to add new features without breaking backward compatibility.

Throughout this chapter, when ADO.NET is mentioned without a version number after it (that is, 1.x, 2.0, or 3.5), the statement applies to all versions of ADO.NET.

ADO.NET 1.x was built upon industry standards such as XML, and it provided a data-access interface to communicate with data sources such as SQL Server and Oracle. ADO.NET 3.5 builds upon these concepts, while increasing performance. Applications can use ADO.NET to connect to these data sources and retrieve, manipulate, and update data. ADO.NET 3.5 does not break any compatibility with ADO.NET 2.0 or 1.x; it only adds to the stack of functionality.

In solutions that require disconnected or remote access to data, ADO.NET 3.5 uses XML to exchange data between programs or with Web pages. Any component that can read XML can make use of ADO.NET components. A receiving component does not even have to be an ADO.NET component if a transmitting ADO.NET component packages and delivers a data set in an XML format. Transmitting information in XML-formatted data sets enables programmers to easily separate the data-processing and user interface components of a data-sharing application onto separate servers. This can greatly improve both the performance and maintainability of systems that support many users.

For distributed applications, ADO.NET 1.x proved that the use of XML data sets provided performance advantages relative to the COM marshaling used to transmit disconnected data sets in ADO. Because transmission of data sets occurred through XML streams in a simple text-based standard accepted throughout the industry, receiving components did not require any of the architectural restrictions required by COM. XML data sets used in ADO.NET 1.x also avoided the processing cost of converting values in the Fields collection of a `Recordset` to data types recognized by COM. Virtually any two components from different systems can share XML data sets, provided that they both use the same XML schema for formatting the data set. This continues to be true in ADO.NET 3.5, but the story gets better. The XML integration in ADO.NET today is even stronger, and extensive work was done to improve the performance of the `DataSet` object, particularly in the areas of serialization and memory usage.

ADO.NET also supports the scalability required by Web-based data-sharing applications. Web applications must often serve hundreds, or even thousands, of users. By default, ADO.NET does not retain lengthy database locks or active connections that monopolize limited resources. This enables the number of users to grow with only a small increase in the demands made on the resources of a system.

In this chapter, you will see that ADO.NET is a very extensive and flexible API for accessing many types of data, and because ADO.NET 3.5 is an incremental change to the previous versions of ADO.NET, all previous ADO.NET knowledge already learned can be leveraged. In fact, to get the most out of this chapter, you should be fairly familiar with earlier versions of ADO.NET and the entire .NET Framework.

This chapter demonstrates how to use the ADO.NET object model in order to build flexible, fast, scalable data-access objects and applications. Specifically, it covers the following:

❑ The ADO.NET architecture

❑ Some of the specific features offered in ADO.NET, including batch updates, `DataSet` performance improvements, and asynchronous processing

❑ Working with the Common Provider Model

❑ Building a data-access component

ADO.NET Architecture

The main design goals of ADO.NET 3.5 are as follows:

❑ Customer-driven features that are still backwardly compatible with ADO.NET 1.x

❑ Improving performance on your data-store calls

❑ Providing more power for power users

❑ Taking advantage of SQL Server 2005/2008 features

ADO.NET addresses a couple of the most common data-access strategies used for applications today. When classic ADO was developed, many applications could be connected to the data store almost indefinitely. Today, with the explosion of the Internet as the means of data communication, a new data technology is required to make data accessible and updateable in a disconnected architecture.

The first of these common data-access scenarios is one in which a user must locate a collection of data and iterate through this data just a single time. This is a popular scenario for Web pages. When a request for data from a Web page that you have created is received, you can simply fill a table with data from a data store. In this case, you go to the data store, grab the data that you want, send the data across the wire, and then populate the table. In this scenario, the goal is to get the data in place as fast as possible.

The second way to work with data in this disconnected architecture is to grab a collection of data and use this data separately from the data store itself. This could be on the server or even on the client. Even though the data is disconnected, you want the capability to keep the data (with all of its tables and relations in place) on the client side. Classic ADO data was represented by a single table that you could iterate through; but ADO.NET can be a reflection of the data store itself, with tables, columns, rows, and relations all in place. When you are done with the client-side copy of the data, you can persist the changes that you made in the local copy of data directly back into the data store. The technology that gives you this capability is the `DataSet`, which is covered shortly.

Although classic ADO was geared for a two-tiered environment (client-server), ADO.NET addresses a multi-tiered environment. ADO.NET is easy to work with because it has a unified programming model. This unified programming model makes working with data on the server the same as working with data on the client. Because the models are the same, you find yourself more productive when working with ADO.NET.

Basic ADO.NET Features

This chapter begins with a quick look at the basics of ADO.NET and then provides an overview of ADO.NET capabilities, namespaces, and classes. It also reviews how to work with the `Connection`, `Command`, `DataAdapter`, `DataSet`, and `DataReader` objects.

Common ADO.NET Tasks

Before jumping into the depths of ADO.NET, step back and make sure that you understand some of the common tasks you might perform programmatically within ADO.NET. This section looks at the process of selecting, inserting, updating, and deleting data.

> *The following example makes use of the `Northwind.mdf` SQL Server Express Database file. To get this database, search for "Northwind and pubs Sample Databases for SQL Server 2000." You can find this link at* `www.microsoft.com/downloads/details.aspx?familyid=06616212-0356-46a0-8da2-eebc53a68034&displaylang=en`*. Once installed, you will find the* `Northwind.mdf` *file in the* `C:\SQL Server 2000 Sample Databases` *directory. To add this database to your ASP.NET application, create an* `App_Data` *folder within your project (if it isn't already there) and right-click on the folder and select Add Existing Item. From the provided dialog, you can browse to the location of the* `Northwind.mdf` *file that you just installed. If you have trouble getting permissions to work with the database, make a data connection to the file from the Visual Studio Server Explorer. You will be asked to be made the appropriate user of the database and VS will make the appropriate changes on your behalf for this to occur.*

Selecting Data

After the connection to the data source is open and ready to use, you probably want to read the data from the data source. If you do not want to manipulate the data, but simply to read it or transfer it from one spot to another, you use the `DataReader` class.

The following example uses the `GetCompanyNameData` function to provide a list of company names from the SQL Northwind database.

```
Imports Microsoft.VisualBasic
Imports System.Collections.Generic
```

```
Imports System.Data
Imports System.Data.SqlClient

Public Class SelectingData
    Public Function GetCompanyNameData() As List(Of String)
        Dim conn As SqlConnection
        Dim cmd As SqlCommand
        Dim cmdString As String = "Select CompanyName from Customers"
        conn = New SqlConnection("Data Source=.\SQLEXPRESS;AttachDbFilename=
            |DataDirectory|\NORTHWND.MDF;Integrated Security=True;
            User Instance=True") ' Put this string on one line in your code
        cmd = New SqlCommand(cmdString, conn)
        conn.Open()

        Dim myReader As SqlDataReader
        Dim returnData As List(Of String) = New List(Of String)
        myReader = cmd.ExecuteReader(CommandBehavior.CloseConnection)

        While myReader.Read()
            returnData.Add(myReader("CompanyName").ToString())
        End While

        Return returnData
    End Function
End Class
```

In this example, you create an instance of both the `SqlConnection` and the `SqlCommand` classes. Then, before you open the connection, you simply pass the `SqlCommand` class a SQL command selecting specific data from the Northwind database. After your connection is opened (based upon the commands passed in), you create a `DataReader`. To read the data from the database, you iterate through the data with the `DataReader` by using the `myReader.Read` method. After the `List(Of String)` object is built, the connection is closed and the object is returned from the function.

Inserting Data

When working with data, you often insert the data into the data source. The next code sample shows you how to do this. This data may have been passed to you by the end user through the XML Web Service, or it may be data that you generated within the logic of your class.

```
Public Sub InsertData()
    Dim conn As SqlConnection
    Dim cmd As SqlCommand
    Dim cmdString As String = "Insert Customers (CustomerID, _
        CompanyName, ContactName) Values ('BILLE', 'XYZ Company', 'Bill Evjen')"
    conn = New SqlConnection("Data Source=.\SQLEXPRESS;AttachDbFilename=
            |DataDirectory|\NORTHWND.MDF;Integrated Security=True;
            User Instance=True") ' Put this string on one line in your code
    cmd = New SqlCommand(cmdString, conn)
    conn.Open()

    cmd.ExecuteNonQuery()
    conn.Close()
End Sub
```

Inserting data into SQL is pretty straightforward and simple. Using the SQL command string, you insert specific values for specific columns. The actual insertion is initiated using the `cmd.ExecuteNonQuery` command. This executes a command on the data when you don't want anything in return.

Updating Data

In addition to inserting new records into a database, you frequently update existing rows of data in a table. Imagine a table in which you can update multiple records at once. In the next example, you want to update an employee table by putting a particular value in the emp_bonus column if the employee has been at the company for five years or longer:

```
Public Function UpdateEmployeeBonus() As Integer
    Dim conn As SqlConnection
    Dim cmd As SqlCommand
    Dim RecordsAffected as Integer
    Dim cmdString As String = "UPDATE Employees SET emp_bonus=1000 WHERE " & _
        "yrs_duty>=5"
    conn = New SqlConnection("Data Source=.\SQLEXPRESS;AttachDbFilename=
            |DataDirectory|\NORTHWND.MDF;Integrated Security=True;
            User Instance=True") ' Put this string on one line in your code
    cmd = New SqlCommand(cmdString, conn)
    conn.Open()

    RecordsAffected = cmd.ExecuteNonQuery()
    conn.Close()

    Return RecordsAffected
End Function
```

This update function iterates through all the employees in the table and changes the value of the emp_bonus field to 1000 if an employee has been with the company for more than five years. This is done with the SQL command string. The great thing about these update capabilities is that you can capture the number of records that were updated by assigning the ExecuteNonQuery command to the RecordsAffected variable. The total number of affected records is then returned by the function.

Deleting Data

Along with reading, inserting, and updating data, you sometimes need to delete data from the data source. Deleting data is a simple process of using the SQL command string and then the ExecuteNonQuery command as you did in the update example. The following bit of code illustrates this:

```
Public Function DeleteEmployee() As Integer
    Dim conn As SqlConnection
    Dim cmd As SqlCommand
    Dim RecordsAffected as Integer
    Dim cmdString As String = "DELETE Employees WHERE LastName='Evjen'"
    conn = New SqlConnection("Data Source=.\SQLEXPRESS;AttachDbFilename=
            |DataDirectory|\NORTHWND.MDF;Integrated Security=True;
            User Instance=True") ' Put this string on one line in your code
    cmd = New SqlCommand(cmdString, conn)
    conn.Open()

    RecordsAffected = cmd.ExecuteNonQuery()
```

```
        conn.Close()

        Return RecordsAffected
    End Function
```

You can assign the `ExecuteNonQuery` command to an `Integer` variable (just as you did for the update function) to return the number of records deleted.

Basic ADO.NET Namespaces and Classes

The six core ADO.NET namespaces are shown in the following table. In addition to these namespaces, each new data provider can have its own namespace. As an example, the Oracle .NET data provider adds a namespace of `System.Data.OracleClient` (for the Microsoft-built Oracle data provider).

Namespace	Description
System.Data	This namespace is the core of ADO.NET. It contains classes used by all data providers. Its classes represent tables, columns, rows, and the `DataSet` class. It also contains several useful interfaces, such as `IDbCommand`, `IDbConnection`, and `IDbDataAdapter`. These interfaces are used by all managed providers, enabling them to plug into the core of ADO.NET.
System.Data.Common	This namespace defines common classes that are used as base classes for data providers. All data providers share these classes. Two examples are `DbConnection` and `DbDataAdapter`.
System.Data.OleDb	This namespace defines classes that work with OLE-DB data sources using the .NET OleDb data provider. It contains classes such as `OleDbConnection` and `OleDbCommand`.
System.Data.Odbc	This namespace defines classes that work with the ODBC data sources using the .NET ODBC data provider. It contains classes such as `OdbcConnection` and `OdbcCommand`.
System.Data.SqlClient	This namespace defines a data provider for the SQL Server 7.0 or later database. It contains classes such as `SqlConnection` and `SqlCommand`.
System.Data.SqlTypes	This namespace defines a few classes that represent specific data types for the SQL Server database.

ADO.NET has three distinct types of classes commonly referred to as *disconnected*, *shared*, and *data providers*. The disconnected classes provide the basic structure for the ADO.NET Framework. A good example of this type of class is the `DataTable` class. The objects of this class are capable of storing data without any dependency on a specific data provider. The `Shared` classes form the base classes for data providers and are shared among all data providers. The data provider classes are meant to work with different kinds of data sources. They are used to perform all data-management operations on specific databases. The `SqlClient` data provider, for example, works only with the SQL Server database.

A data provider contains Connection, Command, DataAdapter, and DataReader objects. Typically, in programming ADO.NET, you first create the Connection object and provide it with the necessary information, such as the connection string. You then create a Command object and provide it with the details of the SQL command that is to be executed. This command can be an inline SQL text command, a stored procedure, or direct table access. You can also provide parameters to these commands if needed.

After you create the Connection and the Command objects, you must decide whether the command returns a result set. If the command doesn't return a result set, then you can simply execute the command by calling one of its several Execute methods. Conversely, if the command returns a result set, you must decide whether you want to retain the result set for future use without maintaining the connection to the database. If you want to retain the result set, then you must create a DataAdapter object and use it to fill a DataSet or a DataTable object. These objects are capable of maintaining their information in a disconnected mode. However, if you don't want to retain the result set, but rather to simply process the command in a swift fashion, then you can use the Command object to create a DataReader object. The DataReader object needs a live connection to the database, and it works as a forward-only, read-only cursor.

ADO.NET Components

To better support the disconnected model as defined above, the ADO.NET components separate data access from data manipulation. This is accomplished via two main components: the DataSet and the .NET Data Provider. Figure 9-1 illustrates the concept of separating data access from data manipulation.

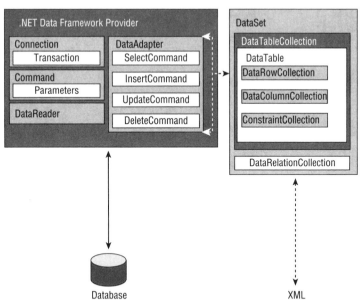

Figure 9-1

The DataSet is the core component of the disconnected architecture of ADO.NET. It is explicitly designed for data access independent of any data source. As a result, it can be used with multiple and differing data sources, with XML data, or even to manage data local to an application such as an in-memory data cache. The DataSet contains a collection of one or more DataTable objects made up of rows and columns of data, as well as primary key, foreign key, constraint, and relation information about the data in the `DataTable` objects. It is basically an in-memory database, but what sets it apart is that it doesn't care whether its data is obtained from a database, an XML file, a combination of the two, or somewhere else. You can apply inserts, updates, and deletes to the `DataSet` and then push the changes back to the data source, no matter where the data source lives! This chapter offers an in-depth look at the `DataSet` object family.

The other core element of the ADO.NET architecture is the .NET Data Provider, whose components are designed for data manipulation (as opposed to data access with the `DataSet`). These components are listed in the following table.

The `DataAdapter` uses `Command` objects to execute SQL commands at the data source, both to load the `DataSet` with data and to reconcile changes made to the data in the `DataSet` with the data source. You will take a closer look at this later in the detailed discussion of the `DataAdapter` object.

.NET Data Providers can be written for any data source, though this topic is beyond the scope of this chapter.

Object	Activity
Connection	Provides connectivity to a data source
Command	Enables access to database commands to return and modify data, run stored procedures, and send or retrieve parameter information
DataReader	Provides a high-performance, read-only stream of data from the data source
DataAdapter	Provides the bridge between the `DataSet` object and the data source

The .NET Framework 3.5 ships with three .NET Data Providers: the SQL Server .NET Data Provider, the Oracle .NET Data Provider, and the OLE DB .NET Data Provider.

Do not confuse the OLE DB .NET Data Provider with generic OLE DB Providers.

The rule of thumb when deciding which data provider to use is to first use a .NET Relational Database Management System (RDBMS)–specific data provider if it is available, and to use the .NET OLE DB Provider when connecting to any other data source. (Most RDBMS vendors are now producing their own .NET Data Providers in order to encourage .NET developers to use their databases.)

For example, if you were writing an application that uses SQL Server, then you would want to use the SQL Server .NET Data Provider. The .NET OLE DB Provider is used to access any data source exposed through OLE DB, such as Microsoft Access, Open DataBase Connectivity (ODBC), and so on. You will be taking a closer look at these later.

.NET Data Providers

.NET Data Providers are used for connecting to a RDBMS-specific database (such as SQL Server or Oracle), executing commands, and retrieving results. Those results are either processed directly (via a `DataReader`) or placed in an ADO.NET `DataSet` (via a `DataAdapter`) in order to be exposed to the user in an ad hoc manner, combined with data from multiple sources, or passed around between tiers. NET Data Providers are designed to be lightweight, to create a minimal layer between the data source and the .NET programmer's code, and to increase performance while not sacrificing any functionality.

Connection Object

To connect to a specific data source, you use a data Connection object. To connect to Microsoft SQL Server 7.0 or later, you need to use the SqlConnection object of the SQL Server .NET Data Provider. You need to use the OleDbConnection object of the OLE DB .NET Data Provider to connect to an OLE DB data source, or the OLE DB Provider for SQL Server (SQLOLEDB) to connect to versions of Microsoft SQL Server earlier than 7.0.

Connection String Format — OleDbConnection

For the OLE DB .NET Data Provider, the connection string format is the same as the connection string format used in ADO, with the following exceptions:

❑ The Provider keyword is required.

❑ The URL, Remote Provider, and Remote Server keywords are not supported.

Here is an example OleDbConnection connection string connecting to an Oracle database:

```
Provider=msdaora;Data Source=MyOracleDB;UserId=myUsername;Password=myPassword;
```

Connection-String Format — SqlConnection

The SQL Server .NET Data Provider supports a connection-string format that is similar to the OLE DB (ADO) connection-string format. The only thing that you need to omit, obviously, is the provider name-value pair, as you know you are using the SQL Server .NET Data Provider. Here is an example of a SqlConnection connection string:

```
Data Source=(local);Initial Catalog=pubs;Integrated Security=SSPI;
```

Command Object

After establishing a connection, you can execute commands and return results from a data source (such as SQL Server) using a Command object. A Command object can be created using the Command constructor, or by calling the CreateCommand method of the Connection object. When creating a Command object using the Command constructor, you need to specify a SQL statement to execute at the data source, and a Connection object. The Command object's SQL statement can be queried and modified using the CommandText property. The following code is an example of executing a SELECT command and returning a DataReader object:

```
` Build the SQL and Connection strings.
Dim sql As String = "SELECT * FROM authors"
Dim connectionString As String = "Initial Catalog=pubs;" _
 & "Data Source=(local);Integrated Security=SSPI;"
` Initialize the SqlCommand with the SQL
` and Connection strings.
Dim command As SqlCommand = New SqlCommand(sql, _
```

```
        New SqlConnection(connectionString))
    ` Open the connection.
    command.Connection.Open()
        ` Execute the query, return a SqlDataReader object.
        ` CommandBehavior.CloseConnection flags the
        ` DataReader to automatically close the DB connection
        ` when it is closed.
    Dim dataReader As SqlDataReader = _
        command.ExecuteReader(CommandBehavior.CloseConnection)
```

The `CommandText` property of the `Command` object executes all SQL statements in addition to the standard `SELECT`, `UPDATE`, `INSERT`, and `DELETE` statements. For example, you could create tables, foreign keys, primary keys, and so on, by executing the applicable SQL from the `Command` object.

The `Command` object exposes several `Execute` methods to perform the intended action. When returning results as a stream of data, `ExecuteReader` is used to return a `DataReader` object. `ExecuteScalar` is used to return a singleton value. In ADO.NET, the `ExecuteRow` method has been added, which returns a single row of data in the form of a `SqlRecord` object. `ExecuteNonQuery` is used to execute commands that do not return rows, which usually includes stored procedures that have output parameters and/or return values. (You will learn about stored procedures in a later section.)

When using a `DataAdapter` with a `DataSet`, `Command` objects are used to return and modify data at the data source through the `DataAdapter` object's `SelectCommand`, `InsertCommand`, `UpdateCommand`, and `DeleteCommand` properties.

> Note that the **DataAdapter** object's **SelectCommand** property must be set before the **Fill** method is called.

The `InsertCommand`, `UpdateCommand`, and `DeleteCommand` properties must be set before the `Update` method is called. You will take a closer look at this when you look at the `DataAdapter` object.

Using Stored Procedures with Command Objects

This section offers a quick look at how to use stored procedures, before delving into a more complex example later in the chapter demonstrating how you can build a reusable data-access component that also uses stored procedures. The motivation for using stored procedures is simple. Imagine you have the following code:

```
SELECT au_lname FROM authors WHERE au_id='172-32-1176'
```

If you pass that to SQL Server using `ExecuteReader` on `SqlCommand` (or any execute method, for that matter), SQL Server has to compile the code before it can run it, in much the same way that VB .NET applications have to be compiled before they can be executed. This compilation takes up SQL Server's time, so it is easy to deduce that if you can reduce the amount of compilation that SQL Server has to do, database performance should increase. (Compare the speed of execution of a compiled application against interpreted code.)

That's what stored procedures are all about: you create a procedure, store it in the database, and because the procedure is recognized and understood ahead of time, it can be compiled ahead of time and ready for use in your application.

Stored procedures are very easy to use, but the code to access them is sometimes a little verbose. The next section demonstrates some code that can make accessing stored procedures a bit more straightforward, but to make things clearer, let's start by building a simple application that demonstrates how to create and call a stored procedure.

Creating a Stored Procedure

To create a stored procedure, you can either use the tools in Visual Studio .NET or you can use the tools in SQL Server's Enterprise Manager if you are using SQL Server 2000, or in SQL Server Management Studio if you are using SQL Server 2005/2008. (Technically, you can use a third-party tool or just create the stored procedure in a good, old-fashioned SQL script.)

This example builds a stored procedure that returns all of the columns for a given author ID. The SQL to do this looks like this:

```
SELECT
    au_id, au_lname, au_fname, phone,
    address, city, state, zip, contract
FROM
    authors
WHERE
    au_id = whatever author ID you want
```

The "whatever author ID you want" part is important. When using stored procedures, you typically have to be able to provide parameters into the stored procedure and use them from within code. This is not a book about SQL Server, so this example focuses only on the principle involved. You can find many resources on the Web about building stored procedures (they have been around a very long time, and they are most definitely not a .NET-specific feature).

Variables in SQL Server are prefixed by the @ symbol, so if you have a variable called au id, then your SQL will look like this:

```
SELECT
    au_id, au_lname, au_fname, phone,
    address, city, state, zip, contract
FROM
    authors
WHERE
    au_id = @au_id
```

In Visual Studio 2008, stored procedures can be accessed using the Server Explorer. Simply add a new data connection (or use an existing data connection), and then drill down into the Stored Procedures folder in the management tree. A number of stored procedures are already loaded. The byroyalty procedure is a stored procedure provided by the sample pubs database developers. Figure 9-2 illustrates the stored procedures of the pubs database in Visual Studio 2008.

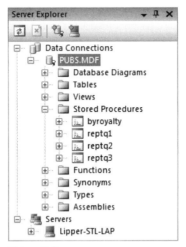

Figure 9-2

To create a new stored procedure, just right-click the Stored Procedures folder in the Server Explorer and select Add New Stored Procedure to invoke the Editor window.

A stored procedure can be either a single SQL statement or a complex set of statements. T-SQL supports branches, loops, and other variable declarations, which can make for some pretty complex stored procedure code. However, your stored procedure is just a single line of SQL. You need to declare the parameter that you want to pass in (@au_id) and the name of the procedure: usp_authors_Get_By_ID. Here's code for the stored procedure:

```
CREATE PROCEDURE usp_authors_Get_By_ID
    @au_id varchar(11)
AS
SELECT
    au_id, au_lname, au_fname, phone,
    address, city, state, zip, contract
FROM
    authors
WHERE
    au_id = @au_id
```

Click OK to save the stored procedure in the database. You are now able to access this stored procedure from code.

Calling the Stored Procedure

Calling the stored procedure is just a matter of creating a SqlConnection object to connect to the database, and a SqlCommand object to run the stored procedure.

The sample code for this chapter demonstrates a solution called Examples.sln, which includes a project called AdoNetFeaturesTest.

> For all of the data-access examples in this chapter, you need the pubs database,
> which can be downloaded from MSDN. In addition, be sure to run the
> `examples.sql` file — available with the code download for this chapter — in SQL
> Server 2005 Management Studio before running the code examples. This creates the
> necessary stored procedures and functions in the pubs database. You can also use
> the SQL Server Express Edition of the pubs database, PUBS.MDF, also found on
> MSDN.

Now you have to decide what you want to return by calling the stored procedure. In this case, you return an instance of the `SqlDataReader` object. The `TestForm.vb` file contains a method called `GetAuthorSqlReader` that takes an author ID and returns an instance of a `SqlDataReader`. Here is the code for the method:

```
Private Function GetAuthorSqlReader(ByVal authorId As String) As SqlDataReader
    ` Build a SqlCommand
    Dim command As SqlCommand = New SqlCommand("usp_authors_Get_By_ID", _
        GetPubsConnection())
    ` Tell the command we are calling a stored procedure
    command.CommandType = CommandType.StoredProcedure
    ` Add the @au_id parameter information to the command
    command.Parameters.Add(New SqlParameter("@au_id", authorId))
    ` The reader requires an open connection
    command.Connection.Open()
    ` Execute the sql and return the reader
    Return command.ExecuteReader(CommandBehavior.CloseConnection)
End Function
```

Notice that in the `SqlCommand`'s constructor call, you have factored out creating a connection to the pubs database into a separate helper method. This is used later in other code examples in your form.

Here is the code for the `GetPubsConnection` helper method:

```
Private Function GetPubsConnection() As SqlConnection
    ` Build a SqlConnection based on the config value.
    Return New _
        SqlConnection(ConfigurationSettings.AppSettings("dbConnectionString"))
End Function
```

The most significant thing this code does is grab a connection string to the database from the application's configuration file, `app.config`. Here is what the entry in the `app.config` file looks like:

```
<appSettings>
    <add key="dbConnectionString" value="data source=(local);initial
        catalog=pubs;Integrated Security=SSPI;" />
</appSettings>
```

Although the helper method does not do much, it is nice to place this code in a separate method. This way, if the code to get a connection to the databases needs to be changed, then the code only has to be changed in one place.

Accessing a stored procedure is more verbose (but not more difficult) than accessing a normal SQL statement through the methods discussed thus far. The approach is as follows:

1. Create a SqlCommand object.

2. Configure it to access a stored procedure by setting the CommandType property.

3. Add parameters that exactly match those in the stored procedure itself.

4. Execute the stored procedure using one of the SqlCommand object's Execute*** methods

There is no real need to build an impressive UI for this application, as we're about to add a button named getAuthorByIdButton that calls the GetAuthorSqlRecord helper method and displays the selected author's name. Here is the button's Click event handler:

```
Private Sub _getAuthorByIdButton_Click(ByVal sender As System.Object, _
    ByVal e As System.EventArgs) Handles _getAuthorByIdButton.Click
    Dim reader As SqlDataReader = Me. GetAuthorSqlReader ("409-56-7008")
    If reader.Read()
        MessageBox.Show(reader("au_fname").ToString() & "  " _
            & reader("au_lname").ToString())
    End If

    reader.Close()
End Sub
```

This has hard-coded an author ID of 409-56-7008. Run the code now and you should see the result shown in Figure 9-3.

Figure 9-3

DataReader Object

You can use the DataReader to retrieve a read-only, forward-only stream of data from the database. Using the DataReader can increase application performance and reduce system overhead because only one buffered row at a time is ever in memory. With the DataReader object, you are getting as close to the raw data as possible in ADO.NET; you do not have to go through the overhead of populating a DataSet object, which sometimes may be expensive if the DataSet contains a lot of data. The disadvantage of using a DataReader object is that it requires an open database connection and increases network activity.

After creating an instance of the Command object, a DataReader is created by calling the ExecuteReader method of the Command object. Here is an example of creating a DataReader and iterating through it to print out its values to the screen:

```
Private Sub TraverseDataReader()

    ` Build the SQL and Connection strings.
    Dim sql As String = "SELECT * FROM authors"
    Dim connectionString As String = "Initial Catalog=pubs;" _
        & "Data Source=(local);Integrated Security=SSPI;"

    ` Initialize the SqlCommand with the SQL query and connection strings.
    Dim command As SqlCommand = New SqlCommand(sql, _
        New SqlConnection(connectionString))
    ` Open the connection.
    command.Connection.Open()
    ` Execute the query, return a SqlDataReader object.
    ` CommandBehavior.CloseConnection flags the
    ` DataReader to automatically close the DB connection
    ` when it is closed.
    Dim reader As SqlDataReader = _
        command.ExecuteReader(CommandBehavior.CloseConnection)
    ` Loop through the records and print the values.
    Do While reader.Read
        Console.WriteLine(reader.GetString(1) & " " & reader.GetString(2))
    Loop
    ` Close the DataReader (and its connection).
    reader.Close()

End Sub
```

This code snippet uses the SqlCommand object to execute the query via the ExecuteReader method. This method returns a populated SqlDataReader object, which you loop through and then print out the author names. The main difference between this code and looping through the rows of a DataTable is that you have to stay connected while you loop through the data in the DataReader object; this is because the DataReader reads in only a small stream of data at a time to conserve memory space.

> At this point, an obvious design question is whether to use the **DataReader** or the **DataSet**. The answer depends upon performance. If you want high performance and you are only going to access the data you are retrieving once, then the **DataReader** is the way to go. If you need access to the same data multiple times, or if you need to model a complex relationship in memory, then the **DataSet** is the way to go. As always, test each option thoroughly before deciding which one is the best.

The Read method of the DataReader object is used to obtain a row from the results of the query. Each column of the returned row may be accessed by passing the name or ordinal reference of the column to the DataReader; or, for best performance, the DataReader provides a series of methods that enable you to access column values in their native data types (GetDateTime, GetDouble, GetGuid, GetInt32, and so on). Using the typed accessor methods when the underlying data type is known reduces the amount of type conversion required (converting from type Object) when retrieving the column value.

The DataReader provides a nonbuffered stream of data that enables procedural logic to efficiently process results from a data source sequentially. The DataReader is a good choice when retrieving large amounts of data; only one row of data is cached in memory at a time. You should always call the Close method when you are through using the DataReader object, as well as close the DataReader object's database connection; otherwise, the connection will not be closed until the garbage collector gets around to collecting the object.

Note how you use the CommandBehavior.CloseConnection enumeration value on the SqlDataReader. ExecuteReader method. This tells the SqlCommand object to automatically close the database connection when the SqlDataReader.Close method is called.

> **If your command contains output parameters or return values, they will not be available until the DataReader is closed.**

Executing Commands Asynchronously

In ADO.NET, additional support enables Command objects to execute their commands asynchronously, which can result in a huge perceived performance gain in many applications, especially in Windows Forms applications. This can come in very handy, especially if you ever have to execute a long-running SQL statement. This section examines how this functionality enables you to add asynchronous processing to enhance the responsiveness of an application.

The SqlCommand object provides three different asynchronous call options: BeginExecuteReader, BeginExecuteNonQuery, and BeginExecuteXmlReader. Each of these methods has a corresponding "end" method — that is, EndExecuteReader, EndExecutreNonQuery, and EndExecuteXmlReader. Now that you are familiar with the DataReader object, let's look at an example using the BeginExecuteReader method to execute a long-running query.

In the AdoNetFeaturesTest project, I have added a Button and an associated Click event handler to the form that will initiate the asynchronous call to get a DataReader instance:

```
Private Sub _testAsyncCallButton_Click(ByVal sender As System.Object, _
        ByVal e As System.EventArgs) Handles _testAsyncCallButton.Click

        ` Build a connection for the async call to the database.
        Dim connection As SqlConnection = GetPubsConnection()
        connection.ConnectionString &= "Asynchronous Processing=true;"

        ` Build a command to call the stored procedure.
        Dim command As New SqlCommand("usp_Long_Running_Procedure", _
          connection)

        ` Set the command type to stored procedure.
        command.CommandType = CommandType.StoredProcedure

        ` The reader requires an open connection.
        connection.Open()
```

```
        ` Make the asynchronous call to the database.
        command.BeginExecuteReader(AddressOf Me.AsyncCallback, _
        command, CommandBehavior.CloseConnection)
    End Sub
```

The first thing you do is reuse your helper method `GetPubsConnection` to get a connection to the pubs database. Next, and this is very important, you append the statement `Asynchronous Processing = true` to your `Connection` object's connection string. This must be set in order for ADO.NET to make asynchronous calls to SQL Server.

After getting the connection set, you then build a `SqlCommand` object and initialize it to be able to execute the `usp_Long_Running_Procedure` stored procedure. This procedure uses the SQL Server 2005 `WAITFOR DELAY` statement to create a 20-second delay before it executes the `usp_Authors_Get_All` stored procedure. As you can probably guess, the `usp_authors_Get_All` stored procedure simply selects all of the authors from the authors table. The delay is added simply to demonstrate that while this stored procedure is executing, you can perform other tasks in your Windows Forms application. Here is the SQL code for the `usp_Long_Running_Procedure` stored procedure:

```
CREATE PROCEDURE usp_Long_Running_Procedure
AS
SET NOCOUNT ON

WAITFOR DELAY '00:00:20'
EXEC usp_authors_Get_All
```

The last line of code in the `Button`'s `Click` event handler is the call to `BeginExecuteReader`. In this call, the first thing you are passing in is a delegate method (`Me.AsyncCallback`) for the `System.AsyncCallback` delegate type. This is how the .NET Framework calls you back once the method is finished running asynchronously. You then pass in your initialized `SqlCommand` object so that it can be executed, as well as the `CommandBehavior` value for the `DataReader`. In this case, you pass in the `CommandBehavior.CloseConnection` value so that the connection to the database will be closed once the `DataReader` has been closed. You will look at the `DataReader` in more detail in the next section.

Now that you have initiated the asynchronous call, and have defined a callback for your asynchronous call, let's look at the actual method that is being called back, the `AsyncCallback` method:

```
Private Sub AsyncCallback(ByVal ar As IAsyncResult)
    ` Get the command that was passed from the AsyncState of the IAsyncResult.
    Dim command As SqlCommand = CType(ar.AsyncState, SqlCommand)
    ` Get the reader from the IAsyncResult.
    Dim reader As SqlDataReader = command.EndExecuteReader(ar)
    ` Get a table from the reader.
    Dim table As DataTable = Me.GetTableFromReader(reader, "Authors")
    ` Call the BindGrid method on the Windows main thread,
    ` passing in the table.
    Me.Invoke(New BindGridDelegate(AddressOf Me.BindGrid), _
        New Object() {table})
End Sub
```

The first line of the code is simply retrieving the `SqlCommand` object from the `AsyncState` property of the `IAsyncResult` that was passed in. Remember that when you called `BeginExecuteReader` earlier, you passed in your `SqlCommand` object. You need it so that you can call the `EndExecuteReader` method on the next line. This method gives you your `SqlDataReader`. On the next line, you then transform the `SqlDataReader` into a `DataTable` (covered later when the `DataSet` is discussed).

The last line of this method is probably the most important. If you tried to just take your `DataTable` and bind it to the grid, it would not work, because right now you are executing on a thread other than the main Windows thread. The helper method named `BindGrid` can do the data binding, but it must be called only in the context of the Windows main thread. To bring the data back to the main Windows thread, it must be marshaled via the `Invoke` method of the `Form` object. `Invoke` takes two arguments: the delegate of the method you want to call and (optionally) any parameters for that method. In this case, you define a delegate for the `BindGrid` method, called `BindGridDelegate`. Here is the delegate declaration:

```
Private Delegate Sub BindGridDelegate(ByVal table As DataTable)
```

Notice how the signature is exactly the same as the `BindGrid` method shown here:

```
Private Sub BindGrid(ByVal table As DataTable)
    ` Clear the grid.
    Me._authorsGridView.DataSource = Nothing
    ` Bind the grid to the DataTable.
    Me._authorsGridView.DataSource = table
End Sub
```

Here is another look at the call to the form's `Invoke` method:

```
Me.Invoke(New BindGridDelegate(AddressOf Me.BindGrid), _
    New Object() {table})
```

You pass in a new instance of the `BindGridDelegate` delegate and initialize it with a pointer to the `BindGrid` method. As a result, the .NET worker thread that was executing your query can now safely join up with the main Windows thread.

DataAdapter Objects

Each .NET Data Provider included with the .NET Framework has a `DataAdapter` object. The OLE DB .NET Data Provider includes an `OleDbDataAdapter` object, and the SQL Server .NET Data Provider includes a `SqlDataAdapter` object. A `DataAdapter` is used to retrieve data from a data source and populate `DataTable` objects and constraints within a `DataSet`. The `DataAdapter` also resolves changes made to the `DataSet` back to the data source. The `DataAdapter` uses the `Connection` object of the .NET Data Provider to connect to a data source, and `Command` objects to retrieve data from, and resolve changes to, the data source from a `DataSet` object.

This differs from the `DataReader`, in that the `DataReader` uses the `Connection` object to access the data directly, without having to use a `DataAdapter`. The `DataAdapter` essentially decouples the `DataSet` object from the actual source of the data, whereas the `DataReader` is tightly bound to the data in a read-only fashion.

The `SelectCommand` property of the `DataAdapter` is a `Command` object that retrieves data from the data source. A nice, convenient way to set the `DataAdapter`'s `SelectCommand` property is to pass in a `Command` object in the `DataAdapter`'s constructor. The `InsertCommand`, `UpdateCommand`, and `DeleteCommand` properties of the DataAdapter are Command objects that manage updates to the data in the data source according to the modifications made to the data in the DataSet. The Fill method of the DataAdapter is used to populate a DataSet with the results of the SelectCommand of the DataAdapter. It also adds or refreshes rows in the DataSet to match those in the data source. The following example code demonstrates how to fill a DataSet object with information from the authors table in the pubs database:

```
Private Sub TraverseDataSet()
    ` Build the SQL and Connection strings.
    Dim sql As String = "SELECT * FROM authors"
    Dim connectionString As String = "Initial Catalog=pubs;" _
        & "Data Source=(local);Integrated Security=SSPI;"

    ` Initialize the SqlDataAdapter with the SQL
    ` and Connection strings, and then use the
    ` SqlDataAdapter to fill the DataSet with data.
    Dim adapter As New SqlDataAdapter(sql, connectionString)
    Dim authors As New DataSet
    adapter.Fill(authors)

    ` Iterate through the DataSet's table.
    For Each row As DataRow In authors.Tables(0).Rows
        Console.WriteLine(row("au_fname").ToString _
            & " " & row("au_lname").ToString)
    Next

    ` Print the DataSet's XML.
    Console.WriteLine(authors.GetXml())
    Console.ReadLine()

End Sub
```

Note how you use the constructor of the SqlDataAdapter to pass in and set the SelectCommand, as well as pass in the connection string in lieu of a SqlCommand object that already has an initialized Connection property. You then just call the SqlDataAdapter object's Fill method and pass in an initialized DataSet object. If the DataSet object is not initialized, then the Fill method raises an exception (System .ArgumentNullException).

Ever since ADO.NET 2.0, a significant performance improvement was made in the way that the DataAdapter updates the database. In ADO.NET 1.x, the DataAdapter's Update method would loop through each row of every DataTable object in the DataSet and subsequently make a trip to the database for each row being updated. In ADO.NET 2.0, batch update support was added to the DataAdapter. This means that when the Update method is called, the DataAdapter batches all of the updates from the DataSet in one trip to the database.

Now let's take a look at a more advanced example. Here, you use a DataAdapter to insert, update, and delete data from a DataTable back to the pubs database:

```
Private Sub _batchUpdateButton_Click(ByVal sender As System.Object, _
        ByVal e As System.EventArgs) Handles _batchUpdateButton.Click

    ` Build insert, update, and delete commands.
```

```
` Build the parameter values.
Dim insertUpdateParams() As String = {"@au_id", "@au_lname", _
    "@au_fname", _
    "@phone", "@address", "@city", "@state", "@zip", "@contract"}
```

The preceding code begins by initializing a string array of parameter names to pass into the Build
SqlCommand helper method:

```
` Insert command.
Dim insertCommand As SqlCommand = _
    BuildSqlCommand("usp_authors_Insert", _
    insertUpdateParams)
```

Next, you pass the name of the stored procedure to execute and the parameters for the stored procedure
to the BuildSqlCommand helper method. This method returns an initialized instance of the SqlCommand
class. Here is the BuildSqlCommand helper method:

```
Private Function BuildSqlCommand(ByVal storedProcedureName As String, _
        ByVal parameterNames() As String) As SqlCommand
    ` Build a SqlCommand.
    Dim command As New SqlCommand(storedProcedureName, GetPubsConnection())
    ` Set the command type to stored procedure.
    command.CommandType = CommandType.StoredProcedure
    ` Build the parameters for the command.
    ` See if any parameter names were passed in.
    If Not parameterNames Is Nothing Then
        ` Iterate through the parameters.
        Dim parameter As SqlParameter = Nothing
        For Each parameterName As String In parameterNames
            ` Create a new SqlParameter.
            parameter = New SqlParameter()
            parameter.ParameterName = parameterName
            ` Map the parameter to a column name in the DataTable/DataSet.
            parameter.SourceColumn = parameterName.Substring(1)
            ` Add the parameter to the command.
            command.Parameters.Add(parameter)
        Next
    End If
    Return command
End Function
```

This method first initializes a SqlCommand class and passes in the name of a stored procedure; it then
uses the GetPubsConnection helper method to pass in a SqlConnection object to the SqlCommand. The
next step is to set the command type of the SqlCommand to a stored procedure. This is important because
ADO.NET uses this to optimize how the stored procedure is called on the database server. You then
check whether any parameter names have been passed (via the parameterNames string array); if so, you
iterate through them. While iterating through the parameter names, you build up SqlParameter objects
and add them to the SqlCommand's collection of parameters.

The most important step in building up the SqlParameter object is setting its SourceColumn property.
This is what the DataAdapter later uses to map the name of the parameter to the name of the column in
the DataTable when its Update method is called. An example of such a mapping is associating the @au_id

parameter name with the `au_id` column name. As shown in the code, the mapping assumes that the stored procedure parameters all have exactly the same names as the columns, except for the mandatory `@` character in front of the parameter. That's why when assigning the `SqlParameter`'s `SourceColumn` property value, you use the `Substring` method to strip off the `@` character to ensure that it maps correctly.

You then call the `BuildSqlCommand` method two more times to build your update and delete `SqlCommand` objects:

```
` Update command.
Dim updateCommand As SqlCommand = _
    BuildSqlCommand("usp_authors_Update", _
    insertUpdateParams)

` Delete command.
Dim deleteCommand As SqlCommand = _
    BuildSqlCommand("usp_authors_Delete", _
    New String() {"@au_id"})
```

Now that the `SqlCommand` objects have been created, the next step is to create a `SqlDataAdapter` object. Once the `SqlDataAdapter` is created, you set its `InsertCommand`, `UpdateCommand`, and `DeleteCommand` properties with the respective `SqlCommand` objects that you just built:

```
` Create an adapter.
Dim adapter As New SqlDataAdapter()

` Associate the commands with the adapter.
adapter.InsertCommand = insertCommand
adapter.UpdateCommand = updateCommand
adapter.DeleteCommand = deleteCommand
```

The next step is to get a `DataTable` instance of the authors table from the pubs database. You do this by calling the `GetAuthorsSqlReader` helper method to first get a `DataReader` and then the `GetTable FromReader` helper method to load a `DataTable` from a `DataReader`:

```
` Get the authors reader.
Dim reader As SqlDataReader = GetAuthorsSqlReader()
` Load a DataTable from the reader.
Dim table As DataTable = GetTableFromReader(reader, "Authors")
```

Once you have your `DataTable` filled with data, you begin modifying it so you can test the new batch update capability of the `DataAdapter`. The first change to make is an insert in the `DataTable`. In order to add a row, you first call the `DataTable`'s `NewRow` method to give you a `DataRow` initialized with the same columns as your `DataTable`:

```
` Add a new author to the DataTable.
Dim row As DataRow = table.NewRow
```

Once that is done, you can set the values of the columns of the `DataRow`:

```
row("au_id") = "335-22-0707"
row("au_fname") = "Bill"
```

```
row("au_lname") = "Evjen"
row("phone") = "800-555-1212"
row("contract") = 0
```

Then you call the Add method of the DataTable's DataRowCollection property and pass in the newly populated DataRow object:

```
table.Rows.Add(row)
```

Now that there is a new row in the DataTable, the next test is to update one of its rows:

```
` Change an author in the DataTable.
table.Rows(0)("au_fname") = "Updated Name!"
```

Finally, you delete a row from the DataTable. In this case, it is the second-to-last row in the DataTable:

```
` Delete the second to last author from the table
table.Rows(table.Rows.Count - 2).Delete()
```

Now that you have performed an insert, update, and delete action on your DataTable, it is time to send the changes back to the database. You do this by calling the DataAdapter's Update method and passing in either a DataSet or a DataTable. Note that you are calling the GetChanges method of the DataTable; this is important, because you only want to send the changes to the DataAdapter:

```
` Send only the changes in the DataTable to the database for updating.
adapter.Update(table.GetChanges())
```

To prove that the update worked, you get back a new DataTable from the server using the same technique as before, and then bind it to the grid with your helper method to view the changes that were made:

```
` Get the new changes back from the server to show that the update worked.
    reader = GetAuthorsSqlReader()
    table = GetTableFromReader(reader, "Authors")
    ` Bind the grid to the new table data.
    BindGrid(table)
End Sub
```

SQL Server .NET Data Provider

The SQL Server .NET Data Provider uses Tabular Data Stream (TDS) to communicate with the SQL Server. This offers a great performance increase, as TDS is SQL Server's native communication protocol. As an example of how much of an increase you can expect, when I ran some simple tests accessing the authors table of the pubs database, the SQL Server .NET Data Provider performed about 70 percent faster than the OLE DB .NET Data Provider.

The SQL Server .NET Data Provider is lightweight and performs very well, thanks to not having to go through the OLE DB or ODBC layer. What it actually does is establish a network connection (usually sockets-based) and drag data from this directly into managed code and vice versa.

> This is very important, as going through the OLE DB or ODBC layers means that the CLR has to marshal (convert) all of the COM data types to .NET CLR data types each time data is accessed from a data source. When using the SQL Server .NET Data Provider, everything runs within the .NET CLR, and the TDS protocol is faster than the other network protocols previously used for SQL Server.

To use this provider, you need to include the `System.Data.SqlClient` namespace in your application. Note that it works only for SQL Server 7.0 and later. I highly recommend using the SQL Server .NET Data Provider any time you are connecting to a SQL Server 7.0 and later database server. The SQL Server .NET Data Provider requires the installation of MDAC 2.6 or later.

OLE DB .NET Data Provider

The OLE DB .NET Data Provider uses native OLE DB through COM interop to enable data access. The OLE DB .NET Data Provider supports both manual and automatic transactions. For automatic transactions, the OLE DB .NET Data Provider automatically enlists in a transaction and obtains transaction details from Windows 2000 Component Services. The OLE DB .NET Data Provider does not support OLE DB 2.5 interfaces. OLE DB Providers that require support for OLE DB 2.5 interfaces will not function properly with the OLE DB .NET Data Provider. This includes the Microsoft OLE DB Provider for Exchange and the Microsoft OLE DB Provider for Internet Publishing. The OLE DB .NET Data Provider requires the installation of MDAC 2.6 or later. To use this provider, you need to include the `System.Data.OleDb` namespace in your application.

The DataSet Component

The `DataSet` object is central to supporting disconnected, distributed data scenarios with ADO.NET. The `DataSet` is a memory-resident representation of data that provides a consistent relational programming model regardless of the data source. The `DataSet` represents a complete set of data, including related tables, constraints, and relationships among the tables; basically, it's like having a small relational database residing in memory.

> *Because the `DataSet` contains a lot of metadata, you need to be careful about how much data you try to stuff into it, as it consumes memory.*

The methods and objects in a `DataSet` are consistent with those in the relational database model. The `DataSet` can also persist and reload its contents as XML, and its schema as XSD. It is completely disconnected from any database connections, so it is totally up to you to fill it with whatever data you need in memory.

Ever since ADO.NET 2.0, there have been several new features to the `DataSet` and the `DataTable` classes, as well as enhancements to existing features. The features covered in this section are as follows:

❑ The binary serialization format option

❑ Additions to make the `DataTable` more of a standalone object

❑   The capability to expose DataSet and DataTable data as a stream (DataReader), and loading stream data into a DataSet or DataTable

DataTableCollection

An ADO.NET DataSet contains a collection of zero or more tables represented by DataTable objects. The DataTableCollection contains all of the DataTable objects in a DataSet.

A DataTable is defined in the System.Data namespace and represents a single table of memory-resident data. It contains a collection of columns represented by the DataColumnCollection, which defines the schema and rows of the table. It also contains a collection of rows represented by the DataRowCollection, which contains the data in the table. Along with the current state, a DataRow retains its original state and tracks changes that occur to the data.

DataRelationCollection

A DataSet contains relationships in its DataRelationCollection object. A relationship (represented by the DataRelation object) associates rows in one DataTable with rows in another DataTable. The relationships in the DataSet can have constraints, which are represented by UniqueConstraint and ForeignKeyConstraint objects. It is analogous to a JOIN path that might exist between the primary and foreign key columns in a relational database. A DataRelation identifies matching columns in two tables of a DataSet.

Relationships enable you to see what links information within one table to another. The essential elements of a DataRelation are the name of the relationship, the two tables being related, and the related columns in each table. Relationships can be built with more than one column per table, with an array of DataColumn objects for the key columns. When a relationship is added to the DataRelationCollection, it may optionally add ForeignKeyConstraints that disallow any changes that would invalidate the relationship.

ExtendedProperties

DataSet (as well as DataTable and DataColumn) has an ExtendedProperties property. ExtendedProperties is a PropertyCollection in which a user can place customized information, such as the SELECT statement that is used to generate the result set, or a date/time stamp indicating when the data was generated. Because the ExtendedProperties contains customized information, this is a good place to store extra user-defined data about the DataSet (or DataTable or DataColumn), such as a time when the data should be refreshed. The ExtendedProperties collection is persisted with the schema information for the DataSet (as well as DataTable and DataColumn). The following code is an example of adding an expiration property to a DataSet:

```
Private Shared Sub DataSetExtended()

    ` Build the SQL and Connection strings.
    Dim sql As String = "SELECT * FROM authors"
    Dim connectionString As String = "Initial Catalog=pubs;" _
        & "Data Source=(local);Integrated Security=SSPI;"

    ` Initialize the SqlDataAdapter with the SQL
    ` and Connection strings, and then use the
    ` SqlDataAdapter to fill the DataSet with data.
```

```
Dim adapter As SqlDataAdapter = _
    New SqlDataAdapter(sql, connectionString)
Dim authors As New DataSet
adapter.Fill(authors)

` Add an extended property called "expiration."
` Set its value to the current date/time + 1 hour.
authors.ExtendedProperties.Add("expiration", _
    DateAdd(DateInterval.Hour, 1, Now))

Console.Write(authors.ExtendedProperties("expiration").ToString)
Console.ReadLine()

End Sub
```

This code begins by filling a DataSet with the authors table from the pubs database. It then adds a new extended property, called expiration, and sets its value to the current date and time plus one hour. You then simply read it back. As you can see, it is very easy to add extended properties to DataSet objects. The same pattern also applies to DataTable and DataColumn objects.

Creating and Using DataSet Objects

The ADO.NET DataSet is a memory-resident representation of the data that provides a consistent relational programming model, regardless of the source of the data it contains. A DataSet represents a complete set of data, including the tables that contain, order, and constrain the data, as well as the relationships between the tables. The advantage to using a DataSet is that the data it contains can come from multiple sources, and it is fairly easy to get the data from multiple sources into the DataSet. In addition, you can define your own constraints between the DataTables in a DataSet.

There are several methods for working with a DataSet, which can be applied independently or in combination:

❑ Programmatically create DataTables, DataRelations, and constraints within the DataSet and populate them with data.

❑ Populate the DataSet or a DataTable from an existing RDBMS using a DataAdapter.

❑ Load and persist a DataSet or DataTable using XML.

❑ Load a DataSet from an XSD schema file.

❑ Load a DataSet or a DataTable from a DataReader.

Here is a typical usage scenario for a DataSet object:

1. A client makes a request to a Web service.

2. Based on this request, the Web service populates a DataSet from a database using a DataAdapter and returns the DataSet to the client.

3. The client then views the data and makes modifications.

4. When finished viewing and modifying the data, the client passes the modified DataSet back to the Web service, which again uses a DataAdapter to reconcile the changes in the returned DataSet with the original data in the database.

5. The Web service may then return a `DataSet` that reflects the current values in the database.

6. Optionally, the client can then use the `DataSet` class's `Merge` method to merge the returned `DataSet` with the client's existing copy of the `DataSet`; the `Merge` method will accept successful changes and mark with an error any changes that failed.

The design of the ADO.NET `DataSet` makes this scenario fairly easy to implement. Because the `DataSet` is stateless, it can be safely passed between the server and the client without tying up server resources such as database connections. Although the `DataSet` is transmitted as XML, Web services and ADO.NET automatically transform the XML representation of the data to and from a `DataSet`, creating a rich, yet simplified, programming model.

In addition, because the `DataSet` is transmitted as an XML stream, non-ADO.NET clients can consume the same Web service consumed by ADO.NET clients. Similarly, ADO.NET clients can interact easily with non-ADO.NET Web services by sending any client `DataSet` to a Web service as XML and by consuming any XML returned as a `DataSet` from the Web service. However, note the size of the data; if your `DataSet` contains a large number of rows, then it will eat up a lot of bandwidth.

Programmatically Creating DataSet Objects

You can programmatically create a `DataSet` object to use as a data structure in your programs. This could be quite useful if you have complex data that needs to be passed around to another object's method. For example, when creating a new customer, instead of passing 20 arguments about the new customer to a method, you could just pass the programmatically created `DataSet` object with all of the customer information to the object's method.

Here is the code for building an ADO.NET `DataSet` object that is comprised of related tables:

```
Private Sub BuildDataSet()

    Dim customerOrders As New Data.DataSet("CustomerOrders")
    Dim customers As Data.DataTable = customerOrders.Tables.Add("Customers")
    Dim orders As Data.DataTable = customerOrders.Tables.Add("Orders")
    Dim row As Data.DataRow

    With customers
        .Columns.Add("CustomerID", Type.GetType("System.Int32"))
        .Columns.Add("FirstName", Type.GetType("System.String"))
        .Columns.Add("LastName", Type.GetType("System.String"))
        .Columns.Add("Phone", Type.GetType("System.String"))
        .Columns.Add("Email", Type.GetType("System.String"))
    End With

    With orders
        .Columns.Add("CustomerID", Type.GetType("System.Int32"))
        .Columns.Add("OrderID", Type.GetType("System.Int32"))
        .Columns.Add("OrderAmount", Type.GetType("System.Double"))
        .Columns.Add("OrderDate", Type.GetType("System.DateTime"))
    End With

    customerOrders.Relations.Add("Customers_Orders", _
    customerOrders.Tables("Customers").Columns("CustomerID"), _
    customerOrders.Tables("Orders").Columns("CustomerID"))
```

```
        row = customers.NewRow()
        row("CustomerID") = 1
        row("FirstName") = "Bill"
        row("LastName") = "Evjen"
        row("Phone") = "555-1212"
        row("Email") = "evjen@yahoo.com"
        customers.Rows.Add(row)

        row = orders.NewRow()
        row("CustomerID") = 1
        row("OrderID") = 22
        row("OrderAmount") = 0
        row("OrderDate") = #11/10/1997#
        orders.Rows.Add(row)

        Console.WriteLine(customerOrders.GetXml())
        Console.ReadLine()

    End Sub
```

Here is what the resulting XML of the DataSet looks like:

```
<CustomerOrders>
  <Customers>
    <CustomerID>1</CustomerID>
    <FirstName>Bill</FirstName>
    <LastName>Evjen</LastName>
    <Phone>555-1212</Phone>
    <Email>evjen@yahoo.com</Email>
  </Customers>
  <Orders>
    <CustomerID>1</CustomerID>
    <OrderID>22</OrderID>
    <OrderAmount>0</OrderAmount>
    <OrderDate>1997-11-10T00:00:00.0000</OrderDate>
  </Orders>
</CustomerOrders>
```

You begin by first defining a DataSet object (CustomerOrders) named CustomerOrders. You then create two tables: one for customers (customers) and one for orders (orders). Then you define the columns of the tables. Note that you call the Add method of the DataSet's Tables collection. You then define the columns of each table and create a relation in the DataSet between the customers table and the orders table on the CustomerID column. Finally, you create instances of Rows for the tables, add the data, and then append the Rows to the Rows collection of the DataTable objects.

If you create a DataSet object with no name, it is given the default name of NewDataSet.

ADO.NET DataTable Objects

A DataSet is made up of a collection of tables, relationships, and constraints. In ADO.NET, DataTable objects are used to represent the tables in a DataSet. A DataTable represents one table of in-memory relational data. The data is local to the .NET application in which it resides, but can be populated from a data source such as SQL Server using a DataAdapter.

The DataTable class is a member of the System.Data namespace within the .NET Framework class library. You can create and use a DataTable independently or as a member of a DataSet, and DataTable objects can be used by other .NET Framework objects, including the DataView. You access the collection of tables in a DataSet through the DataSet object's Tables property.

The schema, or structure, of a table is represented by columns and constraints. You define the schema of a DataTable using DataColumn objects as well as ForeignKeyConstraint and UniqueConstraint objects. The columns in a table can map to columns in a data source, contain calculated values from expressions, automatically increment their values, or contain primary key values.

If you populate a DataTable from a database, then it inherits the constraints from the database, so you don't have to do all of that work manually. A DataTable must also have rows in which to contain and order the data. The DataRow class represents the actual data contained in the table. You use the DataRow and its properties and methods to retrieve, evaluate, and manipulate the data in a table. As you access and change the data within a row, the DataRow object maintains both its current and original state.

You can create parent-child relationships between tables within a database, such as SQL Server, using one or more related columns in the tables. You create a relationship between DataTable objects using a DataRelation, which can then be used to return a row's related child or parent rows.

Advanced ADO.NET Features of the DataSet and DataTable Objects

One of the main complaints developers had about ADO.NET 1.x was related to the performance of the DataSet and its DataTable children — in particular, when they contained a large amount of data. The performance hit comes in two different ways. The first way is the time it takes to actually load a DataSet with a lot of data. As the number of rows in a DataTable increases, the time to load a new row increases almost proportionally to the number of rows. The second way is when the large DataSet is serialized and remoted. A key feature of the DataSet is the fact that it automatically knows how to serialize itself, especially when you want to pass it between application tiers. Unfortunately, the serialization is quite verbose and takes up a lot of memory and network bandwidth. Both of these performance problems have been addressed since ADO.NET 2.0.

Indexing

The first improvement made since ADO.NET 2.0 to the DataSet family was a complete rewrite of the indexing engine for the DataTable, which now scales much better for large DataSets. The addition of the new indexing engine results in faster basic inserts, updates, and deletes, which also means faster Fill and Merge operations. Just as in relational database design, if you are dealing with large DataSets, then it pays big dividends if you first add unique keys and foreign keys to your DataTable. Even better, you don't have to change any of your code at all to take advantage of this new feature.

Serialization

The second improvement made to the DataSet family was adding new options to the way the DataSet and DataTable are serialized. The main complaint about retrieving DataSet objects from Web services and remoting calls was that they were way too verbose and took up too much network bandwidth. In ADO.NET 1.x, the DataSet serializes as XML, even when using the binary formatter. Using ADO.NET, you can also specify true binary serialization by setting the newly added RemotingFormat property to

SerializationFormat.Binary, rather than (the default) SerializationFormat.XML. In the AdoNetFeaturesTest project of the Examples solution, I have added a Button (serializationButton) to the form and its associated Click event handler that demonstrates how to serialize a DataTable in binary format:

```
Private Sub _serializationButton_Click(ByVal sender As System.Object, _
    ByVal e As System.EventArgs) Handles _serializationButton.Click
        ` Get the authors reader.
        Dim reader As SqlDataReader = GetAuthorsSqlReader()
        ` Load a DataTable from the reader
        Dim table As DataTable = GetTableFromReader(reader, "Authors")
```

This code begins by calling the helper methods GetAuthorsSqlReader and GetTableFromReader to get a DataTable of the authors from the pubs database. The next code block, shown here, is where you are actually serializing the DataTable out to a binary format:

```
        Using fs As New FileStream("c:\authors.dat", FileMode.Create)
            table.RemotingFormat = SerializationFormat.Binary
            Dim format As New BinaryFormatter()
            format.Serialize(fs, table)
        End Using

        ` Tell the user what happened.
        MessageBox.Show("Successfully serialized the DataTable!")
    End Sub
```

This code takes advantage of the newly added Using statement for Visual Basic to wrap up creating and disposing of a FileStream instance that will hold your serialized DataTable data. The next step is to set the DataTable's RemotingFormat property to the SerializationFormat.Binary enumeration value. Once that is done, you simply create a new BinaryFormatter instance, and then call its Serialize method to serialize your DataTable into the FileStream instance. You then finish by showing users a message box indicating that the data has been serialized.

DataReader Integration

Another nice feature of the DataSet and DataTable classes is the capability to both read from and write out to a stream of data in the form of a DataReader. You will first take a look at how you can load a DataTable from a DataReader. To demonstrate this, I have added a Button (loadFromReaderButton) and its associated Click event handler to TestForm.vb of the AdoNetFeaturesTest project in the Examples solution:

```
Private Sub _loadFromReaderButton_Click(ByVal sender As System.Object, _
    ByVal e As System.EventArgs) Handles _loadFromReaderButton.Click

        ` Get the authors reader.
        Dim reader As SqlDataReader = GetAuthorsSqlReader()

        ` Load a DataTable from the reader.
        Dim table As DataTable = GetTableFromReader(reader, "Authors")

        ` Bind the grid to the table.
        BindGrid(table)
    End Sub
```

This method is a controller method, meaning that it only calls helper methods. It begins by first obtaining a `SqlDataReader` from the `GetAuthorsReader` helper method. It then calls the `GetTableFromReader` helper method to transform the `DataReader` into a `DataTable`. The `GetTableFromReader` method is where you actually get to see the `DataTable`'s new load functionality:

```
Private Function GetTableFromReader(ByVal reader As SqlDataReader, _
    ByVal tableName As String) As DataTable
    ` Create a new DataTable using the name passed in.
    Dim table As New DataTable(tableName)
    ` Load the DataTable from the reader.
    table.Load(reader)
    ` Close the reader.
    reader.Close()
    Return table
End Function
```

This method begins by first creating an instance of a `DataTable` and initializing it with the name passed in from the `tableName` argument. Once the new `DataTable` has been initialized, you call the new `Load` method and pass in the `SqlDataReader` that was passed into the method via the `reader` argument. This is where the `DataTable` takes the `DataReader` and populates the `DataTable` instance with the column names and data from the `DataReader`. The next step is to close the `DataReader`, as it is no longer needed; and finally, you return the newly populated `DataTable`.

DataTable Independence

One of the most convenient capabilities in ADO.NET is the inclusion of several methods from the `DataSet` class in the `DataTable` class. The `DataTable` is now much more versatile and useful than it was in the early ADO.NET days. The `DataTable` now supports all of the same read and write methods for XML as the `DataSet` — specifically, the `ReadXml`, `ReadXmlSchema`, `WriteXml`, and `WriteXmlSchema` methods.

The `Merge` method of the `DataSet` has now been added to the `DataTable` as well; and in addition to the existing functionality of the `DataSet` class, some of the new features of the `DataSet` class have been added to the `DataTable` class — namely, the `RemotingFormat` property, the `Load` method, and the `GetDataReader` method.

Working with the Common Provider Model

In ADO.NET 1.x, you could either code to the provider-specific classes, such as `SqlConnection`, or the generic interfaces, such as `IDbConnection`. If there was a possibility that the database you were programming against would change during your project, or if you were creating a commercial package intended to support customers with different databases, then you had to use the generic interfaces. You cannot call a constructor on an interface, so most generic programs included code that accomplished the task of obtaining the original `IDbConnection` by means of their own factory method, such as a `GetConnection` method that would return a provider-specific instance of the `IDbConnection` interface.

ADO.NET today has a more elegant solution for getting the provider-specific connection. Each data provider registers a `ProviderFactory` class and a provider string in the .NET `machine.config` file. A base `ProviderFactory` class (`DbProviderFactory`) and a `System.Data.Common.ProviderFactories` class can return a `DataTable` of information about different data providers registered in `machine.config`, and can return the correct `ProviderFactory` given the provider string (called `ProviderInvariantName`) or a `DataRow` from the `DataTable`. Instead of writing your own framework to build connections based on the name of the provider, ADO.NET now makes it much more straightforward, flexible, and easy to solve this problem.

Let's look at an example of using the common provider model to connect to the pubs database and display some rows from the authors table. In the AdoNetFeaturesTest project, on the `TestForm.vb` form, the `providerButton` button's `Click` event handler shows this functionality. The code is broken down into six steps. The first step is get the provider factory object based on a configuration value of the provider's invariant name:

```
Private Sub _providerButton_Click(ByVal sender As System.Object, _
  ByVal e As System.EventArgs) Handles _providerButton.Click
        ` 1. Factory
        ` Create the provider factory from config value.
        Dim factory As DbProviderFactory = DbProviderFactories.GetFactory( _
           ConfigurationSettings.AppSettings("providerInvariantName"))
```

You are able to get the factory via the `DbProviderFactories` object's `GetFactory` method and pass in the string name of the provider invariant that you are storing in the project's `app.config` file. Here is the entry in the `app.config` file:

```
<add key="providerInvariantName" value="System.Data.SqlClient" />
```

In this case, you are using the SQL Server Data Provider. Once you have the factory object, the next step is to use it to create a connection:

```
        ` 2. Connection
        ` Create the connection from the factory.
        Dim connection As DbConnection = factory.CreateConnection()
        ` Get the connection string from config.
        connection.ConnectionString = _
           ConfigurationSettings.AppSettings("dbConnectionString")
```

The connection is created by calling the `DbProviderFactory`'s `CreateConnection` method. In this case, the factory is returning a `SqlConnection`, because you chose to use the `System.Data.SqlClient` provider invariant. To keep your code generic, you will not be directly programming against any of the classes in the `System.Data.SqlClient` namespace. Note how the connection class you declare is a `DbConnection` class, which is part of the `System.Data` namespace.

The next step is to create a `Command` object so you can retrieve the data from the authors table:

```
        ` 3. Command
        ` Create the command from the connection.
        Dim command As DbCommand = connection.CreateCommand()
        ` Set the type of the command to stored procedure.
        command.CommandType = CommandType.StoredProcedure
        ` Set the name of the stored procedure to execute.
        command.CommandText = "usp_authors_Get_All"
```

You begin by declaring a generic DbCommand class variable and then using the DbConnection's CreateCommand method to create the DbCommand instance. Once you have done that, you set the command type to StoredProcedure and then set the stored procedure name.

This example uses a DbDataAdapter to fill a DataTable with the authors' data. Here is how you create and initialize the DbDataAdapter:

```
` 4. Adapter
` Create the adapter from the factory.
Dim adapter As DbDataAdapter = factory.CreateDataAdapter()
` Set the adapter's select command.
adapter.SelectCommand = command
```

Just as you did when you created your DbConnection instance, you use the factory to create your DbDataAdapter. After creating it, you then set the SelectCommand property's value to the instance of the previously initialized DbCommand instance.

After finishing these steps, the next step is to create a DataTable and fill it using the DataAdapter:

```
` 5. DataTable
` Create a new DataTable.
Dim authors As New DataTable("Authors")
` Use the adapter to fill the DataTable.
adapter.Fill(authors)
```

The final step is to bind the table to the form's grid:

```
` 6.  Grid
` Populate the grid with the data.
BindGrid(authors)
```

You already looked at the BindGrid helper method in the asynchronous example earlier. In this example, you are simply reusing this generic method again:

```
Private Sub BindGrid(ByVal table As DataTable)
        ` Clear the grid.
        Me._authorsGridView.DataSource = Nothing
        ` Bind the grid to the DataTable.
        Me._authorsGridView.DataSource = table
    End Sub
```

The main point to take away from this example is that you were able to easily write database-agnostic code with just a few short lines. ADO.NET 1.x required a lot of lines of code to create this functionality; you had to write your own abstract factory classes and factory methods in order to create instances of the generic database interfaces, such as IDbConnection, IDbCommand, and so on.

Connection Pooling in ADO.NET

Pooling connections can significantly enhance the performance and scalability of your application. Both the SQL Client .NET Data Provider and the OLE DB .NET Data Provider automatically pool connections using Windows Component Services and OLE DB Session Pooling, respectively. The only requirement is that you must use the exact same connection string each time if you want a pooled connection.

ADO.NET now enhances the connection pooling functionality offered in ADO.NET 1.x by enabling you to close all of the connections currently kept alive by the particular managed provider that you are using. You can clear a specific connection pool by using the shared `SqlConnection.ClearPool` method or clear all of the connection pools in an application domain by using the shared `SqlConnection.ClearPools` method. Both the SQL Server and Oracle managed providers implement this functionality.

Building a Data-Access Component

To better demonstrate what you have learned so far about ADO.NET, in this section you are going to build a data-access component. This component is designed to abstract the processing of stored procedures. The component you build is targeted at SQL Server, and it is assumed that all data access to the database will be through stored procedures. The idea of only using stored procedures to access data in a database has a number of advantages, such as scalability, performance, flexibility, and security. The only disadvantage is that you have to use stored procedures, and not SQL strings. Through the process of building this component, you will see how stored procedures are implemented in ADO.NET. You will also be building on the knowledge that you have gained from the previous chapters.

This component's main job is to abstract stored procedure calls to SQL Server, and one of the ways you do this is by passing in all of your stored procedure parameter metadata as XML (covered later in this section). The other job of the component is to demonstrate the use of some of the new objects in ADO.NET.

The code for this project is quite extensive, and you will only examine the key parts of it in this chapter. The full source is available in the code download (www.wrox.com).

Let's start with the beginning of the component. The first thing you do is declare your class and the private members of the class:

```
Option Explicit On
Option Strict On

Imports System
Imports System.Data
Imports System.Data.SqlClient
Imports System.Xml
Imports System.Collections
Imports System.Diagnostics

''' <summary>
''' This class wraps stored procedure calls to SQL Server.
''' It requires that all
''' stored procedures and their parameters be defined in an
''' XML document before
''' calling any of its methods. The XML can be passed in as an XmlDocument
''' instance or as a string of XML.  The only exceptions to this rule are
''' stored procedures that do not have parameters. This class also caches
''' SqlCommand objects. Each time a stored procedure is executed, a SqlCommand
''' object is built and cached into memory so that the next time the stored
''' procedure is called the SqlCommand object can be retrieved from memory.
''' </summary>
Public NotInheritable Class StoredProcedureHelper
```

```
Private _connectionString As String = ""
Private _spParamXml As String = ""
Private _spParamXmlDoc As XmlDocument = Nothing
Private _spParamXmlNode As XmlNode = Nothing
Private _commandParametersHashTable As New Hashtable()

Private Const ExceptionMsg As String = _
    "There was an error in the method.  " _
    & "Please see the Windows Event Viewer Application log for details"
```

You begin with your `Option` statements. Note that you are using the `Option Strict` statement. This helps prevent logic errors and data loss that can occur when you work between variables of different types. Next, you import the namespaces that you need for your component. In this case, most of your dependencies are on `System.Data.SqlClient`. You call your class `StoredProcedureHelper` to indicate that it wraps calling stored procedures to SQL Server. Next, you declare your private data members. You use the `ExceptionMsg` constant to indicate a generic error message for any exceptions thrown.

Constructors

Now you get to declare your constructors for the `StoredProcedureHelper` class. This is where you can really take advantage of method overloading, and it gives you a way to pass data to your class upon instantiation. First, you declare a default constructor:

```
''' <summary>
''' Default constructor.
''' </summary>
Public Sub New()

End Sub
```

The default constructor is provided in case users want to pass data to your class through public properties instead of through constructor arguments.

The next constructor you create allows a database connection string to be passed into it. By abstracting the database connection string out of this component, you give users of your component more flexibility regarding how they store and retrieve their database connection strings. Here is the code for the constructor:

```
''' <summary>
''' Overloaded constructor.
''' </summary>
''' <param name="connectionString">The connection string to the
''' SQL Server database.</param>
Public Sub New(ByVal connectionString As String)
    Me._connectionString = connectionString
End Sub
```

The only difference between this constructor and the default constructor is that you are passing in a database connection string.

In the next constructor, you pass in both a database connection string and a string of XML representing the stored procedure parameters for the stored procedures you want to call:

```
''' <summary>
''' Overloaded constructor.
''' </summary>
''' <param name="connectionString">The connection string to the
''' SQL Server database.</param>
''' <param name="spParamXml">A valid XML string which conforms to
''' the correct schema for stored procedure(s) and their
''' associated parameter(s).</param>
Public Sub New(ByVal connectionString As String, ByVal spParamXml As String)
    Me.New(connectionString)
    Me._spParamXml = spParamXml
    Me._spParamXmlDoc = New XmlDocument
    Try
        Me._spParamXmlDoc.LoadXml(spParamXml)
        Me._spParamXmlNode = Me._spParamXmlDoc.DocumentElement
    Catch e As XmlException
        LogError(e)
        Throw New Exception(ExceptionMsg, e)
    End Try
End Sub
```

This constructor sets the database connection string by calling the first overloaded constructor. This handy technique enables you to avoid writing duplicate code in your constructors. The constructor then loads the stored procedure parameter configuration into a private XmlDocument instance variable as well as a private XmlNode instance variable.

The remaining constructors enable you to pass in combinations of database connection strings as well as either a valid XmlDocument instance representing the stored procedure parameters or a valid XmlNode instance that represents the stored procedure parameters.

Properties

Now let's look at the properties of your class. Your object contains the following properties: ConnectionString, SpParamXml, and SpParamXmlDoc. These properties are provided as a courtesy in case the user of your object does not want to supply them via a constructor call. The ConnectionString property provides the same functionality as the first overloaded constructor you looked at. The SpParamXml property enables the user of the object to pass in a valid XML string representing the stored procedures' parameter metadata. All of the properties are read-write. The SpParamXmlDoc property enables users to pass in an XmlDocument instance representing the stored procedures' parameter metadata.

Here is the code for the SpParamXml property:

```
''' <summary>
''' A valid XML string which conforms to the correct schema for
''' stored procedure(s) and their associated parameter(s).
''' </summary>
Public Property SpParamXml() As String
```

```
    Get
        Return Me._spParamXml
    End Get
    Set(ByVal Value As String)
        Me._spParamXml = Value
        ` Set the XmlDocument instance to null, since
        ` an XML string is being passed in.
        Me._spParamXmlDoc = Nothing
        Try
            Me._spParamXmlDoc.LoadXml(Me._spParamXml)
            Me._spParamXmlNode = Me._spParamXmlDoc.DocumentElement
        Catch e As XmlException
            LogError(e)
            Throw New Exception(ExceptionMsg)
        End Try
    End Set
End Property
```

Note that this property resets the XmlDocument instance to Nothing before trying to load the document. This is done in case it was already set in one of the overloaded constructors, or from a previous call to this property. It also sets the XmlNode instance to the DocumentElement property of the XmlDocument instance, thus keeping them both in sync.

Stored Procedure XML Structure

In this case, rather than have the user of this class be responsible for populating the Parameters collection of a Command object, you will abstract it out into an XML structure. The structure is very simple; it basically enables you to store the metadata for one or more stored procedures at a time. This has a huge advantage because you can change all of the parameters on a stored procedure without having to recompile the project. Shown here is the XML structure for the metadata:

```
<StoredProcedures>
 <StoredProcedure name>
  <Parameters>
   <Parameter name size datatype direction isNullable sourceColumn />
  </Parameters>
 </StoredProcedure>
</StoredProcedures>
```

Here is what some sample data for the XML structure looks like:

```
<?xml version="1.0"?>
<StoredProcedures>
 <StoredProcedure name="usp_Get_Authors_By_States">
  <Parameters>
   <Parameter name="@states" size="100" datatype="VarChar"
    direction="Input" isNullable="True" />
   <Parameter name="@state_delimiter" size="1" datatype="Char"
    direction="Input" isNullable="True" />
  </Parameters>
 </StoredProcedure>
</StoredProcedures>
```

The valid values for the `direction` attribute are `Input`, `Output`, `ReturnValue`, and `InputOutput`. These values map directly to the `System.Data.Parameter` enumeration values. The valid values for the data type attribute are `BigInt`, `Binary`, `Bit`, `Char`, `DateTime`, `Decimal`, `Float`, `Image`, `Int`, `Money`, `NChar`, `NText`, `NVarChar`, `Real`, `SmallDateTime`, `SmallInt`, `SmallMoney`, `Text`, `Timestamp`, `TinyInt`, `UniqueIdentifier`, `VarBinary`, `VarChar`, and `Variant`. These values map directly to the `System.Data.SqlDbType` enumeration values.

Methods

That completes our look at the stored procedure XML structure the class expects, as well as the public properties and public constructors for the class. Now let's turn our attention to the public methods of your class.

ExecSpReturnDataSet

This public function executes a stored procedure and returns a `DataSet` object. It takes a stored procedure name (`String`), an optional `DataSet` name (`String`), and an optional list of parameter names and values (`IDictionary`). Here is the code for `ExecSpReturnDataSet`:

```
''' <summary>
''' Executes a stored procedure with or without parameters and returns a
''' populated DataSet object.
''' </summary>
''' <param name="spName">The name of the stored procedure to execute.</param>
''' <param name="dataSetName">An optional name for the DataSet instance.</param>
''' <param name="paramValues">A name-value pair of stored procedure parameter
''' name(s) and value(s).</param>
''' <returns>A populated DataSet object.</returns>
Public Function ExecSpReturnDataSet(ByVal spName As String, _
                ByVal dataSetName As String, _
                ByVal paramValues As IDictionary) As DataSet
    Dim command As SqlCommand = Nothing
    Try
        ' Get the initialized SqlCommand instance.
        command = GetSqlCommand(spName)
        ' Set the parameter values for the SqlCommand.
        SetParameterValues(command, paramValues)
        ' Initialize the SqlDataAdapter with the SqlCommand object.
        Dim sqlDA As New SqlDataAdapter(command)

        ' Initialize the DataSet.
        Dim ds As New DataSet()

        If Not (dataSetName Is Nothing) Then
            If dataSetName.Length > 0 Then
                ds.DataSetName = dataSetName
            End If
        End If

        ' Fill the DataSet.
        sqlDA.Fill(ds)

        ' Return the DataSet.
```

```
            Return ds
      Catch e As Exception
            LogError(e)
            Throw New Exception(ExceptionMsg, e)
      Finally
            ` Close and release resources.
            DisposeCommand(command)
      End Try
End Function
```

This function uses three main objects to accomplish its mission: `SqlCommand`, `SqlDataAdapter`, and `DataSet`. You first wrap everything in a `Try-Catch-Finally` block to ensure that you trap any exceptions that are thrown and to properly close and release the `SqlCommand` and `SqlConnection` resources. You call a helper method, `GetSqlCommand`, in order to get a fully initialized `SqlCommand` instance, to include any `SqlParameter` objects the `SqlCommand` may have based on your object's internal `XmlDocument`. Here is the code for `GetSqlCommand` and its overload:

```
`'` <summary>
`'` Initializes a SqlCommand object based on a stored procedure name
`'` and a SqlTransaction instance. Verifies that the stored procedure
`'` name is valid, and then tries to get the SqlCommand object from
`'` cache. If it is not already in cache, then the SqlCommand object
`'` is initialized and placed into cache.
`'` </summary>
`'` <param name="transaction">The transaction that the stored
`'` procedure will be executed under.</param>
`'` <param name="spName">The name of the stored procedure to execute.</param>
`'` <returns>An initialized SqlCommand object.</returns>
Public Function GetSqlCommand(ByVal transaction As SqlTransaction, _
      ByVal spName As String) As SqlCommand

      Dim command As SqlCommand = Nothing

      ` Get the name of the stored procedure.
      If spName.Length < 1 Or spName.Length > 127 Then
          Throw New ArgumentOutOfRangeException("spName", _
              "Stored procedure name must be from 1 - 128 characters.")
      End If

      ` See if the command object is already in memory.
      Dim hashKey As String = Me._connectionString & ":" & spName
      command = CType(_commandParametersHashTable(hashKey), SqlCommand)
      If command Is Nothing Then
          ` It was not in memory.
          ` Initialize the SqlCommand.
          command = New SqlCommand(spName, GetSqlConnection(transaction))

          ` Tell the SqlCommand that you are using a stored procedure.
          command.CommandType = CommandType.StoredProcedure

          ` Build the parameters, if there are any.
          BuildParameters(command)

          ` Put the SqlCommand instance into memory.
```

```
            Me._commandParametersHashTable(hashKey) = command
        Else
            ` It was in memory, but you still need to set the
            ` connection property.
            command.Connection = GetSqlConnection(transaction)
        End If

        ` Return the initialized SqlCommand instance.
        Return command
    End Function

    ` ` ` <summary>
    ` ` ` Overload. Initializes a SqlCommand object based on a stored
    ` ` ` procedure name, with no SqlTransaction instance.
    ` ` ` Verifies that the stored procedure name is valid, and then tries
    ` ` ` to get the SqlCommand object from cache. If it is not already in
    ` ` ` cache, then the SqlCommand object is initialized and placed into cache.
    ` ` ` </summary>
    ` ` ` <param name="spName">The name of the stored procedure to execute.</param>
    ` ` ` <returns>An initialized SqlCommand object.</returns>
    Public Function GetSqlCommand(ByVal spName As String) As SqlCommand
        ` Return the initialized SqlCommand instance.
        Return GetSqlCommand(Nothing, spName)
    End Function
```

The difference between this method and its overload is that the first method takes in a SqlTransaction instance argument, and the overload does not require the SqlTransaction instance to be passed in. The overload simply calls the first method and passes in a value of Nothing for the SqlTransaction argument.

This method first performs a check to ensure that the stored procedure name is between 1 and 128 characters long, in accordance with SQL Server's object-naming conventions. If it is not, then you throw an exception. The next step this method performs is to try to get an already initialized SqlCommand object from your object's private Hashtable variable, commandParametersHashTable, using your object's database connection string and the name of the stored procedure as the key. If the SqlCommand is not found, then you go ahead and build the SqlCommand object by calling its constructor and passing in the stored procedure name and a SqlConnection instance returned from the GetSqlConnection helper method. The code then sets the SqlCommand's CommandType property. You should ensure that you pass in the CommandType.StoredProcedure enumeration value, as you are executing a stored procedure.

Once the SqlCommand object is properly initialized, you pass it to the BuildParameters method. You will look at this method in more detail later. After this step, the SqlCommand is fully initialized, and you place it into your object's internal cache (the commandParametersHashTable Hashtable variable). Finally, the SqlCommand is returned to the calling code.

Getting back to the ExecSpReturnDataSet method, now that the SqlCommand object has been properly initialized, you need to set the values of the parameters. This is done via another helper method called SetParameterValues. SetParameterValues takes two arguments: a reference to a SqlCommand object and an IDictionary interface. You are using an IDictionary interface instead of a class such as a Hashtable (which implements the IDictionary interface) in order to make your code more flexible. This is a good design practice and works quite well — for example, in situations where the user of your class has built his or her own custom dictionary object that implements the IDictionary interface. It then loops through the `SqlCommand`'s `Parameters` collection and sets each `SqlParameter`'s value based on the corresponding name-value pair in the `IDictionary` object, as long as the parameter's direction is not `Output`. Following is the code for the `SetParameterValues` method:

```
''' <summary>
''' Traverses the SqlCommand's SqlParameters collection and sets the values
''' for all of the SqlParameter(s) objects whose direction is not Output and
''' whose name matches the name in the dictValues IDictionary that was
''' passed in.
''' </summary>
''' <param name="command">An initialized SqlCommand object.</param>
''' <param name="dictValues">A name-value pair of stored procedure parameter
''' name(s) and value(s).</param>
Public Sub SetParameterValues(ByVal command As SqlCommand, _
    ByVal dictValues As IDictionary)
    If command Is Nothing Then
        Throw New ArgumentNullException("command", _
            "The command argument cannot be null.")
    End If
    ` Traverse the SqlCommand's SqlParameters collection.
    Dim parameter As SqlParameter
    For Each parameter In command.Parameters
        ` Do not set Output parameters.
        If parameter.Direction <> ParameterDirection.Output Then
            ` Set the initial value to DBNull.
            parameter.Value = TypeCode.DBNull
            ` If there is a match, then update the parameter value.
            If dictValues.Contains(parameter.ParameterName) Then
                parameter.Value = dictValues(parameter.ParameterName)
            Else
                ` There was not a match.
                ` If the parameter value cannot be null, throw an exception.
                If Not parameter.IsNullable Then
                    Throw New ArgumentNullException(parameter.ParameterName, _
                        "Error getting the value for the " _
                        & parameter.ParameterName & " parameter.")
                End If
            End If
        End If
    Next parameter
End Sub
```

When traversing the `SqlCommand`'s `Parameters` collection, if a `SqlParameter`'s value cannot be found in the `IDictionary` instance, then a check is made to determine whether the `SqlParameter`'s value is allowed to be null or not. If it is allowed, then the value is set to `DBNull`; otherwise, an exception is thrown.

After setting the values of the parameters, the next step is to pass the `SqlCommand` object to the `SqlDataAdapter`'s constructor:

```
` Initialize the SqlDataAdapter with the SqlCommand object.
Dim sqlDA As New SqlDataAdapter(command)
```

Then try to set the name of the `DataSet` using the `dataSetName` method argument:

```
` Try to set the name of the DataSet.
If Not (dataSetName Is Nothing) Then
    If dataSetName.Length > 0 Then
        ds.DataSetName = dataSetName
    End If
End If
```

After doing this, you call the `Fill` method of the `SqlDataAdapter` to fill your `DataSet` object:

```
` Fill the DataSet.
sqlDA.Fill(ds)
```

You then return the `DataSet` object back to the caller:

```
` Return the DataSet.
Return ds
```

If an exception was caught, then you log the exception data to the Windows Application Log via the `LogError` private method, and then throw a new exception with your generic exception message. Nest the original exception inside of the new exception via the `innerException` constructor parameter:

```
Catch e As Exception
    LogError(e)
    Throw New Exception(ExceptionMsg, e)
```

In the `Finally` block, you close and release the `SqlCommand` object's resources via the `DisposeCommand` helper method:

```
Finally
    ` Close and release resources
    DisposeCommand(command)
```

The `DisposeCommand` helper function closes the `SqlCommand`'s `SqlConnection` property and disposes of the `SqlCommand` object:

```
` ´ ` <summary>
` ´ ` Disposes a SqlCommand and its underlying SqlConnection.
` ´ ` </summary>
` ´ ` <param name="command"></param>
Private Sub DisposeCommand(ByVal command As SqlCommand)
    If Not (command Is Nothing) Then
        If Not (command.Connection Is Nothing) Then
            command.Connection.Close()
            command.Connection.Dispose()
        End If
        command.Dispose()
    End If
End Sub
```

BuildParameters

This private method is the heart of this object and does the most work. It is responsible for parsing the stored procedure parameter XML and mapping all of the `SqlParameter` objects into the `Parameters` property of the `SqlCommand` object. Here is the signature of the method:

```
` ' ' <summary>
` ' ' Finds the parameter information for the stored procedure from the
` ' ' stored procedures XML document and then uses that information to
` ' ' build and append the parameter(s) for the SqlCommand's
` ' ' SqlParameters collection.
` ' ' </summary>
` ' ' <param name="command">An initialized SqlCommand object.</param>
Private Sub BuildParameters(ByVal command As SqlCommand)
```

The first thing you do in this method is determine whether any XML is being passed in or not. Here is the code that checks for the XML:

```
` See if there is an XmlNode of parameter(s) for the stored procedure.
If Me._spParamXmlNode Is Nothing Then
    ` No parameters to add, so exit.
    Return
End If
```

The last bit of code simply checks whether there is an `XmlNode` instance of parameter information. If the `XmlNode` has not been initialized, then you exit the method. It is entirely possible that users of this object may have stored procedures with no parameters at all. You choose an `XmlNode` object to parse the XML because loading all of the stored procedure XML into memory will not hurt performance; it is a small amount of data. As an alternative, you could use an `XmlReader` object to load into memory only what you need at runtime.

The next step is to clear the `SqlCommand` object's `Parameters` collection:

```
` Clear the parameters collection for the SqlCommand
command.Parameters.Clear()
```

You then use the name of the stored procedure as the key in your XPath query of the XML, and execute the following XPath query to get the list of parameters for the stored procedure:

```
` Get the node list of <Parameter>'s for the stored procedure.
Dim xpathQuery As String = "//StoredProcedures/StoredProcedure[@name='" _
    & command.CommandText & "']/Parameters/Parameter"
Dim parameterNodes As XmlNodeList = Me._spParamXmlNode.SelectNodes(xpathQuery)
```

This query is executed off the `XmlDocument` object and returns an `XmlNodeList` object. You start the loop through the `Parameter` elements in the XML and retrieve all of the mandatory `Parameter` attributes:

```
Dim parameterNode As XmlElement
For Each parameterNode In parameterNodes
    ` Get the attribute values for the <Parameter> element.

    ` Get the attribute values for the <Parameter> element.
```

368

```vb
` name
Dim parameterName As String = parameterNode.GetAttribute("name")
If parameterName.Length = 0 Then
    Throw New ArgumentNullException("name", "Error getting the 'name' " _
        & "attribute for the <Parameter> element.")
End If

` size
Dim parameterSize As Integer = 0
If parameterNode.GetAttribute("size").Length = 0 Then
    Throw New ArgumentNullException("size", "Error getting the 'size' " _
        & "attribute for the <Parameter> element.")
Else
    parameterSize = Convert.ToInt32(parameterNode.GetAttribute("size"))
End If

` datatype
Dim sqlDataType As SqlDbType
If parameterNode.GetAttribute("datatype").Length = 0 Then
    Throw New ArgumentNullException("datatype", "Error getting the " _
        & "'datatype' attribute for the <Parameter> element.")
Else
    sqlDataType = CType([Enum].Parse(GetType(SqlDbType), _
        parameterNode.GetAttribute("datatype"), True), SqlDbType)
End If

` direction
Dim parameterDirection As ParameterDirection = parameterDirection.Input
If parameterNode.GetAttribute("direction").Length > 0 Then
    parameterDirection = CType([Enum].Parse(GetType(ParameterDirection), _
        parameterNode.GetAttribute("direction"), True), ParameterDirection)
End If
End If
```

Because these attributes are mandatory, if any of them are missing, then you throw an exception. The interesting part of this code is using the Enum.Parse static method to convert the string value from the XML into the correct .NET enumeration data type for the sqlDataType and parameterDirection variables. This is possible because the probable values in your XML for these attributes map directly to the names of their respective enumeration data types in .NET. Next, you get the optional attributes:

```vb
` Get the optional attribute values for the <Parameter> element.
` isNullable
Dim isNullable As Boolean = False
Try
    If parameterNode.GetAttribute("isNullable").Length > 0 Then
        isNullable = Boolean.Parse(parameterNode.GetAttribute("isNullable"))
    End If
Catch
End Try

` sourceColumn  -  This must map to the name of a column in a DataSet.
Dim sourceColumn As String = ""
Try
    If parameterNode.GetAttribute("sourceColumn").Length > 0 Then
```

```
                sourceColumn = parameterNode.GetAttribute("sourceColumn")
        End If
    Catch
    End Try
```

These attributes are optional mainly because of their data types. Because `isNullable` is Boolean, you go ahead and convert it to `False` if it is missing; and if `sourceColumn` is missing, then you just ignore it entirely.

Now you are ready to create the `SqlParameter` object and set its `Direction` property:

```
    ` Create the parameter object.  Pass in the name, datatype,
    ` and size to the constructor.
    Dim sqlParameter As SqlParameter = New SqlParameter(parameterName, _
        sqlDataType, parameterSize)

    'Set the direction of the parameter.
    sqlParameter.Direction = parameterDirection
```

You then set the optional property values of the `SqlParameter` object:

```
    ` If the optional attributes have values, then set them.
    ` IsNullable
    If isNullable Then
        sqlParameter.IsNullable = isNullable
    End If

    ` SourceColumn
    sqlParameter.SourceColumn = sourceColumn
```

Finally, you add the `SqlParameter` object to the `SqlCommand` object's `Parameters` collection, complete your loop, and finish the method:

```
    ` Add the parameter to the SqlCommand's parameter collection.
        command.Parameters.Add(sqlParameter)
    Next parameterNode
End Sub
```

Now it's time to look at `ExecSpReturnDataReader`. This function is almost identical to `ExecSpReturnDataSet` except that it returns a `SqlDataReader` object instead of a `DataSet` object.

ExecSpReturnDataReader

This public function executes a stored procedure and returns a `SqlDataReader` object. Similar to the `ExecSpReturnDataSet` method, it takes a stored procedure name (`String`) and an optional list of parameter names and values (`IDictionary`). Here is the code for `ExecSpReturnDataReader`:

```
    `´ <summary>
    `´ Executes a stored procedure with or without parameters and returns a
    `´ SqlDataReader instance with a live connection to the database. It is
    `´ very important to call the Close method of the SqlDataReader as soon
    `´ as possible after using it.
    `´ </summary>
```

```
`'`     <param name="spName">The name of the stored procedure to execute.</param>
`'`     <param name="paramValues">A name-value pair of stored procedure parameter
`'`     name(s) and value(s).</param>
`'`     <returns>A SqlDataReader object.</returns>
Public Function ExecSpReturnDataReader(ByVal spName As String, _
    ByVal paramValues As IDictionary) As SqlDataReader

  Dim command As SqlCommand = Nothing
  Try
     ` Get the initialized SqlCommand instance.
    command = GetSqlCommand(spName)

     ` Set the parameter values for the SqlCommand.
    SetParameterValues(command, paramValues)

     ` Open the connection.
    command.Connection.Open()

     ` Execute the sp and return the SqlDataReader.
    Return command.ExecuteReader(CommandBehavior.CloseConnection)
  Catch e As Exception
    LogError(e)
    Throw New Exception(ExceptionMsg, e)

  End Try

  End Function
```

This function uses two objects to accomplish its mission: `SqlCommand` and `SqlDataReader`. The only part where this function differs from `ExecSpReturnDataSet` is right after you call the `SetParameterValues` private method. In this case, you have to ensure that the `SqlCommand` object's `SqlConnection` is opened because the `SqlDataReader` requires an open connection. You then call the `ExecuteReader` method of the `SqlCommand` object to get your `SqlDataReader` object, passing in the `CommandBehavior.CloseConnection` value for the method's behavior argument.

Because this method returns a `SqlDataReader` object, which requires an open database connection, you do not close the connection in this method. It is up to the caller to close the `SqlDataReader` and the connection when finished. Because you used the `CommandBehavior.CloseConnection` value for the behavior argument, the user of the method only has to remember to call the `SqlDataReader`'s `Close` method in order to close the underlying `SqlConnection` object.

The next function you are going to look at, `ExecSpReturnXmlReader`, is almost identical to the last two functions, except that it returns an `XmlReader` instead of a `DataSet` or a `SqlDataReader`.

ExecSpReturnXmlReader

This public function executes a stored procedure and returns an `XmlReader` instance. The function requires the stored procedure to contain a `FOR XML` clause in its SQL statement. Once again, it takes a stored procedure name (`String`) and an optional list of parameter names and values (`IDictionary`). Here is the code for `ExecSpReturnXmlReader`:

```
`'`     <summary>
`'`     Executes a stored procedure with or without parameters and returns an
`'`     XmlReader instance with a live connection to the database. It is
```

```
```    very important to call the Close method of the XmlReader as soon
```    as possible after using it. Only use this method when calling stored
```    procedures that return XML results (FOR XML ...).
```    </summary>
```    <param name="spName">The name of the stored procedure to execute.</param>
```    <param name="paramValues">A name-value pair of stored procedure parameter
```    name(s) and value(s).</param>
```    <returns>An XmlReader object.</returns>
Public Function ExecSpReturnXmlReader(ByVal spName As String, _
    ByVal paramValues As IDictionary) As XmlReader

    Dim command As SqlCommand = Nothing
    Try
        ` Get the initialized SqlCommand instance.
        command = GetSqlCommand(spName)
        ` Set the parameter values for the SqlCommand.
        SetParameterValues(command, paramValues)

        ` Open the connection.
        command.Connection.Open()

        ` Execute the sp and return the XmlReader.
        Return command.ExecuteXmlReader()
    Catch e As Exception
        LogError(e)
        Throw New Exception(ExceptionMsg, e)
    End Try
End Function
```

The only difference between this method and `ExecSpReturnDataReader` is that you call the
`ExecuteXmlReader` method of the `SqlCommand` object instead of the `ExecuteReader` method. Like the
`ExecSpReturnDataReader` method, users of this method need to close the returned `XmlReader` after using
it in order to properly release resources.

This method works only with SQL Server 2000 and later.

Next up is the `ExecSp` method, which needs only the `SqlCommand` object to get its work done. Its job is to
execute stored procedures that do not return result sets.

ExecSp

This public method executes a stored procedure and does not return a value. It takes a stored procedure
name (`String`) and an optional list of parameter names and values (`IDictionary`) for its arguments. Here
is the code for `ExecSp`:

```
```    <summary>
```    Executes a stored procedure with or without parameters that
```    does not return output values or a resultset.
```    </summary>
```    <param name="transaction">The transaction that the stored procedure
```    will be executed under.</param>
```    <param name="spName">The name of the stored procedure to execute.</param>
```    <param name="paramValues">A name-value pair of stored procedure parameter
```    name(s) and value(s).</param>
Public Sub ExecSp(ByVal spName As String, ByVal paramValues As IDictionary)
```
```

```
        Dim command As SqlCommand = Nothing
        Try
            ` Get the initialized SqlCommand instance.
            command = GetSqlCommand(transaction, spName)
            ` Set the parameter values for the SqlCommand.
            SetParameterValues(command, paramValues)

            ` Run the stored procedure.
            RunSp(command)

        Catch e As Exception
            LogError(e)
            Throw New Exception(ExceptionMsg, e)
        Finally
            ` Close and release resources.
            DisposeCommand(command)
        End Try
    End Sub
```

It is almost identical to the other `Exec*` functions, except when it executes the stored procedure. The code inside of the private `RunSp` method opens the `SqlCommand`'s `SqlConnection` object and then calls the `SqlCommand` object's `ExecuteNonQuery` method. This ensures that the `SqlCommand` does not return any type of `DataReader` object to read the results. This method is used mostly to execute INSERT, UPDATE, and DELETE stored procedures that do not return any results. It also has an overload that does not include the `SqlTransaction` argument.

Following is the code for `RunSp`:

```
    `` <summary>
    `` Opens the SqlCommand object's underlying SqlConnection and calls
    `` the SqlCommand's ExecuteNonQuery method.
    `` </summary>
    `` <param name="command">An initialized SqlCommand object.</param>
    Private Sub RunSp(ByRef command As SqlCommand)
        ` Open the connection.
        command.Connection.Open()

        `a Execute the stored procedure.
        command.ExecuteNonQuery()
    End Sub
```

Finally, the last public function you are going to create is `ExecSpOutputValues`.

ExecSpOutputValues

This last public function in your component executes a stored procedure and returns an `IDictionary` object that contains output parameter name-value pairs. It is not meant for stored procedures that return result sets. As with the previous examples, this function takes a stored procedure name (`String`) and an optional list of parameter names and values (`IDictionary`) for its arguments. Here is the code for `ExecSpOutputValues`:

```
    `` <summary>
    `` Executes a stored procedure with or without parameters and returns an
```

```
``` IDictionary instance with the stored procedure's output parameter
``` name(s) and value(s).
``` </summary>
``` <param name="transaction">The transaction that the stored procedure
``` will be executed under.</param>
``` <param name="spName">The name of the stored procedure to execute.</param>
``` <param name="paramValues">A name-value pair of stored procedure parameter
``` name(s) and value(s).</param>
``` <returns>An IDictionary object.</returns>
Public Function ExecSpOutputValues(ByVal transaction As SqlTransaction, _
                                   ByVal spName As String, _
                                   ByVal paramValues As IDictionary) As IDictionary

    Dim command As SqlCommand = Nothing
    Try
        ` Get the initialized SqlCommand instance.
        command = GetSqlCommand(transaction, spName)
        ` Set the parameter values for the SqlCommand.
        SetParameterValues(command, paramValues)

        ` Run the stored procedure.
        RunSp(command)

        ` Get the output values.
        Dim outputParams As New Hashtable()
        Dim param As SqlParameter
        For Each param In command.Parameters
            If param.Direction = ParameterDirection.Output _
                Or param.Direction = ParameterDirection.InputOutput Then
                outputParams.Add(param.ParameterName, param.Value)
            End If
        Next param
        Return outputParams
    Catch e As Exception
        LogError(e)
        Throw New Exception(ExceptionMsg, e)
    Finally
        ` Close and release resources.
        DisposeCommand(command)
    End Try
End Function
```

This function is almost identical to ExecSp except that after the SqlCommand.ExecuteNonQuery method is called, you iterate through the SqlCommand object's Parameters collection and look for all of the parameters that are output parameters. Next, you take the values of the output parameters and add the name-value pair to the IDictionary instance that you return. This method also has an overload that does not include the SqlTransaction argument.

## Using DataSet Objects to Bind to DataGrids

Now that you have built your data-access component, it is time to test it. A nice way to do that is to call the ExecSpReturnDataSet method, take the DataSet object that was created, and then bind the DataSet to a DataGrid. You also get to see how easily the DataSet and the DataGrid control integrate together.
```

This exercise uses a Windows Application project called SqlServerWrapperTestHarness, added to the Examples solution. It contains references to System, System.Data, System.Drawing, System.Windows.Forms, and System.Xml, as well as a project reference to the SqlServerWrapper project. Added to the project is a form named TestForm.vb with two buttons, one for testing the ExecSpReturnDataSet method and one for testing the ExecSpReturnSqlRecord method. In this example, you will be looking only at the code for testing the ExecSpReturnDataSet method. Figure 9-4 shows what the test form looks like.

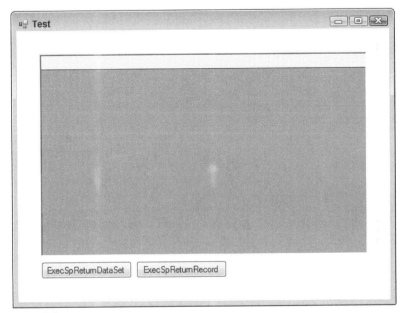

Figure 9-4

Figure 9-5 shows what your references should look like.

Here is the code for the declarations and private members of the form:

```
Option Explicit On
Option Strict On

Imports SqlServerWrapper
Imports System.Data.SqlClient
Imports System.Xml
Imports System.Configuration

Public Class TestForm
    Inherits System.Windows.Forms.Form

    Private _helper As StoredProcedureHelper = Nothing
```

These declarations should look pretty familiar by now. Note that you are declaring a private variable (_helper) for the StoredProcedureHelper class that you are using so you can get to the class from other parts of the form instead of just a Button Click event handler.

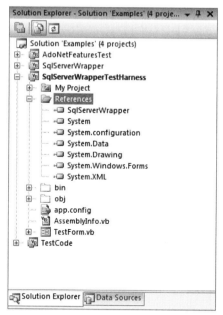

Figure 9-5

Next, you initialize the _helper variable in the form's Load event handler:

```
Private Sub TestForm_Load(ByVal sender As System.Object, _
    ByVal e As System.EventArgs) Handles MyBase.Load
    ` Set the SQL connection string
    Dim connectionString As String = _
       ConfigurationSettings.AppSettings("dbConnectionString")

    ` Call the SqlServer wrapper constructor and
    ` pass the DB connection string and the stored procedures config.
    helper = New StoredProcedureHelper(connectionString, _
        CType(ConfigurationSettings.GetConfig("StoredProcedureSettings"), _
        XmlNode))
End Sub
```

As in the earlier examples, this code begins by retrieving a connection string to the pubs database from the app.config file. You then create a new instance of the StoredProcedureHelper and assign it to the _helper class variable. During the constructor call to the StoredProcedureHelper class, you first pass in your connection string, and then you pass in an XmlNode of the stored procedure metadata for the StoredProcedureHelper class to consume. Note that you are passing the stored procedure metadata in to your class via the GetConfig method of the ConfigurationSettings class. This is because you have created a section inside of your app.config file called StoredProcedureSettings, and you have configured a SectionHandler to let the .NET Framework application configuration functionality consume your XML and give it back to you as an XmlNode. Here is what this section looks like inside of the app.config file:

```
<configSections>
    <section name="StoredProcedureSettings"
    type="SqlServerWrapper.StoredProcedureSectionHandler, SqlServerWrapper" />
```

```
        </configSections>
        <StoredProcedureSettings>
          <StoredProcedures>
            <StoredProcedure name="usp_Get_Authors_By_States">
              <Parameters>
                <Parameter name="@states" datatype="VarChar" direction="Input"
                  isNullable="false" size="100" />
                <Parameter name="@state_delimiter" datatype="Char" direction="Input"
                  isNullable="false" size="1" />
              </Parameters>
            </StoredProcedure>
            <StoredProcedure name="usp_Get_Author_By_ID">
              <Parameters>
                <Parameter name="@au_id" datatype="VarChar" direction="Input"
                  isNullable="false" size="11" />
              </Parameters>
            </StoredProcedure>
          </StoredProcedures>
        </StoredProcedureSettings>
```

This is nice because you don't need to include a separate XML file for your project; you just integrate seamlessly into the app.config file. Note how you are defining what class in what assembly will handle consuming your <StoredProcedureSettings> section in the <section> element. In order for this to work, the class defined must implement the System.Configuration.IConfigurationSectionHandler interface. Here is the code for your section handler:

```
Option Explicit On
Option Strict On

Imports System
Imports System.Configuration
Imports System.Xml
Imports System.Xml.Serialization
Imports System.Xml.XPath

Public Class StoredProcedureSectionHandler
    Implements IConfigurationSectionHandler

    Public Function Create(ByVal parent As Object, _
        ByVal configContext As Object, _
        ByVal section As System.Xml.XmlNode) As Object _
            Implements IConfigurationSectionHandler.Create
        Return section("StoredProcedures")
    End Function
End Class
```

This code is pretty simple; you just return the XML node named StoredProcedures to the caller of your handler.

Back to your Button's Click event handler, once you have the StoredProcedureHelper class instance fully initialized, you then create the parameter values for the stored procedure you want to execute and pass these arguments to the ExecSpReturnDataSet method:

```
` Add the two parameter name-values.
Dim params As New Hashtable
```

```
params.Add("@states", "CA")
params.Add("@state_delimiter", "^")

` Execute the sp, and get the DataSet object back.
Dim ds As DataSet = _helper.ExecSpReturnDataSet("usp_Get_Authors_By_States", _
    "", params)
```

The last step is to actually bind the data to the form's grid:

```
` Bind the DataGrid to the DataSet object.
dgdAuthors.SetDataBinding(ds.Tables(0), Nothing)
```

The results should look like the dialog shown in Figure 9-6.

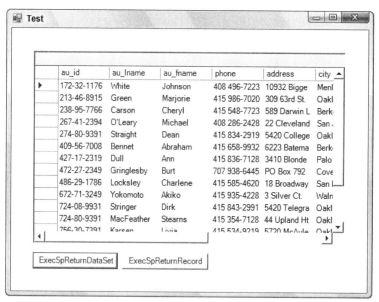

Figure 9-6

Summary

This chapter took a look at ADO.NET and some of its more advanced features. You have seen and used the main objects in ADO.NET that you need to quickly get up and running in order to build data-access into your .NET applications. You took a fairly in-depth look at the DataSet and DataTable classes, as these are the core classes of ADO.NET.

You also looked at stored procedures, including how to create them in SQL Server and how to access them from your code. Finally, you built your own custom data-access component, which makes it easy to call stored procedures, and separate data-access code from the rest of business-logic code in a .NET application.

10

Using XML in Visual Basic 2008

This chapter describes how you can generate and manipulate *Extensible Markup Language (XML)* using Visual Basic 2008. Of course, using XML in Visual Basic is a vast area to cover (more than possibly could be covered in a chapter). The .NET Framework exposes five XML-specific namespaces that contain over a hundred different classes. In addition, dozens of other classes support and implement XML-related technologies, such as ADO.NET, SQL Server, and BizTalk. Consequently, this chapter focuses on the general concepts and the most important classes.

Visual Basic relies on the classes exposed in the following XML-related namespaces to transform, manipulate, and stream XML documents:

❑   System.Xml provides core support for a variety of XML standards, including DTD, namespace, DOM, XDR, XPath, XSLT, and SOAP.

❑   System.Xml.Serialization provides the objects used to transform objects to and from XML documents or streams using serialization.

❑   System.Xml.Schema provides a set of objects that enable schemas to be loaded, created, and streamed. This support is achieved using a suite of objects that support in-memory manipulation of the entities that compose an XML schema.

❑   System.Xml.XPath provides a parser and evaluation engine for the XML Path language (XPath).

❑   System.Xml.Xsl provides the objects necessary when working with Extensible Stylesheet Language (XSL) and XSL Transformations (XSLT).

The XML-related technologies utilized by Visual Basic include other technologies that generate XML documents and enable XML documents to be managed as a data source:

❑   **ADO** — The legacy COM objects provided by ADO can generate XML documents in stream or file form. ADO can also retrieve a previously persisted XML document and manipulate it. (Although ADO is not used in this chapter, ADO and other legacy COM APIs can be accessed seamlessly from Visual Basic.)

❑ **ADO.NET** — This uses XML as its underlying data representation: The in-memory data representation of the ADO.NET `DataSet` object is XML; the results of data queries are represented as XML documents; XML can be imported into a `DataSet` and exported from a `DataSet`. (ADO.NET is covered in Chapter 9.)

❑ **SQL Server 2000** — XML-specific features were added to SQL Server 2000 (`FOR XML` queries to retrieve XML documents and `OPENXML` to represent an XML document as a rowset). Visual Basic can use ADO.NET to access SQL Server's XML-specific features (the documents generated and consumed by SQL Server can then be manipulated programmatically). Recently, Microsoft also released SQLXML, which provides an SQL Server 2000 database with some excellent XML capabilities, such as querying a database using XQuery, getting back XML result sets from a database, working with data just as if it were XML, taking huge XML files and having SQLXML convert them to relational data, and much more. SQLXML enables you to perform these functions and more via a set of managed .NET classes. You can download SQLXML free from the Microsoft SQLXML website at `http://msdn2.microsoft.com/aa286527.aspx`.

❑ **SQL Server 2005** — SQL Server has now been modified with XML in mind. SQL Server 2005 can natively understand XML because it is now built into the underlying foundation of the database. SQL Server 2005 includes an XML data type that also supports an XSD schema validation. The capability to query and understand XML documents is a valuable addition to this database server. SQL Server 2005 also comes in a lightweight (and free) version called SQL Server Express Edition.

❑ **SQL Server 2008** — The latest edition of SQL Server, version 2008, works off of the SQL Server 2005 release and brings to the table an improved XSD schema validation process as well as enhanced support for XQuery.

This chapter makes sense of this range of technologies by introducing some basic XML concepts and demonstrating how Visual Basic, in conjunction with the .NET Framework, can make use of XML. Specifically, in this chapter you will do all of the following:

❑ Learn the rationale behind XML.

❑ Look at the namespaces within the .NET Framework class library that deal with XML and XML-related technologies.

❑ Take a close look at some of the classes contained within these namespaces.

❑ Gain an overview of some of the other Microsoft technologies that utilize XML, particularly SQL Server and ADO.NET.

At the end of this chapter, you will be able to generate, manipulate, and transform XML using Visual Basic.

> *This book also covers LINQ to XML and the new XML objects found in the* `System.Xml.Linq` *namespace. These items are covered in Chapter 11.*

An Introduction to XML

XML is a tagged markup language similar to HTML. In fact, XML and HTML are distant cousins and have their roots in the Standard Generalized Markup Language (SGML). This means that XML leverages one of the most useful features of HTML — readability. However, XML differs from HTML in that XML represents data, whereas HTML is a mechanism for displaying data. The tags in XML describe the data, as shown in the following example:

```
<?xml version="1.0" encoding="utf-8" ?>
<Movies>
  <FilmOrder name="Grease" filmId="1" quantity="21"></FilmOrder>
  <FilmOrder name="Lawrence of Arabia" filmId="2" quantity="10"></FilmOrder>
  <FilmOrder name="Star Wars" filmId="3" quantity="12"></FilmOrder>
  <FilmOrder name="Shrek" filmId="4" quantity="14"></FilmOrder>
</Movies>
```

This XML document represents a store order for a collection of movies. The standard used to represent an order of films would be useful to movie rental firms, collectors, and others. This information can be shared using XML for the following reasons:

❑ The data tags in XML are self-describing.

❑ XML is an open standard and supported on most platforms today.

XML supports the parsing of data by applications not familiar with the contents of the XML document. XML documents can also be associated with a description (a schema) that informs an application as to the structure of the data within the XML document.

At this stage, XML looks simple — it is just a human-readable way to exchange data in a universally accepted format. The essential points that you should understand about XML are as follows:

❑ XML data can be stored in a plain text file.

❑ A document is said to be well formed if it adheres to the XML standard.

❑ Tags are used to specify the contents of a document — for example, `<FilmOrder>`.

❑ XML elements (also called *nodes*) can be thought of as the objects within a document.

❑ Elements are the basic building blocks of the document. Each element contains a start tag and end tag. A tag can be both a start tag and an end tag in one — for example, `<FilmOrder />`. In this case, the tag specifies that there is no content (or inner text) to the element (there isn't a closing tag because none is required due to the lack of inner-text content). Such a tag is said to be *empty*.

❑ Data can be contained in the element (the element content) or within attributes contained in the element.

❑ XML is hierarchical. One document can contain multiple elements, which can themselves contain child elements, and so on. However, an XML document can only have one root element.

This last point means that the XML document hierarchy can be thought of as a tree containing nodes:

❑ The example document has a root node, `<Movies>`.

❑ The branches of the root node are elements of type `<FilmOrder>`.

❑ The leaves of the XML element, `<FilmOrder>`, are its attributes: `name`, `quantity`, and `filmId`.

Of course, we are interested in the practical use of XML by Visual Basic. A practical manipulation of the example XML, for example, is to display (for the staff of a movie supplier) a particular movie order in an application so that the supplier can fill the order and then save the information to a database. This chapter explains how you can perform such tasks using the functionality provided by the .NET Framework class library.

XML Serialization

The simplest way to demonstrate Visual Basic's support for XML is not with a complicated technology, such as SQL Server or ADO.NET, but with a practical use of XML: serializing a class.

The serialization of an object means that it is written out to a stream, such as a file or a socket (this is also known as *dehydrating* an object). The reverse process can also be performed: An object can be deserialized (or rehydrated) by reading it from a stream.

> *The type of serialization described in this chapter is XML serialization, whereby XML is used to represent a class in serialized form.*

To help you understand XML serialization, let's examine a class named `FilmOrder` (which can be found in the code download from www.wrox.com). This class is implemented in Visual Basic and is used by the company for processing a movie order. The class could be instantiated on a firm's PDA, laptop, or even mobile phone (as long as the device had the .NET Framework installed).

An instance of `FilmOrder` corresponding to each order could be serializing to XML and sending over a socket using the PDA's cellular modem. (If the person making the order had a PDA that did not have a cellular modem, then the instance of `FilmOrder` could be serialized to a file.) The order could then be processed when the PDA was dropped into a docking cradle and synced. We are talking about data in a propriety form here, an instance of `FilmOrder` being converted into a generic form — XML — that can be universally understood.

The `System.Xml.Serialization` namespace contains classes and interfaces that support the serialization of objects to XML, and the deserialization of objects from XML. Objects are serialized to documents or streams using the `XmlSerializer` class.

Let's look at how you can use `XmlSerializer`. First, you need to define an object that implements a default constructor, such as `FilmOrder`:

```
Public Class FilmOrder

    ` These are Public because we have yet to implement
    ` properties to provide program access.

    Public name As String
    Public filmId As Integer
    Public quantity As Integer

    Public Sub New()

    End Sub
```

```
    Public Sub New(ByVal name As String, _
                   ByVal filmId As Integer, _
                   ByVal quantity As Integer)
        Me.name = name
        Me.filmId = filmId
        Me.quantity = quantity
    End Sub
End Class
```

This class should be created in a console application. From there, we can move on to the module. Within the module's Sub Main, create an instance of XmlSerializer, specifying the object to serialize and its type in the constructor (you need to make a reference to System.Xml.Serialization for this to work):

```
    Dim serialize As XmlSerializer = _
        New XmlSerializer(GetType(FilmOrder))
```

Create an instance of the same type passed as a parameter to the constructor of XmlSerializer:

```
    Dim MyFilmOrder As FilmOrder = _
        New FilmOrder("Grease", 101, 10)
```

Call the Serialize method of the XmlSerializer instance and specify the stream to which the serialized object is written (parameter one, Console.Out) and the object to be serialized (parameter two, MyFilmOrder):

```
    serialize.Serialize(Console.Out, MyFilmOrder)
    Console.ReadLine()
```

To make reference to the XmlSerializer object, you need to make reference to the System.Xml. Serialization namespace:

```
    Imports System.Xml.Serialization
```

Running the module, the following output is generated by the preceding code:

```
    <?xml version="1.0" encoding="IBM437"?>
    <FilmOrder xmlns:xsd="http://www.w3.org/2001/XMLSchema"
                       xmlns:xsi="http://www.w3.org/2001/XMLSchema-instance">
      <name>Grease</name>
      <filmId>101</filmId>
      <quantity>10</quantity>
    </FilmOrder>
```

This output demonstrates the default way in which the Serialize method serializes an object:

❑   Each object serialized is represented as an element with the same name as the class — in this case, FilmOrder.

❑   The individual data members of the class serialized are contained in elements named for each data member — in this case, name, filmId, and quantity.

Also generated are the following:

❑ The specific version of XML generated — in this case, 1.0

❑ The encoding used — in this case, IBM437

❑ The schemas used to describe the serialized object — in this case, www.w3.org/2001/XMLSchema-instance and www.w3.org/2001/XMLSchema

A schema can be associated with an XML document and describe the data it contains (name, type, scale, precision, length, and so on). Either the actual schema or a reference to where the schema resides can be contained in the XML document. In either case, an XML schema is a standard representation that can be used by all applications that consume XML. This means that applications can use the supplied schema to validate the contents of an XML document generated by the Serialize method of the XmlSerializer object.

The code snippet that demonstrated the Serialize method of XmlSerializer displayed the XML generated to Console.Out. Clearly, we do not expect an application to use Console.Out when it would like to access a FilmOrder object in XML form. The point was to show how serialization can be performed in just two lines of code (one call to a constructor and one call to method). The entire section of code responsible for serializing the instance of FilmOrder is presented here:

```
Try
    Dim serialize As XmlSerializer = _
                New XmlSerializer(GetType(FilmOrder))
    Dim MyMovieOrder As FilmOrder = _
            New FilmOrder("Grease", 101, 10)
    serialize.Serialize(Console.Out, MyMovieOrder)
    Console.Out.WriteLine()
    Console.Readline()
Catch ex As Exception
    Console.Error.WriteLine(ex.ToString())
End Try
```

The Serialize method's first parameter is overridden so that it can serialize XML to a file (the filename is given as type String), a Stream, a TextWriter, or an XmlWriter. When serializing to Stream, TextWriter, or XmlWriter, adding a third parameter to the Serialize method is permissible. This third parameter is of type XmlSerializerNamespaces and is used to specify a list of namespaces that qualify the names in the XML-generated document. The permissible overrides of the Serialize method are as follows:

```
Public Sub Serialize(Stream, Object)
Public Sub Serialize(TextWriter, Object)
Public Sub Serialize(XmlWriter, Object)
Public Sub Serialize(Stream, Object, XmlSerializerNamespaces)
Public Sub Serialize(TextWriter, Object, XmlSerializerNamespaces)
Public Sub Serialize(XmlWriter, Object, XmlSerializerNamespaces)
Public Sub Serialize(XmlWriter, Object, XmlSerializerNamespaces, String)
Public Sub Serialize(XmlWriter, Object, XmlSerializerNamespaces, String, _
    String)
```

An object is reconstituted using the Deserialize method of XmlSerializer. This method is overridden and can deserialize XML presented as a Stream, a TextReader, or an XmlReader. The overloads for Deserialize are as follows:

```
Public Function Deserialize(Stream) As Object
Public Function Deserialize(TextReader) As Object
Public Function Deserialize(XmlReader) As Object
Public Function Deserialize(XmlReader, XmlDeserializationEvents) As Object
Public Function Deserialize(XmlReader, String) As Object
Public Function Deserialize(XmlReader, String, XmlDeserializationEvents) _
    As Object
```

Before demonstrating the Deserialize method, we will introduce a new class, FilmOrder_Multiple. This class contains an array of film orders (actually an array of FilmOrder objects). FilmOrder_Multiple is defined as follows:

```
Public Class FilmOrder_Multiple
    Public multiFilmOrders() As FilmOrder

    Public Sub New()

    End Sub

    Public Sub New(ByVal multiFilmOrders() As FilmOrder)
        Me.multiFilmOrders = multiFilmOrders
    End Sub
End Class
```

The FilmOrder_Multiple class contains a fairly complicated object, an array of FilmOrder objects. The underlying serialization and deserialization of this class is more complicated than that of a single instance of a class that contains several simple types, but the programming effort involved on your part is just as simple as before. This is one of the great ways in which the .NET Framework makes it easy for you to work with XML data, no matter how it is formed.

To work through an example of the deserialization process, first create a sample order stored as an XML file called Filmorama.xml:

```
<?xml version="1.0" encoding="utf-8" ?>
<FilmOrder_Multiple xmlns:xsi="http://www.w3.org/2001/XMLSchema-instance"
 xmlns:xsd="http://www.w3.org/2001/XMLSchema">
    <multiFilmOrders>
        <FilmOrder>
            <name>Grease</name>
            <filmId>101</filmId>
            <quantity>10</quantity>
        </FilmOrder>
        <FilmOrder>
            <name>Lawrence of Arabia</name>
            <filmId>102</filmId>
            <quantity>10</quantity>
        </FilmOrder>
```

```
            <FilmOrder>
                <name>Star Wars</name>
                <filmId>103</filmId>
                <quantity>10</quantity>
            </FilmOrder>
        </multiFilmOrders>
    </FilmOrder_Multiple>
```

In order for this to run, you should either have the .xml file in the location of the executable or define the full path of the file within the code example.

Once the XML file is in place, the next step is to change your console application so it will deserialize the contents of this file. After you have the XML file in place, ensure that your console application has made the proper namespace references:

```
Imports System.Xml
Imports System.Xml.Serialization
Imports System.IO
```

The following code demonstrates an object of type `FilmOrder_Multiple` being deserialized (or rehydrated) from a file, Filmorama.xml. This object is deserialized using this file in conjunction with the `Deserialize` method of `XmlSerializer`:

```
` Open file, ..\Filmorama.xml
Dim dehydrated As FileStream = _
    New FileStream("Filmorama.xml", FileMode.Open)

` Create an XmlSerializer instance to handle deserializing,
` FilmOrder_Multiple
Dim serialize As XmlSerializer = _
    New XmlSerializer(GetType(FilmOrder_Multiple))

` Create an object to contain the deserialized instance of the object.
Dim myFilmOrder As FilmOrder_Multiple = _
    New FilmOrder_Multiple

` Deserialize object
myFilmOrder = serialize.Deserialize(dehydrated)
```

Once deserialized, the array of film orders can be displayed:

```
Dim SingleFilmOrder As FilmOrder

For Each SingleFilmOrder In myFilmOrder.multiFilmOrders
    Console.Out.WriteLine("{0}, {1}, {2}", _
        SingleFilmOrder.name, _
        SingleFilmOrder.filmId, _
        SingleFilmOrder.quantity)
Next

Console.ReadLine()
```

This example is just code that serializes an instance of type `FilmOrder_Multiple`. The output generated by displaying the deserialized object containing an array of film orders is as follows:

```
Grease, 101, 10
Lawrence of Arabia, 102, 10
Star Wars, 103, 10
```

`XmlSerializer` also implements a `CanDeserialize` method. The prototype for this method is as follows:

```
Public Overridable Function CanDeserialize(ByVal xmlReader As XmlReader) _
    As Boolean
```

If `CanDeserialize` returns `True`, then the XML document specified by the `xmlReader` parameter can be deserialized. If the return value of this method is `False`, then the specified XML document cannot be deserialized.

The `FromTypes` method of `XmlSerializer` facilitates the creation of arrays that contain `XmlSerializer` objects. This array of `XmlSerializer` objects can be used in turn to process arrays of the type to be serialized. The prototype for `FromTypes` is shown here:

```
Public Shared Function FromTypes(ByVal types() As Type) As XmlSerializer()
```

Before exploring the `System.Xml.Serialization` namespace, take a moment to consider the various uses of the term "attribute."

Source Code Style Attributes

Thus far, you have seen attributes applied to a specific portion of an XML document. Visual Basic has its own flavor of attributes, as do C# and each of the other .NET languages. These attributes refer to annotations to the source code that specify information, or *metadata*, that can be used by other applications without the need for the original source code. We will call such attributes *Source Code Style attributes*.

In the context of the `System.Xml.Serialization` namespace, Source Code Style attributes can be used to change the names of the elements generated for the data members of a class or to generate XML attributes instead of XML elements for the data members of a class. To demonstrate this, we will use a class called `ElokuvaTilaus`, which contains data members named `name`, `filmId`, and `quantity`. It just so happens that the default XML generated when serializing this class is not in a form that can be readily consumed by an external application.

For example, assume that a Finnish development team has written this external application — hence, the XML element and attribute names are in Finnish (minus the umlauts), rather than English. To rename the XML generated for a data member, `name`, a Source Code Style attribute will be used. This Source Code Style attribute specifies that when `ElokuvaTilaus` is serialized, the `name` data member is represented as an XML element, `<Nimi>`. The actual Source Code Style attribute that specifies this is as follows:

```
<XmlElementAttribute("Nimi")> Public name As String
```

ElokuvaTilaus, which means *MovieOrder* in Finnish, also contains other Source Code Style attributes:

❑ <XmlAttributeAttribute("ElokuvaId")> specifies that filmId is to be serialized as an XML attribute named ElokuvaId.

❑ <XmlAttributeAttribute("Maara")> specifies that quantity is to be serialized as an XML attribute named Maara.

ElokuvaTilaus is defined as follows:

```
Imports System.Xml.Serialization

Public Class ElokuvaTilaus

    ` These are Public because we have yet to implement
    ` properties to provide program access.

    <XmlElementAttribute("Nimi")> Public name As String
    <XmlAttributeAttribute("ElokuvaId")> Public filmId As Integer
    <XmlAttributeAttribute("Maara")> Public quantity As Integer

    Public Sub New()
    End Sub

    Public Sub New(ByVal name As String, _
                   ByVal filmId As Integer, _
                   ByVal quantity As Integer)
        Me.name = name
        Me.filmId = filmId
        Me.quantity = quantity
    End Sub

End Class
```

ElokuvaTilaus can be serialized as follows:

```
Dim serialize As XmlSerializer = _
    New XmlSerializer(GetType(ElokuvaTilaus))
Dim MyMovieOrder As ElokuvaTilaus = _
    New ElokuvaTilaus("Grease", 101, 10)

serialize.Serialize(Console.Out, MyMovieOrder)
Console.Readline()
```

The output generated by this code reflects the Source Code Style attributes associated with the class ElokuvaTilaus:

```
<?xml version="1.0" encoding="IBM437"?>
<ElokuvaTilaus xmlns:xsi="http://www.w3.org/2001/XMLSchema-instance"
 xmlns:xsd="http://www.w3.org/2001/XMLSchema"
 ElokuvaId="101" Maara="10">
    <Nimi>Grease</Nimi>
</ElokuvaTilaus>
```

The value of `filmId` is contained in an XML attribute, `ElokuvaId`, and the value of `quantity` is contained in an XML attribute, `Maara`. The value of `name` is contained in an XML element, `Nimi`.

The example only demonstrates the Source Code Style attributes exposed by the `XmlAttributeAttribute` and `XmlElementAttribute` classes in the `System.Xml.Serialization` namespace. A variety of other Source Code Style attributes exist in this namespace that also control the form of XML generated by serialization. The classes associated with such Source Code Style attributes include `XmlTypeAttribute`, `XmlTextAttribute`, `XmlRootAttribute`, `XmlIncludeAttribute`, `XmlIgnoreAttribute`, and `XmlEnumAttribute`.

System.Xml Document Support

The `System.Xml` namespace implements a variety of objects that support standards-based XML processing. The XML-specific standards facilitated by this namespace include XML 1.0, Document Type Definition (DTD) support, XML namespaces, XML schemas, XPath, XQuery, XSLT, DOM Level 1 and DOM Level 2 (Core implementations), as well as SOAP 1.1, SOAP 1.2, SOAP Contract Language, and SOAP Discovery. The `System.Xml` namespace exposes over 30 separate classes in order to facilitate this level of the XML standard's compliance.

To generate and navigate XML documents, there are two styles of access:

❑ **Stream-based** — `System.Xml` exposes a variety of classes that read XML from and write XML to a stream. This approach tends to be a fast way to consume or generate an XML document because it represents a set of serial reads or writes. The limitation of this approach is that it does not view the XML data as a document composed of tangible entities, such as nodes, elements, and attributes. An example of where a stream could be used is when receiving XML documents from a socket or a file.

❑ **Document Object Model (DOM)-based** — `System.Xml` exposes a set of objects that access XML documents as data. The data is accessed using entities from the XML document tree (nodes, elements, and attributes). This style of XML generation and navigation is flexible but may not yield the same performance as stream-based XML generation and navigation. DOM is an excellent technology for editing and manipulating documents. For example, the functionality exposed by DOM could simplify merging your checking, savings, and brokerage accounts.

XML Stream-Style Parsers

When demonstrating XML serialization, XML stream-style parsers were mentioned. After all, when an instance of an object is serialized to XML, it has to be written to a stream, and when it is deserialized, it is read from a stream. When an XML document is parsed using a stream parser, the parser always points to the current node in the document. The basic architecture of stream parsers is shown in Figure 10-1.

The following classes that access a stream of XML (read XML) and generate a stream of XML (write XML) are contained in the `System.Xml` namespace:

❑ `XmlWriter` — This abstract class specifies a non-cached, forward-only stream that writes an XML document (data and schema).

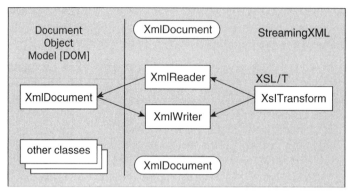

Figure 10-1

❑ XmlReader — This abstract class specifies a non-cached, forward-only stream that reads an XML document (data and schema).

The diagram of the classes associated with the XML stream-style parser referred to one other class, XslTransform. This class is found in the System.Xml.Xsl namespace and is not an XML stream-style parser. Rather, it is used in conjunction with XmlWriter and XmlReader. This class is covered in detail later.

The System.Xml namespace exposes a plethora of additional XML manipulation classes in addition to those shown in the architecture diagram. The classes shown in the diagram include the following:

❑ XmlResolver — This abstract class resolves an external XML resource using a Uniform Resource Identifier (URI). XmlUrlResolver is an implementation of an XmlResolver.

❑ XmlNameTable — This abstract class provides a fast means by which an XML parser can access element or attribute names.

Writing an XML Stream

An XML document can be created programmatically in .NET. One way to perform this task is by writing the individual components of an XML document (schema, attributes, elements, and so on) to an XML stream. Using a unidirectional write-stream means that each element and its attributes must be written in order — the idea is that data is always written at the head of the stream. To accomplish this, you use a writable XML stream class (a class derived from XmlWriter). Such a class ensures that the XML document you generate correctly implements the W3C Extensible Markup Language (XML) 1.0 specification and the Namespaces in XML specification.

Why is this necessary when you have XML serialization? You need to be very careful here to separate interface from implementation. XML serialization works for a specific class, such as the ElokuvaTilaus class. This class is a proprietary implementation and not the format in which data is exchanged. For this one specific case, the XML document generated when ElokuvaTilaus is serialized just so happens to be the XML format used when placing an order for some movies. ElokuvaTilaus was given a little help from Source Code Style attributes so that it would conform to a standard XML representation of a film order summary.

In a different application, if the software used to manage an entire movie distribution business wants to generate movie orders, then it must generate a document of the appropriate form. The movie distribution management software achieves this using the `XmlWriter` object.

Before reviewing the subtleties of `XmlWriter`, note that this class exposes over 40 methods and properties. The example in this section provides an overview that touches on a subset of these methods and properties. This subset enables the generation of an XML document that corresponds to a movie order.

This example builds the module that generates the XML document corresponding to a movie order. It uses an instance of `XmlWriter`, called `FilmOrdersWriter`, which is actually a file on disk. This means that the XML document generated is streamed to this file. Because the `FilmOrdersWriter` variable represents a file, you have to take a few actions against the file. For instance, you have to ensure the file is

❑ **Created** — The instance of `XmlWriter`, `FilmOrdersWriter`, is created by using the `Create` method as well as by assigning all the properties of this object with the `XmlWriterSettings` object.

❑ **Opened** — The file the XML is streamed to, `FilmOrdersProgrammatic.xml`, is opened by passing the filename to the constructor associated with `XmlWriter`.

❑ **Generated** — The process of generating the XML document is described in detail at the end of this section.

❑ **Closed** — The file (the XML stream) is closed using the `Close` method of `XmlWriter` or by simply making use of the `Using` keyword, which ensures that the object is closed at the end of the `Using` statement.

Before you create the `XmlWriter` object, you first need to customize how the object operates by using the `XmlWriterSettings` object. This object, introduced in .NET 2.0, enables you to configure the behavior of the `XmlWriter` object before you instantiate it:

```
Dim myXmlSettings As New XmlWriterSettings()
myXmlSettings.Indent = True
myXmlSettings.NewLineOnAttributes = True
```

You can specify a few settings for the `XmlWriterSettings` object that define how XML creation will be handled by the `XmlWriter` object. The following table details the properties of the `XmlWriterSettings` class:

Property	Initial Value	Description
CheckCharacters	True	This property, if set to `True`, performs a character check on the contents of the `XmlWriter` object. Legal characters can be found at www.w3.org/TR/REC-xml#charsets.
CloseOutput	False	Specifies whether the `XmlWriter` should also close the stream or the `System.IO.TextWriter` object

Property	Initial Value	Description
ConformanceLevel	Conformance Level.Document	Allows the XML to be checked to ensure that it follows certain specified rules. Possible conformance-level settings include Document, Fragment, and Auto.
Encoding	Encoding.UTF8	Defines the encoding of the XML generated
Indent	True	Defines whether the XML generated should be indented or not. Setting this value to False will not indent child nodes from parent nodes.
IndentChars	Two spaces	Specifies the number of spaces by which child nodes are indented from parent nodes. This setting only works when the Indent property is set to True. If you want, you can assign this any string value you choose.
NewLineChars	\r\n	Assigns the characters that are used to define line breaks
NewLineHandling	NewLineHandling. Replace	Defines whether to normalize line breaks in the output. Possible values include Replace, Entitize, and None.
NewLineOn Attributes	True	Defines whether a node's attributes should be written to a new line in the construction. This will occur if set to True.
OmitXml Declaration	False	Defines whether an XML declaration should be generated in the output. This omission only occurs if set to True.
OutputMethod	OutputMethod.Xml	Defines the method to serialize the output. Possible values include Xml, Html, Text, and AutoDetect.

Once the XmlWriterSettings object has been instantiated and assigned the values you deem necessary, the next steps are to invoke the XmlWriter object and make the association between the XmlWriterSettings object and the XmlWriter object.

The basic infrastructure for managing the file (the XML text stream) and applying the settings class is either

```
Dim FilmOrdersWriter As XmlWriter = _
    XmlWriter.Create("..\FilmOrdersProgrammatic.xml", myXmlSettings)

FilmOrdersWriter.Close()
```

or the following, if you are utilizing the Using keyword, which is the recommended approach:

```
Using FilmOrdersWriter As XmlWriter = _
    XmlWriter.Create("..\FilmOrdersProgrammatic.xml", myXmlSettings)
End Using
```

With the preliminaries completed (file created and formatting configured), the process of writing the actual attributes and elements of your XML document can begin. The sequence of steps used to generate your XML document is as follows:

1. Write an XML comment using the `WriteComment` method. This comment describes from whence the concept for this XML document originated and generates the following code:

    ```
    <!-- Same as generated by serializing, ElokuvaTilaus -->
    ```

2. Begin writing the XML element, `<ElokuvaTilaus>`, by calling the `WriteStartElement` method. You can only begin writing this element because its attributes and child elements must be written before the element can be ended with a corresponding `</ElokuvaTilaus>`. The XML generated by the `WriteStartElement` method is as follows

    ```
    <ElokuvaTilaus>
    ```

3. Write the attributes associated with `<ElokuvaTilaus>` by calling the `WriteAttributeString` method twice. The XML generated by calling the `WriteAttributeString` method twice adds to the `<ElokuvaTilaus>` XML element that is currently being written to the following:

    ```
    <ElokuvaTilaus ElokuvaId="101" Maara="10">
    ```

4. Using the `WriteElementString` method, write the child XML element `<Nimi>` contained in the XML element, `<ElokuvaTilaus>`. The XML generated by calling this method is as follows:

    ```
    <Nimi>Grease</Nimi>
    ```

5. Complete writing the `<ElokuvaTilaus>` parent XML element by calling the `WriteEndElement` method. The XML generated by calling this method is as follows:

    ```
    </ElokuvaTilaus>
    ```

Let's now put all this together in the `Module1.vb` file shown here:

```vb
Imports System.Xml
Imports System.Xml.Serialization
Imports System.IO

Module Module1

    Sub Main()

        Dim myXmlSettings As New XmlWriterSettings
        myXmlSettings.Indent = True
        myXmlSettings.NewLineOnAttributes = True

        Using FilmOrdersWriter As XmlWriter = _
            XmlWriter.Create("..\FilmOrdersProgrammatic.xml", myXmlSettings)

            FilmOrdersWriter.WriteComment(" Same as generated " & _
                "by serializing, ElokuvaTilaus ")
            FilmOrdersWriter.WriteStartElement("ElokuvaTilaus")
```

```
            FilmOrdersWriter.WriteAttributeString("ElokuvaId", "101")
            FilmOrdersWriter.WriteAttributeString("Maara", "10")
            FilmOrdersWriter.WriteElementString("Nimi", "Grease")
            FilmOrdersWriter.WriteEndElement() ' End ElokuvaTilaus

        End Using

    End Sub

End Module
```

Once this is run, you will find the XML file `FilmOrdersProgrammatic.xml` created in the same folder as the `Module1.vb` file or in the `bin` directory. The content of this file is as follows:

```
<?xml version="1.0" encoding="utf-8"?>
<!-- Same as generated by serializing, ElokuvaTilaus -->
<ElokuvaTilaus
  ElokuvaId="101"
  Maara="10">
  <Nimi>Grease</Nimi>
</ElokuvaTilaus>
```

The previous XML document is the same in form as the XML document generated by serializing the `ElokuvaTilaus` class. Notice that in the previous XML document, the `<Nimi>` element is indented two characters and that each attribute is on a different line in the document. This was achieved using the `XmlWriterSettings` class.

The sample application covered only a small portion of the methods and properties exposed by the XML stream-writing class, `XmlWriter`. Other methods implemented by this class manipulate the underlying file, such as the `Flush` method; and some methods allow XML text to be written directly to the stream, such as the `WriteRaw` method.

The `XmlWriter` class also exposes a variety of methods that write a specific type of XML data to the stream. These methods include `WriteBinHex`, `WriteCData`, `WriteString`, and `WriteWhiteSpace`.

You can now generate the same XML document in two different ways. You have used two different applications that took two different approaches to generating a document that represents a standardized movie order. However, there are even more ways to generate XML, depending on the circumstances. Using the previous scenario, you could receive a movie order from a store, and this order would have to be transformed from the XML format used by the supplier to your own order format.

Reading an XML Stream

In .NET, XML documents can be read from a stream as well. Data is traversed in the stream in order (first XML element, second XML element, and so on). This traversal is very quick because the data is processed in one direction and features such as write and move backward in the traversal are not supported. At any given instance, only data at the current position in the stream can be accessed.

Before exploring how an XML stream can be read, you need to understand why it should be read in the first place. Returning to our movie supplier example, imagine that the application managing the movie orders can generate a variety of XML documents corresponding to current orders, preorders, and returns.

All the documents (current orders, preorders, and returns) can be extracted in stream form and processed by a report-generating application. This application prints the orders for a given day, the preorders that are going to be due, and the returns that are coming back to the supplier. The report-generating application processes the data by reading in and parsing a stream of XML.

One class that can be used to read and parse such an XML stream is XmlReader. Other classes in the .NET Framework are derived from XmlReader, such as XmlTextReader, which can read XML from a file (specified by a string corresponding to the file's name), a Stream, or an XmlReader. This example uses an XmlReader to read an XML document contained in a file. Reading XML from a file and writing it to a file is not the norm when it comes to XML processing, but a file is the simplest way to access XML data. This simplified access enables you to focus on XML-specific issues.

In creating a sample, the first step is to make the proper imports into the Module1.vb file:

```
Imports System.Xml
Imports System.Xml.Serialization
Imports System.IO
```

From there, the next step in accessing a stream of XML data is to create an instance of the object that will open the stream (the readMovieInfo variable of type XmlReader) and then open the stream itself. Your application performs this as follows (where MovieManage.xml is the name of the file containing the XML document):

```
Dim myXmlSettings As New XmlReaderSettings()
Using readMovieInfo As XmlReader = XmlReader.Create(fileName, myXmlSettings)
```

Note that because the XmlWriter has a settings class, the XmlReader also has a settings class. Though you can make assignments to the XmlReaderSettings object, in this case you do not. Later, this chapter covers the XmlReaderSettings object.

The basic mechanism for traversing each stream is to traverse from node to node using the Read method. Node types in XML include Element and Whitespace. Numerous other node types are defined, but this example focuses on traversing XML elements and the white space that is used to make the elements more readable (carriage returns, linefeeds, and indentation spaces). Once the stream is positioned at a node, the MoveToNextAttribute method can be called to read each attribute contained in an element. The MoveToNextAttribute method only traverses attributes for nodes that contain attributes (nodes of type element). An example of an XmlReader traversing each node and then traversing the attributes of each node follows:

```
While readMovieInfo.Read()
   ` Process node here.
  While readMovieInfo.MoveToNextAttribute()
     ` Process attribute here.
  End While
End While
```

This code, which reads the contents of the XML stream, does not utilize any knowledge of the stream's contents. However, a great many applications know exactly how the stream they are going to traverse is structured. Such applications can use XmlReader in a more deliberate manner and not simply traverse the stream without foreknowledge.

Once the example stream has been read, it can be cleaned up using the End Using call:

```
End Using
```

This ReadMovieXml subroutine takes the filename containing the XML to read as a parameter. The code for the subroutine is as follows (and is basically the code just outlined):

```
Private Sub ReadMovieXml(ByVal fileName As String)
    Dim myXmlSettings As New XmlReaderSettings()
    Using readMovieInfo As XmlReader = XmlReader.Create(fileName, _
        myXmlSettings)
        While readMovieInfo.Read()
            ShowXmlNode(readMovieInfo)
            While readMovieInfo.MoveToNextAttribute()
                ShowXmlNode(readMovieInfo)
            End While
        End While
    End Using

    Console.ReadLine()
End Sub
```

For each node encountered after a call to the Read method, ReadMovieXml calls the ShowXmlNode subroutine. Similarly, for each attribute traversed, the ShowXmlNode subroutine is called. This subroutine breaks down each node into its sub-entities:

❑ **Depth** — This property of XmlReader determines the level at which a node resides in the XML document tree. To understand depth, consider the following XML document composed solely of elements: <A><B></B><C><D></D></C></A>.
Element <A> is the root element, and when parsed would return a Depth of 0. Elements <B> and <C> are contained in <A> and hence reflect a Depth value of 1. Element <D> is contained in <C>. The Depth property value associated with <D> (depth of 2) should, therefore, be one more than the Depth property associated with <C> (depth of 1).

❑ **Type** — The type of each node is determined using the NodeType property of XmlReader. The node returned is of enumeration type, XmlNodeType. Permissible node types include Attribute, Element, and Whitespace. (Numerous other node types can also be returned, including CDATA, Comment, Document, Entity, and DocumentType.)

❑ **Name** — The type of each node is retrieved using the Name property of XmlReader. The name of the node could be an element name, such as <ElokuvaTilaus>, or an attribute name, such as ElokuvaId.

❑ **Attribute Count** — The number of attributes associated with a node is retrieved using the AttributeCount property of XmlReader's NodeType.

❑ **Value** — The value of a node is retrieved using the Value property of XmlReader. For example, the element node <Nimi> contains a value of Grease.

The subroutine ShowXmlNode is implemented as follows:

```
Private Sub ShowXmlNode(ByVal reader As XmlReader)
```

```
      If reader.Depth > 0 Then
         For depthCount As Integer = 1 To reader.Depth
            Console.Write(" ")
         Next
      End If

      If reader.NodeType = XmlNodeType.Whitespace Then

         Console.Out.WriteLine("Type: {0} ", reader.NodeType)

      ElseIf reader.NodeType = XmlNodeType.Text Then

         Console.Out.WriteLine("Type: {0}, Value: {1} ", _
                               reader.NodeType, _
                               reader.Value)

      Else

         Console.Out.WriteLine("Name: {0}, Type: {1}, " & _
                               "AttributeCount: {2}, Value: {3} ", _
                               reader.Name, _
                               reader.NodeType, _
                               reader.AttributeCount, _
                               reader.Value)

      End If

   End Sub
```

Within the ShowXmlNode subroutine, each level of node depth adds two spaces to the output generated:

```
   If reader.Depth > 0 Then
      For depthCount As Integer = 1 To reader.Depth
         Console.Write(" ")
      Next
   End If
```

You add these spaces in order to create human-readable output (so you can easily determine the depth of each node displayed). For each type of node, ShowXmlNode displays the value of the NodeType property. The ShowXmlNode subroutine makes a distinction between nodes of type Whitespace and other types of nodes. The reason for this is simple: A node of type Whitespace does not contain a name or attribute count. The value of such a node is any combination of white-space characters (space, tab, carriage return, and so on). Therefore, it doesn't make sense to display the properties if the NodeType is XmlNodeType.WhiteSpace. Nodes of type Text have no name associated with them, so for this type, subroutine ShowXmlNode only displays the properties NodeType and Value. For all other node types, the Name, AttributeCount, Value, and NodeType properties are displayed.

To finalize this module, add a Sub Main as follows:

```
   Sub Main(ByVal args() As String)
      ReadMovieXml("..\MovieManage.xml")
   End Sub
```

Here is an example construction of the `MovieManage.xml` file:

```xml
<?xml version="1.0" encoding="utf-8" ?>
<MovieOrderDump>

 <FilmOrder_Multiple>
    <multiFilmOrders>
       <FilmOrder>
          <name>Grease</name>
          <filmId>101</filmId>
          <quantity>10</quantity>
       </FilmOrder>
       <FilmOrder>
          <name>Lawrence of Arabia</name>
          <filmId>102</filmId>
          <quantity>10</quantity>
       </FilmOrder>
       <FilmOrder>
          <name>Star Wars</name>
          <filmId>103</filmId>
          <quantity>10</quantity>
       </FilmOrder>
    </multiFilmOrders>
 </FilmOrder_Multiple>

 <PreOrder>
    <FilmOrder>
       <name>Shrek III - Shrek Becomes a Programmer</name>
       <filmId>104</filmId>
       <quantity>10</quantity>
    </FilmOrder>
 </PreOrder>

 <Returns>
    <FilmOrder>
       <name>Star Wars</name>
       <filmId>103</filmId>
       <quantity>2</quantity>
    </FilmOrder>
 </Returns>

</MovieOrderDump>
```

Running this module produces the following output (a partial display, as it would be rather lengthy):

```
Name: xml, Type: XmlDeclaration, AttributeCount: 2, Value: version="1.0"
encoding="utf-8"
Name: version, Type: Attribute, AttributeCount: 2, Value: 1.0
Name: encoding, Type: Attribute, AttributeCount: 2, Value: utf-8
Type: Whitespace
Name: MovieOrderDump, Type: Element, AttributeCount: 0, Value:
 Type: Whitespace
 Name: FilmOrder_Multiple, Type: Element, AttributeCount: 0, Value:
  Type: Whitespace
```

```
Name: multiFilmOrders, Type: Element, AttributeCount: 0, Value:
 Type: Whitespace
 Name: FilmOrder, Type: Element, AttributeCount: 0, Value:
  Type: Whitespace
  Name: name, Type: Element, AttributeCount: 0, Value:
   Type: Text, Value: Grease
```

This example managed to use three methods and five properties of XmlReader. The output generated was informative but far from practical. XmlReader exposes over 50 methods and properties, which means that we have only scratched the surface of this highly versatile class. The remainder of this section looks at the XmlReaderSettings class, introduces a more realistic use of XmlReader, and demonstrates how the classes of System.Xml handle errors.

The XmlReaderSettings Class

Just like the XmlWriter object, the XmlReader object requires settings to be applied for instantiation of the object. This means that you can apply settings specifying how the XmlReader object behaves when it is reading whatever XML you might have for it. This includes settings for dealing with white space, schemas, and more:

Property	Initial Value	Description
CheckCharacters	True	This property, if set to True, performs a character check on the contents of the retrieved object. Legal characters can be found at www.w3.org/TR/REC-xml#charsets.
CloseOutput	False	Specifies whether the XmlWriter should also close the stream or the System.IO.TextWriter object
ConformanceLevel	Conformance Level.Document	Allows the XML to be checked to ensure that it follows certain specified rules. Possible conformance-level settings include Document, Fragment, and Auto.
IgnoreComments	False	Defines whether comments should be ignored or not
IgnoreProcessing Instructions	False	Defines whether processing instructions contained within the XML should be ignored
IgnoreWhitespace	False	Defines whether the XmlReader object should ignore all insignificant white space
LineNumberOffset	0	Defines the line number at which the LineNumber property starts counting within the XML file
LinePosition Offset	0	Defines the position in the line number at which the LineNumber property starts counting within the XML file
NameTable	An empty XmlNameTable object	Enables the XmlReader to work with a specific XmlNameTable object that is used for atomized string comparisons

Property	Initial Value	Description
ProhibitDtd	False	Defines whether the XmlReader should perform a DTD validation
Schemas	An empty XmlSchemaSet object	Enables the XmlReader to work with an instance of the XmlSchemaSet class
ValidationFlags	ValidationFlags .AllowXmlAttributes and validationFlags .ProcessidentityConstraints	Enables you to apply validation schema settings. Possible values include AllowXmlAttributes, ProcessIdentityConstraints, ProcessInlineSchema, ProcessSchemaLocation, ReportValidationWarnings, and None.
ValidationType	None	Specifies whether the XmlReader will perform validation or type assignment when reading. Possible values include Auto, DTD, None, Schema, and XDR.
XmlResolver		A write-only property that enables you to access external documents

An example of using this settings class to modify the behavior of the XmlReader class is as follows:

```
Dim myXmlSettings As New XmlReaderSettings()
myXmlSettings.IgnoreWhitespace = True
myXmlSettings.IgnoreComments = True

Using readMovieInfo As XmlReader = XmlReader.Create(fileName, myXmlSettings)
    ` Use XmlReader object here.
End Using
```

In this case, the XmlReader object that is created ignores the white space that it encounters, as well as any of the XML comments. These settings, once established with the XmlReaderSettings object, are then associated with the XmlReader object through its Create method.

Traversing XML Using XmlTextReader

An application can easily use XmlReader to traverse a document that is received in a known format. The document can thus be traversed in a deliberate manner. You just implemented a class that serialized arrays of movie orders. The next example takes an XML document containing multiple XML documents of that type and traverses them. Each movie order is forwarded to the movie supplier via fax. The document is traversed as follows:

```
Read root element: <MovieOrderDump>
    Process each <FilmOrder_Multiple> element
        Read <multiFilmOrders> element
            Process each <FilmOrder>
                Send fax for each movie order here
```

The basic outline for the program's implementation is to open a file containing the XML document to parse and to traverse it from element to element:

```
Dim myXmlSettings As New XmlReaderSettings()

Using readMovieInfo As XmlReader = XmlReader.Create(fileName, myXmlSettings)
        readMovieInfo.Read()
        readMovieInfo.ReadStartElement("MovieOrderDump")

        Do While (True)
            `***************************************************
            `* Process FilmOrder elements here               *
            `***************************************************

        Loop

        readMovieInfo.ReadEndElement()    '  </MovieOrderDump>

End Using
```

The preceding code opened the file using the constructor of `XmlReader`, and the `End Using` statement takes care of shutting everything down for you. The code also introduced two methods of the `XmlReader` class:

❑   `ReadStartElement(String)` — This verifies that the current in the stream is an element and that the element's name matches the string passed to `ReadStartElement`. If the verification is successful, then the stream is advanced to the next element.

❑   `ReadEndElement()` — This verifies that the current element is an end tab; and if the verification is successful, then the stream is advanced to the next element.

The application knows that an element, `<MovieOrderDump>`, will be found at a specific point in the document. The `ReadStartElement` method verifies this foreknowledge of the document format. After all the elements contained in element `<MovieOrderDump>` have been traversed, the stream should point to the end tag `</MovieOrderDump>`. The `ReadEndElement` method verifies this.

The code that traverses each element of type `<FilmOrder>` similarly uses the `ReadStartElement` and `ReadEndElement` methods to indicate the start and end of the `<FilmOrder>` and `<multiFilmOrders>` elements. The code that ultimately parses the list of movie orders and faxes the movie supplier (using the `FranticallyFaxTheMovieSupplier` subroutine) is as follows:

```
Dim myXmlSettings As New XmlReaderSettings()

Using readMovieInfo As XmlReader = XmlReader.Create(fileName, myXmlSettings)
        readMovieInfo.Read()
        readMovieInfo.ReadStartElement("MovieOrderDump")

        Do While (True)
```

```
        readMovieInfo.ReadStartElement("FilmOrder_Multiple")
        readMovieInfo.ReadStartElement("multiFilmOrders")

        Do While (True)
            readMovieInfo.ReadStartElement("FilmOrder")
            movieName = readMovieInfo.ReadElementString()
            movieId = readMovieInfo.ReadElementString()
            quantity = readMovieInfo.ReadElementString()
            readMovieInfo.ReadEndElement() ' clear </FilmOrder>

            FranticallyFaxTheMovieSupplier(movieName, movieId, quantity)

            ` Should read next FilmOrder node
            ` else quits
            readMovieInfo.Read()

            If ("FilmOrder" <> readMovieInfo.Name) Then
                Exit Do
            End If
        Loop

        readMovieInfo.ReadEndElement() ' clear </multiFilmOrders>
        readMovieInfo.ReadEndElement() ' clear </FilmOrder_Multiple>

        ` Should read next FilmOrder_Multiple node
        ` else you quit
        readMovieInfo.Read() ' clear </MovieOrderDump>

        If ("FilmOrder_Multiple" <> readMovieInfo.Name) Then
            Exit Do
        End If
    Loop

    readMovieInfo.ReadEndElement() '  </MovieOrderDump>

End Using
```

Three lines within the preceding code contain a call to the ReadElementString method:

```
movieName = readMovieInfo.ReadElementString()
movieId = readMovieInfo.ReadElementString()
quantity = readMovieInfo.ReadElementString()
```

While parsing the stream, it was known that an element named <name> existed and that this element contained the name of the movie. Rather than parse the start tag, get the value, and parse the end tag, it was easier to get the data using the ReadElementString method. This method retrieves the data string associated with an element and advances the stream to the next element. The ReadElementString method was also used to retrieve the data associated with the XML elements <filmId> and <quantity>.

The output of this example is a fax (not shown here because the point of this example is to demonstrate that it is simpler to traverse a document when its form is known). The format of the document is still verified by `XmlReader` as it is parsed.

The `XmlReader` class also exposes properties that provide more insight into the data contained in the XML document and the state of parsing: `IsEmptyElement`, `EOF`, and `IsStartElement`.

.NET CLR-compliant types are not 100 percent inline with XML types, so ever since the .NET Framework 2.0 was introduced, the new methods it made available in the `XmlReader` make the process of casting from one of these XML types to .NET types easier.

Using the `ReadElementContentAs` method, you can easily perform the necessary casting required:

```
Dim username As String = _
    myXmlReader.ReadElementContentAs(GetType(String), DBNull.Value)
Dim myDate As DateTime = _
    myXmlReader.ReadElementContentAs(GetType(DateTime), DBNull.Value)
```

Also available is a series of direct casts through new methods such as the following:

- ❏ `ReadElementContentAsBase64()`
- ❏ `ReadElementContentAsBinHex()`
- ❏ `ReadElementContentAsBoolean()`
- ❏ `ReadElementContentAsDateTime()`
- ❏ `ReadElementContentAsDecimal()`
- ❏ `ReadElementContentAsDouble()`
- ❏ `ReadElementContentAsFloat()`
- ❏ `ReadElementContentAsInt()`
- ❏ `ReadElementContentAsLong()`
- ❏ `ReadElementContentAsObject()`
- ❏ `ReadElementContentAsString()`

In addition to these methods, the raw XML associated with the document can also be retrieved, using `ReadInnerXml` and `ReadOuterXml`. Again, this only scratches the surface of the `XmlReader` class, a class quite rich in functionality.

Handling Exceptions

XML is text and could easily be read using mundane methods such as `Read` and `ReadLine`. A key feature of each class that reads and traverses XML is inherent support for error detection and handling. To demonstrate this, consider the following malformed XML document found in the file named `Malformed.xml`:

```
<?xml version="1.0" encoding="IBM437" ?>
<ElokuvaTilaus ElokuvaId="101", Maara="10">
   <Nimi>Grease</Nimi>
<ElokuvaTilaus>
```

This document may not immediately appear to be malformed. By wrapping a call to the method you developed (`ReadMovieXml`), you can see what type of exception is raised when `XmlReader` detects the malformed XML within this document:

```
Try
      ReadMovieXml("Malformed.xml")
Catch xmlEx As XmlException
      Console.Error.WriteLine("XML Error: " + xmlEx.ToString())
Catch ex As Exception
      Console.Error.WriteLine("Some other error: " + ex.ToString())
End Try
```

The methods and properties exposed by the `XmlReader` class raise exceptions of type `System.Xml` `.XmlException`. In fact, every class in the `System.Xml` namespace raises exceptions of type `XmlException`. Although this is a discussion of errors using an instance of type `XmlReader`, the concepts reviewed apply to all errors generated by classes found in the `System.Xml` namespace.

Properties exposed by `XmlException` include the following:

❑ `Data` — A set of key-value pairs that enable you to display user-defined information about the exception

❑ `HelpLink` — The link to the help page that deals with the exception

❑ `InnerException` — The `System.Exception` instance indicating what caused the current exception

❑ `LineNumber` — The number of the line within an XML document where the error occurred

❑ `LinePosition` — The position within the line specified by `LineNumber` where the error occurred

❑ `Message` — The error message that corresponds to the error that occurred. This error took place at the line in the XML document specified by `LineNumber` and within the line at the position specified by `LinePostion`.

❑ `Source` — Provides the name of the application or object that triggered the error

❑ `SourceUri` — Provides the URI of the element or document in which the error occurred

❑ `StackTrace` — Provides a string representation of the frames on the call stack when the error was triggered

❑ `TargetSite` — The method that triggered the error

The error displayed when subroutine `movieReadXML` processes `Malformed.xml` is as follows:

```
XML Error: System.Xml.XmlException: The ',' character, hexadecimal value 0x2C,
  cannot begin a name. Line 2, position 49.
```

The preceding snippet indicates that a comma separates the attributes in element `<FilmOrder>` (`ElokuvaTilaus="101"`, `Maara="10"`). This comma is invalid. Removing it and running the code again results in the following output:

```
XML Error: System.Xml.XmlException: This is an unexpected token. Expected
'EndElement'. Line 5, position 27.
```

Again, you can recognize the precise error. In this case, you do not have an end element, `</ElokuvaTilaus>`, but you do have an opening element, `<ElokuvaTilaus>`.

The properties provided by the `XmlException` class (such as `LineNumber`, `LinePosition`, and `Message`) provide a useful level of precision when tracking down errors. The `XmlReader` class also exposes a level of precision with respect to the parsing of the XML document. This precision is exposed by the `XmlReader` through properties such as `LineNumber` and `LinePosition`.

Using the MemoryStream Object

A very useful class that can greatly help you when working with XML is `System.IO.MemoryStream`. Rather than need a network or disk resource backing the stream (as in `System.Net.Sockets.NetworkStream` and `System.IO.FileStream`), `MemoryStream` backs itself up onto a block of memory. Imagine that you want to generate an XML document and e-mail it. The built-in classes for sending e-mail rely on having a `System.String` containing a block of text for the message body, but if you want to generate an XML document, then you need a stream.

If the document is reasonably sized, then write the document directly to memory and copy that block of memory to the e-mail. This is good from a performance and reliability perspective because you don't have to open a file, write it, rewind it, and read the data back in again. However, you must consider scalability in this situation because if the file is very large, or if you have a great number of smaller files, then you could run out of memory (in which case you have to go the "file" route).

This section describes how to generate an XML document to a `MemoryStream` object, reading the document back out again as a `System.String` value and e-mailing it. What you will do is create a new class called `EmailStream` that extends `MemoryStream`. This new class contains an extra method called `CloseAndSend` that, as its name implies, closes the stream and sends the e-mail message.

First, create a new console application project called "EmailStream." The first task is to create a basic `Customer` object that contains a few basic members and can be automatically serialized by .NET through use of the `SerializableAttribute` attribute:

```
<Serializable()> Public Class Customer

    ` members...
    Public Id As Integer
    Public FirstName As String
    Public LastName As String
    Public Email As String

End Class
```

The fun part is the `EmailStream` class itself. This needs access to the `System.Net.Mail` namespace, so import this namespace into your code for your class. The new class should also extend `System.IO.MemoryStream`, as shown here:

```
Imports System.IO
Imports System.Net.Mail

Public Class EmailStream
    Inherits MemoryStream
```

The first job of `CloseAndSend` is to start putting together the mail message. This is done by creating a new `System.Web.Mail.MailMessage` object and configuring the sender, recipient, and subject:

```
` CloseAndSend - close the stream and send the email...
Public Sub CloseAndSend(ByVal fromAddress As String, _
                        ByVal toAddress As String, _
                        ByVal subject As String)

    ` Create the new message...
    Dim message As New MailMessage()

    message.From = New MailAddress(fromAddress)
    message.To.Add(New MailAddress(toAddress))
    message.Subject = subject
```

This method will be called after the XML document has been written to the stream, so you can assume at this point that the stream contains a block of data. To read the data back out again, you have to rewind the stream and use a `System.IO.StreamReader`. Before you do this, however, call `Flush`. Traditionally, streams have always been buffered — that is, the data is not sent to the final destination (the memory block in this case, but a file in the case of a `FileStream`, and so on) each time the stream is written. Instead, the data is written in (mostly) a nondeterministic way. Because you need all the data to be written, you call `Flush` to ensure that all the data has been sent to the destination and that the buffer is empty.

In a way, `EmailStream` is a great example of buffering. All the data is held in a memory "buffer" until you finally send the data on to its destination in a response to an explicit call to this method:

```
    ` Flush and rewind the stream...

    Flush()
    Seek(0, SeekOrigin.Begin)
```

Once you have flushed and rewound the stream, you can create a `StreamReader` and dredge all the data out into the `Body` property of the `MailMessage` object:

```
    ` Read out the data...

    Dim reader As New StreamReader(Me)
    message.Body = reader.ReadToEnd()
```

After you have done that, close the stream by calling the base class method:

```
` Close the stream...

Close()
```

Finally, send the message:

```
` Send the message...
Dim SmtpMail As New SmtpClient()
SmtpMail.Send(message)

End Sub

End Class
```

To call this method, you need to add some code to the Main method. First, create a new Customer object and populate it with some test data:

```
Imports System.Xml.Serialization

Module Module1

  Sub Main()

    ` Create a new customer...
    Dim customer As New Customer
    customer.Id = 27
    customer.FirstName = "Bill"
    customer.LastName = "Gates"
    customer.Email = bill.gates@microsoft.com
```

After you have done that, you can create a new EmailStream object. You then use XmlSerializer to write an XML document representing the newly created Customer instance to the block of memory that EmailStream is backing to:

```
    ` Create a new email stream...
    Dim stream As New EmailStream

    ` Serialize...
    Dim serializer As New XmlSerializer(customer.GetType())
    serializer.Serialize(stream, customer)
```

At this point, the stream will be filled with data; and after all the data has been flushed, the block of memory that EmailStream backs on to will contain the complete document. Now you can call CloseAndSend to e-mail the document:

```
    ` Send the email...
    stream.CloseAndSend("evjen@yahoo.com", _
       "evjen@yahoo.com", "XML Customer Document")
  End Sub

End Module
```

You probably already have the Microsoft SMTP service properly configured — this service is necessary to send e-mail. You also need to ensure that the e-mail addresses used in your code go to your e-mail address! Run the project and check your e-mail; you should see something similar to what is shown in Figure 10-2.

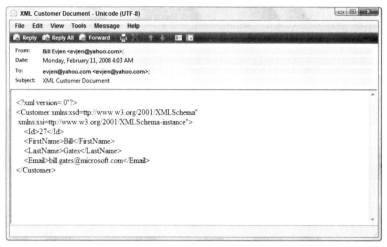

Figure 10-2

Document Object Model (DOM)

The classes of the `System.Xml` namespace that support the Document Object Model (DOM) interact as illustrated in Figure 10-3.

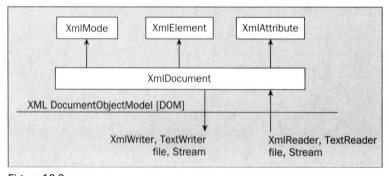

Figure 10-3

Within this diagram, an XML document is contained in a class named `XmlDocument`. Each node within this document is accessible and managed using `XmlNode`. Nodes can also be accessed and managed using a class specifically designed to process a specific node's type (`XmlElement`, `XmlAttribute`, and so on). XML documents are extracted from `XmlDocument` using a variety of mechanisms exposed through such classes as `XmlWriter`, `TextWriter`, `Stream`, and a file (specified by filename of type `String`). XML documents are consumed by an `XmlDocument` using a variety of load mechanisms exposed through the same classes.

A DOM-style parser differs from a stream-style parser with respect to movement. Using the DOM, the nodes can be traversed forward and backward. Nodes can be added to the document, removed from the document, and updated. However, this flexibility comes at a performance cost. It is faster to read or write XML using a stream-style parser.

The DOM-specific classes exposed by `System.Xml` include the following:

❑ `XmlDocument` — Corresponds to an entire XML document. A document is loaded using the `Load` method. XML documents are loaded from a file (the filename specified as type `String`), `TextReader`, or `XmlReader`. A document can be loaded using `LoadXml` in conjunction with a string containing the XML document. The `Save` method is used to save XML documents. The methods exposed by `XmlDocument` reflect the intricate manipulation of an XML document. For example, the following self-documenting creation methods are implemented by this class: `CreateAttribute`, `CreateCDataSection`, `CreateComment`, `CreateDocumentFragment`, `CreateDocumentType`, `CreateElement`, `CreateEntityReference`, `CreateNavigator`, `CreateNode`, `CreateProcessingInstruction`, `CreateSignificantWhitespace`, `CreateTextNode`, `CreateWhitespace`, and `CreateXmlDeclaration`. The elements contained in the document can be retrieved. Other methods support the retrieving, importing, cloning, loading, and writing of nodes.

❑ `XmlNode` — Corresponds to a node within the DOM tree. This class supports data types, namespaces, and DTDs. A robust set of methods and properties is provided to create, delete, and replace nodes: `AppendChild`, `Clone`, `CloneNode`, `CreateNavigator`, `InsertAfter`, `InsertBefore`, `Normalize`, `PrependChild`, `RemoveAll`, `RemoveChild`, `ReplaceChild`, `SelectNodes`, `SelectSingleNode`, `Supports`, `WriteContentTo`, and `WriteTo`. The contents of a node can similarly be traversed in a variety of ways: `FirstChild`, `LastChild`, `NextSibling`, `ParentNode`, and `PreviousSibling`.

❑ `XmlElement` — Corresponds to an element within the DOM tree. The functionality exposed by this class contains a variety of methods used to manipulate an element's attributes: `AppendChild`, `Clone`, `CloneNode`, `CreateNavigator`, `GetAttribute`, `GetAttributeNode`, `GetElementsByTagName`, `GetNamespaceOfPrefix`, `GetPrefixOfNamespace`, `InsertAfter`, `InsertBefore`, `Normalize`, `PrependChild`, `RemoveAll`, `RemoveAllAttributes`, `RemoveAttribute`, `RemoveAttributeAt`, `RemoveAttributeNode`, `RemoveChild`, `ReplaceChild`, `SelectNodes`, `SelectSingleNode`, `SetAttribute`, `SetAttributeNode`, `Supports`, `WriteContentTo`, and `WriteTo`.

❑ `XmlAttribute` — Corresponds to an attribute of an element (`XmlElement`) within the DOM tree. An attribute contains data and lists of subordinate data, so it is a less complicated object than an `XmlNode` or an `XmlElement`. An `XmlAttribute` can retrieve its owner document (property, `OwnerDocument`), retrieve its owner element (property, `OwnerElement`), retrieve its parent node (property, `ParentNode`), and retrieve its name (property, `Name`). The value of an `XmlAttribute` is available via a read-write property named `Value`. Methods available to `XmlAttribute` include `AppendChild`, `Clone`, `CloneNode`, `CreateNavigator`, `GetNamespaceOfPrefix`, `GetPrefixOfNamespace`, `InsertAfter`, `InsertBefore`, `Normalize`, `PrependChild`, `RemoveAll`, `RemoveChild`, `ReplaceChild`, `SelectNodes`, `SelectSingleNode`, `WriteContentTo`, and `WriteTo`.

Given the diverse number of methods and properties exposed by `XmlDocument`, `XmlNode`, `XmlElement`, and `XmlAttribute` (and there are many more than those listed here), it's clear that any XML 1.0 or 1.1-compliant document can be generated and manipulated using these classes. In comparison to their XML stream counterparts, these classes offer more flexible movement within the XML document and through any editing of XML documents.

A similar comparison could be made between DOM and data serialized and deserialized using XML. Using serialization, the type of node (for example, attribute or element) and the node name are specified at compile time. There is no on-the-fly modification of the XML generated by the serialization process.

Other technologies that generate and consume XML are not as flexible as the DOM. This includes ADO.NET and ADO, which generate XML of a particular form. The default install of SQL Server 2000 does expose a certain amount of flexibility when it comes to the generation (`FOR XML` queries) and consumption (`OPENXML`) of XML. SQL Server 2005 has more support for XML and even supports an XML data type. SQL Server 2005 also expands upon the `FOR XML` query with `FOR XML TYPE`. The choice between using classes within the DOM and a version of SQL Server is a choice between using a language such as Visual Basic to manipulate objects or installing SQL Server and performing most of the XML manipulation in SQL.

DOM Traversing Raw XML Elements

The first DOM example loads an XML document into an `XmlDocument` object using a string that contains the actual XML document. This scenario is typical of an application that uses ADO.NET to generate XML, but then uses the objects of the DOM to traverse and manipulate this XML. ADO.NET's `DataSet` object contains the results of ADO.NET data access operations. The `DataSet` class exposes a `GetXml` method that retrieves the underlying XML associated with the `DataSet`. The following code demonstrates how the contents of the `DataSet` are loaded into the `XmlDocument`:

```
Dim xmlDoc As New XmlDocument
Dim ds As New DataSet()

` Set up ADO.NET DataSet() here
xmlDoc.LoadXml(ds.GetXml())
```

This example over the next few pages simply traverses each XML element (`XmlNode`) in the document (`XmlDocument`) and displays the data accordingly. The data associated with this example is not retrieved from a `DataSet` but is instead contained in a string, `rawData`, which is initialized as follows:

```
Dim rawData As String = _
    "<multiFilmOrders>" & _
    "  <FilmOrder>" & _
    "     <name>Grease</name>" & _
    "     <filmId>101</filmId>" & _
    "     <quantity>10</quantity>" & _
    "  </FilmOrder>" & _
    "  <FilmOrder>" & _
    "     <name>Lawrence of Arabia</name>" & _
    "     <filmId>102</filmId>" & _
    "     <quantity>10</quantity>" & _
    "  </FilmOrder>" & _
    "</multiFilmOrders>"
```

410

The XML document in `rawData` is a portion of the XML hierarchy associated with a movie order. The preceding example is what you would do if you were using any of the .NET Framework versions before version 3.5. If you are working on the .NET Framework 3.5, then you can use the new XML literal capability offered. This means that you can now put XML directly in your code as XML and not as a string. This approach is presented here:

```
Dim rawData As String = _
    <multiFilmOrders>
        <FilmOrder>
            <name>Grease</name>
            <filmId>101</filmId>
            <quantity>10</quantity>
        </FilmOrder>
        <FilmOrder>
            <name>Lawrence of Arabia</name>
            <filmId>102</filmId>
            <quantity>10</quantity>
        </FilmOrder>
    </multiFilmOrders>
```

The basic idea in processing this data is to traverse each `<FilmOrder>` element in order to display the data it contains. Each node corresponding to a `<FilmOrder>` element can be retrieved from your `XmlDocument` using the `GetElementsByTagName` method (specifying a tag name of `FilmOrder`). The `GetElementsByTagName` method returns a list of `XmlNode` objects in the form of a collection of type `XmlNodeList`. Using the `For Each` statement to construct this list, the `XmlNodeList` (`movieOrderNodes`) can be traversed as individual `XmlNode` elements (`movieOrderNode`). The code for handling this is as follows:

```
Dim xmlDoc As New XmlDocument
Dim movieOrderNodes As XmlNodeList
Dim movieOrderNode As XmlNode

xmlDoc.LoadXml(rawData)

` Traverse each <FilmOrder>
movieOrderNodes = xmlDoc.GetElementsByTagName("FilmOrder")

For Each movieOrderNode In movieOrderNodes
    `*********************************************************
    ` Process <name>, <filmId> and <quantity> here
    `*********************************************************
Next
```

Each `XmlNode` can then have its contents displayed by traversing the children of this node using the `ChildNodes` method. This method returns an `XmlNodeList` (`baseDataNodes`) that can be traversed one `XmlNode` list element at a time:

```
Dim baseDataNodes As XmlNodeList
Dim bFirstInRow As Boolean

baseDataNodes = movieOrderNode.ChildNodes
```

```
      bFirstInRow = True

      For Each baseDataNode As XmlNode In baseDataNodes
        If (bFirstInRow) Then
          bFirstInRow = False
        Else
          Console.Out.Write(", ")
        End If
        Console.Out.Write(baseDataNode.Name & ": " & baseDataNode.InnerText)
      Next
      Console.Out.WriteLine()
```

The bulk of the preceding code retrieves the name of the node using the Name property and the InnerText property of the node. The InnerText property of each XmlNode retrieved contains the data associated with the XML elements (nodes) <name>, <filmId>, and <quantity>. The example displays the contents of the XML elements using Console.Out. The XML document is displayed as follows:

```
      name: Grease, filmId: 101, quantity: 10
      name: Lawrence of Arabia, filmId: 102, quantity: 10
```

Other, more practical, methods for using this data could have been implemented, including the following:

❑   The contents could have been directed to an ASP.NET Response object, and the data retrieved could have been used to create an HTML table (<table> table, <tr> row, and <td> data) that would be written to the Response object.

❑   The data traversed could have been directed to a ListBox or ComboBox Windows Forms control. This would enable the data returned to be selected as part of a GUI application.

❑   The data could have been edited as part of your application's business rules. For example, you could have used the traversal to verify that the <filmId> matched the <name>. Something like this could be done if you wanted to validate the data entered into the XML document in any manner.

Here is the example in its entirety:

```
      Dim rawData As String = _
         <multiFilmOrders>
            <FilmOrder>
               <name>Grease</name>
               <filmId>101</filmId>
               <quantity>10</quantity>
            </FilmOrder>
            <FilmOrder>
               <name>Lawrence of Arabia</name>
               <filmId>102</filmId>
               <quantity>10</quantity>
            </FilmOrder>
         </multiFilmOrders>

      Dim xmlDoc As New XmlDocument
      Dim movieOrderNodes As XmlNodeList
      Dim movieOrderNode As XmlNode
```

```
Dim baseDataNodes As XmlNodeList
Dim bFirstInRow As Boolean

xmlDoc.LoadXml(rawData)

` Traverse each <FilmOrder>
movieOrderNodes = xmlDoc.GetElementsByTagName("FilmOrder")

For Each movieOrderNode In movieOrderNodes
  baseDataNodes = movieOrderNode.ChildNodes
  bFirstInRow = True
  For Each baseDataNode As XmlNode In baseDataNodes
    If (bFirstInRow) Then
      bFirstInRow = False
    Else
      Console.Out.Write(", ")
    End If
    Console.Out.Write(baseDataNode.Name & ": " & baseDataNode.InnerText)
  Next
  Console.Out.WriteLine()
Next
```

DOM Traversing XML Attributes

This next example demonstrates how to traverse data contained in attributes and how to update the attributes based on a set of business rules. In this example, the XmlDocument object is populated by retrieving an XML document from a file. After the business rules edit the object, the data is persisted back to the file:

```
Dim xmlDoc As New XmlDocument

xmlDoc.Load("..\MovieSupplierShippingListV2.xml")
`**********************************************
` Business rules process document here
`**********************************************


xmlDoc.Save("..\MovieSupplierShippingListV2.xml")
```

The data contained in the file, MovieSupplierShippingListV2.xml, is a variation of the movie order. You have altered your rigid standard (for the sake of example) so that the data associated with individual movie orders is contained in XML attributes instead of XML elements. An example of this movie order data is as follows:

```
<FilmOrder name="Grease" filmId="101" quantity="10" />
```

You already know how to traverse the XML elements associated with a document, so let's assume that you have successfully retrieved the XmlNode associated with the <FilmOrder> element:

```
Dim attributes As XmlAttributeCollection
Dim filmId As Integer
Dim quantity As Integer
```

```
attributes = node.Attributes()

For Each attribute As XmlAttribute In attributes
  If 0 = String.Compare(attribute.Name, "filmId") Then
    filmId = attribute.InnerXml
  ElseIf 0 = String.Compare(attribute.Name, "quantity") Then
    quantity = attribute.InnerXml
  End If
Next
```

The preceding code traverses the attributes of an XmlNode by retrieving a list of attributes using the Attributes method. The value of this method is used to set the attributes' object (data type, XmlAttributeCollection). The individual XmlAttribute objects (variable, attribute) contained in attributes are traversed using a For Each loop. Within the loop, the contents of the filmId and the quantity attribute are saved for processing by your business rules.

Your business rules execute an algorithm that ensures that the movies in the company's order are provided in the correct quantity. This rule specifies that the movie associated with filmId=101 must be sent to the customer in batches of six at a time due to packaging. In the event of an invalid quantity, the code for enforcing this business rule will remove a single order from the quantity value until the number is divisible by six. Then this number is assigned to the quantity attribute. The Value property of the XmlAttribute object is used to set the correct value of the order's quantity. The code performing this business rule is as follows:

```
If filmId = 101 Then
  ` This film comes packaged in batches of six.
  Do Until (quantity / 6) = True
    quantity -= 1
  Loop

  Attributes.ItemOf("quantity").Value = quantity
End If
```

What is elegant about this example is that the list of attributes was traversed using For Each. Then ItemOf was used to look up a specific attribute that had already been traversed. This would not have been possible by reading an XML stream with an object derived from the XML stream reader class, XmlReader.

You can use this code as follows:

```
Sub TraverseAttributes(ByRef node As XmlNode)
    Dim attributes As XmlAttributeCollection
    Dim filmId As Integer
    Dim quantity As Integer

    attributes = node.Attributes()

    For Each attribute As XmlAttribute In attributes
        If 0 = String.Compare(attribute.Name, "filmId") Then
            filmId = attribute.InnerXml
        ElseIf 0 = String.Compare(attribute.Name, "quantity") Then
            quantity = attribute.InnerXml
```

```
        End If
    Next

    If filmId = 101 Then
        ` This film comes packaged in batches of six
        Do Until (quantity / 6) = True
            quantity -= 1
        Loop

        Attributes.ItemOf("quantity").Value = quantity
    End If
End Sub

Sub WXReadMovieDOM()

    Dim xmlDoc As New XmlDocument

    Dim movieOrderNodes As XmlNodeList

    xmlDoc.Load("..\MovieSupplierShippingListV2.xml")

    ` Traverse each <FilmOrder>
    movieOrderNodes = xmlDoc.GetElementsByTagName("FilmOrder")

    For Each movieOrderNode As XmlNode In movieOrderNodes
        TraverseAttributes(movieOrderNode)
    Next

    xmlDoc.Save("..\MovieSupplierShippingListV2.xml")

End Sub
```

XSLT Transformations

XSLT is a language that is used to transform XML documents into another format altogether. One popular use of XSLT is to transform XML into HTML so that XML documents can be presented visually. You have performed a similar task before. When working with XML serialization, you rewrote the `FilmOrder` class. This class was used to serialize a movie order object to XML using nodes that contained English-language names. The rewritten version of this class, `ElokuvaTilaus`, serialized XML nodes containing Finnish names. Source Code Style attributes were used in conjunction with the `XmlSerializer` class to accomplish this transformation. Two words in this paragraph send chills down the spine of any experienced developer: rewrote and rewritten. The point of an XSL transform is to use an alternate language (XSLT) to transform the XML, rather than rewrite the source code, SQL commands, or some other mechanism used to generate XML.

Conceptually, XSLT is straightforward. A file with an `.xslt` extension describes the changes (transformations) that will be applied to a particular XML file. Once this is completed, an XSLT processor is provided with the source XML file and the XSLT file, and performs the transformation. The `System.Xml.Xsl.XslTransform` class is such an XSLT processor. Another processor you will find (introduced in the .NET Framework 2.0) is the `XsltCommand` object found at `SystemXml.Query.XsltCommand`. This section looks at using both of these processors.

There are also some new features to be found in Visual Studio 2008 that deal with XSLT. The new version of the IDE supports items such as XSLT data breakpoints and better support in the editor for loading large documents. Additionally, XSLT stylesheets can be compiled into assemblies even more easily with the new command-line stylesheet compiler, `XSLTC.exe`.

The XSLT file is itself an XML document, although certain elements within this document are XSLT-specific commands. Dozens of XSLT commands can be used in writing an XSLT file. The first example explores the following XSLT elements (commands):

❑   `stylesheet` — This element indicates the start of the style sheet (XSL) in the XSLT file.

❑   `template` — This element denotes a reusable template for producing specific output. This output is generated using a specific node type within the source document under a specific context. For example, the text `<xsl: template match="/">` selects all root notes (`"/"`) for the specific transform template.

❑   `for-each` — This element applies the same template to each node in the specified set. Recall the example class (`FilmOrder_Multiple`) that could be serialized. This class contained an array of movie orders. Given the XML document generated when a `FilmOrder_Multiple` is serialized, each movie order serialized could be processed using `<xsl:for-each select = "FilmOrder_ Multiple/multiFilmOrders/FilmOrder">`.

❑   `value-of` — This element retrieves the value of the specified node and inserts it into the document in text form. For example, `<xsl:value-of select="name" />` would take the value of the XML element `<name>` and insert it into the transformed document.

When serialized, the `FilmOrder_Multiple` class generates XML such as the following (where . . . indicates where additional `<FilmOrder>` elements may reside):

```
<?xml version="1.0" encoding="UTF-8" ?>
<FilmOrder_Multiple>
    <multiFilmOrders>
        <FilmOrder>
            <name>Grease</name>
            <filmId>101</filmId>
            <quantity>10</quantity>
        </FilmOrder>
        ...
    </multiFilmOrders>
</FilmOrder_Multiple>
```

The preceding XML document is used to generate a report that is viewed by the manager of the movie supplier. This report is in HTML form, so that it can be viewed via the Web. The XSLT elements you previously reviewed (`stylesheet`, `template`, and `for-each`) are the only XSLT elements required to transform the XML document (in which data is stored) into an HTML file (data that can be displayed). An XSLT file `DisplayThatPuppy.xslt` contains the following text, which is used to transform a serialized version, `FilmOrder_Multiple`:

```
<?xml version="1.0" encoding="UTF-8" ?>
<xsl:stylesheet xmlns:xsl="http://www.w3.org/1999/XSL/Transform" version="1.0">
 <xsl:template match="/">
        <HTML>
        <TITLE>What people are ordering</TITLE>
        <BODY>
            <TABLE BORDER="1">
```

```
      <TR>
        <TD><B>Film Name</B></TD>
        <TD><B>Film ID</B></TD>
        <TD><B>Quantity</B></TD>
      </TR>
      <xsl:for-each select=
       "FilmOrder_Multiple/multiFilmOrders/FilmOrder">
      <TR>
        <TD><xsl:value-of select="name" /></TD>
        <TD><xsl:value-of select="filmId" /></TD>
        <TD><xsl:value-of select="quantity" /></TD>
      </TR>
      </xsl:for-each>
    </TABLE>
  </BODY>
  </HTML>
  </xsl:template>
</xsl:stylesheet>
```

In the preceding XSLT file, the XSLT elements are marked in bold. These elements perform operations on the source XML file containing a serialized `FilmOrder_Multiple` object and generate the appropriate HTML file. Your file contains a table (marked by the table tag, `<TABLE>`) that contains a set of rows (each row marked by a table row tag, `<TR>`). The columns of the table are contained in table data tags, `<TD>`. The XSLT file contains the header row for the table:

```
<TR>
    <TD><B>Film Name</B></TD>
    <TD><B>Film ID</B></TD>
    <TD><B>Quantity</B></TD>
</TR>
```

Each row containing data (an individual movie order from the serialized object, `FilmOrder_Multiple`) is generated using the XSLT element, `for-each`, to traverse each `<FilmOrder>` element within the source XML document:

```
<xsl:for-each select=
    "FilmOrder_Multiple/multiFilmOrders/FilmOrder">
```

The individual columns of data are generated using the `value-of` XSLT element, in order to query the elements contained within each `<FilmOrder>` element (`<name>`, `<filmId>`, and `<quantity>`):

```
<TR>
    <TD><xsl:value-of select="name" /></TD>
    <TD><xsl:value-of select="filmId" /></TD>
    <TD><xsl:value-of select="quantity" /></TD>
</TR>
```

The code to create a displayable XML file using the `XslTransform` object is as follows:

```
Dim myXslTransform As New XslCompiledTransform()

Dim destFileName As String = "..\ShowIt.html"
```

417

```
myXslTransform.Load("..\DisplayThatPuppy.xsl")
myXslTransform.Transform("..\FilmOrders.xml", destFileName)

System.Diagnostics.Process.Start(destFileName)
```

This consists of only seven lines of code, with the bulk of the coding taking place in the XSLT file. The previous code snippet created an instance of a `System.Xml.Xsl.XslCompiledTransform` object named `myXslTransform`. The `Load` method of this class is used to load the XSLT file you previously reviewed, `DisplayThatPuppy.xslt`. The `Transform` method takes a source XML file as the first parameter, which in this case was a file containing a serialized `FilmOrder_Multiple` object. The second parameter is the destination file created by the transform (`ShowIt.html`). The `Start` method of the `Process` class is used to display the HTML file. This method launches a process that is best suited for displaying the file provided. Basically, the extension of the file dictates which application will be used to display the file. On a typical Windows machine, the program used to display this file is Internet Explorer, as shown in Figure 10-4.

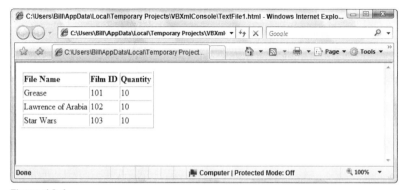

Figure 10-4

Don't confuse displaying this HTML file with ASP.NET. Displaying an HTML file in this manner takes place on a single machine without the involvement of a Web server. Using ASP.NET is more complex than displaying an HTML page in the default browser.

As demonstrated, the backbone of the `System.Xml.Xsl` namespace is the `XslCompiledTransform` class. This class uses XSLT files to transform XML documents. `XslTransform` exposes the following methods and properties:

❑ `XmlResolver` — This get/set property is used to specify a class (abstract base class, `XmlResolver`) that is used to handle external references (import and include elements within the style sheet). These external references are encountered when a document is transformed (the method, `Transform`, is executed). The `System.Xml` namespace contains a class, `XmlUrlResolver`, which is derived from `XmlResolver`. The `XmlUrlResolver` class resolves the external resource based on a URI.

❑ `Load` — This overloaded method loads an XSLT style sheet to be used in transforming XML documents. It is permissible to specify the XSLT style sheet as a parameter of type `XPathNavigator`, filename of XSLT file (specified as parameter type `String`), `XmlReader`, or `IXPathNavigable`. For each type of XSLT supported, an overloaded member is provided that enables an `XmlResolver` to also be specified. For example, it is possible to call Load(String, XmlResolver), where String corresponds to a filename and XmlResolver is an object that handles references in the style sheet of type xsl:import and xsl:include. It would also be permissible to pass in a value of Nothing for the second parameter of the Load method (so that no XmlResolver would be specified).

❑ Transform — This overloaded method transforms a specified XML document using the previously specified XSLT style sheet and an XmlResolver. The location where the transformed XML is to be output is specified as a parameter to this method. The first parameter of each overloaded method is the XML document to be transformed. This parameter can be represented as an IXPathNavigable, XML filename (specified as parameter type String), or XPathNavigator.

The most straightforward variant of the Transform method is Transform(String, String, XmlResolver). In this case, a file containing an XML document is specified as the first parameter, a filename that receives the transformed XML document is specified as the second parameter, and the XmlResolver is used as the third parameter. This is exactly how the first XSLT example utilized the Transform method:

```
myXslTransform.Transform("..\FilmOrders.xml", destFileName)
```

The first parameter to the Transform method can also be specified as IXPathNavigable or XPath-Navigator. Either of these parameter types allows the XML output to be sent to an object of type Stream, TextWriter, or XmlWriter. When these two flavors of input are specified, a parameter containing an object of type XsltArgumentList can be specified. An XsltArgumentList object contains a list of arguments that are used as input to the transform.

When working with a .NET 2.0/3.5 project, it is preferable to use the XslCompiledTransform object instead of the XslTransform object, because the XslTransform object is considered obsolete.

The XslCompiledTransform object uses the same Load and Transform methods to pull the data. The Transform method provides the following signatures:

```
XslCompiledTransform.Transform(IXPathNavigable, XmlWriter)
XslCompiledTransform.Transform(IXPathNavigable, XsltArguementList, XmlWriter)
XslCompiledTransform.Transform(IXPathNavigable, XsltArguementList, TextWriter)
XslCompiledTransform.Transform(IXPathNavigable, XsltArguementList, Stream)
XslCompiledTransform.Transform(XmlReader, XmlWriter)
XslCompiledTransform.Transform(XmlReader, XsltArguementList, XmlWriter)
XslCompiledTransform.Transform(XmlReader, XsltArguementList, TextWriter)
XslCompiledTransform.Transform(XmlReader, XsltArguementList, Stream)
XslCompiledTransform.Transform(XmlReader, XsltArguementList, XmlWriter,
    XmlResolver)
XslCompiledTransform.Transform(String, String)
XslCompiledTransform.Transform(String, XmlWriter)
XslCompiledTransform.Transform(String, XsltArguementList, XmlWriter)
XslCompiledTransform.Transform(String, XsltArguementList, TextWriter)
XslCompiledTransform.Transform(String, XsltArguementList, Stream)
```

In this case, String is a representation of the .xslt file that should be used in the transformation. Here, String represents the location of specific files (whether it is source files or output files). Some of the signatures also allow for output to XmlWriter objects, streams, and TextWriter objects. These can be used by also providing additional arguments using the XsltArgumentList object.

The preceding example used the second signature `XslCompiledTransform.Transform(String, String)`, which asked for the source file and the destination file (both string representations of the location of said files):

```
myXslCompiledTransform.Transform("..\FilmOrders.xml", destFileName)
```

XSLT Transforming between XML Standards

The first example used four XSLT elements to transform an XML file into an HTML file. Such an example has merit, but it doesn't demonstrate an important use of XSLT: transforming XML from one standard into another standard. This may involve renaming elements/attributes, excluding elements/attributes, changing data types, altering the node hierarchy, and representing elements as attributes, and vice versa.

Returning to the example, a case of differing XML standards could easily affect your software that automates movie orders coming into a supplier. Imagine that the software, including its XML representation of a movie order, is so successful that you sell 100,000 copies. However, just as you are celebrating, a consortium of the largest movie supplier chains announces that they are no longer accepting faxed orders and that they are introducing their own standard for the exchange of movie orders between movie sellers and buyers.

Rather than panic, you simply ship an upgrade that includes an XSLT file. This upgrade (a bit of extra code plus the XSLT file) transforms your XML representation of a movie order into the XML representation dictated by the consortium of movie suppliers. Using an XSLT file enables you to ship the upgrade immediately. If the consortium of movie suppliers revises their XML representation, then you are not obliged to change your source code. Instead, you can simply ship the upgraded XSLT file that ensures each movie order document is compliant.

The specific source code that executes the transform is as follows:

```
Dim myXslCompiledTransform As XslCompiledTransform = New XslCompiledTransform

myXslCompiledTransform.Load("..\ConvertLegacyToNewStandard.xslt")
myXslCompiledTransform.Transform("..\MovieOrdersOriginal.xml", _
    "..\MovieOrdersModified.xml")
```

Those three lines of code accomplish the following:

❏   Create an `XslCompiledTransform` object

❏   Use the `Load` method to load an XSLT file (`ConvertLegacyToNewStandard.xslt`)

❏   Use the `Transform` method to transform a source XML file (`MovieOrdersOriginal.xml`) into a destination XML file (`MovieOrdersModified.xml`)

Recall that the input XML document (`MovieOrdersOriginal.xml`) does not match the format required by your consortium of movie supplier chains. The content of this source XML file is as follows:

```
<?xml version="1.0" encoding="utf-8" ?>
<FilmOrder_Multiple>
    <multiFilmOrders>
        <FilmOrder>
```

```
                <name>Grease</name>
                <filmId>101</filmId>
                <quantity>10</quantity>
            </FilmOrder>
            ...
        </multiFilmOrders>
    </FilmOrder_Multiple>
```

The format exhibited in the preceding XML document does not match the format of the consortium of movie supplier chains. To be accepted by the collective of suppliers, you must transform the document as follows:

❑ Remove element `<FilmOrder_Multiple>`.

❑ Remove element `<multiFilmOrders>`.

❑ Rename element `<FilmOrder>` to `<DvdOrder>`.

❑ Remove element `<name>` (the film's name is not to be contained in the document).

❑ Rename element `<quantity>` to `HowMuch` and make `HowMuch` an attribute of `<DvdOrder>`.

❑ Rename element `<filmId>` to `FilmOrderNumber` and make `FilmOrderNumber` an attribute of `<DvdOrder>`.

❑ Display attribute `HowMuch` before attribute `FilmOrderNumber`.

Many of the steps performed by the transform could have been achieved using an alternative technology. For example, you could have used Source Code Style attributes with your serialization to generate the correct XML attribute and XML element name. Had you known in advance that a consortium of suppliers was going to develop a standard, you could have written your classes to be serialized based on the standard. The point is that you did not know and now one standard (your legacy standard) has to be converted into a newly adopted standard of the movie suppliers' consortium. The worst thing you could do would be to change your working code and then force all users working with the application to upgrade. It is vastly simpler to add an extra transformation step to address the new standard.

The XSLT file that facilitates the transform is named `ConvertLegacyToNewStandard.xslt`. A portion of this file is implemented as follows:

```
<?xml version="1.0" encoding="UTF-8" ?>
<xsl:stylesheet version="1.0" xmlns:xsl="http://www.w3.org/1999/XSL/Transform">
  <xsl:template match="FilmOrder">
    <!- rename <FilmOrder> to <DvdOrder> ->
    <xsl:element name="DvdOrder">
      <!- Make element 'quantity' attribute HowMuch
           Notice attribute HowMuch comes before attribute FilmOrderNumber ->
      <xsl:attribute name="HowMuch">
        <xsl:value-of select="quantity"></xsl:value-of>
      </xsl:attribute>
      <!- Make element filmId attribute FilmOrderNumber ->
      <xsl:attribute name="FilmOrderNumber">
        <xsl:value-of select="filmId"></xsl:value-of>
      </xsl:attribute>
    </xsl:element>
```

```
        <!- end of DvdOrder element ->
    </xsl:template>
  </xsl:stylesheet>
```

In the previous snippet of XSLT, the following XSLT elements are used to facilitate the transformation:

❑ `<xsl:template match="FilmOrder">` — All operations in this `template` XSLT element take place on the original document's `FilmOrder` node.

❑ `<xsl:element name="DvdOrder">` — The element corresponding to the source document's `FilmOrder` element will be called `DvdOrder` in the destination document.

❑ `<xsl:attribute name="HowMuch">` — An attribute named `HowMuch` will be contained in the previously specified element, `<DvdOrder>`. This `attribute` XSLT element for `HowMuch` comes before the `attribute` XSLT element for `FilmOrderNumber`. This order was specified as part of your transform to adhere to the new standard.

❑ `<xsl:value-of select='quantity'>` — Retrieve the value of the source document's `<quantity>` element and place it in the destination document. This instance of XSLT element `value-of` provides the value associated with the attribute `HowMuch`.

Two new XSLT elements have crept into your vocabulary: `element` and `attribute`. Both of these XSLT elements live up to their names. Specifying the XSLT element named `element` places an element in the destination XML document. Specifying the XSLT element named `attribute` places an attribute in the destination XML document. The XSLT transform found in `ConvertLegacyToNewStandard.xslt` is too long to review here. When reading this file in its entirety, remember that this XSLT file contains inline documentation to specify precisely what aspect of the transformation is being performed at which location in the XSLT document. For example, the following XML code comments indicate what the XSLT element `attribute` is about to do:

```
<!-- Make element 'quantity' attribute HowMuch
     Notice attribute HowMuch comes before attribute FilmOrderNumber -->
<xsl:attribute name="HowMuch">
    <xsl:value-of select='quantity'></xsl:value-of>
</xsl:attribute>
```

The preceding example spans several pages but contains just three lines of code. This demonstrates that there is more to XML than learning how to use it in Visual Basic and the .NET Framework. Among other things, you also need a good understanding of XSLT, XPath, and XQuery.

Other Classes and Interfaces in System.Xml.Xsl

We just took a good look at XSLT and the `System.Xml.Xsl` namespace, but there is a lot more to it than that. Other classes and interfaces exposed by the `System.Xml.Xsl` namespace include the following:

❑ `IXsltContextFunction` — This interface accesses at runtime a given function defined in the XSLT style sheet.

❑ `IXsltContextVariable` — This interface accesses at runtime a given variable defined in the XSLT style sheet.

❑ XsltArgumentList — This class contains a list of arguments. These arguments are XSLT parameters or XSLT extension objects. The XsltArgumentList object is used in conjunction with the Transform method of XslTransform.

❑ XsltContext — This class contains the state of the XSLT processor. This context information enables XPath expressions to have their various components resolved (functions, parameters, and namespaces).

❑ XsltException, XsltCompileException — These classes contain the information pertaining to an exception raised while transforming data. XsltCompileException is derived from XsltException.

ADO.NET

ADO.NET enables Visual Basic applications to generate XML documents and use such documents to update persisted data. ADO.NET natively represents its DataSet's underlying data store in XML. ADO.NET also enables SQL Server–specific XML support to be accessed. This chapter focuses on those features of ADO.NET that enable the XML generated and consumed to be customized. ADO.NET is covered in detail in Chapter 9.

The DataSet properties and methods that are pertinent to XML include Namespace, Prefix, GetXml, GetXmlSchema, InferXmlSchema, ReadXml, ReadXmlSchema, WriteXml, and WriteXmlSchema. An example of code that uses the GetXml method is shown here:

```
Dim adapter As New _
    SqlClient.SqlDataAdapter("SELECT ShipperID, CompanyName, Phone " & _
                "FROM Shippers", _
                "SERVER=localhost;UID=sa;PWD=sa;Database=Northwind;")
Dim ds As New DataSet()

adapter.Fill(ds)
Console.Out.WriteLine(ds.GetXml())
```

The preceding code uses the sample Northwind database, retrieving all rows from the Shippers table. This table was selected because it contains only three rows of data.

The following example makes use of the Northwind.mdf SQL Server Express Database file. To get this database, please search for "Northwind and pubs Sample Databases for SQL Server 2000." You can find this link at www.microsoft.com/downloads/details.aspx?familyid=06616212-0356-46a0-8da2-eebc53a68034&displaylang=en. Once you've installed it, you'll find the Northwind.mdf file in the C:\SQL Server 2000 Sample Databases directory. To add this database to your application, right-click on the solution you are working with and select Add Existing Item. From the provided dialog, you'll then be able to browse to the location of the Northwind.mdf file that you just installed. If you have trouble getting permissions to work with the database, make a data connection to the file from the Visual Studio Server Explorer. You will be asked to be made the appropriate user of the database, and VS will make the appropriate changes on your behalf for this to occur. When added, you will encounter a Data Source Configuration Wizard. For the purposes of this chapter, simply press the Cancel button when you encounter this dialog.

The XML returned by `GetXml` is as follows (where ... signifies that `<Table>` elements were removed for the sake of brevity):

```
<NewDataSet>
  <Table>
    <ShipperID>1</ShipperID>
    <CompanyName>Speedy Express</CompanyName>
    <Phone>(503) 555-9831</Phone>
  </Table>
  ...
</NewDataSet>
```

What you are trying to determine from this XML document is how to customize the XML generated. The more customization you can perform at the ADO.NET level, the less will be needed later. With this in mind, note that the root element is `<NewDataSet>` and that each row of the `DataSet` is returned as an XML element, `<Table>`. The data returned is contained in an XML element named for the column in which the data resides (`<ShipperID>`, `<CompanyName>`, and `<Phone>`, respectively).

The root element, `<NewDataSet>`, is just the default name of the `DataSet`. This name could have been changed when the `DataSet` was constructed by specifying the name as a parameter to the constructor:

```
Dim ds As New DataSet("WeNameTheDataSet")
```

If the previous version of the constructor were executed, then the `<NewDataSet>` element would be renamed `<WeNameTheDataSet>`. After the `DataSet` has been constructed, you can still set the property `DataSetName`, thus changing `<NewDataSet>` to a name such as `<WeNameTheDataSetAgain>`:

```
ds.DataSetName = "WeNameTheDataSetAgain"
```

The `<Table>` element is actually the name of a table in the `DataSet`'s `Tables` property. Programmatically, you can change `<Table>` to `<WeNameTheTable>`:

```
ds.Tables("Table").TableName = "WeNameTheTable"
```

You can customize the names of the data columns returned by modifying the SQL to use alias names. For example, you could retrieve the same data but generate different elements using the following SQL code:

```
SELECT ShipperID As TheID, CompanyName As CName, Phone
    As TelephoneNumber FROM Shippers
```

Using the preceding SQL statement, the `<ShipperID>` element would become the `<TheID>` element. The `<CompanyName>` element would become `<CName>`, and `<Phone>` would become `<TelephoneNumber>`. The column names can also be changed programmatically by using the `Columns` property associated with the table in which the column resides. An example of this follows, where the XML element `<TheID>` is changed to `<AnotherNewName>`:

```
ds.Tables("WeNameTheTable").Columns("TheID").ColumnName = "AnotherNewName"
```

This XML could be transformed using System.Xml.Xsl. It could be read as a stream (XmlTextReader) or written as a stream (XmlTextWriter). The XML returned by ADO.NET could even be deserialized and used to create an object or objects using XmlSerializer. The point is to recognize what ADO.NET-generated XML looks like. If you know its format, then you can transform it into whatever you like.

ADO.NET and SQL Server 2000's Built-in XML Features

Those interested in fully exploring the XML-specific features of SQL Server should take a look at *Professional SQL Server 2000 Programming* by Robert Vieira (Wrox Press, 2000). However, because the content of that book is not .NET-specific, the next example forms a bridge between *Professional SQL Server 2000 Programming* and the .NET Framework.

Two of the major XML-related features exposed by SQL Server are as follows:

❑   FOR XML — The FOR XML clause of an SQL SELECT statement enables a rowset to be returned as an XML document. The XML document generated by a FOR XML clause is highly customizable with respect to the document hierarchy generated, per-column data transforms, representation of binary data, XML schema generated, and a variety of other XML nuances.

❑   OPENXML — The OPENXML extension to Transact-SQL enables a stored procedure call to manipulate an XML document as a rowset. Subsequently, this rowset can be used to perform a variety of tasks, such as SELECT, INSERT INTO, DELETE, and UPDATE.

SQL Server's support for OPENXML is a matter of calling a stored procedure. A developer who can execute a stored procedure call using Visual Basic in conjunction with ADO.NET can take full advantage of SQL Server's support for OPENXML. FOR XML queries have a certain caveat when it comes to ADO.NET. To understand this caveat, consider the following FOR XML query:

```
SELECT ShipperID, CompanyName, Phone FROM Shippers FOR XML RAW
```

Using SQL Server's Query Analyzer, this FOR XML RAW query generated the following XML:

```
<row ShipperID="1" CompanyName="Speedy Express" Phone="(314) 555-9831" />
<row ShipperID="2" CompanyName="United Package" Phone="(314) 555-3199" />
<row ShipperID="3" CompanyName="Federal Shipping" Phone="(314) 555-9931" />
```

The same FOR XML RAW query can be executed from ADO.NET as follows:

```
Dim adapter As New _
    SqlDataAdapter("SELECT ShipperID, CompanyName, Phone " & _
                   "FROM Shippers FOR XML RAW", _
                   "SERVER=localhost;UID=sa;PWD=sa;Database=Northwind;")
Dim ds As New DataSet

adapter.Fill(ds)
Console.Out.WriteLine(ds.GetXml())
```

The caveat with respect to a FOR XML query is that all data (the XML text) must be returned via a result set containing a single row and a single column named XML_F52E2B61-18A1-11d1-B105- 00805F49916B.

The output from the preceding code snippet demonstrates this caveat (where ... represents similar data not shown for reasons of brevity):

```
<NewDataSet>
  <Table>
    <XML_F52E2B61-18A1-11d1-B105-00805F49916B>
      /&lt;row ShipperID="1" CompanyName="Speedy Express"
      Phone="(503) 555-9831"/&gt;
      ...
    </XML_F52E2B61-18A1-11d1-B105-00805F49916B>
  </Table>
</NewDataSet>
```

The value of the single row and single column returned contains what looks like XML, but it contains /< instead of the less-than character, and /> instead of the greater-than character. The symbols < and > cannot appear inside XML data, so they must be entity-encoded — that is, represented as /> and /<. The data returned in element <XML_F52E2B61-18A1-11d1-B105-00805F49916B> is not XML, but data contained in an XML document.

To fully utilize FOR XML queries, the data must be accessible as XML. The solution to this quandary is the ExecuteXmlReader method of the SQLCommand class. When this method is called, an SQLCommand object assumes that it is executed as a FOR XML query and returns the results of this query as an XmlReader object. An example of this follows:

```
Dim connection As New _
    SqlConnection("SERVER=localhost;UID=sa;PWD=sa;Database=Northwind;")
Dim command As New _
    SqlCommand("SELECT ShipperID, CompanyName, Phone " & _
                 "FROM Shippers FOR XML RAW")
Dim memStream As MemoryStream = New MemoryStream
Dim xmlReader As New XmlTextReader(memStream)

connection.Open()
command.Connection = connection
xmlReader = command.ExecuteXmlReader()
` Extract results from XMLReader
```

You will need to import the System.Data.SqlClient namespace for this example to work.

The XmlReader created in this code is of type XmlTextReader, which derives from XmlReader. The XmlTextReader is backed by a MemoryStream; hence, it is an in-memory stream of XML that can be traversed using the methods and properties exposed by XmlTextReader. Streaming XML generation and retrieval was discussed earlier.

Using the ExecuteXmlReader method of the SQLCommand class, it is possible to retrieve the result of FOR XML queries. What makes the FOR XML style of queries so powerful is that it can configure the data retrieved. The three types of FOR XML queries support the following forms of XML customization:

❑   FOR XML RAW — This type of query returns each row of a result set inside an XML element named <row>. The data retrieved is contained as attributes of the <row> element. The attributes are named for the column name or column alias in the FOR XML RAW query.

❑ FOR XML AUTO — By default, this type of query returns each row of a result set inside an XML element named for the table or table alias contained in the FOR XML AUTO query. The data retrieved is contained as attributes of this element. The attributes are named for the column name or column alias in the FOR XML AUTO query. By specifying FOR XML AUTO, ELEMENTS, it is possible to retrieve all data inside elements, rather than inside attributes. All data retrieved must be in attribute or element form. There is no mix-and-match capability.

❑ FOR XML EXPLICIT — This form of the FOR XML query enables the precise XML type of each column returned to be specified. The data associated with a column can be returned as an attribute or an element. Specific XML types, such as CDATA and ID, can be associated with a column returned. Even the level in the XML hierarchy in which data resides can be specified using a FOR XML EXPLICIT query. This style of query is fairly complicated to implement.

FOR XML queries are flexible. Using FOR XML EXPLICIT and the movie rental database, it would be possible to generate any form of XML movie order standard. The decision that needs to be made is where XML configuration takes place. Using Visual Basic, a developer could use XmlTextReader and XmlTextWriter to create any style of XML document. Using the XSLT language and an XSLT file, the same level of configuration can be achieved. SQL Server and, in particular, FOR XML EXPLICIT, enable the same level of XML customization, but this customization takes place at the SQL level and may even be configured to stored procedure calls.

XML and SQL Server 2005

As a representation for data, XML is ideal in that it is a self-describing data format that enables you to provide your data sets as complex data types. It also provides order to your data. SQL Server 2005 embraces this direction.

More and more developers are turning to XML as a means of data storage. For instance, Microsoft Office enables documents to be saved and stored as XML documents. As an increasing number of products and solutions turn toward XML as a means of storage, this allows for a separation between the underlying data and the presentation aspect of what is being viewed. XML is also being used as a means of communicating data sets across platforms and the enterprise. The entire XML Web Services story is a result of this new capability. Simply said, XML is a powerful alternative to your data storage solutions.

Just remember that the power of using XML isn't only about storing data as XML somewhere (whether that is XML files or not); it is also about the capability to quickly access this XML data and to be able to query the data that is retrieved.

SQL Server 2005 makes a big leap toward XML in adding an XML data type as an option. This enables you to unify the relational aspects of the database and the current desires to work with XML data.

FOR XML has also been expanded from within this latest edition of SQL Server. This includes a new TYPE directive that returns an XML data type instance. In addition, the NET 2.0 Framework introduced a new namespace — System.Data.SqlXml — that enables you to easily work with the XML data that comes from SQL Server 2005. The SqlXml object is an XmlReader-derived type. Another addition is the use of the SqlDataReader object's GetXml method.

XML and SQL Server 2008

SQL Server 2008 continues on this path and introduces some new XML features. First, it supports lax validation using XSD schemas. This wasn't possible prior to this release. Another big change is related to how SQL Server handles the storage of `dateTime` values. In SQL Server 2005, when you stored `dateTime` values, the database would first normalize everything to UTC time, regardless of whether or not you wanted to store the information in a specific time zone. In addition, if you excluded the time in your `dateTime` declaration, SQL Server 2005 would add it back for you so that there was a full `dateTime` stored within the database. SQL Server 2008, conversely, enables you to store the `dateTime` value exactly as you declared it. No modifications or alterations are made to your value as it is stored in the database.

Another new feature of SQL Server 2008 is support of union types that contain list types. This means that you can now work with elements such as the following:

```
<Stocks>INTC MSFT CSCO IBM RTRSY</Stocks>
```

Union types enable you to define multiple items within a single element with a space between the elements, rather than define each as separate elements, as shown here:

```
<Stocks>
    <Item>INTC</Item>
    <Item>MSFT</Item>
    <Item>CSCO</Item>
    <Item>IBM</Item>
    <Item>RTRSY</Item>
</Stocks>
```

XML in ASP.NET 3.5

Most Microsoft-focused Web developers have usually concentrated on either Microsoft SQL Server or Microsoft Access for their data storage needs. Today, however, a considerable amount of data is stored in XML format, so considerable inroads have been made in improving Microsoft's core Web technology to work easily with this format.

The XmlDataSource Server Control

ASP.NET 3.5 contains a series of data source controls designed to bridge the gap between your data stores (such as XML) and the data-bound controls at your disposal. These new data controls not only enable you to retrieve data from various data stores, they also enable you to easily manipulate the data (using paging, sorting, editing, and filtering) before the data is bound to an ASP.NET server control.

With XML being as important as it is, a specific data source control is available in ASP.NET just for retrieving and working with XML data: `XmlDataSource`. This control enables you to connect to your XML data and use this data with any of the ASP.NET data-bound controls. Just like the `SqlDataSource` and the `ObjectDataSource` controls (which are two of the other data source controls), the `XmlDataSource` control enables you to not only retrieve data, but also insert, delete, and update data items. With increasing numbers of users turning to XML data formats, such as Web services, RSS feeds, and more, this control is a valuable resource for your Web applications.

To show the `XmlDataSource` control in action, first create a simple XML file and include this file in your application. The following code reflects a simple XML file of Russian painters:

```xml
<?xml version="1.0" encoding="utf-8" ?>
<Artists>
    <Painter name="Vasily Kandinsky">
        <Painting>
            <Title>Composition No. 218</Title>
            <Year>1919</Year>
        </Painting>
    </Painter>
    <Painter name="Pavel Filonov">
        <Painting>
            <Title>Formula of Spring</Title>
            <Year>1929</Year>
        </Painting>
    </Painter>
    <Painter name="Pyotr Konchalovsky">
        <Painting>
            <Title>Sorrento Garden</Title>
            <Year>1924</Year>
        </Painting>
    </Painter>
</Artists>
```

Now that the `Painters.xml` file is in place, the next step is to use an ASP.NET `DataList` control and connect this `DataList` control to an `<asp:XmlDataSource>` control, as shown here:

```vbnet
<%@ Page Language="VB"%>

<html xmlns="http://www.w3.org/1999/xhtml" >
<head runat="server">
    <title>XmlDataSource</title>
</head>
<body>
    <form id="form1" runat="server">
        <asp:DataList ID="DataList1" Runat="server"
         DataSourceID="XmlDataSource1">
            <ItemTemplate>
                <p><b><%# XPath("@name") %></b><br />
                <i><%# XPath("Painting/Title") %></i><br />
                <%# XPath("Painting/Year") %></p>
            </ItemTemplate>
        </asp:DataList>

        <asp:XmlDataSource ID="XmlDataSource1" Runat="server"
         DataFile="~/Painters.xml" XPath="Artists/Painter">
        </asp:XmlDataSource>
    </form>
</body>
</html>
```

This is a simple example, but it shows you the power and ease of using the `XmlDataSource` control. Pay attention to two attributes in this example. The first is the `DataFile` attribute. This attribute points to

429

the location of the XML file. Because the file resides in the root directory of the application, it is simply `~/Painters.xml`. The next attribute included in the `XmlDataSource` control is the `XPath` attribute. The `XmlDataSource` control uses XPath for the filtering of XML data. In this case, the `XmlDataSource` control is taking everything within the `<Painter>` set of elements. The value `Artists/Painter` means that the `XmlDataSource` control navigates to the `<Artists>` element and then to the `<Painter>` element within the specified XML file.

The `DataList` control next must specify the `DataSourceID` as the `XmlDataSource` control. In the `<ItemTemplate>` section of the `DataList` control, you can retrieve specific values from the XML file by using XPath commands. The XPath commands filter the data from the XML file. The first value retrieved is an element attribute (`name`) contained in the `<Painter>` element. When you retrieve an attribute of an element, you preface the name of the attribute with an @ symbol. In this case, you simply specify `@name` to get the painter's name. The next two XPath commands go deeper into the XML file, getting the specific painting and the year of the painting. Remember to separate nodes with a `/`. When run in the browser, this code produces the results shown in Figure 10-5.

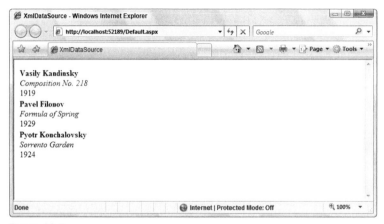

Figure 10-5

Besides working from static XML files such as the `Painters.xml` file, the `XmlDataSource` file can work from dynamic, URL-accessible XML files. One popular XML format pervasive on the Internet today is *blogs*, or *weblogs*. Blogs, or personal diaries, can be viewed either in the browser, through an RSS-aggregator, or just as pure XML.

Figure 10-6 shows blog entries directly in the browser (if you are using IE7). Behind this blog is an actual XML document that can be worked with by your code. You can find a lot of blogs to play with for this example at `weblogs.asp.net`. This screen shot uses the blog found at `www.geekswithblogs.net/evjen`.

Now that you know the location of the XML from the blog, you can use this XML with the `XmlDataSource` control and display some of the results in a `DataList` control. The code for this example is shown here:

```
<%@ Page Language="VB"%>

<html xmlns="http://www.w3.org/1999/xhtml" >
<head runat="server">
```

Figure 10-6

```
    <title>XmlDataSource</title>
</head>
<body>
    <form id="form1" runat="server">
        <asp:DataList ID="DataList1" Runat="server"
        DataSourceID="XmlDataSource1">
            <HeaderTemplate>
                <table border="1" cellpadding="3">
            </HeaderTemplate>
            <ItemTemplate>
                <tr><td><b><%# XPath("title") %></b><br />
                <i><%# XPath("pubDate") %></i><br />
                <%# XPath("description") %></td></tr>
            </ItemTemplate>
            <AlternatingItemTemplate>
                <tr bgcolor="LightGrey"><td><b><%# XPath("title") %></b><br />
                <i><%# XPath("pubDate") %></i><br />
                <%# XPath("description") %></td></tr>
            </AlternatingItemTemplate>
            <FooterTemplate>
                </table>
            </FooterTemplate>
        </asp:DataList>

        <asp:XmlDataSource ID="XmlDataSource1" Runat="server"
         DataFile="http://geekswithblogs.net/evjen/Rss.aspx"
         XPath="rss/channel/item">
        </asp:XmlDataSource>
    </form>
</body>
</html>
```

This example shows that the DataFile points to a URL where the XML is retrieved. The XPath property filters out all the <item> elements from the RSS feed. The DataList control creates an HTML table and pulls out specific data elements from the RSS feed, such as the <title>, <pubDate>, and <description> elements.

Running this page in the browser results in something similar to what is shown in Figure 10-7.

Figure 10-7

This approach also works with XML Web Services, even those for which you can pass in parameters using HTTP-GET. You just set up the DataFile value in the following manner:

```
DataFile="http://www.someserver.com/GetWeather.asmx/ZipWeather?zipcode=63301"
```

The XmlDataSource Control's Namespace Problem

One big issue with using the XmlDataSource control is that when using the XPath capabilities of the control, it is unable to understand namespace-qualified XML. The XmlDataSource control chokes on any XML data that contains namespaces, so it is important to yank out any prefixes and namespaces contained in the XML.

To make this a bit easier, the XmlDataSource control includes the TransformFile attribute. This attribute takes your XSLT transform file, which can be applied to the XML pulled from the XmlDataSource control. That means you can use an XSLT file, which will transform your XML in such a way that the prefixes and namespaces are completely removed from the overall XML document. An example of this XSLT document is illustrated here:

```
<?xml version="1.0" encoding="UTF-8"?>
<xsl:stylesheet version="1.0"
 xmlns:xsl="http://www.w3.org/1999/XSL/Transform">
```

```
<xsl:output method="xml" version="1.0" encoding="UTF-8" indent="yes"/>
<xsl:template match="*">
    <!-- Remove any prefixes -->
    <xsl:element name="{local-name()}">
        <!-- Work through attributes -->
        <xsl:for-each select="@*">
            <!-- Remove any attribute prefixes -->
            <xsl:attribute name="{local-name()}">
                <xsl:value-of select="."/>
            </xsl:attribute>
        </xsl:for-each>
    <xsl:apply-templates/>
    </xsl:element>
</xsl:template>
</xsl:stylesheet>
```

Now, with this XSLT document in place within your application, you can use the `XmlDataSource` control to pull XML data and strip that data of any prefixes and namespaces:

```
<asp:XmlDataSource ID="XmlDataSource1" runat="server"
 DataFile="NamespaceFilled.xml" TransformFile="~/RemoveNamespace.xsl"
 XPath="ItemLookupResponse/Items/Item"></asp:XmlDataSource>
```

The Xml Server Control

Since the very beginning of ASP.NET, there has always been a server control called the `Xml` server control. This control performs the simple operation of XSLT transformation upon an XML document. The control is easy to use: All you do is point to the XML file you wish to transform using the `DocumentSource` attribute, and the XSLT transform file using the `TransformSource` attribute.

To see this in action, use the `Painters.xml` file shown earlier. Create your XSLT transform file, as shown in the following example:

```
<?xml version="1.0" encoding="utf-8"?>

<xsl:stylesheet version="1.0"
     xmlns:xsl="http://www.w3.org/1999/XSL/Transform">

  <xsl:template match="/">
      <html>
      <body>
        <h3>List of Painters &amp; Paintings</h3>
        <table border="1">
          <tr bgcolor="LightGrey">
            <th>Name</th>
            <th>Painting</th>
            <th>Year</th>
          </tr>
          <xsl:apply-templates select="//Painter"/>
        </table>
      </body>
      </html>
  </xsl:template>
```

```
  <xsl:template match="Painter">
    <tr>
      <td>
        <xsl:value-of select="@name"/>
      </td>
      <td>
        <xsl:value-of select="Painting/Title"/>
      </td>
      <td>
        <xsl:value-of select="Painting/Year"/>
      </td>
    </tr>
  </xsl:template>

</xsl:stylesheet>
```

With the XML document and the XSLT document in place, the final step is to combine the two using the Xml server control provided by ASP.NET:

```
<%@ Page Language="VB" %>

<html xmlns="http://www.w3.org/1999/xhtml" >
<head id="Head1" runat="server">
    <title>XmlDataSource</title>
</head>
<body>
    <form id="form1" runat="server">
        <asp:Xml ID="Xml1" runat="server" DocumentSource="~/Painters.xml"
          TransformSource="~/PaintersTransform.xsl"></asp:Xml>
    </form>
</body>
</html>
```

The result is shown in Figure 10-8.

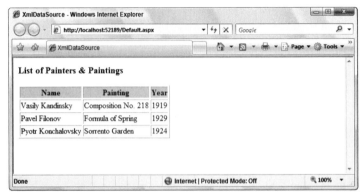

Figure 10-8

Summary

Ultimately, XML could be the underpinning of electronic commerce, banking transactions, and data exchange of almost every conceivable kind. The beauty of XML is that it isolates data representation from data display. Technologies such as HTML contain data that is tightly bound to its display format. XML does not suffer this limitation, and at the same time it has the readability of HTML. Accordingly, the XML facilities available to a Visual Basic application are vast, and a large number of XML-related features, classes, and interfaces are exposed by the .NET Framework.

This chapter showed you how to use `System.Xml.Serialization.XmlSerializer` to serialize classes. Source Code Style attributes were introduced in conjunction with serialization. This style of attributes enables the customization of the XML serialized to be extended to the source code associated with a class. What is important to remember about the direction of serialization classes is that a required change in the XML format becomes a change in the underlying source code. Developers should resist the temptation to rewrite serialized classes in order to conform to some new XML data standard (such as the example movie order format endorsed by your consortium of movie rental establishments). Technologies such as XSLT, exposed via the `System.Xml.Query` namespace, should be examined first as alternatives. This chapter demonstrated how to use XSLT style sheets to transform XML data using the classes found in the `System.Xml.Query` namespace.

The most useful classes and interfaces in the `System.Xml` namespace were reviewed, including those that support document-style XML access: `XmlDocument`, `XmlNode`, `XmlElement`, and `XmlAttribute`. The `System.Xml` namespace also contains classes and interfaces that support stream-style XML access: `XmlReader` and `XmlWriter`.

Finally, you looked at Microsoft's SQL Server 2005, 2008, and XQuery, as well as how to use XML with ASP.NET 3.5. The next chapter takes a look at LINQ, one of the biggest new features related to how the .NET Framework 3.5 works with XML. LINQ, which provides a new means of querying your data, is a lightweight façade over ADO.NET. You will likely find that the new LINQ to XML is a great way to work with XML.

11

LINQ

Probably the biggest and most exciting addition to the .NET Framework 3.5 is the addition of the .NET Language Integrated Query Framework (LINQ) into Visual Basic 2008. Basically, what LINQ provides is a lightweight façade over programmatic data integration. This is a big deal, because *data is king*.

Pretty much every application deals with data in some manner, whether that data comes from memory (in-memory data), databases, XML files, text files, or somewhere else. Many developers find it very difficult to move from the strongly typed, object-oriented world of Visual Basic to the data tier, where objects are second-class citizens. The transition from the one world to the next was a kludge at best and full of error-prone actions.

In VB, programming with objects means a wonderful, strongly typed ability to work with code. You can navigate very easily through the namespaces, work with a debugger in the Visual Studio IDE, and more. However, when you have to access data, you will notice that things are dramatically different.

You end up in a world that is not strongly typed, and debugging is a pain or even nonexistent. You end up spending most of the time sending strings to the database as commands. As a developer, you also have to be aware of the underlying data and how it is structured or how all the data points relate.

Microsoft has provided LINQ as a lightweight façade that provides a strongly typed interface to the underlying data stores. LINQ provides the means for developers to stay within the coding environment they're used to and access the underlying data as objects that work with the IDE, IntelliSense, and even debugging.

With LINQ, the queries that you create now become first-class citizens within the .NET Framework alongside everything else you are used to. When you begin to work with queries for the data store you're working with, you will quickly realize that they now work and behave as if they were types in the system. This means that you can now use any .NET-complaint language and query the underlying data store as you never have before.

Figure 11-1 shows LINQ's place in querying data.

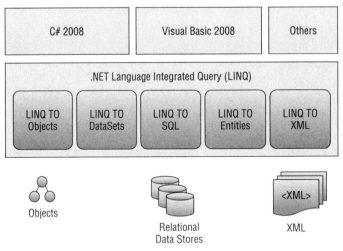

Figure 11-1

Looking at the figure, you can see that different types of LINQ capabilities are available depending on the underlying data you're going to be working with in your application:

❏   LINQ to Objects

❏   LINQ to DataSets

❏   LINQ to SQL

❏   LINQ to Entities

❏   LINQ to XML

As a developer, you are given class libraries that provide objects that, using LINQ, can be queried like any other data store. In fact, objects are nothing more than data that is stored in memory. Indeed, your objects themselves might be querying data. This is where LINQ to Objects comes into play.

LINQ to SQL, LINQ to Entities, and LINQ to DataSets provide the means to query relational data. Using LINQ, you can query directly against your database and even against the stored procedures that your database exposes. The last item in the diagram is the capability to query against your XML using LINQ to XML. What makes LINQ so exciting is that it matters very little what you are querying against, as your queries will be quite similar.

This chapter takes a close look at LINQ to SQL and LINQ to XML. You will get a taste of how to perform LINQ to Object queries via this focus as well.

LINQ to SQL and Visual Studio 2008

LINQ to SQL in particular is a means to have a strongly typed interface against a SQL Server database. You will find that the approach that LINQ to SQL provides is by far the easiest approach there is at present for querying SQL Server. It's not simply about querying single tables within the database; for instance, if you call the Customers table of the Microsoft sample Northwind database and want to pull a customer's specific orders from the Orders table in the same database, then LINQ will use the relations of the tables and make the query on your behalf. LINQ will query the database and load up the data for you to work with from your code (again, strongly typed).

Keep in mind that LINQ to SQL is not only about querying data; you can also perform the `Insert`, `Update`, and `Delete` statements that you need to perform.

In addition, you can interact with the entire process and customize the operations performed to add your own business logic to any of the CRUD operations (`Create/Read/Update/Delete`).

Visual Studio 2008 is highly integrated with LINQ to SQL in that you will find an extensive user interface that enables you to design the LINQ to SQL classes you will work with.

The following section demonstrates how to set up a LINQ to SQL instance and pull items from the Products table of the Northwind database.

Calling the Products Table Using LINQ to SQL: Creating the Console Application

To illustrate using LINQ to SQL, this example begins by calling a single table from the Northwind database and using this table to populate some results to the screen.

First, create a console application (using the .NET Framework 3.5) and add the Northwind database file to this project (`Northwind.MDF`).

> *The following example makes use of the* `Northwind.mdf` *SQL Server Express Database file. To get this database, search for "Northwind and pubs Sample Databases for SQL Server 2000" at* www.microsoft .com/downloads/details.aspx?familyid=06616212-0356-46a0-8da2-eebc53a68034 &displaylang=en. *Once you've installed it, you'll find the* `Northwind.mdf` *file in the* C:\SQL Server 2000 Sample Databases *directory. To add this database to your application, right-click on the solution you are working with and select Add Existing Item. From the provided dialog, you'll then be able to browse to the location of the* `Northwind.mdf` *file that you just installed. If you have trouble getting permissions to work with the database, make a data connection to the file from the Visual Studio Server Explorer. You will be asked to be made the appropriate user of the database, and VS will make the appropriate changes on your behalf for this to occur. When added, you will encounter a Data Source Configuration Wizard. For the purposes of this chapter, simply press the Cancel button when you encounter this dialog.*

By default now, when creating many of the application types provided in the .NET Framework 3.5 within Visual Studio 2008, you will already have the proper references in place to work with LINQ. When creating a console application, you will get the references shown in Figure 11-2.

439

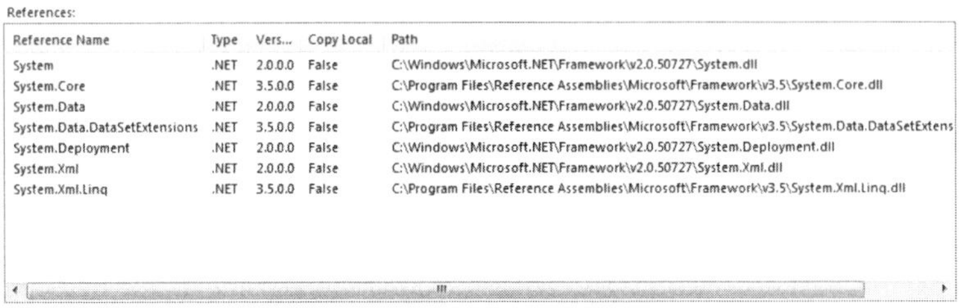
References:
Reference Name
Type
Vers...
Copy Local
Path
System
.NET
2.0.0.0
False
C:\Windows\Microsoft.NET\Framework\v2.0.50727\System.dll
System.Core
.NET
3.5.0.0
False
C:\Program Files\Reference Assemblies\Microsoft\Framework\v3.5\System.Core.dll
System.Data
.NET
2.0.0.0
False
C:\Windows\Microsoft.NET\Framework\v2.0.50727\System.Data.dll
System.Data.DataSetExtensions
.NET
3.5.0.0
False
C:\Program Files\Reference Assemblies\Microsoft\Framework\v3.5\System.Data.DataSetExtens
System.Deployment
.NET
2.0.0.0
False
C:\Windows\Microsoft.NET\Framework\v2.0.50727\System.Deployment.dll
System.Xml
.NET
2.0.0.0
False
C:\Windows\Microsoft.NET\Framework\v2.0.50727\System.Xml.dll
System.Xml.Linq
.NET
3.5.0.0
False
C:\Program Files\Reference Assemblies\Microsoft\Framework\v3.5\System.Xml.Linq.dll

Figure 11-2

The next step is to add a LINQ to SQL class.

Adding a LINQ to SQL Class

When working with LINQ to SQL, one of the big advantages is that Visual Studio 2008 does an outstanding job of making it as easy as possible. VS 2008 provides an object-relational mapping designer, called the Object Relational Designer (O/R Designer), that enables you to visually design the object-to-database mapping.

To start this task, right-click on your solution and select Add New Item from the provided menu. From the items in the Add New Item dialog, select the LINQ to SQL Classes option, shown in Figure 11-3.

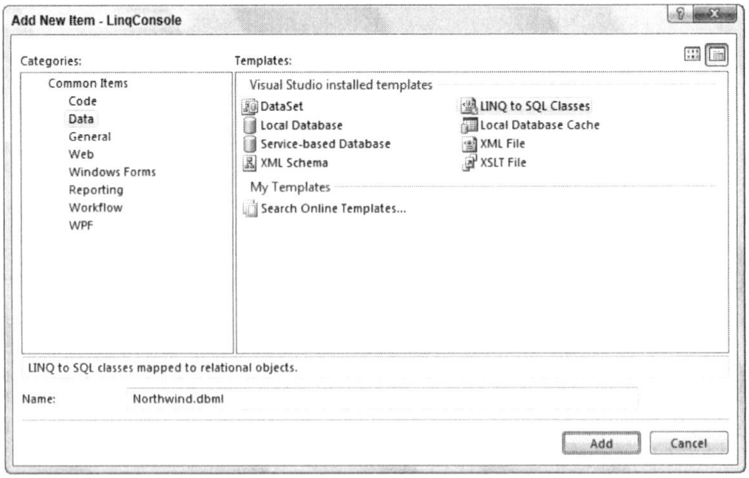
Add New Item - LinqConsole
Categories:
Templates:
Common Items
Code
Data
General
Web
Windows Forms
Reporting
Workflow
WPF
Visual Studio installed templates
DataSet
Local Database
Service-based Database
XML Schema
LINQ to SQL Classes
Local Database Cache
XML File
XSLT File
My Templates
Search Online Templates...
LINQ to SQL classes mapped to relational objects.
Name:
Northwind.dbml
Add
Cancel

Figure 11-3

Because this example uses the Northwind database, name the file `Northwind.dbml`. Click the Add button, which will create a couple of files for you. The Solution Explorer, after adding the `Northwind.dbml` file, is shown in Figure 11-4.

A number of items were added to your project with this action. First, the `Northwind.dbml` file was added, which contains two components. Because the LINQ to SQL class that was added works with LINQ, the `System.Data.Linq` reference was also added on your behalf.

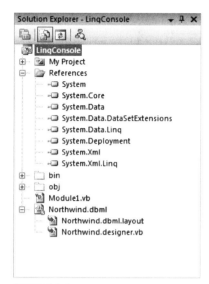

Figure 11-4

Introducing the O/R Designer

Another big addition to the IDE that appeared when you added the LINQ to SQL class to your project (the `Northwind.dbml` file) was a visual representation of the `.dbml` file. The new O/R Designer appears as a tab within the document window directly in the IDE. Figure 11-5 shows a view of the O/R Designer when it is first initiated.

Figure 11-5

The O/R Designer consists of two parts. The first is for data classes, which can be tables, classes, associations, and inheritances. Dragging such items on this design surface will give you a visual representation of the object that can be worked with. The second part (on the right) is for methods, which map to the stored procedures within a database.

When viewing your .dbml file within the O/R Designer, you also have an Object Relational Designer set of controls in the Visual Studio Toolbox, as shown in Figure 11-6.

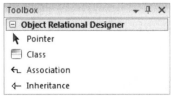

Figure 11-6

Creating the Product Object

For this example, you need to work with the Products table from the Northwind database, which means you need to create a Products table that will use LINQ to SQL to map to this table. Accomplishing this task is simply a matter of opening a view of the tables contained within the database from the Server Explorer dialog within Visual Studio and dragging and dropping the Products table onto the design surface of the O/R Designer. The results of this action are illustrated in Figure 11-7.

Figure 11-7

With this action, a bunch of code is added to the designer files of the .dbml file on your behalf. These classes give you strongly typed access to the Products table. For a demonstration of this, turn your attention to the console application's Module1.vb file. Following is the code required for this example:

```vb
Module Module1

    Sub Main()
        Dim dc As NorthwindDataContext = New NorthwindDataContext()

        Dim query = dc.Products

        For Each item In query
            Console.WriteLine("{0} | {1} | {2}", _
                item.ProductID, item.ProductName, item.UnitsInStock)
        Next

        Console.ReadLine()
    End Sub

End Module
```

This short bit of code is querying the Products table within the Northwind database and pulling out the data to display. It is important to step through this code starting with the first line in the Main method:

```vb
Dim dc As NorthwindDataContext = New NorthwindDataContext()
```

The NorthwindDataContext object is an object of type DataContext. Basically, you can view this as something that maps to a Connection type object. This object works with the connection string and connects to the database for any required operations.

The next line is quite interesting:

```vb
Dim query = dc.Products
```

Here, you are using an implicitly typed variable. If you are unsure of the output type, you can assign a type to the query variable and the type will be set into place at compile time. Actually, the code dc.Products returns a System.Data.Linq.Table(Of ConsoleApplication1.Product) object, and this is what the query type is set as when the application is compiled. Therefore, this means that you could have also just as easily written the statement as follows:

```vb
Dim query As Table(Of Product) = dc.Products
```

This approach is actually better because programmers who look at the application's code later will find it easier to understand what is happening, as just using Dim query by itself has so much of a hidden aspect to it. To use Table(Of Product), which is basically a generic list of Product objects, you should make a reference to the System.Data.Linq namespace (using Imports System.Data.Linq).

The value assigned to the `Query` object is the value of the `Products` property, which is of type `Table(Of Product)`. From there, the next bit of code iterates through the collection of `Product` objects found in `Table(Of Product)`:

```
For Each item In query
    Console.WriteLine("{0} | {1} | {2}", _
        item.ProductID, item.ProductName, item.UnitsInStock)
Next
```

The iteration, in this case, pulls out the `ProductID`, `ProductName`, and `UnitsInStock` properties from the `Product` object and writes them out to the program. Because you are using only a few of the items from the table, the O/R Designer enables you to delete the columns that are you not interested in pulling from the database. The results from the program are presented here:

```
1 | Chai | 39
2 | Chang | 17
3 | Aniseed Syrup | 13
4 | Chef Anton's Cajun Seasoning | 53
5 | Chef Anton's Gumbo Mix | 0

** Results removed for space reasons **

73 | Röd Kaviar | 101
74 | Longlife Tofu | 4
75 | Rhönbräu Klosterbier | 125
76 | Lakkalikööri | 57
77 | Original Frankfurter grüne Soße | 32
```

From this example, you can see just how easy it really is to query a SQL Server database using LINQ to SQL.

How Objects Map to LINQ Objects

The great thing about LINQ is that it gives you strongly typed objects to use in your code (with IntelliSense), and these objects map to existing database objects. Again, LINQ is nothing more than a thin façade over these pre-existing database objects. The following table shows the mappings that exist between the database objects and the LINQ objects:

Database Object	LINQ Object
Database	DataContext
Table	Class and Collection
View	Class and Collection
Column	Property
Relationship	Nested Collection
Stored Procedure	Method

On the left side, you are dealing with your database. The database is the entire entity: the tables, views, triggers, stored procedures — everything that makes up the database. On the right, or LINQ side, you have an object called the `DataContext` object. A `DataContext` object is bound to the database. For the required interaction with the database, it contains a connection string that handles all of the transactions that occur, including any logging. It also manages the output of the data. In short, the `DataContext` object completely manages the transactions with the database on your behalf.

Tables, as you saw in the example, are converted to classes. This means that if you have a Products table, you will have a `Product` class. Note that LINQ is name-friendly in that it changes plural tables to singular to provide the proper name to the class that you are using in your code. In addition to database tables being treated as classes, database views are treated the same. Columns, conversely, are treated as properties. This enables you to manage the attributes (names and type definitions) of the column directly.

Relationships are nested collections that map between these various objects. This gives you the ability to define relationships that are mapped to multiple items.

It's also important to understand the mapping of stored procedures. These actually map to methods within your code off the `DataContext` instance. The next section takes a closer look at the `DataContext` and the table objects within LINQ.

Looking at the architecture of LINQ to SQL, you will notice that there are really three layers: your application, the LINQ to SQL layer, and the SQL Server database. As you saw in the previous examples, you can create a strongly typed query in your application's code:

```
dc.Products
```

This in turn is translated to a SQL query by the LINQ to SQL layer, which is then supplied to the database on your behalf:

```
SELECT [t0].[ProductID], [t0].[ProductName], [t0].[SupplierID],
[t0].[CategoryID], [t0].[QuantityPerUnit], [t0].[UnitPrice],
[t0].[UnitsInStock], [t0].[UnitsOnOrder], [t0].[ReorderLevel],
[t0].[Discontinued]
FROM [dbo].[Products] AS [t0]
```

In return, the LINQ to SQL layer takes the rows coming out of the database from this query and turns them into a collection of strongly typed objects that you can easily work with.

The DataContext Object

In the preceding section, you learned that the `DataContext` object manages the transactions that occur with the database you are working with when working with LINQ to SQL. There is actually a lot that you can do with the `DataContext` object.

In instantiating one of these objects, note that it takes a few optional parameters:

❑   A string that represents the location of the SQL Server Express database file or the name of the SQL Server that is used

❑   A connection string

❑   Another `DataContext` object

The first two string options also provide the option to include your own database mapping file. Once you have instantiated this object, you are then able to programmatically use it for many types of operations.

Using ExecuteQuery

One of the simpler things you can accomplish with the `DataContext` object is running quick commands that you write yourself using the `ExecuteQuery` method. For instance, if you are going to pull all the products from the Products table using the `ExecuteQuery(Of TResult)` method, then your code would be similar to the following:

```
Imports System.Data.Linq

Module Module1

    Sub Main()
        Dim dc As DataContext = New DataContext("Data Source=.\SQLEXPRESS;" & _
            "AttachDbFilename=|DataDirectory|\NORTHWND.MDF;" & _
            "Integrated Security=True;User Instance=True")"

        Dim myProducts As IEnumerable(Of Product) = _
            dc.ExecuteQuery(Of Product)("SELECT * FROM PRODUCTS", "")

        For Each item In myProducts
            Console.WriteLine(item.ProductID & " | " & item.ProductName)
        Next

        Console.ReadLine()
    End Sub

End Module
```

In this case, the `ExecuteQuery(Of TResult)` method is called, passing in a query string and returning a collection of `Product` objects. The query utilized in the method call is a simple `Select` statement that doesn't require any additional parameters to be passed in. Because no parameters are passed in with the query, you instead need to use double quotes as the second required parameter to the method call. If you were going to optionally substitute any values in the query, then you would construct your `ExecuteQuery(Of TResult)` call as follows:

```
Dim myProducts As IEnumerable(Of Product) = _
    dc.ExecuteQuery(Of Product) _
        ("SELECT * FROM PRODUCTS WHERE UnitsInStock > {0}", 50)
```

In this case, the {0} is a placeholder for the substituted parameter value that you are going to pass in, and the second parameter of the `ExecuteQuery(Of TResult)` method is the parameter that will be used in the substitution.

Using Connection

The `Connection` property actually returns an instance of the `System.Data.SqlClient.SqlConnection` that is used by the `DataContext` object. This is ideal if you need to share this connection with other ADO.NET code that you might be using in your application, or if you need to get at any of the `SqlConnection` properties or methods that it exposes. For instance, getting at the connection string is a simple matter:

```
Dim dc As NorthwindDataContext = New NorthwindDataContext()

Console.WriteLine(dc.Connection.ConnectionString)
```

Using Transaction

If you have an ADO.NET transaction that you can use, you are able to assign that transaction to the DataContext object instance using the Transaction property. You can also use Transaction using the TransactionScope object from the .NET 2.0 Framework. You would need to make a reference to the System.Transactions namespace in your References folder for this example to work:

```
Imports System.Transactions

Module Module1

    Sub Main()
        Dim dc As NorthwindDataContext = New NorthwindDataContext()

        Using myScope As TransactionScope = New TransactionScope()
            Dim p1 As Product = New Product() _
                With {.ProductName = "Bill's Product"}
            dc.Products.InsertOnSubmit(p1)

            Dim p2 As Product = New Product() _
                With {.ProductName = "Another Product"}
            dc.Products.InsertOnSubmit(p2)

            Try
                dc.SubmitChanges()

                Console.WriteLine(p1.ProductID)
                Console.WriteLine(p2.ProductID)
            Catch ex As Exception
                Console.WriteLine(ex.ToString())
            End Try

            myScope.Complete()
        End Using


        Console.ReadLine()
    End Sub

End Module
```

In this case, the TransactionScope object is used; and if one of the operations on the database fails, then everything will be rolled back to the original state.

Other Methods and Properties of the DataContext Object

In addition to the items just described, several other methods and properties are available from the DataContext object. The following table shows some of the available methods from DataContext:

Method	Description
CreateDatabase	Enables you to create a database on the server
DatabaseExists	Enables you to determine whether a database exists and can be opened
DeleteDatabase	Deletes the associated database
ExecuteCommand	Enables you to pass in a command to the database to be executed
ExecuteQuery	Enables you to pass queries directly to the database
GetChangeSet	The DataContext object keeps track of changes occurring in the database on your behalf. This method enables you to access these changes.
GetCommand	Provides access to the commands that are performed
GetTable	Provides access to a collection of tables from the database
Refresh	Enables you to refresh your objects from the data stored within the database
SubmitChanges	Executes the insert, update, and delete commands that have been established in your code
Translate	Converts an IDataReader to objects

In addition to these methods, the DataContext object exposes some of the properties shown in the following table:

Property	Description
ChangeConflicts	Provides a collection of objects that caused concurrency conflicts when the SubmitChanges method was called
CommandTimeout	Enables you to set the timeout period for commands against the database. You should set this to a higher value if your query needs more time to execute.
Connection	Enables you to work with the System.Data.SqlClient.SqlConnection object used by the client
DeferredLoadingEnabled	Enables you to specify whether or not to delay the loading of one-to-many or one-to-one relationships
LoadOptions	Enables you to specify or retrieve the value of the DataLoadOptions object
Log	Enables you to specify the location of the output of the command that was used in the query
Mapping	Provides the MetaModel on which the mapping is based
ObjectTrackingEnabled	Specifies whether or not to track changes to the objects within the database for transactional purposes. If you are dealing with a read-only database, then you should set this property to false.
Transaction	Enables you to specify the local transaction used with the database

The Table(TEntity) object

The `Table(TEntity)` object is a representation of the tables that you are working with from the database. For instance, you saw the use of the `Product` class, which is a `Table(Of Product)` instance. As you will see throughout this chapter, several methods are available from the `Table(TEntity)` object. Some of these methods are defined in the following table:

Method	Description
Attach	Enables you to attach an entity to the `DataContext` instance
AttachAll	Enables you to attach a collection of entities to the `DataContext` instance
DeleteAllOnSubmit(TSubEntity)	Enables you to put all the pending actions into a state of readiness for deletion. Everything here is enacted when the `SubmitChanges` method is called off of the `DataContext` object.
DeleteOnSubmit	Enables you to put a pending action into a state of readiness for deletion. Everything here is enacted when the `SubmitChanges` method is called off of the `DataContext` object.
GetModifiedMembers	Provides an array of modified objects. You will be able to access their current and changed values.
GetNewBindingList	Provides a new list for binding to the data store
GetOriginalEntityState	Provides an instance of the object as it appeared in its original state
InsertAllOnSubmit(TSubEntity)	Enables you to put all the pending actions into a state of readiness for insertion. Everything here is enacted when the `SubmitChanges` method is called off of the `DataContext` object.
InsertOnSubmit	Enables you to put a pending action into a state of readiness for insertion. Everything here is enacted when the `SubmitChanges` method is called off of the `DataContext` object.

Working Without the O/R Designer

While the new O/R Designer in Visual Studio 2008 makes the creation of everything you need for LINQ to SQL quite easy, the underlying framework upon which this all rests also enables you to do everything from the ground up yourself. This provides you with the most control over what happens.

Creating Your Own Custom Object

To accomplish the same task, you need to expose your Customers table yourself. The first step is to create a new class in your project called `Customer.vb`. The code for this class is presented here:

```
Imports System.Data.Linq.Mapping

<Table(Name:="Customers")> _
```

```
Public Class Customer
    <Column(IsPrimaryKey:=True)> _
    Public CustomerID As String
    <Column()> _
    Public CompanyName As String
    <Column()> _
    Public ContactName As String
    <Column()> _
    Public ContactTitle As String
    <Column()> _
    Public Address As String
    <Column()> _
    Public City As String
    <Column()> _
    Public Region As String
    <Column()> _
    Public PostalCode As String
    <Column()> _
    Public Country As String
    <Column()> _
    Public Phone As String
    <Column()> _
    Public Fax As String
End Class
```

Here, the Customer.vb file defines the Customer object that you want to use with LINQ to SQL. The class has the Table attribute assigned to it in order to signify the Table class. The Table class attribute includes a property called Name, which defines the name of the table to use within the database that is referenced with the connection string. Using the Table attribute also means that you need to make a reference to the System.Data.Linq.Mapping namespace in your code.

In addition to the Table attribute, each of the defined properties in the class makes use of the Column attribute. As stated earlier, columns from the SQL Server database will map to properties in your code.

Querying with Your Custom Object and LINQ

With only this class in place, you are able to query the Northwind database for the Customers table. The code to accomplish this task is as follows:

```
Imports System.Data.Linq

Module Module1

    Sub Main()
        Dim dc As DataContext = New DataContext("Data Source=.\SQLEXPRESS;
            AttachDbFilename=|DataDirectory|\NORTHWND.MDF;
            Integrated Security=True;User Instance=True") ' Put on one line

        dc.Log = Console.Out ' Used for outputting the SQL used
```

```
            Dim myCustomers As Table(Of Customer) = dc.GetTable(Of Customer)()

            For Each item As Customer In myCustomers
                Console.WriteLine("{0} | {1}", item.CompanyName, item.Country)
            Next

            Console.ReadLine()
        End Sub

End Module
```

In this case, the default `DataContext` object is used, and the connection string to the Northwind SQL Server Express database is passed in as a parameter. A `Table` class of type `Customer` is then populated using the `GetTable(TEntity)` method. For this example, the `GetTable(TEntity)` operation uses your custom-defined `Customer` class:

```
dc.GetTable(Of Customer)()
```

In this example, LINQ to SQL will use the `DataContext` object to make the query to the SQL Server database on your behalf, and will get the returned rows as strongly typed `Customer` objects. This enables you to then iterate through each of the `Customer` objects in the `Table` object's collection and get the information that you need, as is done with the `Console.WriteLine` statements:

```
For Each item As Customer In myCustomers
    Console.WriteLine("{0} | {1}", item.CompanyName, item.Country)
Next
```

Running this code will produce the following results in your console application:

```
SELECT [t0].[CustomerID], [t0].[CompanyName], [t0].[ContactName],
[t0].[ContactTitle], [t0].[Address], [t0].[City], [t0].[Region],
[t0].[PostalCode], [t0].[Country], [t0].[Phone], [t0].[Fax]
FROM [Customers] AS [t0]
-- Context: SqlProvider(Sql2005) Model: AttributedMetaModel Build: 3.5.21022.8

Alfreds Futterkiste | Germany
Ana Trujillo Emparedados y helados | Mexico
Antonio Moreno Taquería | Mexico
Around the Horn | UK
Berglunds snabbköp | Sweden

// Output removed for clarity

Wartian Herkku | Finland
Wellington Importadora | Brazil
White Clover Markets | USA
Wilman Kala | Finland
Wolski  Zajazd | Poland
```

Limiting the Columns Called with the Query

Note that the query grabbed every column specified in your `Customer` class file. If you remove the columns that you are not going to need, you then have a new `Customer` class file:

```
Imports System.Data.Linq.Mapping

<Table(Name:="Customers")> _
Public Class Customer
    <Column(IsPrimaryKey:=True)> _
    Public CustomerID As String
    <Column()> _
    Public CompanyName As String
    <Column()> _
    Public Country As String
End Class
```

In this case, I removed all the columns that are not utilized by the application. Now if you run the console application and look at the SQL query that is produced, you will see the following results:

```
SELECT [t0].[CustomerID], [t0].[CompanyName], [t0].[Country]
FROM [Customers] AS [t0]
```

Now, only the three columns that are defined within the `Customer` class are utilized in the query to the `Customers` table.

The property `CustomerID` is interesting in that you are able to signify that this column is a primary key for the table through the use of the `IsPrimaryKey` setting in the `Column` attribute. This setting takes a `Boolean` value, which in this case is set to `True`.

Working with Column Names

The other important aspect of the columns is that the name of the property that you define in the `Customer` class needs to be the same name as that used in the database. For instance, if you change the name of the `CustomerID` property to `MyCustomerID`, you will get the following exception when you run your console application:

```
System.Data.SqlClient.SqlException was unhandled
  Message="Invalid column name 'MyCustomerID'."
  Source=".Net SqlClient Data Provider"
  ErrorCode=-2146232060
  Class=16
  LineNumber=1
  Number=207
  Procedure=""
  Server="\\\\.\\pipe\\F5E22E37-1AF9-44\\tsql\\query"
```

To get around this, you have to define the name of the column in the custom `Customer` class that you have created. You can do this by using the `Column` attribute, as illustrated here:

```
<Column(IsPrimaryKey:=True, Name:="CustomerID")> _
Public MyCustomerID As String
```

Like the `Table` attribute, the `Column` attribute includes a `Name` property that enables you to specify the name of the column as it appears in the `Customers` table. Doing this will generate a query:

```
SELECT [t0].[CustomerID] AS [MyCustomerID], [t0].[CompanyName], [t0].[Country]
FROM [Customers] AS [t0]
```

This also means that you now need to reference the column using the new name of `MyCustomerID` (e.g., `item.MyCustomerID`).

Creating Your Own DataContext Object

Using the plain-vanilla `DataContext` object probably isn't the best approach; instead, you'll find that you have more control by creating your own `DataContext` class. To accomplish this task, create a new class called `MyNorthwindDataContext.vb` and have the class inherit from `DataContext`. Your class in its simplest form is illustrated here:

```
Imports System.Data.Linq

Public Class MyNorthwindDataContext
    Inherits DataContext

    Public Customers As Table(Of Customer)

    Public Sub New()
        MyBase.New("Data Source=.\SQLEXPRESS;
            AttachDbFilename=|DataDirectory|\NORTHWND.MDF;
            Integrated Security=True;User Instance=True") ' Put on one line
    End Sub
End Class
```

Here, the class `MyNorthwindDataContext` inherits from `DataContext` and provides an instance of the `Table(Of Customer)` object from your `Customer` class that you created earlier. The constructor is the other requirement of this class. This constructor uses a base to initialize a new instance of the object referencing a file (in this case a connection to a SQL database file).

Using your own `DataContext` object enables you to change the code in your application as follows:

```
Imports System.Data.Linq

Module Module1

    Sub Main()
        Dim dc As MyNorthwindDataContext = New MyNorthwindDataContext()

        Dim myCustomers As Table(Of Customer) = dc.Customers

        For Each item As Customer In myCustomers
            Console.WriteLine("{0} | {1}", item.CompanyName, item.Country)
        Next

        Console.ReadLine()
    End Sub

End Module
```

By creating an instance of the MyNorthwindDataContext object, you are enabling the class to manage the connection to the database. Note that now you have direct access to the Customer class through the dc.Customers statement.

The examples provided in this chapter are bare-bones examples, as they don't include all the error handling and logging that would generally be part of building your applications. This abbreviated style enables the examples to highlight the main points being discussed, and nothing more.

Custom Objects and the O/R Designer

In addition to building your custom object in your own .vb file and then tying that class to the DataContext that you have built, you can also use the O/R Designer in Visual Studio 2008 to build your class files. When completed, Visual Studio will create the appropriate .vb file on your behalf, and by using the O/R Designer, you also have a visual representation of the class file and any possible relationships you have established.

For example, when viewing the Designer view of your .dbml file, note the three items in the Toolbox: Class, Association, and Inheritance. Take the Class object from the Toolbox and drop it onto the design surface. You will be presented with an image of the generic class, as shown in Figure 11-8.

Figure 11-8

From here, click on the Class1 name and rename this class to Customer. Then, by right-clicking next to the name, you can add properties to the class file by selecting Add ➪ Property from the provided menu. For this example, give the Customer class three properties: CustomerID, CompanyName, and Country. Highlight the CustomerID property in order to configure the property from the Properties dialog in Visual Studio, changing the Primary Key setting from False to True. Next, highlight the entire class, go to the Properties dialog, and change the Source property to Customers, as this is the name of the table from which this Customer object needs to work. After this is all done, you will have a visual representation of the class, as shown in Figure 11-9.

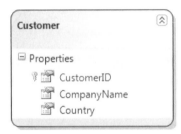

Figure 11-9

As shown in the figure, the `CustomerID` property is properly represented with a primary key icon next to the name. With this in place, expand the plus sign next to the `Northwind.dbml` file. You will find two files here: `Northwind.dbml.layout` and `Northwind.designer.vb`. The `Northwind.dbml.layout` file is an XML file that helps Visual Studio with the visual representation shown in the O/R Designer. The most important file is `Northwind.designer.vb`. This is the `Customer` class file that was created on your behalf. If you open this file, you can see what Visual Studio created for you.

First, you will find the `Customer` class file within the code:

```
<Table(Name:="Customers")> _
Partial Public Class Customer
  Implements System.ComponentModel.INotifyPropertyChanging, _
    System.ComponentModel.INotifyPropertyChanged

    ' Code removed for clarity

End Class
```

The `Customer` class is the name of the class according to what you provided in the designer. The class comes with the `Table` attribute and provides a `Name` value of `Customers`, as this is the name of the database that this object needs to work with when connecting to the Northwind database.

Within the `Customer` class are the three properties you defined. Presented here is just one of the properties, `CustomerID`:

```
<Column(Storage:="_CustomerID", CanBeNull:=false, IsPrimaryKey:=true)> _
Public Property CustomerID() As String
    Get
        Return Me._CustomerID
    End Get
    Set
        If (String.Equals(Me._CustomerID, value) = false) Then
            Me.OnCustomerIDChanging(value)
            Me.SendPropertyChanging
            Me._CustomerID = value
            Me.SendPropertyChanged("CustomerID")
            Me.OnCustomerIDChanged
        End If
    End Set
End Property
```

Like before, when you built a class for yourself, the properties defined here use the `Column` attribute and some of the properties available to this attribute. You can see that the primary key setting is specified using the `IsPrimaryKey` item.

In addition to the `Customer` class is a class that inherits from the `DataContext` object:

```
<System.Data.Linq.Mapping.DatabaseAttribute(Name:="NORTHWND")> _
Partial Public Class NorthwindDataContext
  Inherits System.Data.Linq.DataContext

    ' Code removed for clarity

End Class
```

This `DataContext` object, `NorthwindDataContext`, enables you to connect to the Northwind database and make use of the `Customers` table, as accomplished in the previous examples.

Using the O/R Designer is a process that can make the creation of your database object class files simple and straightforward. However, you have also seen that if you want complete control, you can code everything yourself to get the results you want.

Querying the Database

As you have seen so far in this chapter, there are a number of ways in which you can query the database from the code of your application. In some of the simplest forms, your queries looked like the following:

```
Dim query As Table(Of Product) = dc.Products
```

This command pulled down the entire Products table to your `Query` object instance.

Using Query Expressions

In addition to pulling down a straight table using `dc.Products`, you are about to use a strongly typed query expression directly in your code:

```
Module Module1

    Sub Main()
        Dim dc As NorthwindDataContext = New NorthwindDataContext()

        Dim query = From p In dc.Products Select p

        For Each item In query
            Console.WriteLine(item.ProductID & " | " & item.ProductName)
        Next

        Console.ReadLine()
    End Sub

End Module
```

In this case, a `query` object (again, a `Table(Of Product)` object) is populated with the query value of `From p in dc.Products Select p`.

Query Expressions in Detail

You can use several query expressions from your code. The preceding example is a simple select statement that returns the entire table. The following list of items includes some of the other query expressions that you have at your disposal:

Segmentation	Description
Project	Select *<expression>*
Filter	Where *<expression>*, Distinct
Test	Any(*<expression>*), All(*<expression>*)
Join	*<expression>* Join *<expression>* On *<expression>* Equals *<expression>*
Group	Group By *<expression>*, Into *<expression>*, *<expression>* Group Join *<decision>* On *<expression>* Equals *<expression>* Into *<expression>*
Aggregate	Count([*<expression>*]), Sum(*<expression>*), Min(*<expression>*), Max(*<expression>*), Avg(*<expression>*)
Partition	Skip [While] *<expression>*, Take [While] *<expression>*
Set	Union, Intersect, Except
Order	*Order By <expression>, <expression>[Ascending	Descending]*

Filtering Using Expressions

In addition to straight queries for the entire table, you can filter items using the `Where` and `Distinct` options. The following example queries the Products table for a specific type of record:

```
Dim query = From p In dc.Products _
            Where p.ProductName.StartsWith("L") _
            Select p
```

Here, this query is selecting all the records from the Products table that start with the letter "L." This is done via the `Where p.ProductName.StartsWith("L")` expression. You will find a large selection of methods available off the `ProductName` property that enable you to fine-tune the filtering you need. This operation produces the following results:

```
65 | Louisiana Fiery Hot Pepper Sauce
66 | Louisiana Hot Spiced Okra
67 | Laughing Lumberjack Lager
74 | Longlife Tofu
76 | Lakkalikööri
```

You can add as many of these expressions to the list as you need. For instance, the next example adds two `Where` statements to your query:

```
Dim query = From p In dc.Products _
            Where p.ProductName.StartsWith("L") _
            Where p.ProductName.EndsWith("i") _
            Select p
```

In this case, a filter expression looks for items with a product name starting with the letter "L," and then a second expression is included to ensure that a second criterion is also applied, which states that the items must also end with the letter i. This would give you the following results:

```
76 | Lakkalikööri
```

Performing Joins

In addition to working with one table, you can work with multiple tables and perform joins with your queries. If you drag and drop both the Customers table and the Orders table onto the `Northwind.dbml` design surface, you will get the result shown in Figure 11-10.

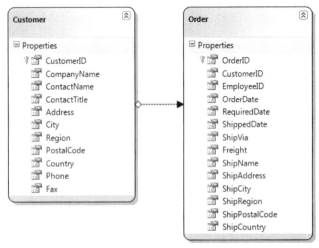

Figure 11-10

After you drag and drop both of these elements onto the design surface, Visual Studio knows that there is a relationship between them and creates this relationship for you in the code and represents it with the black arrow.

From here, you can use a `Join` statement in your query to work with both of the tables, as shown in the following example:

```
Module Module1

    Sub Main()
        Dim dc As NorthwindDataContext = New NorthwindDataContext()

        dc.Log = Console.Out

        Dim query = From c In dc.Customers _
                    Join o In dc.Orders On c.CustomerID Equals o.CustomerID _
                    Order By c.CustomerID _
                    Select c.CustomerID, c.CompanyName, _
                        c.Country, o.OrderID, o.OrderDate
```

```
      For Each item In query
          Console.WriteLine(item.CustomerID & " | " & item.CompanyName _
                  & " | " & item.Country & " | " & item.OrderID _
                  & " | " & item.OrderDate)
      Next

      Console.ReadLine()
   End Sub

End Module
```

This example is pulling from the Customers table and joining on the Orders table where the `CustomerID` columns match. This is done through the `Join` statement:

```
Join o In dc.Orders On c.CustomerID Equals o.CustomerID
```

From here, a new object is created with the `Select` statement; and this new object is comprised of the `CustomerID`, `CompanyName`, and `Country` columns from the Customers table as well as the `OrderID` and `OrderDate` columns from the Orders table.

When it comes to iterating through the collection of this new object, note that the `For Each` statement does not define the variable `item` with a specific type, as the type is not known yet:

```
For Each item In query
    Console.WriteLine(item.CustomerID & " | " & item.CompanyName _
        & " | " & item.Country & " | " & item.OrderID _
        & " | " & item.OrderDate)
Next
```

The `item` object here has access to all the properties specified in the class declaration. Running this example, you will get results similar to what is presented here in this partial result:

```
WILMK | Wilman Kala | Finland | 10695 | 10/7/1997 12:00:00 AM
WILMK | Wilman Kala | Finland | 10615 | 7/30/1997 12:00:00 AM
WILMK | Wilman Kala | Finland | 10673 | 9/18/1997 12:00:00 AM
WILMK | Wilman Kala | Finland | 11005 | 4/7/1998 12:00:00 AM
WILMK | Wilman Kala | Finland | 10879 | 2/10/1998 12:00:00 AM
WILMK | Wilman Kala | Finland | 10873 | 2/6/1998 12:00:00 AM
WILMK | Wilman Kala | Finland | 10910 | 2/26/1998 12:00:00 AM
```

Grouping Items

You can easily group items with your queries. In the `Northwind.dbml` example that you have been working with so far, drag and drop the Categories table onto the design surface. You will then see that there is a relationship between this table and the Products table. The following example demonstrates how to group products by category:

```
Module Module1

    Sub Main()
        Dim dc As NorthwindDataContext = New NorthwindDataContext()
```

```
        Dim query = From p In dc.Products _
                 Order By p.Category.CategoryName Ascending _
                 Group p By p.Category.CategoryName Into Group _
                 Select Category = CategoryName, Products = Group

    For Each item In query
        Console.WriteLine(item.Category)

        For Each innerItem In item.Products
            Console.WriteLine("       " & innerItem.ProductName)
        Next

        Console.WriteLine()
    Next

    Console.ReadLine()
    End Sub

End Module
```

This example creates a new object, which is a group of categories, and packages the entire Product table into this new table, called Group. Before that, the categories are ordered by name using the Order By statement, and the order provided is Ascending (the other option being Descending). The output is the Category (passed in through the CategoryName property) and the Product instance. The iteration with the For Each statements is done once for the categories and again for each of the products that are found in the category.

A partial output of this program is presented here:

```
Beverages
        Chai
        Chang
        Guaraná Fantástica
        Sasquatch Ale
        Steeleye Stout
        Côte de Blaye
        Chartreuse verte
        Ipoh Coffee
        Laughing Lumberjack Lager
        Outback Lager
        Rhönbräu Klosterbier
        Lakkalikööri

Condiments
        Aniseed Syrup
        Chef Anton's Cajun Seasoning
        Chef Anton's Gumbo Mix
        Grandma's Boysenberry Spread
        Northwoods Cranberry Sauce
        Genen Shouyu
        Gula Malacca
```

```
      Sirop d'érable
      Vegie-spread
      Louisiana Fiery Hot Pepper Sauce
      Louisiana Hot Spiced Okra
      Original Frankfurter grüne Soße
```

Many more commands and expressions are available to you beyond what has been presented in this chapter.

Stored Procedures

So far, you have been querying the tables directly and leaving it up to LINQ to create the appropriate SQL statement for the operation. When working with pre-existing databases that make heavy use of stored procedures (and for those who want to follow the best practice of using stored procedures within a database), LINQ is still a viable option.

LINQ to SQL treats working with stored procedures as a method call. As you saw in Figure 11-5, the design surface called the O/R Designer enables you to drag and drop tables onto it so that you can then programmatically work with the table. On the right side of the O/R Designer is a pane in which you can drag and drop stored procedures.

Any stored procedures that you drag and drop onto this part of the O/R Designer become available methods to you off the `DataContext` object. For this example, drag and drop the `TenMostExpensiveProducts` stored procedure onto this part of the O/R Designer. The following code shows how you would call this stored procedure within the Northwind database:

```
    Imports System.Data.Linq

    Module Module1

        Sub Main()
            Dim dc As NorthwindDataContext = New NorthwindDataContext()

            Dim result As ISingleResult(Of Ten_Most_Expensive_ProductsResult) = _
                    dc.Ten_Most_Expensive_Products()

            For Each item As Ten_Most_Expensive_ProductsResult In result
                Console.WriteLine(item.TenMostExpensiveProducts & " | " & _
                        item.UnitPrice)
            Next

            Console.ReadLine()
        End Sub

    End Module
```

The rows coming out of the stored procedure are collected into an `ISingleResult(Of Ten_Most _Expensive_ProductsResult)` object. From here, iteration through this object is simple. As you can see from this example, calling your stored procedures is a straightforward process.

LINQ to XML

As stated earlier, probably the biggest and most exciting addition to the .NET Framework 3.5 is the addition of the .NET Language Integrated Query framework (LINQ) into VB 2008. LINQ comes in many flavors depending on the final data store you are working with in querying your data. The preceding section took a look at using LINQ to SQL to query SQL Server databases. This section takes a quick look at using LINQ to query your XML data sources instead.

Extensible Markup Language (XML) is now in widespread use. Many applications on the Internet or residing on individual computers use some form of XML to run or manage the processes of an application. Earlier books about XML commented that XML was going to be the "next big thing." Now, it *is* the big thing. In fact, there really isn't anything bigger.

Microsoft has been working for years to make using XML in the .NET world as easy as possible. You cannot help but notice the additional capabilities and enhancements to XML usage introduced in each new version of the .NET Framework. In fact, Bill Gates highlighted Microsoft's faith in XML in his keynote address at the Microsoft Professional Developers Conference in 2005 when he stated that XML is being pushed deeper and deeper into the Windows core each year. If you look around the .NET Framework, you will probably agree.

LINQ to XML and .NET 3.5

With the introduction of LINQ to the .NET Framework 3.5, the focus was on easy access to the data that you want to work with in your applications. One of the main data stores in the application space is XML, so it was really a no-brainer to create the LINQ to XML implementation.

Before the LINQ to XML release, working with XML using `System.Xml` was not the easiest thing in the world to achieve. With the inclusion of `System.Xml.Linq`, you now have a series of capabilities that make the process of working with XML in your code much easier to achieve.

New Objects for Creating XML Documents

In creating XML within the application code, many developers turned to the `XmlDocument` object to do this job. This object enables you to create XML documents that in turn enable you to append elements, attributes, and other items in a hierarchical fashion. With LINQ to XML and the inclusion of the new `System.Xml.Linq` namespace, you now have some new objects available that make the creation of XML documents a much simpler process.

Visual Basic 2008 Ventures Down Another Path

An interesting side note to the LINQ to XML feature set is that the Visual Basic 2008 team at Microsoft actually took the LINQ to XML capabilities a little further in some areas. For instance, something you can't accomplish in C# 2008 that you can do in Visual Basic 2008 is include XML as a core part of the language. XML literals are now a true part of the Visual Basic language, and you can paste XML fragments directly in your code for inclusion — the XML is not treated as a string.

Namespaces and Prefixes

One issue that was somewhat ignored in parts of the .NET Framework 2.0 was how the items in the framework dealt with the inclusion of XML namespaces and prefixes in documents. LINQ to XML makes this an important part of the XML story, and you will find the capabilities for working with these types of objects to be quite simple.

New XML Objects from the .NET Framework 3.5

Even if the LINQ querying capability were not around, the new objects available to work with the XML (available in place of working directly with the DOM in this release of the framework) are so good that they can even stand on their own outside LINQ. Within the new `System.Xml.Linq` namespace, you will find a series of new LINQ to XML helper objects that make working with an XML document in memory that much easier. The following sections describe the new objects that are available to you within this new namespace.

> Many of the examples in this chapter use a file called `Hamlet.xml`, which you can find at `http://metalab.unc.edu/bosak/xml/eg/shaks200.zip`. It includes all of Shakespeare's plays as XML files.

XDocument

The `XDocument` is a replacement of the `XmlDocument` object from the pre-.NET 3.5 world. The `XDocument` object is easier to work with when dealing with XML documents. It works with the other new objects in this space, such as the `XNamespace`, `XComment`, `XElement`, and `XAttribute` objects.

One of the more important members of the `XDocument` object is the `Load` method:

```
Dim xdoc As XDocument = XDocument.Load("C:\Hamlet.xml")
```

The preceding example loads the `Hamlet.xml` contents as an in-memory `XDocument` object. You can also pass a `TextReader` or `XmlReader` object into the `Load` method. From here, you are able to programmatically work with the XML:

```
Dim xdoc As XDocument = XDocument.Load("C:\Hamlet.xml")

Console.WriteLine(xdoc.Root.Name.ToString())
Console.WriteLine(xdoc.Root.HasAttributes.ToString())
```

This produces the following results:

```
PLAY
False
```

Another important member to be aware of is the `Save` method, which, like the `Load` method, enables you to save to a physical disk location or to a `TextWriter` or `XmlWriter` object. Note that you need to be running Visual Studio as an administrator for this to work:

```
Dim xdoc As XDocument = XDocument.Load("C:\Hamlet.xml")

xdoc.Save("C:\CopyOfHamlet.xml")
```

XElement

One of the more common objects that you will work with is the `XElement` object. With this object, you can easily create even single-element objects that are XML documents themselves, and even fragments of XML. For instance, here is an example of writing an XML element with a corresponding value:

```
Dim xe As XElement = New XElement("Company", "Lipper")
Console.WriteLine(xe.ToString())
```

When creating a new `XElement` object, you can define the name of the element as well as the value used in the element. In this case, the name of the element will be `<Company>`, while the value of the `<Company>` element will be `Lipper`. Running this in a console application, you will get the following result:

```
<Company>Lipper</Company>
```

You can also create a more complete XML document using multiple `XElement` objects, as shown in the following example:

```
Module Module1

    Sub Main()
        Dim xe As XElement = New XElement("Company", _
            New XElement("CompanyName", "Lipper"), _
            New XElement("CompanyAddress", _
                New XElement("Address", "123 Main Street"), _
                New XElement("City", "St. Louis"), _
                New XElement("State", "MO"), _
                New XElement("Country", "USA")))

        Console.WriteLine(xe.ToString())

        Console.ReadLine()
    End Sub

End Module
```

Running this application yields the results shown in Figure 11-11.

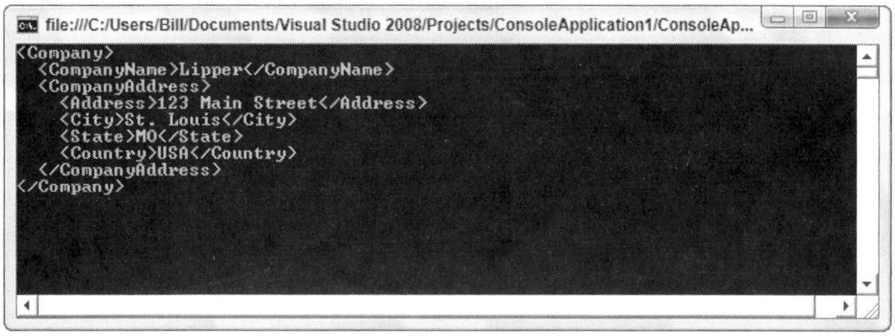

Figure 11-11

XNamespace

The XNamespace is an object that represents an XML namespace; and it is easily applied to elements within your document. For example, you can take the previous example and easily apply a namespace to the root element:

```
Module Module1

    Sub Main()
        Dim ns As XNamespace = "http://www.lipperweb.com/ns/1"

        Dim xe As XElement = New XElement(ns + "Company", _
            New XElement("CompanyName", "Lipper"), _
            New XElement("CompanyAddress", _
                New XElement("Address", "123 Main Street"), _
                New XElement("City", "St. Louis"), _
                New XElement("State", "MO"), _
                New XElement("Country", "USA")))

        Console.WriteLine(xe.ToString())

        Console.ReadLine()
    End Sub

End Module
```

In this case, an XNamespace object is created by assigning it a value of http://www.lipperweb.com/ns/1. From there, it is actually used in the root element <Company> with the instantiation of the XElement object:

```
Dim xe As XElement = New XElement(ns + "Company", _
```

This will produce the results illustrated in Figure 11-12.

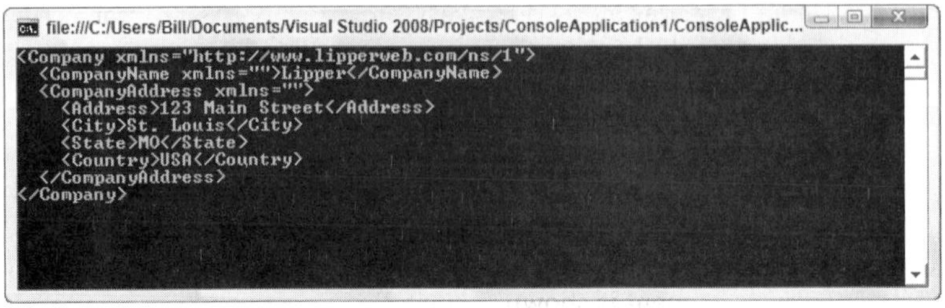

Figure 11-12

Besides dealing with the root element, you can also apply namespaces to all your elements, as shown in the following example:

```
Module Module1

    Sub Main()
        Dim ns1 As XNamespace = "http://www.lipperweb.com/ns/root"
        Dim ns2 As XNamespace = "http://www.lipperweb.com/ns/sub"

        Dim xe As XElement = New XElement(ns1 + "Company", _
            New XElement(ns2 + "CompanyName", "Lipper"), _
            New XElement(ns2 + "CompanyAddress", _
                New XElement(ns2 + "Address", "123 Main Street"), _
                New XElement(ns2 + "City", "St. Louis"), _
                New XElement(ns2 + "State", "MO"), _
                New XElement(ns2 + "Country", "USA")))

        Console.WriteLine(xe.ToString())

        Console.ReadLine()
    End Sub

End Module
```

This produces the results shown in Figure 11-13.

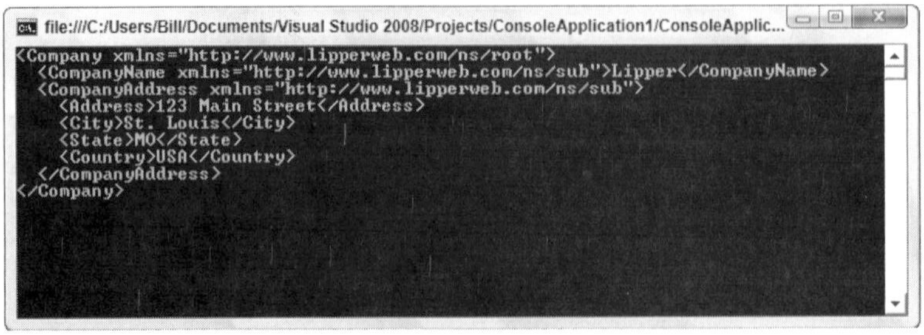

Figure 11-13

In this case, the sub-namespace was applied to everything specified except for the `<Address>`, `<City>`, `<State>`, and `<Country>` elements, because they inherit from their parent, `<CompanyAddress>`, which has the namespace declaration.

XComment

The `XComment` object enables you to easily add XML comments to your XML documents. Adding a comment to the top of the document is shown in the following example:

```
Module Module1

    Sub Main()
        Dim xdoc As XDocument = New XDocument()

        Dim xc As XComment = New XComment("Here is a comment.")
        xdoc.Add(xc)

        Dim xe As XElement = New XElement("Company", _
            New XElement("CompanyName", "Lipper"), _
            New XElement("CompanyAddress", _
                New XComment("Here is another comment."), _
                New XElement("Address", "123 Main Street"), _
                New XElement("City", "St. Louis"), _
                New XElement("State", "MO"), _
                New XElement("Country", "USA")))

        xdoc.Add(xe)

        Console.WriteLine(xdoc.ToString())

        Console.ReadLine()
    End Sub

End Module
```

Here, an `XDocument` object containing two XML comments is written to the console, one at the top of the document and another within the `<CompanyAddress>` element. The output is shown in Figure 11-14.

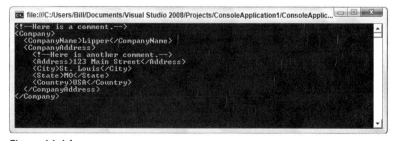

Figure 11-14

XAttribute

In addition to elements, another important aspect of XML is attributes. Adding and working with attributes is done through the use of the XAttribute object. The following example adds an attribute to the root <Customers> node:

```
Module Module1

    Sub Main()
        Dim xe As XElement = New XElement("Company", _
            New XAttribute("MyAttribute", "MyAttributeValue"), _
            New XElement("CompanyName", "Lipper"), _
            New XElement("CompanyAddress", _
                New XElement("Address", "123 Main Street"), _
                New XElement("City", "St. Louis"), _
                New XElement("State", "MO"), _
                New XElement("Country", "USA")))

        Console.WriteLine(xe.ToString())

        Console.ReadLine()
    End Sub

End Module
```

Here, the attribute MyAttribute with a value of MyAttributeValue is added to the root element of the XML document, producing the results shown in Figure 11-15.

Figure 11-15

Visual Basic 2008 and XML Literals

Visual Basic takes LINQ to XML one step further, enabling you to place XML directly in your code. Using XML literals (something not available in C# 2008), you can place XML directly in your code for working with the XDocument and XElement objects. Earlier, the use of the XElement object was presented as follows:

```
Module Module1

    Sub Main()
        Dim xe As XElement = New XElement("Company", _
```

```
                New XElement("CompanyName", "Lipper"), _
                New XElement("CompanyAddress", _
                    New XElement("Address", "123 Main Street"), _
                    New XElement("City", "St. Louis"), _
                    New XElement("State", "MO"), _
                    New XElement("Country", "USA")))

        Console.WriteLine(xe.ToString())

        Console.ReadLine()
    End Sub

End Module
```

Using XML literals, you can use the following syntax:

```
Module Module1

    Sub Main()
        Dim xe As XElement = _
            <Company>
                <CompanyName>Lipper</CompanyName>
                <CompanyAddress>
                    <Address>123 Main Street</Address>
                    <City>St. Louis</City>
                    <State>MO</State>
                    <Country>USA</Country>
                </CompanyAddress>
            </Company>

        Console.WriteLine(xe.ToString())

        Console.ReadLine()
    End Sub

End Module
```

This enables you to place the XML directly in the code (see Figure 11-16). The best part about this is the IDE support for XML literals. Visual Studio 2008 has IntelliSense and excellent color-coding for the XML that you place in your code file.

You can also use inline variables in the XML document. For instance, if you wanted to declare the value of the <CompanyName> element outside the XML literal, then you could use a construct similar to the following:

```
Module Module1

    Sub Main()
        Dim companyName As String = "Lipper"

        Dim xe As XElement = _
            <Company>
                <CompanyName><%= companyName %></CompanyName>
```

```
                    <CompanyAddress>
                        <Address>123 Main Street</Address>
                        <City>St. Louis</City>
                        <State>MO</State>
                        <Country>USA</Country>
                    </CompanyAddress>
                </Company>

        Console.WriteLine(xe.ToString())

        Console.ReadLine()
    End Sub

  End Module
```

In this case, the `<CompanyName>` element is assigned a value of `Lipper` from the `companyName` variable, using the syntax `<%= companyName %>`.

Figure 11-16

Using LINQ to Query XML Documents

Now that you can get your XML documents into an `XDocument` object and work with the various parts of this document, you can also use LINQ to XML to query your XML documents and work with the results.

Querying Static XML Documents

Notice that querying a static XML document using LINQ to XML takes almost no work at all. The following example makes use of the `hamlet.xml` file and queries to get all the players (actors) who appear in a play. Each of these players is defined in the XML document with the `<PERSONA>` element:

```
Module Module1

    Sub Main()
        Dim xdoc As XDocument = XDocument.Load("C:\hamlet.xml")

        Dim query = From people In xdoc.Descendants("PERSONA") _
                    Select people.Value

        Console.WriteLine("{0} Players Found", query.Count())
        Console.WriteLine()

        For Each item In query
            Console.WriteLine(item)
        Next

        Console.ReadLine()
    End Sub

End Module
```

In this case, an XDocument object loads a physical XML file (hamlet.xml) and then performs a LINQ query over the contents of the document:

```
Dim query = From people In xdoc.Descendants("PERSONA") _
            Select people.Value
```

The people object is a representation of all the <PERSONA> elements found in the document. Then the Select statement gets at the values of these elements. From there, a Console.WriteLine method is used to write out a count of all the players found, using query.Count. Next, each of the items is written to the screen in a For Each loop. The results you should see are presented here:

```
26 Players Found

CLAUDIUS, king of Denmark.
HAMLET, son to the late, and nephew to the present king.
POLONIUS, lord chamberlain.
HORATIO, friend to Hamlet.
LAERTES, son to Polonius.
LUCIANUS, nephew to the king.
VOLTIMAND
CORNELIUS
ROSENCRANTZ
GUILDENSTERN
OSRIC
A Gentleman
A Priest.
MARCELLUS
BERNARDO
FRANCISCO, a soldier.
REYNALDO, servant to Polonius.
Players.
Two Clowns, grave-diggers.
FORTINBRAS, prince of Norway.
```

471

```
A Captain.
English Ambassadors.
GERTRUDE, queen of Denmark, and mother to Hamlet.
OPHELIA, daughter to Polonius.
Lords, Ladies, Officers, Soldiers, Sailors, Messengers, and other Attendants.
Ghost of Hamlet's Father.
```

Querying Dynamic XML Documents

Numerous dynamic XML documents can be found on the Internet these days. Blog feeds, podcast feeds, and more provide XML documents by sending a request to a specific URL endpoint. These feeds can be viewed either in the browser, through an RSS-aggregator, or as pure XML:

```vb
Module Module1

    Sub Main()
        Dim xdoc As XDocument = _
                XDocument.Load("http://geekswithblogs.net/evjen/Rss.aspx")

        Dim query = From rssFeed In xdoc.Descendants("channel") _
                    Select Title = rssFeed.Element("title").Value, _
                        Description = rssFeed.Element("description").Value, _
                        Link = rssFeed.Element("link").Value

        For Each item In query
            Console.WriteLine("TITLE: " + item.Title)
            Console.WriteLine("DESCRIPTION: " + item.Description)
            Console.WriteLine("LINK: " + item.Link)
        Next

        Console.WriteLine()

        Dim queryPosts = From myPosts In xdoc.Descendants("item") _
                Select Title = myPosts.Element("title").Value, _
                    Published = _
                      DateTime.Parse(myPosts.Element("pubDate").Value), _
                    Description = myPosts.Element("description").Value, _
                    Url = myPosts.Element("link").Value, _
                    Comments = myPosts.Element("comments").Value

        For Each item In queryPosts
            Console.WriteLine(item.Title)
        Next

        Console.ReadLine()
    End Sub

End Module
```

Here, the `Load` method of the `XDocument` object points to a URL where the XML is retrieved. The first query pulls out all the main sub-elements of the `<channel>` element in the feed and creates new objects called `Title`, `Description`, and `Link` to get at the values of these sub-elements.

From there, a `For Each` statement is run to iterate through all the items found in this query. The results are as follows:

```
TITLE: Bill Evjen's Blog
DESCRIPTION: Code, Life and Community
LINK: http://geekswithblogs.net/evjen/Default.aspx
```

The second query works through all the `<item>` elements and the various sub-elements it contains (these are all the blog entries found in the blog). Though a lot of the items found are rolled up into properties, in the `For Each` loop, only the `Title` property is used. You will see results similar to the following from this query:

```
AJAX Control Toolkit Controls Grayed Out - HOW TO FIX
Welcome .NET 3.5!
Visual Studio 2008 Released
IIS 7.0 Rocks the House!
Word Issue - Couldn't Select Text
Microsoft Releases XML Schema Designer CTP1
Silverlight Book
Microsoft Tafiti as a beta
ReSharper on Visual Studio 2008
Windows Vista Updates for Performance and Reliability Issues
New Version of ODP.NET for .NET 2.0 Released as Beta Today
First Review of Professional XML
Go to MIX07 for free!
Microsoft Surface and the Future of Home Computing?
Alas my friends - I'm *not* TechEd bound
New Book - Professional VB 2005 with .NET 3.0!
An article showing Oracle and .NET working together
My Latest Book - Professional XML
CISCO VPN Client Software on Windows Vista
Server-Side Excel Generation
Scott Guthrie Gives Short Review of Professional ASP.NET 2.0 SE
Windows Forms Additions in the Next Version of .NET
Tag, I'm It
```

Working Around the XML Document

If you have been working with the XML document `hamlet.xml`, you probably noticed that it is quite large. You've seen how you can query into the XML document in a couple of ways, and now this section takes a look at reading and writing to the XML document.

Reading from an XML Document

Earlier you saw just how easy it is to query into an XML document using the LINQ query statements, as shown here:

```
Dim query = From people In xdoc.Descendants("PERSONA") _
            Select people.Value
```

This query returns all the players found in the document. Using the `Element` method of the `XDocument` object, you can also get at specific values of the XML document you are working with. For instance, continuing to work with the `hamlet.xml` document, the following XML fragment shows you how the title is represented:

```
<?xml version="1.0"?>

<PLAY>
    <TITLE>The Tragedy of Hamlet, Prince of Denmark</TITLE>

    <!-- XML removed for clarity -->

</PLAY>
```

As you can see, the `<TITLE>` element is a nested element of the `<PLAY>` element. You can easily get at the title by using the following bit of code:

```
Dim xdoc As XDocument = XDocument.Load("C:\hamlet.xml")

Console.WriteLine(xdoc.Element("PLAY").Element("TITLE").Value)
```

This bit of code writes out the title, The Tragedy of Hamlet, Prince of Denmark, to the console screen. In the code, you were able to work down the hierarchy of the XML document by using two `Element` method calls — first calling the `<PLAY>` element, and then the `<TITLE>` element found nested within the `<PLAY>` element.

Continuing with the `hamlet.xml` document, you can view a long list of players who are defined with the use of the `<PERSONA>` element:

```
<?xml version="1.0"?>

<PLAY>
    <TITLE>The Tragedy of Hamlet, Prince of Denmark</TITLE>

    <!-- XML removed for clarity -->

    <PERSONAE>
        <TITLE>Dramatis Personae</TITLE>

        <PERSONA>CLAUDIUS, king of Denmark. </PERSONA>
        <PERSONA>HAMLET, son to the late,
         and nephew to the present king.</PERSONA>
        <PERSONA>POLONIUS, lord chamberlain. </PERSONA>
        <PERSONA>HORATIO, friend to Hamlet.</PERSONA>
        <PERSONA>LAERTES, son to Polonius.</PERSONA>
        <PERSONA>LUCIANUS, nephew to the king.</PERSONA>

        <!-- XML removed for clarity -->

    </PERSONAE>

</PLAY>
```

Using that, review this bit of the code's use of this XML:

```
Dim xdoc As XDocument = XDocument.Load("C:\hamlet.xml")

Console.WriteLine( _
    xdoc.Element("PLAY").Element("PERSONAE").Element("PERSONA").Value)
```

This bit of code starts at <PLAY>, works down to the <PERSONAE> element, and then makes use of the <PERSONA> element. However, using this you will get the following result:

```
CLAUDIUS, king of Denmark
```

Although there is a collection of <PERSONA> elements, you are only dealing with the first one that is encountered using the Element().Value call.

Writing to an XML Document

In addition to reading from an XML document, you can also write to the document just as easily. For instance, if you wanted to change the name of the first player of the hamlet file, you could make use of the code here to accomplish that task:

```
Module Module1

    Sub Main()
        Dim xdoc As XDocument = XDocument.Load("C:\hamlet.xml")

        xdoc.Element("PLAY").Element("PERSONAE"). _
            Element("PERSONA").SetValue("Bill Evjen, king of Denmark")

        Console.WriteLine(xdoc.Element("PLAY"). _
            Element("PERSONAE").Element("PERSONA").Value)

        Console.ReadLine()
    End Sub

End Module
```

In this case, the first instance of the <PERSONA> element is overwritten with the value of Bill Evjen, king of Denmark using the SetValue method of the Element object. After the SetValue is called and the value is applied to the XML document, the value is then retrieved using the same approach as before. Running this bit of code, you can indeed see that the value of the first <PERSONA> element has been changed.

Another way to change the document (by adding items to it in this example) is to create the element you want as XElement objects and then add them to the document:

```
Module Module1

    Sub Main()
        Dim xdoc As XDocument = XDocument.Load("C:\hamlet.xml")

        Dim xe As XElement = New XElement("PERSONA", _
```

```
                    "Bill Evjen, king of Denmark")

        xdoc.Element("PLAY").Element("PERSONAE").Add(xe)

        Dim query = From people In xdoc.Descendants("PERSONA") _
                    Select people.Value

        Console.WriteLine("{0} Players Found", query.Count())
        Console.WriteLine()

        For Each item In query
            Console.WriteLine(item)
        Next

        Console.ReadLine()
    End Sub

End Module
```

In this case, an XElement document called xe is created. The construction of xe gives you the following XML output:

```
<PERSONA>Bill Evjen, king of Denmark</PERSONA>
```

Then, using the Element().Add method from the XDocument object, you are able to add the created element:

```
xdoc.Element("PLAY").Element("PERSONAE").Add(xe)
```

Next, querying all the players, you will now find that instead of 26, as before, you now have 27, with the new one at the bottom of the list. Besides Add, you can also use AddFirst, which does just that — adds the player to the beginning of the list instead of the end, as is the default.

Using LINQ to SQL with LINQ to XML

When working with LINQ to SQL or LINQ to XML, you are limited to working with the specific data source for which it was designed. In fact, you are able to mix multiple data sources together when working with LINQ. To demonstrate this, this section uses LINQ to SQL to query the customers in the Northwind database and turn the results pulled into an XML document.

Instructions for getting the Northwind sample database file as well as information on working with LINQ to SQL are found earlier in this chapter.

Setting Up the LINQ to SQL Components

If you don't already have it, add the Northwind SQL Server Express Edition database file to your project. From there, right-click on the project to add a new LINQ to SQL class file to your project. Name the file Northwind.dbml.

This operation gives you a design surface to work with. From the Server Explorer, drag and drop both the Customers and the Orders tables onto the design surface. This action establishes a relationship between these two tables. At this point, your view in the IDE should look similar to what is shown in Figure 11-17.

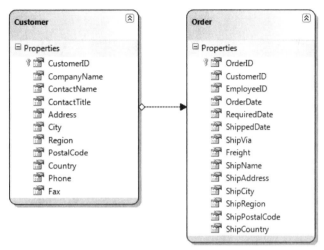

Figure 11-17

Now that you have your Northwind.dbml in place, you are ready to query this database structure and output the results as an XML file.

Querying the Database and Outputting XML

The next step in your console application is to put the following code in your Module1.vb file:

```vb
Module Module1

    Sub Main()
        Dim dc As NorthwindDataContext = New NorthwindDataContext()

        Dim xe As XElement = New XElement("Customer", _
            From c In dc.Customers _
            Select New XElement("Customer", _
                New XElement("CustomerId", c.CustomerID), _
                New XElement("CompanyName", c.CompanyName), _
                New XElement("Country", c.Country), _
                New XElement("OrderNum", c.Orders.Count)))

        xe.Save("C:\myCustomers.xml")
        Console.WriteLine("File created")

        Console.ReadLine()
    End Sub

End Module
```

This example creates a new instance of the `NorthwindDataContext` object, which is created for you automatically with the LINQ to SQL class you created. Then, instead of using the typical

```
Dim query = [query]
```

you populate the query performed in an `XElement` object called `xe`. Within the `select` statement of the query, you also create an iteration of `Customers` objects with the nested elements of `<Customer>`, `<CustomerId>`, `<CompanyName>`, `<Country>`, and `<OrderNum>`. Once queried, the `xe` instance is then saved to disk using `xe.Save`. On disk, looking at the `myCustomers.xml` file, you will see the following results (abbreviated here):

```xml
<?xml version="1.0" encoding="utf-8"?>
<Customer>
  <Customer>
    <CustomerId>ALFKI</CustomerId>
    <CompanyName>Alfreds Futterkiste</CompanyName>
    <Country>Germany</Country>
    <OrderNum>6</OrderNum>
  </Customer>
  <Customer>
    <CustomerId>ANATR</CustomerId>
    <CompanyName>Ana Trujillo Emparedados y helados</CompanyName>
    <Country>Mexico</Country>
    <OrderNum>4</OrderNum>
  </Customer>

  <!-- XML removed for clarity -->

  <Customer>
    <CustomerId>WILMK</CustomerId>
    <CompanyName>Wilman Kala</CompanyName>
    <Country>Finland</Country>
    <OrderNum>7</OrderNum>
  </Customer>
  <Customer>
    <CustomerId>WOLZA</CustomerId>
    <CompanyName>Wolski  Zajazd</CompanyName>
    <Country>Poland</Country>
    <OrderNum>7</OrderNum>
  </Customer>
</Customer>
```

From this, you can see just how easy it is to mix the two data sources using LINQ. Using LINQ to SQL, the customers were pulled from the database, and then using LINQ to XML, an XML file was created and output to disk.

Summary

One of the most exciting features of the .NET Framework 3.5 release is the LINQ capabilities that the platform provides. This chapter focused on using LINQ to SQL and some of the options available to you in querying your SQL Server databases.

Using LINQ to SQL, you are able to have a strongly typed set of operations for performing CRUD operations against your database. In addition, though, you are still able to use pre-existing access capabilities, whether that is interacting with ADO.NET or working with your stored procedures. For example, you can still use your `XmlReader` and `XmlWriter` code along with the new LINQ to XML capabilities.

This chapter also described how to use LINQ to XML and some of the options available to you in reading and writing from XML files and XML sources, whether the source is static or dynamic.

You were also introduced to the new LINQ to XML helper objects `XDocument`, `XElement`, `XNamespace`, `XAttribute`, and `XComment`. These outstanding new objects make working with XML easier than ever before.

12

Security in the .NET Framework

This chapter covers the basics of security and cryptography. It begins with a brief discussion of the .NET Framework's security architecture, because this affects all the solutions you may choose to implement.

The .NET Framework provides you with additional tools and functionality with regard to security. You now have the `System.Security.Permissions` namespace, which enables you to control code access permissions along with role-based and identity permissions. Through your code, you can control access to objects programmatically, as well as receive information on the current permissions of objects. This security framework will assist you in determining whether you have permissions to run your code, instead of getting halfway through execution and having to deal with permission-based exceptions. This chapter covers the following:

❑ Concepts and definitions

❑ Permissions

❑ Roles

❑ Principals

❑ Code access permissions

❑ Role-based permissions

❑ Identity permissions

❑ Managing permissions and policies

❑ Cryptography

Cryptography is the cornerstone of the .NET Web Services security model, so the second half of this chapter discusses the basis of cryptography and how to implement it. Specifically, it covers the following:

- ❏ Hash algorithms
- ❏ SHA
- ❏ MD5
- ❏ Secret key encryption
- ❏ Public key cryptography standard
- ❏ Digital signatures
- ❏ Certification
- ❏ Secure Sockets Layer communications

Let's begin by looking at some security concepts and definitions.

> **As always, the code for this chapter is available for download from www.wrox.com, which you may want in order to follow along.**

Security Concepts and Definitions

The following table describes the different types of security presented in this chapter and how they relate to real-world scenarios:

Security Type	Related Concept in Security.Permissions Namespace or Utility	Purpose
NTFS	None	Allows for detailing of object rights, e.g., locking down of specific files
Security Policies	`Caspol.exe` utility, `PermView.exe` utility	Set up overall security policy for a machine or user from an operating-system level
Cryptographic	Strong name and assembly, generation, `SignCode.exe` utility	Use of public key infrastructure and certificates
Programmatic	Groups and permission sets	For use in pieces of code that are being called into. Provides extra security to prevent users of calling code from violating security measures implemented by the programs that are not provided for on a machine level.

There are many approaches to providing security on your machines where your shared code is hosted. If multiple shared code applications are on one machine, each piece of shared code can be called from many front-end applications. Each piece of shared code will have its own security requirements for accessing environment variables — such as the registry, the file system, and other items — on the machine that it is running on. From an NTFS perspective, the administrator of your server can only lock down those items on the machine that are not required to be accessed from any piece of shared code running on it. Therefore, some applications need additional security built in to prevent any calling code from doing things it is not supposed to do.

The machine administrator can further assist programmers by using the utilities provided with .NET to establish additional machine and/or user policies that programs can implement. Toward that end, the .NET environment provides programmatic security through code access security, role-based security, and identity security. As a final security measure, you can use the cryptographic methods provided to require the use of certificates in order to execute your code.

Security in the .NET infrastructure uses some basic concepts, which are discussed here. Code security is managed and accessed in the .NET environment using security policies. Security policies have a relationship that is fundamentally tied either to the machine that the code is running on or to particular users under whose context the code is running. To this end, any modifications to the policy are done either at the machine level or at the user level.

You establish the security policy on a given set of code by associating it with an entity called a *group*. A group is created and managed within each of the machine- and user-based policies. These group classifications are set up so that you can place code into categories. You want to establish new code groups when you are ready to categorize the pieces of code that would run on a machine, and assign the permissions that users will have to access the code. For instance, if you wanted to group all Internet applications and then group all non-Internet applications, you would establish two groups and associate each of your applications with its respective group.

Once you have the code separated into groups, you can define different permission sets for each group. If you wanted to limit your Internet applications' access to the local file system, you could create a permission set that limits that access and associates the Internet application group with the new permission set. By default, the .NET environment provides one code group named `All Code` that is associated with the `FullTrust` permission set.

Permission sets are unique combinations of security configurations that determine what each user with access to a machine can do on that machine. Each set determines what a user has access to — for instance, whether the user can read environment variables, the file system, or execute other portions of code. Permission sets are maintained at the machine and user levels through the utility `Caspol.exe`. Through this utility, you can create your own permission sets, though the following seven permission sets that ship with the .NET infrastructure are also useful:

Permission Set	Explanation
FullTrust	Allows full access to all resources; adds the assembly to a special list that has `FullTrust` access
Everything	Allows full access to everything covered by default named permission sets, but differs from `FullTrust` in that the group is not added to the `FullTrust` assembly list
Nothing	Denies all access including `Execution`

Permission Set	Explanation
Execution	Allows execution-only access
SkipVerification	Allows objects to bypass all security verification
Internet	Grants default rights that are normal for Internet applications
LocalInternet	Grants rights that are not as restricted as Internet, but not full trust

Security that is used within the programming environment also makes use of permission sets. Through code you can control access to files in a file system, environment variables, file dialogs, isolated storage, reflections, registry, sockets, and UI. Isolated storage and virtual file systems are new operating system–level storage locations that can be used by programs and are governed by the machine security policies. These file systems keep a machine safe from file system intrusion by designating a regulated area for file storage. The main access to these items is controlled through code access permissions.

Although many methods that we use in Visual Basic 2008 provide an identifiable return value, the only time we get a return value from security methods is when the method fails. When a security method succeeds, it does not provide a return value. If it fails, then it returns an exception object reflecting the specific error that occurred.

Permissions in the System.Security .Permissions Namespace

The System.Security.Permissions namespace is the namespace used in the code to establish and use permissions to access many things, such as the file system, environment variables, and the registry within your programs. The namespace controls access to both operating system–level objects as well as code objects. In order to use the namespace in your project, you need to include the Imports System.Security.Permissions line with any of your other Imports statements in your project. Using this namespace gives you access to the CodeAccessPermission and PrincipalPermission classes for using role-based permissions and utilizing information supplied by Identity permissions. CodeAccessPermission is the main class that we will use, as it controls access to the operating system –level objects our code needs in order to function. Role-based permissions and Identity permissions grant access to objects based on the identity of the user of the program that is running (the user context).

In the following table, classes that end with Attribute, such as EnvironmentPermissionAttribute, are classes that enable you to modify the security level at which your code is allowed to interact with each respective object. The attributes that you can specify reflect Assert, Deny, or PermitOnly permissions.

If permissions carry the Assert attribute, you have full access to the object, whereas if you have specified Deny permissions, you are not allowed to access the object through your code. If you have PermitOnly access, only objects within your program's already determined scope can be accessed, and you cannot add any more resources beyond that scope. The table also deals with security in regard to software publishers. A *software publisher* is a specific entity that is using a digital signature to identify itself in a

Web-based application. The following table describes the namespace members that apply to Windows Forms programming, with an explanation of each:

Class	Description
CodeAccessSecurityAttribute	Specifies security access to objects such as the registry and file system
EnvironmentPermission	Controls the capability to see and modify system and user environment variables
EnvironmentPermissionAttribute	Allows security actions for environment variables to be added via code
FileDialogPermission	Controls the capability to open files via a file dialog
FileDialogPermissionAttribute	Allows security actions to be added for file dialogs via code
FileIOPermission	Controls the capability to read and write files in the file system
FileIOPermissionAttribute	Allows security actions to be added for file access attempts via code
GacIdentityPermission	Defines the identity permissions for files that come from the global assembly cache (GAC)
GacIdentityPermissionAttribute	Allows security actions to be added for files that originate from the GAC
HostProtectionAttribute	Allows for the use of security actions to determine host protection requirements
IsolatedStorageFilePermission	Controls access to a private virtual file system within the isolated storage area of an application
IsolatedStorageFilePermission Attribute	Allows security actions to be added for private virtual file systems via code
IsolatedStoragePermission	Controls access to the isolated storage area of an application
IsolatedStoragePermission Attribute	Allows security actions to be added for the isolated storage area of an application
KeyContainerPermission	Controls access to key containers
KeyContainerPermissionAccess Entry	Defines the access rights for particular key containers
KeyContainerPermissionAccess EntryCollection	Represents a collection of KeyContainerPermission-AccessEntry objects
KeyContainerPermissionAccess EntryEnumerator	Represents the enumerators for the objects contained in the KeyContainerPermissionAccessEntryCollection object
KeyContainerPermissionAttribute	Allows security actions to be added for key containers
PermissionSetAttribute	Allows security actions to be added for a permission set

Class	Description
PrincipalPermission	Controls the capability to make checks against an active principal
PrincipalPermissionAttribute	Allows checking against a specific user. Security principals are a user and role combination used to establish security identity.
PublisherIdentityPermission	Allows access based on the identity of a software publisher
PublisherIdentityPermissionAttribute	Allows security actions to be added for a software publisher
ReflectionPermission	Controls access to nonpublic members of a given type
ReflectionPermissionAttribute	Allows security actions to be added for public and nonpublic members of a given type
RegistryPermission	Controls access to registry keys and values
RegistryPermissionAttribute	Allows security actions to be added for registry keys and values
ResourcePermissionBase	Controls the capability to work with the code access security permissions
ResourcePermissionBaseEntry	Allows you to define the smallest part of a code access security permission set
SecurityAttribute	Controls which security attributes are representing code; used to control security when creating an assembly
SecurityPermission	The set of security permission flags for use by .NET; this collection is used when you want to specify a permission flag in your code
SecurityPermissionAttribute	Allows security actions for the security permission flags
StorePermission	Controls access to stores that contain X509 certificates
StorePermissionAttribute	Allows security actions to be added for access stores that contain X509 certificates
UIPermission	Controls access to user interfaces and use of the Windows clipboard
UIPermissionAttribute	Allows security actions to be added for UI interfaces and the use of the clipboard

Code Access Permissions

Code access permissions are controlled through the CodeAccessPermission class within the System .Security namespace, and its members make up the majority of the permissions we'll use in our attempt to secure our code and operating environment. The following table describes the class methods available:

Method	Description
Assert	Sets the permission to full access so that the specific resource can be accessed even if the caller hasn't been granted permission to access the resource
Copy	Copies a permission object
Demand	Returns whether or not all callers in the call chain have been granted the permission to access the resource in a given manner
Deny	Denies all callers access to the resource
Equals	Determines whether a given object is the same instance of the current object
FromXml	Establishes a permission set given a specific XML encoding. This parameter is an XML encoding
GetHashCode	Returns a hash code associated with a given object
GetType	Returns the type of a given object
Intersect	Returns the permissions that two permission objects have in common
IsSubsetOf	Returns a result indicating whether the current permission object is a subset of a specified permission
PermitOnly	Specifies that only those resources within this permission object can be accessed even if code has been granted permission to other objects
RevertAll	Reverses all previous assert, deny or permit-only methods
RevertAssert	Reverses all previous assert methods
RevertDeny	Reverses all previous deny methods
RevertPermitOnly	Reverses all previous permit-only methods
ToString	Returns a string representation of the current permission object
ToXml	Creates an XML representation of the current permission object
Union	Creates a permission that is the union of two permission objects

Role-Based Permissions

Role-based permissions are permissions granted based on the user and the role that code is being called with. Users are generally authenticated within the operating system platform and hold a Security Identifier (SID) that is associated within a security context. The SID can further be associated with a role or a group membership that is established within a security context. The .NET role functionality supports those users and roles associated within a security context and has support for generic and custom users and roles through the concept of principals.

A *principal* is an object that holds the current caller credentials, which is termed the identity of the user. Principals come in two types: Windows principals and non-Windows principals. Windows-based principal objects are objects that store the Windows SID information regarding the current user context associated with the code that is calling into the module role-based permissions that are being used. Non-Windows principals are principal objects that are created programmatically via a custom login methodology and which are made available to the current thread.

Role-based permissions are not set against objects within your environment like code access permissions. They are instead a permission that is checked within the context of the current user and role that a user is part of. Within the System.Security.Permissions namespace, the concepts of principals and the PrincipalPermission class of objects are used to establish and check permissions. If a programmer passes the user and role information during a call as captured from a custom login, then the PrincipalPermission class can be used to verify this information as well. During the verification, if the user and role information is Null, then permission is granted, regardless of the user and role. The PrincipalPermission class does not grant access to objects, but has methods that determine whether a caller has been given permissions according to the current permission object through the Demand method. If a security exception is generated, then the user does not have sufficient permission.

The following table describes the methods in the PrincipalPermission class:

Method	Description
Copy	Copies a permission object
Demand	Returns whether or not all callers in the call chain have been granted the permission to access the resource in a given manner
Equals	Determines whether a given object is the same instance of the current object
FromXml	Establishes a permission set given a specific XML encoding
GetHashCode	Returns a hash code associated with a given object
GetType	Returns the type of a given object
Intersect	Returns the permissions that two permission objects have in common specified in the parameter
IsSubsetOf	Returns a result indicating whether the current permission object is a subset of a specified permission
IsUnrestricted	Returns a result indicating whether the current permission object is unrestricted
ToString	Returns a string representation of the current permission object
ToXml	Creates an XML representation of the current permission object
Union	Creates a permission that is the union of two permission objects

As an example of how you might use these methods, the following code snippet captures the current Windows principal information and displays it on the screen in the form of message box output. Each element of the principal information could be used in a program to validate against, and thus restrict, code execution based on the values in the principal information. This example inserts an Imports System.Security.Pri ncipal line at the top of the module so you can use the identity and principal objects:

```
Imports System.Security.Principal
Imports System.Security.Permissions

Private Sub RoleBasedPermissions_Click(ByVal sender As System.Object, _
    ByVal e As System.EventArgs) Handles RoleBasedPermissions.Click

    Dim objIdentity As WindowsIdentity = WindowsIdentity.GetCurrent
    Dim objPrincipal As New WindowsPrincipal(objIdentity)
    MessageBox.Show(objPrincipal.Identity.IsAuthenticated.ToString())
    MessageBox.Show(objIdentity.IsGuest.ToString())
    MessageBox.Show(objIdentity.ToString())
    objIdentity = Nothing
    objPrincipal = Nothing

End Sub
```

This code illustrates a few of the properties that could be used to validate against when a caller wants to run your code. Sometimes you want to ensure that the caller is an authenticated user, and not someone who bypassed the security of your machine with custom login information. You can achieve that through the following line of code:

```
MessageBox.Show(objPrincipal.Identity.IsAuthenticated.ToString())
```

It outputs in the MessageBox as either True or False depending on whether the user is authenticated or not. Another way to ensure that your caller is not bypassing system security would be to check whether the account is operating as a guest. The following line of code accomplishes that:

```
MessageBox.Show(objIdentity.IsGuest.ToString())
```

IsGuest returns either True or False, depending on whether the caller is authenticated as a guest. The final MessageBox in the example displays the ToString value for the identity object. This value tells you what type of identity it is, either a Windows identity or a non-Windows identity. The line of code that executes it is as follows:

```
MessageBox.Show(objIdentity.ToString())
```

The output from the IsString method is shown in Figure 12-1.

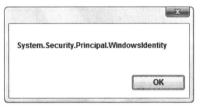

Figure 12-1

Again, the principal and identity objects are used in verifying the identity or aspects of the identity of the caller attempting to execute your code. Based on this information, you can lock down or release certain system resources. You will learn how to lock down and release system resources through the code access permissions examples that follow.

Identity Permissions

Identity permissions are pieces of information, also called *evidence*, by which a piece of code can be identified. Examples of the evidence would be the strong name of the assembly or the digital signature associated with the assembly.

> *A strong name is a combination of the name of a program, its version number, and its associated cryptographic key and digital signature files.*

Identity permissions are granted by the runtime based on information received from the trusted host, or someone who has permission to provide the information. Therefore, they are permissions that you don't specifically request. Identity permissions provide additional information to be used by the runtime when you configure items in the Caspol.exe utility. The additional information that the trusted host can supply includes the digital signature, the application directory, or the strong name of the assembly.

Managing Code Access Permissions

This section looks at the most common type of permissions — programmatic access — and how they are used. This example uses a Windows Form with four buttons on it. This Windows Form illustrates the concept previously mentioned — namely, that when a method fails, an exception object containing your feedback is generated. Note that in the case of a real-world example, you would be setting up permissions for a calling application. In many instances, you don't want a calling application to be able to access the registry, or you want a calling application to be able to read memory variables, but not change them.

However, in order to demonstrate the syntax of the commands, in the examples that follow we have placed the attempts against the objects we have secured in the same module. We first set up the permission that we want and grant the code the appropriate access level we wish it to be able to utilize. Then we use code that accesses our security object to illustrate the effect that our permissions have on the code that accesses the objects. We'll also be tying together many of the concepts discussed so far by way of these examples.

To begin, let's look at an example of trying to access a file in the file system, which illustrates the use of the FileIOPermission class in our Permissions namespace. In the first example, the file C:\testsecurity \testing.txt has been secured at the operating system level so that no one can access it. In order to do this, the system administrator sets the operating system security on the file to no access:

```
Imports System.Security.Principal
Imports System.Security.Permissions
Imports System.IO

Private Sub FileIO_Click(ByVal sender As System.Object, _
    ByVal e As System.EventArgs) Handles FileIO.Click

    Dim oFp As FileIOPermission = New _
        FileIOPermission(FileIOPermissionAccess.Write, _
```

```
        "C:\testsecurity\testing.txt")

    oFp.Assert()

    Try
        Dim objWriter As New IO.StreamWriter _
          (File.Open("C:\testsecurity\testing.txt", IO.FileMode.Open))
        objWriter.WriteLine("Hi there!")
        objWriter.Flush()
        objWriter.Close()
        objWriter = Nothing
    Catch objA As System.Exception
        MessageBox.Show(objA.Message)
    End Try

End Sub
```

Let's walk through the code. In this example, we are going to attempt to open a file in the
`C:\testsecurity` directory called `testing.txt`. We set the file access permissions within our code so
that the method, irrespective of who called it, should be able to get to it with the following lines:

```
Dim oFp As FileIOPermission = New _
    FileIOPermission(FileIOPermissionAccess.Write, _
    "C:\testsecurity\testing.txt")

oFp.Assert()
```

This example used the `Assert` method, which declares that the resource should be accessible even if
the caller has not been granted permission to access the resource. However, in this case, because the
file is secured at the operating system level (by the system administrator), we get the error shown in
Figure 12-2, which was caught by exception handling.

Access to the path 'C:\TestSecurity\testing.txt' is denied.

OK

Figure 12-2

Now let's look at that example again with full operating system rights, but the code permissions
set to `Deny`:

```
Protected Sub btnFileIO_Click(ByVal sender As Object, ByVal e As System.EventArgs)

    Dim oFp As FileIOPermission = New _
        FileIOPermission(FileIOPermissionAccess.Write, _
            "C:\testsecurity\testing.txt")

    oFp.Deny()
```

```
Try
  Dim objWriter As New IO.StreamWriter _
      (File.Open("C:\testsecurity\testing.txt", _
      IO.FileMode.Open))
  objwriter.WriteLine("Hi There!")
  objWriter.Flush()
  objWriter.Close()
  objWriter = Nothing

Catch objA As System.Exception
  messagebox.Show(objA.Message)

End Try

End Sub
```

The Deny method denies all callers access to the object, regardless of whether the operating system granted them permission. This is usually a good thing to put into place, as not every method you implement needs full and unfettered access to system resources. This helps prevent accidental security vulnerabilities that your method may expose. With the Deny method, we catch the error shown in Figure 12-3 in the exception handler.

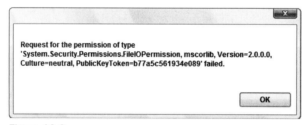

Figure 12-3

As you can see, this error differs from the first by reflecting a System.Security.Permissions .FileIOPermission failure, as opposed to an OS-level exception.

The following example shows how you would use the EnvironmentPermission class of the namespace to look at EnvironmentVariables:

```
Protected Sub TestEnvironmentPermissions_Click _
    (ByVal sender As Object, ByVal e As System.EventArgs) _
    Handles TestEnvironmentPermissions.Click

  Dim oEp As EnvironmentPermission = New EnvironmentPermission _
      (EnvironmentPermissionAccess.Read, "Temp")

  Dim sEv As String
  oEp.Assert()

  Try
      sEv = Environment.GetEnvironmentVariable("Temp")
```

```
            MessageBox.Show("Assert was a success")
        Catch objA As System.Exception
            MessageBox.Show("Assert failed")
        End Try

        System.Security.CodeAccessPermission.RevertAssert()
        oEp.Deny()

        Try
            sEv = Environment.GetEnvironmentVariable("Temp")
            MessageBox.Show("Deny was a success")
        Catch objA As System.Exception
            MessageBox.Show("Deny failed")
        End Try

        MessageBox.Show(oEp.ToString)

    End Sub
```

There is a lot going on in this example, so consider it carefully. We first establish an environment variable permission and use the `Assert` method to ensure access to the code that follows:

```
Dim oEp As EnvironmentPermission = New EnvironmentPermission _
    (EnvironmentPermissionAccess.Read, "Temp")

Dim sEv As String
oEp.Assert()
```

We then try to read the environment variable into a string. If the string read succeeds, then we pop up a message box to reflect the success. If the read fails, then a message box reflects the failure:

```
Try
    sEv = Environment.GetEnvironmentVariable("Temp")
    MessageBox.Show("Assert was a success")
Catch objA As System.Exception
    MessageBox.Show("Assert failed")
End Try
```

Next, we revoke the assert we previously issued by using the `RevertAssert` method, and establish `Deny` permissions:

```
System.Security.CodeAccessPermission.RevertAssert()
oEp.Deny()
```

We then try again to read the variable, and write the appropriate result to a message box:

```
Try
    sEv = Environment.GetEnvironmentVariable("Temp")
    MessageBox.Show("Deny failed")
Catch objA As System.Exception
    MessageBox.Show("Deny was a success")
End Try
```

Finally, we write the `ToString` of the method to another message box. Following is the output of all three message boxes as a result of running this subroutine. The first two message box messages give us the feedback from our `Assert` and `Deny` code, followed by the output of our `ToString` method:

```
Assert was a success

Deny failed

<IPermission class="System.Security.Permissions.EnvironmentPermission, mscorlib,
  Version=2.0.0.0, Culture=neutral, PublicKeyToken=b77a5c561934e089"
  version="1" Read="Temp" />
```

The `ToString` method is an XML representation of the permission object currently in effect. The first and second message boxes that are output reflect the system version information of the Visual Basic security environment that was running at the time the button was clicked. The third message box is the environment variable name surrounded by the `Read` tags, which was the permission in effect when the `ToString` method was executed.

Look at one more example of where the permissions would affect you in your program functionality, that of accessing the registry. You would generally access the registry on the computer that was the central server for a component in your Windows Forms application.

When you use the `EventLog` methods to create entries in the machine Event Logs, you access the registry. To illustrate this concept, the following code example denies permissions to the registry:

```
Protected Sub TestRegistryPermissions_Click(ByVal sender As Object, _
                                            ByVal e As System.EventArgs) _
                                            Handles TestRegistryPermissions.Click

    Dim oRp As New _
        RegistryPermission(Security.Permissions.PermissionState.Unrestricted)
    oRp.Deny()

    Dim objLog As New EventLog
    Dim objLogEntryType As EventLogEntryType

    Try
        Throw (New EntryPointNotFoundException)
    Catch objA As System.EntryPointNotFoundException
        Try
            If Not System.Diagnostics.EventLog.SourceExists("Example") Then
                System.Diagnostics.EventLog.CreateEventSource("Example", "System")
            End If

            objLog.Source = "Example"
            objLog.Log = "System"
            objLogEntryType = EventLogEntryType.Information
            objLog.WriteEntry("Error: " & objA.message, objLogEntryType)
        Catch objB As System.Exception
            MessageBox.Show(objB.Message)
```

```
        End Try
    End Try

End Sub
```

Walking through the code, you begin by specifying the registry permission, setting it to Deny access:

```
Dim oRp As New _
    RegistryPermission(Security.Permissions.PermissionState.Unrestricted)
oRp.Deny()
```

Next, you Throw an exception on purpose in order to set up writing to an Event Log:

```
Throw (New EntryPointNotFoundException)
```

When the exception is caught, it checks the registry to ensure that a specific type of registry entry source already exists:

```
If Not System.Diagnostics.EventLog.SourceExists("Example") Then
    System.Diagnostics.EventLog.CreateEventSource("Example", "System")
End If
```

At this point, the code fails with the error message shown in Figure 12-4.

Figure 12-4

These examples can serve as a good basis for use in developing classes that access the other objects within the scope of the Permissions namespace, such as reflections and UI permissions.

Managing Security Policy

As stated in the introduction to the chapter, two command-line utilities (Caspol.exe and Permview.exe) help in configuring and viewing security policy at both machine and user levels. When you manage security policy at these levels, you are doing so as an administrator of a machine or user policy for a machine that is hosting code that will be called from other front-end applications. Caspol.exe is a command-line utility with many options for configuring your security policies (Caspol stands for Code Access Security Policy). User and machine policy are associated with groups and permission sets. One group is automatically provided, the AllCode group.

The `Caspol` utility has two categories of commands. The first category listed in the following table is the set of commands that provide feedback about the current security policy:

Command	Short Command	Parameters	Effect
-List	-l		
None	This lists the combination of available groups and permission sets.	-ListGroups	-lg
None	This lists only groups.	-ListPset	-lp
None	This lists only permission sets.	-ListFulltrust	-lf
None	This lists only assemblies that have full trust privileges.	-List Description	-ld
None	This lists code group names and descriptions.	-Reset	-rs
None	This resets the machine and user policies to the default for .NET. This is handy if a policy creates a condition that is not recoverable. Use this command carefully, as you will lose all changes made to the current policies.		
--ResolveGroup	-rsg	Assembly File	This lists which groups are associated with a given assembly file.
--ResolvePerm	-rsp	Assembly File	This lists what permission sets are associated with a given assembly file.

This is not the list in its entirety, but some of the more important commands. Now let's look at some examples of output from these commands. If you wanted to list the groups active on your local machine at the Visual Studio command prompt, you would type the following:

```
Caspol -Machine -ListGroups
```

The output looks similar to what is shown in Figure 12-5 (it varies slightly depending on the machine you are working on).

Looking at the output in a bit more detail, you can see some things in addition to what was specifically requested. The fourth line shows that code access security checking is ON. On the following line, the machine is checking for the user's right to execute the Caspol utility, as execution checking is ON. The policy change prompt is also ON, so if the user executes a Caspol command that changes system policy, then a confirmation prompt appears to verify that this is really intentional.

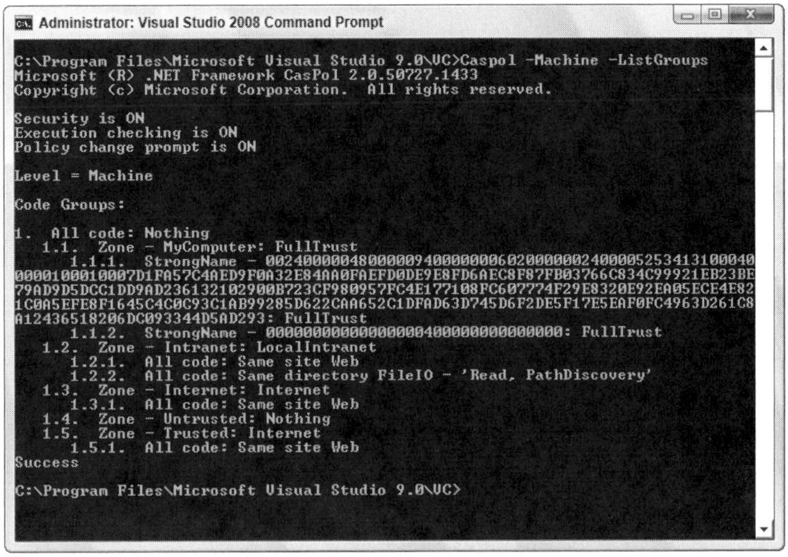

Figure 12-5

The level is also listed on the screen prior to the requested output, which is detailed at the bottom, listing the groups present on the machine. The policies pertain to two levels: the machine and the user. When changing policy, if the user is not an administrator, then the user policy is affected unless the user specifically applies the policy to the machine through use of the -machine switch, as illustrated in the screen shot. If the user is an administrator, then the machine policy is affected unless the user specifically applies the policy to the user level through the use of the -user switch.

Let's now look at another request result example. This time we ask for a listing of all of the permission sets on the machine. At the command prompt, you would type the following:

```
Caspol -machine -listpset
```

This would result in output similar to what is shown in Figure 12-6. The following output has been shortened for space considerations, but it contains a listing of all the code explicitly set to execute against the seven permission sets mentioned in the definitions section. In addition, note that the output is an XML representation of a permission object. The listing details the named permission sets and what each one has as active rights. For instance, the fifth permission set is named LocalIntranet, while the next lines detail the Permission class, an environment permission with read access to the environment variable - USERNAME. The next class detail is regarding FileDialogpermissions, and it lists those as being unrestricted. The output then goes on to detail the effective settings for IsolatedStorage and others.

Figure 12-6

Now consider the second category of commands that go with the `Caspol` utility, shown in the following table. These are the commands that we will use to actually modify policy:

Command	Short Command	Parameters	Effect
-AddFullTrust	-af	Assembly File Name	Adds a given Assembly file to the full trust permission set
-AddGroup	-ag	Parent Label, Membership, Permission Set Name	Adds a code group to the code group hierarchy
-AddPSet	-ap	Permission Set Path, Permission Set Name	Adds a new named permission set to the policy; the permission set should be an XML file
-ChgGroup	-cg	Membership, Permission Set Name	Changes a code group's information
-ChgPset	-cp	File Name, Permission Set Name	Changes a named permission set's information

Command	Short Command	Parameters	Effect
-Force	-f		This option is not recommended. It forces Caspol to accept policy changes even if the change could prevent Caspol itself from being executed.
-Recover	-r		Recovers policy information from a backup file controlled by the utility
-RemFullTrust	-rf	Assembly File Name	Removes a given Assembly file from the full trust permission set
-RemGroup	-rg	Label	Removes a code group
-RemPSet	-rp	Permission Set Name	Removes a permission set. The seven default sets cannot be removed.

As before, this is not a comprehensive list of all the available commands, so consult the MSDN documentation for the complete listing if needed. Let's begin our discussion of these commands with a few more definitions that help clarify the parameters associated with them. An assembly file is created within Visual Basic each time you do a build whereby your version is a release version. An assembly needs to have a strong name associated with it in order to be used in your permissions groupings. It gets a strong name from being associated with a digital signature uniquely identifying the assembly. You carry out this association by right-clicking on your solution within Visual Studio 2008 and selecting Properties from the provided menu. From the available tabs in the Properties dialog, select Signing. Within this page of the Properties dialog, check the "Sign the assembly" check box. You will then need to either choose an already created strong name key file or create a new one. For this example, create a new one (by selecting the New option from the drop-down list). You will then be provided with the dialog shown in Figure 12-7. You will also want to fill out the Create Strong Name Key dialog as shown (though with your own password).

Figure 12-7

After selecting OK in this dialog, you will see a new file in your Solution Explorer called myKey.pfx, as shown in Figure 12-8.

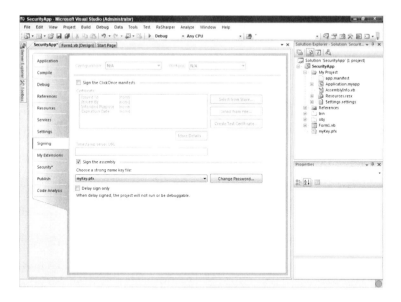

Figure 12-8

During the build, Visual Studio generates the strong name, after which you can add your assembly to your security configuration. Place the executable, SecurityApp.exe (your executable will be the name of your project), which was created from the build, into the C:\testsecurity directory on the local machine for use with the policy method illustrations.

If you wanted to add your assembly to the fulltrust permission set, you would type **Caspol - addfulltrust C:\testsecurity\SecurityApp.exe**.

Figure 12-9 shows the outcome of the command.

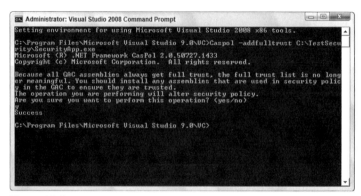

Figure 12-9

Before your command alters your security policy, you are notified that your DLLs can just be placed within the GAC as well to get full trust for them. By typing "**y**" and then pressing Enter, the new application will then be added to the `fulltrust` assembly list. You can confirm it was added by issuing the following command:

```
Caspol -listfulltrust
```

An excerpt of output from the command that includes the new assembly would look like what is shown in Figure 12-10.

Figure 12-10

This shows the application name, version, and key information associated with the `.exe` file when the build was performed. Now let's look at the creation and addition of a permission set to the permission sets in the security policy. Permission sets can be created by hand in any text editor, in an XML format and saved as an `.xml` file (this example saves it as `SecurityExample.xml`). Following is a listing from one such file that was created for this example:

```xml
<PermissionSet class="System.Security.NamedPermissionSet" version="1">
    <Permission class="System.Security.Permissions.FileIOPermission, mscorlib,
            SN=03689116d3a4ae33" version="1">
        <Read> C:\TestSecurity </Read>
```

```
  </Permission>
  <Permission class="System.Security.Permissions.EnvironmentPermission,
          mscorlib, SN=03689116d3a4ae33" version="1">
    <Read> [TEMP] </Read>
  </Permission>
  <Name>SecurityExample</Name>
  <Description>Gives Full File Access</Description>
</PermissionSet>
```

The listing has multiple permissions within the permission set. The listing sets up read file permissions within one set of tags:

```
<Permission class="System.Security.Permissions.FileIOPermission, mscorlib,
        SN=03689116d3a4ae33" version="1">
  <Read> C:\TestSecurity </Read>
</Permission>
```

You then set up read access to the Temp environment variable in the second set of permission tags:

```
<Permission class="System.Security.Permissions.EnvironmentPermission,
        mscorlib, SN=03689116d3a4ae33" version="1">
  <Read> [TEMP] </Read>
</Permission>
```

The listing also gives the custom permission set the name of SecurityExample, with a description:

```
<Name>SecurityExample</Name>
<Description>Gives Full File Access</Description>
```

When you want to add your permission set to your policy, you would type the following command:

```
Caspol -addpset C:\testsecurity\securityexample.xml securityexample
```

The last command issues the -addpset flag to indicate that you want to add a permission set, followed by the XML file containing the permission set, followed finally by the name of the permission set. Figure 12-11 shows the outcome of your command.

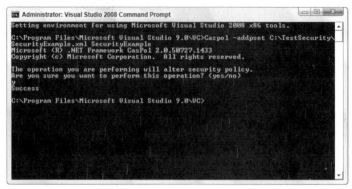

Figure 12-11

You can then list your security permission sets by typing **Caspol -listpset**. Figure 12-12 shows the excerpt of the new security permission set.

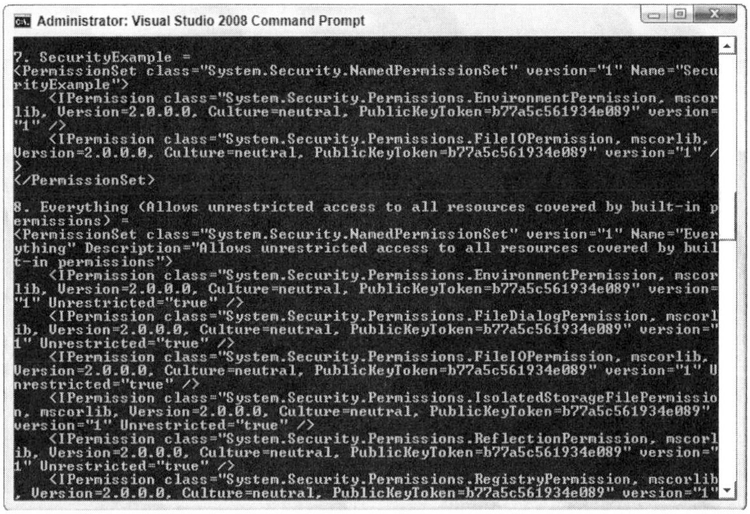

Figure 12-12

This lists just the permission sets within your policy. The named permission set `SecurityExample` shows up under the `Named Permission Sets` heading, and its description is listed just after its name.

Once you have a permission set, you can add a group that your assembly object fits into and which enforces the new permission set. You add this group by using the `AddGroup` switch in `Caspol`. The `AddGroup` switch has a couple of parameters that need more explanation. The first parameter is `parent_label`. As shown in Figure 12-13, the `All` code group has a "1" before it. The labels within code groups have a hierarchy that is established when you add groups, so you need to specify what your parent label would be. In this case, because the only one that exists is "1," that is what you designate.

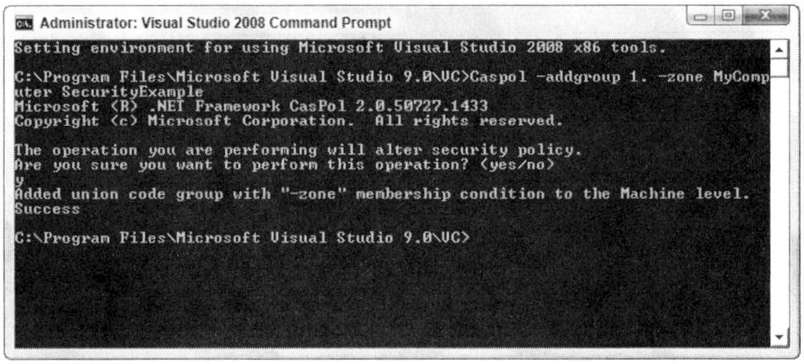

Figure 12-13

Because you designate 1, the new group becomes a child of 1. The second parameter is `membership`. The `membership` parameter has a certain list of options that you can add based on the following table.

Each option designates a piece of information you are providing about the code you will add to your group. For instance, you might state that you will only be adding code that has a specific signature with the -Pub option, or only code in a certain application directory with the -AppDir option.

Option	Description
-All	All code
-Pub	Code that has a specific signature on a certificate file
-Strong	Code that has a specific strong name, as designated by a filename, code name, and version
-Zone	Code that fits into the following zones: MyComputer, Intranet, Trusted, Internet, or Untrusted
-Site	Originating on a website
-Hash	Code that has a specific assembly hash
-AppDir	A specific application directory
-SkipVerif	Code that requests the skipverification permission
-URL	Originating at a specific URL
-Custom	Code that requires a custom membership condition

The third parameter to the AddGroup command is the permission set name that you want to be associated with your group. The group that we will create will be under parent label 1, and we will designate the -Zone parameter as MyComputer because the code lives on a local drive. We will also associate the new group with our SecurityExample permission set by typing the following command:

```
Caspol -addgroup 1. -Zone MyComputer SecurityExample
```

Output from the command was successful, as shown in Figure 12-13.

Figure 12-14 shows the -listgroups command used for listing the new group. You can see that a 1.6 level was added, with the SecurityExample permission set attached to all code that fits into the MyComputer Zone. You can verify that the assembly object fits into the MyComputer Zone by using the resolveperm command, as shown in Figure 12-15.

The bottom of the figure lists which ZoneIdentityPermission the assembly object has been associated with — MyComputer. In addition, each assembly gets a URLIdentityPermission specifying the location of the executable.

Not only do you have a utility that helps with managing security permission sets and groups, you also have a utility that views the security information regarding an assembly, Permview.exe. (Permview stands for Permissions Viewer.)

Permview is not as complex as Caspol because its main purpose is to provide a certain type of feedback regarding the security requests of assemblies. In fact, the Permview utility only has two switches: one for the output location, and one for declarative security to be included in the output. In order to specify an output location, the switch is /Output, and then a file path is appended to the command line after the switch. The Permview utility brings up another concept not covered yet: declarative security.

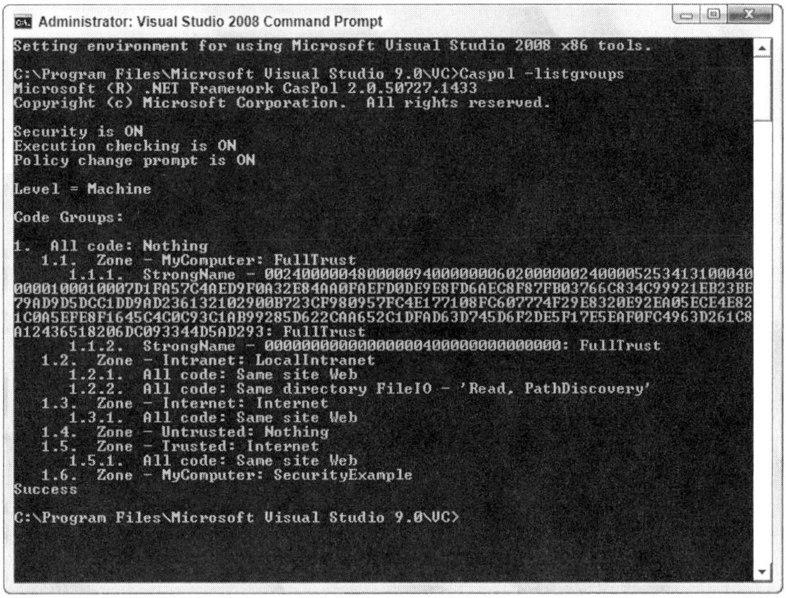

Figure 12-14

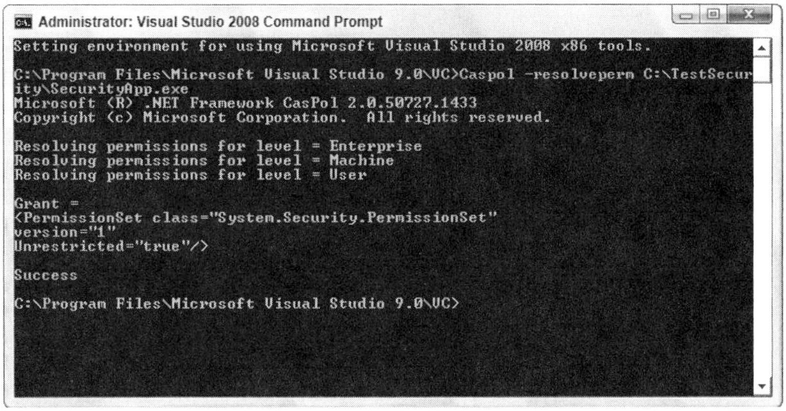

Figure 12-15

505

Declarative security is displayed in the `Permview` utility with the `/Decl` switch; it is security that a piece of code requests at an assembly level. Because it is at the assembly level, the line that requests the security is at the top of the Visual Basic module, even before your `Imports` statements. You can request one of three levels of security, as described in the following table:

Level	Description
RequestMinimum	Permissions the code must have in order to run
RequestOptional	Permissions that code may use, but could run without
RequestRefused	Permissions that you want to ensure are never granted to the code

Requesting permissions at the assembly level helps ensure that the code will be able to run, and won't get permission-based security exceptions. Because you have users calling your code, the declarative security ensures that the callers have proper security to do all that your code requires; otherwise, a security exception is thrown. The following example shows the syntax for requesting minimum permissions; the code would be placed at the top of the procedure. This example also illustrates the syntax described in the table at the beginning of the chapter regarding permissions in the `Security.Permissions` namespace. Moreover, it illustrates the use of a security constant, `SecurityAction.RequestMinimum`, for the type of security you are requesting:

```
<Assembly: SecurityPermissionAttribute(SecurityAction.RequestMinimum)>
```

Once this line is added to the assembly by means of the `AssemblyInfo.vb` file, `Permview` will report on what the assembly requested by listing minimal, optional, and refused permission sets, including the security permission set under the minimal set listing.

Determining an Application's Minimum Permissions

Before the .NET Framework 2.0, a common request from developers who were building and deploying applications was the need for clarification regarding which permissions were required for the application to run. This was sometimes a difficult task, as developers would build their applications under Full Trust and then the applications would be deployed to a machine that didn't have those privileges.

The .NET Framework 2.0 introduced a new tool that can be used to fully understand which permissions your application will need in order to run on another machine. This command-line tool, `PermCalc.exe`, does this by emulating the complete path of your assembly and all the permissions that it would require.

To use `PermCalc.exe`, open the Visual Studio command prompt and navigate to the location of the assembly you want to check. `PermCalc.exe` takes the following command structure:

```
PermCalc.exe [Options] <assembly>
```

You can also have `PermCalc.exe` evaluate more than a single assembly:

```
PermCalc.exe [Options] <assembly> <assembly>
```

For example, running the `PermCalc.exe` tool on the `SecurityApp.exe` resulted in the following:

```xml
<?xml version="1.0"?>
<Assembly>
  <Namespace Name="SecurityApp">
    <Type Name="Form1">
      <Method Sig="void .cctor()" />
      <Method Sig="instance void .ctor()">
        <Demand>
          <PermissionSet version="1" class="System.Security.PermissionSet">
            <IPermission version="1"
             class="System.Security.Permissions.ReflectionPermission,
               mscorlib, Version=2.0.0.0, Culture=neutral,
               PublicKeyToken=b77a5c561934e089" Unrestricted="true" />
            <IPermission version="1"
             class="System.Security.Permissions.SecurityPermission, mscorlib,
               Version=2.0.0.0, Culture=neutral,
               PublicKeyToken=b77a5c561934e089" Flags="UnmanagedCode,
               ControlEvidence" />
            <IPermission Window="AllWindows" version="1"
             class="System.Security.Permissions.UIPermission, mscorlib,
               Version=2.0.0.0, Culture=neutral,
               PublicKeyToken=b77a5c561934e089" />
            <IPermission version="1"
             class="System.Security.Permissions.KeyContainerPermission,
               mscorlib, Version=2.0.0.0, Culture=neutral,
               PublicKeyToken=b77a5c561934e089" Unrestricted="true" />
          </PermissionSet>
        </Demand>
        <Sandbox>
          <PermissionSet version="1" class="System.Security.PermissionSet">
            <IPermission version="1"
             class="System.Security.Permissions.ReflectionPermission,
               mscorlib, Version=2.0.0.0, Culture=neutral,
               PublicKeyToken=b77a5c561934e089" Unrestricted="true" />
            <IPermission version="1"
             class="System.Security.Permissions.SecurityPermission, mscorlib,
               Version=2.0.0.0, Culture=neutral,
               PublicKeyToken=b77a5c561934e089" Flags="UnmanagedCode,
               ControlEvidence" />
            <IPermission Window="AllWindows" version="1"
             class="System.Security.Permissions.UIPermission, mscorlib,
               Version=2.0.0.0, Culture=neutral,
               PublicKeyToken=b77a5c561934e089" />
            <IPermission version="1"
             class="System.Security.Permissions.KeyContainerPermission,
               mscorlib, Version=2.0.0.0, Culture=neutral,
               PublicKeyToken=b77a5c561934e089" Unrestricted="true" />
          </PermissionSet>
        </Sandbox>
      </Method>
    </Type>
  </Namespace>
</Assembly>
```

From this output, you can see the permissions that would be required for the application to run on someone's machine. These results were generated using the following command:

```
PermCalc.exe -under SecurityApp.exe
```

The option -under should be used when you are unsure of the exact permissions, as PermCalc.exe actually overestimates the permissions by default. Using -under forces PermCalc.exe to underestimate the permissions instead.

Using Visual Studio to Figure Minimum Permissions

Looking at the properties of your solution in Visual Studio, note the new Security tab. In the past, one of the problems in testing your application's security and permissioning was that as a developer, you were always forced to develop your programs under Full Trust. This means that you have access to the system's resources in a very open and free manner. This was an issue because typically the programs that you build cannot run under Full Trust and you still have to test the application's abilities to tap into the system's resources where the program is being run.

The Security tab, shown in Figure 12-16, is a GUI to the PermCalc.exe tool that enables you to run your applications under different types of zones.

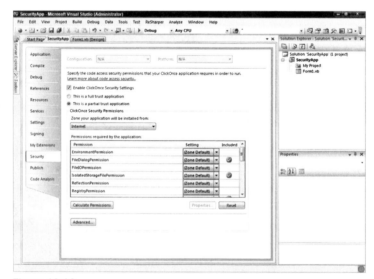

Figure 12-16

After checking the Enable ClickOnce Security Settings check box, you can specify whether the application will run on the client machine under Full Trust or partial trust status. You can also select the zone in which your application will run. The options include the following:

❑   Local Intranet
❑   Internet
❑   Custom

After selecting the zone type, you can examine all the various permissions that are required by the application in order to run.

Clicking the Calculate Permissions button on the form enables you to do just that. Visual Studio examines the assembly (see Figure 12-17) and provides you with information about which permissions for which assemblies would be required to run the application in the zone specified.

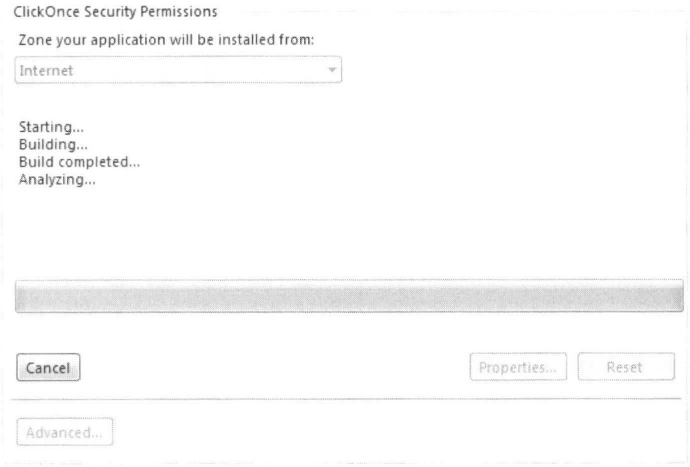

Figure 12-17

After analysis, Visual Studio presents information about what is needed from each of the assemblies in order for the application to function, as shown in Figure 12-18.

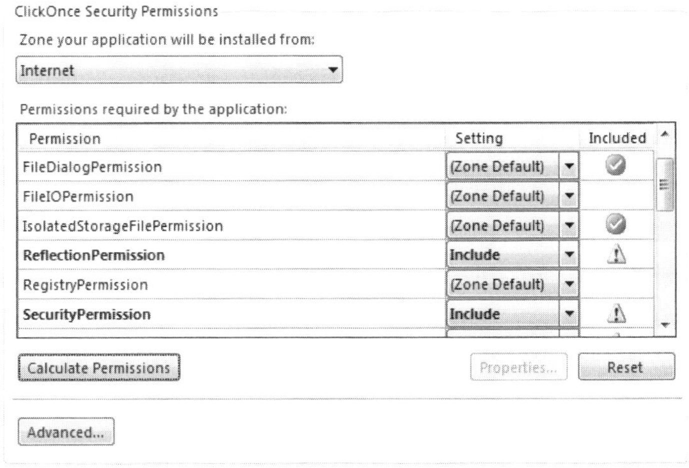

Figure 12-18

What makes this section of the application's property pages even better is that from the text box of assemblies listed, you can highlight selected assemblies and fine-tune their permissions even further — granularizing the permissions the assemblies are allowed to work with. For instance, highlighting the `FileIOPermission` line and changing the drop-down list to Include in the text box and clicking the Properties button enables you to fine-tune the permissioning for this assembly. The Permission Settings dialog that appears is shown in Figure 12-19.

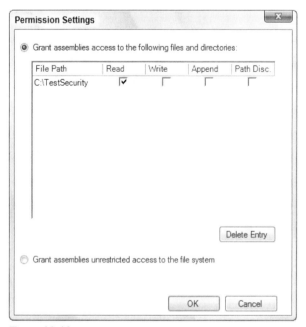

Figure 12-19

The `FileIOPermission` part of the permission settings enables you to specify the file path that the assembly is allowed to access, as well as the actions that the assembly is allowed to take in the path defined.

The capability to examine assemblies is provided not only through the command-line tool, `PermCalc.exe`; even Visual Studio joins in and enables easy management and understanding of your applications.

Security Tools

Microsoft provides many security tools in its .NET SDK. Most of these tools are console-based utility applications. These tools can be used to help implement the security processes outlined earlier. They are not described in great detail, though they do deserve a review. Basically, two groups of tools are provided with the SDK:

❏ Permissions and assembly management tools

❏ Certificate management tools

Permissions and Assembly Management Tools

Program Name	Function
Caspol.exe	Stands for Code Access Security Policy tool. This tool enables you to view and modify security settings.
Signcode.exe	A file signing tool that enables you to digitally sign your executable files
Storeadm.exe	An administrative tool for isolated storage management. It restricts code access to the filing system.
Permcalc.exe	Emulates the complete path of your assembly and all the permissions that it requires. It can also evaluate assemblies and provide information on the permissions an end user would require to run the program.
Permview.exe	Displays an assembly's requested access permissions
Peverify.exe	Checks whether the executable file will pass the runtime test for type-safe coding
Secutil.exe	Extracts a public key from a certificate and puts it in a format that is usable in your source code
Sn.exe	Creates assemblies with strong names — that is, a digitally signed namespace and version information

Certificate Management Tools

Program Name	Function
Makecert.exe	Creates an X.509 certificate for testing purposes
Certmgr.exe	Assembles certificates into a CTL (Certificate Trust List). It can also be used for revoking certificates.
Chktrust.exe	Validates a signed file containing data, its PKCS#7 hash, and a X.509 certificate
Cert2spc.exe	Creates an SPC (Software Publisher Certificate) from an X.509 certificate

Exceptions Using the SecurityException Class

In this latest release of the .NET Framework, the SecurityException class has been greatly expanded to provide considerably more detailed information on the types of exceptions that are encountered in a security context.

In the past, using the .NET Framework versions 1.0/1.1, the SecurityException class provided very little information in terms of actually telling you what was wrong and why the exception was thrown. Due to this limitation, the .NET Framework 2.0 added a number of new properties to the `SecurityException` class. The following table details the properties of the `SecurityException` class:

Properties	Description
Action	Retrieves the security action that caused the exception to occur
Demanded	Returns the permissions, permission sets, or permission set collections that caused the error to occur
DenySetInstance	Returns the denied permissions, permissions sets, or permission set collections that caused the security actions to fail
FailedAssemblyInfo	Returns information about the failed assembly
FirstPermissionThatFailed	Returns the first permission contained in the permissions set or permission set collection that failed
GrantedSet	Returns the set of permissions that caused the security actions to fail
Method	Returns information about the method connected to the exception
PermissionState	Returns the state of the permission that threw the exception
PermissionType	Returns the type of the permission that threw the exception
PermitOnlySetInstance	Returns a permissions set or permission set collection that is part of the permit-only stack frame if a security action has failed
RefusedSet	Returns the permissions that were refused by the assembly
Url	Returns the URL of the assembly that caused the exception
Zone	Returns the zone of the assembly that caused the exception

Clearly, you can get your hands on a lot of information if a security exception is thrown in your application. For instance, you can use something similar to the following `Catch` section of code to check for security errors:

```
Dim myFile as FileInfo

Try
    myFile = _
        My.Computer.FileSystem.GetFileInfo("C:\testingsecurity\testing.txt")
Catch ex As Security.SecurityException
    MessageBox.Show(ex.Method.Name.ToString())
End Try
```

One nice addition to the `SecurityException` class is how Visual Studio so easily works with it. When you encounter a `SecurityException` error while working in the Debug mode of your solution, you will get a warning directly in the IDE, similar to the warning shown in Figure 12-20 .

You can also have Visual Studio provide a detailed view of the error by breaking down the `SecurityException` object in the Locals window of Visual Studio when you catch the error using a `Try-Catch` statement.

Figure 12-20

Cryptography Basics

Rather than present a general exposition of cryptography, this section is meant to familiarize you with basic techniques required to deal with .NET security and protect your Web services through encryption. The three building blocks you need are hashing algorithms, secret key encryption, and an understanding of the Public Key Cryptographic System (PKCS).

Hashing algorithms digest long sequences of data into short footprints, the most popular being 64-bit hash keys. The two most popular hashing algorithms are SHA (Secure Hash Algorithm) and MD5 (Message-Digest algorithm 5). These hash keys are used for signing digital documents; in other words, the hash is generated and encrypted using a private key.

Secret key encryption is commonly used to protect data through passwords and pass phrases (long phrases that would be difficult to guess). Secret key encryption is suitable for situations where the encrypted data needs to be accessed by the same person who protected it.

Public Key Cryptography is most widely used in protecting the data through encryption. It is also used for digital signatures. Public Key Cryptography is based on asymmetric keys, which means you always have a pair of keys. One is known to all and is called the *public key*. The other key of the pair is kept secret and is known only to the owner. This is called the *private key*. If you use the public key to encrypt data, it can only be decrypted using the corresponding private key of the key pair, and vice versa.

Because the public key is known to all, anyone can decrypt the information. However, the private key is known only to the owner, so this process acts as a digital signature. In other words, if the public key decrypts the message, then you know that the sender was the owner of the private key. As suggested earlier, rather than encrypt the whole document using the private key, a hash algorithm is used to digest the data into a compact form, which is then encrypted using the private key. The result of this process is called the *digital signature* of the digital document.

If the data is encrypted using the public key, then it can only be decrypted by the corresponding private key, which means that only the owner of the private key will be able to read the unencrypted data. This can be used for encryption purposes. The cryptographic namespace of the .NET Framework is `System.Security.Cryptography`.

Hash Algorithms

Hash algorithms are also called *one-way functions* because of their mathematical property of nonreversibility. The hash algorithms reduce large binary strings into a fixed-length binary byte array. This fixed-length binary array is used for computing digital signatures, as explained earlier.

To verify a piece of information, the hash is recomputed and compared against a previously computed hash value. If both values match, then the data has not been altered. Cryptographic hashing algorithms map a large stream of binary data to a much shorter fixed length, so it is theoretically possible for two different documents to have the same hash key.

Although it is theoretically possible for two documents to have the same MD5 hash key and a different checksum, it is computationally impossible to create a forged document having the same hash key as the original hash value. Consider the case of a virus attack on an executable code. In the late 1980s, as a protective measure against accidental or malicious damage to the code's integrity, the most sophisticated technique available was to create a checksum or a CRC (cyclic redundancy check).

> *Virus makers drew cunning designs to create viruses that added padding code to the victim's files so that the checksum and CRC remained unchanged in spite of the infection. However, using MD5 hash values, this kind of stealth attack is rendered unfeasible.*

Windows Meta Files (WMF) still use checksums in the file header. For example, the .NET Framework class `System.Drawing.Imaging.WmfPlaceableFileHeader` has a read/write property of type `short` called `Checksum`. However, due to ease of computation, this checksum is used only as a cheap mode of protection against accidental damage, rather than against malicious attacks.

Here is a simple program to calculate a checksum:

```
' Cryptography/Checksum.vb

Imports System
Imports System.IO

Module Module1
```

This is the entry point for the program. Here, you check to see whether you've received the correct argument from the command line to run the program, and stop the program if you haven't:

```
    Public Sub Main(ByVal CmdArgs() As String)
        If (CmdArgs.Length <> 1) Then
            Console.WriteLine("Usage: Checksum <filename>")
            End
        End If
```

First, you open the file for which the checksum is to be computed:

```
        Dim fs As FileStream = File.OpenRead(CmdArgs(0))
```

You then compute the checksum, close the file, and then output the result to the screen:

```
        Dim sum As Short = compute(fs)
        fs.Close()

        Console.WriteLine(sum)
    End Sub
```

The following method computes the checksum:

```
    Function compute(ByVal strm As Stream)
        Dim sum As Long = 0
        Dim by As Integer

        strm.Position = 0
        by = strm.ReadByte

        While (by <> -1)
            sum = (((by Mod &HFF) + sum) Mod &HFFFF)
            by = strm.ReadByte
        End While

        Return CType((sum Mod &HFFFF), Short)
    End Function
End Module
```

Compile this program with the following in the VB compiler (or build and run your application if you are using Visual Studio):

```
vbc Checksum.vb
```

Run it with the following:

```
Checksum <filename>
```

Due to their unsafe nature, checksums and CRCs are sometimes deemed poor cousins of cryptographic hash algorithms. The next section describes classes provided by the .NET Framework to cater to cryptographic-grade algorithms.

Cryptographic Hash Algorithms

The abstract class System.Security.Cryptography.HashAlgorithm represents the concept of crypto-graphic hash algorithms within the .NET Framework. The framework provides eight classes that extend the HashAlgorithm abstract class:

- ❑ MD5CryptoServiceProvider (extends abstract class MD5)
- ❑ RIPEMD160Managed (extends abstract class RIPEMD160)
- ❑ SHA1CryptoServiceProvider (extends abstract class SHA1)
- ❑ SHA256Managed (extends abstract class SHA256)
- ❑ SHA384Managed (extends abstract class SHA384)
- ❑ SHA512Managed (extends abstract class SHA512)

❑   HMACSHA1 (extends abstract class KeyedHashAlgorithm)

❑   MACTripleDES (extends abstract class KeyedHashAlgorithm)

The last two classes belong to a class of algorithm called *keyed hash algorithms*. The keyed hashes extend the concept of the cryptographic hash with the use of a shared secret key. This is used for computing the hash of data transported over an unsecured channel.

The following is an example of computing a hash value of a file:

```
' Cryptography/TestKeyHash.vb

Imports System
Imports System.IO
Imports System.Security.Cryptography
Imports System.Text
Imports System.Runtime.Serialization.Formatters

Module Module1
    Public Sub Main(ByVal CmdArgs() As String)
        If (CmdArgs.Length <> 1) Then
            Console.WriteLine("Usage: TestKeyHash <filename>")
            End
        End If
```

The next snippet creates the object instance of the .NET SDK Framework class with a *salt* (a random secret to confuse a snooper):

```
Dim key() As Byte = Encoding.ASCII.GetBytes("My Secret Key".ToCharArray())
Dim hmac As HMACSHA1 = New HMACSHA1(key)
Dim fs As FileStream = File.OpenRead(CmdArgs(0))
```

The next four lines compute the hash, convert the binary hash into a printable Base64 format, close the file, and then print the Base64 encoded string as the result of hashing to the screen:

```
        Dim hash() As Byte = hmac.ComputeHash(fs)
        Dim b64 As String = Convert.ToBase64String(hash)
        fs.Close()

        Console.WriteLine(b64)
    End Sub
End Module
```

The code can be compiled at the command line using the following:

```
vbc TestKeyHash.vb
```

To execute the code, use the following command at the console prompt:

```
TestKeyHash TestKeyHash.vb
```

This should produce a hashed output:

```
IOEj/D0rOxjEqCD8qHoYm+yWw6I=
```

The previous example uses an instance of the HMACSHA1 class. The output displayed is a Base64 encoding of the binary hash result value. Base64 encoding is widely used in MIME and XML file formats to represent binary data. To recover the binary data from a Base64-encoded string, you could use the following code fragment:

```
Dim orig() As Byte = Convert.FromBase64String(b64)
```

The XML parser, however, does this automatically, as shown in later examples.

SHA

Secure Hash Algorithm (SHA) is a block cipher that operates on a block size of 64 bits. However, the subsequent enhancements of this algorithm have bigger key values, thus increasing the value range and therefore enhancing the cryptographic utility. Note that the bigger the key value sizes, the longer it takes to compute the hash. Moreover, for relatively smaller data files, smaller hash values are more secure. To put it another way, the hash algorithm's block size should be less than or equal to the size of the data itself.

The hash size for the SHA1 algorithm is 160 bits. Similar to the HMACSHA1 code discussed previously, the following code shows how to use it:

```
' Cryptography/TestSHA1.vb

Imports System
Imports System.IO
Imports System.Security.Cryptography
Imports System.Text
Imports System.Runtime.Serialization.Formatters

Module Module1
    Public Sub Main(ByVal CmdArgs() As String)
        If (CmdArgs.Length <> 1) Then
            Console.WriteLine("Usage: TestSHA1 <filename>")
            End
        End If
        Dim fs As FileStream = File.OpenRead(CmdArgs(0))

        Dim sha As SHA1 = New SHA1CryptoServiceProvider()
        Dim hash() As Byte = sha.ComputeHash(fs)
        Dim b64 As String = Convert.ToBase64String(hash)
        fs.Close()

        Console.WriteLine(b64)
    End Sub
End Module
```

The .NET Framework provides bigger key size algorithms as well — namely, SHA256, SHA384, and SHA512. The numbers at the end of the name indicate the block size.

The class SHA256Managed extends the abstract class SHA256, which in turn extends the abstract class HashAlgorithm. The Forms Authentication module of ASP.NET security (System.Web.Security .FormsAuthenticationModule) uses SHA1 as one of its valid formats to store and compare user passwords.

MD5

MD5 stands for Message-Digest algorithm 5. It is a cryptographic, one-way hash algorithm. The MD5 algorithm competes well with SHA. MD5 is an improved version of MD4, devised by Ronald Rivest of RSA fame. In fact, FIPS PUB 180-1 states that SHA-1 is based on principles similar to MD4. The salient features of this class of algorithms are as follows:

❑   It is computationally unfeasible to forge an MD5 hash digest.

❑   MD5 is not based on any mathematical assumption such as the difficulty of factoring large binary integers.

❑   MD5 is computationally cheap, and therefore suitable for low latency requirements.

❑   It is relatively simple to implement.

MD5 is the de facto standard for hash digest computation, due to the popularity of RSA. The .NET Framework provides an implementation of this algorithm through the class MD5CryptoServiceProvider in the System.Security.Cryptography namespace. This class extends the MD5 abstract class, which in turn extends the abstract class HashAlgorithm. This class shares a common base class with SHA1, so the examples previously discussed can be modified easily to accommodate it:

```
Dim fs As FileStream = File.OpenRead(CmdArgs(0))

Dim md5 As MD5 = New MD5CryptoServiceProvider()
Dim hash() As Byte = md5.ComputeHash(fs)

Dim b64 As String = Convert.ToBase64String(hash)
fs.Close()

Console.WriteLine(b64)
```

RIPEMD-160

Based on MD5, RIPEMD-160 started as a project in Europe called RIPE (RACE Integrity Primitives Evaluation Message Digest) in 1996. By 1997, the design of RIPEMD-160 was finalized. RIPEMD-160 is a 160-bit hash algorithm that is meant to be a replacement for MD4 and MD5.

The .NET Framework 2.0 introduced the RIPEMD160 class to work with this iteration of encryption techniques. The following code demonstrates the use of this class:

```
Dim fs As FileStream = File.OpenRead(CmdArgs(0))


Dim myRIPEMD As New RIPEMD160Managed()
```

```
Dim hash() As Byte = myRIPEMD.ComputeHash(fs)

Dim b64 As String = Convert.ToBase64String(hash)

fs.Close()
Console.WriteLine(b64)
```

Secret Key Encryption

Secret key encryption is widely used to encrypt data files using passwords. The simplest technique is to seed a random number using a password, and then encrypt the files with an XOR operation using this random number generator.

The .NET Framework represents the secret key by an abstract base class SymmetricAlgorithm. Four concrete implementations of different secret key algorithms are provided by default:

❑   DESCryptoServiceProvider (extends abstract class DES)

❑   RC2CryptoServiceProvider (extends abstract class RC2)

❑   RijndaelManaged (extends abstract class Rijndael)

❑   TripleDESCryptoServiceProvider (extends abstract class TripleDES)

Let's explore the SymmetricAlgorithm design. As indicated by the following example code, two separate methods are provided to access encryption and decryption. Here is a console application program that encrypts and decrypts a file, given a secret key:

```
' Cryptography/SymEnc.vb

Imports System.Security.Cryptography
Imports System.IO
Imports System

 Module Module1
    Public Sub Main(ByVal CmdArgs() As String)
        If (CmdArgs.Length <> 4) Then
            UsageAndExit()
        End If
```

The following computes the index of the algorithm that we'll use:

```
        Dim algoIndex As Integer = CmdArgs(0)

        If (algoIndex < 0 Or algoIndex >= algo.Length) Then
            UsageAndExit()
        End If
```

The following opens the input and output files (the filename represented by CmdArgs(3) is the output file, and CmdArgs(2) is the input file):

```
        Dim fin As FileStream = File.OpenRead(CmdArgs(2))
        Dim fout As FileStream = File.OpenWrite(CmdArgs(3))
```

We create the symmetric algorithm instance using the .NET Framework class `SymmetricAlgorithm`. This uses the algorithm name indexed by the `CmdArgs(0)` parameter. After this, we set the key parameters and display them onscreen for information:

```
Dim sa As SymmetricAlgorithm = _
    SymmetricAlgorithm.Create(algo(algoIndex))
sa.IV = Convert.FromBase64String(b64IVs(algoIndex))
sa.Key = Convert.FromBase64String(b64Keys(algoIndex))

Console.WriteLine("Key " + CType(sa.Key.Length, String))
Console.WriteLine("IV " + CType(sa.IV.Length, String))
Console.WriteLine("KeySize: " + CType(sa.KeySize, String))
Console.WriteLine("BlockSize: " + CType(sa.BlockSize, String))
Console.WriteLine("Padding: " + CType(sa.Padding, String))
```

At this point, we check which operation is required, and execute the appropriate static method:

```
If (CmdArgs(1).ToUpper().StartsWith("E")) Then
    Encrypt(sa, fin, fout)
Else
    Decrypt(sa, fin, fout)
End If
End Sub
```

Here is where the encryption itself takes place:

```
Public Sub Encrypt(ByVal sa As SymmetricAlgorithm, _
                   ByVal fin As Stream, _
                   ByVal fout As Stream)
    Dim trans As ICryptoTransform = sa.CreateEncryptor()
    Dim buf() As Byte = New Byte(2048) {}
    Dim cs As CryptoStream = _
        New CryptoStream(fout, trans, CryptoStreamMode.Write)
    Dim Len As Integer

    fin.Position = 0
    Len = fin.Read(buf, 0, buf.Length)

    While (Len > 0)
        cs.Write(buf, 0, Len)
        Len = fin.Read(buf, 0, buf.Length)
    End While

    cs.Close()
    fin.Close()
End Sub
```

Here's the decryption method:

```
Public Sub Decrypt(ByVal sa As SymmetricAlgorithm, _
                   ByVal fin As Stream, _
                   ByVal fout As Stream)
    Dim trans As ICryptoTransform = sa.CreateDecryptor()
```

```
        Dim buf() As Byte = New Byte(2048) {}
        Dim cs As CryptoStream = _
            New CryptoStream(fin, trans, CryptoStreamMode.Read)
        Dim Len As Integer

        Len = cs.Read(buf, 0, buf.Length)

        While (Len > 0)
            fout.Write(buf, 0, Len)
            Len = cs.Read(buf, 0, buf.Length)
        End While

        fin.Close()
        fout.Close()
    End Sub
```

This next method prints usage information:

```
Public Sub UsageAndExit()
    Console.Write("Usage SymEnc <algo index> <D|E> <in> <out> ")
    Console.WriteLine("D =decrypt, E=Encrypt")

    For i As Integer = 0 To (algo.Length - 1)
        Console.WriteLine("Algo index: {0} {1}", i, algo(i))
    Next i
    End
End Sub
```

The static parameters used for object creation are indexed by CmdArgs(0). How you arrive at these magic numbers is explained shortly:

```
        Dim algo() As String = {"DES", "RC2", "Rijndael", "TripleDES"}
        Dim b64Keys() As String = {"YE32PGCJ/g0=", _
            "vct+rJ09WuUcR61yfxniTQ==", _
            "PHDPqfwE3z25f2UYjwwfwg4XSqxvl8WYmy+2h8t6AUg=", _
            "Q1/lWoraddTH3IXAQUJGDSYDQcYYuOpm"}
        Dim b64IVs() As String = {"onQX8hdHeWQ=", _
            "jgetiyz+pIc=", _
            "pd5mgMMfDI2Gxm/SKl5I8A==", _
            "6jpFrUh8FF4="}
End Module
```

After compilation, this program can encrypt and decrypt using all four of the symmetric key implementations provided by the .NET Framework. The secret keys and their initialization vectors (IVs) have been generated by a simple source code generator, examined shortly.

The following commands encrypt and decrypt files using the DES algorithm. The first command takes a text file, 1.txt, and uses the DES algorithm to create an encrypted file called 2.bin. The next command decrypts this file and stores it in 3.bin:

```
SymEnc 0 E 1.txt 2.bin
SymEnc 0 D 2.bin 3.bin
```

The first parameter of the SymEnc program is an index to the string array, which determines the algorithm to be used:

```
Dim algo() As String = {"DES", "RC2", "Rijndael", "TripleDES"}
```

The string defining the algorithm is passed as a parameter to the static Create method of the abstract class SymmetricAlgorithm. This class has an abstract factory design pattern:

```
Dim sa As SymmetricAlgorithm = SymmetricAlgorithm.Create(algo(algoIndex))
```

To encrypt, you get an instance of the ICryptoTransform interface by calling the CreateEncryptor method of the SymmetricAlgorithm class extender:

```
Dim trans As ICryptoTransform = sa.CreateEncryptor()
```

Similarly, for decryption, you get an instance of the ICryptoTransform interface by calling the CreateDecryptor method of the SymmetricAlgorithm class instance:

```
Dim trans As ICryptoTransform = sa.CreateDecryptor()
```

You use the class CryptoStream for both encryption and decryption, but the parameters to the constructor differ. Encryption uses the following code:

```
Dim cs As CryptoStream = New CryptoStream(fout, trans, CryptoStreamMode.Write)
```

Similarly, decryption uses this code:

```
Dim cs As CryptoStream = New CryptoStream(fin, trans, CryptoStreamMode.Read)
```

You call the Read and Write methods of the CryptoStream for decryption and encryption, respectively. For generating the keys, you use a simple code generator, as follows:

```
' Cryptography/SymKey.vb

Imports System.IO
Imports System.Security.Cryptography
Imports System.Text

Module Module1
    Public Sub Main(ByVal CmdArgs() As String)
        Dim keyz As StringBuilder = New StringBuilder
        Dim ivz As StringBuilder = New StringBuilder

        keyz.Append("Dim b64Keys() As String = { _" + VbCrLf)
        ivz.Append(VbCrLf + "Dim b64IVs() As String = { _" + VbCrLf )
```

The algorithm names for symmetric keys used by .NET SDK are given the correct index values here:

```
Dim algo() As String = {"DES", "RC2", "Rijndael", "TripleDES"}
```

For each of the algorithms, you generate the keys and IV:

```
Dim comma As String = ", _" + VbCrLf

For i As Integer = 0 To 3
    Dim sa As SymmetricAlgorithm = SymmetricAlgorithm.Create(algo(i))

    sa.GenerateIV()
    sa.GenerateKey()

    Dim Key As String
    Dim IV As String

    Key = Convert.ToBase64String(sa.Key)
    IV = Convert.ToBase64String(sa.IV)

    keyz.AppendFormat(vbTab + """" + Key + """" + comma)
    ivz.AppendFormat(vbTab + """" + IV + """" + comma)

    If i = 2 Then comma = " "
Next i
```

Here, you print or emit the source code:

```
    keyz.Append("}")
    ivz.Append("}")

    Console.WriteLine(keyz.ToString())
    Console.WriteLine(ivz.ToString())
    End Sub
End Module
```

The preceding program creates a random key and an initializing vector for each algorithm. This output can be inserted directly into the SymEnc.vb program. The simplest way to do this is to type the following:

```
SymKey > keys.txt
```

This redirects the information into a file called keys.txt, which you can then use to cut and paste the values into your program. You use the StringBuilder class along with the control character crlf (carriage return and line feed) to format the text so that it can be inserted directly into your program. You then convert the binary data into Base64 encoding using the public instance method ToBase64String of the class Convert. Kerberos, the popular network authentication protocol supported by Windows Server 2003, Windows 2000, and all of the UNIX flavors, uses secret key encryption to implement security.

PKCS

The Public Key Cryptographic System is a type of asymmetric key encryption. This system uses two keys, one private and the other public. The public key is widely distributed, whereas the private key is kept secret. One cannot derive or deduce the private key by knowing the public key, so the public key can be safely distributed.

The keys are different, yet complementary. That is, if you encrypt data using the public key, then only the owner of the private key can decipher it, and vice versa. This forms the basis of PKCS encryption.

If the private key holder encrypts a piece of data using his or her private key, any person with access to the public key can decrypt it. The public key, as the name suggests, is available publicly. This property of the PKCS is exploited along with a hashing algorithm, such as SHA or MD5, to provide a verifiable digital signature process.

The abstract class `System.Security.Cryptography.AsymmetricAlgorithm` represents this concept in the .NET Framework. Two concrete implementations of this class are provided by default:

❑   `DSACryptoServiceProvider`, which extends the abstract class `DSA`

❑   `RSACryptoServiceProvider`, which extends the abstract class `RSA`

DSA (Digital Signature Algorithm) was specified by NIST (National Institute of Standards and Technology) in January 2000. The original DSA standard, however, was issued by NIST much earlier, in August 1991. DSA cannot be used for encryption and is good only for digital signature. Digital signature is discussed in more detail in the next subsection.

RSA algorithms can also be used for encryption as well as digital signatures. RSA is the de facto standard and has much wider acceptance than DSA. RSA is a tiny bit faster than DSA as well.

The RSA algorithm is named after its three inventors: Rivest, Shamir, and Adleman. It was patented in the United States, but the patent expired in September 2000. RSA can be used for both digital signature and data encryption. It is based on the assumption that large numbers are extremely difficult to factor. The use of RSA for digital signatures is approved within the FIPS PUB 186-2 and is defined in the ANSI X9.31 standard document.

To gain some practical insights into RSA implementation of the .NET Framework, consider the following code (for this to compile, you also have to make a reference to the `System.Security` DLL in your project):

```
' Cryptography/TestRSAKey.vb

Imports System.Security.Cryptography.Xml

Module Module1
    Sub Main()
        Dim RSA As RSAKeyValue = New RSAKeyValue
        Dim str As String = RSA.Key.ToXmlString(True)
        System.Console.WriteLine(str)
    End Sub
End Module
```

This code creates a pair of private and public keys and prints it out at the command line in XML format. To compile the preceding code, simply open a console session, run `corvar.bat` (if necessary), set the .NET SDK paths, and compile the program by typing the following command:

```
TestRSAKey.vb
```

This should produce a file called `TestRSAKey.exe`. Execute this program and redirect the output to a file such as `key.xml`:

```
TestRSAKey > key.xml
```

The file `key.xml` contains all the private and public members of the generated RSA key object. You can open this XML file in Internet Explorer 5.5 or later. If you do so, you will notice that the private member variables are also stored in this file. The binary data representing the large integers is encoded in Base64 format.

The preceding program uses an `RSAKeyValue` instance to generate a new key pair. The class `RSAKeyValue` is contained in the `System.Security.Cryptography.Xml` namespace. This namespace can be thought of as the XML face of the .NET cryptographic framework. It contains a specialized, lightweight implementation of XML for the purpose of cryptography, and the model allows XML objects to be signed with a digital signature.

The `System.Security.Cryptography.Xml` namespace classes depend upon the classes contained in the `System.Security.Cryptography` namespace for the actual implementation of cryptographic algorithms.

The `key.xml` file, generated by redirecting the output of the Visual Basic test program `TestRSAKey`, contains both private and public keys. However, you need to keep the private key secret while making the public key widely available. Therefore, you need to separate the public key from the key pair. Here is the program to do that:

```
' Cryptography/TestGetPubKey.vb

Imports System.IO
Imports System.Text
Imports System.Security.Cryptography

Module Module1
    Public Sub Main(ByVal CmdArgs() As String)
        If (CmdArgs.Length <> 1) Then
            Console.WriteLine("Usage: TestGetPubKey <key pair xml>")
            End
        End If

        Dim xstr As String = File2String(CmdArgs(0))
```

The following code creates an instance of the RSA implementation and reinitializes the internal variables through the XML-formatted string:

```
        Dim rsa As RSACryptoServiceProvider = New RSACryptoServiceProvider()
        rsa.FromXmlString(xstr)

        Dim x As String = rsa.ToXmlString(False)
        Console.WriteLine(x)
    End Sub

    Public Function File2String(ByVal fname As String) As String
        Dim finfo As FileInfo = New FileInfo(fname)
        Dim buf() As Byte = New Byte(finfo.Length) {}
```

```
            Dim fs As FileStream = File.OpenRead(fname)

            fs.Read(buf, 0, buf.Length)

            Return (New ASCIIEncoding).GetString(buf)
        End Function
    End Module
```

This program is logically similar to TestRSAKey.vb except that it has to read the key file and pass a different parameter in the ToXmlString method.

The cryptography classes use a lightweight XML implementation, thus avoiding the elaborate ritual of parsing the fully formed generic XML data containing serialized objects. This has another advantage, speed, because it bypasses the DOM parsers. To compile the previous code, type the following:

```
    vbc /r:System.Security.dll TestGetPubKey.vb
```

This should produce the file TestGetPubKey.exe. Run this file, giving key.xml as the name of the input file, and redirect the program's output to pub.xml. This file contains an XML-formatted public key. The binary data, basically binary large integers, are Base64 encoded. You may recall that key.xml contains both the public and private key pairs, and was generated by redirecting the output of TestRSAKey.exe. The following line redirects key.xml's public key to pub.xml:

```
    TestGetPubKey key.xml > pub.xml
```

The following program tests the encrypt and decrypt feature of the RSA algorithm:

```
' Cryptography/TestCrypt.vb

Imports System
Imports System.IO
Imports System.Security.Cryptography
Imports System.Text

Module Module1
    Public Sub Main(ByVal CmdArgs() As String)
        If (CmdArgs.Length <> 4) Then
            Console.WriteLine("Usage: TestCrypt <key xml> <E|D> <in> <out>")
            Console.WriteLine(" E= Encrypt, D= Decrypt (needs private key)")
            End
        End If
```

Here, you read the public or private key into memory:

```
            Dim xstr As String = File2String(CmdArgs(0))
```

You create an instance of an RSA cryptography service provider and initialize the parameters based on the XML lightweight filename passed in CmdArgs(0):

```
            Dim RSA As New RSACryptoServiceProvider()
            RSA.FromXmlString(xstr)
```

Display the key filename:

```
Console.WriteLine("Key File: " + CmdArgs(0))
Dim op As String= "Encrypted"
```

Read the input file and store it into a byte array:

```
Dim info As FileInfo = New FileInfo(CmdArgs(2))
Dim inbuflen As Integer = CType(info.Length, Integer)
Dim inbuf() As Byte = New Byte(inbuflen-1) {}
Dim outbuf() As Byte
Dim fs As FileStream = File.OpenRead(CmdArgs(2))

fs.Read(inbuf, 0, inbuf.Length)
fs.Close()
```

Either encrypt or decrypt depending on the CmdArgs(1) option:

```
If (CmdArgs(1).ToUpper().StartsWith("D")) Then
    op = "Decrypted"
    outbuf = rsa.Decrypt(inbuf, False)
Else
    outbuf = rsa.Encrypt(inbuf, False)
End If
```

Now write the result in the output buffer into the file and display the result:

```
fs = File.OpenWrite(CmdArgs(3))
fs.Write(outbuf, 0, outbuf.Length)
fs.Close()

Console.WriteLine(op + " input [" + CmdArgs(2) + "] to output [" _
            + CmdArgs(3) + "]")
End Sub
```

Here's a helper method to read the filename passed as an argument and convert the content to a string:

```
Public Function File2String(ByVal fname As String)
    Dim finfo As FileInfo = New FileInfo(fname)
    Dim buf() As Byte = New Byte(finfo.Length) {}
    Dim fs As FileStream = File.OpenRead(fname)

    fs.Read(buf, 0, buf.Length)
    fs.Close()

    Return (New ASCIIEncoding).GetString(buf)
End Function
End Module
```

This test program encrypts or decrypts a short file depending on the parameters supplied to it. It takes four parameters: the XML-formatted private or public key file, option E or D, representing the encrypt or decrypt options, respectively, and input and output filenames.

This program can be compiled with the following command:

```
vbc /r:System.Security.dll TestCrypt.vb
```

The preceding command produces a PE file, TestCrypt.exe. To test the encrypt and decrypt functions, create a small plain-text file called 1.txt. Recall that we also created two other files: key.xml and pub.xml. The file key.xml contains a key pair, and pub.xml contains the public key extracted from the file key.xml.

To encrypt the plain-text file plain.txt, use the following command:

```
TestCrypt pub.xml E 1.txt rsa.bin
```

Note that you have used the public key file to encrypt it. You can type the output on the console, but this won't make any sense because it contains binary data. You could use a binary dump utility to dump out the file's content. If you do this, then note that the total number of bytes is 128, compared to the input of 13 bytes. This is because the RSA is a block cipher algorithm and the block size equals the key size, so the output is always in multiples of the block size. You may wish to rerun the preceding examples with larger files to see the resulting encrypted file length.

Now decrypt the file to get back the original text:

```
TestCrypt key.xml D rsa.bin decr.txt
```

The key.xml file, which also contains the private key, is used to decrypt because you use the public key to encrypt, and the private key to decrypt. In other words, anyone may send encrypted documents to you if they know your public key, but only you can decrypt such messages. The reverse is true for digital signatures, covered in the next section.

Digital Signature Basics

Digital signature is the encryption of a hash digest (for example, MD5 or SHA-1) of data using a public key. The digital signature can be verified by decrypting the hash digest and comparing it against a hash digest computed from the data by the verifier.

As noted earlier, the private key is known only to the owner, so the owner can sign a digital document by encrypting the hash computed from the document. The public key is known to all, so anyone can verify the signature by recomputing the hash and comparing it against the decrypted value, using the public key of the signer.

The .NET Framework provides DSA and RSA digital signature implementations by default. This section considers only DSA, as RSA was covered in the preceding section. Both of the implementations extend the same base class, so all programs for DSA discussed here work for RSA as well.

First, go through the same motions of producing a key pair and a public key file and then sign and verify the signature:

```
' Cryptography/GenDSAKeys.vb

Imports System
Imports System.Security.Cryptography
```

```
Imports VB_Security.FileUtil

Module Module1
    Public Sub Main(ByVal CmdArgs() As String)
        Dim dsa As DSACryptoServiceProvider = New DSACryptoServiceProvider()
        Dim prv As String = dsa.ToXmlString(True)
        Dim pub As String = dsa.ToXmlString(False)
        Dim fileutil As FileUtil = New FileUtil()

        fileutil.SaveString("dsa-key.xml", prv)
        fileutil.SaveString("dsa-pub.xml", pub)

        Console.WriteLine("Created dsa-key.xml and dsa-pub.xml")
    End Sub
End Module
```

This code generates two XML-formatted files, dsa-key.xml and dsa-pub.xml, containing private and public keys, respectively. Before you can run this, however, you need to create the FileUtil class used to output the two files:

```
' Cryptography/FileUtil.vb

Imports System.IO
Imports System.Text

Public Class FileUtil
    Public Sub SaveString(ByVal fname As String, ByVal data As String)
        SaveBytes(fname, (New ASCIIEncoding).GetBytes(data))
    End Sub

    Public Function LoadString(ByVal fname As String)
        Dim buf() As Byte = LoadBytes(fname)
        Return (New ASCIIEncoding).GetString(buf)
    End Function

    Public Function LoadBytes(ByVal fname As String)
        Dim finfo As FileInfo = New FileInfo(fname)
        Dim length As String = CType(finfo.Length, String)
        Dim buf() As Byte = New Byte(length) {}
        Dim fs As FileStream = File.OpenRead(fname)

        fs.Read(buf, 0, buf.Length)
        fs.Close()

        Return buf
    End Function

    Public Sub SaveBytes(ByVal fname As String, ByVal data() As Byte)
        Dim fs As FileStream = File.OpenWrite(fname)

        fs.SetLength(0)
        fs.Write(data, 0, data.Length)
        fs.Close()
    End Sub
End Class
```

The following code signs the data:

```
' Cryptography/DSASign.vb

Imports System
Imports System.IO
Imports System.Security.Cryptography
Imports System.Text
Imports VB_Security.FileUtil

Module Module1
    Public Sub Main(ByVal CmdArgs() As String)
        If CmdArgs.Length <> 3 Then
            Console.WriteLine("Usage: DSASign <key xml> <data> <sign>")
            End
        End If

        Dim fileutil As FileUtil = New FileUtil()
        Dim xkey As String = fileutil.LoadString(CmdArgs(0))
        Dim fs As FileStream = File.OpenRead(CmdArgs(1))
```

The following two lines of code create the DSA provider instance and reconstruct the private key from the XML format:

```
        Dim dsa As DSACryptoServiceProvider = New DSACryptoServiceProvider()
        dsa.FromXmlString(xkey)
```

The next line signs the file:

```
        Dim sig() As Byte = dsa.SignData(fs)
        fs.Close()
        fileutil.SaveString(CmdArgs(2), Convert.ToString(sig))
        Console.WriteLine("Signature in {0}} file", CmdArgs(2))
    End Sub
End Module
```

To verify the signature, you can use the following sample code:

```
' Cryptography/DSAVerify.vb

Imports System
Imports System.IO
Imports System.Security.Cryptography
Imports System.Text
Imports VB_Security.FileUtil

Module Module1
    Public Sub Main(ByVal CmdArgs() As String)
        If CmdArgs.Length <> 3 Then
            Console.WriteLine("Usage: DSAVerify <key xml> <data> <sign>")
            End
```

```
                End If

                Dim fileutil As FileUtil = New FileUtil()
                Dim xkey As String = fileutil.LoadString(CmdArgs(0))
                Dim data() As Byte = fileutil.LoadBytes(CmdArgs(1))
                Dim xsig As String = fileutil.LoadString(CmdArgs(2))
                Dim dsa As DSACryptoServiceProvider = New DSACryptoServiceProvider()

                dsa.FromXmlString(xkey)
                Dim xsigAsByte() As Byte = New Byte(xsig) {}

                Dim verify As Boolean
                verify = dsa.VerifyData(data, xsigAsByte)
                Console.WriteLine("Signature Verification is {0}", verify)
        End Sub
    End Module
```

The actual verification is done using the highlighted code fragment. The next four commands compile the source files:

```
    vbc /target:library FileUtil.vb
    vbc /r:FileUtil.dll GenDSAKeys.vb
    vbc /r:FileUtil.dll DSASign.vb
    vbc /r:FileUtil.dll DSAVerify.vb
```

There are many helper classes within the System.Security.Cryptography and the System.Security.Cryptography.Xml namespaces, and they provide numerous features to help deal with digital signatures and encryption. They also provide overlapping functionality, so there is more than one way of doing the same thing.

X.509 Certificates

X.509 is a public key certificate exchange framework. A public key certificate is a digitally signed statement by the owner of a private key, trusted by the verifier (usually a certifying authority), that certifies the validity of the public key of another entity. This creates a trust relationship between two unknown entities. This is an ISO standard specified by the document ISO/IEC 9594-8. X.509 certificates are also used in SSL (Secure Sockets Layer), which is covered in the next section.

Many certifying authority services are available over the Internet. VeriSign (www.verisign.com) is the most popular, and was founded by the RSA trio themselves. You can run your own Certificate Authority (CA) service over an intranet using Microsoft Certificate Server.

The Microsoft .NET Framework SDK also provides tools for generating certificates for testing purposes. The following command generates a test certificate:

```
    makecert -n CN=Test test.cer
```

You can view it by double-clicking the test.cer file from Windows Explorer. The certificate is shown in Figure 12-21. From the same dialog box, you can also install this certificate on your computer by clicking the Install Certificate button.

531

Figure 12-21

Three classes dealing with X.509 certificates are provided in the .NET Framework in the namespace `System.Security.Cryptography.X509Certificates`. The following program loads and manipulates the certificate created earlier:

```
' Cryptography/LoadCert.vb

Imports System
Imports System.Security.Cryptography.X509Certificates

Module Module1
    Public Sub Main(ByVal CmdArgs() As String)
        If CmdArgs.Length <> 1 Then
            Console.Write("Usage loadCert <cert file>")
            End
        End If

        Dim cert As X509Certificate = _
            X509Certificate.CreateFromCertFile(CmdArgs(0))

        Console.WriteLine("Hash= {0}", cert.GetCertHashString())
        Console.WriteLine("Effective Date= {0}", _
                    cert.GetEffectiveDateString())
        Console.WriteLine("Expire Date= {0}", _
                    cert.GetExpirationDateString())
        Console.WriteLine("Issued By= {0}", cert.Issuer.ToString())
```

```
            Console.WriteLine("Issued To= {0}", cert.Subject.ToString())
            Console.WriteLine("Algo= {0}", cert.GetKeyAlgorithm())
            Console.WriteLine("Pub Key= {0}", cert.GetPublicKeyString())
        End Sub
    End Module
```

The static method loads `CreateFromCertFile` (the certificate file) and creates a new instance of the class `X509Certificate`. The next section deals with SSL, which uses X.509 certificates to establish the trust relationship.

Secure Sockets Layer

The SSL (Secure Sockets Layer) protocol provides privacy and reliability between two communicating applications over the Internet. SSL is built over the TCP layer. In January 1999, the IETF (Internet Engineering Task Force) adopted an enhanced version of SSL 3.0 called Transport Layer Security (TLS). TLS is backwardly compatible with SSL, and is defined in RFC 2246. However, the name SSL was retained due to wide acceptance of this Netscape protocol name. This section provides a simplified overview of the SSL algorithm sequence. SSL provides connection-oriented security via the following four properties:

❑ Connection is private and encryption is valid for the current session only.

❑ Symmetric key cryptography, like DES, is used for encryption. However, the session secret key is exchanged using public key encryption.

❑ Digital certificates are used to verify the identities of the communicating entities.

❑ Secure hash functions, such as SHA and MD5, are used for message authentication code (MAC).

The SSL protocol sets the following goals for itself:

❑ **Cryptographic security** — Uses symmetric key for session, and public key for authentication

❑ **Interoperability** — Interpolates OS and programming languages

❑ **Extensibility** — Adds new protocols for encrypting data that are allowed within the SSL framework

❑ **Relative efficiency** — Reduces computation and network activity by using caching techniques

Two entities communicating using SSL protocols must have a public-private key pair, optionally with digital certificates validating their respective public keys.

At the beginning of a session, the client and server exchange information to authenticate each other. This ritual of authentication is called the *handshake protocol*. During this handshake, a session ID, the compression method, and the cipher suite to be used are negotiated. If the certificates exist, then they are exchanged. Although certificates are optional, either the client or the server may refuse to continue with the connection and end the session in the absence of a certificate.

After receiving each other's public keys, a set of secret keys based on a randomly generated number is exchanged by encrypting them with each other's public keys. After this, the application data exchange can commence. The application data is encrypted using a secret key, and a signed hash of the data is sent to verify data integrity.

Microsoft implements the SSL client in the .NET Framework classes. However, the server-side SSL can be used by deploying your service through the IIS Web server. The following code fragment can be used to access SSL-protected Web servers from the .NET platform:

```
Dim req As WebRequest = WebRequest.Create("https://www.reuters.com")
Dim result As WebResponse = req.GetResponse()
```

Note that the preceding URL starts with https, which signals the WebRequest class (part of System.Net) to use the SSL protocol. Interestingly, the same code is useful for accessing unsecured URLs as well.

The following code is a program for accessing a secured URL. It takes care of minor details, such as encoding:

```
' Cryptography/GetWeb.vb

Imports System
Imports System.IO
Imports System.Net
Imports System.Text

Module Module1
    Public Sub Main(ByVal CmdArgs() As String)
        If CmdArgs.Length <> 1 Then
            Console.WriteLine("Usage: GetWeb URL")
            Console.WriteLine("Example: GetWeb https://www.reuters.com")
            End
        End If
        Dim ms As String
```

You call the Create method (shown next) with a URL and an encoding format:

```
    Try
        ms = Create(CmdArgs(0), "utf-8")
        Console.WriteLine(ms)
    Catch x As Exception
        Console.WriteLine(x.StackTrace)
        Console.WriteLine("Bad URL: {0}", CmdArgs(0))
    End Try
End Sub
```

Next is the Create method. Using the .NET Framework WebRequest object, you create an HTTP-secured request object and get its response stream:

```
Function Create(ByVal url As String, ByVal encod As String) As String
    Dim req As WebRequest = WebRequest.Create(url)
    Dim result As WebResponse = req.GetResponse()
    Dim ReceiveStream As Stream = result.GetResponseStream()
```

Create an encoding instance from the .NET Framework object, Encoding:

```
    Dim enc As Encoding = System.Text.Encoding.GetEncoding(encod)
```

The following creates the stream reader:

```
Dim sr As StreamReader = New StreamReader(ReceiveStream, enc)
```

You read the stream fully. The entire Web page or serialized object is read into the `responseString`:

```
Dim response As String = sr.ReadToEnd()
Return response
End Function

Dim MaxContentLength As Integer = 16384 ' 16k
End Module
```

The preceding console application gets a secured (SSL), protected URL and displays the content on the console. To compile the code, use the following command:

```
vbc /r:System.dll GetWeb.vb
```

Summary

This chapter covered the basics of security and cryptography. It began with an overview of the security architecture of the .NET Framework and looked at four types of security: NTFS, security policies, cryptographic, and programmatic.

It went on to examine the security tools and functionality that the .NET Framework provides. You examined the `System.Security.Permissions` namespace and learned how you can control code access permissions, role-based permissions, and identity permissions. You also learned how you can manage code access permissions and security policies for your code. Two tools were used — `Caspol.exe` and `Permview.exe` — to help configure and view security at both the machine and user levels.

The second half of the chapter looked at cryptography, both the underlying theory and how it can be applied within your applications. You looked at the different types of cryptographic hash algorithms, including SHA, MD5, Secret Key Encryption, and PKCS. You should also understand how you can use digital certificates (specifically, X.509 certificates) and Secure Socket Layers (SSL).

13

Visual Studio 2008

It's possible to work with Visual Basic without Visual Studio. In practice, however, the two are almost inseparable; without a version of Visual Studio, you're forced to work from the command line to create project files by hand, to make calls to the associated compilers, and to manually address the tools necessary to build your application. Thus, while it is possible, Visual Studio 2008 is the preferred environment for developing Visual Basic applications.

With the release of Visual Studio 2005, Microsoft expanded on the different versions of Visual Studio available for use. Unlike the early versions, they've expanded what we'll call the high-end and low-end packages associated with Visual Studio. At the low-cost end, currently free, is Visual Basic Express Edition. This tool enables you to build desktop applications with Visual Basic only. Its companion for Web development is Visual Web Developer Express, which enables you to build ASP.NET applications. At the high end, Microsoft offers Visual Studio Team System, available only with a high-cost MSDN subscription, which includes many tools that extend Visual Studio beyond the core Integrated Development Environment (IDE) to help improve design, testing, and collaboration between developers.

Of course, the focus of this chapter is how Visual Studio enables you to use Visual Basic to build applications geared toward "better, faster, cheaper" business goals. To this end, we'll be examining features of Visual Studio starting with those in the core Visual Basic 2008 Express Edition and building up to the full Visual Studio Team Suite. Topics in this chapter include the following:

- ❑ Versions of Visual Studio
- ❑ Project templates
- ❑ Project properties — application, compilation, debug, and so on
- ❑ Setting properties
- ❑ IntelliSense, code expansion, and code snippets
- ❑ Targeting a runtime environment
- ❑ Debugging
- ❑ Recording and using macros
- ❑ The Class Designer

❑ Visual Studio tools for Office

❑ Team System — Team Suite Client Tools

❑ Team Foundation Server — Team Explorer

This chapter provides an overview of many of the capabilities of Visual Studio 2008, with a brief introduction to the features available by using one of the more feature-rich versions of Visual Studio. The goal is to demonstrate how Visual Studio makes you, as a developer, more productive and successful.

Visual Studio 2008: Express through Team Suite

Visual Studio 2003 was focused on .NET 1.1, and Visual Studio .NET (2002) was focused on .NET 1.0, so each version of Visual Studio has been optimized for a particular version of .NET. Similarly, Visual Studio 2005 was optimized for .NET 2.0, and with the exception of unsupported add-ons, didn't support the new features of .NET 3.0.

Fortunately, Microsoft chose to keep Visual Basic and ASP.NET unchanged for the .NET 3.0 Framework release. However, when you looked at the new .NET 3.0 Framework elements, such as Windows Presentation Foundation, Windows Communication Foundation, and Windows Workflow Foundation, you saw those items needed to be addressed outside of Visual Studio. Thus, while Visual Studio 2005 was separate from Visual Basic and .NET development, in practical terms the two were tightly coupled.

With Visual Studio 2008, Microsoft provides robust support for the ability to target any of three different versions of the .NET Framework. Visual Studio 2008 enables you to target an application to run on .NET 2.0, .NET 3.0, or .NET 3.5. However, as you'll discover, this support doesn't mean that Visual Studio 2008 isn't tightly coupled to its own compiler. In fact, the new support for targeting frameworks is designed to support a runtime environment, not a compile-time environment. This is important because Visual Studio 2005 projects are converted to the Visual Studio 2008 format when you open them, after which they cannot be reopened by Visual Studio 2005.

The reason for this is that the underlying build engine used by Visual Studio 2008 accepts syntax changes and even language feature changes such as XML literals, but the Visual Studio 2005 engine does not recognize these new elements of the language. Thus, if you move source code written in Visual Studio 2008 to Visual Studio 2005, you face a strong possibility that it would fail to compile. There are ways to manually work with a project across versions 2005 and 2008 of Visual Studio on the same team, but they are not supported. Bill Sheldon, one of the authors of this book, has a blog post from August 2007 that deals with his experience doing this titled "Working with Both VS 2005 and VS 2008 B2 on the Same Project": http://blogs.interknowlogy.com/billsheldon/archive/2007/08/29/21175.aspx.

Multitargeting support by Visual Studio 2008 ensures that your application will run on a specific version of the framework. Thus, if your organization is not supporting .NET 3.0 or .NET 3.5, you can still use Visual Studio 2008 and be reasonably certain that your application will not reference files from one of those other framework versions. Multitargeting is what enables you to safely deploy without requiring your customers to download additional framework components they don't need.

With those ground rules in place, what versions of Visual Studio 2008 are available and what are the primary differences between them? As already mentioned, Visual Basic 2008 Express is at the bottom tier in terms of price and features. It is accompanied there by Visual Web Developer 2008 Express Edition, for those developers who are developing Web applications, rather than desktop applications. These two tools are separate, but both support developing different types of Visual Basic applications, and coincidentally both are free. Note, however, that neither is extensible; these tools are meant to be introductory, and Microsoft's license prevents vendors from extending these tools with productivity enhancements.

However, each of the Express edition development tools also ships with two additional components covered briefly here: MSDN Express Edition and SQL Server 2005 Express Edition. MSDN is, of course, the Microsoft Developer Network, which has placed most of its content online. It's the source for not only the core language documentation for Visual Basic, but also articles on almost every product oriented to developers using Microsoft technology. Full versions of Visual Studio ship with the full MSDN library so that you can access its content locally. However, the Express Edition tools actually ship with a pared-down 200 MB set of documentation files — of course, that's still a lot of documentation.

Similar to the language and Web-based tools, Microsoft has a SQL Server Express Edition package. This package actually has a history, in that it replaces the MSDE database engine that was available with SQL Server 2000. The SQL Server Express engine provides the core SQL Server 2005 database engine. Unlike MSDE, it also offers a free management application available via a separate download from Microsoft.

When you install Visual Studio 2008, including the Express Editions, you also have the opportunity to install this core database engine. The elements of this engine are freely redistributable, so if you are looking for a set of core database features based on ADO.NET, you can create your application and deploy your SQL Server 2005 Express Edition database without being concerned about licensing. SQL Server is covered in more detail in Chapter 14.

Getting back to the differences in versions, the Express Edition tools provide the core components necessary to create Visual Basic applications (Windows or Web) based on the core IDE. The following table provides a quick summary of what versions are available, including a description of how each extends Visual Studio:

Visual Studio Edition	Description
Visual Basic 2008 Express Edition	This is the core set of functionality required for creating Windows-based applications. It includes the IDE with full local debugging support and support for five project types: Windows Forms Application, Dynamic Link Library, WPF Application, WPF Browser Application, and Console Application.
Visual Web Developer 2008 Express Edition	The core set of functionality required for building Web applications. It supports both Visual Basic and C# and allows for local debugging of your Web application.
Visual Studio 2008 Standard Edition	Provides a combined development language for the core Visual Studio languages (J#, VB, C# and C++). It adds the Object Modeling tool, and provides combined support for both Windows and Web applications. It also provides additional support for application deployment, and support for Mobile Application Development, integration with a source control tool, and macros within Visual Studio; it is also extensible.

Visual Studio Edition	Description
Visual Studio 2008 Professional Edition	Expands on Visual Studio Standard Edition with additional integration to SQL Server and support for XSLTs. It also includes support for Visual Studio Tools for Office, which enables you to create custom client (Word, Excel, Outlook, etc.) and SharePoint Workflow applications. This version also allows for remote debugging of Web applications.
Visual Studio 2008 Team Edition for*	When Visual Studio 2005 was released, Microsoft provided three specialized versions of Visual Studio 2005 Team Suite, each of which contained everything from the previously mentioned versions plus a subset of the Team Suite client tools. The editions were Team Edition for Architects, Team Edition for Developers, and Team Edition for Testers. Since then, Microsoft released a fourth edition that is available with Visual Studio 2008: Team Edition for Database Developers. Each edition contains a subset of the full Team Suite of tools, and includes a client license for Microsoft Team Foundation Server. These must be purchased as part of an annual MSDN package.
Visual Studio 2008 Team Suite	The full Team Suite includes all of the core features of Visual Studio 2008 Professional Edition and Visual Studio Tools for Office. It also includes all the tools from Visual Studio Team Suite: static code analysis, code profiling (performance testing), unit tests (which may be written in Visual Basic), application and deployment graphical design tools, Web and load-testing tools, and a variety of related tools to enhance development. This tool, like the Team Edition versions of Visual Studio, is focused on enabling developers to be productive in a shared collaborative environment. It works best when combined with Microsoft Team Foundation Server for source control and collaboration capabilities.

The Express Edition tools are best described as targeting students and hobbyists, not because you can't create serious applications but because they provide only limited support for team development, have limited extensibility, and offer a standalone environment. The Express Tools are oriented toward developers who work independently, while still providing full access to features of the Visual Basic language. This chapter begins working in the IDE using this version, which is essentially the lowest common denominator, and then extends beyond the capabilities of this free tool.

Eventually, however, a developer needs additional tools and projects. This is where the full versions of Visual Studio 2008 (Standard and Professional) come in. With an increasing level of support for team development, these feature rich versions add macro support, and, more important, provide an Object Modeling tool. As discussed later in this chapter, the Object Modeling tool enables you to create a visual representation of the classes in your solution and then convert that representation into code. Moreover, the tool supports what is known as *round-trip engineering*. This means that not only can you use the graphical model to generate code, you can also take a project's source files and regenerate an updated version of the graphical model — that is, edit that model in its graphical format and then update the associated source files.

For those choosing Visual Studio 2008 Professional or above, Visual Studio Tools for Office (VSTO) is targeted primarily at enterprise developers, those who work in corporate organizations (either as employees or consultant/contractors). This tool provides a way for users of the enterprise editions of Microsoft Office 2003 and Microsoft Office 2007 to extend these office productivity tools with applicationlike features. Many organizations use Microsoft Office for tasks that border on custom applications. This is especially true for Microsoft Excel. VSTO provides project templates based on these Microsoft Office products that enable, for example, a spreadsheet to retrieve its contents from an SQL Server database instead of the local file system. These tools provide the capability not only to manipulate data retrieval and saving, but also to customize the user interface, including direct access to the task pane and custom toolbar options within Microsoft Office products; they are covered in more detail in Chapter 22.

Visual Studio 2008 Team Suite and the various Team Edition products focus on extending a developer's reach beyond just writing code. These tools are used to examine code for flaws, manage the deployment environment, and define relationships between applications. The suite is focused on tools that support repeatable software processes and best practices. They are geared toward examining source code for hidden flaws that might not cause the code to fail but might hide a hidden security flaw or make it difficult to maintain or deploy the application. More important, the suite includes tools for creating unit test tools that attempt to cause the code to fail, whether through bad input data or heavy load. The Team Suite tools are focused on automating software development best practices for application teams, as opposed to actually writing the application.

Complete coverage of all of Team System warrants a book of its own, especially when you take into account all of the collaborative features introduced by Team Foundation Server and its tight integration with both Team Build and SharePoint Server. Team Foundation Server goes beyond just being a replacement for Visual Source Safe. It is the basis for true process-driven development, and it even includes documentation to help train your organization on two process models supported by Microsoft. The Team System extensions to the Microsoft software development suite are nontrivial, and are discussed in more detail at the end of this chapter.

Creating a Project from a Project Template

While it is possible to create a Visual Basic application working entirely outside of Visual Studio 2008, it is much easier to start from Visual Studio 2008. After you install Visual Studio you are presented with a screen similar to the one shown in Figure 13-1 for Visual Studio 2008 Express Edition. The starting default behavior is for the IDE to display the start page in its central section. The start page lists your most recent projects in the upper-left corner, some tips for getting started below that, and a headline section below that. You may or may not immediately recognize that this content is HTML text; more important, the content is based on an RSS feed that retrieves and caches articles appropriate for your version of Visual Studio.

The start page looks similar regardless of which version of Visual Studio 2008 you are running. Conceptually, it provides a generic starting point either to select the application you intend to work on, to quickly receive vital news related to offers, as shown in the figure, or to connect with external resources via the community links.

Once here, the next step is to create your first project. Selecting File ➪ New Project opens the New Project dialog, shown in Figure 13-2. This dialog provides you with a selection of templates customized by application type. One option is to create a Class Library project. Such a project doesn't include a user interface; and instead of creating an assembly with an .exe file, it creates an assembly with a .dll file. The difference, of course, is that an .exe file indicates an executable that can be started by the operating system, whereas a .dll file represents a library referenced by an application.

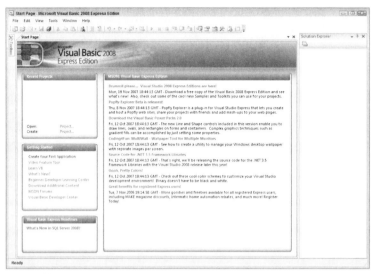

Figure 13-1

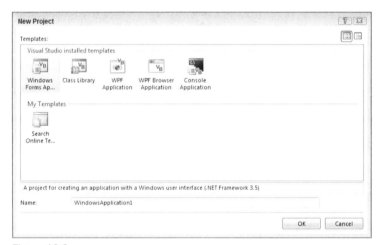

Figure 13-2

One of the ongoing challenges with describing the menu options for Visual Studio is that the various versions have slight differences in look and feel too numerous to mention. For example File ➪ New Project in Visual Basic Express becomes File ➪ New ➪ Project in Visual Studio. Thus, your display may vary slightly from what is shown or described here, although we attempt to showcase significant differences.

Noteworthy in Figure 13-2 is something that is missing: the ability to target different versions of the .NET Framework. With the Express editions, Microsoft has made it so that you will always target the current .NET 3.5 version of the .NET Framework when you create your project. However, as you'll see later in this chapter, you can retarget your application via the Compile Settings.

Another important item to note is that unlike Visual Basic 2005 Express Edition, there are no Starter Kits. These kits went beyond just the basic files associated with a generic project template and included source files associated with a specific application. You'll also note that the dialog includes a reference to My Templates. This section of the New Project window enables you to find and install additional templates. For example, the Microsoft site for Visual Basic enables you to download several additional Starter Kits for everything from PayPal and Amazon.com interfaces to Blackjack and Lego Mindstorms, plus others you can install. Additionally, third parties such as Dot Net Nuke provide custom templates associated with their application. Dot Net Nuke is an excellent example of this type of jump start for your projects.

In order to keep the discussion of project templates in context, Figure 13-3 is an example of the same dialog opened from Visual Studio 2008 Team Suite. In this context, note that not only do you have additional project templates related to Visual Basic, but another pane that groups the templates into project types has been added. Figures 13-2 and 13-3 have different display options selected in the upper-right corner related to the size of the template icons only. The Visual Studio 2008 version of the New Project dialog also includes, in the upper-right corner, an option for you to select which version of the .NET Framework you are targeting.

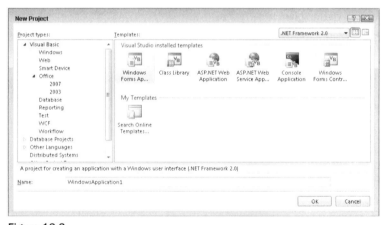

Figure 13-3

A quick note regarding the New Project dialog: In Visual Studio 2005, if you wanted to create an ASP.NET 2.0 website, you needed to start that process by creating a new website instead of creating a new project. Under Visual Studio 2008, the Web projects have been restored to participants as project types; however, to create an ASP.NET website that isn't project-based, you will still want to access the New Website menu item instead of the New Project menu item on the file menu.

Note that in Figure 13-3 the New Project dialog is targeting a .NET 2.0 project, and there are six common project types at the top level of the Visual Basic hierarchy. In Figure 13-4, the target has been changed to .NET 3.5 and the number of available project types has doubled. Targeting keeps you from attempting to create a project for WPF without recognizing that you also need at least .NET 3.0 available on the client. Although you can change your target after you create your project, be very careful when trying to reduce the version number, as the controls to prevent you from selecting dependencies don't check your existing code base for violations. Changing your targeted framework version is covered in more detail later in this chapter.

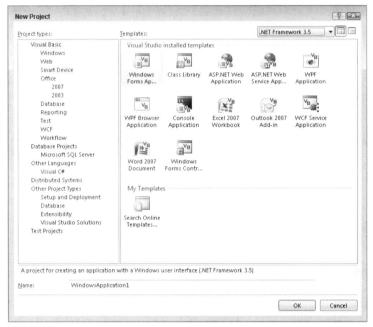

Figure 13-4

Expanding the top level of the Visual Basic tree in Figure 13-4 shows that a project type can be further separated into a series of categories:

❑ **Windows** — These are projects used to create applications that run on the local computer within the CLR. Because such projects can run on any operating system (OS) hosting the framework, the category "Windows" is something of a misnomer when compared to, for example, "Desktop."

❑ **Web** — The original .NET 1.x websites relied on a project file. In .NET 2.0 this project style was briefly removed, but it's back again. You can create these projects, including Web services, from this section of the New Project dialog.

❑ **Smart Device** — These are projects that target the .NET Compact Framework. Such applications may run on one or more handheld devices and make use of a different runtime environment from full .NET applications.

❑ **Office** — Visual Studio Tools for Office (VSTO). These are .NET applications that are hosted under Office. Visual Studio 2008 includes a set of templates you can use to target Office 2003, as well as a separate section for templates that target Office 2007. Note that the project types in Office 2007 include not only client applications but also SharePoint Workflow projects.

❑ **Database** — This template creates a project that supports classes that will run within SQL Server 2005. All versions of SQL Server 2005 (from Express through Enterprise) support the .NET Framework as part of their runtime, and such projects have a unique set of runtime constraints. This is a very different project template from the Database project template provided under the Other Project Types option.

❑ **Reporting** — This is a new project type that enables you to create a Reports application.

❑ **Test** — This section is available only to those using Visual Studio Team Suite. It contains the template for a Visual Basic Unit Test project.

❑ **WCF** — This is the section where you can create Windows Communication Foundation projects.

❑ **Workflow** — This is the section where you can create Windows Workflow Foundation (WF) projects. The templates in this section also include templates for connecting with the SharePoint workflow engine.

Visual Studio has other categories for projects, and you have access to other development languages and far more project types than this chapter has room for. For now, you can select a Windows Application project template to use as an example project for this chapter.

For this example, use ProVB_VS as the project name and then click OK. Visual Studio takes over and uses the Windows Application template to create a new Windows Forms project. The project contains a blank form that can be customized, and a variety of other elements that you can explore. Before customizing any code, let's first look at the elements of this new project.

The Solution Explorer

While the solution window both exists and is applicable for Express Edition users, it will never contain more than a single project. Those with a version of Visual Studio above the Express Edition level have the capability to leverage multiple projects in a single solution. A .NET solution can contain projects of any .NET language and can include the database, testing, and installation projects as part of the overall solution. The advantage of combining these projects is that it is easier to debug projects that reside in a common solution.

Before discussing these files in detail, let's take a look at the next step, which is to reveal a few additional details about your project. Click the second button on the left in Solution Explorer to display all of the project files, as shown in Figure 13-5. As this image shows, many other files make up your project. Some of these, such as those under the My Project grouping, don't require you to edit them directly. Instead, you can double-click on the My Project entry in the Solution Explorer and open the pages to edit your project settings. You do not need to change any of the default settings for this project, but the next section of this chapter walks you through the various property screens.

The `bin` and `obj` directories shown are used when building your project. The `obj` directory contains the first-pass object files used by the compiler to create your final executable file. The "binary" or compiled version of your application is then placed in the `bin` directory by default. Of course, referring to the Microsoft Intermediate Language (MSIL) code as binary is something of a misnomer, as the actual translation to binary does not occur until runtime when your application is compiled by the just-in-time (JIT) compiler. However, Microsoft continues to use the `bin` directory as the default output directory for your project's compilation.

Figure 13-5 also shows that the project does not contain an `app.config` file by default. Most experienced ASP.NET developers are familiar with using `web.config` files. `App.config` files work on the same principle in that they contain XML, which is used to store project-specific settings such as database connection strings and other application-specific settings. Using a `.config` file instead of having your settings in the Windows registry enables your applications to run side by side with another version of the application without the settings from either version impacting the other. Because each version of your application resides in its own directory, its settings are contained in the directory with it, which enables the different versions to run with unique settings. Before we are done going through the project properties, we will add an `App.Config` file to this project.

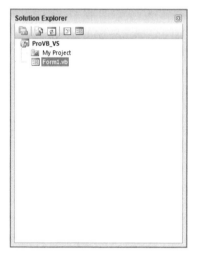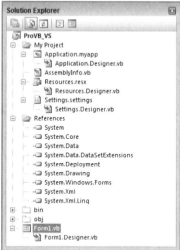

Figure 13-5

Finally, the Solution Explorer includes your actual source file(s). In this case, the `Form1.vb` file is the primary file associated with the default Windows form. You'll be customizing this form shortly, but before looking at that, it would be useful to look at some of the settings available by opening your project properties. An easy way to do this is to double-click on the My Project heading shown in Figure 13-5.

My Project Properties

Visual Studio displays a vertically tabbed display for editing your project settings. The My Project display shown in Figure 13-6, which is the view for users of Express Edition, is the same for all versions of Visual Studio. The project properties give you access to several different aspects of your project. Some, such as Signing, Security, and Publish, are covered in later chapters. For now, just note that this display makes it easier to carry out several tasks that once required engineers to work outside the Visual Studio environment.

Notice that you can customize your assembly name from this screen, as well as reset the type of application and object to be referenced when starting your application. However, resetting the type of your application is not recommended. If you start with the wrong application type, it is better to create a new application, due to all the embedded settings in the application template.

In the next section you will look at a button for changing your assembly information, as well as the capability to define a root namespace for your application classes. Namespaces are covered in detail in Chapter 7. You also have two buttons, one of which is related to Assembly Information, which is covered in the next section. The other button refers to User Access Control settings, which enable you to specify that only certain users can successfully start your application. In short, you have the option to limit your application access to a specific set of users.

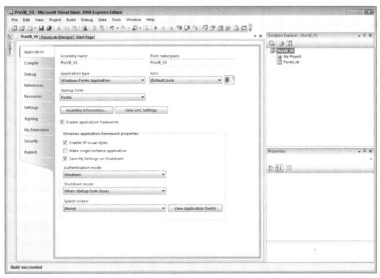

Figure 13-6

Finally, note that there is a section associated with enabling an application framework. The application framework is a set of optional components that enable you to extend your application with custom events and items, such as a splash screen, with minimal effort. Enabling the framework is the default, but unless you want to change the default settings, the behavior is the same as if the framework weren't enabled. Note that the View Application Events button adds a new source file, `ApplicationEvents.vb`, to your project, which includes documentation about which application events are available.

Assembly Information Screen

Selecting the Assembly Information button from within your My Project window opens the Assembly Information dialog box. Within this dialog, shown in Figure 13-7, you can define file properties, such as your company's name and versioning information, which will be embedded in the operating system's file attributes for your project's output. The frame of the assembly file shows that by default it contains several standard values.

Assembly Attributes

The `AssemblyInfo.vb` file contains attribute blocks, which are used to set information about the assembly. Each attribute block has an *assembly modifier*, shown in the following example:

```
<Assembly: AssemblyTitle("")>
```

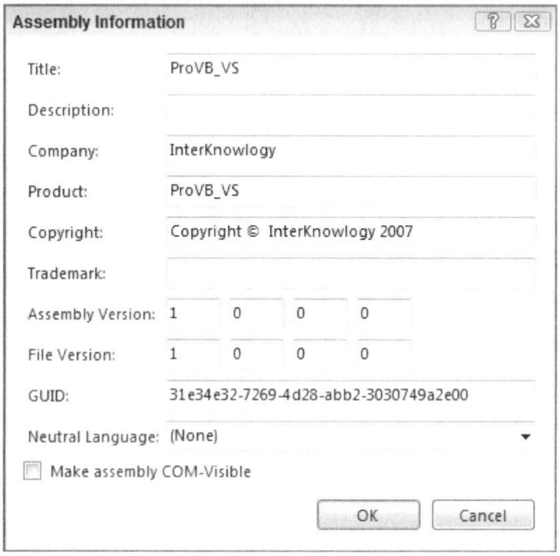

Figure 13-7

All the attributes set within this file provide information that is contained within the assembly metadata. These properties are displayed in the Assembly Information dialog, which is opened from the project's properties page (select the Compile tab and then click the Assembly Information button). The attributes contained within the file are summarized in the following table:

Attribute	Description
Title	This sets the name of the assembly, which appears within the file properties of the compiled file as the description.
Description	This attribute is used to provide a textual description of the assembly, which is added to the Comments property for the file.
Company	This sets the name of the company that produced the assembly. The name set here appears within the Version tab of the file properties.
Product	This attribute sets the product name of the resulting assembly. The product name appears within the Version tab of the file properties.
Copyright	The copyright information for the assembly. This value appears on the Version tab of the file properties.
Trademark	Used to assign any trademark information to the assembly. This information appears on the Version tab of the file properties.
Assembly Version	This attribute is used to set the version number of the assembly. Assembly version numbers can be generated, which is the default setting for .NET applications. This is covered in more detail in Chapter 23.
File Version	This attribute is used to set the version number of the executable files. This and other deployment-related settings are covered in more detail in Chapter 24.

Attribute	Description
COM Visible	This attribute is used to indicate whether this assembly should be registered and made available to COM applications.
Guid	If the assembly is to be exposed as a traditional COM object, then the value of this attribute becomes the ID of the resulting type library.

Compile Settings

The Compile tab (see Figure 13-8) was previously shown in Chapter 1. Visual Basic Express Edition users may have noticed in that original image that near the bottom of this screen is an option to generate XML comments for your assembly. These comments are generated based on the XML comments that you enter for each of the classes, methods, and properties in your source file. Unfortunately, these last settings are not available for Visual Basic 2005 Express Edition developers, although creating such comments, as shown later in this chapter, is possible even for Express Edition users.

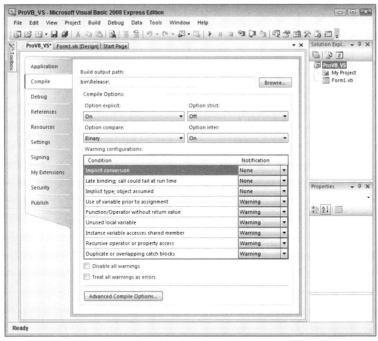

Figure 13-8

Below the grid of individual settings in Figure 13-8 is a series of check boxes. Unlike the full Visual Studio suite of options, Visual Basic Express has fewer check boxes; however, users do have access to the Advanced Compile Options button. This button opens the Advanced Compiler Settings dialog shown in Figure 13-9. Note a couple of key elements on this screen, the first being the Remove Integer Overflow Checks check box. In the past, this was enabled by default, and the result was a performance hit on

Visual Basic applications. The new default matches that of C#, enabling Visual Basic to match C# for performance. The compilation constants are values you shouldn't need to touch normally unless you are into compiler options. Similarly, the generation of serialization assemblies is something that is probably best left in auto mode.

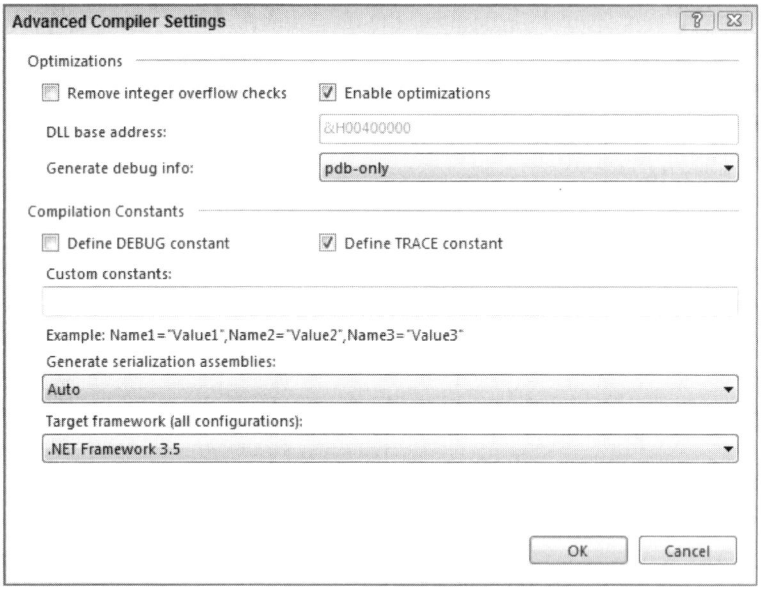

Figure 13-9

However, the last item on the screen enables you to target different environments. The screen shown in Figure 13-9 is taken from the Visual Basic Express Edition, and as you can see this option is available. This means that all Visual Basic developers have the option to target their application at a specific version of the .NET Framework. If you select a version prior to version 3.5, then when you begin to add references, the Add References tab recognizes which version of .NET you are targeting and adjusts the list of available references to exclude those that are part of version 3.5 — or 3.0 if you are targeting .NET 2.0.

Note that this check occurs when adding references; there is no check when you change this value to see whether your updated value conflicts with any existing references. Therefore, if you change this value, then make sure you update any of your existing references to remove any that are part of .NET 3.5. You are bound to have at least one because when the template creates your project it automatically adds a series of references determined in part by the target framework specified when you created your application.

Debug Properties

The Express Edition of Visual Basic 2008 supports local debugging. This means it supports not only the .NET-related Debug and Trace classes discussed in Chapter 8, but also actual breakpoints and the associated interactive debugging available in all versions of Visual Studio. However, as noted, the full versions of Visual Studio provide enhanced debugging options not available in Visual Basic 2008 Express

Edition. Figures 13-10 and 13-11 show the project debugger startup options from Visual Basic Express and Visual Studio 2008 Team Suite, respectively. Note that the Express Edition page has only three of the settings that are part of the more expensive version of Visual Studio.

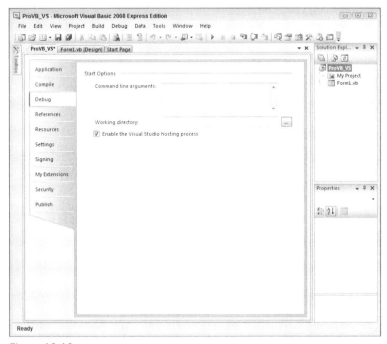

Figure 13-10

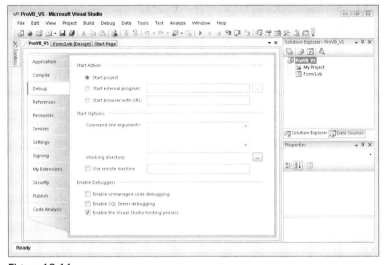

Figure 13-11

As shown in Figure 13-10, Express Edition users have three options related to starting the debugger. The first is to apply command-line arguments to the startup of a given application. This, of course, is most useful for console applications, but in some cases developers add command-line parameters to GUI applications. The second option is to select a different directory to be used to run the application. Generally, this isn't necessary, but it's desirable in some cases because of path or permission requirements or having an isolated runtime area.

Figure 13-11 shows additional options, beginning with Start Action. The default action shown is actually the only option available to Express users — which is to start the current project. However, Visual Studio 2008 developers have two additional options. The first is to start an external program. In other words, if you are working on a DLL or a user control, then you might want to have that application start, which can then execute your assembly. Doing this is essentially a shortcut, rather than needing to bind to a running process.

Similarly for Web development, you can reference a specific URL to start that Web application. This is often a mixed blessing, as with ASP.NET 2.0, Visual Studio automatically attempts to start an ASP.NET application based on the page you are currently editing. This is a change from ASP.NET 1.x, which allowed you to define a start page. Because ASP.NET 2.0 does not use project files, the new behavior was introduced. In most cases it works just fine, but if you have a Web application requiring authentication, then in most cases it makes more sense to actually place that URL into the debug settings for your application.

The next set of options aligns with those of the Express Edition, except for that third item — Use Remote Machine. As noted, Visual Studio 2008 provides support for remote debugging, although such debugging is often more trouble than it's worth. Using the `Debug` and `Trace` classes and effective error handling, it is generally easier to determine remote errors with existing tools. However, for those rare environments where an application only runs on a central server, and for which developers have the necessary permissions to run the debugger but not a copy of Visual Studio on that server, it is possible to leverage remote debugging.

Finally, as might be expected, users of Visual Studio 2008 who work with multiple languages and are given tools to tightly integrate with SQL Server have additional debuggers. The first of these is support for debugging outside of the CLR — what is known as *unmanaged code*. As a Visual Basic developer, the only time you should be using unmanaged code is when you are referencing legacy COM components. The developers most likely to use this debugger work in C++.

The next option turns on support for SQL Server debugging, a potentially useful feature. In short, it's possible, although the steps are not trivial, to have the Visual Studio debugging engine step directly into T-SQL stored procedures so that you can see the interim results as they occur within a complex stored procedure.

References

It's possible to add additional references as part of your project. Similar to the default code files that are created with a new project, each project template has a default set of referenced libraries. Actually, it has a set of imported namespaces and then a subset of the imported namespaces also referenced across the project. This means that while you can easily reference the classes in the referenced namespaces, you still need to fully qualify a reference to, for example, a `System.Collections.Generics.List` class. For

Windows Forms applications, the list of default referenced namespaces that are common from projects that target .NET 2.0 through projects that target .NET 3.5 is fairly short:

Reference	Description
System	Often referred to as the root namespace. All the base data types (`String`, `Object`, and so on) are contained within the `System` namespace. This namespace also acts as the root for all other `System` classes.
System.Data	Classes associated with ADO.NET and database access. This namespace is the root for SQL Server, Oracle, and other data access classes.
System.Deployment	Classes used for One Touch Deployment. This namespace is covered in more detail in Chapter 24.
System.Drawing	Provides access to the GDI+ graphics functionality
System.Windows.Forms	Classes used to create traditional Windows-based applications. This namespace is covered in more detail in Chapters 15 and 16.
System.XML	Root namespace for all of the XML classes

Note that the preceding list is the complete list of references you'll find in a project that was created to target .NET 2.0. If your project was created to target .NET 3.5, then as you'll see in Figure 13-12 your default list of referenced libraries is noticeably larger. Keep in mind that changing your target framework does not update any existing references.

To review the details of the imported and referenced namespaces, select the References tab in your My Project display, as shown in Figure 13-12. This tab enables you to check for unused references and even define reference paths. More important, it is from this tab that you select other .NET class libraries and applications, as well as COM components. Selecting the Add drop-down button gives you the option to add a reference to a local DLL or a Web service.

When referencing DLLs you have three options: reference an assembly from the GAC, reference an assembly based on a file path, or reference another assembly from within your current solution. Each of these options has advantages and disadvantages. The only challenge for assemblies that are in the GAC is that your application is dependent on what is potentially a shared resource. In general, however, for assemblies that are already in the GAC, referencing them is a straightforward, easily maintainable process.

Notice that the list shown in Figure 13-12 reflects what a Visual Basic Express Edition user sees once that user generates a project. If you are going to attempt to target the .NET 2.0 Framework, then you'll want to remove references that have a version higher then 2.0.0.0. References such as `System.Core` enable new features in the `System` namespace that are associated with .NET 3.5.

In addition to referencing libraries, you can reference other assemblies that are part of your solution. If your solution consists of more than a single project, then it is straightforward and highly recommended to use project references to allow those projects to reference each other. While you should avoid circular references — Project A references Project B which references Project A — using project references is preferred over file references. With project references, Visual Studio can map updates to these assemblies as they occur during a build of the solution. It's possible for Visual Studio to automatically update the referenced assemblies in your executable project to be the latest build of the referenced DLLs that are part of the same solution. Note that the target needs to be an executable. Visual Studio will automatically update references between DLL projects in a common solution.

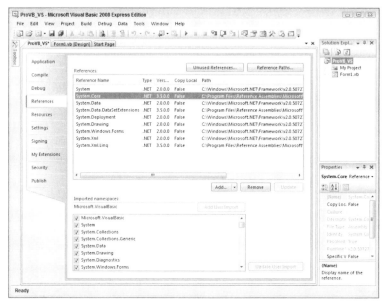

Figure 13-12

This is different from adding a reference to a DLL that is located within a specified directory. When you create a reference via a path specification, Visual Studio can check that path for an updated copy of the reference, but your code is no longer as portable as it would be with a project reference. More important, unless there is a major revision, Visual Studio usually fails to detect the types of changes you are likely to make to that file during the development process. As a result, you'll need to manually update the referenced file in the local directory of the assembly that's referencing it. In general, unless you have only the compiled version of that assembly, it's best to leverage project references versus path-based references.

Resources

In addition to referencing other assemblies, it is quite common for a .NET application to need to reference things such as images, icons, audio, and other files. These files aren't used to provide application logic but are used at runtime to provide support for the look, feel, and even text used to communicate with the application's user. In theory, you can reference a series of images associated with your application by looking for those images based on the installed file path of your application. Doing so, however, places your application's runtime behavior at risk, because a user might choose to replace, copy for profit, or just delete your files.

This is where project references become useful. Instead of placing the raw files onto the operating system alongside your executable, Visual Studio will package these files into your executable so that they are less likely to be lost or damaged. Figure 13-13 shows the Resources tab, which enables you to review and edit all your existing resources within a project, as well as import files for use as resources in your project. It even allows you to create new resources from scratch.

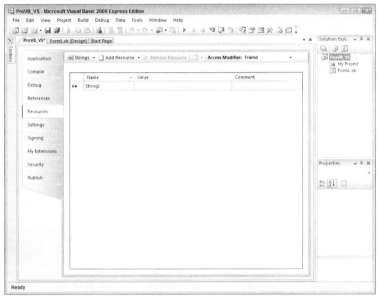

Figure 13-13

Note one little-known feature of this tab: Using the Add Resource drop-down button and selecting an image (not an existing image but one based on one of the available image types) will create a new image file and automatically open Microsoft Paint (for Express Edition developers); this enables you to actually create the image that will be in the image file.

Users of Visual Studio 2008 have additional capabilities not supported by Visual Basic's Express Edition. For one thing, instead of using Paint, Visual Studio provides a basic image editing tool, so when Visual Studio developers add a new image (not from a file), this editor opens within Visual Studio.

Additionally, within the list of Add Resource items, Visual Studio users can select or create a new icon. Choosing to create a new icon opens Visual Studio's icon editor, which provides a basic set of tools for creating custom icons to use as part of your application. This makes working with .ico files easier in that you don't have to hunt for or purchase such files online; instead, you can create your own icons.

However, images aren't the only resources that you can embed with your executable. Resources also apply to the fixed text strings that your application uses. By default, people tend to embed this text directly into the source code so that it is easily accessible to the developer. Unfortunately, this leaves the application difficult to localize for use with a second language. The solution is to group all of those text strings together, thereby creating a resource file containing all of the text strings, which is still part of and easily accessible to the application source code. When the application is converted for use in another language, this list of strings can be converted, making the process of localization easier. Localization is covered in more detail in Chapter 5.

Settings

New support for application settings within .NET 2.0 is a major enhancement that is often overlooked. In .NET 1.x it was possible to create a settings file. As noted earlier in the discussion of the Solution Explorer, the default project template does not create any application settings; accordingly, an `App.Config` file is not needed and not created. `App.Config` files are XML files that define any custom application settings that a developer wants to be able to change without needing to recompile the application. Because these settings live in an XML file, they can be modified in between or even during application execution.

One original goal of .NET was to reduce the version conflict that occurs when a component has registered with global settings and two different applications are attempting to reference two different versions of that component. Because the settings were global and stored in the central system registry, the result was a conflict, as the different applications each wanted its specific component and related settings.

.NET provided the capability to place version-specific project references in a local directory with the application, enabling two different applications to reference the appropriate version of that component. However, the second part of the problem was the central application settings. The `App.config` file provides the same capability, but its goal is allowing for local storage of application settings. Under .NET 1.x, support for application settings was still minimal, as most developers were still looking to the central system registry for this purpose. At the same time, the developer tools associated with settings were also minimal.

Fortunately, under .NET 2.0 this changed dramatically. Visual Basic 2008 provides significant support for application settings, including the Settings tab shown in Figure 13-14. This tab enables Visual Basic developers to identify application settings and automatically create these settings within the `App.config` file.

Figure 13-14

Figure 13-14 illustrates several elements related to the application settings capabilities of Visual Basic. The first setting is of type `String`. Under .NET 1.x, all application settings were seen as strings, and this was considered a weakness. Accordingly, the second setting, `LastLocation`, exposes the Type drop-down, illustrating that under Visual Basic 2008 you can create a setting that has a well-defined type.

However, strongly typed settings are not the most significant set of changes related to application settings. The very next column defines the scope of a setting. There are two possible options: applicationwide or user specific. The settings defined with application scope are available to all users of the application. As shown in Figure 13-14, this example creates a sample connection string to store for the application.

The alternative is a user-specific setting. Such settings have a default value; in this case, the last location defaults to 0,0. However, once a user has read that default setting, the application generally updates and saves the user-specific value for that setting. As noted by the Last Location setting, each user of this application might close the application after having moved it to a new location on the screen, and the goal of such a setting would be to reopen the application in the same location it was last seen. Thus, the application would update this setting value, and Visual Basic makes it easy to do this, as shown in the following code:

```
My.Settings.LastLocation = Me.Location
My.Settings.Save()
```

That's right — all it takes in Visual Basic 2008 is two lines of code that leverage the `My` namespace for you to update a user's application setting and save the new value. Meanwhile, let's take a look at what is occurring within the newly generated `App.config` file. The following XML settings demonstrate how the `App.config` file defines the setting values that you manipulate from within Visual Studio:

```
<?xml version="1.0" encoding="utf-8" ?>
<configuration>
    <configSections>
        <sectionGroup name="userSettings" type="System.Configuration.
UserSettingsGroup, System, Version=2.0.0.0, Culture=neutral,
PublicKeyToken=b77a5c561934e089" >
            <section name="ProVB_VS.My.MySettings" type="System.
Configuration.ClientSettingsSection, System, Version=2.0.0.0, Culture=neutral,
PublicKeyToken=b77a5c561934e089" allowExeDefinition="MachineToLocalUser"
requirePermission="false" />
        </sectionGroup>
        <sectionGroup name="applicationSettings" type="System.Configuration.
ApplicationSettingsGroup, System, Version=2.0.0.0, Culture=neutral,
PublicKeyToken=b77a5c561934e089" >
            <section name="ProVB_VS.My.MySettings" type="System.Configuration.
ClientSettingsSection, System, Version=2.0.0.0, Culture=neutral,
PublicKeyToken=b77a5c561934e089" requirePermission="false" />
        </sectionGroup>
    </configSections>
    <system.diagnostics>
        <sources>
            <!-- This section defines the logging configuration for
My.Application.Log -->
```

```
                <source name="DefaultSource" switchName="DefaultSwitch">
                    <listeners>
                        <add name="FileLog"/>
                        <!-- Uncomment the below section to write to the Application
Event Log -->
                        <!--<add name="EventLog"/>-->
                    </listeners>
                </source>
            </sources>
            <switches>
                <add name="DefaultSwitch" value="Information" />
            </switches>
            <sharedListeners>
                <add name="FileLog"
                    type="Microsoft.VisualBasic.Logging.FileLogTraceListener, Microsoft.
VisualBasic, Version=8.0.0.0, Culture=neutral, PublicKeyToken=b03f5f7f11d50a3a,
processorArchitecture=MSIL"
                    initializeData="FileLogWriter"/>
                <!-- Uncomment the below section and replace APPLICATION_NAME with the
name of your application to write to the Application Event Log -->
                <!--<add name="EventLog"
type="System.Diagnostics.EventLogTraceListener" initializeData="APPLICATION_NAME"/>
-->
            </sharedListeners>
        </system.diagnostics>
        <userSettings>
            <ProVB_VS.My.MySettings>
                <setting name="LastLocation" serializeAs="String">
                    <value>0, 0</value>
                </setting>
            </ProVB_VS.My.MySettings>
        </userSettings>
        <applicationSettings>
            <ProVB_VS.My.MySettings>
                <setting name="ConnectionString" serializeAs="String">
                    <value>server=(local);Database=AdventureWorks</value>
                </setting>
            </ProVB_VS.My.MySettings>
        </applicationSettings>
    </configuration>
```

As shown here, Visual Studio automatically generated all the XML needed to define these settings and save the default values. Note that individual user settings are not saved back into the config file, but rather to a user-specific working directory. It is possible not only to update application settings with Visual Basic, but also to arrange to encrypt those settings, although this action is outside the scope of what you can do from Visual Studio.

There are additional tabs related to your project's properties, but these are primarily associated with deployment. Therefore, in the interest of getting to some code, let's look at the source files that were generated when you created the ProVB_VS project from the Windows application template.

Project ProVB_VS in Visual Studio

The Form Designer opens by default when a new project is created. If you have closed it, then you can easily reopen it by right-clicking `Form1.vb` in the Solution Explorer and selecting View Designer from the pop-up menu. From this window, you can also bring up the Code view for this form. However, Figure 13-15 illustrates the default view you get when your project template completes. On the screen is the design surface upon which you can drag controls from the Toolbox to build your user interface and update properties associated with your form.

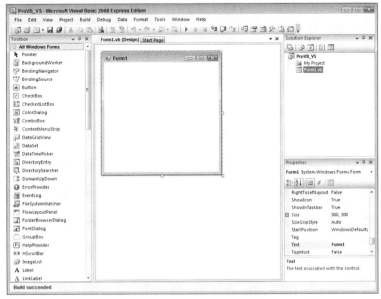

Figure 13-15

The Properties pane, shown in more detail in Figure 13-16, is by default placed in the lower-right corner of the Visual Studio window. Like many of the other windows in the IDE, if you close it, it can be accessed through the View menu. Alternatively, you can use the F4 key to reopen this window. The Properties pane is used to set the properties of the currently selected item control in the display.

Each control you place on your form has its own distinct set of properties. For example, in the design view, select your form. You'll see the Properties window adjust to display the properties of `Form1` (refer to Figure 13-16). This is the list of properties associated with your form. If you want to limit how small a user can reduce the display area of your form, then you can now define this as a property. For your sample, go to the `Text` property and change the default of `Form1` to Professional VB.NET. Once you have accepted the property change, the new value is displayed as the caption of your form. Later in this section, you'll set form properties in code. You'll see that .NET properties are defined within your source file, unlike other environments where properties you edit through the user interface are hidden in some binary or proprietary portion of the project.

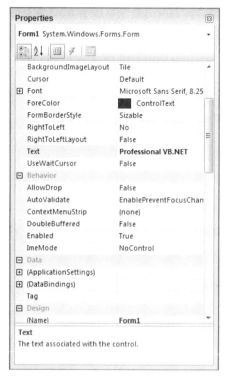

Figure 13-16

Now that you've looked at the form's properties, open the code associated with this file by either right-clicking `Form1.vb` in the Solution Explorer and selecting Code view, or right-clicking the form in the View Designer and selecting View Code from the pop-up menu.

You can see that the initial display of the form looks very simple. There is no code in the `Form1.vb` file. Visual Basic 2005 introduced a capability called *partial classes*. Partial classes are covered briefly in Chapter 2, and Visual Studio leverages them for the code, which is generated as part of the user interface designer.

Visual Studio places all the generated source code for your form in the file `Form1.Designer.vb`. Because the "Designer" portion of this name is a convention that Visual Studio recognizes, it hides these files by default when you review your project in the Solution Explorer. As noted earlier, by asking Visual Studio to "show all files," you can find these generated files. If you open a "Designer.vb" file, you'll see that quite a bit of custom code is generated by the Visual Studio already in your project.

To do this, go to the toolbar located in the Solution Explorer window and select the Show All Files button. This will change your project display and a small plus sign will appear next to the `Form1.vb` file. Expanding this entry displays the `Form1.Designer.vb` file, which you can open within the IDE. Doing this for `Form1.Designer.vb` for the ProVB_VS project you created will result in a window similar to the one shown in Figure 13-17.

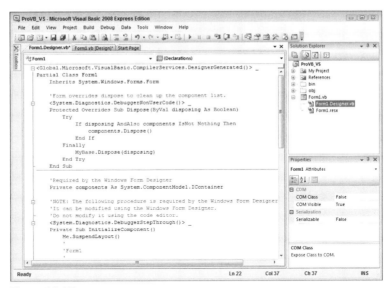

Figure 13-17

Note that the contents of this file are generated. For now, don't try to make any changes. Visual Studio automatically regenerates the entire file when a property is changed, so any changes may be lost. The following lines start the declaration for your form in the file Form1.Designer.vb:

```
<Global.Microsoft.VisualBasic.CompilerServices.DesignerGenerated()> _
Partial Class Form1
    Inherits System.Windows.Forms.Form
```

The first line is an attribute that can be ignored. Next is the line that actually declares a new class called Form1. Note that in spite of the naming convention used by Visual Studio to hide the generated UI class implementation, the name of your class and the file in which it exists are not tightly coupled. Thus, your form will be referenced in the code as Form1 unless you modify the name used in the class declaration. Similarly, you can rename the file that contains the class without changing the actual name of the class.

One powerful result of forms being implemented as classes is that you can now derive one form from another form. This technique is called *visual inheritance*, although the elements that are actually inherited may not be displayed.

Form Properties Set in Code

As noted earlier, Visual Studio keeps every object's custom property values in the source code. To do this, it adds a method to your form class called InitializeComponent. As the name suggests, this method handles the initialization of the components contained on the form. A comment before the procedure warns you that the Form Designer modifies the code contained in the procedure, and that you should not modify the code directly. This module is part of the Form1.Designer.vb source file, and Visual Studio updates this section as changes are made through the IDE.

```
'NOTE: The following procedure is required by the Windows Form Designer
'It can be modified using the Windows Form Designer.
'Do not modify it using the code editor.
<System.Diagnostics.DebuggerStepThrough()> Private Sub _
        InitializeComponent()
Me.SuspendLayout()
'
'Form1
'
Me.AutoScaleDimensions = New System.Drawing.SizeF(6.0!, 13.0!)
Me.AutoScaleMode = System.Windows.Forms.AutoScaleMode.Font
Me.ClientSize = New System.Drawing.Size(292, 266)
Me.Name = "Form1"
Me.Text = "Professional VB.NET"
Me.ResumeLayout(False)

End Sub
```

The seven lines of the `InitializeComponent` procedure assign values to the properties of your `Form1` class. All the properties of the form and controls are now set directly in code. When you change the value of a property of the form or a control through the Properties window, an entry is added to `InitializeComponent` that assigns that value to the property. Previously, while examining the Properties window, you set the `Text` property of the form to Professional VB.NET Intro, which caused the following line of code to be added automatically:

```
Me.Text = "Professional VB.NET"
```

The properties of the form class that are set in `InitializeComponent` by default are shown in the following table:

Property	Description
Suspend Layout	Specifies that the form should not make updates to what is displayed to the user. It is called so that as each change is made, the form doesn't seem to appear in pieces.
AutoScaleDimensions	Initializes the size of the font used to lay out the form at design time. At runtime, the font that is actually rendered is compared with this property, and the form is scaled accordingly.
AutoScaleMode	Indicates that the form will use fonts that are automatically scaled based on the display characteristics of the runtime environment
ClientSize	Sets the area in which controls can be placed (the client area). It is the size of the form minus the size of the title bar and form borders.
Name	This property is used to set the textual name of the form.
ResumeLayout	This tells the form that it should resume the normal layout and displaying of its contents.

Code Regions

Source files in Visual Studio allow you to collapse blocks of code. The idea is that in most cases you can reduce the amount of onscreen code, which seems to separate other modules within a given class, by collapsing the code so it isn't visible; this feature is known as *outlining*. For example, if you are comparing the `load` and `save` methods and in between you have several other blocks of code, then you can effectively "hide" this code, which isn't part of your current focus.

By default, there is a minus sign next to every method (sub or function). This makes it easy to hide or show code on a method-by-method basis. If the code for a method is hidden, the method declaration is still shown and has a plus sign next to it indicating that the body code is hidden. This feature is very useful when a developer is working on a few key methods in a module and wishes to avoid scrolling through many screens of code that are not relevant to the current task.

It is also possible to hide custom regions of code. The `#Region` directive is used for this within the IDE, though it has no effect on the actual application. A region of code is demarcated by the `#Region` directive at the top and the `#End Region` directive at the end. The `#Region` directive that is used to begin a region should include a description. The description appears next to the plus sign shown when the code is minimized.

The outlining enhancement was probably inspired by the fact that the Visual Studio designers generate a lot of code when a project is started. Being able to see the underpinnings of your generated UI does make it is easier to understand what is happening, and possibly to manipulate the process in special cases. However, as you can imagine, it can become problematic; hence the `#Region` directive, which can be used to organize groups of common code and then visually minimize them.

Visual Studio 2008 developers, but not Express Edition developers, can also control outlining throughout a source file. Outlining can be turned off by selecting Edit ➪ Outlining ➪ Stop Outlining from the Visual Studio menu. This menu also contains some other useful functions. A section of code can be temporarily hidden by highlighting it and selecting Edit ➪ Outlining ➪ Hide Selection. The selected code will be replaced by an ellipsis with a plus sign next to it, as if you had dynamically identified a region within the source code. Clicking the plus sign displays the code again.

Tabs versus MDI

You may have noticed in Figure 13-17 that the Code View and Form Designer windows open in a tabbed environment. This environment is the default for working with the code windows inside Visual Studio, but you can toggle this setting, which enables you to work with a more traditional MDI-based interface. Such an interface opens each code window within a separate frame instead of anchoring it to the tabbed display of the integrated development environment (IDE).

To change the arrangement that is used between the tabbed and MDI interface, use the Options dialog box (accessible via Tools ➪ Options); this setting is available as one of the environment settings. You can also force the development environment to use the MDI as opposed to the tabbed interface (for a single session) by using the command-line option `/mdi` when Visual Studio is started.

Running ProVB_VS

Now that you've reviewed the elements of your generated project, let's test the code before continuing. To run an application from within Visual Studio, you have several options; the first is to click the Start button, which looks like the Play button on a tape recorder. Alternatively, you can go to the Debug menu and select Start. Finally, the most common way of launching applications is to press F5.

Once the application starts, an empty form will be displayed with the standard control buttons (in the upper-right corner) from which you can control the application. The form name should be Professional VB.NET Intro, which you applied earlier. At this point, the sample doesn't have any custom code to examine, so the next step is to add some simple elements to this application.

Customizing the Text Editor

In addition to being able to customize the overall environment provided by Visual Studio, you can customize several specific elements related to your development environment. Both Visual Studio 2008 and Visual Basic 2008 Express Edition have a rich set of customizations related to a variety of different environment and developer settings. Admittedly, Visual Studio 2008's feature set results in a larger number of available options for editing, but rest assured that the Express Edition contains many more options for editing than most people expect. A good example that's common to both IDEs is the way the text editor allows for much more customization. If you've ever had to show code to an audience — for example, in a group code review — the capability to adjust things such as font size and other similar options is great.

To leverage Visual Studio's settings, go to the Tools menu and select Options to open the Options dialog box, shown in Figure 13-18. Within the dialog box, make sure the Show All Settings check box is selected. Next, select the Text Editor folder, and then select the All Languages folder. This section enables you to make changes to the text editor that are applied across every supported development language. Additionally, you can select the Basic folder to make changes that are specific to how the text editor will behave when you edit VB source code.

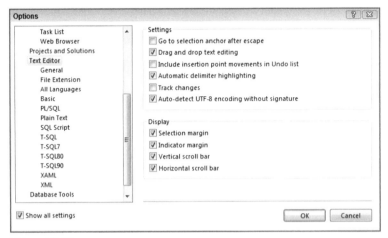

Figure 13-18

From this dialog box, it is possible to modify the number of spaces that each tab will insert into your source code and to manage several other elements of your editing environment. One little-known but useful capability of the text editor is line numbering. Checking the Line numbers check box will cause the editor to number all lines, which provides an easy way to unambiguously reference lines of code.

Visual Studio 2008 also provides a visual indicator so you can track your changes as you edit. Enabling the Track Changes setting under the Text Editor options causes Visual Studio to provide a colored indicator in places where you have modified a file. This indicator is a colored bar at the left margin of your display. It shows which portions of a source file have been recently edited and whether those changes have been saved to disk.

IntelliSense, Code Expansion, and Code Snippets

One of the reasons Microsoft Visual Studio is one of the most popular development environments is that it has been designed to support developer productivity. That sounds really good, but let's back it up. People who are unfamiliar with Visual Studio might just assume that "productivity" refers to organizing and starting projects. Certainly, as shown with the project templates and project settings discussed so far, this is true, but those features don't speed your development after you've created the project.

This section covers three features that target your productivity while writing code. They are of differing value and are specific to Visual Studio. The first, IntelliSense, has always been a popular feature of Microsoft tools and applications. The second feature, code expansion, is another popular feature available since Visual Studio 2005: It enables you to type a keyword, such as "select," and then press the Tab key to automatically insert a generic select-case code block, which you can then customize. Finally, going beyond this, you can use the right mouse button and insert a code snippet at the location of your mouse click. As you can tell, each of these builds on the developer productivity capabilities of Visual Studio.

IntelliSense

IntelliSense has been enhanced in Visual Studio 2008. In the past you needed to first identify a class or property in order to use IntelliSense. With Visual Studio 2008, IntelliSense starts with the first letter you type so that you quickly identify classes, commands, and keywords that you need. Once you've selected a class or keyword, IntelliSense continues, enabling you to not only work with the methods of a class, but also automatically display the list of possible values associated with an enumerated list of properties when one has been defined. IntelliSense also provides a tooltiplike list of parameter definitions when you are making a method call.

Figure 13-19 illustrates how IntelliSense becomes available with the first character you type. Note that the drop-down window has two tabs on the bottom; one is optimized for the items that you are likely to want, while the other shows you everything that is available. In addition, IntelliSense works with multiword commands. For example, if you type **Exit** and a space, IntelliSense displays a drop-down list of keywords that could follow `Exit`. Other keywords that offer drop-down lists to present available options include `Goto`, `Implements`, `Option`, and `Declare`. IntelliSense generally displays more tooltip information in the environment than before and helps developers match up pairs of parentheses, braces, and brackets.

Finally, note that IntelliSense is based on your editing context. While editing a file, there may come a point at which you are looking for a specific item to show up in IntelliSense but when you repeatedly type slightly different versions nothing appears. IntelliSense has recognized that you aren't in a method or are outside of the scope of a class, so it has removed items that are inappropriate for your current location in your source code from the list of items available from IntelliSense.

Code Expansion

Going beyond IntelliSense is code expansion. Code expansion recognizes that certain keywords are consistently associated with other lines of code. At the most basic level, this occurs when you declare a new `Function` or `Sub`: Visual Studio automatically inserts the `End Sub` or `End Function` line once you press Enter. Essentially, Visual Studio is expanding the declaration line to include its matching endpoint. However, real code expansion goes further than this.

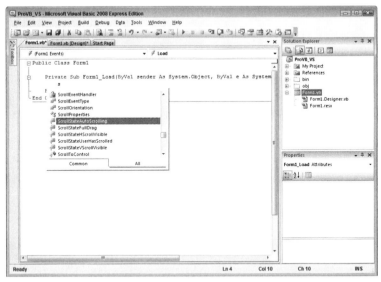

Figure 13-19

With real code expansion, you can type a keyword such as `For`, `ForEach`, `Select`, or any of a number of Visual Basic keywords. If you then use the Tab key, Visual Studio will attempt to recognize that keyword and insert the block of code that you would otherwise need to remember and type yourself. For example, instead of needing to remember how to format the control values of a `Select` statement, you can just type this first part of the command and then press Tab to get the following code block:

```
Select Case VariableName
    Case 1

    Case 2

    Case Else
End Select
```

Unfortunately, this is a case where just showing you the code isn't enough. That's because the code that is inserted has active regions within it that represent key items you will customize. Thus, Figure 13-20 provides a better representation of what is inserted when you expand the `Select` keyword into a full `Select Case` statement.

When the block is inserted the editor automatically positions your cursor in the first highlighted block — `VariableName`. When you start typing the name of the variable that applies, the editor automatically clears that static `VariableName` string, which is acting as a placeholder. Once you have entered the variable name you want, you can just press Tab. At that point the editor automatically jumps to the next highlighted item. This capability to insert a block of boilerplate code and have it automatically respond to your customization is a great feature.

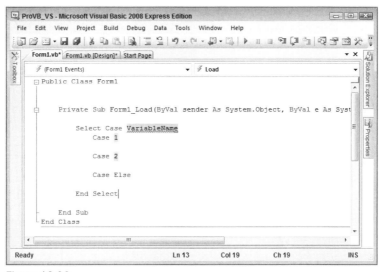

Figure 13-20

Code expansion enables you to quickly shift between the values that need to be customized, but these values are also linked where appropriate, as in the next example. Another code expansion shortcut creates a new property in a class. If at the class level you type the word **property** followed by Tab, you will find the code shown in Figure 13-21 inserted into your code. On the surface this code is very similar to what you see when you expand the `Select` statement. Note that although you type **property**, even the internal value is part of this code expansion.

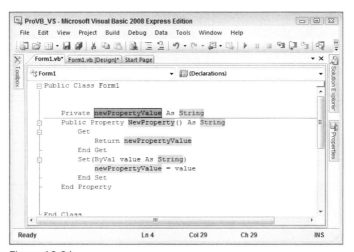

Figure 13-21

The difference, however, is that the same value `String` in Figure 13-21 is repeated for the property. The value you see is actually not the default; the default everywhere you see `String` in Figure 13-21 is `Integer`. However, when you change the first such entry from `Integer` to `String`, Visual Studio automatically updates all three locations because it knows they are linked. Using the code shown in Figure 13-21, update the property value to be m_Count. Press Tab and change the type to Integer; press Tab again and label the new property Count. This gives you a simple property on this form for use later when debugging.

The completed code should look like the following block. Note that one final change was to initialize the value of the m_count value to zero so that it would be initialized when first referenced:

```
Private m_count As Integer = 0
Public Property Count() As Integer
    Get
        Return m_count
    End Get
    Set(ByVal value As Integer)
        m_count = value
    End Set
End Property
```

This capability to fully integrate the template supporting the expanded code with the highlighted elements, helping you navigate to the items you need to edit, makes code expansion such a valuable tool.

Code Snippets

You can, with a click of your mouse, browse a library of code blocks, which, as with code expansion, you can insert into your source file. However, unlike code expansion, these snippets aren't triggered by a keyword. Instead, you right-click and (as shown in Figure 13-22) select Insert Snippet from the context menu. This starts the selection process for whatever code you want to insert.

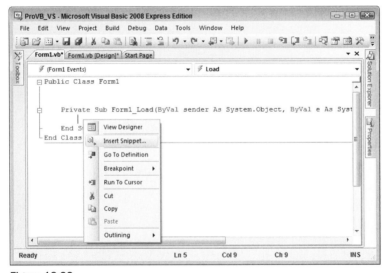

Figure 13-22

The snippet library is installed with Visual Studio and is fully expandable, as discussed later in this chapter. Snippets are categorized by the function on which each is focused. For example, all the code you can reach via code expansion is also available as snippets, but snippets go well beyond that list. There are snippet blocks for XML-related actions, for operating system interface code, for items related to Windows

Forms, and, of course, a lot of data-access-related blocks. The whole idea is that, unlike code expansion, which enhances the language in a way similar to IntelliSense, code snippets are blocks of code focused on functions developers often write from scratch.

As shown in Figure 13-23, the insertion of a snippet triggers the creation of a placeholder tag and a context window showing the categories of snippets. Each of the folders can contain a combination of snippet files or subdirectories containing still more snippet files. Visual Basic 2008 Express contains a subset of the folders provided with Visual Studio 2008. Visual Studio includes additional categories not shown in Figure 13-23. In addition, Visual Studio includes the folder My Code Snippets, to which you can add your own custom snippet files.

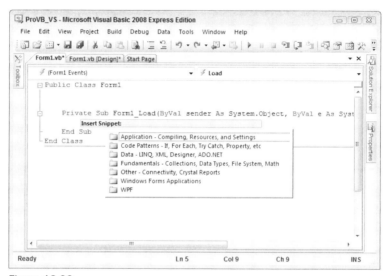

Figure 13-23

Selecting a folder enables you to select from one of its subfolders or a snippet file. Once you select the snippet of interest, Visual Studio inserts the associated code into your source file. Figure 13-24 shows the result of adding an operating system snippet to some sample code. The specific snippet in question is the code within the sub `ReviewAppErrors`. The selected snippet was `Windows Operating System> Event Logs>Read Entries Created by a Particular Application from the Event Log`, which isn't included with Visual Basic 2008 Express, although the code is still valid.

As you can see, this code snippet isn't just a block of code that can be used anywhere. Instead, it is specific to reading the Application Log, and its use in the `ReviewAppErrors` method is based on the idea that many applications log their errors to the Event Log so that they can be reviewed either locally or from another machine in the local domain. The key, however, is that the snippet has pulled in the necessary class references, many of which might not be familiar to you, and has placed them in context. This speeds not only the time spent typing this code, but also the time spent recalling exactly which classes need to be referenced and which methods need to be called and customized.

Finally, it is also possible to shortcut the menu tree. Specifically, if you know the shortcut for a snippet, you can type that and press Tab to have Visual Studio insert that snippet. For example, typing **evReadApp** followed by pressing Tab will insert the same snippet shown in Figure 13-24.

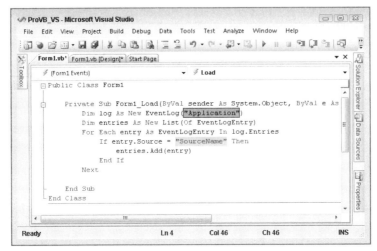

Figure 13-24

Tools such as code snippets and especially code expansion are even more valuable when you work in multiple languages. Keep in mind, however, that Visual Studio isn't limited to the features that come in the box. It's possible to extend Visual Studio not only with additional controls and project templates, but also with additional editing features.

Additional Components for Visual Studio 2008

You might be interested in two additional tools that work with Visual Studio. Even better, both are free. The first is a tool for creating your own Visual Basic snippets. As discussed, snippets can be powerful tools when you need to replicate relatively small but commonly used blocks of code that will be customized. While Visual Studio ships with several such snippets, Microsoft probably hasn't thought of the snippet you want the most.

This is where the first tool comes in: a Snippet Editor for Visual Basic code snippets. This editor doesn't actually live within Visual Studio 2008; it just updates the snippet files you want to use from Visual Studio. Behind the scenes, snippets are actually XML files with embedded text that represents the code used in the snippet. What the Snippet Editor does is read that XML and interpret all of the embedded logic related to things such as replacement blocks. This tool makes it possible for Visual Basic developers to create custom snippets without worrying about the XML formatting details. It is available from MSDN at http://msdn2.microsoft.com/en-us/vbasic/ms789085.aspx.

The second tool is a true add-in to Visual Basic. When Microsoft was announcing features for .NET 2.0, it was apparent that Visual Basic and C# had different feature lists. As time went by, the developers in each community started to better understand what these features represented, and in many cases demanded their inclusion. One such feature was native support in C# for refactoring, the ability to modify a variable name — for example, to take ''i'' and call it ''loopControl'' so that it's more readable. Modifying code to improve structure, performance, and maintainability is referred to generically as *refactoring*.

Traditionally, such changes might make code more maintainable but were often more risk than reward; as a result they seldom were made. The problem, of course, is that a human tends to miss that one remaining reference to the old version of that method or variable name. More important, it was a time-consuming task to find all of the correct references. Fortunately, the compiler knows where these are, and that's the idea behind automated refactoring: You tell Visual Studio what you want to change and it goes through your code and makes all the necessary changes, using the same rules the compiler uses to compile your code.

This is a great maintenance tool; unfortunately, by the time most Visual Basic developers understood what it implied, it was too late for the Visual Basic team to implement a solution in Visual Studio 2005. However, the team did do better than just say, "So sad, too bad." They found a commercial product that actually had more features than what the C# team was developing from scratch. Then they bought a license for every Visual Studio developer, allowing free download of the tool. This solution worked so well for everyone involved that they chose to continue it in Visual Studio 2008. With refactoring, you can quickly clean up gnarly, hard-to-read code and turn it into well-structured logic that's much more maintainable. The free version of the refactoring tool is available at `www.devexpress.com/Products/NET/IDETools/VBRefactor/`.

Enhancing a Sample Application

To start enhancing the application, you are going to use the control Toolbox. Close the `Form1.designer.vb` file and switch your display to the `Form1.vb [Design]` tab. The Toolbox window is available whenever a form is in Design mode. By default, the Toolbox, shown in Figure 13-25, lives on the left-hand side of Visual Studio as a tab. When you click this tab, the control window expands and you can drag controls onto your form. Alternatively, if you have closed the Toolbox tab, you can go to the View menu and select Toolbox.

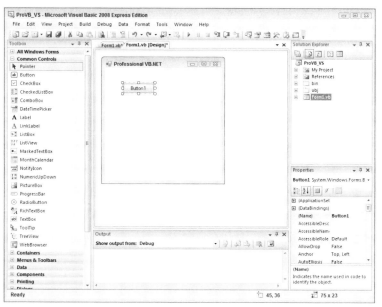

Figure 13-25

If you haven't set up the Toolbox to be permanently visible, it will slide out of the way and disappear whenever focus is moved away from it. This helps maximize the available screen real estate. If you don't like this feature and want the Toolbox to be permanently visible, just click the pushpin icon on the Toolbox's title bar.

The Toolbox contains literally dozens of standard controls, which are categorized so it's easier to find them. Figure 13-25 shows the result of dragging a Button control from the Toolbox and depositing it on the form: a new button displaying the text "Button1." Adding another button would trigger the default naming and text of "Button2."

Before customizing the first control added to this form, take a closer look at the Visual Studio Toolbox. The tools are broken out by category, but this list of categories isn't static. Visual Studio 2005 Standard and above editions enable you to create your own custom controls. When you create such controls, the IDE will — after they have been compiled — automatically add them to the display when you are working in the same solution as the controls. These would be local references to controls that become available within the current solution.

Additionally, depending on whether you are working on a Web or a Windows Forms application, your list of controls in the Toolbox will vary. Windows Forms has a set of controls that leverages the power of the Windows operating system. Web applications, conversely, tend to have controls oriented to working in a disconnected environment.

It's also possible to have third-party controls in your environment. Such controls can be registered with Visual Studio and are then displayed within every project you work on. Controls can add their own categories to the Toolbox so that they are grouped together and therefore easy to find.

Return to the button you've dragged onto the form; it's ready to go in all respects. However, Visual Studio has no way of knowing how you want to customize it. Start by going to the Properties window and changing its text property to "Hello World." You can then change the button's (Name) property to ButtonHelloWorld. Having made these changes, double-click the button in the display view. Double-clicking tells Visual Studio that you want to add an event handler to this control, and by default Visual Studio adds an On_Click event handler for buttons. The IDE then shifts the display to the Code view so that you can customize this handler (Figure 13-26 shows the code for this event handler being edited).

Although the event handler can be added through the designer, it's also possible to add event handlers from Code view. After you double-click the button, Visual Studio will transfer you to code view and display your new event handler. Notice that in Code view there are drop-down lists on the top of the edit window. The boxes indicate the current object on the left — in this case, your new button — and the current method on the right — in this case, the click-event handler. You can add new handlers for other events on your button or form using these drop-down lists.

The drop-down list on the left-hand side contains the objects for which event handlers can be added. The drop-down list on the right-hand side contains all the events for the selected object. For now, you have created a new handler for your button's click event, so let's look at customizing the code associated with this event.

Customizing the Code

With the code window open to the newly added event handler for the "Hello World" button, you can start to customize this handler. Note that adding a control and event handler involves elements of generated code. Visual Studio adds code to the Form1.Designer.vb file. These changes occur in addition to the default method implementation you see in the editable portion of your source code.

Adding XML Comments

One of the features of Visual Studio is the capability to generate an XML comments template for Visual Basic. XML comments are a much more powerful feature than you probably realize, because they are also recognized by Visual Studio for use in IntelliSense. To add a new XML comment to your handler, go to the line before the handler and type three single quotation marks: '''. This triggers Visual Studio to replace your single quotation marks with the following block of comments. You can trigger these comments in front of any method, class, or property in your code:

```
'''  <summary>
'''
'''  </summary>
'''  <param name="sender"></param>
'''  <param name="e"></param>
'''  <remarks></remarks>
```

Note that Visual Studio has provided a template that offers a place to include a summary of what this method does. It also provides placeholders to describe each parameter that is part of this method. Not only are the comments entered in these sections available within the source code, when it's compiled you'll also find an XML file in the project directory, which summarizes all your XML comments and can be used to generate documentation and help files for the said source code. By the way, if you refactor a method and add new parameters, the XML comments also support IntelliSense for the XML tags that represent your parameters.

Customizing the Event Handler

Now customize the code for the button handler, as this method doesn't actually do anything by default. Start by adding a new line of code to increment the Count property you added to the form earlier. Next, use the System.Windows.Forms.MessageBox class to open a message box and show the message indicating the number of times the Hello World button has been pressed. Fortunately, because that namespace is automatically imported into every source file in your project, thanks to your project references, you can reference the MessageBox.Show method directly. The Show method has several different parameters; and as shown in Figure 13-26, not only does the IDE provide a tooltip for the list of parameters, it also provides help regarding the appropriate value for individual parameters.

The completed call to MessageBox.Show should look similar to the following code block. Note that the underscore character is used to continue the command across multiple lines. In addition, unlike previous versions of Visual Basic, for which parentheses were sometimes unnecessary, in .NET the syntax best practice is to use parentheses for every method call:

```
Count += 1
MessageBox.Show(""Hello World shown " + Count.ToString() + " times."", _
                "Hello World Message Box", _
                MessageBoxButtons.OK, _
                MessageBoxIcon.Information)
```

Once you have entered this line of code, you may notice a squiggly line underneath some portions of your text. This occurs when there is an error in the line you have typed. In previous versions of Visual Basic, the development environment would interrupt your progress with a dialog box, but with .NET, the IDE works more like the latest version of Word. Instead of interrupting your progress, it highlights the problem and allows you to continue working on your code. This is a feature of Visual Basic that isn't available in other .NET languages such as C#. Visual Basic is constantly reviewing your code to ensure that it will compile; and when it encounters a problem it immediately notifies you of the location without interrupting your work.

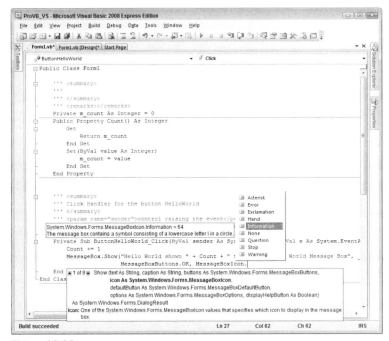

Figure 13-26

Reviewing the Code

Now that you have created a simple Windows application, let's review the elements of the code that have been added by the IDE. Following is the entire `Form1.Designer.vb` source listing. Highlighted in this listing are the lines of code that have changed since the original template was used to generate this project:

```
<Global.Microsoft.VisualBasic.CompilerServices.DesignerGenerated()> _
Partial Class Form1    Inherits System.Windows.Forms.Form

    'Form overrides dispose to clean up the component list.
    <System.Diagnostics.DebuggerNonUserCode()> _
    Protected Overloads Overrides Sub Dispose(ByVal disposing As Boolean)

        If disposing AndAlso components IsNot Nothing Then
                components.Dispose()
        End If
        MyBase.Dispose(disposing)
    End Sub

    'Required by the Windows Form Designer
```

```
        Private components As System.ComponentModel.Icontainer
        'NOTE: The following procedure is required by the Windows Form Designer
        'It can be modified using the Windows Form Designer.
         'Do not modify it using the code editor.
        <System.Diagnostics.DebuggerStepThrough()> _
        Private Sub InitializeComponent()
            Me. ButtonHelloWorld = New System.Windows.Forms.Button()
            Me.SuspendLayout()
            '
            'ButtonHelloWorld
            '
            Me.ButtonHelloWorld.Location = New System.Drawing.Point(112, 112)
            Me.ButtonHelloWorld.Name = "ButtonHelloWorld"
            Me.ButtonHelloWorld.Size = New System.Drawing.Size(75, 23)
            Me.ButtonHelloWorld.TabIndex = 0
            Me.ButtonHelloWorld.Text = "Hello World"
            Me.ButtonHelloWorld.UseVisualStyleBackColor = True
            '
            'Form1
            '
            Me.AutoScaleDimensions = New System.Drawing.SizeF(6.0!, 13.0!)
            Me.AutoScaleMode = System.Windows.Forms.AutoScaleMode.Font    Me.ClientSize =
    New System.Drawing.Size(292, 273)
            Me.Controls.Add(Me.ButtonHelloWorld)

            Me.Name = "Form1"
            Me.Text = "Professional VB.NET"
            Me.ResumeLayout(False)
        End Sub
        Friend WithEvents ButtonHelloWorld As System.Windows.Forms.Button
    End Class
```

After the class declaration in the generated file, the first change made to the code is the addition of a new variable to represent the new button:

```
    Friend WithEvents ButtonHelloWorld As System.Windows.Forms.Button
```

When any type of control is added to the form, a new variable is added to the form class. Controls are represented by variables; and, just as form properties are set in code, form controls are added in code. The Button class in the System.Windows.Forms namespace implements the button control on the Toolbox. Each control added to a form has a class that implements the functionality of the control. For the standard controls, these classes are usually found in the System.Windows.Forms namespace. The WithEvents keyword has been used in the declaration of the new variable so that it can respond to events raised by the button.

The bulk of the code changes are in the InitializeComponent procedure. Eight lines of code have been added to help set up and display the button control. The first addition to the procedure is a line that creates a new instance of the Button class and assigns it to the button variable:

```
    Me.ButtonHelloWorld = New System.Windows.Forms.Button()
```

Before a button is added to the form, the form's layout engine must be paused. This is done using the next line of code:

```
Me.SuspendLayout()
```

The next four lines of code set the properties of the button. The Location property of the Button class sets the location of the top-left corner of the button within the form:

```
Me.ButtonHelloWorld.Location = New System.Drawing.Point(112, 112)
```

The location of a control is expressed in terms of a Point structure. Next, the Name property of the button is set:

```
Me.ButtonHelloWorld.Name = "ButtonHelloWorld"
```

The Name property acts in exactly the same way as it did for the form, setting the textual name of the button. The Name property has no effect on how the button is displayed on the form; it is used to recognize the button's context within the source code. The next three lines of code assign values to the TabIndex, Text, and UseVisualStyleBackColor properties of the button:

```
Me.ButtonHelloWorld.TabIndex = 0
Me.ButtonHelloWorld.Text = "Hello World"
Me.ButtonHelloWorld.UseVisualStyleBackColor = True
```

The TabIndex property of the button is used to set the order in which the control is selected when a user cycles through the controls on the form using the Tab key. The higher the number, the later the control gains focus. Each control should have a unique number for its TabIndex property. The Text property of a button sets the text that appears on the button. Finally, the UseVisualStyleBackColor property indicates that when this button is drawn, it uses the current visual style. This is a Boolean value and typically you can accept this default, but you can customize the background so that a given button doesn't default to the current visual style.

Once the properties of the button have been set, it needs to be added to the form. This is accomplished with the next line of code:

```
Me.Controls.Add(Me.ButtonHelloWorld)
```

The System.Windows.Forms.Form class (from which your Form1 class is derived) has a property called Controls that keeps track of all of the child controls of the form. Whenever you add a control to a form in the designer, a line similar to the preceding one is added automatically to the form's initialization process.

Finally, near the bottom of the initialization logic is the final code change. The form is given permission to resume the layout logic:

```
Me.ResumeLayout(False)
```

In addition to the code that has been generated in the `Form1.Designer.vb` source file, you have created code that lives in the `Form1.vb` source file:

```
Imports System.Windows.Forms
Public Class Form1
    ''' <summary>
    '''
    ''' </summary>
    ''' <param name="sender"></param>
    ''' <param name="e"></param>
    ''' <remarks></remarks>
    Private Sub ButtonHelloWorld_Click (ByVal sender As System.Object, _
                        ByVal e As System.EventArgs) _
                        Handles ButtonHelloWorld.Click
      MessageBox.Show("Hello World", _
                    "Hello World Message Box", _
                    MessageBoxButtons.OK, _
                    MessageBoxIcon.Information)
    End Sub
End Class
```

This code reflects the event handler added for the button. The code contained in the handler was already covered, with the exception of the naming convention for event handlers. Event handlers have a naming convention similar to that in previous versions of Visual Basic: The control name is followed by an underscore and then the event name. The event itself may also have a standard set of parameters. At this point, you can test the application, but let's first look at your build options.

Building Applications

For this example, it is best to build your sample application using the Debug build configuration. The first step is to ensure that Debug is selected as the active configuration in the Configuration drop-down list box discussed in the previous section. Visual Studio provides an entire Build menu with the various options available for building an application. There are essentially two options for building applications:

❑ **Build** — This option uses the currently active build configuration to build the project or solution, depending upon what is available.

❑ **Publish** — For Visual Basic developers, this option starts the process of doing a release build, but note that it also ties in with the deployment of your application, in that you are asked to provide an URL where the application will be published.

The Build menu supports building for either the current project or the entire solution. Thus, you can choose to build only a single project in your solution or all of the projects that have been defined as part of the current configuration. Of course, anytime you choose to test-run your application, the compiler will automatically perform a compilation check to ensure that you run the most recent version of your code.

You can either select Build from the menu or use the Ctrl+Shift+B keyboard combination to initiate a build. When you build your application, the Output window along the bottom edge of the development environment will open. As shown in Figure 13-27, it displays status messages associated with the build process. This window indicates your success in building the application. Once your application has been built successfully, you will find the executable file located in the targeted directory. By default, for .NET applications this is the \bin subdirectory of your project directory.

Figure 13-27

If you encounter any problems building your application, Visual Studio provides a separate window to help track them. If an error occurs, the Task List window will open as a tabbed window in the same region occupied by the Output window shown in Figure 13-27. Each error triggers a separate item in the Task List; if you double-click an error, Visual Studio automatically repositions you on the line with the error. Once your application has been built successfully, you can run it.

Running an Application in the Debugger

As discussed earlier, there are several ways to start your application. Starting the application launches a series of events. First, Visual Studio looks for any modified files and saves those files automatically. It then verifies the build status of your solution and rebuilds any project that does not have an updated binary, including dependencies. Finally, it initiates a separate process space and starts your application with the Visual Studio debugger attached to that process.

When your application is running, the look and feel of Visual Studio's IDE changes, with different windows and button bars becoming visible (see Figure 13-28). While your solution and code remain visible, the IDE displays additional windows such as the Call Stack, Locals, and Watch windows. Not all of these windows are available to users of Visual Studio Express Edition. These windows are used by the debugger for reviewing the current value of variables within your code.

The power of the Visual Studio debugger is its interactive debugging. To demonstrate this, with your application running, select Visual Studio as the active window. Change your display to the Form1.vb Code view (not Design view) and click in the border alongside the line of code you added to increment the count when the button is clicked. Doing this creates a breakpoint on the selected line (refer to Figure 13-28). Return to your application and then click the "Hello World" button. Visual Studio takes the active focus, returning you to the code window, and the line with your breakpoint is now selected.

Breakpoints

You are seeing a breakpoint in action. The key to working with Visual Studio is recognizing the value of the debugger. It is, in fact, more important than any of the other developer productivity features of Visual Studio. Once you are on this breakpoint you have control of every aspect of your running code. By hovering over the property Count, as shown in Figure 13-28, Visual Studio provides a debug tooltip showing you the current value of this property. This "hover over" feature works on any variable in your local environment and is a great way to get a feel for the different values without needing to go to another window. You can do this for any local variable. Windows such as Locals and Autos display similar information on your variables, and you can use these to update those properties while the application is running.

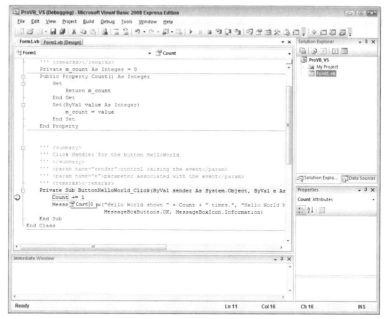

Figure 13-28

Next, move your mouse and hover over the parameter sender and you can see a reference to this object. More important, you see a small plus sign on the right-hand side, which if clicked expands the pop-up to show details about the properties of this object. As shown in Figure 13-29, this is true even for parameters like sender, which you didn't define. However, Figure 13-29 illustrates a key point when looking at variable data. Notice how by expanding the top-level objects you can eventually get to the properties inside those objects. Next to some of those properties, on the right-hand side, is a little magnifying glass. That icon tells you that Visual Studio will open the potentially lengthy string value in any one of three visualization windows. When working with complex XML or other complex data, these visualizers offer significant productivity benefits by enabling you to review data.

Once you are at this breakpoint, you can control your application by leveraging the Debug toolbar buttons. These buttons, shown in Figure 13-30, provide several options for managing the flow of your application. From the left you find the following: a run button, a pause button, a stop button, and a button that looks like a carriage return next to a set of lines. That fourth button represents stepping into code. The toolbar has three buttons showing arrows in relation to a series of lines: Step-In, Step-Over, and Step-Out, respectively.

Step-In tells the debugger to jump to whatever line of code is first within the next method or property you call. Keep in mind that if you pass a property value as a parameter to a method, then the first such line of code is in the Get method of the parameter. Once there, you may want to step out. Stepping out of a method tells the debugger to execute the code in the current method and return you to the line that called this method. Thus, you could step out of the property and then step in again to get into the method you are actually interested in debugging.

Of course, sometimes you don't want to step into a method; this is where the Step-Over button comes in. It enables you to call whatever method(s) are on the current line and step to the next sequential line of code in the method you are currently debugging. The final button, Step-Out, is useful if you know what the code in a method is going to do but want to find out which code called the current method. Stepping out takes you directly to the calling code block.

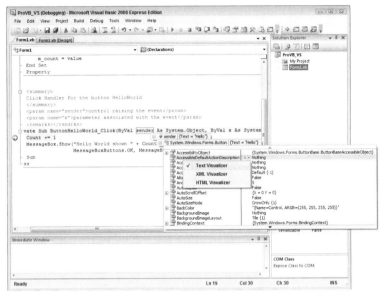

Figure 13-29

Figure 13-30

Each of the buttons shown on the debugging toolbar in Figure 13-30 has an accompanying shortcut key for experienced developers who want to move quickly through a series of breakpoints. Of course, the value of breakpoints goes beyond what you can do with them at runtime. Visual Basic 2008 Express Edition does not support the advanced properties of breakpoints, but Visual Studio provides additional properties for working with them. As shown in Figure 13-31, it's also possible to add specific properties to your breakpoints. The context menu shows several possible options. You can disable breakpoints that you don't currently want to stop your application flow. You can also move a breakpoint, although it's usually easier to just click and delete the current location, and then click and create a new breakpoint at the new location.

More important, it's possible to specify that a given breakpoint should only execute if a certain value is defined (or undefined). In other words, you can make hitting a given breakpoint conditional, and a pop-up window enables you to define this condition. Similarly, if you've ever wanted to stop on, for example, the thirty-seventh iteration of a loop, you know the pain of repeatedly stopping at a breakpoint inside a loop. Visual Studio enables you to specify that a given breakpoint should only stop your application after some specified number of hits.

The next option is one of the more interesting options if you need to carry out a debug session in a live environment. You can create a breakpoint on the debug version of code and then add a filter that

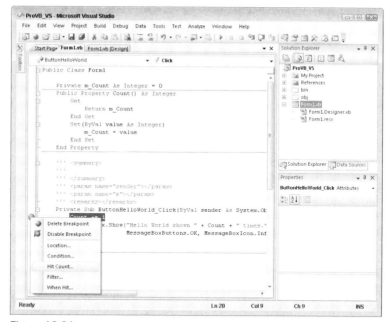

Figure 13-31

ensures you are the only user to stop on that breakpoint. For example, if you are in an environment where multiple people are working against the same executable, then you can add a breakpoint that won't affect the other users of the application.

Similarly, instead of just stopping at a breakpoint, you can also have the breakpoint execute some other code, possibly even a Visual Studio macro, when the given breakpoint is reached. These actions are rather limited and are not frequently used, but in some situations this capability can be used to your advantage.

Note that breakpoints are saved when a solution is saved by the IDE. There is also a Breakpoints window, which provides a common location for managing breakpoints that you may have set across several different source files.

Finally, at some point you are going to want to debug a process that isn't being started from Visual Studio — for example, if you have an existing website that is hosting a DLL you are interested in debugging. In this case you can leverage Visual Studio's capability to attach to a running process and debug that DLL. At or near the top (depending on your settings) of the Tools menu in Visual Studio is the Attach to Process option. (It is visible in Figure 13-35 later in this chapter.) This menu option opens a dialog showing all of your processes. You could then select the process and have the DLL project you want to debug loaded in Visual Studio. The next time your DLL is called by that process, Visual Studio will recognize the call and hit a breakpoint set in your code.

Other Debug-Related Windows

As noted earlier, when you run an application in Debug mode, Visual Studio .NET 2008 can open a series of windows related to debugging. Each of these windows provides a view of a limited set of the overall environment in which your application is running. From these windows, it is possible to find things such as the list of calls (stack) used to get to the current line of code or the present value of all the variables currently available. Visual Studio has a powerful debugger that is fully supported with IntelliSense, and these windows extend the debugger.

Output

Recall that the build process puts progress messages in this window. Similarly, your program can also place messages in it. Several options for accessing this window are discussed in later chapters, but at the simplest level the `Console` object echoes its output to this window during a debug session. For example, the following line of code can be added to your sample application:

```
Console.WriteLine("This is printed in the Output Window")
```

This line of code will cause the string `This is printed in the Output Window` to appear in the Output window when your application is running. You can verify this by adding this line in front of the command to open the message box. Then, run your application and have the debugger stop on the line where the message box is opened. If you check the contents of the Output window, you will find that your string is displayed.

Anything written to the Output window is shown only while running a program from the environment. During execution of the compiled module, no Output window is present, so nothing can be written to it. This is the basic concept behind other objects such as `Debug` and `Trace`, which are covered in more detail in Chapter 8.

Call Stack

The Call Stack window lists the procedures that are currently calling other procedures and waiting for their return. The call stack represents the path through your code that leads to the currently executing command. This can be a valuable tool when you are trying to determine what code is executing a line of code that you didn't expect to execute.

Locals

The Locals window is used to monitor the value of all variables currently in scope. This is a fairly self-explanatory window that shows a list of the current local variables, with the value next to each item. As in previous versions of Visual Studio, this display enables examination of the contents of objects and arrays via a tree-control interface. It also supports the editing of those values, so if you want to change a string from empty to what you thought it would be, just to see what else might be broken, then feel free to do so from here.

Watch Windows

There are four Watch windows, numbered Watch 1 to Watch 4. Each window can hold a set of variables or expressions for which you want to monitor the value. It is also possible to modify the value of a variable from within a Watch window. The display can be set to show variable values in decimal or hexadecimal format. To add a variable to a Watch window, right-click the variable in the code editor and then select Add Watch from the pop-up menu.

Immediate Window

The Immediate window, as its name implies, enables you to evaluate expressions. It becomes available while you are in Debug mode. This is a powerful window, one that can save or ruin a debug session. For example, using the sample from earlier in this chapter, you can start the application and press the button to stop on the breakpoint. Go to the Immediate window and enter **?Button1.Text = "Click Me"** and press return. You should get a response of false as the Immediate window evaluates this statement.

Notice the preceding **?**, which tells the debugger to evaluate your statement, rather than execute it. Repeat the preceding text but omit the question mark: **Button1.Text = "Click Me"**. Press F5 or click the Run button to return control to your application, and notice the caption on your button. From the Immediate window you have updated this value. This window can be very useful if you are working in Debug mode and need to modify a value that is part of a running application.

Autos

Finally, as the chapter prepares to transition to features that are only available in Visual Studio and not Visual Basic 2008 Express, there is the Autos window. The Autos window displays variables used in the statement currently being executed and the statement just before it. These variables are identified and listed for you automatically, hence the window's name. This window shows more than just your local variables. For example, if you are in Debug mode on the line to open the MessageBox in the ProVB_VS sample, then the MessageBox constants referenced on this line are shown in this window. This window enables you to see the content of every variable involved in the currently executing command. As with the Locals window, you can edit the value of a variable during a debug session. However, this window is in fact specific to Visual Studio and not available to users of Visual Basic 2008 Express.

Useful Features of Visual Studio 2008

The focus of most of this chapter has been on creating a simple application, working in either Visual Basic 2008 Express Edition or Visual Studio 2008. It's now time to leave the set of features supported by the Express Edition and move on to some features that are available only to Visual Studio developers. These features include, but are not limited to, the following items, beginning with features available to all Visual Studio 2008 developers.

When Visual Studio 2008 is first started, you configure your custom IDE profile. Visual Studio enables you to select either a language-specific or task-specific profile and then change that profile whenever you desire.

Configuration settings are managed through the Tools ➪ Import and Export Settings menu option. This menu option opens a simple wizard, which first saves your current settings and then allows you to select an alternate set of settings. By default, Visual Studio ships with settings for Visual Basic, Web Development, and C#, to name a few, but by exporting your settings you can create and share your own custom settings files.

The Visual Studio settings file is an XML file that enables you to capture all your Visual Studio configuration settings. This might sound trivial, but it is not. This feature enables the standardization of Visual Studio across different team members. The advantages of a team sharing settings go beyond just a common look and feel.

Build Configurations

Prior to .NET, a Visual Basic project had only one set of properties. There was no way to have one set of properties for a debug build and a separate set for a release build. As a result, you had to manually change any environment-specific properties before you built the application. This has changed with the introduction of *build configurations*, which enable you to have different sets of project properties for debug and release builds. Visual Studio does not limit you to only two build configurations. It's possible to create additional custom configurations. The properties that can be set for a project have been split into two groups: those that are independent of build configuration and therefore apply to all build configurations, and those that apply only to the active build configuration. For example, the Project Name and Project Location properties are the same irrespective of what build configuration is active, whereas the code optimization options vary depending on the active build configuration. This isn't a new concept, and it has been available to Visual C++ developers for some time, but .NET was the first time it was available for VB developers.

The default settings for developers who choose to customize Visual Studio 2008 based on Visual Basic settings do not include the two build configuration settings in the project property pages. By default, Visual Basic applications are built in Debug mode until they are deployed. This enables the Visual Basic developer to be unaware of the build configuration settings. However, if a project's build type is changed, then the VB developer is by default unaware and unable to change the setting.

To display these settings in Visual Studio, select Tools ⇨ Options. On the Options dialog, select the Projects and Solutions tree item; and on the settings for projects and solutions, select the "Show advanced build configurations" check box. This updates the user interface to properly display the build configurations, even though your other settings reflect those of a Visual Basic development environment.

The advantage of multiple configurations is that it's possible to turn off optimization while an application is in development and add symbolic debug information that helps locate and identify errors. When you are ready to ship the application, you can switch to the release configuration and create an executable that is optimized for production.

At the top of Figure 13-32 is a drop-down list box labeled Configuration. Typically, four options are listed in this box: the currently selected configuration, Active; the Debug and Release options; and a final option, All Configurations. When changes are made on this screen, they are applied only to the selected configuration(s). Thus, on the one hand, when Release is selected, any changes are applied only to the settings for the Release build. If, on the other hand, All Configurations is selected, then any changes made are applied to all of the configurations, Debug, and Release. Similarly, if Active is selected, then in the background the changes are made to the underlying configuration that is currently active.

Alongside this is a Platform drop-down. Typically, you should not change this setting; its purpose is to enable you to optimize the generation of your MSIL for a specific processor. For example, 32-bit processors have different optimization than 64-bit AMD processors, which differ from Intel's 64-bit Itanium processors. While the .NET CLR enables you to abstract these differences, Visual Studio enables you to target a specific platform's performance characteristics. In many cases, under Visual Studio 2008 this drop-down no longer has any options because .NET automatically handles processor targeting at JIT compilation.

The window below the two drop-downs displays the individual properties that are dependent on the active build configuration. The first such setting is the location where your project's binary files are sent. Notice that VB now defaults to separate `bin/debug` and `bin/release` directories, so you can keep separate copies of your executables. Below this is the Advanced button, which opens a window containing some low-level compiler optimizations. In most cases, you won't need to change these settings, but they are available for those working with low-level components.

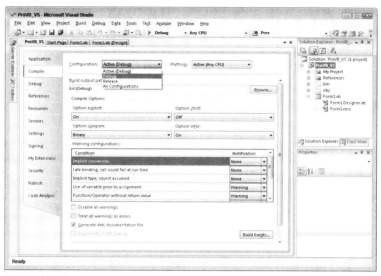

Figure 13-32

Below these settings is the All Configurations section. This label is somewhat misleading, as it actually means "all of the available configuration settings." Of course, that's a bit long, but the point is that while these settings can be different for each configuration, the grid contains all of the primary configuration settings.

All of these settings are project-specific, but when you are working with a solution it is possible to have more than one project in the same solution. Although you are forced to manage these settings independently for each project, there is another form of project configuration related to multiple projects. You are most likely to use this when working with integrated Setup projects, where you might want to build only the Setup project when you are working on a release build.

To customize which projects are included in each build configuration, you need the Configuration Manager for the solution. Projects are assigned to build configurations through the Configuration Manager. You can access the Configuration Manager from the Build menu by selecting Configuration Manager. Alternatively, the Configuration Manager can be opened using the drop-down list box to the right of the Run button on the Visual Studio toolbar. The Active Configuration drop-down box contains the following options: Debug, Release, and Configuration Manager. The first two default options are the currently available configurations. Selecting the bottom option, Configuration Manager, opens the dialog box shown in Figure 13-33.

The Configuration Manager contains an entry for each project in the current solution. You can include or exclude a project from the selected configuration by clearing the check box in the Build column of the grid. This is a valuable capability when a solution has multiple projects, as time isn't wasted waiting while a project that isn't being worked on is recompiled. The build configuration is commonly used when a Setup project is added to a solution. The normal plan is to rebuild only the Setup package when a release version of the actual application project is created. Note that regardless of the build configuration, you can build any assembly by right-clicking that project and selecting the Build option from the pop-up menu.

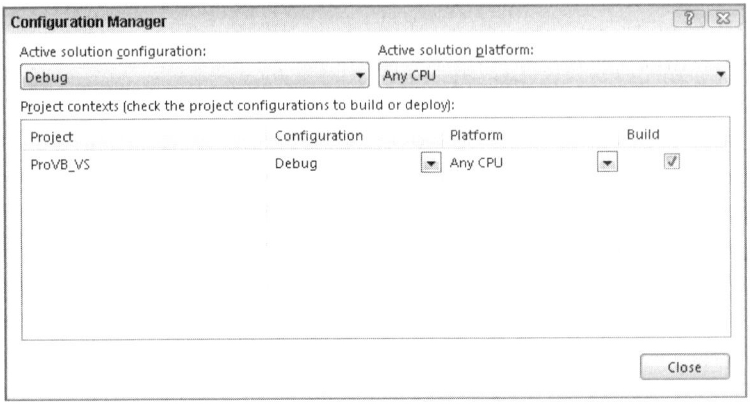

Figure 13-33

The Task List

The Task List is a great productivity tool that tracks not only errors but also pending changes and additions. It's also a good way for the Visual Studio environment to communicate information that the developer needs to know, such as any current errors. The Task List is displayed by selecting Task List from the View menu. It offers two views, Comments and User Tasks, and it displays either group of tasks based on the selection in the drop-down box that is part of this window.

The Comment option is used for tasks embedded in code comments. This is done by creating a standard comment with the apostrophe and then starting the comment with the Visual Studio keyword TODO. The keyword can be followed with any text that describes what needs to be done. Once entered, the text of these comments shows up in the Task List. Note that users can create their own comment tokens in the options for Visual Studio via Tools ⇨ Options ⇨ Environment ⇨ Task List. Other predefined keywords include HACK and UNDONE.

Besides helping developers track these pending coding issues as tasks, leveraging comments embedded in code results in another benefit. Just as with errors, clicking a task in the Task List causes the code editor to jump to the location of the task without hunting through the code for it. Also of note, though we are not going to delve into it, the Task List is integrated with Team Foundation Server if you are using this for your collaboration and source control.

The second type of tasks are user tasks. These may not be related to a specific item within a single file. Examples are tasks associated with resolving a bug, or a new feature. It is possible to enter tasks into the Task List manually. Within the Task List is an image button showing a red check mark. Pressing this button creates a new task in the Task List, where you can edit the description of your new task.

In early versions of Visual Studio, the Task List window was used to display compilation errors, but under Visual Studio 2005 the Error List became a separate window.

The Command Window

The Command window can be opened from the Other Windows section of the View menu. When opened, the window displays a > prompt. This is a command prompt at which you can execute commands — specifically, Visual Studio commands. While Visual Studio is designed to be a GUI environment with limited shortcuts, the Command window enables you to type — with the assistance of IntelliSense — the specific command you want.

The Command window can be used to access Visual Studio menu options and commands by typing them instead of selecting them in the menu structure. For example, type **File.AddNewProject** and press Enter — the dialog box to add a new project will appear. Similarly, if you type **Debug.Start**, you initiate the same build and start actions that you would from the Visual Studio UI.

Server Explorer

As development has become more server-centric, developers have a greater need to discover and manipulate services on the network. The Server Explorer is a feature in Visual Studio that makes this easier. Visual Interdev started in this direction with a Server Object section in the Interdev toolbox. The Server Explorer in Visual Studio is more sophisticated in that it enables you to explore and even alter your application's database or your local registry values. With the assistance of an SQL Database project template (part of the Other Project types), it's possible to fully explore and alter an SQL Server database. You can define the tables, stored procedures, and other database objects as you might have previously done with the SQL Enterprise Manager.

You open the Server Explorer in much the same way you open the control Toolbox. When you hover over or click the Server Explorer's tab, the window expands from the left-hand side of the IDE. Once it is open, you will see a display similar to the one shown in Figure 13-34. Note that this display has two top-level entries. The first, Data Connections, is the starting point for setting up and configuring the database connection. If you installed SQL Server Express, then this database and its connection string have already been loaded into your list of available data connections. You can also right-click on the top-level Data Connections node and define new SQL Server connection settings that will be used in your application to connect to the database. The Server Explorer window provides a way to manage and view project-specific database connections such as those used in data binding.

The second top-level entry, Servers, focuses on other server data that may be of interest to you and your application. When you expand the list of available servers, you have access to several server resources. The Server Explorer even provides the capability to stop and restart services on the server. Note the wide variety of server resources that are available for inspection or use in the project. Having the Server Explorer available means you don't have to go to an outside resource to find, for example, what message queues are available.

By default, you have access to the resources on your local machine; but if you are in a domain, it is possible to add other machines, such as your Web server, to your display. Use the Add Server option to select and inspect a new server. To explore the Event Logs and registry of a server, you need to add this server to your display. Use the Add Server button in the button bar to open the dialog and identify the server to which you would like to connect. Once the connection is made, you can explore the properties of that server.

Recording and Using Macros in Visual Studio 2008

Visual Studio macros are part of the environment and are available to any language. Macro options are accessible from the Tools ➪ Macros menu, as shown in Figure 13-35. The concept of macros is simple: Record a series of keystrokes and/or menu actions, and then play them back by pressing a certain keystroke combination.

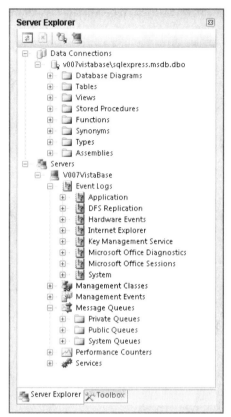

Figure 13-34

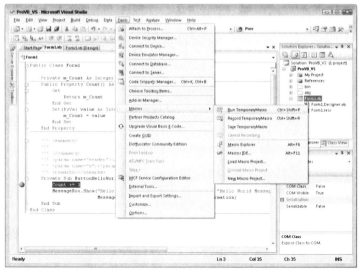

Figure 13-35

For example, suppose that one particular function call with a complex set of arguments is constantly being called on in code, and the function call usually looks the same except for minor variations in the arguments. The keystrokes to code the function call could be recorded and played back as necessary, which would insert code to call the function, which could then be modified as necessary.

Macros can be far more complex than this, containing logic as well as keystrokes. The macro capabilities of Visual Studio are so comprehensive that macros have their own IDE (accessed via Tools ⇨ Macros ⇨ Macros IDE).

Macros can also be developed from scratch in this environment, but more commonly they are recorded using the Record Temporary Macro option on the Macros menu and then renamed and modified in the development environment. Here is an example of recording and modifying a macro:

1. Start a new Windows Application project.

2. In the new project, add a button to `Form1`, which was created with the project.

3. Double-click the button to get to its `Click` event routine.

4. Select Tool ⇨ Macros ⇨ Record Temporary Macro. A small toolbar will appear on top of the IDE with a button to control the recording of a macro (Pause, Stop, and Cancel).

5. Press Enter and then type the following line of code:

   ```
   Console.WriteLine("Macro  test")
   ```

6. Press Enter again.

7. In the small toolbar, press the Stop button.

8. Select Tools ⇨ Macros ⇨ Macro Explorer. The Macro Explorer will appear (in the location normally occupied by the Solution Explorer), with the new macro in it. You can name the macro anything you like.

9. Right-click the macro and select Edit to get to the Macro Editor. You will see the following code in your macro:

   ```
   DTE.ActiveDocument.Selection.NewLine()
   DTE.ActiveDocument.Selection.Text = "Console.WriteLine(""Macro test"")"
   DTE.ActiveDocument.Selection.NewLine()
   ```

The code that appears in step 9 may vary depending on how you typed in the line. For example, if you made a mistake and backspaced, those actions will have their own corresponding lines of code. As a result, after you record a macro, it is worthwhile to examine the code and remove any unnecessary lines.

The code in a macro recorded this way is just standard VB code, and it can be modified as desired. However, there are some restrictions regarding what you can do inside the macro IDE. For example, you cannot refer to the namespace for setting up database connections, because this might constitute a security violation.

To run a macro, you can just double-click it in the Macro Explorer or select Tools ⇨ Macros ⇨ Run Macro. You can also assign a keystroke to a macro in the Keyboard dialog box in the Tools ⇨ Options ⇨ Environment folder.

One final note on macros is that they essentially enable you to generate code that can then be transferred to a Visual Studio Add-In project. An Add-In project is a project designed to extend the properties of

Visual Studio. To create a new Add-In project, open the New Project dialog and select Other Project Types — Extensibility. You can then create a Visual Studio Add-In project. Such a project enables you to essentially share your macro as a new feature of Visual Studio. For example, if Visual Studio 2008 didn't provide a standard way to get formatted comments, you might create an add-in that enables you to automatically generate your comment template so you wouldn't need to retype it repeatedly.

Class Diagrams

One of the features introduced with Visual Studio 2005 was the capability to generate class diagrams. A *class diagram* is a graphical representation of your application's objects. By right-clicking on your project in the Solution Explorer, you can select View Class Diagram from the context menu. Alternatively, you can choose to Add a New item to your project. In the same window where you can add a new class, you have the option to add a new class diagram. The class diagram uses a .cd file extension for its source files. It is a graphical display, as shown in Figure 13-36.

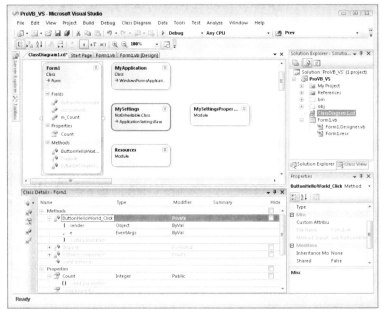

Figure 13-36

Adding such a file to your project creates a dynamically updated representation of your project's classes. As shown in Figure 13-36, the current class structures for even a simple project are immediately represented when you create the diagram. It is possible to add one class diagram per subdirectory in your project. The class diagram graphically displays the relationships between objects — for example, when one object contains another object or even object inheritance. When you change your source code the diagram is also updated. In other words, the diagram isn't something that you create once at the start of your project and then allow to become out of date as your actual implementation changes the class relationships.

More important, you can at any time open the class diagram, make changes to one or more of your existing objects, or create new objects and define their relationship to your existing objects, and when done Visual Studio will automatically update your existing source files and create new source files as necessary for the newly defined objects.

As shown in Figure 13-36, the class diagram files (*.cd) open in the same main display area used for the Visual Studio UI designer and viewing code. They are, however, a graphical design surface that behaves more like Visio than the User Interface designer. Individual objects can be compressed or have their property and method details exposed. Additionally, items such as the relationships between classes can be shown graphically instead of being represented as properties.

In addition to the editing surface, when working with the Class Designer a second window is displayed. As shown in Figure 13-36, the Class Details window is generally located in the same space as your Output, Tasks, and other windows. The Class Details window provides detailed information about each of the properties and methods of the classes you are working with in the Class Designer. You can add and edit methods, properties, fields, and even events associated with your classes. While you can't write code from this window, you can update parameter lists and property types. The Class Diagram tool is an excellent tool for reviewing your application structure.

Team System

The focus of this chapter has been on how you, as a Visual Basic developer, can leverage Visual Studio 2008. At the top end of the Visual Studio 2008 product line is the full Team Suite, and just below that are the various Team Editions. These are part of the umbrella of products referred to as *Team System*. In order to reduce confusion, this section takes a brief look at the tools from Team Suite that are part of the Visual Studio 2008 Team Edition for Software Developers. These tools are focused less on languages and developing code than on managing development and the development of applications.

Architecturally, Team System has two main elements: the server-side components, which operate under Team Foundation Server, and the client components, which are grouped under the Team Suite umbrella. Team Foundation Server (TFS) is in a sense the replacement for Visual Source Safe (VSS), although thinking of it only in those terms is a bit like thinking of the modern automobile as the replacement for the horse and carriage. Note that unlike Visual Source Safe, released in 2005, TFS was updated with a 2008 release and will be updated again in the future as part of the next release of the Team System tools. Understandably, the focus of TFS is on server-side components, but TFS includes a client installation package. This package ships with the server, but includes add-ins to Visual Studio as well as Visual Studio Tools for Office documents that you need in order to work with the server products.

Team Suite is a set of components that are integrated with and ship with Visual Studio 2008. These components were initially categorized into three roles: Architects, Developers, and Testers. Team Suite consolidates the tools appropriate for all these roles in a single product. Since its original release, Microsoft has announced and started offering technology previews for database developers. These tools are also available to users of Team Suite. The underlying concept is that each role needs certain tools in order to better carry out the associated daily tasks, and in some cases these tools overlap between roles.

While having a single product that incorporates all these tools is nice, cost can become an issue. Thus, Microsoft introduced the idea of Team Editions. To minimize the cost to the developer, these provide the same server components access to all of the roles, but on the client side they include only the tools appropriate for a specific role. Thus, from the standpoint of TFS and the server components of Team Suite, there are no differences between Team Suite and a Team Edition. The only differences exist in the tools provided as part of the client's version of Visual Studio.

Team Foundation Server (TFS)

The server components of Team System are not directly integrated into Visual Studio 2008, but it is appropriate to mention a couple of key attributes of TFS that extend it beyond VSS. Similar to VSS, the primary role most developers see for TFS is that of source control. This is the capability to ensure that if multiple people are working on the same project and with the same set of source files, then no two of them can make changes to the same file at the same time.

Actually, that's a bit of an oversimplification. The default mode for TFS is to allow two people to work on the same file, and then have the second person attempting to save changes merge his or her changes with the previously saved changes. The point of this is to ensure that developers check files in and out of source control so that they don't overwrite or lose each other's changes. In terms of its features and usability compared with VSS, TFS is much more capable of supporting remote team members. A project that literally takes hours to download remotely from VSS can download in a few minutes from TFS.

However, that covers just the source control features, and as mentioned previously TFS goes well beyond source control. The most obvious way is that TFS approaches project development from the role of the project manager. It doesn't consider a Visual Studio project file to represent the definition of a project. Instead, it recognizes that a project is based on a customer or contract relationship and may be made up of several seemingly unrelated projects in Visual Studio. Thus, when you define a project you create an area where all of the projects and solutions and their associated source files can be stored.

As part of the creation process you select a process template — and third-party templates are available — and create a SharePoint website based on that template. The SharePoint website becomes the central point of collaboration for the project's team. In addition to hosting the documentation associated with your selected software development process, this site acts as a central location for task lists, requirements, Microsoft project files, and other materials related to your project. In essence, TFS leverages SharePoint to add a group collaboration element to your projects.

As important as this is, an even more important capability TFS supports is that of a build lab. TFS provides another optional product called *Team Build*, which leverages the Visual Studio build engine to enable you to schedule automated builds. This isn't just a simple scheduling service; the Team Build engine not only retrieves and compiles your application files, but also sends update notices regarding the status of the build, and can be instructed to automatically leverage some of the Team Suite tools such as Code Analysis and Unit Testing. The capability to automate your builds and deploy them on a daily basis to a test environment encourages processes that focus on product quality and mirror industry best practices.

Finally, TFS ships with the Team Explorer. This is a Visual Studio add-in on steroids. It includes not only new menu items for Visual Studio, but also a new window similar in concept to the Solution Explorer but that instead provides access to your TFS projects. It also provides a series of windows in Visual Studio, some of which are related to source control, and others related to Tasks. TFS is in many ways the single most important tool in the Team System product line, even though it doesn't truly exist within Visual Studio.

> *Be aware that since TFS 2008 shipped with Visual Studio 2008, there is a new version of both TFS, including Team Build, which was enhanced significantly, and Team Explorer. The Team Explorer 2008 client is what you should integrate with Visual Studio 2008 to connect to either a TFS 2005 or a TFS 2008 server.*

Team Editions

While TFS is available to all users of one of the versions of Team System, on the client side there are several different editions. As noted, Team Suite contains everything, but what about the role-based editions? There are currently three versions of the Team Edition packages: Team Edition for Architects, Team Edition for Software Developers, and Team Edition for Software Testers. These packages are described in detail on Microsoft's website, but here is a thumbnail review of the contents of each.

Team Edition for Architects isn't just focused on software architects. This edition contains tools oriented to the interaction of different applications, and the interaction between physical servers and the components that are installed on those servers. The architect tools essentially work at a level above the Class Designer. These tools enable you to define applications that can then become Visual Studio projects. The designers support designating the security requirements for deploying these applications and enable the architect to compare the requirements of a given application with the settings on a physical server. The goal is to enable an architect to determine quickly whether a new application will work when it is actually deployed into production, and to understand how different applications will interact.

Team Edition for Software Developers is an excellent subset of tools for developers. Details of this edition are the focus of the following sections in this chapter. In short, the Developers edition provides tools to analyze the quality of your source code, to test an application's performance in relation to the system resources it consumes, and to create automated unit tests. This last feature is in many ways the most important feature for improving your code quality.

Team Edition for Software Testers doesn't focus on documenting how an application should work so much as on coding and automating tests. It has all of the same unit testing capabilities of the Developers edition but includes additional test tools for Web applications and for load testing Web applications. It also includes some basic tools for documenting and defining tests; but just as with Team Build, the focus is on creating and customizing automated tests.

Team Edition for Developers

This set of tools, which has been integrated with Visual Studio, is focused on the needs of the application developer. Unlike the Architect tools, those for developers are to a large extent taken from existing, free tools. However, unlike those tools, the Team Suite versions have been fully integrated with Visual Studio and TFS. Don't be fooled by the fact that many of these tools are based on freely available tools; many modifications and improvements are included.

Code Analysis

Code analysis, or static code analysis, is a tool for reviewing your source code — although that's not quite how it works. The basic paradigm reflects the fact that there are certain common best practices when writing code, and that once these best practices have been documented, a tool can be written that examines source code and determines whether these practices have been followed. Visual Studio's static code analysis is incorporated into your project settings for Windows Forms–based projects, as shown in Figure 13-37. For Web applications, there isn't a project file to hold the project settings, so it is possible to configure and run static code analysis from the website menu in Visual Studio.

In fact, the tool doesn't actually look at your source code. Instead, it uses reflection; and once your project has been compiled, it queries the MSIL code your project generates. While this may seem surprising, remember that this tool is looking for several best practices, which may be implemented in different ways in your source code but will always compile in a standard manner.

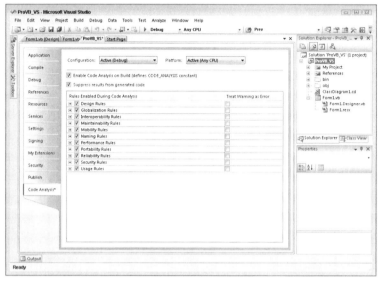

Figure 13-37

Figure 13-37 shows the optional Code Analysis screen. Note that even when you have the code analysis tools available, they are by default not enabled for your project. This is because enabling code analysis significantly extends your compile time. In most cases you'll want to enable these settings for a build or two, and then disable the checks for most of your debug builds. As you can see, to enable analysis you merely check the Enable Code Analysis check box.

Below this check box is a new check box for Visual Studio 2008. One of the code analysis issues for which Microsoft was criticized was that if you used the standard project template to create your project and then ran Code Analysis, you would get certain warnings. The solution Microsoft chose was to enable you to automatically bypass checking their generated code, which at least enables you to avoid having to manually mark all of the issues related to the generated code as being suppressed.

Once you have enabled the code analysis checks, you also have the option to define exactly which rules you want to apply. The checks are divided into different categories of rules. Note that each of the categories can be enabled or disabled as part of your code analysis. You can expand the display to list the rules in each category.

When expanded, next to each category and rule is a check box. By default, Visual Studio issue warnings if your code fails. This enables you to have some rule violations act as compilation errors instead of warnings. You can also enable or disable having the analyzer check individual rules. Outside of the scope of this chapter is the capability to actually identify within your source code those items that may be flagged by the code analyzer but that are valid exceptions to the rule being checked.

Performance Tools

Performance checks are something every developer wants. Visual Studio provides *dynamic code analysis*, or *performance*, tools for your application. These tools are available from the Analyze menu, shown in Figure 13-38. The performance tools provide two runtime environments to measure the performance of your application: Sampling and Instrumented. Note that if you are working within a virtual PC, then you need to use the instrumented version of the performance tools.

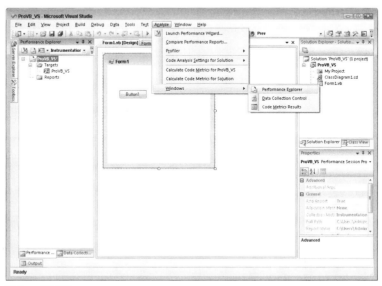

Figure 13-38

Sampling for performance testing is a non-intrusive method of checking your application performance. Essentially, Visual Studio starts your application normally, but behind the scenes it is interfaced into the system performance counters. As your application runs, the performance monitoring engine captures system performance, and when your application completes it provides reports describing that performance. Details about what your application was actually doing to cause a behavior isn't available, but you can get a realistic feel of the impact on the system.

Instrumentation, conversely, is an intrusive form of performance monitoring. Choosing to make an instrumentation run the performance tools triggers the addition of special MSIL commands into your compiled executable. These calls are placed at the start and finish of methods and properties within your executable. Then, as your code executes, the performance engine can gauge how long it takes for specific calls within your application to execute.

Keep in mind that both methods of performance testing affect the underlying performance of the application. It is true that running a performance monitor of any type has built-in overhead that affects your application, but the goal of performance testing isn't to know the exact timing marks of your application, but rather to identify areas that deviate significantly from the norm, and, more important, to establish a baseline from which you can track any significant changes as code is modified.

Unit Tests

Automated unit tests are arguably the most important of the tools provided to the developer as part of Team Edition. To create a new Unit Test, select New Test from the Test menu in Visual Studio. This opens the Add New Test dialog, shown in Figure 13-39. Note that the dialog shown isn't from Visual Studio 2008 Team Edition for Software Developers, but from Visual Studio 2008 Team Suite, the difference being several more project templates, representing the full suite of templates available to a software tester. Developers will normally only see the Unit Test and Unit Test Wizard templates available in this screen. Given this, developers should work with the Unit Test Wizard to generate new tests. This wizard walks you through the process of generating a new test project.

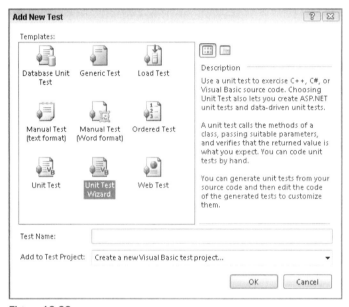

Figure 13-39

Once you have completed the final step in the wizard to define your test project, you are presented with the screen shown in Figure 13-40. This screen shows each of your project's classes, and expands into the methods and properties available in that class. Note that the screen shown is based on the ProVB_VS sample application, which consists of a single form. Displayed are several inherited methods in addition to the custom methods on the form. In fact, the custom methods are not shown in the figure. This screen enables you to review those properties and methods that are part of the My namespace. Specifically, you can run tests against the settings and resources that you expect will be included in your project.

What's missing is any type of review of the actual UI elements with which users of your application would interact. The unit test engine that ships with Team System does not support actual UI testing; it is focused on testing methods that exist in your code. However, this screen enables Visual Studio to generate the source code associated with testing your application. Clicking the OK button triggers the generation of these tests, which are grouped in a new test project. Shown in Figure 13-41 is the newly generated ProVB_VS_Test project.

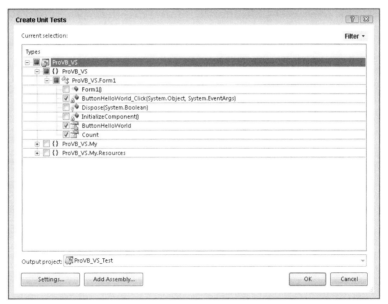

Figure 13-40

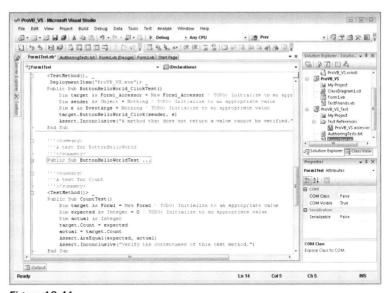

Figure 13-41

The creation of a Unit Test project is not a trivial event. Even though it occurs as quickly as any other project template, the results are significant. First, notice in the Solution Explorer shown in Figure 13-41 that another project has been added to the ProVB_VS solution. This new test project includes a documentation file, AuthoringTests.txt, with tips and instructions for writing unit tests. In addition, this screen shows a subset of the contents of the `Form1Test.vb` source file. It is opened to some of the comments accompanying the methods stubs to implement the tests for your selected methods.

Unit tests present a unique challenge — because you are writing test code, they are an expensive feature to initially implement. Therefore, even though automated unit tests are valuable, organizations often have trouble committing to their development. Nonetheless, a well-written set of tests more than pays for itself. How do you estimate that cost? As a rule of thumb, consider estimating as much time for writing tests as you expect to spend writing the code to be tested.

Summary

In this chapter, you have taken a dive into the versions and features of Visual Studio. This chapter was intended to help you explore the new Visual Studio IDE. It demonstrated how powerful the features of the IDE are, even in the freely available Visual Basic 2008 Express Edition. Following are some of the key points covered in this chapter:

❑ How to create projects, and the different project templates available

❑ Code regions and how you can use them to conceal code

❑ Versions of Visual Studio 2008

❑ The properties and settings of your Visual Studio 2008 projects

❑ Running an application in Debug mode and working with breakpoints

❑ Building configurations and modifying the build configuration of your project

❑ The Class Designer

❑ Team System: Team Foundation Server and Team Suite

❑ Tools in Visual Studio 2008 Team Edition for Developers

❑ Automated unit tests

You've seen that Visual Studio 2008 is highly customizable and comes in a variety of flavors. Numerous windows can be hidden, docked, or undocked. They can be layered in tabs and moved within the IDE. Visual Studio also contains many tools, including some that extend its core capabilities. Keep in mind that whether you are using Visual Basic 2008 Express Edition or Visual Studio 2008 Team Suite, the core elements associated with compiling your application are the same.

14

Working with SQL Server

Most of the relationship between a developer and an SQL Server relates to querying or saving data, but Visual Studio 2008 provides a couple of ways to work with databases: SQL Server Compact Edition and SQL CLR.

While Visual Basic has always included tools for working with the various editions and versions of SQL Server, Visual Studio 2008 includes a new member of the SQL Server family: SQL Server Compact Edition (SQLCE). SQLCE is a lightweight version of the database that requires minimal installation and configuration to use. It runs on both Windows and devices running Windows CE. SQLCE is particularly suited for creating local caches of a larger remote database, which may be used to improve performance when querying rarely changing tables or for the creation of partially connected solutions when working with data. In combination with various synchronization scenarios, SQLCE can provide developers with a powerful tool for enabling their applications to work both connected to the main database and offline (still storing records until the next connection).

SQL Server 2005 added integration with the .NET Framework. This provided two main benefits. First, you can use Visual Basic to create elements in the database, such as user-defined types, stored procedures, and functions. These objects may work alone or in concert with Transact-SQL objects. Second, you can expose Web services from your databases, enabling .NET and other client applications to execute code on the database.

Transact-SQL (T-SQL), while well-featured, lacks a number of features that are common in general-purpose languages such as Visual Basic. VB includes better support for looping and conditional statements than T-SQL. In addition to these language features, the .NET Framework is available for use with Visual Basic, meaning you have access to tools for network access, string handling, mathematical processing, internationalization, and more. Therefore, if your stored procedures need access to features such as these, it may be beneficial to look at using VB as the language, not T-SQL.

This chapter describes how you can use Visual Basic to create applications that save data to SQLCE databases, and how to create database objects in SQL Server 2005. It covers some of the synchronization methods you can take advantage of to create partially connected applications. This chapter also covers the capability of hosting CLR objects and Web services within SQL Server and how you can create these objects using Visual Basic.

SQL Server Compact Edition

The main benefits of SQL Server Compact Edition over its larger cousins are size and ease of deployment. The database engine consists of a set of DLLs with a total size of less than 2MB. Installation can be done either by including these DLLs in the output of your project or by including the SQL Server Compact Edition MSI file as part of your deployment project. This MSI can be included when deploying your application with ClickOnce. After it is installed, you get most of the benefits of SQL Server, including multi-user access, the query processor, and referential integrity. All the data and log files for the database are stored in a single file (with the extension SDF). This file can be encrypted for security purposes with a simple password. The database file will grow as needed to support the stored data and may be compacted if necessary. If these benefits remind you of "the old days" of storing your data in Jet (Microsoft Access) databases, it should. SQLCE provides the same rapid development and deployment model you used to enjoy, along with better compatibility and upgradeability between the server and client databases.

SQLCE is not without its limitations, however. Designed to be small and portable, it does place restrictions on the size and types of data you can store. Those limitations include the following:

❑ The maximum database size is 4GB, although this requires you to change the connection string (see the section "Connecting to a SQL Server Compact Edition Database"). By default, the maximum database size is 256MB (128MB on devices).

❑ Maximum row size is 8060 bytes, although, as with the other editions of SQL Server, this does not include the size of blob or text fields.

❑ By default, SQLCE does not work with ASP.NET. This can be enabled, but it is not recommended, except in cases of simple sites with limited data access needs. This is primarily for concurrency. While SQLCE supports multiple users, it is not quite as reliable as some of the other SQL Server implementations. To enable SQLCE on ASP.NET, you should make the following method call before attempting to open a connection to the SQLCE database:

```
AppDomain.CurrentDomain.SetData("SQLServerCompactEditionUnderWebHosting",
true)
```

❑ No stored procedures, views, functions, or user-defined types

When it is working in a standalone situation, SQLCE is almost identical to its larger SQL versions. You still connect to the database with a class that inherits DbConnection and use classes that inherit from DbDataAdapter and DbCommand to query it. SQLCE differs, however, in that you don't use the classes in System.Data.SqlClient. Instead, you use the classes in the namespace System.Data.SqlServerCe. There you will find SqlCeConnection, SqlCeCommand, and SqlCeDataAdapter. The code that follows shows a simple example of accessing a SQLCE database:

```
Using conn As New SqlCeConnection(My.Settings.productsConnectionString)
    conn.Open()
    Using cmd As _
      New SqlCeCommand("SELECT ProductName, UnitPrice FROM Products", conn)
        Using reader As SqlCeDataReader = cmd.ExecuteReader
            While reader.Read
                Console.WriteLine("{0}: {1:c}", _
                  reader.GetString(0), _
                  reader.GetDecimal(1))
```

```
                End While
            End Using
        End Using
End Using
```

If you use the provider-agnostic classes added in the .NET Framework 2.0, then the code becomes even more like the SQL Server equivalent:

```
Dim fact As DbProviderFactory
Dim prov As String = My.Settings.productsProvider
fact = DbProviderFactories.GetFactory(prov)
Using conn As DbConnection = fact.CreateConnection()
    conn.ConnectionString = My.Settings.productsConnectionString
    conn.Open()
    Using cmd As DbCommand = fact.CreateCommand
        With cmd
            .CommandText = "SELECT ProductName, UnitPrice FROM Products"
            .CommandType = CommandType.Text
            .Connection = conn
            Using reader As DbDataReader = cmd.ExecuteReader
                While reader.Read
                    Console.WriteLine("{0}: {1:c}", _
                        reader.GetString(0), _
                        reader.GetDecimal(1))
                End While
            End Using
        End With
    End Using
End Using
```

The simplest possible way to use a SQL Server Compact Edition database in your application is to use it as a standalone database. While you get none of the benefits of synchronization, you do get the benefit of the simpler (and smaller) deployment for SQLCE. However, the true power of SQLCE comes into play when you use it along with synchronization. This enables you to more easily create applications that work both offline and online.

Connecting to a SQL Server Compact Edition Database

As with other editions of SQL Server, the key to connecting to a SQLCE database is in the connection string. However, because SQLCE does not have the same features in terms of server and integrated security, different options are used to connect to the database, the most important of which are described in the following table. Only the data source and password values can be set within the IDE.

Option	Description
Provider name	`System.Data.SqlServerCe`
Data source	Points to the SDF file. As this file is normally included in the project, the value can be written using the `DataDirectory` shortcut: `DataSource = |DataDirectory|\DatabaseName.sdf;`
Password	The password used to encrypt the database

Option	Description
Max buffer size	The maximum amount of memory that is used before SQLCE flushes the changes to disk, measured in kilobytes. The default value is 640, which should be enough for everyone.
Max database size	The maximum size for the database, measured in megabytes. The default value is 256MB (128MB when SQLCE is running on devices), and the maximum value is 4096MB (4GB).
Mode	How the database file will be opened. This value can be Read only, Read Write, Exclusive, or Shared Read. The default, Read Write, should be used, unless you have particular needs for your database.
Autoshrink threshold	As SQLCE databases will grow on demand, there may be situations when you need them to shrink on demand as well, such as when a large amount of data is deleted or a complex operation needing temporary tables completes. When this occurs, this setting identifies when, and by how much, the database should shrink. By default, SQLCE will shrink a database when 60 percent of the available space is empty. Normally, you will not need to change this setting unless space is at a premium.

Using SQLCE as a local standalone database can be useful when creating small, easily deployed applications. You can see this by creating a simple application to store contact data in a SQLCE database:

1. Create a new Windows Forms project named Contacts, and add a new local database to your application (see Figure 14-1).

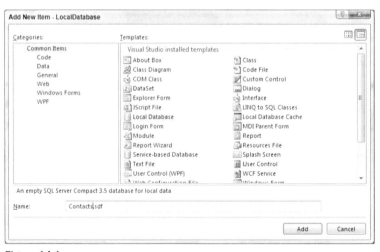

Figure 14-1

2. Once you have added the new database, Visual Studio will also add a new DataSet to the project and start the Data Source Configuration Wizard. As you are not using the database to

retrieve server data, the DataSet will initially be blank (see Figure 14-2). Click Finish to add the new DataSet. You will add the tables later.

Figure 14-2

3. Double-click on the `Contacts.sdf` file in your project to open it in the Server Explorer window. You can now add a new table to the database, as shown in Figure 14-3 and described in the following table.

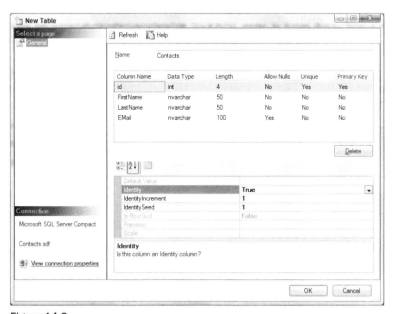

Figure 14-3

Column	Data Type	Comments
Id	Int	This should also be set to not allow null values, and as the primary key for the table. Remember to set Identity to true.
FirstName	NVarChar(50)	Allow nulls should be set to false.
LastName	NVarChar(50)	Allow nulls should be set to false.
Email	NVarChar(100)	Allow nulls should be set to true.

4. Double-click the DataSet added earlier to open the designer and drag the newly created table onto the surface (see Figure 14-4).

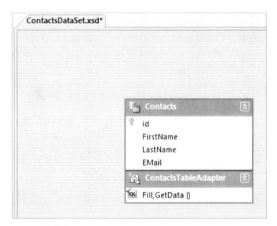

Figure 14-4

5. Open the Data Sources window in Visual Studio. You should see the ContactsDataSet, with the Contacts table. Drag the Contacts table onto the form to create a DataGridView control and a navigator (see Figure 14-5). You should now be able to run the application and add some data.

6. If you look at the contents of the Contacts.sdf file, you may become dismayed, as no data is visible. This is because it is not the database actually being written to. If you look in the /bin/debug folder for the application, you will see the actual database, which contains the data added (see Figure 14-6).

Synchronizing Data

Although you can use SQLCE as a standalone database, it really shines when it is used in combination with a remote database and synchronization. Synchronization enables the developer to reduce the network traffic required when querying the database, while still keeping up-to-date data on the client. It may be one-way synchronization, pulling the most recent server changes down to the client, or it may be bidirectional, keeping both client and server synchronized. The best choice depends on the situation. You would want to use synchronization in your applications in a number of scenarios:

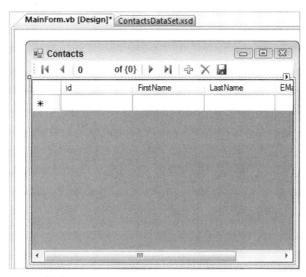

MainForm.vb [Design]*
ContactsDataSet.xsd
Contacts
0
of {0}
id
FirstName
LastName

Figure 14-5

Contacts: Query(I:\...\Contacts.sdf)
MainForm.vb
MainForm.vb [Design]
ContactsDataSet.xsd
id
FirstName
LastName
EMail
1
Bill
Evjen
evjen@yahoo.com
2
Kent
Sharkey
kent@acmebinary.com
NULL
NULL
NULL
NULL

Figure 14-6

- **Remote data mirror applications** — These applications use the local database only as a local copy of the master database, likely as a subset of data. In this scenario, shown in Figure 14-7, data flows only one way: from the server database to the client. Most commonly, this would be product information, news, or customer data that the clients would read but not change.
- **Remote data entry applications** — These include Sales or Field Force Automation (SFA and FFA) applications, such as the classic "traveling salesman" applications. In this scenario, a given data row goes only in a single direction: reference data down, inserts up, as shown in Figure 14-8. As with the remote data mirror applications, a subset of data is typically installed on the client workstation, generally the catalog information and any reference data required, before the application goes off the network. The sales agent then goes out, making sales. Occasionally, the application is reconnected to the network, when new customer and sales data are uploaded to the main database, and updated catalog data is sent to the client.
- **Simple queuing applications** — These applications are a special case of the preceding scenario. The applications write exclusively to the local database and use the synchronization to push the changed data to the server database. The difference here is partly intent; here the local database is used as a temporary holding space. A periodic synchronization moves data between server and client when the two are connected. This scenario, shown in Figure 14-9, improves the overall performance of the application, particularly when you have a slow connection between server and client. It also provides access to the application even when the network is not available.

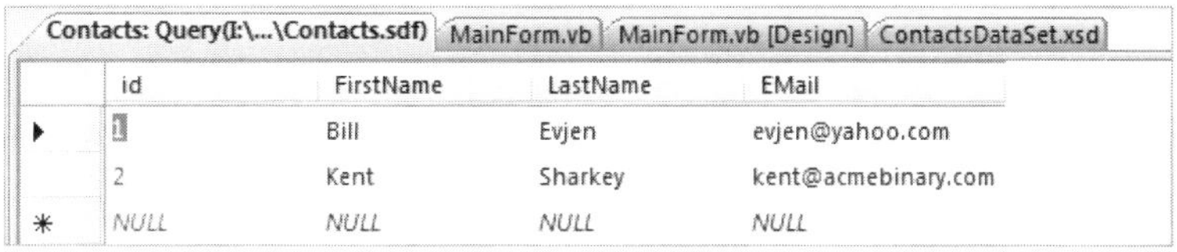

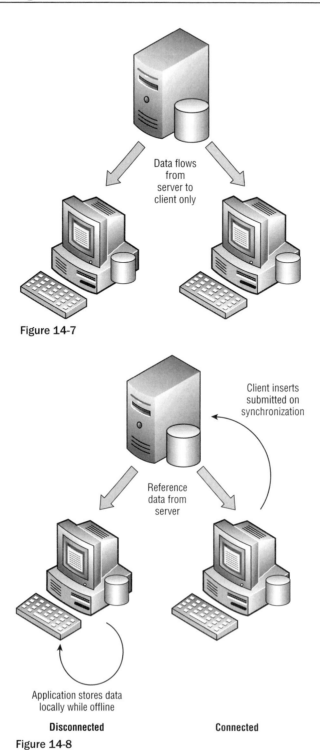

Figure 14-7

Figure 14-8

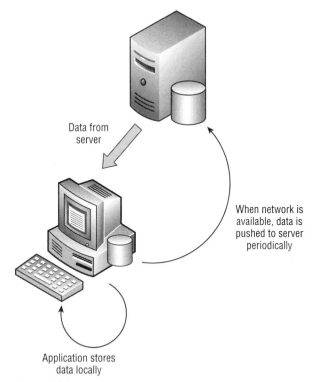

Data from
server

When network is
available, data is
pushed to server
periodically

Application stores
data locally

Figure 14-9

❏ **Remote database applications** — These applications treat the remote database as though it were a "master" copy of the data. In this scenario, shown in Figure 14-10, data may be changed either at the client or the server, and the changes flow in both directions. This is the most dangerous scenario for synchronization clients because the data may have been changed differently in two (or more) locations. Therefore, some form of conflict resolution is required, as well as policies that specify which changes take precedence (for example, last change overrides the data, someone must manually process all conflicts to select the valid data, or the data change made by the highest person in the organization chart wins). It is best to avoid or limit this scenario if at all possible when building a synchronization scenario.

Because each synchronization scenario requires different decisions, SQLCE supports three different technologies for defining the synchronization:

❏ **Remote Data Access (RDA)** — RDA is the simplest means of configuring synchronization between SQLCE and one of its larger brethren. With RDA, you create a new virtual directory under IIS. The virtual directory includes the SQL Server CE Agent DLL. Client applications then initiate the synchronization. Data can be pulled or pushed out of a single table, and you can query for a subset of the data. While this method is tempting, Microsoft has announced that it is unlikely this technology will go much further; they won't be adding any additional features to it. Instead, developers are encouraged to make use of Sync Services.

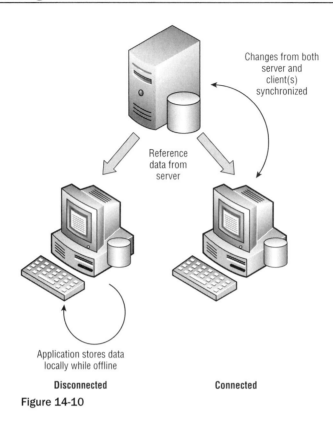

Figure 14-10

❑ **Merge replication** — This is the replication system built into SQL Server. It is a DBA-centric model, whereby the database administrator configures the data shared between the applications. The SQL Server Agent then schedules the synchronization between server and client(s). This form of synchronization is powerful, but it is also the most complex to configure. It requires permissions to create the publications and synchronization schedule on the server, as well as to create the subscriptions on the client. Creating merge replication publications is supported only on SQL Server Standard Edition and higher, so you can't create a merge replication between SQL Server Express and SQLCE.

❑ **Sync Services** — This is a new set of classes that were available separately for earlier versions of Visual Studio but are now included with Visual Studio 2008. Sync Services provide the simplicity of RDA with the robustness of merge replication. They make it incredibly easy to create an application that uses the SQLCE database as a local cache. With a bit of additional code, you can also use it for bidirectional synchronization.

Here's an example of using Sync Services to create a one-way synchronization:

1. Create a new Windows Forms project (here it is called LocalCache).

2. Add a new Local Database Cache item to the project (see Figure 14-11). As this will be used to cache data from the pubs database, it is called PubsCache.

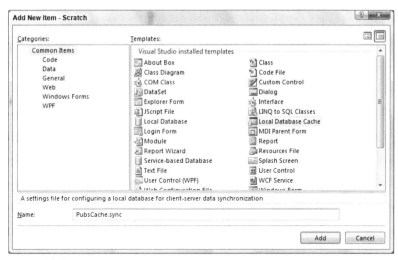

Figure 14-11

3. The Local Database Cache item enables you to easily configure Sync Services, as it starts the Data Synchronization Wizard. The first step of the wizard is to configure the two connection strings: for server and client. Create a new server connection string to the pubs database used in Chapter 9. Once this is done, the wizard will add a new SQLCE database to the project and create the client connection (see Figure 14-12).

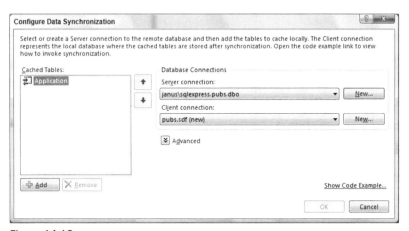

Figure 14-12

4. The next step in configuring the synchronization is to add the tables that will be synchronized. Click the Add button in the lower left-hand corner of the dialog and select the Stores and Titles tables (see Figure 14-13).

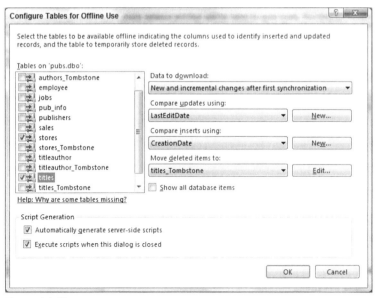

Figure 14-13

5. Sync Services may need to make changes to your database to enable some of its functionality. In order to identify new or updated records, it needs to add fields. By default, these are
called CreationDate and LastEditDate. In addition, deleted records are moved to a tomb-
stone table, rather than completely deleted. If you already have columns defined for these
purposes, you can select them instead. Alternatively, you can have the synchronization pull
down the full copy of the table with each synchronization, which may be a useful alternative
if the tables are fairly small. Click OK to return to the Configure Data Synchronization dialog
(see Figure 14-14).

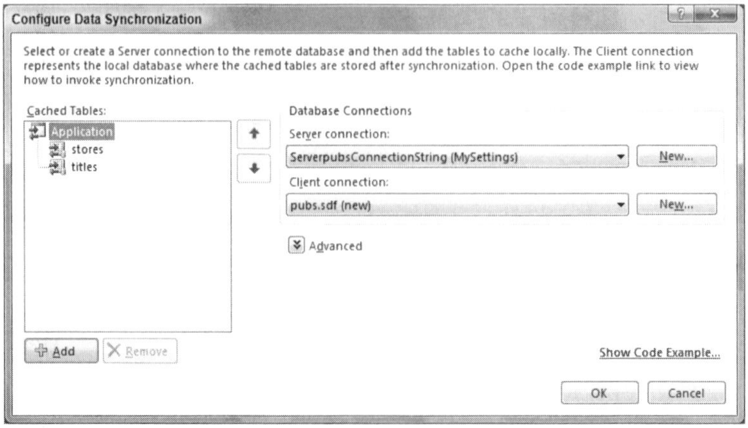

Figure 14-14

6. When you click OK, you should briefly see a dialog appear showing the progress of the synchronization, followed by the appearance of the Data Source Configuration Wizard (see Figure 14-15). Select all the tables and click Finish to create the local DataSet and return to the IDE.

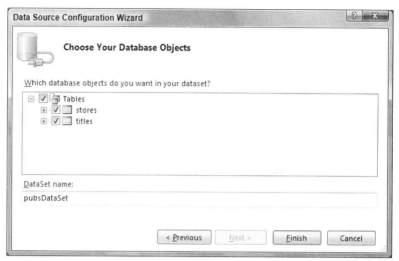

Figure 14-15

You should see a number of changes, including the newly added sync file, as well as the local SQLCE database and the DataSet. If you chose to add the columns and tables for tracking the changes to the database, you will also see two SQL files per table added: one to apply those changes to the database (this has already been run) and one to remove those changes.

7. Open the designer for the DataSet and the Server Explorer. If you have not previously created a connection to the server-side pubs database, add one now. Drag the sales table from the server-side pubs database to the DataSet designer (see Figure 14-16). In this case, you will write to the server-side table, but use the data in the local database as a cache for the less frequently changing stores and titles data. This should improve the overall performance of the application, as it reduces the need to constantly retrieve the data for those two tables.

8. Before adding a control to display the sales data on the form, you must make a few changes to the data source. Open the Data Sources window. Change the control used to display the sales table to a DetailsView, the control for the ord_num column to a Label, and the controls for the stor_id and title_id to ComboBox (see Figure 14-17). This enables you to create a form displaying a single record at a time, with drop-down fields for the two columns that are being synchronized.

9. You can now drag the sales table onto the form from the Data Sources window. This creates the DetailsView control, as well as a BindingNavigator. It also creates the connections

necessary for navigating through the data. Drag the stores table from the Data Sources window onto the stor_id ComboBox. This adds a connection to the local data. It also sets the visible text of the ComboBox to the name of each store, rather than simply displaying the store's id value. Repeat this with the titles table and the title_id ComboBox. The form should now look similar to what is shown in Figure 14-18, and you should be able to run the application and navigate through the data.

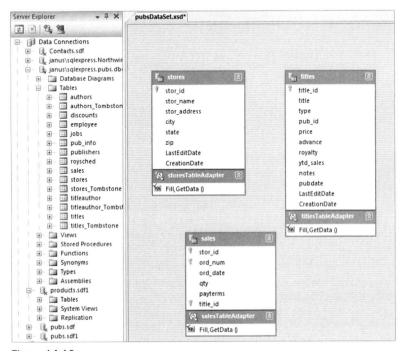

Figure 14-16

Figure 14-17

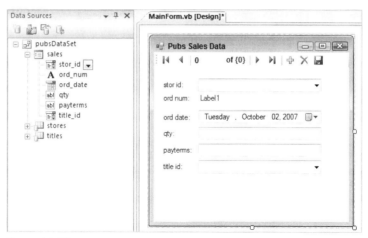

Figure 14-18

10. You're ready to add the synchronization code to the application, but there needs to be some way of triggering it. Add a new button to the Navigator by clicking just after the Save button. Set the properties of the new button as shown in the following table.

Property	Value
Name	SyncButton
DisplayStyle	Text
Text	Sync

11. Double-click the newly created SyncButton to add the code to perform the synchronization. What code do you need to add? Fortunately, the developers have written the majority of it for you. Right-click the PubsCache.sync file and select View Designer to see the designer. Click the Show Code Example link in the lower right corner to display the required code (see Figure 14-19).

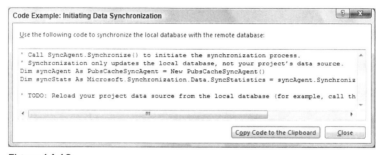

Figure 14-19

12. Click the Copy Code to the Clipboard button to copy the code. Add the code to the
SyncButton click event as shown in the following code. In addition to the code from the dialog that performs the actual synchronization, you need to add the lines to reload your data
into the DataSet (highlighted in the following code):

```
Private Sub SyncButton_Click(ByVal sender As System.Object, _
   ByVal e As System.EventArgs) Handles SyncButton.Click
      Dim syncAgent As PubsCacheSyncAgent = New PubsCacheSyncAgent()
      Dim syncStats As Microsoft.Synchronization.Data.SyncStatistics = _
      syncAgent.Synchronize()

      Me.TitlesTableAdapter.Fill(Me.PubsDataSet.titles)
      Me.StoresTableAdapter.Fill(Me.PubsDataSet.stores)
End Sub
```

13. Run the application (see Figure 14-20). You should be able to view and edit the sales data.
Make a change to one of the stores or titles on the server. You should be able to see the
change only after you have clicked the Sync button.

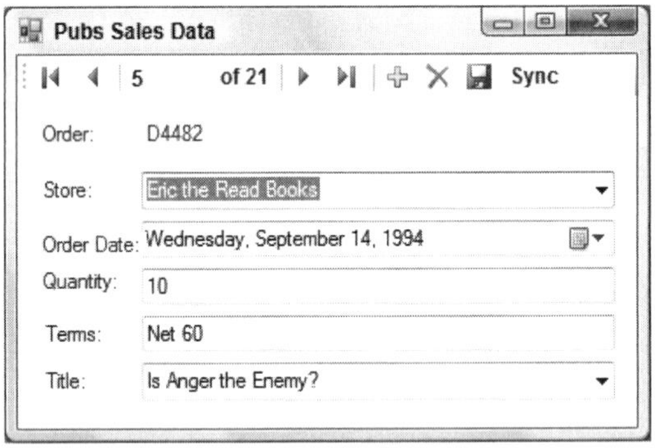

Figure 14-20

While there is no designer support in Visual Studio 2008 for creating bidirectional synchronization,
you can extend the one-way sync created with the Local Database Cache object to provide
two-way sync.

Right-click on the PubsCache.sync file in the Solution Explorer and select View Code. The editor opens
with a newly created partial class for the synchronization agent. Change the SyncDirection property for
each of the synchronized tables that you want to be bidirectional, as shown in the following code. Once
this is done, changes created at the client also appear at the server after synchronization.

```
Partial Public Class PubsCacheSyncAgent
   Private Sub OnInitialized()
         Me.titles.SyncDirection = _
            Microsoft.Synchronization.Data.SyncDirection.Bidirectional
```

```
            ' other tables as desired
      End Sub
End Class
```

The addition of Sync Services and SQL Server Compact Edition provide the Visual Basic developer with yet another client-side tool for configuration and data. You get a powerful and well-tested data storage and query mechanism without sacrificing much in terms of disk or memory overhead.

CLR Integration in SQL Server 2005

As the Developer Division within Microsoft works on the .NET Framework and Visual Basic, other teams within SQL Server work on the new version of SQL Server. The SQL teams wanted to leverage the Framework, so they set about integrating the Common Language Runtime (CLR) into SQL Server 2005. This integration means that developers can use Visual Basic code within the context of SQL Server. It no longer means that success as a DBA is dependent on knowing T-SQL. In addition, it no longer means that complex data access code must be written outside the database. The benefit to both groups is more flexibility in choosing a development language, and more capabilities for your database programming.

CLR integration is disabled by default on SQL Server 2005 and later. This is a safety measure, as most users won't need the features it provides. Not enabling it means one less avenue for attack by hackers. In order to enable creating SQL objects using Visual Basic, you need to enable the integration. This is done by executing the following SQL statement in a query window in the SQL Management console. This is not a decision that should be made lightly. Enabling any feature means that hackers also have the feature available to them. Enabling a feature as powerful as CLR integration means that if compromised, your server can become a dangerous tool. There are limits to the use of the .NET Framework available, however.

```
sp_configure 'clr enabled', 1
GO
RECONFIGURE WITH OVERRIDE
GO
```

Now that you've likely been scared away from enabling CLR integration, be aware that it is an incredibly useful tool in some circumstances. T-SQL, for all of its power, is a relatively limited language compared with Visual Basic. It lacks many of the conditional or looping constructs that developers are used to, such as the `with` statement. In addition, debugging has traditionally been fairly weak with T-SQL. Finally, the ability to use external libraries in T-SQL is limited. You can get around these limits by using Visual Basic to replace T-SQL when appropriate.

Deciding between T-SQL and Visual Basic

Once you have enabled CLR integration with your database, your next set of decisions revolves around when to use T-SQL and the native services of SQL Server versus when to use Visual Basic and the .NET Framework. Your final choice should be based on the needs of the application, rather than because a technology is new or interesting. The following table outlines some of the common scenarios for building applications with SQL Server.

Scenario	T-SQL	Visual Basic
User-defined types	Generally should be the first, if not only, choice	Can be used if you need to integrate with other managed code, or if the UDT needs to provide additional methods. Also a good idea if the UDT will be shared with external VB code.
Functions and stored procedures	Use if the code is to process data in bulk, or with little procedural code	Use if the code requires extensive procedural processing or calculations, or if you need access to external libraries, such as the .NET Framework
Extended stored procedures	Typically, the main method used to provide new functionality to SQL Server. For example, the xp_sendmail procedure enables sending e-mail from T-SQL. Generally, extended stored procedures should be avoided in favor of creating the procedures in managed code. This is partly due to the complexity of creating secure extended procedures, but mostly because they may be removed from a future version of SQL Server.	Use if you need access to external code or libraries, such as the .NET Framework. Depending on your needs, the code may be limited to working within the context of SQL Server, or it may access external resources, such as network services. The benefits of better memory management and security make VB a better choice for creating these extended stored procedures.
Code location	T-SQL code can only exist within SQL Server. This enables optimizations of queries.	VB code may exist either within SQL Server or on the client. This may mean that you can typically take code from the client and adapt it for running within SQL Server. In this case, the code would execute closer to the data, generally increasing performance. In addition, the hardware running SQL Server typically performs better than the average desktop, again meaning that the code will execute faster.
Web services	T-SQL supports the creation of Web services to make any function or stored procedure available via SOAP.	Functions and stored procedures written in VB may be exposed as Web services from SQL Server. The better support for XML handling and procedural logic may mean that it is easier to create these Web services in Visual Basic.

Scenario	T-SQL	Visual Basic
XML handling	T-SQL has been extended to provide some capability for reading and writing XML. These extensions only provide the capability to work with the XML as a whole, however.	Provides excellent XML handling, both for working with the document as a whole and via streaming APIs. Generally, if you need to do a lot of XML handling, using Visual Basic will make your life a lot easier.

Creating User-Defined Types

One feature of SQL Server that does not usually get the attention it deserves is the capability to create user-defined types (UDTs). These enable developers to define new types that may be used in columns, functions, stored procedures, and so on. They can make database development easier by applying specific constraints to values, or simply to better identify the intent of a column. For example, when presented with a table containing a column of type varchar(11), you may still be unsure as to the purpose of the value; but if that column is instead of type ssn, you would recognize this (if you are in the U.S.) as a social security number.

With SQL Server 2005, you can create UDTs using Visual Basic. In addition to the normal benefits of user-defined types, UDTs written in VB have another benefit — they may also provide functionality in the form of methods, which means that you can extend the functionality of your database by providing these methods.

UDTs written using Visual Basic are implemented as structures or classes. Since Visual Studio defaults to creating UDTs as structures, this will be assumed here, but keep in mind that you can create them as classes as well. The properties or fields of the structure become the subtypes of the UDT. Public methods are also accessible, just as they would be in a VB application.

In addition to the normal code used when writing structures, you must also implement other items to make your UDT work with SQL Server. First, your structure should have the attribute Microsoft .SqlServer.Server.SqlUserDefinedType. This attribute identifies the structure as being a SQL Server UDT. In addition, marking the class with the Serializable attribute is highly recommended. The SqlUserDefinedType attribute has a number of parameters that provide information affecting how SQL Server works with the type. These parameters are described in the following table:

Parameter	Value	Description
Format	Native or UserDefined	Identifies the serialization format. If you use Native (the default when you create your UDT with Visual Studio), then it uses the SQL Server serialization model. If you set it to UserDefined, you must also implement Microsoft.SqlServer.Server .IBinarySerialize.

Parameter	Value	Description
		This interface includes methods for reading and writing your data type. Generally, using Native is safe enough unless your data type requires special handling to avoid saving it incorrectly. For example, if you were storing a media stream, you would likely set that as UserDefined to avoid writing the stream incorrectly.
IsByteOrdered	Boolean	True if the data is stored in byte order, false if it is stored using some other order. If this is true, then you can use the default comparison operators with the type, as well as use it as a primary key. The ability to compare two values is a great indicator for how you should use this parameter. If it is possible to define one instance of this UDT as being larger than another, then IsByteOrdered is likely true. If it is not, such as with a latitude value, then IsByteOrdered is false.
IsFixedLength	Boolean	This should be set to true if all instances of this type are the same size. If the UDT includes only fixed-size elements, such as int, double, or char(20), then this is true. If it includes variable-sized elements, such as varchar(50) or text, then it should be false. This is a marker to enable optimizations by the SQL Server query processor.
ValidationMethodName	String	Name of a method to be used to validate the data in the UDT. This method is used when loading the UDT, and should return true if the data is valid.
MaxByteSize	Integer, with a maximum of 8000	Defines the maximum size of the UDT, in bytes

In addition to this attribute, each user-defined type also needs to implement the shared method Parse, and the instance method ToString. These methods enable conversion between your new data type and the interim format, SqlString. Finally, you should also implement INullable in your structure, although this is not a requirement. This interface requires the addition of the IsNull property, which enables your UDT to deal with null values, either stored in the database or passed from the client.

If you are using Visual Studio to create your UDTs, then it's best to create and debug all of your UDTs before you begin to use them, especially if you need to use them in any table columns. This is because VB drops all of the objects you create in a SQL Server project when deploying your project. If you have any tables that use any user-defined types, then you will be unable to drop the UDT, and therefore deploy the changes you've made. If you need to make changes, you may receive an error similar to "Cannot drop type 'Location' because it is currently in use." This error causes the deploy step of your project to fail. If this happens, then change the column type or temporarily drop the table. You can then redeploy the UDT as needed. Don't forget to change the column back, or recreate the table.

While you can write code that integrates with SQL Server using any DLL, Visual Studio provides the SQL Server Project (see Figure 14-21). This project type generates a DLL, but also connects the DLL to the database.

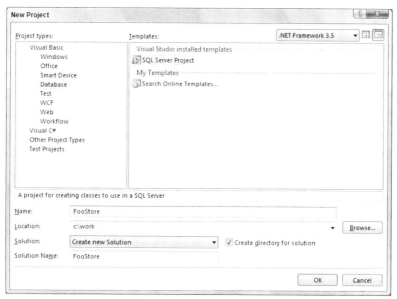

Figure 14-21

When you create a new SQL Server Project, Visual Studio prompts you to identify the database that will host the DLL. At this point, you can either select an existing database connection or create a new one. Visual Studio also asks whether you want to enable SQL/CLR debugging on the connection. Typically, you will want to enable this on development servers, but keep in mind that when debugging, the server is limited to the single connection. Once the project is created, you can add the various database types via the Project menu. Deploying the project loads the created DLL into the database. You can confirm that it is loaded by looking at the Assemblies folder in the Server Explorer (see Figure 14-22).

The following code example shows a simple `Location` user-defined type written in Visual Basic. This type identifies a geographic location. We will use it throughout the remainder of the chapter to track the location of customers and stores. The `Location` type has two main properties: `Latitude` and `Longitude`. Create this file by selecting Add User-defined Type from the Project menu.

SQL Server 2008 includes a new `Geography` data type. This type includes the functionality of the `Location` type, including the ability to calculate the distance between two locations based on latitude and longitude. However, as it would render this demo short, it isn't used here. Instead, included is some information about how the tasks could be accomplished using the `Geography` data type.

Figure 14-22

```vb
Imports System
Imports System.Data
Imports System.Data.SqlClient
Imports System.Data.SqlTypes
Imports Microsoft.SqlServer.Server

<Serializable()> _
<Microsoft.SqlServer.Server.SqlUserDefinedType(Format.Native)> _
Public Structure Location
    Implements INullable

    Public ReadOnly Property IsNull() As Boolean Implements INullable.IsNull
        Get
            If Me.Latitude = Double.NaN OrElse Me.Longitude = Double.NaN Then
                _isNull = True
            Else
                _isNull = False
            End If

            Return _isNull
        End Get
    End Property

    Public Shared ReadOnly Property Null As Location
        Get
            Dim result As Location = New Location
            result._isNull = True
            result.Latitude = Double.NaN
            result.Longitude = Double.NaN
            Return result
        End Get
    End Property

    Public Overrides Function ToString() As String
        Return String.Format("{0}, {1}", Latitude, Longitude)
    End Function
```

```vb
Public Shared Function Parse(ByVal s As SqlString) As Location
    If s.IsNull Then
        Return Null
    End If

    Dim result As Location = New Location
    Dim temp() As String = s.Value.Split(CChar(","))
    If (temp.Length > 1) Then
        result.Latitude = Double.Parse(temp(0))
        result.Longitude = Double.Parse(temp(1))
    End If
    Return result
End Function


Public Function Distance(ByVal loc As Location) As Double
    Dim result As Double
    Dim temp As Double
    Dim deltaLat As Double
    Dim deltaLong As Double
    Const EARTH_RADIUS As Integer = 6378    'kilometers
    Dim lat1 As Double
    Dim lat2 As Double
    Dim long1 As Double
    Dim long2 As Double

    'convert to radians
    lat1 = Me.Latitude * Math.PI / 180
    long1 = Me.Longitude * Math.PI / 180
    lat2 = loc.Latitude * Math.PI / 180
    long2 = loc.Longitude * Math.PI / 180

    'formula from http://mathforum.org/library/drmath/view/51711.html
    deltaLong = long2 - long1
    deltaLat = lat2 - lat1
    temp = (Math.Sin(deltaLat / 2)) ^ 2 + _
        Math.Cos(lat1) * Math.Cos(lat2) * (Math.Sin(deltaLong / 2)) ^ 2
    temp = 2 * Math.Atan2(Math.Sqrt(temp), Math.Sqrt(1 - temp))
    result = EARTH_RADIUS * temp

    Return result
End Function


Private _lat As Double
Private _long As Double
Private _isNull As Boolean
Public Property Latitude() As Double
    Get
        Return _lat
    End Get
    Set(ByVal value As Double)
        _lat = value
    End Set
End Property
```

```
        Public Property Longitude() As Double
            Get
                Return _long
            End Get
            Set(ByVal value As Double)
                _long = value
            End Set
        End Property
    End Structure
```

In addition to the `Latitude` and `Longitude` properties, the `Location` type also defines a `Distance` method. This is used to identify the distance between two locations. It uses the formula for calculating the distance between two points on a sphere to calculate the distance. This formula is clearly described at the "Ask Dr. Math" forum (see `mathforum.org/dr.math`). As the Earth is not a perfect sphere, this calculation is only an estimate, but it should be close enough for our needs.

> The Geography data type includes a number of standard methods defined by the Open Geospatial Consortium. This standard ensures that your code is portable across multiple implementations. In the case of distance, this can be calculated using the `STDistance` method (all of the methods defined in the standard begin with "ST").

Now that you have created the `Location` type, you can use it in the definition of a table. Here we will create part of an e-commerce application to demonstrate the use of `Location` and other SQL Server features.

Imagine that you are creating an application for an online store that also has physical locations. When a customer orders a product, you must obviously ship it from some location. Major online sellers typically have large warehouses that they can use to fulfill these orders. However, they are usually limited to shipping from these warehouses. Other companies have physical stores that stock many of the items available for order. Wouldn't it make sense that if one of those stores has stock and is closer to the customer, you would use the stock in the store to fulfill the order from the website? It would save on shipping costs, and it would get the product to the customer faster. This would save you money, and lead to happier customers who are more likely to order from you again. This hypothetical scenario would likely be called into play many times throughout the day; therefore, moving it to a stored procedure would be useful to improve performance. The calculations would be closer to the data, and the database server itself could perform optimizations on it if needed.

Open the database using SQL Management Studio or the Server Explorer in Visual Studio. Create a table called Stores. This table will be used to track the physical store locations. Figure 14-23 shows the layout of this table. Note that the new Location data type should appear at the bottom of the list of data types; it is not inserted in alphabetical order.

The id column is defined as an identity column and is the primary key. Don't bother adding any data to the table yet, unless you know the appropriate latitude and longitude for each location. We'll create a function for calculating the location in a moment.

In addition to the Stores table, create two other tables: one for products (see Figure 14-24), and the other to track the stock (see Figure 14-25) available in each store.

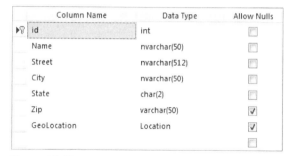

Figure 14-23

Figure 14-24

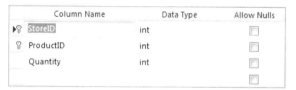

Figure 14-25

As with the Stores table, the id column for the Products table is an identity field. The Name field will contain the name of the product, and Price reflects the unit price of each item. A typical product table would likely have other columns as well; this table has been kept as simple as possible for this example.

The Stock table will provide the connection between the Stores and Products tables. It uses the combination of the two primary keys as its key (see Figure 14-25). This means that each combination of store and product has a single entry, with the quantity of the product per store.

Now that the tables are in place for the sample, we'll turn our attention to creating a way to determine the location, using a SQL Server function written in Visual Basic.

Creating Functions

Functions are a feature of SQL Server that enable a simple calculation that returns either a scalar value or a table of values. These functions differ from stored procedures in that they are typically used to perform some calculation or action, rather than specifically act on a table. You can create functions in either T-SQL or Visual Basic.

When creating functions with Visual Basic, you define a class with one or more methods. Methods that you want to make available as SQL Server functions should be marked with the `Microsoft .SqlServer.Server.SqlFunctionAttribute` attribute. SQL Server will then register the methods, after which they may be used in your database. The `SqlFunction` attribute takes a number of optional parameters, shown in the following table.

Parameter	Value	Description
DataAccess	Either `DataAccessKind.None` or `DataAccessKind.Read`	Set to `DataAccessKind.Read` if the function will access data stored in the database.
SystemDataAccess	Either `SystemDataAccessKind.None` or `SystemDataAccessKind.Read`	Set to `SystemDataAccessKind.Read` if the function will access data in the system tables of the database.
FillRowMethodName	String	The name of the method that will return each row of data. This is only used if the function returns tabular data.
IsDeterministic	Boolean	Set to true if the function is deterministic — that is, if it will always produce the same result, given the same input and database output. (A random function would obviously not be deterministic). The default is false.
IsPrecise	Boolean	Set to true if the function does not use any floating-point calculations. The default is false.
TableDefinition	String	Provides the table definition of the return value. Only needed if the function returns tabular data.

By default, SQL Server 2005 loads Visual Basic objects into a safe environment. This means that they cannot call external code or resources. In addition, Code Access Security (CAS) limits access to some aspects of the .NET Framework. You can change this behavior by explicitly setting the permission level under which the code will run. The following table outlines the available permission levels.

Permission Level	Safe	External	Unsafe
Code access	Limited to code running within the SQL Server context	Ability to access external resources	Unlimited
Framework access	Limited	Limited	Unlimited
Verifiability	Yes	Yes	No
Native code	No	No	Yes

You should use the minimum permission level needed to get your code to run. Typically, this means only the `Safe` level, which enables access to the libraries providing data access, XML handling, mathematic calculations, and other commonly needed capabilities.

If you need access to other network resources, such as the ability to call out to external Web services or SMTP servers, then you should enable the `External` permission level. This also provides all the capabilities provided by the `Safe` permission level.

Only enable the `Unsafe` permission level in the rarest of circumstances, when you need access to native code. Code running within this permission level has full access to any code available to it, so it may represent a potential security hole for your application.

If you attempt to deploy a VB DLL that requires external access, you will receive this lengthy — but not entirely helpful — error message:

```
CREATE ASSEMBLY for assembly 'FooStore' failed because assembly 'FooStore' is not
authorized for PERMISSION_SET = EXTERNAL_ACCESS. The assembly is authorized
when either of the following is true: the database owner (DBO) has EXTERNAL ACCESS
ASSEMBLY permission and the database has the TRUSTWORTHY database property on; or the
assembly is signed with a certificate or an asymmetric key that has a corresponding
login with EXTERNAL ACCESS ASSEMBLY permission.
```

The error message provides the steps required to enable external access. At this point, you have two options:

❑ **Provide the External Access Assembly permission to the user account associated with the database owner** — You should not do this unless the second option is not possible. This creates a dangerous security hole in your database. It would mean that any Visual Basic code running on the server has external access permissions, and complete access to the database.

❑ **Sign the assembly, create an account that uses this signature, and then provide the External Access Assembly permission to that account** — This is the preferred method for enabling safe external access by a Visual Basic assembly. By signing your assembly and giving the assembly (and the user id associated with the signature) permission, you are limiting the amount of code that can access other servers.

The following steps outline how to provide external access permissions to a VB assembly using Visual Studio. First, you set the permission level to External, as shown in Figure 14-26, and provide a name for the owner of the assembly. This is done using the database page of the project's property pages.

Once you have enabled external access for your Visual Basic code, you also need to sign your assembly. Sign the assembly on the Signing tab of the properties dialog (see Figure 14-27). Use an existing key file or create a new one.

Once you have signed and built the assembly, the next steps are to create a key in the database based on the signature of the assembly, and to create a user who will be associated with the key. This is done using a T-SQL query. Run the following query in SQL Management Studio:

```
USE master
GO
CREATE ASYMMETRIC KEY FooStoreKey
```

```
    FROM EXECUTABLE FILE = 'C:\FooStore.dll'
GO

CREATE LOGIN FooUser
  FROM ASYMMETRIC KEY FooStoreKey
GRANT EXTERNAL ACCESS ASSEMBLY TO FooUser
GO
```

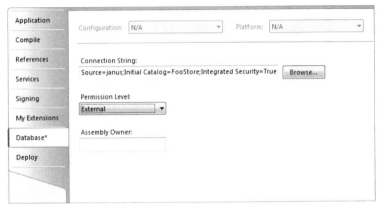

Figure 14-26

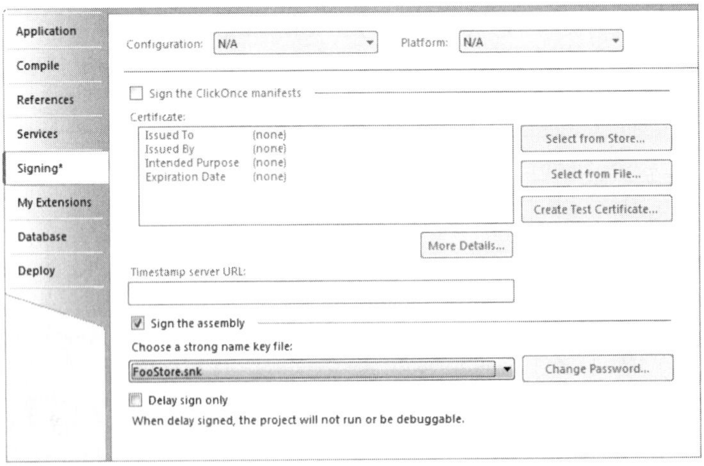

Figure 14-27

Creating a new asymmetric key must be done from the master database. The DLL listed in the FROM EXECUTABLE FILE clause should be the DLL you have just created in Visual Basic; adjust the path in the SQL statement to match the location of your DLL. Once the key is created, you can create a new login based on this key and provide that user with external access. You should also add that login to the database and give it permission to access the desired objects.

Now that the assembly is capable of accessing external sites, we are ready to begin coding the function that will convert the addresses to latitude and longitude (that is, geocode the address). Several companies sell databases or services that provide this capability. However, Yahoo! has a free Web service that will geocode addresses (see the Resources section at the end of this chapter for the URL). It can be called up to 5,000 times a day, more than enough for this sample (but probably not enough for a real store).

The Geocode service is accessed by sending a GET request to `http://api.local.yahoo.com/MapsService/V1/geocode` with the following parameters.

Parameter	Description
appid	(Required) The unique string used to identify each application using the service. Note that this parameter name is case-sensitive. For testing purposes, you can use YahooDemo (used by the Yahoo samples themselves). However, your own applications should have unique application IDs. You can register them at `http://api.search.yahoo.com/webservices/register_application`.
street	(Optional) The street address you are searching for. This should be URL-encoded. That is, spaces should be replaced with + characters, and high ASCII or characters such as < , /, > , etc., should be replaced with their equivalent using '%##' notation.
city	(Optional) The city for the location you are searching for. This should be URL-encoded, although this is really only necessary if the city name contains spaces or high ASCII characters.
state	(Optional) The U.S. state (if applicable) you are searching for. Either the two-letter abbreviation or full name (URL-encoded) will work.
zip	(Optional) The U.S. ZIP code (if applicable) you are searching for. This can be in either 5-digit or 5+4-digit format.
location	(Optional) A free-form field of address information containing the URL-encoded and comma-delimited request. This provides an easier method for querying, rather than setting the individual values listed above. For example: `location=1600+Pennsylvania+Avenue+NW,+Washington,+DC`

The following code shows the full source for the `fnGetLocation` function:

```
Imports System
Imports System.Data
Imports System.Data.SqlClient
Imports System.Data.SqlTypes
Imports Microsoft.SqlServer.Server
Imports System.Xml
Imports System.Text

Partial Public Class UserDefinedFunctions

    'Replace YahooDemo with your key
    Private Const YAHOO_APP_KEY As String = "YahooDemo"
    Private Const BASE_URL As String = _
```

```
                "http://api.local.yahoo.com/MapsService/V1/geocode"

        <Microsoft.SqlServer.Server.SqlFunction()> _
        Public Shared Function fnGetLocation(ByVal street As SqlString, _
            ByVal city As SqlString, _
            ByVal state As SqlString, _
            ByVal zip As SqlString) As Location

            Dim result As New Location
            Dim query As New StringBuilder

            'uses Yahoo geocoder to geocode the location
            'limited to 5000 calls/day

            'construct URL
            ' URL should look like:
            '    http://api.local.yahoo.com/MapsService/V1/geocode?
            '        appid=YahooDemo&street=701+First+Street&city=Sunnyvale&state=CA


            query.AppendFormat("{0}?appid={1}", BASE_URL, YAHOO_APP_KEY)
            If Not street.IsNull Then
                query.AppendFormat("&street={0}", street)
            End If
            If Not city.IsNull Then
                query.AppendFormat("&city={0}", city)
            End If
            If Not state.IsNull Then
                query.AppendFormat("&state={0}", state)
            End If
            If Not zip.IsNull Then
                query.AppendFormat("&zip={0}", zip)
            End If
            'Debug.Print(query.ToString())

            'send request
            Using r As XmlReader = XmlReader.Create(query.ToString())
                'parse output
                While r.Read
                    If r.IsStartElement("Latitude") Then
                        ' longitude directly follows latitude in the result xml
                        result.Latitude = Double.Parse(r.ReadElementString)
                        result.Longitude = Double.Parse(r.ReadElementString)
                        Exit While
                    End If
                End While
            End Using


            Return result
        End Function
    End Class
```

Most of the code in the preceding sample is used to create the appropriate URL to create the query. The query should look as follows:

```
http://api.local.yahoo.com/MapsService/V1/geocode?appid=YahooDemo&street=
701+First+Street&city=Sunnyvale&state=CA&country=USA
```

While the YahooDemo appid will work for testing, there is a good chance that it will not work at times. The query is limited to 5,000 requests for each appid, so if several people call the geocoder in a day, the request will fail. Therefore, you should request your own appid for testing, and replace the preceding appid with your own, which you can request at the following Web page:

```
http://api.search.yahoo.com/webservices/register_application
```

> Notice that the preceding code uses a **StringBuilder** to construct the query. Why not simply concatenate strings to create the query? There are several reasons, but the most important is performance. Because strings in Visual Basic are immutable, concatenation requires the creation of new strings each time. For example, the simple expression **Dim s As String = "Hello" & "world"** actually requires three strings, two of which would be immediately discarded. The **StringBuilder** class has been built for the purpose of avoiding this repeated creation and disposal of objects, and the resulting code offers much better performance than simple concatenation.

Once the query is constructed, an XmlReader is used to execute the query. The resulting XML from a call to Yahoo's geocoder looks like the following:

```
<?xml version="1.0" ?>
<ResultSet xmlns:xsi="http://www.w3.org/2001/XMLSchema-instance"
    xmlns="urn:yahoo:maps"
    xsi:schemaLocation="urn:yahoo:maps
      http://api.local.yahoo.com/MapsService/V1/GeocodeResponse.xsd">
  <Result precision="address"
      warning="The exact location could not be found,
        here is the closest match: 701 First Ave, Sunnyvale, CA 94089">
    <Latitude>37.416384</Latitude>
    <Longitude>-122.024853</Longitude>
    <Address>701 FIRST AVE</Address>
    <City>SUNNYVALE</City>
    <State>CA</State>
    <Zip>94089-1019</Zip>
    <Country>US</Country>
  </Result>
</ResultSet>
```

While you could load all of this into an XmlDocument for processing, the XmlReader is generally faster. In addition, because all that is really needed are the two values for latitude and longitude, using the XmlReader enables the code to extract these two values quickly, and without the overhead of loading all the other data. As the XmlReader class implements IDisposable, you should ensure the correct handling and disposal of the class by either setting the object to nothing in a `Try ... Finally` block, or by using the `Using` statement:

```
Using r As XmlReader = XmlReader.Create(query.ToString())
    'parse output
    While r.Read
        If r.IsStartElement("Latitude") Then
            ' longitude directly follows latitude in the result xml
            result.Latitude = Double.Parse(r.ReadElementString)
            result.Longitude = Double.Parse(r.ReadElementString)
            Exit While
        End If
    End While
End Using
```

As shown in Chapter 10, you create the `XmlReader` using the shared `Create` method. This method has a number of overridden versions. In this case, the string version of the URL is used to create the `XmlReader`. The code then loops through the resulting XML until the start element for the `Latitude` element is found. As we know, the two values are next to each other; the code may then access them and stop reading. Figure 14-28 shows testing this new function in SQL Server Management Studio.

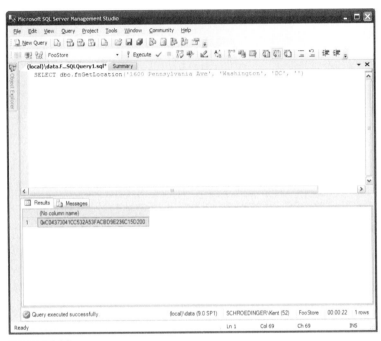

Figure 14-28

Using the User-Defined Function

Even though the `fnGetLocation` function is written in Visual Basic, you can still use this function from T-SQL. This means that you can use either VB or T-SQL for a given SQL Server object, whichever is better suited to the scenario. The following code shows the procedure used to insert new stores.

This procedure is written in T-SQL, but it calls the function written in Visual Basic. Alternately, you could create an insert trigger that calls the function to determine the store's location.

```
CREATE PROCEDURE dbo.procInsertStore
(
   @name nvarchar(50),
   @street nvarchar(512),
   @city nvarchar(50),
   @state char(2),
   @zip varchar(50)
)
AS
   /* need to populate location */
   DECLARE @loc AS Location;

   SET @loc = dbo.fnGetLocation(@street, @city, @state, @zip);

   INSERT INTO Stores (Name, Street, City, State, Zip, GeoLocation)
       OUTPUT INSERTED.id
   VALUES (@name, @street, @city, @state, @zip, @loc);


   RETURN @@IDENTITY
```

The stored procedure uses the function and user-defined type just as it would use the same objects written in T-SQL. Before storing the store data, it calls the Web service to determine the latitude and longitude of the location, and then stores the data in the table.

We are now ready to add data to the three tables. Add a few stores (see Figure 14-29) using the stored procedure. The actual data is not that important, but having multiple stores relatively close to one another will be useful later.

id	Name	Street	City	State	Zip	GeoLocation
1	Store #50	357 108th Ave NE	Bellevue	WA	NULL	47.613399, -122.196403
2	Store #63	15703 NE 56th ...	Redmond	WA	98052	47.658031, -122.130822
3	Store #11	611 Broadway	New York	NY	10012	40.725712, -73.996735
4	Store #23	23 W 60th St	New York	NY	10010	40.769261, -73.982669
5	Store #34	340 W North Ave	Chicago	IL	NULL	41.911237, -87.638002
6	Store #26	2550 N Clark St.	Chicago	IL	NULL	41.928468, -87.642395
NULL	NULL	NULL	NULL	NULL	NULL	NULL

Figure 14-29

Similarly, add a number of items to the Products table (see Figure 14-30). Once again, the data itself is not important, only that you have a variety of items from which to choose.

Finally, add the data to the Stock table (see Figure 14-31). Use a single entry for each combination of store and product. Make certain that you have a variety of quantities on hand for testing.

Now that we have some data to work with, and a function for determining the latitude and longitude of any address, we're ready to examine how to create a stored procedure in Visual Basic to locate the nearest store with available stock to the customer.

id	Name	Price
1	Widget	3.5000
2	Doodad	12.9900
3	Thingie	4.9500
4	Whatchamacallit	52.9800
5	Macguffin	99.9900
NULL	NULL	NULL

Figure 14-30

StoreID	ProductID	Quantity
1	1	0
1	2	0
1	3	0
1	4	4
1	5	2
2	1	0
2	2	2
2	3	0
2	4	0
2	5	1
3	1	1
3	2	4
3	3	2
3	4	4
3	5	2
4	1	0
4	2	2
4	3	3
4	4	0
4	5	1
5	1	4
5	2	0
5	3	4
5	4	2
5	5	0
NULL	NULL	NULL

Figure 14-31

Creating Stored Procedures

Just as with user-defined types and functions, you identify methods as being stored procedures with an attribute. In the case of stored procedures, this is `Microsoft.SqlServer.Server` `.SqlProcedureAttribute`. This attribute is basically a marker attribute; no additional parameters have any dramatic effect on the behavior of the code.

When creating a stored procedure in Visual Basic, you should keep a few considerations in mind. First, and likely most important, is the context. You are no longer running as a separate piece of code, but within SQL Server. Tasks that require long processing mean that whatever resources you are using will be unavailable to other code, which could cause your database to become less responsive, leading to more slowdowns. Therefore, always remain conscious of the resources you are using, and the amount of time you lock them.

The second major consideration when creating stored procedures in VB is the connection to the data. When writing standalone VB code that accesses data, you need to create a connection to a class that implements `IDbConnection`, frequently `SqlConnection` or `OleDbConnection`. The connection string used then identifies the database, user id, and so on. However, in a stored procedure, you are running within the context of SQL Server itself, so most of this information is superfluous, which makes connecting to the datasource much easier.

```
Using connection As New SqlConnection("context connection=true")
...'work with the data here
End Using
```

The connection string is now reduced to the equivalent of "right where the code is running." The user id, database, and other parameters are implied by the context under which the code is running.

Once you have connected to the database, the rest of the code is basically the same as you are used to performing with other ADO.NET code. This means that migrating code that accesses SQL Server to run as a stored procedure is fairly easy: Change the connection string used to connect to the database, and add the `SqlProcedure` attribute.

Returning Data from the Stored Procedure

Once you have performed the manipulations required to get your data, you obviously need to send it back to the user. With normal ADO.NET, you would create a `DataSet` or `SqlDataReader`, and use the methods and properties of the class to extract the data. However, the data access code running within a stored procedure is running in the context of SQL Server, and the stored procedure must behave in the same way as other stored procedures. In addition, your stored procedure may actually be called from T-SQL, which has no knowledge of either the `DataSet` or `IDataReader` data types. Therefore, you must change your code slightly to achieve this behavior.

When returning data using ADO.NET, you typically have a few options. The first option depends on whether you need to return a single value or one or more rows of data.

Returning a Single Value

If you are returning a single value from the stored procedure, then you create your stored procedure as a subroutine. The data you return should be a `ByRef` parameter of the subroutine. Finally, you need to mark this parameter as an out-parameter using the `System.Runtime.InteropServices.Out` attribute. For example, if you were attempting to create a stored procedure that returned the total value of all the items available at a selected store, then you would create something similar to the following procedure:

```
Imports System
Imports System.Data
Imports System.Data.SqlClient
```

```
Imports System.Data.SqlTypes
Imports Microsoft.SqlServer.Server
Imports System.Runtime.InteropServices


Partial Public Class StoredProcedures
    <Microsoft.SqlServer.Server.SqlProcedure()> _
    Public Shared Sub procGetStoreInventoryValue(ByVal storeID As Int32, _
        <Out()> ByRef totalValue As Single)

        Dim query As String = "SELECT SUM(Products.Price * Stock.Quantity) " & _
            "FROM Products INNER JOIN Stock ON " & _
            "Products.id = Stock.ProductID " & _
            "WHERE Stock.StoreID = @storeID"
        Using conn As New SqlConnection("context connection = true")
            conn.Open()
            Using cmd As New SqlCommand(query, conn)
                cmd.Parameters.Add("@storeID", SqlDbType.Int).Value = storeID
                totalValue = CSng(cmd.ExecuteScalar())
            End Using
        End Using
    End Sub
End Class
```

> **Because this stored procedure doesn't really do any processing of the data, or mathematical calculations, it would probably be best created using T-SQL.**

The procedure is fairly basic: It uses the current connection to execute a block of SQL and returns the value from that SQL. As before, the `SqlConnection` and `SqlCommand` values are created using the new `Using` statement. This ensures that they are disposed of, freeing the memory used, when the code block is completed.

Just as when working with `ByRef` parameters in other code, any changes made to the variable within the procedure are reflected outside the method. The `Out` attribute extends this to identify the parameter as a value that needs to be marshaled out of the application. It is needed to change the behavior of the `ByRef` variable. Normally, the `ByRef` variable is an In/Out value. You must at least have it available when you make the call. By marking it with the `Out` attribute, you mark it as not having this requirement.

Returning Multiple Values

Things become slightly more complex if you want to return one or more rows of data. In a sense, your code needs to replicate the data transfer that would normally occur when a stored procedure is executed within SQL Server. The data must somehow be transferred to the TDS (Tabular Data Stream). How do you create this TDS? Fortunately, SQL Server 2005 provides you with a way, via the `SqlPipe` class. The `SqlContext` class provides access to the `SqlPipe` class via its `Pipe` property. As shown in the following table, the `SqlPipe` class has several methods that may be used to return data to the code that called the stored procedure:

Method	Description
ExecuteAndSend	Takes a `SqlCommand`, executes it, and sends back the result. This is the most efficient method that may be used to return data, as it does not need to generate any memory structures.
Send(`SqlDataReader`)	Takes a `SqlDataReader` and streams out the resulting data to the client. This is slightly slower than the preceding method, but recommended if you need to perform any processing on the data before returning.
Send(`SqlDataRecord`)	Returns a single row of data to the client. This is a useful method if you are generating the data and need to send back only a single row.
Send(`String`)	Returns a message to the client. This is not the same as a scalar string value, however. Instead, this is intended for sending informational messages to the client. The information sent back may be retrieved using the `InfoMessage` event of the `SqlConnection`.
SendResultsStart	Used to mark the beginning of a multi-row block of data. This method takes a `SqlDataRecord` that is used to identify the columns that will be sent with subsequent `SendResultsRow` calls. This method is most useful when you must construct multiple rows of data before returning to the client.
SendResultsRow	Used to send a `SqlDataRecord` back to the client. You must already have called `SendResultsStart` using a matching `SqlDataRecord` or an exception will occur.
SendResultsEnd	Marks the end of the transmission of a multi-row block of data. This can only be called after first calling `SendResultsStart`, and likely one or more calls to `SendResultsRow`. If you fail to call this method, then any other attempts to use the `SqlPipe` will cause an exception.

If all you want to do is execute a block of SQL and return the resulting data, then use the `ExecuteAndSend` method. (Actually, in this case, you should probably be using T-SQL, but there may be cases that justify doing this in VB). This method avoids the overhead involved in creating any memory structures to hold the data in an intermediate form. Instead, it streams the data just as it would if the procedure were written in T-SQL.

The next most commonly used method for returning data is the version of the `Send` method that takes a `SqlDataReader`. With this method, your code can return a block of data pointed at by a `SqlDataReader`. This method, as well as the version of `Send` that takes a `SqlDataRecord`, are commonly used when some processing of the data is needed before returning. They do require that some memory structures be created, so they are not as fast at returning data as the `ExecuteAndSend` method.

The version of `Send` taking a `SqlDataRecord` object can be a handy method for constructing and returning a single row of data (or when using `SendResultsRow`).

The `SqlDataRecord` class is new with the `Microsoft.SqlServer.Server` namespace, and represents a single row of data. Why a new data type? Why not just leverage `DataSet`? The creators needed an object that was capable of being converted into the tabular data stream format used by SQL Server, and the DataSet would need to have this functionality added to it. There are two ways to return a SqlDataRecord. If only a single row of data needs to be returned, then you use the Send(SqlDataRecord) method. If multiple records will be returned, then you use the SendResultsStart, SendResultsRow, and SendResultsEnd methods (see below). In each case, you are responsible for creating and populating the values for each column in the SqlDataRecord.

Columns within a SqlDataRecord are defined using the SqlMetaData class. Each column requires the definition of an instance of a separate SqlMetaData object, with the constructor of SqlDataRecord taking a parameter array of these objects. Each SqlMetaData object defines the type, size, and maximum length (if appropriate) of the data for the column. The following code shows the creation of a SqlDataRecord with four columns:

```
Dim rec As SqlDataRecord
rec = New SqlDataRecord( _
    new SqlMetaData("col1", SqlDbType.Int), _
    new SqlMetaData("col2", SqlDbType.VarChar, 25), _
    new SqlMetaData("col3", SqlDbType.Float), _
    new SqlMetaData("col4", SqlDbType.Text, 512))
```

You can retrieve data from each of the columns in two ways. You can use the GetValue method, which returns the value stored in the nth column of the SqlDataRecord as an object, or you can return the data as a particular data type using one of the many GetPNG methods, where PNG is the type required. For example, to return the value stored in the second column of the preceding example as a string, you would use GetString(1). Similarly, there are SetValue and SetPNG methods for setting the value of each column. Once you have created your SqlDataRecord and populated its values, you return it to the client by passing it to the Send method of the SqlPipe, as shown in the following code:

```
rec.SetInt32(0, 42)
rec.SetString(1, "Some string")
rec.SetFloat(2, 3.14)
rec.SetString(3, "Some longer string")

SqlContext.Pipe.Send(rec)
```

The version of the Send method that takes a string is slightly different from the other two variants. Rather than return data, the intent of the Send(String) version is to return information back to the calling application; it's the equivalent of the T-SQL print statement. You can receive this data by adding a handler to the InfoMessage event of the SqlConnection.

The final three methods of the SqlPipe used for returning multiple rows of data are used together. SendResultsStart marks the beginning of a set of rows, SendResultsRow is used to send each row, and SendResultsEnd marks the end of the set of rows.

In addition to marking the start of the block of data, SendResultsStart is used to define the structure of the returned data. This is done by using a SqlDataRecord instance. Once you have called SendResultsStart, the only valid methods of SqlPipe that you can use are SendResultsRow and SendResultsEnd. Calling any other method will cause an exception. The records you send back with each call of SendResultsRow should match the structure defined in the SendResultsStart method. In fact, to conserve server resources, it is a good idea to use the same SqlDataRecord instance for all of these calls. If you create a new SqlDataRecord with each row, then you are wasting memory, as each of these objects will be marked for garbage collection. Therefore, the basic process for using these three methods would work similarly to the following (the `cols` variable points to a prepared collection of `SqlMetaData` objects):

```
Dim rec As New SqlDataRecord(cols)
SqlContext.Pipe.SendResultsStart(rec)
For I As Integer = 1 To 10
    'populate the record
    rec.SetInt32(0, I)
    rec.SetString(1, "Row #" & I.ToString())
    rec.SetFloat(2, I * Math.PI)
    rec.SetString(3, "Information about row #" & I.ToString())
    SqlContext.Pipe.SendResultsRow(rec)
Next
SqlContext.Pipe.SendResultsEnd()
```

The following code shows the complete class, including the stored procedure for determining the nearest store with available stock:

```
Imports System
Imports System.Data
Imports System.Data.SqlClient
Imports System.Data.SqlTypes
Imports Microsoft.SqlServer.Server
Imports System.Collections.Generic

Partial Public Class StoredProcedures
    <Microsoft.SqlServer.Server.SqlProcedure()> _
    Public Shared Sub procGetClosestStoreWithStock(ByVal street As SqlString, _
        ByVal city As SqlString, _
        ByVal state As SqlString, _
        ByVal zip As SqlString, _
        ByVal productID As SqlInt32, _
        ByVal quantity As SqlInt32)

        Dim loc As Location
        Dim query As String = "SELECT id, Name, Street, City, " & _
            "State, Zip, GeoLocation " & _
            "FROM Stores INNER JOIN Stock on Stores.id = Stock.StoreId " & _
            "WHERE Stock.ProductID = @productID " & _
            "AND Stock.Quantity > @quantity " & _
            "ORDER BY Stock.Quantity DESC"
        Dim dr As SqlDataReader
        Dim result As SqlDataRecord = Nothing

        'get location of requested address
        loc = UserDefinedFunctions.fnGetLocation(street, city, state, zip)


        Using connection As New SqlConnection("context connection=true")
            connection.Open()
            'pipe is used to return data to the user
            Dim pipe As SqlPipe = SqlContext.Pipe
```

```vbnet
                    'get stores with stock
                    Using cmd As New SqlCommand(query, connection)
                        With cmd.Parameters
                            .Add("@productID", SqlDbType.Int).Value = productID
                            .Add("@quantity", SqlDbType.Int).Value = quantity
                        End With

                        dr = cmd.ExecuteReader()

                        'find the closest store
                        Dim distance As Double
                        Dim smallest As Double = Double.MaxValue
                        Dim storeLoc As Location
                        Dim rowData(6) As Object
                        While (dr.Read)
                            dr.GetSqlValues(rowData)
                            storeLoc = DirectCast(rowData(6), Location)
                            distance = loc.Distance(storeLoc)
                            If distance < smallest Then
                                result = CopyRow(rowData)
                                smallest = distance
                            End If
                        End While

                        pipe.Send(result)
                    End Using
                End Using

    End Sub

    Private Shared Function CopyRow(ByVal data() As Object) As SqlDataRecord
        Dim result As SqlDataRecord
        Dim cols As New List(Of SqlMetaData)

        'set up columns
        cols.Add(New SqlMetaData("id", SqlDbType.Int))
        cols.Add(New SqlMetaData("Name", SqlDbType.NVarChar, 50))
        cols.Add(New SqlMetaData("Street", SqlDbType.NVarChar, 512))
        cols.Add(New SqlMetaData("City", SqlDbType.NVarChar, 50))
        cols.Add(New SqlMetaData("State", SqlDbType.Char, 2))
        cols.Add(New SqlMetaData("Zip", SqlDbType.VarChar, 50))
        result = New SqlDataRecord(cols.ToArray())

        'copy data from row to record
        result.SetSqlInt32(0, DirectCast(data(0), SqlInt32))
        result.SetSqlString(1, DirectCast(data(1), SqlString))
        result.SetSqlString(2, DirectCast(data(2), SqlString))
        result.SetSqlString(3, DirectCast(data(3), SqlString))
        result.SetSqlString(4, DirectCast(data(4), SqlString))
        result.SetSqlString(5, DirectCast(data(5), SqlString))

        Return result
    End Function
End Class
```

There are three basic steps to the stored procedure. First, it needs to determine the location of the inputted address. Next, it needs to find stores with available stock — that is, with stock greater than the requested amount. Finally, it needs to find the store on that list that is closest to the inputted address.

Getting the location of the address is probably the easiest step, as you already have the fnGetLocation function. Rather than needing to create and use a SqlConnection, however, since the function is a shared method of the UserDefinedFunctions class, you can use it directly from your code. Here you can see another benefit in the way that the VB-SQL interaction was designed. The code is the same that we would have used in a system written completely in VB, but in this case it is actually calling a SQL Server scalar function.

Obtaining the list of stores with stock is simply a matter of creating a SqlCommand and using it to create a SqlDataReader. Again, this is basically the same step you would take in any other VB application. The difference here is that the code will execute within SQL Server. Therefore, the SqlConnection is defined using the connection string "context connection = true".

The final step in the stored procedure — finding the nearest store — requires some mathematical calculations (within the Location.Distance method). While the previous two steps could have been performed easily in straight T-SQL, it is this step that would have been the most awkward to perform using that language. The code loops through each row in the list of stores with available stock. Because all of the values from each row are needed, the GetSqlValues method copies the current row to an array of Object values. Within this array is the GeoLocation column, and we can cast this value to a Location object. After this is done, the Distance method may be used to determine the distance between the input address and the store's address. When the minimum distance has been determined, the Send(SqlDataRecord) method of the SqlPipe class is used to write the data to the output stream, returning it to the calling function.

The CopyRow function is used to create the SqlDataRecord to return. The first step in creating a SqlDataRecord is to define the columns of data. The constructor for the SqlDataRecord requires an array of SqlMetaData objects that define each column. The preceding code uses the List generic collection to make defining this array easier. Once the columns are defined, the data returned from the GetValues method is used to populate the columns of the new SqlDataRecord.

Exposing Web Services from SQL Server

Another new feature of SQL Server 2005 was the addition of support for exposing Web services directly from the server. This means that there is no requirement for IIS on the server, as the requests are received and processed by SQL Server. You define what ports will be used to host the Web service. The structure of the Web service is defined based on the parameters and return data of the function or stored procedure you use as the source of the Web service.

Exposing Web services directly from SQL Server 2005 is supported only on the Standard and higher editions. The Express and Compact editions do not support creating Web services in this manner.

When you are architecting a scenario and plan to expose Web services from SQL Server, you should keep in mind at least one important question: Why do you think you need to expose this database functionality outside of the SQL Server? It's not a trivial question. It means that you plan on hanging data off of the server, possibly for public access. That's a potentially dangerous scenario not to be taken lightly. Most of the scenarios for which it makes sense to provide Web services directly from a SQL Server involve systems entirely behind a firewall, where Web services are used as the conduit between departments. This would be useful if the target departments were using another platform or database, or where security considerations prevented them from directly accessing the SQL Server.

Following is the basic syntax of the CREATE ENDPOINT command. Although both AS HTTP and AS TCP are shown, only one can occur per create endpoint command.

```
CREATE ENDPOINT endPointName [ AUTHORIZATION login ]
STATE = { STARTED | STOPPED | DISABLED }
AS HTTP (
    PATH = 'url',
    AUTHENTICATION =( { BASIC | DIGEST | INTEGRATED | NTLM | KERBEROS } [ ,...n ] ),
    PORTS = ( { CLEAR | SSL} [ ,... n ] )
    [ SITE = {'*' | '+' | 'webSite' },]
    [, CLEAR_PORT = clearPort ]
    [, SSL_PORT = SSLPort ]
    [, AUTH_REALM = { 'realm' | NONE } ]
    [, DEFAULT_LOGON_DOMAIN = { 'domain' | NONE } ]
    [, COMPRESSION = { ENABLED | DISABLED } ]
    )
AS TCP (
    LISTENER_PORT = listenerPort
    [ , LISTENER_IP = ALL | (<4-part-ip> | <ip_address_v6> ) ]
    )
FOR SOAP(
    [ { WEBMETHOD [ 'namespace' .] 'method_alias'
      (   NAME = 'database.owner.name'
        [ , SCHEMA = { NONE | STANDARD | DEFAULT } ]
        [ , FORMAT = { ALL_RESULTS | ROWSETS_ONLY } ]
      )
    } [ ,...n ] ]
    [   BATCHES = { ENABLED | DISABLED } ]
    [ , WSDL = { NONE | DEFAULT | 'sp_name' } ]
    [ , SESSIONS = { ENABLED | DISABLED } ]
    [ , LOGIN_TYPE = { MIXED | WINDOWS } ]
    [ , SESSION_TIMEOUT = timeoutInterval | NEVER ]
    [ , DATABASE = { 'database_name' | DEFAULT }
    [ , NAMESPACE = { 'namespace' | DEFAULT } ]
    [ , SCHEMA = { NONE | STANDARD } ]
    [ , CHARACTER_SET = { SQL | XML }]
    [ , HEADER_LIMIT = int ]
    )
```

The main points to consider when creating an endpoint are as follows:

❑   What stored procedure or function (or UDF) will you be exposing as a Web service? This is identified in the WebMethod clause. There may be multiple Web methods exposed from a single endpoint. If so, each will have a separate WebMethod parameter listing. This parameter identifies the database object you will expose, and allows you to give it a new name.

❑ What authentication will clients need to use? Typically, if your clients are part of the same network, then you use integrated or NTLM authentication. If clients are coming across the Internet or from non-Windows, then you may want to use Kerberos, Digest, or Basic authentication.

❑ What network port will the service use? The two basic options when creating an HTTP endpoint are CLEAR (using HTTP, typically on port 80) or SSL (using HTTPS, typically on port 443). Generally, use SSL if the data transmitted requires security and you are using public networks. Note that Internet Information Services (IIS) and other web servers also use these ports. If you have both IIS and SQL Server on the same machine, you should alternate ports (using CLEAR_PORT or SSL_PORT) for your HTTP endpoints. When creating TCP endpoints, select a LISTENER_-PORT that is unused on your server. HTTP offers the broadest reach and largest number of possible clients, while TCP offers better performance. If you are making the Web service available over the Internet, you would generally use HTTP and TCP within the firewall, where you can control the number and type of clients.

To continue our example, you can make the `procGetClosestStoreWithStock` procedure available as a Web service using the following code:

```
CREATE ENDPOINT store_endpoint
  STATE = STARTED
AS
HTTP(
  PATH = '/fooStore',
  AUTHENTICATION = (INTEGRATED),
  PORTS = (CLEAR),
  CLEAR_PORT = 8888,
  SITE = 'localhost'
  )
FOR
SOAP(
  WEBMETHOD 'GetNearestStore' (name = 'fooStore.dbo.procGetClosestStoreWithStock'),
  WSDL = DEFAULT,
  SCHEMA = STANDARD,
  DATABASE = 'fooStore', NAMESPACE = 'http://fooStore.com/webmethods'
);
```

Endpoints are created within the master database, as they are part of the larger SQL Server system, and not stored within each database. The endpoint defined in the preceding code creates a SOAP wrapper around the `procGetClosestStoreWithStock` stored procedure, making it available as `GetNearestStore`. Integrated security is used, which means that any users need network credentials on the SQL Server. If this service were available over the Internet, you might use Digest or Basic instead. As the server is also running IIS, this example moved the port for the service to 8888.

Once the service has been created you can create clients based on the WSDL of the service.

Accessing the Web Service

SQL Server makes some of the work easier when hosting Web services. The WSDL for the service is automatically generated. Many SOAP tools, such as Visual Studio, enable the creation of wrapper classes based on the WSDL for the service.

The WSDL for a SQL Server Web service may be a little daunting when you first see it, as it's quite lengthy. This is primarily because the WSDL includes definitions for the various SQL Server data types as well as for the Web services you create. Figure 14-32 shows part of the WSDL, the part created for the `procGetClosestStoreWithStock` procedure.

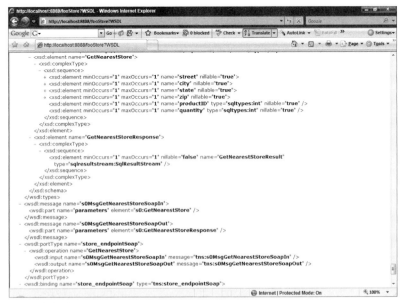

Figure 14-32

As you can see from the WSDL, two main structures are defined: `GetNearestStore` and `GetNearestStoreResponse`. The `GetNearestStore` document is what is sent to the Web service. It includes definitions of each of the columns sent, along with the expected data types and sizes.

`GetNearestStoreResponse` is the return document. In the preceding sample, you can see that it is of type `SqlResultStream`. This type, also defined in the WSDL, is the tabular data stream returned from SQL Server. It consists of the return value from the stored procedure and any result sets of data. This will be converted to an Object array by the SOAP wrapper classes. You can then convert these data blocks to other types.

When creating a Web service, it's a good idea to create a simple form that can be used to test the service. Add a new Windows Forms project to the solution (or create a new Project/Solution). Select the Add Service Reference command from the Solution Explorer. Click the Advanced button on the Add Service Reference dialog and select Add Web Reference. From the Add Web Reference dialog, select the fooStore service (see Figure 14-33).

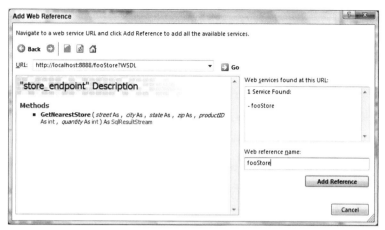

Figure 14-33

Once you have the connection to the Web service, you're ready to begin laying out the fields of the test form. Most of the fields are TextBox controls, with the exception of the Product ComboBox and the DataGridView on the bottom. The following table describes the properties set on the controls:

Control	Property	Value
TextBox	Name	StreetField
TextBox	Name	CityField
TextBox	Name	StateField
	MaxLength	2
TextBox	Name	ZipField
	MaxLength	11
ComboBox	Name	ProductList
TextBox	Name	QuantityField
Button	Name	GetNearestStoreButton
	Text	&Get Nearest Store
DataGridView	Name	ResultGrid
	AllowUserToAddRows	False
	AllowUserToDeleteRows	False
	ReadOnly	True

Organize the controls on the form in any way you find aesthetically pleasing. Figure 14-34 shows one example.

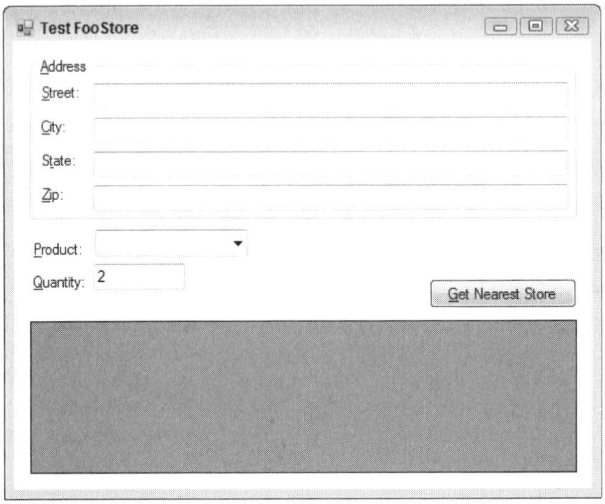

Figure 14-34

The code for the test form is as follows:

```vb
Imports System.Data
Imports System.Data.SqlClient

Public Class MainForm


    Private Sub GetNearestStoreButton_Click(ByVal sender As System.Object, _
      ByVal e As System.EventArgs) Handles GetNearestStoreButton.Click
        Using svc As New fooStore.store_endpoint
            Dim result() As Object
            Dim data As New DataSet

            svc.Credentials = System.Net.CredentialCache.DefaultCredentials
            result = svc.GetNearestStore(Me.StreetField.Text, _
                Me.CityField.Text, _
                Me.StateField.Text, _
                Me.ZipField.Text, _
                CInt(Me.ProductList.SelectedValue), _
                CInt(Me.QuantityField.Text))

            If result IsNot Nothing Then
                data = DirectCast(result(0), DataSet)
                Me.ResultGrid.DataSource = data.Tables(0)
            End If
        End Using
    End Sub

    Private Sub MainForm_Load(ByVal sender As System.Object, _
      ByVal e As System.EventArgs) Handles MyBase.Load
        Dim ds As New DataSet
```

```
Using conn As New SqlConnection(My.Settings.FooStoreConnectionString)
    Using da As New SqlDataAdapter("SELECT id, Name FROM PRODUCTS", conn)
        da.Fill(ds)
        With Me.ProductList
            .DataSource = ds.Tables(0)
            .ValueMember = "id"
            .DisplayMember = "Name"
        End With
    End Using
End Using
        End Sub
End Class
```

The test form consists of two methods. The `Load` method is used to retrieve the data that populates the product drop-down. The call to the Web service takes place in the `Button` click event. This method calls the Web service wrapper, passing in the values entered on the form. Recall that the Web service returns two result sets: the data and the return value.

Run the test application. Enter an address close to one of the stores, and select a product and quantity you know to be available. Click the Get Nearest Store button. After a brief delay, the store's address should appear (see Figure 14-35). Try again with a larger quantity or different product so that another store is returned. Depending on the stock available at each of the store locations, the nearest store may not be all that near.

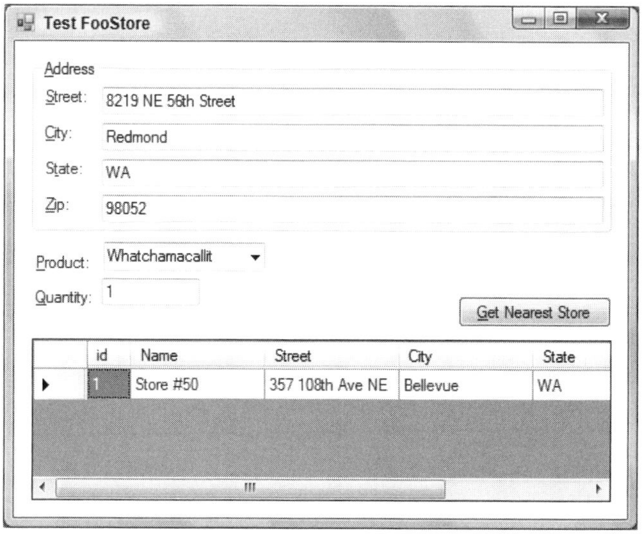

Figure 14-35

Summary

The addition of SQL Server Compact Edition to the SQL family gives you a new, but familiar, place to store data. Rather than create yet another XML file to store small amounts of data, you can make use of the powerful storage and query functionality of SQL Server. In addition, when you combine it with Sync

Services, disconnected and partly connected applications become remarkably easy to create and deploy. One of the most potentially useful changes made to SQL Server lately is the capability to move your code into the database. By integrating the Common Language Runtime with SQL Server, developers now have a choice when creating data access code between T-SQL and VB.

While the implications of having your database run VB code can be a little unnerving, the benefits you receive in terms of flexibility and power may be just what you need in some applications. Visual Basic provides several tools that are not normally available when working with T-SQL, such as access to the .NET Framework's classes. While you should only use VB in stored procedures and other database structures when it's appropriate, in those cases you can dramatically improve the scalability, performance, and functionality of your database applications.

Resources

❑ **SQL Server Developer Center** (http://msdn.microsoft.com/sql) — Main developer resource for information on the features of SQL Server

❑ **Ask Dr. Math** (http://mathforum.org/library/drmath) — Great resource for mathematic algorithms

❑ **Yahoo! Developer Center** (http://developer.yahoo.com/dotnet) — Information on accessing Yahoo!'s services using Visual Basic

15

Windows Forms

Windows Forms is a part of the .NET Framework that is used to create user interfaces for local applications, often called Win32 clients. Windows Forms does not change in moving from Visual Basic 2005 to Visual Basic 2008. Accordingly, the version number used for Windows Forms in Visual Studio 2008 is still 2.0.

The pace of change in Windows Forms is slowing because of the advent of Windows Presentation Foundation (WPF). Visual Studio 2008 is the first version of Visual Studio with a capable visual designer for WPF. Going forward, you can expect continued innovation in WPF, but not much in Windows Forms. However, that does not imply that you should abandon Windows Forms or be reluctant to write programs in it. Windows Forms still has many advantages over WPF.

Those advantages include a more complete set of controls and a mature, easy-to-use designer. The result is faster development in Windows Forms compared to WPF. WPF has advantages of its own, of course. These are discussed in Chapter 17, which provides an introduction to WPF.

This chapter summarizes the changes in Windows Forms 2.0 compared to the earlier 1.0 and 1.1 versions that were present in Visual Studio 2002 and 2003. This enables those with some experience in previous versions of Windows Forms to quickly identify key changes. Then the chapter looks at the behavior of forms and controls, with emphasis on those elements that are most important for routine application development.

Chapter 16 includes more advanced treatment of certain aspects of Windows Forms. After gaining a basic understanding of the key capabilities in this chapter, you'll be ready to go on to the more advanced concepts in that chapter.

Changes in Windows Forms Version 2.0

If you have already used Windows Forms 1.0 or 1.1, much of the material in this chapter will be familiar to you. To help you quickly focus on the new capabilities in Windows Forms 2.0, here is a summary of changes and additions.

Changes to Existing Controls

Changes to existing controls in Windows Forms 2.0 are minor, but are helpful additions of functionality. Some changes apply to all controls because they are part of the base `Control` class in Windows Forms 2.0. Other changes apply only to specific controls.

Smart Tags

Many controls in Windows Forms 2.0 display a small triangle, or glyph, toward the top, right side of the control when highlighted in the visual designer. This is a new feature called a *smart tag*. If you click this glyph, you get a pop-up dialog with common operations for the control. Many of the features that you access through the property box can also be accessed through the smart tag. In general, this chapter uses the Properties window for manipulating properties, but you should be aware of the smart tag shortcut for commonly used features.

AutoCompletion in Text Boxes and Combo Boxes

Text boxes and combo boxes have new properties for autocompletion of text entries. This capability could be added manually or with third-party controls in previous versions, but is now built in. The `AutoCompleteMode` property controls how autocompletion works in the control, while the `AutoCompleteSource` and `AutoCompleteCustomSource` properties tell the control where to get entries for autocompletion.

An example of autocompletion in action is shown later, in the section entitled "Advanced Capabilities for Data Entry."

New Properties for All Controls

The base `Control` class, which is a base class for all Windows Forms controls, has several new properties in Windows Forms 2.0. Because all controls inherit from this class, all Windows Forms controls gain these new properties and the new functionality that goes along with them.

Two of the new properties, `Padding` and `Margin`, are most useful when used in conjunction with some new controls, `TableLayoutPanel` and `FlowLayoutPanel`. Those two properties are discussed later in the chapter. The other new properties are discussed here. They include `MaximumSize`, `MinimumSize`, and `UseWaitCursor`.

MaximumSize and MinimumSize Properties

The `MaximumSize` and `MinimumSize` properties specify the control's maximum and minimum height and width, respectively. Forms had these properties in Windows Forms 1.0 and 1.1, but now all controls have them.

If the maximum height and width are both set to the default value of 0, then there is no maximum. Similarly, if the minimum height and width are set to zero, then there is no minimum. The form or control can be any size.

If these properties are set to anything else, then the settings become limits on the size of the control. For example, if the `MaximumSize` height and width are both set to 100, then the control cannot be bigger than 100×100 pixels. The visual designer will not make the control any larger on the form design surface. Attempting to set the height or width of the control in code at runtime to a value greater than 100 will cause it to be set to 100 instead.

The `MaximumSize` and `MinimumSize` properties can be reset at runtime to enable sizing of the controls outside the limits imposed at design time. However, the properties have a return type of `Size`, so resetting either property requires creating a `Size` structure. For example, you can reset the `MinimumSize` property for a button named `Button1` with the following line of code:

```
Button1.MinimumSize = New Size(20, 20)
```

This sets the new minimum width and height to 20 pixels.

The `Size` structure has members for `Height` and `Width`, which can be used to fetch the current minimum or maximum sizes for either height or width. For example, to find the current minimum height for `Button1`, use the following line of code:

```
Dim n As Integer = Button1.MinimumSize.Height
```

UseWaitCursor Property

Windows Forms interfaces can use threading or asynchronous requests to allow tasks to execute in the background. When a control is waiting for an asynchronous request to finish, it is helpful to indicate that to the user by changing the mouse cursor when the mouse is inside the control. Normally, the cursor used is the familiar hourglass, which is called the `WaitCursor` in Windows Forms.

For any control, setting the `UseWaitCursor` property to `True` causes the cursor to change to the hourglass (or whatever is being used for the `WaitCursor`) while the mouse is positioned inside the control. This allows a control to visually indicate that it is waiting for something. The typical usage is to set `UseWaitCursor` to `True` when an asynchronous process is begun and then set it back to `False` when the process is finished and the control is ready for normal operation again.

New Controls

Windows Forms 2.0 includes a number of new controls. Some are brand-new controls that offer completely new functionality. Others are replacements for existing controls, offering additional functionality.

WebBrowser Control

Even smart client applications often need to display HTML or browse websites. Windows Forms 1.0 or 1.1 did not include a true Windows Forms control for browsing. The legacy ActiveX browsing control built into Windows could be used via interoperability, but this had drawbacks for deployment and versioning.

The legacy ActiveX control is still the ultimate foundation for browsing capability, but Windows Forms 2.0 includes an intelligent Windows Forms wrapper that makes it much easier to use and deploy the control.

MaskedTextbox Control

Windows Forms 1.0 offered replacements for almost all of the controls available in Visual Basic 6, but one notable exception was the `MaskedEdit` control. In Windows Forms 1.0 and 1.1, masked edit capabilities were available only through third-party controls or by doing your own custom development.

That omission has now been rectified. The `MaskedTextbox` control resembles the old `MaskedEdit` control in functionality. It allows a mask for input and a variety of useful properties to control user interaction with the control. More information on this control is available in the section "Advanced Capabilities for Data Entry."

TableLayoutPanel and FlowLayoutPanel Controls

Browser-based user interfaces are good at dynamically arranging controls at runtime, because browser windows can be different sizes for different users. Forms-based interfaces have traditionally lacked such capabilities. Dynamic positioning can be done in forms, but it requires writing a lot of sizing and positioning logic.

Two new controls in Windows Forms 2.0 mimic layout capabilities in a browser, offering better options for dynamic positioning of controls: FlowLayoutPanel and TableLayoutPanel. Both are containers than can automatically reposition controls that are placed in them, based on the current space available in the container.

An example illustrating usage of both controls is included in the section "Dynamic Sizing and Positioning of Controls."

Replacements for Older Windows Forms Controls

The Toolbar, MainMenu, ContextMenu, and StatusBar controls in Windows Forms 1.0 and 1.1 offered basic functionality. These controls are still available in Windows Forms 2.0, but in most cases you won't want to use these controls because new replacements offer significantly enhanced capabilities. Because the old versions are still available, the new versions have different names. The table that follows summarizes these replacements:

Old Control	New Control	Most Important New Capabilities
Toolbar	ToolStrip	Enables many new types of controls on the toolbar. Supports *rafting*, which enables the toolbar to be detached by the user and float over the application. It also enables users to add or remove buttons or other toolbar elements, and includes new cosmetics, enabling toolbars to look like those in Office 2003.
MainMenu	MenuStrip	Both new menu controls inherit from ToolStrip, which enables new cosmetics and more flexible placement.
ContextMenu	ContextMenuStrip	
StatusBar	StatusStrip	Inherits from ToolStrip, which allows new cosmetics and makes it easier to embed other controls in a status bar
Splitter	SplitContainer	Less difficult to set up

The old versions no longer show up by default in the Toolbox. If you want to use them in new projects, then you must add them to the Toolbox by right-clicking on the Windows Forms Toolbox tab, selecting Choose Items, and placing a check mark on the older control that you want added to the Toolbox. However, you'll probably only want to use the older controls for compatibility with older projects, using the improved versions for new development.

These controls are covered in more detail, including examples, in the sections "Toolbars and the New ToolStrip Control," "Menus," and "Dynamic Sizing and Positioning of Controls."

Default Instances of Forms

In VB6 and earlier, a form named `Form1` could be shown by merely including the following line:

```
Form1.Show
```

This capability was not available in Visual Basic 2002 and 2003. Instead, a form was treated like any other class, and had to be instantiated before use. Typical code to show a form in Windows Forms 1.0 and 1.1 looked like this:

```
Dim f As New Form1()
f.Show
```

This technique is still recommended because it fits object-oriented conventions, but the first form returned to Visual Basic starting with the 2005 version, with the minor change of parentheses at the end of the call:

```
Form1.Show()
```

Showing a form without instancing it, as in the first form shown, is referred to as using the default instance of the form. That default instance is available from anywhere in a project containing a form. There is only one default instance, and any reference to it will bring up the same underlying instance of the form.

Another way to get to the default instance of a form is through the new `My` namespace. The following line has exactly the same effect, showing the default instance of a form:

```
My.Forms.Form1.Show()
```

The System.Windows.Forms Namespace

You've already seen how namespaces are used to organize related classes in the .NET Framework. The main namespace used for Windows Forms classes is `System.Windows.Forms`. The classes in this namespace are contained in the `System.Windows.Forms.dll` assembly.

If you choose a Windows application project or Windows Control Library project in VS.NET, a reference to `System.Windows.Forms.dll` is added by default. In some other cases, such as creating a library that will work with controls, you need to add that reference manually. (You can learn more about creating controls in Windows Forms in Chapter 16.)

Using Forms

A form is just a special kind of class in Windows Forms. A class becomes a form based on inheritance. A form must have the `System.Windows.Forms` class in its inheritance tree, which causes the form to have the behavior and object interface a form requires.

The previous section on changes to Windows Forms 2.0 mentioned that forms can be used by referring to a default instance. However, the preferred technique is to treat a form like any other class, which means creating an instance of the form and using the instance. Typical code would look like this:

```
Dim f As New Form1
f.Show()
```

There is one circumstance in which loading a form the same way as a class instance yields undesirable results. Let's cover that next.

Showing Forms via Sub Main

When a form is instanced via the technique just described, it is referenced by an object variable, which establishes an object reference to the instance. References are covered in detail in Chapter 2.

References can disappear as object variables go out of scope or are set to other references or to Nothing. When all object references to a form are gone, the form is disposed of and therefore vanishes. This is particularly apparent if you want to start your application with a Sub Main, and then show your first form inside Sub Main. You might think the following would work:

```
' This code will not work in any .NET version of VB!!
Sub Main()

    ' Do start up work here
    ' After start up work finished, show the main form...
    Dim f As New Form1
    f.Show()

End Sub
```

If you try this, however, Form1 briefly appears and then immediately vanishes, and the application quits. That's because the object variable f went out of scope, and it was the only reference to the form that was shown. Therefore, the form was destroyed because it had no references pointing to it.

To get around this behavior, you could use the default instance as the startup form, but there's a better way that stays within good object-oriented conventions. Replace the line that shows the form, as shown here:

```
' This code will work fine in VB 2008
Sub Main()

    ' Do start up work here
    Dim f As New Form1
    Application.Run(f)

End Sub
```

Now Sub Main will transfer control to the form, and the form won't vanish when Sub Main ends.

Setting the Startup Form

Instead of using `Sub Main` as your application entry point, you can also define a startup form, which is the form that is loaded first when your application begins. To define the startup form, open the Properties dialog box for the project and set the Startup form setting. Do this using the Project ⇨ Properties menu. You can also invoke the window by right-clicking the project name in the Solution Explorer and selecting Properties from the context menu. The Properties dialog for a Windows application is shown in Figure 15-1.

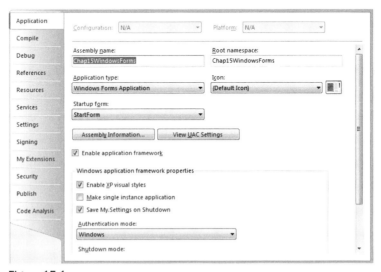

Figure 15-1

If the Properties menu item doesn't appear under your Project menu, open the Solution Explorer (Ctrl+Alt+L), highlight the project name (it will be in bold font), and then try again.

Startup Location

Often, you'll want a form to be centered on the screen when it first appears. VB.NET does this automatically for you when you set the `StartPosition` property. The following table shows the settings and their meanings:

StartPosition Value	Effect
`Manual`	Shows the form positioned at the values defined by the form's `Location` property
`CenterScreen`	Shows the form centered on the screen
`WindowsDefaultLocation`	Shows the form at the window's default location

StartPosition Value	Effect
WindowsDefaultBounds	Shows the form at the window's default location, with the window's default bounding size
CenterParent	Shows the form centered in its owner

Form Borders

Forms have a number of border options in Windows Forms. The FormBorderStyle property is used to set the border option, and the options can affect the way a form can be manipulated by the user. The options available for FormBorderStyle include the following:

❑   None — No border, and the user cannot resize the form

❑   FixedSingle — Single 3-D border, and the user cannot resize the form

❑   Fixed3D — 3-D border, and the user cannot resize the form

❑   FixedDialog — Dialog-box-style border, and the user cannot resize the form

❑   Sizeable — Same as FixedSingle, except that the user can resize the form

❑   FixedToolWindow — Single border, and the user cannot resize the form

❑   SizeableToolWindow — Single border, and the user can resize the form

Each of these has a different effect on the buttons that appear in the title bar of the form. For details, check the help topic for the FormBorderStyle property.

Always on Top — The TopMost Property

Some forms need to remain visible at all times, even when they don't have the focus, e.g., floating toolbars and tutorial windows. In Windows Forms, forms have a property called TopMost. Set it to True to have a form overlay other forms even when it does not have the focus.

Note that a form with TopMost set to True is on top of all applications, not just the hosting application. If you need a form to only be on top of other forms in the application, then this capability is provided by an owned form.

Owned Forms

As with the TopMost property, an owned form floats above the application but it does not interfere with using the application. An example is a search-and-replace box. However, an owned form is not on top of all forms, just the form that is its owner.

When a form is owned by another form, it is minimized and closed with the owner form. Owned forms are never displayed behind their owner form, but they do not prevent their owner form from gaining the focus and being used. However, if you want to click on the area covered by an owned form, the owned form has to be moved out of the way first.

A form can only have one "owner" at a time. If a form that is already owned by `Form1` is added to the owned forms collection for `Form2`, then the form is no longer owned by `Form1`.

There are two ways to make a form owned by another form. It can be done in the owner form or in the owned form.

AddOwnedForm Method

In the owner form, another form can be made owned with the `AddOwnedForm` method. The following code makes an instance of `Form2` become owned by `Form1`. This code would reside somewhere in `Form1` and would typically be placed just before the line that shows the instance of `Form2` to the screen:

```
Dim frm As New Form2
Me.AddOwnedForm(frm)
```

Owner Property

The relationship can also be set up in the owned form. This is done with the `Owner` property of the form. Here is a method that would work inside `Form2` to make it owned by a form that is passed in as an argument to the function:

```
Public Sub MakeMeOwned(frmOwner As Form)
    Me.Owner = frmOwner
End Sub
```

Because this technique requires a reference to the owner inside the owned form, it is not used as often as using the `AddOwnedForm` method in the `Owner` form.

OwnedForms Collection

The owner form can access its collection of owned forms with the `OwnedForms` property. Here is code to loop through the forms owned by a form:

```
Dim frmOwnedForm As Form
For Each frmOwnedForm In Me.OwnedForms
  Console.WriteLine(frmOwnedForm.Text)
Next
```

The owner form can remove an owned form with the `RemoveOwnedForm` property. This could be done in a loop like the previous example, with code like the following:

```
Dim frmOwnedForm As Form
For Each frmOwnedForm In Me.OwnedForms
  Console.WriteLine(frmOwnedForm.Text)
  Me.RemoveOwnedForm(frmOwnedForm)
Next
```

This loop would cause an owner form to stop owning all of its slaved forms. Note that those "deslaved" forms would not be unloaded, they would simply no longer be owned.

Making Forms Transparent and Translucent

Windows Forms offers advanced capabilities to make forms translucent, or parts of a form transparent. You can even change the entire shape of a form.

The Opacity Property

The Opacity property measures how opaque or transparent a form is. A value of 0 percent makes the form fully transparent. A value of 100 percent makes the form fully visible. Any value greater than 0 and less than 100 makes the form partially visible, as if it were a ghost. Note that an opacity value of 0 percent disables the capability to click the form.

Very low levels of opacity, in the range of 1 or 2 percent, make the form effectively invisible, but still allow the form to be clickable. This means that the Opacity property has the potential to create mischievous applications that sit in front of other applications and "steal" their mouse clicks and other events.

Percentage values are used to set opacity in the Properties window, but if you want to set the Opacity property in code, you must use values between 0 and 1 instead, with 0 equivalent to 0 percent and 1 equivalent to 100 percent.

Tool and dialog windows that should not completely obscure their background are one example of a usage for Opacity. Setting expiration for a "free trial" by gradually fading out the application's user interface is another.

The following block of code shows how to fade a form out and back in when the user clicks a button named Button1. You may have to adjust the Step value of the array, depending on your computer's performance:

```
Private Sub Button1_Click(ByVal sender As System.Object, _
                          ByVal e As System.EventArgs) _
                          Handles Button1.Click
    Dim i As Double
    For i = -1 To 1 Step 0.005
      ' Note - opacity is a value from 0.0 to 1.0 in code
      ' Absolute value is used to keep us in that range
      Me.Opacity = System.Math.Abs(i)
      Me.Refresh
    Next i
End Sub
```

The TransparencyKey Property

Instead of making an entire form translucent or transparent, the TransparencyKey property enables you to specify a color that will become transparent on the form. This enables you to make some sections of a form transparent, while other sections are unchanged.

For example, if TransparencyKey is set to a red color and some areas of the form are that exact shade of red, then they will be transparent. Whatever is behind the form shows through in those areas; and if you click in one of those areas, you are actually clicking the object behind the form.

TransparencyKey can be used to create irregularly shaped "skin" forms. A form can have its BackgroundImage property set with an image, and by just painting a part of the image with the TransparencyKey color, you can make parts of the form disappear.

The Region Property

Another way to gain the capability of "skins" is by using the Region property of a form. The Region property allows a shape for a form to be encoded as a "graphics path," thereby changing the shape from the default rectangle to another shape. A path can contain line segments between points, curves, and arcs, and outlines of letters, in any combination.

The following example changes the shape of a form to an arrow. Create a new Windows application. Set the FormBorderStyle property of Form1 to None. Then place the following code in the Load event for Form1:

```
Dim PointArray(6) As Point
PointArray(0) = New Point(0, 40)
PointArray(1) = New Point(200, 40)
PointArray(2) = New Point(200, 0)
PointArray(3) = New Point(250, 100)
PointArray(4) = New Point(200, 200)
PointArray(5) = New Point(200, 160)
PointArray(6) = New Point(0, 160)
Dim myGraphicsPath As _
System.Drawing.Drawing2D.GraphicsPath = _
        New System.Drawing.Drawing2D.GraphicsPath

myGraphicsPath.AddPolygon(PointArray)
Me.Region = New Region(myGraphicsPath)
```

When the program is run, Form1 will appear in the shape of a right-pointing arrow. If you lay out the points in the array, you will see that they have become the vertices of the arrow.

Visual Inheritance

By inheriting from System.Windows.Forms.Form, any class automatically gets all the properties, methods, and events that a form based on Windows Forms is supposed to have. However, a class does not have to inherit directly from the System.Windows.Forms.Form class to become a Windows form. It can become a form by inheriting from another form, which itself inherits from System.Windows.Forms.Form. In this way, controls originally placed on one form can be directly inherited by a second form. Not only is the design of the original form inherited, but also any code associated with these controls (the processing logic behind an Add New button, for example). This means you can create a base form with processing logic required in a number of forms, and then create other forms that inherit the base controls and functionality.

VB 2008 provides an Inheritance Picker tool to aid in this process. Note, however, that a form must be compiled into either an .exe or .dll file before it can be used by the Inheritance Picker. Once that is done, adding a form that inherits from another form in the project can be achieved by selecting Project ➪ Add Windows Form and then choosing the template type of Inherited Form in the resulting dialog.

Scrollable Forms

Some applications need fields that will fit on a single screen. While you could split the data entry into multiple screens, an alternative is a scrollable form.

You can set your forms to automatically have scrollbars when they are sized smaller than the child controls they contain. To do so, set the `AutoScroll` property of your form to `True`. When you run your program, resize the form to make it smaller than the controls require and presto — instant scrolling.

> You cannot have both `Autoscroll` and `IsMdiContainer` set to `True` at the same time. MDI containers have their own scrolling functionality. If you set `Autoscroll` to `True` for an MDI container, then the `IsMdiContainer` property will be set to `False`, and the form will cease to be an MDI container.

MDI Forms

MDI (Multiple Document Interface) forms are forms that are created to hold other forms. The MDI form is often referred to as the *parent*, and the forms displayed within the MDI parent are often called *children*. Figure 15-2 shows a typical MDI parent with several children displayed within it.

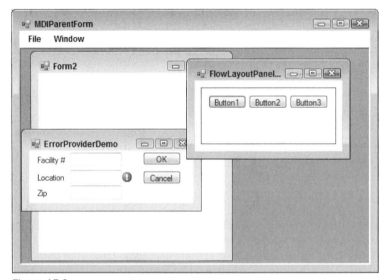

Figure 15-2

Creating an MDI Parent Form

In Windows Forms, a regular form is converted to an MDI parent form by setting the `IsMDIContainer` property of the form to `True`. This is normally done in the Properties window at design time.

A form can also be made into an MDI parent at runtime by setting the `IsMDIContainer` property to `True` in code, but the design of an MDI form is usually different from that of a normal form, so this approach is not often needed.

Differences in MDI Parent Forms between VB6 and VB 2008

In VB6, an MDI parent form can only contain controls that have a property called Align, which is similar to the Dock property in Windows Forms. These controls, such as a PictureBox, can then contain other controls.

In Windows Forms, an MDI parent can contain any control that a regular form can contain. Buttons, labels, and the like can be placed directly on the MDI surface. Such controls appear in front of any MDI child forms that are displayed in the MDI client area.

It is still possible to use controls such as PictureBoxes to hold other controls on a Windows Forms MDI parent. These controls can be docked to the side of the MDI form with the Dock property, which is discussed in the section "Dynamic Sizing and Positioning of Controls."

MDI Child Forms

In Windows Forms, a form becomes an MDI child at runtime by setting the form's MDIParent property to point to an MDI parent form. This makes it possible to use a form as either a standalone form or an MDI child in different circumstances. In fact, the MDIParent property cannot be set at design time — it must be set at runtime to make a form an MDI child. (Note that this is completely different from VB6, where it was necessary to make a form an MDI child at design time.)

Any number of MDI child forms can be displayed in the MDI parent-client area. The currently active child form can be determined with the ActiveForm property of the MDI parent form.

An MDI Example in VB 2008

To see these changes to MDI forms in action, try the following exercise. It shows the basics of creating an MDI parent and making it display an MDI child form:

1. Create a new Windows application. It will have an empty form named Form1. Change both the name of the form and the form's Text property to MDIParentForm.

2. In the Properties window, set the IsMDIContainer property for MDIParentForm to True. This designates the form as an MDI container for child windows. (Setting this property also causes the form to have a different default background color.)

3. From the Toolbox, drag a MenuStrip control to the form. Create a top-level menu item called File with submenu items called New MDI Child and Quit. Also create a top-level menu item called Window. The File ⇨ New MDI Child menu option creates and shows new MDI child forms at runtime; the Window menu keeps track of the open MDI child windows.

4. In the Component Tray at the bottom of the form, click the MenuStrip item and select Properties. In the Properties window, set the MDIWindowListItem property to WindowToolStripMenuItem. This enables the Window menu to maintain a list of open MDI child windows, with a check mark next to the active child window.

5. Create an MDI child form to use as a template for multiple instances. Select Project ⇨ Add Windows Form and click the Add button in the Add New Item dialog box. That results in a new blank form named Form2. Place any controls you like on the form. As an alternative, you can reuse any of the forms created in previous exercises in this chapter.

6. Return to `MDIParentForm`. In the menu editing bar, double-click the New MDI Child option under File. The Code Editor will appear, with the cursor in the event routine for that menu option. Place the following code in the event:

```
Protected Sub NewMdiChildToolStripMenuItem _Click(ByVal sender As Object,
                            ByVal e As System.EventArgs)

    ' This line may change if you are using a form with a different name.
    Dim NewMDIChild As New Form2()
    'Set the Parent Form of the Child window.
    NewMDIChild.MDIParent = Me
    'Display the new form.
    NewMDIChild.Show()

End Sub
```

7. In the menu editing bar for `MDIParentForm`, double-click the Quit option under File. The Code Editor will appear, with the cursor in the event routine for that menu option. Place the following code in the event:

```
Protected Sub QuitToolStripMenuItem_Click(ByVal sender As Object, _
                            ByVal e As System.EventArgs)
    End
End Sub
```

8. Run and test the program. Use the File ➪ New MDI Child option to create several child forms. Note how the Window menu option automatically lists them with the active one checked and allows you to activate a different one.

Arranging Child Windows

MDI parent forms have a method called `LayoutMDI` that automatically arranges child forms in the familiar cascade or tile layout. For the preceding example, add a menu item to your Windows menu called Tile Vertical and insert the following code into the menu item's `Click` event to handle it:

```
Me.LayoutMdi(MDILayout.TileVertical)
```

To see an example of the rearrangement, suppose that the MDI form in Figure 15-2 is rearranged with the `MDILayout.TileVertical` option. It would then look similar to the image in Figure 15-3.

Dialog Forms

In VB6 and earlier, forms were shown with the `Show` method, and this technique is still used in Windows Forms. In both VB6 and VB 2008, the `Show` method by default displays modeless forms, which are forms that enable the user to click off them onto another form in the application.

Applications also sometimes need forms that retain control until their operation is finished. That is, you can't click off such a form onto another form. Such a form is called a *modal form*.

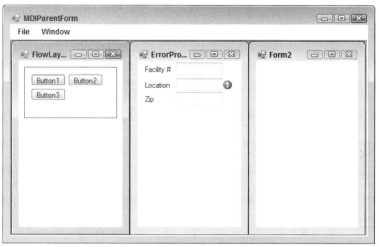

Figure 15-3

In VB6, showing a modal form required using a special parameter on the Show method. Showing a form modally is done differently in Windows Forms, with the ShowDialog method. The following code shows a modal dialog in Windows Forms, assuming the project contains a form with a type of DialogForm:

```
Dim frmDialogForm As New DialogForm
frmDialogForm.ShowDialog()
```

DialogResult

When showing a dialog form, you'll often need to get information about what action the user selected. This was often done with a custom property in VB6, but Windows Forms has a built-in property for that purpose. When a form is shown with the ShowDialog method, the form has a property called DialogResult to indicate its state.

The DialogResult property can take the following enumerated results:

- ❏ DialogResult.Abort
- ❏ DialogResult.Cancel
- ❏ DialogResult.Ignore
- ❏ DialogResult.No
- ❏ DialogResult.None
- ❏ DialogResult.OK
- ❏ DialogResult.Retry
- ❏ DialogResult.Yes

When the DialogResult property is set, the dialog is hidden as a byproduct. That is, setting the DialogResult property causes an implicit call to the Hide method of the dialog form, so that control is released back to the form that called the dialog.

The `DialogResult` property of a dialog box can be set in two ways. The most common way is to associate a `DialogResult` value with a button. Then, when the button is pressed, the associated value is automatically placed in the `DialogResult` property of the form.

To set the `DialogResult` value associated with a button, the `DialogResult` property of the button is used. If this property is set for the button, then it is unnecessary to set the `DialogResult` in code when the button is pressed.

Here is an example that uses this technique. In Visual Studio 2008, start a new VB Windows application. On the automatic blank form that comes up (named `Form1`), place a single button and set its `Text` property to `Dialog`.

Now add a new Windows form by selecting Project ⇨ Add Windows Form and name it `DialogForm.vb`. Place two buttons on `DialogForm` and set the following properties for the buttons:

Property	Value for First Button	Value for Second Button
Name	OKButton	CancelButton
Text	OK	Cancel
DialogResult	OK	Cancel

Do not put any code in `DialogForm` at all. The form should look like the one shown in Figure 15-4.

Figure 15-4

On the first form, `Form1`, place the following code in the `Click` event for `Button1`:

```
Private Sub Button1_Click(ByVal sender As System.Object, _
   ByVal e As System.EventArgs) Handles Button1.Click
   Dim frmDialogForm As New DialogForm()
   frmDialogForm.ShowDialog()

   ' You're back from the dialog - check user action.
   Select Case frmDialogForm.DialogResult
     Case DialogResult.OK
       MsgBox("The user pressed OK")
     Case DialogResult.Cancel
       MsgBox("The user pressed cancel")
   End Select
   frmDialogForm = Nothing
End Sub
```

Run and test the code. When a button is pressed on the dialog form, a message box should be displayed (by the calling form) indicating the button that was pressed.

The second way to set the `DialogResult` property of the form is in code. In a `Button_Click` event, or anywhere else in the dialog form, a line like the following can be used to set the `DialogResult` property for the form and simultaneously hide the dialog form, returning control to the calling form:

```
Me.DialogResult = DialogResult.Ignore
```

This particular line sets the dialog result to `DialogResult.Ignore`, but setting the dialog result to any of the permitted values also hides the dialog form.

Forms at Runtime

The life cycle of a form is like that of all objects. It is created and later destroyed. Forms have a visual component, so they use system resources, such as handles. These are created and destroyed at interim stages within the lifetime of the form. Forms can be created and will hold state as a class, but will not appear until they are activated. Likewise, closing a form doesn't destroy its state.

The following table summarizes the states of a form's existence, how you get the form to that state, the events that occur when the form enters a state, and a brief description of each:

Code	Events Fired	Notes
MyForm = New Form1	Load	The form's `New` method will be called (as will `InitializeComponent`).
MyForm.Show or	HandleCreated	Use `Show` for modeless display.
MyForm.ShowDialog	Load	Use `ShowDialog` for modal display.
	VisibleChanged	The `HandleCreated` event only fires the first time the form is shown or after it has previously been closed.
	Activated	
MyForm.Activate	Activated	A form can be activated when it is visible but does not have the focus.
MyForm.Hide	Deactivate	Hides the form (sets the `Visible` property to `False`).
	VisibleChanged	
MyForm.Close	Deactivate	Closes the form and calls `Dispose` to release the window's resources
	Closing	During the `Closing` event, you can set the `CancelEventArgs.Cancel` property to `True` to abort the close.
	Closed	
	VisibleChanged	
	HandleDestroyed	Also called when the user closes the form using the control box or X button
	Disposed	The `Deactivate` event will only fire if the form is currently active.

Code	Events Fired	Notes
		Note: There is no longer an `Unload` event. Use the `Closing` or `Closed` event instead.
`MyForm.Dispose`	None	Use the `Close` method to finish using your form.
`MyForm = Nothing`	None	Releasing the reference to the form flags it for garbage collection. The garbage collector calls the form's `Finalize` method.

Controls

The controls included in Windows Forms provide basic functionality for a wide range of applications. This section covers the features that all controls use (such as docking) and summarizes the standard controls available to you. Important changes from pre-.NET versions of Visual Basic (VB6 and earlier) are briefly mentioned.

Control Tab Order

The VS 2008 design environment enables you to set the tab order of the controls on a form simply by clicking them in sequence. To activate the feature, open a form in the designer and select View ⇨ Tab Order. This will place a small number in the upper-left corner of each control on your form, representing the tab index of that control.

To set the values, simply click on each control in the sequence you want the tab flow to operate. The screen shot in Figure 15-5 shows a simple form with the tab order feature enabled.

In Windows Forms 2.0, it is possible to have two or more controls with the same tab index value. At runtime, Visual Basic will break the tie by using the z-order of the controls. The control that is highest in the z-order receives the focus first. The z-order is a ranking number that determines which controls are in front of or behind other controls. (The term comes from the z-axis, which is an axis perpendicular to the traditional x-axis and y-axis.) The z-order can be changed by right-clicking the control and selecting Bring to Front.

Figure 15-5

Dynamic Sizing and Positioning of Controls

Windows Forms 2.0 includes a variety of ways to enable dynamic user interfaces. Not only can controls be set to automatically stretch and reposition themselves as a form is resized, they can also be dynamically arranged inside some special container controls intended for that purpose. This section covers all these ways of enabling dynamic sizing and positioning of controls.

Docking

Docking refers to gluing a control to the edge of a parent control. Good examples of docked controls are menu bars and status bars, which are typically docked to the top and bottom of a form, respectively. All visual controls have a `Dock` property.

To work through an example, create a new Windows application and place a `Textbox` on a form. Set the `Text` property of the `TextBox` to `I'm Getting Docked`. The result when you show the form should look something like Figure 15-6.

Figure 15-6

Suppose that you need to glue this `TextBox` to the top of the form. To do this, view the `Dock` property of the label. If you pull it down, you'll see a small graphic like the one shown in Figure 15-7.

Figure 15-7

Simply click the top section of the graphic to stick the label at the top of the form. The other sections give you other effects. (A status bar would use the bottom section, for example. Clicking the box in the middle causes the control to fill the form.) The `TextBox` control will immediately "stick" to the top of your form. When you run your program and stretch the window sideways, you'll see the effect shown in Figure 15-8.

> If you try to dock multiple controls to the same edge, Windows Forms must decide how to break the tie. Precedence is given to controls in reverse z-order. That is, the control that is furthest back in the z-order will be the first control next to the edge. If you dock two controls to the same edge and want to switch them, then right-click the control you want docked first and select Send to Back.

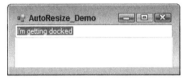

Figure 15-8

If you want a gap between the edge of your form and the docked controls, set the DockPadding property of the parent control. You can set a different value for each of the four directions (Left, Right, Top, Bottom). You can also set all four properties to the same value using the All setting.

Anchoring

Anchoring is similar to docking except that you can specifically define the distance that each edge of your control will maintain from the edges of a parent. To see it in action, add a button to the form in the docking example. The result should look like what is shown in Figure 15-9.

Figure 15-9

Dropping down the Anchor property of the button gives you the graphic shown in Figure 15-10.

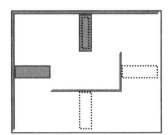

Figure 15-10

The four rectangles surrounding the center box enable you to toggle the anchor settings of the control. Figure 15-10 shows the default anchor setting of Top, Left for all controls.

When the setting is on (dark gray), the edge of the control maintains its original distance from the edge of the parent as the parent is resized. If you set the anchor to two opposing edges (such as the left and right edges), the control stretches to accommodate this, as shown in Figure 15-11.

Figure 15-11

One of the most common uses of anchoring is to set the `Anchor` property for buttons in the lower-right portion of a form. Setting the `Anchor` property of a button to `Bottom, Right` causes the button to maintain a constant distance from the bottom-right corner of the form.

You can also set the `Anchor` property in code. The most common scenario for this would be for a control created on-the-fly. To set the `Anchor` property in code, you must add the anchor styles for all the sides to which you need to anchor. For example, setting the `Anchor` property to `Bottom, Left` would require a line of code like this:

```
MyControl.Anchor = Ctype(AnchorStyles.Bottom + AnchorStyles.Right, AnchorStyles)
```

Sizable Containers

Early versions of Windows Forms used the `Splitter` control to allow resizing of containers. This control is still available in Windows Forms 2.0, but it doesn't appear by default in the Toolbox. In its place is a replacement control, `SplitContainer`, that provides the same functionality with less work on your part.

A single `SplitContainer` acts much like two panels with an appropriately inserted `Splitter`. You can think of it as a panel with two sections separated by a movable divider so that the relative sizes of the sections can be changed by a user.

To use a `SplitContainer`, simply drop it on a form, resize it, and position the draggable divider to the appropriate point. If you want the divider to be horizontal instead of vertical, you change the `Orientation` property. Then you can place controls in each subpanel in any way you like. It is common to insert a control such as a `TreeView` or `ListBox`, and then dock it to its respective subpanel. This enables users to resize such contained controls. A typical example of a `SplitContainer` in action is shown in Figure 15-12.

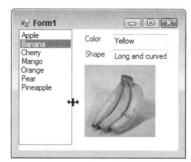

Figure 15-12

The cursor in Figure 15-12 shows that the mouse is hovering over the divider, allowing repositioning of the divider by dragging the mouse. A SplitContainer may be nested inside another SplitContainer. This enables you to build forms in which several parts are resizable relative to each other.

FlowLayoutPanel Control

The FlowLayoutPanel enables the dynamic layout of controls contained within it, based on the size of the FlowLayoutPanel. This is quite a departure from traditional Windows Forms layout, in which controls in a container are positioned solely according to their Top and Left properties.

FlowLayoutPanel works conceptually much like a simple HTML page shown in a browser. The controls placed in the FlowLayoutPanel are positioned in sequence horizontally until there's not enough space for the next control, which then wraps further down for another row of controls. The following walk-through demonstrates this capability.

Start a new Windows application project. On the blank Form1 included in the new project, place a FlowLayoutPanel control toward the top of the form, making it a bit less wide than the width of the form. Set the Anchor property for the FlowLayoutPanel to Top, Left, and Right. Set the BorderStyle property for the FlowLayoutPanel to FixedSingle so it's easy to see.

Place three Button controls in the FlowLayoutPanel, keeping their default sizes. The form you create should look like the one shown in Figure 15-13.

Figure 15-13

Run the application. The initial layout will be similar to the design-time layout. However, if you resize the form to about two thirds of its original width, the layout of the buttons changes. Because there is no longer enough room for them to be arranged side by side, the arrangement automatically switches. Figure 15-14 shows the form in three configurations: first with its original width, then narrower so that only two buttons fit in the FlowLayoutPanel, and finally so narrow that the buttons are all stacked in the FlowLayoutPanel.

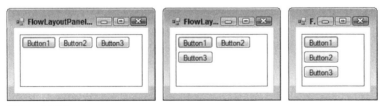

Figure 15-14

Note that no logic of any kind was added to the form — the `FlowLayoutPanel` handles the repositioning of the buttons automatically. In fact, any position information you set for the button controls is ignored if they are placed in a `FlowLayoutPanel`.

Padding and Margin Properties

To assist in positioning controls in the `FlowLayoutPanel`, all controls have a new property called `Margin`. There are settings for `Margin.Left`, `Margin.Right`, `Margin.Top`, and `Margin.Bottom`. These settings determine how much space is reserved around a control when calculating its automatic position in a `FlowLayoutPanel`.

You can see the `Margin` property in action by changing the `Margin` property for one or more of the buttons in the previous example. If you change all the `Margin` settings for the first `Button` to 10 pixels, for example, and run the application, the form will look like the one shown in Figure 15-15.

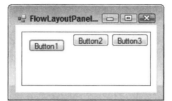

Figure 15-15

The first button now has a 10-pixel separation from all the other controls in the `FlowLayoutPanel`, as well as a 10-pixel separation from the edges of the `FlowLayoutPanel` itself.

The `Padding` property is for the `FlowLayoutPanel` or other container control. When a control is embedded into a `FlowLayoutPanel`, the `Padding.Left`, `Padding.Right`, `Padding.Top`, and `Padding.Bottom` properties of the `FlowLayoutPanel` determine how far the control should be positioned from the inside edge of the container.

You can see the `Padding` property in action by changing the `Padding` property for the `FlowLayoutPanel` in the previous example. If you set all `Padding` settings to 20 pixels, and reset the `Margin` property for the first `Button` back to the default, then the form will look like what is shown in Figure 15-16 in the visual designer.

Figure 15-16

Notice that all the controls in the `FlowLayoutPanel` are now at least 20 pixels from the edges.

The `Padding` property is also applicable to other container controls, if the contained controls have their `Dock` property set. If the settings for `Padding` are not zero, then a docked control will be offset from the edge of the container by the amount specified by the `Padding` property.

TableLayoutPanel Control

Another control that uses dynamic layout of child controls is the `TableLayoutPanel`. This control consists of a table of rows and columns, resulting in a rectangular array of cells. You can place one control in each cell. However, that control can itself be a container, such as a `Panel` or `FlowLayoutPanel`.

The dimensions of the columns and rows can be controlled by setting some key properties. For columns, set the number of columns with the `ColumnCount` property, and then control each individual column with the `ColumnStyles` collection. When you click the button for the `ColumnStyles` collection, you get a designer window that enables you to set two key properties for each column: `SizeType` and `Width`.

`SizeType` can be set to one of the following enumerations:

❑ `Absolute` — Sets the column width to a fixed size in pixels

❑ `AutoSize` — Indicates that the size of the column should be managed by the `TableLayoutPanel`, which allocates width to the column depending on the widest control contained in the column

❑ `Percent` — Sets what percentage of the `TableLayoutPanel` to use for the width of the column

The `Width` property is only applicable if you do not choose a `SizeType` of `AutoSize`. It sets either the number of pixels for the width of the column (if the `SizeType` is `Absolute`) or the percentage width for the column (if the `SizeType` is `Percent`).

Similarly, for rows, there is a `RowCount` property to set the number of rows, and a `RowStyles` collection to manage the size of the rows. Each row in `RowStyles` has a `SizeType`, which works the same way as `SizeType` does for `Columns` except that it manages the height of the row instead of the width of a column. The `Height` property is used for rows instead of a `Width` property, but it works in a corresponding way. `Height` is either the number of pixels (if `SizeType` is `Absolute`) or a percentage of the height of the `TableLayoutPanel` (if `SizeType` is `Percent`). If `SizeType` is `AutoSize`, then a row is sized to the height of the tallest control in the row.

An advanced UI layout technique is to first create a `TableLayoutPanel`, and then embed a `FlowLayoutPanel` in some of the cells of the `TableLayoutPanel`. This allows several controls to be contained in a cell and repositioned as the size of the cell changes.

A step-by-step example of using a `TableLayoutPanel`, with an embedded `FlowLayoutPanel`, is included in the next chapter in the section "Creating a Composite UserControl."

Panel and GroupBox Container Controls

Of course, not all applications need the dynamic layout of the containers just discussed. Windows Forms includes two controls that are static containers, in which the positions and layout of the contained controls are not adjusted at all.

In VB6, the `Frame` control was used for this purpose. However, Windows Forms has two such containers, with minor differences between them: the `GroupBox` control and the `Panel` control.

These two are similar in the following ways:

❑ They can serve as a container for other controls.

❑ If they are hidden or moved, then the action affects all the controls in the container.

The GroupBox control is the one that most closely resembles an old VB6 Frame control visually. It acts much like a VB6 Frame control too, with one significant exception: There is no way to remove its border. It always has a border, and it can have a title, if needed. The border is always set the same way. Figure 15-17 shows a form with a GroupBox control containing three RadioButtons.

Figure 15-17

The Panel control has three major differences from GroupBox:

❑ It has options for displaying its border in the BorderStyle property, with a default of no border.

❑ It has the capability to scroll if its AutoScroll property is set to True.

❑ It cannot set a title or caption.

Figure 15-18 shows a form containing a Panel control with its BorderStyle property set to FixedSingle, with scrolling turned on by setting AutoScroll to True, and with a CheckedListBox that is too big to display all at once (which forces the Panel to show a scrollbar).

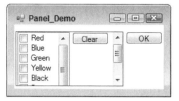

Figure 15-18

Extender Providers

Windows Forms has a family of components that can only be used in association with visual controls. These components are known as *extender providers*. They work with the Visual Studio IDE to cause new properties to appear in the Properties window for controls on the form.

Extender providers have no visible manifestation except in conjunction with other controls, so they appear in the component tray. The three extender providers available with Windows Forms 2.0 are the HelpProvider, the ToolTip, and the ErrorProvider. All three work in basically the same way. Each extender provider implements the properties that are "attached" to other controls. The best way to see how this works is to go through an example, so let's do that with a ToolTip component.

ToolTip

The ToolTip is the simplest of the built-in extender providers. It adds just one property to each control: ToolTip on ToolTip1 (assuming the ToolTip control has the default name of ToolTip1). This property works in very much the same way the ToolTipText property works in VB6, and in fact replaces it.

To see this in action, create a Windows Forms application. On the blank Form1 that is created for the project, place a couple of buttons. Take a look at the Properties window for Button1. Notice that it does not have a ToolTip property of any kind.

Drag over the ToolTip control, which will be placed in the component tray. Go back to the Properties window for Button1. A property named ToolTip on ToolTip1 is now present. Set any string value you like for this property.

Run the project and hover the mouse pointer over Button1. You will see a tooltip containing the string value you entered for the ToolTip on ToolTip1 property.

Other properties of the ToolTip component enable you to control other characteristics of the tooltip, such as the initial delay before the tooltip appears.

New in Windows Forms 2.0 is the capability to change the shape of tooltips to a "balloon." This is done by setting the IsBalloon property of the Tooltip component to True. Instead of a hovering rectangular tooltip, the tooltip has a rounded rectangular outline with a pointer to the control it is associated with, not unlike the dialog balloons in a comic strip. Figure 15-19 shows an example.

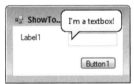

Figure 15-19

HelpProvider

The HelpProvider enables controls to have associated context-sensitive help available by pressing F1. When a HelpProvider is added to a form, all controls on the form get the following new properties, which show up in the controls' Properties window:

Property	Usage
HelpString on HelpProvider1	Provides a pop-up tooltip for the control when F1 is pressed while the control has the focus. If the HelpKeyword and HelpNavigator properties (described later) are set to provide a valid reference to a help file, then the HelpString value is ignored in favor of the help file information.
HelpKeyword onHelpProvider1	Provides a keyword or other index to use in a help file for context-sensitive help for this control. The HelpProvider1 control has a property that indicates which help file to use. This replaces the HelpContextID property in VB6.

Property	Usage
HelpNavigator onHelpProvider1	Contains an enumerated value that determines how the value in HelpKeyword is used to refer to the help file. There are several possible values for displaying such elements as a topic, an index, or a table of contents in the help file.
ShowHelp onHelpProvider1	Determines whether the HelpProvider control is active for this control

Filling in the HelpString property immediately causes the control to provide tooltip help when F1 is pressed while the control has the focus. The HelpProvider control has a property to point to a help file (either an HTML help file or a Win32 help file), and the help topic in the HelpTopic property points to a topic in this file.

ErrorProvider

The ErrorProvider component presents a simple, visual way to indicate to a user that a control on a form has an error associated with it. The added property for controls on the form when an ErrorProvider is used is called Error on ErrorProvider1 (assuming the ErrorProvider has the default name of ErrorProvider1). Setting this property to a string value causes the error icon to appear next to a control. In addition, the text appears in a tooltip if the mouse hovers over the error icon.

Figure 15-20 shows a screen with several text boxes, and an error icon next to one (with a tooltip). The error icon and tooltip are displayed and managed by an ErrorProvider.

Figure 15-20

The ErrorProvider component's default icon is a red circle with an exclamation point. When the Error property for the text box is set, the icon blinks for a few moments, and hovering over the icon causes the tooltip to appear. Writing your own code to set the Error property is explained in the section "Working with Extender Providers in Code."

Properties of Extender Providers

In addition to providing other controls with properties, extender providers also have properties of their own. For example, the ErrorProvider has a property named BlinkStyle. When it is set to NeverBlink, the blinking of the icon is stopped for all controls affected by the ErrorProvider.

Other properties of the ErrorProvider enable you to change things such as the icon used and where the icon appears in relation to the field containing the error. For instance, you might want the icon to appear on the left side of a field instead of the default right side. You can also have multiple error providers on your form. For example, you might wish to give users a warning, rather than an error. A second error provider with a yellow icon could be used for this feature.

Working with Extender Providers in Code

Setting the `Error` property in the previous example can be done with the Properties window, but this is not very useful for on-the-fly error management. However, setting the `Error` property in code is not done with typical property syntax. By convention, extender providers have a method for each extended property they need to set, and the arguments for the method include the associated control and the property setting. To set the `Error` property in the previous example, the following code was used:

```
ErrorProvider1.SetError(txtName, "You must provide a location!")
```

The name of the method to set a property is the word `Set` prefixed to the name of the property. The preceding line of code shows that the `Error` property is set with the `SetError` method of the `ErrorProvider`.

There is a corresponding method to get the value of the property, and it is named with `Get` prefixed to the name of the property. To determine the current `Error` property setting for `txtName`, you would use the following line:

```
sError = ErrorProvider1.GetError(txtName)
```

Similar syntax is used to manipulate any of the properties managed by an extender provider. The discussion of the tooltip provider earlier mentioned setting the tooltip property in the Properties window. To set that same property in code, the syntax would be as follows:

```
ToolTip1.SetToolTip(Button1, "New tooltip for Button1")
```

Advanced Capabilities for Data Entry

Windows Forms 2.0 includes some advanced capabilities for data entry that were not available in earlier versions. `Textbox` and `Combobox` controls in 2.0 have autocompletion capabilities, and a `MaskedTextbox` control allows entry of formatted input such as phone numbers.

Autocompletion

Responsive user interfaces help users accomplish their purposes, thereby making them more productive. One classic way to do this is with *autocompletion.*

An example of autocompletion is IntelliSense in Visual Studio. Using IntelliSense, the user only has to type in a few letters, and Visual Studio presents a list of probable entries matching those letters. If the desired entry is found, the user only needs to select it, rather than type the entire entry.

Autocompletion is available in Windows Forms 2.0 with text boxes and combo boxes. Both use a set of properties to control how autocompletion works and from where the list of entries available to the user comes.

To see autocompletion in action, create a Windows application project. Drag a `Textbox` from the toolbox onto the blank `Form1` created for the project. Set the `AutoCompleteMode` for the text box to `Suggest` in the Properties window. Then set the `AutoCompleteSource` to `CustomSource`. Finally, click the button in the setting window for `AutoCompleteCustomSource`. You'll see a window for adding entries that is very similar to the window for entering items for a list box or combo box.

Enter the following items into the dialog:

```
Holder
Holland
Hollis
Holloway
Holly
Holstein
Holt
```

Start the project and type **Hol** into the text box. As soon as you start typing, a drop-down will appear that contains entries matching what you've typed, including all seven elements in the list. If you then type another 1, the list will decrease to four elements that begin with Holl. If you then type an o, the list will contain only the entry Holloway.

The AutoCompleteMode has two other modes. The Append mode does not automatically present a drop-down, but instead appends the rest of the closest matching entry to the text in the Textbox or ComboBox, and highlights the untyped characters. This allows the closest matching entry to be placed in the text area without the user explicitly selecting an entry.

The SuggestAppend mode combines Suggest and Append. The current best match is displayed in the text area, and the drop-down with other possibilities is automatically displayed. This mode is the one most like IntelliSense.

You can also set the list of items to be included in the autocompletion list at runtime, which is the most common usage scenario. A list of items from a database table would typically be loaded for autocompletion. Here is typical code to create a list of items and attach the list to a combo box:

```
Dim autoCompleteStringCollection1 As New AutoCompleteStringCollection
Dim nReturn As Integer
nReturn = autoCompleteStringCollection1.Add("Holder")
nReturn = autoCompleteStringCollection1.Add("Holland")
nReturn = autoCompleteStringCollection1.Add("Hollis")
nReturn = autoCompleteStringCollection1.Add("Holloway")
ComboBox1.AutoCompleteCustomSource = autoCompleteStringCollection1
```

For this sample to work properly, the Combobox control's AutoCompleteSource property must be set to CustomSource.

Several built-in lists are available for use with autocompletion. Instead of setting AutoCompleteSource to CustomSource, you can set it to sources such as files in the file system, or URLs recently used in Internet Explorer. See the documentation for AutoCompleteSource for additional options; or, if you are using AutoCompleteSource in code, IntelliSense will show the options available.

MaskedTextbox Control

The MaskedTextbox control fulfills the same function as the old VB6 MaskedEdit control. If you have used MaskedEdit in VB6, the MaskedTextbox will feel quite familiar.

After dragging a MaskedTextbox control to a form, you typically want to first set the mask associated with the control. You can do this in the Properties window by selecting the Mask property, but you can also click the smart tag (right-pointing arrow) on the right side of the MaskedTextbox. In either case, you can either construct a mask manually or select one of the commonly used masks from a list.

If you need to create your own mask, you need to design it based on the following set of formatting characters:

Mask Character	Description
#	Digit placeholder
.	Decimal placeholder. The actual character used is the one specified as the decimal placeholder in your international settings. This character is treated as a literal for masking purposes.
,	Thousands separator. The actual character used is the one specified as the thousands separator in your international settings. This character is treated as a literal for masking purposes.
:	Time separator. The actual character used is the one specified as the time separator in your international settings. This character is treated as a literal for masking purposes.
/	Date separator. The actual character used is the one specified as the date separator in your international settings. This character is treated as a literal for masking purposes.
\	Treat the next character in the mask string as a literal. This enables you to include the #, &, A, and ? characters in the mask. This character is treated as a literal for masking purposes.
&	Character placeholder. Valid values for this placeholder are ANSI characters in the following ranges: 32–126 and 128–255.
>	Converts all the characters that follow to uppercase
<	Converts all the characters that follow to lowercase
A	Alphanumeric character placeholder (entry required), e.g., a–z, A–Z, or 0–9
a	Alphanumeric character placeholder (entry optional)
9	Digit placeholder (entry optional), e.g., 0–9
C	Character or space placeholder (entry optional). This operates exactly like the & placeholder and ensures compatibility with Microsoft Access.
?	Letter placeholder, e.g., a–z or A–Z
Literal	All other symbols are displayed as literals — that is, as themselves.

Literal characters are simply inserted automatically by the MaskedTextbox control. If you have literal characters for the parentheses in a phone number, for example, the user need not type these in order for them to show up in the text area of the control.

As an example of a mask, suppose that you have an account number that must consist of exactly two uppercase letters and five digits. You could construct a mask of >??00000. The first character forces all letters to uppercase. The two question marks specify two required alphabetic characters, and the five zeros specify five required digits.

Once you have set the `Mask` for the `MaskedTextbox`, all entries in the control will be coerced to the `Mask` pattern. Keystrokes that don't conform will be thrown away.

Validating Data Entry

Most controls that you place on a form require that its content be validated in some way. A text box might require a numeric value only or simply require that the user provide any value and not leave it blank.

The `ErrorProvider` component discussed earlier makes this task significantly easier than it was in previous versions. To illustrate the use of an `ErrorProvider` in data validation, create a new Windows application project and change the `Text` property for the blank `Form1` to `Data Validation Demo`. Then place two text boxes on the form that will hold a user ID and password, as shown in Figure 15-21.

Figure 15-21

Name the first text box `UserNameTextBox` and name the second text box `PasswordTextBox`. Drag an `ErrorProvider` onto the form, which will cause it to appear in the component tray. In the next section, you'll add the code that simply verifies that the user has filled in both text boxes and gives a visual indication, via the `ErrorProvider`, if either of the fields has been left blank.

The Validating Event

The `Validating` event fires when your control begins its validation. It is here that you need to place the code that validates your control, and set a visual indication for an error. Insert the following code to see this in action:

```
Private Sub UserNameTextBox_Validating(ByVal sender As Object, _
                        ByVal e As System.ComponentModel.CancelEventArgs) _
                        Handles UserNameTextBox.Validating
    If userNameTextbox.Text = "" Then
        ErrorProvider1.SetError(UserNameTextBox, "User Name cannot be blank")
    Else
        ErrorProvider1.SetError(UserNameTextBox, "")
    End If
End Sub
```

```
Private Sub PasswordTextBox_Validating(ByVal sender As Object, _
                        ByVal e As System.ComponentModel.CancelEventArgs) _
                        Handles PasswordTextBox.Validating
    If passwordTextbox.Text = "" Then
        ErrorProvider1.SetError(PasswordTextBox, "Password cannot be blank")
    Else
        ErrorProvider1.SetError(PasswordTextBox, "")
    End If
End Sub
```

Run the program and then tab between the controls without entering any text to get the error message. You'll see an icon blink next to each of the text box controls; and if you hover over an error icon, you'll see the appropriate error message.

There is also a Validated event that fires after a control's Validating event. It can be used, for example, to do a final check after other events have manipulated the contents of the control.

The CausesValidation Property

The CausesValidation property determines whether the control will participate in the validation events on the form. A control with a CausesValidation setting of True (it is True by default) has two effects:

❏   The control's Validating/Validated events fire when appropriate.

❏   The control triggers the Validating/Validated events for other controls.

It is important to understand that the validation events fire for a control not when the focus is lost but when the focus shifts to a control that has a CausesValidation value of True.

To see this effect, set the CausesValidation property of the password text box in your application to False (be sure to leave it True for the user ID and OK button). When you run the program, tab off the user ID text box and again to the OK button. Notice that it isn't until the focus reaches the OK button that the validating event of the user ID text box fires. Also notice that the validating event of the Password field never fires.

Ultimately, if you determine that the control is not valid, you need to specify what happens. That may include setting the focus to the control that needs attention (as well as indicating the error with an ErrorProvider).

Toolbars and the New ToolStrip Control

As mentioned in the summary of new features in Windows Forms 2.0, the ToolStrip control replaces the Toolbar control from Windows Forms 1.0 and 1.1. ToolStrip has many improvements. It supports movement to sides of a form other than the place where it was laid out, and you have much more flexibility in placing items on the toolbar. It also integrates better with the IDE to assist in creating toolbars and manipulating the many settings available.

The ToolStrip does not sit alone on a form. When a ToolStrip is dragged onto a form, the container that actually sits on the form is called a RaftingContainer. This container handles the positioning so that the toolbar created by a ToolStrip can be dragged to other parts of the form.

The `ToolStrip` sits inside the `RaftingContainer` and is the container for toolbar elements. It handles the sizing of the toolbar, movement of toolbar elements, and other general toolbar functions.

The items on the toolbar must be from a set of controls specially designed to serve as toolbar items. All of these items inherit from the `ToolStripItem` base class. The controls available for toolbar items are as follows:

Control	Description
ToolStripButton	Replicates the functionality of a regular `Button` for a toolbar
ToolStripLabel	Replicates the functionality of a regular `Label` for a toolbar
ToolStripSeparator	A visual toolbar element that displays a vertical bar to separate other groups of elements (no user interaction)
ToolStripComboBox	Replicates the functionality of a regular `ComboBox` for a toolbar. This item must be contained within a `ToolStripControlHost` (see below).
ToolStripTextBox	Replicates the functionality of a regular `TextBox` for a toolbar. This item must be contained within a `ToolStripControlHost` (see below).
ToolStripControlHost	A hosting container for other controls that reside on a `ToolStrip`. It can host any of the following controls: `ToolStripComboBox`, `ToolStripTextBox`, other Windows Forms controls, or user controls.
ToolStripDropDownItem	A hosting container for toolbar elements that feature drop-down functionality. It can host a `ToolStripMenuItem`, a `ToolStripSplitButton`, or a `ToolStripDropDownButton`.
ToolStripDropDownButton	A button that supports drop-down functionality. Clicking the button shows a list of options from which the user must select the one desired. This item is used when the user needs to select from a group of options, none of which is used a large majority of the time.
ToolStripSplitButton	A combination of a regular button and a drop-down button. This item is often used when there is a frequently used option to click, but you also need to offer users other options that are less frequently used.
ToolStripMenuItem	A selectable option displayed on a menu or context menu. This item is typically used with the menu controls that inherit from the `ToolStrip`, discussed later in this chapter in the section "Menus."

Note that almost any control can be hosted on a toolbar using the `ToolStripControlHost`. However, for buttons, text boxes, labels, and combo boxes, it is much easier to use the `ToolStrip` version instead of the standard version.

Creating a ToolStrip and Adding Toolbar Elements

Try an example to see how to build a toolbar using the `ToolStrip` control. Create a new Windows application. Add a `ToolStrip` control to the blank `Form1` that is included with the new project. Make the form about twice its default width so that you have plenty of room to see the `ToolStrip` as you work on it.

The `ToolStrip` is positioned at the top of the form by default. It does not contain any elements, although if you highlight the `ToolStrip` control in the component tray, a "menu designer" will appear in the `ToolStrip`.

The easiest way to add multiple elements to the `ToolStrip` is to use the designer dialog for the `ToolStrip`. Highlight the `ToolStrip` in the component tray and click the button in the Properties window for the `Items` property. You'll see a designer dialog like the one shown in Figure 15-22.

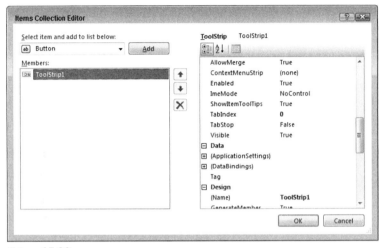

Figure 15-22

The drop-down in the upper-left corner contains the different types of items that can be placed on the toolbar. The names in the drop-down are the same as the names in the table of controls except that the "Toolstrip" prefix is not present. Add one each of the following types, with the setting specified:

❑   `Button` — Set the `Text` property to `Go`. Set the `DisplayStyle` property to `Text`.

❑   `ComboBox` — Leave the `Text` property blank. Set `DropDownStyle` to `DropDownList`. Open the Items dialog and add the names of some colors.

❑   `SplitButton` — Set the `Text` property to `Options`. Set the Display property to `Text`.

❑   `TextBox` — Leave the `Text` property blank.

Click OK. The `ToolStrip` will look like the one shown in Figure 15-23.

You can now handle events on any of these toolbar elements the same way you would any other controls. You can double-click to get a `Click` event routine or access the event routines through the drop-downs in the Code Editor.

To make the `Toolstrip` more dynamic, it must be embedded in a `ToolStripContainer`. You can do that manually by dragging one over and putting the `Toolstrip` in it, but the easy way to do it is to click the smart tag on the `Toolstrip` and then select Embed in ToolStripContainer. This causes a `ToolStripContainer` to appear on your form. Set the `Dock` property for the `ToolStripContainer` to `Fill` and it will provide a surface for the `Toolstrip` that includes all four edges of the form.

Run your program. Using the mouse, grab the dotted handle on the far left edge of the toolbar. If you drag this to the right, then the toolbar will be repositioned. If you drag it to other positions on the form, then the entire toolbar will dock to different edges of the form.

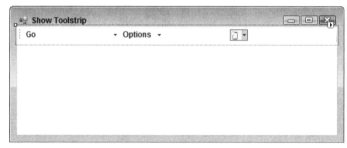

Figure 15-23

Allowing the User to Move Toolbar Elements

By default, the `AllowItemReorder` property of the `ToolStrip` is set to `False`. If you change that to `True`, then the elements on the toolbar can be moved around in relation to one another (reordered) at runtime.

Change the `AllowItemReorder` property to `True` for the `ToolStrip` and run your program again. Hold down the Alt key and drag elements on the toolbar around. They will assume new positions on the toolbar when you drop them.

Creating a Standard Set of Toolbar Elements

If you need a toolbar that has the typical visual elements for cut, copy, paste, and so on, it is not necessary to create the elements. The designer will do it for you.

Create a new form in your project and drag a `ToolStrip` onto it. As before, it will be positioned at the top and will not contain any elements. With the `ToolStrip` highlighted in the component tray, click the `Item` property. Below the properties in the Properties window, a link named Insert Standard Items will appear. Click that link; elements will be inserted into the `ToolStrip`, making it look like the one shown in Figure 15-24.

Figure 15-24

Menus

Menus are added to a form in Windows Forms 2.0 by dragging controls called `MenuStrip` or `ContextMenuStrip` onto your form. `MenuStrip` implements a standard Windows-style menu at the top of the form. `ContextMenuStrip` allows a pop-up menu with a right mouse button click.

These controls are actually subclasses of the `ToolStrip`, so much of the information you learned earlier in this chapter about working with the `ToolStrip` also applies to the `MenuStrip` and `ContextMenuStrip`. When dragged onto the form, these controls appear in the component tray just as the `ToolStrip` does, and you access the designer for these controls the same way you do for the `ToolStrip`. However, because these are menus, the most common way to add items is to type them directly into the menu designer that appears when the control is highlighted.

The menu designer is extremely intuitive — the menu appears on your form just as it would at runtime, and you simply fill in the menu items you need. Each item can be renamed, and each can have a `Click` event associated with it.

Adding Standard Items to a Menu

If your form's menu needs to have the standard top-level options (File, Edit, and so on) and the typical options under these items, then you can have all these usual options inserted for you automatically.

To see this capability in action, drag a `MenuStrip` to a form and then click the smart tag (the right arrow at the right edge) for the `MenuStrip` to bring up the designer dialog. Click the Insert Standard Items link at the bottom of the dialog.

Icons and Checkmarks for Menu Items

Each menu item has an `Image` property. Setting this property to an image causes the image to appear on the left side of the text for the menu option. You can see this property in use by looking at the standard items inserted in the preceding example. The File ⇨ Save option has an icon of a diskette, which is produced by setting the image property of that item.

Items can also have check marks beside them. This is done by changing the `Checked` property of the item to `True`. You can do this at design time or runtime, enabling you to manipulate the check marks on menus as necessary.

Context Menus

To implement a context menu for a form or any control on a form, drag a `ContextMenuStrip` to the form and add the menu items. Items are added and changed the same way as they are with the `MenuStrip`.

To hook a context menu to a control, set the control's `ContextMenuStrip` property to the `ContextMenuStrip` menu control you want to use. Then, when your program runs and you right-click in the control, the context menu will pop up.

Dynamically Manipulating Menus at Runtime

Menus can be adjusted at runtime using code. Context menus, for instance, may need to vary depending on the state of your form. The following walk-through shows how to add a new menu item to a context menu and how to clear the menu items.

Create a new Windows application. On the blank `Form1` for the project, drag over a `MenuStrip` control. Using the menu designer, type in a top-level menu option of `File`. Under that option, type in options for `Open` and `Save`.

Now place a button on the form. Double-click the button to get its `Click` event, and place the following code into the event:

```
Dim NewItem As New ToolStripMenuItem
NewItem.Text = "Save As"
' Set any other properties of the menu item you like.
```

```
FileToolStripMenuItem.DropDownItems.Add(NewItem)
AddHandler NewItem.Click, _
    AddressOf Me.NewMenuItem_Click
```

Add the event handler referenced in this code at the bottom of the form's code:

```
Private Sub NewMenuItem_Click(ByVal sender As System.Object, _
                            ByVal e As System.EventArgs)
    MessageBox.Show("New menu item clicked!")
End Sub
```

If you now run the program and look at the menu, it will only have File and Save options. Clicking the button will cause a new Save As item to be added to the menu, and it will be hooked to the event routine called `NewMenuItem_Click`.

Common Dialogs

Windows Forms provides you with seven common dialog controls. Each control opens a predefined form that is identical to the one used by the operating system.

These dialogs cannot be shown modeless. They have a `ShowDialog` method to show them modally. That method returns one of the standard `DialogResult` values, as discussed earlier in this chapter.

OpenFileDialog and SaveFileDialog

These two controls open the standard dialog control that enables users to select files on the system. They are quite similar except for the buttons and labels that appear on the actual dialog box when it is shown to the user. Each prompts the user for a file on the system by allowing the user to browse the files and folders available.

Use the following properties to set up the dialog boxes:

Property	Comments
InitialDirectory	Defines the initial location that is displayed when the dialog opens, e.g., `OpenFileDialog1.InitialDirectory = "C:\Program Files"`
Filter	String that defines the Files of Type list. Separate items using the pipe character. Items are entered in pairs; the first of each pair is the description of the file type, and the second half is the file wildcard, e.g., `OpenFileDialog1.Filter = "All Files$|*.* |Text Files|*.txt|Rich Text Files|*.rtf"`
FilterIndex	Integer that specifies the default filter item to use when the dialog box opens. For example, with the preceding filter used, defaults to text files as follows: `OpenFileDialog1.FilterIndex = 2`
RestoreDirectory	Boolean value that, when `True`, forces the system's default directory to be restored to the location it was in when the dialog box was first opened. This is `False` by default.

Property	Comments
Filename	Holds the full name of the file that the user selected, including the path
ShowDialog	Displays the dialog

The following code opens the standard dialog box, asking the user to select a file that currently exists on the system, and simply displays the choice in a message box upon return:

```
OpenFileDialog1.InitialDirectory = "C:\"
OpenFileDialog1.Filter = "Text files|*.txt|All files|*.*"
OpenFileDialog1.FilterIndex = 1
OpenFileDialog1.RestoreDirectory = True
If OpenFileDialog1.ShowDialog() = Windows.Forms.DialogResult.OK Then
    MessageBox.Show("You selected """ & OpenFileDialog1.FileName & """")
End If
```

ColorDialog Control

As the name implies, this control gives the user a dialog box from which to select a color. Use the following properties to set up the dialog boxes as follows:

```
ColorDialog1.Color = TextBox1.BackColor
ColorDialog1.AllowFullOpen = True
If ColorDialog1.ShowDialog()= Windows.Forms.DialogResult.OK Then
    TextBox1.BackColor = ColorDialog1.Color
End If
```

Property	Comments
Color	The `System.Drawing.Color` that the user selected. You can also use this to set the initial color selected when the user opens the dialog.
AllowFullOpen	Boolean value that, when `True`, allows the user to select any color. If `False`, then the user is restricted to the set of default colors.
ShowDialog	Displays the dialog

FontDialog Control

This control displays the standard dialog box, allowing a user to select a font. Use the following properties to set up the dialog boxes:

Property	Comments
Font	The `System.Drawing.Font` that the user selected. Also used to set the initial font.
ShowEffects	Boolean value that, when `True`, makes the dialog box display the text effects options of underline and strikeout.

Property	Comments
ShowColor	Boolean value that, when True, makes the dialog box display the combo box of the font colors. The ShowEffects property must be True for this to have an effect.
FixedPitchOnly	Boolean value that, when True, limits the list of font options to only those that have a fixed pitch (such as Courier or Lucida console).
ShowDialog	Displays the dialog

Using these properties looks like this:

```
FontDialog1.Font = TextBox1.Font
FontDialog1.ShowColor = True
FontDialog1.ShowEffects = True
FontDialog1.FixedPitchOnly = False
If FontDialog1.ShowDialog()= Windows.Forms.DialogResult.OK Then
    TextBox1.Font = FontDialog1.Font
End If
```

Printer Dialog Controls

There are three more common dialog controls: PrintDialog, PrintPreviewDialog, and PageSetup-Dialog. They can all be used to control the output of a file to the printer, and you can use these in conjunction with the PrintDocument component to run and control print jobs.

Drag and Drop

Implementing a drag-and-drop operation in the .NET Framework is accomplished by a short sequence of events. Typically, it begins in a MouseDown event of one control, and always ends with the DragDrop event of another.

To demonstrate the process, begin with a new Windows application. Add two list boxes to your form, and add three items to the first using the Items Property Designer. This application enables you to drag the items from one list box into the other.

The first step in making drag and drop work is specifying whether or not a control will accept a drop. By default, all controls reject such an act and do not respond to any attempt by the user to drop something onto them. In this case, set the AllowDrop property of the second list box (the one without the items added) to True.

The next item of business is to invoke the drag-and-drop operation. This is typically done in the MouseDown event of the control containing the data you want to drag (although you're not restricted to it). The DoDragDrop method is used to start the operation. This method defines the data that will be dragged and the type of dragging that is allowed. Here, you'll drag the text of the selected list box item, and permit both a move and a copy of the data to occur.

Switch over to the code window of your form and add the following code to the MouseDown event of ListBox1:

```
Private Sub ListBox1_MouseDown(ByVal sender As Object, _
                               ByVal e As System.Windows.Forms.MouseEventArgs) _
                               Handles ListBox1.MouseDown
    Dim DragDropResult As DragDropEffects
    If e.Button = MouseButtons.Left Then
       DragDropResult = ListBox1.DoDragDrop( _
                   ListBox1.Items(ListBox1.SelectedIndex), _
                   DragDropEffects.Move Or DragDropEffects.Copy)
       ' Leave some room here to check the result of the operation
       ' (You'll fill it in next).
    End If
End Sub
```

Notice the comment about leaving room to check the result of the operation. You'll fill that in shortly. For now, calling the DoDragDrop method has gotten you started.

The next step involves the recipient of the data — in this case, ListBox2. Two events here are important to monitor: DragEnter and DragDrop.

As you can guess by the name, the DragEnter event occurs when the user first moves over the recipient control. The DragEnter event has a parameter of type DragEventArgs that contains an Effect property and a KeyState property.

The Effect property enables you to set the display of the drop icon for the user to indicate whether a move or a copy occurs when the mouse button is released. The KeyState property enables you to determine the state of the Ctrl, Alt, and Shift keys. It is a Windows standard that when both a move or a copy can occur, a user is to indicate the copy action by holding down the Ctrl key. Therefore, in this event, you check the KeyState property and use it to determine how to set the Effect property.

Add the following code to the DragEnter event of ListBox2:

```
Private Sub ListBox2_DragEnter(ByVal sender As Object, _
                               ByVal e As DragEventArgs) _
                               Handles ListBox2.DragOver
    If e.KeyState = 9 Then ' Control key
       e.Effect = DragDropEffects.Copy
    Else
       e.Effect = DragDropEffects.Move
    End If
End Sub
```

Note that you can also use the DragOver event if you want, but it will fire continuously as the mouse moves over the target control. In this situation, you only need to trap the initial entry of the mouse into the control.

The final step in the operation occurs when the user lets go of the mouse button to drop the data at its destination. This is captured by the DragDrop event. The parameter contains a property holding the data that is being dragged. It's now a simple process of placing it into the recipient control as follows:

```
Private Sub ListBox2_DragDrop(ByVal sender As Object, _
                           ByVal e As System.Windows.Forms.DragEventArgs) _
                           Handles ListBox2.DragDrop
    ListBox2.Items.Add(e.Data.GetData(DataFormats.Text))
End Sub
```

One last step: You can't forget to manipulate ListBox1 if the drag and drop was a move. Here's where you'll fill in the hole you left in the MouseDown event of ListBox1. Once the DragDrop has occurred, the initial call that invoked the procedure returns a result indicating what ultimately happened. Go back to the ListBox1_MouseDown event and enhance it to remove the item from Listbox1 if it was moved (and not simply copied):

```
Private Sub ListBox1_MouseDown(ByVal sender As Object, _
            ByVal e As System.Windows.Forms.MouseEventArgs) _
            Handles ListBox1.MouseDown
    Dim DragDropResult As DragDropEffects

    If e.Button = MouseButtons.Left Then
        DragDropResult = ListBox1.DoDragDrop( _
                    ListBox1.Items(ListBox1.SelectedIndex), _
                    DragDropEffects.Move Or DragDropEffects.Copy)
        ' If operation is a move (and not a copy), then remove then
        ' remove the item from the first list box.
        If DragDropResult = DragDropEffects.Move Then
            ListBox1.Items.RemoveAt(ListBox1.SelectedIndex)
        End If
    End If
End Sub
```

When you're done, run your application and drag the items from Listbox1 into Listbox2. Try a copy by holding down the Ctrl key when you do it. The screen shot in Figure 15-25 shows the result after Item1 has been moved and Item3 has been copied a few times.

Figure 15-25

Summary of Standard Windows.Forms Controls

Windows Forms, of course, contains most of the controls that you are accustomed to using in pre-.NET versions of Visual Basic. This section lists the basic controls that are generally quite intuitive and don't warrant a full example to explain. Where appropriate, the important differences from pre-.NET versions of Visual Basic are noted.

❑   Button

    ❑   Known as CommandButton in VB6 and earlier

    ❑   Now uses the Text property instead of Caption

    ❑   Can now display both an icon and text simultaneously. The image is set using the Image property (instead of Picture). The image position can be set using the ImageAlign property (left, right, center, and so on).

    ❑   Text on the button can be aligned using the TextAlign property.

    ❑   Can now have different appearances using the FlatStyle property

    ❑   No longer has the Default and Cancel properties. These are now managed by the form itself using the AcceptButton and CancelButton properties.

❑   CheckBox

    ❑   Now uses the Text property instead of Caption

    ❑   Can now appear as a toggle button using the Appearance property

    ❑   Check box and text can now be positioned within the defined area using the CheckAlign and TextAlign properties

    ❑   Uses the CheckState property instead of Value

    ❑   Has a FlatStyle property controlling the appearance of the check box

❑   CheckedListBox

    ❑   A list box that has check boxes beside each item (see Listbox)

❑   ComboBox

    ❑   Like the new ListBox control, it can now hold a collection of objects instead of an array of strings (see ListBox).

    ❑   Now has a MaxDropDownItems property that specifies how many items to display when the list opens

❑   DateTimePicker

    ❑   Formerly known as a DTPicker in VB6 and earlier

❑   DomainUpDown

    ❑   A simple one-line version of a list box

    ❑   Can hold a collection of objects and will display the ToString result of an item in the collection

    ❑   Can wrap around the list to give a continuous scrolling effect using the Wrap property

❏ HScrollBar

  ❏ Unchanged

❏ ImageList

  ❏ Same as previous versions, but with an improved window for managing the images within the list. The MaskColor property is now TransparentColor.

❏ Label

  ❏ Essentially the same as previous versions

  ❏ Caption is now Text

  ❏ Can now display an image and text

  ❏ Has automatic sizing capability. Set the AutoSize property to True for automatic horizontal sizing (this is the default value of the property).

  ❏ The TextAlign property is especially useful. The text of a label beside a text box in VB6 would always be a few pixels higher than the text in the text box. Now, by setting the label's TextAlign property so that the vertical alignment is Middle, this problem is solved.

  ❏ Can now specify whether a mnemonic should be interpreted (if UseMnemonic is True, then the first ampersand (&) in the Text property specifies underlining the following character and having it react to the Alt key shortcut, placing the focus on the next control in the tab order that can hold focus, such as a text box).

❏ LinkLabel

  ❏ Identical to a label, but behaves like a hyperlink with extra properties, such as LinkBehavior (for example, HoverUnderline), LinkColor, and ActiveLinkColor

❏ ListBox

  ❏ A list box can now hold a collection of objects, instead of an array of strings. Use the DisplayMember property to specify what property of the objects to display in the list, and the ValueMember property to specify what property of the objects to use as the values of the list items. (This is similar to the ItemData array from previous versions.) For example, a combo box could store a collection of employee objects, and display to the user the Name property of each, as well as retrieve the EmployeeId as the value of the item currently selected.

  ❏ Can no longer be set to display check boxes using a Style property. Use the CheckedListBox control instead.

❏ ListView

  ❏ Same functionality as the VB6 version but with an improved Property Editor that enables you to define the list view item collection and its sub-items at design time

  ❏ Sub-items can have their own font display properties.

  ❏ New HeaderStyle property instead of HideColumnHeaders

❏ MonthCalendar

  ❏ Formerly known as MonthView

❑ NotifyIcon

    ❑ Gives a form an icon in the system tray

    ❑ Tooltip of the icon is set by the Text property of the control

    ❑ Pop-up menus are set using a ContextMenu control (see the "Menus" section earlier in chapter).

❑ NumericUpDown

    ❑ A single-line text box that displays a number and up/down buttons that increment /decrement the number when clicked

❑ PictureBox

    ❑ Image property defines the graphic to display instead of Picture

    ❑ Use the SizeMode property to autostretch or center the picture.

❑ ProgressBar

    ❑ Now has a Step method that automatically increments the value of the progress bar by the amount defined in the Step property

❑ RadioButton

    ❑ Formerly known as OptionButton

    ❑ Use the Checked property to specify value (formerly Value).

    ❑ Use CheckAlign and TextAlign to specify where the radio button and text appear in relation to the area of the control.

❑ RichTextBox

    ❑ Has properties not available in VB6, such as ZoomFactor, WordWrap, DetectURLs, and AutoWordSelection

    ❑ Use the Lines array to get or set specific individual lines of the control's text.

❑ TabControl

    ❑ Formerly known as the TabStrip control

    ❑ Now has a TabPages collection of TabPage objects. A TabPage object is a subclass of the Panel control specialized for use in the TabControl.

    ❑ Uses the Appearance property to display the tabs as buttons, if desired (formerly the Style property of the TabStrip control)

*❑ TextBox

    ❑ Now has a CharacterCasing property that can automatically adjust the text entered into uppercase or lowercase

    ❑ ReadOnly property now used to prevent the text from being edited. This used to be the Locked property. (The Locked property now determines whether the control can be moved or resized.)

    ❑ Now has Cut, Copy, Paste, Undo, and ClearUndo methods

❑   Timer

   ❑   This is essentially unchanged from previous versions.

   ❑   The timer is now disabled by default.

   ❑   You cannot set the interval to zero to disable it.

❑   TrackBar

   ❑   Formerly known as the Slider control in VB6, it is essentially unchanged.

❑   TreeView

   ❑   Same functionality as in VB6 but with a new Node Tree Editor that enables you to visually design the tree

❑   VScrollBar

   ❑   Unchanged

Retired Controls

The following list outlines the controls from VB6 that you won't find in Windows Forms and how to reproduce their functionality:

❑   Spinner

   ❑   Use the DomainUpDown or NumericUpDown control.

❑   Line and Shape

   ❑   Windows Forms has no Line or Shape control, nor any immediate equivalent. A "cheap" way of reproducing a horizontal or vertical line is to use a label control. Set its background color to that of the line you want, and then set either the Size.Height or Size.Width value to 1.

   ❑   Diagonal lines and shapes must be drawn using GDI+ graphics methods.

❑   DirListBox, FileListBox, DriveListBox

   ❑   You would typically use these controls to create a file system browser similar to Windows Explorer. Windows Forms has no equivalent controls. You can use the OpenFileDialog and SaveFileDialog (see the previous section) to meet your needs in most circumstances.

❑   Image

   ❑   Use the PictureBox control.

Handling Groups of Related Controls

Occasionally it is necessary for a set of controls to be treated as a group. For example, a set of RadioButton controls might be related, and you might want to channel the Click event for all the controls in the group to the same event handler.

In VB6 and earlier, that functionality required a control array, but Windows Forms 2.0 does not support control arrays. However, .NET offers greatly enhanced control over event handling, and it's easy to route events from multiple controls to a single handler.

To have a single method handle multiple events from controls, you must attach those controls' events to the handler. You can do that with multiple controls specified in a `Handles` clause or by using `AddHandler` for each control. Unless controls are being added to your form on-the-fly, using additional controls in the `Handles` clause is usually preferable. Here is an example of a declaration for a `Click` event that handles three `RadioButton` controls:

```
Private Sub RadioButton3_Click(ByVal sender As Object, _
        ByVal e As EventArgs) _
        Handles RadioButton1.Click, _
        RadioButton2.Click, RadioButton3.Click
```

There is no `Index` property as in old-style control arrays in VB6. Instead, simply use the `Sender` parameter of the event handler to determine which control originated the event.

A simple example is helpful to see how to set this up. Create a new Windows application and set the `Text` property of the blank `Form1` to `Add Dynamic Control Demo`. Then add two buttons to the form, as shown in Figure 15-26.

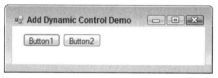

Figure 15-26

Double-click `Button1` to switch over to the code that handles the `Button1.Click` event. To make this method respond to the `Button2.Click` event as well, simply add the `Button2.Click` event handler to the end of the `Handles` list, and then add some simple code to display a message box indicating what button triggered the event:

```
' Note the change in the method name from Button1_Click. Since
' two objects are hooked up, it's a good idea to avoid having the
' method specifically named to a single object.
Private Sub Button_Click(ByVal sender As System.Object, _
                ByVal e As System.EventArgs) _
        Handles Button1.Click, Button2.Click
    Dim buttonClicked As Button
    buttonClicked = CType(sender, Button)
    ' Tell the world what button was clicked
    MessageBox.Show("You clicked " & buttonClicked.Text)
End Sub
```

Run the program and click the two buttons. Each one will trigger the event and display a message box with the appropriate text from the button that was clicked.

Adding Controls at Runtime

Another capability that control arrays provided in VB6 and earlier was making it easy to add controls to a form at runtime. That's also easy to do in Windows Forms, even without control arrays. Here is an example that enhances the preceding program to add a third button dynamically at runtime. Add another button to your form that will trigger the addition of Button3, as shown in Figure 15-27.

Figure 15-27

Name the new button AddNewButton and add the following code to handle its Click event:

```
Private Sub AddNewButton_Click(ByVal sender As System.Object, _
                ByVal e As System.EventArgs) _
                Handles addNewButton.Click

    Dim newButton As Button

    ' Create the new control
    newButton = New Button()

    ' Set it up on the form
    newButton.Location = New System.Drawing.Point(184, 12)
    newButton.Size = New System.Drawing.Size(75, 23)
    newButton.Text = "Button3"

    ' Add it to the form's controls collection
    Me.Controls.Add(newButton)

    ' Hook up the event handler.
    AddHandler newButton.Click, AddressOf Me.Button_Click
End  Sub
```

When the AddNewButton button is clicked, the code creates a new button, sets its size and position, and then does two essential things. First, it adds the button to the form's controls collection; second, it connects the Click event of the button to the method that handles it.

With this done, run the program and click the AddNewButton button. Button3 will appear. Then, simply click Button3 to prove that the Click event is being handled. You should get the result shown in Figure 15-28.

Figure 15-28

Other Handy Programming Tips

Here are some other handy programming tips for using Windows Forms:

❏ **Switch the focus to a control** — Use the .Focus method. To set the focus to TextBox1, for example, use the following code:

```
TextBox1.Focus()
```

❏ **Quickly determine the container control or parent form** — With the use of group boxes and panels, controls are often contained many times. You can now use the FindForm method to immediately get a reference to the form. Use the GetContainerControl method to access the immediate parent of a control.

❏ **Traverse the tab order** — Use the GetNextControl method of any control to get a reference to the next control on the form in the tab order.

❏ **Convert client coordinates to screen coordinates (and back)** — Want to know where a control is in screen coordinates? Use the PointToScreen method. Convert back using the PointToClient method.

❏ **Change the z-order of controls at runtime** — Controls now have both BringToFront and SendToBack methods.

❏ **Locate the mouse pointer** — The control class now exposes a MousePosition property that returns the location of the mouse in screen coordinates.

❏ **Manage child controls** — Container controls, such as a group box or panel, can use the HasChildren property and Controls collection to determine the existence of, and direct references to, child controls, respectively.

❏ **Maximize, minimize, or restore a form** — Use the form's WindowState property.

Summary

Windows Forms is still an excellent technology for the development of rich client and smart client interfaces. While Windows Presentation Foundation will experience more innovation in coming generations of the .NET platform, at present it's significantly easier to develop on Windows Forms. The maturity of the designer and control set in Windows Forms makes it a good choice for many client-based applications, and Windows Forms will be supported indefinitely on the .NET platform.

Becoming a capable Windows Forms developer requires becoming familiar with the controls that are available, including their properties, events, and methods. This takes time. If you are inexperienced with form-based interfaces, you can expend a fair amount of time using the reference documentation to find the control capabilities you need. However, that investment is worthwhile, both because it allows you to be a proficient Windows Forms developer and also because many of the concepts will carry over into WPF.

Many professional Windows Forms developers need to go beyond just creating forms and laying out controls. Complex applications often also require creating new controls or enhancing built-in controls. Accordingly, the next chapter discusses how to create and modify Windows Forms controls, along with some additional advanced Windows Forms topics.

16

Windows Forms
Advanced Features

The previous chapter discussed the basics of Windows Forms 2.0. These capabilities are sufficient for straightforward user interfaces for systems written in VB 2008, along with the built-in capabilities of forms and controls available in Windows Forms 2.0.

However, as applications become larger and more complex, it becomes more important to use the advanced capabilities of the .NET environment to better structure the application. Poorly structured large systems tend to have redundant code. Repeated code patterns end up being used (in slightly different variations) in many, many places in an application, which has numerous bad side effects — longer development time, less reliability, more difficult debugging and testing, and tougher maintenance.

Examples of needs that often result in repeated code include ensuring that fields are entered by the user, that the fields are formatted correctly, and that null fields in the database are handled correctly. Proper object-oriented design can encapsulate such functionality, making it unnecessary to use repeated code. Using the full object-oriented capabilities of the .NET environment, plus additional capabilities specific to Windows Forms programming, you can componentize your logic, allowing the same code to be used in numerous places in your application.

This chapter discusses techniques for componentizing code in Windows Forms applications. It is assumed that you have already read Chapters 2 and 3 on inheritance and other object-oriented techniques available in .NET before working with this chapter.

Packaging Logic in Visual Controls

As shown in the last chapter, Windows Forms user interfaces are based on using controls. A control is simply a special type of .NET class (just as forms are). As a fully object-oriented programming environment, VB 2008 gives you the capability to inherit and extend classes, and controls are no exception. Therefore, it is possible to create new controls that extend what the built-in controls can do.

There are four primary sources of controls for use on Windows Forms interfaces:

❑ Controls packaged with the .NET Framework (referred to in this chapter as *built-in controls*)

❑ Existing ActiveX controls that are imported into Windows Forms (these are briefly discussed in Chapter 25)

❑ Third-party .NET-based controls from a software vendor

❑ Custom controls that are created for a specific purpose in a particular project or organization

If you can build your application with controls from the first three categories, so much the better. Using prewritten functionality that serves the purpose is generally a good idea. However, this chapter assumes you need more than such prepackaged functionality.

If you are primarily familiar with versions of Visual Basic before the .NET era (VB6 and earlier), you know that the only technique available then for such packaging was the UserControl class. While UserControl is also available in Windows Forms (and is much improved), this is only one of several techniques available for writing visual controls.

Custom Controls in Windows Forms

There are three basic techniques for creating custom Windows Forms controls in .NET, corresponding to three different starting points. This range of options offers the flexibility to choose a technique that allows an appropriate balance between simplicity and flexibility:

❑ You can inherit from an existing control.

❑ You can build a composite control (using the UserControl class as your starting point).

❑ You can write a control from scratch (using the very simple Control class as your starting point).

These options are in rough order of complexity, from simplest to most complex. Let's look at each one with a view to understanding the scenarios in which each one is useful.

Inheriting from an Existing Control

The simplest technique starts with a complete Windows Forms control that is already developed. A new class is created that inherits the existing control. This new class has all the functionality of the base class from which it inherits, and the new logic can be added to create additional functionality in this new class or, indeed, to override functionality from the parent (when permitted).

Here are some typical scenarios where it might make sense to extend an existing Windows Forms control:

❑ A text box used for entry of American-style dates

❑ A self-loading list box, combo box, or data grid

❑ A Combobox control that had a mechanism to be reset to an unselected state

❑ A NumericUpDown control that generates a special event when it reaches 80 percent of its maximum allowed value

Each of these scenarios starts with an existing control that simply needs some additional functionality. The more often such functionality is needed in your project, the more sense it makes to package it in a custom control. If a text box that needs special validation or editing will be used in only one place, then it probably doesn't make sense to create an inherited control. In that case, it's probably sufficient to simply add some logic in the form where the control is used to handle the control's events and manipulate the control's properties and methods.

Building a Composite Control

In some cases, a single existing control does not furnish the needed functionality, but a combination of two or more existing controls does. Here are some typical examples:

❑ A set of buttons with related logic that are always used together (such as Save, Delete, and Cancel buttons on a file maintenance form)

❑ A set of text boxes to hold a name, address, and phone number, with the combined information formatted and validated in a particular way

❑ A set of option buttons with a single property exposed as the chosen option

As with inherited controls, composite controls are only appropriate for situations that require the same functionality in multiple places. If the functionality is only needed once, then simply placing the relevant controls on the form and including appropriate logic right in the form is usually better.

Composite controls are the closest relative to VB6 UserControls, and they are sometimes referred to as UserControls. In fact, the base class used to create composite controls is the UserControl class in Windows Forms.

Writing a Control from Scratch

If a control needs special functionality not available in any existing control, then it can be written from scratch to draw its own visual interface and implement its own logic. This option requires more work, but it enables you to do just about anything within .NET and Windows Forms, including very sophisticated user interfaces.

To write a control from scratch, it is necessary to inherit from the Control class, which provides basic functionality such as properties for colors and size. With this basic functionality already built in, your required development tasks include adding any specific properties and methods needed for the control, writing rendering logic that will paint the control to the screen, and handling mouse and keyboard input to the control.

Inheriting from an Existing Control

With this background on the options for creating custom controls, the next step is to look in depth at the procedures used for their development. First up is creating a custom control by inheriting from an existing control and extending it with new functionality. This is the simplest method for the creation of new controls, and the best way to introduce generic techniques that apply to all new controls.

After you look at the general steps needed to create a custom control via inheritance, an example illustrates the details. It is important to understand that many of the techniques described for working with a control created through inheritance also apply to the other ways that a control can be created. Whether inheriting from the `Control` class, the `UserControl` class, or from an existing control, a control is a .NET class. Creating properties, methods, and events, and coordinating these members with the Visual Studio designers, is done in a similar fashion, regardless of the starting point.

Process Overview

Here are the general stages involved in creating a custom control via inheritance from an existing control. This is not a step-by-step recipe, just an overview. A subsequent example provides more detail on the specific steps, but those steps follow these basic stages:

1. Create or open a Windows Control Library project and add a new custom control to the project. The class that is created will inherit from the `System.Windows.Forms.Control` base class. The line that specifies the inherited class must be changed to inherit from the control that is being used as the starting point.

2. The class file gets new logic added as necessary to add new functionality. Then the project is compiled with a `Build` operation in order to create a DLL containing the new control's code.

3. The control is now ready to be used. It can be placed in the Windows Forms Toolbox with the Choose Items option in Visual Studio 2008. From that point forward, it can be dragged onto forms like any other control.

Stage 2, of course, is where the effort lies. New logic for the custom control may include new properties, methods, and events. It may also include intercepting events for the base control and taking special actions as necessary. These tasks are done with standard .NET coding techniques.

Several coding techniques are specific to developing Windows Forms controls, such as using particular .NET attributes. While our example includes adding routine properties and events, we focus on these special techniques for programming controls.

Writing Code for an Inherited Control

This section discusses how to place new logic in an inherited control, with special emphasis on techniques that go beyond basic object orientation. A detailed example using the techniques follows this section.

Creating a Property for a Custom Control

Creating a property for a custom control is just like creating a property for any other class. It is necessary to write a property procedure, and to store the value for the property somewhere, most often in a module-level variable, which is often called a *backing field*.

Properties typically need a default value — that is, a value the property takes on automatically when the control is instantiated. Typically, this means setting the backing field that holds the property value to some initial value. That can be done when the backing field is declared, or it can be done in the constructor for the control.

Here's the code for a typical simple property for a custom control:

```
Dim _nMaxItemsSelected As Integer = 10
Public Property MaxItemsSelected() As Integer
```

```
Get
   Return _nMaxItemsSelected
End Get
Set(ByVal Value As Integer)
   If Value < 0 Then
      Throw New ArgumentException("Property value cannot be negative")
   Else
      _nMaxItemsSelected = Value
   End If
End Set
End Property
```

After a property is created for a control, it automatically shows up in the Properties window for the control. If your Properties window is arranged alphabetically, you will see it in the list. If your window is arranged by category, then the new property will appear in the Misc category. However, you can use some additional capabilities to make the property work better with the designers and the Properties window in Visual Studio.

Coordinating with the Visual Studio IDE

Controls are normally dragged onto a visual design surface, which is managed by the Visual Studio IDE. In order for your control to work effectively with the IDE, it must be able to indicate the *default value* of its properties. The IDE needs the default value of a property for two important capabilities:

❑   To reset the value of the property (done when a user right-clicks the property in the Properties window and selects Reset)

❑   To determine whether to set the property in designer-generated code. A property that is at its default value does not need to be explicitly set in the designer-generated code.

There are two ways for your control to work with the IDE to accomplish these tasks. For properties that take simple values, such as integers, Booleans, floating-point numbers, or strings, .NET provides an attribute. For properties that take complex types, such as structures, enumerated types, or object references, two methods need to be implemented.

Attributes

You can learn more about attributes in Chapter 4, but a short summary of important points is included here. Attributes reside in namespaces, just as components do. The attributes used in this chapter are in the System.ComponentModel namespace. To use attributes, the project must have a reference to the assembly containing the namespace for the attributes. For System.ComponentModel, that's no problem — the project automatically has the reference.

However, the project will not automatically have an Imports statement for that namespace. Attributes could be referred to with a full type name, but that's a bit clumsy. To make it easy to refer to the attributes in code, put the following line at the beginning of all modules that need to use the attributes discussed in this chapter:

```
Imports System.ComponentModel
```

That way, an attribute can be referred to with just its name. For example, the DefaultValue attribute, discussed in detail below, can be declared like this:

```
< DefaultValue(4)> Public Property MyProperty() As Integer
```

All the examples in this chapter assume that the Imports *statement has been placed at the top of the class, so all attributes are referenced by their short name. If you get a compile error on an attribute, then it's likely that you've omitted that line.*

An attribute for a property must be on the same line of code as the property declaration. Of course, line continuation characters can be used so that an attribute is on a separate physical line but still on the same logical line in the program. For example, the last example could also be written as follows:

```
< DefaultValue(4)> _
Public Property MyProperty() As Integer
```

Setting a Default Value with an Attribute

The .NET Framework contains many attributes. Most are used to tag classes, properties, and methods with metadata — that is, information that some other entity, such as a compiler or the Visual Studio IDE, might need to know.

For example, the DefaultValue attribute tells the Visual Studio IDE the default value of a property. We can change the preceding code for a simple property to include a DefaultValue attribute. Here are the first few lines, showing the change to the property declaration that applies the attribute:

```
Dim mnMaxItemsSelected As Integer = 10
  <DefaultValue(10)> Public Property MaxItemsSelected() As Integer
    Get
      Return mnMaxItemsSelected
...
```

Including the DefaultValue attribute enables the Properties window to reset the value of the property back to the default value. That is, if you right-click the property in the Properties window and select Reset from the pop-up context menu, the value of the property returns to 10 from any other value to which it was set.

Another effect of the attribute can be seen in the code generated by the visual designer. If the preceding property is set to any value that is not the default, a line of code appears in the designer-generated code to set the property value. This is called *serializing* the property.

For example, if the value of MaxItemsSelected is set to 5, then a line of code something like this appears in the designer-generated code:

```
MyControl.MaxItemsSelected = 5
```

If the property has the default value of 10 (because it was never changed or it was reset to 10), then the line to set the property value is not present in the designer-generated code. That is, the property does not need to be serialized in code if the value is at the default.

To see serialized code, you need to look in the partial class that holds the Windows Forms designer-generated code. This partial class is not visible in the Solution Explorer by default. To see it, press the Show All Files button in the Solution Explorer.

Alternate Techniques for Working with the IDE

The last sample property returned an `Integer`. Some custom properties return more complex types, such as structures, enumerated types, or object references. These properties cannot use a simple `DefaultValue` attribute to take care of resetting and serializing the property. An alternate technique is needed.

For complex types, designers check to see whether a property needs to be serialized by using a method on the control containing the property. The method returns a Boolean value that indicates whether a property needs to be serialized (`True` if it does, `False` if it does not).

For the following examples, suppose a control has a property named `MyColor`, which is of type `Color`. The `Color` type is a structure in Windows Forms, so the normal `DefaultValue` attribute can't be used with it. Further suppose the backing variable for the property is named `_MyColor`.

In this case, the method to check serialization would be called `ShouldSerializeMyColor`. It would typically look something like the following code:

```
Public Function ShouldSerializeMyColor() As Boolean
  If Color.Equals(_MyColor, Color.Red) Then
    Return False
  Else
    Return True
  End If
End Function
```

This is a good example of why a `DefaultValue` attribute can't work for all types. There is no equality operator for the `Color` type, so you have to write appropriate code to perform the check to determine whether the current value of the `MyColor` property is the default. In this case, that's done with the `Equals` method of the `Color` type.

If a property in a custom control does not have a related `ShouldSerializeXXX` method or a `DefaultValue` attribute, then the property is always serialized. Code for setting the property's value is always included by the designer in the generated code for a form, so it's a good idea to always include either a `ShouldSerializeXXX` method or a `DefaultValue` attribute for every new property created for a control.

Providing a Reset Method for a Control Property

The `ShouldSerialize` method only takes care of telling the IDE whether to serialize the property value. Properties that require a `ShouldSerialize` method also need a way to reset a property's value to the default. This is done by providing a special reset method. In the case of the `MyColor` property, the reset method is named `ResetMyColor`. It would look something like the following:

```
Public Sub ResetMyColor()
  _MyColor = Color.Red
End Sub
```

Other Useful Attributes

`DefaultValue` is not the only attribute that is useful for properties. The `Description` attribute is also one that should be used consistently. It contains a text description of the property, and that description

703

shows up at the bottom of the Properties windows when a property is selected. To include a `Description` attribute, the declaration of the preceding property would appear as follows:

```
<DefaultValue(100), _
Description("This is a pithy description of my property")> _
Public Property MyProperty() As Integer
```

Such a property will look like Figure 16-1 when highlighted in the Properties window.

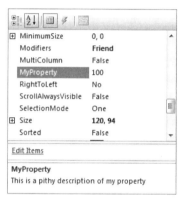

Figure 16-1

Another attribute you will sometimes need is the `Browsable` attribute. As mentioned earlier, a new property appears in the Properties window automatically. In some cases, you may need to create a property for a control that you do not want to show up in the Properties window. In that case, you use a `Browsable` attribute set to `False`. Here is code similar to the last, making a property nonbrowsable in the Properties window:

```
<Browsable(False)> _
Public Property MyProperty() As Integer
```

One additional attribute you may want to use regularly is the `Category` attribute. Properties can be grouped by category in the Properties window by pressing a button at the top of the window. Standard categories include Behavior, Appearance, and so on. You can have your property appear in any of those categories, or you can make up a new category of your own. To assign a category to a property, use code like this:

```
<Category("Appearance")> _
Public Property MyProperty() As Integer
```

There are other attributes for control properties that are useful in specific circumstances. If you understand how the common ones discussed here are used, then you can investigate additional attributes for other purposes in the documentation.

Defining a Custom Event for the Inherited Control

Events in .NET are covered in Chapter 2. To recap, for controls, the process for creating and handling an event includes these steps:

1. Declare the event in the control. The event can have any arguments that are appropriate, but it cannot have named arguments, optional arguments, or arguments that are `ParamArrays`. Though not required, normally you will want to follow the same convention as events in the .NET Framework, which means an event declaration similar to this:

```
Public Event MyEvent(ByVal sender As Object, e As EventArgs)
```

2. Elsewhere in the control's code, implement code to raise the event. The location and circumstances of this code vary depending on the nature of the event, but a typical line that raises the preceding event looks like the following code:

```
RaiseEvent MyEvent(Me, New EventArgs)
```

3. The form that contains the control can now handle the event. The process for doing that is the same as handling an event for a built-in control.

As the preceding example shows, the standard convention in .NET is to use two arguments for an event: `Sender`, which is the object raising the event, and `e`, which is an object of type `EventArgs` or a type that inherits from `EventArgs`. This is not a requirement of the syntax (you can actually use any arguments you like when you declare your event), but it's a consistent convention throughout the .NET Framework, so it is used in this chapter. It is suggested that you follow this convention as well, because it will make your controls consistent with the built-in controls in their operation.

The following example illustrates the concepts discussed. In this example, you create a new control that contains a custom property and a custom event. The property uses several of the attributes discussed.

A CheckedListBox Limiting Selected Items

This example inherits the built-in `CheckedListBox` control and extends its functionality. If you are not familiar with this control, it works just like a normal `ListBox` control except that selected items are indicated with a check in a check box at the front of the item, rather than by highlighting the item.

To extend the functionality of this control, the example includes the creation of a property called `MaxItemsToSelect`. This property holds a maximum value for the number of items that a user can select. The event that fires when a user checks an item is then monitored to determine whether the maximum has already been reached.

If selection of another item would exceed the maximum number, then the selection is prevented, and an event is fired to let the consumer form know that the user has tried to exceed the maximum limit. The code that handles the event in the form can then do whatever is appropriate. In this case, a message box is used to tell the user that no more items can be selected.

The `DefaultValue`, `Description`, and `Category` attributes are placed on the `MaxItemsToSelect` property to coordinate with the IDE.

Here is the step-by-step construction of our example:

1. Start a new Windows Control Library project in Visual Studio and name it MyControls. In the Solution Explorer, select the `UserControl1.vb` file, right-click it, and delete it.

2. Select Project ➪ Add New Item, and select the item template called Custom Control. Name the item `LimitedCheckedListBox`.

3. Click the button in the Solution Explorer to show all files for the project. Bring up the file `LimitedCheckedListBox.Designer.vb`, which is found by clicking the plus sign next to `LimitedCheckedListBox.vb`. (If you don't see a plus sign next to `LimitedChecked ListBox.vb`, click the Show All Files button at the top of the Solution Explorer.)

4. At the top of the `LimitedCheckedListbox.Designer.vb` code, look for the line that reads `Inherits System.Windows.Forms.Control`.

5. Change that line to read `Inherits System.Windows.Forms.CheckedListbox`.

6. Add the following declarations at the top of the code (before the line declaring the class):

```
Imports System.ComponentModel
```

This enables you to utilize the attributes required from the `System.ComponentModel` namespace.

7. The code for `LimitedCheckedListBox.vb` will contain an event for painting the control. Since you are not using a control that draws its own surface, delete that event. (It won't hurt to leave it, but you don't need it.)

8. Begin adding code specifically for this control. First, implement the `MaxItemsToSelect` property. A module-level variable is needed to hold the property's value, so insert this line just under the class declaration line:

```
Private _nMaxItemsToSelect As Integer = 4
```

9. Create the code for the property itself. Insert the following code into the class just above the line that says `End Class`:

```
<DefaultValue(4), Category("Behavior"), _
Description("The maximum number of items allowed to be checked")> _
Public Property MaxItemsToSelect() As Integer
  Get
    Return _nMaxItemsToSelect
  End Get
  Set(ByVal Value As Integer)
    If Value < 0 Then
      Throw New ArgumentException("Property value cannot be negative")
    Else
      _nMaxItemsToSelect = Value
    End If
  End Set
End Property
```

This code sets the default value of the `MaxItemsToSelect` property to 4, and sets a description for the property to be shown in the Properties window when the property is selected there. It also specifies that the property should appear in the Behavior category when properties in the Properties window are sorted by category.

10. Declare the event that will be fired when a user selects too many items. The event is named MaxItemsExceeded. Just under the code for step 9, insert the following line:

```
Public Event MaxItemsExceeded(Sender As Object, e As EventArgs)
```

11. Insert code into the event routine that fires when the user clicks on an item. For the CheckedListBox base class, this is called the ItemCheck property. Open the left-hand drop-down box in the code window and select the option LimitedCheckedListBox Events. Then, select the ItemCheck event in the right-hand drop-down box of the code window. The following code will be inserted to handle the ItemCheck event:

```
Private Sub LimitedCheckedListBox_ItemCheck(ByVal sender As Object, _
        ByVal e As System.Windows.Forms.ItemCheckEventArgs) _
        Handles MyBase.ItemCheck

End Sub
```

12. The following code should be added to the ItemCheck event to monitor it for too many items:

```
Private Sub LimitedCheckedListBox_ItemCheck(ByVal sender As Object, _
        ByVal e As System.Windows.Forms.ItemCheckEventArgs) _
        Handles MyBase.ItemCheck

If (Me.CheckedItems.Count >= _nMaxItemsToSelect) _
    And (e.NewValue = CheckState.Checked) Then
    RaiseEvent MaxItemsExceeded(Me, New EventArgs)
    e.NewValue = CheckState.Unchecked
End If

End Sub
```

13. Build the project to create a DLL containing the LimitedCheckedListBox control.

14. Add a new Windows Application project to the solution (using the File ⇨ Add Project ⇨ New Project menu) to test the control. Name the new project anything you like. Right-click the project in the Solution Explorer, and select Set as Startup Project in the pop-up menu. This will cause your Windows application to run when you press F5 in Visual Studio.

15. Scroll to the top of the controls in the Toolbox. The LimitedCheckedListBox control should be there.

16. The Windows Application will have a Form1 that was created automatically. Drag a LimitedCheckedListBox control onto Form1, just as you would a normal list box. Change the CheckOnClick event for the LimitedCheckedListBox to True (to make testing easier). This property was inherited from the base CheckedListBox control.

17. In the Items property of the LimitedCheckedListBox, click the button to add some items. Insert the following list of colors: Red, Yellow, Green, Brown, Blue, Pink, and Black. At this point, your Windows Application Project should have a Form1 that looks something like Figure 16-2.

Figure 16-2

18. Bring up the code window for Form1. In the left-hand drop-down box above the code window, select LimitedCheckedListBox1 to get to its events. Then, in the right-hand drop-down box, select the MaxItemsExceeded event. The empty event will look like the following code:

```
Private Sub LimitedCheckedListBox1_MaxItemsExceeded( _
          ByVal sender As System.Object, e As System.EventArgs) _
          Handles LimitedCheckedListBox1.MaxItemsExceeded

    End Sub
```

19. Insert the following code to handle the event:

```
MsgBox("You are attempting to select more than " & _
      LimitedCheckedListBox1.MaxItemsToSelect & _
      " items. You must uncheck some other item " & _
      " before checking this one.")
```

20. Start the Windows Application project. Check and uncheck various items in the list box to verify that the control works as intended. You should get a message box whenever you attempt to check more than four items. (Four items is the default maximum, and it was not changed.) If you uncheck some items, then you can check items again until the maximum is once again exceeded. When finished, close the form to stop execution.

21. If you want to check the serialization of the code, look at the designer-generated code in the partial class for Form1 (named LimitedCheckedListBox.Designer.vb), and examine the properties for LimitedCheckedListBox1. Note that there is no line of code that sets MaxSelectedItems. Remember that if you don't see the partial class in the Solution Explorer, then you'll need to press the Show All button at the top of the Solution Explorer.

22. Go back to the Design view for Form1 and select LimitedCheckedListBox1. In the Properties window, change the MaxSelectedItems property to 3.

23. Return to the partial class and look again at the code that declares the properties for LimitedCheckedListBox1. Note that there is now a line of code that sets MaxSelectedItems to the value of 3.

24. Go back to the Design view for Form1 and select LimitedCheckedListBox1. In the Properties window, right-click the MaxSelectedItems property. In the pop-up menu, select Reset. The property will change back to a value of 4, and the line of code that sets the property you looked at in the last step will be gone.

These last few steps showed that the DefaultValue attribute is working as it should.

The Control and UserControl Base Classes

In the earlier example, a new control was created by inheriting from an existing control. As is standard with inheritance, this means the new control began with all the functionality of the control from which it inherited. Then new functionality was added.

This chapter didn't discuss the base class for this new control (`CheckedListBox`) because you probably already understand a lot about the properties, methods, events, and behavior of that class. However, you are not likely to be as familiar with the base classes used for the other techniques for creating controls, so it's appropriate to discuss them now.

Two generic base classes are used as a starting point to create a control. It is helpful to understand something about the structure of these classes to know when the use of each is appropriate.

> *The classes discussed in this chapter are all in the* `System.Windows.Forms` *namespace. There are similarly named classes for some of these in the* `System.Web.UI` *namespace (which is used for Web Forms), but these classes should not be confused with anything discussed in this chapter.*

The Control Class

The `Control` class is contained within the `System.Windows.Forms` namespace and contains base functionality to define a rectangle on the screen, provide a handle for it, and process routine operating system messages. This enables the class to perform such functions as handling user input through the keyboard and mouse. The `Control` class serves as the base class for any component that needs a visual representation on a Win32-type graphical interface. Besides built-in controls and custom controls that inherit from the `Control` class, the `Form` class also ultimately derives from the `Control` class.

In addition to these low-level windowing capabilities, the `Control` class also includes such visually related properties as `Font`, `ForeColor`, `BackColor`, and `BackGroundImage`. The `Control` class also has properties that are used to manage layout of the control on a form, such as docking and anchoring.

> *The* `Control` *class does not contain any logic to paint to the screen except to paint a background color or show a background image. While it does offer access to the keyboard and mouse, it does not contain any actual input processing logic except for the ability to generate standard control events such as* `Click` *and* `KeyPress`. *The developer of a custom control based on the* `Control` *class must provide all of the functions for the control beyond the basic capabilities provided by the* `Control` *class.*

A standard set of events is also furnished by the `Control` class, including events for clicking the control (`Click`, `DoubleClick`), for keystroke handling (`KeyUp`, `KeyPress`, `KeyDown`), for mouse handling (`MouseUp`, `MouseHover`, `MouseDown`, etc.), and drag-and-drop operations (`DragEnter`, `DragOver`, `DragLeave`, `DragDrop`). Also included are standard events for managing focus and validation in the control (`GotFocus`, `Validating`, `Validated`). See the help files on the `Control` class for details on these events and a comprehensive list.

The UserControl Class

The built-in functionality of the `Control` class is a great starting point for controls that will be built from scratch, with their own display and keyboard handling logic. However, the `Control` class has limited capability for use as a container for other controls.

That means that composite controls do not typically use the `Control` class as a starting point. Composite controls combine two or more existing controls, so the starting point must be able to manage contained controls. The class that meets this requirement is the `UserControl` class. Because it ultimately derives from the `Control` class, it has all of the properties, methods, and events discussed earlier for that class.

However, the `UserControl` class does not derive directly from the `Control` class. It derives from the `ContainerControl` class, which, in turn, derives from the `ScrollableControl` class.

As the name suggests, the `ScrollableControl` class adds support for scrolling the client area of the control's window. Almost all the members implemented by this class relate to scrolling. They include `AutoScroll`, which turns scrolling on or off, and controlling properties such as `AutoScrollPosition`, which gets or sets the position within the scrollable area.

The `ContainerControl` class derives from `ScrollableControl` and adds the capability to support and manage child controls. It manages the focus and the capability to tab from control to control. It includes properties such as `ActiveControl` to point to the control with the focus, and `Validate`, which validates the most recently changed control that has not had its validation event fired.

Neither `ScrollableControl` nor `ContainerControl` are usually inherited from directly; they add functionality that is needed by their more commonly used child classes: `Form` and `UserControl`.

The `UserControl` class can contain other child controls, but the interface of `UserControl` does not automatically expose these child controls in any way. Instead, the interface of `UserControl` is designed to present a single, unified interface to outside clients such as forms or container controls. Any object interface that is needed to access the child controls must be specifically implemented in your custom control. The following example demonstrates this.

A Composite UserControl

Our earlier example showed inheriting an existing control, which was the first of the three techniques for creating custom controls. The next step up in complexity and flexibility is to combine more than one existing control to become a new control. This is similar to the process of creating a `UserControl` in VB6, but it is easier to do in Windows Forms.

The main steps in the process of creating a `UserControl` are as follows:

1. Start a new Windows Control Library project and assign names to the project and the class representing the control.

2. The project will contain a design surface that looks a lot like a form. You can drag controls onto this surface just as you would a form. Writing code that works with the controls, such as event routines, is done the same way as with a form, but with a few extra considerations that don't apply to most forms. In particular, it is important to handle resizing when the `UserControl` is resized. This can be done by using the `Anchor` and `Dock` properties of the constituent controls, or you can create resize logic that repositions and resizes the controls on your `UserControl` when it is resized on the form containing it. Another option is to use `FlowLayoutPanel` and/or `TableLayoutPanel` controls to do automatic layout.

3. Create properties of the UserControl to expose functionality to a form that will use it. This typically means creating a property to load information into and get information out of the control. Sometimes properties to handle cosmetic elements are also necessary.

4. Build the control and use it in a Windows application exactly as you did for the inherited controls discussed earlier.

There is a key difference between this type of development and inheriting a control, as shown in the preceding examples. A UserControl *will not by default expose the properties of the controls it contains. It exposes the properties of the* UserControl *class plus any custom properties that you give it. If you want properties for contained controls to be exposed, you must explicitly create logic to expose them.*

Creating a Composite UserControl

To demonstrate the process of creating a composite UserControl, the next exercise builds one that is similar to what is shown in Figure 16-3. The control is named ListSelector.

Figure 16-3

This type of layout is common in wizards and other user interfaces that require selection from a long list of items. The control has one list box holding a list of items that can be chosen (on the left), and another list box containing the items chosen so far (on the right). Buttons enable items to be moved back and forth.

Loading this control means loading items into the left list box, which we will call SourceListBox. Getting selected items back out involves exposing the items that are selected in the right list box, named TargetListBox.

The buttons in the middle that transfer elements back and forth are called AddButton, AddAllButton, RemoveButton, and ClearButton, from top to bottom, respectively.

There are several ways to handle this kind of interface element in detail. A production-level version would have the following characteristics:

❑   Buttons would gray out (disable) when they are not appropriate. For example, btnAdd would not be enabled unless an item were selected in lstSource.

❑   Items could be dragged and dropped between the two list boxes.

❏　　Items could be selected and moved with a double-click.

Such a production-type version contains too much code to discuss in this chapter. For simplicity, the exercise has the following limitations:

❏　　Buttons do not gray out when they should be unavailable.

❏　　Drag-and-drop is not supported. (Implementation of drag-and-drop is discussed in Chapter 15, if you are interested in adding it to the example.)

❏　　No double-clicking is supported.

This leaves the following general tasks to make the control work, which are detailed in the step-by-step exercise that follows:

1.　　Create a `UserControl` and name it `ListSelector`.

2.　　Add the list boxes and buttons to the `ListSelector` design surface, using a `TableLayoutPanel` and a `FlowLayoutPanel` to control layout when the control is resized.

3.　　Add logic to transfer elements back and forth between the list boxes when buttons are pressed. (More than one item may be selected for an operation, so several items may need to be transferred when a button is pressed.)

4.　　Expose properties to enable the control to be loaded, and for selected items to be fetched by the form that contains the control.

Resizing the Control

As shown in Figure 16-3, there are three main areas of the control: the two `Listbox` controls and a vertical strip between them that holds the buttons. As the control is resized, these areas need to also be appropriately resized.

If the `ListSelector` control gets too small, then there won't be enough room for the buttons and the list boxes to display properly, so it needs to have a minimum size. That's enforced by setting the `MinimumSize` property for the `UserControl` in the designer. The `MinimumSize` property is inherited from the `Control` class (as discussed in the previous chapter).

The rest of the resizing is handled by using a `TableLayoutPanel` that contains three columns, one for each of the three areas. That is, the first column of the `TableLayoutPanel` will hold `SourceListBox`, the second column will hold the buttons, and the third column will hold `TargetListBox`. The capabilities of the `TableLayoutPanel` enable the middle column to be a fixed size, and the left and right columns to share all remaining width.

The middle column could contain a standard `Panel` to hold the buttons, but it's a bit easier to use a `FlowLayoutPanel` because it automatically stacks the buttons.

Exposing Properties of Contained Controls

Most of the controls contained in the composite control in this exercise do not need to expose their interfaces to the form that will use the composite control. The buttons, for example, are completely private to the `ListSelector` — none of their properties or methods need to be exposed.

The easiest way to load up the control is to expose the Items property of the source list box. Similarly, the easiest way to allow access to the selected items is to expose the Items property of the target list box. The Items property exposes the entire collection of items in a list box, and can be used to add, clear, or examine items. No other properties of the list boxes need to be exposed.

The exercise also includes a Clear method that clears both list boxes simultaneously. This allows the control to be easily flushed and reused by a form that consumes it.

Stepping Through the Example

Here is the step-by-step procedure to build our composite UserControl:

1. Start a new Windows Control Library project and name it ListSelector.

2. Right-click on the UserControl1.vb module that is generated for the project and select Rename. Change the name of the module to ListSelector.vb. This automatically changes the name of your class to ListSelector.

3. Go to the design surface for the control. Increase the size of the control to about 300 x 200. Then drag a TableLayoutPanel onto the control and set the Dock property of the TableLayoutPanel to Fill.

4. Click the smart tag (the triangular glyph in the upper-right corner) of the TableLayoutPanel. A menu will appear. Select Edit Rows and Columns.

5. Highlight Column2 and click the Insert button. The TableLayoutPanel will now have three columns. In the new column just inserted (the new Column2), the width will be set to an absolute size of 20 pixels. Change that width to 100 pixels. The dialog containing your column settings should now look like Figure 16-4.

6. Click the Show drop-down menu in the upper-left corner and select Rows. Press the Delete button to delete a row because you need only one row in the control. Click OK. The design surface for the control should now look similar to Figure 16-5.

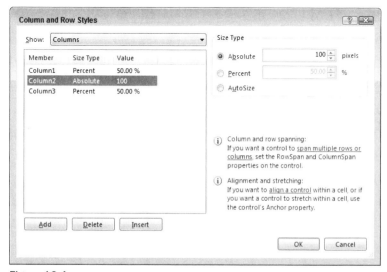

Figure 16-4

713

Figure 16-5

7. Drag a Listbox into the first cell and another one into the third cell. Drag a FlowLayoutPanel into the middle cell. For all three of these, set the Dock property to Fill.

8. Drag four buttons into the FlowLayoutPanel in the middle. At this point your control should look like the one shown in Figure 16-6.

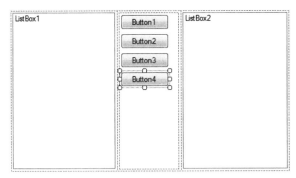

Figure 16-6

9. Change the names and properties of these controls as shown in the following table:

Original Name	New Name	Properties to Set for Control
Listbox1	SourceListBox	
Listbox2	TargetListBox	
Button1	AddButton	Text = "Add >" Size.Width = 90
Button2	AddAllButton	Text = "Add All >>" Size.Width = 90
Button3	RemoveButton	Text = "< Remove" Margin.Top = 20 Size.Width = 90
Button4	ClearButton	Text = "<< Clear" Size.Width = 90

10. In the Properties window, click the drop-down at the top and select `ListSelector` so that the properties for the `UserControl` itself appear in the Properties window. Set the `MinimumSize` height and width to 200 pixels each.

11. Create the public properties and methods of the composite control. In this case, you need the following members:

Member	Purpose
`Clear` method	Clears both list boxes of their items
`SourceItems` property	Exposes the items collection for the source list box
`SelectedItems` property	Exposes the items collection for the target list box

The code for these properties and methods is as follows:

```
<Browsable(False)> _
Public ReadOnly Property SourceItems() As ListBox.ObjectCollection
    Get
        Return SourceListBox.Items
    End Get
End Property

<Browsable(False)> _
Public ReadOnly Property SelectedItems() As ListBox.ObjectCollection
    Get
        Return TargetListBox.Items
    End Get
End Property

Public Sub Clear()
    SourceListBox.Items.Clear()
    TargetListBox.Items.Clear()
End Sub
```

Remember that your class must have an `Imports` for `System.ComponentModel` at the top so that the attributes can be identified by the compiler.

12. Put logic in the class to transfer items back and forth between the list boxes and clear the target list box when the Clear button is pressed. This logic manipulates the collections of items in the list boxes, and is fairly brief. You need one helper function to check whether an item is already in a list box before adding it (to avoid duplicates). Here are the click events for each of the buttons, with the helper function at the top:

```
Private Function ItemInListBox(ByVal ListBoxToCheck As ListBox, _
                               ByVal ItemToCheck As Object) As Boolean
    Dim bFound As Boolean = False
    For Each Item As Object In ListBoxToCheck.Items
        If Item Is ItemToCheck Then
            bFound = True
            Exit For
        End If
    Next
    Return bFound
```

```
        End Function

        Private Sub AddButton_Click(ByVal sender As System.Object, _
                                ByVal e As System.EventArgs) _
                                Handles AddButton.Click
            For Each SelectedItem As Object In SourceListBox.SelectedItems
                If Not ItemInListBox(TargetListBox, SelectedItem) Then
                    TargetListBox.Items.Add(SelectedItem)
                End If
            Next
        End Sub

        Private Sub AddAllButton_Click(ByVal sender As System.Object, _
                                ByVal e As System.EventArgs) _
                                Handles AddAllButton.Click
            For Each SelectedItem As Object In SourceListBox.Items
                If Not ItemInListBox(TargetListBox, SelectedItem) Then
                    TargetListBox.Items.Add(SelectedItem)
                End If
            Next
        End Sub

        ' For both the following operations, we have to go through the
        ' collection in reverse because we are removing items.

        Private Sub RemoveButton_Click(ByVal sender As System.Object, _
                                ByVal e As System.EventArgs) _
                                Handles RemoveButton.Click
            For iIndex As Integer = TargetListBox.SelectedItems.Count - 1 To 0
        Step -1
                TargetListBox.Items.Remove(TargetListBox.SelectedItems(iIndex))
            Next iIndex
        End Sub

        Private Sub ClearButton_Click(ByVal sender As System.Object, _
                                ByVal e As System.EventArgs) _
                                Handles ClearButton.Click
            For iIndex As Integer = TargetListBox.Items.Count - 1 To 0 Step -1
                TargetListBox.Items.Remove(TargetListBox.Items(iIndex))
            Next iIndex
        End Sub
```

The logic in the Click events for RemoveButton and ClearButton needs a bit of explanation. Because items are being removed from the collection, it is necessary to go through the collection in reverse. Otherwise, the removal of items will confuse the looping enumeration and a runtime error will be generated.

13. Build the control. Then create a Windows Application project to test it in. You can drag the control from the top of the Toolbox, add items in code (via the Add method of the SourceItems collection), resize, and so on. When the project is run, the buttons can be used to transfer items back and forth between the list boxes, and the items in the target list box can be read with the SelectedItems property.

Keep in mind that you can also use the techniques for inherited controls in composite controls, too. You can create custom events, apply attributes to properties, and create ShouldSerialize and Reset methods to make properties work better with the designer. (That wasn't necessary here because our two properties were `ReadOnly`.)

Building a Control from Scratch

If your custom control needs to draw its own interface, you should use the `Control` class as your starting point. Such a control gets a fair amount of base functionality from the `Control` class. A partial list of properties and methods of the `Control` class was included earlier in the chapter. These properties arrange for the control to automatically have visual elements such as background and foreground colors, fonts, window size, and so on.

However, such a control does not automatically use any of that information to actually display anything (except for a `BackgroundImage`, if that property is set). A control derived from the `Control` class must implement its own logic for painting the control's visual representation. In all but the most trivial examples, such a control also needs to implement its own properties and methods to gain the functionality it needs.

The techniques used in the earlier example for default values and the `ShouldSerialize` and `Reset` methods all work fine with the controls created from the `Control` class, so that capability is not discussed again. Instead, this section focuses on the capability that is very different in the `Control` class — the logic to paint the control to the screen.

Painting a Custom Control with GDI+

The base functionality used to paint visual elements for a custom control is in the part of .NET called GDI+. A complete explanation of GDI+ is too complex for this chapter, but an overview of some of the main concepts is needed here.

What Is GDI+?

GDI+ is an updated version of the old GDI (Graphics Device Interface) functions provided by the Windows API. GDI+ provides a new API for graphics functions, which then takes advantage of the Windows graphics library.

The System.Drawing Namespace

The GDI+ functionality can be found in the `System.Drawing` namespace and its subnamespaces. Some of the classes and members in this namespace will look familiar if you have used the Win32 GDI functions. Classes are available for such items as pens, brushes, and rectangles. Naturally, the `System.Drawing` namespace makes these capabilities much easier to use than the equivalent API functions.

With the `System.Drawing` namespace, you can manipulate bitmaps and use various structures for dealing with graphics such as `Point`, `Size`, `Color`, and `Rectangle`. Also included are numerous classes for use in drawing logic. The first three such classes you need to understand represent the surface on which drawing takes place, and the objects used to draw lines and fill shapes:

- ❏ **Graphics** — Represents the surface on which drawing is done. Contains methods to draw items to the surface, including lines, curves, ellipses, text, and so on.

- ❏ **Pen** — Used for drawing line-based objects

- ❏ **Brush** — Used for filling shapes (includes its subclasses)

The `System.Drawing` namespace includes many other classes and some subsidiary namespaces. Let's look at the `Graphics` class in a bit more detail.

The System.Drawing.Graphics Class

Many of the important drawing functions are members of the `System.Drawing.Graphics` class. Methods such as `DrawArc`, `FillRectangle`, `DrawEllipse`, and `DrawIcon` have self-evident actions. More than 40 methods provide drawing-related functions in the class.

Many drawing members require one or more points as arguments. A point is a structure in the `System.Drawing` namespace. It has X and Y values for horizontal and vertical positions, respectively. When a variable number of points are needed, an array of points may be used as an argument. The next example uses points.

The `System.Drawing.Graphics` class cannot be directly instantiated. It is only supposed to be manipulated by objects that can set the `Graphics` class up for themselves. There are several ways to get a reference to a `Graphics` class, but the one most commonly used in the creation of Windows controls is to get one out of the arguments in a `Paint` event. That technique is used in a later example. For now, to understand the capabilities of GDI+ a little better, let's do a quick example on a standard Windows Form.

Using GDI+ Capabilities in a Windows Form

Here is an example of a form that uses the `System.Drawing.Graphics` class to draw some graphic elements on the form's surface. The example code runs in the `Paint` event for the form, and draws an ellipse, an icon (which it gets from the form itself), and two triangles: one in outline and one filled.

Start a Windows Application project in VB 2008. On the `Form1` that is automatically created for the project, place the following code in the `Paint` event for the form:

```
' Need a pen for the drawing. We'll make it violet.
Dim penDrawingPen As New _
        System.Drawing.Pen(System.Drawing.Color.BlueViolet)

' Draw an ellipse and an icon on the form
e.Graphics.DrawEllipse(penDrawingPen, 30, 100, 30, 60)
e.Graphics.DrawIcon(Me.Icon, 90, 20)

' Draw a triangle on the form.
' First have to define an array of points.
Dim pntPoint(2) As System.Drawing.Point

pntPoint(0).X = 150
pntPoint(0).Y = 100

pntPoint(1).X = 150
pntPoint(1).Y = 150

pntPoint(2).X = 50
pntPoint(2).Y = 70

e.Graphics.DrawPolygon(penDrawingPen, pntPoint)

' Do a filled triangle.
' First need a brush to specify how it is filled.
```

```
Dim bshBrush As System.Drawing.Brush
bshBrush = New SolidBrush(Color.Blue)

' Now relocate the points for the triangle.
' We'll just move it 100 pixels to the right.
pntPoint(0).X += 100
pntPoint(1).X += 100
pntPoint(2).X += 100
e.Graphics.FillPolygon(bshBrush, pntPoint)
```

Start the program. The form that appears will look like the one shown in Figure 16-7.

Figure 16-7

To apply GDI+ to control creation, you create a custom control that displays a "traffic light," with red, yellow, and green signals that can be displayed via a property of the control. GDI+ classes will be used to draw the traffic light graphics in the control.

Start a new project in VB 2008 of the Windows Control Library type and name it TrafficLight. The created module has a class in it named UserControl1. We want a different type of control class, so you need to get rid of this one. Right-click on this module in the Solution Explorer and select Delete.

Next, right-click on the project and select Add New Item. Select the item type of Custom Control and name it TrafficLight.vb.

As with the other examples in this chapter, it is necessary to include the Imports statement for the name-space containing the attribute you will use. This line should go at the very top of the code module for TrafficLight.vb:

```
Imports System.ComponentModel
```

The TrafficLight control needs to know which "light" to display. The control can be in three states: red, yellow, or green. An enumerated type will be used for these states. Add the following code just below the previous code:

```
Public Enum TrafficLightStatus
    statusRed = 1
```

```
            statusYellow = 2
            statusGreen = 3
    End Enum
```

The example also needs a module-level variable and a property procedure to support changing and retaining the state of the light. The property is named Status. To handle the Status property, first place a declaration directly under the last enumeration declaration that creates a module-level variable to hold the current status:

```
    Private mStatus As TrafficLightStatus = TrafficLightStatus.statusGreen
```

Then, insert the following property procedure in the class to create the Status property:

```
    <Description("Status (color) of the traffic light")> _
    Public Property Status() As TrafficLightStatus
        Get
            Status = mStatus
        End Get
        Set(ByVal Value As TrafficLightStatus)
            If mStatus <> Value Then
                mStatus = Value
                Me.Invalidate()
            End If
        End Set
    End Property
```

The Invalidate method of the control is used when the Status property changes, which forces a redraw of the control. Ideally, this type of logic should be placed in all of the events that affect the rendering of the control.

Now add procedures to make the property serialize and reset properly:

```
    Public Function ShouldSerializeStatus() As Boolean
        If mStatus = TrafficLightStatus.statusGreen Then
            Return False
        Else
            Return True
        End If
    End Function

    Public Sub ResetStatus()
        Me.Status = TrafficLightStatus.statusGreen
    End Sub
```

Place code to do painting of the control, to draw the "traffic light" when the control repaints. We will use code similar to that used previously. The code generated for the new custom control will already have a blank OnPaint method inserted. You just need to insert the following highlighted code into that event, below the comment line that says Add your custom paint code here:

```
    Protected Overrides Sub OnPaint(ByVal pe As _
                        System.Windows.Forms.PaintEventArgs)
```

```
MyBase.OnPaint(pe)

'Add your custom paint code here
Dim grfGraphics As System.Drawing.Graphics
grfGraphics = pe.Graphics

' Need a pen for the drawing the outline. We'll make it black.
Dim penDrawingPen As New _
    System.Drawing.Pen(System.Drawing.Color.Black)

' Draw the outline of the traffic light on the control.
 ' First have to define an array of points.
 Dim pntPoint(3) As System.Drawing.Point

pntPoint(0).X = 0
pntPoint(0).Y = 0

pntPoint(1).X = Me.Size.Width - 2
pntPoint(1).Y = 0

pntPoint(2).X = Me.Size.Width - 2
pntPoint(2).Y = Me.Size.Height - 2

pntPoint(3).X = 0
pntPoint(3).Y = Me.Size.Height - 2

grfGraphics.DrawPolygon(penDrawingPen, pntPoint)

' Now ready to draw the circle for the "light"
Dim nCirclePositionX As Integer
Dim nCirclePositionY As Integer
Dim nCircleDiameter As Integer
Dim nCircleColor As Color

nCirclePositionX = Me.Size.Width * 0.02
nCircleDiameter = Me.Size.Height * 0.3
Select Case Me.Status
    Case TrafficLightStatus.statusRed
        nCircleColor = Color.OrangeRed
        nCirclePositionY = Me.Size.Height * 0.01
    Case TrafficLightStatus.statusYellow
        nCircleColor = Color.Yellow
        nCirclePositionY = Me.Size.Height * 0.34
    Case TrafficLightStatus.statusGreen
        nCircleColor = Color.LightGreen
        nCirclePositionY = Me.Size.Height * 0.67
End Select

Dim bshBrush As System.Drawing.Brush
bshBrush = New SolidBrush(nCircleColor)
' Draw the circle for the signal light
 grfGraphics.FillEllipse(bshBrush, nCirclePositionX, _
         nCirclePositionY, nCircleDiameter, nCircleDiameter)
End Sub
```

Build the control library by selecting Build from the Build menu. This will create a DLL in the /bin directory where the control library solution is saved.

Next, start a new Windows Application project. Drag a TrafficLight control from the top of the Toolbox onto the form in the Windows Application project. Notice that its property window includes a Status property. Set that to statusYellow. Note that the rendering on the control on the form's design surface changes to reflect this new status. Change the background color of the TrafficLight control to a darker gray to improve its contrast. (The BackColor property for TrafficLight was inherited from the Control class.)

At the top of the code for the form, place the following line to make the enumerated value for the traffic light's status available:

```
Imports TrafficLight.TrafficLight
```

Add three buttons (named btnRed, btnYellow, and btnGreen) to the form to make the traffic light control display as red, yellow, and green. The logic for the buttons looks something like the following:

```
Private Sub btnRed_Click(ByVal sender As System.Object, _
              ByVal e As System.EventArgs) Handles btnRed.Click
    TrafficLight1.Status = TrafficLightStatus.statusRed
End Sub

Private Sub btnYellow_Click(ByVal sender As System.Object, _
              ByVal e As System.EventArgs) Handles btnYellow.Click
    TrafficLight1.Status = TrafficLightStatus.statusYellow
End Sub

Private Sub btnGreen_Click(ByVal sender As System.Object, _
              ByVal e As System.EventArgs) Handles btnGreen.Click
    TrafficLight1.Status = TrafficLightStatus.statusGreen
End Sub
```

In the Solution Explorer, right-click your test Windows Application, and select Set as Startup Project. Then press F5 to run. When your test form comes up, you can change the "signal" on the traffic light by pressing the buttons. Figure 16-8 shows a sample screen.

Of course, you can't see the color in a black-and-white screen shot, but as you might expect from its position, the circle is red. The "yellow light" displays in the middle of the control, and the "green light" displays at the bottom. These positions are all calculated in the Paint event logic, depending on the value of the Status property.

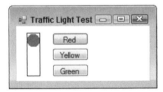

Figure 16-8

For a complete example, it would be desirable for the control to allow the user to change the `Status` by clicking on a different part of the "traffic light." That means including logic to examine mouse clicks, calculate whether they are in a given area, and change the `Status` property if appropriate. In the code available for download for this book, the `TrafficLight` example includes such functionality.

Attaching an Icon for the Toolbox

By default, the icon that appears in the Toolbox next to your control's name is a gear-shaped icon. However, you can attach an icon to a control for the Toolbox to display. There are two ways to do that.

Windows Forms includes a `ToolboxBitmap` attribute that can specify an icon for a class. It can be used in several ways, and you can see examples in the help file for the `ToolboxBitmap` attribute.

The easy way to attach an icon to your control is to let Visual Studio do it for you. Simply locate or draw the icon you want to use, and add it to the project containing your control. Then rename the icon so that it has the same name as your control but an extension of `ico` instead of `vb`.

For example, to attach an icon to the `TrafficLight` control in the preceding example, find an icon you like, place it in your project, and name it `TrafficLight.ico`. Then Visual Studio will attach the icon to your control during the compilation process; and when your control is added to the Toolbox, your icon will be used instead of the gear-shaped one.

> *Custom icons are displayed for a control in the Toolbox only when the control is added with the Toolbox's Choose Items option. Controls that appear in the Toolbox at the top because their project is currently loaded do not exhibit custom icons. They always have a blue, gear-shaped icon.*

Embedding Controls in Other Controls

Another valuable technique for creating custom controls is to embed other controls. In a sense, the `UserControl` does this; but when a `UserControl` is used as the base class, by default it only exposes the properties of the `UserControl` class. Instead, you may want to use a control such as `Textbox` or `Grid` as the starting point, but embed a `Button` in the `Textbox` or `Grid` to obtain some new functionality.

The embedding technique relies on the fact that in Windows Forms, all controls can be containers for other controls. Visual Basic developers are familiar with the idea that `Panels` and `GroupBoxes` can be containers, but in fact a `TextBox` or a `Grid` can also be a container of other controls.

This technique is best presented with an example. The standard `ComboBox` control does not have a way for users to reset to a "no selection" state. Once an item is selected, setting to that state requires code that sets the `SelectedIndex` to -1.

This exercise creates a `ComboBox` that has a button to reset the selection state back to "no selection." That enables users to access that capability directly. Now that you have worked with several controls in the examples, rather than proceed step by step, we'll just show the code for such a `ComboBox` and discuss how the code works:

```
Public Class SpecialComboBox
    Inherits ComboBox
```

```vb
    Dim WithEvents btnEmbeddedButton As Button

    Public Sub New()

        Me.DropDownStyle = ComboBoxStyle.DropDownList

        ' Fix up the embedded button.
        btnEmbeddedButton = New Button
        btnEmbeddedButton.Width = SystemInformation.VerticalScrollBarWidth
        btnEmbeddedButton.Top = 0
        btnEmbeddedButton.Height = Me.Height - 4
        btnEmbeddedButton.BackColor = SystemColors.Control
        btnEmbeddedButton.FlatStyle = FlatStyle.Popup
        btnEmbeddedButton.Text = "t"
        Dim fSpecial As New Font("Wingdings 3", Me.Font.Size - 1)
        btnEmbeddedButton.Font = fSpecial

        btnEmbeddedButton.Left = Me.Width - btnEmbeddedButton.Width - _
            SystemInformation.VerticalScrollBarWidth

        Me.Controls.Add(btnEmbeddedButton)
        btnEmbeddedButton.Anchor = CType(AnchorStyles.Right _
            Or AnchorStyles.Top Or AnchorStyles.Bottom, AnchorStyles)
        btnEmbeddedButton.BringToFront()

    End Sub

    Private Sub btnEmbeddedButton_Click(ByVal sender As Object, _
            ByVal e As System.EventArgs) Handles btnEmbeddedButton.Click
        Me.SelectedIndex = -1
        Me.Focus
    End Sub

    Private Sub BillysComboBox_DropDownStyleChanged(ByVal sender As Object, _
            ByVal e As System.EventArgs) Handles MyBase.DropDownStyleChanged
        If Me.DropDownStyle <> ComboBoxStyle.DropDownList Then
            Me.DropDownStyle = ComboBoxStyle.DropDownList
            Throw New _
                InvalidOperationException("DropDownStyle must be DropDownList")
        End If
    End Sub
End Class
```

As in the first example in the chapter, this example inherits from a built-in control. Thus, it immediately gets all the capabilities of the standard ComboBox. All you need to add is the capability to reset the selected state.

To do that, you need a button for the user to press. The class declares the button as a private object named btnEmbeddedButton. Then, in the constructor for the class, the button is instantiated, and its properties are set as necessary. The size and position of the button need to be calculated. This is done using the size of the ComboBox and a special system parameter called SystemInformation.VerticalScrollBarWidth. This parameter is chosen because it is also used to calculate the size of the button used to drop down a combo box. Thus, your new embedded button will be the same width as the button that the regular ComboBox displays for dropping down the list.

Of course, you need to display something in the new button to indicate its purpose. For simplicity, the preceding code displays a lowercase "t" using the WingDings 3 font (which all Windows systems should have installed). This causes a left-pointing triangle to appear, as shown in Figure 16-9, which is a screen shot of the control in use.

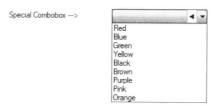

Special Combobox --->

Red
Blue
Green
Yellow
Black
Brown
Purple
Pink
Orange

Figure 16-9

The button is then added to the `Controls` collection of the `ComboBox`. You may be surprised to learn that a `ComboBox` even has a `Controls` collection for embedded controls, but all controls in Windows Forms have one.

Finally, the `Anchor` property of the new button is set to maintain the position if the `SpecialComboBox` is resized by its consumer.

Besides the constructor, only a couple of small routines are needed. The `click` event for the button must be handled, and in it the `SelectedIndex` must be set to -1. In addition, because this functionality is only for combo boxes with a style of `DropDownList`, the `DropDownStyleChanged` event of the `ComboBox` must be trapped, and the style prevented from being set to anything else.

Summary

This chapter discussed how to create custom controls in Windows Forms, enabling you to consolidate logic used throughout your user interfaces. The full inheritance capabilities in .NET and the classes in the Windows Forms namespace allow several options for creating controls. It is probably best to start by overriding these controls in order to learn the basics of creating properties and coordinating them with the designer, building controls and testing them, and so on. These techniques can then be extended by creating composite controls, as illustrated by the examples in the chapter.

We also discussed creating a control from scratch, using the base `Control` class. In the course of writing a control from scratch, it was necessary to discuss the basics of GDI+, but if you are going to do extensive work with GDI+, you will need to seek out additional resources to aid in that effort.

The key concept that you should take away from this chapter is that Windows Forms controls are a great way both to package functionality that will be reused across many forms and to create more dynamic, responsive user interfaces much more quickly with much less code.

17

Windows Presentation Foundation

Windows Presentation Foundation (WPF) — previously known as Avalon — is the next-generation presentation library and development paradigm for user interfaces. It was introduced with Windows Vista as a key architectural component in the .NET 3.0 Framework. This chapter introduces you to the WPF programming model and discusses key elements you'll need to know in order to work with WPF. Rest assured you will be creating applications that leverage the features of WPF in the future. Visual Studio introduces a fully enabled development environment for creating and customizing WPF-based applications.

The libraries that make up WPF were released in conjunction with the release of Windows Vista — not the commercial and much-publicized public launch of Vista in January 2007, but the initial release of Vista to enterprise partners in November 2006. The libraries shipped with Vista and coincidentally with Microsoft Office 2007, but what you may or may not have noticed at the time was the lack of development tools.

However, with Visual Studio 2008, not only are there tools for the .NET 3.5 libraries, but also tools for all of the .NET 3.0 libraries. Additionally, Microsoft released the Expression suite of tools, in particular Blend, which you'll also need if you are going to create custom WPF applications.

This chapter covers several key areas, including the following:

- ❑ The WPF strategy
- ❑ Why you should use WPF
- ❑ Creating a WPF application
- ❑ XAML
- ❑ Implementing a custom WPF application
- ❑ Customizing the user interface
- ❑ Using Blend for custom graphics and behavior

This chapter introduces a basic WPF application and then focuses on the underlying XAML that's used to declare WPF and other applications. Then it picks up with a custom WPF Windows framework application that you can leverage. The goal is to introduce you to WPF in a manner that should be familiar to Windows Forms developers and then expand on what additional items WPF brings to the equation. This chapter will not make you an expert WPF developer — WPF is too large a topic to fully cover in a single chapter — but it does provide a good starting place.

What, Where, Why, How — WPF Strategy

When .NET was released, most people realized that in terms of application development, a paradigm shift was occurring. The release of WPF was the first step in yet another paradigm shift, this one focusing on how user interfaces are designed and implemented. Therefore, it's appropriate to take a little time to look at not only where the user interface models are coming from, but also where they are going. Understanding that will enable you to see how WPF fits in, and not only why you'll want WPF in the future, but also how you can start leveraging it today.

The original user interfaces were punch cards for input and hard copy text for output. OK, maybe that's going a little too far back. Instead, let's jump ahead to the part of the user interface's resume that applies to where we're going today. The 1980s through 1990s saw several computer and software manufacturers introduce the graphical user interface (GUI). These GUI environments, while implemented differently on different platforms, became a part of the operating system. For Windows, this is the User32.dll and its companion UI classes. The original Visual Basic 1.0 was designed to enable developers to interact in a simple manner with these files, unlike C++, which referenced the raw User32.dll interfaces for everything.

Over time, Visual Basic's simple drag-and-drop approach to creating the forms users would access as part of an application in that GUI environment helped make it the most popular development language. However, with Web migrations, the paradigm started to shift. The Web introduced its own way of creating forms — one that used HTML. The HTML model is more declarative and doesn't guarantee the behavior of the components in the user interface. For example, the HTML page may declare it wants a text box, but it's up to the browser to interpret and provide the code that creates the actual object. The HTML control model is supported on Windows by Internet Explorer and by third-party tools such as Firefox and Netscape.

.NET ushered in the next stage of client UI implementation with ASP.NET and Windows Forms. Changing the UI model wasn't a primary focus of .NET; .NET introduced new tools for the UI. .NET shipped with two user-interface implementations: ASP.NET's HTML-based UI and the desktop-centric Windows Forms. It's important to realize that Windows Forms isn't based on the same code that User32 windows are, even though the programming model whereby the designer adds the code to a portion of the application's source is similar. The managed environment represents both the second and third programming models for developing user interfaces under Windows. Of course, other platforms include still other GUI models, but these three GUI models — User32.dll, ASP.NET, and Windows Forms — represent the ones Microsoft supported as of .NET 2.0.

Thus, Microsoft was left repeating many user-interface controls with three distinct implementations, a cost noticeable to even an organization as large as Microsoft. For developers, including those at Microsoft, the pain starts with the fact that a user interface can't be transported seamlessly between a Web-based version of an application and a local desktop version of the same application, or across platforms. For example, Microsoft can't design a UI for Outlook and reuse it for Outlook Web Access (OWA). Instead, it needs a different team of developers with different skills to create the OWA interface, and have you seen a remotely downloadable Windows Forms–based OWA application?

Let's face it: There wasn't much economic incentive to create both a Windows Forms–based and ASP .NET-based user interface for the same application. Until such a task is almost painless, people will continue to select an environment and then build their application targeting that model. In some cases where an application is successful, a follow-up task may be to attempt to reproduce the user interface for another target UI, but that is the exception, not the rule. Thus, while there are several options for creating a user interface, they represent "either-or" decisions.

This is where the WPF model comes in. WPF is a more declarative way of designing interfaces. The idea is that you can use a declaration to describe your user interface and then compile or include that definition with either a desktop or Web or even another operating system version of your application. WPF uses XML to declare the user-interface elements, relying on a standard known as the *Extensible Application Markup Language (XAML)*. This standard is pronounced "zamel" (rhymes with camel). It enables you to layer elements and include elements such as colors and 3-D shapes.

XAML goes well beyond what you normally expect to find in an HTML UI, yet at the same time the format should feel somewhat familiar to those who know HTML and/or XML. As for the implementation of code to interpret XAML UI declarations, Microsoft introduced the components that make up WPF with the release of Vista.

Raster Graphics and Vector Graphics

Currently, when you create a Windows Forms control you decide how large, in pixels, that button should be. A similar action is taken with regard to HTML forms, where you can specify either a size in pixels or a percentage of the screen. In both cases, the computer simply lays out a square or rounded square based on a flat set of pixels. It does the same with other images you use, working with what are known as *raster graphics*. Raster graphics are a collection of points on the surface of a screen that represent an image.

The alternative form of graphics is known as *vector graphics*. A vector is a line with a point of origin that continues forward in space from that point of origin. Vector graphics aren't based on a collection of points, but rather on a series of vectors. A plane representing the surface of your screen is placed in the path of these vectors, which define a set of points, and that is what you see on your screen. Vector graphics provide much better and more realistic image manipulation. Note that while you can incorporate a raster image with vector graphics, because you can place the raster image in your virtual plane, the reverse isn't feasible.

WPF is the first forms-based engine that relies on this vector-based model. The good news is that you can create user interfaces that truly look fantastic. The bad news is that you need to account for the fact that computing a series of vectors and the plane that intersects those vectors requires more CPU or Graphical Processing Unit (GPU) cycles. Thus, like the Vista UI, all WPF user interfaces require a bit more computing horsepower. However, unlike Vista, for which certain graphical features are disabled if your computer doesn't natively have that horsepower, for WPF that isn't the case. Because WPF is compatible with Windows XP, it isn't limited to those scenarios in which a powerful GPU is available to offload that processing. After all, Windows Vista was the first operating system to support leveraging the GPU, so system performance only degrades when you run a WPF application on Windows XP or an older computer that isn't able to support something such as the Glass display settings.

However, those concerns aside, one of the main appeals of the WPF model is the graphical capabilities. Built around raster graphics and enhanced GPU processor support, WPF enables a much more appealing user interface. You can hide the native Windows frame, as you'll see later in this chapter, make round buttons, and essentially begin to create a truly custom user interface, one that in an artistically designed application has the user saying "wow" in a truly memorable experience.

Should Your Next Windows Project Use WPF?

Microsoft will, of course, need to support all its previous GUI models in addition to WPF for the foreseeable future. However, Microsoft is motivated by the same aspects the rest of us can leverage — better graphics and the idea that a single application can have a UI that runs in multiple environments. Accordingly, Microsoft announced that enhancements to the .NET-based Windows Forms class libraries would not be occurring. While this UI model would receive maintenance and security-related updates, there would be no future new development on that set of libraries.

Does this mean you should automatically plan on moving to WPF for your next Windows application? Well, that depends on several factors. If you want to target a desktop that isn't running Windows XP or Windows Vista, then you can't use WPF. In addition, as noted earlier regarding the change related to graphics, if you don't want to see a performance drop for clients running operating systems such as Windows XP or Windows Server 2003, then you again need to target Windows Forms instead of WPF. Moreover, unlike Windows Forms — which has a mature control set, including items such as `DataGridView`, Timers, `ErrorProvider`, and common dialog controls — the WPF control gallery is still in its first release. The array of controls added since the original release of .NET 3.0 with the release of Visual Studio 2008 is rather impressive, but you may still find yourself returning to these standard dialogs or to the `WindowsFormsHost` control to encapsulate a Windows Forms user control.

You'll also see in this chapter that many of the really cool graphic capabilities that WPF provides come at the cost of limited behavior support. Thus, a simple setting such as Transparency expects you to provide a lot of manual code to implement standard Windows behavior. Additionally, in order to achieve a fancy design, you'll need — not want, but need — a XAML generation tool such as Microsoft Blend. Complex graphics are still complex, and a tool is required to create these items. The Blend tool, although available to developers, is really focused on graphic designers and doesn't provide a Visual Studio look and feel.

Overall, unless you are looking to leverage high-end graphics, you may find that even though WPF is the UI model of the future, the next version of your application is best served by using Windows Forms and perhaps leveraging the WPF interop libraries described in Chapter 18. However, this chapter is going to help you get started with WPF so that you can continue to work toward this next-generation application interface, which is based on a powerful graphic engine and includes built-in multimedia support.

Creating a WPF Application

The previous edition of this book, *Professional Visual Basic 2005 with .NET 3.0*, focused on going through the manual steps of creating a basic WPF application and manually updating the build file to create that application. These steps were appropriate because at the time WPF didn't have a native IDE and code-generation toolset. Most early WPF applications were built by hand or with minor conversation tools that could output graphics as XAML. With the release of Visual Studio 2008, WPF, like the other .NET 3.0 technologies, gained a true IDE and, with the availability of Blend, a powerful design tool. The focus is now on creating applications with Visual Studio 2008 and then customizing the design surface with Blend.

Be aware that while working in Blend it is very easy to spend a lot of time adjusting colors or fades, or adding simple animations. This can chew up an application development budget in nothing flat. In addition, it is possible to create design elements in Blend that are, unfortunately, incompatible or difficult to manipulate once you are trying to hook that design into your application logic. Accordingly, it is recommended that you define the initial application layout and then get the application operational. Only after you have completed the business integration and gotten the control elements working as required should you return to the design surface to provide complex graphics and behavior on top of your application.

Thus, the next step is to use Visual Studio to generate your WPF application and then go from a basic application into Blend to enhance graphic support. This application will go through three phases in this chapter, so three different projects are associated with it. For now we will create the first project, after which we transition to either the _Step_2 or _Step_3 version of the sample project. In each case, the project will contain the completed code for that portion of the project, but because this code is going to transform rather dramatically over the course of the chapter, this format provides you with a series of check points while going through this chapter yourself.

Begin by using the File menu in Visual Studio 2008 and select the option to create a new project. Navigate to the new Visual Basic Window section of the New Project dialog, as shown in Figure 17-1.

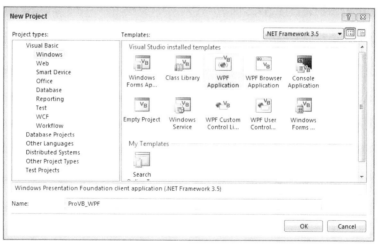

Figure 17-1

For the purposes of this chapter you can create a .NET 3.5 application called ProVB_WPF. This application could also be created as a .NET 3.0 application, but in that case we wouldn't have access to .NET 3.5 features such as LINQ. Additionally, note that the list of available templates for WPF applications disappears if you choose to target a .NET 2.0 baseline.

Similar to other project templates, Visual Studio opens in the main window you've just declared, but unlike Windows Forms, this isn't just a design surface. The first thing to notice is that there isn't a line of VB code in this project, just a few XAML snippets. As shown in Figure 17-2, the default application does not look entirely different from that of a Windows Form, except when it comes to the design surface. In Windows Forms, the design surface generates code that is placed in the myWindow.Designer.vb file. The generated file *.designer.vb is a partial class definition that Visual Studio uses to hold the definition of each control you place onto the form, as well as the form itself.

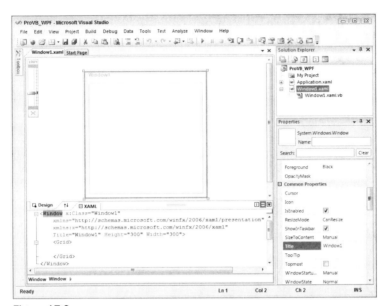

Figure 17-2

However, with WPF and XAML, that partial class definition is instead a collection of XML declarations that define your window and its behavior. More important, although parts may be generated, that XAML file isn't considered generated code; instead, it is a fully editable definition, and as such is available in the same display as the graphical representation of your display. You'll find that as you work with your design surface, Visual Studio 2008 automatically updates the XAML file; and similarly when you edit the XAML file, Visual Studio 2008 automatically updates the design surface.

The design surface shown in Figure 17-2 has several features specific to WPF. The first you'll find in the upper left-hand corner as you look at the screen. That scrollbar enables you to zoom in on a specific portion of your interface. You can choose to limit your view to just a portion of the overall window by zooming in for a closer look at how elements are aligned. Alternatively, you can "back" away from your overall window to look at the entire display, even when that design is larger then the design area available on your screen.

The second item to note about the display relates to the relationship between the currently top design surface in the display and the XAML tab located below it. Between these two tabs, in the middle of the screen, is a pair of up and down arrows. These arrows aren't just there for decoration to indicate that these two surfaces are related, but rather to swap the location of each of these two surfaces. Thus, if you are working with the XAML and directly making changes to it, you can shift that to the top of the display and reduce the graphical display.

However, having the code located above or below your design surface may not be your preferred display. That's where the three little icons located on the tab bar come in. The first two are a vertical line and a horizontal line, respectively. These buttons indicate that you can choose to place the XAML code and the design surface in a side-by-side display mode or in a top-bottom design mode, respectively. The third button, which shows double down arrows, enables you to collapse the combined display so that the tabs are along the bottom or the right side of the design display. Thus, if you prefer to maximize the available display surface, you can create a display similar to what you have when editing ASP.NET Web pages.

Of course, you are probably wondering about the XAML that is shown in Figure 17-2 and that defines your main window. This is one of two XAML files that are generated with your project. This XAML file has a top-level node of Window that tells the compiler that it defines a window. The top-level node ties this window to the class Window1, which matches the default filename, as shown in the following code:

```
<Window x:Class="Window1"
    xmlns="http://schemas.microsoft.com/winfx/2006/xaml/presentation"
    xmlns:x="http://schemas.microsoft.com/winfx/2006/xaml"
    Title="Window1" Height="300" Width="300">
    <Grid>

    </Grid>
</Window>
```

Because the XML namespace declarations are shared between this file and the second XAML file, let's jump to the remaining attributes of the window. By default, the window is given a title that matches the class same, as in Windows Forms, and the default size is a Height of 300 and a Width of 300. In addition to these attributes, the Window node that declares the actual main window contains a single control, a grid. The grid is the default control in the window because it provides developers with the most consistent design experience from Windows Forms.

Next, let's review the second XAML file, application.xaml. This file contains the application definition. Like your Visual Basic Windows Forms code, the Application object represents the application to the CLR. It is this object that represents the base reference for things such as garbage collection, and it is registered as the primary process. Because the Application object is implemented as an object in the System.Windows namespace, it supports properties, methods, and events just like any other class. The contents of application.xaml are shown in the following:

```
<Application x:Class="Application"
    xmlns="http://schemas.microsoft.com/winfx/2006/xaml/presentation"
    xmlns:x="http://schemas.microsoft.com/winfx/2006/xaml"
    StartupUri="Window1.xaml">
    <Application.Resources>

    </Application.Resources>
</Application>
```

This file is a good place to take a moment to discuss the basics of XAML. As you can see, this file starts with a reference to an x:Class declaration as an attribute of the Application node. The x: represents an alias similar to what you find in Visual Basic, where the x: indicates that Class is defined in the schema http://schemas.microsoft.com/winfx/2006/xaml, the XAML schema. You'll notice there is a second declaration for http://schemas.microsoft.com/winfx/2006/xaml/presentation. This second declaration is the one that references the actual WPF libraries. The last item in the attributes of the Application node is a StartupUri. This property tells the compiler that when this application is started, the next step is to open the file Window1.xaml in order to find the definition of the window to be displayed.

Similar to a traditional Windows Forms application, the application doesn't actually define a window; instead, it defines the application context, and then it calls another class to create the window. However, this file is a great place to add XAML resources that will apply across your application. Resources refers to the fact that in WPF it is possible to declare the color, shape, and behavior (in terms of hover over, mouse down, etc.) of your controls. Placing these XAML declarations in the Application.Resources section of the application definition is a natural way to share them across all of that type of control in your application. However, before continuing with this discussion of shared resources, it's important to understand XAML itself so that you'll have a better understanding of the XML node declarations.

Leveraging WPF with XAML

The ProVB_WPF example doesn't have much purpose yet, but it makes it easier to keep the discussion of XAML in context. The next step is to take a more detailed look at just what XAML is and how it relates to WPF. XAML is a markup-based protocol. Similar to SOAP and several other XML-based formats, the XAML specification describes a potentially open standard for describing user-interface elements. WPF is Microsoft's implementation of this standard. Currently, XAML isn't an open standard and it's unknown whether XAML will ever be a true open standard. However, the .NET implementation separates the definition of the XAML elements from the implementation of WPF, which means that creating an open standard is a possibility for XAML.

Regardless of whether XAML ever actually becomes an open standard, Microsoft has implemented WPF using a minimum of two XML namespaces. As noted in the application.xaml file, one namespace is focused on the definition of XAML, and the second is focused on WPF's custom classes. Returning to the ProVB_WPF Application.xaml file, the following namespace declaration is included:

```
xmlns="http://schemas.microsoft.com/winfx/2006/xaml/presentation"
```

The preceding line is similar to an Imports statement for XML in that it indicates a set of nodes and keywords that will be used within the associated XML file. In this case, the winfx/2006/xaml/presentation namespace contains the definition of WPF — not the definition of XAML keywords, but rather the definition of WPF, which is why you see statements such as Application.Window in that XML. The classes contained in the presentation namespace are the .NET implementation of WPF. The XAML file contains declarations referencing these classes, either as part of the XAML standard or as part of WPF. To start working with commands and controls that are part of the XAML standard, a second namespace reference is needed:

```
xmlns:x=http://schemas.microsoft.com/winfx/2006/xaml
```

This second reference is used throughout all XAML files to declare the actual XAML language standard. By convention, it is aliased as x:. For those of you who may not have done much XML development, this means that within the XAML you'll see things such as x:Class, x:Code, and other similar nodes. The x: is required to indicate that what follows is an element of the XAML languages, as opposed to, for example, WPF or some other .NET library. The x: nodes are the actual XAML declarations. What is important to remember is that the XAML namespace can be and is used for things other than just WPF. As you'll see in Chapter 27, Windows Workflow Foundation is based on XAML; it has its own /workflows namespace.

XAML Language Basics

XAML is defined as a language consisting of a collection of elements, attributes, and related objects. These objects are referenced from the XAML namespace, which by convention precedes each class with an x:. .NET extends and maps these declarative structures into .NET.

Before getting to the syntax, take a look at the three categories of XML statement you will find within the XAML namespace: attribute, markup extension, and XAML directive. Each is a separate category of language element.

Within XML, attributes refer to named properties that are associated with a given XML node. Thus, the XML node `object` might have several attributes such as `ID`, `Name`, `Text`, and so on associated with it. These attributes in XML live within the definition of the XML node. They are not contained within the XML node but its definition, as shown here:

```
<object id="myObject"></object>
```

Within XAML, the list of attributes includes those in the following table. Be aware that the term "object" in the following snippets can be replaced with one of several WPF objects, including `Application`, `Window`, `Button`, `Brush`, and so on:

XAML Attributes	Description and Example
x:Class	Used to reference the root class for an XAML document. Each document can be associated with a single root object. `<object x:Class="Window"></object>`
x:ClassModifier	Modifies the class definition for a given XAML document. Specifically, it enables you to indicate that a given class doesn't provide a public interface. Public is the default. `<object x:Class="Window" x:ClassModifier="Friend"></object>`
x:FieldModifier	Unlike classes, which are by default public, fields within objects are by default assigned with the `modifier Friend`. If you have added an object within XAML that you want available to other classes (within your code behind), then the `FieldModifier` needs to declare this field with the modifier of `Friend`. This property can only be used with objects that also have the `x:Name` attribute shown here: `<object x:Name="LoginWindow" x:FieldModifier="Public"></object>`
x:Key	Some objects, such as the `Dictionary` object and other collection objects, allow items to be indexed via a key. Such a key must be named, and this attribute is used to provide a unique key name. Note that most XAML applications leverage a resource dictionary, which is a common use of this attribute. Keys need to be unique within the scope of the object to which they are applicable. `<object.Resources> <SolidColorBrush x:Key="string"/> </object.Resources>`
x:Name	Similar to a key, but used more for the naming of objects within the scope of an application. Such objects are not public by default, but typically represent the controls and related user-interface objects used by your application. `<object x:Name="LoginWindow"> </object>`

XAML Attributes	Description and Example
x:Shared	This actually maps to what Visual Basic users understand the keyword Shared to mean. By default, if your application requests an object from your XAML resources, then you will get the same instance of the requested resource. You can use this property such that each time a given object is requested, a new instance of that object is created. `<ResourceDictionary><object x:shared="false"/>` `</ResourceDictionary>`
x:Subclass	This attribute can be used in conjunction with an x:Class declaration. It essentially enables your XAML to inherit from another class; however, as a Visual Basic user you won't use this attribute because you can do this in a much more natural manner in the code-behind source file associated with your class. `<object x:Class="class" x:Subclass="namespace.subclass"></object>`
x:TypeArguments	This attribute enables you to create a collection of x:Type markup extensions. This collection acts as the parameters to the constructor for a generic class to ensure that the associated types are defined with the constructor. This attribute must be used with a class declaration, and the associated class must be a generic. `<object x:class="PageFunction" x:TypeArguments="{x:Type=type1}">` `</object>`

Notice that none of the preceding attributes are actually referenced as a node within XML. Instead, they modify the properties associated with a node. Thus, the attributes are modifiers, as opposed to the next category of elements: markup extensions. As implied by the word "extensible" in the name Extensible XML, one of the features of this model is that the format allows for the definition of extensions. These extensions expand on the base elements associated with that markup definition. XAML includes a limited number of such extensions. Unlike an attribute, a markup extension can be used to create an XML node or a collection of XML attributes. When used to create a node, the markup extension allows for the definition of property values within this node. When used to allow for the creation of a collection of attributes, it can be recognized by the surrounding curly braces, as shown in the preceding TypeArguments definition. Markup extensions for XAML are shown in the following table:

XAML Markup Extension	Description and Example
x:Array	Used to provide support for arrays. The array declaration allows for the assignment of a data type, to support strong typing and the inclusion of a series of elements.`<x:Array Type="object"> <myObject1/> <myObject2/></x:Array>`
x:Null	Nothing in Visual Basic, but the extension is implemented based on the C#/C++ keyword of null. Will set an object property to null, which may or may not be the default state when that object property is created. x:Null has no additional modifiers and is typically implemented as a node, as opposed to an attribute, as it references the value of its parent node. `<object><object.property><x:Null/></object.property></object>`

XAML Markup Extension	Description and Example
x:Static	Supports the reference of constant values, shared properties of objects, and enumeration values. Similar to an attribute, it is most commonly used as an attribute with the format X:static "{namespace.class}" This extension is used to gain access to common values that are defaults for your application — for example, to the system colors used by the operating system. `<object Background= "{x:Static SystemColors.ControlBrush}"></object>`
x:Type	As previously introduced with the x:Typename attribute, the x:Type extension allows for the specification of a type when creating an object that is a generic. However, it has a second use: the specification of a property type. Thus, if you create an object that has properties, then the x:Type extension is used to specify the type associated with that property. `<object><object.property> <x:Type TypeName="namespace.class"/></object.property></object>`

Don't let that last extension confuse you; there are two ways that markup extensions are used — either as attributes contained within curly braces or as nodes that may contain their own attributes and properties. Some, such as x:Static, always appear as attributes; others, such as x:Null and x:Array, always appear as nodes; and of course x:Type can be found in either location. Up until now, all the XAML language elements have been used to operate within the definition of XML. That is, they define attributes and nodes, and as long as you understand the definition of the keyword, you can understand the data it references.

However, at times you need to truly reference data. For example, none of the preceding extensions would support embedding other XML data into your XAML file or referencing code directly from within your XAML file. These two capabilities are available based on XAML directives. XAML directives enable you to embed elements that don't follow the XML formatting rules. There are two such directives:

XAML Directive	Description and Example
x:Code	Enables you to embed Visual Basic code directly into your XAML file. However, although you can do it, you shouldn't: It's considered a very poor coding practice — not only because it isolates code outside of a code-behind file, but also because such code makes the XAML dependent on a language for compilation, and is isolated and more difficult to debug and maintain. However, you may come across such an element. In general, it is considered best to further nest any embedded code within an x:Code block within a CDATA block, as shown in the following sample, so that the XAML parsing engine doesn't attempt to parse the code. Thus, a code block will look similar to this: `<object><x:Code> <![CDATA[ // code instructions, usually enclosed by CDATA ... Sub MyMethod() End Sub ]]></x:Code></object>`

XAML Directive	Description and Example

x:XData	The second item that isn't standard XAML that you might want to embed within your XAML document is another XML document. For example, you might want to display an e-mail message or a Word document that has been converted to XML, so you might want this data to be within your XAML document. The key point is that you don't want this additional XML to accidentally use the same tag information associated with your XAML. Thus, you need to provide an x:XData directive containing your root data node, which contains your custom data. Note that in most cases the "object"' node in this sample will be a System.Windows.Data.XMLDataProvider as opposed to a Window or some other object. A sample of this is shown here:
	 `<object><x:XData> <dataItems xmlns="yourNamespace">...`
	 `</dataItems><elementDataRoot></x:XData></object>`

As you can see, the scope of the XML definition for what you're going to see within a XAML file is not that complex. You're probably wondering where all the controls, windows, and even the application object that we've already seen in action are. These items, while defined as part of the WPF implementation, are not part of the core XAML language definition. They are the WPF extensions, and the reason why you added a second namespace reference to the Presentation folder. Everything else you see in XAML that falls into this second category is also available for reference from your .NET application, so let's take a look at the integration of XAML and Visual Basic.

Implementing a Custom WPF Application

It is possible to do much of your WPF programming using XAML, but the next step is to examine how XAML can be integrated with code. After all, at some point you probably expect to start seeing some Visual Basic code again. Until now the ProVB_WPF sample has been a pure XAML application, so first we will make a quick plan for what this application will do and then we will create a first-cut implementation. For demonstration purposes, we will create a simple photo-viewing application. The user should be able to select a folder containing one or more images and then view those images, moving forward and backward through the list.

For now, that will be the limit of the requirements; later, after the basic application is operational, you can expand the scope to customize the look and feel further. Begin by modifying the "empty" window. Of course, it's not really empty. The window actually has a grid within it, so you can start with that and create three sections. After selecting the grid, hover over the left-hand border of your window. You'll see a point appear within the border that sends a guide line horizontally across the window. Select a point about 40 pixels from the top and a second point around 40 pixels from the bottom, dividing your grid into three sections.

Don't worry about being exactly on 40, because after you've selected your two points you are going to switch to the XAML view. Now, instead of the previous default display, you have code similar to what appears in the following block:

```
<Window x:Class="Window1"
    xmlns="http://schemas.microsoft.com/winfx/2006/xaml/presentation"
    xmlns:x="http://schemas.microsoft.com/winfx/2006/xaml"
```

```
    Title="ProVB_WPF" Height="335" Width="415" Name="MainWindow">
<Grid>
    <Grid.RowDefinitions>
        <RowDefinition Height="45" />
        <RowDefinition Height="215*" />
        <RowDefinition Height="40" />
    </Grid.RowDefinitions>
</Grid>
</Window>
```

This may look familiar because the preceding code includes a few edits that you can reproduce at this point. Note that the title of the window has been modified to match the project name. On this same line, you can see that the default size of the window has changed, and that the name of this instance of the Window1 class is now MainWindow. These are relatively minor in comparison to the newly added lines in this file.

The XAML now includes a new section related to the Grid.RowDefinitions. This section contains the specification of sections within the points in the grid. When you selected those points in the designer, you were defining these sections. The default syntax associated with the height of each section is the number of pixels followed by an asterisk. The asterisk indicates that when the window is resized, this row should also resize. For this application, only the center section should resize, so the asterisk has been removed from the top and bottom row definitions.

This provides a set of defined regions that can be used to align controls within this form. Thus, the next step is to add some controls to the form and create a basic user interface. In this scenario, the actions should be very familiar to any developer who has worked with either Windows Forms or ASP.NET forms.

Controls

WPF provides an entirely different set of libraries for developing applications. However, although these controls exist in a different library, how you interact with them from Visual Basic is generally the same. Each control has a set of properties, events, and methods that you can leverage. The XAML file may assign these values in the declarative format of XML, but you can still reference the same properties on the instances of the objects that the framework creates within your Visual Basic code.

Starting with the top section, drag the following from the Toolbox onto the form: a label, a text box, and a button control. These can be aligned into this region in the same order they were added. Ensure that the label is bound to the left side and top of the window, while the button is bound to the right side and top of the window. Meanwhile, the text box should be bound to the top and both sides of the window so that as the window is stretched, the width of the text box increases. The resulting XAML should be similar to this:

```
<Window x:Class="Window1"
  xmlns="http://schemas.microsoft.com/winfx/2006/xaml/presentation"
  xmlns:x="http://schemas.microsoft.com/winfx/2006/xaml"
    Title="ProVB_WPF" Height="335" Width="415" Name="MainWindow">
    <Grid>
        <Grid.RowDefinitions>
            <RowDefinition Height="45" />
```

```
            <RowDefinition Height="215*" />
            <RowDefinition Height="40" />
        </Grid.RowDefinitions>
        <Label Margin="0,11,0,0" Name="Label1" HorizontalAlignment="Left" Width="80"
Height="23" VerticalAlignment="Top">Image Path:</Label>

        <TextBox Margin="81,13,92,0" Name="TextBox1" Height="21"
VerticalAlignment="Top" />

        <Button HorizontalAlignment="Right" Margin="0,11,9,11" Name="ButtonBrowse"
Width="75">Images ...</Button>
    </Grid>
</Window>
```

As shown in the newly added lines, each control is assigned a name and defines a set of editable properties. Note that these names can be addressed from within the code and that you can handle events from each control based on that control's named instance. For now, however, just adjust the text within the label to indicate that the text box to its immediate right will contain a folder path for images, and adjust the `button` control. Place a new label on the `button` control's `Images` and rename the control to `ButtonBrowse`. There is obviously more to do with this button, but for now you can finish creating the initial user interface.

Next, add the following controls in the following order. First, add an `Image` control. To achieve a design surface similar to the one shown in Figure 17-3, drop the `Image` control so that it overlaps both the middle and bottom sections of the grid display. Now add three buttons to the bottom portion of the display. At this point the controls can be aligned. You can do this through a combination of editing the XAML directly and positioning things on the screen. For example, expand the `image` control to the limits of the two bottom grid rows using the design surface; similarly, align the buttons visually on the design surface.

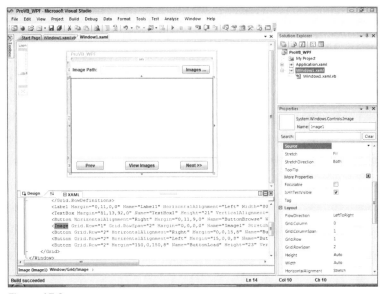

Figure 17-3

As shown in the figure, the separations for the two row definitions are described in the design surface, and each of the buttons has a custom label. Note that the Next button is followed by a pair of greater than symbols, but the Prev button is missing a matching set of less than symbols. The problem is that the less than and greater than symbols have special meaning in XAML, so it can be difficult to use them in the XAML. Therefore, one of the changes to be made in the Visual Basic code is the addition of these symbols to the button label.

First, however, review the XAML code and ensure that, for example, the `Image` control is assigned to `Grid.Row` 1 and that the property `Grid.RowSpan` is 2. Unlike the items that were in `Grid.Row` 0, the items in other rows of the grid must be explicitly assigned. Similarly, the name and caption of each button in the bottom row of the grid are modified to reflect that control's behavior. These and similar changes are shown in the following XAML:

```
<Window x:Class="Window1"
  xmlns="http://schemas.microsoft.com/winfx/2006/xaml/presentation"
  xmlns:x="http://schemas.microsoft.com/winfx/2006/xaml"
    Title="ProVB_WPF" Height="335" Width="415" Name="MainWindow">
    <Grid>
        <Grid.RowDefinitions>
            <RowDefinition Height="45" />
            <RowDefinition Height="215*" />
            <RowDefinition Height="40" />
        </Grid.RowDefinitions>
        <Label Margin="0,11,0,0" Name="Label1" HorizontalAlignment="Left" Width="80"
Height="23" VerticalAlignment="Top">Image Path:</Label>

        <TextBox Margin="81,13,92,0" Name="TextBox1" Height="21"
VerticalAlignment="Top" />

        <Button HorizontalAlignment="Right" Margin="0,11,9,11" Name="ButtonBrowse"
Width="75">Images ...</Button>


        <Image Grid.Row="1" Grid.RowSpan="2" Margin="0,0,0,0" Name="Image1"
Stretch="Fill" />

        <Button Grid.Row="2" HorizontalAlignment="Right" Margin="0,0,15,8"
Name="ButtonNext" Width="75" Height="23" VerticalAlignment="Bottom">Next >>
</Button>

        <Button Grid.Row="2" HorizontalAlignment="Left" Margin="15,0,0,8"
Name="ButtonPrev" Width="75" Height="23" VerticalAlignment="Bottom">
Prev</Button>

        <Button Grid.Row="2" Margin="150,0,150,8" Name="ButtonLoad" Height="23"
VerticalAlignment="Bottom">View Images</Button>
    </Grid>
</Window>
```

Note in the shaded sections the description of the new controls. The `Image` control is first, and it is positioned in `Grid.Row` number 1, which, because .NET arrays are always zero-based, is the second row. The second attribute on this node indicates that it will span more then a single row in the grid. For now, this control uses the default name, and it has been set so that it will stretch to fill the area that contains it.

Following the `Image` control are the definitions for the three buttons along the bottom of the display. For now, these buttons will control the loading of images; over the course of this chapter, these buttons will be either removed or redone significantly. The order of these buttons isn't important, so following their order in the file, the first button is like the others positioned in the final row of the grid. This button has been placed on the right-hand side of this area and is bound to the bottom and right corners of the display. Its name has been changed to `ButtonNext` and its label is `Next >>`.

The next button is the Prev button, which has been placed and bound to the left-hand side and bottom of the display. Its name has been changed to `ButtonPrev`, and its display text has been changed to read `Prev`. As noted, the arrow symbols are not in the button name; and, as you can test in your own code, attempting to add them here causes an error.

Finally, there is the `ButtonLoad` button, which is centered in the display area. It has been bound to both sides of the display to maintain its position in the center. The label for this button is `View Images`, which is, of course, the goal of this application. However, in order for that to happen, you need an event handler for this button; in fact, you need several event handlers in order to get the basic behavior of the application in place.

Event Handlers

Begin by adding some event handlers to the application. In previous versions of Visual Studio you could click on a control and Visual Studio would automatically generate the default event handler for that control in your code. Fortunately, WPF also provides this behavior, so generate the following event handlers:

❑ Double-click on the title bar of the form to generate the `Window1_Loaded` event handler.

❑ Double-click on the Images button to create the `ButtonBrowse_Click` handler.

❑ Double-click on the Load button to create the `ButtonLoad_Click` handler.

❑ Double-click on the Prev button to create the `ButtonPrev_Click` handler.

❑ Double-click on the Next button to create the `ButtonNext_Click` handler.

To create each of these handlers, you need to return to the design display and click on the associated control, but after they are created you can stay in code mode for most of this section. Take a look at the `ButtonBrowse_Click` event handler's method stub:

```
Private Sub ButtonBrowse_Click(ByVal sender As System.Object, _
    ByVal e As System.Windows.RoutedEventArgs) _
    Handles ButtonBrowse.Click
End Sub
```

The preceding code was reformatted with line extension characters to improve readability, but this is essentially what each of your event handlers looks like. As a Visual Basic developer, you should find this syntax very familiar. Note that the method name has been generated based on the control name and the event being handled. The parameter list is generated with the "sender" and e parameter values, although the e value now references a different object in the `System.Windows` namespace. Finally, defined here is the VB-specific `Handles` syntax that indicates this method is an event handler and which specific event or events it handles.

While this is a very familiar, powerful, and even recommended way of defining event handlers with VB and WPF, it isn't the only way. WPF allows you to define event handlers within your XAML code. To be honest, if this were a book on C#, we would probably spend a fair amount of time covering the advantages of that type of event handler declaration. After all, C# doesn't support the direct association of the event handler declaration with the method handling the event; as a result, C# developers prefer to declare their event handlers in XAML.

Visual Basic provides a default implementation of WPF that encourages less coupling of the UI and business logic than C# does.

However, one of the goals of XAML is the separation of the application logic from the UI, and placing the names of event handlers in the UI actually couples the UI to the business logic. It shouldn't matter to the UI whether the `Click` event or the `DoubleClick` or any other event is being handled by custom logic. Therefore, although this section introduces the way to define events directly in XAML, the recommendation is to define event handlers with the code that implements the handler.

In order to demonstrate this in the code, return to the design view for your form. Select the Images button and position your cursor just after the word Button, which names this node. Press the spacebar. You'll see that you have IntelliSense, indicating which properties and events are available on this control. Typing a **c** adjusts the IntelliSense display so that you see the `Click` event. Select this event by pressing Tab and you'll see the display shown in Figure 17-4.

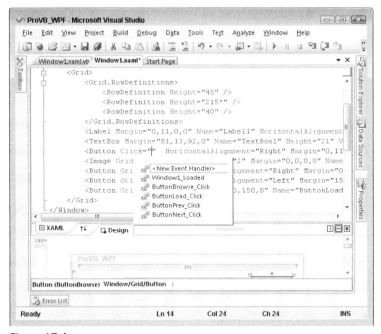

Figure 17-4

As shown here, not only does the XAML editor support full IntelliSense for selecting properties and events on a control, when an event is selected, it displays a list of possible methods that can handle this event. Of particular note is the first item in the list, which enables you to request that a new event handler be created in your code. Selecting this item tells Visual Studio to generate the same event handler stub that you created by double-clicking on the control; however, instead of placing the `Handles` clause on this method, the definition of this method as an event handler is kept in the XAML.

This causes two issues. First, if you are looking only at the code, then nothing explicitly indicates whether a given method in your code is in fact an event handler. This makes maintaining the code a bit (not a lot) more difficult to maintain. Second, if you have handled an event that is specific to Windows as opposed to the Web, then your XAML won't be portable. Neither of these side effects is desirable. Thus, given the VB syntax for defining events as part of the method declaration, the code in this chapter avoids the embedded XAML style of declaring standard Windows event handlers. At this point, you could run your application. It won't do anything except allow you to close it, but you can verify that it behaves as expected and save your work.

Adding Behavior

It's almost time to make this UI do something, but there is one more step before you start working with code. As part of this application, you want to allow users to select the directory from which images should be displayed. In theory, you could (and in practice, at some time probably would) write a custom interface for selecting or navigating to the images directory. However, for this application that isn't important, and you want a quick and easy solution.

Unfortunately, WPF doesn't offer any native control that supports providing a quick and easy view into the file system. However, Windows Forms does, and in this case you want to leverage this control. The good news is that you can, and the even better news is that you don't need the Windows interop library in order to do so. Because something like the Browse Folders dialog isn't a control hosted on your form, you can reference it from your code. Thus, although you need the Windows Forms Integration Library and the `WindowsFormsHost` control discussed in Chapter 18 for any UI-based controls, in this case the code just needs to reference the `System.Windows.Forms` library.

Because the `System.Windows.Forms` library isn't automatically included as a reference in a WPF application, you need to manually add a reference to this library. Open the My Project display and select the References tab. Click the Add button to open the Add Reference dialog and then select the `System .Windows.Forms` library, as shown in Figure 17-5. You can't add controls to your WPF form without leveraging the `Windows.Forms.Integration` library, but you can, behind the scenes, continue to reference controls and features of Windows Forms.

With this additional reference, you can begin to place some code into this application. Start with the `window_loaded` event. This event is where you'll define the default path for the image library, set up the label for the Prev button, and change the default property of the `grid` control so that it handles the images the way you want:

```vb
Private Sub Window1_Loaded(ByVal sender As System.Object, _
                           ByVal e As System.Windows.RoutedEventArgs) _
                           Handles MyBase.Loaded
    ' Append the << to the text for the button since these are _
    ' reserved characters within XAML
    ButtonPrev.Content = "<< " + ButtonPrev.Content.ToString()
    ' Set the default path from which to load images
    TextBox1.Text = _
        Environment.GetFolderPath(Environment.SpecialFolder.MyPictures)
```

```
' Have the images maintain their aspect ration
    Image1.Stretch = Stretch.Uniform
End Sub
```

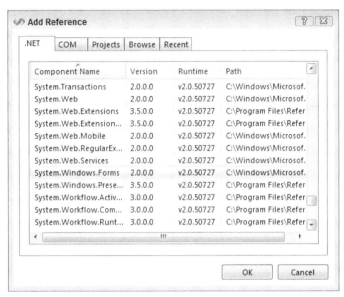

Figure 17-5

The preceding implementation handles these three tasks. It takes the content of the `ButtonPrev` control and appends the two less than symbols to the front of the string so that both buttons are displayed uniformly. Of course, long term, this code is going to be disposed of, but for now it helps illustrate that while controls such as `Button` may seem familiar from Windows Forms, these controls are in fact different. The WPF version of the `Button` control doesn't have a `text` property; it has a `content` property. The `content` property is, in fact, an untyped object reference. In the case of this application, you know this content is a string to which you can append additional text. However, this code is neither a good idea nor easily maintained, so this is just a temporary solution.

Next, the code updates the `text` property of the `TextBox` control used on the form. This text box displays the folder for the images to display. In order to provide a dynamic path, the code leverages the `Environment` class to get a folder path. To this shared method the code passes a shared environment variable: `Environment.SpecialFolder.MyPictures`. This variable provides the path to the current user's My Pictures folder (on Vista, the Pictures folder). By using this value, the code automatically points to a directory where the current user would be expected to have images.

Finally, to again demonstrate that any of the WPF classes can in fact be modified within your code, this code sets a property on the image control. Specifically, it updates the `Stretch` property of the `Image` control to ensure that images are resized with their aspect maintained. Thus, if an image is square, then when your image control becomes a rectangle, the image remains square. The `Stretch.Uniform` value indicates that aspect should be maintained, while other members of the `Windows.Stretch` enumeration provide alternative behavior.

The next step is to implement your first button handler, the `ButtonBrowse_Click` handler. When this button is clicked, the application should open the Folder Browse dialog, displaying the currently selected folder as the default. The user should be allowed to navigate to an existing folder or create a new folder. When the dialog is closed, the application should, if the user selected a new folder, update the folder's text box to display this new location:

```
Private Sub ButtonBrowse_Click(ByVal sender As System.Object, _
                            ByVal e As System.Windows.RoutedEventArgs) _
                            Handles ButtonBrowse.Click
    Dim folderDialog As System.Windows.Forms.FolderBrowserDialog = _
                        New System.Windows.Forms.FolderBrowserDialog()
    folderDialog.Description = "Select the folder for images."
    folderDialog.SelectedPath = TextBox1.Text
    Dim res As System.Windows.Forms.DialogResult = _
                                        folderDialog.ShowDialog()
    If res = System.Windows.Forms.DialogResult.OK Then
        TextBox1.Text = folderDialog.SelectedPath
    End If
End Sub
```

The preceding code block declares an instance of the `System.Windows.Forms.FolderBrowserDialog` control. As noted when the reference was added, this control isn't part of your primary window display, so you can create an instance of this dialog without needing the `Windows.Forms.Interface` library. It then sets a description indicating to users what they should do while in the dialog, and updates the current path for the dialog to reflect the currently selected folder. The dialog is then opened and the result assigned directly into the variable `res`. This variable is of type `System.Windows.Forms.DialogResult` and is checked to determine whether the user selected the OK or Cancel button. If OK was selected, then the currently selected folder is updated.

Now it's time to start working with the images. That means you need to retrieve a list of images and manipulate that list as the user moves forward and backward through it. You could constantly return to the source directory to find the next and previous images, but you will get much better performance by capturing the list locally and keeping your current location in the list. This implies two local variables; and because you want these variables available across different events, you need to declare them as member variables to your class:

```
Class Window1
    Private m_imageList As String() = {}
    Private m_curIndex As Integer = 0

    Private Sub Window1_Loaded(ByVal sender As System.Object, _
                            ByVal e As System.Windows.RoutedEventArgs) _
                            Handles MyBase.Loaded
        ' Append the << to the text for the button since these are _
        ' reserved characters within XAML
        ButtonPrev.Content = "<< " + ButtonPrev.Content.ToString()
        ' Set the default path from which to load images
        TextBox1.Text = _
                Environment.GetFolderPath(Environment.SpecialFolder.MyPictures)
        ' Have the images maintain their aspect ration
        Image1.Stretch = Stretch.Uniform
    End Sub
```

```
Private Sub ButtonBrowse_Click(ByVal sender As System.Object, _
                            ByVal e As System.Windows.RoutedEventArgs) _
                            Handles ButtonBrowse.Click
    Dim folderDialog As System.Windows.Forms.FolderBrowserDialog = _
                        New System.Windows.Forms.FolderBrowserDialog()
    folderDialog.Description = "Select the folder for images."
    folderDialog.SelectedPath = TextBox1.Text
    Dim res As System.Windows.Forms.DialogResult = _
                                            folderDialog.ShowDialog()
    If res = System.Windows.Forms.DialogResult.OK Then
        TextBox1.Text = folderDialog.SelectedPath
    End If
End Sub


Private Sub ButtonLoad_Click(ByVal sender As System.Object, _
                            ByVal e As System.Windows.RoutedEventArgs) _
                            Handles ButtonLoad.Click
    Image1.Source = Nothing
    m_imageList = System.IO.Directory.GetFiles(TextBox1.Text, "*.jpg")
    m_curIndex = 0
    If m_imageList.Count > 0 Then
        Image1.Source = _
                    New System.Windows.Media.Imaging.BitmapImage( _
                        New System.Uri(m_imageList(m_curIndex)))
    End If
End Sub
```

The beginning of the preceding code adds two new properties to class Window1. Both values are private variables that have not been exposed as public properties. They are being made available for use in the image-handling buttons. Your code should look similar to the preceding code. The second shaded section is an implementation of the ButtonLoad event handler. This event handler is called when the user clicks ButtonLoad, and the first thing it does is clear the current image from the display. It then leverages the System.IO.Directory class, calling the shared method GetFiles to retrieve a list of files. For simplicity, this call screens out all files that don't have the extension .jpg. In a full production application, this call would probably use a much more complex screening system to gather all types of images and potentially feed a folder navigation control so that users could change the selected folder or even add multiple folders at once.

Once the list of files is retrieved and assigned to the private variable m_imageList, the code clears the current index and determines whether any files were returned for the current directory. The screenshots in this chapter have three images in the folder in order to obtain a small array; however, if no images are present, then the code exists without displaying anything. Here, presume an image is available. The code uses the System.Windows.Media.Imaging class to load an image file as a bitmap. It does this by accepting the URI or path to that image, a path that was returned as an array from your call to GetFiles. Note that the BitmapImage call doesn't need an image formatted as a bitmap, but instead converts the chosen image to a bitmap format that can then be directly referenced by the source property of the Image control:

```
Private Sub ButtonPrev_Click(ByVal sender As System.Object, _
                            ByVal e As System.Windows.RoutedEventArgs) _
                            Handles ButtonPrev.Click
    If m_imageList.Count > 0 Then
```

```
                    m_curIndex -= 1
                    If m_curIndex < 0 Then
                        m_curIndex = m_imageList.Count - 1
                    End If
                    Image1.Source = New System.Windows.Media.Imaging.BitmapImage( _
                                        New System.Uri(m_imageList(m_curIndex)))
                End If
            End Sub

        Private Sub ButtonNext_Click(ByVal sender As System.Object, _
                                ByVal e As System.Windows.RoutedEventArgs) _
                                Handles ButtonNext.Click
            If m_imageList.Count > 0 Then
                m_m_curIndex += 1
                If m_curIndex > m_imageList.Count - 1 Then
                    m_curIndex = 0
                End If
                Image1.Source = New System.Windows.Media.Imaging.BitmapImage( _
                                    New System.Uri(m_imageList(m_curIndex)))
            End If
        End Sub
    End Class
```

After the code to load an image has been added, implementing the ButtonPrev and ButtonNext event handlers is fairly simple. In both cases the code first checks to ensure that one or more images are available in the m_imageList. If so, then the code either decrements or increments the m_curIndex value, indicating the image that should currently be displayed. In each case the code ensures that the new index value is within the limits of the array. For example, if it is below 0, then it is reset to the last image index; and if it is greater than the last used index, the counter is reset to 0 to return it to the start of the list.

The next logical step is to run the application. Clicking the Run button within Visual Studio ensures that your application starts. If you have images loaded in your Pictures folder, then you can open the first of these images in the application. If not, then you can navigate to another directory such as the Samples folder using the Images button. At this point, you'll probably agree that the sample application shown in Figure 17-6 looks just like a typical Windows Forms application — so much so in fact that the next steps are included to ensure that this doesn't look like a Windows Forms application.

However, before adding new features, there is a possibility that when you loaded your image, your application didn't display the image quite like the one shown in Figure 17-6; in fact, it might look more like the image shown in Figure 17-7. If, when you worked on your own code, you added the Image control after adding the View, Prev, and Next buttons, then your buttons — in particular, the View Images button — might be completely hidden from view. This is caused by the way in which WPF layers and loads controls, and to resolve it you need to change the order in which the controls are loaded in your XAML. Before doing that, however, this is a good place to discuss layers and the WPF layering and layout model.

Layout

WPF supports a very robust model for control layout, which it achieves by leveraging the capability to layer controls and by providing a set of controls directly related to layout. Combined with the capability to define a reasonable set of layout information for each control, what you wind up with is an adaptable environment that can, at the extreme, provide unique behavior.

Figure 17-6

How does the process work? Within each control are the basic elements associated with the sizing of that control. As with past versions of Windows Forms, included is the concept of height and width and the four associated limitations: MaxHeight, MaxWidth, MinHeight, and MinWidth. Additionally, as shown in this chapter, it is possible to bind controls to window borders.

The layout properties aren't the focus of this section, however. More important is the concept of *layered controls*. What happens when you layer an image on top of something such as a grid? Recall how the Image control you defined was bound to the four borders of its display area. In fact, the control isn't bound to the limits of the window per se; it is bound to the limits of the grid control upon which it is explicitly layered. This layering occurs because the Image control is defined as part of the content of the grid. That content is actually a collection containing each of the layered controls for the selected control.

When it comes to layout and layering, keep in mind that if a control is explicitly layered on top of another control as part of its content, then its display boundaries are by default limited by the containing control's boundaries.

You can override this behavior using the ClipToBounds property, the LayoutClip property, and the GetLayoutClip method of the container. Note, however, that the default behavior of WPF controls is to set ClipToBounds to false and then use the LayoutClip property and the GetLayoutClip method to specify the actual clipping bounds. Resetting and manually managing the clipping behavior enables a control to be drawn outside the bounds of its parent container. That behavior is beyond the scope of this chapter, as the process is somewhat involved and the preferred behavior, when available, is to clip within the region of the parent control.

The fact that your control can be drawn beyond the limits of its container is an important concept. It means your controls are no longer "contained," but rather are truly layered. This may sound trivial, but the implications are significant. Under previous UI models, an object had a container of some sort. For example, a panel could contain other controls of certain types, but not necessarily all types. A button's content was generally text unless you had a button configured for images, but you couldn't really find a button configured to contain, for example, a drop-down list box, unless you wrote a custom display implementation.

By moving to a more layered approach, you can create a single control that handles text, images, and other controls. The technique chosen to accomplish that was for those controls that support layering to include a *content presenter control*. Thus, when you indicated that the Image control in ProVB_WPF should stretch, it stretched in accordance with the grid control. Were you to change the XAML definition of the grid control and give it a fixed height or width, then even though the window might change, the Image control would still be bound to the limits of the grid control.

This behavior is explicit layering, and it is only available with certain control types. For example, WPF provides a series of different "panel" controls that are used to provide a framework for control layout. The grid is probably the one most familiar to .NET Windows Forms developers because it maps most closely to the default behavior of Windows Forms. Other similar controls include StackPanel, Canvas, DockPanel, ToolBar, and Tab-related controls. Each of these provides unique layout behavior. Because these are available as controls, which you can nest, you can combine these different layout paradigms within different sections of a single form, which enables you to group controls and achieve a common layout behavior of related controls.

To be clear, however, explicit layering or nesting isn't just available with panel controls; another WPF example is the Button control. The button has a layer of generic button code — background color, border, size, and so on — that is managed within the display for the button. Then the button has a content presenter within its definition that takes whatever was placed into the button's content property and calls the presentation logic for that control. This enables the button and many other controls to contain other controls of any type.

You can place a button on a form and bind it to the form's borders, and then place other controls on the form. Because the button exposes a content property, it supports explicit layering, and other controls can in fact be placed within the content of the button. Thus, whenever a user clicks on the surface of the form, a click event is raised to the underlying button that is the owner of that content. The fact that WPF controls forward events up the chain of containers is an important factor to consider when capturing events and planning for application behavior. The formal name for this behavior is *routed events*.

Routed events are a key new concept introduced with WPF, and they are important in the sense that as you add controls to your UI, you create a hierarchy. In the example thus far, this hierarchy is rather flat: There is a window, and then a grid, and each of the controls is a child of the grid. However, you can make this hierarchy much deeper, and routed events enable the controls at the top of the hierarchy to be notified when something changes in the controls that are part of their content structure.

In addition to these explicit concepts of layering, hierarchy, and routed events, WPF also has the concept of implicit layering. An *implicit layer* describes the scenario when you have two different controls defined to occupy the same space on your form. In the case of the example code, recall that the image was defined to overlay both of the row definitions, including the one containing the three Image control buttons. Thus, these controls were defined to display in the same area, which isn't a problem for WPF, but which in the current design isn't ideal for display purposes either.

The key idea is that there is implicit layering and explicit layering. In case you didn't see the same behavior that's been described in terms of the loaded image hiding the control buttons, you'll need to modify the XAML code. Note that the code available for download implements the solution correctly, so if you are following along with the sample code you'll need to modify the XAML in Window1.xaml. The *incorrect* version of this XAML is as follows:

```
<Grid>
    <Grid.RowDefinitions>
```

```
        <RowDefinition Height="45" />
        <RowDefinition Height="215*" />
        <RowDefinition Height="40" />
    </Grid.RowDefinitions>
    <Label Margin="0,11,0,0" Name="Label1" HorizontalAlignment="Left" Width="80"
Height="23" VerticalAlignment="Top">Image Path:</Label>
    <TextBox Margin="81,13,92,0" Name="TextBox1" Height="21"
VerticalAlignment="Top" />
    <Button HorizontalAlignment="Right" Margin="0,11,9,0" Name="ButtonBrowse"
Width="75" Height="23" VerticalAlignment="Top">Images ...</Button>
    <Button Grid.Row="2" HorizontalAlignment="Right" Margin="0,0,15,8"
Name="ButtonNext" Width="75" Height="23" VerticalAlignment="Bottom">Next >></Button>
    <Button Grid.Row="2" HorizontalAlignment="Left" Margin="15,0,0,8"
Name="ButtonPrev" Width="75" Height="23" VerticalAlignment="Bottom"> Prev</Button>
    <Button Grid.Row="2" Margin="150,0,150,8" Name="ButtonLoad" Height="23"
VerticalAlignment="Bottom">View Images</Button>
    <Image Grid.Row="1" Grid.RowSpan="2" Margin="0,0,0,0" Name="Image1"
Stretch="Fill" />
</Grid>
```

In the preceding XAML, the buttons are defined and loaded, and the image control isn't defined until later. As a result, the Image control is considered to be layered on top of the button controls. When the application starts, you might expect that Image control to immediately block the buttons, but it doesn't. That's because there is no image to display, so the Image control essentially stays out of the way, enabling the controls that would otherwise be behind it to both be displayed and receive input. WPF fully supports the concept of transparency, as demonstrated later in this chapter.

When there is something to display, the resulting image can block the same buttons that were used to load it, as shown in Figure 17-7. Because the image isn't part of the content for any of these buttons, none of the click events that would occur on the image at this point are raised to those buttons, so the buttons that are hidden don't respond. This is different behavior from what you get when you layer controls, and much closer to what a Windows Forms developer might expect. As a result, you need to be aware, just as with other user interfaces, of which order controls overlap in the same display area that's loaded.

Figure 17-7

Thus, everything you've done in the past, both with Windows Forms and ASP.NET, is still possible. On the surface, the WPF controls have more in common with existing programming models than might at first seem apparent.

Now that we have uttered heresy against this new UI paradigm, it's time to examine what is meant by a paradigm shift with the XAML model. As noted, it starts with a new set of classes and a new declarative language, but it continues with being able to have much finer control over your application's UI behavior.

Customizing the User Interface

While you can create a user interface that looks disappointingly similar to a Windows Forms application, the real power of WPF is the customization it enables you to create for your application. At this point, our example moves from the `ProVB_WPF` application to the second application, `ProVB_WPF_Step_2`. The goal here is to provide, through Visual Studio 2008, an even cleaner interface — not one that leverages all of WPF's power, but one that at least reduces the Windows Forms look and feel of this application.

The first step is to change some of the application, so for starters, a text box with the name of the selected directory is redundant. You don't expect users to type that name, but rather to select it, so you can instead display the currently selected directory on the actual button label. Accordingly, the current label and text box controls in the form can be removed. Additionally, both at load and following a change to the selected folder, instead of waiting for the user to request the image folder, just have the application query and pull the initial image into the application.

Carrying out these changes is relatively simple. The first step is to adjust the existing button handler for the View Images button. Because this button will be deleted but the actions that the handler implements are still needed, change the method definition from being an event handler with associated parameters to being a private method that doesn't require any parameters:

```
Private Sub LoadImages()
```

Next, this method needs to be called when a new directory is chosen, so update the event handler for the `ButtonBrowse_Click` to include a call to this method when the name of the directory is updated.

Now you can get rid of the `Label` and `TextBox` controls. Eliminating the `Label` control is easy, as it isn't referenced in the code, but the `TextBox` poses a challenge. You can replace the `TextBox` control with a reference to the content of the `Button` control, but in this case you've jumped from the frying pan into the fire in terms of maintenance. Face it: The button content over time could be anything.

From a coding standpoint, it makes much more sense to store the current path as part of your local business data. Then, if the goal is to have the label of that button display the current path, fine; but if for some reason that changes, then you can minimize the changes required to your application code. Therefore, add a new private value to your class:

```
Private m_curImagePath As String = ""
```

Now replace all of the references to `TextBox1.Text` with the new value of `m_curImagePath` in your code. There are likely more than you would expect, and not using the button's label for this task should make more sense at this point. Next, you need to update the button label for when the `m_curImagePath` value changes. This occurs only in two places: in the `Window1_Loaded` event handler and in the `ButtonBrowse_ Click` event handler.

Finally, update the code in the `load` event. There are three actions in the current method, and two of them should be eliminated. The first is where the code is adding the "<<" to the `ButtonPrev` label. This label is going to become an image, so get rid of this assignment statement. Similarly, setting the `Stretch` property of the `Image` control within this event is duplicate effort. Instead, update the XAML and set that property to the desired value directly in the XAML. When you are done, the code for your class and its first three methods should look similar to the following code, given that there were no changes to the event handlers for `ButtonPrev` and `ButtonNext`:

```
Class Window1
    Private m_imageList As String() = {}
    Private m_curIndex As Integer = 0

    Private m_curImagePath As String = ""

    Private Sub Window1_Loaded(ByVal sender As System.Object, _
                            ByVal e As System.Windows.RoutedEventArgs) _
                        Handles MyBase.Loaded
        ' Set the default path from which to load images and load them
        m_curImagePath = _
            Environment.GetFolderPath(Environment.SpecialFolder.MyPictures)
        ButtonBrowse.Content = m_curImagePath
        LoadImages()
    End Sub

    Private Sub ButtonBrowse_Click(ByVal sender As System.Object, _
                            ByVal e As System.Windows.RoutedEventArgs) _
                        Handles ButtonBrowse.Click
        Dim folderDialog As System.Windows.Forms.FolderBrowserDialog = _
                        New System.Windows.Forms.FolderBrowserDialog()
        folderDialog.Description = "Select the folder for images."
        folderDialog.SelectedPath = m_curImagePath
        Dim res As System.Windows.Forms.DialogResult = _
                                            folderDialog.ShowDialog()
        If res = System.Windows.Forms.DialogResult.OK Then
            m_curImagePath = folderDialog.SelectedPath
            ButtonBrowse.Content = m_curImagePath
            LoadImages()
        End If
    End Sub

    Private Sub LoadImages()
        Image1.Source = Nothing
        m_imageList = System.IO.Directory.GetFiles(m_curImagePath, "*.jpg")
        m_curIndex = 0
        If m_imageList.Count > 0 Then
            Image1.Source = New System.Windows.Media.Imaging.BitmapImage( _
                            New System.Uri(m_imageList(m_curIndex)))
        End If
    End Sub
```

Now that you have updated your code, it's time to clean up the XAML. First, delete the `Label` and `TextBox` controls and move the button that is currently on the right-hand side of the top section to the left-hand side. Next, bind the window to both sides of the display and expand its size to allow it to display the full path. Of course, this is ugly, which means it will be changed as part of the upcoming UI changes. Next, delete the ShowImages button from the design surface. At this point you could stop, but to help prepare for other design changes you are going to make, review the placement of the Prev and Next buttons. Currently, these buttons are tied to the bottom portion of the grid; instead, get rid of that third grid row definition and center the Prev and Next buttons on the side of the image. At this point, the designer should look similar to what is shown in Figure 17-8.

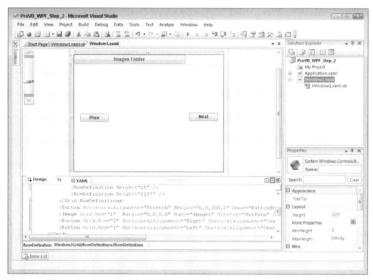

Figure 17-8

This is a much simpler and cleaner interface. The XAML is as follows:

```
<Grid>
    <Grid.RowDefinitions>
        <RowDefinition Height="25" />
        <RowDefinition Height="215*" />
    </Grid.RowDefinitions>
    <Button HorizontalAlignment="Stretch" Margin="0,0,100,2" Name="ButtonBrowse" >
Images Folder</Button>
    <Image Grid.Row="1" Margin="0,0,0,0" Name="Image1" Stretch="Uniform" />
    <Button Grid.Row="1" HorizontalAlignment="Right" Name="ButtonNext"
VerticalAlignment="Center" Margin="0,0,15,8" Width="75">Next</Button>
    <Button Grid.Row="1" HorizontalAlignment="Left" Name="ButtonPrev"
VerticalAlignment="Center" Margin="17,113,0,116" Width="75"> Prev</Button>
    </Grid>
```

This indicates that the `Grid` now has only two row definitions, and the `Image` control was updated to be located in row 1, as were the Prev and Next buttons.

Now you are ready to address the next set of changes to make this application look and behave more like a WPF application. One is to get rid of the "ugly" Windows frame around the application. (Your designer may want to skin this application later, and that frame just won't support the look desired.) Second, the designer wants the Prev and Next buttons modified so that they are circular instead of square and use images instead of text; and just to be consistent, the designer would like those buttons hidden except when the user hovers over them.

Removing the Frame

Removing the Windows frame from your application is actually fairly easy to do, as you only need to set two properties on your form. The first is `WindowStyle`, which is set to `"None"`; the second is `AllowTransparency`, which is set to `"True"`. You can accomplish that by adding the following line before the closing bracket of your window attributes:

```
WindowStyle="None" AllowsTransparency="True">
```

Once you've added this line to your XAML, run the application in the debugger. This is a good point to test not only what happens based on this change, but also the other changes you made to reduce the number of controls in your application. The result is shown in Figure 17-9. You probably notice that there are no longer any controls related to moving, resizing, closing, or maximizing your window. In fact, if you don't start the application within the Visual Studio debugger, you'll need to go to the Task Manager in order to end the process, as you haven't provided any way to end this application through the user interface.

Figure 17-9

In order to be able to skin this application, you need to provide some controls that implement many of the baseline window behaviors that most form developers take for granted. This isn't as hard as it might sound. The main challenge is to add a series of buttons for maximizing and restoring your application window, closing the application, and, of course, resizing the application. Because your designer wants to skin the application, you decide that the best way to handle the resize capability is with a single hotspot in the bottom right corner that represents the resize capability.

However, your first task is to provide a way to move the window. To do that you are going to add a rectangular area that maps to the top `Grid.Row`. This rectangle supports capturing the mouse down event and then responds if the user drags the window with the mouse button down. Because moving the window is essentially a mouse down and drag activity, as opposed to a `click` event, the `Rectangle` is a quick and easy way to implement this feature. It takes only a single line of XAML added as the first control in the grid:

```
<Rectangle Name="TitleBar" HorizontalAlignment="Stretch" Margin="0,0,0,0"
Stroke="Black" Fill="Green" VerticalAlignment="Stretch" />
```

Now, of course, you've filled the default rectangle with a beautiful green color to help with visibility, leaving the black border around the control. These two elements help you see where the rectangle is prior to taking this XAML into a designer and cleaning it up. Aside from this, however, having a control is only half the equation; the other half is detecting and responding to the drag event.

This is done with the following event handler, which is added using VB:

```
Private Sub Rectangle_MouseLeftButtonDown(ByVal sender As Object, _
                    ByVal e As System.Windows.Input.MouseButtonEventArgs) _
                    Handles TitleBar.MouseLeftButtonDown
        Me.DragMove()
End Sub
```

To recap, that's a single line of code in the handler calling the built-in method on the Window base class — `DragMove`. This method handles dragging the window to a new location. Right now the handler only looks for the dragging to occur from a control named `TitleBar`, but you could change this to something else or even change which control was called `Titlebar`.

Having resolved the first issue, you can move to the second: implementing the three buttons required for Minimize, Maximize, and Close. In each case the action required only occurs after a `Click` event. One of the unique characteristics of a button is that it detects a `Click` event, so it is the natural choice for implementing these actions. The buttons in this case should be images, so the first step is to create a few simple images.

Four image references have been added to the example project. Yes, these images are ugly, but the goal here isn't to create flashy design elements. You can literally spend days tweaking minor UI elements, which shouldn't be your focus. The focus here is on creating the elements that can be used in the UI. The color of the buttons, whether the Close button looks like the Windows icon, and so on are irrelevant at this point. What you care about here is providing a button with basic elements that a designer can later customize. As a rule, don't mix design and implementation.

The simplest way for an engineer to create graphics is with the world-famous Paint program. That's right, nothing fancy but reasonably meaningful. Create the four necessary `.jpg` files as 24 × 24 pixel images, and include an image for the resize handle for the window. Next, access the MyProject page and select the Resources tab. Then, select each of your `.jpg` files and add them as Image resources to the project, as shown in Figure 17-10.

Note that Visual Studio automatically places these items in the Resources folder for your project. Next, verify that in the properties for each file, the Build Action property is set to Resource. In order for these resources to be referenced from within your XAML, they need to be designated as resources, not just located in this folder. Now do a complete build of your project so the resources are compiled.

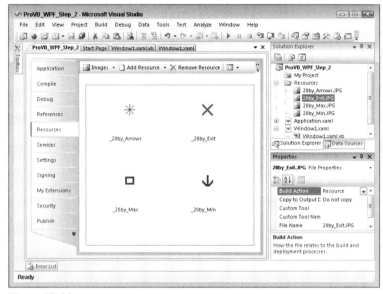

Figure 17-10

At this point you can move back to the XAML designer and add the three buttons for Minimize, Maximize, and Close. For your purposes, they should reside in the upper-right corner of the display and be around the same size as your new graphics. Drag a button onto the design surface and then edit the XAML to place it in the upper-right corner and size it to a height and width of 20 pixels. After doing this, one easy way to proceed is to simply copy that first button and paste two more buttons just like it into the XAML. Then all you need to do is change the button names and locations. Voilà — three buttons.

Of course, your goal is for these buttons to have images on them, so you need to add an Image control to the form and then move it so that it becomes the content for the first button. In this case, just bind the button to the borders of the button and then add a source to the button. Here, the source is the local reference to your .jpg resource, so in the case of ButtonClose, the source value is set to /Resources/20by_Exit.jpg. Add an Image control to the other two buttons and reference the associated resource in order to get the XAML here:

```
<Button Height="20" Width="20" HorizontalAlignment="Right" Margin="0,1,1,0"
                            Name="ButtonClose" VerticalAlignment="Top">
    <Image Margin="0,0,0,0" Name="Image2" Stretch="Fill"
            Source="/Resources/20by_Exit.JPG"/>
</Button>
<Button Height="20" Width="20" HorizontalAlignment="Right" Margin="0,1,25,0"
                            Name="ButtonMax" VerticalAlignment="Top" >
    <Image Margin="0,0,0,0" Name="Image3" Stretch="Fill"
            Source="/Resources/20by_Max.JPG"/>
</Button>
```

```
<Button Height="20" Width="20" HorizontalAlignment="Right" Margin="0,1,47,0"
                              Name="ButtonMin" VerticalAlignment="Top" >
    <Image Margin="0,0,0,0" Name="Image4" Stretch="Fill"
                              Source="/Resources/20by_Min.JPG"/>
</Button>
```

At this point the basic XAML elements needed in order to implement a custom shell on this application are in place. Note that each button has a specific name: ButtonClose, ButtonMax, and ButtonMin. You'll need these, and the design can't change them because you'll use the button names to handle the Click event for each button. In each case, you need to carry out a simple action:

```
Private Sub ButtonMin_Click(ByVal sender As Object, _
                        ByVal e As RoutedEventArgs) _
                        Handles ButtonMin.Click
    Me.WindowState = WindowState.Minimized
End Sub

Private Sub ButtonMax_Click(ByVal sender As Object, _
                        ByVal e As RoutedEventArgs) _
                        Handles ButtonMax.Click
    If (Me.WindowState = WindowState.Maximized) Then
        Me.WindowState = WindowState.Normal
    Else
        Me.WindowState = WindowState.Maximized
    End If
End Sub

Private Sub ButtonClose_Click(ByVal sender As Object, _
                        ByVal e As RoutedEventArgs)
                        Handles ButtonClose.Click
    Me.Close()
End Sub
```

The code is fairly simple. After all, it's not as if the methods you need aren't still available; all you are doing is providing part of the plumbing that will enable your custom UI to reach these methods. Thus, to minimize the button's Click event, merely reset the window state to minimized. The real plumbing, however, was prebuilt for you as part of the way WPF layers controls. Keep in mind that when users click the minimize button, they are actually clicking on an image. WPF routes the Click event that occurred on that image.

When you hear about routed events and how powerful they are, remember that they are a capability built into the way that WPF layers and associates different controls. The routing mechanism in this case is referred to as *bubbling* because the event bubbles up to the parent; however, note that routed events can travel both up and down the control hierarchy.

For the ButtonMax event handler, the code is significantly more complex. Unlike minimizing a window, which has only one action when the button is pressed, the maximize button has two options. The first time it is pressed it takes the window from its current size and fills the display. If it is then pressed again, it needs to detect that the window has already been maximized and instead restore that original size. As a result, this event handler has an actual If statement that checks the current window state and then determines which value to assign.

Finally, the `ButtonClose` event handler has that one line of code that has been with VB developers pretty much since the beginning: `Me.Close`, telling the current window it's time to close. As noted, there isn't much magic here; the actual "magic" occurs with resizing.

Up until this point, changing the default window frame for a set of custom controls has been surprisingly easy. Now, however, if you are working on your own, you are about to hit a challenge. You need a control that will respond to the user's drag action and enable the user to drag the window frame while providing you with updates on that status.

There isn't a tool in the Visual Studio Toolbox for WPF that does this, but there are things such as splitter windows and other resizable controls that have this behavior. WPF was written in such a way that most of what you consider "controls" are actually an amalgamation of primitive single-feature controls. In this case, the primitive you are looking for is called a `Thumb`. The `Thumb` control is a WPF control, and it is located in the `System.Windows.Controls.Primitives` namespace.

Fortunately, you can directly reference this control from within your XAML, and once you have added it to your XAML, handling the events is just as simple as it is with your other custom UI elements. However, this control can't contain another control, and its default look is blank. For the moment, examine the XAML that is used to create an instance of this control on your form:

```
<Thumb Grid.Row="1" Cursor="ScrollAll" Name="ThumbResize" Height="20" Width="20"
HorizontalAlignment="Right" VerticalAlignment="Bottom" Margin="0,0,0,0" />
```

Note a few items of customization. Because the typical location to resize from in most UI models is the lower right corner, this control is placed in the lower right corner and aligned to the bottom and left edges of the bottom grid row. The control itself is sized to match the other buttons used to control the window's behavior. The name `ThumbResize` is used to indicate the control, and in this case the property `Cursor` is set. The `Cursor` property enables you to control the display of the mouse cursor when it moves over the control. There are several options in the enumeration of standard mouse cursors, and for this control arrows are displayed in every direction.

Before you change the default display any further, it makes sense to wire up an event handler. This enables you to test the control's behavior. Just as with the other event handlers, double-clicking on the control in the designer generates a default event handler for the control. In this case, the event to be handled is the `DragDelta` event. As the name implies, this event fires every time the potential size of the display area is changed. There are multiple ways to handle resizing. For this application, having the window redisplay as the user drags the mouse is feasible because the amount of time to update the display is short.

If that weren't the case, then you would want to override two additional events: `DragStarted` and `DragOver`. These events enable you to catch the window's start size and the final size based on the end of the user's action. You would then only resize the form in the `DragOver` event instead of in the `DragDelta` event. You would still need to override `DragDelta` because it is in this event that you monitor whether the window's minimum and/or maximum size constraints have been met:

```
Private Sub ThumbResize_DragDelta(ByVal sender As System.Object, _
                        ByVal e As Primitives.DragDeltaEventArgs) _
                        Handles ThumbResize.DragDelta
    Me.Height += e.VerticalChange
    If (Me.Height < Me.MinHeight) Then
```

```
            Me.Height = Me.MinHeight
        End If
        Me.Width += e.HorizontalChange
        If (Me.Width < Me.MinWidth) Then
            Me.Width = Me.MinWidth
        End If
    End Sub
```

The preceding block of code illustrates the code for this event handler. Notice that in this case the parameter e is specific to the DragDeltaEventArgs structure. This structure enables you to retrieve the current totals for both the vertical and horizontal change of the current drag location from the current window's frame.

This code enables you to see the visible window as the window is dragged because each time the event is fired, the Height and Width of the window are updated with the changes so that the window is resized. Note that this code handles checking the minimum height and width of your window. The code to check for the maximum size is similar. At this point, you can rerun the application to verify that the event is handled correctly and that as you drag the thumb, the application is resized.

Once you have the ThumbResize control working, the next step is to customize the display of this control. Unlike a button or other more advanced controls, this control won't allow you to associate it with an image or have content. As one of the primitive control types, you are limited to working with things such as the background color; and just assigning a color to this control really doesn't meet your needs. Thus, this is an excellent place to talk about another WPF feature: resources.

Resources

Typically, there comes a point where you want to include one or more resources with your application. A resource can be anything, including a static string, an image, a graphics element, and so on. In this case, you want to associate an image with the background of a control that would otherwise not support an image. Resources enable you to set up a more complex structure than just a color that can then be assigned to a control's property. For this simple example you'll create a simple application-level resource that uses an image brush, and then have your control reference this resource.

As noted in the introduction to XAML syntax, the definition for x:Key included the label object. Resources. The implication is that objects of different types can include resources. The scope of a resource, then, is defined by the scope of the object with which it is defined. For a resource that will span your application, you can in fact define that resource within your application XAML. Resources that are to be available within a given window are defined in the XAML file for that window. The following XAML demonstrates adding a resource to the application file of the sample application created earlier:

```
<Application x:Class="Application"
    xmlns="http://schemas.microsoft.com/winfx/2006/xaml/presentation"
    xmlns:x="http://schemas.microsoft.com/winfx/2006/xaml"
        StartupUri="Window1.xaml">
    <Application.Resources>
        <ImageBrush x:Key="ResizeImage"
                               ImageSource="/Resources/20by_Arrows.JPG">
        </ImageBrush>
```

```
        </Application.Resources>
    </Application>
```

Here, you are going to create a new `ImageBrush`. An image brush, as you would expect, accepts an image source and then it "paints" this image onto the surface where it is applied. In the XAML, notice that you assign an `x:Key` value. As far as XAML is concerned, this name is the identity of the resource. Once this has been assigned, other controls and objects within your XAML can reference this resource and apply it to an object or property. Thus, you need to add a reference to this resource to your definition of the `ThumbResize` control. This should result in a change to your XAML similar to this:

```
<Thumb Grid.Row="1" Cursor="ScrollAll" HorizontalAlignment="Right" Height="20"
Background="{StaticResource ResizeImage}" Name="ThumbResize"
Margin="0,0,0,0" Width="20" VerticalAlignment="Bottom" />
```

This change involves what is assigned to the background property of your `Thumb` control. As you look through XAML files, you will often see references to items such as `StaticResources`, and these can become fairly complex when you start to work with a tool such as Blend. However, this example should help you recognize what you are seeing when you look at more complex XAML files. You will also see references to dynamic resources, which are discussed later in this chapter in conjunction with dependency properties.

Resources can be referenced by several different controls and even other resources. However, resources aren't the only, or most maintainable, resource in all instances. Because a resource must be referenced within each object that uses it, it doesn't scale well across several dozen controls. In addition, during maintenance, each time someone edited a XAML file that applied resources to every control, they would also need to be careful to add that resource to any new controls. Fortunately, XAML borrows other resource types based on the basic idea of style sheets. WPF supports other types of resources, including templates and styles, which are discussed later in this chapter. Unlike styles and resources, templates are applied to all objects of the same type. Coverage of templates is beyond the scope of this chapter, but they work similarly to resources except that the settings they define are automatically applied to every control of a given type.

This juncture is an excellent point to test your application. When you start the application, you should see something similar to Figure 17-11. As noted earlier, at this point the application isn't exactly going to win a beauty contest (although the baby might). What you have achieved is a custom framework that enables you to literally treat an application UI as a blank slate, while still providing the standard Windows services that users have come to expect. This is important as you start to create applications that truly push the UI design envelope.

Customizing the Buttons

Your next task is to adjust the buttons in the application. Recall that the `ButtonPrev` and `ButtonNext` controls need to be round and only appear when the mouse is over them. This requires both XAML updates and new event handlers to hide the buttons. The second task results from the fact that when the mouse hovers over a button, Windows automatically changes the color of that button. This is a problem because the graphic guru doesn't want Windows changing the color of elements in the display.

We'll begin with making the current buttons round and changing them to use images instead of text. Making the buttons round in Visual Studio isn't as hard as it sounds. You can clip the button display and thus quickly create a round button. The easiest way to do this is to place the button on a `Panel` control and then clip the display region of the panel. You might be tempted to clip the button or place it within a border region, but neither of these actions will work as expected.

Figure 17-11

What you need to leverage is the capability to layer controls and a `panel` control for each of these buttons. In this case, placing a panel on the display and then telling the panel that its contents have been clipped to fit within a geometric shape enables the clipped control to be displayed with the desired shape. Additionally, when it comes to hiding the button and only showing it when the mouse is over the control, the container is the control you need to detect the `MouseEnter` event. Instead of adding a panel to your application window, you are welcome to try the following: Go to the `ButtonPrev` XAML and set its visibility to `Hidden`. Next, from within the XAML, add a new event handler for the `MouseEnter` event and generate the stub. Within this stub, add a single line of code to make the button visible and set a breakpoint on this line of code.

Now start your application. Do you see any good way of knowing when the mouse is over the area where the control should be? No matter how many times you move across the area where the control should be, your `MouseEnter` event handler isn't called. Similarly, you can stop your application and change the visibility setting on the button from `Hidden` to `Collapsed`. Restart the application. You'll get the same result. In fact, short of attempting to track where the mouse is over your entire application and then computing the current location of the buttons to determine whether the mouse's current position happens to fall in that region, there isn't a good way to handle this aside from adding another control. If you chose to run this experiment, you should remove the reference to the event handler from your XAML — you can leave the button visibility set to either `Hidden` or `Collapsed` — and the event handler code.

The UI trick is that the panel, or in this case the `StackPanel` control that you use, supports true background transparency. Thus, even though it doesn't display, it does register for handling events. Thus, the `StackPanel` acts not only as a way to clip the display area available to the button, but also as the control that knows when the button should be visible. You'll create `MouseEnter` and `MouseLeave` event handlers for the `StackPanel`, and these will then tell `ButtonNext` when to be visible and when to be hidden.

First, add a `StackPanel` control to your display. This stack panel, once it has been added to your design surface, will be easier to manipulate from within the XAML display. Ensure that the `StackPanel` was created in the second grid row. Then ensure that it has both an open and a close tag, and position these tags so they encapsulate your existing `ButtonNext` declaration. At this point, the `ButtonNext` declaration is constrained by the `StackPanel`'s display region. Next, ensure that most of the layout settings previously associated with the button are instead associated with the `StackPanel`:

```
<StackPanel Background="Transparent" Margin="0,0,25,0" Height="75" Width="75"
Name="StackPanelNext" Grid.Row="1" HorizontalAlignment="Right"
VerticalAlignment="Center" >
        <Button Grid.Row="1" Height="75" Width="75" HorizontalAlignment="Center"
VerticalAlignment="Center" Name="ButtonNext" Visibility="Hidden">Next</Button>
</StackPanel>
```

The preceding snippet shows how the `Margin` property that was set on the button is now associated with the `StackPanel`. Similarly, the `StackPanel` has the `VerticalAlignment` and `HorizontalAlignment` settings that were previously defined on the button. The `Button` now places both its vertical and horizontal alignment settings to `Stretch` because it is mainly concerned with filling the available area. Finally, note that both the `ButtonNext` control and the `StackPanelNext` control are given a `Height` and `Width` of 75 pixels, making them square.

Before you address that issue, it makes sense to set up the event handlers to show and hide `ButtonNext`; otherwise, there won't be anything in the display. Within the code you can create an event handler for the `MouseLeave` event and associate it with `Handles StackPanelNext.MouseLeave`. If you previously attempted to capture the `MouseEnter` event with the button itself, you already have that method and all you need to do is add the `Handles` clause to the event definition:

```
Private Sub StackPanelNext_MouseEnter(ByVal sender As System.Object, _
                       ByVal e As System.Windows.Input.MouseEventArgs) _
                       Handles StackPanelNext.MouseEnter
    ButtonNext.Visibility = Windows.Visibility.Visible
End Sub

Private Sub StackPanelNext_MouseLeave(ByVal sender As System.Object, _
                       ByVal e As System.Windows.Input.MouseEventArgs) _
                       Handles StackPanelNext.MouseLeave
    ButtonNext.Visibility = Windows.Visibility.Hidden
End Sub
```

At this point, test your code and ensure that it compiles. If so, make a test run and see whether the button is hidden and reappears as you mouse over the area where it should be located. If everything works, you are almost ready to repeat this logic for `ButtonPrev`. First, however, add the clip region to your `StackPanel` control so that the button displays as a circle instead of as a square.

The `Clip` property wants a geometry for the display region. Creating this requires that you define another object and then assign this object to that property. Since you'll want to report this geometric definition for both buttons, the most efficient way of doing this is to add a resource to your window. Go to the top of your `Window1` XAML, just below the attributes for the window. Add a new XML node for `<Window.Resources></Window.Resources>`. Between the start and end tags, create a new `EllipseGeometry` object. A radius is the distance from the center to the edge of a circle, so define your X and Y radius properties as `34`. This is less than the distance between any edge and the center of your stack panel. Next, center the ellipse on the point `36, 36` — placing it near the center of your `StackPanel` and far enough from the edges that neither radius reaches all the way to one of the edges. The resulting XAML is shown in the following code block:

```
<Window.Resources>
    <EllipseGeometry x:Key="RoundPanel" Center="36, 36" RadiusX="34" RadiusY="34">
</EllipseGeometry>
    </Window.Resources>
```

Define the `Clip` property for your `StackPanel` to reference this new resource. As shown in the sample code, the name for this resource is `RoundPanel`. Then, add the following property definition to your `StackPanelNext` control:

```
Clip="{StaticResource RoundPanel}"
```

Next, add the images that will be used on these buttons. From the Resources tab of the MyProject screen, add two new images: `LeftArrow.jpg` and `RightArrow.jpg`. The images here were created with Microsoft Paint. Of course, both images are also square, but from the standpoint of what will be visible this doesn't matter. Once the images have been loaded, the last step is to add an `Image` control to the `ButtonNext` content, similar to what was done earlier for your Minimize, Maximize, and Close buttons:

```
<Image Margin="0,0,0,0" Stretch="Fill"
                          Source="/Resources/RightArrow.jpg"></Image>
```

Once you have defined this you can then copy the `StackPanel` definition you've set up around `ButtonNext` and replicate it around `ButtonPrev`. You'll need to customize the location settings and then create event handlers for the `StackPanelPrev` mouse events that update the visibility of the `ButtonPrev` control. The code block that follows shows the complete XAML file to this point:

```
<Window x:Class="Window1"
    xmlns="http://schemas.microsoft.com/winfx/2006/xaml/presentation"
    xmlns:x="http://schemas.microsoft.com/winfx/2006/xaml"
    Title="ProVB_WPF" Height="335" Width="415" Name="MainWindow"
    WindowStyle="None" AllowsTransparency="True">
    <Window.Resources>
        <EllipseGeometry x:Key="RoundPanel" Center="36, 36" RadiusX="34" RadiusY="34">
</EllipseGeometry>
    </Window.Resources>
    <Grid>
        <Grid.RowDefinitions>
            <RowDefinition Height="25" />
            <RowDefinition Height="215*" />
        </Grid.RowDefinitions>
        <Rectangle Name="TitleBar" HorizontalAlignment="Stretch" Margin="0,0,0,0"
Stroke="Black" Fill="Green" VerticalAlignment="Stretch" />
        <Button HorizontalAlignment="Stretch" Margin="0,0,130,2" Name="ButtonBrowse"
>Images Folder</Button>
```

```
                <Button Height="20" Width="23" HorizontalAlignment="Right" Margin="0,1,1,0"
Name="ButtonClose" VerticalAlignment="Top">
                    <Image Margin="0,0,0,0" Name="Image2" Stretch="Fill" Source="/Resources/
20by_Exit.JPG"/>
            </Button>
                <Button Height="20" Width="20" HorizontalAlignment="Right" Margin="0,1,25,0"
Name="ButtonMax" VerticalAlignment="Top" >
                    <Image Margin="0,0,0,0" HorizontalAlignment="Center" Name="Image3"
Stretch="Fill" Source="/Resources/20by_Max.JPG"/>
            </Button>
                <Button Height="20" Width="20" HorizontalAlignment="Right" Margin="0,1,47,0"
Name="ButtonMin" VerticalAlignment="Top" >
                    <Image Margin="0,0,0,0" Name="Image4" Stretch="Fill" Source="/Resources/
20by_Min.JPG"/>
            </Button>
            <Image Grid.Row="1"  Margin="0,0,0,0" Name="Image1" Stretch="Uniform" />
                <StackPanel Background="Transparent" VerticalAlignment="Center"
Margin="0,0,25,0" Height="75" Name="StackPanelNext" Grid.Row="1"
HorizontalAlignment="Right" Width="75" Clip="{StaticResource RoundPanel}">
                    <Button Grid.Row="1" HorizontalAlignment="Stretch"
VerticalAlignment="Stretch" Name="ButtonNext" Height="75" Width="75"
Visibility="Hidden">
                        <Image Margin="0,0,0,0" Stretch="Fill" Source="/Resources/
RightArrow.jpg"></Image>
                </Button>
            </StackPanel>
                <StackPanel Background="Transparent" VerticalAlignment="Center"
Margin="25,0,0,0" Height="75" Name="StackPanelPrev" Grid.Row="1"
HorizontalAlignment="Left" Width="75" Clip="{StaticResource RoundPanel}">
                <Button Grid.Row="1" HorizontalAlignment="Left" VerticalAlignment="Center"
Name="ButtonPrev" Height="75" Width="75" Visibility="Hidden">
                        <Image Margin="0,0,0,0" Stretch="Fill" Source="/Resources/↵
LeftArrow.jpg"></Image>
                </Button>
            </StackPanel>
                <Thumb Grid.Row="1" Cursor="ScrollAll"  Background="{StaticResource
ResizeImage}" Height="20" Width="20" HorizontalAlignment="Right" Margin="0,0,0,0"
Name="ThumbResize" VerticalAlignment="Bottom" />
        </Grid>
</Window>
```

Next, test run the application. Figure 17-12 shows the application with the mouse over the Prev button, causing that button to appear.

That completes the steps for the code in the `ProVB_WPF_Step_2` project.

Expression Blend

The remaining task is to enable the mouse cursor to move over one of the buttons without highlighting it. This task illustrates two things about WPF. The first is how styles work. More important, however, this task illustrates a key point: If you want to create a customer user interface with WPF, you need Blend.

As you'll see, it is almost a requirement for you to have Blend in order to accomplish what might on the surface seem like a simple task.

Before proceeding, save a backup copy of your application thus far. The sample code that is provided for download branches at this point, and moving forward the changes that are shown are available from the `ProVB_WPF_Step_3` project.

Figure 17-12

What probably isn't obvious is that every project has an implicit style definition if you don't override it. For example, when you added a button to your form, how did it know that its background should be a gradient silver-like color? Where did those hover over and mouse down effects come from?

Dependency Properties

The answer is that every control is associated with one or more styles. As part of your work, you can create a style just as you created a resource. Styles can be assigned similarly to resources — that is, either by referencing them by name when assigning a new style to an instance of a control, or by creating a style that is associated with all instances of a given type. In either case, the `Style` property of a control is what is known as a *dependency property*.

When you hear the term *dependency* your initial reaction may be that this means the property has a dependency on some other item. However, in the context of WPF, a better way to think of the term *dependency* is that "it depends on who set that specific value in the object that defines that property." A dependency property isn't dependent on some external item; the property's value varies over time depending upon the last update to the property.

Going into the details of why this occurs is beyond the scope of this chapter. However, dependency properties are coupled with change notification logic, and play a significant role in things such as animation and 3-D layout. For the purposes of this chapter, it's only necessary to understand a few things about dependency properties. First, they reference resources and styles as dynamic resources, not static resources. Second, they are identified in the documentation of the WPF components. Finally, as stated already, the `Style` property is in fact a dependency property.

Styles

Styles essentially leverage the concept of resources. With a style you have the option of either referencing all objects of a common type and setting the default style for that control type or creating a custom style that is specific to those control instances that reference it. In short, styles provide a mechanism for you to apply a theme across an application and to override that theme in those specific instances where you want to. If another developer later adds new elements to your application, the default styles are automatically applied.

Styles are defined like resources; in fact, they are defined within the same section of your XAML file in which resources are defined. As with resources, when you define a style at the application level, the style can be applied across all of the windows in the application. Conversely, if a style is meant to target only the objects in a given window, page, or user control, then it makes sense to define them at that level.

Rather than provide a simple example of a style, in this case the goal is to understand where the hover effect for a standard button comes from, so the following code block provides the default style assigned to each control of type `Button`. As you might guess, this style was retrieved using Blend; it isn't available via Visual Studio. With Blend, you can request that it allow you to edit these default templates, and you can do so such that your changes will be used only on those controls for which you explicitly assign your custom style.

```xml
<Style x:Key="ButtonFocusVisual">
  <Setter Property="Control.Template">
    <Setter.Value>
      <ControlTemplate>
        <Rectangle SnapsToDevicePixels="true" Stroke="Black" StrokeDashArray="1 2"
StrokeThickness="1" Margin="2"/>
      </ControlTemplate>
    </Setter.Value>
  </Setter>
</Style>
<LinearGradientBrush x:Key="ButtonNormalBackground" EndPoint="0,1" StartPoint="0,0">
  <GradientStop Color="#F3F3F3" Offset="0"/>
  <GradientStop Color="#EBEBEB" Offset="0.5"/>
  <GradientStop Color="#DDDDDD" Offset="0.5"/>
  <GradientStop Color="#CDCDCD" Offset="1"/>
</LinearGradientBrush>
<SolidColorBrush x:Key="ButtonNormalBorder" Color="#FF707070"/>
<Style x:Key="ButtonStyle1" TargetType="{x:Type Button}">
  <Setter Property="FocusVisualStyle" Value="{StaticResource ButtonFocusVisual}"/>
  <Setter Property="Background" Value="{StaticResource ButtonNormalBackground}"/>
  <Setter Property="BorderBrush" Value="{StaticResource ButtonNormalBorder}"/>
  <Setter Property="BorderThickness" Value="1"/>
  <Setter Property="Foreground" Value="{DynamicResource {x:Static SystemColors.
ControlTextBrushKey}}"/>
  <Setter Property="HorizontalContentAlignment" Value="Center"/>
  <Setter Property="VerticalContentAlignment" Value="Center"/>
  <Setter Property="Padding" Value="1"/>
  <Setter Property="Template">
    <Setter.Value>
      <ControlTemplate TargetType="{x:Type Button}">
```

```
            <Microsoft_Windows_Themes:ButtonChrome SnapsToDevicePixels="true"
x:Name="Chrome" Background="{TemplateBinding Background}" BorderBrush="{
TemplateBinding BorderBrush}" RenderDefaulted="{TemplateBinding IsDefaulted}"
RenderMouseOver="{TemplateBinding IsMouseOver}" RenderPressed="{TemplateBinding
IsPressed}">
                <ContentPresenter SnapsToDevicePixels="{TemplateBinding
SnapsToDevicePixels}" HorizontalAlignment="{TemplateBinding
HorizontalContentAlignment}" Margin="{TemplateBinding Padding}"
VerticalAlignment="{TemplateBinding VerticalContentAlignment}"
RecognizesAccessKey="True"/>
            </Microsoft_Windows_Themes:ButtonChrome>
            <ControlTemplate.Triggers>
                <Trigger Property="IsKeyboardFocused" Value="true">
                  <Setter Property="RenderDefaulted" TargetName="Chrome" Value="true"/>
                </Trigger>
                <Trigger Property="ToggleButton.IsChecked" Value="true">
                  <Setter Property="RenderPressed" TargetName="Chrome" Value="true"/>
                </Trigger>
                <Trigger Property="IsEnabled" Value="false">
                  <Setter Property="Foreground" Value="#ADADAD"/>
                </Trigger>
            </ControlTemplate.Triggers>
        </ControlTemplate>
      </Setter.Value>
    </Setter>
</Style>
```

There are two lines of interest in the preceding code block. The first concerns the actual button style defined. Styles often reference other resources, and similar to early C compilers, references must be defined before they are actually referenced. Thus, the `Style` defined in the preceding code block is actually the last `Style` entry that starts thus:

```
<Style x:Key="ButtonStyle1" TargetType="{x:Type Button}">
```

This line indicates that this set of resources defines a style with the key `ButtonStyle1`. Because this style is defined with a key, it is not a default style applied to all controls of the target type. Styles always define a target type because different control types expect different specific values defined within all of the detailed elements of a style.

To have every control button use the same style, instead of providing a key for the style `ButtonStyle1`, you provide only the type definition. If at some point you want objects of different types to share certain characteristics, this can be done by defining a resource and then applying it to the style for each of the types. If these styles are then designated without a key, then they are by default applied to every object of that type.

All of that is great, but the goal is to find a way to remove the default highlight that occurs as you mouse over a button. The good news is that the hook that causes that behavior is in fact included in this file; the bad news is that it references a template that is then assigned to that behavior. The following line of XAML shows that the `RenderMouseOver` property is being associated with the template `IsMouseOver`:

```
RenderMouseOver="{TemplateBinding IsMouseOver}"
```

It is this template that causes the button to change its look to reflect this state. Thus, to have a button without this default behavior, you need to either define a new template or delete this line of XAML from your custom style.

You could, of course, take the preceding code block, make the necessary change, and paste it into your application's XAML. Certainly that will work if you also carry out the other steps that you need. However, long term, the preceding block of XAML is specific to controls of the type `Button`. Moreover, all of the preceding code was in fact generated from within Blend, so if you needed to customize the runtime behavior of another control type, you would have to find some way to generate the default style for that control.

This is where Blend becomes a requirement. Blend enables you to open your application directly. If, as assumed here, you are using Visual Studio 2008, then you can't open your projects using the current release of Blend. Blend 1.0 targets project files based on the Visual Studio 2005 format. In order to directly open your projects, you must have installed Service Pack 1 for Blend 1.0, which can open Visual Studio 2008 projects.

Normally when you open Blend, you can select any control in your application and generate the XAML for the default style. Blend will automatically integrate this style information into your XAML file, enabling you to proceed efficiently. However, in order to better understand styles, you are going to manually extract some style information generated by Blend for use within Visual Studio 2008.

Figure 17-13 shows the startup screen for Expression Blend. The only reason this screen is being shown is to highlight the fact that, of the three potential tabs in this window, the Samples tab is selected. This tab shows the list of samples that ship with Blend. These samples are not installed on disk with Blend. If you choose to open one of these samples, Blend generates the associated project at that time. What you need to know is that if you then modify anything in that project, even something as simple as adding a space to a XAML file, Blend will ask whether you want to create a copy of that sample on your local disk.

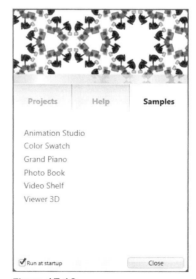

Figure 17-13

Once Blend opens, you are presented with what is probably best described as a rather dark and busy user interface. Fortunately, you can change the coloring. From the Tools menu, select Options. As shown in Figure 17-14, this opens the Options window. The first screen is the Theme setting. Changing this from Expression Dark to Expression Light enables you to see the interface in the same format for which the screens are being captured for this chapter. There don't seem to be any settings to reduce how much information the tool presents at once. In fact, this is one tool that, as these screenshots will demonstrate, isn't actually usable at 1024 × 768.

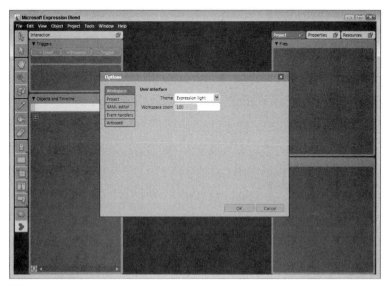

Figure 17-14

Once you've opened the tool, the next step is to open or create a project. Although you have a Visual Studio 2008 project, you'll want to create a new project to follow this demonstration on the default styling of a button. Use the File menu and select a new project. When the New Project dialog opens, you have the option to select a language, but because you only care about the XAML that will be generated, it doesn't matter which language or project name you select.

Once you have a new project, the main display area presents a clean white canvas, as shown in Figure 17-15. In order to add a button to this canvas, ensure that the Button control is selected in the toolbar. Unlike the Visual Studio toolbar, which lists each control, Blend groups the controls by category, from which you select a control. When you want to add that control to your display, you first click and hold the mouse button on that category to open the list of controls for that category. You then verify or select the control you wish to create.

Once you have selected the control, it displays above that category in the toolbar. You then take your mouse and draw that control onto your form. The Blend interface is not a drag and drop interface for adding controls. For this example, you'll select the button control and then draw that control onto your user interface.

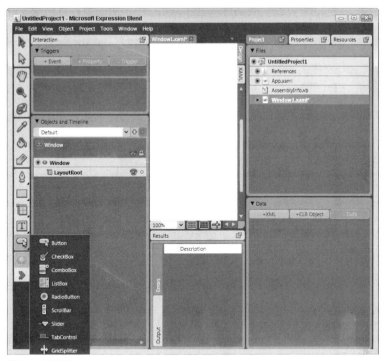

Figure 17-15

Notice that unlike the Visual Studio editor that places both the design surface and the source XAML in the same display, Blend has room for only one of these surfaces. On the right-hand side of the display are the tabs that enable you to move between the design surface and the source XAML. You could edit a complete XAML file through this interface, but for now the only goal is to generate and retrieve the default style information associated with your control. Therefore, once you've added your button to this display, the next step is to ensure that it is selected on the design surface.

After you've added a button to your display surface, as shown in Figure 17-16, it is time to look for the XAML associated with the default style of that button. To generate this XAML, you need to first ensure that the control is selected. Next, as shown in Figure 17-16, open the Object menu, select the Edit Style menu option, and then select the Edit a Copy menu option.

Once you have selected this menu item, you'll be taken to the Create Style Resource dialog shown in Figure 17-17. This dialog enables you to customize the type of style declaration that is generated and to determine what level of scope this resource should have.

As Figure 17-17 shows, when you generate your style to include a key, it is specific to those controls that reference it. However, you can choose to generate a style that applies to all instances of a given control. The other option allows you to generate a resource that is defined at and within your application scope. The default is to create a resource at the level of the current window. Both of these options are acceptable;

however, the designers of Blend foresaw that in the case of very large projects these files could start to become extremely large and unwieldy. As a result, Blend allows you to create a resource dictionary as part of your project.

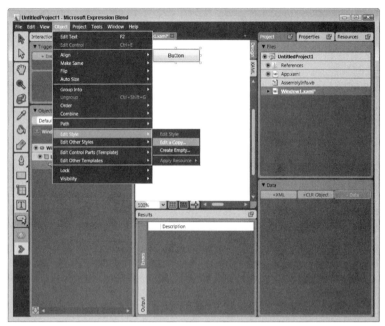

Figure 17-16

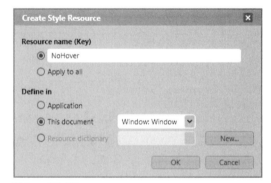

Figure 17-17

In short, you can choose to create a new file that is referenced by either your application or window XAML file, and that contains and isolates your custom style and other resource definitions. The advantages of this method include not only a smaller file size for your key files, but the capability to separate the different resources into different files for scenarios in which multiple people are working on the same project. For example, one designer could work on customizing the style for buttons while another person is customizing the style of the drop-down lists.

For this example, call the new style NoHover and click OK. Once you complete this dialog, Blend generates the same style definition that was included earlier. You'll need to use the XAML tab, shown earlier in Figure 17-16, to switch to the source view; and just as you've seen previously when you created a resource manually, Blend adds all of the XAML for your default button behavior into this file.

Copy this text from Blend and return to Visual Studio. In Visual Studio, paste the text from Blend directly into the XAML for Window1.XAML. This places the new style definition into your project and immediately triggers an error. Typically when this is generated, and in fact in the sample project you just created in Blend, the Blend engine takes care of hooking your custom style into the project. The first step in this process is adding a reference to the classes that define that style. Thus, you need to add a new reference to your project. Figure 17-18 shows the MyProject References page with a newly added reference.

Figure 17-18

The reference at the project level to the PresentationFramework.Aero libraries allows you various source files to reference this library. However, there is still one more step. You need to reference this library from within the XAML for Window1. Go to the definition of the window and its attributes at the top of your XAML file and add another xmlns, also known as an *XML namespace declaration*:

```
<Window x:Class="Window1"
    xmlns="http://schemas.microsoft.com/winfx/2006/xaml/presentation"
    xmlns:x="http://schemas.microsoft.com/winfx/2006/xaml"

    xmlns:Microsoft_Windows_Themes="clr-namespace:Microsoft.Windows.Themes;
assembly=PresentationFramework.Aero"

    Title="ProVB_WPF" Height="335" Width="415" Name="MainWindow"
    WindowStyle="None" AllowsTransparency="True">
```

The highlighted line is the line that needs to be added to your source file. Once this line is added you'll find that the XAML errors that occurred when you pasted the new style definition into your window go away. This is the same reference that you added to your project, but in this case you are defining for the XML compiler where to find things such as the definition for Chrome. As with the project reference, Blend typically handles this automatically for you.

At this point there is only one more manual step in this process. Although you've added a new style to your project, you haven't referenced that style anywhere. For the purpose of this version, you are just going to add that style definition to the ButtonBrowse definition. Doing so works just like other resources you've referenced, but in this case the assignment to the Style property is for a dynamic resource:

```
        <Button Style="{DynamicResource NoHover}" HorizontalAlignment="Stretch"
    Margin="0,0,130,2" Name="ButtonBrowse" >Images Folder</Button>
```

You should then be able to compile and run the application and get a result similar to what is shown in Figure 17-19. Notice that many of the graphics have been updated to be less stark, and include some basic color gradients. I did this by closing Visual Studio and reopening the project in Blend. Just as with Visual Studio, you can open the solution file for ProVB_WPF_Step_3. Blend displays your project on the right-hand side, in a window just like the Visual Studio Solution Explorer, although the tab is named Project. Open your Window1.xaml file. On the right-hand side you'll see the tree that represents the controls used in your XAML.

Figure 17-19

Selecting, for example, the button, you want to then select the Properties tab, which is located next to your Project tab. Once you have opened this, you have access to many of the display properties of your control. In the case of ButtonBrowse, I modified its background brush to be transparent. I did this by first selecting the Brushes section and then selecting the background. I then made certain that a solid brush was selected from the row of buttons so that I would see the color selector. There are four color options: Red, Green, and Blue (RGB) are self-explanatory. The remaining value is the A channel, which reflects transparency. Setting this to 100 means that you can't see through that item; setting this to 0 means that a given value is invisible.

I set the button background to be transparent, and then repositioned it to be centered better in the title bar. Next, I selected that rectangle called Title Bar to edit its display properties. I went to the brushes section of the Properties again, but this time I selected a gradient brush for the background. This results in the color display, but below it you have what looks similar to the ruler in Word. The ruler in Word is where you manage page elements such as page borders and tabs, and setting gradient colors works similarly.

On the left side of the toolbar is a little tag; if you drag this tag to the right, the default black color continues and the gradient section of the display decreases. Similarly, on the right-hand side of the display is a tag is associated with white. To change the default colors, you select that tag and then edit the color resources, just as you edit the A channel for transparency, only this time you focus on the RGB values. However, a gradient brush isn't limited to two color tags; in the ProVB_WPF_Step_3 project, the left corner of the title bar is green and the right side is blue.

To replicate this requires four tags on your gradient bar, and to add those tags you simply click on the bar. Just like adding tabs in Word, you can easily define additional color transition points. By defining the two inner tags as white and adjusting their position near the edges of the ButtonBrowse display, you can create a white background for the button while creating a gradient on either side of the title bar.

For the three control buttons, I first created a blue gradient background for each button. However, because the buttons actually display images, this background isn't visible, so I expanded each button and selected the image associated with the display of that button. Each image has an opacity property. The opacity property is another way of referencing the A channel for the color system, and by reducing the opacity from 100 percent to 50 percent, the blue background for each button is visible. The result is a version of the application that matches the final code in ProVB_WPF_Step_3 and looks similar to what is shown in Figure 17-19.

The next step is to separate out the custom window framework that was the focus of the ProVB_WPF_Step_2 project created earlier in this chapter. This can act as a base set of application classes that can be reused across multiple different applications. You can leverage the main application in Window1 just for managing your window and take the logic associated with its contents for displaying images and move that into a user control.

WPF User Controls

As for the specific controls available in WPF, you've seen in this chapter that several are available, although even those like the button that seem familiar may not work as expected. The fact is that WPF controls need to fit a different paradigm than the old Windows Forms model. In that model, a control could be associated with data, and in some cases undergo minor customization to its look and feel. Under WPF, the concept of a grid is used. It isn't, however, similar to the old Windows Forms DataGridView in any way. The WPF grid is a much more generic grid that enables you to truly customize almost everything about its behavior.

Part of the goal of WPF is to make it immaterial which environment your application will work in, Web or desktop. For example, consider a couple of the bottom-layer elements. The one used most in this chapter is the Window control. As demonstrated in the first ProVB_WPF example, a window includes a frame and a title in addition to its content area. You might want to apply a layout grid or a panel — for example, a stack panel — within this content area. Conversely, you could take a different tack and place a user control within this window. In fact, in most cases this is the recommended path because of the other low-level WPF element — the `Page`.

A `Page` control is, of course, the base UI element for a Web application, so it's easy to see how this paradigm of the content area can support the layering of two different user-interface implementations. Once you have defined the base elements of your user interface you can leverage user controls, which are equally happy on the desktop or in the browser. Of course, creating applications that flexible is a bit more challenging, unless you are leveraging services. In other words, instead of targeting the file system, you would target a service that might be local or remote and that would be focused on the appropriate file system. Then the application is running on a local computer. It can encapsulate the pages in a `Window` control; and when hosted in a browser, it can use those same user controls within the framework of a `Page`.

Aside from some standard user interface controls, the WPF Toolbox contains nearly all of the controls that you can find in every other Windows-based user interface model, such as tabs, toolbars, tooltips, text boxes, drop downs, expanders, and so on. It should also be noted that the WPF namespace consists of several graphics, ink, and even data and data-bound controls.

Accordingly, the key to working with WPF is taking these basic controls and using WPF user control projects to create the building blocks that you will then use to create your custom user interfaces. If the example in this chapter demonstrated anything, it is how time consuming making changes to the XAML can be.

Summary

A good exercise moving forward with the demonstration code from this chapter is to combine this code with the Photo Book example provided with Blend. You could combine these elements for a dynamic page-turning image viewer. The Photo Book sample application includes an excellent user control, `Photobook.xaml`, that encapsulates the page-turning effect. Of course, that control is currently implemented to reference local resources, and the application relies on the Windows default frame. The challenge isn't just to leverage this control but to enhance it, to perhaps leverage the full `Windows.Media.MediaPlayer` control so that you could display not only saved images but also recordings.

This chapter focused on familiarizing you with WPF and XAML. WPF implements a new application development paradigm for user interfaces. You can start designing and planning the next versions of your applications to use these new controls. Keep in mind that this single chapter hasn't covered all the new features you can potentially leverage with WPF — that would require an entire book. Instead, you should now have an understanding of the base principals of the WPF programming model and how it integrates with Visual Basic.

WPF is the user interface paradigm of the future for .NET developers. However, while the graphic support is more powerful, certain elements of this model require you to handle more of what traditionally was thought of as standard window behavior. It is hoped that this chapter has clarified several key concepts that you need to know when working with WPF:

❏   XAML is a declarative standard for defining your user interface.

❏   WPF-based applications leverage traditional programming languages such as Visual Basic.

❏   WPF separates the UI creator from the business logic developer.

❏   Creating the custom window behaviors, while sometimes required, is not especially difficult.

❏   Visual Basic is uniquely positioned with literal XML strings to dynamically generate and display XAML elements as part of your application.

❏   Blend is a required tool if you are trying to design a custom user interface that includes custom display characteristics.

This chapter focused on the WPF libraries within the context of building new applications. At this point you are probably wondering about your existing applications. Chapter 18 continues working with the WPF libraries, but looks at how to leverage WPF elements in an existing application.

18

Integrating WPF and Windows Forms

Windows Presentation Foundation (WPF) was introduced in the preceding chapter as Microsoft's next-generation solution to graphical user-interface development. In terms of user interfaces, the transition to this new model will be similar in significance and paradigm shift to the shift from COM-based Visual Basic to Visual Basic .NET. In other words, the paradigms and syntax familiar to developers of Windows applications are changing, and most of the changes are not backwardly compatible. Currently, there are no plans for an automated migration from any existing user-interface paradigm, forms, or Web, to the new WPF format.

You will need to transition existing application source code to a new technology paradigm. Perhaps not this year or next, but at some point the WPF paradigm will be used to update the look and feel of existing applications. How will this transition compare to the last major .NET-related transition — the one from COM? The original version of Visual Studio .NET included a tool to aid in migrating code from the COM-based world to .NET. No migration tool will be provided to transition existing user interfaces to WPF, which should be considered a good thing, considering the history of the current migration tools.

Instead, Microsoft learned the lesson that migration is both difficult and time consuming and is best done at the developer's pace. This is seen in the new Power Pack tools for Visual Basic, which Microsoft first released in 2006. These tools, which are now on version 2.0, are covered in Appendix B and are similar in concept to the interop methodology that Microsoft has chosen to follow with WPF. Microsoft is providing libraries that enable user-interface developers to integrate these two interface models. In the long run, this integration will probably go the way of COM-Interop, which is to say it will be available but carry such a stigma that people will only use it when absolutely necessary.

This chapter takes you through several key areas of Windows Forms integration, including the following:

- ❏ The Integration Library — code-named Crossbow
- ❏ Using WPF controls in Windows Forms

❑　Using Windows Forms controls in WPF

❑　Interop limitations

The focus of this chapter is how to use these libraries to best enable you to both leverage WPF with your existing code and leverage your existing code and related Forms-based code with your new WPF applications. Just as with COM-Interop, the point of this tool is to help you, the developer, transition your application from Windows Forms to WPF over time, while working with time and budget constraints that all developers face and potentially waiting on the availability of a control that isn't available in WPF.

The Integration Library

Crossbow was the code name for the project to provide a library that enables WPF applications to host Windows Forms controls and vice versa. The Crossbow project's focus was to provide a .NET library that developers could leverage; what it created was the `WindowsFormsIntegration` library. `WindowFormsIntegration.dll` supports the `Windows.Forms.Integration` namespace. This namespace provides the tools necessary for using WPF and Windows Forms in a single application. At the core of this namespace are the two classes `ElementHost` and `WindowsFormHost`. These two classes provide for interoperability in the WPF and the Windows Forms environment, respectively.

With Visual Studio 2008, the `WindowsFormsIntegration.dll` is located with the other .NET library classes and is imported like any other common namespace. It's the last item in the list of .NET references for most Windows Forms applications. Once it's imported, you'll find that the appropriate control class
for your project type — `ElementHost` or `WindowsFormHost` — is available in its respective designer.

The next step in looking at this library is to review a list of the classes and the delegate that make up the `Windows.Forms.Integration` namespace:

Class	Description
`ChildChangedEventArgs`	This class is used when passing event arguments to the `ChildChanged` event. This event occurs on both the `WindowsFormsHost` and `ElementHost` classes when the content of the `Child` property is changed.
`ElementHost`	This is the core class for embedding WPF controls within Windows Forms. Using the `Child` property, you identify the top-level object (probably some type of panel) that will be hosted, and via this object define an area that will be controlled by that object. The object referenced by the host can contain other controls, but the host references only this one.
`IntegrationExceptionEventArgs`	This is the base class for the `Integration` and `Property Mapping` exception classes. It provides the common implementation used by these classes.
`LayoutExceptionEventArgs`	This class enables you to return information related to a Layout error within a host class to the hosting environment, Windows Forms, or WPF.

Class	Description
PropertyMap	A property on each of the host classes. It provides a way for a Windows Form to handle a change that occurs to one of the properties of a hosted control — for example, if the size of the ElementHost control has changed and the form needs to carry out some other action due to this change. The same capability exists for WPF applications hosting a WindowsFormHost control.
PropertyMappingExceptionEventArgs	Similar to the layout exception class, this enables a hosted control to return information related to an exception to the hosting environment.
WindowsFormsHost	This is the primary control when a WPF application wants to host Windows Forms controls. Similar to ElementHost, the actual Windowsformshost object contains only a single child — typically, a user control. This control can then contain an array of controls, but it is this class that acts as the virtual Windows Form that is referencing the user control.
PropertyTranslator	This is the only delegate in this namespace. It is used within your Visual Basic code to enable you to translate properties from a WindowsFormsHost control to a WPF ElementHost control (and vice versa). Essentially, you provide it with the property to be updated and the value to update that property with, and this method passes that value across the boundary from one UI model to the other. It works in conjunction with the PropertyMap class.

These classes enable your application to host controls within its display area. As noted, when you add the appropriate host class to your display area, the host class contains a child control. Each host contains only a single child control. The 1-to-1 relationship enables the integration library to assign the display area allocated to the host directly to the child and not be concerned with maintaining positioning multiple children but instead be focused on a single target child. Thus, when you assign a control to a WindowsFormsHost, behind the scenes the Margin, Docking, AutoSizing, and Location properties of the WindowsFormsHost control are automatically applied to the Child control. The host controls don't contain a great deal of logic on the workings of what they are hosting; instead, they just act as an interop layer. The properties of the child are controlled via the host, and that control can, via user controls and panels, act as a native host for the other controls that you want to display within the host control.

Similar to the WindowsFormsHost, the ElementHost control automatically controls the display characteristics associated, including the following properties: Height, Width, Margin, HorizontalAlignment, and VerticalAlignment. In both cases, the host control acts as the virtual display area for the hosted control, and you should manage that display area via the host control, not the child it contains. Even though both controls are targeted at area controls such as user controls and panels, their purpose is to access controls and features across the UI display models.

Hosting WPF Controls in Windows Forms

Hosting WPF controls within your existing Windows Forms–based applications enables you to introduce new functionality that requires the capabilities of WPF without forcing you to entirely rewrite your application. This way, even as you work on upgrading an existing application to WPF, you aren't forced to take on a single large project. As for the integration itself, it isn't page- or window-based, although you can introduce new WPF windows to an existing application. The integration is focused on enabling you to incorporate new user controls into your existing Windows Forms application.

Accordingly, the model is based around the idea that you can encapsulate the functionality of a set of WPF UI features as a user control. This has a couple of key advantages, the first being that if you've been working with .NET, you are already familiar with user controls and how they function. Once again, the paradigms of previous user-interface models appear and are reused within WPF. The second big advantage to modeling this around user controls is that as more of your application moves to WPF, you don't have to rewrite the user controls you create today when later they are used within a pure WPF environment.

With this goal in mind of creating a control that can later be moved from being hosted within a Windows Form application to running unchanged within a WPF application, you can turn your attention to creating a sample solution.

Creating a WPF Control Library

The first step is to open Visual Studio 2008 and go to the New Project dialog. From here, select the Windows category of Templates and create a new Windows Forms application. For example purposes, you can name this ProVBWinForm_Interop. As discussed in Chapter 13, Visual Studio uses the template to create a new Windows Forms project, and you can accept the default of targeting .NET 3.5. At this point, using the File menu, add a second project to your solution.

Again select the Windows category of Templates and create a new WPF user control library. For demonstration purposes, use the name WpfInteropCtrl. When you are done, the Visual Studio Solution Explorer will look similar to what is shown in Figure 18-1. The next step is to add the customization to the newly created WPF library, after which the Windows Form application will be updated to reference the integration library and the new WPF user control.

The first customization is to the grid, which is by default in the display area. For this example, you will change the background color of the grid that fills your control's display. You will also add a new Image control to the grid and bind it to the edges using the margin property, not the height or width properties.

The complete XAML is shown in the following code block:

```
<UserControl x:Class="UserControl1"
    xmlns="http://schemas.microsoft.com/winfx/2006/xaml/presentation"
    xmlns:x="http://schemas.microsoft.com/winfx/2006/xaml"
    Height="300" Width="300">
    <Grid Background="LightSteelBlue">
            <Image Margin="10,10,10,10" Name="Image1" />
    </Grid>
</UserControl>
```

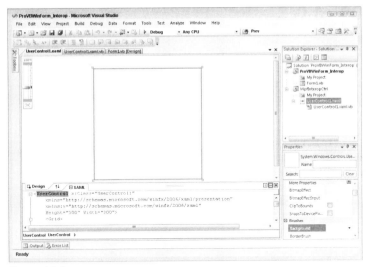

Figure 18-1

Now that you have completed your work in XAML, it's time for some code to accompany your control. As you can imagine, this WPF control is fairly simple in that you merely want it to display an image. This means you need a property that represents the path to the image to be displayed, some logic to load that image, the capability to respond to changes in size, and, for the purposes of custom code, the capability to prevent increasing the size of the image beyond its original size.

To meet these requirements you add a public property Image to your control that represents the path to the image that will be loaded. Within the Set logic for this property, you load the image. As noted in the following code block, the internal value has been set to a specific picture, but to be thorough, take a minute to review the accessors.

The Get and Set property accessors have been defined, with the Set accessor being customized. Note that after assigning the path for the current image to the internal value, this accessor then creates a new local image object and attempts to load the selected image path as a bitmap. WPF comes with converters for several common image types, but because this is demo code, no real checking is done to ensure the validity of the path passed in.

Thus, this logic is located within a Try-Catch block, and if the image load fails, the image value in the control is set to nothing. However, if a valid image path is provided, then the code loads the image and calls the local ResizeMargins method to handle adding margins based on the size of the image. Similarly, the SizeChanged event has been handled in this code, and it calls the same private method to ensure that the image is not stretched beyond its original size:

```
<UserControl x:Class="UserControl1"
Class UserControl1
    ' The default directory and image path are native to Windows Vista.
    ' On other operating systems select an appropriate directory.
    Private m_Image As String = _
            "C:\Users\Public\Pictures\Sample Pictures\Green Sea Turtle.jpg"

    Public Property Image() As String
```

```
            Get
                Return m_Image
            End Get
            Set(ByVal value As String)
                m_Image = value
                Dim image As BitmapImage
                Try
                    image = New Windows.Media.Imaging.BitmapImage( _
                       New Uri("file:///" + m_Image))
                    ' Add path validation prior to loading the selected file...
                    Image1.Source = image
                    ' Resize Margins if appropriate
                    ResizeMargins(image)
                Catch
                    Image1.Source = Nothing
                    Return
                End Try
            End Set
        End Property


        Private Sub UserControl1_SizeChanged(ByVal sender As Object, _
                            ByVal e As System.Windows.SizeChangedEventArgs) _
                            Handles Me.SizeChanged
            If Image1.Source IsNot Nothing Then
                ResizeMargins(CType(Image1.Source, _
                                        Windows.Media.Imaging.BitmapImage))
            End If
        End Sub


        Public Sub ResizeMargins(ByVal image As Windows.Media.Imaging.BitmapImage)
            ' ActualHeight and ActualWidth represent the size of the image control
            ' whether margin is set or not. If the actual size is greater than the
            ' size of the image reset margins to the max size of the image.
            Dim imgH As Double = image.Height
            Dim ctrlH As Double = Me.ActualHeight
            Dim marginHorizontal As Double
            If imgH > ctrlH Then
                marginHorizontal = 0
            Else
                marginHorizontal = (ctrlH - imgH) / 2
            End If

            Dim imgW As Double = image.Width
            Dim ctrlW As Double = Me.ActualWidth
            Dim marginSide As Double
            If imgW > ctrlW Then
                marginSide = 0
            Else
                marginSide = (ctrlW - imgW) / 2
            End If
            Image1.Margin = New Thickness(marginSide, marginHorizontal, _
                                    marginSide, marginHorizontal)
        End Sub
    End Class</UserControl>
```

The remaining custom code is in fact the `ResizeMargins` method. This method is reasonably simple. It takes the size of the image itself and compares this to the size of the control `Image1`. Note that this code references the `ActualHeight` property. Unlike the `Height` property, which for controls that are docked doesn't provide a valid size, the `ActualHeight` property reflects the current size of the `Image1` control. If the control size is larger than the original size of the image, then the code adjusts the margins to fill in around the image.

This completes the definition of your sample WPF control library, so compile your application to ensure that no errors are pending.

The Windows Forms Application

The next step is to customize the Windows Forms application. Begin by adding the five required references that enable you to embed and manipulate this control. They are the four framework libraries — `Windows.Forms.Integration`, `PresentationCore`, `PresentationFramework`, and `WindowsBase` — and a project reference to your custom `WpfInteropCtrl` library. Open the project properties for your `ProVBWinForm_Interop` project and go to the References tab.

Choose Add References, and in the list of available .NET libraries you'll find all four framework references available. Other presentation libraries are also available from this screen, and depending on what you intend to do in your application you can choose to add other library references to your project as well. Finally, switch to the Project References tab and add a reference to your local project.

Laying Out Controls on the Form

Now go to the Design mode for the `Form1.vb` file that was created by the Windows Forms template when you created this project. Extend the default size of the design surface with the size of your control in mind, allocating enough room to align three rows of Windows Forms controls above your custom user control.

Starting at the top, you are going to add a new `Button` control to the upper-right corner of the display. The label on this button will be "Select Folder," and the button should be resized to display its full size. Next, add a `FolderBrowserDialog` control to your window; this control doesn't have a display element and will be shown below your form. Now add a `Label` control below your button and change its display text to "Image:". Once this is in place, add a `ComboBox` control to the right of this label. Accept the default name of `ComboBox1` and specify that this control should expand as the form widens.

Next, add a `Label` control to the right of your button, and use the text "Mask:". To the right of the "Mask:" label, add a new combo box, `ComboBox2`, in the sample code. Go to the context menu for this `ComboBox` and select Edit Items to open the edit window. Within this screen add the three options that will make up the image mask options: No Mask, Ellipse, and Rectangle. Ensure that this control is also bound to the form's width.

Below the image `ComboBox`, in a third row on your Windows Form. add a `Label` control with the text "Margin:" and a `TextBox` control with the name `TextBoxMargin`. Set the default value for this `TextBox` to 10 and limit its length to 4 characters in the properties display. Similarly, alongside this text box, add another `Label` control with the text "Corner Radius," and a second `TextBox` control called `TextBoxRounding`. Set the default value for this second text box to 50.

At this point, add the `ElementHost` control to your form. Your first reaction might be to drag and drop your `UserControl1` directly onto the form surface. Doing this will appear to work until the first time you run your project, at which point an error will occur in the designer. This may be repaired in a future release, but for now the correct step is to go to the Toolbox and drag and drop the control `ElementHost1` onto your form. Resize the control to fill up the area in the display. Next, drag and drop your custom `UserControl1` onto the display area of `ElementHost1` and use the control's context menu to have it dock with the parent container.

The design view for `Form1` should look similar to the one shown in Figure 18-2. Note the expanded Properties pane. This is currently set to display/edit the properties for `ElementHost1`, focusing on its reference to the user control.

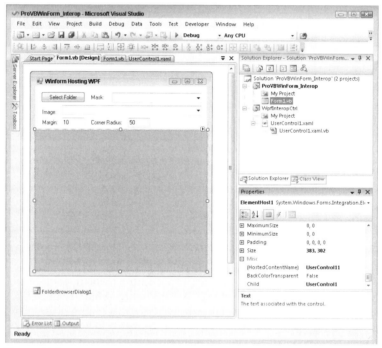

Figure 18-2

Adding Custom Code to the Form

The next step is to add some custom code to this form. The form will allow you to select a folder containing images and then display any of those images. Additionally, you will have the capability to place a mask over the image to provide a custom "frame" around the displayed image. The goal is to demonstrate not only adding a control, but also a scenario in which you need to map one of the `ElementHost`'s properties within your code.

The next listing provides the basis for your customization. The first item is to hold onto the current directory path. The private value is defined on the form class, and a default path for images on Vista is assigned to this property. Next, the `Load` event for the form is handled. Within the `Load` event the code will get the list of files from the default directory and then load `ComboBox1` with this list of files. It will select the first file from the list, and then ensure that no mask is selected. Finally, the sample code calls the method `AddPropertyMapping`. This call is currently commented on, and you will uncomment it after the reason for mapping a property is illustrated.

The next method shown in this code block is the event handler for the button's `Click` event. This event handler opens a folder browsing dialog using the control `FolderBrowserDialog1`. It uses the current path as the default for this dialog, and if the user selects a new directory for images, it loads the new list of files into the `ComboBox`. Note that it doesn't change the selected image, so a user won't see a new image automatically displayed when the list of files is loaded.

```vb
Public Class Form1
    ' The default directory path is native to Windows Vista.
    ' On other operating systems select an appropriate directory.
    Private m_path As String = "C:\Users\Public\Pictures\Sample Pictures"
    Private Sub Form1_Load(ByVal sender As System.Object, _
                        ByVal e As System.EventArgs) _
                        Handles MyBase.Load

        For Each filename As String In System.IO.Directory.GetFiles(m_path)
            ComboBox1.Items.Add(filename)
        Next
        ComboBox1.SelectedIndex = 0
        Me.ComboBox2.SelectedIndex = 0

        'AddPropertyMapping()
    End Sub

    Private Sub Button1_Click(ByVal sender As System.Object, _
                            ByVal e As System.EventArgs) _
                            Handles Button1.Click
        FolderBrowserDialog1.SelectedPath = m_path
        If (FolderBrowserDialog1.ShowDialog() = _
                                Windows.Forms.DialogResult.OK) Then
            If Not m_path = FolderBrowserDialog1.SelectedPath Then
                m_path = FolderBrowserDialog1.SelectedPath
                ComboBox1.Items.Clear()
                For Each filename As String In _
                                    System.IO.Directory.GetFiles(m_path)
                    ComboBox1.Items.Add(filename)
                Next
            End If
        End If
    End Sub

    Private Sub ComboBox1_SelectedIndexChanged( _
                ByVal sender As System.Object, ByVal e As System.EventArgs) _
                Handles ComboBox1.SelectedIndexChanged
        Dim x As WpfInteropCtrl.UserControl1 = _
                    CType(ElementHost1.Child, WpfInteropCtrl.UserControl1)
        x.Image = ComboBox1.SelectedItem.ToString
    End Sub
End Class
```

Finally, the preceding code includes the `SelectedIndexChanged` event handler, which is called when a user selects a new item from the list of available image files. This event handler retrieves the selected image path and passes this path to the child of the `ElementHost1` control. Because the child object is in fact an instance of the class `WpfInteropCtrl.UserControl`, the generic child property can be cast to this object, which supports the public property defined as part of the user control's definition, discussed earlier.

At this point, if you are following along with the text, you should save, build, and run your project. The project will work, although to be honest at this point it isn't doing too much. It illustrates that you can, in fact, host classes from the `System.Windows.Controls` namespace in an `ElementHost` control.

Custom Display Masking

The next part of this demonstration involves altering the display of the `ElementHost` content based on code located within the Windows form. Accordingly, the next block of code uses a geometric shape to overlay a mask above the selected display, making it possible to round the corners or the entire image. The application of the mask occurs based on the second `ComboBox` control that was added to the form.

This control was assigned three values, and when one of the values is selected, it triggers the `ComboBox2`.`SelectedIndexChanged` event, which has been handled in this code. The code follows a best practice and calls a private method that implements the appropriate action based on which value was selected. The method `ApplyMask` uses a `Select Case` statement to identify which of the three fixed maps has been selected and then either disables the clipping region or enables a clipping region of the appropriate shape.

The clipping region is a WPF property available on WPF controls. The `Clip` property enables you to overlay a given control with a geometric shape that masks out portions of the targeted control. This example implements two simple masks: an ellipse and a rectangle. Selecting to not have a mask sets the `Clip` property for the `Child` object within the control `ElementHost1` to `Nothing`. However, selecting a mask to screen out a portion of the display results in the code calling one of a pair of methods, `EllipseMask` and `RectMask`, each of which is focused on a single geometric shape.

These two methods share the majority of their logic, first getting the available display area from `ElementHost1`'s `Child` property. Both then use the `TextBoxMargin` to allow the user to change the size of the margin surrounding the clip region. Note that in both cases the margin isn't applied in the same manner as setting a margin in WPF was.

Under WPF, a `Margin` property is defined as a thickness or distance between the edge of the control and the edge of the display for each of the four sides. Thus, both the left and right or top and bottom values are the same. However, in the case of a clipping region, the code is defining the size of a rectangle. Thus, the size of the rectangle needs to account for the fact that moving the top of the image 10 pixels lower means that the box needs to be 20 pixels smaller on the length of the side so that the 10 pixels from the top balance the 10 matching pixels on the bottom. This is why the margin is doubled when describing the height and width and not doubled when defining the upper-left corner location.

```
Private Sub ComboBox2_SelectedIndexChanged(ByVal sender As System.Object, _
                              ByVal e As System.EventArgs) _
                              Handles ComboBox2.SelectedIndexChanged
        ApplyMask()
End Sub

Private Sub ApplyMask()
```

```vb
        Select Case ComboBox2.SelectedIndex
            Case 0
                ElementHost1.Child.Clip = Nothing
                TextBoxMargin.Enabled = False
                TextBoxRounding.Enabled = False
            Case 1
                EllipseMask()
                TextBoxMargin.Enabled = True
                TextBoxRounding.Enabled = False
            Case 2
                RectMask()
                TextBoxMargin.Enabled = True
                TextBoxRounding.Enabled = True
            Case Else
                ' An error has occurred. Pick the top entry and try again...
                ComboBox2.SelectedIndex = 0
        End Select
    End Sub

    Private Sub EllipseMask()
        Dim width As Double = ElementHost1.Child.RenderSize.Width
        Dim height As Double = ElementHost1.Child.RenderSize.Height
        Dim margin As Double = Convert.ToDouble(TextBoxMargin.Text)

        If width = 0 Then
            width = ElementHost1.Width
        End If

        If height = 0 Then
            height = ElementHost1.Height
        End If
        If (margin * 2) > height Or (margin * 2) > width Then
            ElementHost1.Child.Clip = Nothing
        Else
            ElementHost1.Child.Clip = New Windows.Media.EllipseGeometry( _
                            New Windows.Rect(margin, margin, _
                            width - (margin * 2), height - (margin * 2)))
        End If
    End Sub

    Private Sub RectMask()
        Dim width As Double = ElementHost1.Width
        Dim height As Double = ElementHost1.Height
        Dim margin As Double = Convert.ToDouble(TextBoxMargin.Text)

        If (margin * 2) > height Or (margin * 2) > width Then
            ElementHost1.Child.Clip = Nothing
        Else
            Dim rect As New Windows.Media.RectangleGeometry( _
                            New Windows.Rect(margin, margin, _
                            width - (margin * 2), height - (margin * 2)))
            rect.RadiusX = Convert.ToDouble(TextBoxRounding.Text)
            rect.RadiusY = rect.RadiusX
            ElementHost1.Child.Clip = rect
        End If
```

```
        End Sub

        Private Sub TextBoxMargin_TextChanged(ByVal sender As System.Object, _
                                              ByVal e As System.EventArgs) _
                                              Handles TextBoxMargin.TextChanged
            Dim margin As Double
            If Double.TryParse(TextBoxMargin.Text, margin) Then
                ApplyMask()
            Else
                TextBoxMargin.Text = 0
            End If
        End Sub

        Private Sub TextBoxRounding_TextChanged(ByVal sender As System.Object, _
                                                ByVal e As System.EventArgs) _
                                                Handles TextBoxRounding.TextChanged
            Dim margin As Double
            If Double.TryParse(TextBoxRounding.Text, margin) Then
                ApplyMask()
            Else
                TextBoxRounding.Text = 0
            End If
        End Sub
```

Aside from the margin, note that in the `RectMask` function the code also applies the value from the `TextBoxRounding` control to the `RadiusX` and `RadiusY` properties on the rectangle. These properties cause the corners of the rectangle to be rounded, so when the rectangle mask is selected, the user is able to apply a value that changes the amount of corner rounding.

Figure 18-3

Finally, the preceding code block includes two additional event handlers, one for each of the two text boxes on the form. The first one handles events related to the margin's width, and the second event is related to the radius for rounded corners on your rectangle map. In both cases they call the same `ApplyMask` method, which is called when you select a mask.

Now it's time to build and run your application. After building and running your control, you should see a display similar to the one shown in Figure 18-3. Superficially, this application works and allows you to apply different masks and resize these masks. Notice that you are now modifying your WPF controls from within your Windows Forms application.

However, apply a mask and then resize your main frame. Notice how even though the image was resized, the mask remained static. Your application isn't recognizing a change in the size of control `ElementHost1` or the need to recalculate the size and location of the mask.

Using a Mapped Property of a WPF Control

There are a couple of potential solutions to this problem; however, for the purposes of this chapter, which focuses on demonstrating the features of the `WindowsFormsIntegration` library, the solution described here uses a mapped property on your control. The ability to access the mapped properties of WPF controls is one of the features of this library that provides you with greater flexibility. One of the available properties on control `ElementHost1`, the `PropertyMap` collection, enables you to select one or more of the `ElementHost1` properties and essentially register for a custom event handler. This is not an event handler in the traditional Windows Forms sense of the word, but rather the assignment of a delegate that is called when that property is changed.

The first step is to go to the load event described earlier in this chapter and uncomment the line that is calling the method `AddPropertyMapping`. Once you have uncommented this line, add the functions shown in the block of code that follows. The first of these is, in fact, the custom function `AddPropertyMapping`. This function simply calls the `Add` method on the `PropertyMap` collection to assign a new delegate in the form of a `PropertyTranslator` from the `Windows.Forms.Integration` library that will be called when the `Size` property of control `ElementHost1` is changed. Note that by assigning this value at the end of the `Form1_Load` event handler, your application will now make this call whenever the size of the control changes.

```
' The AddPropertynMapping method assigns a custom
' mapping for the Size property.
Private Sub AddPropertyMapping()
    ElementHost1.PropertyMap.Add( _
        "Size", _
        New Integration.PropertyTranslator(AddressOf OnEHSizeChange))
End Sub


''' <summary>
''' Called when the ElementHost control's size is changed
''' </summary>
''' <param name="h"></param>
''' <param name="propertyName"></param>
''' <param name="value"></param>
''' <remarks>A change of this property requires the form hosting this
''' control to adjust the clipping region, so the Property Mapper
''' in the Integration library is used to map an "event" handler.</remarks>
```

791

```
        Private Sub OnEHSizeChange(ByVal h As Object, _
                    ByVal propertyName As String, ByVal value As Object)
            ApplyMask()
        End Sub
```

The second method in the preceding block of code is the actual OnEHSizeChange method. Note that this method has three parameters:

❑ The first is the actual object that has been changed.

❑ The second is the name of the property, so multiple properties could call the same delegate in your Windows Forms code.

❑ The third is the new value of that property.

For the purposes of this demonstration, because this method will only be called for a single property on a single object, and because the new value will already be assigned within the control, the only thing this method needs to do is call the same ApplyMask method that is called elsewhere to correctly apply the mask to the image. Save, build, and run your example code again and notice how the mapping of the property has allowed your form to detect when a property on control ElementHost1, or potentially even on one of the WPF controls within your ElementHost control, has changed. As an exercise, consider changing this example to detect when the image hosted in control Image1 changes.

This example illustrates how you can create a new WPF component that can be incorporated into an existing Windows Forms application. You can start the process of migrating your application to WPF while still focusing the majority of your available resources on adding new capabilities to your existing application. Migration in this context means you are not forced to attempt to spend the majority of your cycles rewriting your entire existing interface. Instead, you can integrate these two display methodologies. The preceding example demonstrates one way of working with a WPF control within a Windows Forms application.

Other methods for carrying out the same tasks, including adding WPF controls within the context of the same project, are also possible. However, defining WPF controls within a Windows Forms project reduces your ability to migrate your control into a larger WPF model. Using the method demonstrated in this chapter makes that transition easy, as you'll just be hosting Windows Forms controls in WPF.

Hosting Windows Forms Controls in WPF

In the case of WPF hosting Windows Forms controls, you might choose to do this if you have an existing application that relies on certain controls that have not yet been implemented in WPF. For example, the following table lists some of the controls that are not directly supported in WPF:

BindingNavigator	DataGridView	DateTimePicker
ErrorProvider	HelpProvider	ImageList
LinkLable	MaskedTextBox	MonthCalendar
NotifyIcon	PrintDocument	PropertyGrid

In addition to these controls that aren't directly supported, still other controls may behave differently in this release. For example, the `ComboBox` control in WPF doesn't provide built-in support for `AutoComplete`. In other cases, such as the `HelpProvider` (F1 Help), a control isn't supported because the WPF provides an alternative implementation. Even if you have an application in which the existing user interface takes advantage of one of the preceding control's features, it is understandable that you might be interested in integrating your existing investment in the next version of your application.

However, there is a real possibility that if you have heavily leveraged a `DataGridView` control, you will want to reuse your existing control, rather than attempt to design a custom replacement.

To walk through the process of using the `WindowsFormsHost` control, create a new WPF Windows Application called ProVBWPFInterop. Once you have that application, go to the File menu and use the Add option to add a second project to this solution. This time, pick a Windows Control Library called `WinFormInteropCtrl`. Again, Visual Studio will execute the template to create a new project. At this point you will have access to a new control called `UserControl1`. Go to the designer for this new user control and add a `Button` control and a `DataGridView` control to the design surface, as shown in Figure 18-4.

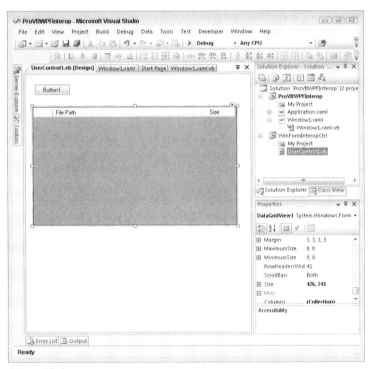

Figure 18-4

Figure 18-4 shows one way to arrange these controls. For the purposes of this demonstration, the `Button` control is static; it is there to demonstrate a formatting issue. Next, manually add the two columns shown in the grid through Visual Studio 2008. The first column will wind up holding string values representing the available images; this control represents a complex grid but is not meant to be one. Resize the grid to fit within the display area of your user control. This demonstration focuses on display characteristics, so there is no need to edit the default code-behind or provide an action for the `click` event of the button.

After you have created a new `UserControl1`, build the project so that the WinFormInteropCtrl has been compiled and then close this window. The next step is to update your WPF project with the appropriate references. Three references need to be added. From the Project Settings window, select the References tab. Add references to the .NET assemblies `System.Windows.Forms` and `Windows.Forms.Integration`. Finally, add a reference to the WinFormInteropCtrl project. After adding these three references, close the Project Settings window and recompile the project.

Having created a new user control and added the references, open the `Window1.xaml` file that's created with this template. In that XAML file you'll see the "Window" declaration. This declaration in Visual Studio imports two namespaces, as discussed in Chapter 17. You'll want to change the title of the form to reflect the new form title.

Next, switch to design view and add a button to the upper-right corner of the display. This button will illustrate two concepts. First, just as with the Windows Forms example, where the code leveraged some of the WPF classes outside the context of the interop form, this WPF form is going to leverage the same `FolderBrowseDialog` that was used in the preceding Windows form. Second, it will help show that although WPF and Windows Forms share the same control, a button, the default display of that control is very different, a problem that can be corrected. Label this button `Select Folder` and add an event handler for its `click` event.

Next, add a second button to the upper-right corner of the display. Align the buttons, label this as a `Close` button, and then set up an event handler for this button's `click` event. Next, drag and drop a `WindowsFormsHost` control onto the display. The control should be docked to the bottom bounds of the display below the two buttons.

Unlike the Windows Forms project earlier in this chapter, the WPF design surface currently does not support adding your custom user control to this display. At this point you can review the XAML view within Visual Studio to compare your XAML to the XAML shown in the following listing. Additionally, your overall display should look similar to Figure 18-5.

```
<Window x:Class="Window1"
    xmlns="http://schemas.microsoft.com/winfx/2006/xaml/presentation"
    xmlns:x="http://schemas.microsoft.com/winfx/2006/xaml"
  Title="ProVB WPF Interop" Height="300" Width="450" Name="Window1">
    <Grid>
        <Button Height="23" HorizontalAlignment="Left" Margin="14,14,0,0"
            Name="Button1" VerticalAlignment="Top"
            Width="100">Select Folder</Button>
        <Button Height="23" HorizontalAlignment="Right" Margin="0,14,26,0"
            Name="Button2" VerticalAlignment="Top"
            Width="75">Close</Button>
        <my:WindowsFormsHost Margin="0,50,0,0" Name="WindowsFormsHost1"
xmlns:my="clr-namespace:System.Windows.Forms.Integration;assembly=
WindowsFormsIntegration" />
    </Grid>
</Window>
```

Once you have set up your application's look, it's time to start handling some of the code. You'll notice in the code that follows there is again a default directory that is the images directory on Vista. The next method is the `Window1_Loaded` method. This method is called once when your form is initially loaded, and it's a great place to create an instance of your custom user control and assign it as the child

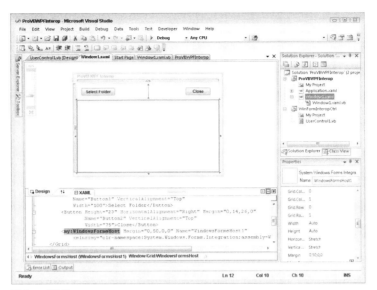

Figure 18-5

of `WindowsFormsHost1`. There is also a line that has been commented out in this initial listing; you will uncomment that line after the first time you test run your application.

The majority of this code is associated with the `Button1.Click` event handler. In this case, for brevity, the application doesn't automatically load the contents of the directory. Instead when you first click `Button1`, you'll be allowed to select the default folder and then have it load the contents of that folder. Notice that although the grid was created with two columns, this sample code merely loads the document name for demonstration purposes into the grid that is part of your custom user control:

```vb
Class Window1
    ' The default directory path is native to Windows Vista.
    ' On other operating system's select an appropriate directory.
    Private m_path As String = "C:\Users\Public\Pictures\Sample Pictures"

    Private Sub Window1_Loaded(ByVal sender As System.Object, _
                            ByVal e As System.Windows.RoutedEventArgs) _
                            Handles MyBase.Loaded
        WindowsFormsHost1.Child = New WinFormInteropCtrl.UserControl1()
        'System.Windows.Forms.Application.EnableVisualStyles()
    End Sub

    Private Sub Button1_Click(ByVal sender As System.Object, _
                            ByVal e As System.Windows.RoutedEventArgs) _
                            Handles Button1.Click
        Dim FolderBrowserDialog1 As New System.Windows.Forms.FolderBrowserDialog()
        FolderBrowserDialog1.SelectedPath = m_path
        If (FolderBrowserDialog1.ShowDialog() = Windows.Forms.DialogResult.OK) Then
            m_path = FolderBrowserDialog1.SelectedPath
            Dim uc As WinFormInteropCtrl.UserControl1 = _
                CType(WindowsFormsHost1.Child, WinFormInteropCtrl.UserControl1)
            Dim roid As Integer
```

```
        For Each control As System.Windows.Forms.Control In uc.Controls
            If TypeOf control Is System.Windows.Forms.DataGridView Then
                Dim grid As System.Windows.Forms.DataGridView = control
                grid.Rows.Clear()
                For Each filename As String In _
                                    System.IO.Directory.GetFiles(m_path)
                    roid = grid.Rows.Add()
                    grid.Rows(roid).Cells(0).Value = filename
                Next
            End If
        Next
    End If
End Sub

Private Sub Button2_Click(ByVal sender As System.Object, _
                    ByVal e As System.Windows.RoutedEventArgs) _
                    Handles Button2.Click
    Me.Close()
End Sub
End Class
```

Finally, note that the last method is the event handler for the Button2.Click event. As you might expect, this event handles closing the window, an important capability if you hide the outer frame of your window.

At this point you can run the application. If you are using the downloadable package, you should see the results shown in Figure 18-6. If you are creating your own copy of the project, you should see similar results; however, the button in WindowsFormsHost1 should have the incorrect styling.

Figure 18-6

The first item that should jump out at you is that the `WinFormInteropCtrl` has lost the Windows XP visual styling. Referring back to Figure 18-6, you can confirm that this styling was present in the designer for this control. To resolve this issue, go to the code-behind file for your `Window1.xaml` file, `Window1.xaml.vb`. Within the `Window1_Loaded` method, either before or after the call to create your user control as the child of the control `WindowsFormsHost1`, add the following line of code:

```
System.Windows.Forms.Application.EnableVisualStyles()
```

Rerun the application. The visual styling is now correct, but you should also be able to see that WPF and Windows Forms render this style differently on a similar control. Thus, you'll want to ensure that you minimize the number of similar controls you reference on different sides of the host boundary. In this case, you simply needed to manually reset the display settings for your control to indicate that it should use the XP styling; however, this styling issue provides an excellent introduction to the next topic.

```
Private Sub Window1_Initialized(ByVal sender As Object, _
                    ByVal e As System.EventArgs) Handles Me.Initialized
    Me.WindowStyle = Windows.WindowStyle.None
    Me.AllowsTransparency = True
End Sub
```

One of the options discussed in the preceding chapter that focused on WPF was the capability to change the window style so that the traditional border and controls in the frame were hidden. Once this is done, it is possible to enable transparency and really work on creating a custom look and feel for your application. However, you'll note that the preceding code is commented out in the online materials. That's because this code is there to illustrate one of the limitations of the `WindowsFormsHost` control.

If you enable this code, you'll find that instead of getting your interop control to display, the WPF rendering engine does not render anything. Thus, while the limitations include not being able to use certain types of transparency with the control, this provides a much better illustration of how using a `WindowsFormsHost` control can impact your overall application look and feel.

Integration Limitations

The challenge with integration is that these two display models don't operate under the same paradigm. The Windows Forms world and the `WindowsFormsHost` are based on window handles, also known as `HWnd` structures. WPF, conversely, has only a single `HWnd` to define its display area for the operating system and then avoids using `HWnd`s. The thing to remember, then, is that when you are working with encapsulating a control, that control — be it WPF or Windows Forms — will be affected by the environment in which it is hosted.

For example, if you host a WPF control inside a Windows Forms application, then the ability to control low-level graphical display characteristics such as opacity or background may be limited by the rules for Windows Forms. Unlike WPF, which layers control characteristics supporting the display of a control at a layer below the current control, Windows Forms controls are contained; when the control doesn't paint a background on your WPF control, the display may see that region as not painted and use a black or white background instead. Note that setting the `AllowTransparency` property for a control is supported when hosting WPF controls on a Windows Form. You can play with the background color used for the `ElementHost` control introduced earlier in this chapter to get a feel for this issue.

Recognizing that the host control is often limited by the underlying environment containing it is a good guide to predicting limitations. Although sometimes the actual characteristics of the parent application framework might come as a surprise, as you gain more experience with WPF you'll be able to predict where issues are likely to exist. For example, you can create both window- and page-based WPF applications, but these applications work on entirely different models. For example, a page-based WPF application is stateless. To support this stateless nature in those instances where it finds itself used in a page-based WPF application, the WindowsFormsHost control fully refreshes the contained control each time the page is refreshed — losing any user input that you might expect to remain within a Windows Forms control.

Another issue can arise with the advanced scaling capabilities of WPF. While Windows Forms controls are scalable, Windows Forms doesn't support the concept of scaling down to 0 and then restoring properly.

Similarly, be aware of the message loop, current control focus, and property mapping of hosted controls. The host controls support passing messages to the controls they contain, but across the application the ordering of messages may not occur in the expected order. Similarly, when a WindowsFormsHost control has passed focus to a contained control and then the form is minimized, the host control may lose track of which control within its Child has that focus. As a result, even though the unseen host has the current focus within your WPF application, there is no visible control with that focus. Finally, there are additional potential issues with property mapping other than the background color issue described earlier, so you need to watch the behavior of these controls carefully and be prepared to manually map properties as shown in this chapter's first example.

The preceding list is not a complete list of potential issues you may encounter when attempting to integrate these two distinct user-interface implementations. One final warning is that you can't nest host controls. Both Windows Forms and WPF can contain multiple-host controls within a given window, but each of these host controls must be separate and of the same type. Thus, you can't create a WPF application containing a WindowsFormsHost control that contains an ElementHost control. If you're integrating controls, try to minimize the number of user controls or panels containing the host controls so that you don't accidentally attempt to nest the embedded host controls in another layer of integration.

Summary

This chapter extended the coverage of WPF with regard to how you can leverage WPF within your Windows Forms applications and, conversely, how you can leverage existing Forms based components to work with WPF applications. The chapter introduced the Windows.Forms.Integration library and the ability to have WPF and Windows Forms components provide an application user interface. This library is similar to other transitional libraries in that the focus is on supporting business needs and not on complete support for the features of WPF by Windows Forms components within the WPF environment. Key points from this chapter include the following:

❑   It is possible to start a migration to a WPF-based application interface using the Windows.Forms .Integration library and the ElementHost class.

❑   Such an interface enables you to embed enhanced image processing into an existing Windows Forms application.

❑ Using the `WindowsFormsHost` class enables you to embed a complex business or third-party control that you are not ready to replace within a WPF application.

❑ Using the integration library, you can support key business-driven components, but it may affect the visual appeal of your user interface.

While this chapter introduced the Windows Forms integration library, you may have noticed that the overall tone isn't describing this as the next great feature. This isn't because the integration library didn't require significant effort to create or wasn't well designed. This library is an excellent resource — in the limited area for which it was designed: to support your transition from Windows Forms to WPF. Using this library across a few releases of your application as you migrate to a WPF-based user interface is an excellent way to manage complexity, but always remember that you want to fully commit to the WPF-based paradigms, which means moving beyond this library.

Finally, if you do have the opportunity to create a complete new user interface and can avoid the added complexity associated with working with this integration class, then you should.

19

Working with ASP.NET 3.5

The introduction of ASP.NET 1.0/1.1 changed the Web programming model, and ASP.NET 3.5 is just as revolutionary in the way it increases the productivity of .NET developers. The primary goal of ASP.NET is to enable you to build powerful, secure, and dynamic applications using the least possible amount of code. This chapter covers some of the exciting features provided by ASP.NET 3.5 and most of what the ASP.NET technology offers.

The Goals of ASP.NET

ASP.NET 3.5 is a substantial release of the product and an integral part of the .NET Framework 3.5. This release of ASP.NET heralds a new wave of development for AJAX-enabled applications and provides a new means of coding a rich application.

ASP.NET 3.5 has specific goals to achieve. These goals are focused around developer productivity, administration, and management, as well as performance and scalability. After working with ASP.NET, you will find that these goals have indeed been achieved.

Developer Productivity

Much of ASP.NET's focus is on productivity. Huge productivity gains were made with the release of ASP.NET 1.*x* — could it be possible to expand further on those gains?

The ASP.NET development team's ongoing goal has been to eliminate much of the tedious coding that ASP.NET originally required and to make common ASP.NET tasks easier. After the release of the first version of ASP.NET, the Microsoft team developing ASP.NET has had the goal of reducing by two-thirds the number of lines of code required for an ASP.NET application. It succeeded: you will be amazed at how quickly you can create your applications in ASP.NET 3.5.

Administration and Management

The initial release of ASP.NET focused on the developer, and little thought was given to the people who had to administer and manage all the ASP.NET applications that were built and deployed. Instead of working with consoles and wizards as they did in the past, administrators and managers of these new applications now had to work with unfamiliar XML configuration files such as `machine.config` and `web.config`.

To remedy this situation, if you are using Windows XP, ASP.NET includes a Microsoft Management Console (MMC) snap-in that enables Web application administrators to edit configuration settings easily on-the-fly through IIS. If you are using Windows Vista, the IIS Manager has been enhanced to give you the same capabilities that the MMC snap-in included.

Performance and Scalability

The Microsoft team set out to provide the world's fastest Web application server. One of the most exciting performance features of ASP.NET 3.5 is the caching capability aimed at exploiting Microsoft's SQL Server. This feature is called *SQL cache invalidation*. Before ASP.NET 2.0, it was possible to cache the results that came from SQL Server and to update the cache based on a time interval — for example, every 15 seconds or so. This meant that end users might see stale data if the result set changed sometime during that 15-second interval.

In some cases, this time interval result set is unacceptable. Ideally, the result set stored in the cache is destroyed if any underlying change occurs in the source from which the result set is retrieved — in this case, SQL Server. Ever since ASP.NET 2.0, you can make this happen with the use of SQL cache invalidation. When the result set from SQL Server changes, the output cache is triggered to change, and the end user always sees the latest result set. The data presented is never stale.

ASP.NET 3.5 provides 64-bit support, which means you can run your ASP.NET applications on 64-bit Intel or AMD processors. In addition, because ASP.NET 3.5 is fully backwardly compatible with ASP.NET 1.0/1.1 and 2.0, you can now take any former ASP.NET application, recompile it on the .NET Framework 3.5, and run it on a 64-bit processor.

The ASP.NET Compilation System

In ASP.NET, code is constructed and compiled in an interesting way. Compilation in ASP.NET 1.0 was always tricky. You could build an application's code-behind files using ASP.NET and Visual Studio, deploy it, and then watch as the `.aspx` files were compiled page by page as each page was requested. If you made any changes to the code-behind file in ASP.NET 1.0, it was not reflected in your application until the entire application was rebuilt, which meant that the same page-by-page request had to be done again before the entire application was recompiled.

Everything regarding how ASP.NET 1.0 worked with classes and compilation changed with the release of ASP.NET 2.0. The mechanics of the ASP.NET compilation system actually begin with how a page is structured. In ASP.NET 1.0, you constructed your pages either by using the code-behind model or by placing all the server code inline between `<script>` tags on your `.aspx` page. Most pages were constructed using the code-behind model because this was the default when using Visual Studio .NET 2002 or 2003. It was quite difficult to create your page using the inline style in these IDEs. If you did, then you were deprived of the use of IntelliSense, which can be quite a lifesaver when working with the tremendously large collection of classes that the .NET Framework offers.

ASP.NET 3.5 offers a code-behind model because the .NET Framework 2.0 (the core of the .NET Framework 3.5) offers the capability to work with *partial classes* (also called *partial types*). Upon compilation, the separate files are combined into a single offering. This gives you much cleaner code-behind pages. The code that was part of the Web Form Designer Generated section of your classes is separated from the code-behind classes that you create yourself. Contrast this with the ASP.NET 1.0 .aspx file's requirement to derive from its own code-behind file to represent a single logical page.

ASP.NET 3.5 applications can include an \App_Code directory in which you place your class's source. Any class placed here is dynamically compiled and reflected in the application. Unlike ASP.NET 1.0, you do not use a separate build process when you make changes. This enables a "just save and hit" deployment model like the one in classic ASP 3.0. Visual Studio Web Developer also automatically provides IntelliSense for any objects placed in the \App_Code directory, whether you are working with the code-behind model or are coding inline.

ASP.NET 3.5 provides you with tools that enable you to precompile your ASP.NET applications — both .aspx pages and code-behind — so that no page within your application experiences latency when it is retrieved for the first time. This is also a great way to discover any errors in the pages without invoking every page. Precompiling your ASP.NET 3.5 applications is as simple as using aspnet_compiler.exe and employing some of the available flags. As you precompile your entire application, you receive error notifications if errors are found anywhere within it. Precompilation also enables you to deliver only the created assembly to the deployment server, thereby protecting your code from snooping, unwanted changes, and tampering after deployment.

Health Monitoring for Your ASP.NET Applications

The built-in health-monitoring capabilities are rather significant features designed to make it easier to manage a deployed ASP.NET application. Health monitoring provides what the term implies — the capability to monitor the health and performance of your deployed ASP.NET applications.

ASP.NET health monitoring is built around various health-monitoring events (referred to as *Web events*) occurring in your application. Using the health-monitoring system enables you to perform event logging for Web events such as failed logins, application starts and stops, or any unhandled exceptions. The event logging can occur in more than one place, so you can log to the Event Log or even back to a database. In addition to performing this disk-based logging, you can also use the system to e-mail health-monitoring information.

Besides working with specific events in your application, you can use the health-monitoring system to take health snapshots of a running application. As with most systems built into ASP.NET 3.5, you can extend the health-monitoring system and create your own events for recording application information.

Reading and Writing Configuration Settings

Using the WebConfigurationManager class, you can read from and write to the server or application configuration files. This means that you can write and read settings in the machine.config or the web.config files that your application uses.

The capability to read and write to configuration files is not limited to working with the local machine in which your application resides. You can also perform these operations on remote servers and applications.

Of course, a GUI technique exists for performing these read or change operations on the configuration files at your disposal. Most exciting, however, is that the built-in GUI tools that provide this functionality (such as the ASP.NET MMC snap-in available for Windows XP) use the `WebConfigurationManager` class that is also available for building custom administration tools.

Localization

ASP.NET 3.5 makes it easy to localize applications. In addition to using Visual Studio, you can create resource files (`.resx`) that enable you to dynamically change the pages you create based upon the culture settings of the requester.

ASP.NET also provides the capability to provide resources either application-wide or just to particular pages in your application through the use of two application folders: `App_GlobalResources` and `App_LocalResources`.

The items defined in any `.resx` files you create are then accessible directly in the ASP.NET server controls or programmatically, using expressions such as the following:

```
<%= Resources.Resource.Question %>
```

This system is straightforward and simple to implement.

Objects for Accessing Data

One of the more code-intensive tasks in ASP.NET 1.0 was data retrieval. In many cases, this meant working with several objects. If you have been working with ASP.NET for a while, you know that it is an involved process to display data from a Microsoft SQL Server table within a `DataGrid` server control. For instance, you first had to create a number of new objects, including a `SqlConnection` object followed by a `SqlCommand` object. When those objects were in place, you then created a `SqlDataReader` to populate your `DataGrid` by binding the result to the `DataGrid`. In the end, a table appeared containing the contents of the data you were retrieving (such as the Customers table from the Northwind database).

Ever since version 2.0, ASP.NET eliminates this intensive procedure with the inclusion of a set of objects that work specifically with data access and retrieval. These data controls are so easy to use that you can access and retrieve data to populate your ASP.NET server controls without writing any code. Even better, this functionality is not limited to Microsoft's SQL Server. In fact, several data-source server controls are at your disposal, and you can create your own. In addition to the `SqlDataSource` server control, ASP.NET 3.5 includes the `AccessDataSource`, `XmlDataSource`, `ObjectDataSource`, and `SiteMapData Source` server controls. ASP.NET 3.5 also introduces the new `LinqDataSource` control, which enables you to work with the LINQ configurations that you design within your applications.

The IDE for Building ASP.NET 3.5 Pages

With ASP.NET 1.0/1.1, you can build your ASP.NET application using Notepad, Visual Studio .NET 2002 and 2003, as well as the hobbyist-focused ASP.NET Web Matrix. In ASP.NET 2.0, you were able to use Visual Studio 2005. ASP.NET 3.5 adds another IDE to the Visual Studio family — Visual Studio 2008. Visual Studio 2008 offers some dramatic enhancements to how you build your ASP.NET applications.

Visual Studio 2008 now enables you to target the version of the framework for which you are building (see Figure 19-1).

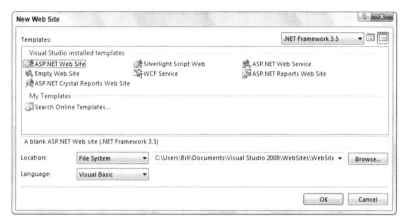

Figure 19-1

In the New Web Site dialog, you are provided with a drop-down list in the top right-hand corner that enables you to choose which version of the framework your ASP.NET should be compiled against.

In addition to this change, AJAX has now become an integrated part of Visual Studio. Prior to Visual Studio 2008, ASP.NET AJAX Extensions was available only as a separate add-on that would be integrated with Visual Studio 2005. It is now completely built into the IDE with the release of Visual Studio 2008.

IntelliSense has always been an important tool used by .NET developers to help them quickly build their applications. With the release of Visual Studio 2008, this capability has also been extended; VS 2008 now supports JavaScript IntelliSense as well as inline JavaScript validation. This means that if your JavaScript is not correct in the document window, then you will see red and green squiggly lines under the corresponding code.

In addition to enhanced support for JavaScript and CSS, the IDE now has full support for WCF. This is true not only for building new WCF services, but also for consuming them. For instance, in addition to the Add Reference and Add Web Reference capabilities, a new Add Service option is available when you right-click on the project within the VS 2008 Solution Explorer.

Note that like Visual Studio 2005, the new Visual Studio 2008 builds applications using a *file-based system*, not the project-based system used by Visual Studio .NET. When using Visual Studio .NET in the past, you had to create new projects (for example, an ASP.NET Web Application project). This process created a number of project files in your application in addition to the `Default.aspx` page. Because everything was based on a singular project, it was very difficult to develop applications in a team environment.

Conversely, Web projects in Visual Studio 2008 are based on a file-system approach. No project files are included in your project, which makes it easy for multiple developers to work on a single application without bumping into each other. Other changes are those to the compilation system discussed earlier. You can build your ASP.NET pages using either the inline model or the code-behind model. Both offer full IntelliSense capabilities. This, in itself, is powerful and innovative. Figure 19-2 shows IntelliSense running from an ASP.NET page that is being built using the inline model.

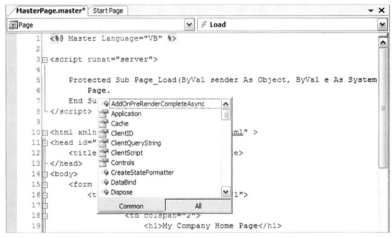

Figure 19-2

Another feature of Visual Studio 2008 borrowed from the ASP.NET Web Matrix is that you do not need IIS on your development machine. Visual Studio 2008 has a built-in web server that enables you to launch pages from any folder in your system with relative ease.

Building ASP.NET Applications

If you are new to ASP.NET and are building your first set of applications in ASP.NET 3.5, you may be amazed by all the wonderful new server controls it provides. You may marvel at how it enables you to work with data more effectively using the new data providers, and you are sure to be impressed with how easily you can build in security and personalization.

The outstanding capabilities of ASP.NET 3.5 do not end there, however. This section looks at many exciting additions that facilitate working with ASP.NET pages and applications. One of the first steps you, as the developer, should take when starting a project is to become familiar with the foundation you are building on and the options available for customizing that foundation.

Application Location Options

With ASP.NET 3.5, you have the option — using Visual Studio 2008 — to create an application with a virtual directory mapped to IIS, or a standalone application outside the confines of IIS. Whereas Visual Studio .NET forced developers to use IIS for all Web applications, Visual Studio 2008 includes a built-in web server that you can use for development, much like the one used in the past with the ASP.NET Web Matrix.

> *This built-in web server was previously presented to developers as a code sample called Cassini. In fact, the code for this mini web server is freely downloadable from the ASP.NET team website found at* `www.asp.net`*.*

The Built-in Web Server

By default, Visual Studio 2008 builds applications without the use of IIS. You can see this when you select File ➪ New Web Site in the IDE. By default, the location provided for your application is `C:\Users\<username>\Documents\Visual Studio 2008\WebSites` if you are using Windows Vista (shown in Figure 19-3). It is not `C:\Inetpub\wwwroot\` as it would have been in Visual Studio .NET 2002/2003. By default, any site that you build and host inside `C:\Users\<username>\Documents\Visual Studio 2008\WebSites` (or any other folder you create) uses the built-in web server that is part of Visual Studio 2008. If you use the built-in web server from Visual Studio 2008, you are not locked into the `WebSites` folder; you can create any folder you want in your system.

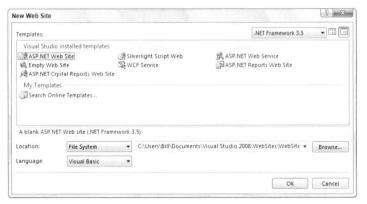

Figure 19-3

To change this default, you have a handful of options. Click the Browse button in the New Web Site dialog. This brings up the Choose Location dialog, shown in Figure 19-4.

If you continue to use the built-in web server that Visual Studio 2008 provides, you can choose a new location for your Web application from this dialog. To do so, select a new folder and save your `.aspx` pages and any other associated files to this directory. When using Visual Studio 2008, you can run your application completely from this location. This way of working with the ASP.NET pages you create is ideal if you don't have access to a web server, as you can build applications that don't reside on a machine with IIS. This means that you can even develop ASP.NET applications on operating systems such as Windows XP Home Edition.

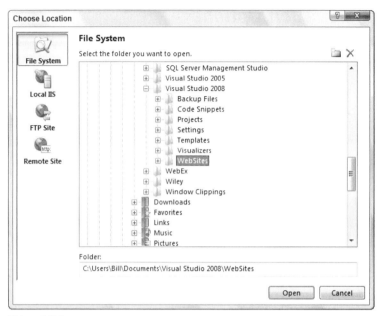

Figure 19-4

IIS

From the Choose Location dialog, you can also change where your application is saved and which type of web server your application employs. To use IIS (as you probably did when you used Visual Studio .NET 2002/2003), select the Local IIS button in the dialog. This changes the results in the text area to display a list of all the virtual application roots on your machine.

To create a new virtual root for your application, highlight Default Web Site. Three buttons appear at the top of the dialog (see Figure 19-5). From left to right, the first button in the top-right corner of the dialog is for creating a new Web application — or a virtual root. This button is shown as a globe inside a box. The second button enables you to create virtual directories for any of the virtual roots you created. The third button is a Delete button, which you can use to delete any selected virtual directories or virtual roots on the server.

After you have created the virtual directory you want, click the Open button. Visual Studio 2008 then goes through the standard process to create your application. Now, however, instead of depending on the built-in web server from ASP.NET 3.5, your application will use IIS. When you invoke your application, the URL now consists of something like `http://localhost/MyWeb/Default.aspx`, which means it is using IIS.

FTP

Not only can you choose the type of web server for your Web application when you create it using the Choose Location dialog, you can also decide where to locate your application. The previous options built applications that resided on your local server. The FTP option enables you to actually store and even code your applications while they reside on a server somewhere else in your enterprise — or on the other side of the planet. You can also use the FTP capabilities to work on different locations within the same server. This built-in capability provides a wide range of possible options and represents a major enhancement to the IDE. Previously difficult to accomplish, this task is now quite simple, as illustrated in Figure 19-6.

Figure 19-5

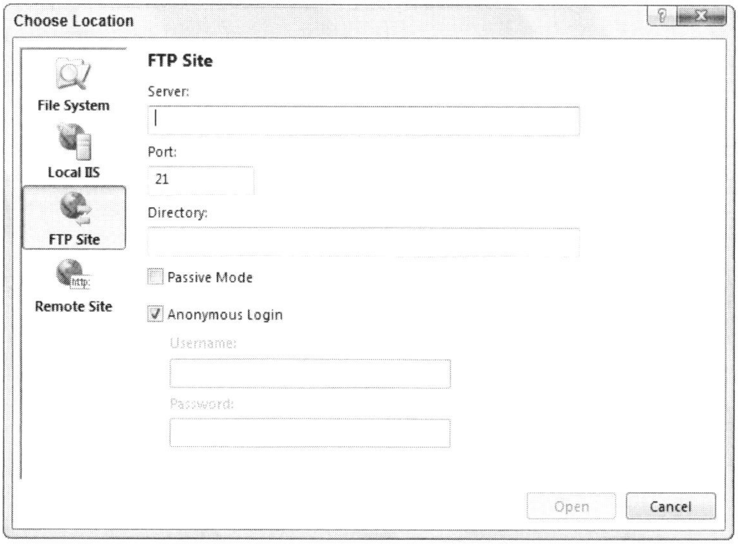

Figure 19-6

To create your application on a remote server using FTP, simply provide the server name, the port to use, and the directory — as well as any required credentials. If the correct information is provided, then Visual Studio 2008 accesses the remote server and creates the appropriate files for the start of your application, just as if it were doing the job locally. From this point on, you can open your project and connect to the remote server using FTP.

Websites Requiring FrontPage Extensions

The last option in the Choose Location dialog is the Remote Site option (see Figure 19-7). Clicking this button provides a dialog that enables you to connect to a remote or local server that utilizes FrontPage Extensions.

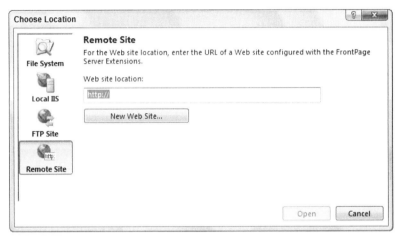

Figure 19-7

The ASP.NET Page Structure Options

ASP.NET 3.5 provides two paths for structuring the code of your ASP.NET pages. The first path utilizes the code-inline model. This model should be familiar to classic ASP 2.0/3.0 developers because all the code is contained within a single `.aspx` page. The second path uses ASP.NET's code-behind model, which enables the separation of the page's business logic from its presentation logic. In this model, the presentation logic for the page is stored in an `.aspx` page, whereas the logic piece is stored in a separate class file: `.aspx.vb` or `.aspx.cs`.

One of the major complaints about Visual Studio .NET 2002 and 2003 is that it forces you to use the code-behind model when developing your ASP.NET pages because it does not understand the code-inline model. The code-behind model in ASP.NET was introduced as a new way to separate the presentation code and business logic. Example 1 (named because it is referred to later) shows a typical `.aspx` page generated using Visual Studio .NET 2002 or 2003:

Example 1

```
<%@ Page Language="vb" AutoEventWireup="false" Codebehind="WebForm1.aspx.vb"
    Inherits="WebApplication.WebForm1"%>
<!DOCTYPE HTML PUBLIC "-//W3C//DTD HTML 4.0 Transitional//EN">
<HTML>
 <HEAD>
    <title>WebForm1</title>
    <meta name="GENERATOR" content="Microsoft Visual Studio .NET 7.1">
    <meta name="CODE_LANGUAGE" content="Visual Basic .NET 7.1">
```

```
      <meta name="vs_defaultClientScript" content="JavaScript">
      <meta name="vs_targetSchema"
        content="http://schemas.microsoft.com/intellisense/ie5">
  </HEAD>
  <body>
      <form id="Form1" method="post" runat="server">
        <P>What is your name?<br>
        <asp:TextBox id="TextBox1" runat="server"></asp:TextBox><BR>
        <asp:Button id="Button1" runat="server" Text="Submit"></asp:Button></P>
        <P><asp:Label id="Label1" runat="server"></asp:Label></P>
      </form>
  </body>
</HTML>
```

Example 2, shown next, shows the code-behind file created within Visual Studio .NET 2002/2003 for the `.aspx` page:

Example 2

```
Public Class WebForm1
    Inherits System.Web.UI.Page

#Region " Web Form Designer Generated Code "

    'This call is required by the Web Form Designer.
    <System.Diagnostics.DebuggerStepThrough()> _
      Private Sub InitializeComponent()

    End Sub
    Protected WithEvents TextBox1 As System.Web.UI.WebControls.TextBox
    Protected WithEvents Button1 As System.Web.UI.WebControls.Button
    Protected WithEvents Label1 As System.Web.UI.WebControls.Label

    'NOTE: The following placeholder declaration is required by the Web Form
        Designer.
    'Do not delete or move it.
    Private designerPlaceholderDeclaration As System.Object

    Private Sub Page_Init(ByVal sender As System.Object, ByVal e As
      System.EventArgs) Handles MyBase.Init
        'CODEGEN: This method call is required by the Web Form Designer
        'Do not modify it using the code editor.
        InitializeComponent()
    End Sub

#End Region

    Private Sub Page_Load(ByVal sender As System.Object, ByVal e As
      System.EventArgs) Handles MyBase.Load
        'Put user code to initialize the page here
    End Sub
```

```
        Private Sub Button1_Click(ByVal sender As System.Object, ByVal e As
          System.EventArgs) Handles Button1.Click
            Label1.Text = "Hello " & TextBox1.Text
        End Sub
    End Class
```

In this code-behind page from ASP.NET 1.0/1.1, you can see that a lot of the code that developers never have to deal with is hidden in the #Region section of the page. Because ASP.NET 3.5 is built on top of .NET 3.5, which in turn is utilizing the core .NET 2.0 Framework, it can take advantage of the .NET Framework's partial class capability. Partial classes enable you to separate your classes into multiple class files, which are then combined into a single class when the application is compiled. Because ASP.NET 3.5 combines all this page code for you behind the scenes when the application is compiled, the code-behind files you work with in ASP.NET 3.5 are simpler in appearance and the model is easier to use. You are presented with only the pieces of the class that you need.

Inline Coding

With the .NET Framework 1.0/1.1, developers went out of their way (and outside Visual Studio .NET) to build their ASP.NET pages inline and avoid the code-behind model that was so heavily promoted by Microsoft and others. Visual Studio 2008 (as well as Visual Web Developer 2008) enables you to build your pages easily using this coding style. To build an ASP.NET page inline instead of using the code-behind model, you simply select the page type from the Add New Item dialog and ensure that the Place Code in Separate File check box is unchecked. You can access this dialog by right-clicking the project or the solution in the Solution Explorer and selecting Add New Item (see Figure 19-8).

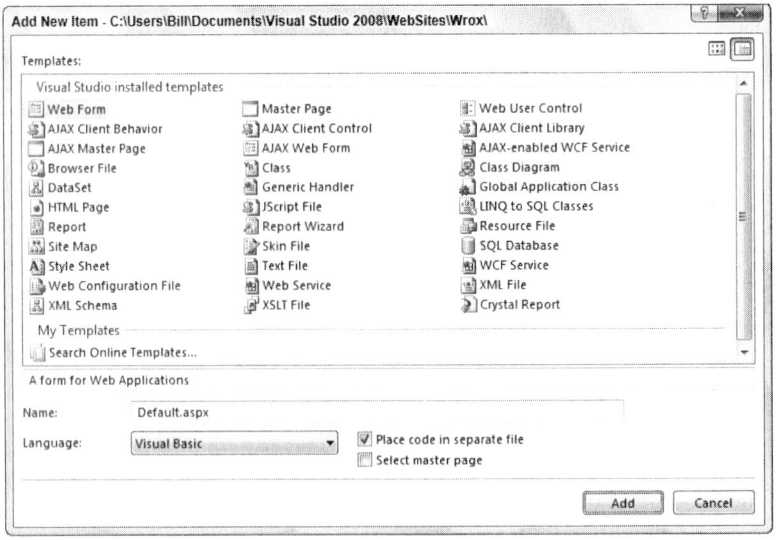

Figure 19-8

In fact, many page types have options for both inline and code-behind styles. The following table shows your inline options when selecting files from this dialog:

File Options Using Inline Coding	File Created
Web Form	.aspx file
AJAX Web Form	.aspx file
Master Page	.master file
AJAX Master Page	.master file
Web User Control	.ascx file
Web Service	.asmx file

By using the Web Form option with a few controls, you get a page that encapsulates not only the presentation logic, but also the business logic:

```
<%@ Page Language="VB" %>

<!DOCTYPE html PUBLIC "-//W3C//DTD XHTML 1.1//EN"
 "http://www.w3.org/TR/xhtml11/DTD/xhtml11.dtd">

<script runat="server">
    Protected Sub Button1_Click(ByVal sender As Object, _
        ByVal e As System.EventArgs)

        Label1.Text = "Hello " & Textbox1.Text
    End Sub
</script>

<html xmlns="http://www.w3.org/1999/xhtml" >
<head runat="server">
    <title>Simple Page</title>
</head>
<body>
    <form id="form1" runat="server">
        What is your name?<br />
        <asp:Textbox ID="Textbox1" Runat="server"></asp:Textbox><br />
        <asp:Button ID="Button1" Runat="server" Text="Submit"
         OnClick="Button1_Click" />
        <p><asp:Label ID="Label1" Runat="server"></asp:Label></p>
    </form>
</body>
</html>
```

From this example, you can see that all the business logic is encapsulated in between `<script>` tags. The nice feature of the inline model is that the business logic and the presentation logic are contained within the same file. Some developers find that having everything in a single viewable instance makes working with the ASP.NET page easier.

Visual Studio 2008 also provides IntelliSense when working with the inline coding model and ASP.NET 3.5. Before .NET 2.0, this capability did not exist. Visual Studio .NET 2002/2003 forced you to use the code-behind model; and even if you rigged it so your pages were using the inline model, you lost all IntelliSense capabilities.

Code-Behind Model

The other option for constructing your ASP.NET 3.5 pages is to build your files using the new code-behind model. We say "new" because even though the concept of the code-behind model is the same as it was in previous versions, the code-behind model used in ASP.NET 3.5 is quite different.

The preferred method is the code-behind model, rather than the inline model. Using this method employs the proper segmentation between presentation and business logic in many cases. Many of the examples in the ASP.NET chapters use an inline coding model because the inline model works well for showing an example in a book in one listing. Therefore, even though the example uses an inline coding style, it is recommended that you employ the code-behind model.

To create a new page in your ASP.NET solution that uses the code-behind model, select the page type you want from the New File dialog. To build a page using the code-behind model, first select the page in the Add New Item dialog and ensure that the Place Code in Separate File check box is checked. The following table shows the options for pages that use the code-behind model:

File Options Using Code-Behind	File Created
Web Form	.aspx file .aspx.vb or .aspx.cs file
AJAX Web Form	.aspx file .aspx.vb or .aspx.cs file
Master Page	.master file .master.vb or .master.cs file
AJAX Master Page	.master.vb or .master.cs file
Web User Control	.ascx file .ascx.vb or .ascx.cs file
Web Service	.asmx file .vb or .cs file

The idea of using the code-behind model is to separate the business logic and presentation logic into separate files. This makes it easier to work with your pages, especially if you are working in a team environment where visual designers work on the UI of the page and coders work on the business logic that sits behind the presentation pieces. In the earlier code labeled Examples 1 and 2, you saw how pages using the code-behind model in ASP.NET 1.0/1.1 were constructed. To see the difference in ASP.NET 3.5, look at how its code-behind pages are constructed in the following two examples, the first for the presentation piece and the second for the code-behind piece:

```
<%@ Page Language="VB" AutoEventWireup="false" CodeFile="Default.aspx.vb"
    Inherits="_Default" %>

<!DOCTYPE html PUBLIC "-//W3C//DTD XHTML 1.1//EN"
 "http://www.w3.org/TR/xhtml11/DTD/xhtml11.dtd">

<html xmlns="http://www.w3.org/1999/xhtml">
```

```
<head runat="server">
    <title>Simple Page</title>
</head>
<body>
    <form id="form1" runat="server">
        What is your name?<br />
        <asp:Textbox ID="Textbox1" Runat="server"></asp:Textbox><br />
        <asp:Button ID="Button1" Runat="server" Text="Submit"
         OnClick="Button1_Click" />
        <p><asp:Label ID="Label1" Runat="server"></asp:Label></p>
    </form>
</body>
</html>
```

Code-behind example:

```
Partial Class _Default
    Inherits System.Web.UI.Page

    Protected Sub Button1_Click(ByVal sender As Object, _
        ByVal e As System.EventArgs) Handles Button1.Click

        Label1.Text = "Hello " & TextBox1.Text
    End Sub
End Class
```

The .aspx page using this ASP.NET 3.5 code-behind model has some attributes in the Page directive that you should pay attention to when working in this mode. The first is the CodeFile attribute. This is an attribute in the Page directive and is meant to point to the code-behind page used with this presentation page. In this case, the value assigned is Default.aspx.vb or Default.aspx.cs. The second attribute needed is the Inherits attribute. This attribute was available in previous versions of ASP.NET but was infrequently used before ASP.NET 2.0. This attribute specifies the name of the class that is bound to the page when the page is compiled. The directives are simple enough in ASP.NET 3.5.

Take another look at the preceding code-behind page. It is rather simple in appearance because of the partial class capabilities that .NET 3.5 provides. You can see that the class created in the code-behind file uses partial classes, employing the Partial keyword in Visual Basic 2008. This enables you to simply place the methods that you need in your Page class. In this case, you have a button-click event and nothing else.

ASP.NET 3.5 Page Directives

ASP.NET directives are part of every ASP.NET page. You can control the behavior of your ASP.NET pages by using these directives. Here is an example of the Page directive:

```
<%@ Page Language="VB" AutoEventWireup="false" CodeFile="Default.aspx.vb"
    Inherits="_Default" %>
```

Eleven directives are at your disposal in your ASP.NET pages or user controls. You use these directives in your applications whether the page uses the code-behind model or the inline coding model. Basically, these directives are commands that the compiler uses when the page is compiled. Directives are simple to incorporate into your pages, and are written in the following format:

```
<%@ [Directive] [Attribute=Value] %>
```

A directive is opened with `<%@` and closed with `%>`. It is best to put these directives at the top of your pages or controls because this is traditionally where developers expect to see them (although the page still compiles if the directives are located elsewhere. Of course, you can also add more than a single attribute to your directive statements, as shown here:

```
<%@ [Directive] [Attribute=Value] [Attribute=Value] %>
```

The following table describes the directives at your disposal in ASP.NET 3.5:

Directive	Description
Assembly	Links an assembly to the page or user control to which it is associated
Control	Page directive meant for use with user controls (.ascx)
Implements	Implements a specified .NET Framework interface
Import	Imports specified namespaces into the page or user control
Master	Enables you to specify a master page — specific attributes and values to use when the page parses or compiles. This directive can be used only with master pages (.master).
MasterType	Associates a class name to a page in order to get at strongly typed references or members contained within the specified master page
OutputCache	Controls the output caching policies of a page or user control
Page	Enables you to define page-specific attributes and values to use when the page parses or compiles. This directive can be used only with ASP.NET pages (.aspx).
PreviousPageType	Enables an ASP.NET page to work with a postback from another page in the application
Reference	Links a page or user control to the current page or user control
Register	Associates aliases with namespaces and class names for notation in custom server control syntax

ASP.NET Page Events

ASP.NET developers consistently work with various events in their server-side code. Many of the events that they work with pertain to specific server controls. For instance, if you want to initiate an action when the end user clicks a button on your Web page, you create a button-click event in your server-side code, as shown in the following example:

```
Protected Sub Button1_Click(sender As Object, e As EventArgs) _
    Handles Button1.Click

    Label1.Text = TextBox1.Text
End Sub
```

In addition to the server controls, developers also want to initiate actions at specific moments when the ASP.NET page is being either created or destroyed. The ASP.NET page itself has always had a number of events for these instances. Following is a list of all the page events you could use in ASP.NET 1.0/1.1:

- ❑ AbortTransaction
- ❑ CommitTransaction
- ❑ DataBinding
- ❑ Disposed
- ❑ Error
- ❑ Init
- ❑ Load
- ❑ PreRender
- ❑ Unload

One popular page event from this list is Load, which is used in VB as shown in the following code (called Example 4 for later reference):

Example 3

```
Protected Sub Page_Load(ByVal sender As Object, ByVal e As System.EventArgs)
    Handles Me.Load

    Response.Write("This is the Page_Load event")
End Sub
```

Besides the page events just shown, ASP.NET 3.5 provides the following events beyond the ones offered in ASP.NET 1.0/1.1:

- ❑ **InitComplete** — Indicates that initialization of the page is completed
- ❑ **LoadComplete** — Indicates that the page has been completely loaded into memory
- ❑ **PreInit** — Indicates the moment immediately before a page is initialized
- ❑ **PreLoad** — Indicates the moment before a page has been loaded into memory
- ❑ **PreRenderComplete** — Indicates the moment directly before a page has been rendered in the browser

You construct these page events just as you did the previously shown page events. For example, you use the PreInit event as follows:

```vb
<script runat="server" language="vb">
    Protected Sub Page_PreInit(ByVal sender As Object, _
      ByVal e As System.EventArgs)

        Page.Theme = Request.QueryString("ThemeChange")
    End Sub
</script>
```

If you create an ASP.NET 3.5 page and turn on tracing, you can see the order in which the main page events are initiated:

1. PreInit
2. Init
3. InitComplete
4. PreLoad
5. Load
6. LoadComplete
7. PreRender
8. PreRenderComplete
9. Unload

With the addition of these options, you can work with the page and the controls on the page at many different points in the page-compilation process.

ASP.NET Application Folders

When you create ASP.NET applications, note that ASP.NET 3.5 uses a file-based approach. You can add as many files and folders as you want within your application without recompiling each and every time a new file is added to the overall solution. ASP.NET 3.5 includes the capability to automatically precompile your ASP.NET applications dynamically.

ASP.NET 1.0/1.1 compiled everything in your solution into a DLL. This is no longer necessary be-cause ASP.NET applications now have a defined folder structure. By using the ASP.NET defined folders, you can have your code automatically compiled for you, your application themes accessible through-out your application, and your globalization resources available whenever you need them. The following sections show how these defined folders work.

\App_Code Folder

The \App_Code folder is meant to store your classes, .wsdl files, and typed datasets. Any of these items stored in this folder are then automatically available to all the pages within your solution. The nice thing about the \App_Code folder is that when you place something inside it, Visual Studio 2008 automatically detects this and compiles it if it is a class (such as a .vb file), automatically creates your XML Web service proxy class (from the .wsdl file), or automatically creates a typed dataset for you from your .xsd files.

After the files are automatically compiled, these items are then immediately available to any of your ASP.NET pages in the same solution. Let's look at how to employ a simple class in your solution using the \App_Code folder. Create an \App_Code folder by right-clicking the solution and choosing Add ASP.NET Folder ➪ App_Code. Note that Visual Studio 2008 treats this folder differently than the other folders in your solution. The \App_Code folder appears in a different color (gray), with a document pictured next to the folder icon (see Figure 19-9).

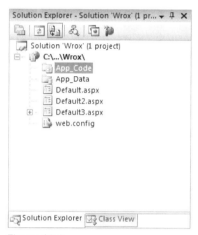

Figure 19-9

After the \App_Code folder is in place, right-click the folder and select Add New Item. The Add New Item dialog that appears provides a few options for the types of files that you can place within this folder. These include an AJAX-enabled WCF Service, a Class file, a LINQ to SQL Class, a Text file, a DataSet, a Report, and a Class Diagram if you are using Visual Studio 2008. Visual Web Developer 2008 offers only the Class file, the Text file, and the DataSet file. For the first example, select the file of type Class and name the class Calculator.vb or Calculator.cs. The following listing shows how the Calculator class should appear:

```
Imports Microsoft.VisualBasic

Public Class Calculator
    Public Function Add(ByVal a As Integer, ByVal b As Integer) As Integer
        Return (a + b)
    End Function
End Class
```

Simply save this file and it is now available for use in any pages in your solution. To see this in action, create a simple .aspx page that contains a single Label server control. The following example shows the code to place within the Page_Load event to make this new class available:

```
<%@ Page Language="VB" %>

<!DOCTYPE html PUBLIC "-//W3C//DTD XHTML 1.1//EN"
  "http://www.w3.org/TR/xhtml11/DTD/xhtml11.dtd">
```

```
<script runat="server">
    Protected Sub Page_Load(ByVal sender As Object, _
      ByVal e As System.EventArgs)

        Dim myCalc As New Calculator()
        Label1.Text = myCalc.Add(12, 12)
    End Sub
</script>
```

When you run this .aspx page, note that it utilizes the Calculator class without any problem, with no need to compile the class before use. In fact, right after saving the Calculator class in your solution or moving the class to the \App_Code folder, you also immediately receive IntelliSense capability on the methods that the class exposes (as illustrated in Figure 19-10).

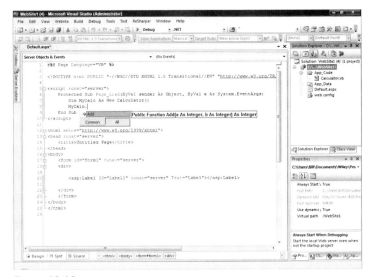

Figure 19-10

To see how Visual Studio 2008 works with the \App_Code folder, open the Calculator class again in the IDE and add a Subtract method. Your class should now appear as shown here:

```
Imports Microsoft.VisualBasic

Public Class Calculator
    Public Function Add(ByVal a As Integer, ByVal b As Integer) As Integer
        Return (a + b)
    End Function

    Public Function Subtract(ByVal a As Integer, ByVal b As Integer) _
        As Integer

        Return (a - b)
    End Function
End Class
```

After adding the `Subtract` method to the `Calculator` class, save the file and return to your `.aspx` page. Note that the class has been recompiled by the IDE, and the new method is now available to your page (see Figure 19-11). You see this directly in IntelliSense.

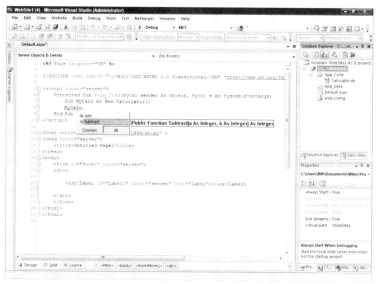

Figure 19-11

Everything placed in the `\App_Code` folder is compiled into a single assembly. The class files placed within the `\App_Code` folder are not required to use a specific language. For example, even if all the pages of the solution are written in Visual Basic 2008, the `Calculator` class in the `\App_Code` folder of the solution can be built in C# (`Calculator.cs`).

Because all the classes contained in this folder are built into a single assembly, you *cannot* have classes of different languages sitting in the root `\App_Code` folder, as in the following example:

```
\App_Code
    Calculator.cs
    AdvancedMath.vb
```

Having two classes made up of different languages in the `\App_Code` folder (as shown here) causes an error to be thrown. It is impossible for the assigned compiler to work with two different languages. Therefore, in order to work with multiple languages in your `\App_Code` folder, you must make some changes to the folder structure and the `web.config` file.

First, add two new subfolders to the `\App_Code` folder: a `\VB` folder and a `\CS` folder. This gives you the following folder structure:

```
\App_Code
    \VB
        Add.vb
    \CS
        Subtract.cs
```

This still will not correctly compile these class files into separate assemblies, at least not until you make some additions to the web.config file. Most likely, you do not have a web.config file in your solution at the moment, so add one through the Solution Explorer. After it is added, change the <compilation> node so that it is structured as shown here:

```
<compilation>
    <codeSubDirectories>
        <add directoryName="VB"></add>
        <add directoryName="CS"></add>
    </codeSubDirectories>
</compilation>
```

Now that this is in place in your web.config file, you can work with each of the classes in your ASP.NET pages. In addition, any C# class placed in the CS folder is now automatically compiled just like any of the classes placed in the VB folder. Because you can add these directories in the web.config file, you are not required to name them VB and CS; you can use whatever names you want.

\App_Data Folder

The \App_Data folder holds the data stores used by the application. It is a good spot to centrally store all the data stores your application might use. The \App_Data folder can contain Microsoft SQL Express files (.mdf files), Microsoft Access files (.mdb files), XML files, and more.

The user account utilized by your application has read and write access to any of the files contained within the \App_Data folder. By default, this is the ASP.NET account. Another reason to store all your data files in this folder is that much of the ASP.NET system — from the membership and role management systems to the GUI tools such as the ASP.NET MMC snap-in, the new IIS Manager, and ASP.NET Web Site Administration Tool — is built to work with the \App_Data folder.

\App_Themes Folder

Themes are a way of providing a common look and feel to your site across every page. You implement a theme by using a .skin file, CSS files, and images used by the server controls of your site. All these elements can make a *theme*, which is then stored in the \App_Themes folder of your solution. By storing these elements within the \App_Themes folder, you ensure that all the pages within the solution can take advantage of the theme and easily apply its elements to the controls and markup of the page.

\App_GlobalResources Folder

Resource files are string tables that can serve as data dictionaries for your applications when they require changes to content based on things such as changes in culture. You can add Assembly Resource files (.resx) to the \App_GlobalResources folder, and they are dynamically compiled and made part of the solution for use by all your .aspx pages in the application. When using ASP.NET 1.0/1.1, you had to use the resgen.exe tool and compile your resource files to a .dll or .exe for use within your solution.

It is considerably easier to deal with resource files in ASP.NET 3.5. Simply place your application-wide resources in this folder to make them instantly accessible.

\App_LocalResources

Even if you are not interested in constructing application-wide resources using the `\App_Global Resources` folder, you may want resources that can be used for a single `.aspx` page. You can do this very simply by using the `\App_LocalResources` folder.

Add page-specific resource files to the `\App_LocalResources` folder by constructing the name of the `.resx` file in the following manner:

- ❑   `Default.aspx.resx`
- ❑   `Default.aspx.fi.resx`
- ❑   `Default.aspx.ja.resx`
- ❑   `Default.aspx.en-gb.resx`

The resource declarations used on the `Default.aspx` page are retrieved from the appropriate file in the `\App_LocalResources` folder. By default, the `Default.aspx.resx` resource file is used if another match is not found. If the client is using a culture specification of `fi-FI` (Finnish), however, then the `Default.aspx.fi.resx` file is used instead.

\App_WebReferences

The `\App_WebReferences` folder is a new name for the `Web References` folder used in earlier versions of ASP.NET. Using the `\App_WebReferences` folder, you have automatic access to the remote Web services referenced from your application.

\App_Browsers

The `\App_Browsers` folder holds `.browser` files, which are XML files used to identify the browsers making requests to the application, and to understand the capabilities of these browsers. You can find a list of globally accessible `.browser` files at `C:\Windows\Microsoft.NET\Framework\v2.0.50727\CONFIG\ Browsers`. If you want to change any part of these default browser definition files, just copy the appropriate `.browser` file from the `Browsers` folder to your application's `\App_Browsers` folder and change the definition.

Global.asax

To add a new item to your ASP.NET application, you use the Add New Item dialog. From here, you can add a Global Application Class to your applications. This adds a `Global.asax` file, which is used by the application to hold application-level events, objects, and variables — all of which are accessible application-wide. Active Server Pages developers had something similar with the `Global.asa` file.

Your ASP.NET applications can have only a single `Global.asax` file, which supports a number of items. When it is created, you are given the following template:

```
<%@ Application Language="VB" %>

<script runat="server">

    Sub Application_Start(ByVal sender As Object, ByVal e As EventArgs)
        ' Code that runs on application startup
    End Sub

    Sub Application_End(ByVal sender As Object, ByVal e As EventArgs)
        ' Code that runs on application shutdown
    End Sub

    Sub Application_Error(ByVal sender As Object, ByVal e As EventArgs)
        ' Code that runs when an unhandled error occurs
    End Sub

    Sub Session_Start(ByVal sender As Object, ByVal e As EventArgs)
        ' Code that runs when a new session is started
    End Sub

    Sub Session_End(ByVal sender As Object, ByVal e As EventArgs)
        ' Code that runs when a session ends.
        ' Note: The Session_End event is raised only when the sessionstate mode
        ' is set to InProc in the Web.config file. If session mode is
        ' set to StateServer
        ' or SQLServer, the event is not raised.
    End Sub

</script>
```

Just as you can work with page-level events in your `.aspx` pages, you can work with overall application events from the `Global.asax` file. In addition to the events listed in this code example, the following list details some of the events you can structure inside this file:

❑ **Application_Start** — Called when the application receives its first request. This is an ideal spot in your application to assign any application-level variables or state that must be maintained across all users.

❑ **Session_Start** — Similar to the `Application_Start` event except that this event is fired when an individual user accesses the application for the first time. For instance, the `Application_Start` event fires once when the first request comes in, which gets the application going, but `Session_Start` is invoked for each end user who requests something from the application for the first time.

❑ **Application_BeginRequest** — Although it is not listed in the preceding template provided by Visual Studio 2008, the `Application_BeginRequest` event is triggered before each and every request that comes its way. This means that before a request coming into the server is processed, `Application_BeginRequest` is triggered and dealt with before any processing of the request occurs.

❑ **Application_AuthenticateRequest** — This is triggered for each request and enables you to set up custom authentications for a request.

❑ **Application_Error** — Triggered when an error is thrown anywhere in the application by any user. This is an ideal spot to provide application-wide error handling or an event recording an error to the server's Event Logs.

❑ **Session_End** — When running in `InProc` mode, this event is triggered when an end user leaves the application.

❑ **Application_End** — Triggered when the application comes to an end. Most ASP.NET developers won't often use this event because ASP.NET does such a good job of closing and cleaning up any objects left around.

In addition to the global application events to which the `Global.asax` file provides access, you can also use the following directives in this file, just as you can with other ASP.NET pages:

❑ `@Application`

❑ `@Assembly`

❑ `@Import`

These directives perform in the same way when they are used with other ASP.NET page types. An example of using the `Global.asax` file is shown in the next code example. It demonstrates how to log when the ASP.NET application domain shuts down. When this happens, the ASP.NET application abruptly comes to an end, so place any logging code in the `Application_End` method of the `Global.asax` file:

```
<%@ Application Language="VB" %>
<%@ Import Namespace="System.Reflection" %>
<%@ Import Namespace="System.Diagnostics" %>

<script runat="server">

    Sub Application_End(ByVal sender As Object, ByVal e As EventArgs)
        Dim MyRuntime As HttpRuntime = _
            GetType(System.Web.HttpRuntime).InvokeMember("_theRuntime", _
            BindingFlags.NonPublic Or BindingFlags.Static Or _
            BindingFlags.GetField, _
            Nothing, Nothing, Nothing)

        If (MyRuntime Is Nothing) Then
            Return
        End If
        Dim shutDownMessage As String = _
            CType(MyRuntime.GetType().InvokeMember("_shutDownMessage", _
            BindingFlags.NonPublic Or BindingFlags.Instance Or _
            BindingFlags.GetField, _
            Nothing, MyRuntime, Nothing), System.String)
```

```
Dim shutDownStack As String = _
    CType(MyRuntime.GetType().InvokeMember("_shutDownStack", _
    BindingFlags.NonPublic Or BindingFlags.Instance Or _
    BindingFlags.GetField, _
    Nothing, MyRuntime, Nothing), System.String)

If (Not EventLog.SourceExists(".NET Runtime")) Then
    EventLog.CreateEventSource(".NET Runtime", "Application")
End If

Dim logEntry As EventLog = New EventLog()
logEntry.Source = ".NET Runtime"
logEntry.WriteEntry(String.Format( _
    "shutDownMessage={0}\r\n\r\n_shutDownStack={1}", _
    shutDownMessage, shutDownStack), EventLogEntryType.Error)
End Sub

</script>
```

With this code in place in your `Global.asax` file, start your ASP.NET application. Next, do something to cause the application to restart. For example, you could make a change to the `web.config` file while the application is running. This triggers the `Application_End` event, resulting in the addition to the Event Log shown in Figure 19-12.

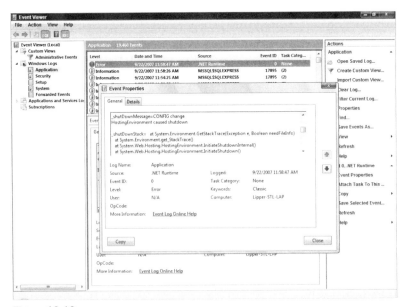

Figure 19-12

ASP.NET Server Controls

In the past, one of the difficulties in working with classic ASP was that you were completely in charge of the entire HTML output from the browser by virtue of the server-side code you wrote. Although this might seem ideal, it created a problem because each browser interpreted the HTML given to it in a slightly different way.

The two main browsers at the time were Internet Explorer and Netscape Navigator. This meant that not only did developers have to be cognizant of the browser type to which they were outputting HTML, they also had to take into account which versions of those particular browsers might be making a request to their application. Some developers resolved the issue by creating two separate applications. When an end user made an initial request to the application, the code made a browser check to see what browser type made the request. Then, the ASP page redirected the request: down one path for an IE user or down another path for a Netscape user.

Because requests came from so many different versions of the same browser, developers typically designed for the lowest possible version that might be used to visit the site. Everyone loses when the lowest common denominator is used as the target. This technique ensures that the page is rendered properly in most browsers making a request, but it forces developers to dumb down their applications. If applications are built for the lowest common denominator, then developers can't take advantage of the more advanced features offered by newer browser versions.

ASP.NET server controls overcome these obstacles. When using the server controls provided by ASP.NET, you are not specifying the HTML to be output from your server-side code. Rather, you are specifying the functionality you want to see in the browser, letting the ASP.NET determine the output to be sent to the browser.

When a request comes in, ASP.NET examines the request to see which browser type is making it, as well as the version of the browser, and then it produces HTML output specific to that browser. This process is accomplished by processing a User Agent header retrieved from the HTTP request to *sniff* the browser. This means that you can now build for the best browsers out there without worrying about whether features will work in the different browsers making requests to your applications. Because of these capabilities, these server controls are often referred to as *smart controls*.

Types of Server Controls

ASP.NET provides two distinct types of server controls: HTML server controls and web server controls. Each type of control is quite different; and as you work with ASP.NET, you will see that much of the focus is on the web server controls. This does not mean that HTML server controls have no value. They do provide you with many capabilities — some that web server controls do not.

If you are wondering which is the better control type to use, it depends on what you are trying to achieve. HTML server controls map to specific HTML elements. You can place an `HtmlTable` server control on your ASP.NET page that works dynamically with a `<table>` element. On the other hand, web server controls map to specific functionality that you want on your ASP.NET pages. This means an `<asp:Panel>` control might use a `<table>` or an `<IFrame>` element — it depends on the capability of the requesting browser.

The following table summarizes some advice regarding when to use HTML server controls and when to use web server controls:

Control Type	Use This Control Type . . .
HTML Server	When converting traditional ASP 3.0 Web pages to ASP.NET Web pages and speed of completion is a concern. It is a lot easier to change your HTML elements to HTML server controls than it is to change them to web server controls.
	When you prefer a more HTML-type programming model.
	When you want to explicitly control the code that is generated for the browser.
Web Server	When you require a richer set of functionality to achieve complicated page requirements.
	When you are developing Web pages that will be viewed by a multitude of browser types and that require different code based upon these types.
	When you prefer a more Visual Basic–type programming model that is based on the use of controls and control properties.

Of course, some developers like to separate certain controls from the rest and place them in their own categories. For instance, you may see references to the following types of controls:

❑ **List controls** — Enable data to be bound to them for display purposes of some kind

❑ **Rich controls** — Controls, such as the Calendar control, that display richer content and capabilities than other controls

❑ **Validation controls** — Controls that interact with other form controls to validate the data that they contain

❑ **Mobile controls** — Specific to output to devices such as mobile phones, PDAs, and more

❑ **User controls** — Not really controls, but page templates that you can work with as you would a control on your ASP.NET page

❑ **Custom controls** — Controls that you build yourself and use in the same manner as the supplied ASP.NET server controls that are included with the default install of ASP.NET 3.5

When you are deciding between HTML server controls and web server controls, remember that no hard-and-fast rules exist about which type to use. You might find yourself working with one control type more than another, but certain features are available in one control type that might not be available in the other. If you are trying to accomplish a specific task and do not see a solution with the control type you are using, another control type may very well hold the answer. Keep in mind that you can mix and match these control types. Nothing prevents you from using both HTML server controls and web server controls on the same page or within the same application.

Building with Server Controls

You have a couple of ways to use server controls to construct your ASP.NET pages. You can use tools that are specifically designed to work with ASP.NET 3.5 that enable you to visually drag and drop controls onto a design surface and manipulate the behavior of the control, or you can work with server controls directly through code input.

Working with Server Controls on a Design Surface

Visual Studio 2008 enables you to visually create an ASP.NET page by dragging and dropping visual controls onto a design surface. You can get to this visual design option by clicking the Design tab at the bottom of the IDE when viewing your ASP.NET page. You can also show the Design mode and the Source code view in the same document window. This is a new feature available in Visual Studio 2008. When the Design view is present, you can place the cursor on the page in the location where you want the control to appear and then double-click the control you want in the Toolbox window of Visual Studio. Unlike the 2002 and 2003 versions of Visual Studio, Visual Studio 2008 (like Visual Studio 2005) does an excellent job of not touching your code when switching between the Design and Source tabs.

In the Design view of your page, you can highlight a control, and the properties for the control appear in the Properties window. For example, Figure 19-13 shows a `Button` control selected, with its properties displayed in the Properties window on the right.

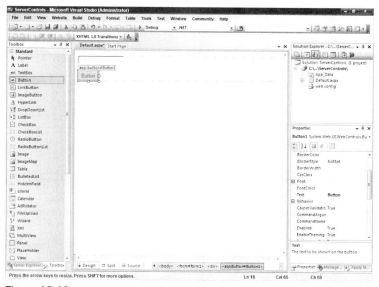

Figure 19-13

Changing the properties in the window changes the appearance or behavior of the highlighted control. Because all controls inherit from a specific base class (`WebControl`), you can highlight multiple controls at the same time and change the base properties of all the controls at once by holding down the Ctrl key as you make your control selections.

Coding Server Controls

You also can work from the code page directly. Because many developers prefer this, it is the default when you first create your ASP.NET page. Hand-coding your own ASP.NET pages may seem to be a slower approach than simply dragging and dropping controls onto a design surface, but it isn't as slow as you might think. You get plenty of assistance in coding your applications from Visual Studio 2008. As you start typing in Visual Studio, the IntelliSense features kick in and help you with code auto-completion. Figure 19-14, for example, shows an IntelliSense drop-down list of possible code completion statements that appeared as the code was typed.

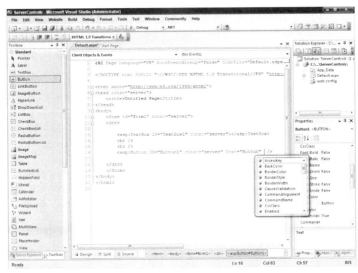

Figure 19-14

The IntelliSense focus is on the most commonly used attribute or statement for the control or piece of code that you are working with. Using IntelliSense effectively as you work is a great way to code with speed.

Like Design view, the Source view of your page enables you to drag and drop controls from the Toolbox onto the code page itself. For example, dragging and dropping a TextBox control onto the code page produces the same results as dropping it on the design page:

```
<asp:TextBox ID="TextBox1" Runat="server"></asp:TextBox>
```

You can also highlight a control in Source view, or simply place your cursor in the code statement of the control, and the Properties window displays the properties of the control. You can apply properties directly in the Properties window of Visual Studio, and these properties are dynamically added to the code of your control.

Working with Server Control Events

ASP.NET uses more of a traditional Visual Basic event model than classic ASP. Instead of working with interpreted code, you are actually coding an event-based structure for your pages. Classic ASP used an interpreted model: When the server processed the Web page, the code of the page was interpreted line by line in a linear fashion whereby the only "event" implied was the page loading. This meant that occurrences you wanted to initiate early in the process were placed at the top of the page.

Today, ASP.NET uses an event-driven model. Items or coding tasks are initiated only when a particular event occurs. A common event in the ASP.NET programming model is Page_Load, shown here:

```
Protected Sub Page_Load(ByVal sender As Object, ByVal e As System.EventArgs)
    ' Code actions here
End Sub
```

Not only can you work with the overall page — as well as its properties and methods at particular moments in time via page events — you can also work with the server controls contained on the page through particular control events. For example, one common event for a button on a form is Button_Click, illustrated here:

```
Protected Sub Button1_Click(ByVal sender As Object, ByVal e As System.EventArgs)
    ' Code actions here
End Sub
```

The event shown here is fired only when the end user actually clicks the button on the form that has an OnClick attribute value of Button1_Click. Therefore, not only does the event handler exist in the server-side code of the ASP.NET page, but that handler is also hooked up using the OnClick property of the server control in the associated ASP.NET page markup, as shown here:

```
<asp:Button ID="Button1" Runat="server" Text="Button"
 OnClick="Button1_Click" />
```

How do you fire these events for server controls? You have a couple of ways to go about it. The first way is to pull up your ASP.NET page in Design view and double-click the control for which you want to create a server-side event. For instance, double-clicking a Button server control in Design view creates the structure of the Button1_Click event within your server-side code, whether the code is in a code-behind file or inline. This creates a stub handler for that server control's most popular event.

That said, be aware that a considerable number of additional events are available to the Button control that you cannot access by double-clicking the control. To access them, pull up the page that contains the server-side code, select the control from the first drop-down list at the top of the IDE, and then choose the particular event you want for that control in the second drop-down list. Figure 19-15 shows the event drop-down list displayed. You might, for example, want to work with the Button control's PreRender event, rather than its Click event. The handler for the event you choose is placed in your server-side code.

The second way to create server-side events for your server controls is from the Properties window of Visual Studio. This works only from Design view of the page. In Design view, highlight the server control that you want to work with. The properties for the control will appear in the Properties window, along with an icon menu. One of the icons, the Events icon, is represented by a lightning bolt within the IDE (see Figure 19-16).

Clicking the Events icon pulls up a list of events available for the control. Simply double-click one of the events to have that event structure created in your server-side code. After you have an event structure in place, you can program specific actions you want to occur when the event is fired.

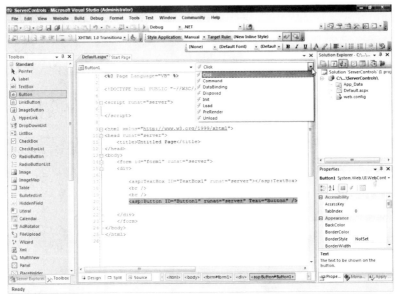

Figure 19-15

Figure 19-16

Manipulating Pages and Server Controls with JavaScript

Developers generally like to include some of their own custom JavaScript functions in their ASP.NET pages. You have a couple of ways to do this. The first is to apply JavaScript directly to the controls on your ASP.NET pages. For example, the following simple Label server control displays the current date and time:

```
Protected Sub Page_Load(ByVal sender As Object, ByVal e As System.EventArgs)
    TextBox1.Text = DateTime.Now.ToString()
End Sub
```

The problem is that the date and time displayed are correct for the web server that generated the page. If the user is in the Pacific time zone (PST) and the web server is in the Eastern time zone (EST), the page won't be correct for that viewer. To ensure that the time is correct for anyone visiting the site, regardless of where they reside in the world, you can employ JavaScript to work with the TextBox control:

```
<%@ Page Language="VB" %>

<html xmlns="http://www.w3.org/1999/xhtml" >
<head runat="server">
    <title>Using JavaScript</title>
</head>
<body onload="javascript:document.forms[0]['TextBox1'].value=Date();">
    <form id="form1" runat="server">
    <div>
        <asp:TextBox ID="TextBox1" Runat="server" Width="300"></asp:TextBox>
    </div>
    </form>
</body>
</html>
```

In this example, even though you are using a standard TextBox server control from the web server control family, you can access this control using JavaScript that is planted in the onload attribute of the <body> element. The value of the onload attribute actually points to the specific server control via an anonymous function by using the value of the ID attribute from the server control: TextBox1. You can get at other server controls on your page by employing the same methods. This bit of code produces a text box with the current date and time inside of it.

ASP.NET uses the Page.ClientScript property to register and place JavaScript functions on your ASP .NET pages. Three of these methods are reviewed here. Other methods and properties are available through the ClientScript object (which references an instance of System.Web.UI.ClientScript Manager), but these are the most useful ones. You can find the rest in the SDK documentation.

The Page.RegisterStartupScript *and* Page.RegisterClientScriptBlock *methods from the .NET Framework 1.0/1.1 are now considered obsolete. Both of these options for registering scripts required a key/script set of parameters. Because two separate methods were involved, key name collisions were common. The* Page.ClientScript *property is meant to bring all the script registrations under one umbrella, making your code less error-prone.*

Using Page.ClientScript.RegisterClientScriptBlock

The `RegisterClientScriptBlock` method enables you to place a JavaScript function at the top of the page. This means that the script is in place for the startup of the page in the browser. Its use is shown here:

```
<%@ Page Language="VB" %>

<script runat="server">
    Protected Sub Page_Load(ByVal sender As Object, _
      ByVal e As System.EventArgs)

      Dim myScript As String = _
         "function AlertHello() { alert('Hello ASP.NET'); }"
      Page.ClientScript.RegisterClientScriptBlock(Me.GetType(), "MyScript", _
         myScript, True)
    End Sub
</script>

<html xmlns="http://www.w3.org/1999/xhtml" >
<head runat="server">
    <title>Adding JavaScript</title>
</head>
<body>
    <form id="form1" runat="server">
    <div>
        <asp:Button ID="Button1" Runat="server" Text="Button"
        OnClientClick="AlertHello()" />
    </div>
    </form>
</body>
</html>
```

You create the JavaScript function `AlertHello` as a string called `myScript`. Then, using the `Page.Client Script.RegisterClientScriptBlock` method, you program the script to be placed on the page. The two possible constructions of the `RegisterClientScriptBlock` method are as follows:

❑   `RegisterClientScriptBlock` (*type*, *key*, script)

❑   `RegisterClientScriptBlock` (*type*, *key*, *script*, script tag specification)

The preceding example specifies the type as `Me.GetType`, the key, the script to include, and then a `Boolean` value setting of `True` so that .NET places the script on the ASP.NET page with <script> tags automatically. When running the page, you can view the source code for the page to see the results:

```
<html xmlns="http://www.w3.org/1999/xhtml" >
<head><title>
    Adding JavaScript
</title></head>
<body>
    <form method="post" action="JavaScriptPage.aspx" id="form1">
<div>
<input type="hidden" name="__VIEWSTATE"
```

```
         value="/wEPDwUKMTY3NzE5MjIyMGRkiyYSRMg+bcXi9DiawYlbxndiTDo=" />
      </div>


      <script type="text/javascript">
      <!--
      function AlertHello() { alert('Hello ASP.NET'); }// -->
      </script>

          <div>
              <input type="submit" name="Button1" value="Button"
              onclick="AlertHello();"
              id="Button1" />
          </div>
          </form>
      </body>
      </html>
```

From this, you can see that the script specified was indeed included on the ASP.NET page before the page code. Not only were the `<script>` tags included, but the proper comment tags were added around the script (so older browsers will not break).

Using Page.ClientScript.RegisterStartupScript

The `RegisterStartupScript` method is similar to the `RegisterClientScriptBlock` method. The big difference is that the `RegisterStartupScript` places the script at the bottom of the ASP.NET page instead of at the top. In fact, the `RegisterStartupScript` method even takes the same constructors as the `RegisterClientScriptBlock` method:

❑   `RegisterStartupScript` (*type*, *key*, script)

❑   `RegisterStartupScript` (*type*, *key*, *script*, script tag specification)

What difference does it make where the script is registered on the page? A lot, actually! If you have a bit of JavaScript that is working with one of the controls on your page, in most cases you want to use the `RegisterStartupScript` method instead of `RegisterClientScriptBlock`. For example, you would use the following code to create a page that includes a simple `<asp:TextBox>` control that contains a default value of `Hello ASP.NET`:

```
<asp:TextBox ID="TextBox1" Runat="server">Hello ASP.NET</asp:TextBox>
```

Then use the `RegisterClientScriptBlock` method to place a script on the page that utilizes the value in the `TextBox1` control:

```
Protected Sub Page_Load(ByVal sender As Object, ByVal e As System.EventArgs)
    Dim myScript As String = "alert(document.forms[0]['TextBox1'].value);"
    Page.ClientScript.RegisterClientScriptBlock(Me.GetType(), "myKey", myScript, _
        True)
End Sub
```

Running this page results in the JavaScript error shown in Figure 19-17.

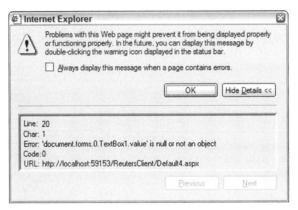

Figure 19-17

The error occurs because the JavaScript function fired before the text box was even placed on the screen. Therefore, the JavaScript function did not find TextBox1, which caused an error to be thrown by the page. Now try the RegisterStartupScript method shown here:

```
Protected Sub Page_Load(ByVal sender As Object, ByVal e As System.EventArgs)
    Dim myScript As String = "alert(document.forms[0]['TextBox1'].value);"
    Page.ClientScript.RegisterStartupScript(Me.GetType(), "myKey", myScript, _
        True)
End Sub
```

This approach puts the JavaScript function at the bottom of the ASP.NET page, so when the JavaScript actually starts, it finds the TextBox1 element and works as planned, as shown in Figure 19-18.

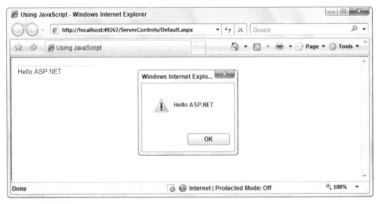

Figure 19-18

Using Page.ClientScript.RegisterClientScriptInclude

The final method is RegisterClientScriptInclude. Many developers place their JavaScript inside a .js file, which is considered a best practice because it makes it very easy to make global JavaScript changes to the application. You can register the script files on your ASP.NET pages using the `RegisterClientScript Include` method, shown here:

```
Dim myScript As String = "myJavaScriptCode.js"
Page.ClientScript.RegisterClientScriptInclude("myKey", myScript)
```

This creates the following construction on the ASP.NET page:

```
<script src="myJavaScriptCode.js" type="text/javascript"></script>
```

Summary

This chapter covered a lot of ground. It discussed many aspects of ASP.NET applications as a whole and the options you have when building and deploying these applications. With the help of Visual Studio 2008, you have a number of options regarding which web server to use when building your application and whether to work locally or remotely through the built-in FTP capabilities.

ASP.NET 3.5 and Visual Studio 2008 make it easy to build your pages using an inline coding model or a code-behind model that is simpler to use and easier to deploy. You also learned about the fixed folders that ASP.NET 3.5 has to make your life easier. These folders make their resources available dynamically with no work on your part. Finally, you saw some of the outstanding JavaScript options that you have at your disposal. The next chapter examines some of the more advanced systems available to you in ASP.NET 3.5.

20

ASP.NET 3.5 Advanced Features

ASP.NET is an exciting technology. It enables the creation and delivery of remotely generated applications (Web applications) accessible via a simple browser — a container that many are rather familiar with. The purpose of Web-based applications (in our case, ASP.NET applications) is to deliver only a single instance of the application to the end user over HTTP. This means that the end users viewing your application will always have the latest and greatest version at their disposal. Because of this, many companies today are looking at ASP.NET to not only deliver the company's website, but also to deliver some of their latest applications for their employees, partners, and customers.

The last chapter looked at some of the basics of ASP.NET 3.5. This chapter continues that exploration, showing you some additional and exciting technologies that you will find in ASP.NET 3.5, including master pages, configuration, data access, and more.

This chapter touches upon many topics, as ASP.NET has become a rather large offering with many possibilities and capabilities. Sit back, pull up that keyboard, and enjoy!

Applications and Pages

The previous chapter looked at the structure of ASP.NET pages and their life cycle. You can do quite a bit with the applications and pages in ASP.NET to change how they behave or how you compile and deliver them. This section looks at some of these possibilities.

Cross-Page Posting

In Active Server Pages 2.0/3.0 (also called *classic ASP*), values from forms were usually posted to other pages. These pages were typically steps in a process that the end user worked through. With the introduction of ASP.NET, pages in this environment posted back results to themselves in a step called a *postback*. One of the most frequent requests of Web developers in the ASP.NET world has been the capability to do postbacks, not only to the page from which the values originated, but also to other pages within the application. You can easily accomplish this *cross-page posting* functionality in ASP.NET 3.5, which makes it possible to post page values from one page (Page1.aspx) to an entirely different page (Page2.aspx). Normally, when posting to the same page (as with ASP.NET 1.0/1.1), you could capture the postback in a postback event, as shown here:

```
If Page.IsPostBack Then
    ' do work here
End If
```

Now look at Page1.aspx and see how you accomplish cross-page posting with ASP.NET 3.5:

```
<%@ Page Language="VB" %>

<script runat="server">
    Protected Sub Button1_Click(ByVal sender As Object, _
        ByVal e As System.EventArgs)

        Label1.Text = "Your name is: " & TextBox1.Text & "<br>" & _
            "Your appointment is on: " & _
            Calendar1.SelectedDate.ToLongDateString()
    End Sub
</script>

<html xmlns="http://www.w3.org/1999/xhtml" >
<head runat="server">
    <title>Cross-Page Posting</title>
</head>
<body>
    <form id="form1" runat="server">
    <div>
        What is your name?<br />
        <asp:TextBox ID="TextBox1" runat="server"></asp:TextBox>
        <br />
        <br />
        When is your appointment?<br />
        <asp:Calendar ID="Calendar1" runat="server">
        </asp:Calendar><br />
        <asp:Button ID="Button1" OnClick="Button1_Click" runat="server"
         Text="Do a PostBack to this Page" />
        <br />
        <br />
        <asp:Button ID="Button2" runat="server"
         Text="Do a PostBack to Another Page" PostBackUrl="~/Page2.aspx" />
        <br />
        <br />
        <asp:Label ID="Label1" runat="server"></asp:Label>
    </div>
    </form>
</body>
</html>
```

With `Page1.aspx`, there is nothing really different about this page — except for the `Button2` server control. This page contains a new attribute, which you will find with the `Button`, `ImageButton`, and `LinkButton` controls — the `PostBackUrl` attribute. The value of this attribute points to the location of the file that this page should post to. In this case, the `PostBackUrl` attribute states that this page should post to `Page2.aspx`. This is the only thing needed on the `Page1.aspx` to cause it to post back to another page. As for `Button1`, this is a simple button that causes the page to post back to itself, as was the case even in ASP.NET 1.x. The event handler for this postback is in the `OnClick` attribute within the `Button1` control. Pressing this button causes the page to post back to itself and to populate the `Label1` control at the bottom of the page.

Clicking on the second button, though, will post to the second page, which is shown here:

```
<%@ Page Language="VB" %>

<script runat="server">
    Protected Sub Page_Load(ByVal sender As Object, _
     ByVal e As System.EventArgs)

        Dim pp_TextBox1 As TextBox
        Dim pp_Calendar1 As Calendar

        pp_TextBox1 = CType(PreviousPage.FindControl("TextBox1"), TextBox)
        pp_Calendar1 = CType(PreviousPage.FindControl("Calendar1"), Calendar)

        Label1.Text = "Your name is: " & pp_TextBox1.Text & "<br>" & _
            "Your appointment is on: " & _
            pp_Calendar1.SelectedDate.ToLongDateString()
    End Sub
</script>

<html xmlns="http://www.w3.org/1999/xhtml" >
<head runat="server">
    <title>Second Page</title>
</head>
<body>
    <form id="form1" runat="server">
    <div>
        <asp:Label ID="Label1" runat="server"></asp:Label>
    </div>
    </form>
</body>
</html>
```

In this page, the first step is the creation in the `Page_Load` event of instances of both the `TextBox` and `Calendar` controls. From here, these instances are populated with the values of these controls on the previous page (`Page1.aspx`) by using the `PreviousPage.FindControl` method. The `String` value assigned to the `FindControl` method is the `ID` value of the ASP.NET server control from the originating page (in this case, `TextBox1` and `Calendar1`). Once you have assigned the values to these control instances, you can then start working with the new controls and their values as if they were posted from the same page.

You can also expose the server controls and other items as properties from `Page1.aspx`, as illustrated in this partial code sample:

```
<%@ Page Language="VB" %>

<script runat="server">

    Public ReadOnly Property pp_TextBox1() As TextBox
        Get
            Return TextBox1
        End Get
    End Property

    Public ReadOnly Property pp_Calendar1() As Calendar
        Get
            Return Calendar1
        End Get
    End Property


    Protected Sub Button1_Click(ByVal sender As Object, _
        ByVal e As System.EventArgs)

        Label1.Text = "Your name is: " & TextBox1.Text & "<br>" & _
            "Your appointment is on: " & Calendar1.SelectedDate.ToLongDateString()
    End Sub
</script>
```

Once you have exposed the properties you want from `Page1.aspx`, you can easily get at these properties in the cross-page postback by using the new `PreviousPageType` page directive, as shown in the following example:

```
<%@ Page Language="VB" %>
<%@ PreviousPageType VirtualPath="~/Page1.aspx" %>

<script runat="server">
    Protected Sub Page_Load(ByVal sender As Object, _
        ByVal e As System.EventArgs)

        Label1.Text = "Your name is: " & PreviousPage.pp_TextBox1.Text & _
            "<br>" & _
            "Your appointment is on: " & _
            PreviousPage.pp_Calendar1.SelectedDate.ToLongDateString()
    End Sub
</script>
```

After your properties are on `Page1.aspx`, you can access them easily by strongly typing the `PreviousPage` property on `Page2.aspx` by using the `PreviousPageType` directive. The `PreviousPageType` directive specifies the page from which the post will come. Using this directive enables you to specifically point at `Page1.aspx`. This is done using the `VirtualPath` attribute of the `PreviousPageType` directive. The `VirtualPath` attribute takes a `String` whose value is the location of the directing page.

Once this association has been made, you can then use the `PreviousPage` property. The `pp_TextBox1` and `pp_Calendar1` properties that were created on `Page1.aspx` are now present in Visual Studio 2008's

IntelliSense (see Figure 20-1). Working with the `PreviousPage` property is a bit easier and is less error prone than using weak typing.

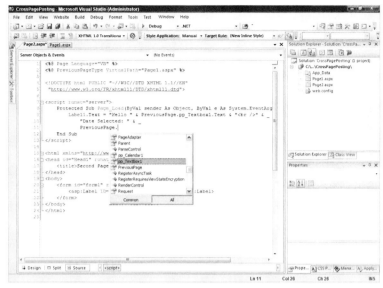

Figure 20-1

One thing to guard against is a browser hitting a page that is expecting information from a cross-page post; this action causes errors if the information the second page is expecting is not there. You have always had to guard against pages that were looking for postback information — even when dealing with ASP.NET pages (1.0/1.1) that performed postbacks to themselves. With standard pages that are not cross-page posting, you could protect your code from this postback behavior through the use of the `Page.IsPostBack` property, as shown here:

```
If Page.IsPostBack Then
    ' code here
End If
```

When cross-page posting, use the `Page.IsCrossPagePostBack` property:

```
<%@ Page Language="VB" %>
<%@ PreviousPageType VirtualPath="~/Page1.aspx" %>

<script runat="server">
    Protected Sub Page_Load(ByVal sender As Object, _
        ByVal e As System.EventArgs)

        If Not PreviousPage Is Nothing And _
            PreviousPage.IsCrossPagePostBack Then

            Label1.Text = "Your name is: " & PreviousPage.pp_TextBox1.Text & _
                "<br>" & _
                "Your appointment is on: " & _
                PreviousPage.pp_Calendar1.SelectedDate.ToLongDateString()
```

```
        Else
            Response.Redirect("Page1.aspx")
        End If
    End Sub

</script>
```

In this example, if someone hits this page without going to Page1.aspx first to get cross-posted to Page2.aspx, then the request will be checked to determine whether the request is a cross post. If it is (checked using the Page.IsCrossPagePostBack property), then the code is run; otherwise, the request is redirected to Page1.aspx.

ASP.NET Compilation

With ASP.NET, you can observe this compilation process and how it works when you hit one of the ASP.NET pages you have built for the first time. You will notice that it takes a few seconds for the page to be generated. When an ASP.NET page is referenced in the browser for the first time, the request is passed to the ASP.NET parser that creates the class file in the language of the page. It is passed to the parser based on the file's extension (.aspx) because ASP.NET realizes that this file extension type is meant for its handling and processing. After the class file has been created, it is compiled into a DLL and then written to the disk of the Web server. At this point, the DLL is instantiated and processed, and output is generated for the initial requester of the ASP.NET page. This process is detailed in Figure 20-2.

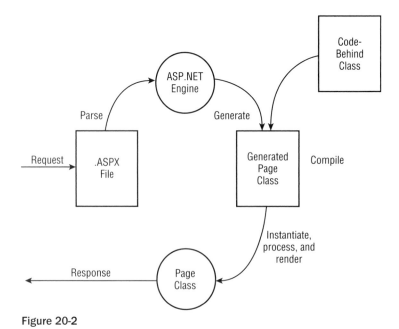

Figure 20-2

On the next request, great things happen. Instead of going through the entire process again for the second and subsequent requests, the request simply causes an instantiation of the already created DLL, which sends out a response to the requester (see Figure 20-3).

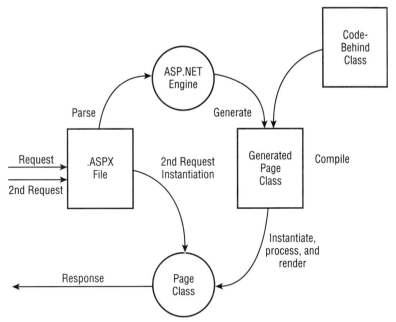

Figure 20-3

Previously, because of the mechanics of this process, if you made changes to your `.aspx` code-behind pages, then it was necessary to recompile your application. This was quite a pain if you had a larger site and didn't want your end users to experience the extreme lag that occurs when an `.aspx` page is referenced for the first time after compilation. Many developers, consequently, began to develop their own tools that automatically hit every single page within the application to remove this first-time lag hit from the end user's browsing experience.

ASP.NET 3.5 provides a few ways to precompile your entire application with a single command that you can issue through a command line. One type of compilation is referred to as *in-place precompilation*. In order to precompile your entire ASP.NET application, you must use the `aspnet_compiler.exe` tool that comes with ASP.NET. To do so, open the command prompt window and navigate to `C:\Windows\Microsoft.NET\Framework\v2.0.50727\`. From there you can work with the `aspnet_compiler` tool. You can also access this tool directly by pulling up the Visual Studio 2008 command prompt window. Choose Start ➪ All Programs ➪ Microsoft Visual Studio 2008 ➪ Visual Studio Tools ➪ Visual Studio 2008 Command Prompt.

After you get the command prompt, use the `aspnet_compiler.exe` tool to perform an in-place precompilation using the following command:

```
aspnet_compiler -p "C:\Inetpub\wwwroot\WROX" -v none
```

In the example just shown, `-v` is a command for the virtual path of the application, which is provided by using `\WROX`. The next command is `-p`, which points to the physical path of the application. In this case, it is `C:\Websites\WROX`. Finally, the last bit, `C:\Wrox`, is the location of the compiler output. The following table describes the possible commands for the `aspnet_compiler.exe` tool:

Command	Description
-m	Specifies the full IIS metabase path of the application. If you use the -m command, then you cannot use the -v or -p command.
-v	Specifies the virtual path of the application to be compiled. If you also use the -p command, then the physical path is used to find the location of the application.
-p	Specifies the physical path of the application to be compiled. If this is not specified, then the IIS metabase is used to find the application.
-u	When this command is utilized, it specifies that the application is updateable.
-f	Specifies overwriting the target directory if it already exists
-d	Specifies that the debug information should be excluded from the compilation process
[targetDir]	Specifies the target directory in which the compiled files should be placed. If this is not specified, then the output files are placed in the application directory.

After compiling the application, you can go to C:\Wrox to see the output. Here you see all the files and file structures that were in the original application, but if you look at the content of one of the files, the file is simply a placeholder. In the actual file is the following comment:

```
This is a marker file generated by the precompilation tool
and should not be deleted!
```

In fact, you find a Code.dll file in the bin folder where all the page code is located. Because it is in a DLL file, it provides great code obfuscation as well. From here on, all you do is move these files to another server using FTP or Windows Explorer, and you can run the entire Web application from these files. When you have an update to the application, you simply provide a new set of compiled files. Sample output is displayed in Figure 20-4.

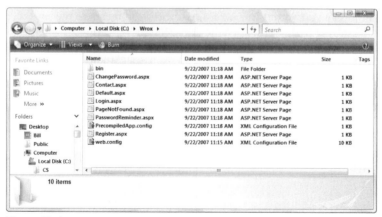

Figure 20-4

Note that this compilation process does not compile *every* type of Web file. In fact, it compiles only the ASP.NET-specific file types, omitting from the compilation process the following types of files:

❑   HTML files

❑   XML files

❑   XSD files

❑   web.config files

❑   Text files

You cannot do much to get around this, except in the case of the HTML files and the text files. For these file types, just change the file extensions of these file types to .aspx; they are then compiled into the Code.dll like all the other ASP.NET files.

Master Pages

Many Web applications are built so that each page of the application has some similarities. For instance, a common header might be used on every page of your application. Similarly, there may be other common page elements, including navigation sections, advertisements, footers, and more. In fact, individual Web pages rarely have their own unique look and feel. Most people prefer uniformity in their applications in order to give end users a consistent experience in a multi-paged application.

What is needed for these types of applications is a way to provide a template that can be used by your pages — a sort of visual inheritance (such as you can achieve with Windows Forms). With a feature that was first introduced in ASP.NET 2.0 called *master pages*, you can now employ visual inheritance in your Web applications.

The use of master pages means that you are working with a template file (the master page), which has a .master extension. Once a .master page is created, you can then take a *content page*, with an .aspx extension, and create an association between the two files. Doing this enables ASP.NET to combine the two files into a single Web page to display in a browser, as illustrated in Figure 20-5.

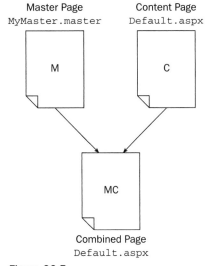

Figure 20-5

847

The following sections describe how you make this work, beginning with the master page.

Creating a Master Page

The first step is to create a template that will end up being your master page. You can build a master page using any text editor (such as Notepad), but it is far easier to use Visual Studio 2008 or Visual Web Developer, as described here.

Start within the Solution Explorer. Right-click on the solution and select Add New Item. In the Add New Item dialog is an option to add a master page to the solution, as shown in Figure 20-6.

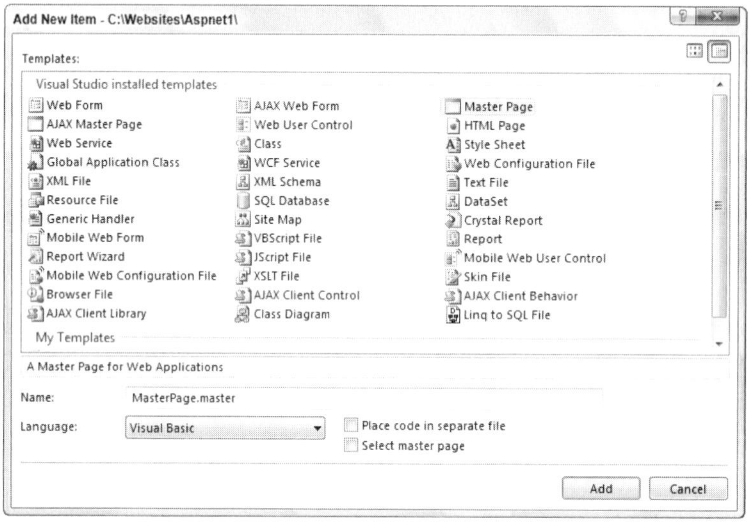

Figure 20-6

Your master page options are quite similar to those when working with a standard .aspx page. You can create master pages to be inline or you can have master pages that utilize the code-behind model. If you wish to use the code-behind model, then make sure that you have the "Place code in separate file" check box checked in the dialog — otherwise, leave it blank. Creating an inline master page produces a single .master file. Using the code-behind model produces a .master file in addition to a .master.vb or .master.cs file. You also have the option of nesting your master page within another master page by selecting the Select Master Page option.

A master page should be built so that it contains one or more content regions that are utilized by the content pages. The following master page example (named Wrox.master) contains two of these content areas:

```
<%@ Master Language="VB" %>

<!DOCTYPE html PUBLIC "-//W3C//DTD XHTML 1.1//EN"
  "http://www.w3.org/TR/xhtml11/DTD/xhtml11.dtd">

<script runat="server">
```

```
    </script>

    <html xmlns="http://www.w3.org/1999/xhtml" >
    <head runat="server">
        <title>Wrox</title>
        <asp:ContentPlaceHolder id="head" runat="server">
        </asp:ContentPlaceHolder>
    </head>
    <body>
        <form id="form1" runat="server">
        <div>
            <table cellpadding="3" border="1">
                <tr bgcolor="silver">
                    <td colspan="2"><h1>The Wrox Company Homepage</h1></td>
                </tr>
                <tr>
                    <td>
                        <asp:ContentPlaceHolder ID="ContentPlaceHolder1"
                         runat="server">
                        </asp:ContentPlaceHolder>
                    </td>
                    <td>
                        <asp:ContentPlaceHolder ID="ContentPlaceHolder2"
                         runat="server">
                        </asp:ContentPlaceHolder>
                    </td>
                </tr>
                <tr>
                    <td colspan="2">Copyright 2008 - Wrox</td>
                </tr>
            </table>
        </div>
        </form>
    </body>
    </html>
```

The first thing to notice is the `< % Master % >` directive at the top of the page instead of the standard `< % Page % >` directive. This specifies that this is a master page and cannot be generated without a content page associated with it. It is not a page that you can pull up in the browser. In this case, the `Master` directive simply uses the `Language` attribute and nothing more, but it has a number of other attributes at its disposal to fine-tune the behavior of the page.

The idea is to code the master page as you would any other `.aspx` page. This master page contains a simple table and two areas that are meant for the content pages. These areas are defined with the use of the `ContentPlaceHolder` server control. This page contains two such controls. It is *only* in these two specified areas where content pages will be allowed to interject content into the dynamically created page (as shown shortly).

The nice thing about working with master pages is that you are not limited to working with them in the Code view of the IDE; Visual Studio 2008 also enables you to work with them in Design view as well, as shown in Figure 20-7. In this view, you can work with the master page by simply dragging and dropping controls onto the design surface, just as you would with any typical .aspx page.

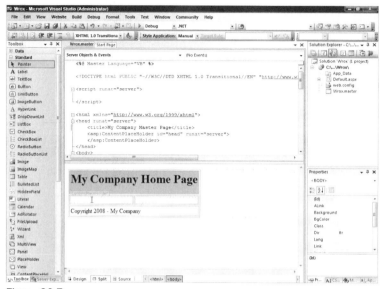

Figure 20-7

Creating the Content Page

Now that there is a master page in your project that you can utilize, the next step is to create a content page that does just that. Right-click on the solution from within the Solution Explorer of Visual Studio 2008 and select Add New Item. This time, though, you are going to add a typical Web Form to the project. However, before you click the Add button, be sure to check the Select Master Page check box in the dialog. This informs VS 2008 that you are going to build a content page that will be associated with a master page. Doing this pulls up a new dialog that enables you to select a master page to associate with this new file, as shown in Figure 20-8.

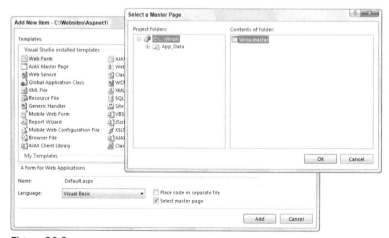

Figure 20-8

In this case, if you have been following along with the example, you should only have a single master page available in the dialog, though it is possible to have as many different master pages as you wish in a single project. Select the `Wrox.master` page and press the OK button.

The page created has only a single line of code to it:

```
<%@ Page Language="VB" MasterPageFile="~/Wrox.master" Title="Untitled Page" %>
```

This file is quite a bit different from a typical `.aspx` page. First, there is none of the default HTML code, script tags, and `DOCTYPE` declarations that are the norm. Second, note the addition of the `MasterPageFile` attribute in the `Page` directive. This new attribute makes the association to the master page that will be used for this content page. In this case, it is the `Wrox.master` file created earlier.

There isn't much to show while in the Source view of Visual Studio when looking at a content page; the real power of master pages can be seen when you switch to the Design view of the same page (see Figure 20-9).

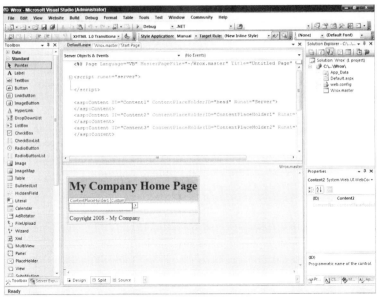

Figure 20-9

This view shows you the entire template and the two content areas that this content page is allowed to deal with. All the grayed-out areas are off-limits and do not allow for any changes from the content page, whereas the available areas allow you to deal with any type of content you wish. For instance, not only can you place raw text in these content areas, you can also add anything that you would normally place into a typical `.aspx` page. For example, create a simple form in one of the content areas and place an image in the other. The code is shown here:

```
<%@ Page Language="VB" MasterPageFile="~/Wrox.master" Title="My Content Page" %>

<script runat="server">
```

```
    Protected Sub Button1_Click(ByVal sender As Object, _
       ByVal e As System.EventArgs)
         Label1.Text = "Hello " & Textbox1.Text
    End Sub
</script>

<asp:Content ID="Content1" ContentPlaceHolderID="ContentPlaceHolder1"
 runat="server">
    <b>Enter in your name:<br />
    <asp:TextBox ID="TextBox1" runat="server"></asp:TextBox>
    <asp:Button ID="Button1" runat="server" Text="Submit"
     OnClick="Button1_Click" />
    <br />
    <br />
    <asp:Label ID="Label1" runat="server" Font-Bold="True"></asp:Label>
    </b>
</asp:Content>

<asp:Content ID="Content2" ContentPlaceHolderID="ContentPlaceHolder2"
 runat="server">
     <asp:Image ID="Image1" runat="server" ImageUrl="wrox_logo.gif" />
</asp:Content>
```

Even from this simple example, you can see the differences between a content page and a regular `.aspx` page. Most important, this page does not contain any `<form>` element or any of the `<html>` structure that you would normally see in a typical Web form. All of this content is instead stored inside the master page itself.

This content page contains two `Content` server controls. Each of these `Content` server controls maps to a specific `<asp:ContentPlaceHolder>` control from the master page. This association is made through the use of the `ContentPlaceHolderID` attribute of the `Content` control:

```
<asp:Content ID="Content1" ContentPlaceHolderID="ContentPlaceHolder1"
 runat="Server"> ... </asp:Content>
```

Just as with typical `.aspx` pages, you can create any event handlers you may need for your content page. This particular example uses a button-click event for when the end user submits the form. Running this example produces the results shown in Figure 20-10.

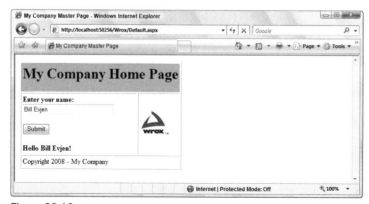

Figure 20-10

Declaring the Master Page Application-Wide

As shown in the examples thus far, we have been declaring the master page from the content page through the use of the `MasterPageFile` attribute of the `Page` directive:

```
<%@ Page Language="VB" MasterPageFile="~/Wrox.master" Title="My Content Page" %>
```

You can apply this attribute to each of your content pages or you can make this declaration in the `web.config` file of your application, as shown here:

```
<configuration>
    <system.web>
        <pages masterPageFile="~/Wrox.master"></pages>
    </system.web>
</configuration>
```

From the `<pages>` node in the `web.config` file, you declare that all your content pages will use a specific master page using the `masterPageFile` attribute. Doing this means that your content pages can simply use the following `Page` directive construction:

```
<%@ Page Language="VB" Title="My Content Page" %>
```

The nice thing about making the master page declaration in the `web.config` file is you do not have to make this declaration on any of your solution's content pages; if you later decide to change the template and associate all the content pages to a brand-new master page, you can change every content page instantaneously in one spot.

Doing this has no effect on the regular .aspx pages in your solution. They will still function as normal. Moreover, if you have a content page that you wish to associate with a master page other than the one specified in the `web.config` file, then you simply use the `MasterPageFile` attribute in the `Page` directive of the page. This will override any declaration that you may have in the `web.config` file.

Providing Default Content in Your Master Page

Earlier, you saw how to use a basic `ContentPlaceHolder` control. In addition to using it as shown, you can also create `ContentPlaceHolder` controls that contain default content:

```
<asp:ContentPlaceHolder ID="ContentPlaceHolder1" runat="server">
  Here is some default content!
</asp:ContentPlaceHolder>
```

For default content, you can again use whatever you want, including any other ASP.NET server controls. A content page that uses a master page containing one of these `ContentPlaceHolder` controls can then either override the default content — by just specifying content (which overrides the original content declared in the master page) — or keep the default content contained in the control.

Data-Driven Applications

ASP.NET 3.5 provides some unique data-access server controls that make it easy for you to get at the data you need. As data for your applications finds itself in more and more types of data stores, it can sometimes be a nightmare to figure out how to get at and aggregate these information sets onto a Web page in a simple and logical manner. ASP.NET data source controls are meant to work with a specific type of data store by connecting to the data store and performing operations such as inserts, updates, and deletes — all on your behalf. The following table details the new data source controls at your disposal:

Data Source Control	Description
SqlDataSource	Enables you to work with any SQL-based database, such as Microsoft SQL Server or even Oracle
AccessDataSource	Enables you to work with a Microsoft Access file (.mbd)
ObjectDataSource	Enables you to work with a business object or a Visual Studio 2008 data component
LinqDataSource	Enables you to use LINQ to query everything from in-memory collections to databases. This is a new control of ASP.NET 3.5.
XmlDataSource	Enables you to work with the information from an XML file or even a dynamic XML source (e.g., an RSS feed)
SiteMapDataSource	Enables you to work with the hierarchical data represented in the site map file (.sitemap)

ASP.NET itself provides a number of server controls that you can use for data-binding purposes. That means you can use these data source controls as the underlying data systems for a series of controls with very little work on your part. These data-bound controls in ASP.NET include the following:

- ❑   `<asp:GridView>`
- ❑   `<asp:DataGrid>`
- ❑   `<asp:DetailsView>`
- ❑   `<asp:FormView>`
- ❑   `<asp:TreeView>`
- ❑   `<asp:Menu>`
- ❑   `<asp:DataList>`
- ❑   `<asp:ListView>`
- ❑   `<asp:Repeater>`
- ❑   `<asp:DropDownList>`
- ❑   `<asp:BulletedList>`
- ❑   `<asp:CheckBoxList>`
- ❑   `<asp:RadioButtonList>`
- ❑   `<asp:ListBox>`
- ❑   `<asp:AdRotator>`

The newest control in this group is the ListView control, introduced in ASP.NET 3.5. Another popular control in this group is the GridView control, which, when introduced in the .NET Framework 2.0, made the `DataGrid` control more or less obsolete. The `GridView` control enables paging, sorting, and editing with very little work on your part. The next section looks at using the `GridView` control with SQL Server and taking advantage of these advanced features.

Using the GridView and SqlDataSource Controls

For an example of using these two controls together to display some information, let's turn to Visual Studio 2008. Start a new page and drag and drop a `GridView` control onto the design surface of the page. Pulling up the smart tag for the control on the design surface, you can click the Auto Format link to give your `GridView` control a better appearance, rather than the default provided.

Next, drag and drop an `SqlDataSource` control onto the design surface. This control is a middle-tier component, so it appears as a gray box on the design surface. The first step is to configure the `SqlDataSource` control to work with the data you want from your Microsoft SQL Server instance (see Figure 20-11).

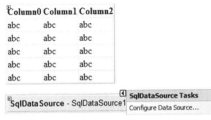

Figure 20-11

Working through the configuration process for the `SqlDataSource` control, you must choose your data connection and then indicate whether you want to store this connection in the `web.config` file (shown in Figure 20-12), which is highly advisable.

Within this configuration process, you also choose the table you are going to work with, and test out the queries that the wizard generates. For this example, choose the Customers table and select every row by checking the * check box, as shown in Figure 20-13.

After working through the configuration process, you will notice that your `web.config` file has changed to include the connection string:

```
<configuration>
```

```
    <connectionStrings>
        <add name="NorthwindConnectionString"
         connectionString="Data Source=.\SQLEXPRESS;
           AttachDbFilename=|DataDirectory|\NORTHWND.MDF;
           Integrated Security=True;User Instance=True"
         providerName="System.Data.SqlClient" />
    </connectionStrings>
```

```
    <system.web>
       ...
    </system.web>
</configuration>
```

Figure 20-12

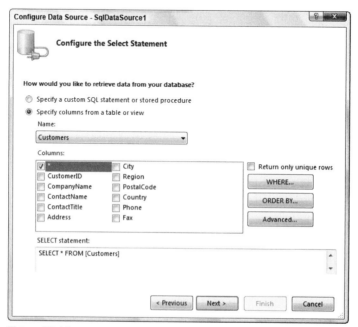

Figure 20-13

Once you have configured the `SqlDataSource` control, the next step is to tie the `GridView` control to this `SqlDataSource` control instance. This can be done through the `GridView` control's smart tag, as shown in Figure 20-14. You can also enable paging and sorting for the control in the same form.

Figure 20-14

The code generated by the wizard (it is also how you would code it yourself) is shown here:

```
<%@ Page Language="VB" %>

<script runat="server">

</script>

<html xmlns="http://www.w3.org/1999/xhtml" >
<head runat="server">
    <title>GridView Example</title>
</head>
<body>
    <form id="form1" runat="server">
    <div>
        <asp:GridView ID="GridView1" runat="server" BorderWidth="1px"
         BackColor="White" GridLines="Vertical"
         CellPadding="3" BorderStyle="Solid" BorderColor="#999999"
         ForeColor="Black" DataSourceID="SqlDataSource1"
         DataKeyNames="CustomerID" AutoGenerateColumns="False"
         AllowPaging="True"
         AllowSorting="True">
            <FooterStyle BackColor="#CCCCCC"></FooterStyle>
            <PagerStyle ForeColor="Black" HorizontalAlign="Center"
             BackColor="#999999"></PagerStyle>
            <HeaderStyle ForeColor="White" Font-Bold="True"
             BackColor="Black"></HeaderStyle>
            <AlternatingRowStyle BackColor="#CCCCCC"></AlternatingRowStyle>
            <Columns>
                <asp:BoundField ReadOnly="True" HeaderText="CustomerID"
                 DataField="CustomerID"
                 SortExpression="CustomerID"></asp:BoundField>
                <asp:BoundField HeaderText="CompanyName"
                 DataField="CompanyName"
                 SortExpression="CompanyName"></asp:BoundField>
                <asp:BoundField HeaderText="ContactName"
```

```
                          DataField="ContactName"
                          SortExpression="ContactName"></asp:BoundField>
                        <asp:BoundField HeaderText="ContactTitle"
                          DataField="ContactTitle"
                          SortExpression="ContactTitle"></asp:BoundField>
                        <asp:BoundField HeaderText="Address" DataField="Address"
                          SortExpression="Address"></asp:BoundField>
                        <asp:BoundField HeaderText="City" DataField="City"
                          SortExpression="City"></asp:BoundField>
                        <asp:BoundField HeaderText="Region" DataField="Region"
                          SortExpression="Region"></asp:BoundField>
                        <asp:BoundField HeaderText="PostalCode" DataField="PostalCode"
                          SortExpression="PostalCode"></asp:BoundField>
                        <asp:BoundField HeaderText="Country" DataField="Country"
                          SortExpression="Country"></asp:BoundField>
                        <asp:BoundField HeaderText="Phone" DataField="Phone"
                          SortExpression="Phone"></asp:BoundField>
                        <asp:BoundField HeaderText="Fax" DataField="Fax"
                          SortExpression="Fax"></asp:BoundField>
                    </Columns>
                    <SelectedRowStyle ForeColor="White" Font-Bold="True"
                     BackColor="#000099"></SelectedRowStyle>
                </asp:GridView>
                <asp:SqlDataSource ID="SqlDataSource1" runat="server"
                 SelectCommand="SELECT * FROM [Customers]"
                ConnectionString="<%$ ConnectionStrings:NorthwindConnectionString %>">
                </asp:SqlDataSource>
            </div>
            </form>
    </body>
    </html>
```

First, consider the SqlDataSource control, which has some important attributes to pay attention to. The first is the SelectCommand attribute. This is the SQL query that you will be using. In this case, it is a Select * From [Customers] query (meaning you are grabbing everything from the Customers table of the Northwind database). The second attribute to pay attention to is the ConnectionString attribute. The interesting aspect of this attribute is the use of < %$ ConnectionStrings:NorthwindConnectionString % > to get at the connection string. This value points at the settings placed inside the web.config file for those who do not want to hard-code their connection strings directly in the code of their pages. If you did want to do this, you would use something similar to the following construction:

```
ConnectionString="Data Source=.\SQLEXPRESS;
    AttachDbFilename=|DataDirectory|\NORTHWND.MDF;
    Integrated Security=True;User Instance=True"
```

Looking now at the GridView control, you can see how easy it is to add paging and sorting capabilities to the control. It is simply a matter of adding the attributes AllowPaging and AllowSorting to the control and setting their values to True (they are set to False by default):

```
<asp:GridView ID="GridView1" runat="server" BorderWidth="1px"
 BackColor="White" GridLines="Vertical"
 CellPadding="3" BorderStyle="Solid" BorderColor="#999999"
```

```
    ForeColor="Black" DataSourceID="SqlDataSource1"
    DataKeyNames="CustomerID" AutoGenerateColumns="False" AllowPaging="True"
    AllowSorting="True">
      <!-- Inner content removed for clarity -->
  </asp:GridView>
```

Each of the columns from the Customers table of the Northwind database is defined in the control through the use of the `<asp:BoundField>` control, a subcontrol of the `GridView` control. The `BoundField` control enables you to specify the header text of the column through the use of the `HeaderText` attribute. The `DataField` attribute actually ties the values displayed in this column to a particular value from the Customers table, and the `SortExpression` attribute should use the same values for sorting — unless you are sorting on a different value than what is being displayed.

Ultimately, your page should look similar to what is shown in Figure 20-15.

Figure 20-15

Allowing Editing and Deleting of Records with GridView

Now let's expand upon the previous example by allowing for the editing and deleting of records that are displayed in the `GridView`. If you are using the Visual Studio 2008 `SqlDataSource` Configuration Wizard to accomplish these tasks, then you need to take some extra steps beyond what was shown in the preceding `GridView` example.

Go back to the `SqlDataSource` control on the design surface of your Web page and pull up the control's smart tag. Select the Configure Data Source option to reconfigure the `SqlDataSource` control to enable the editing and deletion of data from the Customers table of the Northwind database.

When you come to the Configure the Select Statement screen (see Figure 20-16), click the Advanced button.

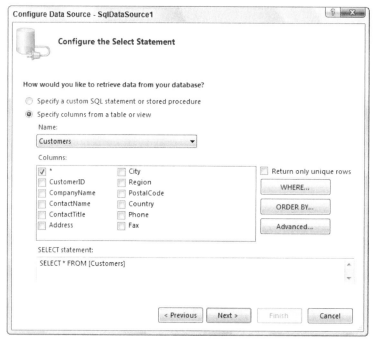

Figure 20-16

This will pull up the Advanced SQL Generation Options dialog, shown in Figure 20-17.

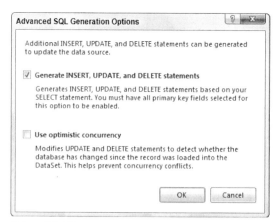

Figure 20-17

As shown in this dialog, select the Generate Insert, Update, and Delete statements check box. This will instruct the SqlDataSource control to not only handle the simple Select query, but also the Update and Delete queries. Press OK and then work through the rest of the wizard.

Return to the GridView control's smart tag and select Refresh Schema. You will also now find check boxes in the smart tag for editing and deleting rows of data. Make sure both of these check boxes are checked, as shown in Figure 20-18.

Figure 20-18

Now look at what changed in the code. First, the SqlDataSource control has changed to allow for the updating and deletion of data:

```
<asp:SqlDataSource ID="SqlDataSource1" runat="server"
 SelectCommand="SELECT * FROM [Customers]"
 ConnectionString="<%$ ConnectionStrings:AppConnectionString1 %>"
 DeleteCommand="DELETE FROM [Customers] WHERE [CustomerID] =
    @original_CustomerID"
 InsertCommand="INSERT INTO [Customers] ([CustomerID], [CompanyName],
    [ContactName], [ContactTitle], [Address], [City], [Region], [PostalCode],
    [Country], [Phone], [Fax]) VALUES (@CustomerID, @CompanyName,
    @ContactName, @ContactTitle, @Address, @City,
    @Region, @PostalCode, @Country, @Phone, @Fax)"
 UpdateCommand="UPDATE [Customers] SET [CompanyName] = @CompanyName,
    [ContactName] = @ContactName,
    [ContactTitle] = @ContactTitle, [Address] = @Address, [City] =
    @City, [Region] = @Region, [PostalCode] = @PostalCode,
    [Country] = @Country, [Phone] = @Phone,
    [Fax] = @Fax WHERE [CustomerID] = @original_CustomerID">
        <DeleteParameters>
            <asp:Parameter Type="String" Name="CustomerID">
            </asp:Parameter>
        </DeleteParameters>
        <UpdateParameters>
            <asp:Parameter Type="String" Name="CompanyName">
            </asp:Parameter>
            <asp:Parameter Type="String" Name="ContactName">
            </asp:Parameter>
            <asp:Parameter Type="String" Name="ContactTitle">
            </asp:Parameter>
            <asp:Parameter Type="String" Name="Address"></asp:Parameter>
            <asp:Parameter Type="String" Name="City"></asp:Parameter>
            <asp:Parameter Type="String" Name="Region"></asp:Parameter>
            <asp:Parameter Type="String" Name="PostalCode">
            </asp:Parameter>
            <asp:Parameter Type="String" Name="Country"></asp:Parameter>
            <asp:Parameter Type="String" Name="Phone"></asp:Parameter>
            <asp:Parameter Type="String" Name="Fax"></asp:Parameter>
            <asp:Parameter Type="String" Name="CustomerID">
```

```
                    </asp:Parameter>
                </UpdateParameters>
                <InsertParameters>
                    <asp:Parameter Type="String" Name="CustomerID">
                    </asp:Parameter>
                    <asp:Parameter Type="String" Name="CompanyName">
                    </asp:Parameter>
                    <asp:Parameter Type="String" Name="ContactName">
                    </asp:Parameter>
                    <asp:Parameter Type="String" Name="ContactTitle">
                    </asp:Parameter>
                    <asp:Parameter Type="String" Name="Address"></asp:Parameter>
                    <asp:Parameter Type="String" Name="City"></asp:Parameter>
                    <asp:Parameter Type="String" Name="Region"></asp:Parameter>
                    <asp:Parameter Type="String" Name="PostalCode">
                    </asp:Parameter>
                    <asp:Parameter Type="String" Name="Country"></asp:Parameter>
                    <asp:Parameter Type="String" Name="Phone"></asp:Parameter>
                    <asp:Parameter Type="String" Name="Fax"></asp:Parameter>
                </InsertParameters>
        </asp:SqlDataSource>
```

Second, other queries have been added to the control. Using the `DeleteCommand`, `InsertCommand`, and `UpdateCommand` attributes of the `SqlDataSource` control, these functions can now be performed just as `Select` queries were enabled through the use of the `SelectCommand` attribute. As you can see in the queries, many parameters are defined within them. These parameters are then assigned through the `<DeleteParameters>`, `<UpdateParameters>`, and `<InsertParameters>` elements. Within each of these subsections, the actual parameters are defined through the use of the `<asp:Parameter>` control, where you also assign the data type of the parameter (through the use of the `Type` attribute) and the name of the parameter.

Besides these changes to the `SqlDataSource` control, only one small change has been made to the `GridView` control:

```
<Columns>

    <asp:CommandField ShowDeleteButton="True"
     ShowEditButton="True"></asp:CommandField>
    <asp:BoundField ReadOnly="True" HeaderText="CustomerID"
     DataField="CustomerID"
     SortExpression="CustomerID"></asp:BoundField>
    <asp:BoundField HeaderText="CompanyName" DataField="CompanyName"
     SortExpression="CompanyName"></asp:BoundField>
    <asp:BoundField HeaderText="ContactName" DataField="ContactName"
     SortExpression="ContactName"></asp:BoundField>
    <asp:BoundField HeaderText="ContactTitle" DataField="ContactTitle"
     SortExpression="ContactTitle"></asp:BoundField>
    <asp:BoundField HeaderText="Address" DataField="Address"
     SortExpression="Address"></asp:BoundField>
    <asp:BoundField HeaderText="City" DataField="City"
     SortExpression="City"></asp:BoundField>
```

```
        <asp:BoundField HeaderText="Region" DataField="Region"
          SortExpression="Region"></asp:BoundField>
        <asp:BoundField HeaderText="PostalCode" DataField="PostalCode"
          SortExpression="PostalCode"></asp:BoundField>
        <asp:BoundField HeaderText="Country" DataField="Country"
          SortExpression="Country"></asp:BoundField>
        <asp:BoundField HeaderText="Phone" DataField="Phone"
          SortExpression="Phone"></asp:BoundField>
        <asp:BoundField HeaderText="Fax" DataField="Fax"
          SortExpression="Fax"></asp:BoundField>
    </Columns>
```

The only change needed for the `GridView` control is the addition of a new column from which editing and deleting commands can be initiated. This is done with the `<asp:CommandField>` control. From this control, you can see that we also enabled the Edit and Delete buttons through a `Boolean` value. Once built and run, your new page will look like the one shown in Figure 20-19.

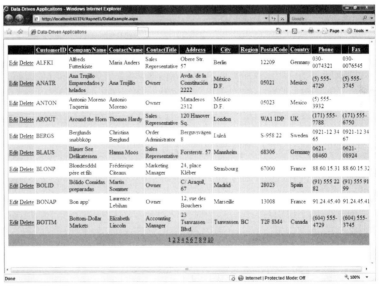

Figure 20-19

Don't Stop There!

Due to limited space, this chapter can only present one example, but many other `DataSource` controls are at your disposal. The `ObjectDataSource` control is rather powerful for those who wish to enforce a strict *n*-tier model and separate the data retrieval logic into an object that the `GridView` and other data-bound controls can work with. The `XmlDataSource` control is one control that you will most likely find yourself using a lot, as more and more data is being stored as XML, including dynamic data (such as Web logs via RSS). These `DataSource` controls are fine-tuned for the type of data stores for which they are targeted, so you will find a lot of benefit in exploring their capabilities in detail.

Navigation

Developers rarely build Web applications that are made up of just a single page instance. Instead, applications are usually made up of multiple pages that are all related to each other in some fashion. Some applications have a workflow through which end users can work from page to page, while other applications have a navigation structure that allows for free roaming throughout the pages. Sometimes the navigation structure of a site becomes complex, and managing this complexity can be rather cumbersome.

ASP.NET includes a way to manage the navigational structure of your Web applications. Using this system, you first define your navigational structure through an XML file that can then be bound to a couple of different server controls focused on navigation.

This makes it relatively easy when you have to introduce changes to the structure of your navigation or make name changes to pages contained within this structure. Instead of going from page to page throughout your entire application, changing titles or page destinations, you can now make these changes in one place — an XML file — and the changes are instantaneously reflected throughout your application.

The first step in working with the ASP.NET navigation system is to reflect your navigational structure in the `web.sitemap` file, the XML file that will contain the complete site structure. For instance, suppose you want the following site structure:

```
Home
        Books
        Magazines
                U.S. Magazines
                European Magazines
```

This site structure has three levels to it, with multiple items in the lowest level. You can reflect this in the `web.sitemap` file as follows:

```
<?xml version="1.0" encoding="utf-8" ?>
<siteMap xmlns="http://schemas.microsoft.com/AspNet/SiteMap-File-1.0" >
    <siteMapNode url="default.aspx" title="Home"
     description="The site homepage">
        <siteMapNode url="books.aspx" title="Books"
         description="Books from our catalog" />
        <siteMapNode url="magazines.aspx" title="Magazines"
         description="Magazines from our catalog">
            <siteMapNode url="magazines_us.aspx" title="U.S. Magazines"
             description="Magazines from the U.S." />
            <siteMapNode url="magazines_eur.aspx" title="European Magazines"
             description="Magazines from Europe" />
        </siteMapNode>
    </siteMapNode>
</siteMap>
```

To create a `web.sitemap` file in Visual Studio 2008, go to the Add New Items dialog and select the Site Map option. You can place the preceding content in this file. To move a level down in the hierarchy, nest `<siteMapNode>` elements within other `< siteMapNode >` elements. A `<siteMapNode>` element can contain several different attributes, as defined in the following table:

Attribute	Description
Title	The `title` attribute provides a textual description of the link. The `String` value used here is the text used for the link.
Description	The `description` attribute not only reminds you what the link is for, it is also used for the `ToolTip` attribute on the link. The `ToolTip` attribute is the yellow box that appears next to the link when the end user hovers the cursor over the link for a couple of seconds.
Url	The `url` attribute describes where the file is located in the solution. If the file is in the root directory, then simply use the filename, such as `default.aspx`. If the file is located in a subfolder, then be sure to include the folders in the `String` value used for this attribute, e.g., `MySubFolder/MyFile.aspx`.
Roles	If ASP.NET security trimming is enabled, you can use the `roles` attribute to define which roles are allowed to view and click the provided link in the navigation.

Using the SiteMapPath Server Control

One of the available server controls that works with a `web.sitemap` file is the `SiteMapPath` control. This control provides a popular structure found on many Internet websites. Sometimes called *breadcrumb navigation*, this feature is simple to implement in ASP.NET.

To see an example of this control at work, we'll create a page that would be at the bottom of the site map structure. Within the project that contains your `web.sitemap` file, create an ASP.NET page named `magazines_us.aspx`. On this page, simply drag and drop a `SiteMapPath` control onto the page. You will find this control under the Navigation section in the Visual Studio Toolbox. This control's code looks as follows:

```
<asp:SiteMapPath ID="SiteMapPath1" runat="server"></asp:SiteMapPath>
```

What else do you need to do to get this control to work? Nothing. Simply build and run the page to see the results shown in Figure 20-20.

Figure 20-20

The `SiteMapPath` control defines the end user's place in the application's site structure. It shows the current page the user is on (U.S. Magazines), as well as the two pages above it in the hierarchy.

The `SiteMapPath` control requires no `DataSource` control, as it automatically binds itself to any `.sitemap` file it finds in the project, and nothing is required on your part to make this happen. The `SiteMapPath`'s smart tag enables you to customize the control's appearance too, so you can produce other results, as shown in Figure 20-21.

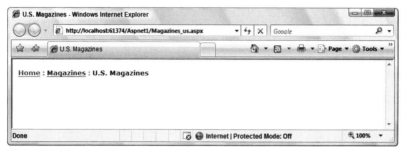

Figure 20-21

The code for this version of the `SiteMapPath` control is as follows:

```
<asp:SiteMapPath ID="SiteMapPath1" runat="server" PathSeparator=" : "
 Font-Names="Verdana" Font-Size="0.8em">
   <PathSeparatorStyle Font-Bold="True"
    ForeColor="#507CD1"></PathSeparatorStyle>
   <CurrentNodeStyle ForeColor="#333333"></CurrentNodeStyle>
   <NodeStyle Font-Bold="True" ForeColor="#284E98"></NodeStyle>
   <RootNodeStyle Font-Bold="True" ForeColor="#507CD1"></RootNodeStyle>
</asp:SiteMapPath>
```

This example illustrates that a lot of style elements and attributes can be used with the `SiteMapPath` control. Many options at your disposal enable you to create breadcrumb navigation that is unique.

Menu Server Control

Another navigation control enables end users of your application to navigate throughout the pages based upon information stored within the `web.sitemap` file. The `Menu` server control produces a compact navigation system that pops up sub-options when the user hovers the mouse over an option. The result of the `Menu` server control when bound to the site map is shown in Figure 20-22.

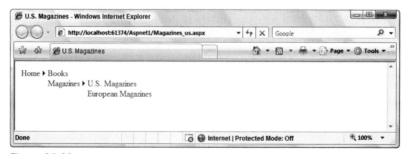

Figure 20-22

To build this, you must be working off of the web.sitemap file created earlier. After the web.sitemap file is in place, place a Menu server control on the page, along with a SiteMapDataSource control:

```
<asp:Menu ID="Menu1" runat="server" DataSourceID="SiteMapDataSource1">
</asp:Menu>
<asp:SiteMapDataSource ID="SiteMapDataSource1" runat="server" />
```

The SiteMapDataSource control automatically works with the application's web.sitemap file. In addition to the SiteMapDataSource control, the other item included is the Menu server control, which uses the typical ID and runat attributes, in addition to the DataSourceID attribute, to connect this control with what is retrieved from the SiteMapDataSource control.

Like the other controls provided by ASP.NET, you can easily modify the appearance of this control. By clicking the Auto Format link in the control's smart tag, you can give the control the "classic" look and feel. This setting produces the result shown in Figure 20-23.

Figure 20-23

As with the other controls, a lot of sub-elements contribute to the changed look of the control's style:

```
<asp:Menu ID="Menu1" runat="server" DataSourceID="SiteMapDataSource1"
 Font-Names="Verdana" Font-Size="0.8em" BackColor="#B5C7DE"
 ForeColor="#284E98"
 StaticSubMenuIndent="10px" DynamicHorizontalOffset="2">
   <StaticSelectedStyle BackColor="#507CD1"></StaticSelectedStyle>
   <StaticMenuItemStyle HorizontalPadding="5"
    VerticalPadding="2"></StaticMenuItemStyle>
   <DynamicMenuStyle BackColor="#B5C7DE"></DynamicMenuStyle>
   <DynamicSelectedStyle BackColor="#507CD1"></DynamicSelectedStyle>
   <DynamicMenuItemStyle HorizontalPadding="5"
    VerticalPadding="2"></DynamicMenuItemStyle>
   <DynamicHoverStyle ForeColor="White" Font-Bold="True"
    BackColor="#284E98"></DynamicHoverStyle>
   <StaticHoverStyle ForeColor="White" Font-Bold="True"
    BackColor="#284E98"></StaticHoverStyle>
</asp:Menu>
```

The TreeView Server Control

The last navigation server control to look at is the TreeView control. This control enables you to render a hierarchy of data. The TreeView control is not only meant for displaying what is contained within the

.sitemap file; you can also use this control to represent other forms of hierarchical data, such as data that you might store in a standard XML file.

You may have encountered a similar TreeView control in .NET when using the IE Web controls, which also contained a TreeView control. That previous TreeView control was limited to working only in Microsoft's Internet Explorer, whereas the new TreeView control works in a wide variety of browsers.

The TreeView control is similar to the Menu control in that it will not bind automatically to the web.sitemap file, but instead requires an underlying DataSource control. The code for displaying the contents of the .sitemap file is shown in the following example:

```
<asp:TreeView ID="TreeView1" runat="server" DataSourceID="SiteMapDataSource1">
</asp:TreeView>
<asp:SiteMapDataSource ID="SiteMapDataSource1" runat="server" />
```

As with the Menu control example, a SiteMapDataSource is needed. After a basic SiteMapDataSource control is in place, position a TreeView control on the page and set the DataSourceId property to SiteMapDataSource1. This simple construction produces the result shown in Figure 20-24.

Figure 20-24

Remember that by using the Auto Format link from the control's smart tag, you can format the TreeView control in a wide variety of ways.

The TreeView is not meant only for site maps; as mentioned, it can build upon any underlying hierarchical data set. For instance, you can display a hierarchical data structure from a standard XML file just as easily. Suppose you have the following XML file:

```
<?xml version="1.0" encoding="utf-8" ?>
<Hardware>
    <Item Category="Motherboards">
        <Option Choice="Asus" />
        <Option Choice="Abit" />
    </Item>
    <Item Category="Memory">
        <Option Choice="128mb" />
        <Option Choice="256mb" />
        <Option Choice="512mb" />
    </Item>
```

```
    <Item Category="Hard Drives">
       <Option Choice="40GB" />
       <Option Choice="80GB" />
       <Option Choice="100GB" />
    </Item>
    <Item Category="Drives">
       <Option Choice="CD" />
       <Option Choice="DVD" />
       <Option Choice="DVD Burner" />
    </Item>
</Hardware>
```

It's obvious that this XML file is not meant for site navigation, but for options from which end users can make selections. As stated, the TreeView control is quite extensible. For example, the following code creates a page that uses the preceding XML file:

```
<%@ Page Language="VB" %>

<script runat="server">
    Protected Sub Button1_Click(ByVal sender As Object, _
        ByVal e As System.EventArgs)

        If TreeView1.CheckedNodes.Count > 0 Then
            Label1.Text = "We are sending you information on:<p>"

            For Each node As TreeNode In TreeView1.CheckedNodes
                Label1.Text += node.Text & " " & node.Parent.Text & "<br>"
            Next
        Else
            label1.Text = "You didn't select anything. Sorry!"
        End If
    End Sub
</script>

<html xmlns="http://www.w3.org/1999/xhtml" >
<head runat="server">
    <title>The TreeView Control</title>
</head>
<body>
    <form id="form1" runat="server">
    <div>
        Please select the following items that you are interesting in:
        <br />
        <br />
        <asp:TreeView ID="TreeView1" runat="server"
         DataSourceID="XmlDataSource1" ShowLines="True">
            <DataBindings>
                <asp:TreeNodeBinding TextField="Category"
                 DataMember="Item"></asp:TreeNodeBinding>
                <asp:TreeNodeBinding ShowCheckBox="True" TextField="Choice"
                 DataMember="Option"></asp:TreeNodeBinding>
            </DataBindings>
        </asp:TreeView> <br />
        <br />
```

```
        <asp:Button ID="Button1" runat="server"
         Text="Submit Choices" OnClick="Button1_Click" />
        <br />
        <br />
        <asp:Label ID="Label1" runat="server"></asp:Label>
        <asp:XmlDataSource ID="XmlDataSource1" runat="server"
         DataFile="~/Hardware.xml">
        </asp:XmlDataSource>
      </div>
      </form>
  </body>
  </html>
```

This example uses an `XmlDataSource` control instead of the `SiteMapDataSource` control. The `XmlDataSource` control associates itself with the XML file shown earlier (`Hardware.xml`) through the use of the `DataFile` attribute.

The `TreeView` control then binds itself to the `XmlDataSource` control through the use of the `DataSourceID` attribute, which here is pointed to `XmlDataSource1`. Another interesting addition in the root `TreeView` node is the `ShowLines` attribute, set to `True`. This feature of the `TreeView` causes every node in the hierarchy to show its connection to its parent node through a visual line.

When working with XML files, which can basically be of any construction, you must bind the nodes of the `TreeView` control to specific values that come from the XML file. This is done through the use of the `<DataBindings>` element. This element encapsulates one or more `TreeNodeBinding` objects. Two of the more important available properties of a `TreeNodeBinding` object are `DataMember` and `TextField`. The `DataMember` property points to the name of the XML element that the `TreeView` control should look for. The `TextField` property specifies the XML attribute of that particular XML element. If you do this correctly with the use of the `<DataBindings>` construct, you get the result shown in Figure 20-25.

In the button `click` event from our example, you can see how easy it is to iterate through each of the checked nodes from the `TreeView` selection by creating instances of `TreeNode` objects. These selections are made from one of the `TreeNodeBinding` objects, which sets the `ShowCheckBox` property to `True`.

Membership and Role Management

ASP.NET contains a built-in membership and role management system that can be initiated either through code or through the ASP.NET Web Site Administration Tool. This is an ideal system for authenticating users to access a page or even your entire site. This management system not only provides a new API suite for managing users, but also provides you with some server controls that interact with this API.

As the first step in setting up your site's security and the user roles, open the ASP.NET Web Site Administration Tool. You can launch this tool through a button in the Visual Studio 2008 Solution Explorer or by clicking Website ➪ ASP.NET Configuration in the Visual Studio menu. When the tool opens in the document window, click the Security tab, shown in Figure 20-26.

Click the link to start the Security Setup Wizard, shown in Figure 20-27.

Figure 20-25

Figure 20-26

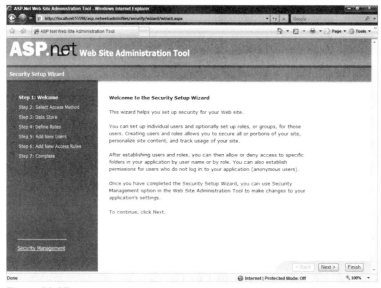

Figure 20-27

The wizard first asks whether your application will be available on the public Internet or hosted on an intranet. If you select Internet, then your website will be enabled with Forms Authentication. If you select Intranet, then your site will be configured to work with Windows Integrated Authentication. For our example, select the Internet option.

Working through the wizard, you are also asked whether you are going to work with role management. Enable role management by checking the appropriate check box and add a role titled Manager. After this step, you can begin to enter users into the system. Fill out information for each user you want in the system, as shown in Figure 20-28.

The next step is to create the access rules for your site. You can pick specific folders and apply the rules for the folder. In this example, anyone in the Manager role would have access to the site, while anonymous users would be denied access (see Figure 20-29).

Click the Finish button to exit the wizard. If you refresh the Solution Explorer in Visual Studio, a new data store (an SQL Server Express Edition .mdf file) appears in the App_Data folder. This is where all of the user and role information is stored. Note that you can configure both of the systems (the membership and role management systems) to work with other data stores besides these SQL Express data files. For example, you can configure these systems to work with a full-blown version of Microsoft's SQL Server. Notice in the Solution Explorer that if you didn't already have a web.config file, you have one now. The contents added to the web.config file includes the following:

```xml
<?xml version="1.0" encoding="utf-8"?>
<configuration>
    <system.web>
        <authorization>
            <allow roles="Manager" />
            <deny users="?" />
        </authorization>
```

```
        <roleManager enabled="true" />
        <authentication mode="Forms" />
    </system.web>
</configuration>
```

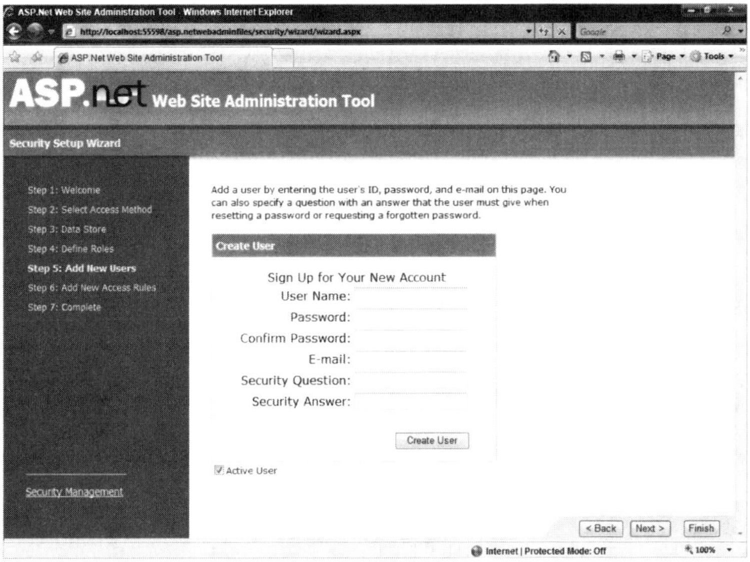

Figure 20-28

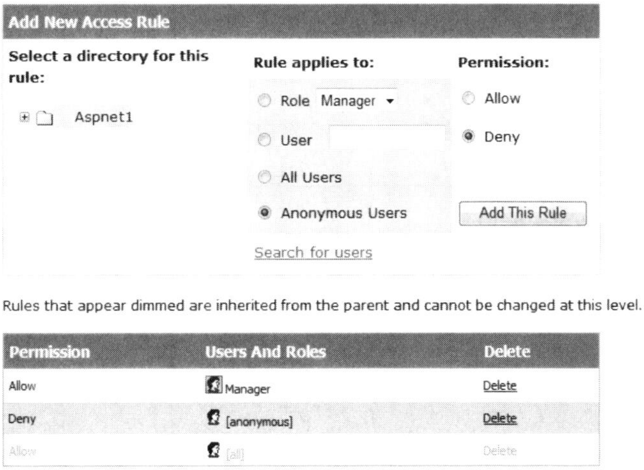

Figure 20-29

This shows all the settings that were enabled. The `<authorization>` section allows for users who are in the role of `Manager`, and denies all anonymous users (defined with a question mark). The `<roleManager>` element turns on the role management system, while the `<authentication>` element turns on forms authentication. Now, let's utilize these configurations.

Create a login page, as everyone will access any page in this application as an anonymous user first. The login page enables people to enter their credentials in order to be authorized in the `Manager` role created earlier.

ASP.NET includes a slew of controls that make working with the membership and role management systems easier. On the login page (`Login.aspx`), place a simple `Login` server control:

```
<asp:Login ID="Login1" runat="server"></asp:Login>
```

The nice thing here is that you have to do absolutely nothing to tie this `Login` control to the .mdf database created earlier through the wizard. Now access another page in the application (other than the `Login.aspx` page) and start up that page. This example starts up `Default.aspx` (which only contains a simple text statement), but looking at Figure 20-30 you can see from the URL specified in the browser that I was redirected to `Login.aspx` because I wasn't yet authenticated.

Figure 20-30

The `Login.aspx` page enables me to enter my credentials, which then authorize me in the `Manager` role. Pressing the Login button causes the browser to redirect me to the appropriate page. I am now authenticated and authorized for the site!

Personalization

Many Web applications have features that allow for personalization of some kind. This might be as simple as greeting a user by name, or it might deal with more advanced issues such as content placement. Whatever the case, personalization techniques have always been tricky. Developers have used anything from cookies, sessions, or database entries to control the personalization that users can perform on their pages.

ASP.NET includes an easy to use and configure personalization system. It is as simple as making entries in the `web.config` file to get the personalization system started. Like the membership and role management systems, the personalization system also uses an underlying data store. The next example continues to work with the SQL Server Express Edition .mdb file.

This example creates two properties, `FirstName` and `LastName`, both of type `String`. First, alter the `web.config` file as shown here:

```
<?xml version="1.0"?>
<configuration>
   <system.web>
      <profile>
         <properties>
            <add name="FirstName" type="System.String" />
            <add name="LastName" type="System.String" />
         </properties>
      </profile>
   </system.web>
</configuration>
```

Now that the profile properties we are going to store for each user are configured in the web.config file, the next step is to build a simple ASP.NET page that utilizes these property settings. Create a simple page that contains two TextBox controls that ask end users for their first and last name. We will then input the values collected into the personalization engine via a button Click event. The code for this page is as follows:

```
<%@ Page Language="VB" %>

<script runat="server">
    Protected Sub Button1_Click(ByVal sender As Object, _
       ByVal e As System.EventArgs)

        Profile.FirstName = TextBox1.Text
        Profile.LastName = TextBox1.Text

        Label1.Text = "First name: " & Profile.FirstName & _
            "<br>Last name: " & Profile.LastName
    End Sub
</script>

<html xmlns="http://www.w3.org/1999/xhtml" >
<head runat="server">
    <title>Welcome Page</title>
</head>
<body>
    <form id="form1" runat="server">
    <div>
        First name:<br />
        <asp:TextBox ID="TextBox1" runat="server"></asp:TextBox>
        <br />
        Last name:<br />
        <asp:TextBox ID="TextBox2" runat="server"></asp:TextBox>
        <br />
        <asp:Button ID="Button1" runat="server" Text="Submit Information"
         OnClick="Button1_Click" />
        <br />
        <br />
        <asp:Label ID="Label1" runat="server"></asp:Label>
    </div>
    </form>
</body>
</html>
```

When this page is posted back to itself, the values placed into the two text boxes are placed into the personalization engine and associated with this particular user through the use of the `Profile` object. When working with the `Profile` object in Visual Studio, note that the custom properties you created are provided to you through IntelliSense. Once stored in the personalization engine, they are then available to you on any page within the application through the use of the same `Profile` object.

Configuring ASP.NET in IIS on Vista

If you are using IIS as the basis of your ASP.NET applications, you will find that it is quite easy to configure the ASP.NET application directly through the Internet Information Services (IIS) Manager if you are using Windows Vista. To access the ASP.NET configurations, open IIS and expand the `Web Sites` folder, which contains all the sites configured to work with IIS. Remember that not all your websites are configured to work in this manner because it is also possible to create ASP.NET applications that make use of the new ASP.NET built-in Web server.

Once you have expanded the IIS `Web Sites` folder, right-click one of the applications in this folder. You will notice that the available options for configuration appear in the IIS Manager (see Figure 20-31).

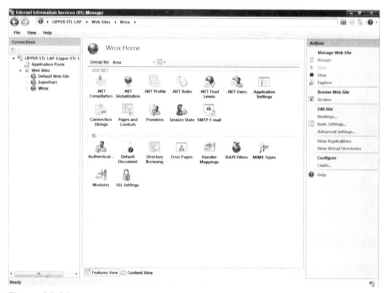

Figure 20-31

The options available to you enable you to completely configure ASP.NET or even configure IIS itself. The focus of this chapter is on the ASP.NET section of the options. In addition to the options you can select from the available icons, you can also configure some basic settings of the application by clicking the Basic Settings link in the Actions pane on the right-hand side of the IIS Manager. When clicking the Basic Settings link, you will get the Edit Web Site dialog box shown in Figure 20-32.

Changes you make in the IIS Manager are actually being applied to the `web.config` *file of your application; making changes to the Default website (the root node) enables you edit the* `machine.config` *file.*

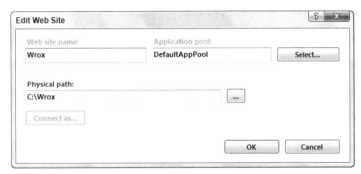

Figure 20-32

This dialog enables you to change the following items:

❑ **Web site name:** The name of the website. In the case of Figure 20-32, naming the website "Wrox" means that the URL will be http://[IP address or domain name]/Wrox.

❑ **Application pool:** The application pool you are going to use for the application. Note that you have three options by default: DefaultAppPool (which uses the .NET Framework 2.0 and an integrated pipeline mode), Classic .NET AppPool (which uses the .NET Framework 2.0 and a classic pipeline mode), and ASP.NET 1.1 (which uses the .NET Framework 1.1 as it states and a classic pipeline mode).

❑ **Physical path:** The folder location where the ASP.NET application can be found. In this case, it is C:\Wrox.

The sections that follow describe some of the options available to you through the icons in the IIS Manager.

Working with the ASP.NET Provider Model

Ever since the beginning days of ASP.NET, users wanted to be able to store sessions by means other than the three methods: InProc, StateServer, and SQLServer. One such request was for a provider that could store sessions in an Oracle database. This might seem like a logical thing to add to ASP.NET in the days of ASP.NET 1.1, but if the team added a provider for Oracle, they would soon get requests to add even more providers for other databases and data storage methods. For this reason, instead of building providers for every possible scenario, the developers designed a provider model that enabled them to add any providers they wished. Thus was born the new provider model introduced in ASP.NET 2.0.

ASP.NET includes a lot of systems that require state storage of some kind. In addition, instead of recording state in a fragile mode (the way sessions are stored by default), many of these new systems require their state to be stored in more concrete data stores such as databases or XML files. This also enables a longer-lived state for the users visiting an application — something else that is required by these new systems.

The systems found in ASP.NET today that require advanced state management include the following:

❑ Membership
❑ Role management

❑   Site navigation

❑   Personalization

❑   Health-monitoring Web events

❑   Web parts personalization

❑   Configuration file protection

The membership system enables ASP.NET to work from a user store of some kind to create, delete, or edit application users. Because it is apparent that developers want to work with an unlimited amount of different data stores for their user store, they need a means to easily change the underlying user store for their ASP.NET applications. The provider model found in ASP.NET is the answer.

Out of the box, ASP.NET provides two membership providers that enable you to store user information: SQL Server and the Active Directory membership providers (found at `System.Web.Security.SqlMembershipProvider` and `System.Web.Security.ActiveDirectoryMembershipProvider`, respectively). In fact, for each of the systems (as well as for some of the ASP.NET 1.x systems), a series of providers is available to alter the way the state of that system is recorded. Figure 20-33 illustrates these providers.

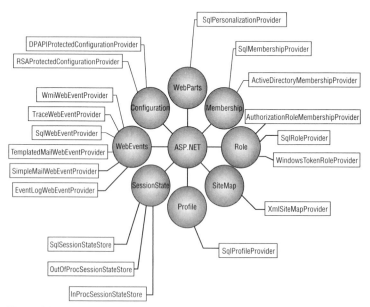

Figure 20-33

As shown in the diagram, ASP.NET provides a large number of providers out of the box. Some systems have only a single provider (such as the profile system, which includes only a provider to connect to SQL Server), whereas other systems include multiple providers (such as the WebEvents provider, which includes six separate providers). The next section describes how to set up SQL Server to work with several of the providers presented in this chapter. You can use SQL Server 7.0, 2000, 2005, or 2008 for the back-end data store for many of the providers presented (although not all of them). After this explanation is an overview of the available providers built into ASP.NET.

Working with Microsoft SQL Server from 7.0 to 2008

Quite a number of providers work with SQL Server. For instance, the membership, role management, personalization, and other systems work easily with SQL Server. However, all these systems work with the new Microsoft SQL Server Express Edition file (.mdf) by default instead of with one of the full-blown versions of SQL Server, such as SQL Server 7.0, SQL Server 2000, SQL Server 2005, or SQL Server 2008.

To work with either Microsoft SQL Server 7.0, 2000, 2005, or 2008, you must set up the database using the aspnet_regsql.exe tool. Working with aspnet_regsql.exe creates the necessary tables, roles, stored procedures, and other items needed by the providers. To access this tool, open the Visual Studio 2008 command prompt by selecting Start ➪ All Programs ➪ Visual Studio 2008 ➪ Visual Studio Tools ➪ Visual Studio 2008 Command Prompt. This gives you access to the ASP.NET SQL Server Setup Wizard. The ASP.NET SQL Server Setup Wizard is an easy to use tool that facilitates setup of SQL Server to work with many of the systems built into ASP.NET, such as the membership, role management, and personalization systems. The Setup Wizard provides two ways for you to set up the database: using a command-line tool or using a GUI tool.

The ASP.NET SQL Server Setup Wizard Command-Line Tool

The command-line version of the Setup Wizard gives developers optimal control over how the database is created. Working from the command line using this tool is not difficult, so don't be intimidated by it.

You can get at the actual tool, aspnet_regsql.exe, from the Visual Studio command prompt if you have Visual Studio 2008. At the command prompt, type **aspnet regsql.exe -?** to get a list of all the command-line options at your disposal for working with this tool.

The following table describes some of the available options for setting up your SQL Server instance to work with the personalization framework:

Command Option	Description
-?	Displays a list of available option commands
-W	Uses the Wizard mode. This uses the default installation if no other parameters are used.
-S <server>	Specifies the SQL Server instance to work with
-U <login>	Specifies the username for logging in to SQL Server. If you use this, then you also use the -P command.
-P <password>	Specifies the password to use for logging in to SQL Server. If you use this, then you also use the -U command.
-E	Provides instructions for using the current Windows credentials for authentication
-C	Specifies the connection string for connecting to SQL Server. If you use this, then you don't need to use the -U and -P commands because they are specified in the connection string itself.

Command Option	Description
-A all	Adds support for all the available SQL Server operations provided by ASP.NET, including membership, role management, profiles, site counters, and page/control personalization
-A p	Adds support for working with profiles
_R all	Removes support for all the available SQL Server operations that have been previously installed. These include membership, role management, profiles, site counters, and page/control personalization.
-R p	Removes support for the profile capability from SQL Server
-d <database>	Specifies the database name to use with the application services. If you don't specify a database name, then aspnetdb is used.
/sqlexportonly <filename>	Instead of modifying an instance of a SQL Server database, use this command in conjunction with the other commands to generate a SQL script that adds or removes the features specified. This command creates the scripts in a file that has the name specified in the command.

To modify SQL Server to work with the personalization provider using this command-line tool, you enter a command such as the following:

```
aspnet_regsql.exe -A all -E
```

After you enter the preceding command, the command-line tool creates the features required by all the available ASP.NET systems. The results are shown in the tool itself, as illustrated in Figure 20-34.

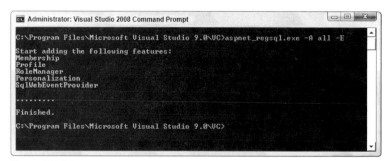

Figure 20-34

When this action is completed, you can see that a new database, aspnetdb, has been created in the SQL Server Enterprise Manager of Microsoft SQL Server 2005 (the database used for this example). You now have the appropriate tables for working with all the ASP.NET 3.5 systems that are able to work with SQL Server (see Figure 20-35).

One advantage of using the command-line tool, rather than the GUI-based version of the ASP.NET SQL Server Setup Wizard, is that you can install in the database just the features you're interested in working with, instead of installing everything (as the GUI-based version does). For instance, if you want only the membership system to interact with SQL Server 2005 — not any of the other systems (such as role management and personalization) — then you can configure the setup so that only the tables, roles, stored procedures, and other items required by the membership system are established in the database. To set up the database for the membership system only, use the following on the command line:

```
aspnet_regsql.exe -A m -E
```

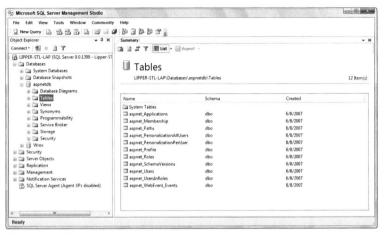

Figure 20-35

The ASP.NET SQL Server Setup Wizard GUI Tool

Instead of working with the tool through the command line, you can also work with a GUI version of the same wizard. To access the GUI version, type the following at the Visual Studio command prompt:

```
aspnet_regsql.exe
```

At this point, the ASP.NET SQL Server Setup Wizard welcome screen appears, as shown in Figure 20-36.

Figure 20-36

Clicking the Next button gives you a new screen that offers two options: one to install management features into SQL Server and the other to remove them (see Figure 20-37).

Figure 20-37

From here, choose "Configure SQL Server for application services" and click Next. The third screen (see Figure 20-38) asks for the login credentials to SQL Server and the name of the database to perform the operations. The Database option is <default> — meaning the wizard creates a database called aspnetdb. If you want to choose a different folder, such as the application's database, choose the appropriate option.

After you have made your server and database selections, click Next. The screen shown in Figure 20-39 asks you to confirm your settings. If everything looks correct, click the Next button — otherwise, click Previous and correct your settings.

When this is complete, you get a notification that everything was set up correctly.

Connecting Your Default Provider to a New SQL Server Instance

After you set up the full-blown Microsoft SQL Server to work with the various systems provided by ASP.NET 3.5, you create a connection string to the database in your machine.config or web.config file, as shown in the following code:

```
<configuration>

    <connectionStrings>
        <add name="LocalSql2005Server"
          connectionString="Data Source=127.0.0.1;Integrated Security=SSPI" />
    </connectionStrings>

</configuration>
```

Figure 20-38

Figure 20-39

You may want to change the values provided if you are working with a remote instance of SQL Server, rather than an instance that resides on the same server as the application. Changing this value in the `machine.config` file changes how each ASP.NET application uses this provider. Applying this setting in the `web.config` file causes only the local application to work with this instance.

After the connection string is set up, look further in the `<providers>` area of the section you are going to work with. For instance, if you are using the membership provider, then you want to work with the `<membership>` element in the configuration file. The settings to change SQL Server are shown here:

```
<configuration>

  <connectionStrings>
    <add name="LocalSql2005Server"
      connectionString="Data Source=127.0.0.1;Integrated Security=SSPI" />
```

```
        </connectionStrings>

        <system.web>

                <membership defaultProvider="AspNetSql2005MembershipProvider">
                    <providers>
                        <add name="AspNetSql2005MembershipProvider"
                            type="System.Web.Security.SqlMembershipProvider,
                                System.Web, Version=2.0.0.0, Culture=neutral,
                                PublicKeyToken=b03f5f7f11d50a3a"
                            connectionStringName="LocalSql2005Server"
                            enablePasswordRetrieval="false"
                            enablePasswordReset="true"
                            requiresQuestionAndAnswer="true"
                            applicationName="/"
                            requiresUniqueEmail="false"
                            passwordFormat="Hashed"
                            maxInvalidPasswordAttempts="5"
                            minRequiredPasswordLength="7"
                            minRequiredNonalphanumericCharacters="1"
                            passwordAttemptWindow="10"
                            passwordStrengthRegularExpression="" />
                    </providers>
                </membership>

        </system.web>

    </configuration>
```

With these changes in place, the SQL Server 2005 instance is now one of the providers available for use with your applications. The name of this instance is `AspNetSql2005MembershipProvider`. You can see that this instance also uses the connection string of `LocalSql2005Server`, which was defined earlier.

Pay attention to some important attribute declarations in the preceding configuration code. For example, the provider used by the membership system is defined via the `defaultProvider` attribute found in the main `<membership>` node. Using this attribute, you can specify whether the provider is one of the built-in providers or whether it is a custom provider that you have built yourself or received from a third party. With the code in place, the membership provider now works with Microsoft SQL Server 2005 (as shown in this example) instead of the Microsoft SQL Server Express Edition files.

ASP.NET AJAX

AJAX is definitely the current hot buzzword in the Web application world. AJAX is an acronym for *Asynchronous JavaScript and XML*, and in Web application development it signifies the capability to build applications that make use of the `XMLHttpRequest` object.

The creation and inclusion of the `XMLHttpRequest` object in JavaScript and the fact that most upper-level browsers support it led to the creation of the AJAX model. AJAX applications, although they have been around for a few years, gained popularity after Google released a number of notable, AJAX-enabled applications such as Google Maps and Google Suggest. These applications clearly demonstrated the value of AJAX.

Shortly thereafter, Microsoft released a beta for a new toolkit that enabled developers to incorporate AJAX features in their Web applications. This toolkit, code-named *Atlas* and later renamed ASP.NET AJAX, makes it extremely simple to start using AJAX features in your applications today.

The ASP.NET AJAX toolkit was *not* part of the default .NET Framework 2.0 install. If you are using the .NET Framework 2.0, it is an extra component that you must download from the Internet.

Understanding the Need for AJAX

Today, if you are going to build an application, you have the option of creating either a thick-client or a thin-client application. A *thick-client* application is typically a compiled executable that end users can run in the confines of their own environment — usually without any dependencies elsewhere (such as an upstream server). Generally, the technology to build this type of application is the Windows Forms technology, or MFC in the C++ world. A *thin-client* application is typically one that has its processing and rendering controlled at a single point (the upstream server), and the results of the view are sent down as HTML to a browser to be viewed by a client. To work, this type of technology generally requires that the end user be connected to the Internet or an intranet of some kind.

Each type of application has its pros and cons. The thick-client style of application is touted as more fluid and more responsive to an end user's actions. In a Web-based application, for many years the complaint has been that every action by an end user takes numerous seconds and results in a jerky page refresh. In turn, the problem with a thick-client style of application has always been that the application sits on the end user's machine and any patches or updates to the application require you to somehow upgrade each and every machine upon which the application sits. In contrast, the thin-client application, or the Web application architecture, includes only one instance of the application. The application in this case is installed on a Web server, and any updates that need to occur happen only to this instance. End users who are calling the application through their browsers always get the latest and greatest version of the application. That change model has a lot of power to it.

With this said, it is important to understand that Microsoft is making huge inroads into solving this thick- or thin-client problem, and you now have options that completely change this model. For instance, the Windows Presentation Foundation technology recently offered by Microsoft and the new Silverlight technology blur the lines between the two traditional application styles.

Even with the existing Windows Forms and ASP.NET technologies to build the respective thick- or thin-client applications, each of these technologies is advancing to a point where it is even blurring the lines further. ASP.NET AJAX in particular is further removing any of the negatives that would have stopped you from building an application on the Web.

ASP.NET AJAX makes your Web applications seem more fluid than ever before. AJAX-enabled applications are highly responsive and give the end user immediate feedback and direction through the workflows that you provide. The power of this alone makes the study of this new technology and its incorporation into your projects of the utmost importance.

Before AJAX

So, what is AJAX doing to your Web application? First, let's take a look at what a Web page does when it *does not* use AJAX. Figure 20-40 shows a typical request and response activity for a Web application.

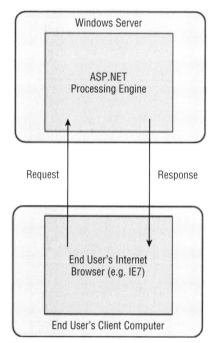

Figure 20-40

In this case, an end user makes a request from his or her browser to the application that is stored on your Web server. The server processes the request, and ASP.NET renders a page, which is then sent to the requestor as a response. The response, once received by the end user, is displayed within the end user's browser.

From here, many events that take place within the application instance as it sits within the end user's browser cause the complete request and response process to reoccur. For instance, the end user might click a radio button, a check box, a button, a calendar, or anything else, and this action causes the entire Web page to be refreshed or a new page to be provided.

AJAX Changes the Story

Conversely, an AJAX-enabled Web page includes a JavaScript library on the client that takes care of issuing the calls to the Web server. It does this when it is possible to send a request and get a response for just part of the page and using script; the client library updates that part of the page without updating the entire page. An entire page is a lot of code to send down to the browser to process each and every time. With only part of the page being processed, the end user experiences what some people term "fluidity" in the page, which makes the page seem more responsive. The amount of code required to update just a portion of a page is less and produces the responsiveness the end user expects. Figure 20-41 shows a diagram of how this works.

First, the entire page is delivered in the initial request and response. From there, any partial updates required by the page are performed using the client script library. This library can make asynchronous page requests and update just the portion of the page that needs updating. One major advantage to this is that a minimal amount of data is transferred for the updates to occur. Updating a partial page is better than recalling the entire page for what is just a minor change.

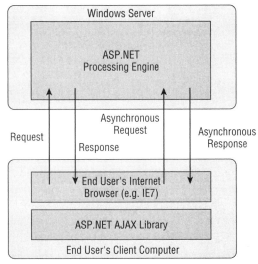

Figure 20-41

AJAX is dependent upon a few technologies in order for it to work:

❑   The first is the XMLHttpRequest object. This object enables the browser to communicate to a back-end server and has been available in the Microsoft world since Internet Explorer 5 through the MSXML ActiveX component.

❑   The other major component is JavaScript. This technology provides the client-side initiation to communication with the back-end services and takes care of packaging a message to send to any server-side services.

❑   Another aspect of AJAX is support for DHTML and the Document Object Model (DOM). These are the pieces that will change the page when the asynchronous response is received from the server.

❑   The last piece is the data being transferred from the client to the server. This is done in XML or, more important, JavaScript Object Notation (JSON).

Support for the XMLHttpRequest object gives JavaScript functions within the client script library the capability to call server-side events. As stated, typically HTTP requests are issued by a browser. It is also the browser that takes care of processing the server's response, and then usually regenerates the entire Web page in the browser after a response is issued.

If you use the XMLHttpRequest object from your JavaScript library, you do not actually issue full-page requests from the browser. Instead, you use a client-side script engine (which is basically a JavaScript function) to initiate the request and to receive the response. Because you are not issuing a request and response to deal with the entire Web page, you can skip a lot of the page processing because it is not needed. This is the essence of an AJAX Web request.

This opens the door to a tremendous number of possibilities. Microsoft has provided the necessary script engines to automate much of the communication that must take place in order for AJAX-style functionality to occur.

ASP.NET AJAX and Visual Studio 2008

Prior to Visual Studio 2008, the ASP.NET AJAX product used to be a separate installation that you were required to install on your machine and the Web server that you were working with. This release gained in popularity quite rapidly and is now a part of the Visual Studio 2008 offering. Not only is it a part of the Visual Studio 2008 IDE, the ASP.NET AJAX product is also baked into the .NET Framework 3.5. This means that to use ASP.NET AJAX, you don't need to install anything if you are working with ASP.NET 3.5.

> *If you are using an ASP.NET version prior to the ASP.NET 3.5 release, then you need to visit* www.asp.net/AJAX *to get the components required to work with AJAX.*

Because ASP.NET AJAX is now part of the ASP.NET framework, when you create a new Web application you don't have to create a separate type of ASP.NET application. Instead, all ASP.NET applications that you create are AJAX-enabled.

If you have already worked with ASP.NET AJAX prior to this 3.5 release, there is really nothing new to learn. The entire technology is seamlessly integrated.

Overall, Microsoft has fully integrated the entire ASP.NET AJAX experience so you can easily use Visual Studio and its visual designers to work with your AJAX-enabled pages and even have the full debugging story that you would want to have with your applications. Using Visual Studio 2008, you can now debug the JavaScript that you are using in the pages.

In addition, note that Microsoft focused a lot of attention on cross-platform compatibility with ASP.NET AJAX. The AJAX-enabled applications that you build upon the .NET Framework 3.5 can work within all the major up-level browsers available (e.g., Firefox and Opera).

Client-Side Technologies

There are actually two parts to the ASP.NET AJAX story. The first is a client-side framework and a set of services that are completely on the client-side. The other part of the story is a server-side framework. Remember that the client side of ASP.NET AJAX is all about the client communicating asynchronous requests to the server side of the offering.

For this reason, Microsoft offers a Client Script Library, which is a JavaScript library that takes care of the required communications. The Client Script Library is presented in Figure 20-42.

The Client Script Library provides a JavaScript, object-oriented interface that is reasonably consistent with aspects of the .NET Framework. Because browser compatibility components are built in, any work that you build in this layer or (in most cases) work that you let ASP.NET AJAX perform for you here will function with a multitude of different browsers. In addition, several components support a rich UI infrastructure capable of producing many things that would otherwise take some serious time to build yourself.

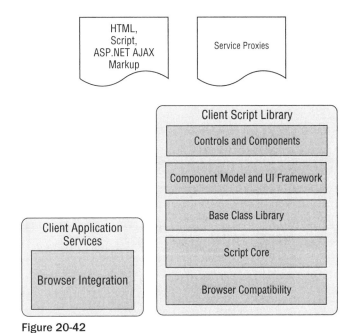

Figure 20-42

The interesting thing about the client-side technologies provided by ASP.NET AJAX is that they are completely independent of ASP.NET. In fact, any developer can freely download the Microsoft AJAX Library (again from asp.net/AJAX) and use it with other Web technologies such as PHP (www.php.net) and Java Server Pages (JSP). That said, the entire Web story is actually a lot more complete with the server-side technologies provided with ASP.NET AJAX.

Server-Side Technologies

As an ASP.NET developer, you will most likely be spending most of your time on the server-side aspect of ASP.NET AJAX. Remember that ASP.NET AJAX is all about the client-side technologies talking back to the server-side technologies. You can actually perform quite a bit on the server side of ASP.NET AJAX.

The server-side framework knows how to deal with client requests, such as putting responses in the correct format. The server-side framework also takes care of the marshalling of objects back and forth between JavaScript objects and the .NET objects that you are using in your server-side code. Figure 20-43 illustrates the server-side framework provided by ASP.NET AJAX.

When you have the .NET Framework 3.5, you have the ASP.NET AJAX Server Extensions on top of the core ASP.NET 2.0 Framework, the Windows Communication Foundation, as well as ASP.NET-based Web services (.asmx).

Developing with ASP.NET AJAX

Some Web developers are used to working with ASP.NET, and have experience working with server-side controls and manipulating these controls on the server-side. Other developers concentrate on the client side and work with DHTML and JavaScript to manipulate and control the page and its behaviors.

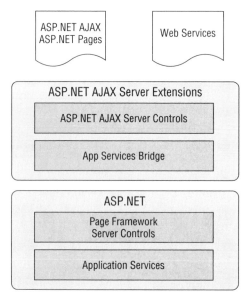

Figure 20-43

ASP.NET AJAX was designed for both types of developers. If you want to work more on the server side of ASP.NET AJAX, you can use the new `ScriptManager` control and the new `UpdatePanel` control to AJAX-enable your current ASP.NET applications with little work on your part. All this work can be done using the same programming models that you are quite familiar with in ASP.NET. In turn, you can also use the Client Script Library directly and gain greater control over what is happening on the client's machine. In the next section, you'll build a simple Web page that makes use of AJAX.

Building a Simple ASP.NET Page with AJAX

For this example, you will be adding some simple controls. Two of the controls to add are typical ASP.NET server controls — another `Label` and `Button` server control. In addition to these controls, you are going to add some ASP.NET AJAX controls.

In the Visual Studio 2008 Toolbox is a new section titled AJAX Extensions, as shown in Figure 20-44.

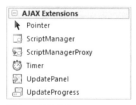

Figure 20-44

From AJAX Extensions, add a `ScriptManager` server control to the top of the page and include the second `Label` and `Button` control inside the `UpdatePanel` control. The `UpdatePanel` control is a template server control that enables you to include any number of items within it (just as other templated ASP.NET server controls). When you have your page set up, it should look something like what is shown in Figure 20-45.

890

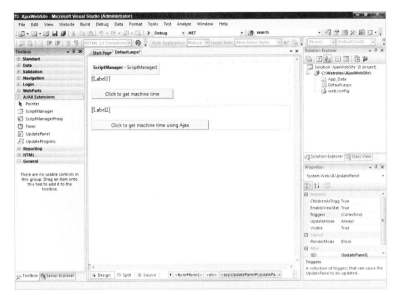

Figure 20-45

The code for this page is as follows:

```vb
<%@ Page Language="VB" %>

<script runat="server">
    Protected Sub Button1_Click(ByVal sender As Object, _
        ByVal e As System.EventArgs)
         Label1.Text = DateTime.Now.ToString()
    End Sub

    Protected Sub Button2_Click(ByVal sender As Object, _
        ByVal e As System.EventArgs)
         Label2.Text = DateTime.Now.ToString()
    End Sub
</script>

<html xmlns="http://www.w3.org/1999/xhtml">
<head runat="server">
    <title>My ASP.NET AJAX Page</title>
</head>
<body>
    <form id="form1" runat="server">
    <div>
        <asp:ScriptManager ID="ScriptManager1" runat="server">
        </asp:ScriptManager>
        <asp:Label ID="Label1" runat="server"></asp:Label>
        <br />
        <br />
        <asp:Button ID="Button1" runat="server"
         Text="Click to get machine time"
         onclick="Button1_Click" />
```

```
        <br />
        <br />
        <asp:UpdatePanel ID="UpdatePanel1" runat="server">
            <ContentTemplate>
                <asp:Label ID="Label2" runat="server" Text=""></asp:Label>
                <br />
                <br />
                <asp:Button ID="Button2" runat="server"
                 Text="Click to get machine time using AJAX"
                 onclick="Button2_Click" />
            </ContentTemplate>
        </asp:UpdatePanel>
    </div>
    </form>
</body>
</html>
```

When this page is pulled up in the browser, it has two buttons. The first button causes a complete page postback and updates the current time in the Label1 server control. Clicking on the second button causes an AJAX asynchronous postback. Clicking this second button updates the current server time in the Label2 server control. When you click the AJAX button, the time in Label1 will not change at all, as it is outside of the UpdatePanel. The result is presented in Figure 20-46.

Figure 20-46

When you first pull up the page from the preceding listing, the code is quite different from the page that would be built if you weren't using AJAX. The following code listing shows the page results that you see by using AJAX:

```
<html xmlns="http://www.w3.org/1999/xhtml">
<head><title>
 My ASP.NET AJAX Page
</title></head>
<body>
    <form name="form1" method="post" action="Default.aspx" id="form1">
<div>
<input type="hidden" name="__EVENTTARGET" id="__EVENTTARGET" value="" />
<input type="hidden" name="__EVENTARGUMENT" id="__EVENTARGUMENT" value="" />
<input type="hidden" name="__VIEWSTATE" id="__VIEWSTATE"
 value="/wEPDwULLTE4NzE5NTc5MzRkZDRIzHpPZg4GaO9Hox9A/RnOflkm" />
```

```
</div>

<script type="text/javascript">
//<![CDATA[
var theForm = document.forms['form1'];
if (!theForm) {
    theForm = document.form1;
}
function __doPostBack(eventTarget, eventArgument) {
    if (!theForm.onsubmit || (theForm.onsubmit() != false)) {
        theForm.__EVENTTARGET.value = eventTarget;
        theForm.__EVENTARGUMENT.value = eventArgument;
        theForm.submit();
    }
}
//]]>
</script>

<script src="/AJAXWebSite/WebResource.axd?d=o84znEj-
 n4cYi0Wg0pFXCg2&amp;t=633285028458684000" type="text/javascript"></script>

<script src="/AJAXWebSite/ScriptResource.axd?
 d=FETsh5584DXpx8XqIhEM50YSKyR2GkoMoAqraYEDU5_
 gi1SUmL2Gt7rQTRBAw56lSojJRQe0OjVI8SiYDjmpYmFP0
 CO8wBFGhtKKJwm2MeE1&amp;t=633285035850304000"
 type="text/javascript"></script>
<script type="text/javascript">
//<![CDATA[
if (typeof(Sys) === 'undefined') throw new Error('ASP.NET AJAX client-side
  framework failed to load.');
//]]>
</script>

<script src="/AJAXWebSite/ScriptResource.axd?
 d=FETsh5584DXpx8XqIhEM50YSKyR2GkoMoAqraYEDU5_
 gi1SUmL2Gt7rQTRBAw56l7AYfmRViCoO2lZ3XwZ33TGiC
 t92e_UOqfrP30mdEYnJYs09ulU1xBLj8TjXOLR1k0&amp;t=633285035850304000"
 type="text/javascript"></script>
    <div>
        <script type="text/javascript">
//<![CDATA[
Sys.WebForms.PageRequestManager._initialize('ScriptManager1',
document.getElementById('form1'));
Sys.WebForms.PageRequestManager.getInstance()._updateControls(['tUpdatePanel1'],
[], [], 90);
//]]>
</script>
        <span id="Label1"></span>
        <br />
        <br />
        <input type="submit" name="Button1" value="Click to get machine time"
         id="Button1" />
        <br />
        <br />
        <div id="UpdatePanel1">
```

```
                    <span id="Label2"></span>
                    <br />
                    <br />
                    <input type="submit" name="Button2"
                     value="Click to get machine
                     time using AJAX" id="Button2" />
</div>
    </div>
<div>

 <input type="hidden" name="__EVENTVALIDATION" id="__EVENTVALIDATION"
value="/wEWAwLktbDGDgKM54rGBgK7q7GGCMYnNq57VIqmVD2sRDQqfnOsgWQK" />
</div>

<script type="text/javascript">
//<![CDATA[
Sys.Application.initialize();
//]]>
</script>
</form>
</body>
</html>
```

From there, if you click Button1 and perform the full-page postback, you get this entire bit of code back in a response — even though you are interested in updating only a small portion of the page! However, if you click Button2 — the AJAX button — you send the request shown here:

```
POST /AJAXWebSite/Default.aspx HTTP/1.1
Accept: */*
Accept-Language: en-US
Referer: http://localhost.:62203/AJAXWebSite/Default.aspx
x-microsoftAJAX: Delta=true
Content-Type: application/x-www-form-urlencoded; charset=utf-8
Cache-Control: no-cache
UA-CPU: x86
Accept-Encoding: gzip, deflate
User-Agent: Mozilla/4.0 (compatible; MSIE 7.0; Windows NT 6.0; SLCC1; .NET CLR
2.0.50727; Media Center PC 5.0; .NET CLR 1.1.4322; .NET CLR 3.5.21004; .NET CLR
3.0.04506)
Host: localhost.:62203
Content-Length: 334
Proxy-Connection: Keep-Alive
Pragma: no-cache

ScriptManager1=UpdatePanel1%7CButton2&__EVENTTARGET=&__EVENTARGUMENT=&__
VIEWSTATE=%2FwEPDwULLTE4NzE5NTc5MzQPZBYCAgQPZBYCAgMPDxYCHgRUZXh0BRQxMS8zLzI
wMDcgMjoxNzo1NSBQTWRkZHZxUyYQG0M25t8U7vLbHRJuKlcS&__
EVENTVALIDATION=%2FwEWAwKCxdk9AoznisYGArursYYI1844
hk7V466AsW31G5yIZ73%2Bc6o%3D&Button2=Click%20to%20get%20machine
%20time%20using%20Ajax
```

The response for this request is shown here:

```
HTTP/1.1 200 OK
Server: ASP.NET Development Server/9.0.0.0
Date: Sat, 03 Nov 2007 19:17:58 GMT
X-AspNet-Version: 2.0.50727
Cache-Control: private
Content-Type: text/plain; charset=utf-8
Content-Length: 796
Connection: Close

239|updatePanel|UpdatePanel1|
                <span id="Label2">11/3/2007 2:17:58 PM</span>
                <br />
                <br />
                <input type="submit" name="Button2"
                 value="Click to get machine
                 time using AJAX" id="Button2" />
            |172|hiddenField|__VIEWSTATE|/wEPDwULLTE4NzE5NTc5MzQPZBYCAgQPZBYEAgM
PDxYCHgRUZXh0BRQxMS8zLzIwMDcgMjoxNzo1NSBQTWRkAgcPZBYCZg9kFgICAQ8PFgI
fAAUUMTEvMy8yMDA3IDI6MTc6NTggUE1kZGQ4ipZIg91+XSI/dqxFueSUwcrXGw==|56
|hiddenField|__EVENTVALIDATION|/wEWAwKCz4mbCAK7q7GGCAKM54rGBj8b4/mkK
NKhV59qX9SdCzqU3AiM|0|asyncPostBackControlIDs|||0|postBackControlIDs
|||13|updatePanelIDs||tUpdatePanel1|0|childUpdatePanelIDs|||12|panels
ToRefreshIDs||UpdatePanel1|2|asyncPostBackTimeout||90|12|formAction||
Default.aspx|22|pageTitle||My ASP.NET AJAX Page|
```

Clearly, the response is much smaller than an entire Web page! In fact, the main part of the response is only the code contained within the UpdatePanel server control and nothing more. The items at the bottom deal with the ViewState of the page (as it has now changed) and some other small page changes.

Summary

This chapter and the previous chapter offered a whirlwind tour of ASP.NET 3.5 and some of the application features that you can provide to the projects you develop. ASP.NET is highly focused on the area of developer productivity, and works very hard at providing you access to the features and functions that most websites need to employ today. This chapter covered the following ASP.NET technologies:

❑   Cross-page posting

❑   ASP.NET compilation techniques

❑   Master pages

❑   The data source controls

❑   The navigation system and some of the navigation server controls

❑   Membership and role management

❑   The new ASP.NET AJAX capabilities

A nice aspect of the features presented is that you can either utilize the wizards that are built into the underlying technology or simply skip these wizards and employ the technologies yourself. Either way is fine. Another useful aspect of the technologies introduced is that they all enable a huge amount of customization. You can alter the behavior and output of these technologies to achieve exactly what you need. If you want to dig deeper into ASP.NET, be sure to take a look at *Professional ASP.NET 3.5* (Wiley, 2008).

Silverlight Development

One of the newer technologies out there is Silverlight 1.0, which was released in September of 2007. At the time of this writing, Silverlight 1.0 is the only production release of the product. However, Silverlight 2.0 will be released in the first half of 2008.

Silverlight is a lightweight browser plug-in from Microsoft that, much like Adobe's Flash, will allow for greater fluidity in your applications, thereby providing a rich user experience like no other in ASP.NET. The base of Silverlight is XAML — a new markup language for creating applications by Microsoft, such as WPF (Windows Presentation Foundation) applications.

You can build Silverlight applications using Microsoft's new Expression Blend IDE, as well as the new Visual Studio 2008. This chapter looks at the basics of Silverlight and how to build a Silverlight application.

Looking at Silverlight

Silverlight is not tied to Microsoft's Internet Explorer. It cannot be. If an application is going to work on the Web, then it has to work in a multitude of browsers. For this reason, Silverlight is a cross-browser platform for the applications you build. It is a standalone environment and has no dependency for items, such as the .NET Framework, on the client machine.

However, even though you are using XAML to build your Silverlight applications, you're not required to have the .NET Framework 3.0 or 3.5 on the client. Instead, the XAML is loaded into the browser and run in the context of the Silverlight plug-in.

Silverlight browser requirements

Silverlight will not run in every browser on the market. The following list shows which popular browsers Silverlight 1.0 can work with today:

- ❑ Microsoft's Internet Explorer 6 and later
- ❑ Firefox 1.5.0.8 and later (running on Windows or the Mac)
- ❑ Safari 2.0.4 and later (running on the Mac)

Following are the operating systems that can run Silverlight:

❑ Windows XP SP2

❑ Windows Vista

❑ Mac OS X (10.4.8 or better)

You might be wondering why Linux is not on this list. Novell is building a Silverlight plug-in for the Linux environment called Moonlight — a Mono-based implementation of Silverlight.

You can find more information on Moonlight at `www.mono-project.com/Moonlight`.

Two versions of Silverlight

At the time of writing, Silverlight 1.0 has been out for a couple of months. Though revolutionary, this first version of the product supports a model that uses JavaScript programming to interact with the Silverlight objects.

The big change coming with Silverlight 2.0 is that you are going to be able to use managed code (such as Visual Basic) to interact with the Silverlight objects.

Both versions use XAML to control the output to the browser. The difference between the two versions of Silverlight is that JavaScript is used to control the behaviors on the page for version 1.0, and managed code is used for version 2.0.

Installing Silverlight

If you are an end user and you access a Silverlight application (a page on the Internet that makes use of the Silverlight plug-in), then you will be prompted to download the Silverlight plug-in. Obviously, this only occurs when end users don't have the plug-in installed yet on their machines.

For instance, if you direct your browser to the URL `www.silverlight.net`, which is the URL for the main Silverlight page, you will be prompted to install Silverlight, as shown in Figure 21-1.

Installing Silverlight is quick and simple. It takes about 20 seconds to perform this 1.3 MB install. Pressing the Click to Install button on the page will give you a File Download security warning (as shown in Figure 21-2). In this case, simple press the Run button.

The Silverlight application will install, and you will get a notification of the install process, as shown in Figure 21-3.

This install process shows what percentage you have installed as well as the version of Silverlight that you are installing (shown in the lower right-hand corner of the dialog).

Once you've installed it, you'll be able to right-click on any Silverlight component on the page and view the Silverlight configuration by making the appropriate selection from the provided menu. On the Silverlight Web page, you can see this by right-clicking on the upper menu. You will then see the Silverlight Configuration dialog, shown in Figure 21-4.

Figure 21-1

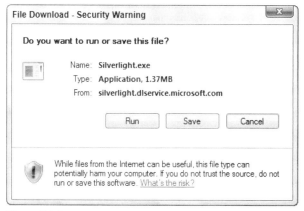

Figure 21-2

Figure 21-3

Figure 21-4

Developing Silverlight Applications

When you open Visual Studio 2008, you won't find a Silverlight application template in the list of available options when you create a new project. In order to get that, you need to download the Silverlight SDK from the Silverlight.net website.

On the Silverlight.net website, click the Get Started option in the menu at the top of the page. The window shown in Figure 21-5 will appear.

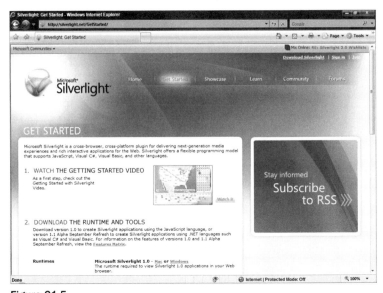

Figure 21-5

From this site, the following items can be downloaded:

Runtimes:

- ❏ Microsoft Silverlight 1.0 for the Mac or Windows
- ❏ A version of Microsoft Silverlight 2.0

Developer Tools:

- ❏ Microsoft Visual Studio 2008
- ❏ The Microsoft Silverlight Tools for Visual Studio 2008

Designer Tools:

- ❏ Microsoft's Expression Blend
- ❏ Expression Encoder
- ❏ Expression Design

Software Development Kits:

- ❏ Microsoft Silverlight 1.0 Software Development Kit
- ❏ Microsoft Silverlight 2.0 Software Development Kit

Assuming you have already installed Visual Studio 2008, you need to install the Silverlight Tools for Visual Studio. Installing this toolset will add the Silverlight Project option to your instance of Visual Studio 2008.

Building a simple Silverlight application

Now that you have installed everything that's needed to build a Silverlight application, the next step is to build a simple application that makes use of the Silverlight plug-in. The first step is select the Silverlight Project template that is now available in Visual Studio 2008 from the install you just did of the Silverlight Tools for Visual Studio.

Choosing the Silverlight Project Template

Within Visual Studio 2008, select File ➪ New Project. You will find the Silverlight Project option in the New Project dialog that appears, as shown in Figure 21-6.

The Silverlight Project option is only available as a .NET Framework 3.5 project, and the default name of the project is SilverlightProject1, as shown in the figure. Selecting the OK button will create the project for you.

The Silverlight Solution

Once you have created your application, you will find a series of files contained within the project. The SilverlightProject1 solution is presented in Figure 21-7.

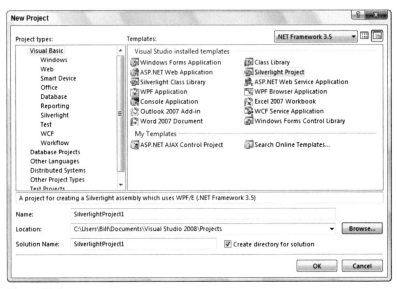

Figure 21-6

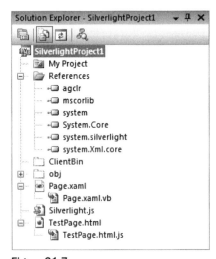

Figure 21-7

Within this solution are references to `agclr` (the CLR imbedded in the Silverlight container), `mscorlib`, `System`, `System.Core`, `System.Silverlight`, and `System.Xml.Core`. The Silverlight parts to focus on within this application are the `Page.xaml` and `Page.xaml.vb` files. These are embedded in the container on the client. The test client, in this case, is the `TestPage.html` page. Here is a description of the pages included in the solution shown in Figure 21-7.

File	Description
Page.xaml	The default XAML file that contains the XAML-markup needed for the page. The object defined in this file is what is presented in the Silverlight container.
Page.xaml.vb	The code-behind page for the XAML file
Silverlight.js	Contains the core JavaScript library that works with the client to ensure that the Silverlight plug-in is installed on the machine. If not, then an Install Silverlight button will be presented to the client.
TestPage.html	A test Web page that hosts the Silverlight plug-in and contains the appropriate references to the required JavaScript files
TestPage.html.js	The JavaScript page that is associated with the TestPage.html page

Looking at the Page.xaml file, you will see the following:

```
<Canvas x:Name="parentCanvas"
        xmlns="http://schemas.microsoft.com/client/2007"
        xmlns:x="http://schemas.microsoft.com/winfx/2006/xaml"
        Loaded="Page_Loaded"
        x:Class="SilverlightProject1.Page;
            assembly=ClientBin/SilverlightProject1.dll"
        Width="640"
        Height="480"
        Background="White"
        >

</Canvas>
```

The Canvas control is the container in which you can place any number of child elements. From this bit of code, you can see that the Canvas control has an assigned name:

```
X:Name="parentCanvas"
```

There is also an event handler in the code with the Loaded attribute:

```
Loaded="Page_Loaded"
```

Finally, other points to pay attention to are the style attributes of Width, Height, and Background:

```
Width="640"
Height="480"
Background="White"
```

In version 2.0 of Silverlight, the code-behind page for the .xaml file is a .xaml.vb file. In version 1.0 of Silverlight, you use JavaScript as your code-behind page, so your code-behind file would be .xaml.js.

The example in this chapter uses the 2.0 version of Silverlight, and the code for the `Page.xaml.vb` file is presented here:

```
Partial Public Class Page
    Inherits Canvas

    Public Sub Page_Loaded(ByVal o As Object, ByVal e As EventArgs)
        ' Required to initialize variables
        InitializeComponent()

    End Sub

End Class
```

In this case, you have a `Page` class that inherits from `Canvas`. Any page events that you are going to put on your page would happen here on this code-behind page.

The `Page.xaml` and the `Page.xaml.vb` files are the files that constitute the Silverlight portion of the application. The other two pages, `TestPage.html` and `TestPage.html.js`, are sample pages used to host the Silverlight player. The `TestPage.html` page is presented in the following code:

```
<!DOCTYPE html PUBLIC "-//W3C//DTD XHTML 1.0 Transitional//EN"
 "http://www.w3.org/TR/xhtml1/DTD/xhtml1-transitional.dtd">

<html xmlns="http://www.w3.org/1999/xhtml" >
<head>
    <title>Silverlight Project Test Page </title>

    <script type="text/javascript" src="Silverlight.js"></script>
    <script type="text/javascript" src="TestPage.html.js"></script>
    <style type="text/css">
        .silverlightHost { width: 640px; height: 480px; }
    </style>
</head>

<body>
    <div id="SilverlightControlHost" class="silverlightHost" >
        <script type="text/javascript">
            createSilverlight();
        </script>
    </div>
</body>
</html>
```

This page loads two JavaScript files: `Silverlight.js` and `TestPage.html.js`. Keep in mind that the `Silverlight.js` file is used to detect whether or not the client has Silverlight installed on his or her computer, whereas `TestPage.html.js` is used for any JavaScript functions that you need on the page. The `TestPage.html.js` file is presented here:

```
// JScript source code

//contains calls to silverlight.js, example below loads Page.xaml
```

```
function createSilverlight()
{
 Silverlight.createObjectEx({
        source: "Page.xaml",
        parentElement: document.getElementById("SilverlightControlHost"),
        id: "SilverlightControl",
        properties: {
                width: "100%",
                height: "100%",
                version: "1.1",
                enableHtmlAccess: "true"
        },
        events: {}
 });

 // Give the keyboard focus to the Silverlight control by default
    document.body.onload = function() {
       var silverlightControl = document.getElementById('SilverlightControl');
       if (silverlightControl)
       silverlightControl.focus();
    }

}
```

This page works with the Silverlight player and assigns the page that this player is to work with when the object is created.

The Silverlight Canvas

You can view the canvas you are working with by changing the background color of the `<Canvas>` element, as shown in the following example:

```
<Canvas x:Name="parentCanvas"
        xmlns="http://schemas.microsoft.com/client/2007"
        xmlns:x="http://schemas.microsoft.com/winfx/2006/xaml"
        Loaded="Page_Loaded"
        x:Class="SilverlightProject1.Page;
           assembly=ClientBin/SilverlightProject1.dll"
        Width="350"
        Height="350"
        Background="Black"

        >

</Canvas>
```

In this case, the `Width` and `Height` properties were changed to 350 pixels, and the `Background` property value was changed to `Black`. This would produce the results shown in Figure 21-8.

This shows the Silverlight canvas as it is presented in the browser. In this case, the entire canvas is represented as a black square.

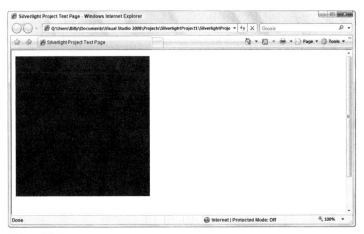

Figure 21-8

Silverlight Examples

Silverlight's capabilities enable you to do quite a bit, including video, animation, vector-based graphics, and much more — obviously more than what can be represented in a single chapter. The next few sections provide an overview of Silverlight through some basic examples that will help you understand your Silverlight application.

A simple Hello World! example

This example creates a Hello World! application. The only requirement here is that you change the Page.xaml file as follows:

```
<Canvas x:Name="parentCanvas"
        xmlns="http://schemas.microsoft.com/client/2007"
        xmlns:x="http://schemas.microsoft.com/winfx/2006/xaml"
        Loaded="Page_Loaded"
        x:Class="SilverlightProject1.Page;
            assembly=ClientBin/SilverlightProject1.dll"
        Width="640"
        Height="480"
        Background="White"
        >

  <Ellipse Height="200" Width="200" Canvas.Left="30" Canvas.Top="30"
      Stroke="Black" StrokeThickness="10" Fill="Yellow">
  </Ellipse>

  <TextBlock Canvas.Left="5" Canvas.Top="5" Text="Hello World!"
    FontFamily="Arial" FontSize="20" FontWeight="Bold"></TextBlock>

</Canvas>
```

In this example, the canvas contains two elements. The first is a circle represented with the <Ellipse> element. The ellipse, or circle, is given a size with the Height and Width attributes. Both of these attributes are assigned a value of 200.

Important attributes to understand are the `Canvas.Left` and `Canvas.Top` attributes used in this example. These attributes define the location of the element on the page. Figure 21-9 shows how these attributes work.

Canvas.Top 30 PIXELS FROM THE TOP

Canvas.Left 30 PIXELS FROM THE LEFT

CANVAS

Figure 21-9

As shown in Figure 21-9, `Canvas.Left` defines the number of pixels that the element is positioned from the left side of the canvas. `Canvas.Top` defines the number of pixels that the element is positioned from the top of the canvas.

The `Stroke` and `StrokeThickness` attributes work with the border of the ellipse. The `Stroke` attribute is given a value of `Black` and the `StrokeThickness` is set at 10 pixels. Finally, the `Fill` attribute defines the color used inside of the ellipse itself. This attribute is set to `Yellow`.

In addition to the yellow ellipse defined with the `<Ellipse>` element, there is a second element — a `<TextBlock>` element. Here, a series of attributes works with the text that appears in the element itself:

```
<TextBlock Canvas.Left="5" Canvas.Top="5" Text="Hello World!"
  FontFamily="Arial" FontSize="20" FontWeight="Bold"></TextBlock>
```

Just like the `<Ellipse>` element, this element also contains `Canvas.Left` and `Canvas.Top` attributes to define its position within the canvas. When this page is run, you will get what is presented in Figure 21-10.

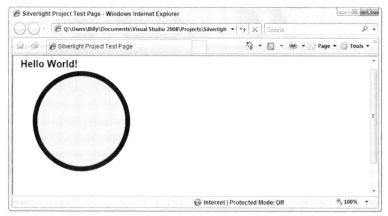

Figure 21-10

Both elements are positioned as defined in the example.

Working with multiple elements

As shown in the preceding example, the canvas contains two elements — an `Ellipse` control and a `TextBlock` control. Each of these controls was laid onto the canvas using various attributes. The following example demonstrates what happens when these elements overlap:

```
<Canvas x:Name="parentCanvas"
        xmlns="http://schemas.microsoft.com/client/2007"
        xmlns:x="http://schemas.microsoft.com/winfx/2006/xaml"
        Loaded="Page_Loaded"
        x:Class="SilverlightProject1.Page;
            assembly=ClientBin/SilverlightProject1.dll"
        Width="640"
        Height="480"
        Background="White"
        >

    <Ellipse Height="200" Width="200" Canvas.Left="30" Canvas.Top="30"
        Stroke="Black" StrokeThickness="10" Fill="Yellow">
    </Ellipse>

    <Ellipse Height="200" Width="200" Canvas.Left="60" Canvas.Top="60"
        Stroke="Black" StrokeThickness="10" Fill="Blue">
    </Ellipse>

    <Ellipse Height="200" Width="200" Canvas.Left="90" Canvas.Top="90"
        Stroke="Black" StrokeThickness="10" Fill="Red">
    </Ellipse>

</Canvas>
```

In this case, there are three `<Ellipse>` elements of different colors (yellow, blue, and red), and each has a different position on the canvas defined. Running this page will result in the image shown in Figure 21-11 (without the color, of course).

In order to fully appreciate Figures 21-11 through 21-14, you need to see them in color, which can only be indicated here with callouts. However, if you are following along and creating these code samples yourself, you will be able to see the colored ellipses discussed here.

In this example, three elements overlap one another. A stack order determines how these elements are laid upon the canvas, with the yellow ellipse at the back and the red ellipse at the front.

The purpose of this example is to demonstrate that in addition to positioning your elements within the `<Canvas>` element, there is also a process for determining how the elements are drawn onto the screen. The order of the elements is what is important to understand. The first element encountered in the `.xaml` document will be drawn first (the yellow ellipse), followed by the second ellipse (blue). The last element (red) in the document is drawn last.

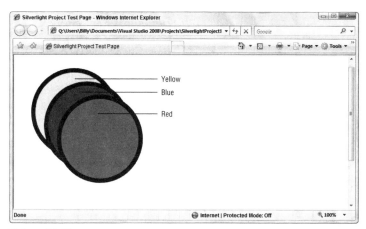

Figure 21-11

To see this in action, consider the following code:

```
<Canvas x:Name="parentCanvas"
        xmlns="http://schemas.microsoft.com/client/2007"
        xmlns:x="http://schemas.microsoft.com/winfx/2006/xaml"
        Loaded="Page_Loaded"
        x:Class="SilverlightProject1.Page;
            assembly=ClientBin/SilverlightProject1.dll"
        Width="640"
        Height="480"
        Background="White"
        >

    <Ellipse Height="200" Width="200" Canvas.Left="90" Canvas.Top="90"
        Stroke="Black" StrokeThickness="10" Fill="Red">
    </Ellipse>

    <Ellipse Height="200" Width="200" Canvas.Left="30" Canvas.Top="30"
        Stroke="Black" StrokeThickness="10" Fill="Yellow">
    </Ellipse>

    <Ellipse Height="200" Width="200" Canvas.Left="60" Canvas.Top="60"
        Stroke="Black" StrokeThickness="10" Fill="Blue">
    </Ellipse>

</Canvas>
```

In this case, the `<Ellipse>` element (the red ellipse) that was at the bottom is now at the top, meaning that this element will be drawn before the other two. Running this page will produce the results illustrated in Figure 21-12.

From this image, you can see that the red ellipse is now at the back of the bunch. The red ellipse is drawn first, followed by the yellow ellipse, and then the third ellipse (blue) is drawn last and put on top of the stack.

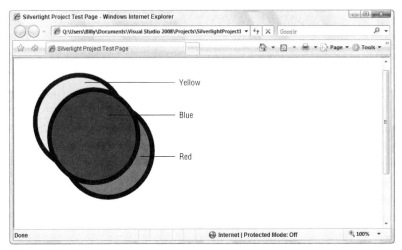

Figure 21-12

Events and Silverlight

Now that you can draw items directly onto the canvas for a Silverlight application, the next step is to enable some type of end-user interaction with the elements on this canvas. For this you will find a series of attributes for your elements that can be directly tied to specific events in the `Page.xaml.vb` code-behind page.

The first step for this example is to create a rectangle on the canvas using the `<Rectangle>` element:

```
<Canvas x:Name="parentCanvas"
        xmlns="http://schemas.microsoft.com/client/2007"
        xmlns:x="http://schemas.microsoft.com/winfx/2006/xaml"
        Loaded="Page_Loaded"
        x:Class="SilverlightProject1.Page;
            assembly=ClientBin/SilverlightProject1.dll"
        Width="640"
        Height="480"
        Background="White"
        >

  <Rectangle Opacity="1" Canvas.Left="100" Canvas.Top="100" Width="200"
  Height="200" x:Name="myRec"
  MouseLeftButtonDown="RectangleClick">
    <Rectangle.Fill>
      <LinearGradientBrush StartPoint="0.9, 0.05" EndPoint="0.9, 0.9">
        <LinearGradientBrush.GradientStops>
          <GradientStop Color="Black" Offset="0"/>
          <GradientStop Color="Blue" Offset="0.50"/>
          <GradientStop Color="Purple" Offset="1"/>
        </LinearGradientBrush.GradientStops>
      </LinearGradientBrush>
    </Rectangle.Fill>
    <Rectangle.Stroke>
```

```
    <SolidColorBrush Color="Black"></SolidColorBrush>
  </Rectangle.Stroke>
</Rectangle>

</Canvas>
```

This is a normal `<Rectangle>` element. Instead of a standard use of the `Fill` attribute with something like `Fill = "Yellow"`, this uses a `<LinearGradientBrush>` element to provide a gradient of color from black, to blue, and finally to purple. Then a stroke (border) is set to black around the entire rectangle.

Earlier, you saw that the `<Canvas>` element had a name value that was provided with the `x:Name` attribute:

```
x:Name="parentCanvas"
```

Note that in this example the `<Rectangle>` element is also provided a name:

```
x:Name="myRec"
```

This action makes it possible to reference the element in the code-behind of the `Page.xaml` page.

Next is a series of attributes geared to working with code-behind events. This example makes use of the `MouseLeftButtonDown` attribute and is provided a value of `RectangleClick`, which is the name of the event you will use in the code-behind page.

The available attributes you can use here include the following:

- ❑ KeyDown
- ❑ KeyUp
- ❑ Loaded
- ❑ LostFocus
- ❑ MouseEnter
- ❑ MouseLeave
- ❑ MouseLeftButtonDown
- ❑ MouseLeftButtonUp
- ❑ MouseMove

Now that the `<Rectangle>` element has a `MouseLeftButtonDown` attribute in it, the next step is to change the `Page.xaml.vb` code-behind page to make use of this declaration. Currently, your code-behind page should appear as follows:

```
Partial Public Class Page
    Inherits Canvas

    Public Sub Page_Loaded(ByVal o As Object, ByVal e As EventArgs)
        ' Required to initialize variables
        InitializeComponent()
```

```
        End Sub

    End Class
```

You first need to wire the event handler that will be built shortly. This can be done within the Page_Loaded subroutine:

```
    Partial Public Class Page
        Inherits Canvas

        Public Sub Page_Loaded(ByVal o As Object, ByVal e As EventArgs)
            ' Required to initialize variables
            InitializeComponent()

            AddHandler myRec.MouseLeftButtonDown, AddressOf RectangleClick
        End Sub

    End Class
```

Here, an AddHandler is utilized to add an event handler for the myRec.MouseLeftButtonDown property. This is then assigned a value of RectangleClick. Remember that the myRec value comes from the name of the <Rectangle> element that was defined in the Page.xaml page. The RectangleClick routine can then be added to the code-behind page:

```
    Partial Public Class Page
        Inherits Canvas

        Public Sub Page_Loaded(ByVal o As Object, ByVal e As EventArgs)
            ' Required to initialize variables
            InitializeComponent()

            AddHandler myRec.MouseLeftButtonDown, AddressOf RectangleClick
        End Sub

        Private Sub RectangleClick(ByVal sender As Object, _
            ByVal args As MouseEventArgs)

            Dim rectanglePaintBrush As New SolidColorBrush()
            rectanglePaintBrush.Color = Colors.Red

            myRec.Fill = rectanglePaintBrush
            myRec.Width = 300
            myRec.StrokeThickness = 10
        End Sub

    End Class
```

In this case, a subroutine called RectangleClick() is created, which then changes the structure of the <Rectangle> element. First, an instance of a SolidColorBrush object is created and assigned a color of Color.Red. Then the Fill property of the myRec rectangle is assigned this instance, meaning the rectangle on the page should turn red when the end user clicks the left mouse button on the rectangle itself.

In addition to changing the color of the rectangle, the width and the stroke's thickness are altered using `myRec.Width` and `myRec.StrokeThickness`, respectively. When the page is first loaded, the end user will see what is presented in Figure 21-13.

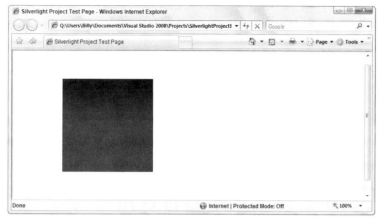

Figure 21-13

The rectangle is positioned on the page as specified using `Canvas.Top` and `Canvas.Left`. It contains a gradient of color from black to blue to purple. Finally, there is a thin, black border around the rectangle.

The next step requires an end user to interact with the rectangle. Clicking on the rectangle with your left mouse button will instantly change the rectangle as shown in Figure 21-14.

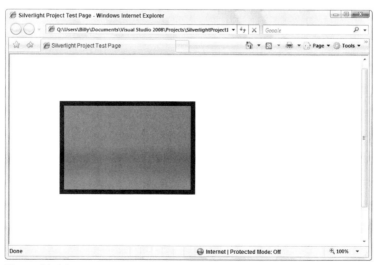

Figure 21-14

In this case, the rectangle is extended, the color changes, and the thickness of the border is changed. The change happens instantly when the mouse button is clicked.

Summary

Silverlight is an outstanding way to bring a rich user experience to your browser-based applications. It is a browser plug-in designed to compete with Flash. This chapter took a look at Silverlight from a developer's perspective, while a designer would instead focus on the user of Microsoft's Expression Blend (for better graphics than what was achieved in this chapter).

Silverlight 1.0 focuses on the use of JavaScript as the code-behind of the XAML pages that you build, whereas Silverlight 2.0 brings a more "managed" experience to the developer. In Silverlight 2.0, you will be able to build XAML pages that have a managed .vb file behind them, as demonstrated in this chapter.

22

Visual Studio Tools for Office

This chapter introduces the Visual Studio Tools for Office (VSTO) project templates. VSTO has been around as an add-in to Visual Studio for several releases. Visual Studio 2008 includes it as part of the standard installation of all versions of Visual Studio Professional and above. The VSTO package isn't so much a set of new menus as it is templates and DLLs that enable you to integrate custom business logic into Microsoft Office products.

VSTO has been somewhat neglected in the .NET development world. The main Office client applications that most people think about to target, Word and Excel, have supported customization through Visual Basic for Applications (VBA) since long before .NET, so for most developers the power of VSTO hasn't really been leveraged. With the release of Office 2007 and the new project types available in Visual Studio 2008, you can expect Outlook to start to take center stage in terms of Office-based application customization.

More important, Visual Studio 2008 not only introduces VSTO as a mainline set of tools with Visual Studio Professional Edition and above, but also provides one of the largest deltas in terms of new features from previous versions of anything in Visual Studio 2008. These new features are intended to provide much more end-to-end use of VSTO to enable the creation of business applications.

This chapter introduces you to the role of the VSTO family of tools and demonstrates three different implementation examples. The topics in this chapter include the following:

- ❑   VSTO releases
- ❑   Office business application architecture
- ❑   VBA-VSTO interop
- ❑   Creating a document template (Word)
- ❑   Creating an Office add-in (Excel)
- ❑   Outlook form regions

These tools are available as part of Visual Studio 2008 Professional and are focused on enabling you to move from a goal of "this project will create a custom grid with the following capabilities" to a goal of "this project will enable users to leverage Excel 2007 and surface our business application data in the robust Excel table management system, where users can customize and save the data back into our custom line-of-business data store." Developers and customers often talk about how nice it would be to embed Excel in their application. Now, as you'll see in this chapter, the real solution is the reverse — your application can be embedded in Excel.

Examining the VSTO Releases

With Visual Studio 2005, the VSTO package was available as an add-in to Visual Studio. VSTO has been around since early in the .NET tools life cycle. That original package targeted Office 2003, which was the most recent version of Office at the time Visual Studio 2007 was released. There were five templates, two each for Word and Excel document-level customizations and then a single template for creating Outlook add-ins.

With the release of Office 2007, Microsoft provided an update to the Visual Studio 2005 environment called VSTO 2005 SE, where SE stood for Second Edition. This update essentially enabled VSTO to access some of the same templates for Office 2007; however, access to, say, the Office 2007 Ribbon was limited in this set of tools. The requirement to manually create and edit an XML file to define a custom Ribbon bar made approaching this solution somewhat intimidating. However, VSTO 2005 SE was just an interim release until the VSTO team could put together a more complete package for Visual Studio 2008.

With the release of Visual Studio 2008, the number of available options enabling you to extend the standard features of Office VSTO has exploded. As shown in Figure 22-1, the number of project templates referencing the Microsoft Office System far exceeds the five offered in 2005. Moreover, note that Visual Studio 2008 supports templates for both Office 2003 and Office 2007. There are in fact twice as many Office 2003 templates in Visual Studio 2008 as there were in VSTO 2005.

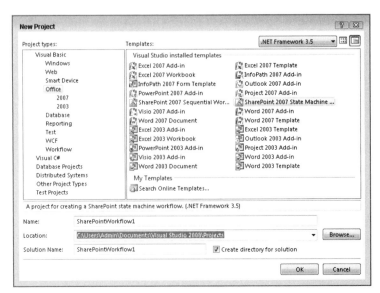

Figure 22-1

Figure 22-1 shows a template for creating a workflow project that targets SharePoint 2007. Note that under Visual Studio 2008, the types of VSTO projects available include not only client-based templates, but also server-based templates. The two workflow templates available in the Office 2007 collection are also available as part of the template collection in the Workflow category.

This chapter bypasses working with examples of the Office 2003 packages, not because there is anything wrong with them but simply to devote the most coverage to the current version of Office. Note that the project templates can all be created while targeting the .NET 2.0 Framework. Conversely, all the Office 2007 projects require you to target .NET 3.5; there are no .NET 3.0 targeted projects in the package.

Office Automation versus VSTO

In any discussion of VSTO, it's important to distinguish between Office automation and VSTO. *Office automation* is a term that actually refers to your ability to create a custom application that references Word or Excel or some other Office application. In this case, the user of your custom application can start and send data to your application. This type of automation does not necessarily involve VSTO or VBA.

Office automation relies on the custom application having a reference to Office and then sending information into or retrieving information from that application without Office being customized. This type of automation leverages COM-based interop to the Office components and doesn't fall into the same category of application as VSTO. A VSTO application is one in which the actual Office application is aware of and connected to the custom logic. Thus, when a user of an application that supports Office automation wants to retrieve data from an Excel spreadsheet, that user exits Excel, goes to that custom application, asks it to connect to the currently running instance of Excel, and attempts to retrieve the data. This type of automation tends to treat Office as more of a black box.

VSTO applications are built into Office. They can and do display UI elements directly within applications such as Word, and they can and do leverage the same automation elements and interop assemblies that Office automation clients leverage. The key difference is that VSTO applications are directly integrated with the application process (threads) and have direct access to UI elements that are part of the application.

When it comes to the Office Primary Interop Assemblies (PIA) for Office 2003, the Office installer did not automatically include these when Office 2003 was installed. As a result, if at some point you choose to do either a VSTO or Office automation project for an Office 2003 project, you'll want to include the redistributable for these assemblies. The PIA for Office 2003 is available from Microsoft Downloads, currently located at `www.microsoft.com/downloads/details.aspx?familyid = 3c9a983a-ac14-4125-8ba0-d36d67e0f4ad&displaylang = en`.

VSTO Project Types

While the difference between a Word project and an Excel project is no doubt self-evident to you, the difference between an Add-In and a Document project might not be. In short, each of the different VSTO project types targets not only a given client or server Office application, but also a different way of customizing that application. In the case of Add-In projects, the project type enables you to customize the application. The main project types for VSTO are as follows:

❑　**Add-In** — This template enables you to create an extension to an Office project that is loaded every time that product is started. Add-ins, as with Visual Studio add-ins, are code that is registered with the application and started every time that application is started. Add-ins are needed for some applications such as Outlook in which an inbound customized message would need the add-in support on the client to recognize the customizations in order to load the document (mail message) correctly.

❑ **Document/Workbook** — These are two separate templates, associated with Word and Excel, respectively. The key aspect of these templates is that the code associated with your custom logic is embedded in a specific document file. The model is much closer to the model exposed by the original VBA customization in these products. In fact, there is even a way to interoperate between Document/Workbook projects and VBA projects. If you open Word or Excel and select a new document or a document that doesn't include this logic, the custom code isn't loaded. On the one hand, this makes these projects lower risk in that you are less likely to disable a client's system. On the other hand, without a central location such as SharePoint to host these custom documents, the application model is much weaker.

❑ **Template** — These projects are similar to the Document/Workbook model in that you are defining code that lives in a single template. This template and code are loaded only when a user chooses to use it from within Office.

❑ **Workflow** — These templates target the SharePoint workflow engine. This chapter doesn't go into much detail on these project types, as the process of creating custom workflow projects is described in Chapter 27. The templates in this section are not generic Windows Workflow Foundation (WF) templates, but rather are specific to creating workflows installed and run on MOSS 2007 (SharePoint 3.0).

A Word Add-In template is a project template that enables you to create a custom actions pane and a custom menu and/or ribbon bar for Word. The Add-In project types host code that will run each time that Word (or the selected application) is started. Thus, it doesn't matter which document the user chooses to open or the underlying template that is part of the current document — the code in the Add-In will be loaded.

This doesn't mean that an Add-In template can't be document specific. In the case of Outlook, the only available template is an Add-In template. This is because of the nature of the extensions to Outlook, which loads a complete collection of "documents" (i.e., e-mail messages) when it is started. As such, the document model isn't directly used in Outlook, although Outlook does support custom Outlook Form Regions.

What makes an Outlook Form Region (OFR) different from a Document or Template model VSTO extension? Well, the OFR is part of an add-in to Outlook, so if a new message is received that references that custom OFR, Outlook is ready to load the custom application logic. The potential challenges of OFR messages are discussed later in this chapter. The OFR customization provides a very powerful, compelling application model, but as a result it also has key requirements in order for it to function correctly.

Office Business Application Architecture

The Office Business Application (OBA) model is one that Microsoft is beginning to promote as a product. Indeed, if you go to www.microsoft.com/oba, you'll find yourself redirected to the OBA product site at Microsoft. However, there isn't a license or a product called OBA that you can order in a box. Rather, the OBA model is conceptual, explaining how you can leverage the components that make up Microsoft Office to create a custom business logic solution. Instead of building applications from scratch, you can integrate the functionality of Excel for managing table data into your business logic using VSTO (not that VSTO is the only enabling technology associated with an OBA).

The OBA model has been made possible by a combination of several changes to Microsoft Office that have occurred over the years. When products such as Word and Excel were originally rolled into the larger "Office" product group, it was primarily a licensing arrangement. The original Office designation was a little like MSDN in that it enabled you to purchase a group of products for a lower price than purchasing each independently. Aside from some limited integration points, such as using the Word engine to edit Outlook messages, these products were independent.

However, over time integration has gone beyond COM-based document integration. Arguably one of the key enabling technologies within the Office integration and collaboration framework is SharePoint. Other servers in the Office suite also fill this role in specialized areas — for example, Office Communication Server. This chapter doesn't cover SharePoint in depth, or its far more functional upgrade, Microsoft Office SharePoint Server (MOSS).

SharePoint provides a central location from which you can host customized Office documents. It also enables you to host custom workflow logic and provides a central location for e-mail and notification messages related to business processes. Feature-rich versions of MOSS include capabilities such as Excel Services and other advanced capabilities.

Because of these benefits, the OBA model builds around a central server. As noted, this might be a Share-Point server if the goal is to create a custom workflow to monitor an internal business process. However, it doesn't have to be SharePoint. As shown in Figure 22-2, you might choose to create your OBA to leverage data stored in a line-of-business (LOB) system such as SAP, PeopleSoft, SQL Server, or any of several other business and data systems. Often these systems have either limited or no custom user interface. As a result, the user interface may or may not include features that your customers are familiar with from Office. Given that millions of people are familiar with Office and its interface, taking this data and placing it into that interface is the OBA model.

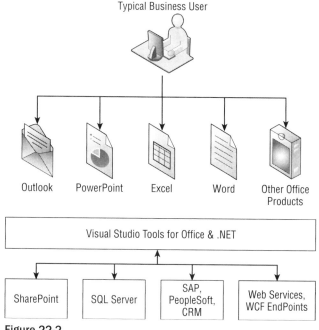

Figure 22-2

This brings up the second key enabling technology: the ease with which you can now import and export data and behavior to the Office client applications via VSTO. In fact, even with SharePoint it is the VSTO piece that truly enables you to integrate your custom business application into the Office client tools. VSTO enables you to retrieve data either from a database via ADO.NET or LINQ or to communicate with XML Web Services and WCF. Once you have the data, you can enable your users to leverage their experience with the Office user interface to manipulate that data. As you'll see in this chapter, with the release of Visual Studio 2008 on top of Office 2007, you can now interface your LOB processes and data into every one of the Microsoft Office client applications.

This should give you a better idea of what an OBA is and how it provides an architectural pattern that you can use to create a business application using VSTO. In addition to the Microsoft.com line provided at the start of this section, you can also find more information at the Microsoft-sponsored site www.obacentral.com.

Finally, if you want to see an example of an OBA built against Office 2003 and Windows SharePoint Services (WSS) 2.0, take a look at Team System. The Team Explorer install for Team Foundation Server not only provides a set of add-ins for Visual Studio, but also provides support for a set of custom VSTO document applications. Every time you create a new Team Foundation Server (TFS) project, a new WSS project site is created. The site will contain several VSTO-based documents for Word and Excel. These illustrate how to use VSTO and the OBA model for your custom applications.

Of course, VSTO wasn't the original or even now the only way to create custom logic within an Office client application. Since the early days of COM, both Microsoft Word and Microsoft Excel have supported Visual Basic for Applications (VBA). Fortunately, ongoing improvements occurring within VSTO can be integrated with existing VBA.

Working with Both VBA and VSTO

The VBA model for Office document customization was limited at best. For starters, it is only available in Word and Excel. However, the VBA application model is not yet retired. That bears repeating: VBA is still a viable and supported set of tools for customizing the Microsoft Office experience. As with all such changes in technology, there are certain things that VSTO does that VBA wasn't designed to do and to a certain degree is not capable of doing. However, there are also certain VBA optimizations within the existing tools with which VSTO can't currently compete.

Office 2007 is also known as Office version 12. Microsoft has committed to keeping VBA through Office version 14, which is still quite a way off. Thus, instead of doing a blanket conversion, you'll be able to interoperate with existing code. Just like the WPF interop library and the Visual Basic 6.0 interop library, VSTO and VBA have an interop library. Microsoft suggests that companies with complex VBA solutions will probably want to update these Document/Workbook style solutions with VSTO features, but not necessarily attempt to convert working code and features. Thus, your new VSTO code may call existing VBA functions; and similarly, your existing VBA code may start calling your VSTO objects.

There are, of course, limitations to this model, and it isn't one that's recommended for new development. When it comes to the ability to call VBA from VSTO, you can call the Run method on the Office object model. This method accepts the name of a VBA method and a list of parameters. There is no IntelliSense, as what you are doing is making a dynamic runtime call. An example of this call is as follows:

```
Dim result As Integer = Me.Application.Run("MyFunctionAdd", 1, 2)
```

That's it — no special steps or hoops, just a standard call. Of course, your document or workbook needs to actually include the VBA function MyFunctionAdd, but that should be apparent. Also note that when you combine VBA and VSTO, you have to handle permissions for both, so plan to spend a little more time building your installation package and permissions. In addition, when you create your first custom VSTO Document or Workbook project, you'll get the warning shown in Figure 22-3.

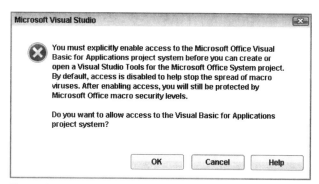

Figure 22-3

At this point, you may not know whether you want to enable VBA interop within Visual Studio and your VSTO projects. If you've worked with VBA in the past or think you might need to do any VBA, consider enabling access to the VBA project system. As noted in the dialog, while turning this off completely is meant to act as a first layer of defense against the spread of macro viruses, your project will still maintain protection via other layers of security. Keep in mind that this option is available only to Word Document and Excel Workbook templates.

While this chapter isn't going to focus on security, sometimes — such as when you are enabling VBA macro interop — you do require a few specific settings. While it's possible to call VSTO from VBA in Office 2007, it isn't the default. Note the reference to "Office 2007." With Office 2007 it's possible to enable macros, and as part of the creation of a VSTO project on a macro-enabled document, by changing a couple of document properties in your VSTO project you can reference your VSTO methods and properties from VBA code. This process only begins after you have enabled macros within your document.

Your first step in enabling macros in a document is to ensure that the file is saved as a .docm file instead of a .docx file. The same is true for Excel, where the file type needs to be .xlsm as opposed to .xlsx. By default, documents saved with the extension .docx do not allow macros, so open Word 2007 and press Alt + F11 to open the VBA editor for your document. You can add an actual macro or something as simple as a comment inside a default event handler. Alternatively, you can select a document that already contains a macro. Once this is complete, you need to save your document. For this example, call your document VBAInterop. Then, select the .docm document type, as shown in Figure 22-4.

If you accidentally attempt to save your document as a .docx, the file system should warn you that it is about to clear your macros. The message box will allow you to return to the Save As window and change the document type to a macro-enabled document.

Next, you need to ensure that Word considers your macro available whenever the document is opened. This demo was written on the Vista operating system with Office 2007. In this environment you need to change your Trust settings for Office. Once you have added your comment macro and saved your .docm file, within Word (you may need to reopen the document) you should see a notification that a macro in the document has been prevented from running.

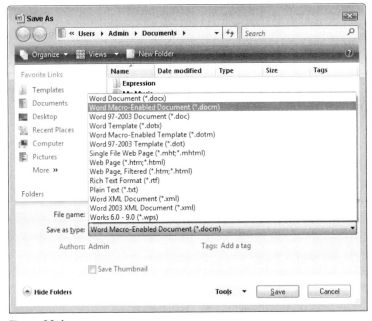

Figure 22-4

At this point you can choose to enable the macro. However, that choice is for the currently running instance only. If you closed and reopened the document, you would again be presented with that prompt. To make the change permanent, you need to either use the link in the lower-left corner of that display or traverse the menus to access the Trust Center for Word.

To traverse the menus, go to the Office button in the upper-left corner of your document and open the menu associated with this button. On the bottom of the menu is a button labeled Word Options. Select this button to open the Word Options dialog. On the left side of that dialog is an item labeled Trust Center that is similar to the link mentioned earlier. This opens the Trust Center dialog, shown in Figure 22-5

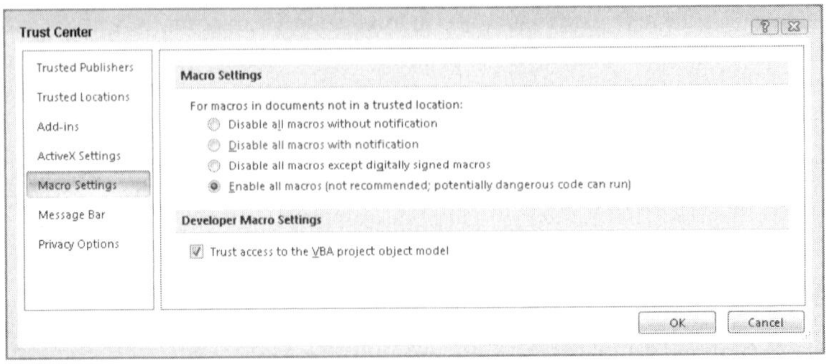

Figure 22-5

For the VBA interop to work, go to the Macro Settings in the Word/Excel Trust Center and update the Macro Settings to always enable all macros. Yes, you essentially need to turn off the security for macros on your development machine (unless you are using digitally signed macros — which isn't the case for this example).

Once you have saved your document, it's time to open Visual Studio 2008 and create a new Office 2007 Word Document project, which in this case you can also name VBAInterop, as shown in Figure 22-6.

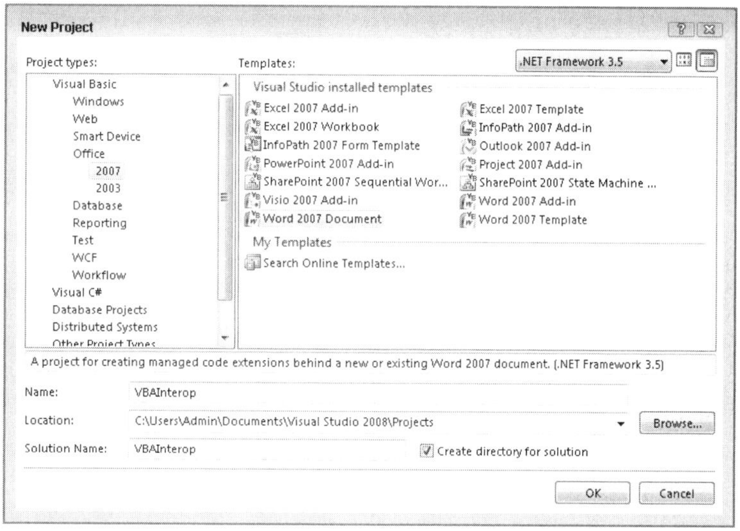

Figure 22-6

This brings up a second dialog, which is where you need to change from the default process. Normally, you would create a new document in the dialog shown in Figure 22-7. However, in this case you actually want to import your macro-enabled document VBAInterop.docm. By default, the Browse button limits the display of available files to those with the .docx extension, so you need to change the default in the file browse window to .docm in order to see your document.

Clicking OK triggers Visual Studio to generate your project. When the generation is complete, Visual Studio will display your Word document within the main window, and in the lower right-hand corner you should have your Properties window. This window, shown in Figure 22-8, has two new Interop properties at the bottom. You need to modify both these properties from their default of False to the new value of True.

These properties cause your VSTO project to regenerate and insert a new property within your project's macro file. To test this, you can start your project; once the project builds, you'll see Word start and it will open your custom document. Once your document is open, press Alt-F11 to open the Macro Editor. Above your custom code should be the newly generated property value. The resulting code if you merely entered a comment should look similar to the following:

```
Property Get CallVSTOAssembly() As VBAInterop.ThisDocument
    Set CallVSTOAssembly = GetManagedClass(Me)
End Property
```

```
Private Sub Document_New()
    ' This is a placeholder comment.
End Sub
```

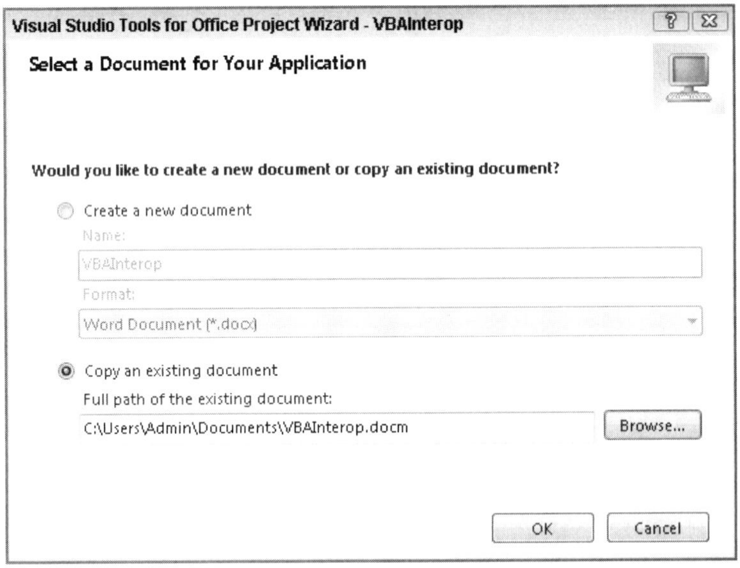

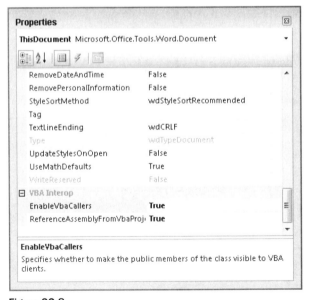

Figure 22-7

Figure 22-8

The code in this block shows the newly generated property that associates your VBA environment with the VSTO code that you are creating. You can then proceed to the placeholder comment in the Document_New method where you initially entered a comment to maintain your macro's existence. Within this method, on a new line, make a call to CallVSTOAssembly, and you'll see that you have full IntelliSense for the list of available methods and properties, as shown in Figure 22-9. Note that because you didn't create any custom code in your VSTO solution during this process, the options shown in Figure 22-9 reflect those which are generated as part of your project template.

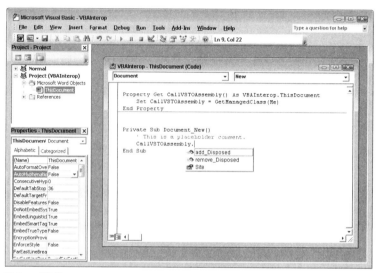

Figure 22-9

There are a few additional steps in order to enable VBA to connect to VSTO, but for those who are already working with VBA these steps won't be a significant challenge. After all, it is the development experience and ability to continue to leverage existing resources that really drive this interop feature. The fact that this feature is so natural for a VBA developer — who may want to leverage key new capabilities such as WCF, WF, or possibly even WPF-based graphics in Excel — means that you can expect to be able to leverage your existing VBA code for several more years. When you do "migrate," the process is one that you control and can carry out in stages based on your requirements and decisions, not some overriding conversion process.

Creating a Document Template (Word)

The previous section introduced you to creating a document template from the standpoint of interoperating with VBA, but unless you have an existing VBA application, in most cases you'll just create a new, clean Word Document project. These projects focus on a specific document. They are self-contained in the sense that your changes only affect the user's system when the user chooses to open a document that specifically includes your changes.

This is great, as it isolates your changes. When users open Word or Excel they don't automatically load your customization. This way, your code won't impact the overall performance of their system — not that most developers care about this. The model also means that customizations for Application A aren't competing with Application B, which is in some ways a bigger challenge with add-ins.

However, this model (shared by VBA) has a limitation. The user must open a copy of the correct document to access your custom code. In an uncontrolled environment it may be difficult for a user to find the most recent version of that code. Sure, the first time your document customization is sent out to 10, 20, or 200,000 users, it's easy to locate and update the source documents. However, when you need to update some element of that standalone document, you have a problem.

Fortunately, this is where the OBA model and SharePoint become invaluable. By placing your documents onto SharePoint, you now have a controlled location from which users can access your VSTO application. In fact, with SharePoint 3.0 and MOSS 2007 you can actually create a library for copies of your custom document that uses your document as what is known as a *content type*. By using your VSTO document as a SharePoint content type, when users access that SharePoint library and request a "new" document, they'll automatically open a new document that leverages your customizations.

An alternative to leveraging SharePoint is illustrated by another way to leverage document-based VSTO solutions. Your document might be included in a Microsoft or Windows Installer (MSI) package that is part of a larger installed application. In fact, you might not want users to directly open your customizations. Instead, your custom application might install your custom document via an MSI, so that updates can occur in conjunction with your application updates. Then, when a user needs to modify data in a grid, you might open a custom Excel document, which, rather then save data in Excel automatically, places the data back into your application data store when the user asks to save.

The first step in creating such a solution is to create a new project. In this case the sample project will be named "ProVB_WordDocument." Once you have changed the default name, click OK in the New Project dialog. This will take you to the Office Project Wizard dialog shown in Figure 22-10.

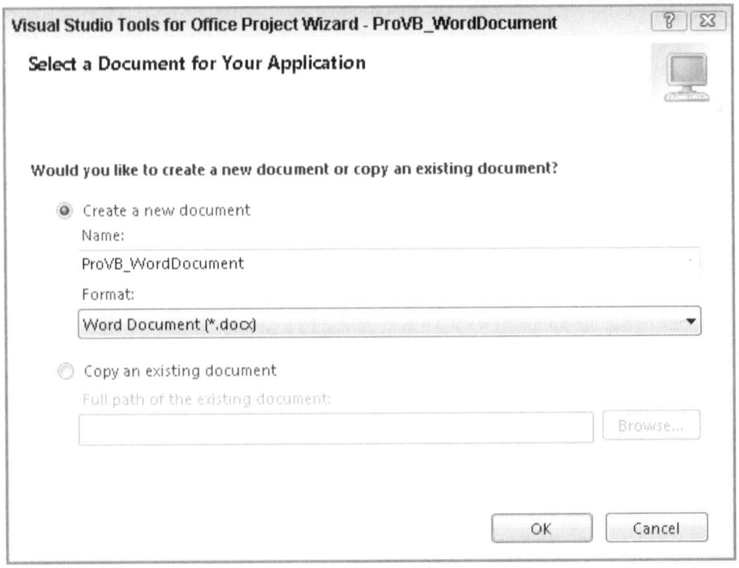

Figure 22-10

Note that you can specify a name for the document but it defaults to the project name you've chosen. That's because as part of this process, Visual Studio is going to generate a new Office 2007 document and place that .docx file in your solution directory. When you work on this project, you'll be customizing that document. Thus, in many cases you may want to give the document that will host your customization an end-user-friendly name instead of your project name.

Once this is complete you are returned to the main Visual Studio window with a new project. Unlike other project types, however, in this case the template creates a Word document and then opens that document within Visual Studio. As shown in Figure 22-11, within the Solution Explorer, on the upper-right side of the display, your project contains a .docx file. Associated with this file is a second .vb file, which is where some of your custom code may be placed. As shown in Figure 22-11, the Visual Studio user interface actually encapsulates this document. The Properties window shows the properties for this document. Note that unlike when you created your VSTO project from an existing VBA document, there are no properties to support integration with VBA.

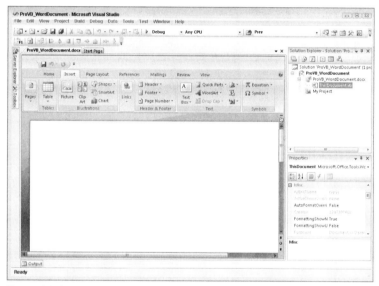

Figure 22-11

Also noteworthy (although not shown) is that if you were to open your project's properties and review the references, you'd find that all the Office Primary Interop assemblies you need in order to work with the Office object model have automatically been added to your project. You no longer need to try to figure out which COM interop assemblies you'll need for accessing that interface from Word.

Adding Content to the Document

Of course, the main feature of Figure 22-11 is that Visual Studio has fully encapsulated the Word user interface. Note how the Insert tab has been selected in the document. You have full access to all the features in Word in this mode; and to demonstrate this, let's adjust the default contents of this document. Choose the Smart Art category. Then, from within its dialogs, go to the Process tab of the SmartArt

Graphic dialog, scroll down, and select the circular equation image. This will add that item to your document and automatically open an equation editor, as shown in Figure 22-12.

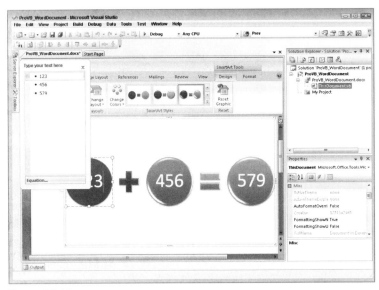

Figure 22-12

You can enter some numbers into the text box for this equation, but there is no built-in adding logic. Close that text window and return to Visual Studio. Of course, at this point you haven't actually added any code to your document, so switch to the code view. By default, VSTO inserts two event handlers when your project is created. Note that as long as the .docx file is displayed, you can't access the ThisDocument.vb file for that document. To switch the view, close the default .docx display and then right-click on the ThisDocument.vb file in the Solution Explorer and select Code View from the context menu. Now you should be able to see the code that was created as part of your project:

```
Public Class ThisDocument

    Private Sub ThisDocument_Startup(ByVal sender As Object, _
                          ByVal e As System.EventArgs) Handles Me.Startup

    End Sub

    Private Sub ThisDocument_Shutdown(ByVal sender As Object, _
                          ByVal e As System.EventArgs) Handles Me.Shutdown

    End Sub

End Class
```

As the preceding code illustrates, the document has two events available within VSTO. The first handles the startup event; the second handles the shutdown event. These are the only two that are added to your project by default. You'll learn more about these shortly, but first add another event. This is the `BeforeSave` event, and as you might expect, it fires just before your document is saved:

```
Private Sub ThisDocument_BeforeSave(ByVal sender As Object, _
                ByVal e As Microsoft.Office.Tools.Word.SaveEventArgs) _
                Handles Me.BeforeSave
    Dim res As DialogResult = MessageBox.Show( _
                "Should I save?", "Before Save", _
                MessageBoxButtons.YesNo)
    If res = DialogResult.No Then
        ' This code could call a backend data store and then
        ' not save the associated document so the document would remain
        ' unchanged.
        e.Cancel = True
    Else
        ' This code would allow you to encourage the user to
        ' always save a new copy of the document
        e.ShowSaveAsDialog = True
    End If
End Sub
```

The preceding code illustrates a custom override of the `BeforeSave` event on the document. Note that after the event handler is declared, the code creates a local variable to hold a dialog result. It then shows a message box asking the user if it should save. Normally this isn't something you would do on this event, but in this case it enables you to see two of the attributes of the `SaveEventArgs` class.

If the user chooses not to save, then you have the option to not save data. Alternatively, you don't have to offer a choice to the user; instead you can simply add code ensuring that the user simultaneously saves data to a backend data store. Whether you need to call a Web service or update a database, this is a good place to call that logic. You then can save to the database and decide whether or not you actually want to update the underlying document. In some cases you might quietly save the data to the database and never save the document; then, when the document is next opened, you retrieve the data from the database as part of the startup. This is a particularly useful trick if you don't trust the file system's read-only privileges or want to ensure that data from multiple different users is properly refreshed each time the document is opened.

Alternatively, you can force the user to perform a "save as" instead of a typical save. This uses the self-explanatory `ShowSaveAsDialog` property. The idea, again, is that you might not want the user to save over the original; to keep that from happening, you can have Word automatically prompt the user to save the document with a different name. You can also save data to a database or other data store during this process.

Adding a Ribbon and an Actions Pane

The preceding work provides some baseline code in your application, but it doesn't provide either a custom ribbon or custom task pane. Therefore, before testing this, let's add one of each of these items to the project. To add either of these controls, right-click on your project in the Solution Explorer and then select the Add button to open the Add New Item dialog.

As shown in Figure 22-13, when this dialog opens you can select from one or more categories. In order to manage the available selections, select the Office category. This will reduce the number of available options from dozens to the three that are appropriate for a Word Document project. Start by adding a new ribbon bar. There are two options: XML and Visual Designer. Select Visual Designer and provide "DocRibbon" for your control's name.

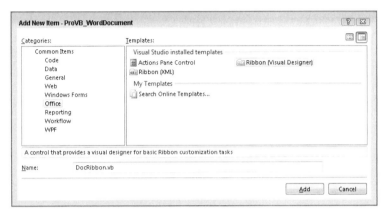

Figure 22-13

Figure 22-13 shows two alternatives for the Ribbon control, for backward compatibility. If you were customizing a ribbon bar for Office 2007 under Visual Studio 2007 and VSTO 2005 SE, then you didn't have access to a visual designer for the ribbon bar. Instead, you needed to create and edit an XML file, which would define your ribbon and the controls that were placed on it. There was neither a designer, nor a tool customized for this task.

With the release of Visual Studio 2008, the VSTO team had an opportunity to create a visual designer for the ribbon bar. Thus, unless you are working with a legacy XML definition file, you should always select the ribbon with visual design support. Once you have modified the name of the new control to DocRibbon, select OK and return to Visual Studio. The control template will generate the control and open in Design mode.

In Design mode, note that if you open the control Toolbox, you have a new category of controls available at the top. The Office Ribbon Controls, shown in Figure 22-14, provide a list of controls that you can add to the default ribbon. Note that these controls are Windows Forms controls, not WPF controls.

Add a button to the default Group1 in the designer. Once the button has been added, go to its properties and change the label for the button to Hide/Show the Actions Pane. You can optionally add an icon to the button. For this I went into the Visual Studio directory to retrieve one of the icons that ship with Visual Studio 2008. If you navigate to the folder where you installed Visual Studio 9.0 and navigate the folder tree: Common7\VS2008ImageLibrary\1033, within this folder you'll find a zip file: VS2008ImageLibrary.zip. Within this zip file are several thousand different images and icons that you can leverage within your application. Shown in Figure 22-14 is one similar to the shape of the task pane.

For now, skip implementing a handler for this button, as you want to see the default behavior of the ribbon and the actions pane. Instead, right-click on your project and again request to add a new item. In the Add New Item dialog, select an actions pane and name it "DocActionPane." Once you have created your new actions pane you'll again be in Visual Studio, this time in the designer for your new pane.

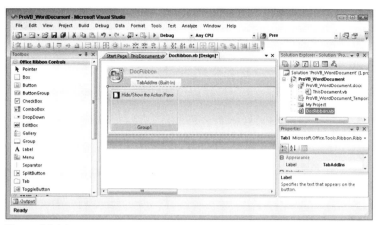

Figure 22-14

Unlike the Ribbon control, the designer for the actions pane doesn't require a special set of controls and by default has a white background. Unfortunately, I've had trouble delineating the edges of the control in a white-on-white scenario. Therefore, before doing anything else, I proceed to the properties for the control and select the Background Color property. Visual Studio 2008 opens a small window with three tabs, as shown in Figure 22-15.

Figure 22-15

This illustrates the default setting for the background, which is the system-defined color for control surfaces. Specifically, the System tab colors are those defined for your system based on setting your own visual preferences. The other two tabs present color options the developer has selected. Because I only want to change the display color while I am working on the design and layout, it's good to capture the original color and then go to the highlighted Custom tab and select a nice bright color such as red to highlight the actual surface area of my actions pane.

Now it's time to add a simple control to this panel. Once again, drag a button onto the design surface. Orient it in the upper-left corner and change the label to "Load." Eventually this button will be used to load some data into the document, but this is a good time to test run your project using F5. Your project starts and Visual Studio starts Microsoft Word. When Word opens you'll see your document with the image that you've embedded displayed, as shown in Figure 22-16.

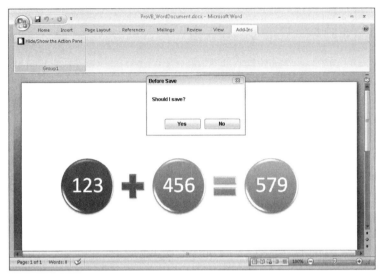

Figure 22-16

Figure 22-16 shows your custom document in Word. Note a few things about the running application at this point. First, the tab Add-Ins is set to display the custom ribbon bar. This isn't an error; even though you have created a custom VSTO Document solution, the customizations you made to the ribbon bar were automatically placed in this section.

Next, Figure 22-16 also captures the message box that was added to the `BeforeSave` event earlier. The Save button in the upper-left corner of the title bar was selected and as a result the event was fired. Below this you see the custom smart graphics that were added to the document itself. So far, so good, but where is the document's actions pane?

Unlike the ribbon bar, which is automatically associated with your custom document when you add it to your project, the document actions pane needs to be manually associated with your document. As a result, Figure 22-16 does not show your custom actions pane, so your next step is to add that pane to your document, and in this case have it shown or hidden based on the selection of the toggle button added to the ribbon bar. Close the running document and return to Visual Studio once the debugger has stopped.

Activating the Actions Pane

If you choose to view all files in your project, you can select and open your `DocActionPane.Designer.vb` source file. Within this file you'll find that your `DocActionPane` class inherits from `System.Windows` `.Forms.UserControl`. That's right; the document actions pane is just a customized user control.

Knowing this tells you that you can in fact include not only individual controls but also panel controls, such as a tab panel, or other custom user controls in this display area. More important, you can take a user control that you might be using in your current application logic and use it with no significant changes within the document's actions pane. However, anticipating your probable question, the reason the panel didn't show up is that both Word and Excel expect you to associate a user control with the ActionsPane property of your document.

Because the actions pane is actually open for use by any user control in your project, it is up to you to tell Word which control to assign. View the code for your document in the ThisDocument.vb file. Earlier you saw that the template created the Startup event handler by default. Add to this handler the following line:

```
Private Sub ThisDocument_Startup(ByVal sender As Object, _
                          ByVal e As System.EventArgs) Handles Me.Startup

    ActionsPane.Controls.Add(New DocActionPane())
End Sub
```

That line of code takes the built-in actions pane associated with your document and adds a control to that pane. Of course, you could also add items such as buttons and text boxes directly to your document's actions pane. However, as the control you added demonstrated, the preferred method is to create a custom user control and add this one control to the embedded actions pane in your document. The New DocActionPane() literally creates a new instance of your user control and places it onto the actions pane.

However, this isn't very flexible, in that you want users to be able to show or hide that pane. Instead of relying on the built-in controls for displaying or hiding the pane, you want to be able to toggle the actions pane on and off, which is why you have already added a button to the ribbon. That means customizing the Click handler for your toggle button. Before leaving the ThisDocument.vb display, make sure you close this file's editor so that later you'll be able to get to the document itself.

Next, select DocRibbon and double-click your button to add an event handler for your ToggleButton1 control's Click event. This is where you want to alter the status of your actions pane's display. The way to access the actions pane from the ribbon bar is through the application's Globals collection. Within VSTO you'll find a reference to the current document or workbook within this collection. From here you have access to objects such as the actions pane. In fact, you can type **Globals.ThisDocument.ActionsPane** to get access to the actions pane to which you assigned your user control.

However, while this does give you access to the user control, that control in your display is hosted by a frame, so even if you add code that sets the Visibility property on the ActionsPane attribute of your document, it probably won't have the desired effect. Setting the visibility status on the control only hides the control; it does not hide the now empty frame that was hosting the control. However, keep in mind that you can access the actions pane directly, as there may be a point when you want to do more then just hide and show the actions pane. For example, if you wanted to pass data or set a custom property on your user control, then you would leverage this object and retrieve your control from the Controls collection.

For this task you want to hide the entire Document Actions frame, not just the control it contains. The secret to this is the fact that the frame is considered by Word to be a CommandBar. Therefore, you need to access the `CommandBars` collection. However, the `CommandBars` collection has multiple different controls in it, so you need to retrieve the Document Actions pane from this collection. The most reliable way to do that is by name, so your `Click` event handler code should look similar to the following:

```
Private Sub ToggleButton1_Click(ByVal sender As System.Object, _
        ByVal e As Microsoft.Office.Tools.Ribbon.RibbonControlEventArgs) _
        Handles ToggleButton1.Click
    If ToggleButton1.Checked = True Then
        Globals.ThisDocument.CommandBars("Document Actions").Visible = _
                                                            True
        ToggleButton1.Label = "Hide Action Pane"
    Else
        Globals.ThisDocument.CommandBars("Document Actions").Visible = _
                                                            False
        ToggleButton1.Label = "Show Action Pane"
    End If
End Sub
```

The preceding code is called when the toggle button on your ribbon is clicked. It first determines whether the toggle button is selected or unselected. The `Checked` property provides this, and if the button is being selected, then the next step is to ensure that the Document Actions command bar is visible. Next, the code updates the text label on the button to "Hide Action Pane." This provides the user with initial feedback regarding what the button will do if it is clicked again.

Similarly, the code does the reverse, hiding the command bar and updating the text on the toggle button to indicate that in order to restore the command bar, the user should press the button again.

Now there is only one other thing to do. By default, because you are assigning a control to the actions pane, your pane should be displayed. However, it may not be; the user might load an add-in that suppresses the Document Actions command bar. Additionally, your toggle button is by default not selected, which is the state normally associated with the command bar being hidden.

To resolve these issues, you can override the `Load` event on your ribbon. Within the `Load` event, check the visibility status of the command bar and set the appropriate values for the display text and checked status of your toggle button:

```
Private Sub DocRibbon_Load(ByVal sender As System.Object, _
                        ByVal e As RibbonUIEventArgs) _
                        Handles MyBase.Load
    If Globals.ThisDocument.CommandBars("Document Actions").Visible Then
        ToggleButton1.Checked = True
        ToggleButton1.Label = "Hide Action Pane"
    Else
        ToggleButton1.Label = "Show Action Pane"
    End If
End Sub
```

Now that you have created the appropriate handlers for your ribbon bar, which will enable you to show and hide the actions pane, it's a good time to again test your application. Figure 22-17 shows your custom document. It shows the Add-Ins ribbon, and your Show/Hide toggle button is selected with the caption "Hide Action Pane." This correctly reflects that the next time that button is toggled, the display of the actions pane will be hidden. Notice how the toggle button gives you the visual state by applying the

Office color scheme for a selected control. When working with a custom Office application, it's often said that your UI will be more intuitive to a user familiar with the workings of Office; this example demonstrates that.

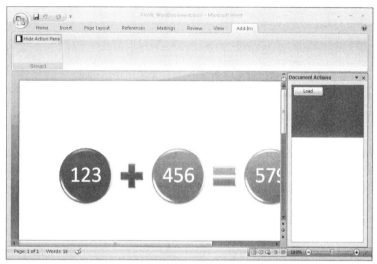

Figure 22-17

The other item that Figure 22-17 displays is the actual Document Actions window with your actions pane. You may recall that I changed the background color of the `DocActionPane` control to red. This should leave you a little concerned about why that red background (invisible in the figure here in the book) is near only the top of the window. This challenge is one for which there is only a partial resolution.

Unfortunately, the layout of a .NET control within the Document Actions host is limited. You can ask that your control fill the display, but this value is ignored. You can ask that it stretch, but this setting determines whether the size of the control should by default match the display area of its contents. There simply isn't a good way to automatically resize your custom display area.

You can return to Visual Studio and increase the height of your background. In fact, you can make the background tall enough and wide enough to account for a display area of almost any size, but the real challenge is related to the controls that you place in your display. Unfortunately, you can't be certain that as the user resizes Word, the key controls you've chosen to place on the actions pane will always be displayed. However, right now there is only a single button on this control and it isn't doing anything, so it's time to add some logic for placing data into the Word document.

Updating a Content Control

Until now the only thing placed in your Word document was a simple graphic. While this made it apparent that you can in fact customize the content of this VSTO document, it didn't really demonstrate the capability to dynamically update the content of the document. The first step is to look at one of the new features of Office 2007 — content controls. Return to the designer view of your Word document, as shown in Figure 22-18, and notice the Toolbox. Within this Toolbox is a section titled Word Controls, which has been expanded.

Figure 22-18

The controls shown in this section of the Toolbox are controls that you can apply to your document. Let's look at a couple of simple examples. Add some text similar to what you see in Figure 22-18 (the actual content isn't that important). Then, on a new line within the document, add the text "Document Name:" followed by a tab or two. Drag a `PlainTextContentControl` onto your document. On the next line, add the label "Application Name:" followed by a tab. Then drag a `RichTextContentControl` onto the document. These two controls will provide a simple example of working with content controls.

On the lower right-hand side of Figure 22-18, you'll notice the Properties window. It is currently selected for the second control, but it provides an illustration of a few key content control properties. The first two are the capability to lock the control or to lock the contents of the control. Locking the control prevents users of your document from being able to delete the control. Locking the contents enables you to ensure that the text within the control can't be modified by the user. Of the other properties shown, the `Text` property represents the text that should be displayed in the control, which is customized along with the `Title` property.

I customized the `Title` property because of how you can reference these controls within your code. Keep in mind that these are controls, which means you can data bind these controls to data you have retrieved, and you can handle events on these controls. Several chapters have already covered handling events, so this demo code focuses on having the actions pane interface with these controls.

With that in mind, switch to the Design view for your `DocActionPane` control. Not that you are going to make changes to this beautiful design — you just want to double-click your Load button to create an event handler for the `Click` event. This will take you to the code view, where you can enter the custom code to update your content controls. The code block that follows includes two methods for accessing these controls, one of which has been commented out:

```
Public Class DocActionPane
    Private Sub Button1_Click(ByVal sender As System.Object, _
                            ByVal e As System.EventArgs) _
                            Handles Button1.Click
        'This code could make database calls, process user input etc.
        'For Each ctrl As Word.ContentControl In _
                                    Globals.ThisDocument.ContentControls
        '    'This will retrieve all of the embedded content controls.
        '    'Cycle through the list looking for those of interest
        '    Select Case ctrl.Title
        '        Case "PlainText1"
        '            ctrl.Range.Text = My.User.Name
        '        Case "RichText1"
        '            ctrl.Range.Text = My.Application.Info.ProductName
        '        Case Else
        '    End Select
        'Next

        Globals.ThisDocument.PlainTextContentControl1.Text = _
                                        Globals.ThisDocument.Name
        Globals.ThisDocument.PlainTextContentControl1.LockContentControl = _
                                        True
        Globals.ThisDocument.PlainTextContentControl1.LockContents = True
        Globals.ThisDocument.RichTextContentControl1.Text = _
                                        My.Application.Info.ProductName
    End Sub
End Class
```

The event handler starts with a comment related to the fact that at this point you are essentially working within the confines of a user control. Thus, you can add any data access code or XML processing code you want into this class. (Because those have already been covered in other chapters, this code focuses on the content controls.)

The first block of code, which is associated with a For loop, has been commented out because it isn't needed or even the preferred solution in this scenario. However, if instead of working with Word this solution were focused on Excel, and if you were working with cells, each of which might contain a content control, then the odds are good you would want an efficient way to access this large array of controls. This loop leverages the Content Controls collection. It also serves to illustrate a couple of key idiosyncrasies of this control collection.

Unlike what you might expect after the controls are retrieved from the collection, they do not directly expose all of their properties. In fact, the first missing property is the Name property. Thus, for this code to work based on identifying specific controls, you would need to use a separate identifier such as Title. In fact, a title has been added to each of the controls in the document, so if you want to you can uncomment and run this code. However, in typical scenarios where you use this code, you would be processing an array of controls and be primarily interested in control type and control location.

Control location would be related in Excel to the range associated with that control. Specifically, the Range property and its property Cells would tell you where on the spreadsheet you were. The Range property is important for a second reason. Like the control's Name property, the controls in this array don't expose a Text property. Instead, you can access the Text property of the Range in order to update the text in that control. As noted, however, this code has been commented out because there is a more direct way to access named properties.

The uncommented lines of code leverage the Globals.ThisDocument object to access by name the controls in your document. This code is not limited to Word and will work for Excel if you have only a small number of controls in your workbook. Note that the first line updates the value displayed in the PlainTextContentControl. It replaces the default text (which was formatted with a larger font and colored red) with the current document name.

Next, the code locks the control and its content. Not that you would necessarily wait until this point to set those properties, but this is just an illustration of accessing these properties and seeing the results when you run your document. The final line updates the RichTextContentControl using the My namespace, this time to retrieve the application name for your project.

At this point you can build and run your code. Once your document is displayed, go to the actions pane and use the Load button. Your results should look similar to what is shown in Figure 22-19. Note that the formatting for both the plain text and rich-text controls, which was applied in your source code, has remained unchanged.

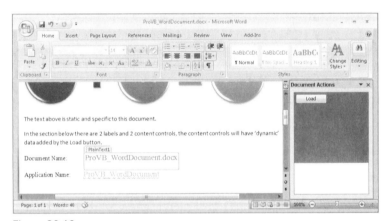

Figure 22-19

Note also that the highlight around your content control is by default visible to the end user. This is why you may want to lock these controls. In fact, you can attempt to delete or edit the document name to get a feel for the end-user experience. In case it wasn't clear, the work shown in this section can be replicated in an Excel workbook. In fact, the next section looks at using Excel, but instead of doing another VSTO document, the focus is on creating an add-in.

Creating an Office Add-In (Excel)

Unlike the Document/Workbook project, the Add-In project type is installed on the user's computer and then loaded for every document that is opened. This introduces a set of different issues and concerns. For starters, unlike the document project, where you focused on the content of the document or workbook, in an add-in scenario you don't have an associated document in your project. Nor can you access the actions pane, although the Add-In project allows you to access not only the ribbon bar but also a similar UI feature called the task pane.

Of course, the most important difference is the fact that once your add-in is registered, it will be loaded for every document that the user accesses. This means that even if the user opens a VSTO document project, your add-in will be loaded alongside the customizations associated with that document. Similarly, if the user has multiple add-ins installed, then each one will be loaded for every document the user accesses. In short, your code has to play well with others and should load with minimal delay. Keep in mind when working with an add-in that you probably aren't alone.

Create a new project of the type Excel 2007 Add-In. While in the New Project dialog, name your project ProVB_ExcelAddIn and select OK. You'll notice that, unlike when you created a document project and were deposited within your Office client inside Visual Studio, you are now in a code page. As shown in Figure 22-20, the code associated with your document looks very similar to what you had with your document project. However, unlike that project, you don't have access to the document itself.

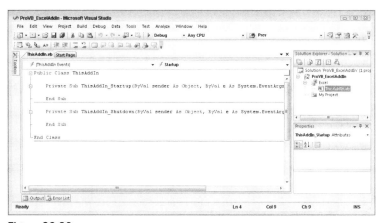

Figure 22-20

Just like the document-based project, you have the Startup and Shutdown event handlers and no others, but you can create any that are available for your application. To begin, access the ribbon bar and task pane by right-clicking on your project. Select Add New Item to open the Add New Item dialog and select the Office category. This is where the next difference for an Add-In project becomes apparent: As illustrated in Figure 22-21, only the two Ribbon templates are available.

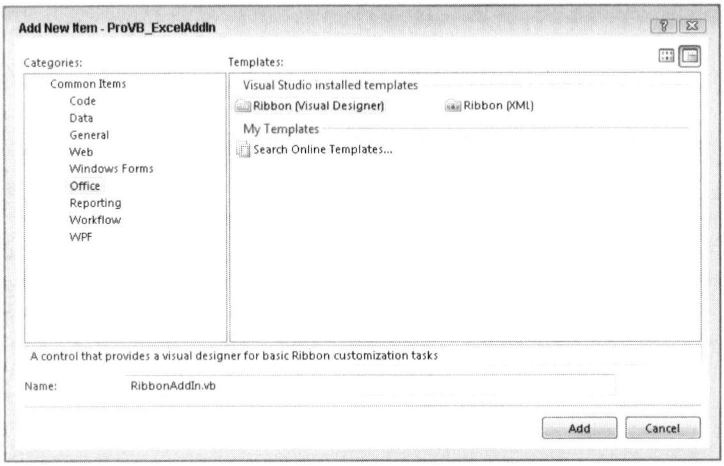

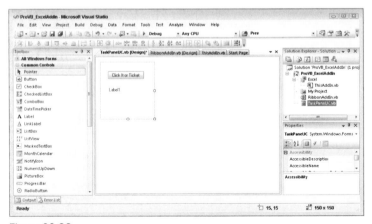

Figure 22-21

Select the Ribbon (Visual Designer) template and name your new control "RibbonAddIn." Selecting Add will add this control to your project; and just as with the document project, you'll be in the designer for your ribbon. Leaving the ribbon alone for now, return to your project and again select Add New Item and return to the dialog shown in Figure 22-21. This time select the Common Items category.

Earlier in this chapter, the Actions Pane template was described as a customized user control. The template took a common user control and added some custom properties to enable it to work with the actions pane. The task pane, conversely, doesn't need much in the way of customization for the user control it will use, so simply select the User Control template, use "TaskPaneUC" for your control name, and click Add.

After you are returned to Visual Studio, drag a button and a label into your new user control's design surface. The result should look similar to what is displayed in Figured 22-22. You can provide a custom label for your button if you choose, but once you have reviewed the layout of your controls, go ahead and double-click your button to create the event handler for the Click event.

Figure 22-22

After adding the event handler, add a simple call to reset the text displayed by the label control, which is in your user control. In theory, you could add any code you wanted, but in keeping with the idea that you don't want to necessarily target or count on anything existing within your document, the goal is just to ensure that your code is accessible:

```
Public Class TaskPaneUC
    Private Sub Button1_Click(ByVal sender As System.Object, _
                              ByVal e As System.EventArgs) _
                              Handles Button1.Click
        Label1.Text = "Clicked it."
    End Sub
End Class
```

You could run your project and look for your custom task pane at this point, but by now you can probably guess that you won't find it. Just as with the actions pane, you need to associate your custom control with the collection of available task panes. Unlike the actions pane, for which there is only a single instance, each Add-In project could in theory want access to its own task pane. To resolve this, when you create an instance of a task pane, you create an item in a collection and assign it a unique name. This is significant, because although it wasn't mentioned earlier, regardless of how badly you want to change the name of the Document Actions pane, it isn't possible.

To associate your control with the task pane, switch to your document and take two steps. First, declare a property for your document that will hold a copy of your task pane. Note that this property has been declared as a "Friend" member so that other classes in the same project can access it. This will be important when you want to reference that control from within your ribbon bar.

Second, code is added to the Startup event handler. The first line assigns your custom user control as a new entry in the list of available task panes, and passes a copy of that control to the member variable you created. The second line is temporary; it indicates that your task pane should be visible, so you can ensure that you are seeing what you expect:

```
Public Class ThisAddIn
    Private m_ProVBTaskPane As Microsoft.Office.Tools.CustomTaskPane

    Friend Property ProVBTaskPane() As Microsoft.Office.Tools.CustomTaskPane
        Get
            Return m_ProVBTaskPane
        End Get
        Set(ByVal value As Microsoft.Office.Tools.CustomTaskPane)
            m_ProVBTaskPane = value
        End Set
    End Property

    Private Sub ThisAddIn_Startup(ByVal sender As Object, _
                                  ByVal e As System.EventArgs) _
                                  Handles Me.Startup
        ProVBTaskPane = Me.CustomTaskPanes.Add(New TaskPaneUC(), _
                                               "Do Not Push Me")
        ProVBTaskPane.Visible = True
    End Sub
End Sub
```

Once you've added the preceding code to your project, it's time to test run your application. Using F5, build and start your project. Excel 2007 will open and then a blank spreadsheet will open. Your custom task pane should appear on the left-hand side, and once you click the button, your display should look similar to Figure 22-23.

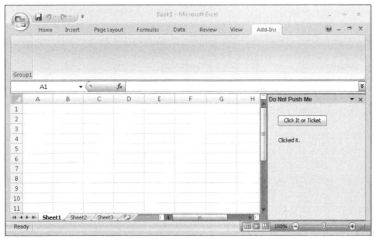

Figure 22-23

Notice that your custom title for the task pane is displayed. Of course, you could exit Visual Studio right now and open an Excel spreadsheet that was completely unrelated to your current project. However, your code has been registered for COM interop, so if you do this your custom task pane appears within your totally unrelated spreadsheet. This would quickly become annoying, which is why you'll want to display your custom task pane only when the user asks for it.

The next step is to customize your ribbon so that it can control your task pane. First, within your `ThisAddIn.vb` logic, remove the `ProVBTaskPane.Visible = True` line of code. Next, go to the designer for your ribbon and add a new `ToggleButton`. You can label this button with some descriptive text. Additionally, select the group control that is already on your ribbon and change the text shown as the label for that control to something such as "ProVB Add-In." Double-click on your new button and add the event handler for the `Click` event. Within this event you are going to again hide and show the control and update the display text of the button:

```vb
Private Sub ToggleButton1_Click(ByVal sender As System.Object, _
        ByVal e As Microsoft.Office.Tools.Ribbon.RibbonControlEventArgs) _
                                        Handles ToggleButton1.Click
    If ToggleButton1.Checked = True Then
        Globals.ThisAddIn.ProVBTaskPane.Visible = True
        ToggleButton1.Label = "Hide Push Me Pane"
    Else
        Globals.ThisAddIn.ProVBTaskPane.Visible = False
        ToggleButton1.Label = "Show Push Me Pane"
    End If
End Sub
```

The preceding code block should in fact look very similar to what you did within your Document project earlier in this chapter. However, there is a key difference when it comes to referencing the task pane.

Notice that instead of accessing the `Command Bars` collection to make the entire pane display clear correctly, you are instead referencing the local `Friend` property that you declared in your `ThisAddIn` class. In addition, instead of a global reference to `ThisDocument`, you access the `ThisAddIn` object.

Similar to working with the earlier project, you will want to modify the `Load` event. However, there is an additional consideration here. When your add-in is loaded by Excel, the ribbon bar is loaded before the core add-in's `Startup` event fires. This is important because you can't just check to see whether your task pane is visible. First you need to determine whether the task pane exists. Then, if it does, you check whether it is visible. To do this you create an `If` statement, which as shown in the following code block leverages the conditional `AndAlso`:

```
Imports Microsoft.Office.Tools.Ribbon

Public Class RibbonAddIn

    Private Sub RibbonAddIn_Load(ByVal sender As System.Object, _
                                 ByVal e As RibbonUIEventArgs) _
                                 Handles MyBase.Load
        If Globals.ThisAddIn.ProVBTaskPane IsNot Nothing AndAlso _
           Globals.ThisAddIn.ProVBTaskPane.Visible Then
            ToggleButton1.Checked = True
            ToggleButton1.Label = "Hide Push Me Pane"
        Else
            ToggleButton1.Label = "Show Push Me Pane"
        End If

    End Sub
    Private Sub ToggleButton1_Click(ByVal sender As System.Object, _
        ByVal e As Microsoft.Office.Tools.Ribbon.RibbonControlEventArgs) _
                                            Handles ToggleButton1.Click
        If ToggleButton1.Checked = True Then
            Globals.ThisAddIn.ProVBTaskPane.Visible = True
            ToggleButton1.Label = "Hide Push Me Pane"
        Else
            Globals.ThisAddIn.ProVBTaskPane.Visible = False
            ToggleButton1.Label = "Show Push Me Pane"
        End If
    End Sub
End Class
```

If you fail to add that check, you'll throw an exception as Excel is trying to load. Excel won't appreciate this, and it remembers. The next time Excel starts it will warn the user that your add-in caused an error the last time it tried to load it, and suggest that the user disable your add-in — not exactly the result you want for your code.

If your code is working, your display should look similar to what is shown in Figure 22-24, which shows the user interface with the mouse hovering over your new ribbon bar button. If you leave the mouse there, then you'll get an Office tip telling you that you can select F1 for help about this control. Using the F1 key starts the help system and Excel opens a help page describing how you can manage add-ins within Excel.

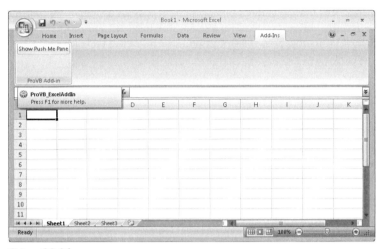

Figure 22-24

The available help page is a good resource for Office 2007, for which you may need a bit of help finding the options. You can test the add-in at this point to ensure that it opens and closes the task pane correctly. However, just as you can manage add-ins from Excel, it is difficult to dispose of them from within Excel. This is important, because if you start creating add-ins for several different customers, you could wind up with ten or twenty such add-ins taking up residence on your system. Excel would open only after a longer and longer delay.

Of course, it's bad enough that during testing, every time you debug, you're paying a price to ensure that your current code is registered properly. Having add-ins piling up could be even more of a problem. Fortunately, Visual Studio has an easy solution (see Figure 22-25).

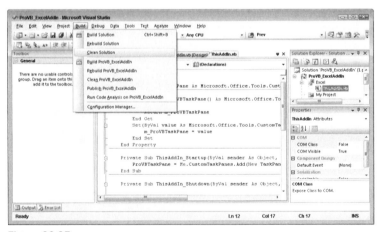

Figure 22-25

This same menu option is available across all the different Add-In project types. Selecting this enables you to easily remove from your system the test add-ins that you make. As annoying as this might be for

Excel or Word, when you see the implications of an Outlook Form Region, which relies on an Outlook add-in, you'll understand why this clean option is important.

Outlook Form Regions

As previously noted, Visual Studio 2008 VSTO provides templates for every client application in the Microsoft Office 2007 suite. Some of these, such as Word and Excel, are the traditional favorites for customization. Others, such as Power Point, may see very little automation. However, there is a new kid on the block. Outlook supports an add-in template and as part of this template provides what is sure to become one of the more popular extension models.

Outlook Form Regions (OFR) provide you with the capability to customize what users see when they open an e-mail message or a contact or any of several other components within Outlook. As you'll see in this section, the OFR is a very flexible framework that enables you to embed anything from an HTML view to a custom WPF user control in Outlook. Because Outlook is as popular as almost any other Office client application, this feature will have a broad reach.

OFR provides a canvas that isn't simply visible alongside your primary focus; the OFR provides a very configurable UI that enables you to extend or replace the default interface associated with typical components in Outlook. Because e-mail has become the ubiquitous office and home communication tool, being able to customize how key business data is presented in this medium is powerful.

To get started, create a new Outlook add-in project with the name "ProVB_OFR." Not shown here are screenshots of the New Project dialog or the initial view in Visual Studio after the template has run, as the Outlook add-in looks very similar to the Excel add-in discussed earlier. You'll find yourself in the code view for your add-in, with the `Startup` and `Shutdown` event handlers.

At this point, add your OFR to your project. Right-click on your project and select the Add option from the context menu to open the Add New Item dialog. As before, go to the Office category to review the available templates, where you'll find an Outlook Form Region template (see Figure 22-26). Give it a meaningful name, such as "AdjoiningOFR," to reflect the type of form region you'll create.

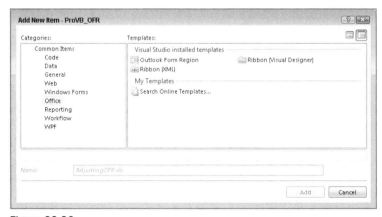

Figure 22-26

After clicking the Add button, instead of being returned to Visual Studio, you'll be presented with the first screen in the wizard for the New Outlook Form Region. This wizard walks you through several different options related to your OFR. The first choice, shown in Figure 22-27, is whether you want to generate your form from scratch or would like to import one of the standard templates that ship with Outlook.

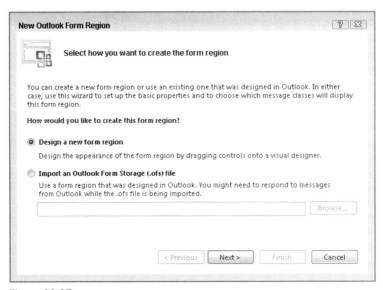

Figure 22-27

The current example will go through the steps to create a new form region. (Take some time to explore one or more of the standard forms on your own, as a complete discussion is beyond the scope of this chapter.) Click Next to be taken to the second step of the wizard — selecting a type of form.

The dialog shown in Figure 22-28 lists four different types of potential region. As you move between the different options, the wizard will display a graphic to better illustrate how each one affects the default display. These four options can actually be grouped in two sets. The first two options — Separate and Adjoining — are form types that modify the built-in components of Excel. At their core, these forms continue to display the underlying components associated with whatever class they are associated with. The second group consists of the Replacement and Replace-all regions. These form types replace the object that would normally display within Outlook.

As noted in the naming of your OFR, the plan is to demonstrate creating an Adjoining form region, but to demonstrate how Replacement and Replace-all forms actually work, select one of these two options and click Next. This will take you to a screen where you can name and set some options related to your OFR. You will return to this screen when you revert to the Adjoining OFR type. Instead of discussing this now, click Next a second time and move to the next step in the wizard. This will take you to the screen shown in Figure 22-29, defining the object(s) that will be associated with your OFR.

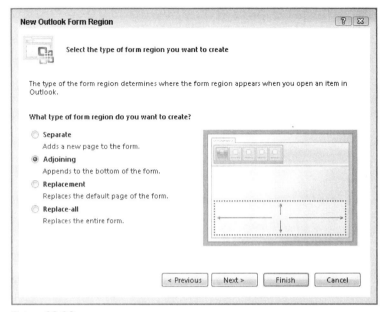

New Outlook Form Region

Select the type of form region you want to create

The type of the form region determines where the form region appears when you open an item in Outlook.

What type of form region do you want to create?

○ **Separate**
Adds a new page to the form.

◉ **Adjoining**
Appends to the bottom of the form.

○ **Replacement**
Replaces the default page of the form.

○ **Replace-all**
Replaces the entire form.

[< Previous] [Next >] [Finish] [Cancel]

Figure 22-28

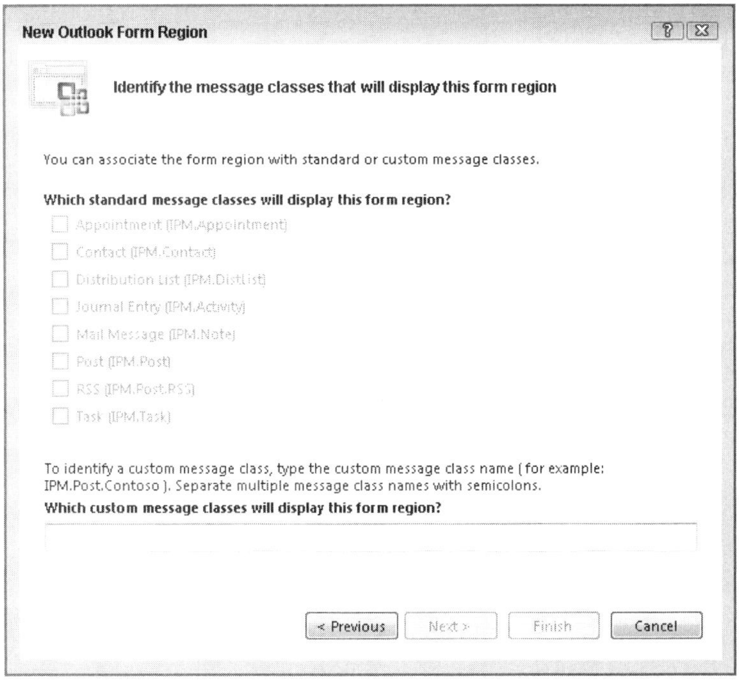

New Outlook Form Region

Identify the message classes that will display this form region

You can associate the form region with standard or custom message classes.

Which standard message classes will display this form region?

☐ Appointment (IPM.Appointment)
☐ Contact (IPM.Contact)
☐ Distribution List (IPM.DistList)
☐ Journal Entry (IPM.Activity)
☐ Mail Message (IPM.Note)
☐ Post (IPM.Post)
☐ RSS (IPM.Post.RSS)
☐ Task (IPM.Task)

To identify a custom message class, type the custom message class name (for example: IPM.Post.Contoso). Separate multiple message class names with semicolons.
Which custom message classes will display this form region?

[< Previous] [Next >] [Finish] [Cancel]

Figure 22-29

Keep in mind that Figure 22-29 shows this dialog as it looks when you have selected either a Replacement or Replace-all OFR type. As noted, these form types replace the underlying class. In Figure 22-29, each of the built-in classes has been disabled, so you can't ask to apply your change to one of those existing types. Instead, your only option is to define a custom class or classes — the best practice is to define a single class.

This custom message class is one that you would define within your custom add-in. To better explain what is occurring, let's use a mail message as an example. Typically, when Outlook receives a mail message, the message is assigned to the class IPM.Note. The IPM.Note class is what provides all of the typical display elements that you see in a message within Outlook. If you create a replacement form, then when that form is sent it is flagged not as a typical message, but instead as an instance of your custom class.

In other words, the sender of the message needs to be aware of the name of the class used for this type of OFR. In theory, this is all that the sender needs to be aware of — however, that's only a theory. The Replacement and Replace-all form types work fine as long as the initial message is sent to the Microsoft Exchange Server. However, if you are attempting to trigger a message from, say, SharePoint, there is a problem. Typically, when SharePoint is installed and configured, the e-mail options are set up such that SharePoint handles its own messages. However, SharePoint doesn't allow for sending messages with custom message types, so when your code attempts to trigger this custom message type from within SharePoint, the message is sent only if you have configured your SharePoint server to communicate with an Exchange Server.

There are other unique features to Replacement and Replace-all forms. On the positive side, unlike the OFRs that modify an existing object type, Replacement and Replace-all forms are only instantiated when a message of that specific class is received. As discussed later in this section, Adjoining and Separate forms need to have custom code added that screens when that OFR should be displayed.

Another advantage of Replacement and Replace-all forms is that they give you more control over the message content. Any text in the underlying body is hidden, which means that you can embed information in the message body that will later be used in the form. In addition, these form types also hide enclosures, so it is possible to enclose, for example, an XML file containing application data and then retrieve and process this data when the message is opened.

However, for this example you are creating a new Adjoining OFR, so use the Previous button twice in order to return to the screen shown in Figure 22-27. Change your OFR type from Replacement to Adjoining and click Next. This should bring you to the screen shown in Figure 22-30. Here you have the option to provide a display name for your OFR. In order to see the effect of this, place the word "My" at the start of your class name so that you'll be able to see where this value is used.

The three check boxes in this dialog represent times when this OFR will, by default, be available in Outlook. In the case of the first one at least, you might not want to accept that default. "Inspectors that are in compose mode," enables you to determine whether someone who is creating a new message or contact should also see your OFR region by default.

Although the setting is present for all OFR types, it in fact is not applicable to Replacement and Replace-all. In the case of Replacement and Replace-all forms, Outlook doesn't automatically offer these as an option for creating a new message. Instead, users need to access the File menu and select the Forms option to tell Outlook that they are attempting to send a message defined by the custom type.

However, for Separate and Adjoining forms, Outlook will, if you leave this checked, automatically add your custom region to the standard new message, contact, appointment, and so on, window. This could get quite annoying if your users aren't going to be placing data into that OFR and it is for display only. Thus, in many cases you'll clear this first check box. However, if you are customizing a contact to capture and update new data elements, you would probably want to leave this check box selected.

As for the other two check boxes in Figure 22-30, these refer to displaying your custom OFR, and typically these remain selected so that your OFR will be visible to display data.

Figure 22-30

Clicking Next takes you to the dialog shown in Figure 22-31. This dialog enables you to select from any of the standard classes that are used within Outlook. The goal is to enable you to create a custom OFR for one or more of these classes, although typically you'll select just one. For now, select just Mail Message and click Finish to complete the creation of your OFR and return to Visual Studio.

On your return to Visual Studio you'll be in the designer for your AdjoiningOFR user control. That's right, once again you are working with a Windows Forms user control that has been customized by the VSTO team to provide the characteristics you defined in the preceding wizard. At this point you can open the Toolbox and drag and drop controls onto the form.

Figure 22-31

Figure 22-32 illustrates a few changes that you can make so that your form will be both visible and have some simple elements you can manipulate. The user control shown in Figure 22-32 has had a new background color assigned, and has had two label controls dragged onto the form. Label1 has had its font changed to a much larger size and the background changed to white. The default text in Label1 is now a zero. To the left of Label1 is Label2, which has had its text updated to read "Attachment Count."

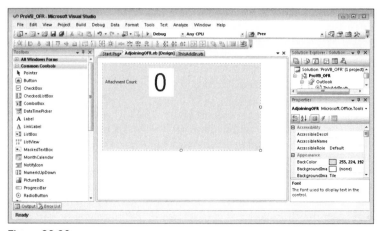

Figure 22-32

You still haven't written any actual code, so this is a great time to test your application. Use F5 to build and run it. Once the build is complete, Outlook will automatically open. You should see something similar to what is shown in Figure 22-33.

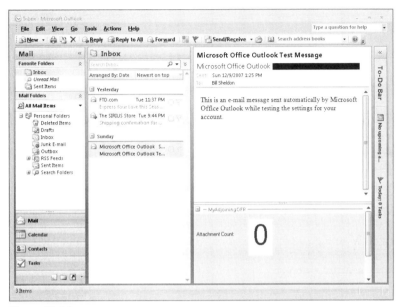

Figure 22-33

Note that even the original Outlook test message, which was received two days ago, now includes your custom OFR. In fact, you'll find that every message you open includes the OFR — which could easily become annoying, given that in a real application your OFR would probably be targeting a single message type. Similarly, if you choose to create a new message, there it is again — an OFR that has only display information. Once you have satisfied yourself with the impact of this region on Outlook, close Outlook and return to Visual Studio.

Figure 22-34 provides a view of the default generated code for your OFR. Your goal is to carry out two tasks: first, make it so that this OFR only displays if the associated message includes one or more attachments. Second, update Label1 so that the number of attachments is shown in the OFR.

The first item to note is the Form Region Factory code block, which has been collapsed. There are actually three generated methods, and it is the method hidden inside this code block where you'll want to put the custom logic specifying when this OFR should be visible. When expanded, as shown in the following code block, not only do you have your `AdjoiningOFR` class, but within this collapsed block is a second partial class definition that defines an implementation to create your OFR as part of a factory. Factories are a well-known software pattern wherein the calling application might not know the details of which class is being created, but only the base-class OFR and the methods and properties exposed at the base-class level.

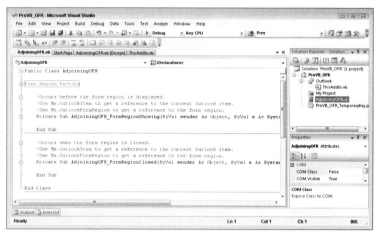

Figure 22-34

Software patterns are outside the scope of this chapter, but in short, the factory patterns indicate that there will be a `FormRegionInitializing` event handler, and that the calling application will be able to create several different types of OFRs based on which factory has been implemented within each OFR.

```
Public Class AdjoiningOFR
#Region "Form Region Factory"
  <Microsoft.Office.Tools.Outlook.FormRegionMessageClass
  (Microsoft.Office.Tools.Outlook.FormRegionMessageClassAttribute.Note)> _
  <Microsoft.Office.Tools.Outlook.FormRegionName("ProVB_OFR.AdjoiningOFR")> _
    Partial Public Class AdjoiningOFRFactory

    ' Occurs before the form region is initialized.
    ' To prevent the form region from appearing, set e.Cancel to true.
    ' Use e.OutlookItem to get a reference to the current Outlook item.
        Private Sub AdjoiningOFRFactory_FormRegionInitializing( _
                    ByVal sender As Object, _
                    ByVal e As _
            Microsoft.Office.Tools.Outlook.FormRegionInitializingEventArgs) _
                    Handles Me.FormRegionInitializing

    End Sub

    End Class

#End Region

    'Occurs before the form region is displayed.
    'Use Me.OutlookItem to get a reference to the current Outlook item.
    'Use Me.OutlookFormRegion to get a reference to the form region.
    Private Sub AdjoiningOFR_FormRegionShowing(ByVal sender As Object, _
                                        ByVal e As System.EventArgs) _
                                        Handles MyBase.FormRegionShowing

    End Sub
```

```
'Occurs when the form region is closed.
'Use Me.OutlookItem to get a reference to the current Outlook item.
'Use Me.OutlookFormRegion to get a reference to the form region.
Private Sub AdjoiningOFR_FormRegionClosed(ByVal sender As Object, _
                                    ByVal e As System.EventArgs) _
                                    Handles MyBase.FormRegionClosed


    End Sub

End Class
```

In order to prevent your OFR from being displayed, you need to add custom code to the `FormRegionInitializing` event handler. In this case you simply want to determine whether the message has one or more attachments. If it doesn't have any attachments, then you want the OFR to remain hidden:

```
Private Sub AdjoiningOFRFactory_FormRegionInitializing( _
                        ByVal sender As Object, _
    ByVal e As Microsoft.Office.Tools.Outlook.FormRegionInitializingEventArgs) _
                        Handles Me.FormRegionInitializing

        Try
            Dim mail = CType(e.OutlookItem, Outlook.MailItem)
            If Not mail.Attachments.Count > 0 Then
                e.Cancel = True
                Return
            End If
        Catch
            e.Cancel = True
        End Try
    End Sub
```

The preceding code illustrates some of the key elements to screening your OFR. The first thing to note is that you can access the inbound e-mail message by retrieving the `OutlookItem` object from the parameter e. Of course, you need to cast this item, as it is passed as type `Object`. Once you've done this, you have full access to the Outlook object model for e-mail messages. Thus, you can quickly determine the number of attachments; and if there are none, you can set the `Cancel` property to `True`.

Next up is getting the number of attachments in your message into the OFR. This is a fairly easy task. Unlike the decision about whether to display the OFR, which occurs when the code is looking to create that OFR, your ability to influence what is displayed doesn't occur until the `FormRegionShowing` event handler is called. In the code block that follows, instead of retrieving the current e-mail object from a parameter, it is one of the member values for your OFR:

```
Private Sub AdjoiningOFR_FormRegionShowing(ByVal sender As Object, _
                                ByVal e As System.EventArgs) _
                                Handles MyBase.FormRegionShowing

        Dim mail = CType(Me.OutlookItem, Outlook.MailItem)
        Me.Label1.Text = mail.Attachments.Count
    End Sub
```

Thus, the code to get the number of attachments and assign that as the contents of the label boils down to two lines of custom code. At this point you can rerun the application to test your code. Once Outlook opens, you should see that the `MyAdjoiningPane`, which was previously displayed for all messages, is now gone except in the case of those that have attachments.

What this means is that when you now create a new message, the OFR is still not shown. However, if you add an attachment and then save that message before sending, you can reopen the saved message and you'll see the OFR displayed. Keep in mind that the determination of whether the OFR should be displayed occurs during the creation of the OFR, and once the OFR has been hidden you can't change that setting while the object remains open.

Summary

This chapter looked at VSTO and introduced many of its new features and where it is headed in the future. It didn't spend a lot of time talking about how you can add controls and logic to user controls, but instead focused on how to work with the custom task pane or actions pane, and how to leverage new capabilities such as content controls. Overall, VSTO's enhancements are some of the most significant in Visual Studio 2008. VSTO isn't just a simple set of extensions that mirrors what you could do in VBA. In fact, VSTO extends every client in the Office system and provides multiple templates. It provides flexibility with Word and Excel to customize either at the document level or by creating a custom add-in; and if you do customize at the document level, it provides the option to interoperate with any existing VBA code you have in your document.

In addition to Word and Excel, you've been introduced to Windows Outlook Form Regions. The OFR model enables you to send business data directly into the application that everyone uses. The various OFR models have differing advantages and disadvantages, but each is based on an underlying user control, which enables you to leverage everything that is available via Windows Forms, including WPF interop.

Highlights of this chapter included the following:

❑ Office Business Application Architecture as the target of VSTO solutions

❑ How SharePoint can provide additional capabilities when used as the central document store for document-based VSTO applications

❑ VSTO-VBA interop and the steps to enable VBA to call new VSTO capabilities

❑ A document-based VSTO solution

❑ Customizing the Document Actions pane and the ribbon bar and enabling them to communicate

❑ Working with content controls

❑ Creating an Excel add-in solution and customizing the ribbon bar and task pane

❑ Differences between the OFR types

While the concept of an OBA is relatively recent, you learned that the OBA model is becoming an increasingly important focus for Microsoft. The ability to tie your business logic into applications such as Word, Excel, and Outlook means that your developers can spend less time creating and maintaining custom grid controls, and your end users can get started with less time spent in training.

23

Assemblies

By now, you've probably developed some programs in .NET, so you've seen the modules produced by the .NET compilers, which have file extensions of .dll or .exe. Most .NET modules are DLLs, including class libraries and those that serve as code-behind for ASP.NET. Windows applications, console applications, and Windows Services are examples of .NET modules that are executables and thus have an extension of .exe.

These .NET-compiled modules, both DLLs and EXEs, are referred to as *assemblies*. Assemblies are the unit of deployment in .NET, containing both compiled code and metadata that is needed by the .NET common language runtime (CLR) to run the code. Metadata includes information such as the code's identity and version, dependencies on other assemblies, and a list of types and resources exposed by the assembly.

Basic development in .NET doesn't require you to know any more than that. However, as your applications become more complex, and as you begin considering such issues as deployment and maintenance of your code, you need to understand more about assemblies. This chapter addresses that need, including the following:

- ❑ What assemblies are and how they are used

- ❑ The general structure of an assembly

- ❑ How assemblies can be versioned

- ❑ The global application cache (GAC), including how and when to use it

- ❑ How assemblies are located and loaded by the CLR

After you are familiar with these essentials, Chapter 24 uses this information to discuss deployment in depth.

Assemblies

The assembly is used by the CLR as the smallest unit for the following:

❑ Deployment
❑ Version control
❑ Security
❑ Type grouping
❑ Code reuse

An assembly must contain a *manifest*, which tells the CLR what else is in the assembly. The other elements can be any of the following three categories:

❑ Type metadata
❑ Microsoft Intermediate Language (MSIL) code
❑ Resources

An assembly can be just one file. Figure 23-1 details the contents of a single-file assembly.

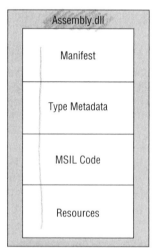

Figure 23-1

Alternatively, the structure can be split across multiple files, as shown in Figure 23-2. This is just one example of a multiple-file assembly configuration.

An assembly can only have one manifest section across all the files that make up the assembly. There is nothing stopping you, however, from having a resource section (or any of the other sections of type `Metadata` and MSIL code) in each of the files that make up an assembly.

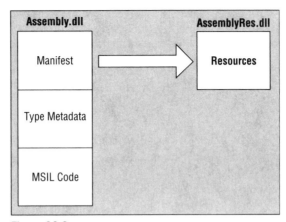

Figure 23-2

The Manifest

The manifest is the part of the assembly that contains a list of the other elements contained in the assembly and basic identification information for the assembly. The manifest contains the largest part of the information that enables the assembly to be self-describing. Elements listed in the manifest are placed in appropriate sections. The manifest includes the sections displayed in Figure 23-3. These sections are covered later in the chapter.

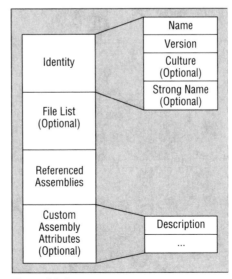

Figure 23-3

To look at the manifest for a particular assembly, you can use the IL Disassembler (`Ildasm.exe`), which is included with Visual Studio 2008. There is no shortcut on the Programs menu for `ildasm.exe`, but you can run it by going to Start ⇨ Programs ⇨ Microsoft Visual Studio 2008 ⇨ Visual Studio Tools ⇨ Visual Studio 2008 Command Prompt, and then typing `Ildasm` on the resulting command line.

The version of `Ildasm.exe` in the SDK for .NET Framework 3.5 can examine assemblies created with earlier versions of the .NET Framework.

When `Ildasm.exe` loads, you can browse for an assembly to view by selecting File ⇨ Open. Once an assembly has been loaded into `Ildasm.exe`, it disassembles the metadata contained within the assembly and presents you with a tree-view layout of the data. Initially, the tree view shows only top-level elements, as illustrated in Figure 23-4. This example has only one namespace element in the tree, but if an assembly contains classes in more than one namespace, then additional elements will be shown.

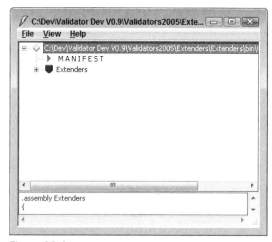

Figure 23-4

The full path of the assembly you are viewing represents the root node. The first node below the root is called MANIFEST, and as you've probably guessed, it contains all the information about the assembly's manifest. If you double-click this node, a new window is displayed with the information contained within the manifest. The manifest for a complex assembly can be rather long. For our example, three sections of a manifest are shown in Figures 23-5, 23-6, and 23-7. Figure 23-5 shows the top of the manifest, which contains the external references needed by this assembly, such as other .NET assemblies on which this assembly depends. If the assembly depends on COM libraries, those will be shown as external modules and listed before the external assemblies.

Figure 23-6 shows a portion of the manifest further down, containing the beginning of the section for the actual assembly. The first items listed in the manifest for the assembly itself are the attributes that apply to the assembly.

Further down are items such as resources that reside in the assembly. Figure 23-7 shows a bitmap named `checkmark8.bmp` that is used by this particular assembly.

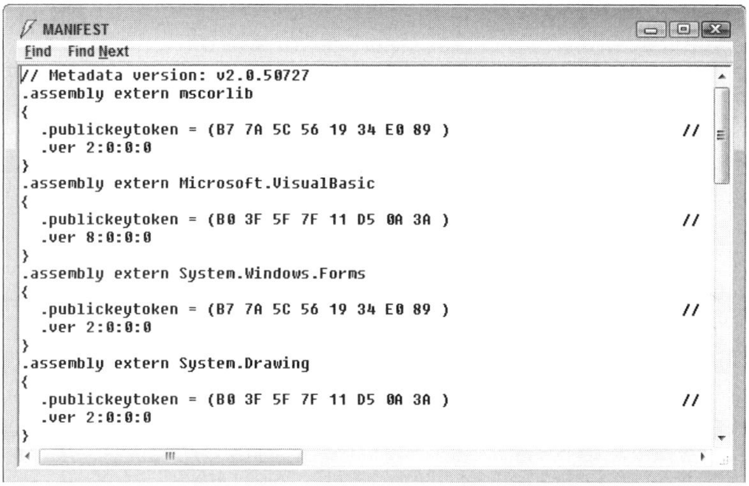

Figure 23-5

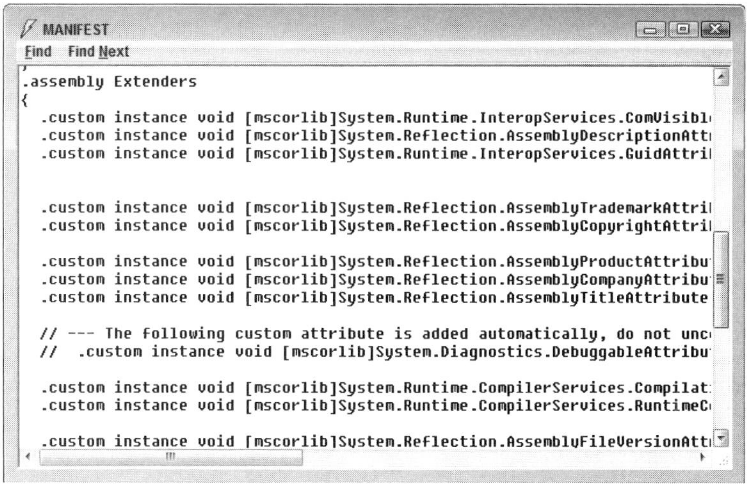

Figure 23-6

Assembly identity

The section of the manifest for an assembly also contains information used to uniquely identify the assembly. This section contains some standard information, such as the version number, and may also contain some optional elements, such as a strong name for the assembly. Assemblies come in two types: application-private and shared (differences between the two types are covered shortly), and they have slightly different identity information.

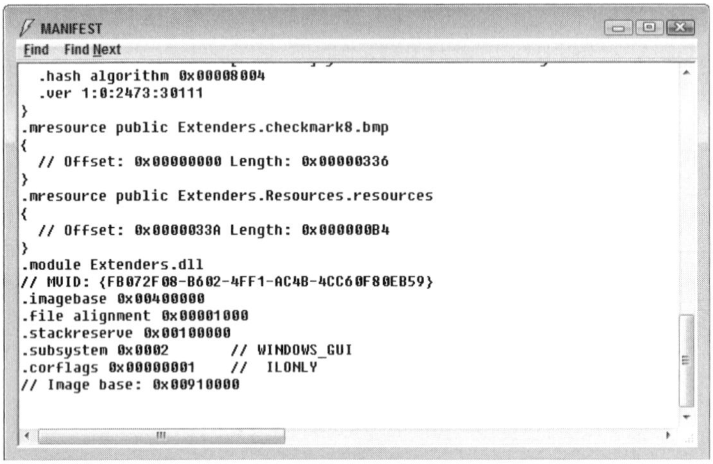

Figure 23-7

The Version Number

The section of the manifest for an assembly contains a version number, which is indicated by the `.ver` directive in `Ildasm.exe`. Figure 23-7, shown earlier, includes a `.ver` directive on the following line in the `.assembly` section:

```
.ver 1.0.2473.30111
```

A version number contains four parts:

```
Major : Minor : Build : Revision
```

Assemblies that have the same name but different version numbers are treated as completely different assemblies. If you have an assembly on your machine that has a version number of 1.5.2.3 and another version of the same assembly with a version number of 1.6.0.1, then the CLR treats them as different assemblies. The version number of an assembly is part of what is used to define dependencies between assemblies.

Strong Names

The manifest can also contain an optional *strong name* for an assembly. The strong name is not a name per se, but a public key that has been generated by the author of the assembly to uniquely identify it. A strong name is used to ensure that your assembly has a unique signature compared to other assemblies that may have the same name. Strong names were introduced to combat DLL hell by providing an unambiguous way to differentiate among assemblies.

A strong name is based on public-private key encryption and creates a unique identity for your assembly. The public key is stored in the identity section of the manifest. A signature of the file containing the assembly's manifest is created and stored in the resulting PE file. The .NET Framework uses these two signatures when resolving type references to ensure that the correct assembly is loaded at runtime. A strong name is indicated in the manifest by the `.publickey` directive in the `.assembly` section.

Signing an Assembly with a Strong Name

As mentioned above, applying a strong name to an assembly is based on public-private key encryption. The public and private keys are related, and a set is called a public-private *key pair*. Applying a strong name to an assembly is usually called *signing* the assembly with the strong name.

You can create a key pair with the sn.exe utility. At the Visual Studio command prompt, enter the following command:

```
sn -k pairname.snk
```

You should replace *pairname* with an appropriate name, often the name of your product or system. The same key pair can be used to apply a strong name to all the assemblies in your system.

Once you have a key pair, you need to add it to any projects in Visual Studio that need to generate a strong-named assembly. To do that, just select Project ↪ Add Existing Item, and browse to the key pair.

The final step is to change the module AssemblyInfo.vb to apply the strong name. AssemblyInfo.vb was automatically created when your project was created, and is under the My Project area in the Solution Explorer. If you can't see a plus sign to expand My Project, press the Show All Files button at the top of the Solution Explorer.

In AssemblyInfo.vb, insert a line that looks like this:

```
<Assembly: AssemblyKeyFile("pairname.snk")>
```

Again, you should replace *pairname* with the name you actually used for the key pair file earlier. The next time your project is built, the resulting assembly will have a strong name, generated by using the key pair you have indicated.

You can also sign an assembly with a strong name by compiling at the command line. This might be the case if you want to sign the assembly outside of Visual Studio. A typical command line to compile and sign a Visual Basic assembly looks like this:

```
vbc /reference:Microsoft.VisualBasic.dll /reference:System.Windows.Forms.dll
/target:library /keyfile:c:\mykeys\keypair.snk /out:MyAssembly.dll
/rootnamespace:MyAssembly *.vb
```

The separate elements of the command line have been placed on different lines for ease of reading, but they should all be on the same line in actual use. The preceding is just a template. You would need to change the /reference options to include any references needed by your assembly. You would also need to specify the correct file path for your own key pair file (.snk file) and apply your assembly and root namespace names.

Finally, strong names can be applied with a technique called *delay signing*. That's beyond the scope of this chapter, but the Visual Studio help files include step-by-step instructions. Delayed signing is helpful when assemblies need to be properly strong-named during development (so that any problems with strong names are detected at that point), but it is undesirable for all the developers to have a copy of the key pair that will be used for signing the final compiled version of the assembly.

The Culture

The final part of an assembly's identity is its *culture*, which is optional. Cultures are used to define the country/language for which the assembly is targeted.

The combination of name, strong name, version number, and culture is used by the CLR to enforce version dependencies. For example, you could create one version of your assembly targeted at English users, another for German users, another for Finnish users, and so on.

Cultures can be general, as in the case of English, or more specific, as in the case of US-English. Cultures are represented by a string that can contain two parts: primary and secondary (optional). The culture for English is en, and the culture for US-English is en-us. See Chapter 5 for more about cultures in .NET.

If a culture is not indicated in the assembly, then it is assumed that the assembly can be used for any culture. Such an assembly is said to be *culture neutral*. You can assign a culture to an assembly by including the attribute AssemblyCulture from the System.Reflection namespace in your assembly's code (usually within the AssemblyInfo.vb file):

```
<Assembly: AssemblyCulture("en")>
```

The culture of an assembly is represented in the manifest by the .locale directive in the .assembly section.

Referenced assemblies

It was mentioned earlier that the first section of the manifest contains referenced assemblies. An assembly reference is indicated in the manifest with the .assembly extern directive (refer to Figure 23-5).

The first piece of information included is the name of the referenced assembly. Figure 23-5 shows a reference to the mscorlib assembly. This name is used to determine the name of the file that contains the actual assembly. The CLR takes the name of the assembly reference and appends .dll. For instance, in the last example, the CLR will look for a file called mscorlib.dll. The assembly mscorlib is a special assembly in .NET that contains all the definitions of the base types used in .NET, and is referenced by all assemblies.

The .publickeytoken Directive

If the assembly being referenced contains a strong name, then a hash of the public key of the referenced assembly is stored as part of the record to the external reference. This hash is stored in the manifest using the .publickeytoken directive as part of the .assembly extern section. The assembly reference shown in Figure 23-5 contains a hash of the strong name of the mscorlib assembly. The stored hash of the strong name is compared at runtime to a hash of the strong name (.publickey) contained within the referenced assembly to help ensure that the correct assembly is loaded. The value of the .publickeytoken is computed by taking the lower 8 bytes of a hash (SHA1) of the strong name of the referenced assemblies.

The .ver Directive

The version of the assembly being referenced is also stored in the manifest. This version information is used with the rest of the information stored about a reference to ensure that the correct assembly is loaded (this is discussed later). If an application references version 1.1.0.0 of an assembly, it will not load version 2.1.0.0 of the assembly unless a version policy (also discussed later) exists to indicate otherwise. The version of the referenced assembly is stored in the manifest using the `.ver` directive as part of an `.assembly extern` section.

The .locale Directive

If an assembly that is being referenced has a culture, then the culture information is also stored in the external assembly reference section, using the `.locale` directive. The combination of name, strong name (if it exists), version number, and culture are what make up a unique version of an assembly.

Assemblies and Deployment

The information in the manifest enables the reliable determination of the identity and version of an assembly. This is the basis for the deployment options available in .NET, and for the side-by-side execution of assemblies that helps .NET overcome DLL hell. This section looks at these issues in detail.

Application-private assemblies

It was mentioned earlier that assemblies can be of two types. The first is an application-private assembly. As the name implies, this type of assembly is used by one application only and is not shared. This is the default style of assembly in .NET and is the main mechanism by which an application can be independent of changes to the system.

Application-private assemblies are deployed into the application's own directory. Because application-private assemblies are not shared, they do not need a strong name. This means that, at a minimum, they only need to have a name and version number in the identity section of the manifest. Because the assemblies are private to the application, the application does not perform version checks on the assemblies, as the application developer has control over the assemblies that are deployed to the application directory. If strong names exist, however, the CLR will verify that they match.

If all the assemblies that an application uses are application-private and the CLR is already installed on the target machine, then deployment is quite simple. Chapter 24 discusses this implication in more detail.

Shared assemblies

The second type of assembly is the shared assembly. As the name suggests, this type of assembly can be shared among several different applications that reside on the same server. This type of assembly should only be used when it is important to share assemblies among many applications. For example, a Windows Forms control purchased as part of a package may be used in many of your applications, and thus it is better to install a shared version of the assembly, rather than copies of it, for each application. The .NET Framework assemblies themselves are also examples of shared assemblies.

Certain requirements are placed upon shared assemblies. The assembly needs to have a globally unique name, which is not a requirement of application-private assemblies. As mentioned earlier, a strong name is used to create a globally unique name for an assembly. As the assembly is shared, all references to the shared assembly are checked to ensure that the correct version is being used by an application.

Shared assemblies are stored in the global assembly cache (GAC), which is usually located in the `assembly` folder in the `Windows` directory (in a typical Windows XP or Vista installation, `C:\Windows\assembly`). However, it's not enough to just copy an assembly into that directory. In fact, if you browse to that directory using Windows Explorer, you'll find that you can't just drag files in and out of it. The process for placing an assembly in the GAC is similar in concept to registering a COM DLL. That process is discussed in detail later in this chapter.

No other changes to the code of the assembly are necessary to differentiate it from that of an application-private assembly. In fact, just because an assembly has a strong name does not mean that it has to be deployed as a shared assembly; it could just as easily be deployed in the application directory as an application-private assembly.

Installing a shared assembly into the GAC requires administrator rights on the machine. This is another factor complicating deployment of shared assemblies. Because of the extra effort involved in the creation and deployment of shared assemblies, you should avoid this type of assembly unless you really need it.

The Global Assembly Cache

Each computer that has the .NET runtime installed has a global assembly cache (GAC). However, assemblies in the GAC are always stored in the same folder, no matter which version of .NET you have. The folder is a subfolder of your main Windows folder, and it is named `Assembly`. If you have multiple versions of the .NET Framework, assemblies in the GAC for all of them are stored in this directory.

As previously noted, a strong name is required for an assembly placed in that GAC. That strong name is used to identify a particular assembly. However, another piece of metadata is also used for verification of an assembly. When an assembly is created, a hash of the assembly is placed in the metadata. If an assembly is changed (with a binary editor, for example), the hash of the assembly will no longer match the hash in the metadata. The metadata hash is checked against the actual hash when an assembly is placed in the GAC with the `gacutil.exe` utility (described later). If the two hash codes do not match, the installation cannot be completed.

The strong name is also used when an application resolves a reference to an external assembly. It checks whether the public key stored in the assembly is equal to the hash of the public key stored as part of the reference in the application. If the two do not match, then the application knows that the external assembly has not been created by the original author of the assembly.

You can view the assemblies contained within the GAC by navigating to the directory using the Windows Explorer.

The `gacutil.exe` utility that ships with .NET is used to add and remove assemblies from the GAC. To add an assembly into the GAC using the `gacutil.exe` tool, use the following command line:

```
gacutil.exe /i myassembly.dll
```

Recall that the assembly being loaded must have a strong name.

To remove an assembly, use the `/u` option, like this:

```
gacutil.exe /u myassembly.dll
```

`gacutil.exe` has a number of other options. You can examine them and see examples of their usage by typing in the following command:

```
gacutil.exe /?
```

Versioning Issues

In COM, the versioning of DLLs had some significant limitations. For example, a different DLL with the same nominal version number could be indistinguishable from the one desired.

.NET's versioning scheme was specifically designed to alleviate the problems of COM. The major capabilities of .NET that solve versioning issues are as follows:

❑ Application isolation

❑ Side-by-side execution

❑ Self-describing components

Application isolation

For an application to be isolated, it should be self-contained and independent. This means that the application should rely on its own dependencies for ActiveX controls, components, or files, and not have those files shared with other applications. The option of having application isolation is essential for a good solution to versioning problems.

If an application is isolated, components are owned, managed, and used by the parent application alone. If a component is used by another application, even if it is the same version, the other application must have its own copy. This ensures that each application can install and uninstall dependencies and not interfere with other applications.

> **Does this sound familiar? This is what most early Windows and DOS applications did until COM required registration of DLLs in the registry and placement of shared DLLs in the system directory. The wheel surely does turn!**

The .NET Framework enables application isolation by allowing developers to create application-private assemblies. These are in the application's own directory, and if another application needs the same assembly, it can be duplicated in that application's directory.

This means that each application is independent from the others. This isolation works best for many scenarios. It is sometimes referred to as a *zero-impact deployment* because when you either install or uninstall such an application, you are in no danger of causing problems for any other application.

Side-by-side execution

Side-by-side execution occurs when multiple versions of the same assembly can run at the same time. Side-by-side execution is performed by the CLR. Components that are to execute side by side must be installed within the application directory or a subdirectory of it.

965

With application assemblies, versioning is not much of an issue. The interfaces are dynamically resolved by the CLR. If you replace an application assembly with a different version, the CLR will load it and make it work with the other assemblies in the application as long as the new version doesn't have any interface incompatibilities. The new version may even have elements of the interface that are new and that don't exist in the old version (new properties or methods). As long as the existing class interface elements used by the other application assemblies are unchanged, the new version will work fine. In the following discussion of exactly how the CLR locates a referenced assembly, you'll learn more about how this works.

Self-describing

In the earlier section on the manifest, the self-describing nature of .NET assemblies was mentioned. The term "self-describing" means that all the information the CLR needs to know to load and execute an assembly is inside the assembly itself.

Self-describing components are essential to .NET's side-by-side execution. Once the extra version is known by the CLR to be needed, everything else about the assembly needed to run side by side is in the assembly itself. Each application can get its own version of an assembly, and all the work to coordinate the versions in memory is performed transparently by the CLR.

Versioning becomes more important with shared assemblies. Without good coordination of versions, .NET applications with shared assemblies are subject to some of the same problems as COM applications. In particular, if a new version of a shared assembly is placed in the GAC, then there must be a means to control which applications get which version of a shared assembly. This is accomplished with a *versioning policy*.

Version policies

As discussed earlier, a version number includes four parts: major, minor, build, and revision. The version number is part of the identity of the assembly. When a new version of a shared assembly is created and placed in the GAC, any of these parts can change. Which ones change affects how the CLR views compatibility for the new assembly.

When the version number of a component only changes according to its build and revision parts, it is compatible. This is often referred to as *Quick Fix Engineering (QFE)*. It's only necessary to place the new assembly in the GAC, and it will automatically be considered compatible with applications that were created to use the older version that had different numbers for the build and revision.

If either the major or minor build number changes, however, compatibility is not assumed by the CLR. In that case, there are manual ways to indicate compatibility if necessary, and these are covered later in this section.

When an application comes across a type that is implemented in an external reference, the CLR has to determine what version of the referenced assembly to load. What steps does the CLR go through to ensure that the correct version of an assembly is loaded? To answer this question, you need to look at version policies and how they affect which version of an assembly is loaded.

The Default Versioning Policy

Let's start by looking at the default versioning policy. This policy is followed in the absence of any configuration files that would modify the versioning policy. The runtime default behavior is to consult the manifest for the name of the referenced assembly and the version of the assembly to use.

If the referenced assembly does not contain a strong name, then it is assumed that the referenced assembly is application-private and is located in the application's directory. The CLR takes the name of the referenced assembly and appends `.dll` to create the filename that contains the referenced assembly's manifest. The CLR then searches in the application's directory for the filename; if it's found, it uses the version indicated, even if the version number is different from the one specified in the manifest. Therefore, the version numbers of application-private assemblies are not checked, because the application developer, in theory, has control over which assemblies are deployed to the application's directory. If the file cannot be found, the CLR raises a `System.IO.FileNotFoundException`.

Automatic Quick Fix Engineering Policy

If the referenced assembly contains a strong name, then the process by which an assembly is loaded is different:

1. The three different types of assembly configuration files (discussed later) are consulted, if they exist, to see whether they contain any settings that will modify which version of the assembly the CLR should load.

2. The CLR then checks whether the assembly has been requested and loaded in a previous call. If it has, it uses the loaded assembly.

3. If the assembly is not already loaded, then the GAC is queried for a match. If a match is found, it is used by the application.

4. If any of the configuration files contains a `codebase` (discussed later) entry for the assembly, then the assembly is looked for in the location specified. If the assembly cannot be found in the location specified in the `codebase`, then a `TypeLoadException` is raised to the application.

5. If there are no configuration files or if there are no `codebase` entries for the assembly, then the CLR probes for the assembly starting in the application's base directory.

6. If the assembly still isn't found, then the CLR asks the Windows Installer service if it has the assembly in question. If it does, then the assembly is installed and the application uses it. This is a feature called *on-demand installation*.

If the assembly hasn't been found by the end of this entire process, then a `TypeLoadException` is raised.

Although a referenced assembly contains a strong name, this does not mean that it has to be deployed into the GAC. This enables application developers to install a version with the application that is known to work. The GAC is consulted to see whether it contains a version of an assembly with a higher `build.revision` number to enable administrators to deploy an updated assembly without having to reinstall or rebuild the application. This is known as the *Automatic Quick Fix Engineering Policy*.

Configuration files

The default versioning policy described earlier may not be the most appropriate policy for your requirements. Fortunately, you can modify this policy through the use of XML configuration files to meet your specific needs. Two types of configuration files can hold versioning information:

❑ The first is an application configuration file, and it is created in the application directory. As the name implies, this configuration file applies to a single application only. You need to create the application configuration file in the application directory with the same name as the application filename and append .config. For example, suppose that you have a Windows Forms application called HelloWorld.exe installed in the C:\HelloWorld directory. The application configuration file would be C:\HelloWorld\HelloWorld.exe.config.

❑ The second type of configuration file is called the machine configuration file. It is named machine.config and can be found in the C:\Windows\Microsoft.NET\Framework\v2.0.xxxx\ CONFIG directory. The machine.config file overrides any other configuration files on a machine and can be thought of as containing global settings.

The main purpose of the configuration file is to provide binding-related information to the developer or administrator who wishes to override the default policy handling of the CLR.

Specifically, the configuration file, as it's written in XML, has a root node named <configuration>, and it must have the end node of </configuration> present to be syntactically correct. The configuration file is divided into specific types of nodes that represent different areas of control. These areas are as follows:

❑ Startup

❑ Runtime

❑ Remoting

❑ Crypto

❑ Class API

❑ Security

Although all of these areas are important, this chapter covers only the first two. All of the settings discussed can be added to the application configuration file. Some of the settings (these are pointed out) can also be added to the machine configuration file. If a setting in the application configuration file conflicts with one in the machine configuration file, then the setting in the machine configuration file is used. When we talk about assembly references in the following discussion of configuration settings, we are talking exclusively about *shared assemblies* (which implies that the assemblies have a strong name, as assemblies in the GAC are required to have one).

Startup Settings

The <startup> node of the application and machine configuration files has a <requiredRuntime> node that specifies the runtime version required by the application. This is because different versions of the CLR can run on a machine side by side. The following example shows how you would specify the version of the .NET runtime inside the configuration file:

```
<configuration>
  <startup>
```

```
        <requiredRuntime version ="2.0.xxxx" safemode ="true"/>
    </startup>
</configuration>
```

Runtime Settings

The runtime node, which is written as `<runtime>` (not to be confused with `<requiredRuntime>`), specifies the settings that manage how the CLR handles garbage collection and versions of assemblies. With these settings, you can specify which version of an assembly the application requires, or redirect it to another version entirely.

Loading a particular version of an assembly

The application and machine configuration files can be used to ensure that a particular version of an assembly is loaded. You can indicate whether this version should be loaded all the time or should only replace a specific version of the assembly. This functionality is supported through the use of the `<assemblyIdentity>` and `<bindingRedirect>` elements in the configuration file, as shown in the following example:

```
<configuration>
  <runtime>
    <assemblyBinding xmlns="urn:schemas-microsoft-com:asm.v1">
      <dependentAssembly>
        <assemblyIdentity name="AssemblyName"
                          publickeytoken="b77a5c561934e089"
                          culture="en-us"/>
          <bindingRedirect oldVersion="*"
                          newVersion="2.0.50.0"/>
      </dependentAssembly>
    </assemblyBindings>
  </runtime>
</configuration>
```

The `<assemblyBinding>` node is used to declare settings for the locations of assemblies and redirections via the `<dependentAssembly>` node and the `<probing>` node (which you will look at shortly).

In the last example, when the CLR resolves the reference to the assembly named `AssemblyName`, it loads version 2.0.50.0 instead of the version that appears in the manifest. If you want to load only version 2.0.50.0 of the assembly when a specific version is referenced, then you can replace the value of the `oldVersion` attribute with the version number that you would like to replace (for example, 1.5.0.0). The `publickeytoken` attribute is used to store the hash of the strong name of the assembly to replace. This ensures that the correct assembly is identified. The same is true of the `culture` attribute.

Defining the location of an assembly

The location of an assembly can also be defined in both the application and machine configuration files. You can use the `<codeBase>` element to inform the CLR of the location of an assembly. This enables you to distribute an application and have the externally referenced assemblies downloaded the first time they are used (on-demand downloading):

```
<configuration>
  <runtime>
    <assemblyBinding xmlns="urn:schemas-microsoft-com:asm.v1">
```

```
        <dependentAssembly>
          <assemblyIdentity name="AssemblyName"
                            publickeytoken="b77a5c561934e089"
                            culture="en-us"/>
          <codeBase version="2.0.50.0"
                    href="http://www.wrox.com/AssemblyName.dll/>
        </dependentAssembly>
      </assemblyBindings>
    </runtime>
  </configuration>
```

You can see from this example that whenever a reference to version 2.0.50.0 of the assembly
AssemblyName is resolved (and the assembly isn't already on the user's computer), the CLR will try
to load the assembly from the location defined in the href attribute. The location defined in the href
attribute is a standard URL and can be used to locate a file across the Internet or locally.

If the assembly cannot be found or the details in the manifest of the assembly defined in the href attribute
do not match those defined in the configuration file, then the loading of the assembly will fail and you
will receive a TypeLoadException. If the version of the assembly in the preceding example were actually
2.0.60.0, then the assembly would load because the version number is only different by build and revision
number.

Providing the search path

The final use of configuration files to consider is that of providing the search path to use when locating
assemblies in the application's directory. This setting only applies to the application configuration file.
By default, the CLR searches for an assembly only in the application's base directory — it will not look
in any subdirectories. You can modify this behavior by using the <probing> element in an application
configuration file, as shown in the following example:

```
  <configuration>
    <runtime>
      <assemblyBinding xmlns="urn:schemas-microsoft-com:asm.v1">
        <probing privatePath="regional"/>
      </assemblyBinding>
    </runtime>
  </configuration>
```

The privatePath attribute can contain a list of directories relative to the application's directory (separated by a semicolon) that you would like the CLR to search in when trying to locate an assembly. The
privatePath attribute cannot contain an absolute pathname.

As part of resolving an assembly reference, the CLR checks in the application's base directory for it. If it
cannot find it, then it looks through, in order, all the subdirectories specified in the privatePath variable,
as well as looking for a subdirectory with the same name as the assembly. If the assembly being resolved
is called AssemblyName, then the CLR also checks for the assembly in a subdirectory called AssemblyName,
if it exists.

This isn't the end of the story, though. If the referenced assembly being resolved contains a culture
setting, then the CLR also checks for culture-specific subdirectories in each of the directories it searches
in. For example, if the CLR is trying to resolve a reference to an assembly named AssemblyName with

a culture of en and a `privatePath` equal to that in the last example, and the application being run has a home directory of `C:\ExampleApp`, then the CLR will look in the following directories (in the order shown):

❑ C:\ExampleApp

❑ C:\ExampleApp\en

❑ C:\ExampleApp\en\AssemblyName

❑ C:\ExampleApp\regional\en

❑ C:\ExampleApp\regional\en\AssemblyName

As you can see, the CLR can probe quite a number of directories to locate an assembly. When an external assembly is resolved by the CLR, it consults the configuration files first to determine whether it needs to modify the process by which it resolves an assembly. As discussed, you can modify the resolution process to suit your needs.

Dynamic Loading of Assemblies

The preceding discussion about locating and loading assemblies refers to assemblies that are known at compile time through the application's references. There is an alternative method of locating and loading an assembly that is useful for certain scenarios.

In this technique, the location of the assembly is supplied by the application, using a URL or filename. The normal rules for locating the assembly do not apply — only the location specified by the application is used.

The location is just a string variable, so it may come from a configuration file or a database. In fact, the assembly to be loaded may be newly created, and perhaps did not even exist when the original application was compiled. Because the information to load the assembly can be passed into the application on-the-fly at runtime, this type of assembly loading is called *dynamic loading*.

The Assembly class

References to assemblies, and operations to be performed on assemblies in code, are mostly contained in a .NET Framework class called the `Assembly` class. It is part of the `System.Reflection` namespace. In the code examples that follow, assume that the following `Imports` statement is at the top of the code module:

```
Imports System.Reflection
```

The `Assembly` class has a shared method called `LoadFrom`, which takes a URL or filename and returns a reference to the assembly at that location. Here's a code example of `LoadFrom` in action, getting an assembly reference from a URL:

```
Dim asmDynamic As [Assembly]
asmDynamic = [Assembly].LoadFrom("http://www.dotnetmasters.com/loancalc2.dll")
```

The brackets around `Assembly` are needed because it is a reserved keyword in Visual Basic. The brackets indicate that the word applies to the `Assembly` class, and the keyword is not being used.

After these lines are executed, the code contains a reference to the assembly at the given location. That enables other operations on the assembly to take place. One such operation is getting a reference to a particular type (which could be a class, structure, or enumeration) in the assembly. The reference to a type is needed to instantiate the type when an assembly is loaded dynamically. The `GetType` method of the `Assembly` class is used to get the reference, using a string that represents the identification of the type. The identification consists of the full namespace path that uniquely identifies the type within the current application.

For example, suppose that you wanted to get an instance of a certain form in the assembly, with a namespace path of `MyProject.Form1`. The following line of code would get a reference to the type for that form:

```
Dim typMyForm As Type = formAsm.GetType("MyProject.Form1")
```

The type reference can then be used to generate an instance of the type. To do this, you need another class in `System.Reflection` called the `Activator` class. This class has a shared method called `CreateInstance`, which takes a type reference and returns an instance of that type. (If you are familiar with Active Server Pages and older versions of Visual Basic, `CreateInstance` is functionally similar to the `CreateObject` function in those environments.) You could, therefore, get an instance of the form with these lines:

```
Dim objForm As Object
objForm = Activator.CreateInstance(typeMyForm)
```

`CreateInstance` always returns a generic object. That means it may be necessary to coerce the returned reference to a particular type to gain access to the type's interface. For example, assuming that you knew the object was actually a Windows Form, you could coerce the preceding instance into the type of `System.Windows.Forms.Form` and then do normal operations that are available on a form:

```
Dim FormToShow As Form = CType(objForm, System.Windows.Forms.Form)
FormToShow.MdiParent = Me
FormToShow.Show()
```

At this point, the form will operate normally. It will behave no differently from a form that was in a referenced assembly (except for potential code access security limitations, as discussed in Chapter 12).

If the newly loaded form needs to load other classes in the dynamic assembly, nothing special needs to be done. For example, suppose that the form just shown needs to load an instance of another form, named `Form2`, that resides in the same dynamically loaded assembly. The standard code to instantiate a form will work fine. The CLR will automatically load the `Form2` type because it already has a reference to the assembly containing `Form2`.

Furthermore, suppose that the dynamically loaded form needs to instantiate a class from another DLL that is not referenced by the application. For example, suppose that the form needs to create an instance of a `Customer` object, and the `Customer` class is in a different DLL. As long as that DLL is in the same folder as the dynamically loaded DLL, the CLR will automatically locate and load the second DLL.

Dynamic loading example

To see dynamic loading in action, try the following step-by-step example:

1. Open a new Windows Application in Visual Studio and name it DynamicLoading. On the blank Form1 that appears, drag a Button from the Toolbox, and set its Text property to Load.

2. Double-click the Load button to get to its Click event in the code editor. Then go to the top of the code module and insert the following Imports statement:

   ```
   Imports System.Reflection
   ```

3. Insert the following code into the button's Click event:

   ```
   Dim sLocation As String = "C:\Deploy\DynamicForms.dll"
   If My.Computer.FileSystem.FileExists(sLocation) Then

       Dim sType As String = "DynamicForms.Form1"
       Dim DynamicAssembly As [Assembly] = _
               [Assembly].LoadFrom(sLocation)
       Dim DynamicType As Type = DynamicAssembly.GetType(sType)
       Dim DynamicObject As Object
       DynamicObject = Activator.CreateInstance(DynamicType)

       ' We know it's a form - cast to form type
       Dim FormToShow As Form = CType(DynamicObject, Form)
       FormToShow.Show()
   Else
       MsgBox("Unable to load assembly " & sLocation & _
               " because the file does not exist")

   End If
   ```

4. Run the program and click the Load button. You should get a message box with the message "Unable to load assembly C:\Deploy\DynamicForms.dll because the form does not exist." Leave this program running while you carry out the next few steps.

5. Start another, separate Visual Studio instance, and create a new Windows Application project named DynamicForms. On the blank Form1 that appears, drag over a few controls. It doesn't really matter what controls you drag onto Form1. The version that can be downloaded for the book includes some labels, buttons, and text boxes.

6. In the properties for DynamicForms, change the application type to Class Library.

7. Build the DynamicForms project by selecting Build ⇨ Build DynamicForms from the Visual Studio menu. This will place a file named DynamicForms.dll in the project's \bin\Debug directory (or the \bin\Release directory if you happen to have the Release configuration set in Visual Studio).

8. Create a directory named C:\Deploy and copy the DynamicForms.dll file to that directory.

9. Return to the running program DynamicLoading. Click the Load button again. This time, it should load the assembly from the DLL you just copied and launch an instance of Form1 from the DynamicForms project.

Notice that the DynamicForms.dll was created and compiled after the DynamicLoading.exe project that loaded it. It is not necessary to recompile or even restart DynamicLoading.exe to load a new assembly dynamically, as long as DynamicLoading.exe knows the location of the assembly and the type to be loaded from it.

Putting assemblies to work

The previous code examples include hard-coded strings for the location of the assembly and the identification of the type. There are uses for such a technique, such as certain types of Internet deployment of an application. However, when using dynamic loading, it is common for these values to be obtained from outside the code. For example, a database table or an XML-based configuration file can be used to store the information.

This enables you to add new capabilities to an application on-the-fly. A new assembly with new functionality can be written, and then the location of the assembly and the identity of the type to load from the assembly can be added to the configuration file or database table.

Unlike application assemblies automatically located by the CLR, which must be in the application's directory or a subdirectory of it, dynamically loaded assemblies can be anywhere the application knows how to access. Possibilities include the following:

❑ A website

❑ A directory on the local machine

❑ A directory on a shared network machine

The security privileges available to code vary, depending on where the assembly was loaded from. Code loaded from a URL via HTTP, as shown earlier, has a very restricted set of privileges by default compared to code loaded from a local directory. Chapter 12 has details on code access security, default security policies, and how default policies can be changed.

Summary

Assemblies are the basic unit of deployment and versioning in .NET. Simple applications can be written and installed without knowing much about assemblies. More complex applications require an in-depth understanding of the structure of assemblies, the metadata they contain, and how assemblies are located and loaded by the CLR.

You have learned how the identity of an assembly is used to allow multiple versions of an assembly to be installed on a machine and run side by side. This chapter explained how an assembly is versioned, the process by which the CLR resolves an external assembly reference, and how you can modify this process through the use of configuration files.

You also learned about how an assembly stores information, such as version number, strong name, and culture, about any external assemblies that it references, information checked at runtime to ensure that the correct version of the assembly is referenced. You saw how you can use versioning policies to override this in the case of a buggy assembly. The assembly is the single biggest aid in reducing the errors that can occur due to DLL hell, and in helping with deployment.

The chapter also discussed the capability to load an assembly dynamically, based on a location that is derived at runtime. This capability is useful for some special deployment scenarios, such as simple Internet deployment. Understanding all these elements helps you understand how to structure an application, when and how to use shared assemblies, and the deployment implications of your choices for assemblies.

Simple applications are usually created with no strong names or shared assemblies, and all assemblies for the application are deployed to the application directory. Versioning issues are rare as long as class interfaces are consistent.

Complex applications may require shared assemblies to be placed in the GAC, which means that those assemblies must have strong names, and you must control your version numbers. You also need to understand your options for allowing an application to load a version of an assembly other than the one it would load by default, or for loading assemblies dynamically using an application-specific technique to determine the assembly's location. This chapter has covered the basics for all of these needs.

24

Deployment

Applications developed with the .NET Framework have a host of deployment options that were not available for older, COM-based software. These options completely change the economics of deployment. The changes are so important that they can even alter the preferred architecture for a system written in .NET.

Deployment encompasses many activities required to place an application into a production environment, including setting up databases, placing software in appropriate directories on servers, and configuring options for a particular installation. Deployment also includes handling changes and upgrades to the application.

This chapter covers the major deployment options for .NET applications. The previous chapter on assemblies should be considered a prerequisite for this chapter, as assemblies are the basic unit of deployment.

First, you'll look at some of the problems that can occur when you deploy applications, along with a number of terms that are used when talking about application deployment. Then you'll learn how .NET addresses many of these deployment issues. The remainder of the chapter covers the following:

❑ Creating deployment projects in Visual Studio 2008 that enable initial installation of applications

❑ Deployment of the .NET Framework itself on systems where it does not already reside

❑ Updating applications on servers, including components and ASP.NET applications

❑ Installing and updating Windows Forms applications on client machines with ClickOnce

Deployment in .NET is a huge topic that can't be covered completely within one chapter. This chapter should provide you with a basic understanding of the options available, and a desire to learn more about them.

Application Deployment

In the context of this chapter, *application deployment* includes two principal functions:

❑ The process of taking an application, packaging it up, and installing it on another machine

❑ The process of updating an already installed application with new or changed functionality

Deployment can, in some cases, also include placing the .NET Framework itself on a particular machine. This chapter assumes that the .NET Framework is installed on any machines in question. During the discussion of creating deployment projects, you will learn what to do if the .NET Framework is not available on a system.

Why Deployment Is Straightforward in .NET

As covered in the previous chapter, assemblies in .NET are self-describing. All the information needed to execute an assembly is normally contained in the assembly itself. There is no need to place any information in the Windows registry. If the CLR can find an assembly needed by an application (the process of location was discussed in the previous chapter), then the assembly can be run.

The previous chapter also discussed side-by-side execution of .NET assemblies. Multiple versions of an assembly can be executed by .NET, even if they have exactly the same interface and nominal version number. The implication for deployment is that each application can deploy the assemblies it needs and be assured that there will be no conflict with assemblies needed by other applications.

These .NET capabilities provide a range of deployment possibilities, from simple to complex. Let's start by looking at the simplest method of deployment, which harkens back to the days of DOS-XCOPY deployment.

XCOPY Deployment

The term *XCOPY deployment* was coined to describe an ideal deployment scenario. Its name derives from the DOS xcopy command. XCOPY deployment means that the only thing you need to do in order to deploy an application is copy the directory (including all child directories) to the computer on which you want to run the program.

XCOPY deployment is fine for very simple applications, but most business applications require other dependencies (such as databases and message queues) to be created on the new computer. .NET cannot help with those, so applications that have them need more sophisticated deployment.

Using the Windows Installer

The *Windows Installer* service is available on all operating systems that support .NET Framework 3.0. It was specifically created for installing applications onto a Windows system.

The Windows Installer service uses a file, called a *Windows Installer package file*, to install an application. Such files have an extension of .msi, an abbreviation derived from "Microsoft Installer." The files that make up a product can be packaged inside the .msi file, or externally in a number of cabinet files.

When the user requests that a particular application be installed, he or she can just double-click the .msi file. The Windows Installer service reads the file and determines what needs to be done (such as which files need to be copied and where they need to be copied to) to install the application. All the installation rules are implemented centrally by the service and do not need to be distributed as part of a setup executable. The Windows Installer package file contains a list of actions (such as *copy file mfc40.dll to the Windows system folder*) and what rules need to be applied to these actions.

The Windows Installer service also has a rollback method to handle failed installations. If the installation fails for some reason, the Windows Installer service will roll back the computer to its original state.

You can manually create a Windows Installer package file using the Windows Installer SDK tools, but it's much easier to use Visual Studio. Several templates in VS 2008 create projects that output .msi files, as discussed in detail in the section "Visual Studio Deployment Projects," later in this chapter.

ClickOnce Deployment

An alternative to Windows Installer for Windows Forms and WPF applications is *ClickOnce*. This deployment technology was first included in Visual Studio 2005. Creating ClickOnce deployments is simpler than creating .msi files, but the most important ClickOnce advantage is that it is designed to deploy over the Internet. ClickOnce is discussed later in the chapter in the section "Internet Deployment of Windows Applications."

New in Visual Studio 2008

Previous versions of Visual Studio have always been associated with a single version of the .NET Framework. As such, you had no choice regarding which version of the framework should be associated with your projects; if you used Visual Studio 2005, for example, then you automatically used the 2.0 version of the Framework.

Visual Studio 2008 enables you to target a particular version of the framework. You can choose to base your application on the 2.0, 3.0, or 3.5 version of the framework by selecting it from the Advanced Compiler Settings dialog, which is available by selecting the properties for a project, navigating to the Compile page, and clicking the Advanced Compile Options button. The Advanced Compiler Settings dialog is shown in Figure 24-1, and the last option in the dialog is a drop-down list for the version of the .NET Framework you want to target.

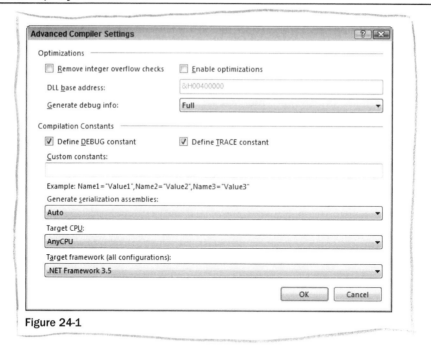

Figure 24-1

Visual Studio Deployment Projects

Visual Studio 2008 provides a set of project templates that can be used to help package your application and deploy it. Most of these templates use Windows Installer technology. Before looking at the project templates, however, it is important to understand the difference between setup and deployment. *Setup* is the process that you use to package your application. *Deployment* is the process of installing an application on another machine, usually through a setup application/process.

Project Templates

The deployment project templates available within Visual Studio 2008 can be created by the same means as any other project type, by using the New Project dialog box, shown in Figure 24-2.

As shown in the figure, you first select the Other Project Types node, and then the Setup and Deployment Projects node from the tree view of project types on the left of the dialog box. Of the six available project templates, five are actual project templates:

- ❏ CAB Project
- ❏ Merge Module Project
- ❏ Setup Project
- ❏ Web Setup Project
- ❏ Smart Device CAB Project

The sixth is a wizard (called the Setup Wizard) that can be used to help create any of the project templates listed except the Smart Device CAB Project.

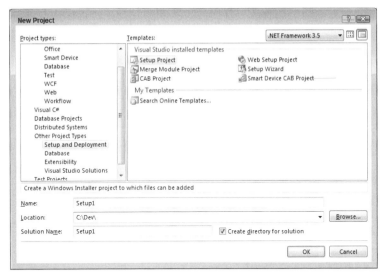

Figure 24-2

The CAB Project Template

The CAB Project template is used to create a *cabinet file*. A cabinet file (.cab) can contain any number of files. It is often used to package a set of related components in an application.

Controls hosted within Internet Explorer are often packaged into a cabinet file, with a reference added to the file in the Web page that uses the control. When Internet Explorer encounters this reference, it confirms that the control isn't already installed on the user's computer, at which point it downloads the cabinet file, extracts the control, and installs it to a protected part of the user's computer.

You can compress cabinet files to reduce their size and consequently the amount of time it takes to download them.

The Merge Module Project Template

The Merge Module Project template is used to create a *merge module*, which is similar to a cabinet file in that it can be used to package a group of files. The difference is that a merge module file (.msm) cannot be used by itself to install the files that it contains. The merge module file created by this project template can only be used within another setup project.

Merge modules were introduced as part of the Microsoft Windows Installer technology to enable a set of files to be packaged into an easy-to-use file that could be reused and shared between Windows-Installer-based setup programs. The idea is to package all the files and any other resources (e.g., registry entries, bitmaps, and so on) that are dependent on each other into the merge module.

This type of project can be very useful for packaging a component and all its dependencies. The resulting merge file can then be used in the setup program of each application that uses the component. This enables applications such as Crystal Reports to have a prepackaged deployment set that can be integrated into the deployment of other applications.

The Setup Project Template

The Setup Project template is used to create a standard Windows Installer setup for an application, which is normally installed in the `Program Files` directory of a user's computer.

The Web Setup Project Template

The Web Setup Project template is used to create a Windows Installer setup program that can be used to install a project into a virtual directory of a web server. It is intended to be used to create a setup program for a Web application, which may contain ASP.NET Web Forms or Web services.

The Smart Device CAB Project Template

The Smart Device CAB Project template is used to create a CAB file for an application that runs on a device containing the .NET Compact Framework, such as a Pocket PC device. Such applications are often referred to as *mobile applications*, and they have many capabilities and limitations that do not apply to other .NET-based applications. This book does not discuss mobile applications, so this template isn't covered here.

The Setup Wizard

The Setup Wizard can be used to help guide you through the creation of any of the previous setup and deployment project templates except the Smart Device CAB template.

Creating a Deployment Project

A deployment project can be created in exactly the same way as any other project in Visual Studio 2008. It can be standalone, or it can be part of a solution that contains other projects.

To illustrate a typical deployment project, the following section contains a simple walk-through of one of the most commonly used templates for a deployment project — the Setup Project, which is used to deploy a Windows application.

Walk-through

First create an application that will serve as the desktop application you want to deploy. Create a new project and choose Windows Application from the list of available Visual Basic project templates. Name the project SampleForDeployment and don't add any code to it yet.

Next, add a new project to the solution and choose Setup Project from the list of available Setup and Deployment Project templates. You now have a Visual Studio solution containing two projects.

When created, the deployment project does not contain any files. It has a folder called Detected Dependencies, which is discussed later. You will need to add the executable file from your Windows application SampleForDeployment to the deployment project.

You add files to a setup deployment project using the Add function, which is available in two places: You can select the deployment project in the Solution Explorer and use the Add option from the Project menu, or you can right-click the setup project file in the Solution Explorer and choose Add from the pop-up menu. Both methods enable you to choose from one of four options:

- ❏ If you select File from the submenu, you are presented with a dialog box that enables you to browse for and select a particular file to add to the setup project. This method is suitable if a file needed by the application is not the output from another project within the solution.

- ❏ The Merge Module option enables you to include a merge module in the deployment project. Third-party vendors can supply merge modules or you can create your own with Visual Studio.

- ❏ The Assembly option can be used to select a .NET component (assembly) to be included in the deployment project.

- ❏ If the deployment project is part of a solution (as in this walk-through), you can use the Project ➪ Add ➪ Project Output submenu item. This enables you to add the output from any of the projects in the solution to the setup project.

Add the output of the Windows application project to the setup project. Select the Project Output menu item to bring up the dialog box shown in Figure 24-3.

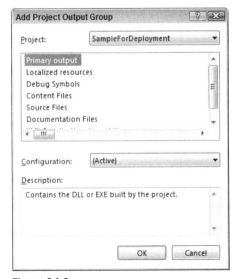

Figure 24-3

The Add Project Output Group dialog box is divided into several parts:

- ❏ The combo box at the top contains a list of names of all the nondeployment projects in the current solution. In your case, there is only one project: SampleForDeployment.

- ❏ Below the combo box is a list box containing all the possible outputs from the selected project. You are interested in the Primary output, so make sure that this is selected. (Other options for output are described in the MSDN for Visual Studio help files.)

- ❏ Below the list of possible outputs is a combo box from which you can select the configuration to use for the selected project. You will use the (Active) option here, because this uses whatever configuration is in effect when the project is built.

Click OK to return to the solution.

At this point, not only has the output from the Windows application been added to the Setup project, but the Detected Dependencies folder also contains an entry.

Whenever you add a .NET component to this deployment project, its dependencies are added to this folder. The dependencies of the dependencies are also added, and so on until all the required files have been added. The files listed in the Detected Dependencies folder are included in the resulting setup and, by default, are installed into the application's directory as application-private assemblies. This default behavior helps reduce the possible effects of DLL hell by making the application use its own copies of dependent files.

If you don't want a particular dependency file to be included in the resulting setup, you can exclude it by right-clicking the file entry under Detected Dependencies and selecting Exclude from the pop-up menu. For example, you may decide that you want to exclude a detected dependency from the setup of an application because you know that the dependency is already installed on the target computer. The dependency will then have a small "circle and slash" icon before its name to indicate that it has been excluded.

> *Dependencies can also be excluded by selecting the particular dependency and using the Properties window to set the* Exclude *property to* True. *The listed dependencies are refreshed whenever a .NET file is added to or removed from the setup project, taking into account any files that have already been excluded.*

You can select an item in the setup project in the Solution Explorer and that particular item's properties will be displayed in the Properties window. Because there are too many properties to discuss them all, we will take a look at the properties from the root setup node and each of the two different project items. First, however, make sure that the root setup node is selected, and take some time to browse the list of available properties.

The root setup node represents the output from this deployment project type: a Windows Installer package (.msi). Therefore, the Properties window contains properties that affect the resulting .msi that is produced.

Important Properties of the Root Setup Node

The ProductName property is used to set the text name of the product that this Windows Installer package is installing. By default, it is set to the name of the setup project (in this case Setup1). The value of this property is used throughout the steps of the resulting setup. For instance, it is used for the text of the title bar when the resulting .msi file is run. The property is used along with the Manufacturer property to construct the default installation directory: C:\ProgramFiles\ < Manufacturer > \ < ProductName > . The ProductName property is also used within the control panel by the Add/Remove Programs applet to show that the application is installed.

The AddRemoveProgramsIcon property enables you to set the icon that appears in the Add/Remove Programs control panel applet. The default of (None) means that the default icon will be used. You can select an icon with the (Browse) option. The icon can be a standalone icon file or you can select an executable or DLL that contains an icon you want to use.

The Title property is used to set the textual title of the application that is installed. By default, this property has the same name as the setup project.

In addition, you may need to set several additional properties of the root node. The remaining properties for the root setup node are for various advanced options and are not discussed in this walk-through.

Properties of the Primary Output Project Item

Previously, you added the primary output from the SampleForDeployment Windows application to your deployment project. It should now appear as an item in that project. Primary Output project items also have several important properties that you should know about, including the following:

Property	Description
Condition	This enables you to enter a condition that will be evaluated when the installation is run. If the condition evaluates to True, then the file is installed; if the condition evaluates to False, then the file is not installed. If you only want a particular file to be installed and the installation is being run on Microsoft Windows 2000 or better, you could enter the following for the condition: VersionNT >= 5.
Dependencies	Selecting this property displays a window showing all the dependencies of the selected project output.
Exclude	You can use this property to indicate whether you want the project output to be excluded from the resulting Windows Installer package.
Folder	This property enables you to select the target folder for the project outputs.
KeyOutput	This property expands to provide information about the main file that makes up the project output. In your case, it will show information for the WindowsApplication.exe file.
Outputs	Selecting this property displays a window listing all the files that are part of the project output, and indicates where these files are located on the development machine.
Permanent	This property is used to indicate whether the files that make up the project output should be removed when the application is uninstalled (False) or left behind (True). It is advisable to remove all the files installed by an application when the application is uninstalled. Therefore, this property should be set to False, which is the default.
ReadOnly	This property is used to set the read-only file attribute of all the files that make up the project output. As the name suggests, this makes the file read-only on the target machine.
Register	This property enables you to instruct the Windows Installer to register the files contained within the project output as COM objects. This only applies to projects (for example, the Class Library project template) that have been compiled with the Register for COM Interop project property set.
Vital	This property is used to indicate that the files contained within the project output are vital to the installation — if the installation of these files fails, then the installation as a whole should fail. The default value is True.

Properties of the Detected Dependency Items

Items that reside in the `DetectedDependencies` folder have some of the preceding properties, and they also have some read-only properties that provide you with detailed information about the item. This chapter does not include a detailed discussion of those informational properties.

This has been only a brief look at the Setup Project template. It uses all the project defaults and provides a standard set of steps to users when they run the Windows Installer package. Of course, a real application needs more than a single application file and its dependencies. You can customize the setup project extensively to meet those additional needs.

Besides adding more files to the deployment project, you may need to create shortcuts, directories, registry entries, and so on. These customizations and more can be accomplished using the set of built-in editors, which are covered in the section "Modifying the Deployment Project."

Creating a Deployment Project for an ASP.NET Web Application

Another commonly used deployment scenario is that of a Web application that has been created using the ASP.NET Web Application Project template. Typically, the Web application is developed on a development web server, and you need to create a deployment project to transfer the finished application to a production web server.

For this scenario, the template to use is the Web Setup Project template. There is one major difference between this template and the previously described Setup Project template: The Web Setup Project will, by default, deploy the application to a virtual directory of the web server on which the setup is run, whereas a Setup Project deploys the application to the `Program Files` folder on the target machine by default.

There are substantial similarities between producing a deployment project for this scenario and producing a Windows application deployment project as shown in the walk-through. They both produce a Windows Installer package and have the same set of project properties discussed earlier.

As in the previous walk-through, you need to add the output of the Web application to the deployment project. This is accomplished in much the same way as earlier, by right-clicking on a Web Setup project and selecting Add — Project Output. There is one key difference: When you add the project representing the website, the only option you have for the type of files to add is Content Files, which encompasses the files that make up the website.

As before, if you build such a project, then the result in an .msi file, which can be used in this case to deploy a website.

Modifying the Deployment Project

In the walk-through, you created a default Windows Installer package for a particular project template. You didn't customize the steps or actions that were performed when the package was run. What if you want to add a step to the installation process in order to display a `ReadMe` file to the user? Or what if you need to create registry entries on the installation computer?

This section focuses on additional capabilities for deployment projects. Most of these capabilities are accessed by using a series of "editors" to change parts of the deployment project. You can use six editors to customize a Windows-Installer-based deployment project:

- ❑ File System Editor
- ❑ Registry Editor
- ❑ File Types Editor
- ❑ User Interface Editor
- ❑ Custom Actions Editor
- ❑ Launch Conditions Editor

The editors are accessible through the View ➪ Editor menu option or by using the corresponding buttons at the top of the Solution Explorer.

You can also modify the resulting Windows Installer package through the project's Properties window. This section takes a brief look at each of the six editors and the project properties, and describes how you can use them to modify the resulting Windows Installer package. You will use the project created in the Windows application walk-through.

Project Properties

The first step to take in customizing the Windows Installer package is to use the project's property pages. The Property Pages dialog box is accessed by right-clicking the root of the setup project in the Solution Explorer and selecting Properties from the pop-up menu. You can also select the Properties item from the Project menu when the setup project is the active project. Both of these methods will bring up the dialog box shown in Figure 24-4.

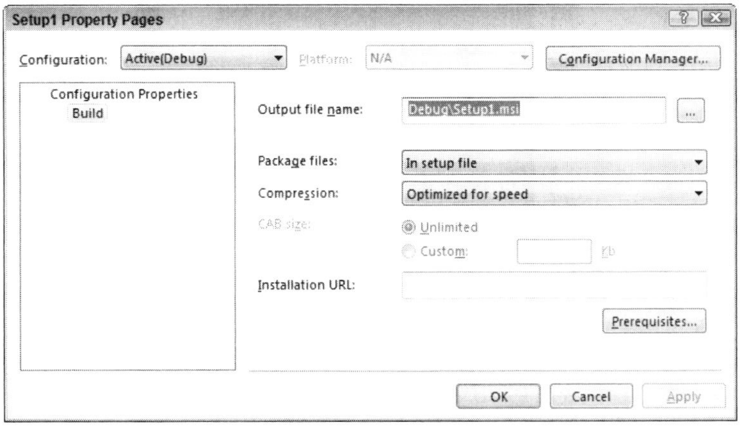

Figure 24-4

The Build Page

The only page available from the Property Pages dialog is the Build page. The options on this page can be used to affect the way that the resulting Windows Installer package is built.

As with most other projects in VS 2008, you can create different build configurations. Use the Configuration combo box to select the build configuration for which you want to alter properties. In Figure 24-4, notice that you are modifying the properties for the currently active build configuration: Debug. The button labeled Configuration Manager enables you to add, remove, and edit the build configurations for this project.

The Output File Name setting can be used to modify where the resulting Windows Installer package (.msi) file is created. You can modify the filename and path directly or you can click the Browse button.

Package Files

The next setting, Package Files, enables you to specify how the files that make up the installation are packaged. The following table describes the possible options:

Package	Description
As loose uncompressed files	When you build the project, the files that are to be included as part of the installation are copied to the same directory as the resulting Windows Installer package (.msi) file. As mentioned earlier, this directory can be set using the Output File Name setting.
In setup file	When the project is built, the files that are to be included as part of the installation are packaged in the resulting Windows Installer package file. When you use this method, you have only one file to distribute. This is the default setting.
In cabinet file(s)	With this option, when the project is built, the files that are to be included as part of the installation are packaged into a number of cabinet files.

Prerequisites

Prerequisites are standard components that may be needed to install or run the application but are not a part of the application. There are several of these, as shown in Figure 24-5, which shows the dialog that is displayed when the Prerequisites button is clicked.

The .NET Framework is checked by default, and so is the Windows Installer. You should only uncheck these if you are sure that all the machines upon which your application will be installed already have the correct versions of these prerequisites installed. As mentioned earlier in this chapter, Visual Studio 2008 allows targeting of the .NET Framework version you would like to use (2.0, 3.0, or 3.5), so the targeted version of the framework needs to be coordinated with the prerequisites.

If the box for any of these prerequisites is checked, then the resulting installation package will automatically check for the presence of that prerequisite and install it if required. If you are installing from a CD or network share, then it is common for the packages that install these prerequisites to be placed in the same location as your installation package. The default settings assume that this is true and install the prerequisites from that location.

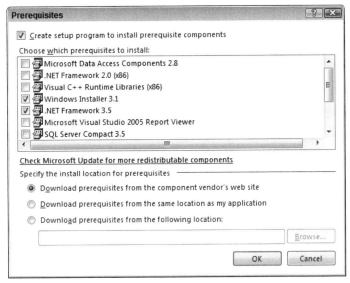

Figure 24-5

However, you can specify a different location for packages that install prerequisites. You can select the "Download prerequisites from the following location:" option at the bottom of the dialog and then specify the URL at which the packages are located. Alternately, you can select "Download prerequisites from the component vendor's web site," and then the Installation URL on the previous dialog will be used (refer to Figure 24-5).

Compression

You also have the option to modify the compression used when packaging the files that are to be contained within the installation program. The three options (Optimized for Speed, Optimized for Size, and None) are self-explanatory and are not covered. The default is Optimized for Speed.

Setting the Cabinet File Size

If you want to package the files in cabinet files, then you have the option to specify the size of those resulting cabinet file(s):

❑ The first option is to let the resulting cabinet file be of an unlimited size. What this effectively means is that all the files are packaged into one big cabinet file. The resulting size of the cabinet file depends on the compression method selected.

❑ If you are installing from floppy disks or CDs, then creating one large cabinet file may not be wise. In this case, you can use the second option to specify the maximum size of the resulting cabinet file(s). If you select this option, then you need to specify the maximum allowed size for a cabinet file (this figure is in KB). If all the files that need to be contained within this installation exceed this size, then multiple cabinet files are created.

The File System Editor

The File System Editor is automatically displayed for you in VS 2008's document window when you first create the Setup project. You can also access this editor (and the other editors that are available) via the View ➪ Editor menu option in the VS 2008 IDE. The File System Editor is used to manage all the file system aspects of the installation, including the following:

❑ Creating folders on the user's machine

❑ Adding files to the folders defined

❑ Creating shortcuts

Basically, this is the editor that you use to define what files need to be installed and where they should be installed on the user's machine. The File System Editor is divided into two main panes in the document window (see Figure 24-6).

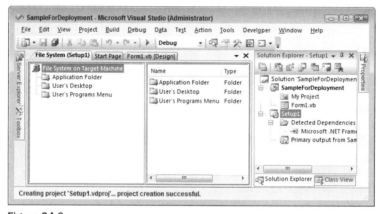

Figure 24-6

The left pane shows a list of the folders that have been created automatically for the project. When you select a folder in the left pane, two things happen: first, the right pane of the editor displays a list of the files to be installed into the selected folder, and second, the Properties window will change to show you the properties of the currently selected folder. Depending on the size of the Visual Studio 2008 window, you might not see the right-hand pane unless you widen the screen.

Adding Items to a Folder

To add an item that needs to be installed to a folder, you can either right-click the folder in the left pane and choose Add from the pop-up menu or you can select the required folder, right-click in the right pane, and again choose Add from the pop-up menu. You will be presented with four options, three of which were discussed earlier in the walk-through:

❑ Project output

❑ File

❑ Assembly

The fourth option (Folder) enables you to add a subfolder to the currently selected folder. This subfolder then becomes a standard folder that can be used to add files. If you add any .NET components or executables, the dependencies of these components are also added to the installation automatically.

Adding Special Folders

When you create a new deployment project, a set of standard folders is created for you (listed in the desktop application section). If the folders created do not match your requirements, you can also use the File System editor to add special folders. To add a special folder, right-click anywhere in the left pane (other than on a folder), and you will be presented with a pop-up menu containing one item: Add Special Folder. This menu item expands to show you a list of folders that you can add to the installation (folders already added to the project are grayed out).

You can choose from several system folders, which are summarized in the following table:

Name	Description	Windows Installer Property
Common Files Folder	Files (nonsystem) that are shared by multiple applications are usually installed to this folder.	[CommonFilesFolder]
Common Files Folder (64-bit)	Same as Common Files Folder, but for 64-bit systems	[CommonFiles64Folder]
Fonts Folder	Used to contain all the fonts that are installed on the computer. If your application used a specific font, then you should install it in this folder.	[FontsFolder]
Program Files Folder	Most applications are installed in a directory below the Program Files Folder. This acts as root directory for installed applications.	[ProgramFilesFolder]
Program Files Folder (64-bit)	Same as Program Files Folder, but for 64-bit systems	[ProgramFiles64Folder]
System Folder	This folder is used to store shared system files. The folder typically holds files that are part of the OS.	[SystemFolder]
System Folder (64-bit)	Same as System Folder, but for 64-bit systems	[System64Folder]
User's Application Data Folder	This folder is used to store data on a per-application basis, specific to a user.	[CommonAppDataFolder]
User's Desktop	This folder represents the user's desktop. It can be used to create and display a shortcut that users can use to start your application.	[DesktopFolder]

Continued

Name	Description	Windows Installer Property
User's Favorites Folder	Used as a central place to store links to the user's favorite websites, documents, folders, and so on	[FavoritesFolder]
User's Personal Data Folder	This folder is where a user stores important files. It is normally referred to as My Documents.	[PersonalFolder]
User's Programs Menu	This folder is where shortcuts are created to applications that appear on the user's Program menu. This is an ideal place to create a shortcut to your application.	[ProgramMenuFolder]
User's Send To Menu	Stores all the user's send-to shortcuts. A send-to shortcut is displayed when you right-click a file in the Windows Explorer and choose Send To. The send-to shortcut usually invokes an application, passing in the pathname of the files it was invoked from.	[SendToFolder]
User's Start Menu	This folder can be used to add items to the user's Start menu. This is not often used.	[StartMenuFolder]
User's Startup Folder	Used to start applications whenever the user logs in to the computer. If you want your application to start every time the user logs in, then you can add a shortcut to your application in this folder.	[StartupFolder]
User's Template Folder	This folder contains templates specific to the logged-in user. Templates are usually used by applications such as Microsoft Office 2000.	[TemplateFolder]
Windows Folder	The Windows root folder. This is where the OS is installed.	[WindowsFolder]
Global Assembly Cache Folder	Used to store all shared assemblies on the user's computer	

If none of the built-in folders match your requirements, you can create your own custom folder. Right-click in the left pane of the File Editor and choose Custom Folder from the pop-up menu.

The new folder is created in the left pane of the editor. The folder name appears in edit mode, so enter the name of the folder and press Enter. The folder will now be selected, and the Properties window will change to show the properties of the new folder. The properties of a folder are summarized in the following table:

Property	Description
(Name)	The name of the selected folder. The name property is used within the setup project as the means by which you select a folder.
AlwaysCreate	Indicates whether this folder should be created on installation even if it's empty (True). If the value is False and no files are to be installed into the folder, then the folder isn't created. The default is False.
Condition	This enables you to enter a condition that will be evaluated when the installation is run. If the condition evaluates to True then the folder is created; if the condition evaluates to False, then the folder won't be created.
DefaultLocation	This is where you define where the folder is going to be created on the target machine. You can enter a literal folder name (such as C:\Temp), or you can use a Windows Installer property, or a combination of the two. A Windows Installer property contains information that is filled in when the installer is run. The preceding table of special folders contains a column called Windows Installer property. The property defined in this table is filled in with the actual location of the special folder at runtime. Therefore, if you enter [WindowsFolder] as the text for this property, the folder created represents the Windows special folder.
Property	Defines a Windows Installer property that can be used to override the DefaultLocation property of the folder when the installation is run
Transitive	Indicates whether the condition specified in the condition property is reevaluated on subsequent (re)installs. If the value is True, then the condition is checked on each additional run of the installation. A value of False causes the condition to be run only the first time the installation is run on the computer. The default value is False.

Suppose you name your folder "Wrox Press" and you set the DefaultLocation property for your folder to [FavoritesFolder]\Wrox Press. You could add some shortcuts to this folder using the technique described in the following section. When the installation is run, a new folder is added to the user's Favorites folder called Wrox Press, and those shortcuts are placed in it.

Creating Shortcuts

The first step in creating a shortcut is to locate the file that is the target of the shortcut. Select the target file and right-click it. The pop-up menu that appears includes an option to create a shortcut to the selected file, which is created in the same folder. Select this option.

To add the shortcut to the user's desktop, you need to move this shortcut to the folder that represents the user's desktop. Likewise, you could move this shortcut to the folder that represents the user's Programs menu. Cut and paste the new shortcut to the User's Desktop folder in the left pane of the editor. The shortcut will be added to the user's desktop when the installation is run. You should probably rename the shortcut, which is easily accomplished via the Rename option of the pop-up menu.

This has been only a brief tour of the File System Editor. There are many additional capabilities that you can explore.

The Registry Editor

You can use the Registry Editor to do the following:

❑ Create registry keys

❑ Create values for registry keys

❑ Import a registry file

Like the File System Editor, the Registry Editor is divided into two panes, as illustrated in Figure 24-7.

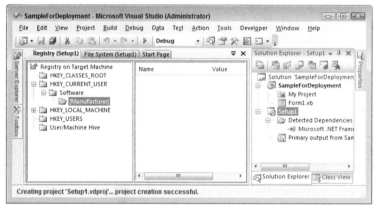

Figure 24-7

The left pane of the editor represents the registry keys on the target computer. When you select a registry key, two things happen. One, the right pane of the editor is updated to show the values that are to be created under the selected registry key. Two, if the registry key selected is not a root key in the left pane, then the Properties window is updated with a set of properties for this registry key.

When you create a new deployment project, a set of registry keys is created for you that correspond to the standard base registry keys of Windows. Notice in Figure 24-7 that there is a key defined with a name of [Manufacturer]. When the installation is run, this will be replaced with the value of the Manufacturer property described earlier in the chapter. [Manufacturer] is a property of the installation and can be used elsewhere within the installation. Several of these properties are defined and can be used in much the same way (consult the "Property Reference" topic in the MSDN documentation for a full list).

Adding a Value to a Registry Key

Before adding a value, you must select (or create) the registry key that will hold the value. There are several ways to add the registry value:

❏   Right-click the registry key and use the resulting pop-up menu.

❏   Right-click in the right-hand pane and use the resulting pop-up menu.

❏   Use the Action menu.

For illustrational purposes here, select one of the Software registry keys. The Action menu contains one item, New, which contains a number of submenu items:

❏   Key

❏   String value

❏   Environment string value

❏   Binary value

❏   DWORD value

Using this menu, you can create a new registry key below the currently selected key (via Key), or you can create a value for the currently selected registry key using one of the four Value types: String, Environment String, Binary, and DWORD.

For example, suppose you need to create a registry entry that informs the application whether or not to run in Debug mode. The registry value must be applicable to a particular user, must be called Debug, and must contain the text True or False.

The first step is to select the following registry key in the left pane of the editor:

```
HKEY_CURRENT_USER\Software [Manufacturer].
```

The registry key HKEY>_CURRENT>_USER is used to store registry settings that apply to the currently logged-in user.

Now you want to create a value that it is applicable to only this application, not all applications created by you. You need to create a new registry key below the HKEY>_CURRENT>_USER Software Manufacturer] key that is specific to this product, so select the Action ⇨ New ⇨ Key menu item.

When the key is created, the key name is editable, so give it a name of [ProductName] and press Enter. This creates a key that is given the name of the product contained within this Windows Installer package. The ProductName property of the setup was discussed earlier in this chapter.

Now that you have created the correct registry key, the next step is to create the actual registry value. Make sure that your new registry key is selected, and choose String Value from the Action ⇨ New menu and give the new value a name of "Debug".

Once the value has been created, you can set a default value for it in its Properties window; in this case `False`. When the Windows Installer package is run in the Debug registry, the value will be created. If a value already exists in the registry, then the Windows Installer package will overwrite the existing value with what is defined in the Registry Editor.

You can move around most keys and values in the Registry Editor by using cut and paste or simply by dragging and dropping the required item.

The alternative to creating registry entries during installation is to have your application create registry entries the first time they are needed. However, this has one significant difference from registry keys created with a Windows Installer package. The uninstall corresponding to a Windows Installer installation automatically removes any registry keys created during the install. If the registry entries are created by the application instead, then the uninstall has no way of knowing that these registry entries should be removed.

Importing Registry Files

If you already have a registry file containing the registry settings that you would like to be created, you can import the file into the Registry Editor. To import a registry file, you need to ensure that the root node (Registry on Target Machine) is selected in the left pane of the editor. You can then use the Import item of the Action menu to select the registry file to import.

> *Registry manipulation should be used with extreme caution. Windows relies heavily on the registry, so you can cause yourself a great number of problems if you delete, overwrite, or change registry values and keys without knowing the full consequences of the action.*

If you want to create the registry entries that are required to create file associations, then use the editor covered next.

The File Types Editor

The File Types Editor can be used to create the required registry entries to establish a *file association* for the application being installed. A file association is simply a link between a particular file extension and a particular application. For example, the file extension .doc is normally associated with Microsoft WordPad or Microsoft Word.

When you create a file association, not only do you create a link between the file extension and the application, you also define a set of actions that can be performed from the context menu of the file with the associated extension. For example, when you right-click a document with an extension of .doc, you get a context menu that can contain any number of actions, such as Open and Print. The action in bold (Open, by default) is the default action to be called when you double-click the file, so in the example, double-clicking a Word document starts Microsoft Word and loads the selected document.

Let's walk through the creation of a file extension for the application. Suppose that the application uses a file extension of .set and that the file is to be opened in the application when it is double-clicked. Start the File Types editor, which contains a single pane. In a new deployment project, this pane will only contain a root node called "File Types on Target Machine."

To add a new file type, make sure the root element is selected in the editor. You can then choose Add File Type from the Action menu, or right-click on the root node and select Add File Type. Give the new file type the name "Example File Type."

Next, you must set the extension and application for this file type. Use the Properties window (shown in Figure Figure 24-8). Enter .set as the value for the Extensions property.

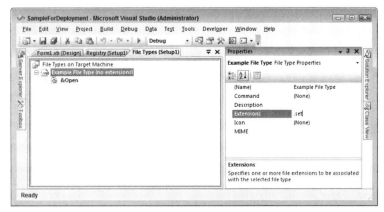

Figure 24-8

To associate an application with this file type, use the Command property. The ellipsis button for this property presents you with a dialog box from which you can select an executable file contained within any of the folders defined in the File System Editor. In this case, you'll select Primary Output from WindowsApplication (active) from the Application Folder as the value for Command.

When this new file type was first created, a default action was added for you called &Open — select it. Now take a look at the Properties window again. Notice the Arguments property: You can use this to add command-line arguments to the application defined in the last step. In the case of the default action that has been added for you, the arguments are "%1", where the value "%1" will be replaced by the filename that invoked the action. You can add your own hard-coded arguments (such as /d). You can set an action to be the default by right-clicking it and selecting Set as Default from the pop-up menu.

The User Interface Editor

The User Interface Editor is used to manage the interface that is shown during the installation of the application. This editor enables you to define the dialog boxes that are displayed to the user and in what order they are shown. The User Interface Editor appears in Figure 24-9.

The editor uses a tree view with two root nodes: Install and Administrative Install. Below each of these nodes are three nodes that represent the stages of installation: Start, Progress, and End. Each of the three stages can contain a number of dialog boxes that are displayed to the user when the resulting Windows Installer package is run. A default set of dialog boxes is predefined when you create the deployment project. Which default dialog boxes are present depends on the type of deployment project: Setup Project or Web Setup Project. Figure 24-9 shows the dialog boxes that were added by default to a Setup Project. However, if you are creating a Web Setup Project, the Installation Folder dialog box will be replaced by an Installation Address dialog box.

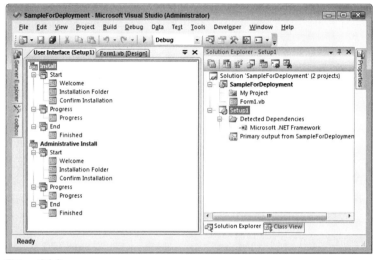

Figure 24-9

Using Figure 24-9, the following section discusses the two modes in which the installer can be run, and explains the three stages of the installation.

Installation Modes

The installation can run in two modes, which correspond to the two root nodes of the editor: Install and Administrative Install. These distinguish between an end user installing the application and a system administrator performing a network setup.

> To use the Administrative Install mode of the resulting Windows Installer package, you can use `msiexec.exe` with the `/a` command-line parameter: `msiexec.exe /a < PACKAGE > .msi`.

The Install mode is most frequently used and is what you will use in this exercise. As mentioned earlier, the installation steps are divided into three stages, represented as subnodes of the parent installation mode.

The Start Stage

The Start stage is the first stage of the installation. It contains the dialog boxes that need to be displayed to the user before the actual installation of the files begins. The Start stage should be used to gather any information from the user that may affect what is installed and where it is installed.

This stage is commonly used to ask the user to select the base installation folder for the application and which parts of the system should be installed. Another common task at this stage is asking users for their name and organization. At the end of this stage the Windows Installer service determines how much disk space is required on the target machine and checks whether this amount of space is available. If the space is not available, then the user receives an error and the installation will not continue.

The Progress Stage

The Progress stage is the second stage of the installer. This is where the actual installation of the files occurs. There isn't usually any user interaction in this stage of installation, and typically one dialog box indicates the current progress of the install, which is calculated automatically.

The End Stage

Once the actual installation of the files has finished, the installer moves into the End stage. The most common use of this stage is to inform the user that the installation has been completed successfully. It is also often used to provide the option to run the application immediately or to view any release notes.

Customizing the Order of Dialog Boxes

The order in which the dialog boxes appear within the tree view determines the order in which they are presented to the user during an installation. Dialog boxes cannot be moved between different stages.

The order of the dialog boxes can be changed by dragging the respective dialog boxes to the position in which you want them to appear. You can also move a particular dialog box up or down in the order by right-clicking the dialog box and selecting either Move Up or Move Down.

Adding Dialog Boxes

A set of predefined dialog boxes has been added to the project for you, enabling actions such as prompting a user for a registration code. If these do not match your requirements, you can add or remove dialog boxes in any of the stages.

When adding a dialog box, you have the choice of using a built-in dialog box or importing one. To illustrate how to add a dialog box, consider an example of adding a dialog box to display a ReadMe file to the user of a Windows Installer package. The ReadMe file needs to be displayed before the actual installation of the files occurs.

The first step is to choose the mode in which the dialog box is to be shown: Install or Administrative Install. In this example, you will use the Install mode. Next, you need to determine the stage at which the dialog box is to be shown. In the example, you want to display the ReadMe file to the user before the actual installation of the files occurs, which means you have to show the ReadMe file in the Start stage. Make sure the Start node is selected below the Install parent node.

You are now ready to add the dialog box. Using the Action menu again, select the Add Dialog menu item, which will display a dialog box (see Figure 24-10) from which you can choose the desired dialog box.

As you can see, several built-in dialog boxes are available. Each dialog box includes a short description that appears at the bottom of the window to inform you of its intended function. In this case, you want to use the Read Me dialog box, so select it and click OK.

New dialog boxes are always added as the last dialog box in the stage that they are added to, so now you need to move it into the correct position. In this case, you want the Read Me dialog box to be shown immediately after the Welcome dialog box, so drag and drop it into position.

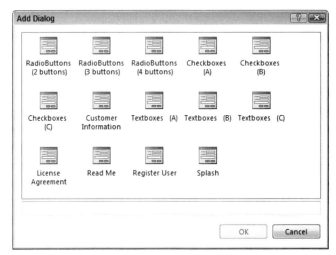

Figure 24-10

Properties of the Dialog Boxes

Like most other project items in Visual Studio, dialog boxes have a set of properties that you can change to suit your needs using the Properties window. If you make sure a dialog box is selected, you will notice that the Properties window changes to show the properties of the selected dialog box. The properties that appear vary according to the dialog box selected. Details of all the properties of the built-in dialog boxes can be found by looking at the "Properties of the User Interface Editor" topic in the MSDN documentation.

The Custom Actions Editor

The Custom Actions Editor (see Figure 24-11) is used for fairly advanced installations. It enables you to define actions that are to be performed due to one of the following installation events: Install, Commit, Rollback, and Uninstall. For example, you can use this editor to define an action that creates a new database when the installation is committed.

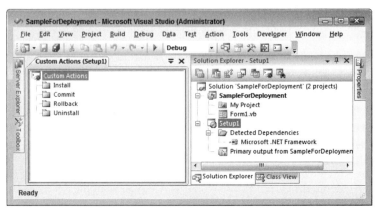

Figure 24-11

The custom actions that are added using this editor can be Windows script-based, compiled executables, or DLLs. Load the editor by right-clicking on the Setup1 project and selecting View ⇨ Custom Actions. The editor uses a tree view to represent the information. The four nodes in the tree view represent each of the four installation events to which you can add custom actions.

As with the User Interface Editor, the order in which the actions appear determines the order in which they are run, but you can modify this by dragging and dropping the actions or using the context menus of the actions to move them up or down.

Adding a Custom Action

To add a custom action you must select the node of the event into which you want to install the action. You can then use the Action menu to select the executable, DLL, or script that implements the custom action. The four actions defined in the editor are described in the following table:

Event	Description
Install	The actions defined for this event will be run when the installation of the files has finished, but before the installation has been committed.
Commit	The actions defined for this event will be run when the installation has been committed and has therefore been successful.
Rollback	The actions defined for this event will be run when the installation fails and rolls back the machine to the state it was in before the install was started.
Uninstall	The actions defined for this event will be run when the application is being uninstalled from the machine.

Suppose that you want to start your application as soon as the installation is completed successfully. Use the following process to accomplish this.

First, decide when the action must occur. Using the preceding table, you can see that the Commit event will be run when the installation has been successful. Ensure that this node is selected in the editor. You are now ready to add the actual action you want to occur when the Commit event is called. Using the Action menu again, select the Add Custom Action menu item, which will display a dialog box that you can use to navigate to and select a file (.exe, .dll, or Windows script) from any that are included in the File System Editor. For this example, select Primary output from WindowsApplication (Active), which is contained within the Application Folder.

As with most items in the editors, the new custom action has a number of properties. Here are some of the properties you are most likely to need:

Property	Description
(Name)	This is the name given to the selected custom action.
Arguments	This property enables you to pass command-line arguments into the executable that makes up the custom action. This only applies to custom actions that are implemented in executable files (.exe).

Continued

Property	Description

	By default, the first argument passed in indicates what event caused the action to run. It can have the following values:
	
	`/Install`
	
	`/Commit`
	
	`/Rollback`
	
	`/Uninstall`

`Condition`	This enables you to enter a condition that will be evaluated before the custom action is run. If the condition evaluates to `True`, then the custom action will run; if the condition evaluates to `False`, then the custom action will not run.
`CustomActionData`	This property enables you to pass additional information to the custom action.
`InstallerClass`	If the custom action is implemented by an `Installer` class in the selected component, then this property must be set to `True`. If not, it must be set to `False` (consult the MSDN documentation for more information on the `Installer` class, which is used to create special installers for such .NET applications as Windows Services. The `Installer` class is located in the `System.Configuration.Install` namespace)

Set the `InstallClass` property to equal `False` because your application does not contain an `Installer` class.

That's it. When you run the Windows Installer package and the installation is successful, the application will automatically start. The custom action that you implemented earlier is very simple, but custom actions can be used to accomplish any customized installation actions that you could want. Take some time to play around with what can be accomplished using custom actions. For instance, try creating a custom action that writes a short file into the application directory.

The Launch Conditions Editor

The Launch Conditions Editor can be used to define a number of conditions for the target machine that must be met before the installation will run. For example, if your application relies on the fact that users must have Microsoft Word 2000 installed on their machine, you can define a launch condition that will check this.

You can define a number of searches that can be performed to help create launch conditions:

- ❑ File search
- ❑ Registry search
- ❑ Windows Installer search

As with the Custom Actions Editor, the Launch Conditions Editor (shown in Figure 24-12) uses a tree view to display the information contained within it. The example shows a Custom Actions Editor that has had an item added. The steps for adding that item are covered later.

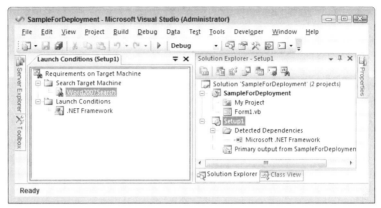

Figure 24-12

There are two root nodes. The first (Search Target Machine) is used to display the searches that have been defined. The second (Launch Conditions) contains a list of the conditions that will be evaluated when the Windows Installer package is run on the target machine.

As with many of the other editors, the order in which the items appear below these two nodes determines the order in which the searches are run and the order in which the conditions are evaluated. If you wish, you can modify the order of the items in the same way that you did with the previous editors.

The searches are run and then the conditions are evaluated as soon as the Windows Installer package is run, before any dialog boxes are shown to the user.

We are now going to look at an example of adding a file search and launch condition to a setup project. For this exercise, suppose that you want to make sure that your users have Microsoft Word 2007 installed on their machine before they are allowed to run the installation for your application.

Adding a File Search

To add a file search, you begin by searching for the Microsoft Word 2007 executable. Making sure the Search Target Machine node is currently selected in the editor, add a new file search by selecting the Add File Search item from the Action menu. The new item should be given a meaningful name, so enter `Word2007Search`. The end result is shown in Figure 24-12.

Modifying the File Search Properties

Like most items contained within the editors mentioned in this chapter, the new file search item has a set of properties that you can modify using the Properties window. The properties of the file search item determine the criteria that will be used when searching for the file. Most of the properties are self-explanatory and have been covered in previous sections, so they are not covered in this chapter.

In this example, you need to search for the Microsoft Word 2007 executable, which means that a number of these properties need to be modified to match your own search criteria.

The first property that requires modification is `FileName`. In this case, you are searching for the Microsoft Word 2007 executable, so enter `winword.exe` as the value for this property. Previous versions of Microsoft Word used the same filename.

There is no need to search for the file from the root of the hard drive. The `Folder` property can be used to define the starting folder for the search. By default, the value is `[SystemFolder]`, which indicates that the search will start from the Windows `system` folder. There are several of these built-in values; if you are interested, you can look up what these folders correspond to in the section "Adding Special Folders."

In this example, you do not want to search the Windows `system` folder because Microsoft Word is usually installed in the `Program Files` folder. Set the value of the `Folder` property to `[ProgramFilesFolder]` to indicate that this should be your starting folder.

When the search starts, it will only search the folder specified in the `Folder` property, as indicated by the default value (`0`) of the `Depth` property. The `Depth` property is used to specify how many levels of subfolders the search will look in for the file in question, beginning from the starting folder specified. Note that there are performance issues associated with the `Depth` property. If a search is performed for a file that is very deep in the file system hierarchy, then it can take a long time to find the file. Therefore, wherever possible, use a combination of the `Folder` and `Depth` properties to decrease the possible search range. The file that you are searching for in your example will probably be at a depth of greater than 1, so change the value to `3`.

There may be different versions of the file that you are searching for on a user's machine. You can use the remaining properties to specify a set of requirements for the file that must be met in order for it to be found, such as minimum version number or minimum file size.

You are searching for the existence of Microsoft Word 2007, which means you need to define the minimum version of the file that you want to find. To search for the correct version of `winword.exe`, you need to enter `12.0.0.0` as the value for the `MinVersion` property. This ensures that the user has Microsoft Word 2007 or later installed and not an earlier version.

To use the results of the file search, there must be a name for the results. This name is assigned to a Windows Installer property and is normally used to create a launch condition later. The `Property` property is where this name is specified.

For our example, enter `WORDEXISTS` as the value for the `Property` property. If the file search is successful, then the full path to the found file will be assigned to this Windows Installer property; otherwise, it will be left blank. At this point, the Properties window should look like the window shown in Figure 24-13.

Creating a Launch Condition

A file search alone is pretty useless. The second step of the process of ensuring that the user has Microsoft Word 2007 installed is creating a launch condition that uses the results of the file search.

Make sure that the Launch Conditions node is selected in the editor, and add a new launch condition to the project by selecting Add Launch Condition from the Action menu. You need to give this new item a meaningful name; in this case, give it a name of `Word2007Exists` (see Figure 24-14).

This new item has a number of properties that you will need to modify. The first property you will change is called `Message`, and it is used to set the text of the message box that appears if this condition is not met. Enter any meaningful description that explains why the installation cannot continue.

Figure 24-13

Figure 24-14

The next property that you need to change is called `Condition`. It is used to define a valid deployment condition that is evaluated when the installation runs. The deployment condition entered must evaluate to `True` or `False`. When the installer is run, the condition is evaluated; if the result of the condition is `False`, then the message defined is displayed to the user and the installation stops.

For this example, you need to enter a condition that takes into account whether the `winword.exe` file was found. You can use the Windows Installer property defined earlier (`WORDEXISTS`) as part of the condition. Because the property is empty if the file was not found, and non-empty if the file was found, you can perform a simple test to determine whether the property is empty to create the condition. Enter `WORDEXISTS <> ""` as the value for the `Condition` property.

It is hoped that based on the preceding discussion of this search, you will be able to understand how to use the other searches and create your own launch conditions. That completes our brief tour of the editors that you can use to modify the resulting Windows Installer package to suit your needs. Although you have looked only briefly at the functionality of the editors, you have seen that they are extremely powerful, and worth investment of your time for further investigation.

Building

The final step is to build the deployment or setup project you have created. There is no difference between how you build a Visual Basic .NET application and a deployment/setup project. If the project is the only project contained within the solution, then you can just use the Build item from the Build menu, which will cause the project to be built. As with the other projects, you are informed of what is happening during the build through the Output window.

The deployment/setup project can also be built as part of a multiproject solution. If the Build Solution item is chosen from the Build menu, then all the projects in the solution will be built. Any deployment or setup projects are built last. This ensures that if they contain the output from another project in the solution, they pick up the latest build of that project.

Internet Deployment of Windows Applications

The earlier discussions of creating an installation package for your application assumed that you were able to transfer the MSI file to each machine that needed installation, either electronically or via some storage medium such as a CD-ROM. This works well for installations within an organization and can work acceptably for initial installation from CD-ROMs on distributed systems.

However, the availability of the Internet has raised the bar for acceptable deployment of Windows-based client applications. Perhaps the most important advantage of browser-based applications has been their ease of deployment for the user. For Windows Forms applications to be cost-competitive with browser-based applications, low-cost deployment over the Internet is needed.

Fortunately, there are several ways to achieve low-cost deployment over the Internet, including the following:

❑   "No-touch" deployment

❑   Deployment with ClickOnce, a capability added to Visual Studio 2008

❑   Components or libraries that contain deployment capabilities, such as the Application Updater Application Block

Different deployment techniques are suitable for different applications. The following sections describe each technique and how it works, and what kinds of applications it is suitable for use with.

No-Touch Deployment

Built into all versions of the .NET Framework is the capability to run applications from a web server instead of from the local machine. There are two ways to do this, depending on how the application is launched.

First, an application EXE that exists on a web server can be launched via a standard HTML hyperlink. For example, an application named `MyApp.exe` that is located at `www.mycompany.com/apps` can be launched with the following HTML in a Web page:

```
<a href="http://www.mycompany.com/apps/MyApp.exe">Launch MyApp</a>
```

When the hyperlink is clicked on a system with the .NET Framework installed, Internet Explorer transfers control to the .NET Framework to launch the program. The Framework then tries to load the EXE assembly, which does not yet exist on the client. At that point, the assembly is automatically fetched from the deployment web server and placed on the local client machine. It resides on the client machine in an area called the *application download cache*, which is a special directory on the system managed by the .NET Framework.

If the EXE tries to load a class from another application assembly (typically, a DLL), then that assembly is assumed to be in the same directory on the web server as the EXE. The application assembly is also transferred to the application download cache and loaded for use. This process continues for any other application assemblies needed. The application is said to *trickle-feed* to the client system.

Automatic Updating

Whenever an assembly in the application download cache is needed, the .NET Framework automatically checks for a new version in the appropriate directory on the web server. Thus, the application can be updated for all client machines by simply placing an assembly on the web server.

Using a Launch Application

One drawback of this technique for deploying the application is that it can be launched only from a Web page or some other means of accessing a URL (such as a shortcut or the Start ➪ Run dialog).

To get around this limitation, you can get a similar deployment capability by using a small launching application that uses dynamic loading to start the main application. Dynamic loading was discussed in the previous chapter. In this case, the location for the assembly used in dynamic loading will be the URL of the assembly on the web server. An application that uses this technique still gets all the trickle feeding and auto-update features of an application launched straight from a URL.

Limitations of No-Touch Deployment

No-touch deployment is useful for simple applications, but it has some serious drawbacks for more complex applications:

❑ An active Internet connection is required to run the application — no offline capability is available.

❑ Only assemblies can be deployed via no-touch deployment — application files such as configuration files cannot be included.

❑ Applications deployed via no-touch deployment are subject to code-access security limitations, as discussed in Chapter 12.

❑ No-touch deployment has no capability to deploy any prerequisites for the application or any COM components that it may need.

Given the limitations of no-touch deployment, in the 2.0 version of the .NET Framework Microsoft added an alternative called ClickOnce. It is essentially a complete replacement for no-touch deployment. Thus, while no-touch deployment is still supported in .NET Framework 2.0 and higher, it is no longer recommended for use and is not covered here.

ClickOnce Deployment

ClickOnce has several advantages over alternatives such as no-touch deployment, including the following:

❑ **Updating from a web server with a user control** — No-touch deployment allows only completely automatic updating from the web server. ClickOnce can be configured for completely automatic updates from a web server, but can also be set up to allow more control by the user regarding when the application is installed and uninstalled.

❑ **Offline access** — Applications deployed with ClickOnce can be configured to run in an offline condition also. Applications that can be run offline have a shortcut installed on the Start menu.

ClickOnce also has advantages over applications installed with Windows Installer. These include auto-updating of the application from the deployment server, and installation of the application by users who are not administrators. (Windows Installer applications require the active user to be an administrator of the local machine. ClickOnce applications can be installed by users with fewer permissions.)

ClickOnce deployment can be done from a web server, a network share, or read-only media such as a CD-ROM or DVD-ROM. The following discussion assumes you are using a web server for deployment, but you can substitute a network share if you do not have access to a web server.

> ClickOnce does not require any version of the .NET Framework to be installed on the web server you use for ClickOnce deployment. However, it does require that the web server understand how to handle files with extensions .application and .manifest. The configuration for these extensions is done automatically if the Framework is installed on the web server. On servers that don't contain the .NET Framework, you will probably have to do the configuration manually.
>
> Each extension that a web server can handle must be associated with an option called a *MIME type* that tells the web server how to handle that file extension when serving a file. The MIME type for each extension used by ClickOnce should be set to "application/x-ms-application." If you don't know how to configure MIME types for your web server, ask a network administrator or other professional who can do so.

Configuring an Application for ClickOnce

For a simple case, no special work is needed to prepare a typical Windows application to be deployed via ClickOnce. Unlike the deployment options discussed earlier, it is not necessary to add additional projects to the solution. If you use standard options in ClickOnce, then it is also unnecessary to add any custom logic to your application. All of the work to enable ClickOnce deployment for an application can be performed by selecting options in the IDE.

It is possible to control the ClickOnce deployment by writing your own custom logic controlling the ClickOnce deployment processes, but that capability is beyond the scope of this book and is not covered here. Instead, this chapter explains the basic configuration of ClickOnce and common options that don't require you to write any code.

Online versus Locally Installed Applications

Applications installed via ClickOnce are one of two types:

❑   Online applications, which can be accessed by the user only when the system has a connection to the website used to deploy the application

❑   Offline applications, which can be used when no connection is available

Online applications must be launched with a URL (Uniform Resource Locator), a standard filename, or a UNC (Universal Naming Convention) filename. This may be done in various ways, such as clicking a link in a Web page, typing a URL into the Address text box of a browser, typing a filename into the Address text box of Windows Explorer, or selecting a shortcut on the local machine that contains the URL or filename. However, ClickOnce does not automatically add any such mechanisms to a user's machine to access the application. That is up to you.

Offline applications can also be launched with a URL or UNC, and are always launched that way the first time. The differences are as follows:

❑   When ClickOnce performs the initial install of the application on the user's machine, by default it places a shortcut to the application on the user's Start ➪ Programs menu.

❑   The application can be started from the shortcut, and will run with no connection to the original location used for installation. Of course, any functionality of the application that depends on a network or Internet connection will be affected if the system is not online. It is your responsibility to build the application in such a way that it functions properly when offline.

Deploying an Online Application

A deployment walk-through for a simple Windows application will demonstrate the basics of ClickOnce. This first walk-through deploys an online application to a web server, which is one of the simpler user scenarios for ClickOnce.

First, create a simple Windows Application in Visual Studio, and name it SimpleApp. On the blank Form1 that is created as part of the application, place a single button.

To enable ClickOnce deployment, access the Build menu and select the Publish SimpleApp option. The ClickOnce Publish Wizard will appear. The first screen of the wizard is shown in Figure 24-15.

Figure 24-15

The location defaults to a local web server if you have one, but as discussed earlier, deployment can be done on a remote website, a network share, or even a local directory. You should change the location if the default is not appropriate for your circumstances. Once you've verified the location to publish to, click Next.

Select one of the two types of ClickOnce applications discussed earlier. Because this example is for an online application, click the second option to make the application available online only, as shown in Figure 24-16.

Figure 24-16

Click Next to see a summary of your selections, and then click Finish. The ClickOnce deployment process will begin. A new item will be added to your project called "SimpleApp_TemporaryKey.pfx," a complete build will be done, a new virtual directory will be created for the application on the web server, and the files needed to deploy the application will be copied to that virtual directory. (The new item is discussed later in the chapter, in the section "Signing the Manifest.")

> *If your publish operation fails, look in the Output window for Visual Studio to determine the reason. Usually, either Internet Information Server (IIS) is not running or you don't have the appropriate permissions to publish to a website.*
>
> *IIS is not installed by default on Windows Vista or Windows XP. Under Vista, you need to ensure that the account in which you are developing with Visual Studio has appropriate security permissions to create new websites under IIS.*

When the process is complete, a Web page will be generated that contains the link needed to deploy the application. The Web page has a Run button that activates the link. If you click this button, the application will be deployed by ClickOnce. (You may wish to view the source for this Web page to obtain the HTML needed to launch the application from your own Web pages.)

First, the prerequisites for the application are verified. In this case, that just means the .NET Framework. If the website is remote, then you will see a Security Warning dialog much like you would get if you attempted to download a file, and you'll need to select the Run option.

Next, an Application Run - Security Warning dialog is displayed, asking if it is acceptable to run the application, as shown in Figure 24-17. You can run the application by selecting the Run button, or select Don't Run, which aborts the process. For now, select Run, and after a short delay you will see the application's form appear.

If you now make any changes to the SimpleApp application, you must publish the application again to make the changes available via ClickOnce. You can do that by stepping through the Publish Wizard once again. More details about automatic updating of ClickOnce applications are provided later in this chapter in the section "The Update Process."

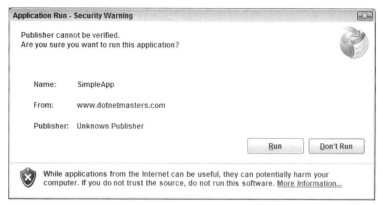

Figure 24-17

Deploying an Application That Is Available Offline

In the second screen of the Publish Wizard, if you select the first option, then the installation process has some differences:

❑ The Web page that ClickOnce generates to test the deployment has an Install button instead of a Run button.

❑ When the button is pressed, a shortcut to the application is added to the user's Start ➪ Programs menu. The shortcut is in the program folder named for the company name that was entered when Visual Studio was installed.

❑ The application is launched at the end of the install process, as it was with an online application, but future launches can be accomplished with the same URL or via the shortcut in the Start menu.

Files and Directories Produced by ClickOnce

The virtual directory used by ClickOnce to deploy your application contains a number of files for different aspects of the deployment. Figure 24-18 shows what the directory for SimpleApp looks like after ClickOnce has finished copying all needed files.

Figure 24-18

The virtual directory contains a folder for the first version of SimpleApp, which by default is version 1.0.0.0. It also contains the Web page that was displayed after ClickOnce finished, which is named publish.htm.

The next file is Setup.exe. This is an executable that does not need the .NET Framework to run. It is used during the ClickOnce process for all the activities that must take place before the application is launched. This includes activities such as checking for the presence of the .NET Framework. It is discussed further later in the chapter in the section "The Bootstrapper."

The next file is SimpleApp.application. The ".application" extension is specific to ClickOnce, and indicates the special file called a manifest, introduced in the last chapter. This is an XML-based file that contains all the information needed to deploy the application, such as what files are needed and what options have been chosen. There is also a file named `SimpleApp_1_0_0_0.application`, which is the manifest specifically associated with version 1.0.0.0.

Each version of the application has its own manifest, and the one named SimpleApp.application (with no embedded version number) is typically the currently active one. (Thus, the link to the application does not need to change when the version number changes.)

Other files associated with a version are in the folder for that version.

Signing the Manifest

Because the manifest controls the update process, it is essential that ClickOnce be assured that the manifest is valid. This is done by signing the manifest, using a public-private key pair. As long as a third party does not have the key pair, that party cannot "spoof" a manifest, preventing any malicious interference in the ClickOnce deployment process.

A key pair is automatically generated when you publish with ClickOnce. However, you can supply your own key pair if you like. Options for signing the application are discussed later in the section "ClickOnce Configuration Options."

Note that your application assemblies do not need to be signed in order for them to be used in a Click-Once deployment. Only the manifest must be signed. The manifest contains hash codes of all the assemblies involved, and those hash codes are checked before assemblies are used. This prevents malicious third parties from inserting their own versions of your assemblies.

The Update Process

By default, all ClickOnce applications check for updates each time the application is launched. This is done by getting the current version of the manifest and checking whether any changes were made since the last time the application was launched. This process is automatic, so there's nothing you need to do to make it happen, but it's helpful for you to understand the steps that are taken.

For an online application, if a change is detected, then it is immediately applied by downloading any changed files. Then the application is launched. This is conceptually similar to a browser-based application because the user has no option to use an older version.

For an application available offline, if changes are detected, then the user is asked whether the update should be made. The user can choose to decline the update. A configuration option enables you to specify a minimum version number, and that can force a user to accept an update. You will look at ClickOnce configuration options later.

If an update is made for an offline application, then the previous version is kept. The user can then roll back to that version using the Add/Remove Programs option in the control panel. A user can also uninstall the ClickOnce-deployed application from that same location.

Only one previous version is kept. Older versions are removed when a new version is installed, so the only versions available at any point in time are the current version and the one immediately before it. A rollback can be made to the immediately preceding version, but not to any earlier versions.

You can control the update process by including code in your application that detects when changes have been made and applies the changes as necessary. As previously mentioned, this chapter does not cover writing such logic. You can find samples in the MSDN documentation for this capability.

ClickOnce Configuration Options

In Visual Studio 2008, the properties for a Windows Application project include several pages that affect ClickOnce. (You can get to the properties for a project by right-clicking on it in the Solution Explorer and selecting Properties.)

The Signing tab page includes options for signing the ClickOnce manifest. There are buttons to select a particular certificate from a store or a file, or to generate a new test certification for signing. This page also contains an option to sign the assembly that is compiled from the project, but as mentioned previously, this is not necessary for ClickOnce to operate.

The Security tab page provides settings related to the code access security permissions needed by the application to run. Because the application is being deployed from a source other than the local machine, if you use ClickOnce, code access security limitations are in effect, as described in Chapter 12. A typical example of the Security tab page is shown in Figure 24-19.

Figure 24-19

Using the options on the Security tab page, you can calculate the permissions needed by the application, using the Calculate Permissions button. You can also arrange to test your application against a particular set of permissions. To do that, change from the default option "This is a full trust application" to the option immediately below it, labeled "This is a partial trust application." Then select the zone from which the application will be installed. When the application is run by Visual Studio, permission for that zone will be enforced.

All of the other ClickOnce configuration options are on the Publish tab, shown in Figure 24-20.

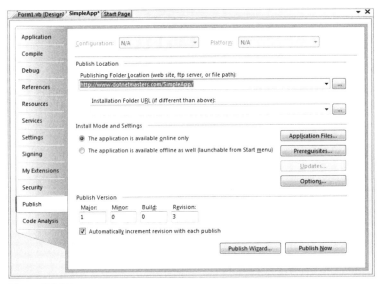

Figure 24-20

You can set many options with the Publish page, but here are some of the most important:

Property/Option	Purpose	Where to set it on the page
Publishing Location	Specifies the virtual directory, network directory, or local directory to which the application will be published by ClickOnce	Textbox labeled "Publishing Location." (Note that this can also be set in the first screen of the Publish Wizard.)
Installation URL	Specifies the location from which your application will be deployed by users. By default, this is the same as the Publishing Location, but may be set to be elsewhere.	Textbox labeled "Installation URL"
Install Mode	Selects the online only vs. offline mode for the application.	Option buttons under "Install Mode and Settings." (Note that this can also be set in the second screen of the Publish Wizard.)
Publish Version	Sets the version of the application for publishing purposes. ClickOnce requires version changes to properly auto-update the application.	The textboxes under "Publish Version." If the check box under those boxes is checked, the publish version will be automatically incremented each time the application is published.

Property/Option	Purpose	Where to set it on the page
Prerequisites	Specifies the software that must be installed before your application can itself be installed, including elements such as the .NET Framework	The Prerequisites button brings up a dialog box that enables standard prerequisites to be checked off. The .NET Framework is checked by default. The dialog also enables you to specify the location for downloading prerequisites. See the next section, "The Bootstrapper," for more information on prerequisites.
Miscellaneous options	Options for various purposes such as the product name	The Options button brings up a dialog box in which these options can be set.
Update options	Options that control the update process, including when the application updates (before or after it starts), the minimum version number required, etc.	These options are available only for applications that can run offline. The Updates button brings up a dialog box controlling these options.

The Bootstrapper

Because applications deployed by ClickOnce are a part of the .NET Framework, the .NET Framework must be available on the user's machine before your application can be installed and run. In addition, your application may require other items, such as a database or COM component, to be installed.

To provide for such needs, ClickOnce includes a *bootstrapper* that runs as the first step in the ClickOnce process. The bootstrapper is not a .NET program, so it can run on systems that do not yet have the .NET Framework installed. The bootstrapper is contained in a program called Setup.exe, which is included by ClickOnce as part of the publishing process.

When setup.exe runs, it checks for the prerequisites needed by the application, as specified in the Prerequisites options discussed previously. If needed, these options are then downloaded and installed. Only if the user's system contains installed prerequisites does ClickOnce attempt to install and run your Windows application.

The MSDN documentation includes more details on configuring and using the ClickOnce bootstrapper.

Manual Editing of ClickOnce Manifests

Sometimes an application manifest created by ClickOnce needs to be manually changed. For example, if the application contains dynamically loaded .NET DLLs (as discussed in the previous chapter), then such DLLs are not automatically included in a ClickOnce manifest.

In creating a manifest for an installation, ClickOnce relies on the compile-time references for the application being deployed. It will place any application assemblies that have compile-time references into the manifest.

However, dynamically loaded assemblies do not have a compile time reference, which means Click-Once can't put them in the manifest automatically. If you have dynamically loaded assemblies in your Windows Forms application, then you must add them to the manifest manually.

ClickOnce includes a tool for manually editing the manifest. Named MAGE.exe, it can be started from the Visual Studio 2008 command prompt. It offers a UI to open a manifest and perform various manual operations on it. MAGE.exe can also be used from the command line, so you can create batch files or PowerShell scripts to automate insertion of files in a ClickOnce manifest.

How to use MAGE.exe is beyond the scope of this chapter, but the help files for MAGE.exe are extensive, and you can find MSDN samples on using it.

Rolling Back or Uninstalling ClickOnce Applications

In addition to deploying an application for use, ClickOnce also provides the capability to uninstall or roll back applications that are deployed with the offline option. Such applications will have an entry in the Add/Remove Programs section of the control panel. That entry will offer an uninstall option; and if a rollback version is present, an option to roll back the last update.

Only one level of rollback is available. If multiple updates have occurred, then the user can only roll back to the most recent one. Once a rollback is done, no further rollback is possible until another update has been deployed.

ClickOnce versus Other Deployment Technologies

ClickOnce is a complete replacement for no-touch deployment. However, there are other deployment scenarios for which ClickOnce may not be the ideal solution. For example, ClickOnce can deploy only a per-user installation. It cannot install an application once to be used by all users on the system.

ClickOnce may be used in combination with technologies such as the Windows Installer. If you create .msi files, as discussed earlier in the chapter, you may include them as part of ClickOnce's bootstrapper process. This is an advanced technique not discussed in this book, but you can learn more about this capability in the MSDN documentation.

For cases in which ClickOnce is not appropriate, you may wish to use more customized deployment technologies, which are discussed next.

Custom Deployment Options

If an application needs deployment capabilities not covered by the technologies discussed so far, it may be necessary to use alternative technologies, or even develop them yourself. For example, you can create a deployment function that checks, via a Web service, whether updating needs to take place and that uses FTP to transfer files from a web server to a client machine.

Updater Application Block

Rather than start from scratch on such a deployment/installation technology, you can look at starting points such as the Updater Application Block. Created by Microsoft's Patterns and Practices Group, the Updater Application Block can be downloaded from Microsoft's website. It includes manifest-based checking of modules for updating, and background transfer of new modules using the same transfer technology as Windows Update.

You can use the Updater Application Block as is, or customize it for your own needs. For example, you could create a version that enables different classes of users to have different update strategies, so that new updates are sent to a select group of users first.

Summary

An application must be deployed to be useful. How an individual application should be deployed depends heavily on circumstances. Factors such as the geographic distribution of the application, its complexity, and how often it will be updated must all be considered when choosing an appropriate strategy.

The main possibilities for deployment are as follows:

❑ XCOPY deployment

❑ Installation via the Windows Installer

❑ No-touch deployment

❑ ClickOnce deployment

❑ Deployment with other technologies such as the Application Updater Block

This chapter has covered each of these, with some discussion of their applicability. It will be helpful for you to understand all of these options to make appropriate decisions for the deployment of individual applications.

On the one hand, simple utilities, for example, might be best installed by simply copying files. On the other hand, standalone applications that have many dependencies on COM-based components will more often use Windows Installer technology. Applications that depend on Web services for data will often be best deployed with ClickOnce. Corporate applications with special needs for security during installation, or that need to install an application once for multiple users, may be better off using the Application Updater Block.

You should also be aware that these options are not mutually exclusive. You might have an application with COM dependencies that needs to use an .msi file for an initial install, but gets the rest of the application and future updates via ClickOnce or the Application Updater Block. Whatever your application, the plethora of application deployment technologies available for .NET-based applications means you should be able to find an option or combination that suits your needs.

Working with Classic COM and Interfaces

However much we try, we just cannot ignore the vast body of technology surrounding Microsoft's Component Object Model (COM). Over the years, this model has been the cornerstone of so much Microsoft-related development that we have to take a long, hard look at how we are going to integrate all that technology into the world of .NET.

This chapter begins by taking a brief backward glance at COM, and then compares it with the way that components interact in .NET. It also takes a look at the tools Microsoft provides to help link the two together. Having looked at the theory, you then try it out by building a few example applications. First you take a legacy basic COM object and run it from a Visual Basic 2008 program. Then you repeat the trick with a full-blown ActiveX control. Finally, you run some Visual Basic code in the guise of a COM object.

> More information on how to make COM and VB6 code interoperate with the .NET platform can be found in Professional Visual Basic Interoperability: COM and VB6 to .NET (Wiley, 2002).

As you do all that, keep in mind one thing: COM is, to a large extent, where .NET came from. In addition, with all the time and resources that have been invested in this technology, it is important to consider the best ways to both maintain these investments and integrate them into new investments you make.

Understanding COM

Before looking into the COM-.NET interoperability story, it is important to understand COM's main concepts. This section does not attempt to do more than skim the surface, however. While the basic concepts are fundamentally simple, the underlying technology is anything but simple. Some of the most impenetrable books on software ever written have COM as their subject, and we have no wish to add to these.

COM was Microsoft's first full-blown attempt to create a language-independent standard for programming. The idea was that interfaces between components would be defined according to a binary standard. This means that you could, for the first time, invoke a VB component from a VC++ application, and vice versa. It would also be possible to invoke a component in another process or even on another machine, via Distributed COM (DCOM). You will not be looking at out-of-process servers here, however, because the vast majority of components developed to date are in process. Largely, DCOM was fatally compromised by bandwidth, deployment, and firewall problems, and never achieved a high level of acceptance.

A COM component implements one or more *interfaces*, some of which are standards provided by the system, and some of which are custom interfaces defined by the component developer. An interface defines the various members that an application may invoke. Once specified, an interface definition is supposed to be inviolate, so that even when the underlying code changes, applications that use the interface do not need to be rebuilt. If the component developers find that they have left something out, then they should define a new interface containing the extra functionality in addition to that in the original interface. This has, in fact, happened with a number of standard Microsoft interfaces. For example, the `IClassFactory2` interface extends the `IClassFactory` interface by adding features for managing the creation of licensed objects.

The key to getting applications and components to work together is *binding*. COM offers two forms of binding, early and late:

❑ In *early binding*, the application uses a *type library* at compile time to determine how to link in to the methods in the component's interfaces. A type library can exist as a separate file, with the extension `.tlb`, or as part of the DLL containing the component code.

❑ In *late binding*, no connection is made between the application and its components at compile time. Instead, the COM runtime searches through the component for the location of the required member when the application is actually run. This has two main disadvantages: it is slower and unreliable. If a programming error is made (e.g., the wrong method is called, or the right method with the wrong number of arguments), then it is not caught at compile time.

When a type library is not explicitly referred to, there are two ways to identify a COM component: by *class ID*, which is actually a GUID, and by *ProgID*, which is a string and looks something like `"MyProject .MyComponent"`. These are all cross-referenced in the registry. In fact, COM makes extensive use of the registry to maintain links between applications, their components, and their interfaces. All experienced COM programmers know their way around the registry blindfolded.

VB6 has a lot of COM features embedded into it, to the extent that many VB6 programmers are not even aware that they are developing COM components. For instance, if you create a DLL containing an instance of a VB6 class, then you have in fact created a COM object without even asking for one. The relative ease of this process is demonstrated in this chapter.

There are clearly similarities between COM and .NET, so to a large extent, all you have to do to make them work together is put a wrapper around a COM object to turn it into an assembly, and vice versa.

COM and .NET in Practice

It is time to get serious and see whether all this seamless integration really works. To do so, we have to simulate a legacy situation. Suppose your enterprise depends on a particular COM object that was written for you a long time ago by staff who are no longer in the organization. All you know about the component is that the code within it works perfectly and you need to employ it for your .NET application.

You have one, possibly two, options in this case. If you have the source code of the COM component (which is not always the case) and you have sufficient time (that is, money), then you can upgrade the object to .NET and continue to maintain it under Visual Studio 2008. For the purist, this is the ideal solution for going forward. However, maintaining the source as it exists under Visual Studio is not really a viable option. Visual Studio does offer an upgrade path, but it does not cope well with COM objects using interfaces specified as abstract classes.

If upgrading the object to a .NET component is not an option for you, then all you really can do is include the DLL as it stands as a COM object, register it on the server containing the .NET Framework, and use the .NET interoperability tools to integrate the two technologies. This is the path that this chapter takes for the example.

Therefore, what you need for this example is a genuine legacy COM object. This chapter uses a genuine legacy VB6 component to integrate within a .NET application. For the next section, this chapter steps back in time and uses VB6 for the classic component required. If you are not very interested in VB6, then feel free to skip this section. In any case, the DLL created is available as part of the code download from this book.

A Legacy Component

For the legacy component, imagine that you have some kind of analytics engine that requires a number of calculations. Because of the highly complex nature of these calculations, their development has been given to specialists, while the user interface for the application has been given to some UI specialists. A COM interface has been specified to which all calculations must conform. This interface has the name IMegaCalc and has the following methods:

Method	Description
Sub AddInput(InputValue as Double)	Adds the input value to the calculation
Sub DoCalculation( )	Performs the calculation
Function GetOutput( ) as Double	Gets the output from the calculation
Sub Reset( )	Resets the calculation for the next time

Step 1: Defining the Interface

When building any component, the first thing you have to do is define your interface. In VB6, the way to do this is to create an abstract class — that is, one without any implementation. Therefore, create an ActiveX DLL project called MegaCalculator. You do this by creating a new project and then changing its name to MegaCalculator by means of the Project⇨Project1 Properties dialog box. Then, create a class called IMegaCalc. This is what the code should look like:

```
Option Explicit

Public Sub AddInput(InputValue As Double)
End Sub
```

```
Public Sub DoCalculation()
End Sub

Public Function GetOutput() As Double
End Function

Public Sub Reset()
End Sub
```

From the main menu, select File⇨Make MegaCalculator.dll to define and register the interface.

Step 2: Implementing the Component

For the purposes of this demonstration, the actual calculation that you are going to perform is fairly mundane. In fact, the component will calculate the mean of a series of numbers. Create another ActiveX DLL project called MeanCalculator. Add a reference to the type library for the interface that you are going to implement by selecting the MegaCalculator DLL via the References dialog box that appears when you select Project⇨References.

Having done that, go ahead and write the code for the mean calculation. You do that in a class called MeanCalc:

```
Option Explicit

Implements IMegaCalc

Dim mintValue As Integer
Dim mdblValues() As Double
Dim mdblMean As Double

Private Sub Class_Initialize()
  IMegaCalc_Reset
End Sub

Private Sub IMegaCalc_AddInput(InputValue As Double)
  mintValue = mintValue + 1
  ReDim Preserve mdblValues(mintValue)
  mdblValues(mintValue) = InputValue
End Sub

Private Sub IMegaCalc_DoCalculation()
  Dim iValue As Integer
  mdblMean = 0#
  If (mintValue = 0) Then Exit Sub

  For iValue = 1 To mintValue
    mdblMean = mdblMean + mdblValues(iValue)
  Next iValue

  mdblMean = mdblMean / mintValue
End Sub

Private Function IMegaCalc_GetOutput() As Double
  IMegaCalc_GetOutput = mdblMean
```

```
End Function

Private Sub IMegaCalc_Reset()
  mintValue = 0
End Sub
```

As before, you select File⇨Make MeanCalculator.dll to build and register the component. It has a default interface called MeanCalc (which contains no methods, and is thus invisible to the naked eye), plus an implementation of IMegaCalc.

Step 3: Registering the Legacy Component

If you have made it this far, then you should now have your legacy component. When developing your new .NET application on the same machine, you do not need to do anything more because your component is already registered by the build process. However, if you are working on an entirely new machine, then you must register it there. To do that, open a command window and register it with the following command using regsvr32.exe found at C:\Windows\system32:

```
regsvr32 MeanCalculator.dll
```

You should then see the result shown in Figure 25-1.

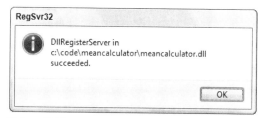

Figure 25-1

Because MeanCalculator implements an interface from MegaCalculator, you have to repeat the trick with that DLL:

```
regsvr32 MegaCalculator.dll
```

That action should yield the results shown in Figure 25-2. You are now ready to use your classic component from a .NET application.

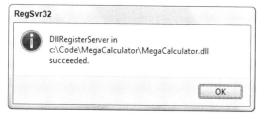

Figure 25-2

The .NET Application

For the .NET application used in this chapter, you only need to instantiate an instance of the MeanCalc object and get it to figure out a mean calculation for you. In order to accomplish this task, create a .NET Windows Application project in Visual Basic called CalcApp. Laid out, the form looks like what is shown in Figure 25-3.

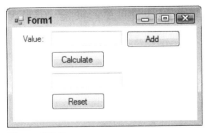

Figure 25-3

The two text boxes are called txtInput and txtOutput, respectively; the second one is not enabled for user input. The three command buttons are btnAdd, btnCalculate, and btnReset, respectively.

Referencing the Legacy COM Component from .NET

Before you dive into writing the code behind the buttons on the form, you first need to make your new application aware of the MeanCalculator component. Add a reference to the component via the Project➪ Add Reference menu item. This brings up the Add Reference dialog box, which contains five tabs: .NET, COM, Projects, Browse, and Recent. From the COM tab, select MeanCalculator and MegaCalculator in turn (see Figure 25-4).

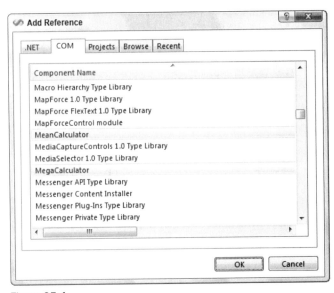

Figure 25-4

Press OK after you highlight both of the required components. Note that in the list of references in the Solution Explorer, you can now see the `MeanCalculator` and `MegaCalculator` components. If you don't see these items, be sure to press the Show All Files button in the Solution Explorer's toolbar. This view is presented in Figure 25-5.

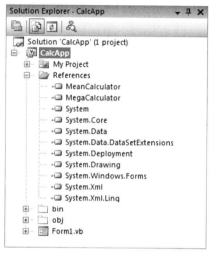

Figure 25-5

Inside the .NET Application

Now that you have successfully referenced the components in the .NET application, you can finish coding the application, using the functionality provided via the COM components. To start making use of the new capabilities provided from the COM component, add to the code a global variable (`mobjMean`) that will hold a reference to an instance of the mean calculation component, as shown here:

```
Public Class Form1

    Dim mobjMean As MegaCalculator.IMegaCalc
```

Next, create a `Form1_Load` event to which you will add the following instruction, which creates the component you are going to use:

```
Private Sub Form1_Load(ByVal sender As System.Object, _
    ByVal e As System.EventArgs) Handles MyBase.Load

    mobjMean = New MeanCalculator.MeanCalc()

End Sub
```

Finally, add the code behind the form's buttons. First, working with the Add button, add the following code that calls the COM component:

```
Private Sub btnAdd_Click(ByVal sender As System.Object, _
                         ByVal e As System.EventArgs) _
```

```
                              Handles btnAdd.Click

        mobjMean.AddInput(CDbl(txtInput.Text))

    End Sub
```

This adds whatever is in the input text box into the list of numbers for the calculation. Next, here's the code-behind for the Calculate button:

```
    Private Sub btnCalculate_Click(ByVal sender As System.Object, _
                             ByVal e As System.EventArgs) _
                             Handles btnCalculate.Click

        mobjMean.DoCalculation()
        txtOutput.Text = mobjMean.GetOutput()

    End Sub
```

This performs the calculation, retrieves the answer, and puts it into the output text box — all of this from the COM component. Finally, the code behind the Reset button simply resets the calculation:

```
    Private Sub btnReset_Click(ByVal sender As System.Object, _
                  ByVal e As System.EventArgs) Handles btnReset.Click

        mobjMean.Reset()

    End Sub
```

Trying It All Out

Of course, the proof of the pudding is in the eating, so let's see what happens when you run your application. Compile and run the application and place a value in the first text box — for example, 2 — and click the Add button on the form. Next, enter another value — for example, 3 — and click the Add button again. When you click Calculate, you'll get the mean of the two values (2.5 in this case), as shown in Figure 25-6.

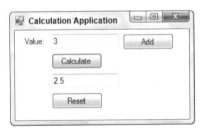

Figure 25-6

Using TlbImp Directly

In the preceding example, there is actually quite a lot going on under the hood. Every time you import a COM DLL into Visual Studio, it creates a *default interop assembly*, which is basically a .NET assembly that acts as a wrapper for the COM object. If you are doing this a lot, then it might be better to do the wrapping once and for all, and then let your application developers import the resulting .NET assembly instead. Let's see how you might accomplish this task.

The process that creates the default interop assembly on behalf of Visual Studio is called TlbImp.exe. The name stands for *Type Library Import*, and that's pretty much what the process does. It is included in the .NET Framework SDK, and you might find it convenient to extend the PATH environment variable to include the \bin directory of the .NET Framework SDK.

TlbImp takes a COM DLL as its input and generates a .NET assembly DLL as its output. By default, the .NET assembly has the same name as the type library, which will — in the case of VB6 components — always be the same as the COM DLL. This means you have to explicitly specify a different output file. You do this by using the /out: switch. If you want to see what's going on at each step in the process, then you should also specify the /verbose flag:

```
tlbimp MegaCalculator.dll /out:MegaCalculatorNet.dll /verbose
```

For this example, start with MegaCalculator, because MeanCalculator has a reference to MegaCalculator. If you start with MeanCalculator, you get an error indicating that there is a reference to MegaCalculator and that TlbImp will not be able to overwrite the MegaCalculator.dll. The way to get around this is to start with MegaCalculator by giving TlbImp the command, as shown previously. Once this is accomplished, TlbImp will inform you of the success or failure in creating a .NET assembly of the name MegaCalculatorNet.dll.

Now that you have MegaCalculatorNet.dll in place, you can work with MeanCalculator and make sure that the reference now points to the new MegaCalculatorNet.dll. You can accomplish this by using the following command:

```
tlbimp MeanCalculator.dll /out:MeanCalculatorNet.dll
    reference:MegaCalculatorNet.dll /verbose
```

The result of this command is shown in Figure 25-7.

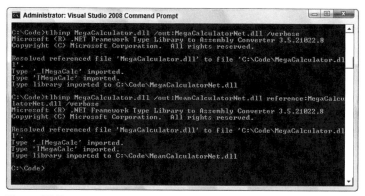

Figure 25-7

Notice that TlbImp has encountered a reference to another COM type library, MegaCalculator, and it has very kindly in turn imported MegaCalculatorNet instead. Having converted your COM DLLs into .NET assemblies, you can now reference them in an application as you would any other .NET DLL.

Late Binding

You've seen that you can successfully do early binding on COM components within a .NET application, but what if you want to do late binding instead? Suppose you don't have access to a type library at application development time. Can you still make use of the COM component? Does the .NET equivalent of late binding even exist?

The answer is yes, it does, but it is not as transparent as it is with VB6. Let's take a look at what occurred in VB6. If you wanted to do early binding, you would do this:

```
Dim myObj As MyObj
Set myObj = New MyObj

MyObj.MyMethod (...)
```

For late binding, it would look like this instead:

```
Dim myObj As Object
Set myObj = CreateObject ("MyLibrary.MyObject")
MyObj.MyMethod (...)
```

There is actually an enormous amount of activity going on under the hood here; and if you are interested in looking into this further, try *Building N-Tier Applications with COM and Visual Basic 6.0* by Ash Rofail and Tony Martin (Wiley, 1999).

An Example for Late Binding

For the sample being built in this chapter, let's extend the calculator to a more generic framework that can feed inputs into a number of different calculation modules, rather than just the fixed one it currently implements. For this example, you'll keep a table in memory of calculation ProgIDs and present the user with a combo box to select the correct one.

The Sample COM Object

The first problem you encounter with late binding is that you can only late bind to the default interface, which in this case is `MeanCalculator.MeanCalc`, not `MeanCalculator.IMegaCalc`. Therefore, you need to redevelop your COM object as a standalone library, with no references to other interfaces.

As before, you'll build a DLL under the VB6 IDE, copy it over to your .NET environment, and reregister it there. Call this new VB6 DLL `MeanCalculator2.dll`; the code in the class (called `MeanCalc`) should look as follows:

```
Option Explicit

Dim mintValue As Integer
Dim mdblValues() As Double
Dim mdblMean As Double

Private Sub Class_Initialize()
  Reset
End Sub
```

```
Public Sub AddInput(InputValue As Double)
  mintValue = mintValue + 1
  ReDim Preserve mdblValues(mintValue)
  mdblValues(mintValue) = InputValue
End Sub

Public Sub DoCalculation()
  Dim iValue As Integer
  mdblMean = 0#

  If (mintValue = 0) Then Exit Sub

  For iValue = 1 To mintVal
    mdblMean = mdblMean + mdblValues(iValue)
  Next iValue

  mdblMean = mdblMean / mintValue
End Sub

Public Function GetOutput() As Double
  GetOutput = mdblMean
End Function

Public Sub Reset()
  mintValue = 0
End Sub
```

As before, move this across to your .NET server and register it using RegSvr32.

The Calculation Framework

For your generic calculation framework, you'll create a new application in Visual Basic 2008 called CalcFrame. You will basically use the same dialog box as before, but with an extra combo box at the top of the form. This new layout is illustrated in Figure 25-8.

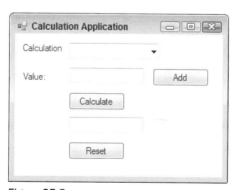

Figure 25-8

The new combo box is called cmbCalculation. For this to work, you also need to disable the controls txtInput, btnAdd, btnCalculate, and btnReset until you know whether the selected calculation is valid. Begin your application by importing the `Reflection` namespace, which you need for handling the application's late binding:

```
Imports System.Reflection
```

Once the form is in place, add a few member variables to the code of your application:

```
Public Class Form1
    Inherits System.Windows.Forms.Form
    Private mstrObjects() As String
    Private mnObject As Integer
    Private mtypCalc As Type
    Private mobjcalc As Object
```

From there, add a few new lines to `Form1_Load`:

```
Private Sub Form1_Load(ByVal sender As System.Object, _
    ByVal e As System.EventArgs) Handles MyBase.Load

    mnObject = 0
    AddObject("Mean", "MeanCalculator2.MeanCalc")
    AddObject("StdDev", "StddevCalculator.StddevCalc")

    If (mnObject > 0) Then
        cmbCalculation.SelectedIndex = 0
    End If
End Sub
```

What you are doing here is building a list of calculations. When you're finished, you select the first one in the list. Let's take a look at that subroutine `AddObject`:

```
Private Sub AddObject(ByVal strName As String, ByVal strObject As String)
    cmbCalculation.Items.Add(strName)
    mnObject = mnObject + 1
    ReDim Preserve mstrObjects(mnObject)
    mstrObjects(mnObject - 1) = strObject
End Sub
```

The preceding code segment adds the calculation name to the combo box, and its ProgID to an array of strings. Neither of these is sorted, so you get a one-to-one mapping between them. Check out what happens when you select a calculation via the combo box:

```
Private Sub cmbCalculation_SelectedIndexChanged(ByVal sender As System.Object, _
                                ByVal e As System.EventArgs) _
                    Handles cmbCalculation.SelectedIndexChanged

    Dim intIndex As Integer
    Dim bEnabled As Boolean

    intIndex = cmbCalculation.SelectedIndex
    mtypCalc = Type.GetTypeFromProgID(mstrObjects(intIndex))

    If (mtypCalc Is Nothing) Then
        mobjcalc = Nothing
```

```
                 bEnabled = False
        Else
             mobjcalc = Activator.CreateInstance(mtypCalc)
             bEnabled = True
        End If

        txtInput.Enabled = bEnabled
        btnAdd.Enabled = bEnabled
        btnCalculate.Enabled = bEnabled
        btnReset.Enabled = bEnabled
    End Sub
```

There are two key calls in this example. The first is to `Type.GetTypeFromProgID`. This takes the incoming ProgID string and converts it to a `Type` object. This process either succeeds or fails; if it fails, then you disable all the controls and let the user try again. If it succeeds, however, then you create an instance of the object described by the type. You do this in the call to the static method `Activator.CreateInstance()`.

For this example, assume that the user has selected a calculation that you can successfully instantiate. What next? The user enters a number and clicks the Add button on the form:

```
Private Sub btnAdd_Click(ByVal sender As System.Object, _
    ByVal e As System.EventArgs) Handles btnAdd.Click

    Dim objArgs() As [Object] = {CDbl(txtInput.Text)}
    mtypCalc.InvokeMember("AddInput", BindingFlags.InvokeMethod, _
        Nothing, mobjcalc, objArgs)

End Sub
```

The important call here is to the `InvokeMember()` method. Let's take a closer look at what is going on. Five parameters are passed into the `InvokeMember()` method:

❑   The first parameter is the name of the method that you want to call: `AddInput` in this case. There-fore, instead of going directly to the location of the routine in memory, you ask the .NET runtime to find it for you.

❑   The value from the `BindingFlags` enumeration tells it to invoke a method.

❑   The next parameter provides language-specific binding information, which is not needed in this case.

❑   The fourth parameter is a reference to the COM object itself (the one you instantiated using `Activator.CreateInstance`).

❑   Finally, the fifth parameter is an array of objects representing the arguments for the method. In this case, there is only one argument, the input value.

Something very similar to this is going on underneath VB6 late binding, except that here it is exposed in all its horror. In some ways, that's not a bad thing, because it should highlight the point that late binding is something to avoid if possible. Anyway, let's carry on and complete the program. Here are the remaining event handlers for the other buttons:

```
Private Sub btnCalculate_Click(ByVal sender As System.Object, _
        ByVal e As System.EventArgs) Handles btnCalculate.Click
```

```
        Dim objResult As Object
        mtypCalc.InvokeMember("DoCalculation", BindingFlags.InvokeMethod, _
                        Nothing, mobjcalc, Nothing)
        objResult = mtypCalc.InvokeMember("GetOutput", _
                    BindingFlags.InvokeMethod, Nothing, mobjcalc, Nothing)
        txtOutput.Text = objResult

    End Sub

    Private Sub btnReset_Click(ByVal sender As System.Object, _
                ByVal e As System.EventArgs) Handles btnReset.Click

        mtypCalc.InvokeMember("Reset", BindingFlags.InvokeMethod, _
            Nothing, mobjcalc, Nothing)

    End Sub
```

Running the Calculation Framework

Let's quickly complete the job by running the application. Figure 25-9 shows what happens when you select the nonexistent calculation StdDev.

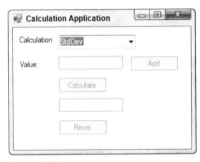

Figure 25-9

As shown in the screen shot, the input fields have been disabled, as desired. Figure 25-10 shows what happens when you repeat the earlier calculation using Mean. This time, the input fields are enabled, and the calculation can be carried out as before.

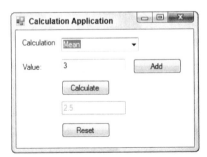

Figure 25-10

One final word about late binding. You took care to ensure that you checked whether the object was successfully instantiated. In a real-life application, you also need to ensure that the method invocations are successful and that all exceptions are caught — you do not have the luxury of having the compiler find all your bugs for you.

ActiveX Controls

Let's move on from basic COM objects to ActiveX controls. You are going to do pretty much the same thing you did with the basic COM component (apart from late binding, which has no relevance to ActiveX controls): build a legacy control using VB6 and then import it into your .NET Visual Basic project.

The Legacy ActiveX Control

For your legacy ActiveX control, you are going to build a simple button-like object that is capable of interpreting a mouse click and can be one of two colors according to its state. To accomplish this task, you will take a second foray into VB6, so if you don't have VB6 handy, feel free to skip the next section, download the OCX file, and pick it up when you start developing your .NET application.

Step 1: Creating the Control

This time, within the VB6 IDE, you need to create an ActiveX Control project. For this example, call the project Magic, and the control class `MagicButton`, to reflect its remarkable powers. From the Toolbox, select a `Shape` control and place it on the `UserControl` form that VB6 provides for you. Rename the shape provided on the form to `shpButton`, and change its properties as follows:

Property	Value
FillStyle	0 — Solid
Shape	4 — Rounded Rectangle
FillColor	Gray (&H00808080&)

Add a label on top of the `Shape` control and rename it to `lblText`. Change this control's properties to the following:

Property	Value
BackStyle	0 — Solid 0Transparent
Alignment	2Center

Switch to the code view of the `MagicButton` component. Within the code presented, add two properties called `Caption` and `State`, and an event called `Click()`, as well as code to handle the initialization of the properties and persisting them, to ensure that the shape resizes correctly and that the label is centered.

You also need to handle mouse clicks within the code. The final code of the `MagicButton` class should look as follows:

```
Option Explicit

Public Event Click()

Dim mintState As Integer

Public Property Get Caption() As String
  Caption = lblText.Caption
End Property

Public Property Let Caption(ByVal vNewValue As String)
  lblText.Caption = vNewValue
  PropertyChanged ("Caption")
End Property

Public Property Get State() As Integer
  State = mintState
End Property

Public Property Let State(ByVal vNewValue As Integer)
  mintState = vNewValue
  PropertyChanged ("State")

  If (State = 0) Then
    shpButton.FillColor = &HFFFFFF&
  Else
    shpButton.FillColor = &H808080&
  End If
End Property

Private Sub UserControl_InitProperties()
  Caption = Extender.Name
  State = 1
End Sub

Private Sub UserControl_ReadProperties(PropBag As PropertyBag)
  Caption = PropBag.ReadProperty("Caption", Extender.Name)
  State = PropBag.ReadProperty("State", 1)
End Sub

Private Sub UserControl_WriteProperties(PropBag As PropertyBag)
  PropBag.WriteProperty "Caption", lblText.Caption
  PropBag.WriteProperty "State", mintState
End Sub

Private Sub UserControl_Resize()
  shpButton.Move 0, 0, ScaleWidth, ScaleHeight
  lblText.Move 0, (ScaleHeight - lblText.Height) / 2, ScaleWidth
End Sub

Private Sub lblText_Click()
```

```
      RaiseEvent Click
End Sub

Private Sub UserControl_MouseUp(Button As Integer, Shift As Integer, _
                               X As Single, Y As Single)
   RaiseEvent Click
End Sub
```

If you build this, you'll get an ActiveX control called Magic.ocx.

Step 2: Registering Your Legacy Control

You now have your legacy control. As before, if you are developing your new .NET application on the same machine, then you don't need to do anything more, because your control will already be registered by the build process. However, if you are working on an entirely new machine, then you need to register it there. As before, open a command window and register it as follows:

```
      regsvr32 Magic.ocx
```

Having done that, you are ready to build your .NET application.

A .NET Application, Again

This .NET application is even more straightforward than the last one. All you are going to do this time is display a button that changes color whenever the user clicks it. To begin, create a .NET Windows Application project in Visual Basic called "ButtonApp." Before you start to develop it, however, extend the Toolbox to incorporate your new control by selecting Tools⇨Choose Toolbox Items. Figure 25-11 shows the resulting dialog.

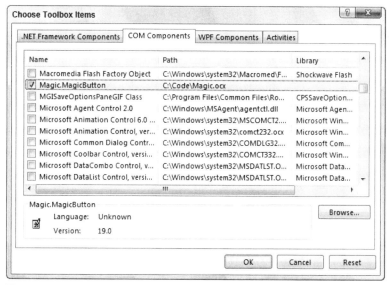

Figure 25-11

1035

When you click the OK button, your `MagicButton` class is now available to you in the Toolbox (see Figure 25-12). Add the `Magic.MagicButton` control to your form, as shown in Figure 25-13, by checking the box next to the control name. Note that references to `AxMagic` and `Magic` are added to the project in the Solution Explorer window within the References folder, as shown in Figure 25-14.

Figure 25-12

Figure 25-13

All you need to do now is initialize the `Caption` property to `ON`, change the `Text` of the form to `Button Application`, and code up a handler for the mouse `Click` event:

```
Private Sub AxMagicButton1_ClickEvent(ByVal sender As System.Object, _
        ByVal e As System.EventArgs) Handles AxMagicButton1.ClickEvent
```

```
    AxMagicButton1.CtlState = CType(1 - AxMagicButton1.CtlState, Short)
    If (AxMagicButton1.CtlState = 0) Then
        AxMagicButton1.Caption = "OFF"
    Else
```

```
            AxMagicButton1.Caption = "ON"
       End If

   End Sub
```

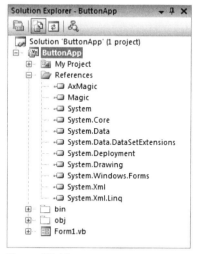

Figure 25-14

Note something slightly peculiar happening here. In the course of importing the control into .NET, the variable State mutated into CtlState. This is because there is already a class in the AxHost namespace called State, which is used to encapsulate the persisted state of an ActiveX control.

Trying It All Out, Again

When you run this application, note the control in the ON position, as shown in Figure 25-15. If you click the control, it changes to the OFF position, as shown in Figure 25-16.

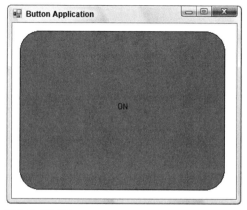

Figure 25-15

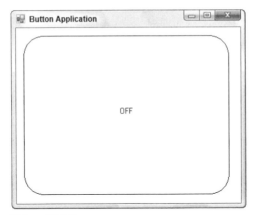

Figure 25-16

Using .NET Components in the COM World

So far, this chapter has established, through a couple of examples, that you can use your COM legacy components within any of your .NET-based applications. You do not have to throw everything out *quite* yet. Now it's time to consider the opposite question: Can you run .NET components in the COM world?

Why on earth would you want to run .NET components in the COM world? It is not immediately obvious, in fact, because migration to .NET would almost certainly be application-led in most cases, rather than component-led. However, it is possible (just) to imagine a situation in which a particularly large application remains not based on .NET, while component development moves over to .NET. Let's assume that's the case for the next section. The technology is quite cool, anyway.

A .NET Component

Let's take a look at the .NET component. Here, you will implement an exact copy of the functionality created earlier with the `MegaCalculator` and `MeanCalculator` components, except you will use Visual Basic, rather than VB6.

Begin by creating a Class Library project called MegaCalculator2. Here is the entire code of the interface for the class library:

```
Public Interface IMegaCalc

  Sub AddInput(ByVal InputValue As Double)

  Sub DoCalculation()
  Function GetResult() As Double
  Sub Reset()

End Interface
```

Now create another Class Library project called MeanCalculator3. This will contain a class called `MeanCalc` that is going to implement the `IMegaCalc` interface, in a precise analog of the `MeanCalc` in your original VB6 MeanCalculator project. As before, you need to add a reference to MegaCalculator2 first, although this time it will be a true .NET Framework reference, and you'll have to browse for it (see Figure 25-17).

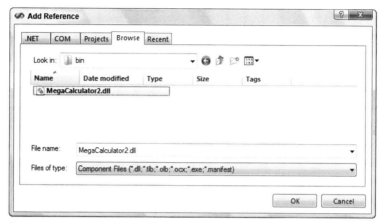

Figure 25-17

Here is the code:

```
Public Class MeanCalc
  Implements MegaCalculator2.IMegaCalc

  Dim mintValue As Integer
  Dim mdblValues() As Double
  Dim mdblMean As Double

  Public Sub AddInput(ByVal InputValue As Double) _
      Implements MegaCalculator2.IMegaCalc.AddInput
    mintValue = mintValue + 1
    ReDim Preserve mdblValues(mintValue)
    mdblValues(mintValue - 1) = InputValue
  End Sub

  Public Sub DoCalculation() _
      Implements MegaCalculator2.IMegaCalc.DoCalculation
    Dim iValue As Integer

    mdblMean = 0

    If (mintValue = 0) Then Exit Sub

    For iValue = 0 To mintValue - 1 Step 1
      mdblMean = mdblMean + mdblValues(iValue)
    Next iValue

    mdblMean = mdblMean / iValue
  End Sub
```

```
Public Function GetResult() As Double Implements _
                MegaCalculator2.IMegaCalc.GetResult
  GetResult = mdblMean
End Function

Public Sub Reset() Implements MegaCalculator2.IMegaCalc.Reset
  mintValue = 0
End Sub

Public Sub New()
  Reset()
End Sub

End Class
```

Before compiling this application, make the component that you are building COM-visible. To do this, right-click on the MeanCalculator3 solution within Visual Studio 2008 and select Properties from the provided menu.

From the Properties dialog, select the Compile tab, where you will find a check box called Register for COM Interop (see Figure 25-18). Make sure that this is checked and then compile the application.

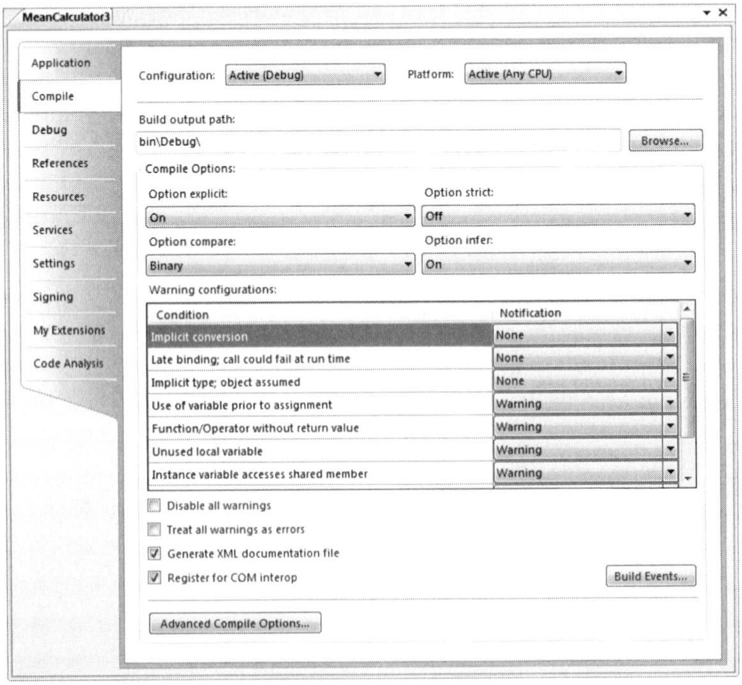

Figure 25-18

This component is quite similar to the VB6 version, apart from the way in which Implements is used. After this is all in place, build the assembly. If you have security issues with this compilation, then you need to ensure that you are running Visual Studio as an Administrator. Now we come to the interesting part: How do you register the resulting assembly so that a COM-enabled application can make use of it?

RegAsm

The tool provided with the .NET Framework SDK to register assemblies for use by COM is called RegAsm. This tool is very simple to use. If all you are interested in is late binding, then you simply run it as presented in Figure 25-19.

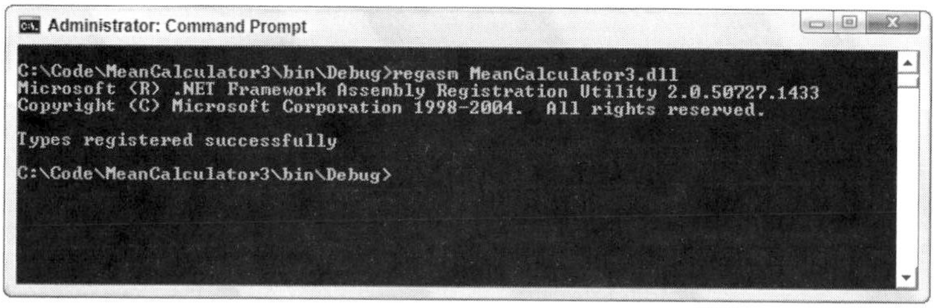

Figure 25-19

The only challenge with RegAsm is finding the thing. It is usually found lurking in C:\Windows\Microsoft .NET\Framework\2.0.50727, even if you are working with the .NET Framework 3.0 or 3.5. You might find it useful to add this to your path in the system environment. You can also use the Visual Studio command prompt to directly access this tool.

However, there is probably even less reason for late binding to an exported .NET component than there is for early binding, so we'll move on to look at early binding. For this, you need a type library, so add another parameter, /tlb (see Figure 25-20).

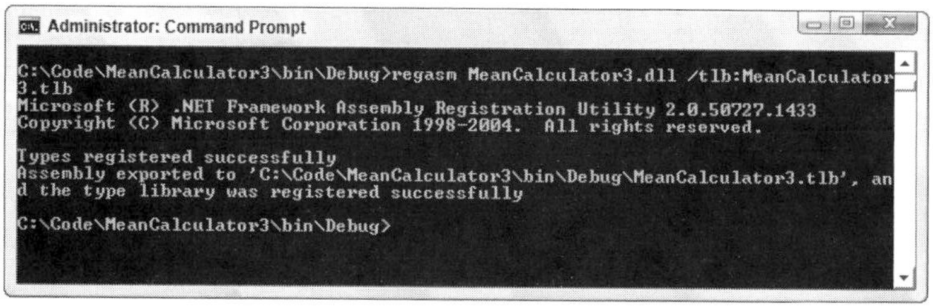

Figure 25-20

Now when you look in the target directory, not only do you have the original MeanCalculator3.dll, but you've also acquired a copy of the MegaCalculator2.dll and two type libraries: MeanCalculator3.tlb and MegaCalculator2.tlb. You need both of these, so it was good of RegAsm to provide them for you. You need the MegaCalculator2 type library for the same reason that .NET needed the MegaCalculator assembly: because it contains the definition of the IMegaCalc interface that MeanCalculator is using.

Testing with a VB6 Application

Turning the tables again, build a VB6 application to see whether this is really going to work. Copy the type libraries over to your pre-.NET machine (if that is where VB6 is running) and create a Standard EXE project in VB6. Call this project "CalcApp2." Within this project, you need to create references to the two new type libraries, so go to the References dialog box, browse to find them, and select them, as shown in Figure 25-21.

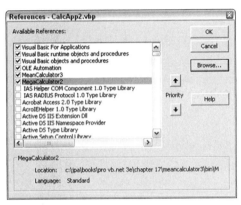

Figure 25-21

At this point, you have everything you need to create the application. Create it as you did for the Visual Basic CalcApp (see Figure 25-22). As before, the text boxes are txtInput and txtOutput, respectively, and the command buttons are btnAdd, btnCalculate, and btnReset.

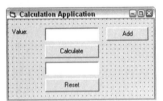

Figure 25-22

Here's the code behind it:

```
Option Explicit

Dim mobjCalc As MeanCalculator3.MeanCalc
Dim mobjMega As MegaCalculator2.IMegaCalc

Private Sub btnAdd_Click()
  mobjMega.AddInput (txtInput.Text)
End Sub

Private Sub btnCalculate_Click()
  mobjMega.DoCalculation
  txtOutput.Text = mobjMega.GetResult
End Sub

Private Sub btnReset_Click()
  mobjMega.Reset
```

```
End Sub

Private Sub Form_Load()
   Set mobjCalc = New MeanCalculator3.MeanCalc
   Set mobjMega = mobjCalc
End Sub
```

Notice that this time you have to explicitly get a reference to the interface IMegaCalc. The default interface of the component, MeanCalc, is entirely empty.

Make the executable via the File⇨Make CalcApp2.exe menu item, and then move it back to your .NET machine (unless, of course, you are already there). Run it up and see what happens (see Figure 25-23).

Figure 25-23

Well, that's not what you expected. What's happened here? In COM, the location of the DLL containing the component is available via the registry. In .NET, the assembly always has to be in either the current directory or the global assembly. All the registry is doing for you here is converting a COM reference to a .NET one; it is not finding the .NET one for you.

Fortunately, this is easy to sort out. To resolve the problem, move the two assemblies, MegaCalculator3 and MeanCalculator2, to your current directory and try again (see Figure 25-24).

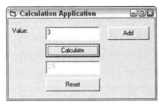

Figure 25-24

That's better. You've established that in the unlikely event of having to run .NET from a COM-oriented application, Microsoft has provided you with the tools necessary to do the job.

TlbExp

In fact, Microsoft provides you with not one, but *two* alternative tools. The other one is TlbExp, which, as its name suggests, is the counterpart of TlbImp. You can use TlbExp to achieve the same result as RegAsm in the previous section.

Summary

COM is not going to go away for quite some time, so .NET applications have to interoperate with COM, and they have to do it well. By the end of this chapter, you have achieved several things:

❑ You made a .NET application early bind to a COM component, using the import features available in Visual Basic.

❑ You looked at the underlying tool, Tlbimp.

❑ You managed to make the application late bind as well, although it wasn't a pleasant experience.

❑ You incorporated an ActiveX control into a .NET user interface, again using the features of Visual Basic.

❑ You looked at using Regasm and TlbExp to export type libraries from .NET assemblies, in order to enable VB6 applications to use .NET assemblies as if they were COM components.

## 26

Threading

One of the results of the move from 16-bit to 32-bit computing was the ability to write code that made use of threads, but although Visual C++ developers have been able to use threads for some time, Visual Basic developers have not had a truly reliable way to do so, until now. Previous techniques involved accessing the threading functionality available to Visual C++ developers. Although this worked, actually developing multithreaded code without adequate debugger support in the Visual Basic environment was nothing short of a nightmare.

For most developers, the primary motivation for multithreading is the ability to perform long-running tasks in the background while still providing the user with an interactive interface. Another common scenario is when building server-side code that can perform multiple long-running tasks at the same time. In that case, each task can be run on a separate thread, enabling all the tasks to run in parallel.

This chapter introduces you to the various objects in the .NET Framework that enable any .NET language to be used to develop multithreaded applications.

What Is a Thread?

The term *thread* really refers to *thread of execution*. When your program is running, the CPU is actually running a sequence of processor instructions, one after another. You can think of these sequential instructions as forming a thread that is being executed by the CPU. A thread is, in effect, a pointer to the currently executing instruction in the sequence of instructions that make up the application. This pointer starts at the top of the program and moves through each line, branching and looping when it comes across decisions and loops. When the program is no longer needed, the pointer steps outside of the program code and the program is effectively stopped.

Most applications have only one thread, so they are only executing one sequence of instructions. Some applications have more than one thread, so they can simultaneously execute more than one sequence of instructions. It is important to realize that each CPU in your computer can only execute one thread at a time, with the exception of hyperthreaded processors that essentially contain multiple CPUs inside a single CPU. If you have only one CPU, then your computer can execute only one thread at a time. Even when an application has several threads, only one can run at a time in this case. If your computer has two or more CPUs, then each CPU will run a different thread at the same time. In this case, more than one thread in your application may run at the same time, each on a different CPU.

Of course, when you have a computer with only one CPU, on which several programs can be actively running at the same time, the statements in the previous paragraph fly in the face of visual evidence. Yet it is true that only one thread can execute at a time on a single-CPU machine. What you *perceive* to be simultaneously running applications is really an illusion created by the Windows operating system through a technique called *preemptive multithreading*, which is discussed later in the chapter.

All applications have at least one thread — otherwise, they could not do any work, as there would be no pointer to the thread of execution. The principle of a thread is that it enables your program to perform multiple actions, potentially at the same time. Each sequence of instructions is executed independently of other threads.

The classic example of *multithreaded* functionality is Microsoft Word's spell checker. When the program starts, the execution pointer begins at the top of the program and eventually gets itself into a position where you are able to start writing code. However, at some point Word starts another thread and creates another execution pointer. As you type, this new thread examines the text and flags any spelling errors as you go, encircling them with a red oval (see Figure 26-1).

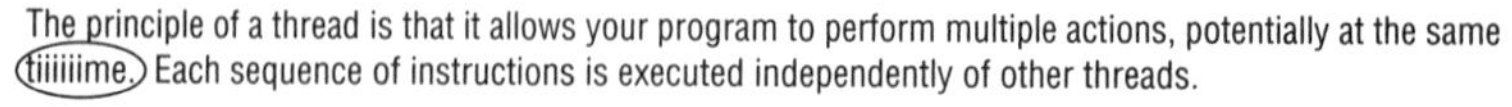

The principle of a thread is that it allows your program to perform multiple actions, potentially at the same (tiiiiiime.) Each sequence of instructions is executed independently of other threads.

Figure 26-1

Every application has one primary thread, which serves as the main process thread through the application. Imagine you have an application that starts up, loads a file from disk, performs some processing on the data in the file, writes a new file, and then quits. Functionally, it might look like Figure 26-2.

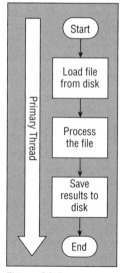

Figure 26-2

This simple application needs only a single thread. When the program is told to run, Windows creates a new process and creates the *primary thread*. To understand more about exactly what it is that a thread does, you need to understand how Windows and the computer's processor deal with different processes.

Processes, AppDomains, and Threads

Windows is capable of keeping many programs in memory at once and enabling the user to switch between them. Windows can also run programs in the background, possibly under different user identities. The capability to run many programs at once is called *multitasking*.

Each of the programs that your computer keeps in memory runs in a single *process*. A process is an isolated region of memory that contains a program's code and data. All programs run within a process, and code running in one process cannot access the memory within any other process. This prevents one program from interfering with any other program.

The process is started when the program starts, and exists for as long as the program is running. When a process is started, Windows sets up an isolated memory area for the program and loads the program's code into that area of memory. It then starts the main thread for the process, pointing it at the first instruction in the program. From that point, the thread runs the sequence of instructions defined by the program.

Windows supports *multithreading*, so the main thread might execute instructions that create more threads within the same process. These other threads run within the same memory space as the main thread — all sharing the same memory. Threads within a process are not isolated from each other. One thread in a process can tamper with data being used by other threads in that same process. However, a thread in one process cannot tamper with data being used by threads in any other processes on the computer.

At this point, you should understand that Windows loads program code into a process and executes that code on one or more threads. The .NET Framework adds another concept to the mix: the *AppDomain*. An AppDomain is very much like a process in concept. Each AppDomain is an isolated region of memory, and code running in one AppDomain cannot access the memory of another AppDomain.

The .NET Framework introduced the AppDomain to make it possible to run multiple, isolated programs within the same Windows process. It turns out to be relatively expensive to create a Windows process in terms of time and memory. It is much cheaper to create a new AppDomain within an existing process.

Remember that Windows has no concept of an AppDomain; it only understands the concept of a process. The only way to get *any* code to run under Windows is to load it into a process. This means that each .NET AppDomain exists within a process. The result is that all .NET code runs within an AppDomain *and* within a Windows process (see Figure 26-3).

In most cases, a Windows process contains one AppDomain, which contains your program's code. The main thread of the process executes your program's instructions, so the existence of the AppDomain is largely invisible to your program.

In some cases, most notably ASP.NET, a Windows process will contain multiple AppDomains, each with a separate program loaded (see Figure 26-4).

ASP.NET uses this technique to isolate Web applications from each other without having to start an expensive new Windows process for each virtual root on the server.

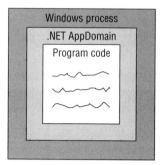

Figure 26-3

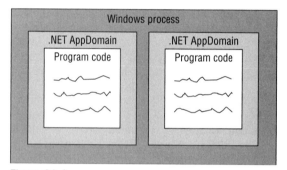

Figure 26-4

Note that AppDomains do not change the relationship between a process and threads. Each process has a main thread and may have other threads. Therefore, even in the ASP.NET process, with multiple AppDomains, there is only one main thread. Of course, ASP.NET creates other threads, so multiple Web applications can execute simultaneously, but there is only a single main thread in the entire process.

Thread Scheduling

It was noted earlier that visual evidence suggests that multiple programs, and thus multiple threads, execute simultaneously, even on a single-CPU computer. Again, this is an illusion created by the operating system, through the use of a concept called *time slicing* or *time sharing*.

In reality, only one thread runs on each CPU at a time, with the exception of hyperthreaded processors, which are essentially multiple CPUs in one. In a single-CPU machine, this means that only one thread is ever executing at any one time. To provide the illusion that many things are happening at the same time, the operating system never lets any one thread run for very long, giving other threads a chance to get a bit of work done as well. As a result, it *appears* that the computer is executing several threads at the same time.

The length of time each thread is allowed to run is called a *quantum*. Although a quantum can vary, it is typically around 20 milliseconds. After a thread has run for its quantum, the OS stops the thread and allows another thread to run. When that thread reaches its quantum, yet another thread is allowed to run, and so on. A thread can also give up the CPU before it reaches its quantum. This happens frequently, as most I/O operations and numerous other interactions with the Windows operating system cause a thread to give up the CPU.

Because the length of time each thread can run is so short, it isn't noticeable that threads are being started and stopped. This is the same concept animators use when creating cartoons or other animated media. As long as the changes happen faster than you can perceive them, you have the illusion of motion, or, in this case, simultaneous execution of code.

The technology used by Windows is called *preemptive multitasking*. It is preemptive because no thread is ever allowed to run beyond its quantum. The operating system always intervenes and allows other threads to run. This ensures that no single thread can consume all the processing power on the machine to the detriment of other threads.

It also means that you can never be sure when your thread will be interrupted and another thread allowed to run. This is the primary source of multithreading's complexity, as it can cause race conditions when two threads access the same memory. If you attempt to solve a race condition with a lock, it can cause deadlock conditions when two threads attempt to access the same lock. You will learn more about these concepts later. For now, understand that writing multithreaded code can be exceedingly difficult.

The entity that executes code in Windows is the thread. Therefore, the operating system is primarily focused on scheduling threads to keep the CPU or CPUs busy at all times. The operating system does not schedule either processes or AppDomains. Processes and AppDomains are merely regions of memory that contain your code — threads are what execute the code.

Threads have priorities, and Windows always allows higher priority threads to run before lower priority threads. In fact, if a higher priority thread is ready to run, Windows will cut short a lower priority thread's quantum to allow the higher priority thread to execute sooner. In short, Windows has a bias toward threads of higher priority.

Setting thread priorities can be useful in situations where you have a process that requires a lot of processor muscle but it doesn't matter how long the process takes to do its work. Setting a program's thread to a low priority allows that program to run continuously with little impact on other programs, so if you need to use Word or Outlook or another application, Windows gives more processor time to these applications and less time to the low-priority program. This enables the computer to work smoothly and efficiently for the user, letting the low-priority program only use otherwise wasted CPU power.

Threads may also voluntarily suspend themselves before their quantum is complete. This happens frequently — for example, when a thread attempts to read data from a file. It takes significant time for the I/O subsystem to locate the file and start retrieving the data. You cannot have the CPU sitting idle during that time, especially when other threads could be running. Instead, the thread enters a wait state to indicate that it is waiting for an external event. The Windows scheduler immediately locates and runs the next ready thread, keeping the CPU busy while the first thread waits for its data.

Windows also automatically suspends and resumes threads depending on perceived processing needs, the various priority settings, and so on. Suppose you are running one AppDomain containing two threads. If you can somehow mark the second thread as dormant (in other words, tell Windows that it has nothing to do), then there's no need for Windows to allocate time to it. Effectively, the first thread receives 100 percent of the processor horsepower available to that process. When a thread is marked as dormant, it is said to be in a *wait state*.

Windows is particularly good at managing processes and threads. It is a core part of Windows' functionality, so its developers have spent a lot of time ensuring that it is super-efficient and as bug-free as possible. This means that creating and spinning up threads is very easy to do and happens very quickly. In addition, threads only consume a small amount of system resources. However, there is a caveat you should be aware of.

The act of stopping one thread and starting another is called *context switching*. This switching happens relatively quickly, but only if you are careful with the number of threads you create. Remember that this happens for each active thread at the end of each quantum (if not before) — so after at most 20 milliseconds. If you spin up too many threads, the operating system spends all its time switching between different threads, perhaps even getting to a point where the code in the thread doesn't get a chance to run because as soon as you've started the thread it's time for it to stop again.

Creating thousands of threads is not the right solution. What you need is a balance between the number of threads that your application requires and the number of threads that Windows can handle. There is no magic number or right answer to the question of how many threads you should create. Just be aware of context switching and experiment a little.

Consider the Microsoft Word spell check example. The thread that performs the spell check is around all the time. Imagine you have a blank document containing no text. At this point, the spell check thread is in a wait state. If you type a single word into the document and then pause, Word will pass that word over to the thread and signal it to start working. The thread uses its own slice of the processor power to examine the word. If it finds something wrong with it, then it tells the primary thread that a spelling problem was found and that the user needs to be alerted. At this point, the spell check thread drops back into a wait state until more text is entered into the document. Word does not spin up the thread whenever it needs to perform a check — rather, the thread runs all the time, but if it has nothing to do, it drops into this efficient wait state. (You will learn about how the thread starts again later.)

Again, this is an oversimplification. Word actually "wakes up" the thread at various times, but the basic principle is sound — the thread is given work to do, it reports the results, and then it starts waiting for the next chunk of work to do. So why is all this important? If you plan to author multithreaded applications, then you need to understand how the operating system will be scheduling your threads, as well as the threads of all other processes on the system. Most important, you need to recognize that your thread can be interrupted at any time so that another thread can run.

Thread Safety and Thread Affinity

Most of the .NET Framework base class library is not *thread safe*. Thread-safe code is code that can be called by multiple threads at the same time without negative side effects. If code is not thread safe, then calling that code from multiple threads at the same time can result in unpredictable and undesirable side effects, potentially even crashing your application. When dealing with objects that are not thread safe, you must ensure that multiple threads never simultaneously interact with the same object.

For example, suppose you have a `ListBox` control (or any other control) on a Windows Form and you start updating that control with data from multiple threads. You will find that your results are undependable. Sometimes you will see all your data in order, but other times it will be out of order, and other times some data will be missing. This is because Windows Forms controls are not thread safe and don't behave properly when used by multiple threads at the same time.

To determine whether any specific method in the .NET Base Class Library is thread safe, refer to the online help. If no mention of threading appears in association with the method, then the method is *not* thread safe.

The Windows Forms subset of the .NET Framework is not only not thread safe, it also has *thread affinity*. Thread affinity means that objects created by a thread can only be used by that thread. Other threads should never interact with those objects. In the case of Windows Forms, this means that you must ensure that multiple threads never interact with Windows Forms objects (such as forms and controls). This is important because when you are creating interactive, multithreaded applications, you must ensure that only the thread that created a form interacts directly with that form.

As you will see, Windows Forms includes technology by which a background thread can safely make method calls on forms and controls by transferring the method call to the thread that owns the form.

When to Use Threads

If we regard computer programs as being either application software or service software, we find there are different motivators for each one. Application software uses threads primarily to deliver a better user experience. Common examples are as follows:

❑ **Microsoft Word** — Background spell checker

❑ **Microsoft Word** — Background printing

❑ **Microsoft Outlook** — Background sending and receiving of e-mail

❑ **Microsoft Excel** — Background recalculation

In all of these cases, threads are used to do "something in the background." This provides a better user experience. For example, you can still edit a Word document while Word is spooling another document to the printer. Similarly, you can still read e-mails while Outlook is sending your new e-mail. As an application developer, you should use threads to enhance the user experience. At some point during the application startup, code running in the primary thread will have spun up another thread to be used for spell checking. As part of the "allow user to edit the document" process, you give the spell checker thread some words to check. This thread separation means that the user can continue to type, even though spell checking is still taking place.

Service software uses threads to both deliver scalability and improve the service offered. For example, imagine you have a web server that receives six incoming connections simultaneously. That server needs to service each of the requests in parallel; otherwise, the sixth thread would have to wait for you to finish threads one through five before it was even started. Figure 26-5 shows how IIS might handle incoming requests.

The primary motivation for multiple threads in a service like this is to keep the CPU busy servicing user requests even when other user requests are blocked waiting for data or other events. If you have six user requests, the odds are high that some or all of them will read from files or databases and thus will spend many milliseconds in wait states. While some of the user requests are in wait states, other user requests need CPU time and can be scheduled to run. The result is higher scalability because the CPU, I/O, and other subsystems of the computer are kept as busy as possible at all times.

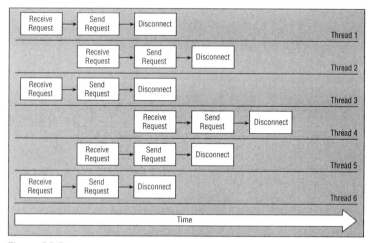

Figure 26-5

Designing a Background Task

The specific goals and requirements for background processing in an interactive application are quite different from a server application. By "interactive application" we are talking about Windows Forms or Console applications. While a Web application might be somewhat interactive, in fact, all your code runs on the server, and so Web applications are server applications when it comes to threading.

Interactive Applications

In the case of interactive applications (typically, Windows Forms applications), your design must center on having the background thread do useful work, but also interact appropriately (and safely) with the thread managing the UI. After all, you usually want to let the user know when the background process starts, stops, and does interesting things over its life. The following list summarizes the basic requirements for the background thread:

- ❑ Indicate that the background task has started.
- ❑ Provide periodic status or progress information.
- ❑ Indicate that the background task has completed.
- ❑ Enable the user to request that the background task be canceled.

While every application is different, these four requirements are typical for background threads in an interactive application.

As noted earlier, most of the .NET Framework is not thread safe, and Windows Forms is even more restrictive by having thread affinity. You want your background task to be able to notify the user when it starts, stops, and provides progress information. The fact that Windows Forms has thread affinity complicates this, because your background thread can never directly interact with Windows Forms objects. Fortunately, Windows Forms provides a formalized mechanism by which code in a background thread can send messages to the UI thread so that the UI thread can update the display for the user.

This is done using the `BackgroundWorker` control, which is found in the Components tab of the Toolbox. The purpose of the `BackgroundWorker` control is to start, monitor, and control the execution of background tasks. The control makes it easy for code on the application's primary thread to start a task on a background thread. It also makes it easy for the code running on the background thread to notify the primary thread of progress and completion. Finally, it provides a mechanism by which the primary thread can request that the background task be canceled, and for the background thread to notify the primary thread when it has completed the cancellation.

All this is done in a way that safely transfers control between the primary thread (which can update the UI) and the background thread (which cannot update the UI).

Server Applications

In the case of server programs, your design should focus on making the background thread as efficient as possible. Server resources are precious, so the quicker the task can complete, the fewer resources you will consume over time. Interactivity with a UI is not a concern, as your code is running on a server, detached from any UI. The key to success in server coding is to avoid or minimize locking, thus maximizing throughput because your code is never stopped by a lock.

For example, Microsoft went to great pains to design and refine ASP.NET to minimize the number of locks required from the time a user request hits the server to the time an ASPX page's code is running. After the page code is running, no locking occurs, so the page code can just run, top to bottom, as fast and efficiently as possible.

Avoiding locking means avoiding shared resources or data. This is the dominant design goal for server code — designing programs to avoid scenarios in which multiple threads need access to the same variables or other resources. Anytime multiple threads may access the same resource, you need to implement locking to prevent the threads from colliding with one another. You'll learn about locking later in the chapter, as sometimes it is simply unavoidable.

Implementing Threading

At this point, you should have a basic understanding of threads and how they relate to the process and AppDomain concepts. You should also realize that for interactive applications, multithreading is not a way to improve performance, but rather a way to improve the end user experience by providing the illusion that the computer is executing more code simultaneously. In the case of server-side code, multithreading enables higher scalability by enabling Windows to better utilize the CPU, along with other subsystems such as I/O.

A Quick Tour

When a background thread is created, it points to a method or procedure that will be executed by the thread. Remember that a thread is just a pointer to the current instruction in a sequence of instructions to be executed. In all cases, the first instruction in this sequence is the start of a method or procedure.

When using the `BackgroundWorker` control, this method is always the control's `DoWork` event handler. Keep in mind that this method can't be a function. There is no mechanism by which a method running on one thread can return a result directly to code running on another thread. This means that anytime you design a background task, you should start by creating a `Sub` in which you write the code to run on the background thread.

In addition, because the goals for interactive applications and server programs are different, your designs for implementing threading in these two environments are different. This means that the way you design and code the background task will vary.

To demonstrate this, let's work with a simple method that calculates prime numbers. This implementation is naive, and can take quite a lot of time when run against larger numbers, so it serves as a useful example of a long-running background task. Do the following:

1. Create a new Windows Forms Application project named Threading.

2. Add two Button controls, a ListBox and a ProgressBar control to Form1.

3. Add a BackgroundWorker control to Form1.

4. Set its WorkerReportsProgress and WorkerSupportsCancellation properties to True.

5. Add the following to the form's code:

```
Public Class Form1

#Region " Shared data "

  Private mMin As Integer
  Private mMax As Integer
  Private mResults As New List(Of Integer)

#End Region

#Region " Primary thread methods "

  Private Sub btnStart_Click(ByVal sender As System.Object, _
    ByVal e As System.EventArgs) Handles btnStart.Click

    ProgressBar1.Value = 0
    ListBox1.Items.Clear()
    mMin = 1
    mMax = 10000
    BackgroundWorker1.RunWorkerAsync()

  End Sub


  Private Sub btnCancel_Click(ByVal sender As System.Object, _
    ByVal e As System.EventArgs) Handles btnCancel.Click

    BackgroundWorker1.CancelAsync()

  End Sub


  Private Sub BackgroundWorker1_ProgressChanged( _
    ByVal sender As Object, ByVal e As _
    System.ComponentModel.ProgressChangedEventArgs) _
    Handles BackgroundWorker1.ProgressChanged

    ProgressBar1.Value = e.ProgressPercentage
```

```vbnet
    End Sub

    Private Sub BackgroundWorker1_RunWorkerCompleted( _
      ByVal sender As Object, ByVal e As _
      System.ComponentModel.RunWorkerCompletedEventArgs) _
      Handles BackgroundWorker1.RunWorkerCompleted

      For Each item As String In mResults
        ListBox1.Items.Add(item)
      Next

    End Sub

#End Region

#Region " Background thread methods "

    Private Sub BackgroundWorker1_DoWork(ByVal sender As Object, _
      ByVal e As System.ComponentModel.DoWorkEventArgs) _
      Handles BackgroundWorker1.DoWork

      mResults.Clear()

      For count As Integer = mMin To mMax Step 2
        Dim isPrime As Boolean = True

        For x As Integer = 1 To CInt(count / 2)
          For y As Integer = 1 To x
            If x * y = count Then
              ' the number is not prime
              isPrime = False
              Exit For
            End If
          Next
          ' short-circuit the check
          If Not isPrime Then Exit For
        Next

        If isPrime Then
          mResults.Add(count)
        End If

        Me.BackgroundWorker1.ReportProgress( _
          CInt((count - mMin) / (mMax - mMin) * 100))

        If Me.BackgroundWorker1.CancellationPending Then
          Exit Sub
        End If

      Next

    End Sub

#End Region

End Class
```

The `BackgroundWorker1_DoWork` method implements the code to find the prime numbers. This method is automatically run on a background thread by the `BackgroundWorker1` control. Notice that the method is a `Sub`, so it returns no value. Instead, it stores its results in a variable — in this case, a `List(Of Integer)`. The idea is that once the background task is complete, you can do something useful with the results.

When `btnStart` is clicked, the `BackgroundWorker` control is told to start the background task. In order to initialize any data values before launching the background thread, the `mMin` and `mMax` variables are set before the task is started.

Of course, you want to display the results of the background task. Fortunately, the `BackgroundWorker` control raises an event when the task is complete. In this event handler you can safely copy the values from the `List(Of Integer)` into the `ListBox` for display to the user.

Similarly, the `BackgroundWorker` control raises an event to indicate progress as the task runs. Notice that the `DoWork` method periodically calls the `ReportProgress` method. When this method is called, the progress is transferred from the background thread to the primary thread via the `ProgressChanged` event.

Finally, you may have the need to cancel a long-running task. It is never wise to directly terminate a background task. Instead, you should send a request to the background task, asking it to stop running. This enables the task to cleanly stop running so it can close any resources it might be using and shut down properly.

To send the cancel request, call the `BackgroundWorker` control's `CancelAsync` method. This sets the control's `CancellationPending` property to `True`. Notice how this value is periodically checked by the `DoWork` method; and if it is `True`, you exit the method, effectively canceling the task.

Running the code now demonstrates that the UI remains entirely responsive while the background task is running, and the results are displayed when available.

Threading Options

Now that you have learned the basics of threading in an interactive application, let's look at the various threading options at your disposal. The .NET Framework offers two ways to implement multithreading. Regardless of which approach you use, you must specify the method or procedure that the thread will execute when it starts.

First, you can use the thread pool provided by the .NET Framework. The thread pool is a managed pool of threads that can be reused over the life of your application. Threads are created in the pool on an as-needed basis, and idle threads in the pool are reused, thus keeping the number of threads created by your application to a minimum. This is important because threads are an expensive operating system resource.

> **The thread pool should be your first choice in most multithreading scenarios.**

Many built-in .NET Framework features already use the thread pool. In fact, you have already used it, because the `BackgroundWorker` control runs its background tasks on a thread from the thread pool. In addition, anytime you do an asynchronous read from a file, URL, or TCP socket, the thread pool is used on your behalf; and anytime you implement a remoting listener, a website, or a Web service, the thread pool is used. Because the .NET Framework itself relies on the thread pool, it is an optimal choice for most multithreading requirements.

Second, you can create your own thread object. This can be a good approach if you have a single, long-running background task in your application. It is also useful if you need fine-grained control over the background thread. Examples of such control include setting the thread priority or suspending and resuming the thread's execution.

Using the Thread Pool

The .NET Framework provides a thread pool in the `System.Threading` namespace. This thread pool is self-managing. It creates threads on demand and, if possible, reuses idle threads that already exist in the pool.

The thread pool will not create an unlimited number of threads. In fact, it creates at most 25 threads per CPU in the system. If you assign more work requests to the pool than it can handle with these threads, your work requests are queued until a thread becomes available. This is typically a good feature, as it helps ensure that your application will not overload the operating system with too many threads.

There are five primary ways to use the thread pool: through the `BackgroundWorker` control, by calling `BeginXYZ` methods, via `Delegates`, manually via the `ThreadPool.QueueUserWorkItem` method, or by using a `System.Timers.Timer` control. Of the five, the easiest is to use the `BackgroundWorker` control.

Using the BackgroundWorker Control

The previous quick tour of threading explored the `BackgroundWorker` control, which enables you to easily start a task on a background thread, monitor that task's progress, and be notified when it is complete. It also enables you to request that the background task cancel itself. All this is done in a safe manner, with control transferred from the primary thread to the background thread and back again without you having to worry about the details.

Using BeginXYZ Methods

Many of the .NET Framework objects support both synchronous and asynchronous invocation. For instance, you can read from a TCP socket by using the `Read` method or the `BeginRead` method. The `Read` method is synchronous, so you're blocked until the data is read.

The `BeginRead` method is asynchronous, so you are not blocked. Instead, the read operation occurs on a background thread in the thread pool. You provide the address of a method that is called automatically when the read operation is complete. This *callback* method is invoked by the background thread, so your code also ends up running on the background thread in the thread pool.

Behind the scenes, this behavior is all driven by delegates. Rather than explore TCP sockets or some other specific subset of the .NET Framework class library, let's move on and look at the underlying technology itself.

Using Delegates

A *delegate* is a strongly typed pointer to a function or method. Delegates are the underlying technology used to implement events within Visual Basic, and they can be used directly to invoke a method, given just a pointer to that method.

Delegates can be used to launch a background task on a thread in the thread pool. They can also transfer a method call from a background thread to the UI thread. The BackgroundWorker control uses this technology behind the scenes on your behalf, but you can use delegates directly as well.

To use delegates, your worker code must be in a method, and you must define a delegate for that method. The delegate is a pointer for the method, so it must have the same method signature as the method itself:

```
Private Delegate Sub TaskDelegate(ByVal min As Integer, ByVal max As Integer)

Private Sub FindPrimesViaDelegate(ByVal min As Integer, ByVal max As Integer)

    mResults.Clear()

    For count As Integer = min To max Step 2
      Dim isPrime As Boolean = True

      For x As Integer = 1 To CInt(count / 2)
        For y As Integer = 1 To x
          If x * y = count Then
            ' the number is not prime
            isPrime = False
            Exit For
          End If
        Next
        ' short-circuit the check
        If Not isPrime Then Exit For
      Next

      If isPrime Then
        mResults.Add(count)
      End If

    Next
  End Sub
```

Running background tasks via delegates enables you to pass strongly typed parameters to the background task, thus clarifying and simplifying your code. Now that you have a worker method and corresponding delegate, you can add a new button and write code in its click event handler to use it to run FindPrimes on a background thread:

```
Private Sub btnDelegate_Click(ByVal sender As System.Object, _
        ByVal e As System.EventArgs) Handles btnDelegate.Click
    ' run the task
    Dim worker As New TaskDelegate(AddressOf FindPrimesViaDelegate)
    worker.BeginInvoke(1, 10000, AddressOf TaskComplete, Nothing)
  End Sub
```

First, you create an instance of the delegate, setting it up to point to the FindPrimesViaDelegate method. Next, you call BeginInvoke on the delegate to invoke the method.

The `BeginInvoke` method is the key here. `BeginInvoke` is an example of the `BeginXYZ` methods discussed earlier; recall that they automatically run the method on a background thread in the thread pool. This is true for `BeginInvoke` as well, meaning that `FindPrimes` runs in the background and the UI thread is not blocked, so it can continue to interact with the user.

Notice all the parameters passed to `BeginInvoke`. The first two correspond to the parameters defined on the delegate — the `min` and `max` values that should be passed to `FindPrimes`. The next parameter is the address of a method that is automatically invoked when the background thread is complete. The final parameter (to which you have passed `Nothing`) is a mechanism by which you can pass a value from your UI thread to the method that is invoked when the background task is complete.

This means that you need to implement the `TaskComplete` method. This method is invoked when the background task is complete. It runs on the background thread, not on the UI thread, so remember that this method cannot interact with any Windows Forms objects. Instead, it will contain the code to invoke an `UpdateDisplay` method on the UI thread via the form's `BeginInvoke` method:

```
Private Sub TaskComplete(ByVal ar As IAsyncResult)

  Dim update As New UpdateDisplayDelegate(AddressOf UpdateDisplay)
  Me.BeginInvoke(update)

End Sub

Private Delegate Sub UpdateDisplayDelegate()

Private Sub UpdateDisplay()

  For Each item As String In mResults
    ListBox1.Items.Add(item)
  Next

End Sub
```

Notice how a delegate is used to invoke the `UpdateDisplay` method as well, thus illustrating how delegates can be used with a `Form` object's `BeginInvoke` method to transfer control back to the primary thread. The same technique could be used to enable the background task to notify the primary thread of progress as the task runs.

Now when you run the application, you'll have a responsive UI, with the `FindPrimesViaDelegate` method running in the background within the thread pool.

Manually Queuing Work

The final option for using the thread pool is to manually queue items for the thread pool to process. This is done by calling `ThreadPool.QueueUserWorkItem`. This is a `Shared` method on the `ThreadPool` class that directly places a method into the thread pool to be executed on a background thread.

This technique does not allow you to pass arbitrary parameters to the worker method. Instead, it requires that the `worker` method accept a single parameter of type `Object`, through which you can pass an arbitrary value. You can use this to pass multiple values by declaring a class with all your parameter types. Add the following class *inside* the Form1 class:

```
Private Class params
   Public min As Integer
   Public max As Integer

   Public Sub New(ByVal min As Integer, ByVal max As Integer)
     Me.min = min
     Me.max = max
   End Sub

End Class
```

Then you can make FindPrimes accept this value as an Object:

```
Private Sub FindPrimesInPool(ByVal state As Object)
   Dim params As params = DirectCast(state, params)
   mResults.Clear()

   For count As Integer = params.min To params.max Step 2
     Dim isPrime As Boolean = True

     For x As Integer = 1 To CInt(count / 2)
       For y As Integer = 1 To x
         If x * y = count Then
           ' the number is not prime
           isPrime = False
           Exit For
         End If
       Next
       ' short-circuit the check
       If Not isPrime Then Exit For
     Next

     If isPrime Then
       mResults.Add(count)
     End If

   Next

   Dim update As New UpdateDisplayDelegate(AddressOf UpdateDisplay)
   Me.BeginInvoke(update)

End Sub
```

This is basically the same method used with delegates, but it accepts an object parameter, rather than the strongly typed parameters. Notice that the method uses a delegate to invoke the UpdateDisplay method on the UI thread when the task is complete. When you manually put a task on the thread pool, there is no automatic callback to a method when the task is complete, so you must do the callback in the worker method itself.

Now you can manually queue the worker method to run in the thread pool within the Click event handler:

```
Private Sub btnPool_Click(ByVal sender As System.Object, _
        ByVal e As System.EventArgs) Handles btnPool.Click

  ' run the task
  System.Threading.ThreadPool.QueueUserWorkItem( _
    AddressOf FindPrimesInPool, New params(1, 10000))
End Sub
```

The QueueUserWorkItem method accepts the address of the worker method — in this case, FindPrimes. This worker method must accept a single parameter of type Object or you will get a compile error here.

The second parameter to QueueUserWorkItem is the object to be passed to the worker method when it is invoked on the background thread. In this case, you're passing a new instance of the params class defined earlier. This enables you to pass your parameter values to FindPrimes.

When you run this code, you will again find that you have a responsive UI, with FindPrimes running on a background thread in the thread pool.

Using System.Timers.Timer

Beyond BeginXYZ methods, delegates, and manually queuing work items, there are various other ways to get your code running in the thread pool. One of the most common is using a special Timer control. The Elapsed event of this control is raised on a background thread in the thread pool.

This is different from the System.Windows.Forms.Timer control, where the Tick event is raised on the UI thread. The difference is very important to understand, because you can't directly interact with Windows Forms objects from background threads. Code running in the Elapsed event of a System.Timers.Timer control must be treated like any other code running on a background thread.

The exception to this is if you set the SynchronizingObject property on the control to a Windows Forms object such as a Form or a Control. In this case, the Elapsed event is raised on the appropriate UI thread, rather than on a thread in the thread pool. The result is basically the same as using System.Windows.Forms.Timer instead.

Manually Creating a Thread

Thus far, we have been working with the .NET thread pool. You can also manually create and control background threads through code. To manually create a thread, you need to create and start a Thread object. This looks something like the following:

```
  ' run the task
  Dim worker As New Thread(AddressOf FindPrimes)
  worker.Start()
```

While this seems like the obvious way to do multithreading, the thread pool is typically the preferred approach because there is a cost to creating and destroying threads, and the thread pool helps avoid that cost by reusing threads when possible. When you manually create a thread as shown here, you must pay the cost of creating the thread each time or implement your own scheme to reuse the threads you create.

However, manual creation of threads can be useful. The thread pool is designed to be used for background tasks that run for a while and then complete, thus enabling the background thread to be reused for subsequent background tasks. If you need to run a background task for the entire duration of your application, the thread pool is not ideal because that thread would never become available for reuse. In such a case, you are better off creating the background thread manually.

An example of this is the aforementioned spell checker in Word, which runs as long as you're editing a document. Running such a task on the thread pool would make little sense, as the task will run as long as the application, so instead it should be run on a manually created thread, leaving the thread pool available for shorter-running tasks.

The other primary scenario for manually creating threads is when you want to be able to interact with the Thread object as it is running. You can use various methods on the Thread object to interact with and control the background thread. These are described in the following table:

Method	Description
Abort	Stops the thread. This is not recommended, as no cleanup occurs. This is not a graceful shutdown of the thread.
ApartmentState	Sets the COM apartment type used by this thread — important if you're using COM interop in the background task
Join	Blocks your current thread until the background thread is complete
Priority	Enables you to raise or lower the priority of the background thread so Windows will schedule it to get more or less CPU time relative to other threads
Sleep	Causes the thread to be suspended for a specified period of time
Suspend	Suspends a thread — temporarily stopping it without terminating the thread
Resume	Restarts a suspended thread

Many other methods are available on the Thread object as well; consult the online help for more details. You can use these methods to control the behavior and lifetime of the background thread, which can be useful in advanced threading scenarios.

Shared Data

In most multithreading scenarios, you have data in your main thread that needs to be used by the background task on the background thread. Likewise, the background task typically generates data that is needed by the main thread. These are examples of *shared data*, or data that is used by multiple threads.

Remember that multithreading means you have multiple threads within the same process, and in .NET within the same AppDomain. Because memory within an AppDomain is common across all threads in that AppDomain, it is very easy for multiple threads to access the same objects or variables within your application.

For example, in our original prime example, the background task needed the `min` and `max` values from the main thread, and all the implementations have used a `List(Of Integer)` to transfer results back to the main thread when the task was complete. These are examples of shared data. Note that we did not do anything special to make the data shared — the variables were shared by default.

When you are writing multithreaded code, the trickiest issue is managing access to shared data within your AppDomain. You do not want, for example, two threads writing to the same piece of memory at the same time. Equally, you do not want a group of threads reading memory that another thread is in the process of changing. This management of memory access is called *synchronization*. It is properly managing synchronization that makes writing multithreaded code difficult.

When multiple threads want to simultaneously access a common bit of shared data, use synchronization to control things. This is typically done by blocking all but one thread, so only one thread can access the shared data. All other threads are put into a wait state by using a blocking operation of some sort. Once the nonblocked thread is done using the shared data, it releases the block, enabling another thread to resume processing and to use the shared data.

The process of releasing the block is often called an *event*. When we say "event," we are *not* talking about a Visual Basic event. Although the naming convention is unfortunate, the principle is the same — something happens and we react to it. In this case, the nonblocked thread causes an event, which releases some other thread so it can access the shared data.

Although blocking can be used to control the execution of threads, it is primarily used to control access to resources, including memory. This is the basic idea behind synchronization — if you need something, you block until you can access it.

Synchronization is expensive and can be complex. It is expensive because it stops one or more threads from running while another thread uses the shared data. The whole point of having multiple threads is to do more than one thing at a time, and if you are constantly blocking all but one thread, then you lose this benefit.

It can be complex because there are many ways to implement synchronization. Each technique is appropriate for a certain class of synchronization problem, and using the wrong one in the wrong place increases the cost of synchronization.

It is also quite possible to create *deadlocks*, whereby two or more threads end up *permanently* blocked. You have undoubtedly seen examples of this. Pretty much anytime a Windows application totally locks up and must be stopped by the Task Manager, you are seeing an example of poor multithreading implementation. The fact that this happens even in otherwise high-quality commercial applications (such as Microsoft Outlook) is confirmation that synchronization can be very hard to get right.

Avoid Sharing Data

Because synchronization has so many downsides in terms of performance and complexity, the best thing you can do is avoid or minimize its use. If at all possible, design your multithreaded applications to avoid reliance on shared data, and to maintain tight control over the use of any shared data that is required.

Typically, some shared data is unavoidable, so the question becomes how to manage that shared data to avoid or minimize synchronization. Two primary schemes are used for this purpose.

Transferring Data Copies

The first approach is to avoid sharing of data by always passing references to the data between threads. If you also ensure that neither thread uses the same reference, then each thread has its own copy of the data, and no thread needs access to data being used by any other threads.

This is exactly what you did in the prime example where you started the background task via a delegate:

```
Dim worker As New TaskDelegate(AddressOf FindPrimesViaDelegate)
worker.BeginInvoke(1, 10000, AddressOf TaskComplete, Nothing)
```

The min and max values are passed as ByVal parameters, meaning they are copied and provided to the indPrimes method. No synchronization is required here because the background thread never tries to access the values from the main thread. We passed copies of the values a different way when we manually started the task in the thread pool:

```
System.Threading.ThreadPool.QueueUserWorkItem( _
    AddressOf FindPrimesInPool, New params(1, 10000))
```

In this case, we created a params object into which we put the min and max values. Again, those values were copied before they were used by the background thread. The FindPrimesInPool method never attempted to access any parameter data being used by the main thread.

Transferring Data Ownership

What we have done so far works great for variables that are *value types*, such as Integer, and *immutable* objects, such as String. It will not work for *reference types*, such as a regular object, because reference types are never passed by value, only by reference.

To use reference types, we need to change our approach. Rather than return a copy of the data, we will return a reference to the object containing the data. Then we ensure that the background task stops using *that* object, and starts using a new object. As long as different threads are not simultaneously using the same objects, there's no conflict.

You can enhance the prime application to provide the prime numbers to the UI thread as it finds them, rather than in a batch at the end of the process. To see how this works, we will alter the original code based on the BackgroundWorker control. That is the easiest, and typically the best, way to start a background task, so we will use it as a base implementation.

The first thing to do is alter the DoWork method so it periodically returns results. Rather than use the shared mResults variable, we'll use a local List(Of Integer) variable to store the results. Each time we have enough results to report, we'll return that List(Of Integer) to the UI thread, and create a new List(Of Integer) for the next batch of values. This way, we are never sharing the same object between two threads. The required changes are highlighted:

```vb
Private Sub BackgroundWorker1_DoWork(ByVal sender As Object, _
  ByVal e As System.ComponentModel.DoWorkEventArgs) _
  Handles BackgroundWorker1.DoWork

  'mResults.Clear()
  Dim results As New List(Of Integer)

  For count As Integer = mMin To mMax Step 2
    Dim isPrime As Boolean = True

    For x As Integer = 1 To CInt(count / 2)
      For y As Integer = 1 To x
        If x * y = count Then
          ' the number is not prime
          isPrime = False
          Exit For
        End If
      Next
      ' short-circuit the check
      If Not isPrime Then Exit For
    Next

    If isPrime Then
      'mResults.Add(count)
      results.Add(count)
      If results.Count >= 10 Then
        BackgroundWorker1.ReportProgress( _
          CInt((count - mMin) / (mMax - mMin) * 100), results)
        results = New List(Of Integer)
      End If
    End If

    BackgroundWorker1.ReportProgress( _
      CInt((count - mMin) / (mMax - mMin) * 100))

    If BackgroundWorker1.CancellationPending Then
      Exit Sub
    End If

  Next

  BackgroundWorker1.ReportProgress(100, results)

End Sub
```

The results are now placed into a local List(Of Integer). Anytime the list has 10 values, we return it to the primary thread by calling the BackgroundWorker control's ReportProgress method, passing the List(Of Integer) as a parameter.

The important thing here is to then immediately create a new `List(Of Integer)` for use in the `DoWorker` method. This ensures that the background thread is never trying to interact with the same `List(Of Integer)` object as the UI thread.

Now that the `DoWork` method is returning results, alter the code on the primary thread to use those results:

```
Private Sub BackgroundWorker1_ProgressChanged( _
    ByVal sender As Object, _
    ByVal e As System.ComponentModel.ProgressChangedEventArgs) _
    Handles BackgroundWorker1.ProgressChanged

    ProgressBar1.Value = e.ProgressPercentage
    If e.UserState IsNot Nothing Then
        For Each item As String In CType(e.UserState, List(Of Integer))
            ListBox1.Items.Add(item)
        Next
    End If

End Sub
```

Anytime the `ProgressChanged` event is raised, the code checks to see whether the background task provided a state object. If it did, then you cast it to a `List(Of Integer)` and update the UI to display the values in the object.

At this point, you no longer need the `RunWorkerCompleted` method, so it can be removed or commented out. If you run the code at this point, not only is the UI continually responsive, but the results from the background task are displayed as they are discovered, rather than in a batch at the end of the process. As you run the application, resize and move the form while the prime numbers are being found. Although the *displaying* of the data may be slowed down as you interact with the form (because the UI thread can only do so much work), the *generation* of the data continues independently in the background and is not blocked by the UI thread's work.

When you rely on transferring data ownership, you ensure that only one thread can access the data at any given time by ensuring that the background task never uses an object once it returns it to the primary thread.

Sharing Data with Synchronization

So far, you have seen ways to avoid the sharing of data, but sometimes you'll have a requirement for data sharing, in which case you'll be faced with the complex world of synchronization.

As discussed earlier, incorrect implementation of synchronization can cause performance issues, deadlocks, and application crashes. Success is dependent on serious attention to detail. Problems may not manifest in testing, but when they happen in production, they are often catastrophic. You cannot *test* to ensure proper implementation; you must prove it in the same way mathematicians prove mathematical truths — by careful logical analysis of all possibilities.

Built-In Synchronization Support

Some objects in the .NET Framework have built-in support for synchronization, so you don't need to write it yourself. In particular, most of the collection-oriented classes have optional support for synchronization, including Queue, Stack, Hashtable, ArrayList, and more.

Rather than transfer ownership of List (Of Integer) objects from the background thread to the UI thread as shown in the last example, you can use the synchronization provided by the ArrayList object to help mediate between the two threads.

To use a synchronized ArrayList, you need to change from the List (Of Integer) to an ArrayList. Additionally, the ArrayList must be created a special way:

```
Private Sub BackgroundWorker1_DoWork(ByVal sender As Object, _
  ByVal e As System.ComponentModel.DoWorkEventArgs) _
  Handles BackgroundWorker1.DoWork

  'mResults.Clear()
  'Dim results As New List(Of Integer)
  Dim results As ArrayList = ArrayList.Synchronized(New ArrayList)
```

What you are doing here is creating a normal ArrayList, and then having the ArrayList class "wrap" it with a synchronized wrapper. The result is a thread-safe ArrayList object that automatically prevents multiple threads from interacting with the data in invalid ways.

Now that the ArrayList is synchronized, you don't need to create a new one each time you return the values to the primary thread. Comment out the following line in the DoWork method:

```
    If results.Count >= 10 Then
      BackgroundWorker1.ReportProgress( _
        CInt((count - mMin) / (mMax - mMin) * 100), results)
      'results = New List(Of Integer)
    End If
```

Finally, update the code on the primary thread to properly display the data from the ArrayList:

```
  Private Sub BackgroundWorker1_ProgressChanged( _
    ByVal sender As Object, _
    ByVal e As System.ComponentModel.ProgressChangedEventArgs) _
    Handles BackgroundWorker1.ProgressChanged

    ProgressBar1.Value = e.ProgressPercentage
    If e.UserState IsNot Nothing Then
      Dim result As ArrayList = CType(e.UserState, ArrayList)
      For index As Integer = ListBox1.Items.Count To result.Count - 1
        ListBox1.Items.Add(result(index))
      Next
    End If

  End Sub
```

Because the entire list is accessible at all times, you need only copy the new values to the ListBox, rather than loop through the entire list. This works out well anyway, because the For Each statement isn't thread safe even with a synchronized collection. To use the For Each statement, you would need to enclose the entire loop inside a SyncLock block:

```
Dim result As ArrayList = CType(e.UserState, ArrayList)
SyncLock result.SyncRoot
  For Each item As String in result
    ListBox1.Items.Add(item)
  Next
End SyncLock
```

The SyncLock statement in Visual Basic is used to provide an exclusive lock on an object. Here it is being used to get an exclusive lock on the ArrayList object's SyncRoot. This means all the code within the SyncLock block can be sure that it is the only code interacting with the contents of the ArrayList. No other threads can access the data while your code is in this block.

Synchronization Objects

While many collection objects optionally provide support for synchronization, most objects in the .NET Framework or in third-party libraries are not thread safe. To safely share these objects and classes in a multithreaded environment, you must manually implement synchronization.

To manually implement synchronization, you must rely on help from the Windows operating system. The .NET Framework includes classes that wrap the underlying Windows operating system concepts, so you don't need to call Windows directly. Instead, you use the .NET Framework synchronization objects.

Synchronization objects have their own special terminology. Most of these objects can be acquired and released. In other cases, you wait on an object until it is signaled.

For objects that can be acquired, the idea is that when you have the object, you have a lock. Any other threads trying to acquire the object are blocked until you release the object. These types of synchronization objects are sort of like a hot potato — only one thread has it at any given time and other threads are waiting for it. No thread should hold onto such an object any longer than necessary, as that slows down the whole system.

The other class of objects comprises those that wait on the object — which means your thread is blocked. Some other thread will signal your object, which releases you (to become unblocked). Many threads can be waiting on the same object, and when the object is signaled, all the blocked threads are released. This is basically the exact opposite of an acquire/release type object. The following table lists the primary synchronization objects in the .NET Framework:

Object	Model	Description
AutoResetEvent	Wait/Signal	Allows a thread to release other threads that are waiting on the object
Interlocked	N/A	Allows multiple threads to safely increment and decrement values that are stored in variables accessible to all the threads

Object	Model	Description
ManualResetEvent	Wait/Signal	Allows a thread to release other threads that are waiting on the object
Monitor	Acquire/Release	Defines an exclusive application-level lock whereby only one thread can hold the lock at any given time
Mutex	Acquire/Release	Defines an exclusive systemwide lock whereby only one thread can hold the lock at any given time
ReaderWriterLock	Acquire/Release	Defines a lock whereby many threads can read data, but only a single writer is allowed
ReaderWriterLockSlim	Acquire/Release	Defines a lock whereby many threads can read data, but exclusive access is provided to one thread for writing data. This is a new object in the .NET Framework 3.5.

Exclusive Locks and the SyncLock Statement

Perhaps the easiest type of synchronization to understand and implement is an *exclusive lock*. When one thread holds an exclusive lock, no other thread can obtain that lock. Any other thread attempting to obtain the lock is blocked until the lock becomes available.

There are two primary technologies for exclusive locking: the monitor and mutex objects. The monitor object allows a thread in a process to block other threads in the same process. The mutex object allows a thread in any process to block threads in the same process or in other processes. Because a mutex has systemwide scope, it is a more expensive object to use and should only be used when cross-process locking is required.

Visual Basic includes the SyncLock statement, which is a shortcut to access a monitor object. While it is possible to directly create and use a System.Threading.Monitor object, it is far simpler to just use the SyncLock statement (briefly mentioned in the ArrayList object discussion), so that is what we will do here.

Exclusive locks can be used to protect shared data so that only one thread at a time can access the data. They can also be used to ensure that only one thread at a time can run a specific bit of code. This exclusive bit of code is called a *critical section*. While critical sections are an important concept in computer science, it is far more common to use exclusive locks to protect shared data, and that is what this chapter focuses on.

You can use an exclusive lock to lock virtually any shared data. For example, you can change your code to use the SyncLock statement instead of a synchronized ArrayList. To do so, change the declaration of the ArrayList in the DoWork method so it is global to the form and no longer synchronized:

```
Private results As New ArrayList
```

This means you are responsible for managing all synchronization yourself. First, in the DoWork method, protect all access to the results variable:

```
If isPrime Then
    Dim numberOfResults As Integer
    SyncLock results.SyncRoot
        results.Add(count)
        numberOfResults = results.Count
    End SyncLock
    If numberofresults >= 10 Then
        BackgroundWorker1.ReportProgress( _
            CInt((count - mMin) / (mMax - mMin) * 100), results)
    End If
End If
```

Notice how the code has changed so both the Add and Count method calls are contained within a SyncLock block. This ensures that no other thread can be interacting with the ArrayList while you make these calls. The SyncLock statement acts against an object — in this case, results.SyncRoot.

The trick to making this work is to ensure that all code throughout the application wraps any access to results within the SyncLock statement. If any code doesn't follow this protocol, then there will be conflicts between threads!

Because SyncLock acts against a specific object, you can have many active SyncLock statements, each working against a different object:

```
SyncLock obj1
    ' blocks against obj1
End SyncLock

SyncLock obj2
    ' blocks against obj2
End SyncLock
```

Note that neither obj1 nor obj2 is altered or affected by this at all. The only thing you are saying here is that while you're within a SyncLock obj1 code block, any other thread attempting to execute a SyncLock obj1 statement will be blocked until you've executed the End SyncLock statement.

Next, change the UI update code in the ProgressChanged method:

```
ProgressBar1.Value = e.ProgressPercentage
If e.UserState IsNot Nothing Then
    Dim result As ArrayList = CType(e.UserState, ArrayList)
    SyncLock result
        For index As Integer = ListBox1.Items.Count To result.Count - 1
            ListBox1.Items.Add(result(index))
        Next
    End SyncLock
End If
```

Again, notice how the interaction with the ArrayList is contained within a SyncLock block. While this version of the code will operate just fine, it is very slow. In fact, you can pretty much stall out the whole processing by continually moving or resizing the window while it runs. This is because the UI thread is blocking the background thread via the SyncLock call, and if the UI thread is totally busy moving or resizing the window, then the background thread can be entirely blocked during that time as well.

Reader-Writer Locks

While exclusive locks are an easy way to protect shared data, they are not always the most efficient. Your application will often contain some code that is updating shared data, and other code that is only reading from shared data. Some applications do a great deal of data reading and only periodic data changes.

Because reading data does not change anything, there is nothing wrong with having multiple threads read data at the same time, as long as you can ensure that no threads are *updating* data while you are trying to read. In addition, you typically only want one thread updating at a time.

What you have then is a scenario in which you want to allow many concurrent readers, but if the data is to be changed, then one thread must temporarily gain exclusive access to the shared memory. This is the purpose behind the ReaderWriterLock and ReaderWriterLockSlim objects.

Using a ReaderWriterLock, you can request either a read lock or a write lock. If you obtain a read lock, you can safely read the data. Other threads can simultaneously obtain read locks and safely read the data.

Before you can update data, you must obtain a write lock. When you request a write lock, any other threads requesting either a read or write lock are blocked. If any outstanding read or write locks are in progress, then you will be blocked until they are released. When there are no outstanding locks (read or write), you will be granted the write lock. No other locks are granted until you release the write lock, so your write lock is an exclusive lock.

After you release the write lock, any pending requests for other locks are granted, allowing either another single writer to access the data or multiple readers to simultaneously access the data. You can adapt the sample code to use a System.Threading.ReaderWriterLock object. Start by using the code that was just created based on the SyncLock statement, with a Queue object as shared data. First, create an instance of the ReaderWriterLock in a form-wide variable:

```
' lock object
Private mRWLock As New System.Threading.ReaderWriterLock
```

Because a ReaderWriterLock is just an object, you can have many lock objects in an application if needed. You could use each lock object to protect different bits of shared data. Then you can change the DoWork method to make use of this object instead of the SyncLock statement:

```
If isPrime Then
    Dim numberOfResults As Integer
    mRWLock.AcquireWriterLock(100)
    Try
        results.Add(count)
    Finally
        mRWLock.ReleaseWriterLock()
    End Try
    mRWLock.AcquireReaderLock(100)
    Try
```

```
         numberOfResults = results.Count
      Finally
         mRWLock.ReleaseReaderLock()
      End Try
      If numberOfResults >= 10 Then
         BackgroundWorker1.ReportProgress( _
            CInt((count - mMin) / (mMax - mMin) * 100), results)
      End If
   End If
```

Before you write or alter the data in the `ArrayList`, you need to acquire a writer lock. Before reading any data from the `ArrayList`, you need to acquire a reader lock.

If any thread holds a reader lock, then attempts to get a writer lock are blocked. When any thread requests a writer lock, any *other* requests for a reader lock are blocked until after that thread gets (and releases) its writer lock. In addition, if any thread has a writer lock, then other threads requesting a reader (or writer) lock are blocked until that writer lock is released.

The result is that there can be only one writer, and while the writer is active, there are no readers. However, if no writer is active, then there can be many concurrent reader threads running at the same time.

Note that all work done while a lock is held is contained within a `Try..Finally` block. This ensures that the lock is released regardless of any exceptions you might encounter.

> It is critical to always release locks you are holding. Failure to do so may cause your application to become unstable and crash or lock up unexpectedly.

Failure to release a lock will almost certainly block other threads, possibly forever — causing a deadlock situation. The alternate fate is that the other threads will request a lock and time out, throwing an exception and causing the application to fail. Either way, when you do not release your locks, you cause application failure.

Now update the code in the `ProgressChanged` method:

```
      ProgressBar1.Value = e.ProgressPercentage
      If e.UserState IsNot Nothing Then
         Dim result As ArrayList = CType(e.UserState, ArrayList)
         mRWLock.AcquireReaderLock(100)
         Try
            For index As Integer = ListBox1.Items.Count To result.Count - 1
               ListBox1.Items.Add(result(index))
            Next
         Finally
            mRWLock.ReleaseReaderLock()
         End Try
      End If
```

Again, before reading from `results`, you get a reader lock, releasing it in a `Finally` block once you're done. This code will run a bit smoother than the previous implementation, but the UI thread can be kept busy with resizing or moving the window, thus causing it to hold the reader lock and preventing the background thread from running, as it will not be able to acquire a writer lock.

A brand-new lock available to you in version 3.5 of the .NET Framework is the ReaderWriterLockSlim object. This new lock was introduced to allow for upgradeable reads. The previous ReaderWriterLock has some issues associated with it, such as a poorly designed non-atomic upgrade method. In addition to this, the lock was considered to have rather poor performance. The new ReaderWriterLock also gives precedence to locks in a write mode, rather than a read or an upgradable read mode. The reasoning for this is that it is assumed that write locks are going to occur less frequently, so this precedence structure would allow for better overall performance.

Microsoft was unable to fix the ReaderWriterLock in the previous .NET Framework and thus introduced a brand-new lock. The new ReaderWriterLockSlim supports the methods shown in the following table:

Method	Description
Dispose	Releases all the resources held by the object
EnterReadLock	Tries to acquire a read lock
EnterUpgradeableReadLock	Tries to acquire a lock in an upgradable mode
EnterWriteLock	Tries to acquire a write lock
ExitReadLock	Exits the read lock
ExitUpgradeableReadLock	Exits the upgradable read lock
ExitWriteLock	Exits the write lock
TryEnterReadLock	Tries to enter a lock in read mode. You can optionally set a timeout period on the try.
TryEnterUpgradeableReadLock	Tries to enter a lock in an upgradable read mode. You can optionally set a timeout period on the try.
TryEnterWriteLock	Tries to enter a lock in a write mode. You can optionally set a timeout period on the try.

As you can see from the list of methods, the new ReaderWriterLockSlim supports three modes: read, upgradable read, and write. The new upgradable read mode enables your code to safely transition from read to write modes. This lock supports an atomic upgrade path and won't cause deadlocks like the older ReaderWriterLock. Note that only one thread is allowed in the upgradeable read mode no matter how many threads are contained in a read mode. This is what enables the atomic upgrade path.

The following code shows an example of using the new ReaderWriterLockSlim object:

```
Imports System.Threading

Module Module1
    Dim rwl As New ReaderWriterLockSlim()

    Sub Main()
```

```
        Dim th1 As New Thread(AddressOf Read)
        th1.Start("1")

        Dim th2 As New Thread(AddressOf Read)
        th2.Start("2")

        Dim th3 As New Thread(AddressOf Write)
        th3.Start("3")

        Dim th4 As New Thread(AddressOf Write)
        th4.Start("4")

        Dim th5 As New Thread(AddressOf Write)
        th5.Start("5")

    End Sub

    Sub Read(ByVal ThreadID As String)
        While (True)
            Console.WriteLine("Thread " & ThreadID & _
                " has entered the ReadLock")
            rwl.EnterReadLock()
            Thread.Sleep(100)
            Console.WriteLine("Thread " & ThreadID & _
                " has exited the ReadLock")
            rwl.ExitReadLock()
        End While
    End Sub

    Sub Write(ByVal ThreadID As String)
        While (True)
            rwl.EnterUpgradeableReadLock()
            Console.WriteLine("Thread " & ThreadID & _
                " has entered the UpgradeableReadLock")
            rwl.EnterWriteLock()
            Console.WriteLine("Thread " & ThreadID & _
                " has entered the WriteLock")
            Console.WriteLine("Thread " & ThreadID & _
                " has the write lock.")
            rwl.ExitWriteLock()
            Console.WriteLine("Thread " & ThreadID & _
                " has exited the WriteLock")
            rwl.ExitUpgradeableReadLock()
            Console.WriteLine("Thread " & ThreadID & _
                " has exited the UpgradeableReadLock")
            Thread.Sleep(1000)
        End While
    End Sub

End Module
```

From this example, threads can very easily obtain a read lock. Getting a write lock requires the thread to enter the UpgradableReadLock method, and the thread waits in the read mode until it is able to enter into the upgradeable read mode (as only one thread is allowed in this mode at any given time). From there, it can enter into the write mode; and upon exiting, not only does the thread have to exit from the write mode, but it also must exit from the upgradeable read mode.

AutoReset Events

Both the `Monitor` (`SyncLock`) and `ReaderWriterLock` objects follow the acquire/release model, whereby threads are blocked until they can acquire control of the appropriate lock.

You can flip the paradigm by using the `AutoResetEvent` and `ManualResetEvent` objects. With these objects, threads voluntarily wait on the event object. While waiting, they are blocked and do no work. When another thread signals (raises) the event, any threads waiting on the event object are released and do work.

You can signal an event object by calling the object's `Set` method. To wait on an event object, a thread calls that object's `WaitOne` method. This method blocks the thread until the event object is signaled (the event is raised).

Event objects can be in one of two states: signaled or not signaled. When an event object is signaled, threads waiting on the object are released. If a thread calls `WaitOne` on an event object that is signaled, then the thread isn't blocked and continues running. However, if a thread calls `WaitOne` on an event object that is not signaled, then the thread is blocked until some other thread calls that object's `Set` method, thus signaling the event.

`AutoResetEvent` objects automatically reset themselves to the not signaled state as soon as any thread calls the `WaitOne` method. In other words, if an `AutoResetEvent` is not signaled and a thread calls `WaitOne`, then that thread will be blocked. Another thread can then call the `Set` method, thus signaling the event. This both releases the waiting thread and immediately resets the `AutoResetEvent` object to its not signaled state.

You can use an `AutoResetEvent` object to coordinate the use of shared data between threads. Change the `ReaderWriterLock` declaration to declare an `AutoResetEvent` instead:

```
Dim mWait As New System.Threading.AutoResetEvent(False)
```

By passing `False` to the constructor, you are telling the event object to start out in its not signaled state. Were you to pass `True`, it would start out in the signaled state, and the first thread to call `WaitOne` would *not* be blocked, but would trigger the event object to automatically reset its state to not signaled.

Next, you can update `DoWork` to use the event object. In order to ensure that both the primary and background threads do not simultaneously access the `ArrayList` object, use the `AutoResetEvent` object to block the background thread until the UI thread is done with the `ArrayList`:

```
If isPrime Then
  Dim numberOfResults As Integer
  results.Add(count)
  numberOfResults = results.Count
  If numberOfResults >= 10 Then
    BackgroundWorker1.ReportProgress( _
      CInt((count - mMin) / (mMax - mMin) * 100), results)
    mWait.WaitOne()
  End If
End If
```

This code is much simpler than using the ReaderWriterLock. In this case, the background thread assumes it has exclusive access to the ArrayList until the ReportProgress method is called to invoke the primary thread to update the UI. When that occurs, the background thread calls the WaitOne method, so it is blocked until released by the primary thread.

In the UI update code, change the code to release the background thread:

```
ProgressBar1.Value = e.ProgressPercentage
If e.UserState IsNot Nothing Then
    Dim result As ArrayList = CType(e.UserState, ArrayList)
    For index As Integer = ListBox1.Items.Count To result.Count - 1
        ListBox1.Items.Add(result(index))
    Next
    mWait.Set()
End If
```

This is done by calling the Set method on the AutoResetEvent object, thus setting it to its signaled state. This releases the background thread so it can continue to work. Notice that the Set method isn't called until after the primary thread is completely done working with the ArrayList object.

As with the previous examples, if you continually move or resize the form, then the UI thread becomes so busy it will never release the background thread.

ManualReset Events

A ManualResetEvent object is very similar to the AutoResetEvent just used. The difference is that with a ManualResetEvent object, you are in total control over whether the event object is set to its signaled or not signaled state. The state of the event object is never altered automatically.

This means you can manually call the Reset method, rather than rely on it to occur automatically. The result is that you have more control over the process and can potentially gain some efficiency.

To see how this works, change the declaration to create a ManualResetEvent:

```
' wait object
Dim mWait As New System.Threading.ManualResetEvent(True)
```

Notice that you're constructing it with a True parameter. This means that the object will initially be in its signaled state. Until it is reset to a nonsignaled state, WaitOne calls won't block on this object.

Change the DoWork method as follows:

```
If isPrime Then
    mWait.WaitOne()
    Dim numberOfResults As Integer
    results.Add(count)
    numberOfResults = results.Count
    If numberOfResults >= 10 Then
        mWait.Reset()
        BackgroundWorker1.ReportProgress( _
            CInt((count - mMin) / (mMax - mMin) * 100), results)
    End If
End If
```

This is quite different from the previous code. Before interacting with the `ArrayList` object, the code calls `WaitOne`. This causes it to block if the primary thread is active. Remember that initially the lock object is signaled, so the `WaitOne` call will *not* block.

Then, before transferring control to the primary thread to update the UI, you call `mWait.Reset`. The `Reset` event sets the lock object to its nonsignaled state. Until its `Set` method is called, any `WaitOne` methods will block. No changes are required to the UI update code. It already calls the `Set` method when it is done interacting with the `ArrayList`.

The result is that the background thread can continue to search for prime numbers while the UI is being updated. The only time the background thread will block is when it finds a prime number before the UI is done with its update process.

Summary

This chapter took an involved look at the subject of threading in .NET and demonstrated the rich set of threading functionality now available to Visual Basic developers.

Proper implementation of multithreaded code is very difficult, and proving that multithreaded code will always run as expected requires careful code walk-throughs, as it cannot be proven through testing. For that reason, it is best to avoid the use of multithreading when possible.

However, multithreading can be a useful way to run lengthy tasks in the background while continuing to provide the user with an interactive experience. When you do use multithreading, try to avoid using shared data and instead relay data between the UI and background threads using messaging techniques, as shown in this chapter.

If you must share data between multiple threads, be sure to use appropriate synchronization primitives to ensure that only one thread interacts with the data at any given time. Be aware of the performance implications of using synchronization objects, and design carefully to avoid deadlocks.

Threading can be useful in specialized situations, although its use should be limited whenever possible.

27

Windows Workflow Foundation

While Windows Communication Foundation and Windows Presentation Foundation enjoy much of the attention, the .NET Framework 3.0 also comes with another "Foundation": Windows Workflow Foundation (usually abbreviated WF). WF can be a powerful tool in developing applications, as it provides a standard means of adding workflow to an application. *Workflow* refers to the steps involved in an application. Most business applications contain one or more workflows, such as the approval steps in an expense-tracking application or the steps involved in paying for a cart full of items at an online store. Normally, a workflow is created in code and is inextricably bound to the application. WF enables developers to graphically build the workflow, keeping it logically separated from the code itself. It also enables the workflow to change as the needs of the business change. These workflows may be as complex as needed and may integrate human processes or Web services.

This chapter looks at how you can take advantage of WF in your applications: how you can add and edit workflows, how you can integrate workflows into an existing business process, and how the graphical tools used to build workflows with Visual Studio can help you communicate with business users and avoid errors caused by mistakes in the workflow.

Workflow in Applications

Just what is workflow? It's a very heavily used word, and many developers use it in multiple contexts. For our purposes, it is the description of the steps involved in some process performed at least partially by a computer. Workflows are common in many types of business applications. For example, if you were building an application for tracking employee expense reports, the workflow might look something like the following:

1. The employee completes a form and submits it into the system.

2. The employee prints the expense report form, attaches original invoices, and sends it to accounting for a permanent record.

3. The system examines the data in the expense report:

    a. Depending on the rules defined by the company, it may be automatically approved, require management approval, or require investigation by the accounting department. Some of the rules that may come into play would likely be the expense types, the amount of each expense, how the expense was paid, and so on.

    b. Copies of the expense report are e-mailed if additional approval is required.

    c. If approved, the expense report continues in the workflow; otherwise, it is returned to the submitting employee for correction (or to complain to the employee's manager).

4. Expense report values are recorded in the accounting system.

5. A check is printed and sent to the happy employee. This step may be delayed if the originals have not been received. Alternatively, the company may delay future expense reimbursement requests.

The steps in a workflow may be carried out by a human or computer; they may require custom code or calculations, or may need to integrate with an external application. Building workflows into an application is frequently a difficult process. Unless a developer completely understands the process (and they rarely do), identifying the true workflow used for a process requires interviewing multiple people at one or more companies. This often results in conflicting descriptions of the steps involved, or of the actions required at each step, requiring someone to decide on the actual intent.

Even after the exact workflow has been defined, it frequently changes. This may be due to some new legal requirements, a company merger, or even (frequently) the whims of management. In traditional applications, this would likely mean that a developer would have to change the code for one or more steps of the process, ideally without introducing any new bugs into the system. In short, developing workflow applications using traditional tools can be a difficult, time-consuming process. WF makes building and maintaining these workflows easier by abstracting away the logic of the workflow, and by providing several of the common services required.

Building Workflows

The actual workflow files in WF are XML files written in a version of XAML. This is the same XAML used to describe Windows Presentation Foundation (WPF) files. (See Chapter 17 for more details on WPF.) They describe the actions to perform within the workflow, and the relationship between those actions. You can create a workflow using only a text editor, but Visual Studio makes creating these workflows much easier. It provides a graphical designer that enables developers to visually design the workflow, creating the XAML in the background. See the following code:

```
<RuleDefinitions xmlns="http://schemas.microsoft.com/winfx/2006/xaml/workflow">
  <RuleDefinitions.Conditions>
    <RuleExpressionCondition Name="TranslationCallWorked">
      <RuleExpressionCondition.Expression>
        <ns0:CodeBinaryOperatorExpression Operator="ValueEquality"
          xmlns:ns0="clr-namespace:System.CodeDom;Assembly=System, Version=2.0.0.0,
```

```
                Culture=neutral, PublicKeyToken=b77a5c561934e089">
                <ns0:CodeBinaryOperatorExpression.Left>
                  <ns0:CodeBinaryOperatorExpression Operator="ValueEquality">
                    <ns0:CodeBinaryOperatorExpression.Left>
                      <ns0:CodeMethodInvokeExpression>
                        <ns0:CodeMethodInvokeExpression.Parameters>
                          <ns0:CodeFieldReferenceExpression
                            FieldName="OutputTextProperty">
                            <ns0:CodeFieldReferenceExpression.TargetObject>
                              <ns0:CodeTypeReferenceExpression
                                Type="TranslateActivity.TranslateActivity" />
                            </ns0:CodeFieldReferenceExpression.TargetObject>
                          </ns0:CodeFieldReferenceExpression>
                        </ns0:CodeMethodInvokeExpression.Parameters>
                        <ns0:CodeMethodInvokeExpression.Method>
                          <ns0:CodeMethodReferenceExpression MethodName="GetValue">
                            <ns0:CodeMethodReferenceExpression.TargetObject>
                              <ns0:CodeThisReferenceExpression />
                            </ns0:CodeMethodReferenceExpression.TargetObject>
                          </ns0:CodeMethodReferenceExpression>
                        </ns0:CodeMethodInvokeExpression.Method>
                      </ns0:CodeMethodInvokeExpression>
                    </ns0:CodeBinaryOperatorExpression.Left>
                    <ns0:CodeBinaryOperatorExpression.Right>
                      <ns0:CodePrimitiveExpression />
                    </ns0:CodeBinaryOperatorExpression.Right>
                  </ns0:CodeBinaryOperatorExpression>
                </ns0:CodeBinaryOperatorExpression.Left>
                <ns0:CodeBinaryOperatorExpression.Right>
                  <ns0:CodePrimitiveExpression>
                    <ns0:CodePrimitiveExpression.Value>
                      <ns1:Boolean xmlns:ns1="clr-namespace:System;Assembly=mscorlib,
                        Version=2.0.0.0, Culture=neutral,
                        PublicKeyToken=b77a5c561934e089">false</ns1:Boolean>
                    </ns0:CodePrimitiveExpression.Value>
                  </ns0:CodePrimitiveExpression>
                </ns0:CodeBinaryOperatorExpression.Right>
              </ns0:CodeBinaryOperatorExpression>
            </RuleExpressionCondition.Expression>
          </RuleExpressionCondition>
        </RuleDefinitions.Conditions>
      </RuleDefinitions>
```

The workflow comprises a number of rule definitions. Each definition includes activities, conditions, and expressions. Activities are the steps involved in the workflow. They are executed based on the workflow's design and the conditions included. Controlling the behavior of the workflow are conditions, which are evaluated and may result in code running. Finally, expressions describe the individual tests used as part of the conditions. For example, each side of an equality condition would be expressions. When building the workflow by hand, you are responsible for creating the markup. Fortunately, Visual Studio writes it as you design your workflow.

Adding Workflow with Windows Workflow Foundation

Windows Workflow Foundation is composed of a number of components that work together with your application to carry out the desired workflow. Six main components make up any WF application:

❑ **Host process** — This is the executable that will host the workflow. Typically, this is your application, and is usually a Windows Form, ASP.NET, or a Windows service application. The workflow is hosted and runs within this process. All normal rules of application design apply here: If another application needs to communicate with the workflow, then you need to use Web services or remoting to enable communication between the two applications.

❑ **WF runtime services** — Windows Workflow Foundation provides several essential services to your application. Most notable, of course, is the capability to execute workflows. This service is responsible for loading, scheduling, and executing your workflows within the context of the host process. In addition to this service, WF provides services for persistence and tracking. The persistence service enables saving the state of a workflow as needed. Because a workflow may take a long time to complete, having multiple workflows in process can use a lot of the computer's memory. The persistence services enable the workflow to be saved for later use. When there is more to complete, the workflow can be reactivated and continue, even after weeks of inactivity. The tracking services enable the developer to monitor the state of the workflows. This is particularly useful when you might have multiple workflows active at any given time (such as in a shopping checkout workflow). The tracking services enable the creation of applications to monitor the health of your workflow applications.

❑ **Workflow runtime engine** — The runtime engine is responsible for executing each workflow instance. It runs in process within the host process. Each engine may execute multiple workflow instances simultaneously, and multiple engines may be running concurrently within the same host process.

❑ **Workflow** — The workflow is the list of steps required to carry out an action. It may be created graphically using a tool such as Visual Studio, or manually. Each workflow is composed of one or more activities, and may consist of workflow markup and/or code. Multiple instances of a workflow may be active at any given moment in an application.

❑ **Activity library** — The activity library is a collection of the standard actions used to create workflows. There are several different types of activities. Some are used to communicate with outside processes, while others affect the flow of a workflow.

❑ **Custom activities** — In addition to the standard activities that exist within the activity library, developers can create custom activities. This may be to support a particular application you need to integrate with WF, or as a simplification of a complex composite activity. Creating custom activities is done mostly through attributes and inheritance.

Figure 27-1 shows how the main components of WF fit together.

Windows Workflow Foundation supports two main styles of creating workflows: *sequential* and *state machine*. Sequential workflows (see Figure 27-2) are the classic flowchart style of process. They begin when some action initiates the workflow, such as the submission of an expense report or a user decision to check out a shopping cart. The workflow then continues stepwise through the activities until it reaches the end. There may be branching or looping, but generally the flow moves down the workflow. Sequential workflows are best when a set series of steps is needed for the workflow.

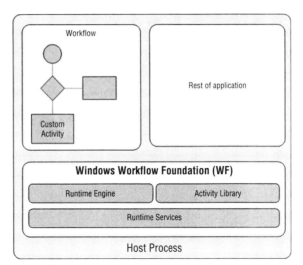

Figure 27-1

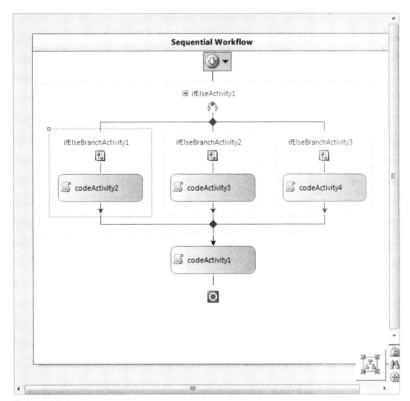

Figure 27-2

State machine workflows (see Figure 27-3) are less linear than sequential workflows. They are typically used when the data moves through a series of steps toward completion. At each step, the state of the application has a particular value. Transitions move the state between steps. One example of a state machine workflow that most people are familiar with (unfortunately) is voice mail. Most voice-mail systems are collections of states, represented by a menu. You move between the states by pressing the keys of your phone. State machine workflows can be useful when the process you are modeling is not necessarily linear. There may still be some required steps, but generally the flow may iterate between the steps for some time before completion.

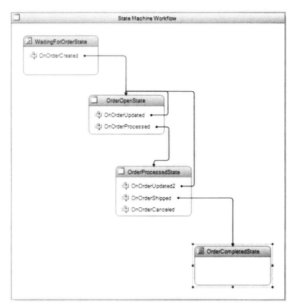

Figure 27-3

A good way to identify a candidate for a state machine workflow is determining whether the process is better defined in terms of modes, rather than a linear series of steps. For example, a shopping site is a classic example of a state machine. The user is either in browse mode or cart view mode. Selecting check-out would likely initiate a sequential workflow, as the steps in that process are more easily described in a linear fashion.

A Simple Workflow

As with any other programming endeavor, the best way to understand WF is to create a simple workflow and extend it with additional steps. Start Visual Studio and create a new Sequential Workflow Console application (see Figure 27-4) called HelloWorkflow.

This project creates two files: a module that includes the `Main` file for the application and the workflow. The sequential workflow begins life with only two steps: start and finish, as shown in Figure 27-5. You build the workflow by adding steps between these two.

To begin, drag a `Code` activity between the start and finish markers. Note the red exclamation mark on the new activity in the diagram (shown without color in Figure 27-6). WF makes heavy use of these tips to help you set required properties.

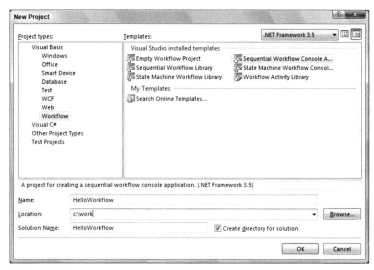

Figure 27-4

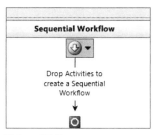

Figure 27-5

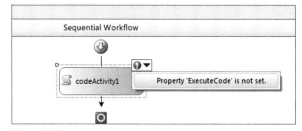

Figure 27-6

Click the code tip and select the menu item "Property 'ExecuteCode' is not set." This will bring up the Properties window for the Code activity. Enter **SayGreetings** and press Enter. This brings up the code window for the activity. Add the following code:

```
Private Sub SayGreetings(ByVal sender As System.Object, _
    ByVal e As System.EventArgs)
        Console.WriteLine("Hello world, from workflow")
        Console.WriteLine("Press enter to continue")
        Console.ReadLine()
End Sub
```

Notice that coding the action for the activity is the same as any other event. Run the project to see the console window (see Figure 27-7), along with the message you should be expecting.

Figure 27-7

While trivial, the project makes a useful test bed for experimenting with the various activities. Add an `IfElse` activity before the `Code` activity. `IfElse` activities are one of the main ways to add logic and control of flow to your workflows. They have a condition property that determines when each half of the flow will be executed. The condition may be code that executes or a declarative rule. For this example, declarative rules are enough. You create these rules in the Select Condition Editor (see Figure 27-8). To display the Select Condition Editor, select `Declarative Rule Condition` for the `Condition` property of the `ifElseBranchActivity` component. Once you have selected `Declarative Rule Condition`, you can click the ellipsis on the `ConditionName` property to display the dialog.

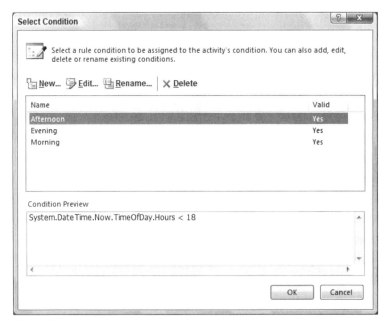

Figure 27-8

Clicking New brings up the Rule Condition Editor (see Figure 27-9). This enables you to create simple expressions that will be used by the `IfElse` activity to determine flow.

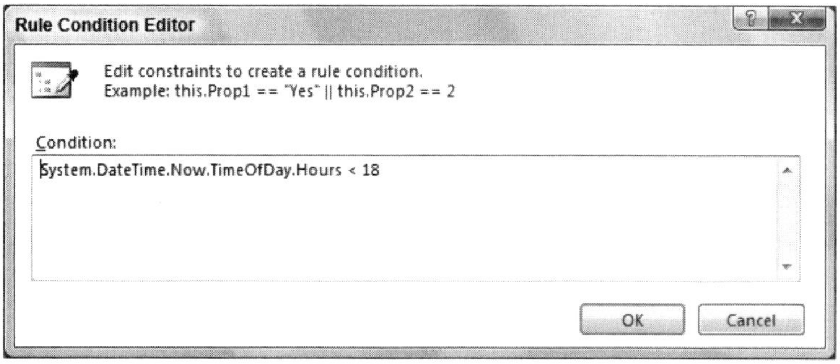

Figure 27-9

Set the rule on the `If` half of the `IfElse` activity to determine whether the current time is before noon:

```
System.DateTime.Now.TimeOfDay.Hours < 12
```

Right-click on the activity and select Add Branch to create a third branch to the `IfElse` activity. Set the condition for this one as you did for the first activity, but use 18 for the value to check for hours.

Add a `Code` activity to each of the three sections of the diagram (see Figure 27-10). You will use these activities to affect the message that is displayed. Assign the properties as follows:

Activity	Property	Value
codeActivity2	ExecuteCode	SetMessageMorning
codeActivity3	ExecuteCode	SetMessageAfternoon
codeActivity4	ExecuteCode	SetMessageEvening

Finally, change the code in the workflow to the following (note that this replaces the `SayGreetings` method created earlier):

```
Public class Workflow1
    Inherits SequentialWorkflowActivity

    Private Message As String
    Private Sub SayGreetings(ByVal sender As System.Object, _
        ByVal e As System.EventArgs)
        Console.WriteLine(Message & ", from workflow")
        Console.WriteLine("Press enter to continue")
        Console.ReadLine()
    End Sub

    Private Sub SetMessageMorning(ByVal sender As System.Object, _
      ByVal e As System.EventArgs)
```

```
            Message = "Good morning"
        End Sub
        Private Sub SetMessageAfternoon(ByVal sender As System.Object, _
          ByVal e As System.EventArgs)
            Message = "Good afternoon"
        End Sub
        Private Sub SetMessageEvening(ByVal sender As System.Object, _
          ByVal e As System.EventArgs)
            Message = "Good night"
        End Sub
End Class
```

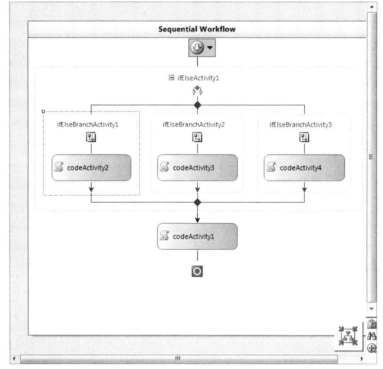

Figure 27-10

Each of the three SetMessage methods changes the greeting as appropriate. The final greeting is displayed in the SayGreetings method. Run the project again. You should be greeted appropriately for the time of day.

While this workflow is probably overkill to generate a simple message, the example does show many of the common steps used in defining a workflow. Workflows are composed of multiple activities. Many activities can in turn be composed of other activities. Activities may use declarative properties, or code may be executed as needed.

Standard Activities

The standard WF activities can be divided into five major categories:

❑ **Activities that communicate with external code** — These activities are either called by external code to initiate a workflow or used to call to external code as part of a workflow.

❑ **Control of flow activities** — These activities are the equivalent of Visual Basic's `If` statement or `While` loop. They enable the workflow to branch or repeat as needed to carry out a step.

❑ **Scope activities** — These activities group a number of other activities together into some logical element. This is usually done to mark a number of activities that participate in a transaction.

❑ **State activities** — These activities are used exclusively in state machine workflows. They represent the state of the process involved as part of the overall state machine.

❑ **Action activities** — These activities perform some action as part of the overall workflow.

In order for a workflow to begin, there must be some way for external code to initiate it. In addition, a workflow would be limited if there were no way for the workflow to execute external code and/or Web services. The standard activities that are used to communicate with external code include the following:

Activity	Description
CallExternalMethod	As the name implies, this activity calls an external method. The activity requires two properties. The first identifies an interface shared by the workflow and the external code. The second identifies the method on that interface that will be called. If the method requires additional parameters, then they appear on the property grid after setting the other two properties. This method is frequently used in combination with the HandleExternalEvent activity. This activity executes the external method synchronously, so be cautious when calling external methods that take a long time to execute.
HandleExternalEvent	Receives a trigger from an external block of code. This is a commonly used activity to initiate a workflow when the workflow is running in the context of a Windows Forms or ASP.NET application. As with the CallExternalMethod activity, it requires at least two properties. The first identifies a shared interface and the second identifies the event on that interface that will be received.
InvokeWebService	Calls an external Web service. You assign a WSDL file to the activity and it generates a proxy class for the Web service. You must also identify the method on the class that will be called. The SessionId property is used to identify the session that will be used for the requests. All requests with the same SessionId value share the session. If the SessionId is blank, then this activity creates a new session per request.

Activity	Description
InvokeWorkflow	Calls another workflow. This is a useful activity for chaining multiple workflows together, reducing the complexity of each workflow. The external workflow must complete before the current workflow continues.
WebServiceInput	Receives an incoming Web service request. You must publish the workflow containing this activity for it to work. You publish the workflow by selecting Publish as Web Service from the Project menu. This generates a new Web Service project that includes the output from the workflow project as well as an ASMX file that serves as the address for the workflow.
WebServiceOutput	Produces the output for a Web service request. This activity is used in partnership with the WebServiceInput activity.
WebServiceFault	Triggers a Web service error. This is used in partnership with the WebServiceInput activity to signal an error with the Web service call.

All programming languages need some form of flow control to regulate the applications. Visual Basic includes language elements such as If..Else, Do..While, For..Next, and Select Case to perform these actions. WF includes a number of activities to perform similar actions, although the options are more limited:

Activity	Description
IfElse	Provides for executing two or more different workflow paths based on the status of a condition. The condition may be code or an expression. This is a commonly used activity to branch a workflow.
Listen	Provides for executing two or more different workflow paths based on an event. The path chosen is selected by the first event that occurs. This is a useful activity for monitoring a class that could generate multiple events (such as a class that could either approve or reject a request).
Policy	Provides for executing multiple rules. Each rule is a condition with some resulting action. This activity provides a way to group multiple related rules into a single activity.
Replicator	Enables the workflow to create multiple instances of an activity for processing. The resulting child activities may run serially or in parallel. This is an excellent way to divide a large task: For example, you could have the Replicator activity create multiple child activities that are responsible for mailing a newsletter to a large list. The child activities could run in parallel, dividing the list into smaller groups for faster processing.
While	Loops the workflow until a condition has been met. The condition may be the result of code or an expression. This is typically used to receive multiple input values or to process multiple requests, such as a batch job.

Several composite activities may cooperate to complete a single logical action by grouping other activities:

Activity	Description
CompensatableSequence	Similar to the Sequence activity (see below), this activity differs in that it supports "undoing" the child activities. You can think of this in terms of a transaction: If one child activity fails, then the completed activities must be undone. The CompensatableSequence activity includes handles that enable the developer to perform this correction.
ConditionedActivityGroup	Includes a number of child activities that are run based on a condition. All child activities will execute until some defined condition occurs. This provides a means of grouping a number of related activities into a single activity.
EventDriven	Responds to an external event to initiate a set of activities. This is similar to the HandleExternalEvent activity, but the events are internal to the workflow. This activity is commonly used in a state-machine workflow to move between the states.
FaultHandler	Enables handling an error within a workflow. You use the FaultHandler activity to either correct or report the error gracefully. For example, a timeout may occur, triggering a fault condition in the workflow. This handler would contain other activities that are responsible for an alternate method of processing the item.
Parallel	Contains a series of child activities that run concurrently. You should only use this if either the child activities do not affect the data or the order of change is not important.
Sequence	Contains a series of child activities that run in order. This is the default model for a workflow. Each child activity must complete before the next one begins.

State activities represent the current state of the data and process for the workflow. They are only used within state-machine workflows:

Activity	Description
State	Represents the current state of the workflow. For example, in a workflow driving a voice-mail system, the state would represent the current menu that the client is on.
StateFinalization	Provides an activity to handle the actions needed as a given state is completed. This would provide a place to record the user's selection or to free up resources used by the state.
StateInitialization	Provides an activity to handle the actions needed before the given state is entered. This would enable the creation of any data or code needed to prepare for the state functioning.

The final group of activities are those that perform some action. You already saw this activity type in the form of the `CodeActivity`. These activities are the cornerstone of any workflow. The standard activities in this group include the following:

Activity	Description
Code	Enables custom Visual Basic code to be performed at a stage in the workflow. You can use these wherever you need to perform some action not done by another activity. Whenever you use one of these — especially if you use the same type of code frequently — you should consider moving the code into a custom activity.
Compensate	Enables custom code to undo a previous action. This is typically done if an error occurs within the workflow.
Delay	Pauses the flow of the workflow. This is typically used to schedule some event. For example, you might have a workflow that is responsible for printing a daily report. The `Delay` activity could be used to schedule this printout so that it is ready as the workers come in to read it. You can either set the delay explicitly by setting the `TimeoutDuration` property or set it via code using the event identified in the `InitializeTimeoutDuration` property.
Suspend	Temporarily stops the workflow. This is usually due to some extraordinary event that you would want an administrator or developer to correct. The workflow will continue to receive requests, but not complete them past the `Suspend` activity. The administrator may then resume the workflow to complete processing.
Terminate	Ends the workflow immediately. This should only be done in extreme situations such as when the workflow is not capable of any further processing (e.g., it has lost the connection to a database or other needed resource).
Throw	Creates an exception that can be caught by the code hosting the workflow. This provides a means of propagating an error from the workflow to the containing code.

Building Custom Activities

In addition to the standard activity library, WF supports extensibility through the creation of custom activities. Creating custom activities is a matter of creating a new class that inherits from `Activity` (or one of the existing child classes). Several available attributes enable customization of the activity and how it appears when you use it in your workflows.

Creating custom activities is the primary means of extending WF. You might use custom activities to simplify a complex workflow, grouping a number of common activities into a single new activity.

Alternatively, custom activities can create a workflow that is easier to understand, using terms that are more familiar to the developers and business experts. Finally, custom activities can be used to support software used within the business, such as activities to communicate with a CRM or ERP system.

So you can see the steps required for creating a custom activity, the next exercise creates a simple activity that wraps the Google translation service. Create a new project using the Workflow Activity Library template. This project will create a DLL that contains the activities you create. Name the project TranslationActivity. It will include a single custom activity initially. This activity inherits from `SequenceActivity`, so it might include multiple child activities. You can change this as needed, but it's a good enough default for most activities. Drag a `Code` activity onto the designer. This activity does the actual translation work.

Because the new activity will be used to convert between a number of set language pairs, create an enumeration containing the valid options. This enumeration can be expanded as new options become available. You can either add this enumeration to a new class file or add it to the bottom of the current module (after the `End Class` statement):

```
Public Enum TranslationOptions As Integer
    EnglishToFrench
    EnglishToSpanish
    EnglishToGerman
    EnglishToItalian
    EnglishToRussian
    EnglishToChinese
    FrenchToEnglish
    SpanishToEnglish
    GermanToEnglish
    ItalianToEnglish
    RussianToEnglish
    ChineseToEnglish
End Enum
```

The new activity has three properties: the input text, a language pair that defines the source and target languages, and the output text (the latter being a read-only property). You can create properties normally in an activity, but it is beneficial to create them so that they participate in the workflow and are available to other activities. In order to do this, use the following pattern to describe your properties:

```
Public Shared SomeProperty As DependencyProperty = _
    DependencyProperty.Register("PropertyName", _
    GetType(ReturnType), _
    GetType(ClassName))

    Public Property PropertyName () As ReturnType
    Get
        Return CType(MyBase.GetValue(SomeProperty), _
            ReturnType)
    End Get
    Set(ByVal value As ReturnType)
        MyBase.SetValue(SomeProperty, value)
    End Set
End Property
```

The initial shared field of type DependencyProperty identifies the field that will be used to communicate with other activities. DependencyProperty is a common type used in WPF programming, enabling easier communication between nested types. The Public property enables the more common use of the property. Notice that it stores the data in the shared property between all instances of the type.

As described, there are three properties in the translate activity:

```
Public Shared InputTextProperty As DependencyProperty = _
     DependencyProperty.Register("InputText", _
     GetType(System.String), _
     GetType(TranslateActivity))
  Public Shared TranslationTypeProperty As DependencyProperty = _
     DependencyProperty.Register("TranslationType", _
     GetType(TranslationOptions), _
     GetType(TranslateActivity))
  Public Shared OutputTextProperty As DependencyProperty = _
     DependencyProperty.Register("OutputText", _
     GetType(System.String), _
     GetType(TranslateActivity))

  <DesignerSerializationVisibilityAttribute(DesignerSerializationVisibility.
Visible)> _
     <BrowsableAttribute(True)> _
     <DescriptionAttribute("Text to be translated")> _
     Public Property InputText() As String
     Get
          Return CStr(MyBase.GetValue(InputTextProperty))
     End Get
     Set(ByVal value As String)
          MyBase.SetValue(InputTextProperty, value)
     End Set
  End Property

  <DesignerSerializationVisibilityAttribute(DesignerSerializationVisibility.
Visible)> _
  <BrowsableAttribute(False)> _
  <DescriptionAttribute("Translated text")> _
  Public ReadOnly Property OutputText() As String
     Get
          Return CStr(MyBase.GetValue(OutputTextProperty))
     End Get
  End Property

  <DesignerSerializationVisibilityAttribute(DesignerSerializationVisibility.
Visible)> _
  <BrowsableAttribute(True)> _
  <DescriptionAttribute("Language pair to use for the translation")> _
  Public Property TranslationType() As TranslationOptions
     Get
          Return CType(MyBase.GetValue(TranslationTypeProperty), TranslationOptions)
     End Get
     Set(ByVal value As TranslationOptions)
```

```
                MyBase.SetValue(TranslationTypeProperty, value)
          End Set
     End Property
```

Attributes are added to the properties to enable communication with the designer. The core translation method is assigned to the `ExecuteCode` property of the `Code` activity. It calls the Google translation service and extracts the result from the returned HTML:

```
Private Const SERVICE_URL As String = _
   "http://translate.google.com/translate_t"

Private Sub Translate(ByVal sender As System.Object, _
     ByVal e As System.EventArgs)
         Dim reqString As String = _
           String.Format("{0}?hl=en&ie=UTF8&text={1}&langpair={2}", _
           SERVICE_URL, _
           Encode(Me.InputText), _
           BuildLanguageClause(Me.TranslationType))
         Dim respString As String
         Dim req As System.Net.HttpWebRequest

         Try
             req = CType(Net.WebRequest.Create(reqString), Net.HttpWebRequest)
             req.ProtocolVersion = Net.HttpVersion.Version10

             Dim resp As Net.WebResponse
             resp = req.GetResponse()
             Using reader As _
               New IO.StreamReader(resp.GetResponseStream(), Encoding.UTF8)
                 respString = reader.ReadToEnd
             End Using

             If Not String.IsNullOrEmpty(respString) Then
                 MyBase.SetValue(OutputTextProperty, _
                   Decode(ExtractText(respString)))
             End If
         Catch ex As Exception
             Console.WriteLine("Error translating text: " & ex.Message)
         End Try
     End Sub
```

A typical request to the Google translation service is performed using the service's Web page, available at www.google.com/translate_t. However, you can make the same type of request the Web page would, and parse the resulting HTML to extract the returned text. The request is made using a POST, to enable sending large blocks of text. For safety, the text is URL encoded using the HttpUtility class.

The routines used by the Translate method are as follows:

```
Private _langOptions As New List(Of String)()

Public Sub New()
```

```
        ' This call is required by the Windows Form Designer.
        InitializeComponent()

        ' Add any initialization after the InitializeComponent() call.
        _langOptions.Add("en|fr")
        _langOptions.Add("en|es")
        _langOptions.Add("en|de")
        _langOptions.Add("en|it")
        _langOptions.Add("en|zn-CH")
        _langOptions.Add("en|ru")
        _langOptions.Add("fr|en")
        _langOptions.Add("es|en")
        _langOptions.Add("de|en")
        _langOptions.Add("it|en")
        _langOptions.Add("ru|en")
        _langOptions.Add("zn-CH|en")

    End Sub


    Private Function Encode(ByVal value As String) As String
        Return Web.HttpUtility.UrlEncode(value)
    End Function
    Private Function Decode(ByVal value As String) As String
        Return Web.HttpUtility.HtmlDecode(value)
    End Function

    Private Function BuildLanguageClause( _
        ByVal languages As TranslationOptions) As String

        Dim result As String = String.Empty
        result = _langOptions.Item(languages)
        Return result
    End Function

    Private Function ExtractText(ByVal value As String) As String
        Dim result As String = String.Empty
        Dim r As RegularExpressions.Regex
        Dim m As RegularExpressions.Match

        r = New RegularExpressions.Regex("<div?[^>]*>(?<result>[^<]*)</div", _
            RegularExpressions.RegexOptions.IgnoreCase Or _
            RegularExpressions.RegexOptions.Multiline Or _
            RegularExpressions.RegexOptions.IgnorePatternWhitespace)
        m = r.Match(value)
        If m IsNot Nothing Then
            result = m.Groups.Item("result").Value
        End If

        Return result
    End Function
```

The _langOptions list is used to track the strings needed by the various language pairs. This is used by the BuildLanguageClause method to write the appropriate pair to the posted data. The order of the items in the `TranslationOptions` enumeration matches the order in which items are added to the list, so the `BuildLanguageOptions` method simply does a lookup into the list.

The `ExtractText` function uses a regular expression to extract the translated text. The translated text appears in a `<div>` tag within the resulting HTML. Fortunately, it is the only `<div>`, although you could modify the regular expression to look for a div with the id of `result_box`:

```
<div id=result_box dir=ltr>Bonne chance, Mandrin. Je pense que ceci pourrait juste
fonctionner </div>
```

The resulting activity can now be compiled and included in other workflows. Just as with custom controls, you can add this DLL to the Toolbox using the Choose Toolbox Items dialog after it has been compiled. If the Workflow Activity project is in the same solution as the workflow, it will be automatically added to the Toolbox after it has been compiled. Figure 27-11 shows the `Translate` activity added to the earlier example.

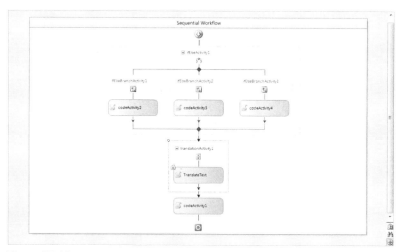

Figure 27-11

Recall that the Message field was used to store the message you wanted the workflow to generate. This is the text you want to translate. Click the ellipsis button on the `InputText` property in the property grid to bring up the Bind property dialog (see Figure 27-12). This enables you to visually connect the `Message` field to the input of the `TranslateActivity`.

The last change to the workflow is to update the text you output. Change the code for the `SayGreetings` method to display the `OutputText` of the `TranslateActivity`, as shown here:

```
Private Sub SayGreetings(ByVal sender As System.Object, _
    ByVal e As System.EventArgs)
    Console.WriteLine(Message & ", from workflow")
    Console.WriteLine("Press enter to continue")
    Console.ReadLine()
End Sub
```

Figure 27-12

Select the `TranslationType` and run the test project. Depending on the time of day and the language selected, you should see something similar to what is shown in Figure 27-13.

Figure 27-13

Using Workflows with Other Applications

Workflows are not typically standalone applications, or run as part of a console application, although this is an excellent way to develop them initially. Usually workflows are created to work within some larger application, so you need to integrate your workflow with the rest of your application, whether it is a Windows Forms application or ASP.NET.

Using Workflow Foundation with Windows Forms

When combining WF with Windows Forms, there are three main points of contact: hosting (and starting) the workflow, setting parameters for the workflow, and getting data out of the workflow.

Recall that the workflow runs within a host process. This process may be the Windows Forms process itself or an external one. If the Windows Forms process is hosting the workflow, then the workflow only exists as long as the application is running. The alternative is a workflow hosted within a Windows Service or another Windows Forms application. In this case, your application needs to use some form of interprocess communication to communicate with the workflow. Typically, this would take the form of remoting between the two applications. The application that hosts the workflow needs to initialize the WF runtime, load the workflow, and start it. In addition, the workflow host may initialize event handlers for the events that the WF runtime will throw. The following code shows an example of hosting the WF runtime and loading a workflow:

```vb
Imports System.Workflow.Activities
Imports System.Workflow.ComponentModel
Imports System.Workflow.Runtime

Public Class MainForm

    Private WithEvents wr As WorkflowRuntime
    Private wf As WorkflowInstance

    Private Sub TranslateButton_Click(ByVal sender As System.Object, _
        ByVal e As System.EventArgs) _
        Handles TranslateButton.Click
        If wr Is Nothing Then
            wr = New WorkflowRuntime
            wr.StartRuntime()
        End If
        'load a new instance of the workflow
        Me.EventList.Items.Add("Translating: " & Me.MessageField.Text)
        Dim parms As New Dictionary(Of String, Object)
        parms.Add("Message", Me.MessageField.Text)
        wf = wr.CreateWorkflow(GetType(HelloWorkflowDLL.SimpleWorkflow), parms)
        'start the workflow
        wf.Start()
    End Sub

    Private Sub MainForm_FormClosing(ByVal sender As Object, _
        ByVal e As System.Windows.Forms.FormClosingEventArgs) _
        Handles Me.FormClosing

        If wr IsNot Nothing Then
            If wr.IsStarted Then
                wr.StopRuntime()
            End If
        End If
    End Sub
```

In addition, you have to load references to the three workflow DLLs, and to the assembly that holds the workflow you want to create. Notice that you must create and start the WF runtime before you can load and start workflows. While the preceding code only creates a single instance of a workflow, you can create multiple instances from a single application. Stopping the runtime is not absolutely necessary, but gives you better control when the resources used by the WF runtime are freed.

The second step in working with WF and Windows Forms is providing parameters to the workflow. This is done by supplying a `Dictionary` when you create the workflow. The items in the `Dictionary` should match the public properties of the workflow. This changes the code used to create the workflow in the preceding sample as follows:

```
'load a new instance of the workflow
Dim parms As New Dictionary(Of String, Object)
parms.Add("Message", Me.MessageField.Text)
wf = wr.CreateWorkflow(GetType(TranslatedWorkflowDLL.SimpleWorkflow), parms)
```

By using a `Dictionary` with an `Object` value, any type of data can be supplied to the workflow. This provides flexibility in terms of the number and type of parameters you supply to the workflow, including changing the parameters over time.

The final step when working with WF and Windows Forms is retrieving data from the workflow. This is slightly more difficult than it may first seem because the workflow runs on a separate thread from the Windows Forms code. Therefore, the workflow can't directly access the controls on a form, and vice versa. The communication between the two is best performed by having the workflow generate events. The following code receives the `WorkflowCompleted` event and updates the `ListBox` on the form:

```
Private Sub wr_WorkflowCompleted(ByVal sender As Object, _
    ByVal e As System.Workflow.Runtime.WorkflowCompletedEventArgs) _
    Handles wr.WorkflowCompleted

    If Me. EventList.InvokeRequired Then
        Me. EventList.Invoke(New EventHandler(Of WorkflowCompletedEventArgs)( _
                AddressOf Me.wr_WorkflowCompleted), _
                New Object() {sender, e})
    Else
        Me.EventList.Items.Add("Translation: " & _
            e.OutputParameters("Message").ToString())
    End If

End Sub
```

Recall that the workflow runtime is actually running on a separate thread. Therefore, any attempts to access the `EventList` directly throw an exception. The first time through this code, the `InvokeRequired` property of the `EventList` is `true`. This means that the running code is executing on a separate thread. In this case, the code invokes a new instance of the event, passing in copies of the sender and `EventArgs`. This has the side effect of marshalling the data across to the thread containing the form. In this case, `InvokeRequired` is `false`, and you can retrieve the data from the workflow. Figure 27-14 shows the result.

Using Workflow Foundation with ASP.NET

Combining ASP.NET with Windows Workflow Foundation raises many of the same issues involved in using WF with other technologies. That is, you still need to host the services and the runtime of WF within the host process under which ASP.NET runs. However, developing solutions using ASP.NET offers more features and requires more decisions than other solutions. In particular, it is possible to publish workflows as ASP.NET Web services. Hosting workflows within ASP.NET solutions is similar to hosting workflows with Windows Forms, but an ASP.NET solution might actually be supporting multiple concurrent users. This means that you must be more aware of where the runtime is created and how instances are created and freed.

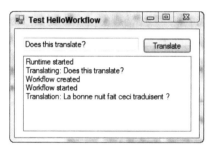

Figure 27-14

You can host a workflow as a Web service if it has one or more WebServiceInput activities. This activity represents a SOAP endpoint. The WebServiceInput activity needs two properties set: InterfaceType and MethodName. Communication between the client code and the Web service is achieved via a shared interface. This interface is the value needed for the InterfaceType property. It represents the contract between the client code and the WebServiceInput activity. The MethodName identifies the method on the interface that will initiate the Web service call. The first WebServiceInput activity should have the IsActivating property set to true. In addition to the WebServiceInput activity, the workflow should also include a WebServiceOutput activity if the method includes a return value. Including a WebServiceFault activity is also useful if you need to return an error to the client code. If the Web service has parameters or return values, these may be mapped to the properties of the workflow using the Bind property dialog (refer to Figure 27-12).

Once you have built the workflow, including the WebServiceInput and WebServiceOutput activities (see Figure 27-15), you must publish it as a Web service. This adds an additional ASP.NET Web Service project to the solution. The wizard creates the ASMX file that wraps the workflow and adds the required settings to the web.config file. The ASMX wrapper does nothing but delegate to the workflow class.

```
<%@WebService Class="TranslatedWorkflowDLL.SimpleWorkflow_WebService" %>
```

The additional settings in the configuration file add a new section for configuring the WorkflowRuntime and load the workflow HTTP handler that translates the incoming request:

```
<?xml version="1.0"?>
<configuration>
  <configSections>
    <section name="WorkflowRuntime"
      type="System.Workflow.Runtime.Configuration.WorkflowRuntimeSection,
      System.Workflow.Runtime, Version=3.0.00000.0, Culture=neutral,
      PublicKeyToken=31bf3856ad364e35"/>
  </configSections>
  <WorkflowRuntime Name="WorkflowServiceContainer">
    <Services>
    <add type="System.Workflow.Runtime.Hosting.ManualWorkflowSchedulerService,
        System.Workflow.Runtime, Version=3.0.0.0, Culture=neutral,
        PublicKeyToken=31bf3856ad364e35"/>
    <add
      type="System.Workflow.Runtime.Hosting.DefaultWorkflowCommitWorkBatchService,
        System.Workflow.Runtime, Version=3.0.0.0, Culture=neutral,
        PublicKeyToken=31bf3856ad364e35"/>
    </Services>
  </WorkflowRuntime>
```

```
<appSettings/>
<connectionStrings/>
<system.web>
  <httpModules>
    <add type="System.Workflow.Runtime.Hosting.WorkflowWebHostingModule,
       System.Workflow.Runtime, Version=3.0.0.0, Culture=neutral,
       PublicKeyToken=31bf3856ad364e35" name="WorkflowHost"/>
  </httpModules>
</system.web>
</configuration>
```

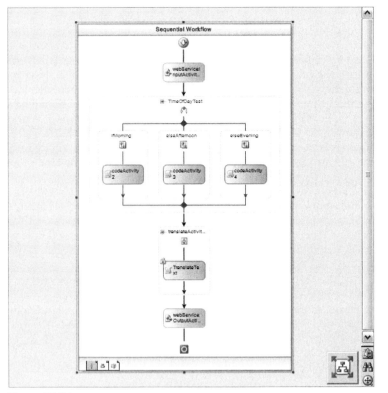

Figure 27-15

The resulting Web service works just like any other created by Visual Studio: You can access it in a browser to receive a test form (see Figure 27-16), request the WSDL, and access it using Web service clients.

Beyond Web services, ASP.NET applications can also host and access regular workflows. When hosting workflows in ASP.NET, keep in mind that your application may be accessed by many concurrent users, so you must be aware of when you create the runtime instance. In addition, remember that each workflow instance can use a good deal of memory. Therefore, limit the creation of workflows to when they are needed and free them quickly when they are no longer needed.

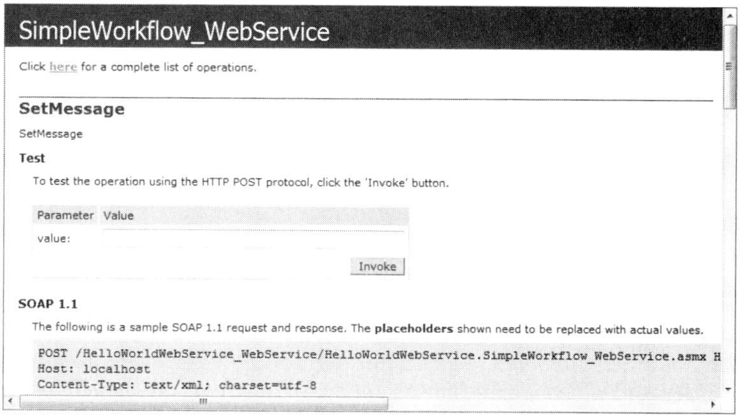

Figure 27-16

As you will probably want a single workflow runtime instance supporting all of your workflows, the best place to create the workflow runtime is when the application first starts. You can do this in the application's `Start` event in the `global.asax` file:

```
Sub Application_Start(ByVal sender As Object, ByVal e As EventArgs)
    Dim wfRun As New System.Workflow.Runtime.WorkflowRuntime
    Dim wfSked As _
      New System.Workflow.Runtime.Hosting.ManualWorkflowSchedulerService

    wfRun.AddService(wfSked)
    wfRun.StartRuntime()
    Application.Item("WorkflowRuntime") = wfRun
End Sub
```

This ensures that the same runtime is available to all sessions. Next, free up the resources used by the runtime when the application ends:

```
Sub Application_End(ByVal sender As Object, ByVal e As EventArgs)
    Dim wfRun As System.Workflow.Runtime.WorkflowRuntime
    wfRun = CType(Application.Item("WorkflowRuntime"), _
        System.Workflow.Runtime.WorkflowRuntime)
    wfRun.StopRuntime()

End Sub
```

Running a workflow instance is now a matter of retrieving the runtime instance and using it to execute the workflow. This leads to another issue related to the way Web pages are handled. Recall that the workflow typically runs asynchronously. This could mean that the workflow instance continues to run in the background after the Web page has returned. Therefore, you must run the workflow instance synchronously, so that it completes before returning data to the Web page:

```
Dim wfRun As WorkflowRuntime
wfRun = CType(Application.Item("WorkflowRuntime"), WorkflowRuntime)
```

```
Dim wfSked As ManualWorkflowSchedulerService
wfSked = wfRun.GetService(GetType(ManualWorkflowSchedulerService))

Dim wfInst As WorkflowInstance
wfInst = wfRun.CreateWorkflow(GetType(SimpleWorkflow))
wfInst.Start()

wfSked.RunWorkflow(wfInst.InstanceId)
```

The preceding code extracts the workflow runtime from the `Application` storage. It then retrieves the workflow scheduling service that was associated with the runtime as part of the `Application_Start` event handler. This scheduling service executes the workflows synchronously. This ensures that the entire workflow runs before the Web page is returned. The runtime is also used to create a new instance of the workflow desired, which is then started and associated with the scheduler. You could provide parameters to the workflow just as you did with the Windows Forms sample, by creating a `Dictionary` and populating it with the properties. This `Dictionary` would then be provided as a second parameter on the `CreateWorkflow` call. Similarly, you could retrieve the result of the workflow using the `OutputParameters` property in the `Completed` event handler for the workflow, just as you did with Windows Forms.

Summary

While Windows Workflow Foundation does not have the visual glitz of WPF or the broad reach of WCF, it is a highly useful addition to the .NET Framework 3.0. Most business applications have some need for workflows, and having a standard means of creating this workflow ensures that the workflow is fully featured and accurately reflects business needs. As WF is readily available with the .NET Framework, developers no longer need to recreate a core business rules engine with each application. WF is extensible, so developers can take advantage of it in their applications, without being limited to the designed features.

As with the other components of the .NET Framework, WF integrates well into other applications, including Windows Forms and ASP.NET applications. It provides the means to extract the frequently complex workflow from those applications and to graphically design it. This graphical representation can be used to communicate the process to business users, increasing the chance that the workflow is represented correctly. Finally, as business needs change, it is a simple process to update the workflow, without requiring changes to the core application.

Resources

While Windows Workflow Foundation is a relatively new component of the .NET Framework, you can already find useful websites for information:

❑ **Microsoft .NET Framework 3.0 Community** (http://wf.netfx3.com) — The main community site for WF and the other frameworks added with .NET Framework 3.0. This site has a number of useful samples, custom activities, and forums available.

❑ **WF on MSDN** (http://msdn.microsoft.com/workflow) — Articles, documentation, and more assistance on the main MSDN site.

XML Web Services

This chapter begins with a short history of multi-tier architecture and network operating systems, a discussion of the early days of the "network as the computer," and a discussion of where system architecture is heading today. The reason for this diversion is to understand the rationale behind Web services.

The chapter next looks at a sample Web service and walks through the process of making it accessible to the Internet as well as accessing it from a client application — both with the Visual Studio IDE and using command-line tools. From there, the chapter moves on to a key feature of Web services: the *Service Repository*, *Discovery*, and *Universal Description, Discovery, and Integration (UDDI)* features that enable remote programmers to correctly access Web services.

Finally, the chapter delves into more in-depth topics during discussion of the four namespaces found in the .NET Framework class library that deal with Web services and how to utilize them with Visual Basic 2008. Moving on, the chapter covers topics such as security, transactions, and the downsides of any distributed architecture (including any downsides associated with the Web services model), followed by a short discussion of where you go from here and how to get there.

Introduction to Web Services

A Web service is a means of exposing application logic or data via standard protocols such as XML, or, more specifically, SOAP (Simple Object Access Protocol). A Web service comprises one or more functions, packaged together for use in a common framework throughout a network. This idea is illustrated in Figure 28-1, where Web services provide access to information through standard Internet protocols, such as HTTP. By using a Web Services Description Language (WSDL) contract, consumers of the Web service can learn about the structure of the data the Web service provides, as well as all the details about how to actually consume it. A WSDL is a description of the remote interface offered from the Web service.

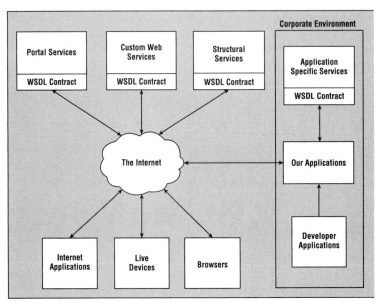

Figure 28-1

This simple concept provides for a very wide variety of potential uses by developers of Internet and intranet applications alike, as presented in Figure 28-1. Today, the Web services model is often the heart of the next generation of systems architecture because it is all of the following:

❑ **Architecturally neutral** — Web services do not depend on a proprietary wire format, schema description, or discovery standard.

❑ **Ubiquitous** — Any service that supports the associated Web service standards can support the service.

❑ **Simple** — Creating Web services is easy, quick, and can be free. The data schema is human readable. Any programming language can participate.

❑ **Interoperable** — Because the Web services all conform to the same standards, they can all speak to one another.

In basic terms, a Web service is an object with an XML document describing all of the methods, properties, and events sitting between the code and the caller. Any body of code written in just about any programming language can be described with this XML document, and any application that understands XML (or SOAP) over the assigned protocol (such as HTTP) can access the object. That's because the parameters you type after the function name are passed via XML to the Web service, and because SOAP is an open standard.

Microsoft has put a wrapper around all of the XML schemas that support Web services (including SOAP and WSDL), so they end up looking like .NET or COM objects. The following sections look at how the world views a Web service, and how Microsoft views Web services.

Early Architectural Designs

Understanding the history of the search for a decent *remote method invocation (RMI)* protocol is imperative to an understanding of why Web services are so important. Each of the RMI systems created before the current Web services model solved a particular set of problems, and you will see how current Web services represent the next stage in the evolution of these cross-platform boundaries to solve the problems that former technologies tried to address.

The Network Angle

Throughout the history of computing, networking operations were largely handled by the operating system. UNIX, the networking host of early computing, featured a body of shell operations that provided remarkable user control over network operations. Personal computing was slower to catch up: Microsoft and Apple software didn't inherently support networking protocols until the mid-1990s. Third-party add-ons by Novell and Banyan were available earlier, but they were only an adjunct to the operating system. The concept of the network being the computer did not fully infiltrate the development community until the expansion of the World Wide Web.

Application Development

Let's break away from networking for a minute and look at how application development evolved until now. Early time-sharing operating systems enabled several people to use the same application with its built-in data. These single-tier systems didn't allow for growth in the system's size, and data redundancy became the standard, with nightly batch jobs to synchronize the data becoming commonplace through the 1970s and early '80s.

Eventually, the opportunity presented by networks became the overriding factor in systems development, and enterprise network developers began offering the loosely termed *Object Request Brokers (ORBs)* on their systems: Microsoft's *Transaction Server (MTS)*, *Common Object Request Broker Architecture (CORBA)*, and the like. These ORBs enabled the separation of the user interface from the business logic using tightly coupled method pooling. This three-tier architecture brings you to the present in development terms, so let's step back and let networking catch up.

Merging the Two with the Web

The HTTP protocol was born in 1990. There were several other information delivery protocols before, such as Gopher, but HTTP was different because of the extensibility of the related language, HTML, and the flexibility of the transport layer, TCP/IP. Suddenly, movement of many formats of data was possible in a stateless, distributed way. Software as a service was born.

Over the next decade, low-level protocols supported by network systems and the Internet became a staple in applications, with SMTP and FTP providing file and information transfer among distributed servers. *Remote procedure calls (RPCs)* took things to the next level, but they were platform specific, with UNIX implementations in CORBA and Microsoft's Distributed COM (DCOM) leading the pack.

Enterprise development took a clue from the emerging technologies in wide area network (WAN) networking and personal computing, and development for these large-scale business systems began to mature. As usage of networks grew, developers began to solve problems of scalability, reliability, and adaptability with the traditional flat-format programming model. Multi-tier development began to spread the data, processing, and user interface of applications over several machines connected by local area networks (LANs).

This made applications more scalable and reliable by accommodating growth and providing redundancy. Gradually, vendor compliance and the Java programming language provided adaptability, enabling applications to run in a variety of circumstances on a variety of platforms.

However, there was a dichotomy between the capabilities of the network and the features of the programming environment. Specifically, after the introduction of XML, there still existed no "killer app" using its power. XML is a subset of Standard Generalized Markup Language (SGML), an international standard that describes the relationship between a document's content and its structure. It enables developers to create their own tags for hierarchical data transport in an HTML-like format. With HTTP as a transport and SOAP as a protocol, still needed was an interoperable, ubiquitous, simple, broadly supported system for the execution of business logic throughout the world of Internet application development.

The Foundations of Web Services

The hunt began with a look at the existing protocols. As had been the case for years, the Microsoft versus Sun Alliance debate was heating up among RPC programmers. CORBA versus DCOM was a source of continuing debate for developers using those platforms for distributed object development. After Sun added Remote Method Invocation to Java with Java-RMI, there were three distributed object protocols that fit none of the requirements.

Because DCOM and RMI are manufacturer-specific, it makes sense to start with those. CORBA is centrally managed by the Object Management Group, so it is a special case and should be considered separately.

RMI and DCOM provide distributed object invocation for their respective platforms — extremely important in this era of distributed networks. Both accommodate enterprisewide reuse of existing functionality, which dramatically reduces cost and time-to-market. Both provide encapsulated object methodology, preventing changes made to one set of business logic from affecting another. Finally, similar to ORB-managed objects, maintenance and client weight are reduced by the simple fact that applications using distributed objects are by nature multi-tier.

DCOM

DCOM's best feature is the fact that it is based on COM, one of the most prevalent desktop object models in use today. COM components are shielded from one another, and calls between them are so well defined by the OS-specific languages that there is practically no overhead to the methods. Each COM object is instantiated in its own space, with the necessary security and protocol providers. When an object in one process needs to call an object in another process, COM handles the exchange by intercepting the call and forwarding it through one of the network protocols.

When you use DCOM, all you are doing is making the wire a bit longer. With Windows NT4, Microsoft added the TCP/IP protocol to the COM network architecture and essentially made DCOM Internet-savvy. Aside from the setup on the client and server, the inter-object calls are transparent to the client, and even to the programmer.

Any Microsoft programmer can tell you, though, that DCOM has its problems. First, because there is a customer wire transport function, most firewalls do not allow DCOM calls to get through, even though they are by nature quite benign. There is no way to query DCOM about the methods and properties available, unless you have the opportunity to get the source code or request the remote component locally. In addition, there is no standard data transfer protocol (though that is less of a problem because DCOM is mostly for Microsoft networks).

Remote Method Invocation in Java

RMI is Sun's answer to DCOM. Java relies on a really neat, but very proprietary, protocol called *Java Object Serialization*, which protects objects marshaled as a stream. The client and server both need to be constructed in Java for this to work, but it further simplifies RMI because Java doesn't care whether the serialization takes place on one machine or across a continent. Similarly to DCOM, RMI enables the object developer to define an interface for remote access to certain methods.

CORBA

CORBA uses the *Internet Inter-ORB Protocol* to provide remote method invocation. It is remarkably similar to Java Object Serialization in this regard. Because it is only a specification, though, it is supported by a number of languages on diverse operating systems. With CORBA, the ORB does all the work, such as finding the pointer to the parent, instantiating it so that it can receive remote requests, carrying messages back and forth, and disputing arbitration and garbage collecting. The CORBA objects use specially designed sub-ORB objects called *basic* (or *portable*) *object adapters* to communicate with remote ORBs, giving developers more leeway in code reuse.

At first glance, CORBA would seem to be your ace in the hole. Unfortunately, it doesn't actually work that way. CORBA suffers from the same problem web browsers do — poor implementations of the standards — which causes lack of interoperability between ORBs. With IE and Netscape, minor differences in the way pages are displayed is written off as cosmetic. When there is a problem with the CORBA standard, however, it is a *real* problem. Not only is appearance affected, but also network interactions, as if there were 15 different implementations of HTTP.

The Problems

The principal problem of the DCOM/CORBA/RMI methods is complexity of implementation. The transfer protocol of each is based on manufacturers' standards, generally preventing interoperability. In essence, the left hand has to know what the right hand is doing. This prevents a company using DCOM from communicating with a company using CORBA.

First, there is the problem of wire format. Each of these three methods uses an OS-specific wire format that encompasses information supplied only by the operating system in question. This means two diverse machines cannot usually share information. The benefit is security: Because the client and server can make assumptions about the availability of functionality, data security can be managed with API calls to the operating system.

The second problem is the number of issues associated with describing the format of the protocol. Apart from the actual transport layer, there must be a schema, or layout, for the data that moves back and forth. Each of the three contemporary protocols makes numerous assumptions between the client and server. DCOM, for instance, provides ADO/RDS for data transport, whereas RMI has JDBC. While we can endlessly debate the merits of one over the other, we can at least agree that they don't play well together.

The third problem is knowing where to find broadly available services, even within your own network. We have all faced the problem of having to call up the COM + MMC panel so that we could remember how to spell this component or that method. When the method is resident on a server ten buildings away and you don't have access to the MMC console, the next step is digging through the text documentation, if there is any.

The Other Players

On a path to providing these services, we stumble across a few other technologies. While Java applets and Microsoft's client-side ActiveX technically are not distributed object invocations, they do provide distributed computing and provide important lessons. Fortunately, we can describe both in the same section because they are largely the same, with different operating systems as their backbone.

Applets and client-side ActiveX are both attempts to use the HTTP protocol to send thick clients to the end user. In circumstances where a user can provide a platform previously prepared to maintain a thicker-than-HTML client base to a precompiled binary, the ActiveX and applet protocols pass small applications to the end user, usually running a Web browser. These applications are still managed by their servers, at least loosely, and usually provide custom data transmission, utilizing the power of the client to manage the information distributed, as well as display it.

This concept was taken to the extreme with *Distributed Applet-Based Massively Parallel Processing*, a strategy that used the power of the Internet to complete processor-intense tasks, such as 3-D rendering or massive economic models, with a small application installed on the user's computer. If you view the Internet as a massive collection of parallel processors, sitting mostly unused, you have the right idea. An example of this type of processing is provided by United Devices (www.ud.com).

In short, HTTP can provide distributed computing. The problem is that the tightly coupled connection between the client and server has to go, given the nature of today's large enterprises. The HTTP angle did show developers that using an industry-recognized transport method solved problem number one, wire format. Using HTTP meant that regardless of the network, the object could communicate. The client still had to know a lot about the service being sent, but the network did not.

The goal? Distributed Object Invocation meets the World Wide Web. The problems are wire format, protocol, and discovery. The solution is a standards-based, loosely coupled method invocation protocol with a huge catalog. Microsoft, IBM, and Ariba set out in 1999 to create just that, and generated the RFC for Web services.

What All the Foundations Missed

You may notice that in reviewing the majority of the earlier services there has been little mention of language. That's because it was a problem overlooked by the foundations. Even RMI failed to recognize that you can't make everyone use the same language, even a great language.

HTTP — A Language-Independent Protocol

What we need is a language-independent protocol that accommodates a standard wire transfer, protocol language, and catalog service. Java with Remote Scripting and ActiveX taught us that HTTP is the wire transfer of choice. Why? What does HTTP do that is so great? First, it is simple. The header added to a communication by HTTP is straightforward enough that power users can type it at a command prompt if they have to. Second, it doesn't require a special data protocol; it just uses ASCII text. Third, HTTP traffic can easily get through firewalls (port 80 is usually open). Finally, it is extensible. Additional headers can be added to the HTTP header for application-specific needs, and any intermediary software can just ignore it.

XML — Cross-Language Data Markup

Now that we have a standard wire transfer protocol that we know works, we need a language and a transport mechanism. Existing languages don't really have data description functions, aside from the data management object models such as ADO. XML fits the bill because it is self-describing. The left hand doesn't need to know what the right hand is doing. An XML file transported over HTTP does not need to know the answering system's network protocol or its data description language. The concepts behind XML are so light and open that everyone can agree to support them. In fact, almost everyone has. XML has become the ASCII of the Web.

XML is important to Web services because it provides a universal format for information to be passed from system to system. We knew that, but Web services actually uses XML as the object invocation layer, changing the input and output to tightly formatted XML, making it platform and language independent.

SOAP — The Transfer You Need

Enter Simple Object Access Protocol (SOAP), which uses HTTP to package essentially one-way messages from service to service in such a way that business logic can interpolate a request/response pair. For your Web page to get an example, you'd make a SOAP request that would look something like this:

```
POST /Directory HTTP/1.1
Host: Ldap.companyname.com
Content-Type: text/xml; charset="utf-8"
Content-Length: 33
SOAPAction: "Some-URI"\vs

<SOAP-ENV:Envelope
 xmlns:SOAP-ENV="http://schemas.xmlsoap.org/soap/envelope/"
 SOAP-ENV:encodingStyle="http://schemas.xmlsoap.org/soap/encoding/">
 <SOAP-ENV:Body>
   <m:FindPerson xmlns:m="Some-URI">
     <NAME>Gates</NAME>
   </m: FindPerson>
 </SOAP-ENV:Body>
</SOAP-ENV:Envelope>
```

This is an HTTP page request, just like one you'd see for an HTML page except that the Content-Type specifies XML, and there is the addition of the SOAPAction header. SOAP has made use of the two most powerful parts of HTTP: content neutrality and extensibility. Here is the response statement from the server:

```
HTTP/1.1 200 OK
Content-Type: text/xml;
charset="utf-8"
Content-Length: 66
```

```
<SOAP-ENV:Envelope
 xmlns:SOAP-ENV="http://schemas.xmlsoap.org/soap/envelope/"
 SOAP-ENV:encodingStyle="http://schemas.xmlsoap.org/soap/encoding/"/>
  <SOAP-ENV:Body>
     <m:FindPersonResponse xmlns:m="Some-URI">
       <DIRECTORY>Employees
       <PERSON>
          <NAME>Bill Gates</NAME>
          <FUNCTION>Architect
             <TYPE>Web Services</TYPE>
          </FUNCTION>
          <CONTACT>
             <PHONE TYPE=CELL>123-456-7890</PHONE>
             <PHONE TYPE=HOME>555-111-2222</PHONE>
          </CONTACT>
       </PERSON>
       </DIRECTORY>
     </m: FindPersonResponse >
  </SOAP-ENV:Body>
</SOAP-ENV:Envelope>
```

SOAP enables you to send the XML files back and forth among remote methods. It is similar to XML-RPC, a protocol developed by Dave Winer in parallel with the SOAP protocol. Both protocols provide similar structures, but the official SOAP protocol is used by Visual Basic and the entire .NET platform.

SOAP is not specific to .NET either. The SOAP Toolkit is another set of tools that Microsoft's Web Services Team provides free of charge. It contains a wonderful WSDL editor, retrofit objects for Windows 2000 and Windows NT4 servers, and more. You can find it at `http://msdn.microsoft.com/webservices`.

Web Services Description Language

A Web Services Description Language (WSDL) document is a set of definitions that is utilized to describe the interface of any of your Web services. Six elements are defined and used by the SOAP protocol: `types`, `message`, `portType`, `binding`, `port`, and `service`. Essentially adding another layer of abstraction, the purpose of WSDL is to isolate remote method invocations from their wire transport and data definition language. Once again, it is a specification, not a language, so it is much easier to get companies to agree to its use.

Because WSDL is just a set of descriptions in XML, it is not so much a protocol as a grammar. Following is the sample service contract for the `HelloWorld` Web service you will be building shortly. You can see this file by visiting `http://localhost/HelloWorldExample/Service.asmx?WSDL` using your Web browser after you create the examples:

```
<?xml version="1.0" encoding="utf-8" ?>
<wsdl:definitions xmlns:soap="http://schemas.xmlsoap.org/wsdl/soap/"
  xmlns:tm="http://microsoft.com/wsdl/mime/textMatching/"
  xmlns:soapenc="http://schemas.xmlsoap.org/soap/encoding/"
  xmlns:mime="http://schemas.xmlsoap.org/wsdl/mime/"
  xmlns:tns="http://localhost/webservice" xmlns:s="http://www.w3.org/2001/XMLSchema"
  xmlns:soap12="http://schemas.xmlsoap.org/wsdl/soap12/"
  xmlns:http="http://schemas.xmlsoap.org/wsdl/http/"
  targetNamespace="http://localhost/webservice"
```

```
xmlns:wsdl="http://schemas.xmlsoap.org/wsdl/">
  <wsdl:types>
     <s:schema elementFormDefault="qualified"
       targetNamespace="http://localhost/webservice">
        <s:element name="HelloWorld">
           <s:complexType />
        </s:element>
        <s:element name="HelloWorldResponse">
           <s:complexType>
              <s:sequence>
                 <s:element minOccurs="0" maxOccurs="1" name="HelloWorldResult"
                   type="s:string" />
              </s:sequence>
           </s:complexType>
        </s:element>
     </s:schema>
  </wsdl:types>
  <wsdl:message name="HelloWorldSoapIn">
     <wsdl:part name="parameters" element="tns:HelloWorld" />
  </wsdl:message>
  <wsdl:message name="HelloWorldSoapOut">
     <wsdl:part name="parameters" element="tns:HelloWorldResponse" />
  </wsdl:message>
  <wsdl:portType name="WebServiceSoap">
     <wsdl:operation name="HelloWorld">
        <wsdl:input message="tns:HelloWorldSoapIn" />
        <wsdl:output message="tns:HelloWorldSoapOut" />
     </wsdl:operation>
  </wsdl:portType>
  <wsdl:binding name="WebServiceSoap" type="tns:WebServiceSoap">
     <wsdl:documentation>
        <wsi:Claim conformsTo="http://ws-i.org/profiles/basic/1.0"
          xmlns:wsi="http://ws-i.org/schemas/conformanceClaim/" />
     </wsdl:documentation>
     <soap:binding transport="http://schemas.xmlsoap.org/soap/http"
       style="document" />
     <wsdl:operation name="HelloWorld">
        <soap:operation soapAction="http://localhost/webservice/HelloWorld"
          style="document" />
        <wsdl:input>
           <soap:body use="literal" />
        </wsdl:input>
        <wsdl:output>
           <soap:body use="literal" />
        </wsdl:output>
     </wsdl:operation>
  </wsdl:binding>
  <wsdl:binding name="WebServiceSoap12" type="tns:WebServiceSoap">
     <soap12:binding transport="http://schemas.xmlsoap.org/soap/http"
       style="document" />
     <wsdl:operation name="HelloWorld">
        <soap12:operation soapAction="http://localhost/webservice/HelloWorld"
          style="document" />
        <wsdl:input>
           <soap12:body use="literal" />
```

```
                </wsdl:input>
                <wsdl:output>
                    <soap12:body use="literal" />
                </wsdl:output>
            </wsdl:operation>
        </wsdl:binding>
        <wsdl:service name="WebService">
            <wsdl:port name="WebServiceSoap" binding="tns:WebServiceSoap">
                <soap:address location="http://localhost:40718/Reuters/WebService.asmx" />
            </wsdl:port>
            <wsdl:port name="WebServiceSoap12" binding="tns:WebServiceSoap12">
                <soap12:address
                 location="http://localhost:40718/Reuters/WebService.asmx" />
            </wsdl:port>
        </wsdl:service>
    </wsdl:definitions>
```

This is what makes it all work. Notice that each of the inputs and outputs of the `HelloWorldResponse` function is defined as an element in the schema. The .NET Framework uses this to build library files that understand how best to format the outgoing requests, so no matter what operating system develops the WSDL, as long as it is well formed according to the WSDL specification, any type of application (it doesn't necessarily need to be a .NET application) can consume it with a simple SOAP request.

In fact, IIS with the .NET Framework is set up to use the WSDL document in order to provide a great auto-generated user interface for developers and consumers to check out and test Web services. After removing the `?wsdl` from the preceding URL, you'll see a very nicely formatted documentation screen for the service. Click the function name and you will get the screen shown in Figure 28-2. This is all dynamically generated based upon the contents of the WSDL document, which is itself dynamically generated by .NET.

Figure 28-2

The WSDL document can also be expanded in order to define your own descriptions. You can use the `Description` property of both the `WebService` and `WebMethod` attributes to provide more details for this .NET-generated test page for your XML Web services.

Building a Web Service

Building Web services with Visual Studio 2008 is *incredibly* easy. Microsoft has made it a cakewalk to put together a new Web service application and expose methods off that Web service.

To get started, create an ASP.NET Web Service application. Find this option by clicking File ➪ New Web Site in Visual Studio. From there, Visual Studio will ask you for the location of the Web server. Enter this as `C:\Documents and Settings\Bill\My Documents\Visual Studio 2008\WebSites\HelloWorldExample`.

Unlike an ASP.NET Web Application project, Visual Studio creates an .asmx file, rather than an .aspx file. The .asmx file extension is short for Active Server Methods, derived from the fact that it contains methods that will be exposed through the Web service.

By default, Visual Studio creates the Web service using the code-behind model for the Web service page. In addition to the .asmx file, Visual Studio also creates a `Service.vb` file and places this file in the `App_Code` folder of the project.

Open the `Service.asmx` file in Visual Studio. It contains only the `WebService` page directive, as shown here:

```
<%@ WebService Language="VB" CodeBehind="~/App_Code/Service.vb"
    Class="Service" %>
```

You use the `@WebService` directive instead of the `@Page` directive. The simple `WebService` directive has only four possible attributes:

- ❑ `Class` — This required attribute specifies the class used to define the methods and data types visible to the XML Web Service clients.

- ❑ `CodeBehind` — Required only when you are working with an XML Web Service file using the code-behind model, this enables you to work with Web services in two separate and more manageable pieces instead of a single file. The `CodeBehind` attribute takes a string value representing the physical location of the second piece of the Web Service — the class file containing all the Web service logic. In ASP.NET 2.0, it is best to place the code-behind files in the `App_Code` folder, starting with the default Web Service created by Visual Studio when you initially opened the Web Service project.

- ❑ `Debug` — This optional attribute takes a setting of either `True` or `False`. If the `Debug` attribute is set to `True`, then the XML Web Service is compiled with debug symbols in place; setting the value to `False` ensures that the Web service is compiled without the debug symbols in place.

- ❑ `Language` — This required attribute specifies the language used for the Web Service.

Instead of focusing on the `Service.asmx` page, double-click on the `Service.vb` file to open the file in the document window of Visual Studio. With the `Service.vb` file in the document window, notice that the single method on the page is decorated with the `<WebMethod()>` attribute. This attribute (`System.Web.Services.WebMethodAttribute`) is used to tell ASP.NET to expose this particular method through the Web service.

Directly after the `WebServiceBinding` attribute, place the `WebService` attribute in code to define a custom namespace, which the industry recommends you always provide. The value of the namespace can be whatever you see fit; it does not have to be an actual URL, just a unique identifier:

```
Imports System.Web
Imports System.Web.Services
Imports System.Web.Services.Protocols

<WebService(Namespace:="http://localhost/HelloWorldExample")> _
<WebServiceBinding(ConformsTo:=WsiProfiles.BasicProfile1_1)> _
<Global.Microsoft.VisualBasic.CompilerServices.DesignerGenerated()> _
Public Class Service
    Inherits System.Web.Services.WebService

    <WebMethod()> _
    Public Function HelloWorld() As String
        Return "Hello World"
    End Function

End Class
```

Now add a new method called `GoodbyeWorld`, without a `WebMethod` attribute:

```
Public Function GoodbyeWorld() As String
  Return "Goodbye World"
End Function
```

Run the project. Visual Studio will open the `Service.asmx` file. By default, Web services display a test interface (see Figure 28-3) that enables you to see which methods are available and to execute them.

Figure 28-3

Notice that only the `HelloWorld` method is displayed. This is the only method decorated with the `WebMethod` attribute, and hence the reason why `GoodbyeWorld` and all of the inherited methods on the `Service` class were not displayed. Clicking the link enables you to invoke the method, as shown in Figure 28-4.

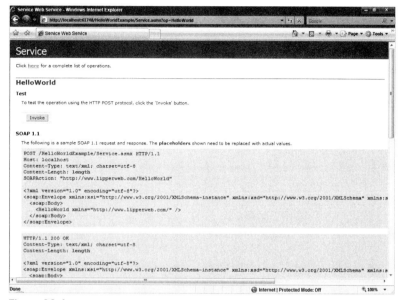

Figure 28-4

If you do this, the URL `http://localhost:#####/HelloWorldExample/Service.asmx/HelloWorld` is requested, which happens to be the URL for this specific method (running with the built-in web server provided with Visual Studio). You will then see the payload of the SOAP document directly in the browser, which contains the results of the call, as shown in Figure 28-5.

Figure 28-5

That is pretty much all there is to Web services from an implementation perspective when working with the .NET Framework. The .NET Framework deals with all of the plumbing (SOAP, WSDL, and so on) discussed in the first part of this chapter on your behalf, so you only have to add properly decorated methods to the service.

1117

A Realistic Example

Although the previous example was very easy to implement, it does not demonstrate a real-world application of Web services. Let's take a look at a more realistic example by building a Web service that provides a richer set of data from a database instead. For this example, imagine that a third-party provider hosts the site. The SQL server is behind a firewall, and the IIS server is in a demilitarized zone — a safe, though exposed, network position, as shown in Figure 28-6.

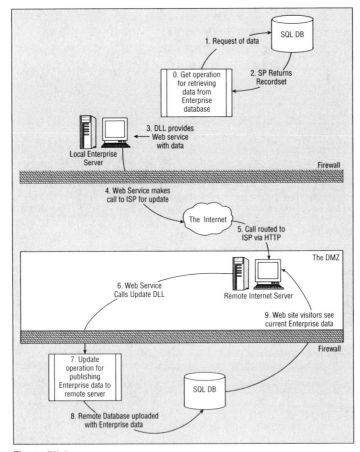

Figure 28-6

To get the data from your site to the remote site, you need to call a Web service on the remote web server from your intranet. The SOAP envelope is sent via HTTP, so the firewall allows it to pass through, and ADO.NET on the IIS server handles the actual database manipulation. The remote firewall allows database calls only from the IIS server, and the data is updated safely because of the security.

In real life, the method `GetEmployees` would be local to your intranet server, and the database file would be a SQL server on a second server. Across the Internet, as shown in Figure 28-6, the Web service would be on an IIS server sitting outside the network firewall. The DLL that actually provides the data functions would be on an application server inside the firewall, and the database would again be on a separate server.

For this application, though, you need to create a Web service that exposes some of the Contact table, as well as some of the Employee table, from the sample AdventureWorks database, across the intranet, which will later be consumed by a Web application. Keep in mind that Web services not only expose simple values, but also a richer data set of values, such as entire tables from a data store (for example, SQL Server).

Start this example by first creating a new Web Service project in Visual Studio called WebService1.

Using Visual Studio 2008 to Build Web Services

The Visual Studio 2008 IDE shows a marked improvement from the add-ins provided for Visual Studio 6 in the SOAP Toolkit. For instance, Web services are shown as references on a project, rather than in a separate dialog box. The discovery process, discussed later, is used to its fullest, providing much more information to the developer. In short, it is nearly as easy to consume a Web service with Visual Basic as it is to use DLLs.

Producing a Typed DataSet

For simplicity, you will use Visual Studio to first create a typed DataSet, which will be returned from the WebMethod that you later produce. This IDE enables you to quickly and easily create the needed data access without having to dig through a lot of ADO.NET code.

Right-click the WebService1 project in the Solution Explorer and select Add New Item. From the provided menu of file options, select DataSet. Change the name of this file to MyDataComponent.xsd. This creates an already strongly typed DataSet on the fly. In addition, Visual Studio requests to place this file in the App_Code folder of your solution. Confirm this request, because having it in the App_Code folder allows for programmatic access to the DataSet (see Figure 28-7).

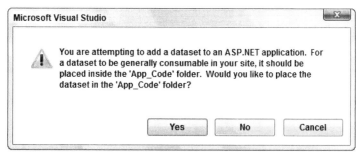

Figure 28-7

Once created, the MyDataComponent.xsd file opens itself in Visual Studio. This file appears as a blue screen in the document window. The first step is to drag and drop a single TableAdapter onto this design surface. Once you do this, the TableAdapter Configuration Wizard opens, as shown in Figure 28-8.

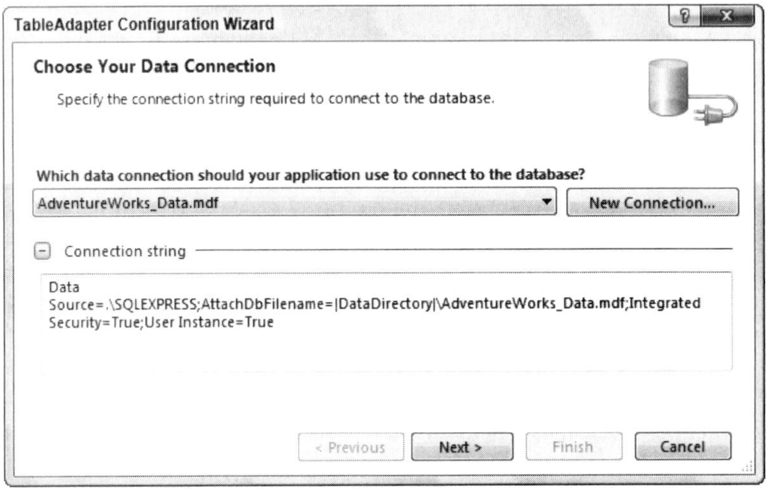

Figure 28-8

The first step in the TableAdapter Configuration Wizard is establishing a data connection. If a connection is not already in place, then create one by clicking the New Connection button. Using this dialog, make a new connection to the sample AdventureWorks_Data.mdf database, which is a SQL Server Express Edition database file. You can find this and other SQL Server 2005 samples online on the Microsoft CodePlex website (www.codeplex.com/MSFTDBProdSamples/Release/ProjectReleases.aspx?ReleaseId = 4004). Download the file AdventureWorksDB.msi.

Once the connection is defined in the TableAdapter Configuration Wizard, the next step of the wizard asks you to store the connection in the web.config file, which is always a good option to choose. Choosing both of these actions will copy the AdventureWorks_Data.mdf database file to the App_Data folder in your project, and the connection to this database file will now be named and placed within the web.config file of your ASP.NET Web Service project.

```
<connectionStrings>
   <add name="AdventureWorks_DataConnectionString"
     connectionString="Data Source=.\SQLEXPRESS;AttachDbFilename=|DataDirectory|
       \AdventureWorks_Data.mdf;Integrated Security=True;Connect Timeout=30;
       User Instance=True"
     providerName="System.Data.SqlClient" />
</connectionStrings>
```

Once the connection to the data store is established, click Next. In the dialog that appears, pick the command type that you want to work with. Typically, the options are working with either direct SQL commands, existing stored procedures, or stored procedures that you can create directly in the wizard. For this example, choose the first option: Use SQL Statements.

The next page in the wizard asks for the query that you want to use to load the table data. Input the following:

```
SELECT HumanResources.Employee.EmployeeID, HumanResources.Employee.Title,
    HumanResources.Employee.Gender,
```

```
        HumanResources.Employee.HireDate, Person.Contact.Title AS EXPR1,
        Person.Contact.FirstName, Person.Contact.MiddleName,
        Person.Contact.LastName, Person.Contact.EmailAddress, Person.Contact.Phone
FROM Person.Contact INNER JOIN
        HumanResources.Employee ON Person.Contact.ContactID =
            HumanResources.Employee.ContactID
```

Clicking the Next button results in a page from which you can select the methods that the wizard will generate (as shown in Figure 28-9). These are the methods used in your Web service to load data into data sets for transmission. In this case, the `Fill` and `GetData` methods are specified with the first two options in the dialog. In some cases, you might want to also select the last check box, which creates the additional `Insert`, `Update`, and `Delete` methods that you might want to later expose via a Web service. When you are done, click Next again to proceed to the next step in the wizard.

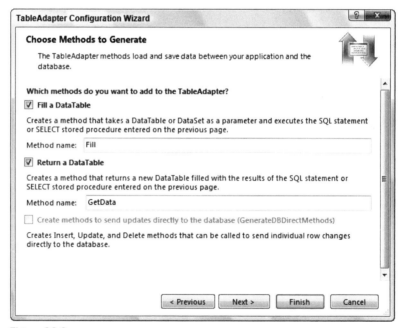

Figure 28-9

Figure 28-10 shows the last page of the wizard. This final page just shows the results of all the actions taken in the preceding steps.

After clicking the Finish button, note that the design surface of the `MyDataComponent.xsd` file changes to reflect the data that comes from the two tables of the AdventureWorks database (see Figure 28-11).

At this point, your typed data set is now in place and ready for use by the Web service. Looking at the results on the design surface of the `.xsd` file, you can see that indeed the typed `MyDataComponent` data set is in place and contains a single `DataTable` called `DataTable1`. There is also a `DataTable1TableAdapter` object with `Fill` and `GetData` methods in place.

Figure 28-10

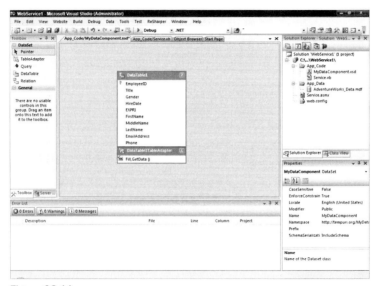

Figure 28-11

Building the Service

Right-click `Service.asmx` from within the Solution Explorer in Visual Studio and select View Code. Rename the `HelloWorld` function to `GetEmployees`. From here, simply retrieve data from the `DataTable1TableAdapter` that was created when you created the `.xsd` file earlier:

```
Imports System.Web
Imports System.Web.Services
Imports System.Web.Services.Protocols

<WebService(Namespace:="http://www.lipperweb.com/namespace")> _
<WebServiceBinding(ConformsTo:=WsiProfiles.BasicProfile1_1)> _
```

```
<Global.Microsoft.VisualBasic.CompilerServices.DesignerGenerated()> _
Public Class Service
    Inherits System.Web.Services.WebService

    <WebMethod()> _
    Public Function GetEmployees() As MyDataComponent.DataTable1DataTable
        Dim da As New MyDataComponentTableAdapters.DataTable1TableAdapter
        Dim ds As New MyDataComponent.DataTable1DataTable

        da.Fill(ds)

        Return ds
    End Function
End Class
```

> If you are having trouble getting the **MyDataComponent** object recognized by Visual Studio, before adding this code, be sure to build your application, and then you will find that it is recognized.

Right-click the `Service.asmx` file in the Solution Explorer and select View in Browser. If there are no errors, then a simple screen listing `GetEmployees` as the sole method of the service appears. Click the Service Description line. You will get a screen like the one shown earlier in Figure 28-2.

Consuming the Service

Although the Web service is in place, you really have seen only half the story. Exposing data and logic as SOAP to disparate systems across the enterprise or across the world is a simple task using .NET, and particularly ASP.NET. The other half of the story is the actual consumption of an XML Web Service into another application.

Keep in mind that you are not limited to consuming Web services only into ASP.NET applications, as shown shortly. Consuming Web services into other types of applications is not that difficult; in fact, it is rather similar to how you would consume them using ASP.NET. Remember that the Web services you come across can be consumed in Window Forms, Windows Presentation Foundation applications, mobile applications, other databases, and more. You can even consume Web services with other Web services, resulting in a single Web service made up of what is basically an aggregate of other Web services.

For this consuming application, provide a Web application called WSEmployees by creating a new ASP.NET Web Site project with that name. For this example, create this new project within your current solution: Right-click on the WebService1 solution and select Add ➪ New Web Site from the menu. Once complete, your solution will now contain two projects: `WebService1` and `WSEmployees`. The first step to take within your WSEmployees project is to create a Web reference to the remote XML Web Service that was created in the WebService1 project.

Adding a Web Reference

The only bit of magic here is the adding of a Web reference to the project using the Visual Studio IDE. As described later, you are really creating a proxy based upon the WSDL file of the service and referencing the proxy in the project, but the IDE makes this all quite simple.

To create the proxy needed by the consuming application, right-click the WSCustomers project in the Solution Explorer and select Add Web Reference from the list of options. In this form, enter the WSDL file of the Web service to which you want to make a reference. If the Web service is a .NET Web Service (with an .asmx file extension), simply input the URL of the .asmx file and nothing more because the wizard automatically adds ?wsdl at the end of the input. If you are referencing a Java Web Service, then place the URL for the .wsdl file in this wizard. In most cases, you would simply enter the URL of the service you are interested in consuming in the address bar of the Add Web Reference dialog. For this example, click the "Web Services found at this URL" link. The dialog box shown in Figure 28-12 should appear.

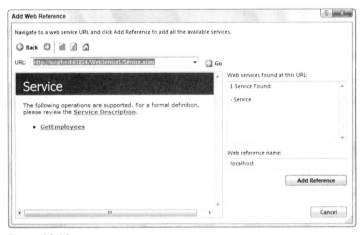

Figure 28-12

The service description page you see when you build your service appears in the left pane of the wizard, with .NET-specific information in the right. Click the Add Reference button at the right of the window to add this reference to your project. The service appears in a new folder called Web References within the Solution Explorer, as shown in Figure 28-13.

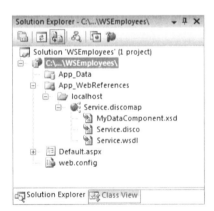

Figure 28-13

In making the reference, you can see that the .wsdl file was copied over, as well as the typed DataSet, MyDataComponent. The power of this Web services model is that it can work with the GetEmployees method as if it were now local to your machine, when in fact it is hosted in an entirely different application.

Building the Consumer

The COM architecture continually promised "one line of code" to generate great results. Web services live up to the promise, minus the declarations. Now the only thing left to do is call the referenced Web service and pass the generated `DataTable` that comes from the `DataSet`. Compared to the scores of lines of XML needed to pass the `DataSet` in the existing Microsoft technologies, this is a breeze.

The first step to consuming an .aspx page is simply to make a reference to the proxy that Visual Studio created and then call the `GetEmployees` WebMethod through this instantiated object. The results pulled from the `GetEmployees` method are then displayed in a `GridView` control, which is placed on a Web form.

You have a couple of ways to achieve this. The first method is to use an `ObjectDataSource` control, which does the work of invoking the `GetEmployees` WebMethod and then displaying the results in the `GridView` control. (The second method, discussed a bit later, is to manually write the required code.) To work through this example, drop a `GridView` and an `ObjectDataSource` server control onto the design surface of the Web form. Open the smart tag of the `ObjectDataSource` control and select Configure Data Source. You are then presented with the Configure Data Source Wizard.

In the first page of this wizard, uncheck the Show Only Data Components check box and select `localhost.Service` from the drop-down list. Click the Next button to choose the `SELECT` method for that `ObjectDataSource` control to use (shown in Figure 28-14).

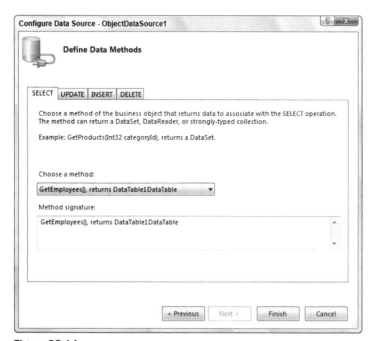

Figure 28-14

From the drop-down list on this page of the wizard, select `GetEmployees()`, returns `DataTable1DataTable` and click Finish to progress to the next step of binding the `GridView` control to the returned `DataTable` from this `ObjectDataSource` control.

Now turn your attention to the `GridView` control. In configuring this control, open the control's smart tag. From the drop-down list, select `ObjectDataSource1` as the data source control for this control. Note that once you do this, the `GridView` control expands to include all the appropriate columns from the result set you specified earlier from the AdventureWorks database.

Now, in the same smart tag, enable paging by selecting the appropriate check boxes. The code generated by Visual Studio is shown here:

```
<%@ Page Language="VB" AutoEventWireup="false" CodeFile="Default.aspx.vb"
    Inherits="_Default" %>

<!DOCTYPE html PUBLIC "-//W3C//DTD XHTML 1.0 Transitional//EN"
  "http://www.w3.org/TR/xhtml1/DTD/xhtml1-transitional.dtd">

<html xmlns="http://www.w3.org/1999/xhtml">
<head runat="server">
    <title>Consuming Application</title>
</head>
<body>
    <form id="form1" runat="server">
    <div>
        <asp:GridView ID="GridView1" runat="server" AllowPaging="True"
         AutoGenerateColumns="False"
         DataKeyNames="EmployeeID" DataSourceID="ObjectDataSource1">
            <Columns>
                <asp:BoundField DataField="EmployeeID" HeaderText="EmployeeID"
                 InsertVisible="False"
                 ReadOnly="True" SortExpression="EmployeeID" />
                <asp:BoundField DataField="Title" HeaderText="Title"
                 SortExpression="Title" />
                <asp:BoundField DataField="Gender" HeaderText="Gender"
                 SortExpression="Gender" />
                <asp:BoundField DataField="HireDate" HeaderText="HireDate"
                 SortExpression="HireDate" />
                <asp:BoundField DataField="EXPR1" HeaderText="EXPR1"
                 SortExpression="EXPR1" />
                <asp:BoundField DataField="FirstName" HeaderText="FirstName"
                 SortExpression="FirstName" />
                <asp:BoundField DataField="MiddleName" HeaderText="MiddleName"
                 SortExpression="MiddleName" />
                <asp:BoundField DataField="LastName" HeaderText="LastName"
                 SortExpression="LastName" />
                <asp:BoundField DataField="EmailAddress" HeaderText="EmailAddress"
                 SortExpression="EmailAddress" />
                <asp:BoundField DataField="Phone" HeaderText="Phone"
                 SortExpression="Phone" />
            </Columns>
        </asp:GridView>
        <asp:ObjectDataSource ID="ObjectDataSource1" runat="server"
         SelectMethod="GetEmployees"
```

```
        TypeName="localhost.Service"></asp:ObjectDataSource>
    </div>
    </form>
</body>
</html>
```

Once the page is complete, build and run it. That's it. There is now a table in the Web form with all the data from a remote SQL Server Express Edition file that can be paged — and you did not have to write *any* code to achieve this functionality! The page results are shown in Figure 28-15.

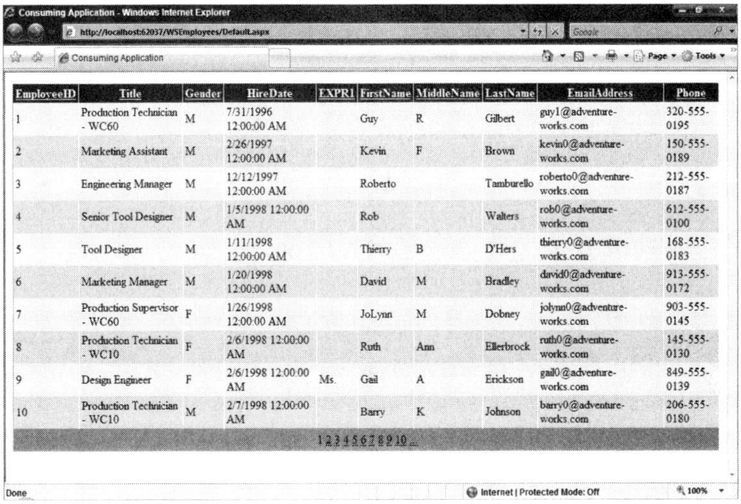

Figure 28-15

Now consider doing the same thing but instead spending a little time writing some code. This is a good exercise because it offers more control over the situation (if desired), and it teaches you more about what is going on.

Create a page that includes only a GridView server control. From here, you get at the data that comes from the Web service in the Page_Load event, as shown in the following example:

```
<%@ Page Language="VB" %>

<script runat="server">
    Sub Page_Load(ByVal sender As Object, ByVal e As System.EventArgs)
        Dim ws As New localhost.Service

        GridView1.DataSource = ws.GetEmployees()
        GridView1.DataBind()
    End Sub
</script>

<html xmlns="http://www.w3.org/1999/xhtml">
<head runat="server">
    <title>Consuming Application</title>
```

```
    </head>
    <body>
        <form id="form1" runat="server">
        <div>
            <asp:GridView ID="GridView1" Runat="server"
             AllowPaging="True" AllowSorting="True">
            </asp:GridView>
        </div>
        </form>
    </body>
    </html>
```

The first line of code contained in the `Page_Load` event instantiates the proxy object that was created for you. The next line assigns the `DataSource` property of the `GridView` server control to the result set from the `GetEmployees` WebMethod call. Finally, you close everything by calling the `DataBind` method of the `GridView` control. By compiling and running the XML Web Service, you can retrieve from the database the view of the Employees table that you created earlier from the AdventureWorks database. A returned dataset contains a wealth of information, including the following:

❑   An XSD definition of the XML contained in the `DataSet`

❑   The employee information from the Employees table of the AdventureWorks database

On the consumption side, consumers of this XML Web Service can easily use the XSD definition and the XML contained within the `DataTable` within their own applications. If users are then consuming this `DataTable` into .NET applications, they can easily bind this data to a `GridView` and use it within their applications with minimal lines of code.

Overloading WebMethods

In the object-oriented world of .NET, it is quite possible to use method overloading in the code you develop. A true object-oriented language has support for *polymorphism*, of which method overloading is a part. Method overloading enables you to have multiple methods that use the same name but have different signatures. With method overloading, one method can be called, but the call is routed to the appropriate method based on the full signature of the request. An example of standard method overloading is illustrated in the following code listing:

```
Public Function HelloWorld() As String
    Return "Hello"
End Function

Public Function HelloWorld(ByVal FirstName As String) As String
    Return "Hello " & FirstName
End Function
```

In this example, both methods have the same name, `HelloWorld`. Which one is called when you invoke `HelloWorld` depends on the signature you pass to the method. For instance, you might provide the following:

```
Label1.Text = HelloWorld()
```

This yields a result of just `Hello`. However, you might invoke the `HelloWorld` method using the following signature:

```
Label1.Text = HelloWorld("Bill Evjen")
```

This returns a result of `Hello Bill Evjen`. As you can see, method overloading is a great feature that can be effectively utilized by your ASP.NET applications — but how do you go about overloading `WebMethods`?

If you have already tried to overload any of your `WebMethods`, you probably got the following error when you pulled up the Web service in the browser:

```
Both System.String HelloWorld(System.String) and System.String HelloWorld() use the
message name 'HelloWorld'. Use the MessageName property of the WebMethod custom
attribute to specify unique message names for the methods.
```

As this error shows, the extra step you have to take to overload `WebMethods` is to use the `MessageName` property. The following bit of code shows how:

```
<WebMethod(MessageName:="HelloWorld")> _
Public Function HelloWorld() As String
    Return "Hello"
End Function

<WebMethod(MessageName:="HelloWorldWithFirstName")> _
Public Function HelloWorld(ByVal FirstName As String) As String
    Return "Hello " & FirstName
End Function
```

In addition to adding the `MessageName` property of the `WebMethod` attribute, you have to disable your Web service's adherence to the WS-I Basic Profile 1.0 specification — that it would not be doing if you perform `WebMethod` overloading with your Web services. You can disable conformance to the WS-I Basic Profile specification in a couple of ways. The first way is to add the `<WebServiceBinding>` attribute to your code, as illustrated here:

```
<WebServiceBinding(ConformsTo := WsiProfiles.None)> _
Public Class MyOverloadingExample
    ' Code here
End Class
```

The other option is to turn off the WS-I Basic Profile 1.0 capability in the `web.config` file:

```
<configuration>
  <system.web>
    <webServices>
      <conformanceWarnings>
        <remove name="BasicProfile1_1" />
      </conformanceWarnings>
    </webServices>
  </system.web>
</configuration>
```

1129

After you have enabled your Web service to overload WebMethods, you can see both WebMethods defined by their MessageName value properties when you pull up the Web service's interface test page in the browser (see Figure 28-16).

Figure 28-16

Although the names of the WebMethods are distinct (based on the MessageName property values you assigned in your code through the Web service's test page), when the developer consuming the Web service makes a Web reference to your Web service, he or she sees only a single method name available (in this example, HelloWorld). This is evident in the IntelliSense of Visual Studio 2008 in the application consuming these methods (see Figure 28-17).

```
Default2.aspx*                                                    ▾ ✕
Server Objects & Events                    ▾   (No Events)         ▾
   1   <%@ Page Language="VB" %>
   2
   3   <!DOCTYPE html PUBLIC "-//W3C//DTD XHTML 1.0 Transitional//EN" "http://www
   4
   5 ⊟ <script runat="server">
   6       Protected Sub Page_Load(ByVal sender As Object, ByVal e As System.Even
   7           Dim ws As New WroxOverloading.Overloading()
   8           ws.HelloWorld(
   9       End  ▲2 of 2▼  HelloWorld (FirstName As String) As String
  10 └ </script>
  11
  12 ⊟ <html xmlns="http://www.w3.org/1999/xhtml">
  13 ⊟ <head runat="server">
  14       <title>Untitled Page</title>
  15 └ </head>
  16 ⊟ <body>
  17 ⊟     <form id="form1" runat="server">
  18 ⊟     <div>
  19
  20 └     </div>
  21 └     </form>
  22 └ </body>
  23 └ </html>
  24
  ▣ Design  ▢ Split  ▣ Source   ◀ <script>
```

Figure 28-17

In the yellow box that pops up to guide developers on the signature structure, two options are available — one is an empty signature and the other requires a single string.

Caching Web Service Responses

Caching is an important feature in almost every application that you build with .NET. Although many features in the .NET Framework provide different vehicles for caching, a feature of Web services in .NET enables you to cache the SOAP response sent to any of the service's consumers.

First, by way of review, remember that caching is the capability to maintain an in-memory store where data, objects, and various items are stored for reuse. This feature increases the responsiveness of the applications you build and manage. Sometimes, returning cached results can greatly affect performance.

XML Web Services use an attribute to control caching of SOAP responses — the `CacheDuration` property. The following bit of code shows its use:

```
<WebMethod(CacheDuration:=60)> _
Public Function GetServerTime() As String
    Return DateTime.Now.ToLongTimeString()
End Function
```

As you can see, `CacheDuration` is used within the `WebMethod` attribute much like the `Description` and `Name` properties. `CacheDuration` takes an `Integer` value that is equal to the number of seconds during which the SOAP response is cached.

When the first request comes in, the SOAP response is cached by the server, and the consumer gets the same time stamp in the SOAP response for the next minute. After that minute is up, the stored cache is discarded, and a new response is generated and stored in the cache again for servicing all other requests for the next minute.

Among the many benefits of caching your SOAP responses, you will find that your application's performance is greatly improved when you have a response that is repeatedly recreated without any change.

SOAP Headers

One of the more common forms of extending the capabilities of SOAP messages is to add metadata of the request to the SOAP message itself. The metadata is usually added to a section of the SOAP envelope called the *SOAP header*. Figure 28-18 shows the structure of a SOAP message.

Figure 28-18

The entire SOAP message is referred to as a *SOAP envelope*. Contained within the SOAP message is the *SOAP body* — a piece of the SOAP message that you have been working with in every example thus far. It is a required element of the SOAP message.

The one optional component of the SOAP message is the SOAP header, which is the part of the SOAP message where you can place any metadata about the overall SOAP request instead of incorporating it into the signature of any of your WebMethods. It is important to keep metadata separate from the actual request.

It terms of the information it contains, it could include a lot of things. One of the more common items placed in the SOAP header is any authentication/authorization functionality required to consume your Web service or to get at specific pieces of logic or data. Usernames and passwords are good examples of what you might include inside the SOAP headers of your messages.

Building a Web Service with SOAP Headers

You can build upon the sample HelloWorld Web service presented in the default .asmx page when it is first pulled up in Visual Studio. Name the new .asmx file HelloSoapHeader.asmx. Add a class that is an object representing what is to be placed in the SOAP header by the client, as shown in the following example:

```
Public Class HelloHeader
    Inherits System.Web.Services.Protocols.SoapHeader

    Public Username As String
    Public Password As String
End Class
```

The class, representing a SOAP header object, has to inherit from the SoapHeader class from System.Web.Services.Protocols.SoapHeader. The SoapHeader class serializes the payload of the <soap:header> element into XML for you. In this example, the SOAP header requires two elements — a username and a password, both of type String. The names you create in this class are those used for the sub-elements of the SOAP header construction, so it is important to name them descriptively.

The following code shows the Web service class that instantiates an instance of the HelloHeader class:

```
<WebService(Namespace:="http://www.wrox.com/helloworld")> _
<WebServiceBinding(ConformsTo:=WsiProfiles.BasicProfile1_1, _
  EmitConformanceClaims:=True)> _
Public Class HelloSoapHeader
    Inherits System.Web.Services.WebService

    Public myHeader As HelloHeader

    <WebMethod(), SoapHeader("myHeader")> _
    Public Function HelloWorld() As String
        If (myHeader Is Nothing) Then
            Return "Hello World"
        Else
            Return "Hello " & myHeader.Username & ". " & _
                "<br>Your password is: " & myHeader.Password
        End If
    End Function

End Class
```

The Web service, `HelloSoapHeader`, has a single `WebMethod` — `HelloWorld`. Within the Web service class, but outside of the `WebMethod` itself, create an instance of the `SoapHeader` class:

```
Public myHeader As HelloHeader
```

Now that you have an instance of the `HelloHeader` class that you created earlier, `myHeader`, you can use that instantiation in your `WebMethod`. Because Web services can contain any number of `WebMethods`, it is not necessary for all `WebMethods` to use an instantiated SOAP header. You specify whether a `WebMethod` uses a particular instantiation of a SOAP header class by placing the `SoapHeader` attribute before the `WebMethod` declaration:

```
<WebMethod(), SoapHeader("myHeader")> _
Public Function HelloWorld() As String
    ' Code here
End Function
```

Here, the `SoapHeader` attribute takes a `string` value of the name of the instantiated `SoapHeader` class — in this case, `myHeader`.

The `WebMethod` actually makes use of the `myHeader` object. If the `myHeader` object is not found (meaning the client did not send a SOAP header with the constructed SOAP message), then a simple "`Hello World`" is returned. However, if values are provided in the header of the SOAP request, then those values are used in the returned `string` value.

Consuming a Web Service Using SOAP Headers

It is not difficult to build an ASP.NET application that makes a SOAP request to a Web service using SOAP headers. As with Web services that do not include SOAP headers, you make a Web reference to the remote Web service directly in Visual Studio.

For the ASP.NET page, create a simple page with a single `Label` control. The output of the Web service is placed in this control. Following is the code for the ASP.NET page:

```
<%@ Page Language="VB" %>

<script runat="server">
    Protected Sub Page_Load(ByVal sender As Object, ByVal e As System.EventArgs)
        Dim ws As New localhost.HelloSoapHeader()
        Dim wsHeader As New localhost.HelloHeader()

        wsHeader.Username = "Bill Evjen"
        wsHeader.Password = "Bubbles"
        ws.HelloHeaderValue = wsHeader

        Label1.Text = ws.HelloWorld()
    End Sub
</script>

<html xmlns="http://www.w3.org/1999/xhtml">
<head runat="server">
    <title>Working with SOAP headers</title>
```

```
    </head>
    <body>
        <form id="form1" runat="server">
        <div>
            <asp:Label ID="Label1" Runat="server"></asp:Label>
        </div>
        </form>
    </body>
</html>
```

Two objects are instantiated. The first is the actual Web service, `HelloSoapHeader`. The second, which is instantiated as `wsHeader`, is the `SoapHeader` object. After both of these objects are instantiated and before making the SOAP request in the application, you construct the SOAP header. This is as easy as assigning values to the `Username` and `Password` properties of the `wsHeader` object. After these properties are assigned, you associate the `wsHeader` object to the `ws` object through the use of the `HelloHeaderValue` property. After you have made the association between the constructed SOAP header object and the actual `WebMethod` object (`ws`), you can make a SOAP request, just as you would normally do:

```
Label1.Text = ws.HelloWorld()
```

Running the page produces the result shown in Figure 28-19.

Figure 28-19

Note that the SOAP request reveals that the SOAP header was indeed constructed into the overall SOAP message, as shown in the following SOAP request:

```
<?xml version="1.0" encoding="utf-8" ?>
<soap:Envelope xmlns:soap="http://schemas.xmlsoap.org/soap/envelope/"
 xmlns:xsi="http://www.w3.org/2001/XMLSchema-instance"
 xmlns:xsd="http://www.w3.org/2001/XMLSchema">
    <soap:Header>
        <HelloHeader xmlns="http://www.wrox.com/helloworld/">
            <Username>Bill Evjen</Username>
            <Password>Bubbles</Password>
        </HelloHeader>
    </soap:Header>
    <soap:Body>
        <HelloWorld xmlns="http://www.wrox.com/helloworld/" />
    </soap:Body>
</soap:Envelope>
```

This returns the SOAP response shown here:

```
<?xml version="1.0" encoding="utf-8" ?>
<soap:Envelope xmlns:soap="http://schemas.xmlsoap.org/soap/envelope/"
 xmlns:xsi="http://www.w3.org/2001/XMLSchema-instance"
 xmlns:xsd="http://www.w3.org/2001/XMLSchema">
    <soap:Body>
        <HelloWorldResponse xmlns="http://www.wrox.com/helloworld/">
            <HelloWorldResult>Hello Bill Evjen. Your password is:
             Bubbles</HelloWorldResult>
        </HelloWorldResponse>
    </soap:Body>
</soap:Envelope>
```

Requesting Web Services Using SOAP 1.2

Most Web services use SOAP version 1.1 for the construction of their messages. However, SOAP 1.2 became a W3C Recommendation in June 2003 (see www.w3.org/TR/soap12-part1/). The nice thing about XML Web Services in the .NET Framework platform is that they are capable of communicating in both the 1.1 and 1.2 versions of SOAP.

In an ASP.NET application that is consuming a Web service, you can control whether the SOAP request is constructed as a SOAP 1.1 message or a 1.2 message. The next example changes the previous example to use SOAP 1.2 instead of the default setting of SOAP 1.1:

```
<%@ Page Language="VB" %>

<script runat="server">
    Protected Sub Page_Load(ByVal sender As Object, ByVal e As System.EventArgs)
        Dim ws As New localhost.HelloSoapHeader()
        Dim wsHeader As New localhost.HelloHeader()

        wsHeader.Username = "Bill Evjen"
        wsHeader.Password = "Bubbles"
        ws.HelloHeaderValue = wsHeader

        ws.SoapVersion = System.Web.Services.Protocols.SoapProtocolVersion.Soap12

        Label1.Text = ws.HelloWorld()
    End Sub
</script>
```

This example first provides an instantiation of the Web service object and uses the new `SoapVersion` property. The property takes a value of `System.Web.Services.Protocols.SoapProtocolVersion`.`Soap12` to work with SOAP 1.2 specifically. With this bit of code in place, the SOAP request takes the structure shown here:

```
<?xml version="1.0" encoding="utf-8"?>
<soap:Envelope xmlns:soap="http://www.w3.org/2003/05/soap-envelope"
 xmlns:xsi="http://www.w3.org/2001/XMLSchema-instance"
 xmlns:xsd="http://www.w3.org/2001/XMLSchema">
    <soap:Header>
```

1135

```
        <HelloHeader xmlns="http://www.wrox.com/helloworld/">
            <Username>Bill Evjen</Username>
            <Password>Bubbles</Password>
        </HelloHeader>
    </soap:Header>
    <soap:Body>
        <HelloWorld xmlns="http://www.wrox.com/helloworld/" />
    </soap:Body>
</soap:Envelope>
```

One difference between the two examples is the `xmlns:soap` namespace that is used. The difference actually resides in the HTTP header. Comparing the SOAP 1.1 and SOAP 1.2 messages, you can see a difference in the `Content-Type` attribute. In addition, the SOAP 1.2 HTTP header does not use the `soapaction` attribute because this is now combined with the `Content-Type` attribute.

You can turn off either SOAP 1.1 or SOAP 1.2 capabilities with the Web services that you build by making the proper settings in the `web.config` file, as illustrated here in this snippet of configuration code:

```
<configuration xmlns="http://schemas.microsoft.com/.NetConfiguration/v2.0">
    <system.web>
        <webServices>
            <protocols>
                <remove name="HttpSoap"/> <!-- Removes SOAP 1.1 abilities -->
                <remove name="HttpSoap1.2"/> <!-- Removes SOAP 1.2 abilities -->
            </protocols>
        </webServices>
    </system.web>
</configuration>
```

Visual Basic and System.Web.Services

The SOAP Toolkit provides a number of wizards to navigate most of the obstacle course required to set up a Web service, but the .NET Framework class library provides the abstract classes. The `System.Web.Services` namespace provides four classes and three other namespaces that enable programmatic exposure of methods to the Web.

System.Web.Services Namespace

The `System.Web.Services` namespace includes the following component classes:

❑   `WebService`

❑   `WebMethodAttribute`

❑   `WebServiceAttribute`

❑   `WebServicesBindingAttribute`

The `WebService` class is the base class from which all the ASP.NET services are derived, and it includes access to the public properties for `Application`, `Context`, `Server`, `Session`, `Site`, and `User`. ASP programmers will recognize these objects from the ASP namespace. Web services can access the IIS object model from the `WebService` class, including application-level variables:

```
Imports System.Web
Imports System.Web.Services
Imports System.Web.Services.Protocols

<WebService(Namespace:="http://www.lipperweb.com/namespace")> _
<WebServiceBinding(ConformsTo:=WsiProfiles.BasicProfile1_1)> _
Public Class Util
    Inherits System.Web.Services.WebService

  <WebMethod(Description:="Application Hit Counter", EnableSession:=False)> _
   Public Function HitCounter() As String

      Dim HitCounter As Integer

      If (Application("HitCounter") Is DBNull.Value) Then
         Application("HitCounter") = 1
      Else
         Application("HitCounter") = Application("HitCounter") + 1
      End If

      HitCounter = Application("HitCounter")

      Return HitCounter

   End Function

End Class
```

`WebService` is an optional base class, used only if access to ASP.NET objects is desired. The `WebMethodAttribute` class, however, is a necessity if the class needs to be available over the Web.

The `WebServiceAttribute` class is similar to the `WebMethodAttribute` class in that it enables the addition of the description string to an entire class, rather than method by method. We recommend adding it before the previous class declaration:

```
<WebService(Description:="Common Server Variables")> _
Public Class ServerVariables
    Inherits System.Web.Services.WebService
```

Instead of using WSDL in the contract to describe these services, the `System.Web.Services` namespace provides programmatic access to these properties. IIS Service Discovery uses these descriptions when queried. This way, you have removed the necessity to struggle with myriad protocols surrounding Service Contract Language and SOAP.

System.Web.Services.Description Namespace

The `System.Web.Services.Description` namespace provides a host of classes that provide total management of the WSDL descriptions for your Web service. This object manages every element in the WSDL schema as a class property.

For example, the preceding discussion on the benefits of WSDL description mentioned being able to query a Web service about its methods and parameters. The `System.Web.Services.Description` namespace provides methods for the discovery of methods and parameters, gathering the information from the service contract and providing it to the object model in Visual Basic code.

When working on the HTTP GET protocol (as opposed to SOAP, for instance), simply pass in the required `sEmail` parameter through the use of a `querystring`. You can find details about this in the Web service's WSDL description. In the successive `<wsdl:message>` sections, you can find all parameter information for all three protocols, including HTTP GET (if enabled via the `web.config` file):

```
<wsdl:message name="IsValidEmailHttpGetIn">
   <wsdl:part name="sEmail" type="s:string" />
</wsdl:message>
<wsdl:message name="IsValidEmailHttpGetOut">
   <wsdl:part name="Body" element="tns:boolean" />
</wsdl:message>
```

Invoking this Web service using HTTP GET, use the following construct:

```
http://localserver/Validate.asmx?sEmail=evjen@yahoo.com
```

Note that HTTP GET is disabled by default because it is deemed a security risk. If you wish to enable HTTP GET for your XML Web Services, then configure it for this in the `web.config` file of your Web service solution, as shown here:

```
<configuration>
   <system.web>
      <webServices>
         <protocols>
            <add name="HttpGet"/>
         </protocols>
      </webServices>
   </system.web>
</configuration>
```

System.Web.Services.Discovery Namespace

The `System.Web.Services.Discovery` namespace provides access to all of the wonderful features of the `.disco` files on a dynamic basis. Because Microsoft is currently trying to integrate Web services as a remoting protocol and is not pushing the public service side as much, you don't see the use of `.disco` files as often in the Microsoft side of things. Your business partner might be using them, though, so this namespace proves useful. For instance, you can access the `DiscoveryDocument` using the `Discovery` class:

```
Imports System.Web.Services.Discovery

ReadOnly Property DiscoveryDocument(strURL As String) As DiscoveryDocument
   Get
      DiscoveryDocument = DiscoveryClientProtocol.Discover(strURL)
   End Get
End Property
```

Like the `System.Web.Services.Description` namespace, the `System.Web.Services.Discovery` namespace provides many tools to build a .disco document on the fly.

System.Web.Services.Protocols Namespace

All of the wire service problems solved with HTTP and SOAP are handled in the `System.Web.Services.Protocols` namespace. When handling references to classes also referenced in other Web service namespaces, the `System.Web.Services.Protocols` namespace proves to be a handy tool. Objects referenced by the `System.Web.Services.Protocols` namespace include the following (among others):

❑ Cookies, per RFC 2019

❑ HTML forms

❑ HTTP request and response

❑ MIME

❑ Server

❑ SOAP, including `SoapException`, the only error-handling mechanism

❑ URIs and URLs

❑ XML

The `System.Web.Services.Protocols` namespace is particularly handy for managing the connection type by a client. A consumer of a Web service can use the HTTP GET or HTTP POST protocol to call a service, as well as the HTTP SOAP protocol. Microsoft's .NET initiative focuses on SOAP as the ultimate means of connecting disparate data sources. The `System.Web.Services.Protocols` `.SoapDocumentMethodAttribute` class enables developers to set special attributes of a public method for when a client calls it using SOAP:

```
Imports System.Web
Imports System.Web.Services
Imports System.Web.Services.Protocols

<WebService(Namespace:="http://www.lipperweb.com/namespace")> _
<WebServiceBinding(ConformsTo:=WsiProfiles.BasicProfile1_1)> _
Public Class Util
    Inherits System.Web.Services.WebService

  <SoapDocumentMethod(Action:="http://MySoapMethod.org/Sample", _
   RequestNamespace:="http://MyNamespace.org/Request", _
   RequestElementName:="GetUserNameRequest", _
   ResponseNamespace:="http://MyNamespace.org/Response", _
   ResponseElementName:="GetUserNameResponse")> _
   WebMethod(Description:="Obtains the User Name")> _
  Public Function GetUserName()
    '...
  End Function

End Class
```

Architecting with Web Services

Web services impart two remarkable benefits to users — one rather obvious, the other less so. First, they replace common binary RPC formats, such as DCOM, CORBA, and RMI. Because these use a proprietary communication protocol, they are significantly less architecturally flexible than Web services. As devices utilize more and more of the Internet, platform neutrality will be a great advantage.

Less obvious but more important, Web services will be used to transfer structured business communications in a secure manner, potentially ending the hold that Sterling has on the Electronic Data Interchange (EDI) market. HTTPS with 128-bit SSL can provide the security necessary for intracompany information transfer. Furthermore, Microsoft has recently (as of this writing) released Web Services Enhancements 3.0 (WSE), as well as the Windows Communication Foundation (WCF), which enables you to easily use WS-Security and other advanced protocols to apply credentials, encryption, and digital signing to your SOAP messages in an easy and straightforward manner.

Why Web Services?

Web services are remarkably easy to deploy with Visual Basic. The key to remoting with Web services is the WSDL contract — written in the dense WSDL protocol shown earlier. IIS 5.0, 6.0, and 7.0 does that in conjunction with the .NET Framework, analyzing the VB code and dynamically generating the WSDL code for the contract.

In addition, Web services are inherently cross-platform, even when created with Microsoft products. Yes, you have heard this before, but so far it seems to be true. The standard XML schemas are centrally managed, and IBM mostly built the WSDL specification, so Microsoft seems to have been up to standard on this one.

Finally, they best represent where the Internet is heading — toward an architecturally neutral collection of devices, rather than millions of PCs surfing the World Wide Web. Encapsulating code so that you can simply and easily allow cell phones to use your logic is a major boon to developers, even if they do not know it yet.

How This All Fits Together

Note that Web services are not a feature of the .NET Framework per se. In fact, Web services run fine on Windows NT4 SP6, with the SOAP Toolkit installed. You can do most anything you are doing here with VB6 and IIS 4.0.

However, the .NET Framework encapsulates the Web service protocol into objects. It is now an integrated part of the strategy, rather than an add-on. If you are currently working in a VB6 environment, look at the SOAP Toolkit (downloadable from MSDN at `http://msdn.microsoft.com/webservices`), and understand that the services you build are available not only to different flavors of Windows, but also to IBM and Sun platforms.

The goal of Web services is to provide a loosely coupled, ubiquitous, universal information exchange format. Toward that end, SOAP is not the only mechanism for communicating with Web services — the HTTP GET and HTTP POST protocols are also supported by the .NET Framework. Response is via HTTP, just like normal RPCs with SOAP. This enables legacy Web applications to make use of Web services without the benefit of the .NET Framework.

State Management for XML Web Services

The Internet is *stateless* by nature. Many of the techniques used for managing state in ASP.NET Web applications are the same techniques you can use within the XML Web Services built on the .NET platform. Remember that XML Web Services are part of the ASP.NET model, and both application types have the same objects at their disposal.

Therefore, just like an ASP.NET application, XML Web Services can also use the `Application` object or the `Session` object. These sessions can also be run in the same process as the XML Web Services application itself — out of process, using the .NET `StateServer` or by storing all the sessions within SQL Server.

To use sessions within XML Web Services built on the .NET platform, you must turn on this capability within the `WebMethod` attribute by using the `EnableSession` property. By default, the `EnableSession` property is set to `False`, so to use the `HTTPSessionState` object, set this property to `True`, as shown here:

```
Imports System.Web
Imports System.Web.Services
Imports System.Web.Services.Protocols

<WebService(Namespace:="http://www.lipperweb.com/namespace")> _
<WebServiceBinding(ConformsTo:=WsiProfiles.BasicProfile1_1)> _
Public Class Service
    Inherits System.Web.Services.WebService

    <WebMethod(EnableSession:=True)> _
    Public Function SessionCounter() As Integer
        If Session("Counter") Is Nothing Then
            Session("Counter") = 1
        Else
            Session("Counter") = CInt(Session("Counter")) + 1
        End If

        Return CInt(Session("Counter"))
    End Function

End Class
```

The `EnableSession` property goes directly in the parentheses of the `WebMethod` declaration. This property takes a Boolean value and needs to be set to `True` in order to work with the `Session` object.

Security in Web Services

Opening up a procedure call to remoting makes applications vulnerable to accidents, poor end-user implementation, and crackers. Any application design needs to include some level of security. Web services demand the inclusion of security.

Security problems with Web services fall into two categories: interception and unauthorized use. SOAP messages intercepted by crackers potentially expose private information, such as account numbers and passwords, to the public. At best, unauthorized use costs money, and at worst it wreaks havoc within a system.

Very few of the concepts discussed here are things we would like to see in the hands of those wearing the black hats. Even the simple validation service handles e-mail addresses — a valuable commodity in this world of "opt in" spamming. If you add social security or account numbers to the service, then this becomes even more of a concern. Fortunately, the wire transport of choice — HTTPS — provides a 128-bit solution.

In addition, as mentioned earlier, by using Microsoft's Web Services Enhancements (WSE) and the Windows Communication Foundation capabilities, you now can easily apply security standards such as WS-Security to your SOAP messages.

The Secure Sockets Layer

The Secure Sockets Layer (SSL) is a protocol consumed by HTTP in the transfer of Internet data from the web server to the browser. On the Web, the process works like this:

1. The user calls a secure Web document, and a unique public key is generated for the client browser, using the server's root certificate.

2. A message encrypted with the server's public key is sent from the browser.

3. The server can decrypt the message using its private key.

The protocol in the URI represents how HTTP would appear if it were changed to HTTPS:

```
<address uri="https://aspx.securedomains.com/evjen/Validate.asmx" />
```

The service would then make an SSL call to the server. Remember that SSL is significantly slower than HTTP, so you will suffer a performance hit. Given the sensitivity of much of the information passing over Web services, however, it is probably worth the slowdown.

Directory-Level Security

You also have the option to code security into your applications. This solves different problems from SSL, and in fact you may want to combine the two services for a complete security solution.

Unauthorized access is a potential problem for any remote system, but even more so for Web services. The open architecture of the system provides crackers with all the information they need to plan an attack. Fortunately, simplicity is often the best defense. Using the NT security options already on the server is the best way to defend against unauthorized users.

You can use NTFS permissions for individual directories within an application and require users to provide a valid username and password combination if they want to access the service.

> *Web service security is a large area to cover. For more information, refer to the documentation included with the .NET Framework SDK.*

The best approach to security is to use SSL and directory-level security together. It is slow, and at times inconvenient, but this is a small price to pay for the heightened level of security. Though this is different from the traditional role-based COM + security, it is still very effective for running information across the wire.

Other Types of Security

The Windows platform also provides for other forms of security. For instance, the Windows CryptoAPI supplies access to most of the commonly used encryption algorithms — aside from the protocols used in the Secure Sockets Layer. Digital certificates (sort of a personal form of SSL `ServerCertificates`) are now rapidly becoming a powerful force in security.

The Downside

There is a downside to any distributed architecture. We've covered most of them in this chapter and suggested workarounds — security, state, speed, and connectivity. Let's go over them once more to ensure that Web services are the way to go.

Security

The key to the issue and solution of security problems is the management of client expectations. If Web services are built securely to begin with, then you won't face situations that draw concern or scrutiny. Consider the security of everything you write. It's fairly easy, and the payoff is great.

State

State is less of a problem in a distributed architecture because in Windows DNA, Microsoft has been saying for years that *n*-tier statefulness has to go. Most developers are used to the idea, but if you are not, then you need to get on the boat with the rest of us. Architect your solutions to be loosely coupled, which is what Web services are designed to do.

Transactions

Web services are not made for transactional systems. If the web server at `MyCompany.com` were to access a database at UPS, for example, and the connection dropped in the middle, the lock on the database would remain without giving the network system at UPS a chance to solve the problem. Web services are by nature loosely coupled. They are not designed for tight transactional integration.

A common use of Web services, communication between differing systems, prompted a number of technology architects to design several XML transaction protocols, such as 2PC. These packages provide the two systems with an understanding that the network link will remain stable.

Speed and Connectivity

Speed and connectivity are going to be a continuing problem until we have the ubiquitous bandwidth George Gilder talks about in his book *Telecosm* (Free Press, 2000). Right now, the majority of Internet devices that could really benefit from Web services — cell phones, PDAs, and the like — are stuck at the paltry 14,000 bits per second currently supported by most wireless providers.

For application development, this is a concern because when the router goes down, the application goes down. Right now, intranets continue to function when the ISP drops the ISDN. With Web services running the links to customers and suppliers, that ISDN line becomes the company lifeline. Redundancy of connections and a firm partnership with your service provider are the only solution.

Where We Go from Here

The cell phone is a listening device. It listens for a call to its network address from the cell network. When it receives one, it follows some logic to handle the call. Sound familiar? This works just like the RPC architecture and will be the format for a new host of devices that listen for Web service calls over the G3 wireless network.

The first lines of the W3C XML group's charter state the following:

> "Today, the principal use of the World Wide Web is for interactive access to documents and applications. In almost all cases, such access is by human users, typically working through web browsers, audio players, or other interactive front-end systems. The Web can grow significantly in power and scope if it is extended to support communication between applications, from one program to another."

New business communication will be via XML and Web services, rather than EDI and VANs. Micropayment may actually become a reality. Scores of promises that the Internet has made since its inception can be fulfilled with Web services and XML. It won't stop there, though. The power of listening devices will bring Web services development into user-to-user markets from business-to-business ones.

It sounds far-fetched, but it is hoped that you can see how the power of Web services on .NET could make this possible. SOAP is not just about replacing the RPC architecture already out there. It is a fundamentally different way to think about the network as the platform.

Summary

This chapter looked at the need for an architecturally neutral, ubiquitous, easy to use, and interoperable system to replace DCOM, RMI, and CORBA. It discussed how Web services fill the gaps successfully because HTTP is used as the language-independent protocol, XML is its language (in WSDL) and transport mechanism, and SOAP enables you to package messages for sending over HTTP.

The chapter also described how to create and consume Web services programmatically using Visual Basic, and discussed the abstract classes provided by the .NET Framework class library to set up and work with Web Services. In particular, it looked at the `WebService`, `WebServiceAttribute`, `WebMethodAttribute`, and `WebServiceBindingAttribute` component classes of the `System.Web.Services` namespace, in addition to the `System.Web.Services.Description`, `System.Web.Services.Discovery`, and `System.Web.Services.Protocols` namespaces.

Finally, it outlined some of the downsides to using any distributed architecture (Web services included), but it finished with an optimistic note regarding where Web services might take us in the future.

29

Remoting

Remoting is the .NET technology that enables code in one application domain (`AppDomain`) to call into the methods and properties of objects running in another application domain. A major use of remoting is in the classic *n*-tier desktop approach, where presentation code on the desktop needs to access objects running on a server somewhere on the network. Another primary use for remoting is when code in ASP.NET Web Forms or Web Services needs to call objects running on an application server somewhere else on the network. In short, remoting is the technology to use when your *n*-tier code needs to talk to the business or data tier that is running on an application server.

Remoting is conceptually somewhat similar to Web services. Both remoting and Web services are TCP/IP-based technologies that enable communication between different machines over an IP network. This means that they both pass through firewalls, and they both provide stateless and connectionless communication between machines. These two technologies share many of the same principles.

> It is important to recognize that Microsoft has merged the functionality of remoting, Web services, enterprise services, and MSMQ (Microsoft Message Queue) into the Windows Communication Foundation (WCF) — the next generation of the technologies. You can find more information on WCF in Chapter 32.

When working with XML Web Services, you will find that the biggest problem with SOAP — Simple Object Access Protocol — is that it is not lightweight. It is designed with maximum platform interoperability in mind, and this puts certain limits on how data can be transferred. For example, imagine that Platform A stores `Integer` variables as a 4-byte block of memory, with the lowest-value byte appearing first. Now imagine that Platform B also uses a 4-byte block of memory, but this time the highest-value byte appears first. The encoding of the value is different. Without some form of conversion, if you copy that block of bytes from Platform A to Platform B, the platforms will not be able to agree on what the number actually is. In this scenario, one platform thinks it has the number 4, whereas the other thinks that the number is actually `536870912`.

SOAP gets around this problem by representing numbers (and everything else) as strings of ASCII characters — since ASCII is a text-encoding standard that most platforms can understand. However, this means that the native binary representations of the numbers have to be converted to text each time the SOAP document has to be constructed. In addition, the values themselves have to be packaged in something that you can read (with a little bit of effort). This leads to two problems: massive bloat (a 4-byte value starts taking hundreds of bytes to store) and wasted CPU cycles used in converting from native encoding to text encoding and back again.

You can live with all these problems if you only want to run your web service on, say, Windows 2000, and have it accessed through a client running on a cell phone. SOAP is designed to do this kind of thing. However, if you have a Windows XP desktop application that wants to use objects hosted on a Windows 2000 server (using the same platform), the bloated network traffic and wastage in terms of conversion is sub-optimal at best and ridiculous at worst.

Remoting enables you to enjoy the power of Web services but without the downside. If you want, you can connect directly to the server over TCP and send binary data without having to do any conversions. If one Windows computer has a 4-byte block of memory holding a 32-bit integer value, you can safely copy the bit pattern to another Windows computer and both will agree on what the number is. In effect, network traffic sanity is restored and processor time is not wasted doing conversions.

Now that you know what remoting is, you're ready to look at its architecture.

Remoting Overview

It is important to understand several fundamental aspects of remoting, including the basic terms and related objects, which are covered in the following sections.

Basic Terminology

A normal object is not accessible via remoting. By default, .NET objects are only accessible to other code running within the same .NET `AppDomain`.

A *remote object* is an object that has been made available over remoting by inheriting from `System.MarshalByRefObject`. These objects are often also called MBROs. Remote objects are the same kinds of objects that you build normally, except they inherit from `MarshalByRefObject` and you register them with the `Remoting` subsystem to make them available to clients. Remote objects are anchored to the machine and `AppDomain` where they were created, and you communicate with them over the network. The wonderful part of this scenario is that the client is working with a proxy object, instantiated by the client, that enables programmatic access to the remote object just as if it were in the same process as your client application, even though it actually resides in a completely separate process — even on a completely separate machine.

A *serializable object* is an object that's been made available over remoting by marking the class with the `<Serializable()>` attribute. These objects will move from machine to machine or `AppDomain` to `AppDomain`. They are not anchored to any particular location, so they are known as unanchored objects. A common example of a serializable object is the `DataSet`, which can be returned from a server to a client across the network. The `DataSet` physically moves from server to client via the serialization technology in the .NET Framework.

A *remoting host* is a server application that configures remoting to listen for client requests. Remoting runs within the host process, using the memory and threads of the host process to handle any client requests. The most common remoting host is IIS. You can create custom remoting hosts, which are typically created as a Windows service, so they can run even when no user is logged in to the server. It is also possible to have any .NET application be a remoting host, which enables you to emulate ActiveX EXE behaviors to some degree. This last technique is most commonly used when creating peer-to-peer-style applications.

A *channel* is a way of communicating between two machines. In order for two separate application processes to communicate with each other, a *transport channel* is opened between the processes. A transport channel is a combination of underlying technologies required to open a network connection and use a particular protocol to send the bytes to the receiving application. A channel works with a stream of data and creates an object based upon the transport protocol. Out of the box, .NET comes with two channels: TCP and HTTP.

The TCP channel is a lightweight channel designed for transporting binary data between two computers. (The TCP channel is different from the TCP protocol that HTTP also uses.) It works using sockets, something discussed in much more detail in Chapter 31. TCP is more suited for an intranet environment because an intranet sits behind a firewall, and TCP does not always cross firewalls easily. Using TCP also means that a binary formatter is used by default, which actually reduces the size of the object that is being transported. Having smaller packages to transport allows for better and faster network communications.

HTTP, as you already know, is the protocol that web servers use. The HTTP channel hosted in IIS is the recommended approach by Microsoft. HTTP is a firewall-friendly transport because HTTP traffic generally flows directly through firewalls over port 80 (which is generally open on most computers).

After a channel is established through a specific port, a *formatter* object is needed to initiate the serialization or deserialization of the object. A formatter object is used to serialize or marshal an object's data into a format in which it can be transferred down the channel. In order for an object to move through the channel from one process to another, the formatter must take the object that you are sending and serialize it into the network stream. Out of the box, you have two formatter objects: `BinaryFormatter` and `SoapFormatter`. The `BinaryFormatter` is more efficient and is recommended. The `SoapFormatter` is not recommended and may be discontinued in future versions of the .NET Framework.

A *message* is a communication between the client and server. It holds the information about the remote object and the method or property that is being invoked, as well as any parameters.

A *proxy* is used on the client side to call into the remote object. To use remoting, you do not typically have to worry about creating the proxy — .NET can do it all for you. However, there is a slightly confusing split between something called a *transparent proxy* and a *real proxy*. A transparent proxy is so called because "you can't see it." When you request a remote object, a transparent proxy is what you get. It looks like the remote object (that is, it has the same properties and methods as the original). This means that your client code can use the remote object or a local copy of the would-be-remote object without you having to make any changes and without you knowing there is any difference. The transparent proxy defers the calls to the real proxy. The real proxy is what actually constructs the message, sends it to the server, and waits for the response. You can think of the transparent proxy as a "fake" object that contains the same methods and properties that the real object contains. The real proxy is effectively a set of helper functions that manages the communications. You don't use the real proxy directly; instead, the transparent proxy calls into the real proxy on your behalf.

A *message sink* is an "interceptor object." Before messages go into the channel, these are used to do some further processing on them, perhaps to attach more data, reformat data before it is sent, route debugging information, or perform security checking. On the client side, you have an *envoy sink*. On the server side, you have a *server context sink* and an *object context sink*. In typical use, you can ignore these.

Message sinks are a pretty advanced topic and allow for some powerful extensions to the remoting model. It is not recommended that you create custom sinks, channels, or formatters, so they are not covered in this book. Creating them is not recommended because they will not transfer directly to WCF, the next generation of the technology from Microsoft. If you do opt to create your own custom sink, formatter, or channel, you must expect to rewrite it from scratch when you upgrade to WCF. Figures 29-1 and 29-2 show how these concepts fit together.

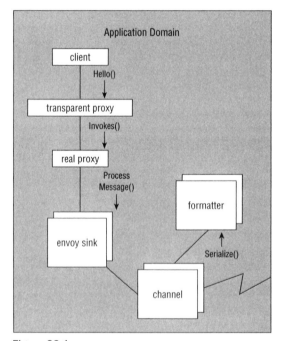

Figure 29-1

Figure 29-1 shows how a client calls the `Hello` method of a transparent proxy object. The transparent proxy looks just like the real object, so the client doesn't even realize that remoting is involved. The transparent proxy then invokes the real proxy, which converts the method call into a generic remoting message.

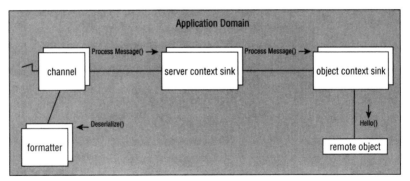

Figure 29-2

This message is sent through any messaging sinks configured on the client. These messaging sinks may transform the message in various ways, including adding encryption or compressing the data.

The message is then serialized by the formatter object. The result is a byte stream that is sent to the server by using the channel configured for use on the client.

Figure 29-2 shows how the server handles the message. The message comes into the server via a channel. The message is then deserialized by the formatter object and run through any messaging sinks configured on the server. These messaging sinks typically mirror those on the client, unencrypting or decompressing the data as appropriate.

Finally, the message is decoded by the object context sink, which uses the information in the message to invoke the method on the actual object. The object itself has no idea that it was invoked via remoting, as the method call was merely relayed from the client.

SingleCall, Singleton, and Activated Objects

The next step is to look at the way that remoting treats objects. In remoting, objects are divided into three camps: *well-known* objects, *client-activated* objects, and *serializable* objects.

❏   The well-known (`wellknown`) objects run on the server and perform a service for the remote application, such as "give me a list of all the customers" or "create an invoice." They can be configured to act similarly to a Web service or use what is called a *singleton pattern* (which is discussed shortly).

❏   Client-activated (`Activated`) objects are created for each client and maintain state on the server over time. In many ways, these objects act similarly to COM objects you may have accessed via DCOM in the past.

❏   Serializable objects can move from machine to machine as needed. For instance, a serializable object can be created on the server (by a `wellknown` or `Activated` object) and then returned to a client. When the object is returned to the client, it is physically copied *to the client machine*, where it can be used by client code.

The following table summarizes the types of object:

Type	Calling Semantics	Key Attributes
SingleCall (wellknown)	An object is created for each client method call made to the server.	Stateless, per-method lifetime, atomic methods, no threading issues, anchored to AppDomain where created
Singleton (wellknown)	One object exists on the server and is used to handle all method calls from all clients.	Stateful, long-lived, shared instance, thread synchronization required, anchored to AppDomain where created
Activated	The client creates Activated objects on the server. The client can create many such objects. Activated objects are available only to the client that created the object.	Stateful, long-lived, per-client instances, threading issues only if client is multithreaded, anchored to AppDomain where created
Serializable	The object is automatically copied from machine to machine when it is passed as a parameter or returned as the result of a function.	Stateful, long-lived, no threading issues, non-anchored (moves across network automatically)

The following sections discuss each object in a bit more detail.

SingleCall Objects

SingleCall objects act much like typical Web service objects. Each time a client calls a method on a SingleCall object, an object is created specifically to handle that method call. Once the method call is complete, the object is not reused and is garbage collected by the .NET runtime.

SingleCall objects also work the way a JIT (just-in-time) Activated object does in COM+, and matches the way most people use MTS or COM+ objects. In those environments, good developers typically create a server-side object, make a method call, and then release the object.

These objects must inherit from System.MarshalByRefObject, so they are MBROs. This means that they always run in the AppDomain and Windows process where they are created. If they are created on a server in a host process, then that is where they live and run. Clients interact with them across the network.

The most commonly used type of service object in remoting is the SingleCall object. Not only do these objects provide semantics similar to Web services, MTS, and COM+, they also provide the simplest programming model.

Because an object is created for each method call, these objects are inherently stateless. Even if an object tried to keep state between calls, it would fail because the object is destroyed after each method is complete. This helps ensure that no method call can be affected by previous method calls or contaminate subsequent method calls.

Each method call runs on its own thread (from the .NET thread pool, as discussed in Chapter 26). However, because each method call also gets its own object, there's typically no contention between threads. This means you don't need to worry about writing synchronization or locking code in your SingleCall code.

Technically, it is possible to encounter synchronization issues if there are shared stateful objects on the server. Creating and accessing such shared objects requires substantial work and is a topic outside the scope of this book. Typically, this type of model is not used, so threading is a non-issue with SingleCall *objects.*

Because of their automatic isolation, statelessness, and threading simplicity, SingleCall objects are the preferred technology for creating server code in remoting.

Singleton Objects

Singleton objects are quite different from SingleCall objects. Only one Singleton object exists at a time, and it may exist for a long time and maintain state. All client method calls from all users are routed to this one Singleton object. This means that all clients have equal, shared access to any state maintained by the Singleton object.

These objects must inherit from System.MarshalByRefObject, so they are MBROs. This means that they always run in the AppDomain and Windows process where they are created. If they are created on a server in a host process, then that is where they live and run. Clients interact with them across the network.

As with the SingleCall scenario, all method calls are run on threads from the .NET thread pool. This means that multiple simultaneous method calls can be running on different threads at the same time. As discussed in Chapter 26, this can be complex, as you have to write multithreaded synchronization code to ensure that these threads do not collide as they interact with your Singleton object.

Singleton objects have a potentially unpredictable life span. When the first client makes the first method call to the object, it is created. From that point forward, it remains in memory for an indeterminate period of time. As long as it remains in memory, all method calls from all the clients will be handled by this one object. However, if the object is idle for a long time, then remoting may release it to conserve resources. In addition, some remoting hosts may recycle their AppDomain objects, which automatically causes the destruction of all your objects.

Because of this, you can never be certain that the data stored in memory in the object will remain available over time. This means that any long-term state data must be written to a persistent store such as a database.

Due to the complexity of shared memory, thread synchronization, and dealing with object lifetime issues, Singleton objects are more complex to design and code than SingleCall objects. While they can be useful in specialized scenarios, they are not as widely used as SingleCall objects.

Activated Objects

Client-activated (or Activated) objects are different from both SingleCall and Singleton objects. Activated objects are created by a client application, and they remain in memory on the server over time. They are associated with just that one client, so they are not shared between clients. They are stateful objects, meaning that they can maintain data in memory during their lifetime.

These objects must inherit from System.MarshalByRefObject, so they are MBROs. This means that they always run in the AppDomain and Windows process where they are created. If they are created on a server in a host process, then that is where they live and run. Clients interact with them across the network.

A client can create multiple `Activated` objects on the server. The objects remain on the server until the client releases them or the server `Appdomain` is reset (which can happen with some types of remoting host). In addition, if the client does not contact the server for several minutes, then the server assumes the client abandoned the objects and it will release them.

`Activated` objects typically do not have any threading issues. The only way multiple threads will be running in the same `Activated` object is if the client is multithreaded, and multiple client threads simultaneously make method calls to the same server-side `Activated` object. If this is the case in your application, then you have to deal with shared data and synchronization issues as discussed in Chapter 26.

While long-lived, stateful, per-client objects can be useful in some specialized scenarios; they are not commonly used in most client/server or *n*-tier application environments. By storing per-client state in an object on the server, this type of design reduces the scalability and fault tolerance of a system.

Serializable Objects

While `SingleCall`, `Singleton`, and `Activated` objects are always anchored to the `Appdomain`, Windows process, and machine where they are created, this is not the case with serializable objects.

`Serializable` objects can move from machine to machine as needed. The classic example of this is the ADO.NET `DataSet`, which can be returned as a result of a function on a server. The `DataSet` physically moves to the client machine, where it can be used by client code. When the client wants to update the `DataSet`, it simply passes the object to the server as a parameter, causing the `DataSet` to physically move to the server machine.

These objects *do not* inherit from `System.MarshalByRefObject`. Instead, they are decorated with the `< Serializable() >` attribute and may optionally implement the `ISerializable` interface. The following is a very basic implementation of a `< Serializable() >` object:

```
<Serializable()> _
Public Class Customer
  Private mName As String = ""

  Public Property Name() As String
    Get
      Return mName
    End Get
    Set(ByVal value As String)
      mName = value
    End Set
  End Property

  Public Sub Load()
    ' Load data here.
  End Sub
End Class
```

`<Serializable()>` objects are not anchored to the `Appdomain` or Windows process where they were created. The remoting subsystem automatically serializes the data of these objects and transfers it across the network to another machine. On that other machine, a new instance of the objects is created and loaded with the data, effectively cloning the objects across the network.

When working with serializable objects, it's typically a good idea to use a `SingleCall` object on the server to create the serializable object and call any server-side methods (such as ones to load the object with data from a database). The `SingleCall` object will then return the serializable object to the client as a function result, so the client can then interact with the object. The `SingleCall` object's method might look like the following:

```
Public Function GetCustomer(ByVal ID As Integer) As Customer

  Dim cust As New Customer()
  cust.Load(ID)
  Return cust

End Function
```

The client code might look as follows:

```
Dim cust As Customer

cust = myService.GetCustomer(123)
TextBox1.Text = cust.Name()
```

Note that both server and client code have direct, local access to the `Customer` object, because it is automatically copied from the server to the client as a result of the `GetCustomer` method call.

Serializable objects can be very useful in many client/server scenarios, especially if the application is created using object-oriented application design principles.

Implementing Remoting

When you implement an application using remoting, there are three key components to the application:

Client	The application calling the server
Server Library	The DLL containing the objects to be called by the client
Host	The application running on the server that hosts remoting and the Server Library

Basically, you create your server-side objects in a Visual Basic Class Library project. Then you expose the classes in that DLL from your server-side remoting host application. With the objects exposed on the server, you can then create client applications that call the objects in the Server Library DLL.

You might also have some other optional components to support various scenarios:

Interface	A DLL containing interfaces that are implemented by the objects in the Server Library
Proxy	A DLL containing generated proxy code based on the objects in the Server Library
Shared Library	A DLL containing serializable objects that must be available to both the Server Library and the client

Each of these is discussed in detail as it is used later in the chapter. Now it is time to get into some code and see how remoting works.

A Simple Example

This exercise has you create a simple remoting application consisting of a library DLL that contains the server-side code, a remoting host application, and a client to call the library DLL on the server.

Note that both the host and the client need access to the type information that describes the classes in the library DLL. The type information includes the name of the classes in the DLL and the methods exposed by those classes.

The host needs the information because it will be exposing the library DLL to clients via remoting. The client needs the information in order to know which objects to create and what methods are available on those objects.

You know that the library DLL will be on the server, so it is easy enough for the host application to just reference the DLL to get the type information. The client is a bit trickier because the library DLL will not necessarily be on the client machine. You have three options for getting the type information to the client:

Reference the library DLL	This is the simplest approach, as the client just references the DLL directly and therefore has all the type information. The drawback is that the DLL must be installed on the client along with the client application.
Use an interface DLL	This approach is more complex. The classes in the library DLL must implement formal interfaces as defined in this interface DLL. The client can then reference just the interface DLL, so the library DLL doesn't need to be installed on the client machine. The way the client invokes the server is different when using interfaces.
Generate a proxy DLL	This approach is of moderate complexity. The server must expose the objects via HTTP, so you can run the `soapsuds.exe` command-line utility. The utility creates an assembly containing the type information for the library DLL classes exposed by the server. The client then references this proxy assembly, rather than the library DLL.

You will implement all three options in this chapter, starting with the simplest — referencing the library DLL directly from the client application.

Library DLL

To begin, create the library DLL. This is just a regular Class Library project, so open Visual Studio .NET (Visual Studio) and create a new class library named SimpleLibrary. Remove `Class1.vb` and add a new class named `Calculator.vb`. Because you are creating a well-known remoting object, it must inherit from `MarshalByRefObject`:

```
Public Class Calculator
    Inherits MarshalByRefObject
End Class
```

That's really all there is to it. At this point, the `Calculator` class is ready to be exposed from a server via remoting. Of course, you need to add some methods that clients can call.

Any and all `Public` methods written in the `Calculator` class will be available to clients. How you design the methods depends entirely on whether you plan to expose this class as `SingleCall`, `Singleton`, or `Activated`. For `SingleCall` you know that an instance of `Calculator` will be created for *each method call*, so there is absolutely no point in using any class-level variables. After all, they will be destroyed along with the object when each method call is complete.

It also means that you cannot have the client call a sequence of methods on your object. Each method call gets its own object, so each method call is entirely isolated from any previous or subsequent method calls. In short, each method must stand alone.

For illustration purposes, you need to prove that the server-side code is running in a different process from the client code. The easiest way to prove this is to return the `thread ID` where the code is running. You can compare this `thread ID` to the `thread ID` of the client process. If they are different, then you know that the server-side code is actually running on the server (or at least in another process on your machine).

Add the following method:

```
Public Function GetThreadID() As Integer

  Return Threading.Thread.CurrentThread.ManagedThreadId

End Function
```

You can add other `Public` methods as well if you would like, such as the following:

```
Public Function Add(ByVal a As Integer, ByVal b As Integer) As Integer

  Return a + b

End Function
```

As this is a `Calculator` class, it seems appropriate that it should do some calculations. At this point, you have a simple but functional `Calculator` class. Build the solution to create the DLL. Your remoting host application will use this DLL to provide the calculator functionality to clients.

Host Application

With the server-side library complete, you can create a remoting host. It is recommended that you use IIS as a remoting host, but it is possible to create a custom host as well. You will use IIS later in the chapter, but for now let's see how you can create a custom host in a `Console` Application for testing.

Most custom hosts are created as a Windows Service so the host can run on the server even when no user is logged into the machine. However, for testing purposes, a console application is easier to create and run.

The advantage to a custom host is that you can host a remoting server on any machine that supports the .NET Framework. This includes Windows 98 and later. If you use IIS as a host, then you can only host on Windows 2000 and later, which is a bit more restrictive (but not much).

The drawback to a custom host is that it is not as robust and capable as IIS, at least not without a lot of work. For this chapter's example, you are not going to attempt to make your host as powerful as IIS. You will just stick with the basic process of creating a custom host.

Setting Up the Project

Create a new solution in Visual Studio, with a console application named SimpleServer. Because the remoting host will be interacting with remoting, you need to reference the appropriate framework DLL. Use the Add Reference dialog box to add a reference to `System.Runtime.Remoting`, as shown in Figure 29-3.

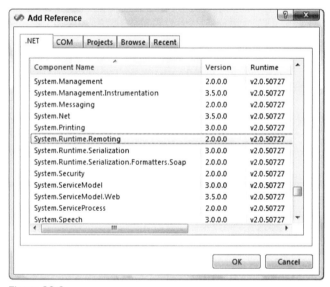

Figure 29-3

Then, in `Module1` you need to import the appropriate namespace:

```
Imports System.Runtime.Remoting
```

At this point, you can configure and use remoting. However, before you do that, you need to have access to the DLL containing the classes you plan to expose via remoting — in this case, `SimpleLibrary.dll`.

Referencing the Library DLL

There are two ways to configure remoting: via a configuration file or via code. If you opt for the configuration file approach, then the only requirement is that `SimpleLibrary.dll` be in the same directory as your host application. You don't even need to reference `SimpleLibrary.dll` from the host. However, if you opt to configure remoting via code, then your host must reference `SimpleLibrary.dll`.

Even if you go with the configuration file approach, referencing `SimpleLibrary.dll` from the host project enables Visual Studio to automatically keep the DLL updated in your project directory, and any setup project you might create will automatically include `SimpleLibrary.dll`. In general, it is a good idea to reference the library DLL from the host, and that is what you will do here.

Add a reference to `SimpleLibrary.dll` by clicking the Browse button in the Add References dialog box and navigating to the `SimpleLibrary\bin\Release` directory, as shown in Figure 29-4. Note that if you are running in Debug mode, then you will find the DLL in the Debug folder, rather than the Release folder.

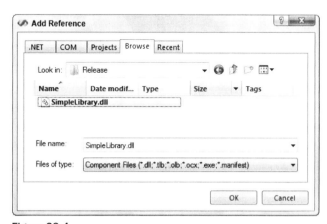

Figure 29-4

All that remains now is to configure remoting.

Configuring Remoting

The typical way to do this is with a configuration file. Open the `app.config` file (add this file to your project if it isn't already present) in the `SimpleServer` project. In this `config` file, you'll add a section to configure remoting. Remember that XML is case sensitive, so the slightest typo here will prevent remoting from being properly configured:

```xml
<?xml version="1.0" encoding="utf-8" ?>
<configuration>
  <system.runtime.remoting>
    <application>
      <!-- The following section defines the classes you're
           exposing to clients from this host. -->
      <service>
        <wellknown mode="SingleCall"
            objectUri="Calculator.rem"
            type="SimpleLibrary.Calculator, SimpleLibrary" />
      </service>

      <channels>
        <channel ref="tcp" port="49341" />
      </channels>
```

```
        </application>
      </system.runtime.remoting>
    </configuration>
```

Notice that all configuration is within the `< system.runtime.remoting >` element, and then within an `<application>` element. The real work happens first inside the `<service>` element. The `<service>` element tells remoting that you're configuring server-side components. It is within this block that you define the classes you want to make available to clients. You can define both `wellknown` and `Activated` classes here. In this case you're defining a `wellknown` class:

```
<wellknown mode="SingleCall"
      objectUri="Calculator.rem"
      type="SimpleLibrary.Calculator, SimpleLibrary" />
```

The mode will be either `SingleCall` or `Singleton` as discussed earlier in the chapter.

The `objectUri` is the "end part" of the URL that clients will use to reach your server. You'll revisit this in a moment, but this is basically how it fits (depending on whether you're using the TCP or HTTP protocol):

```
tcp://localhost:49341/Calculator.rem
```

or

```
http://localhost:49341/Calculator.rem
```

The `.rem` extension on the `objectUri` is important. This extension indicates that remoting should handle the client request, and it is used by the networking infrastructure to route the request to the right location. You can optionally use the .soap extension to get the same result. The .rem and .soap extensions are totally equivalent.

Finally, the type defines the full type name and assembly where the actual class can be found. Remoting uses this information to dynamically load the assembly and create the object when requested by a client.

You can have many `<wellknown>` blocks here to expose all the server-side classes you want to make available to clients.

The other key configuration block is where you specify which remoting channel (protocol) you want to use. You can choose between the TCP and HTTP channels.

| TCP | Slightly faster than HTTP, but less stable (not recommended) |
| HTTP | Slightly slower than TCP, but more stable (recommended) |

You'll look at the HTTP channel later, so you'll use the TCP channel now. Either way, you need to specify the IP port number on which you'll be listening for client requests. When choosing a port for a server, keep the following port ranges in mind:

❑ **0–1023** — Well-known ports reserved for specific applications such as web servers, mail servers, and so on

❑ **1024–49151** — Registered ports that are reserved for various widely used protocols such as DirectPlay

❑ **49152–65535** — Intended for dynamic or private use, such as for applications that might be performing remoting with .NET

You're setting remoting to use a TCP channel, listening on port 49341:

```
<channels>
  <channel ref="tcp" port="49341" />
</channels>
```

With the .config file created, the only thing remaining is to tell remoting to configure itself based on this information. To do this you need to add the following code to Sub Main:

```
Sub Main()
  RemotingConfiguration.Configure( _
    AppDomain.CurrentDomain.SetupInformation.ConfigurationFile, False)
  Console.Write("Press <enter> to exit")
  Console.Read()
End Sub
```

The Console.Write and Console.Read statements are there to ensure that the application stays running until you are ready for it to terminate. The line that actually configures remoting is as follows:

```
RemotingConfiguration.Configure( _
  AppDomain.CurrentDomain.SetupInformation.ConfigurationFile)
```

You are calling the Configure method, which tells remoting to read a .config file and to process the <system.runtime.remoting> element in that file. You want it to use your application configuration file, so you pass that path as a parameter. Fortunately, you can get the path from your AppDomain object so you don't have to worry about hard-coding the filename.

Configuring Remoting via Code

Your other option is to configure the remoting host via code. To do this you'd write different code in Sub Main:

```
Sub Main()

  RemotingConfiguration.RegisterWellKnownServiceType( _
    GetType(SimpleLibrary.Calculator), _
    "Calculator.rem", _
    WellKnownObjectMode.SingleCall)

  System.Runtime.Remoting.Channels.ChannelServices.RegisterChannel( _
    New System.Runtime.Remoting.Channels.Tcp.TcpServerChannel(49341), False)
  Console.Write("Press <enter> to exit")
  Console.Read()
End Sub
```

As shown in the preceding snippet, you're providing the exact same information here as you did in the `.config` file, only via code. You call `RegisterWellKnownServiceType`, passing the mode, `objectUri`, and type data just as you did in the `.config` file. Then you call `RegisterChannel`, passing a new instance of the `TcpServerChannel` configured to use the port you chose earlier.

The result is the same as using the `.config` file. Most server applications use a `.config` file to configure remoting because it enables you to change things such as the channel and the port without having to recompile the host application.

Build the solution. At this point, your host is ready to run. Open a command prompt window, navigate to the `bin` directory, and run `SimpleServer.exe`.

The Client Application

The final piece of the puzzle is to create a client application that calls the server.

Setting Up the Project

Here is how to create a new Visual Studio solution with a Windows Application named SimpleClient. As discussed earlier, the client needs access to the type information for the classes it wants to call on the server. The easiest way to get this type information is to have it reference `SimpleLibrary.dll`. Because you will be configuring remoting, you also need to reference the remoting DLL. Then import the remoting namespace in `Form1`:

```
Imports System.Runtime.Remoting
```

Now you can write code to interact with the `Calculator` class. Add controls to the form as shown in Figure 29-5.

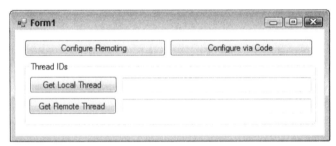

Figure 29-5

Name the controls (in order): `ConfigureButton`, `CodeConfigureButton`, `LocalThreadButton`, `LocalThread`, `RemoteThreadButton`, and `RemoteThread`. First, write the code to get the `thread ID` values for each object:

```
Private Sub LocalThreadButton_Click( _
    ByVal sender As System.Object, ByVal e As System.EventArgs) _
    Handles LocalThreadButton.Click
```

```
        LocalThread.Text = CStr(Threading.Thread.CurrentThread.ManagedThreadId)

    End Sub

    Private Sub RemoteThreadButton_Click( _
        ByVal sender As System.Object, ByVal e As System.EventArgs) _
        Handles RemoteThreadButton.Click

      Dim calc As New SimpleLibrary.Calculator

      RemoteThread.Text = CStr(calc.GetThreadID)

    End Sub
```

Displaying the thread ID of the local process is easily accomplished. More interesting, though, is that your code to interact with the Calculator class does not look special in any way. Where is the remoting code?

This example reflects the idea of *location transparency*, whereby it is possible to write "normal" code that interacts with an object whether it is running locally or remotely. This is an important and desirable trait for distributed technologies, and remoting supports the concept. Looking at the code you've written, you can't tell whether the Calculator object is local or remoting; its location is transparent.

All that remains is to configure remoting so that it knows that the Calculator object should, in fact, be created remotely. As with the server, you can configure clients either via a config file or through code.

Before you configure remoting, note something important: If remoting is not configured before the first usage of SimpleLibrary.Calculator, then the Calculator object will be created locally. If that happens, then configuring remoting will not help, and you'll never create remote Calculator objects.

To prevent this from happening, you need to ensure that you cannot interact with the class until after remoting is configured. Typically, this is done by configuring remoting as the application starts up, either in Sub Main or in the first form's Load event. In this case, however, you are going to configure remoting behind some buttons, so a different approach is required.

In Form_Load, add the following code:

```
    Private Sub Form1_Load( _
      ByVal sender As System.Object, ByVal e As System.EventArgs) _
      Handles MyBase.Load

      RemoteThreadButton.Enabled = False

    End Sub
```

This prevents you from requesting the remote thread. You won't enable this button until after remoting has been configured through either the config file or code.

Configuring Remoting

To configure remoting via a `config` file, you first need to add a `config` file to the project. Use the Project ⇨ Add New Item menu to add an Application Configuration File. Be sure to keep the default name of `App.config`. In this file, add the following code:

```
<?xml version="1.0" encoding="utf-8" ?>
<configuration>
  <system.runtime.remoting>
    <application>
      <!-- The following section defines the classes you're
           getting from the remote host. -->
      <client>
        <wellknown mode="SingleCall"
             type="SimpleLibrary.Calculator, SimpleLibrary"
             url="tcp://localhost:49341/Calculator.rem" />
      </client>
    </application>
  </system.runtime.remoting>
</configuration>
```

In this case, you are using the `<client>` element, telling remoting that you are configuring a client. Within the `<client>` block, you define the classes that should be run on a remote server, both `wellknown` and `Activated`. In your case, you have a `wellknown` class:

```
<wellknown
        type="SimpleLibrary.Calculator, SimpleLibrary"
        url="tcp://localhost:49341/Calculator.rem" />
```

On the client, you only need to provide two bits of information. You need to tell remoting the class and assembly that should be run remotely. This is done with the `type` attribute, which specifies the full type name and assembly name for the class, just as you did on the server. You also need to provide the full URL for the class on the server.

You defined this URL when you created the server, though it might not have been clear that you did so. When you defined the class for remoting on the server, you specified an `objectUri` value (`Calculator.rem`). In addition, on the server you specified the channel (TCP) and port (49341) on which the server will listen for client requests. Combined with the server name itself, you have a URL:

```
tcp://localhost:49341/Calculator.rem
```

The channel is `tcp://`, the server name is `localhost` (or whatever the server name might be), the port is 49341, and the object's URI is `Calculator.rem`. This is the unique address of your `SimpleLibrary.Calculator` class on the remote server.

As with the server configuration, you might have multiple elements in the .config file, one for each server-side object you wish to use. These can be a mix of `<wellknown>` and `<activated>` elements.

With the configuration set up, you just need to tell remoting to read the file. You'll do this behind the `ConfigureButton` control:

```
Private Sub ConfigureButton_Click( _
  ByVal sender As System.Object, ByVal e As System.EventArgs) _
```

```
   Handles ConfigureButton.Click

   RemotingConfiguration.Configure( _
     AppDomain.CurrentDomain.SetupInformation.ConfigurationFile, True)

   ConfigureButton.Enabled = False
   CodeConfigureButton.Enabled = False
   RemoteThreadButton.Enabled = True

 End Sub
```

Once remoting is configured in an application, you cannot configure it again, so you're disabling the two configuration buttons. In addition, you're enabling the button to retrieve the remote thread ID. Now that remoting has been configured, it is safe to interact with SimpleLibrary.Calculator.

The line of code that configures remoting is the same as it was in the server:

```
   RemotingConfiguration.Configure( _
     AppDomain.CurrentDomain.SetupInformation.ConfigurationFile)
```

Again, you are telling remoting to read your application configuration file to find the < system.runtime.remoting > element and process it.

Configuring Remoting via Code

Another option for configuring remoting is to do it via code. You must provide the same information in your code as you did in the .config file. Put this behind the CodeConfigureButton control:

```
   Private Sub CodeConfigureButton_Click( _
     ByVal sender As System.Object, ByVal e As System.EventArgs) _
     Handles CodeConfigureButton.Click
     RemotingConfiguration.RegisterWellKnownClientType( _
       GetType(SimpleLibrary.Calculator), "tcp://localhost:49341/Calculator.rem")

     ConfigureButton.Enabled = False
     CodeConfigureButton.Enabled = False
     RemoteThreadButton.Enabled = True

   End Sub
```

The RegisterWellKnownClientType method requires that you specify the type of the class to be run remotely, in this case SimpleLibrary.Calculator. It also requires that you provide the URL for the class on the remote server, just as you did in the .config file.

Regardless of whether you do the configuration via code or the .config file, the result is that the .NET runtime now knows that any attempt to create a SimpleLibrary.Calculator object should be routed through remoting, so the object will be created on the server.

Compile and run the application. Try configuring remoting both ways. In either case, you should discover that the local thread ID and the remote thread ID are different, proving that the Calculator code is running on the server, not locally in the Windows application, as shown in Figure 29-6.

Figure 29-6

Of course, your specific thread ID values will be different from those shown here. The important point is that they are different from each other, establishing that the local code and remote code are running in different places.

Using IIS as a Remoting Host

You have learned how to create a very basic custom host. In most production environments, however, such a basic host is not directly useful. You'd need to create a Windows Service, add management and logging facilities, implement security, and so forth.

Alternatively, you could just use IIS as the host and get all those things automatically, so it is often better to use IIS as a remoting host than to try to create your own.

Creating the Host

Using IIS as a host is a straightforward exercise. First, create a web project. To do this, create a new solution in Visual Studio with an Empty Web Site template, as shown in Figure 29-7. Name it SimpleHost. When you click OK, Visual Studio will properly create and configure the virtual root on your server.

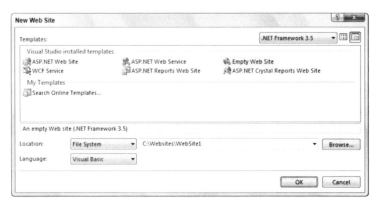

Figure 29-7

The next task is to ensure that the SimpleLibrary.dll is in the bin directory under the virtual root. While you could copy the DLL there by hand, it is often easier to simply add a reference to the DLL from the website. This enables Visual Studio to automatically copy the DLL to the right location, and it has the added benefit that if you create a deployment project, then the DLL will be automatically included as part of the setup.

Add a reference to `SimpleLibrary.dll` using the Add References dialog box as you did previously in the SimpleServer and SimpleClient projects. This way, Visual Studio will ensure that the DLL is available as needed.

All that remains now is to configure remoting. Within an IIS host, add the `< system.runtime.remoting >` section to the `web.config` file. Remoting is automatically configured based on `web.config` by ASP.NET.

Use the Project ➪ Add New Item menu to add a Web Configuration File. Be sure to use the default name of `web.config`. This adds a `web.config` file to the project with a series of default settings. You may opt to change some of these settings for your environment. In particular, these settings enable you to control security options and so forth.

More important, however, add the remoting configuration to the file:

```xml
<?xml version="1.0" encoding="utf-8" ?>
<configuration>
  <system.runtime.remoting>
    <application>
      <!-- The following section defines the classes you're
           exposing to clients from this host. -->
      <service>
        <wellknown mode="SingleCall"
            objectUri="Calculator.rem"
            type="SimpleLibrary.Calculator, SimpleLibrary" />
      </service>

    </application>
  </system.runtime.remoting>
</configuration>
```

An IIS host can only support the HTTP channel. In addition, the port on which the host listens is defined by IIS, not by your configuration file. This means that all you need to do here is define the classes you want to expose to clients. This is done within the `<service>` element, just like with a custom host. Again, you use a `<wellknown>` element to define your class:

```xml
<wellknown mode="SingleCall"
    objectUri="Calculator.rem"
    type="SimpleLibrary.Calculator, SimpleLibrary" />
```

The `<wellknown>` element shown here is the exact same definition used with the custom host, and you'll get the same result.

The primary difference between your custom host and the IIS host is that IIS cannot use the TCP channel, but only uses the HTTP channel. This means that the URL for your server-side class is different:

```
http://localhost/SimpleHost/Calculator.rem
```

The channel defines the protocol, which is `http://`. The server name is `localhost` (or whatever your server name might be). The virtual root within IIS is `SimpleHost`, named just as it is with any Web project. Finally, the `objectUri` value for your class (`Calculator.rem`) rounds out the URL.

Again, the `.rem` extension is important. This extension (or the equivalent `.soap` extension) tells IIS to route the client request to ASP.NET, and it tells ASP.NET to route the request to remoting so it can be properly handled by invoking your `Calculator` class.

At this point, the remoting host is done and ready to go. Because it is using the HTTP protocol, you can test it with the browser by navigating to the following URL:

```
http://localhost/SimpleHost/Calculator.rem?wsdl
```

This should return an XML description of the host service and all the classes exposed from the host.

Updating the Client Application

With a new host set up, you can change the client application to use this IIS host instead of the custom host. To do this, all you need to do is change the URL for the object when you configure remoting.

If you were using the `.config` file to configure remoting, you would make the following change:

```xml
<?xml version="1.0" encoding="utf-8" ?>
<configuration>
  <system.runtime.remoting>
    <application>
      <!- the following section defines the classes you're
           getting from the remote host ->
      <client>
        <wellknown
              type="SimpleLibrary.Calculator, SimpleLibrary"
              url="http://localhost/SimpleHost/Calculator.rem" />
      </client>
    </application>
  </system.runtime.remoting>
</configuration>
```

After making this change to `App.config`, be sure to rebuild the project so Visual Studio copies the new `.config` file to the `bin` directory and renames it `SimpleClient.exe.config`.

When configuring remoting via code, change the code to the following:

```vb
Private Sub CodeConfigureButton_Click( _
  ByVal sender As System.Object, ByVal e As System.EventArgs) _
  Handles CodeConfigureButton.Click

  RemotingConfiguration.RegisterWellKnownClientType( _
    GetType(SimpleLibrary.Calculator), _
    "http://localhost/SimpleHost/Calculator.rem")
  ConfigureButton.Enabled = False
  CodeConfigureButton.Enabled = False
  RemoteThreadButton.Enabled = True

End Sub
```

In either case, you are simply changing the URL, so remoting now routes your calls to the IIS host instead of your custom host.

Using the Binary Formatter in IIS

One thing to note about using IIS as a host is that it always uses the HTTP channel. The HTTP channel defaults to using the SoapFormatter instead of the BinaryFormatter to encode the data sent across the network. While SOAP is a fine format, it is extremely verbose. The BinaryFormatter generates about one-third the number of bytes as the SoapFormatter to send the same data.

As stated, the SoapFormatter class is the default formatter when using an HTTP channel with .NET remoting, and this class serializes any objects that it receives into a SOAP 1.1-compliant text format. The HTTP channel uses the SoapFormatter to serialize the objects that it sends through the channel. After the object is received and serialized into XML, this formatter also adds any appropriate SOAP headers to the message before it is sent through the channel.

Besides the SoapFormatter, the BinaryFormatter class is typically used when sending an object through a TCP network protocol. When objects are sent using the BinaryFormatter, these objects are more compact and therefore require less network utilization.

For production code, it is good practice to use the BinaryFormatter to reduce the amount of data sent across the network and to improve performance. The formatter is controlled by the client, so you need to update the client configuration of remoting.

Change the .config file as follows:

```xml
<?xml version="1.0" encoding="utf-8" ?>
<configuration>
  <system.runtime.remoting>
    <application>
      <!- the following section defines the classes you're
          getting from the remote host ->
      <client>
        <wellknown
            type="SimpleLibrary.Calculator, SimpleLibrary"
            url="http://localhost/SimpleHost/Calculator.rem" />
      </client>
      <!-- use the binary formatter over the
          http channel ->
      <channels>
        <channel ref="http">
         <clientProviders>
           <formatter ref="binary" />
         </clientProviders>
        </channel>
      </channels>
    </application>
  </system.runtime.remoting>
</configuration>
```

The highlighted XML configures remoting, so when it initializes the HTTP channel, it does so with a BinaryFormatter instead of the default SoapFormatter.

To do the equivalent to the XML configuration in code, you'll want to import two namespaces into Form1:

```
Imports System.Runtime.Remoting.Channels
Imports System.Runtime.Remoting.Channels.Http
```

This also requires that the SimpleClient project reference the System.Runtime.Remoting.dll assembly. Do this using the Add References dialog as you did earlier in the SimpleLibrary project.

Then add the following when configuring remoting:

```
Private Sub CodeConfigureButton_Click( _
  ByVal sender As System.Object, ByVal e As System.EventArgs) _
  Handles CodeConfigureButton.Click

  RemotingConfiguration.RegisterWellKnownClientType( _
    GetType(SimpleLibrary.Calculator), _
    "http://localhost/SimpleHost/Calculator.rem")

    ' Use the binary formatter with the
    ' HTTP channel.
    Dim clientFormatter As New BinaryClientFormatterSinkProvider
    Dim channel As New HttpChannel(Nothing, clientFormatter, Nothing)
    ChannelServices.RegisterChannel(channel)
    ConfigureButton.Enabled = False
    CodeConfigureButton.Enabled = False
    RemoteThreadButton.Enabled = True

End Sub
```

As with the .config file approach, you're specifically creating the HttpChannel object, specifying that it should use a BinaryFormatter, rather than the default.

At this point, you have explored the basic use of remoting. You have created a library DLL, a client that uses the library DLL, and two different types of remoting hosts, so the library DLL can run on the server.

There are many other facets of remoting to explore, more than what can fit into this single chapter. The remainder of the chapter explores some of the more common features that you might encounter or use in your applications. You will have to take them pretty fast, but the complete code for each is available in the code download for the book, so you can get the complete picture there.

Using Activator.GetObject

In your simple client, you configured remoting so that all attempts to use SimpleLibrary.Calculator were automatically routed to a specific server. If you want more control and flexibility, you can take a different approach by using the System.Activator class. The full code for this example is in the ActivatorClient project.

Instead of configuring remoting to always know where to find the remote class, you can specify it as you create the remote object. As you will not be configuring remoting, you don't need a reference to System.Runtime.Remoting.dll, nor do you need any of the remoting configuration code you had in the client to this point.

All you do is replace the use of the New keyword with a call to Activator.GetObject. To use the custom host, you would use the following code to retrieve the remote thread ID:

```
Private Sub RemoteThreadButton_Click( _
  ByVal sender As System.Object, ByVal e As System.EventArgs) _
  Handles RemoteThreadButton.Click

  Dim calc As SimpleLibrary.Calculator

  calc = CType(Activator.GetObject( _
    GetType(SimpleLibrary.Calculator), _
    "tcp://localhost:49341/Calculator.rem"), _
    SimpleLibrary.Calculator)
  RemoteThread.Text = CStr(calc.GetThreadID)

End Sub
```

For this to work, the SimpleServer application must be running before the RemoteThread button is clicked.

The Activator.GetObject method accepts the type of object to create (SimpleLibrary.Calculator) and the URL where the object can be found. To use the IIS host, you would change the URL:

```
calc = CType(Activator.GetObject( _
  GetType(SimpleLibrary.Calculator), _

  "http://localhost/SimpleHost/Calculator.rem"), _
  SimpleLibrary.Calculator)
```

Using this approach, you lose location transparency because it is obvious looking at your code that you're using a remote object. However, you gain explicit control over where the remote object will be created. This can be useful in some cases, such as when you want to programmatically control the URL on a per-call basis.

Interface-Based Design

One drawback to the simple implementation you have used thus far is that the library DLL (SimpleLibrary.dll) must be installed on the client machine. Sometimes this is not desirable, because you don't want clients to have access to the server-side code. You have two options in this case: use an interface DLL or use a generated proxy.

Interface DLL

To use this approach, you need to create a new DLL containing interface definitions for your server-side classes and their methods. For instance, in the SimpleInterface project, you have the following interface defined:

```
Public Interface <code> ICalculator
  Function GetThreadID() As Integer
  Function Add(ByVal a As Integer, ByVal b As Integer) As Integer
End Interface
```

This interface defines the methods on your `Calculator` class. You need to update the `Calculator` class to implement this interface. The SimpleLibrary project must reference the `SimpleInterface` DLL; then you can do the following in your `Calculator` class:

```
Public Class Calculator
  Inherits MarshalByRefObject

 Implements SimpleInterface.ICalculator
 Public Function GetThreadID() As Integer _
   Implements SimpleInterface.ICalculator.GetThreadID

   Return AppDomain.GetCurrentThreadId

 End Function

 Public Function Add(ByVal a As Integer, ByVal b As Integer) As Integer _
   Implements SimpleInterface.ICalculator.Add

      Return a + b

  End Function

End Class
```

At this point, the `SimpleLibrary.Calculator` class can be invoked either directly or via the `ICalculator` interface.

Be sure to rebuild the custom and IIS host projects so that the new SimpleLibrary and the SimpleInterface DLLs are both copied to the host directories. Note that because `SimpleLibrary.Calculator` is still available natively, your existing client applications (SimpleClient and ActivatorClient) will continue to run just fine.

Updating the Client Application

The InterfaceClient project only references `SimpleInterface.dll`, not `SimpleLibrary.dll`. This means that the client machine doesn't need to install `SimpleLibrary.dll` for the client to run, which means the client has no access to the actual server-side code.

Because you don't have access to the types in `SimpleLibrary`, you can't use them in your code. The only types you can use come from SimpleInterface. This means that your code to retrieve the remote thread ID is a bit different. To use the custom host, you do the following:

```
Private Sub RemoteThreadButton_Click( _
   ByVal sender As System.Object, ByVal e As System.EventArgs) _
   Handles RemoteThreadButton.Click

   Dim calc As SimpleInterface.ICalculator

   calc = CType(Activator.GetObject( _
     GetType(SimpleInterface.ICalculator), _
     "tcp://localhost:49341/Calculator.rem"), _
     SimpleInterface.ICalculator)

   RemoteThread.Text = CStr(calc.GetThreadID)

End Sub
```

Note that the `calc` variable is now declared as type `ICalculator`, rather than `Calculator`. Notice too that you're using `Activator.GetType`. This is required when using interfaces, because you can't use the `New` keyword at all. That is, you can't do the following:

```
calc = New SimpleInterface.ICalculator()
```

The result is a compiler error because it isn't possible to create an instance of an interface. Therefore, you can't just configure remoting and use location transparency; you must use `Activator.GetObject` to have remoting create an instance of the object on the server.

Remoting knows how and where to create the object based on the URL you provide. It then converts the object to the right type (`SimpleInterface.ICalculator`) based on the type you provide in the `GetObject` call. If the remote object doesn't implement this interface, then you'll get a runtime exception.

Using Generated Proxies

Another way to create a client that does not reference the library DLL is to use the `soapsuds.exe` command-line utility to create a proxy assembly for the service and the classes it exposes. This proxy assembly is then referenced by the client application, giving the client access to the server type information so that it can interact with the server objects.

Proxy DLL

To create the proxy DLL, you just run the `soapsuds.exe` utility with the following command line:

```
> soapsuds -url:http://localhost/SimpleHost/Calculator.rem?wsdl -oa:SimpleProxy.dll
```

Note that you are going against the IIS host here because it uses the HTTP protocol. This won't work against your current custom host, as the `soapsuds.exe` utility doesn't understand the `tcp://` prefix. To use this against a custom host, you would have to ensure that the custom host used the HTTP protocol.

Creating the Client Application

The code download includes a ProxyClient project, which is a Windows application that references only `SimpleProxy.dll`. There is no reference to `SimpleLibrary.dll` or `SimpleInterface.dll` — this client relies entirely on the generated proxy assembly to interact with the server.

The best part of this is that the generated proxy contains the same namespace and class names as the service on the server. In other words, it appears that you are working with `SimpleLibrary.Calculator` because the proxy is set up with that same namespace and class name. To get the remote thread ID, write the following code:

```
Private Sub RemoteThreadButton_Click( _
  ByVal sender As System.Object, ByVal e As System.EventArgs) _
  Handles RemoteThreadButton.Click

  Dim calc As New SimpleLibrary.Calculator()
  RemoteThread.Text = CStr(calc.GetThreadID)

End Sub
```

1171

Note that this is the same code used in the original simple example. You've come full circle at this point, but now the client application doesn't directly reference your library DLL.

Summary

Remoting is a powerful technology that provides many of the capabilities of Web services and DCOM, plus some new capabilities of its own. Using remoting, you can create both Windows and Web applications that interact with objects on an application server across the network.

On the server you can create SingleCall, Singleton, and Activated objects. These three object types provide a great deal of flexibility in terms of *n*-tier application design and should be able to meet almost any need. SingleCall gives you behavior similar to Web services or typical COM+ objects. Activated gives you objects that act similar to COM objects exposed via DCOM. Singleton objects are unique to remoting and enable all your clients to share a single stateful object on the server.

You can also create serializable objects, which can move from machine to machine as needed. Using this type of object enables you to easily move data and business logic from server to client and back again. This technology is particularly exciting for object-oriented development in a distributed environment.

In this chapter, you created a library DLL and exposed it to clients from both a custom and IIS remoting host. You then created client applications to use your server-side code by referencing the library DLL directly, using an interface DLL and using the soapsuds.exe utility to create a proxy DLL. These techniques apply not only to SingleCall objects but also to Singleton and Activated objects, so you should have a good grounding in the techniques available for using remoting in your environment.

30

Enterprise Services

Chapter 25 explored the vast hinterland of legacy software known as COM. This chapter looks at "what COM did next" and how it fits into the world of .NET, in the form of *.NET Enterprise Services*.

To understand Enterprise Services, you must go back in time (all the way to the last century!) when a number of technologies began to emerge from Microsoft, including *Microsoft Transaction Server (MTS)*, *Microsoft Message Queuing (MSMQ)*, and *Microsoft Clustering Services*. The aim of these developments was to increase the scalability, performance, and reliability of applications.

Handling transactions involved a considerable extension to the NT/COM runtime. It also involved the introduction of several new standard COM interfaces, some to be used or implemented by transactional components and some to be used or implemented by the underlying resource managers, such as SQL Server. These additions, along with some other innovations relating to areas such as asynchronous COM, came to be known as *COM+*.

This chapter explores the .NET Enterprise Services. In particular, it looks at transaction processing and queued components using the classes of the `System.EnterpriseServices` and `System.Transactions` namespaces. This is an enormous subject that could easily fill a whole book by itself, so this chapter only scratches the surface of it. However, by the end of the chapter, you will understand how all the pieces fit together. Let's begin by looking at what transactions are, and how they fit into Visual Basic 2008.

Transactions

A *transaction* is one or more linked units of processing placed together as a single unit of work, which either succeeds or fails. If the unit of work succeeds, then all the work is committed. If the unit fails, then every item of processing is rolled back and the process is returned to its original state.

The standard transaction example involves transferring money from account A to account B. The money must either end up in account B (and nowhere else), or — if something goes wrong — stay in account A (and go nowhere else). This avoids the very undesirable case in which we have taken money from account A but haven't put it in account B.

The ACID Test

Transaction theory starts with *ACID*, an acronym describing the following properties that all transactions should have:

❑ **Atomicity** — A transaction is *atomic*; that is, everything is treated as one unit. However many different components the transaction involves, and however many different method calls are made on those components, the system treats it as a single operation that either entirely succeeds or entirely fails. If it fails, then the system is left in the state it was in before the transaction was attempted.

❑ **Consistency** — All changes are done in a consistent manner. The system goes from one valid state to another.

❑ **Isolation** — Transactions that are going on at the same time are isolated from each other. If transaction A changes the system from state 1 to state 2, transaction B will see the system in either state 1 or 2, but not some half-baked state in between the two.

❑ **Durability** — If a transaction has been committed, the effect is permanent, even if the system fails.

Let's illustrate this with a concrete example. Imagine that after spending a happy afternoon browsing in your favorite bookstore, you decide to shell out some of your hard-earned dollars for a copy of, yes, *Professional Visual Basic 2008* (a wise choice). You take the copy to the checkout and exchange a bit of cash for the book. A transaction is going on here: You pay money and the store provides you with a book.

The important aspect of this transaction isn't the exchange of money, but that only two reasonable outcomes are possible — either you get the book and the store gets its money or you don't get the book and the store doesn't get its money. If, for example, there is insufficient credit on your credit card, then you'll leave the shop without the book. In that case, the transaction doesn't happen. The only way for the transaction to complete is both for you to get the book and the store to get its money. This is the principle of *atomicity*.

If the store provides you with a copy of some other book instead, then you would reasonably feel that you ended up with an outcome that was neither anticipated nor desirable. This would be a violation of the principle of *consistency*.

Now imagine that there is one copy of the book in the store, and another potential buyer of that book has gone up to the cashier next to you. As far as the person at the other checkout is concerned, your respective transactions are *isolated* from each other (even though you are competing for the same resource). Either your transaction succeeds or the other person's does. What definitely *doesn't* happen is that the bookstore decides to exert the wisdom of Solomon and give you half each.

Now suppose you take the book home and the bookstore calls you to ask if they can have the book back. Apparently, an important customer (well, far more important than you, anyway) needs a copy. You would find this a tad unreasonable, and a violation of the principle of *durability*.

At this point, it's worth considering what implications all this is likely to have on the underlying components. How can you ensure that all of the changes in the system can be unwound if the transaction is aborted at some point? Perhaps you're in the middle of updating dozens of database files and something goes wrong.

There are three aspects to rescuing this situation with transactions:

❑ Knowledge that something has gone wrong

❑ Knowledge to perform the recovery

❑ Coordination of the recovery process

The middle part of the process is handled by the resource managers themselves. The likes of SQL Server and Oracle are fully equipped to deal with transactions and rollback (even if the resource manager in question is restarted partway through a transaction), so you don't need to worry about any of that. The last part of the process, coordination, is handled by the .NET runtime (or at least the Enterprise Services part of it). The first part, knowing that something is wrong, is shared between the components themselves and the .NET runtime. This isn't at all unusual: Sometimes a component can detect that something has gone wrong itself and signal that recovery is necessary, while on other occasions it may not be able to do so, because it has crashed.

Later, you will see how all this works as you build a transactional application.

Transactional Components

To understand what components are actually managed by Enterprise Services and what purpose they serve, you need to consider what a typical real-world *n*-tier application looks like. The bottom tier is the persistent data store, typically a database such as SQL Server or Oracle. However, there are other possible data stores, including the file system (on Windows NT and above). These are termed *resource managers* because they manage resources. The software here is concerned with maintaining the integrity of the application's data and providing rapid and efficient access to it.

The top tier is the user interface. This is a completely different specialization, and the software here is concerned with presenting a smooth, easy-to-follow front end to the end user. This layer shouldn't actually do any data manipulation at all, apart from whatever formatting is necessary to meet each user's presentational needs. The interesting stuff is in the tiers in between — in particular, the business logic. In the .NET/COM+ transactional model, the software elements that implement this are components running under the control of the Enterprise Services runtime.

Typically, these components are called into being to perform some sort of transaction and then, to all intents and purposes, disappear again. For example, a component might be called into play to transfer information from one database to another in such a way that the information is either in one database or the other, but not both. This component might have a number of different methods, each of which does a different kind of transfer. However, each method call would carry out a complete transfer:

```
Public Sub TransferSomething()
  TakeSomethingFromA
  AddSomethingToB
End Sub
```

Crucially, this means that most transaction components have no concept of *state*; there are no properties that hold values between method calls. You can see the reason for this if you imagine what would happen if you had a number of instances of the preceding components all vying for the attention of the database. If instance one of the control started the transfer, remembering the state or current values of A and B just after instance two had done the same, you could end up with the state being different between the two instances. This would violate the isolation of the transaction. Persistence is left to the outside data stores in this model.

The business logic is the area of the system that requires all the transactional management. Anything that happens here needs to be monitored and controlled to ensure that all the ACID requirements are met. The neatest way to do this in a component-oriented framework is to develop the business logic as components that are required to implement a standard interface. The transaction management framework can then use this interface to monitor and control how the logic is implemented from a transactional point of view. The transaction interface is a means for the business logic elements to talk to the transaction framework and for the transaction framework to reply to the logic elements.

So what's all this about not having state? Well, if you maintain state inside your components, then you immediately have a scaling problem. The middle tiers of your application are now seriously resource-hungry. If you want an analogy from another area of software, consider why the Internet scales so well: because HTTP is a stateless protocol. Every HTTP request stands in isolation, so no resources are tied up in maintaining any form of session. It's the same with transactional components.

This is not to say that you can never maintain state inside your transactional components. You can, but it's not recommended, and the examples in this chapter don't illustrate it.

An Example of Transactions

For our transaction example, we're going to build a simple business-logic component that transfers data from one bank account to another account. The current balance in the bank account will be represented by a row in one database, while the other will be represented by a row in another database.

Before beginning, note one important point: You can't have transactions without any resource managers. It's very tempting to assume that you can experiment with transactional component services without actually involving, say, a database, because (as you shall see) none of the methods in the transactional classes make any explicit references to one. However, if you do try to do this, then you will find that your transactions don't actually trouble the system's statistics. Fortunately, you don't need to lay out your hard-earned cash for a copy of SQL Server (nice though that is), because Visual Studio 2008 comes with a lightweight (but fully functional) copy of SQL Server, which goes under the name of *SQL Server 2005 Express Edition*, or more simply *SQL Express*. In addition, SQL Express is available separately, so you can even work with databases if you use Visual Basic Express.

Creating the Databases

First, set up the databases. Check whether the Server Explorer tab is visible in Visual Studio 2008 (see Figure 30-1). If not, then open it by selecting View➪ Server Explorer. Create a new database in the Data Connections tree.

Right-click Data Connections and select New Database from the menu. Alternately, you can click the icon that looks like a plus sign over a can with a plug (not quite the universal symbol for a database, but it will have to do). The Add Connection dialog box appears (see Figure 30-2).

Figure 30-1

Figure 30-2

Enter the database name (BankOfWrox) and select Use Windows Authentication. After clicking OK, you are prompted to create the database if it doesn't exist. You should now see BankOfWrox in the list of data connections (see Figure 30-3).

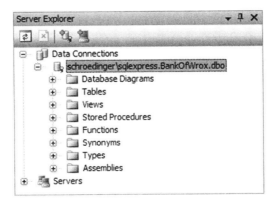

Figure 30-3

Set up the database. If you open the new node, you will see several other nodes, including Tables. Right-click this and then select New Table from the menu. Another dialog box should appear (see Figure 30-4). Create two columns, Name and Amount, as shown. Make sure that Name is set up to be the primary key. When you click Close, you'll be asked whether you want to save the changes to Table1. Select Yes, and the Choose Name dialog box will appear (see Figure 30-5).

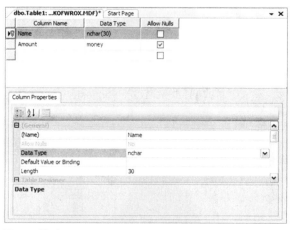

Figure 30-4

Figure 30-5

Use the name Accounts for the table. You should now see a child node called Accounts below Tables in the tree. That completes the creation of BankOfWrox. Repeat the process for BankOfMe. The structure is exactly the same (although it doesn't need to be for the purposes of this example). Don't forget to set Name as the primary key. We could have created these two as separate rows in the same database, but it doesn't really simulate the scenario where Enterprise Services is intended (inter-application communication).

Populating Your Databases

The next thing to do is populate the databases. If you right-click over Accounts for either database and select Show Table Data from Table from the menu, you will see a grid that enables you to add rows and initialize the values of their columns (see Figure 30-6).

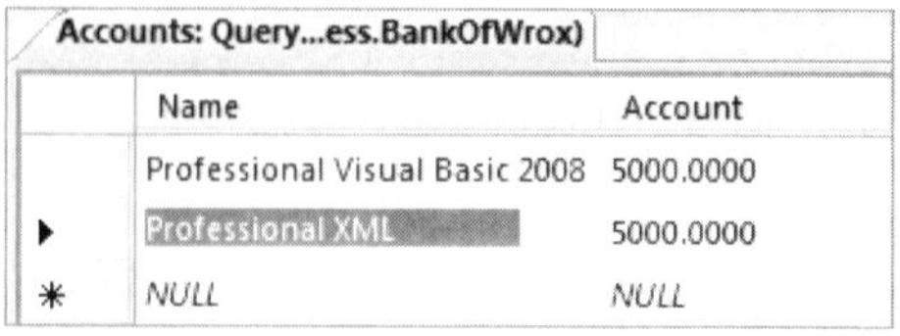

Accounts: Query...ess.BankOfWrox)		
	Name	Account
	Professional Visual Basic 2008	5000.0000
▶	Professional XML	5000.0000
*	NULL	NULL

Figure 30-6

Enter two accounts in BankOfWrox — Professional Visual Basic 2008 and Professional XML — and allocate $5,000 to each. Now repeat the process for BankOfMe, setting up one account, Me, with $0 in it.

The Business Logic

The next step is to create the transactional component to support the business logic. Create a new Class Library project called "Transactions." Then, add a reference to `System.EnterpriseServices` (see Figure 30-7).

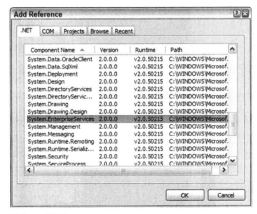

Figure 30-7

This reference is needed because in order to come under the control of the Enterprise Services runtime, the component must inherit from the `System.EnterpriseServices.ServicedComponent` class:

```vb
Imports System.EnterpriseServices
Imports System.Configuration
Imports System.Data.SqlClient

<Assembly: ApplicationName("WroxTransactions")>
<Assembly: ApplicationAccessControl(True)>
Public Class BankTransactions
    Inherits ServicedComponent
```

Here's the main function in the component, `TransferMoney`:

```vb
Public Sub TransferMoney(ByVal amount As Decimal, _
  ByVal sourceBank As String, _
  ByVal sourceAccount As String, _
  ByVal destinationBank As String, _
  ByVal destinationAccount As String)

    Try
        Withdraw(sourceBank, sourceAccount, amount)
        Try
            Deposit(destinationBank, destinationAccount, amount)
        Catch ex As Exception
            'deposit failed
            Throw New _
            ApplicationException("Error transfering money, deposit failed.", _
              ex)
        End Try
```

1179

```
            'both operations succeeded
            ContextUtil.SetComplete()
        Catch ex As Exception
            'withdraw failed
            Throw New _
            ApplicationException("Error transfering money, withdrawal failed.", _
            ex)
        End Try
    End Sub
```

Ignoring for the moment the references to ContextUtil, we have effectively divided the logic into two halves: the half that takes money from the Wrox account (represented by the private function Withdraw), and the half that adds it to your account (represented by the private function Deposit). In order for the function to complete successfully, each of the two halves must complete successfully.

The ContextUtil class represents the context of the transaction. Within that context are basically two bits that control the behavior of the transaction from the point of view of each participant: the *consistent* bit and the *done* bit. The done bit determines whether or not the transaction is finished, so that resources can be reused. The consistent bit determines whether or not the transaction was successful from the point of view of the participant. This is established during the first phase of the two-phase commit process. In complex distributed transactions involving more than one participant, the overall consistency and completeness are voted on, so that a transaction is only consistent or done when everyone agrees that it is. If a transaction completes in an inconsistent state, then it is not allowed to proceed to the second phase of the commit.

In this case, there is only a single participant, but the principle remains the same. We can determine the overall outcome by setting these two bits, which is done via SetComplete and SetAbort, which are static methods in the ContextUtil class. Both of these set the done bit to True. SetComplete also sets the consistent bit to True, whereas SetAbort sets the consistent bit to False. In this example, SetComplete is only set if both halves of the transaction are successful.

The First Half of the Transaction

Now it's time to see what's going on in the two halves of the transaction itself. The component is responsible for reading from and writing to the two databases, so it needs two connection strings. You could hard-code these into the component, but a better solution is to use the new My Settings feature to include them. Double-click My Project in the Solution Explorer and navigate to the Settings tab. Add the two connection strings using the names BankOfWrox and BankOfMe, as shown in Figure 30-8.

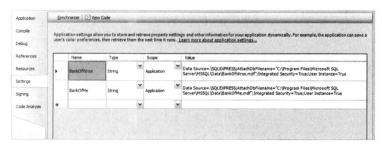

Figure 30-8

1. Here's the function that removes money from the Wrox account:

```
Private Sub Withdraw(ByVal bank As String, _
   ByVal account As String, _
   ByVal amount As Decimal)
```

2. Establish a connection to the database and retrieve the current account balance from it:

```
Dim ConnectionString As String
Dim SQL As String
Dim conn As SqlConnection = Nothing
Dim cmdCurrent As SqlCommand
Dim currentValue As Decimal
Dim cmdUpdate As SqlCommand

ConnectionString = My.Settings.Item(bank).ToString
SQL = String.Format("SELECT Amount FROM Accounts WHERE Name = '{0}'", _
   account)
```

3. The call to `ExecuteScalar` retrieves a single value from the database — in this case, the amount for the requested account. Note that we have started an exception handler with the `Try` keyword. We'll finish the `Try` block in a moment:

```
Try
    conn = New SqlConnection(ConnectionString)
    conn.Open()

    cmdCurrent = New SqlCommand(SQL, conn)
    currentValue = CDec(cmdCurrent.ExecuteScalar())
```

4. Note the current balance and determine whether you can afford to transfer the amount asked for. If not, raise an `Exception`:

```
'check for overdrafts
        If amount > currentValue Then
            Throw New ArgumentException("Attempt to overdraft account")
        End If
```

5. Otherwise, subtract the amount and update the table accordingly:

```
'otherwise, we're good to withdraw
SQL = _
    String.Format("UPDATE Accounts SET Amount = {0} WHERE Name = '{1}'", _
    currentValue - amount, account)
cmdUpdate = New SqlCommand(SQL, conn)
cmdUpdate.ExecuteNonQuery()
```

6. Close the exception handler and the database:

```
Catch ex As Exception
        Throw New DataException("Error withdrawing", ex)
    Finally
```

```
                    If Not conn Is Nothing Then
                        conn.Close()
                    End If
                End Try
            End Sub
```

The Second Half of the Transaction

The second half of the transaction is similar, except that the failure conditions are slightly different. First, we stipulate that we don't want any transfer of less than $50. Second, we've inserted a bug such that an attempt to transfer a negative amount will cause a divide by zero. (You'll see why we added this rather bizarre act of sabotage in a moment.) Here's the code:

```
Private Sub Deposit(ByVal bank As String, _
  ByVal account As String, _
  ByVal amount As Decimal)

    Dim ConnectionString As String
    Dim SQL As String
    Dim conn As SqlConnection = Nothing
    Dim cmdCurrent As SqlCommand
    Dim currentValue As Decimal
    Dim cmdUpdate As SqlCommand

    ConnectionString = My.Settings.Item(bank).ToString
    SQL = String.Format("SELECT Amount FROM Accounts WHERE Name = '{0}'", _
      account)

    If amount < 0 Then
        amount = amount / 0
    ElseIf amount < 50 Then
        Throw New ArgumentException("Value of deposit must be greater than $50")
    Else
        Try
            conn = New SqlConnection(ConnectionString)
            conn.Open()

            'get the current value
            cmdCurrent = New SqlCommand(SQL, conn)
            currentValue = CDec(cmdCurrent.ExecuteScalar())

            SQL = _
              String.Format("UPDATE Accounts SET Amount = {0} WHERE Name = '{1}'", _
                currentValue + amount, account)

            cmdUpdate = New SqlCommand(SQL, conn)
            cmdUpdate.ExecuteNonQuery()
        Finally
            If Not conn Is Nothing Then
                conn.Close()
            End If
        End Try
    End If

End Sub
```

The business logic component is complete. Let's see how you can bring it under the control of Enterprise Services. First, of course, you need to build your DLL.

Why did we intentionally add the divide by zero error? This gives you a chance to see what happens to the transaction when an exception occurs in your code. The transaction will automatically fail and roll back, which means that your data will still be in a good state at the end.

Registering Your Component

Because the Enterprise Services infrastructure is COM-oriented, you need to expose the .NET component as a COM component, and register it with Component Services. Component Services handles all transaction coordination; that is, Component Services tracks any changes and restores the data should the transaction fail. First, some changes to the component are needed to enable this COM interaction. Prepare to take a trip down memory lane.

All COM components must have a GUID (globally unique identifier) that uniquely identifies it to the COM infrastructure. This was done for you in Visual Basic 6.0, but .NET requires you to add a value. In addition, your component needs an attribute to make it visible to COM. You can set both of these in the Assembly Information dialog. Double-click My Project in the Solution Explorer. On the Application page, click Assembly Information. There should already be a `Guid` assigned to your component. Check the option Make Assembly COM-Visible. This makes all of the `Public` types accessible to COM (see Figure 30-9).

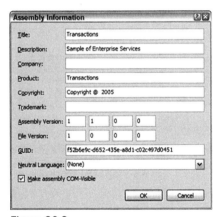

Figure 30-9

You should also update the Assembly Version fields as you make changes to the component.

Chapter 23 contains more information about strong names and assemblies.

The problem is that the assembly is a private assembly. In order to make it available to the transaction framework, it needs to be a shared assembly. To do this, give the assembly a *cryptographically strong name*, generally referred to as its *strong name*.

Cryptographically strong means that the name has been signed with the private key of a dual key pair. This isn't the place to go into a long discussion about dual-key cryptography, but essentially a pair of keys is generated, one public and one private. If something is encrypted using the private key, it can only be decrypted using the public key from that pair, and vice versa. It is therefore an excellent tool for preventing tampering with information. If, for example, the name of an assembly were to be encrypted using the private key of a pair, then the recipient of a new version of that assembly could verify the origin of that new version, and be confident that it was not a rogue version from some other source. This is because only the original creator of the assembly retains access to its private key.

Giving the Assembly a Strong Name

You now need to ensure that your assembly uses the strong name. You can create a new strong name file, or assign an existing strong name file on the Signing tab of the Project Designer dialog (see Figure 30-10).

Figure 30-10

Registering with Component Services

Once you've built the DLL again, you can run RegSvcs to register the DLL with Component Services (see Figure 30-11).

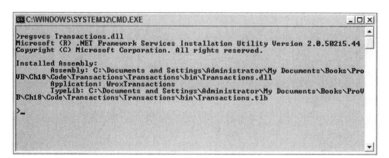

Figure 30-11

RegSvcs does a few things at this point. It creates a COM type library for the DLL, which enables it to communicate with COM, and it creates a COM+ application for the component.

The Component Services Console

The *Component Services Console* is the control interface for Component Services. This is an MMC snap-in, which you can find by selecting Control Panel⇨ Administrative Tools⇨ Component Services (see Figure 30-12).

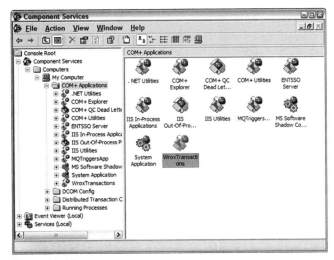

Figure 30-12

You should be able to find the sample under COM+ Applications. A COM+ application is a set of related COM+ components that have been packaged together. RegSvcs creates a new application for every component that it registers. If you want to bundle together a series of components from separate DLLs, you can do so, but only by creating a new application via the Component Services Console (right-click COM+ Applications and then select New). We'll explore the console a little more as we go on.

Now you need a test application. More important, you need to tell Component Services that you're interested in transactions.

Test Application

Create a Windows Application project called TestTransactions and a very simple form (see Figure 30-13).

Figure 30-13

The text field is called TransferField and the command button is called TransferButton. In order to access the transactional component, add references to a couple of DLLs. First, add a reference to the transactional component DLL itself. You'll need to browse for this, as it isn't currently in the global assembly cache. Second, in order to access the objects in this DLL, you also need to make the application aware of the `System.EnterpriseServices` assembly, so add a reference to that as well. Having done that, it's time to import `Transactions` into the application:

```
Imports Transactions
```

Here's the code behind the `TransferButton` button:

```
Private Sub TransferButton_Click(ByVal sender As System.Object, _
    ByVal e As System.EventArgs) Handles TransferButton.Click
    Dim txn As New BankTransactions
    Try
        txn.TransferMoney(CDec(Me.TransferField.Text), _
            "BankOfWrox", "Professional Visual Basic 2008", _
            "BankOfMe", "Me")
        MessageBox.Show(String.Format("{0:C} transfered from {1} to {2}", _
            CDec(Me.TransferField.Text), "BankOfWrox", "BankOfMe"), _
            "Transfer Succeeded", _
            MessageBoxButtons.OK, _
            MessageBoxIcon.Information)

    Catch ex As Exception
        MessageBox.Show(ex.Message, "Transfer failed", _
            MessageBoxButtons.OK, _
            MessageBoxIcon.Error)

    End Try

End Sub
```

The Transaction Attribute

Now it's time to tell Component Services how the component should enter a transaction. There are two ways of doing this: via the Component Services Console or via an attribute in code. To do it via the Component Services Console, open the Explorer tree to locate the Transactions component (as shown in Figure 30-14).

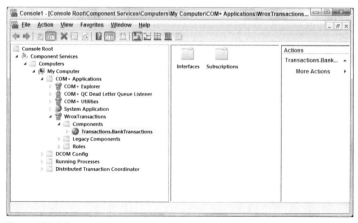

Figure 30-14

Select one of the available options; you'll learn what these all mean in a moment. It's a little tiresome to require the system manager to do this every time, especially if you already know that your component is always going to have the same transaction characteristics. An alternative mechanism is available: You can explicitly set up an attribute in the code for your component.

Attributes are items of declarative information that can be attached to the elements of code, such as classes, methods, data members, and properties. Anything that uses these can query their values at runtime. One such attribute is called `TransactionAttribute`, which, unsurprisingly, is used for specifying the transaction characteristics of a component class. The value of this attribute is taken from an enumeration called `TransactionOption`. Both `TransactionAttribute` and `TransactionOption` are found within the `System.EnterpriseServices` namespace. The enumeration can take the following values:

Value	Description
Disabled	Ignores any transaction in the current context. This is the default.
NotSupported	Creates the component in a context with no governing transaction
Required	Shares a transaction if one exists. Creates a new transaction if necessary.
RequiresNew	Creates the component with a new transaction, regardless of the state of the current context
Supported	Shares a transaction if one exists. If it doesn't, then it creates the component.

The available values are exactly the same as the ones shown in the Transaction tab. This case is a stand-alone transaction, so either `RequiresNew` or `Required` are equally valid. However, you would most commonly select `RequiresNew` to create a component that will participate in an existing transaction or create a new transaction if needed.

Before changing the component, deregister the current version to avoid any confusion. Now return to the `Transactions` project and make the change:

```
<Assembly: ApplicationName("WroxTransactions")>
<Assembly: ApplicationAccessControl(True)>
<Transaction(TransactionOption.RequiresNew)> _

Public Class BankTransactions
    Inherits ServicedComponent
```

Having made the change, rebuild `Transactions` and then register it as before. Now run the test application and start the Component Services Console application. Enter 1000 and click the Confirm button. You might be able to see the number of current active transactions briefly go from none to one (depending on your computer, this may be too fast to see), followed by the number of committed transactions and the total both increasing by one. That's it. You've implemented your first transaction. If you check the two databases, the amount in the `BankOfWrox` Professional Visual Basic account has been reduced to $4,000, whereas the account in `BankOfMe` has been increased by $1,000.

Invalid Data

What happens if you enter a value that you know is invalid? There are two options here: either try to transfer more money than there is in the Professional Visual Basic account, or try to transfer less than the "approved limit." Run the application again and try to transfer $10. As expected, the transaction will fail, and no changes will be made to the accounts. Professional Visual Basic still has $4,000, and your account still has $1,000. This isn't too much of a big deal, because the invalid condition is spotted before any database manipulation is carried out. If you check the transaction statistics, the number of *aborted* transactions has been incremented this time.

Now try to transfer $10,000. This time, the first part of the transaction is successful, but the *second* part fails. Again the number of aborted transactions is incremented, but what's happened to the database? Well, fortunately for everyone concerned, there is still $4,000 in the Professional Visual Basic account, and still $1,000 in your account. The *entire* transaction has failed.

When Something Goes Wrong

Recall that bit of mindless vandalism that we did to the Deposit function so that it would divide by zero if we entered a negative value? Here's where we get to try it out. Run the application again and try to transfer $-1. You should receive an error message. It was halfway through a transaction, but when you look at the transaction statistics, the aborted count has increased by one. More important, if you check the databases, the Pro VB account *still* has $4,000, and the other account still has $1,000, so you're protected against software failures as well.

Other Aspects of Transactions

Dealing with transactions involves several other topics as well, including just-in-time (JIT) activation and object pooling.

Just-In-Time

Creating and deleting components takes time. Instead of discarding the component when finished with it, why not keep it around in case it's needed again? The mechanism by which this is done is called *just-in-time* (JIT) *activation*, and it's set by default for all automatic transactional components (it's unset by default for all other COM+ components, however). This is another reason why holding state is undesirable within components — it limits the ability to share them.

All good transactional components are entirely stateless, but real life dictates differently. For example, you might want to maintain a link to your database, one that would be expensive to set up every time. The JIT mechanism provides a couple of methods that you can override in the ServicedComponent class in this case.

The method that is invoked when a JIT component is activated is called Activate, and the component that is invoked when it is deactivated is called, unsurprisingly, Deactivate. In Activate and Deactivate you put the things that you would normally put in your constructor and deconstructor. JIT can also be activated by adding the JustInTimeActivation attribute to any class within the ServicedComponent class.

Object Pooling

You can, if you want, take this a step further and maintain a pool of objects already constructed and prepared to be activated whenever required. When an object is no longer required (i.e., it's deactivated), it is returned to the pool until the next time it is needed. By retaining objects, you don't have to continually create them anew, which reduces your application's performance costs. You can use the `ObjectPooling` attribute within your class to determine how the pool operates:

```
<Transaction(TransactionOption.RequiresNew), _
ObjectPooling(MinPoolSize:=5, MaxPoolSize:=20, _
                        CreationTimeOut:=30)> _
Public Class BankTransactions
```

Queued Components

The traditional component programming model is very much a *synchronous* one. Put simply, you invoke a method and you get a result. Unfortunately, many real-world problems are inherently *asynchronous*. You can't always wait for a response to your request before moving on to the next task. A real-world analogy is the difference between phoning someone and sending an e-mail. Phoning is a synchronous process; either the phone is answered (a successful transaction) or it isn't (or you've called a wrong number, another form of unsuccessful transaction). E-mailing someone is asynchronous; you have no control over how long the e-mail takes to arrive, or when the person will actually look at it. Therefore, in order to tackle everything that the real world throws at us, we need an asynchronous component model for those scenarios where it is appropriate.

Why only some scenarios? The synchronous model is quite simple to manage, because the three possible outcomes of a request are quite straightforward to handle. First, the request can be successful. Second, the request can fail. Finally, the target of the request can simply not respond at all, in which case it times out. However, when dealing with asynchronous requests, expect all manner of unusual conditions. For example, the target system may not currently be operational, so you have to make a decision regarding how long to wait before it comes back up again. Each outstanding request takes up system resources, so they need to be managed carefully. You need to be able to determine when the response comes back; you need to make certain that the recipient only receives a given message once, and so on. We are, in fact, dealing with a different infrastructure than MTS here, an infrastructure to handle reliable messaging. Microsoft's product to tackle this type of problem is Microsoft Message Queue (MSMQ).

The idea behind reliable messaging is that once you have asked the system to send a message to a given target, you can effectively stop worrying about it. The system handles the storing and forwarding of messages to their target. It also handles retries and timeouts, ensuring a message is received only once, and returning a message to the dead letter queue if all else fails. MSMQ is, in fact, a whole technology in itself, and can seem quite complex. However, Enterprise Services provides a handy, simple abstraction called *queued components*.

Queued components take the sometimes gnarly aspects of working with MSMQ and make them easier to deal with than the raw queue handling. Instead, you have the concepts of recorders, listeners, and players. Recorders create messages that are put on a queue. Eventually, a listener receives the message. This could happen immediately or it could take weeks if the two components are disconnected. Finally, the player does whatever the message requests. Naturally, this places some restrictions on the kind of component that can be used. For example, you can't have any output arguments or return values. If you have either of these, the values can't be set until the action is complete, removing the benefit of the asynchronous aspects of the call. However, there are some cool things that you can do, explored in the next section.

> In order to run the queued components examples, you need MSMQ, which comes with Windows 2000, XP, and Vista. However, you need to install it separately using the Add Windows Components dialog.

An Example of Queued Components

This example creates a very simple logging component that takes a string as its input and writes it out to a sequential file, as well as outputs it in a message box. To keep the example simple, the client and the server are on the same machine; in a production scenario they would be separate. The benefit of using queued components here is that the logging doesn't slow down the main process.

Create a Class Library project called `Reporter` and add a reference to the `System.EnterpriseServices` namespace. First, define an interface:

```
Imports System.IO
Imports System.EnterpriseServices
Public Interface IReporter
   Sub Log(ByVal message As String)
End Interface
```

Notice that the `Log` method follows the requirements listed earlier. There is no return value, and all parameters are input only. We need to separate the interface from the implementation because the implementation, residing on the server, is going to be sitting on another machine somewhere. The client isn't the slightest bit interested in the details of this; it only needs to know how to interface to it.

Take a look at the actual implementation. As with the transactional component, we inherit from `Serviced Component`, and implement the interface just defined. However, notice the `<InterfaceQueuing()>` attribute that indicates to the Component Services runtime that the interface can be queued (we did the same for the interface):

```
<InterfaceQueuing(Interface:="IReporter")> Public Class Reporter
   Inherits ServicedComponent
   Implements IReporter
```

In the logging method, simply output a message box, open a `StreamWriter` component to append to the log file, and then close it:

```
Sub Log(ByVal message As String) Implements IReporter.Log
    MsgBox(strText)
    Using writer As   _
```

```
        New StreamWriter("c:\account.log", True)
           writer.WriteLine(String.Format("{0}: {1}", _
             DateTime.Now, message))
           writer.Close()
      End Using
   End Sub
End Class
```

That's it for the component's code. To enable queuing, click Show All Files on the Solution Explorer to see the hidden files for the project. Open the My Project item and then open the `AssemblyInfo.vb` file. Ensure that it has these attributes:

```
'Enterprise Services attributes
<Assembly: EnterpriseServices.ApplicationAccessControl(False, _
    Authentication:=EnterpriseServices.AuthenticationOption.None)>
<Assembly: EnterpriseServices.ApplicationQueuing(Enabled:=True, _
    QueueListenerEnabled:=True)>
<Assembly: EnterpriseServices.ApplicationName("WroxQueue")>
```

Next, ensure that queuing is correctly enabled for this component. The next line is a special line to enable message queuing to work correctly in a workgroup environment, by switching off authentication. If we didn't do this, we would need to set up an entire domain structure and create specific users for the queues. (In a production scenario, that's exactly what you would use, so you would need to remove this line.) Finally, ensure that the component runs as a server, rather than a library. This was optional for transactional components, but it's mandatory for queued components. You'll soon see why. In addition, add a strong name file to your project, as you did with the `Transactions` component.

Consoles Again

It's time to build your component. Once built, register it using `RegSvcs` just as you did with the `Transactions` component. Take a look at the Component Services Console to see how it's going. Also, look closely at Figure 30-15. It looks fine, but there's one other console to check out: the *Computer Management Console*. Access this either from the system console or by right-clicking the My Computer icon and selecting Manage from the menu. Tucked away at the bottom is the relevant part. Open Services and Applications to find it. Component Services has set up some queues for us. There are five queues feeding into the main one, so the infrastructure is ready. Keep in mind that all this would be running on the server machine in a production scenario, not the client.

Building the Client

The problem is that all the code you've written in this project is built on top of the MSMQ infrastructure, which is, inevitably, a COM infrastructure. Worse, the current tasks involve *marshaling* COM objects into a stream suitable for inserting into a queued message. For the purposes of this discussion, think of marshaling as intelligently serializing the contents of a method invocation on an interface. We do this in such a way that they can then be deserialized at the other end and turned into a successful invocation of the same method in a remote implementation of the interface. We get COM to do this for us by constructing a *moniker*, which is basically an intelligent name.

Begin by creating a Windows Application project called `TestReporter`. Add a reference to the `Reporter` component in the usual manner. Figure 30-16 shows the form.

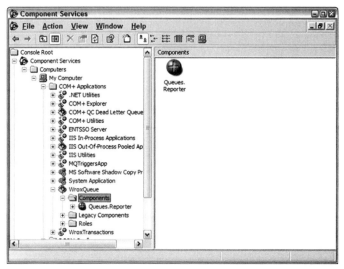

Figure 30-15

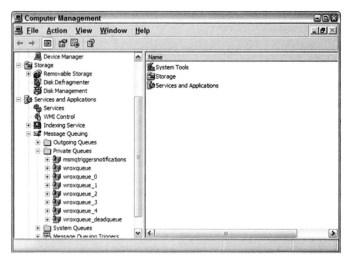

Figure 30-16

The text box is called `MessageField`, and the button is called `SendButton`. Here's the code:

```
Imports System.Runtime.InteropServices
Public Class MainForm
  Inherits System.Windows.Forms.Form
  Private Sub SendButton_Click(ByVal sender As System.Object, _
                       ByVal e As System.EventArgs) _
                       Handles SendButton.Click
```

Here's the crucial section. Note the references to the interface and how the object is instantiated:

```
Dim logger As Queues.IReporter

Try
    logger = _
        CType(Marshal.BindToMoniker("queue:/new:Queues.Reporter"), _
        Queues.IReporter)
```

Once the object is created, you can make the queued call:

```
logger.Log(Me.MessageField.Text)
```

Finally, release the reference to the underlying COM object:

```
        Marshal.ReleaseComObject(logger)
        MessageBox.Show("Message sent")

Catch ex As Exception
        MessageBox.Show(ex.Message, "Error sending message")
End Try
```

It's not pretty, but you only have to do it once to use it repeatedly.

Queuing Invocations

Now try using this application to put a message onto the queue (see Figure 30-17). Run the client application and enter a suitable message, such as "Hello everyone."

Figure 30-17

We've definitely created a message, so that represents our invocation. If we were able to read it, we would see the message you typed in earlier embedded somewhere in it. (Unfortunately, the console only allows us to inspect the start of the message, but we can see the name of the component in there.) Why hasn't anything happened? We haven't actually started our server. Recall that our component has to run as a server; this is why. The server has to sit there all the time, serving the incoming queue. Therefore, return to the Component Services Console, right-click Reporter, select Start from the menu, and you're off. Lo and behold, there's the message box (see Figure 30-18).

Figure 30-18

Now that the message has been delivered, return to the Component Services Console. Right-clicking over the message queue and selecting Refresh confirms that the message has indeed been removed from the queue. Look in `account.log` and notice that it has been updated as well. Running the application results in the message boxes popping up right away, as the server is now running and responding to the messages entering the queue.

Transactions with Queued Components

Why were you instructed to call that file `account.log`? MSMQ, like SQL Server, is a resource manager, and it can take part in transactions. This may seem a little counterintuitive at first because how on earth can anything as asynchronous as MSMQ have anything to do with transactions? The key is that it is *reliable*. Anything you put into a queue is guaranteed to come out the other end. If we take a transaction to the point at which a message is securely in the queue, we definitely have something that can participate. What happens at the other end of the queue is an entirely separate transaction. Of course, if something goes wrong there, you may need to look at setting up a compensating transaction coming back the other way to trigger some kind of rollback.

For the final example, then, we're going to take our original transactional component and add in a queued element, so that not only does the transfer of money take place, but that fact is also logged to a remote file. Use exactly the same queued component as last time.

Begin by making a clone of `TestTransactions` called `TestQueuedTransactions`. Add a reference to Queues and an `Imports` statement:

```
Imports System.Runtime.InteropServices
```

You also need a new private subroutine:

```
Private Shared Sub LogTransaction(ByVal amount As Decimal, _
    ByVal sourceBank As String, ByVal sourceAccount As String, _
    ByVal destinationBank As String, ByVal destinationAccount As String)
```

```
            Dim logger As Queues.IReporter

            Try
                logger = _
                  CType(Marshal.BindToMoniker("queue:/new:Queues.Reporter"), _
                  Queues.IReporter)

                logger.Log(String.Format("{0:c} transfered from {1}:{2} to {3}:{4}", _
                    amount, _
                    sourceBank, sourceAccount, _
                    destinationBank, destinationAccount))

                Marshal.ReleaseComObject(logger)
                MessageBox.Show("Message sent")

            Catch ex As Exception
                MessageBox.Show(ex.Message, "Error sending message")
            End Try
        End Sub
```

This may look similar to the previous queued component example application. Finally, add a call to this subroutine in the Button_Click event handler:

```
        Private Sub TransferButton_Click(ByVal sender As System.Object, _
          ByVal e As System.EventArgs) Handles TransferButton.Click
            Dim txn As New Transactions.BankTransactions
            Try
                txn.TransferMoney(CDec(Me.TransferField.Text), _
                  "BankOfWrox", "Professional VB", _
                  "BankOfMe", "Me")
                LogTransaction(CDec(Me.TransferField.Text), _
                  "BankOfWrox", "Professional VB", _
                  "BankOfMe", "Me")

                MessageBox.Show(String.Format("{0:C} transfered from {1} to {2}", _
                    CDec(Me.TransferField.Text), "BankOfWrox", "BankOfMe"), _
                    "Transfer Succeeded", _
                    MessageBoxButtons.OK, _
                    MessageBoxIcon.Information)

            Catch ex As Exception
                MessageBox.Show(ex.Message, "Transfer failed", _
                  MessageBoxButtons.OK, _
                  MessageBoxIcon.Error)

            End Try
        End Sub
```

Here, we're including a queued component in our transaction. It's been deliberately placed at the beginning to determine whether it genuinely takes part in the two-phase committal. If the transaction fails, then you shouldn't see any messages come through the queue.

You also need to make a small change to the `Reporter` component, but you must shut it down via the Component Services Console first. The change is very simple. To ensure that the queued component takes part in the transaction, it must be marked with the `Transaction` attribute:

```
<InterfaceQueuing(Interface:="Reporter.IReporter"), _
Transaction(TransactionOption.Required)> _
Public Class Reporter
```

If you now transfer $1,000, you'll see the usual "Transfer complete" message box, and if you start up the `Reporter` component, you also see the message box from our queued component (see Figure 30-19).

Figure 30-19

If you try it again, you see the queued message coming through first, so you know it's OK for valid transfers. What happens if you try to transfer $100? As we know from the earlier example, this will fail, and indeed, we see the "Transfer failed" message box from the main component, but not a peep out of the queued component.

Transactions and System.Transactions

While the classes within `System.EnterpriseServices` make working with transactions easier, they are not the only way to define transactions with VB. Visual Basic 2008 includes a set of classes specifically designed for working with transactions: the `System.Transactions` namespace. As the name implies, these classes make it easier to define and work with transactions in your code.

You may well be wondering at this point why we need two sets of classes that work with transactions. The classes of `System.Transaction`, particularly the `Transaction` class itself, abstract the code from the resource managers participating in the transaction. While this is similar to the goal of the COM+ model described earlier, it is subtly different. The classes of Enterprise Services worked with the Distributed Transaction Coordinator (MSDTC) service, which in turn worked with the participating resource managers. The `Transaction` class does not need to work with the MSDTC and can coordinate multiple resource managers itself.

The classes of `System.Transaction` also provide the means to create your own resource managers. These resource managers may then participate in transactions. At first, you may balk at this prospect, wondering how you could write something that manages all the details of a transactional data store. Aren't the details enormous? Fortunately, the classes make it easy to enlist in a transaction and report on your results.

Creating Transactions

`System.Transaction` supports two means of working with transactions: *implicit* and *explicit*. With implicit transactions, you define a boundary for the transaction. Any resource managers you use within this boundary become part of the transaction. That is, if you have defined a boundary and then call a database such as SQL Server, the actions performed on the database are part of the transaction. If the code reaches the boundary without incident, then the transaction is committed. If an exception occurs during this implicit transaction, then the transaction is rolled back. Explicit transactions, as you may have guessed, mean that you explicitly commit or roll back the transaction as needed.

Using the implicit model can greatly simplify the code involved in a transaction. For example, the TransferMoney method used in the preceding sample could be rewritten to use an implicit transaction:

```
Public Sub TransferMoney(ByVal amount As Decimal, _
  ByVal sourceBank As String, _
  ByVal sourceAccount As String, _
  ByVal destinationBank As String, _
  ByVal destinationAccount As String)

    Using scope As New TransactionScope
        Withdraw(sourceBank, sourceAccount, amount)
        Deposit(destinationBank, destinationAccount, amount)
    End Using
End Sub
```

The Using clause wraps the two methods within an implicit transaction. All resource managers that recognize transactions participate in this transaction. The Using clause guarantees that the Transaction Scope object is disposed of when the transaction is complete.

Using explicit transactions requires a bit more code but provides greater control over the transaction. You can use either the Transaction class or the CommittableTransaction class to wrap transactions in this model. CommittableTransaction is a child class of Transaction, and adds the capability to commit a transaction, as the name implies.

Using a CommittableTransaction in the bank sample changes the TransferMoney method as follows:

```
Public Sub TransferMoney(ByVal amount As Decimal, _
    ByVal sourceBank As String, _
    ByVal sourceAccount As String, _
    ByVal destinationBank As String, _
    ByVal destinationAccount As String)

    Using txn As New CommittableTransaction
        Withdraw(sourceBank, sourceAccount, amount, txn)
        Deposit(destinationBank, destinationAccount, amount, txn)
    End Using
End Sub
```

Notice that the Withdraw and Deposit methods now have an additional parameter to receive the transaction. These additions enable the two methods to vote on the transaction:

```
Private Sub Deposit(ByVal bank As String, _
  ByVal account As String, _
  ByVal amount As Decimal, _
```

```
        ByVal txn As CommittableTransaction)

    Dim ConnectionString As String
    Dim SQL As String
    Dim cmdCurrent As SqlCommand
    Dim currentValue As Decimal
    Dim cmdUpdate As SqlCommand


    ConnectionString = My.Settings.Item(bank).ToString
    SQL = String.Format("SELECT Amount FROM Accounts WHERE Name = '{0}'", _
        account)

    If amount < 0 Then
        amount = amount / 0
    ElseIf amount < 50 Then
        Throw New ArgumentException("Value of deposit must be greater than 50")
    Else
        Using conn As New SqlConnection(ConnectionString)
            Try
                conn.Open()
                'join the transaction
                conn.EnlistTransaction(txn)
                'get the current value
                cmdCurrent = New SqlCommand(SQL, conn)
                currentValue = CDec(cmdCurrent.ExecuteScalar())

                SQL = String.Format("UPDATE Accounts SET Amount = " _
                    "{0} WHERE Name = '{1}'", _
                    currentValue + amount, account)

                cmdUpdate = New SqlCommand(SQL, conn)
                cmdUpdate.ExecuteNonQuery()
                txn.Commit()
            Catch ex As Exception
                'deal with transaction here
                txn.Rollback()
                Throw New DataException("Error depositing", ex)
            End Try
        End Using
    End If

End Sub
```

The principal change here is that the SQL connection must be enlisted in the transaction using the EnlistTransaction method (or EnlistDistributedTransaction if the transaction will span multiple computers). Once it is a part of the transaction, it can then use the transaction methods to commit or roll back each part of the transaction.

Using the `TransactionScope` and `Transaction` classes can greatly decrease the amount of effort involved in creating and working with transactions in your applications. Generally, using implicit transactions using `TransactionScope` is easier and less error prone, and should be your first choice.

Creating Resource Managers

In addition to using the classes in `System.Transactions` for managing transactions, you can also use them to define your own resource managers. These resource managers can then participate in transactions with databases, MSDTC, message queues, and more. There are three basic steps to defining a resource manager:

1. Create an enlistment class. This class is used to track the resource manager's participation in the transaction. That is, this is the class that will vote on whether the transaction should complete or be rolled back. This class should implement the `IEnlistmentNotification` interface.

2. Enlist the new enlistment class in the transaction. There are two main ways the class may participate in the transaction: `EnlistDurable` or `EnlistVolatile`. You use `EnlistDurable` if your resource manager stores data permanently, such as in a file or database. `Enlist Volatile` is used if your resource manager stores its information in memory or in some other nonrecoverable location.

3. Implement the methods of the `IEnlistmentNotification` interface to react to the states of the transaction. The `IEnlistmentNotification` interface provides four methods: `Prepare`, `Commit`, `Rollback`, and `InDoubt`. `Commit` and `Rollback` are self-explanatory, used at these two phases of the transaction. `Prepare` is called before `Commit`, to determine whether it is possible to commit the transaction. Finally, `InDoubt` is called if the transaction is questionable. This can happen if the transaction coordinator has lost track of one of the resource managers.

Why would you define your own resource managers and not simply use an existing one such as SQL Server? You might need to store data in another database that does not directly participate in transactions. Alternately, you may want to enable a normally nontransactional component with transactional behavior. For example, the cache in ASP.NET doesn't support the addition of items using transactions. You could create a resource manager that wraps the ASP.NET cache and adds support for commit and rollback of entries. This might be part of a system in which you want to use the cache as an in-memory data store. While this would work without the transactions, adding transactional support would ensure that if the database write fails for any reason, then the entry could be rolled back out of the cache.

Summary

This chapter looked at creating applications using the classes of `System.EnterpriseServices` and `System.Transactions`. We first examined transactions and their importance in maintaining data integrity when multiple simultaneous changes may affect your data. Properly applied, transactions can ensure that even with multiple users editing data, your database always reflects the correct data. We also looked at asynchronous processing using MSMQ and queued components. Many scenarios, such as logging or other "background" processes, are better handled using asynchronous code. Queued components make building these asynchronous handlers much easier. Many other aspects of Enterprise Services were beyond the scope of this chapter, including role-based security, object constructors, and more.

In addition to creating transactions with the Enterprise Services classes, Visual Basic 2008 provides the `System.Transactions` namespace. This namespace provides even more ways of implementing transactions in your code. Beyond their use in creating transactions, they can also be used to create your own resource managers: data stores that can participate in transactions.

## 31

Network Programming

Just as it is difficult to live your life without talking with people, your applications also need to communicate, perhaps with other programs or perhaps with hardware devices. As you have seen throughout this book, you can use a variety of techniques to have your program communicate, including .NET Remoting, Web Services, and Enterprise Services. This chapter looks at yet another way to communicate: using the basic protocols on which the Internet and many networks have been built. You will learn how the classes in System.Net can provide a variety of techniques for communicating with existing applications such as web or FTP servers, or how you can use them to create your own network applications.

Before getting started on writing applications using these classes, however, it would be good to get some background on how networks are bolted together, and how machines and applications are identified.

Protocols, Addresses, and Ports

No discussion of a network is complete without a huge number of acronyms, seemingly random numbers, and the idea of a protocol. For example, the World Wide Web runs using a protocol called HTTP or Hypertext Transfer Protocol. Similarly, there are File Transfer Protocol (FTP), Network News Transfer Protocol (NNTP), and Gopher, also a protocol. Each application you run on a network communicates with another program using a defined protocol. The protocol is simply the expected messages each program will send the other, in the order they should be sent. For a real-world example, consider a scenario in which you want to go see a movie with a friend. A simplified conversation could look like this:

```
You: Dials phone
Friend: Hears phone ringing, answers phone. "Hello?"
You: "Hello. Want to go see 'Freddie and Jason Escape from New York, Part 6'?"
Friend: "No, I saw that one already. What about 'Star Warthogs'?"
You: "OK, 9:30 showing downtown?"
Friend: "Yes."
You: "Later."
Friend: "See you," hangs up
```

Apart from a bad taste in movies, you can see a basic protocol here. Someone initiates a communication channel. The recipient accepts the channel and signals the start of the communication. The initial caller then sends a series of messages to which the recipient replies, either to signify they have been received or as either a positive or a negative response. Finally, one of the messages indicates the end of the communication channel, and the two disconnect.

Similarly, network applications have their own protocols, defined by the application writer. For example, sending an e-mail using SMTP (Simple Mail Transfer Protocol) could look like this:

```
220 schroedinger Microsoft ESMTP MAIL Service, Version: 6.0.2600.2180 ready at Wed,
6 Oct 2004 15:58:28 -0700
HELLO
250 schroedinger Hello [127.0.0.1]
FOO
500 5.3.3 Unrecognized command
MAIL FROM: me
250 2.1.0 me@schroedinger....Sender OK
RCPT TO: him
250 2.1.5 him@schroedinger
DATA
354 Start mail input; end with <CRLF>.<CRLF>
subject: Testing SMTP

Hello World, via mail.
.
250 2.6.0 <SCHROEDINGERKaq65r500000001@schroedinger> Queued mail for delivery
QUIT
221 2.0.0 schroedinger Service closing transmission channel


Connection to host lost.
```

In this case, lines beginning with numbers are coming from the server, while the items in uppercase (and the message itself) were sent from the client. If the client sends an invalid message (such as the FOO message in the preceding example), then it receives a gentle rebuff from the server, while correct messages receive the equivalent of an "OK" or "Go on" reply. Traditionally, for SMTP and many other protocols (including HTTP), the reply is a three-digit number (see the following table) identifying the result of the request. The text after the number, such as 2.1.0 me@schroedinger . . . Sender OK, isn't really needed, and many servers attempt to be overly cute or clever here, so it isn't a good idea to assume anything about this text. The return values for the services generally fall into one of five ranges. Each range identifies a certain family of responses.

Range	Description
100–199	Message is good, but the server is still working on the request
200–299	Message is good, and the server has completed acting on the request
300–399	Message is good, but the server needs more information to work on the request

Range	Description
400–499	Message is good, but the server could not act on the request. You may try the request again to see whether it works in the future.
500–599	The server could not act on the request. Either the message was bad or an error occurred. It likely won't work next time.

Other protocols use this technique as well (leading to the infamous HTTP 404 error for "Page not found"), but they don't have to. Having a good reference is key to your success, and the best reference for existing protocols is the Request for Comments (RFC) for the protocol. These are the definitions that are used by protocol authors to create their implementation of the standard. Many of these RFCs are available at the IETF (`www.ietf.org`) and the World Wide Web Consortium (`www.w3.org`) websites.

Addresses and names

The next important topic necessary to a thorough understanding of network programming is the relationship between the names and addresses of each of the computers involved. Each form of network communication (such as TCP/IP networks such as the Internet) has its own way of mapping the name of a computer (or host) to an address. The reason for this is simple: computers deal with numbers better than text, and humans can remember text better than numbers (generally). Therefore, while you may have named your computer something clever like "l33t_#4x0R," applications and other computers know it by its IP (Internet Protocol) address. This address is a 32-bit value, usually written in four parts (each one a byte that is a number from 0 to 255), such as 192.168.1.39. This is the standard the Internet has operated on for many years. However, as only about four billion unique addresses are possible using this method, another standard, IPv6, has been proposed. It is called IPv6 because it is the sixth recommendation in the series (the older 32-bit addresses are often called IPv4 to differentiate them from this new standard). With IPv6, a 128-bit address is used, leading to a maximum number of about 3×10^{28} unique addresses, which would be more than enough for every Internet-enabled toaster.

This IP address (whether IPv4 or IPv6) must uniquely identify each host on a network (actually subnetwork, but I'm getting ahead of myself). If not, then messages will not be routed to their destination properly, and chaos ensues. The matter gets more complicated when another 32-bit number, the subnet mask, enters the picture. This is a value that is masked (using a Boolean AND operation) over the address to identify the subnetwork of the network on which the computer resides. All addresses on the same subnetwork must be unique. Two subnetworks may have the same address, however, as long as their subnet masks are different.

Many common subnetworks use the value 255.255.255.0 for the subnet mask. When this is applied to the network address, as shown in the following example, only the last address is considered significant. Therefore, the subnetwork can include only 254 unique addresses (0 and 255 are used for other purposes).

```
Network address:      192.168.  1.107
Subnet Mask:          255.255.255.  0
Result:               192.168.  1.  0
```

Because computers and humans use two different means of identifying computers, there must be some way to relate the two. The term for this process is *name resolution*. In the case of the Internet, a common means of name resolution is yet another protocol, the Domain Naming System (DNS). A computer, when faced with an unknown text-based name, will send a message to the closest DNS server. It then determines whether it knows the IP address of that host. If it does, it passes this back to the requester. If not, it asks another DNS server it knows. This process continues until either the IP address is found or you run out of DNS servers. After the IP address is found, all of the servers (and the original computer) store that number for a while in case they are asked again.

Keeping in mind the problems that can ensue during name resolution can often solve many development problems. For example, if you are having difficulty communicating with a computer that should be responding, then it may be that your computer simply can't resolve the name of the remote computer. Try using the IP address instead. This removes any name-resolution problems from the equation, and may allow you to continue developing while someone else fixes the name-resolution problem.

Ports: they're not just for ships

As described earlier, each computer or host on a network is uniquely identified by an address. How does your computer realize which of possibly many applications running are meant to receive a given message arriving on the network? This is determined by the port at which the message is targeted. The port is another number, in this case an integer value from 1 to 32,767. The unique combination of address and port identifies the target application.

For example, assume you currently have a web server (IIS) running, as well as an SMTP server, and a few browser windows open. When a network message comes in, how does the operating system "know" which of these applications should receive the packet? Each of the applications (either client or server) that may receive a message is assigned a unique port number. In the case of servers, this is typically a fixed number, whereas client applications, such as your Web browser, are assigned a random available port.

To make communication with servers easier, they typically use a well-known assigned port. In the case of web servers, this is port 80, while SMTP servers use port 25. You can see a list of common servers and their ports in the file `%windows%sudhasystem32sudhadriverssudhaetcsudhaservices`.

If you're writing a server application, then you can either use these common port numbers (and you should if you're attempting to write a common type of server) or choose your own. If you're writing a new type of server, then you should choose a port that has not been assigned to another server; choosing a port higher than 1024 should prevent any conflicts, as these are not assigned. When writing a client application, there is typically no need to assign a port, as a dynamic port is assigned to the client for communication with a server.

> *Ports below 1024 should be considered secure ports, and applications that use them should have administrative access.*

Firewalls: can't live with them, can't live without them

Many people have a love-hate relationship with firewalls. While they are invaluable in today's network, sometimes it would be nice if they got out of the way. A firewall is a piece of hardware or software that monitors network traffic, either incoming, outgoing, or both. It can be configured to allow only particular ports or applications to transmit information beyond the firewall. Firewalls protect against hackers or viruses that may attempt to connect to open ports, leveraging them to their own ends. They protect against spyware applications that may attempt to communicate out from your machine. However, they also "protect" against any network programming you may attempt to do. You must invariably cooperate with your network administrators, working within their guidelines for network access. If they make only certain ports available, then your applications should use only those ports. Alternately, you may be able to get them to configure the firewalls involved to permit the ports needed by your applications.

Thankfully, creating network messages is a bit easier with Visual Basic 2008. The following sections demonstrate how.

The System.Net Namespace

Most of the functionality used when writing network applications is contained within the `System.Net` and `System.Net.Sockets` namespaces. This chapter covers the following main classes in these namespaces:

❑   `WebRequest` and `WebResponse`, and their subclasses, including `FtpWebRequest`

❑   `WebClient`, the simplified `WebRequest` for common scenarios

❑   `HttpListener`, which enables you to create your own web server

> *Additional classes, methods, properties, and events were added to the* `System.Net` *and* `System.Net.Sockets` *namespaces in the .NET Framework 2.0. You can locate the updated reference for these namespaces at* `http://msdn2.microsoft.com/library/system.net.aspx` *as of this writing.*

Web requests (and responses)

When most people think of network programming these days, they're really thinking of communication via a web server or client. Therefore, it shouldn't be surprising that there is a set of classes for this communication need. In this case, it is the abstract `WebRequest` class and the associated `WebResponse`. These two classes represent the concept of a request/response communication with a web server, or similar server. As these are abstract classes — that is, `MustInherit` classes — they cannot be created by themselves. Instead, you create the subclasses of `WebRequest` that are optimized for specific types of communication.

The most important properties and methods of the `WebRequest` class are shown in the following table:

Member	Description
Create	Method used to create a specific type of `WebRequest`. This method uses the URL (either as a string or as an Uri class) passed to identify and create a subclass of `WebRequest`.
GetRequestStream	Method that allows access to the outgoing request. This enables you to add additional information, such as POST data, to the request before sending.

Member	Description
GetResponse	Method used to perform the request and retrieve the corresponding `WebResponse`
Credentials	Property that enables you to set the user ID and password for the request if they are needed to perform it
Headers	Property that enables you to change or add to the headers for the request
Method	Property used to identify the action for the request, such as GET or POST. The list of available methods is specific to each type of server.
Proxy	Property that enables you to identify a proxy server for the communication if needed. You generally don't need to set this property, as Visual Basic 2008 detects the settings for Internet Explorer and uses them by default.
Timeout	Property that enables you to define the duration of the request before you "give up" on the server

Each subclass of `WebRequest` supports these methods, providing a very consistent programming model for communication with a variety of server types. The basic model for working with any of the subclasses of `WebRequest` can be written in the following pseudo-code:

```
Declare variables as either WebRequest and WebResponse, or the specific child classes
Create the variable based on the URL
Make any changes to the Request object you may need
Use the GetResponse method to retrieve the response from the server
Get the Stream from the WebResponse
Do something with the Stream
```

If you decide to change the protocol (e.g., from HTTP to a file-based protocol), then you only need to change the URL used to retrieve the object.

Working with FileWebRequest and HttpWebRequest

The first two types of `WebRequest` that became available were `FileWebRequest` and `HttpWebRequest`. `FileWebRequest` is used less frequently; it represents a request to a local file, using the "file://" URL format. You have likely seen this type of request if you attempted to open a local file using your Web browser, such as Internet Explorer, Firefox, or Navigator. Generally, however, the subclass most developers will use is `HttpWebRequest`. This class enables you to make HTTP requests to a web server without requiring a browser. This could enable you to communicate with a web server, or, using the time-honored tradition of "screen scraping," to retrieve data available on the Web.

One hurdle many developers encounter when first working with `HttpWebRequest` is that there is no available constructor. Instead, you must use the `WebRequest.Create` method (or the `Create` method of your desired subclass) to create new instances of any of the subclasses. This method uses the URL requested to create the appropriate subtype of `WebRequest`. For example, this would create a new `HttpWebRequest`:

```
Dim req As HttpWebRequest = WebRequest.Create("http://msdn.microsoft.com")
```

Note that if you have `Option Strict` turned on (and you should), the preceding code will produce an error. Instead, you should explicitly cast the return value of `Create` to the desired type:

```
Dim req As HttpWebRequest = _
  DirectCast(WebRequest.Create("http://msdn.microsoft.com"), _
  System.Net.HttpWebRequest)
```

Putting It Together

In order to demonstrate how to use `WebRequest`/`WebResponse`, the following example shows how to wrap a Web call into a Visual Basic class. In this case, we'll wrap Google's `define:` keyword, which enables you to retrieve a set of definitions for a word (e.g., `www.google.com/search?q = define%3A + protocol`), and then use that in a sample application (see Figure 31-1.)

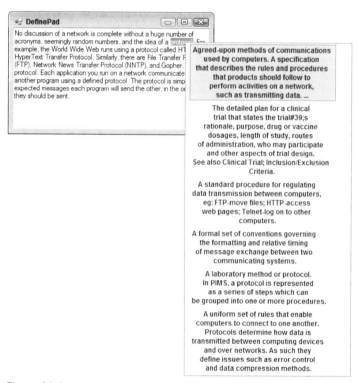

Figure 31-1

1. Create a new Windows application named "DefinePad."

2. Add a new class to the project. This will hold the actual `WebRequest` code. Call it `GoogleClient`.

3. Add a reference to the `System.Web` DLL, as you will need access to some of its functionality later.

4. In the `GoogleClient.vb` file, add `Imports` statements to make the coding a little briefer:

```
Imports System.IO
Imports System.Net
Imports System.Web
Imports System.Collections.Generic
```

5. The main function in `GoogleClient` will be a `Define` function that returns an array of strings. Each string will be one definition returned by Google:

```
Public Function Define(ByVal word As String) As String()
    Dim req As HttpWebRequest = Nothing
    Dim resp As HttpWebResponse
    Dim query As String
    Dim result As New List(Of String)

    query = "http://www.google.com/search?q=define%3A" & _
      HttpUtility.UrlEncode(word)

    Try
        req = DirectCast(WebRequest.Create(query), HttpWebRequest)
        With req
            .Method = "GET"
            resp = req.GetResponse
            If resp.StatusCode = HttpStatusCode.OK Then
                ParseResponse(resp.GetResponseStream, result)
            Else
                MessageBox.Show("Error calling definition service")
            End If
        End With
    Catch ex As Exception

    End Try

    Return result.ToArray()

End Function
```

The first task is to guarantee that no invalid characters appear in the query string when you send the request, such as a space, an accented character, or other non-ASCII characters. The `System.Web.HttpUtility` class has a number of handy shared methods for encoding strings, including the `UrlEncode` method. This replaces characters with a safe representation of the character that looks like `%value`, where the value is the Unicode code for the character. For example, in the definition of the query variable above, the `%3A` is actually the colon character ("`:`"), which has been encoded. Any time you retrieve a URL based on user input, encode it because there is no guarantee the resulting URL is safe to send.

Once the query is ready, you create the `WebRequest`. As the URL is for an HTTP resource, an `HttpWebRequest` is created. While the default method for `WebRequest` is a GET, it's still good practice to set it. You'll create the `ParseResponse` method shortly to process the stream returned from the server.

One other piece of code worth mentioning is the return value for this method, and how it is created. In order to return arrays of a specific type (rather than return actual collections from a method), you must either know the actual size to initialize the array or use the `List` generic type or the older `ArrayList`. These classes behave like the Visual Basic 6.0 `Collection` class, which enables you to add items, and grows as needed. They also have a handy method that enables you to convert the array into an array of any type; you can see this in the return statement. The `ArrayList` requires you to do a bit more work. If you want to use an `ArrayList` for this method, then you must identify the type of array you'd like to return. The resulting return statement would look like this using an `ArrayList`:

```
Return result.ToArray(GetType(String))
```

6. The `ProcessRequest` method parses the stream returned from the server and converts it into an array of items. Note that this is slightly simplified; in a real application, you would likely want to return an array of objects, where each object provides access to the definition and the URL of the site providing it:

```
Private Sub ParseResponse (ByVal input As System.IO.Stream, _
    ByRef output As List(Of String))
            'definitions are in a block beginning with <p>Definitions for...
            'then are marked with <li> tags
            'yes, I should use Regular Expressions for this
            'this format will also likely change in the future.
            Dim reader As New StreamReader(input)
            Dim work As String = reader.ReadToEnd
            Dim blockStart As String = "<p>Definitions of"
            Dim pos As Integer = work.IndexOf(blockStart)
            Dim posEnd As Integer
            Dim temp As String

        Do
            pos = work.IndexOf("<li>", pos + 1)
            If pos > 0 Then
                posEnd = work.IndexOf("<br>", pos)
                temp = work.Substring(pos + 4, posEnd - pos - 4)
                output.Add(ParseDefinition(temp))
                pos = posEnd + 1
            End If
        Loop While pos > 0

    End Sub
```

The code is fairly simple, using the time-honored tradition of *screen scraping* — processing the HTML of a page to find the section you need and then removing the HTML to produce the result.

7. The last part of the `GoogleClient` class is the `ParseDefinition` method that cleans up the definition, removing the link and other HTML tags:

```
Private Function ParseDefinition(ByVal input As String) As String
    Dim result As String = ""
        Dim lineBreak As Integer

        lineBreak = input.IndexOf("<br>")
        If lineBreak > 0 Then
            result = input.Substring(0, input.IndexOf("<br>"))
        Else
```

```
                    result = input
                End If
                Return result.Trim
        End Function
```

8. Now, with the class in hand, you can create a client to use it. In this case, you'll create a simple text editor that adds the capability to retrieve definitions for words. Go back to the Form created for the application and add controls as shown in Figure 31-2.

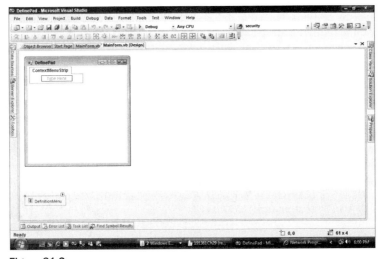

Figure 31-2

9. The user interface for DefinePad is simple: a TextBox and a ContextMenuStrip.

Control	Property	Value
TextBox	Name	TextField
	Multiline	True
	Dock	Fill
	ContextMenuStrip	DefinitionMenu
ContextMenuStrip	Name	DefinitionMenu

10. The only code in the Form is for the Opening event of the ContextMenuStrip. Here, you add the definitions to the menu. Add the following code to the handler for the Opening event:

```
Private Sub DefinitionMenu_Opening(ByVal sender As Object, _
    ByVal e As System.ComponentModel.CancelEventArgs) _
    Handles DefinitionMenu.Opening
    Dim svc As New GoogleClient
```

```
            Dim definitions() As String
            Dim definitionCount As Integer

            DefinitionMenu.Items.Clear()

            Try
                'define the currently selected word
                If TextField.SelectionLength > 0 Then
                    definitions = svc.Define(TextField.SelectedText)

                    'build context menu of returned definitions
                    definitionCount = definitions.Length
                    If definitionCount > 6 Then
                        definitionCount = 6
                    ElseIf definitionCount = 0 Then
                        'we can't do any more, so exit
                        Dim item As New ToolStripButton
                        item.Text = "Sorry, no definitions available"
                        DefinitionMenu.Items.Add(item)
                        Exit Sub
                    End If

                    For i As Integer = 1 To definitionCount
                        Dim item As New ToolStripButton
                        item.Text = definitions(i)
                        DefinitionMenu.Items.Add(item)
                    Next
                End If

            Catch ex As Exception
                MessageBox.Show(ex.Message, "Error getting definitions", _
                    MessageBoxButtons.OK, MessageBoxIcon.Error)

            End Try
        End Sub
```

The bulk of the code in this event is to limit the number of items displayed in the menu. The actual functional part of the routine is the call to the Define method of the GoogleClient. If you trace through the code as you run, you'll see the WebRequest generated, the call made, and the resulting response stream parsed into the individual items as desired. Finally, you can use the returned list to create a set of menu items (that don't actually do anything), and display the "menu." Clicking on any definition closes the menu.

11. To test the application, run it. Type or copy some text into the text box, select a word, and right-click on it. After a brief pause, you should see the definitions for the word (Figure 31-3 shows definitions of "protocol").

While it isn't as sexy as Web services, using this technique (WebRequest, screen scraping of the resulting HTML) can provide access to a great deal of the functionality of the Internet for your applications.

Working with FtpWebRequest

The .NET Framework includes another useful version of WebRequest — the FtpWebRequest. This class, and the related FtpWebResponse, is used to communicate with FTP servers. While the HttpWebRequest/

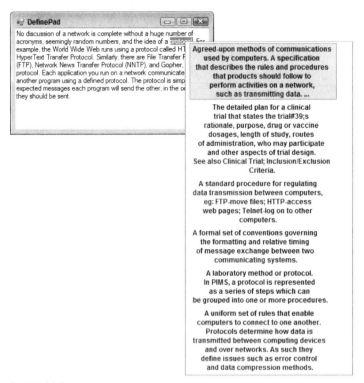

Figure 31-3

`Response` can be used for simple file uploading and retrieving, the `FtpWebRequest` adds the capability to browse or create directories, delete files, and more. The following table describes some of the added functionality of the `FtpWebRequest`:

Member	Description
`Abort`	Used when performing an asynchronous operation. This command terminates the current operation.
`Binary`	A Boolean value that determines whether the data transfer should be treated as binary or text. Set to `true` when you are transferring a binary file, and text otherwise.
`Method`	While not new, the behavior of this method is quite important with the `FtpWebRequest` as it defines the action to perform. See the section below on `WebRequestMethods.Ftp` that defines the possible values.
`Passive`	Boolean value that determines how the client and server should communicate. When set to `true`, the server does not initiate communication back to the client. Instead, it waits until the client initiates the communication. This is typically needed when communicating through a firewall that might not allow the server to open a connection to the client machine.

WebRequestMethods.Ftp

As described above, the actual request made by the `FtpWebRequest` is identified by the `Method` property. This is a string property that can be set to any value recognized by your FTP server, but you will often want to set it to one of the values in the `WebRequestMethods.Ftp` structure.

Field	Description
AppendFile	Adds content to an existing file
DeleteFile	Deletes a file from the server (if you have permission)
DownloadFile	Retrieves a file from the FTP server
GetDateTimeStamp	Gets the date and time the file was last modified
GetFileSize	Gets the size of the file on the FTP server
ListDirectory	Gets the file and directory names for a directory on the FTP server. The data returned is a list of the files, each on a line (that is, separated by CRLF characters). This method doesn't provide an easy way to determine which of the items returned are directories or files.
ListDirectoryDetails	Gets the file and directory information for a directory on the FTP server. This method returns a good deal of information about each item, including attributes, permissions, date of last modification, and size. Like the `ListDirectory` method, each file's (or directory's) information is on a single line.
MakeDirectory	Creates a directory on the server
PrintWorkingDirectory	Gets the current path on the FTP server
RemoveDirectory	Removes a directory from the server (if you have permission)
UploadFile	Uploads a file to the FTP server
UploadFileWithUniqueName	Similar to `UploadFile`, but this method ensures that the new file has a unique filename. This is great when you allow the user to upload files but don't want possible name collisions to occur, or if you don't really care what name the file has (e.g., when the file contents just need processing but not saving).

Creating an FTP Client

In order to demonstrate using the `FtpWebRequest`, this section covers how to create a simple FTP server browser. The application will enable you to connect to a server, browse the available files, and download files (see Figure 31-4).

Even though this application is a Windows Forms application, we separate the FTP handling to a class for use in other applications:

1. Create a new Windows application called "FTP Browser."

2. Before creating the user interface, define the class that will provide the functionality. Add a new class to the project, called `FtpClient.vb`. This class will be used to create wrapper

functionality to make working with `FtpWebRequest` easier. First, add the `Imports` statements for later use:

```
Imports System.IO
Imports System.Net
Imports System.Text
Imports System.Collections.Generic
```

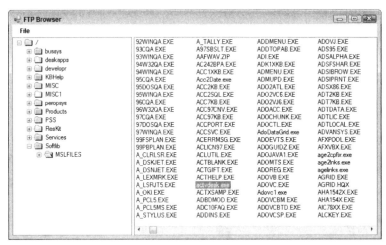

Figure 31-4

3. Add two properties to the class. This is for the user ID and password that will be used by the `FtpClient`:

```
Private _user As String
Private _pwd As String

Public Property UserId() As String
    Get
        Return _user
    End Get
    Set(ByVal value As String)
        _user = value
    End Set
End Property

Public Property Password() As String
    Get
        Return _pwd
    End Get
    Set(ByVal value As String)
        _pwd = value
    End Set
End Property
```

4. The form will use two methods: `GetDirectories` and `GetFiles`. These two methods are basically identical:

```
Public Function GetDirectories(ByVal url As String) As String()
    'line should look like:
    '[DIRECTORY]   developr .  .    [Feb  1  2006]
    Return GetDirectoryEntries(url, "[DIRECTORY]")
End Function

Public Function GetFiles(ByVal url As String) As String()
    'line should look like:
    '[BINARY]      211SP2EI.EXE .  .    [Feb 26  1997]     5M
    Return GetDirectoryEntries(url, "[BINARY]")
End Function
```

5. Obviously, both `GetDirectories` and `GetFiles` simply return the result of another helper routine, `GetDirectoryEntries`. The only difference between the information returned for a file and a directory is that directories have the directory attribute set to "d," whereas files have a blank ("-") in that position:

```
Private Function GetDirectoryEntries(ByVal url As String, _
    ByVal directoryAttribute As String) As String()

    Dim result As New List(Of String)
    Dim str As Stream = Nothing
    Dim temp As String
    Dim words() As String
    Dim splitChars() As Char = {"<"c, ">"c}

    DoFtpRequest(url, _
        WebRequestMethods.Ftp.ListDirectoryDetails, _
        False, str)
    Try
        Using reader As StreamReader = New StreamReader(str)
            Do
                temp = reader.ReadLine

                If Not String.IsNullOrEmpty(temp) Then
                    'split into component parts
                    If temp.StartsWith(directoryAttribute) Then
                        words = temp.Split(splitChars, _
                            StringSplitOptions.RemoveEmptyEntries)
                        If String.Compare(words(2), _
                            "Parent Directory", True) <> 0 Then
                            result.Add(words(2))
                        End If

                    End If
                End If
            Loop While temp <> Nothing
        End Using
    Catch ex As Exception
```

```
                    MessageBox.Show(ex.Message, "Error getting files from " & url)
            End Try

            Return result.ToArray()

    End Function
```

The `GetDirectoryEntries` method uses another helper method you'll create shortly to execute the `WebRequestMethods.Ftp.ListDirectoryDetails` method on the FTP server. This method returns the resulting response stream in the `str` parameter. The code then loops through the returned content. Each of the directory entries appears on a separate line, so `ReadLine` is perfect here. The line is split on spaces, and then added to the return value if it has the desired value for the first character (which represents it if it's a directory or a file).

6. The `GetDirectoryEntries` method calls a helper method that does the actual `FtpWebRequest`. This method returns the resulting stream by way of a `ByRef` parameter:

```
        Private Function DoFtpRequest(ByVal url As String, _
            ByVal method As String, ByVal useBinary As Boolean, _
            ByRef data As Stream) As FtpStatusCode
            Dim result As FtpStatusCode


            Dim req As FtpWebRequest
            Dim resp As FtpWebResponse
            Dim creds As New NetworkCredential(UserId, Password)

            req = DirectCast(WebRequest.Create(url), FtpWebRequest)

            With req
                .Credentials = creds
                .UseBinary = useBinary
                .UsePassive = True
                .KeepAlive = True

                'make initial connection
                .Method = method
                Try
                    resp = .GetResponse()
                Catch ex As Exception
                    MessageBox.Show(ex.Message)
                End Try

                If resp IsNot Nothing Then
                    data = resp.GetResponseStream()
                    result = resp.StatusCode
                End If

            End With

            Return result
        End Function
```

The appropriate type of WebRequest is created, the properties are set, and the final request is sent.

7. With the class created, we can move our attention back to the user interface. Return to the form and add MenuStrip and SplitContainer controls. Leave the names and other properties of these controls at their defaults. Create three items under the File menu: Connect, Download, and Exit. You may also want to add an ImageList control and populate it with appropriate graphics for open and closed folders. The following table lists the properties set on the ImageList in the sample project:

Property	Value
TransparentColor	Transparent
Images – open	Uses the OpenFold.ico graphic from the Visual Studio 2008 Image Library (located in the iconssudhaWin9x directory)
Images – closed	Uses the ClsdFold.ico graphic from the Visual Studio 2008 Image Library (located in the iconssudhaWin9x directory)

8. Add a TreeView control to the left side of the SplitContainer, and a ListView to the right side. Set the properties as shown in the following tables:

TreeView

Property	Value
Name	DirectoryTree
Dock	Fill
PathSeparator	/
ImageList	The name of your ImageList control
SelectedImageKey	The open image's name
ImageKey	The closed image's name

ListView

Property	Value
Name	FileList
Dock	Fill
MultiSelect	False
View	List

9.   Open the Code view for the form. First, add a few private variables to the Form class.

```
Private ftp As New FtpClient
Private baseUrl As String
Private downloadPath As String
```

10.   Add a handler for the Form Load event. This will initialize the TreeView and FtpClient objects:

```
Private Sub MainForm_Load(ByVal sender As Object, _
   ByVal e As System.EventArgs) Handles Me.Load
    'initialize form
    With Me.DirectoryTree
        .Nodes.Add("/")
    End With
    'initialize ftp client
    With ftp
        .UserId = My.Settings.user
        .Password = My.Settings.email
    End With
    downloadPath = My.Settings.downloadPath

End Sub
```

11.   Notice the calls to My.Settings when initializing the FtpClient. The Settings collection is available to the My object when you have created settings values in the My Project dialog. Open the Solution Explorer and double-click on the My Project item. Select the Settings tab and add the three values there (see Figure 31-5).

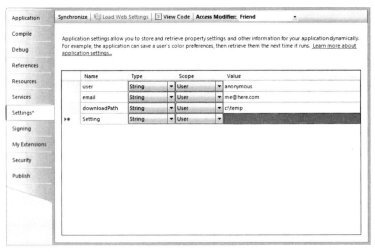

Figure 31-5

12.   You can now return to adding the code to the form. The next step is to enable connecting to the FTP server and retrieving the initial list of directories to add to the TreeView. Add this to the Connect menu item:

```
        Private Sub ConnectToolStripMenuItem_Click(ByVal sender As
    System.Object, _
            ByVal e As System.EventArgs) Handles ConnectToolStripMenuItem.Click
                'makes a new connection to an FTP server

                baseUrl = InputBox("Enter FTP site to open", "FTP Browser", __
                    "ftp://ftp.microsoft.com")
                Me.DirectoryTree.Nodes.Clear()
                'add the base node
                Me.DirectoryTree.Nodes.Add("/")
                AddNodes(Me.DirectoryTree.Nodes(0), baseUrl)

        End Sub
```

13. The event prompts the user for the address of the FTP server to connect with, and then adds it to the `TreeView` via a helper subroutine, `AddNodes`:

```
        Private Sub AddNodes(ByVal parent As TreeNode, ByVal url As String)
                Dim dirs() As String

                Me.Cursor = Cursors.WaitCursor

                dirs = ftp.GetDirectories(url)
                For Each dir As String In dirs
                    With parent.Nodes.Add(dir)
                            .Nodes.Add("NoNodeHere", "empty")
                    End With
                Next

                Me.Cursor = Cursors.Default
        End Sub
```

The `AddNodes` method retrieves the list of directories for the selected URL. In this, the first call for an FTP server, it retrieves the root directory. Later, the same method is used to retrieve subdirectories by requesting a URL containing the full path. Notice the addition of a fake node to each of the directories (the `"NoNodeHere"` item). This ensures that each of the directories added has the plus symbol next to it in the `TreeView`, implying that there is content below it. We will remove the empty node later when we request the actual subdirectories.

14. Initially, each of the directories is empty except for the `"NoNodeHere"` item. You can use the presence of this node to determine whether you need to request subdirectories. If it still exists, then you need to call `AddNodes` when the user attempts to expand the `TreeView` node:

```
        Private Sub DirectoryTree_BeforeExpand(ByVal sender As Object, _
            ByVal e As System.Windows.Forms.TreeViewCancelEventArgs) _
            Handles DirectoryTree.BeforeExpand
            Dim thisNode As TreeNode

            thisNode = e.Node
            If thisNode.Nodes.ContainsKey("NoNodeHere") Then
                'we haven't retrieved this nodes children yet
                'remove the empty node
                thisNode.Nodes("NoNodeHere").Remove()
```

```
                        'get the real children now
                        AddNodes(thisNode, baseUrl + thisNode.FullPath)
                    End If

                End Sub
```

If "NoNodeHere" still exists, then you remove it and call the AddNodes method again, pass-ing this node and its path. This calls the FTP server again, retrieving the child directories of the selected directory. You perform this before the node is expanded, so before the user can see the "NoNodeHere" node. If the subdirectories have already been requested, then the "NoNodeHere" node won't be in the TreeView anymore, and so the code to call the FTP server won't be called again.

15. After the node has been expanded, it is selected. At this time, retrieve the list of files in that directory to display in the ListView control:

```
            Private Sub DirectoryTree_AfterSelect(ByVal sender As System.Object, _
                ByVal e As System.Windows.Forms.TreeViewEventArgs) _
                Handles DirectoryTree.AfterSelect
                Dim thisNode As TreeNode
                Dim files() As String

                thisNode = e.Node

                'we don't want to do this for the root node
                If thisNode.Text <> "/" Then
                    'get files for this directory
                    Me.Cursor = Cursors.WaitCursor
                    'clear the current list
                    Me.FileList.Items.Clear()
                    files = ftp.GetFiles(baseUrl + thisNode.FullPath)
                    For Each fil As String In files
                        Me.FileList.Items.Add(fil)
                    Next

                    Me.Cursor = Cursors.Default
                End If
            End Sub
```

This code is fairly simple. First, the ListView is cleared of existing files. Then the FtpClient is called, retrieving the list of files in the selected directory. These are then added to the ListView.

16. You should now be able to run the application and browse an FTP server (see Figure 31-6). Note that because we haven't added any credentials, only anonymous FTP servers can be browsed. If you want to connect to FTP servers that require authentication, then set the UserId and Password as appropriate, or query them from the user.

17. For a few finishing touches, set the Download menu item to be usable only if a file is selected, and add the code for the Exit menu item. Set the initial value for Enabled to False for the download menu item, and add the following code to the handler for the ListView's SelectedIndexChanged event:

```
            Private Sub FileList_SelectedIndexChanged(ByVal sender As
        System.Object, _
```

```
ByVal e As System.EventArgs) Handles FileList.SelectedIndexChanged
    Me.DownloadToolStripMenuItem.Enabled = _
        CBool(Me.FileList.SelectedItems.Count)
End Sub
```

When an item is selected, the Count will be > 0, which converts to `True`. If 0 items are selected, then this will be `False`.

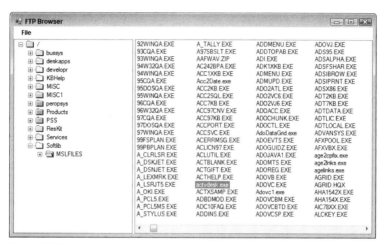

Figure 31-6

18. The code for the Exit menu item is simple enough:

```
Private Sub ExitToolStripMenuItem_Click(ByVal sender As System.Object, _
    ByVal e As System.EventArgs) Handles ExitToolStripMenuItem.Click
        Me.Close()
End Sub
```

19. Finally, add the code for the Download menu item:

```
Private Sub DownloadToolStripMenuItem_Click(ByVal sender As Object, _
    ByVal e As System.EventArgs) Handles DownloadToolStripMenuItem.Click
        'download currently selected file (but only if something is selected)

        ftp.DownloadFile(baseUrl & _
            Me.DirectoryTree.SelectedNode.FullPath & _
            "/" & Me.FileList.SelectedItems(0).Text, _
            downloadPath & Me.FileList.SelectedItems(0).Text)
End Sub
```

20. Obviously, we need to add the `DownloadFile` method to the `FtpClient` class:

```
Public Sub DownloadFile(ByVal url As String, _
    ByVal destination As String)
        Dim str As Stream = Nothing

        DoFtpRequest(url, _
```

```
                    WebRequestMethods.Ftp.DownloadFile, _
                    True, _
                    str)

            Using reader As StreamReader = New StreamReader(str)
                Using writer As StreamWriter = _
                  New StreamWriter(File.OpenWrite(destination))
                    writer.Write(reader.ReadToEnd)
                End Using
            End Using

    End Sub
```

Note the repeat use of the `DoFtpRequest` method. However, this time, we pass `True` for the binary, just in case the file we're transferring is not a text-based file. Using the `Using` block, we create a new `StreamReader` around the output stream of the response, and a new `StreamWriter` to a local output file. By adding the `Using` block, we guarantee that the associated readers, writers, and streams will all be closed when we're done using them. The `Using` block is functionally identical to the following .NET Framework 1.1 code:

```
Dim reader As StreamReader
Try
    reader = New StreamReader(str)
    ...
Finally
    reader.Flush()
    reader.Close()
    reader = Nothing
End Try
```

Now you can test out the new download code. Run the application again, connect to an FTP server, select a file, and then select Download from the File menu. You should see the newly created file appear in your download directory (see Figure 31-7).

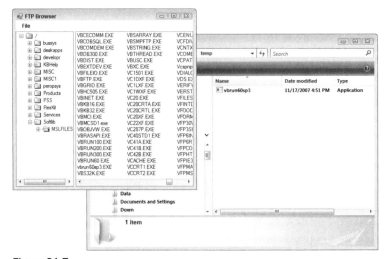

Figure 31-7

While creating a full-blown FTP client would still be a fair bit more work, it is hoped that you can see that the functionality of the `FtpWebRequest` and `FtpWebResponse` classes makes communicating with an FTP server much easier than before, let alone writing the core functionality yourself using sockets.

Simplifying common Web requests with WebClient

When I first saw a demo of `WebRequest` in early 2000, I was delighted. Here was the capability to easily access Internet resources. However, one of the other attendees of the demo asked, "Why is that so difficult? You need to do so much to get it to work." The next time I saw the same `WebRequest` demo, the presenter concluded with, "For those of you doing the common scenarios, we have an even easier way." He then went on to show us how to use `System.Net.WebClient`.

For those times when you just want to send a GET or POST request and download a file or the resulting data, you can forget about `WebRequest`/`WebResponse`. `WebClient` abstracts away all of the little details of making Web requests, and makes it amazingly easy to grab data from the Web. The important methods and properties of the `WebClient` class are described in the following table:

Member	Description
DownloadData	Returns a byte array of data from the server. This is essentially the same as if you had called the Re4ad method on the stream returned from GetResponseStream. You could then save this to a binary file, or convert to text using an appropriate Encoding. However, see DownloadFile and DownloadString below for two easier ways to perform these tasks.
DownloadFile	Retrieves a file from the server and saves it locally
DownloadString	Returns a block of text from the server
OpenRead	Returns a stream providing data from the server. This is essentially the same stream returned from the call to GetResponseStream.
OpenWrite	Returns a stream you can use to write to the server. This is essentially the same as creating a WebRequest and writing to the GetResponse stream.
UploadData	Sends a byte array of data to the server. See UploadFile, UploadString, and UploadValues for easier ways to perform this task.
UploadFile	Sends a local file up to the server for processing
UploadString	POSTs a string to the server. This is very handy when you are simulating HTML form input.
UploadValues	Sends a set of name-value pairs to the server. This is similar to the format used by QueryString values, and this method is quite useful for simulating HTML input.
BaseAddress	The base URL the WebClient will access — e.g., www.example.com.
Credentials	Credentials that will be used when performing any request. You can either create a new NetworkCredential to use this or, alternately, set the UseDefaultCredentials property to true to use the credentials the user has logged in as.

Member	Description
Headers	Collection of headers that will be used for the request
Proxy	Overrides the proxy settings from Internet Explorer if set. You should never need to set this property, as the normal proxy settings are chosen by default.
QueryString	Collection of name-value pairs that will be sent with the request. This represents the values after the ? on a request.
ResponseHeaders	Collection of headers returned by the server after the request is completed

All of the DownloadX and UploadX methods also support an asynchronous version of the method, called DownloadXAsync, such as DownloadFileAsync or UploadValuesAsync. These methods perform the actual request on a background thread, and fire an event when the task is completed. If your application has some form of user interface, such as a form, then you should generally use these methods to keep your application responsive.

As WebClient uses the WebRequest classes to actually perform its magic, it can greatly simplify network coding. For example, just replace the code used in the WebRequest sample created earlier.

Before:

```
Public Function Define(ByVal word As String) As String()
    Dim req As HttpWebRequest = Nothing
    Dim resp As HttpWebResponse
    Dim query As String
    Dim result As New List(Of String)

    query = "http://www.google.com/search?q=define%3A" & _
      HttpUtility.UrlEncode(word)

    Try
        req = DirectCast(WebRequest.Create(query), HttpWebRequest)
        With req
            .Method = "GET"
            resp = req.GetResponse
            If resp.StatusCode = HttpStatusCode.OK Then
                ParseResponse(resp.GetResponseStream, result)
            Else
                MessageBox.Show("Error calling definition service")
            End If
        End With
    Catch ex As Exception

    End Try

    Return result.ToArray()

End Function
```

After:

```
Public Function Define(ByVal word As String) As String()
    Dim client As New WebClient
    Dim query As String
    Dim result As New List(Of String)

    query = "http://www.google.com/search?q=define%3A" & _
      HttpUtility.UrlEncode(word)

    Try
        result = ParseResponse(client.DownloadString(query))
    Catch ex As Exception

    End Try

    Return result.ToArray()

End Function
```

WebClient avoids all of the stream handling required for WebRequest. However, you should still know how WebRequest operates, as this knowledge is directly relatable to WebClient.

Creating your own web server with HttpListener

One exciting feature of the .NET Framework 2.0 was the new HttpListener class (and related classes). This class enables you to very easily create your own web server. While it likely wouldn't be a replacement for IIS, it enables you to add web server functionality to other applications. For example, rather than use remoting or MSMQ to create a communication channel between two applications, why not use HTTP? Each instance could host its own little web server, and then you could use HttpWebRequest or WebClient to communicate between them. Alternately, many applications and hardware devices now provide a built-in Web application, enabling you to configure the device or application via a Web browser.

> *The fine print: The* HttpListener *class relies on the new* Http.sys *functionality built into IIS 6.0, so you must be using an operating system that includes* http.sys *as a systemwide HTTP service. Only Windows Vista, Windows Server 2003, and Windows XP SP2 (and future versions of the operating system) include this functionality. This is yet another reason to upgrade and install Service Packs. Future operating systems should all provide this functionality.*

HttpListener works by registering one or more "prefixes" with http.sys. Once this is done, any requests intercepted by the HTTP subsystem will be passed on to the registered listener. An HttpListenerContext object is created and passed to your listener. This context contains properties for the Request and Response objects, just as the Context object in ASP.NET does. Again, similar to Web applications, you read the request from the Request property, and write the response to the Response property. Closing the Response sends the resulting page to the user's browser. The following table describes the important members of HttpListener:

Member	Description
Abort	Shuts down the server, without finishing any existing requests
Close	Shuts down the server, after finishing handling any existing requests
Start	Starts the listener receiving requests
Stop	Stops the listener from receiving requests
IsListening	Property that determines whether the listener is currently receiving requests
Prefixes	Collection of the types of requests that this listener will respond to. These are the "left-hand side" of the URL, such as http://localhost:8080/ or http://serverName:1234/vrootName/. Note that you must end the prefix in a slash, or you will receive a runtime error. If you have IIS installed on the same server, then you can use port 80, as long as a vroot with the same name is not already defined by IIS.

Creating Your Web Server

To demonstrate using HttpListener, this section describes how to create a Windows Service to host its functionality. This could simulate a management or monitoring interface to a Windows Service that would enable authenticated individuals to use the Windows Service remotely or get other information out of it.

1. Create a new Windows Service application called "MiniServer." The server won't do much on its own, but it will host an HttpListener.

2. From the Components section of the toolbox, add a BackgroundWorker component and call it BackgroundWork. The other properties can remain at their defaults. This BackgroundWorker will be used to process HTTP requests on a background thread, simplifying the handling of the threads.

3. Switch to Code view for the service. Add the Imports statements you need to the top of the file. In addition, add a reference to the System.Web DLL:

```
Imports System.Net
Imports System.IO
Imports System.Web
Imports System.Text
```

4. Add the private members to the class. In addition, add a constant to identify the port number the service will use for listening. Select a port that currently isn't in use. The example uses 9090:

```
Private listener As New HttpListener()
Private theService As String

Private Const PORT As Integer = 9090
```

5. In the OnStart method, set up the list of prefixes to which the server will respond. This can be as simple as adding a port address to the URL, or it can include specific vroots. The sample provides examples of each:

```
Protected Overrides Sub OnStart(ByVal args() As String)
    Dim machineName As String

    machineName = System.Environment.MachineName
    theService = HttpUtility.UrlEncode(Me.ServiceName)

    Me.EventLog.WriteEntry("Service Name: " & Me.ServiceName)

    With listener
        .Prefixes.Add(String.Format("http://{0}:{1}/", _
            "localhost", PORT.ToString))
        .Prefixes.Add(String.Format("http://{0}:{1}/", _
            machineName, PORT.ToString))
        .Prefixes.Add(String.Format("http://{0}/{1}/", _
            "localhost", theService))
        .Prefixes.Add(String.Format("http://{0}/{1}/", _
            machineName, theService))
        .Start()
    End With
    'start up the background thread
    Me.BackgroundWork.RunWorkerAsync()

End Sub
```

In this case, the server will respond to a prefix in any of the formats (the sample computer is called Tantalus):

```
http://localhost:9090/
http://tantalus:9090/
http://localhost/sampleservice/
http://tantalus/sampleservice/
```

Keep one important point in mind as you add prefixes: They must end in a slash ("/") character. Otherwise, you will get a runtime error when the listener attempts to add that prefix.

If you already have a web server listening on port 80, such as IIS, then you shouldn't include the last two prefixes. As only a single application can listen to each port, this service will not be able to start if the other service is already monitoring port 80.

After initializing the Prefixes collection, calling the Start method binds the listener to the appropriate ports and vroots and starts it accepting requests. However, we don't want to actually receive the requests in the OnStart handler. Remember that the service doesn't actually start until after this method has completed, so having a lot of processing in the OnStart will actually prevent the service from completing. Therefore, we use another feature of Visual Basic 2008, the BackgroundWorker component, to handle the requests. Call its RunWorkerAsync to start the background task (in our case, the HttpListener).

6. The OnStop method serves to shut down the HttpListener:

```
Protected Overrides Sub OnStop()
    With listener
        .Stop()
        .Close()
    End With
End Sub
```

7. The background task performed by the BackgroundWorker component can be any process that you don't want to interfere with the normal application's processing. If this were a Windows Forms application, having a long-running loop or other process running might prevent the application from drawing, or responding to, the user's requests. Beyond that, we can do anything we want in the background task, with one exception: because a Windows Forms application works in a single foreground task, one can't directly access the controls on the form from the background task. Instead, if the background task must change properties on the controls, then it should fire events. The controls can then subscribe to those events, where you can access the properties. This Windows Service has no such user interface, so that problem is avoided.

The actual work you want the BackgroundWorker to perform is in the DoWork event handler:

```
Private Sub BackgroundWork_DoWork(ByVal sender As System.Object, _
  ByVal e As System.ComponentModel.DoWorkEventArgs) Handles
BackgroundWork.DoWork
    Dim context As HttpListenerContext
    Dim path As String
    Dim defaultPage As String

    'this is where we actually process requests
    While listener.IsListening
        context = listener.GetContext
        path = context.Request.Url.AbsolutePath.ToLower

        'strip out the serviceName if you're using the URL format:
        'http://server/servicename/path
        If path.StartsWith("/" & theService.ToLower) Then
            path = path.Substring(theService.Length + 1)
        End If
        Me.EventLog.WriteEntry("Received request for " & path)


        Select Case path
            Case "/"
                'this would probably be a resource
                defaultPage = "Available pages<ul>" & _
                    "<li><a href='/time'>Current server time</a></li>" & _
                    "<li><a href='/date'>Current date</a></li>" & _
                    "<li><a href='/random'>Random number</a></li></ul>"
                SendPage(context.Response, defaultPage)
            Case "/time"
                SendPage(context.Response, DateTime.Now.ToLongTimeString)
            Case "/date"
                SendPage(context.Response, DateTime.Now.ToLongDateString)
```

```
                     Case "/random"
                         SendPage(context.Response, New Random().Next.ToString)
                     Case Else
                         'if we don't understand the request, send a 404
                         context.Response.StatusCode = 404
             End Select

      End While
 End Sub
```

The background task performs its work in a loop as long as the `HttpListener` is actively listening. Every developer knows that performing a set of tasks in a (relatively) tight loop is dangerous, possibly leading to computer or application lockup. However, the `BackgroundWorker` performs this on another thread, leaving our application responsive.

For this application, we first get access to the context for the listener. The context groups together one client's set of communication with our listener. Similar to the `HttpContext` in ASP.NET, the `HttpListenerContext` provides access to the `HttpListenerRequest` and `HttpListenerResponse` objects, so the first step in handling a request should always be to get this context. Next, the code uses a very simple means of determining the request URL. In a more full-featured implementation, this could be more complex, separating any query values from the path requested, etc. For this sample, the listener only responds to three main paths, `'/time'`, `'/date'`, and `'/random'`, to receive the current (server) time or date, or a random `Integer` value. If the user requests anything else, then we return a 404.

8. The `SendPage` subroutine simply writes out a basic HTML page and the value determined:

```
Private Sub SendPage(ByVal response As HttpListenerResponse, _
   ByVal message As String)
    Dim sb As New StringBuilder

    'build string
    With sb
        .Append("<html><body>")
        .AppendFormat("<h3>{0}</h3>", message)
        .Append("</body></html>")
    End With

    Me.EventLog.WriteEntry(sb.ToString)

    'set up content headers
    With response
        .ContentType = "text/html"
        .ContentEncoding = Encoding.UTF8
        .ContentLength64 = sb.ToString.Length
        Me.EventLog.WriteEntry(sb.ToString.Length.ToString)

        Try
            Using writer As New StreamWriter(.OutputStream)
                With writer
                    .Write(sb.ToString)
                    .Flush()
                End With
            End Using
```

```
            Catch ex As Exception
                Me.EventLog.WriteEntry(ex.Message, EventLogEntryType.Error)
            Finally
                'close the response to end
                .Close()
            End Try
        End With
    End Sub
```

It is hoped that there aren't any surprises in this code. Using a `StringBuilder`, a response is built. Then the content is written back to the browser (see Figure 31-8) using a `StreamWriter` that is created on top of the `Response.OutputStream`. Remember to close the `Response`, or the request will never close until it times out.

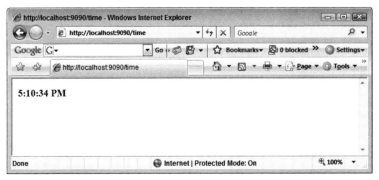

Figure 31-8

9. Before you can test your Windows Service, however, it must be installed. Right-click on the designer and select Add Installer (see Figure 31-9). This adds a new file to the project called `ProjectInstaller.vb`, and adds two components to the file: `ServiceInstaller1` and `ServiceProcessInstaller1`. You can either keep these names or change them. In addition, set the properties as shown in the following table:

Component	Property	Value
ServiceInstaller1	Description	Sample Service from *Wrox Professional Visual Basic 2008*
	DisplayName	Sample Service
	ServiceName	SampleService
ServiceProcessInstaller1	Account	LocalSystem

Most of these properties only affect the display values for the Windows Service. However, the `Account` property of the `ServiceProcessInstaller` deserves special mention. Windows Services run on behalf of the user. Therefore, they can actually run under another user account. By setting the `Account` property to `LocalSystem`, you are setting the resulting Windows Service to run under the local system account. This account has a lot of access to the system, so you may want to instead use an account with more limited system rights; however, you would have to create this account separately.

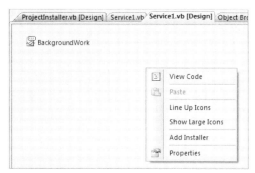

Figure 31-9

10. Build the Windows service. Unfortunately, if you attempt to run the service directly from Visual Basic, you will get an error message (see Figure 31-10).

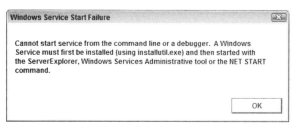

Figure 31-10

A Windows Service can only run if it has been installed into the system, and this task is performed using a command-line utility, `InstallUtil.exe`. Open the Visual Studio command prompt and navigate to the directory where you have built `MiniServer.exe`. Run `installutil miniserver.exe`. It is hoped that you'll be greeted with a success message (see Figure 31-11).

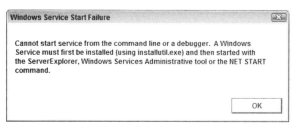

Figure 31-11

If you are running Windows Vista, then you need to run the Visual Studio command prompt as an administrator. To do so, right-click on the Visual Studio 2008 Command Prompt icon and select Run As Administrator.

11. Finally, you can start your new service. Open the Services application from Start ⇨ All Programs ⇨ Administrative Tools. Find the Sample Service in the list (see Figure 31-12) and click Start. You should now be able to request one of the items the service is listening to, such as `http://localhost:9090/time` (see Figure 31-13).

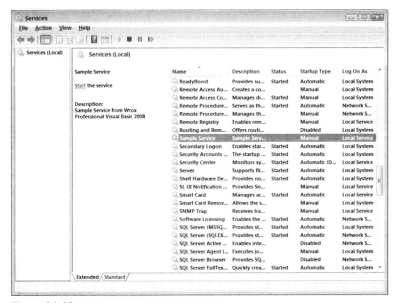

Figure 31-12

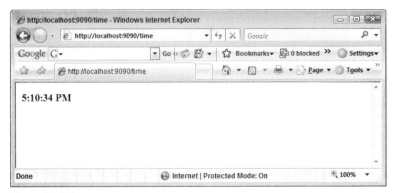

Figure 31-13

Just to confirm that all of the prefixes work, you can also request one of the values using the vroot, rather than using the port (see Figure 31-14).

Figure 31-14

The `HttpListener` adds yet another powerful way for your applications to communicate. It gives you the ability to extend the reach of your applications out to Web browser clients, without requiring the additional administrative and management overhead of IIS to your deployment.

Summary

Programming directly to the network provides a great deal of power and flexibility. Of course, all of that power and flexibility comes at a cost. Many of the services provided by higher-level technologies, such as Web services or remoting, aren't available, and must often be recreated. However, in those situations where you must communicate with an existing application, or when you need the ultimate in control and speed, using the classes in `System.Net` makes life easier than it would be otherwise.

This chapter looked at many of the classes that expose network programming. You've learned how to make Web requests without a browser so you could use the data on the Internet in your applications; you've seen how you can leverage the bare sockets layer to write your own communication protocols, and you've been introduced to some of the classes in Visual Basic 2008 for creating FTP clients and web servers.

32

Windows Communication Foundation

Until now, building components that were required to communicate a message from one point to another was not always the simplest of tasks. This was because Microsoft provided more than one technology that you could have used for such an action.

For instance, you could have used ASP.NET Web Services, Web Service Enhancements 3.0 (WSE), MSMQ, Enterprise Services, .NET Remoting, and even the `System.Messaging` namespace. Each one of these technologies has pros and cons associated with it. ASP.NET Web Services (also known as *ASMX Web Services*) provided the capability to easily build interoperable Web services. The WSE enabled you to easily build services that took advantage of some of the WS-* message protocols. MSMQ enabled the queuing of messages, making it easy to work with solutions that were only intermittently connected. Enterprise Services, provided as a successor to COM+, offered an easy means to build distributed applications. .NET Remoting provided a fast way to move messages from one .NET application to another. Moreover, this is only the Microsoft world — it does not include all the options available in other environments, such as the Java world.

With these options for a Microsoft developer alone, it can be tough to decide what path to take with the applications you are trying to build. With this problem in mind, Microsoft has brought forth the Windows Communication Foundation (WCF).

WCF is a framework for building service-oriented applications. Microsoft wanted to provide its developers with a framework that would provide the fastest means to getting a proper service-oriented architecture up and running. Using the WCF, you can take advantage of all of the items that made the aforementioned distribution technologies powerful. WCF is the answer and the successor to all these other message-distribution technologies.

WCF was introduced as a new component with the .NET Framework 3.0 release. Therefore, to work through the examples in this chapter, you need at least the .NET Framework 3.0 installed on your machine.

The Larger Move to SOA

Looking at what WCF provides, you will find that it is part of a larger move that organizations are making to the much talked-about *service-oriented architecture*, or *SOA*. An SOA is a message-based service architecture that is vendor-agnostic. This means you have the capability to distribute messages across a system, and the messages are interoperable with other systems that would otherwise be considered incompatible with the provider system.

Looking back, you can see the gradual progression to the service-oriented architecture model. In the 1980s, the revolutions arrived amid the paradigm of everything being an object. When object-oriented programming came on the scene, it was enthusiastically accepted as the proper means to represent entities within a programming model. The 1990s took that one step further, and the component-oriented model was born. This enabled objects to be encapsulated in a tightly coupled manner. It was only recently that the industry turned to a service-oriented architecture, once developers and architects needed to distribute components to other points in an organization, to their partners, or to their customers. This distribution system needed to have the means to transfer messages between machines that were generally incompatible with one another. In addition, the messages had to include the capability to express the metadata about how a system should handle a message.

If you ask 10 people what an SOA is, you'll probably get 11 different answers, but there are some common principles that are considered to be the foundation of a service-oriented architecture:

❑ **Boundaries are explicit** — Any data store, logic, or entity uses an interface to expose its data or capabilities. The interface provides the means to hide the behaviors within the service, and the interface front-end enables you to change this behavior as required without affecting downstream consumers.

❑ **Services are autonomous** — All the services are updated or versioned independently of one another. This means that you don't upgrade a system in its entirety; instead, each component of these systems is an individual entity within itself and can move forward without waiting for other components to progress forward. Note that with this type of model, once you publish an interface, that interface must remain unchanged. Interface changes require new interfaces (versioned, of course).

❑ **Services are based upon contracts, schemas, and policies** — All services developed require a contract regarding what is needed to consume items from the interface (usually done through a WSDL document). Along with a contract, schemas are required to define the items passed in as parameters or delivered through the service (using XSD schemas). Finally, policies define any capabilities or requirements of the service.

❑ **Service compatibility that is based upon policy** — The final principle enables services to define policies (decided at runtime) that are required to consume the service. These policies are usually expressed through WS-Policy.

If your own organization is considering establishing an SOA, the WCF is a framework that works on these principles and makes it relatively simple to implement. The next section looks at what the WCF offers. Then you can dive into building your first WCF service.

WCF Overview

As stated, the Windows Communication Foundation is a means to build distributed applications in a Microsoft environment. Though the distributed application is built upon that environment, this does not mean that the consumers are required to be Microsoft clients, nor is any Microsoft component or technology necessary to accomplish the task of consumption. Conversely, building WCF services means you are also building services that abide by the principles set forth in the aforementioned SOA discussion and that these services are vendor-agnostic — that is, they can be consumed by almost anyone.

WCF is part of the .NET Framework 3.0 and is available to your .NET 3.5 applications. The .NET Framework 3.0 also includes the Windows Presentation Foundation and the Windows Workflow Foundation. Because it is part of the .NET Framework, as a developer you are able to use Visual Studio 2008 to build WCF services. Being able to build your services in Visual Studio just as you build any other .NET-based application also means that you can take advantage of the various integrated development systems offered via the IDE, such as debugging, Visual Studio's outstanding IntelliSense capabilities, refactoring, and more.

Note that because this is a .NET Framework 3.0 component, you are actually limited to the operating systems in which you can run a WCF service. While the other Microsoft distribution technologies previously mentioned in this chapter really don't have many limitations on the Microsoft operating systems in which they can run, a .NET Framework 3.0 application can only run on Windows XP SP2, Windows Vista, or Windows Server 2008.

Capabilities of WCF

The WCF framework provides you with the capability to build all kinds of distributed applications. You can build Web services just as you could previously in earlier .NET Framework releases. This means that your services will support SOAP, and therefore will be compatible with older .NET technologies, older Microsoft technologies, and even non-Microsoft technologies (such as any Java-based consumers).

WCF is not about pure SOAP over a wire, but you can work with an Infoset, and create a binary representation of your SOAP message that can then be sent along your choice of protocol. This is for folks who are concerned about the performance of their services and have traditionally turned to .NET Remoting for this binary-based distribution system.

The WCF framework can also work with a message through its life cycle, meaning that WCF can deal with transactions like those of the Enterprise Services mentioned earlier. Along with distributed transactions, WCF can deal with the queuing of messages, and it allows for the intermittent connected nature that an application or process might have to deal with.

When you need to get messages from one point to another, the WCF is the big gun in your arsenal to get the job accomplished. For instance, many developers might consider using WCF primarily to communicate ASP.NET Web Service-like messages (SOAP) from one disparate system to another, but you can use WCF for much more than this. For instance, WCF can be used to communicate messages to components contained on the same machine on which the WCF service is running. This means you can use WCF to communicate with components contained in different processes on the same machine. You can also use WCF to communicate with components on another machine — even if that machine is not a Microsoft-based machine.

Probably the biggest and most exciting part of the WCF model is that it enables you to develop a service once and then expose that service via multiple endpoints (even endpoints on entirely different protocols) via simple configuration changes.

Working with the WS-* protocols

There has not been a larger set of WS-* specifications that any other Microsoft distribution technology can work with but that WCF cannot. WCF understands a framework of WS-* specifications, and these specifications can be enabled to allow for defined ways of dealing with security, reliability, and transactions. For this capability, many previous developers turned to the WSE. Figure 32-1 shows the architectural stack on which the WCF relies.

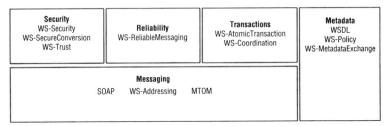

Figure 32-1

WCF can make use of these specifications if the developer wishes. Messages, as defined by the Messaging layer, rely on SOAP (sent as open text or in a binary format). The other advanced WS-* specifications make heavy use of the SOAP header, enabling messages to be self-contained and not have any real reliance on the transport protocol to provide items such as security, reliability, or any other capability beyond the simple transmission of the message itself. *Message Transmission Optimization Mechanism (MTOM)* is a capability to replace *Direct Internet Message Encapsulation (DIME)* as a means to transmit binary objects along with a SOAP message. An example binary object would be a JPEG image that you want to expose through a WCF service.

The Metadata section enables you to define your interface. When you build a service that you want to include in your application, you need to determine which parameters the service requires in order for the consumption process to work. In addition, after you pass the parameters to the service, you need to know what is returned so you can properly use the passed information within your own application. Without this information, using the service would prove rather difficult. Just as there are standard ways to represent the message itself with technologies such as SOAP, there is an industry standard for getting a description of a service that you are attempting to consume.

The WCF framework makes use of the *Web Services Description Language (WSDL)* to describe the service. WSDL is a language that uses XML to describe a service and define the format of the messages a service understands. The other item the WCF provides from the Metadata layer is WS-Policy. This specification provides consumers with an understanding of what is actually required to consume a service.

The Security part of WCF enables you to work with WS-Security. Before WS-Security came along, the initial lack of a security model in Web services kept many companies from massively adopting them companywide and moving to a service-oriented architecture. WS-Security, developed by Microsoft, IBM, and VeriSign, addresses the main areas that are required to keep messages secure — credential exchange, message integrity, and message confidentiality.

WS-Security enables two entities to exchange their security credentials from within the message itself (actually from the SOAP header of the message). The great thing about WS-Security is that it doesn't require a specific type of credential set to be used. Instead, it allows any type of credentials to be used. In addition, because it is possible to send messages through multiple routers and, in effect, bounce messages from here to there before they reach their final destination, you want to ensure that the messages are not tampered with in transport. As messages move from one SOAP router to another, these SOAP nodes can make additions to or subtractions from the messages. If such SOAP nodes were to get into the hands of malicious parties, the integrity of the messages could be compromised. This is where WS-Security comes into play. The other area in which WS-Security helps is when you need to have WS-Security encrypt all or part of your SOAP messages. When your messages are zipping across the virtual world, there is a chance that they might be intercepted and opened for viewing by parties who should not be looking at their contents. That's why it is often beneficial to scramble the contents of the message. When it reaches the intended receiver, the application can then use your encryption key and unscramble the message to read the contents.

WS-SecureConversation works to establish a connection that enables entities to exchange multiple messages and maintain their established security arrangements. WS-Trust, conversely, works in conjunction with WS-Security and allows for the issuance of security tokens and a way in which entities can exchange these tokens. This specification also deals with establishing trust relationships between two entities.

WS-ReliableMessaging allows for reliable end-to-end communications of messages to ensure that they are delivered.

The Transactions section allows for the use of WS-Coordination and WS-AtomicTransaction. WS-Coordination is there for the purpose of addressing the description of the relationships that multiple services have to one another. As a company starts developing a multitude of services within its enterprise, it realizes that many of the services developed have a relationship with one another, and that's where WS-Coordination comes into play. This specification is meant to be expanded by other specifications that will further define particular coordination types.

WS-AtomicTransaction uses WS-Coordination and WS-Security to allow for the definition of a service transaction process. An atomic transaction is a way of creating a transaction process that works on an all-or-nothing basis. These are meant to be short-lived transactions, so when you use them you are locking data resources and holding onto physical resources such as connections, threads, and memory.

The main point of this discussion is that you have a whole slew of WS-* specifications at your disposal. The nice thing about working with WCF is that you really don't have to be aware that these specifications are even there — you can access the capabilities these specifications offer through programmatic or declarative programming.

Building a WCF Service

Building a WCF service is not hard to accomplish. If you are working from a .NET Framework 2.0 environment, you need to install the .NET Framework 3.0. If you have installed the .NET Framework 3.5, then both the .NET Framework 2.0 and 3.0 also have been installed.

From there, it is easy to build WCF services directly in Visual Studio 2008, as it is already geared to work with this application type. If you are working with Visual Studio 2005, then you need to install the Visual Studio 2005 extensions for .NET Framework 3.0 (WCF and WPF). Download these Visual Studio extensions if you are using Visual Studio 2005. Installing the extensions into Visual Studio 2005 will add a WCF project to your IDE. If you are using Visual Studio 2008, then Figure 32-2 shows the view of the project from the New Project dialog.

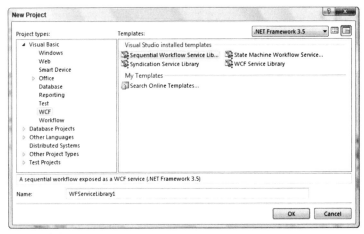

Figure 32-2

When you build a WCF project in this manner, the idea is that you build a traditional class library that is compiled down to a DLL that can then be added to another project. The separation of code and projects is a powerful division on larger projects. That said, though, you can also just as easily build a WCF service directly in your .NET project, whether that is a console application or a Windows Forms application. The approach taken for the examples in this chapter shows you how to build a WCF service that is hosted in a console application. Keep in mind that for the services you actually build and deploy, it is usually better to build them directly as a WCF Service Library project and use the created DLL in your projects or in IIS itself.

Before we jump into building a WCF service, first consider what makes up a service built upon the WCF framework.

What makes a WCF service

A WCF service consists of three parts: the service, one or more endpoints, and an environment in which to host the service.

A service is a class that is written in one of the .NET-compliant languages. The class can contain one or more methods that are exposed through the WCF service. A service can have one or more endpoints, which are used to communicate through the service to the client.

Endpoints themselves are also made up of three parts. These parts are usually defined by Microsoft as the ABC of WCF. Each letter of WCF means something in particular in the WCF model. Similarly,

- ❑ "A" is for address
- ❑ "B" is for binding
- ❑ "C" is for contract

Basically, you can think of this as follows: "A" is the *where*, "B" is the *how*, and "C" is the *what*. Finally, a hosting environment is where the service is contained. This constitutes an application domain and process. All three of these elements (the service, the endpoints, and the hosting environment) together create a WCF service offering, as depicted in Figure 32-3.

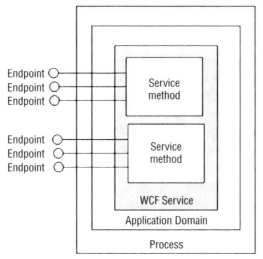

Figure 32-3

The next step is to create a basic service using the WCF framework.

Creating your first WCF service

To build your service, prior to hosting it, two main steps need to occur. First, create a service contract. Then, create a data contract. The service contract is really a class with the methods that you want to expose from the WCF service. The data contract is a class that specifies the structure you want to expose from the interface.

After you have a service class in place, you can host it almost anywhere you want. This example shows you how to host the WCF service inside a console application. Therefore, first create a new console application project called VbWCF_Service1.

To create a WCF service, you need to make a reference to System.ServiceModel.dll. Right-click on the console application project in the Solution Explorer and select Add Reference from the menu. In the .NET tab of the Add Reference dialog, shown in Figure 32-4, is the .NET Framework 3.0 version of the System.ServiceModel.dll (though it has a runtime version v2.0.50727).

Note that we are only going to host the WCF service from the console application. The WCF service is something that you would normally build as its own entity, such as the WCF Class Library project, and then include the created DLL into your host, such as the console application.

This example first demonstrates how to build the WCF service. The next step is the requirements that need to be put into place for the service to be hosted in the console application.

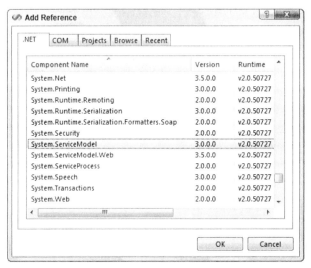

Figure 32-4

Creating the Interface

To create your service, you need a service contract, which is the interface of the service. This consists of all the methods exposed, as well as the input and output parameters that are required to invoke the methods. To accomplish this task, create a class file in your project called `Calculator.vb`. The interface you need to create is presented here:

```vb
Imports System.ServiceModel

<ServiceContract()> _
Public Interface ICalculator
    <OperationContract()> _
    Function Add(ByVal a As Integer, ByVal b As Integer) As Integer

    <OperationContract()> _
    Function Subtract(ByVal a As Integer, ByVal b As Integer) As Integer

    <OperationContract()> _
    Function Multiply(ByVal a As Integer, ByVal b As Integer) As Integer

    <OperationContract()> _
    Function Divide(ByVal a As Integer, ByVal b As Integer) As Integer
End Interface

Public Class Calculator

End Class
```

This is pretty much the normal interface definition you would expect, but with a couple of new attributes included. To gain access to these required attributes, you need to make a reference to the `System .ServiceModel` namespace. This will give you access to the `<ServiceContract()>` and `<OperationContract()>` attributes.

The `<ServiceContract()>` attribute is used to define the class or interface as the service class, and it needs to precede the opening declaration of the class or interface. In this case, the example in the preceding code is based upon an interface:

```
<ServiceContract()> _
Public Interface ICalculator

    ' Code removed for clarity

End Interface
```

Within the interface, four methods are defined. Each of these methods is going to be exposed through the WCF service as part of the service contract, so they all require that the `<OperationContract()>` attribute be applied to them:

```
<OperationContract()> _
Function Add(ByVal a As Integer, ByVal b As Integer) As Integer
```

Utilizing the Interface

The next step is to create a class that implements the interface. Not only is the new class implementing the interface defined, it is also implementing the service contract. You can add this class to the same Calculator.vb file. The following code illustrates the implementation of this interface:

```
Imports System
Imports System.ServiceModel

<ServiceContract()> _
Public Interface ICalculator
    <OperationContract()> _
    Function Add(ByVal a As Integer, ByVal b As Integer) As Integer

    <OperationContract()> _
    Function Subtract(ByVal a As Integer, ByVal b As Integer) As Integer

    <OperationContract()> _
    Function Multiply(ByVal a As Integer, ByVal b As Integer) As Integer

    <OperationContract()> _
    Function Divide(ByVal a As Integer, ByVal b As Integer) As Integer
End Interface

Public Class Calculator
    Implements ICalculator

    Public Function Add(ByVal a As Integer, ByVal b As Integer) As Integer _
        Implements ICalculator.Add

        Return (a + b)
    End Function

    Public Function Subtract(ByVal a As Integer, ByVal b As Integer) As Integer _
        Implements ICalculator.Subtract
```

```
        Return (a - b)
    End Function

    Public Function Multiply(ByVal a As Integer, ByVal b As Integer) As Integer _
        Implements ICalculator.Multiply

        Return (a * b)
    End Function

    Public Function Divide(ByVal a As Integer, ByVal b As Integer) As Integer _
        Implements ICalculator.Divide

        Return (a / b)
    End Function
End Class
```

From these new additions, you can see that nothing is done differently with the Calculator class than what you might do otherwise. It is a simple class that implements the ICalculator interface and provides implementations of the Add, Subtract, Multiply, and Divide methods.

With the interface and the class available, you now have your WCF service built and ready to go. The next step is to get the service hosted. This is a simple service. One of the simplicities of the service is that it only exposes simple types, rather than a complex type. This enables you to build only a service contract and not have to deal with construction of a data contract. Constructing data contracts is presented later in this chapter.

Hosting the WCF Service in a Console Application

The next step is to take the service just developed and host it in some type of application process. You have many available hosting options, including the following:

- ❏ Console applications
- ❏ Windows Forms applications
- ❏ Windows Presentation Foundation applications
- ❏ Managed Windows Services
- ❏ Internet Information Services (IIS) 5.1
- ❏ Internet Information Services (IIS) 6.0
- ❏ Internet Information Services (IIS) 7.0 and the Windows Activation Service (WAS)

As stated earlier, this example hosts the service in a simple console application. There are a couple of ways to activate hosting — either through the direct coding of the hosting behaviors or through declarative programming (usually done via the configuration file).

For this example, the console application will define the host through coding the behaviors of the host environment directly. Following is the code for the console application, through the Module1.vb file (this block is referred to later in the chapter as the console-application code example):

```
Imports System
Imports System.ServiceModel
Imports System.ServiceModel.Description

Module Module1

    Sub Main()
        Using serviceHost As ServiceHost = New ServiceHost(GetType(Calculator))
            Dim ntb As NetTcpBinding = New NetTcpBinding(SecurityMode.None)
            serviceHost.AddServiceEndpoint(GetType(ICalculator), ntb, _
                New Uri("net.tcp://192.168.1.102:8080/Calculator/"))

            Dim smb As New ServiceMetadataBehavior()
            smb.HttpGetEnabled = True
            smb.HttpGetUrl = New Uri("http://localhost:8000/docs")

            serviceHost.Description.Behaviors.Add(smb)

            serviceHost.Open()

            Console.WriteLine("Press the <ENTER> key to close the host.")
            Console.ReadLine()
        End Using
    End Sub

End Module
```

A couple of things are going on in this file. First, to gain access to working with any of the WCF framework pieces, you need a reference to the System.ServiceModel and the System.ServiceModel .Description namespaces in the file. The System.ServiceModel gives you access to defining things such as the endpoints that you need to create, while the System.ServiceModel.Description namespace reference gives you access to defining things such as the WSDL file.

Remember that creating endpoints uses the ABC model (address, binding, and contract). The address part here is net.tcp://192.168.1.102:8080/Calculator. The binding is a TCP binding — NetTcpBinding — while the contract part is the ICalculator interface.

*The 192.168.1.102 IP address is specific to my machine; you should use your own IP address for the example. You can get your IP address by typing **ipconfig** at a command prompt.*

Many different bindings are available to you when coding WCF services. Here, this example makes use of the NetTcpBinding. The full list of available bindings is as follows:

❑   System.ServiceModel.BasicHttpBinding

❑   System.ServiceModel.Channels.CustomBinding

❑   System.ServiceModel.MsmqBindingBase

❑   System.ServiceModel.NetNamedPipeBinding

❑   System.ServiceModel.NetPeerTcpBinding

❑ System.ServiceModel.NetTcpBinding

❑ System.ServiceModel.WSDualHttpBinding

❑ System.ServiceModel.WSHttpBindingBase

Clearly, several bindings are available. In the preceding example, the NetTcpBinding class is the named pipe being used. This means that the service being built will be delivered over TCP.

In the first step of the example, for console-application code, a ServiceHost is established:

```
Using serviceHost As ServiceHost = New ServiceHost(GetType(Calculator))

    ' Code removed for clarity

End Using
```

By working with the Using keyword, when the End Using statement is encountered, the ServiceHost object is destroyed. In the creation of the host, the Calculator type is assigned. From there, the endpoint is established. In this case, a NetTcpBinding object is created with a security setting of None through the command SecurityMode.None:

```
Dim ntb As NetTcpBinding = New NetTcpBinding(SecurityMode.None)
```

This means that no security is applied to the message. The other options include Message, Transport, and TransportWithMessageCredential. The Message option signifies that the security credentials are included in the message itself (in the SOAP header, for instance), whereas the Transport option signifies that the transport protocol takes care of the security implementation. The last option, TransportWithMessageCredential, means that the message contains some security credentials along with the transport protocol working for the same cause.

Once the NetTcpBinding object is in place, the next step is to finalize the endpoint creation. This is done through the use of the ServiceHost object's AddServiceEndpoint method:

```
serviceHost.AddServiceEndpoint(GetType(ICalculator), ntb, _
              New Uri("net.tcp://192.168.1.102:8080/Calculator/"))
```

From this, you can see that the entire ABC statement is used in the creation of the endpoint, although not necessarily in ABC order; in fact, the first item defined is actually the "C" — the contract. This is done through the GetType(ICalculator) setting. The "B" is next (the binding) with the reference to the NetTcpBinding object. Then, finally, the "A" is defined through an instantiation of a Uri object pointing to net.tcp://192.168.1.102:8080/Calculator/.

The next step is a process to bring forth the WSDL document so that it can be viewed by the developer consuming this service:

```
Dim smb As New ServiceMetadataBehavior()
smb.HttpGetEnabled = True
smb.HttpGetUrl = New Uri("http://localhost:8000/docs")

serviceHost.Description.Behaviors.Add(smb)
```

This bit of code is the reason why the System.ServiceModel.Description namespace is imported into the file at the beginning. Here, a ServiceMetadataBehavior object is created, the object's HttpGetEnabled property is set to True, and the HttpGetUrl property is provided an address of http://localhost:8000/docs. The documents can be located anywhere you like.

Once the ServiceMetadataBehavior object is created as you wish, the next step is to associate this object to the ServiceHost through the serviceHost.Description.Behaviors.Add method.

After all of these items are defined, you only need to open the ServiceHost for business, using the serviceHost.Open method. The console application is kept alive through the use of a Console.ReadLine method call, which waits for the end user to press the Enter key before shutting down the application. You want the Console.ReadLine command there because you want to keep the host open.

Compiling and running this application produces the results illustrated in Figure 32-5.

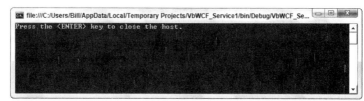

Figure 32-5

Reviewing the WSDL Document

The preceding console-application code provides an instantiation of the ServiceMetadataBehavior object and defines a Uri object for it as well. You can simply type in that address to get at the WSDL file for the service you just built. Therefore, calling http://localhost:8000/docs provides the WSDL file shown in Figure 32-6.

Figure 32-6

With this WSDL file, you can now consume the service it defines through TCP. Note the following element at the bottom of the document:

```
<wsdl:service name="Calculator">
    <wsdl:port name="NetTcpBinding_ICalculator"
     binding="tns:NetTcpBinding_ICalculator">
        <soap12:address location="net.tcp://192.168.1.102:8080/Calculator/" />
        <wsa10:EndpointReference>
            <wsa10:Address>net.tcp://192.168.1.102:8080/Calculator/</wsa10:Address>
        </wsa10:EndpointReference>
    </wsdl:port>
</wsdl:service>
```

This element in the XML document indicates that in order to consume the service, the end user needs to use SOAP 1.2 over TCP. This is presented through the use of the `<soap12:address>` element in the document. The `<wsa10:EndpointReference>` is a WS-Addressing endpoint definition.

Using this simple WSDL document, you can now build a consumer that makes use of this interface.

Building the WCF Consumer

Now that a TCP service is out there, which you built using the WCF framework, the next step is to build a consumer application that uses the simple `Calculator` service. The consumer sends its request via TCP using SOAP. Using TCP means that the consumption can actually occur with a binary encoding of the SOAP message on the wire, substantially decreasing the size of the payload being transmitted.

This section describes how to consume this service. First, open Visual Studio 2008 and create a new Windows Forms application. Though we are using a Windows Forms application, you can make this consumer call through any other application type within .NET as well.

Call the new Windows Forms application WCF_Consumer. This application will consume the `Calculator` service, so it should be laid out as shown in Figure 32-7.

Adding a service reference

After you have laid out the form, make a reference to the new WCF service. You do this in a manner quite similar to how it is done with XML Web Service references. Right-click on the solution name from the Solution Explorer in Visual Studio and select Add Service Reference from the dialog. This capability to add a service reference is new to Visual Studio — previously, you only had the Add Reference and Add Web Reference options.

After selecting Add Service Reference, you are presented with the dialog shown in Figure 32-8.

The Add Service Reference dialog asks you for two things: the Service URI (basically a pointer to the WSDL file) and the name you want to give to the reference. The name you provide the reference is the name that will be used for the instantiated object that enables you to interact with the service.

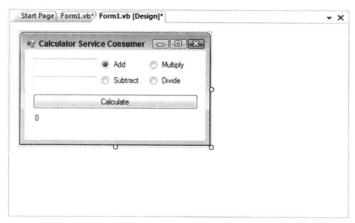

Figure 32-7

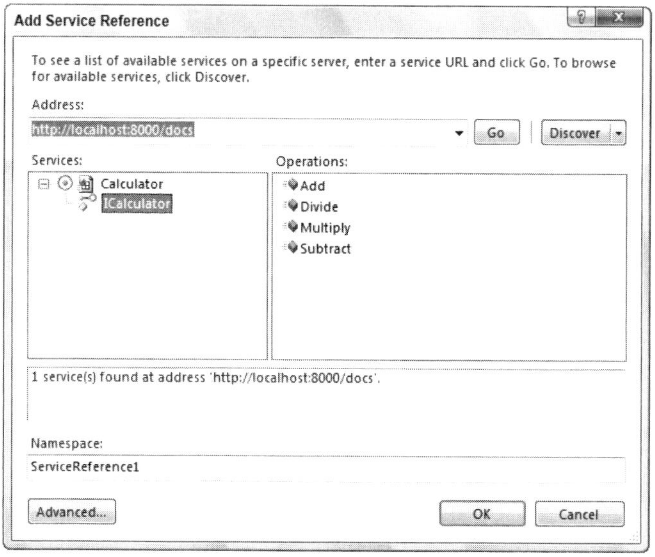

Figure 32-8

Referring to Figure 32-8, you can see that the name provided for the Address text box is http://localhost:8000/docs. Remember that this is the location you defined earlier when you built the service. This URI was defined in code directly in the service:

```
Dim smb As New ServiceMetadataBehavior()
smb.HttpGetEnabled = True
smb.HttpGetUrl = New Uri("http://localhost:8000/docs")

serviceHost.Description.Behaviors.Add(smb)
```

Rename the service reference to `CalculatorService` from `ServiceReference1`. Press the OK button in the Add Service Reference dialog. This adds to your project a Service References folder containing some proxy files, as shown in Figure 32-9.

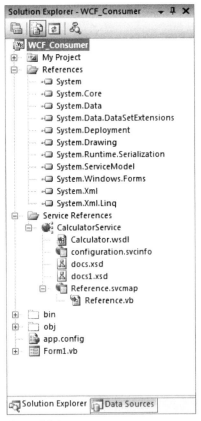

Figure 32-9

Digging down into these files, you will find `Reference.svcmap` and `Reference.vb`. The other important addition to note is the `System.ServiceModel` reference, made for you in the References folder. This reference was not there before you made reference to the service through the Add Service Reference dialog.

Reviewing the reference

Looking at the `Reference.svcmap` file, you can see that it is a simple XML file that provides some information about where the WSDL file is located, as well as the location of the service (referenced through the `configuration.svcinfo` file):

```
<?xml version="1.0" encoding="utf-8"?>
<ReferenceGroup xmlns:xsi="http://www.w3.org/2001/XMLSchema-instance"
 xmlns:xsd="http://www.w3.org/2001/XMLSchema"
```

```
  ID="95adc6e4-181d-4b1e-8b65-765821ccec25"
  xmlns="urn:schemas-microsoft-com:xml-wcfservicemap">
   <ClientOptions>
     <GenerateAsynchronousMethods>false</GenerateAsynchronousMethods>
     <EnableDataBinding>true</EnableDataBinding>
     <ExcludedTypes />
     <ImportXmlTypes>false</ImportXmlTypes>
     <GenerateInternalTypes>false</GenerateInternalTypes>
     <GenerateMessageContracts>false</GenerateMessageContracts>
     <NamespaceMappings />
     <CollectionMappings />
     <GenerateSerializableTypes>true</GenerateSerializableTypes>
     <Serializer>Auto</Serializer>
     <ReferenceAllAssemblies>true</ReferenceAllAssemblies>
     <ReferencedAssemblies />
     <ReferencedDataContractTypes />
     <ServiceContractMappings />
   </ClientOptions>
   <MetadataSources>
     <MetadataSource Address="http://localhost:8000/docs"
      Protocol="http" SourceId="1" />
   </MetadataSources>
   <Metadata>
     <MetadataFile FileName="docs.xsd" MetadataType="Schema"
      ID="8a563b41-2340-4c5e-832d-c775e182e9bf" SourceId="1"
      SourceUrl="http://localhost:8000/docs?xsd=xsd0" />
     <MetadataFile FileName="Calculator.wsdl" MetadataType="Wsdl"
      ID="f81b212f-9c59-45d6-bbca-1bee58a6700f" SourceId="1"
      SourceUrl="http://localhost:8000/docs" />
     <MetadataFile FileName="docs1.xsd" MetadataType="Schema"
      ID="76d57f76-4409-48d7-9122-6c2eb500b69a" SourceId="1"
      SourceUrl="http://localhost:8000/docs?xsd=xsd1" />
   </Metadata>
   <Extensions>
     <ExtensionFile FileName="configuration.svcinfo"
      Name="configuration.svcinfo" />
   </Extensions>
 </ReferenceGroup>
```

This file provides the capability to later update the reference to the service if needed, due to a change in the service interface. You can see this capability by right-clicking on the CalculatorService reference; an Update Service Reference option appears in the provided menu.

The other file in the reference collection of files, the Reference.vb file, is your proxy to interact with the service. This file is presented here:

```
Option Strict Off
Option Explicit On

Namespace CalculatorService

    <System.CodeDom.Compiler.GeneratedCodeAttribute("System.ServiceModel", _
        "3.0.0.0"), _
     System.ServiceModel.ServiceContractAttribute( _
```

```vbnet
          ConfigurationName:="CalculatorService.ICalculator")>  _
    Public Interface ICalculator
      <System.ServiceModel.OperationContractAttribute( _
      Action:="http://tempuri.org/ICalculator/Add", _
      ReplyAction:="http://tempuri.org/ICalculator/AddResponse")>  _
      Function Add(ByVal a As Integer, ByVal b As Integer) As Integer

      <System.ServiceModel.OperationContractAttribute( _
      Action:="http://tempuri.org/ICalculator/Subtract", _
      ReplyAction:="http://tempuri.org/ICalculator/SubtractResponse")>  _
      Function Subtract(ByVal a As Integer, ByVal b As Integer) As Integer

      <System.ServiceModel.OperationContractAttribute( _
      Action:="http://tempuri.org/ICalculator/Multiply", _
      ReplyAction:="http://tempuri.org/ICalculator/MultiplyResponse")>  _
      Function Multiply(ByVal a As Integer, ByVal b As Integer) As Integer

      <System.ServiceModel.OperationContractAttribute( _
      Action:="http://tempuri.org/ICalculator/Divide",  _
      ReplyAction:="http://tempuri.org/ICalculator/DivideResponse")>  _
      Function Divide(ByVal a As Integer, ByVal b As Integer) As Integer
    End Interface

    <System.CodeDom.Compiler.GeneratedCodeAttribute( _
      "System.ServiceModel", "3.0.0.0")>  _
    Public Interface ICalculatorChannel
        Inherits CalculatorService.ICalculator, _
            System.ServiceModel.IClientChannel
    End Interface

    <System.Diagnostics.DebuggerStepThroughAttribute(),  _
     System.CodeDom.Compiler.GeneratedCodeAttribute("System.ServiceModel", _
      "3.0.0.0")>  _
    Partial Public Class CalculatorClient
        Inherits System.ServiceModel.ClientBase(Of _
            CalculatorService.ICalculator)
        Implements CalculatorService.ICalculator

        Public Sub New()
            MyBase.New
        End Sub

        Public Sub New(ByVal endpointConfigurationName As String)
            MyBase.New(endpointConfigurationName)
        End Sub

        Public Sub New(ByVal endpointConfigurationName As String, _
           ByVal remoteAddress As String)
            MyBase.New(endpointConfigurationName, remoteAddress)
        End Sub

        Public Sub New(ByVal endpointConfigurationName As String, _
           ByVal remoteAddress As System.ServiceModel.EndpointAddress)
            MyBase.New(endpointConfigurationName, remoteAddress)
        End Sub
```

```
        Public Sub New(ByVal binding As System.ServiceModel.Channels.Binding, _
            ByVal remoteAddress As System.ServiceModel.EndpointAddress)
            MyBase.New(binding, remoteAddress)
        End Sub

        Public Function Add(ByVal a As Integer, ByVal b As Integer) As Integer _
            Implements CalculatorService.ICalculator.Add
            Return MyBase.Channel.Add(a, b)
        End Function

        Public Function Subtract(ByVal a As Integer, ByVal b As Integer) _
            As Integer Implements CalculatorService.ICalculator.Subtract
            Return MyBase.Channel.Subtract(a, b)
        End Function

        Public Function Multiply(ByVal a As Integer, ByVal b As Integer) _
            As Integer Implements CalculatorService.ICalculator.Multiply
            Return MyBase.Channel.Multiply(a, b)
        End Function

        Public Function Divide(ByVal a As Integer, ByVal b As Integer) _
            As Integer Implements CalculatorService.ICalculator.Divide
            Return MyBase.Channel.Divide(a, b)
        End Function
    End Class
End Namespace
```

Here, an interface is defining the four methods and the implementing class `CalculatorClient`, which contains the functions that in turn call the service built earlier in the chapter.

Configuration file changes

Another addition to your project is the `app.config` file. After the service reference is made, the `app.config` file contains several .NET 3.0 configuration settings. These configuration settings were automatically added by the Visual Studio WCF extensions. The new `app.config` file is presented in the following code block:

```
<?xml version="1.0" encoding="utf-8" ?>
<configuration>
    <system.diagnostics>

        <!-- XML removed for clarity -->

    </system.diagnostics>
    <system.serviceModel>
        <bindings>
            <netTcpBinding>
                <binding name="NetTcpBinding_ICalculator"
                    closeTimeout="00:01:00"
                    openTimeout="00:01:00" receiveTimeout="00:10:00"
                    sendTimeout="00:01:00"
                    transactionFlow="false" transferMode="Buffered"
                    transactionProtocol="OleTransactions"
```

```
                          hostNameComparisonMode="StrongWildcard" listenBacklog="10"
                          maxBufferPoolSize="524288" maxBufferSize="65536"
                          maxConnections="10"
                          maxReceivedMessageSize="65536">
                          <readerQuotas maxDepth="32" maxStringContentLength="8192"
                              maxArrayLength="16384"
                              maxBytesPerRead="4096"
                              maxNameTableCharCount="16384" />
                          <reliableSession ordered="true"
                              inactivityTimeout="00:10:00"
                              enabled="false" />
                          <security mode="None">
                              <transport clientCredentialType="Windows"
                               protectionLevel="EncryptAndSign" />
                              <message clientCredentialType="Windows" />
                          </security>
                      </binding>
                  </netTcpBinding>
              </bindings>
              <client>
                  <endpoint address="net.tcp://192.168.1.102:8080/Calculator/"
                      binding="netTcpBinding"
                      bindingConfiguration="NetTcpBinding_ICalculator"
                      contract="CalculatorService.ICalculator"
                      name="NetTcpBinding_ICalculator" />
              </client>
          </system.serviceModel>
      </configuration>
```

The important part of this configuration document is the `<client>` element. This element contains a child element called `<endpoint>` that defines the *where* and *how* of the service consumption process.

The `<endpoint>` element provides the address of the service — `net.tcp://192.168.1.102:8080 /Calculator` — and it specifies which binding of the available WCF bindings should be used. In this case, the `netTcpBinding` is the required binding. Although you are using an established binding from the WCF framework, from the client side you can customize how this binding behaves. The settings that define the behavior of the binding are specified using the `bindingConfiguration` attribute of the `<endpoint>` element. In this case, the value provided to the `bindingConfiguration` attribute is `NetTcpBinding_ICalculator`, which is a reference to the `<binding>` element contained within the `<netTcpBinding>` element:

```
<binding name="NetTcpBinding_ICalculator" closeTimeout="00:01:00"
 openTimeout="00:01:00" receiveTimeout="00:10:00"
 sendTimeout="00:01:00"
 transactionFlow="false" transferMode="Buffered"
 transactionProtocol="OleTransactions"
 hostNameComparisonMode="StrongWildcard" listenBacklog="10"
 maxBufferPoolSize="524288" maxBufferSize="65536"
 maxConnections="10"
 maxReceivedMessageSize="65536">
   <readerQuotas maxDepth="32" maxStringContentLength="8192"
```

```
        maxArrayLength="16384"
        maxBytesPerRead="4096" maxNameTableCharCount="16384" />
      <reliableSession ordered="true" inactivityTimeout="00:10:00"
      enabled="false" />
      <security mode="None">
        <transport clientCredentialType="Windows"
        protectionLevel="EncryptAndSign" />
        <message clientCredentialType="Windows" />
      </security>
    </binding>
```

As demonstrated, the Visual Studio 2008 capabilities for WCF make the consumption of these services fairly trivial. The next step is to code the consumption of the service interface to the GUI that was created as one of the first steps.

Writing the consumption code

The code to consume the interface is quite minimal. End users will merely select the radio button of the operation that they are interested in performing. The default radio button selected is Add. The user places a number in each of the two text boxes provided and clicks the Calculate button to call the service to perform the designated operation on the provided numbers. Here is the code for the form:

```
Public Class Form1

    Private Sub Button1_Click(ByVal sender As System.Object, _
       ByVal e As System.EventArgs) Handles Button1.Click

        Dim result As Integer
        Dim svc As New CalculatorService.CalculatorClient()

        svc.Open()

        If RadioButton1.Checked = True Then
            result = svc.Add(Integer.Parse(TextBox1.Text), _
                Integer.Parse(TextBox2.Text))
        ElseIf RadioButton2.Checked = True Then
            result = svc.Subtract(Integer.Parse(TextBox1.Text), _
                Integer.Parse(TextBox2.Text))
        ElseIf RadioButton3.Checked = True Then
            result = svc.Multiply(Integer.Parse(TextBox1.Text), _
                Integer.Parse(TextBox2.Text))
        ElseIf RadioButton4.Checked = True Then
            result = svc.Divide(Integer.Parse(TextBox1.Text), _
                Integer.Parse(TextBox2.Text))
        End If

        svc.Close()

        Label1.Text = result.ToString()
    End Sub
End Class
```

This is quite similar to what is done when working with Web references from the XML Web Services world. First is an instantiation of the proxy class, as shown with the creation of the svc object:

```
Dim svc As New CalculatorService.CalculatorClient()
```

Working with the ws object now, the IntelliSense options provide you with the appropriate Add, Subtract, Multiply, and Divide methods. Running this application provides results similar to those presented in Figure 32-10.

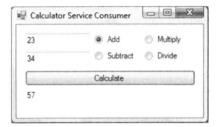

Figure 32-10

In this case, the Add method is invoked from the service when the form's Calculate button is pressed. If you add some kind of TCP trace on your machine, you will see results similar to the following:

```
00000000  0B 06 92 01 55 2A 68 74   74 70 3A 2F 2F 74 65 6D   ....U*ht tp://tem
00000010  70 75 72 69 2E 6F 72 67   2F 49 43 61 6C 63 75 6C   puri.org /ICalcul
00000020  61 74 6F 72 2F 41 64 64   52 65 73 70 6F 6E 73 65   ator/Add Response
00000030  0B 41 64 64 52 65 73 70   6F 6E 73 65 13 68 74 74   .AddResp onse.htt
00000040  70 3A 2F 2F 74 65 6D 70   75 72 69 2E 6F 72 67 2F   p://temp uri.org/
00000050  09 41 64 64 52 65 73 75   6C 74 56 02 0B 01 73 04   .AddResu ltV...s.
00000060  0B 01 61 06 56 08 44 0A   1E 00 82 AB 01 44 12 AD   ..a.V.D. .....D..
00000070  A1 8F 9D 89 5A B0 FF 45   A1 D5 29 A9 F4 57 2B A3   ....Z..E ..)..W+.
00000080  44 0C 1E 00 82 AB 14 01   56 0E 42 03 0A 05 42 07   D....... V.B...B.
00000090  8B 00 01 01 01 01                                   ......
```

The response will return something such as the following:

```
00000000  00 01 00 01 02 02 28 6E   65 74 2E 74 63 70 3A 2F   ......(n et.tcp:/
00000010  2F 31 39 32 2E 31 36 38   2E 31 2E 31 30 32 3A 38   /192.168 .1.102:8
00000020  30 38 30 2F 43 61 6C 63   75 6C 61 74 6F 72 2F 03   080/Calc ulator/.
00000030  08 0C 06 B0 01 68 22 68   74 74 70 3A 2F 2F 74 65   .....h"h ttp://te
00000040  6D 70 75 72 69 2E 6F 72   67 2F 49 43 61 6C 63 75   mpuri.or g/ICalcu
00000050  6C 61 74 6F 72 2F 41 64   64 28 6E 65 74 2E 74 63   lator/Ad d(net.tc
00000060  70 3A 2F 2F 31 39 32 2E   31 36 38 2E 31 2E 31 30   p://192. 168.1.10
00000070  32 3A 38 30 38 30 2F 43   61 6C 63 75 6C 61 74 6F   2:8080/C alculato
00000080  72 2F 03 41 64 64 13 68   74 74 70 3A 2F 2F 74 65   r/.Add.h ttp://te
00000090  6D 70 75 72 69 2E 6F 72   67 2F 01 61 01 62 56 02   mpuri.or g/.a.bV.
000000A0  0B 01 73 04 0B 01 61 06   56 08 44 0A 1E 00 82 AB   ..s...a. V.D.....
000000B0  01 44 1A AD A1 8F 9D 89   5A B0 FF 45 A1 D5 29 A9   .D...... Z..E..).
000000C0  F4 57 2B A3 44 2C 44 2A   AB 14 01 44 0C 1E 00 82   .W+.D,D* ...D....
000000D0  AB 03 01 56 0E 42 05 0A   07 42 09 89 17 42 0B 8B   ...V.B.. .B...B..
000000E0  E9 00 01 01 01                                      .....
```

As before, the requests and responses are sent over TCP as binary, dramatically decreasing the size of the payload for large messages. This is something that .NET Remoting was used for prior to the release of the WCF framework. This concludes the short tutorial demonstrating how to build your own WCF service using the TCP protocol and consume this service directly into a .NET Windows Forms application.

Working with Data Contracts

When building the WCF services so far, the data contract that was defined depended upon simple types or primitive data types. In the case of the earlier WCF service, a .NET type of Integer was exposed, which in turn was mapped to an XSD type of int. You might not have noticed the input and output types actually defined in the WSDL document that was provided via the WCF-generated one, but they are there. These types are actually exposed through an imported .xsd document (a dynamic document). This bit of the WSDL document is presented here:

```
<wsdl:types>
  <xsd:schema targetNamespace="http://tempuri.org/Imports">
  <xsd:import schemaLocation="http://localhost:8000/docs?xsd=xsd0"
   namespace="http://tempuri.org/" />
  <xsd:import schemaLocation="http://localhost:8000/docs?xsd=xsd1"
   namespace="http://schemas.microsoft.com/2003/10/Serialization/" />
  </xsd:schema>
</wsdl:types>
```

Typing in the XSD location of http://localhost:8000/docs?xsd=xsd0 gives you the input and output parameters of the service. For instance, looking at the definition of the Add method, you will see the following bit of code:

```
<xs:element name="Add">
   <xs:complexType>
      <xs:sequence>
         <xs:element minOccurs="0" name="a" type="xs:int" />
         <xs:element minOccurs="0" name="b" type="xs:int" />
      </xs:sequence>
   </xs:complexType>
</xs:element>
<xs:element name="AddResponse">
   <xs:complexType>
      <xs:sequence>
         <xs:element minOccurs="0" name="AddResult" type="xs:int" />
      </xs:sequence>
   </xs:complexType>
</xs:element>
```

This bit of XML code indicates that there are two required input parameters (a and b) that are of type int; in return, the consumer gets an element called <AddResult>, which contains a value of type int.

As a builder of this WCF service, you didn't have to build the data contract, mainly because this service uses simple types. When using complex types, you have to create a data contract in addition to your service contract.

Building a service with a data contract

For an example of working with data contracts, create a new WCF service (again within a Console Application project) called WCF_WithDataContract. In this case, you still need an interface that defines your service contract, and then another class that implements that interface. In addition to these items, you need another class that defines the data contract.

Like the service contract, which makes use of the <ServiceContract()> and the <OperationContract()> attributes, the data contract uses the <DataContract()> and <DataMember()> attributes. To gain access to these attributes, you have to make a reference to the System.Runtime.Serialization namespace in your project and import this namespace into the file.

The full WCF definition is presented here:

```
Imports System
Imports System.ServiceModel
Imports System.Runtime.Serialization

<DataContract()> _
Public Class Customer
    <DataMember()> _
    Public FirstName As String

    <DataMember()> _
    Public LastName As String
End Class

<ServiceContract()> _
Public Interface IHelloCustomer
    <OperationContract()> _
    Function HelloFirstName(ByVal cust As Customer) As String

    <OperationContract()> _
    Function HelloFullName(ByVal cust As Customer) As String
End Interface

Public Class HelloCustomer
    Implements IHelloCustomer

    Public Function HelloFirstName(ByVal cust As Customer) As String _
      Implements IHelloCustomer.HelloFirstName
        Return "Hello " & cust.FirstName
    End Function

    Public Function HelloFullName(ByVal cust As Customer) As String _
      Implements IHelloCustomer.HelloFullName
        Return "Hello " & cust.FirstName & " " & cust.LastName
    End Function
End Class
```

Here, you can see that the System.Runtime.Serialization namespace is also imported, and the first class in the file is the data contract of the service. This class, the Customer class, has two members: FirstName and LastName. Both of these properties are of type String. You specify a class as a data contract through the use of the <DataContract()> attribute:

```
<DataContract()> _
Public Class Customer

    ' Code removed for clarity

End Class
```

Now, any of the properties contained in the class are also part of the data contract through the use of the `<DataMember()>` attribute:

```
<DataContract()> _
Public Class Customer
    <DataMember()> _
    Public FirstName As String

    <DataMember()> _
    Public LastName As String
End Class
```

Finally, the `Customer` object is used in the interface, as well as the class that implements the `IHelloCustomer` interface.

Building the host

The next step is the same as before: change the `Module1.vb` file so that it becomes the host of the WCF service you just built. This task is illustrated in the following example:

```
Imports System
Imports System.ServiceModel
Imports System.ServiceModel.Description

Module Module1

    Sub Main()
        Using serviceHost As ServiceHost = _
          New ServiceHost(GetType(HelloCustomer))

            Dim ntb As NetTcpBinding = New NetTcpBinding(SecurityMode.None)
            serviceHost.AddServiceEndpoint(GetType(IHelloCustomer), ntb, _
               New Uri("net.tcp://192.168.1.102:8080/HelloCustomer/"))

            Dim smb As New ServiceMetadataBehavior()
            smb.HttpGetEnabled = True
            smb.HttpGetUrl = New Uri("http://localhost:8000/docs")

            serviceHost.Description.Behaviors.Add(smb)

            serviceHost.Open()

            Console.WriteLine("Press the <ENTER> key to close the host.")
            Console.ReadLine()
        End Using
    End Sub

End Module
```

This host uses the `IHelloCustomer` interface and builds an endpoint at `net.tcp://192.168.1.102:8080` `/HelloCustomer`. Next, let's look at consuming this service from another console application.

Building the consumer

Now that the service is running and in place, the next step is to build the consumer. To begin, build a new console application from Visual Studio 2008 and call the project HelloWorldConsumer. Right-click on the solution and select Add Service Reference from the options provided.

From the Add Service Reference dialog, add `http://localhost:8000/docs` as the service URI and `HelloCustomerService` as the service reference name, as shown in Figure 32-11.

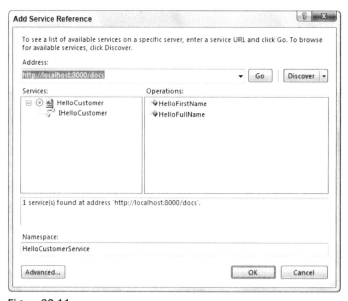

Figure 32-11

This will add the changes to the references and the `app.config` file just as before, enabling you to consume the service. The following code shows what is required:

```
Module Module1

    Sub Main()
        Dim svc As New HelloCustomerService.HelloCustomerClient()
        Dim cust As New HelloCustomerService.Customer()

        Dim result As String

        svc.Open()

        Console.WriteLine("What is your first name?")
```

```
            cust.FirstName = Console.ReadLine()

            Console.WriteLine("What is your last name?")
            cust.LastName = Console.ReadLine()

            result = svc.HelloFullName(cust)

            svc.Close()

            Console.WriteLine(result)
            Console.ReadLine()
        End Sub

    End Module
```

As a consumer, once you make the reference, the service reference doesn't just provide a HelloCustomerClient object; you will also find the Customer object that was defined through the service's data contract.

Therefore, the preceding code block just instantiates both of these objects and builds the Customer object before it is passed into the HelloFullName method provided by the service. Running this bit of code will return the results shown in Figure 32-12.

Figure 32-12

Looking at WSDL and the schema for HelloCustomerService

When you make a reference to the HelloCustomer service, looking at the WSDL, you will find the following XSD imports:

```
<wsdl:types>
    <xsd:schema targetNamespace="http://tempuri.org/Imports">
        <xsd:import schemaLocation="http://localhost:8000/docs?xsd=xsd0"
         namespace="http://tempuri.org/" />
        <xsd:import schemaLocation="http://localhost:8000/docs?xsd=xsd1"
         namespace="http://schemas.microsoft.com/2003/10/Serialization/" />
        <xsd:import schemaLocation="http://localhost:8000/docs?xsd=xsd2"
         namespace="http://schemas.datacontract.org/2004/07/WCF_WithDataContract" />
    </xsd:schema>
</wsdl:types>
```

`http://localhost:8000/docs?xsd=xsd2` provides the details on your `Customer` object. The code from this file is shown here:

```xml
<?xml version="1.0" encoding="utf-8" ?>
<xs:schema elementFormDefault="qualified"
 targetNamespace="http://schemas.datacontract.org/2004/07/WCF_WithDataContract"
 xmlns:xs="http://www.w3.org/2001/XMLSchema"
 xmlns:tns="http://schemas.datacontract.org/2004/07/WCF_WithDataContract">
    <xs:complexType name="Customer">
        <xs:sequence>
            <xs:element minOccurs="0" name="FirstName"
             nillable="true" type="xs:string" />
            <xs:element minOccurs="0" name="LastName"
             nillable="true" type="xs:string" />
        </xs:sequence>
    </xs:complexType>
    <xs:element name="Customer" nillable="true" type="tns:Customer" />
</xs:schema>
```

This is an XSD description of the `Customer` object. Making a reference to the WSDL that includes the XSD description of the `Customer` object causes the auto-generated proxy class to create the following class as part of the proxy:

```vb
<System.CodeDom.Compiler.GeneratedCodeAttribute( _
    "System.Runtime.Serialization", _
    "3.0.0.0"),  _
    System.Runtime.Serialization.DataContractAttribute( _
    [Namespace]:= _
      "http://schemas.datacontract.org/2004/07/WCF_WithDataContract"),  _
    System.SerializableAttribute()>  _
  Partial Public Class Customer
      Inherits Object
      Implements System.Runtime.Serialization.IExtensibleDataObject

      <System.NonSerializedAttribute()>  _
      Private extensionDataField As _
          System.Runtime.Serialization.ExtensionDataObject

      <System.Runtime.Serialization.OptionalFieldAttribute()>  _
      Private FirstNameField As String

      <System.Runtime.Serialization.OptionalFieldAttribute()>  _
      Private LastNameField As String

      Public Property ExtensionData() As _
          System.Runtime.Serialization.ExtensionDataObject Implements _
            System.Runtime.Serialization.IExtensibleDataObject.ExtensionData
          Get
              Return Me.extensionDataField
          End Get
          Set
              Me.extensionDataField = value
          End Set
      End Property
```

```
        <System.Runtime.Serialization.DataMemberAttribute()> _
        Public Property FirstName() As String
            Get
                Return Me.FirstNameField
            End Get
            Set
                Me.FirstNameField = value
            End Set
        End Property

        <System.Runtime.Serialization.DataMemberAttribute()> _
        Public Property LastName() As String
            Get
                Return Me.LastNameField
            End Get
            Set
                Me.LastNameField = value
            End Set
        End Property
    End Class
```

Using this model, you can easily build your services with your own defined types.

Namespaces

Note that the services built in the chapter have no defined namespaces. If you looked at the WSDL files that were produced, you would see that the namespace provided is `http://tempuri.org`. Obviously, you do not want to go live with this default namespace. Instead, you need to define your own namespace.

To accomplish this task, the interface's `<ServiceContract()>` attribute enables you to set the namespace, as shown here:

```
<ServiceContract(Namespace:="http://www.lipperweb.com/ns/")> _
Public Interface IHelloCustomer
    <OperationContract()> _
    Function HelloFirstName(ByVal cust As Customer) As String

    <OperationContract()> _
    Function HelloFullName(ByVal cust As Customer) As String
End Interface
```

Here, the `<ServiceContract()>` attribute uses the `Namespace` property to provide a namespace.

Touching on Security

The WCF framework offers a multitude of different WS-* specifications that you can take advantage of in your services without really needing to know how to code for those specifications, as the framework takes care of this for you on your behalf.

To see an example of this, consider the VbWCF_Service1 solution from the console-application code earlier in this chapter. Take that code and modify it to add a requirement that the service makes use of WS-Security and that the client can only consume the service using WS-Security by supplying their Windows credentials as the user context. The code for this modified service is provided here:

```
Imports System
Imports System.ServiceModel
Imports System.ServiceModel.Description

Module Module1

    Sub Main()
        Using serviceHost As ServiceHost = _
          New ServiceHost(GetType(Calculator))

            Dim ntb As NetTcpBinding = New NetTcpBinding(SecurityMode.Message)
            ntb.Security.Message.ClientCredentialType = _
                MessageCredentialType.Windows
            serviceHost.AddServiceEndpoint(GetType(ICalculator), ntb, _
                New Uri("net.tcp://192.168.1.102:8080/Calculator/"))

            Dim smb As New ServiceMetadataBehavior()
            smb.HttpGetEnabled = True
            smb.HttpGetUrl = New Uri("http://localhost:8000/docs")

            serviceHost.Description.Behaviors.Add(smb)

            serviceHost.Open()

            Console.WriteLine("Press the <ENTER> key to close the host.")
            Console.ReadLine()
        End Using
    End Sub

End Module
```

Instead of the SecurityMode.None property, you can also use the SecurityMode.Message property. This forces the SOAP message to include a WS-Security header. The next line of code specifies that the credential type that the service needs to make use of is a Windows credential, set with the MessageCredentialType.Windows property.

Making a client reference to this service gives you a different app.config file than what you had before. Here is the <system.serviceModel> element of the app.config file:

```
<system.serviceModel>
    <bindings>
        <netTcpBinding>
            <binding name="NetTcpBinding_ICalculator" closeTimeout="00:01:00"
              openTimeout="00:01:00" receiveTimeout="00:10:00"
              sendTimeout="00:01:00"
              transactionFlow="false" transferMode="Buffered"
              transactionProtocol="OleTransactions"
              hostNameComparisonMode="StrongWildcard" listenBacklog="10"
```

```
              maxBufferPoolSize="524288" maxBufferSize="65536" maxConnections="10"
              maxReceivedMessageSize="65536" >
                <readerQuotas maxDepth="32" maxStringContentLength="8192"
                 maxArrayLength="16384"
                 maxBytesPerRead="4096" maxNameTableCharCount="16384" />
                <reliableSession ordered="true" inactivityTimeout="00:10:00"
                 enabled="false" />
                <security mode="Message">
                    <transport clientCredentialType="Windows"
                     protectionLevel="EncryptAndSign" />
                    <message clientCredentialType="Windows" />
                </security>
            </binding>
        </netTcpBinding>
    </bindings>
    <client>
        <endpoint address="net.tcp://192.168.1.102:8080/Calculator/"
         binding="netTcpBinding"
         bindingConfiguration="NetTcpBinding_ICalculator"
         contract="CalculatorService.ICalculator"
         name="NetTcpBinding_ICalculator">
            <identity>
                <userPrincipalName value="Bill-PC\Bill" />
            </identity>
        </endpoint>
    </client>
</system.serviceModel>
```

Note that the `<security>` element defines the client credential type as a Windows credential set, and that the credentials provided in the WS-Security SOAP header need to be encrypted and signed.

From the `<client>` element, you have a user principal defined as the credentials provided in the request. Now when the request and response occur, you will find a WS-Security header, which is present in the SOAP header of the message.

Summary

This chapter looked at one of the more outstanding capabilities provided to the Visual Basic world. VB 2008 using the .NET Framework 3.5 is a great combination for building advanced services that take ASP.NET Web Services, .NET Remoting, Enterprise Services, and MSMQ to the next level.

Though not exhaustive, this chapter broadly outlined the basics of the framework. As you start to dig deeper in the technology, you will find capabilities that are strong and extensible.

## 33

Windows Services

Modern, multitasking operating systems often need to run applications that operate in the background and that are independent of the user who is logged in. From Windows NT to Windows Vista, such applications are called *Windows Services* (formerly known as NT Services). The tasks carried out by Windows Services are typically long-running tasks and have little or no direct interaction with a user (so they don't usually have user interfaces). Such applications may be started when the computer is booted and often continue to run until the computer is shut down.

This chapter covers the following:

- ❏ The characteristics of a Windows Service

- ❏ How to interact with a Windows Service using Visual Studio 2008 and the management applets in the Windows Control Panel

- ❏ How to create, install, and communicate with a Windows Service using Visual Basic

- ❏ How to debug a Windows Service from within Visual Studio 2008

As VB6 did not offer direct support for the creation of Windows Services, you might be unfamiliar with such applications. To help you understand the variety of such applications, this chapter examines some scenarios for which a Windows Service application is a good solution.

Example Windows Services

Microsoft SQL Server, Exchange Server, Internet Information Server (IIS), and antivirus software all use Windows Services to perform tasks in response to events that occur on the system overall. Only a background service, or Windows Service, that runs no matter which user is logged in, could perform such operations. For example, consider these potential Windows Services:

- ❏ **A file watcher** — Suppose you are running an FTP server that enables users to place files in a particular directory. You could use a Windows Service to monitor and process files within that directory as they arrive. The service runs in the background and detects when files are changed or added within the directory, and then extracts information from these files in order to process orders, or update address and billing information. You will see an example of such a Windows Service later in this chapter.

❏ **An automated stock price reporter** — You could build a system that extracts stock prices from a Web service or website and then e-mails the information to users. You could set thresholds such that an e-mail is sent only when the stock price reaches a certain price. This Windows Service can be automated to extract the information every 10 minutes, every 10 seconds, or whatever you choose. Because a Windows Service can contain any logic that does not require a user interface, you have a lot of flexibility in constructing such applications.

❏ **Microsoft Transaction Server (MTS)** — Part of COM+ Services in Windows 2000 and later, this is an object broker that manages instances of components. It is used regularly by professional developers. This service runs constantly in the background and manages components as soon as the computer is booted, just like IIS or Exchange Server.

Characteristics of a Windows Service

To properly design and develop a Windows Service, it is important to understand how it differs from a typical Windows program. Here are the most important characteristics of a Windows Service:

❏ It can start before a user logs on. The system maintains a list of Windows Services, which can be set to start at boot time. Services can also be installed such that they require a manual startup and will not start at bootup.

❏ It can run under a different account from that of the current user. Most Windows Services provide functionality that needs to be running all the time, and some load before a user logs on, so they cannot depend on a user being logged on to run.

❏ It has its own process. It does not run in the process of a program communicating with it (Chapter 29 has more information on processes).

❏ It typically has no user interface. This is because the service may be running under a different account from that of the current user, or the service may start at bootup, which means that calls to put up a user interface might fail because they are out of context (it's possible to create a Windows Service with a user interface, but Visual Basic 2008 can't be used to do it; you will learn why later).

❏ It requires a special installation procedure; just clicking on a compiled EXE will not run it. The program must run in a special context in the operating system, and a specific installation process is required to do the configuration necessary for a Windows Service to be run in this special context.

❏ It works with a *Service Control Manager* (discussed shortly). The Service Control Manager is required to provide an interface to the Windows Service. External programs that want to communicate with a Windows Service (for example, to start or stop the service) must go through the Service Control Manager. The Service Control Manager is an operating-system-level program, but it has a user interface that can be used to start and stop services, and this interface can be accessed through the Computer Management section of the Control Panel.

Interacting with Windows Services

You can view the services that are used on your computer by opening the Service Control Manager user interface. To do so in Windows 2000, select Administrative Tools ➪ Services in the Control Panel. In Windows XP Professional, select Start ➪ All Programs ➪ Administrative Tools ➪ Services. In Windows

Vista, select Start ➪ Control Panel ➪ System and Maintenance ➪ Administrative Tools. Using the Service Control Manager, a service can be set to automatically start when the system is booted, or it can be started manually. Services can also be stopped or paused. The list of services contained in the Service Control Manager includes the current state for each service. Figure 33-1 shows the Service Control Manager in Windows Vista.

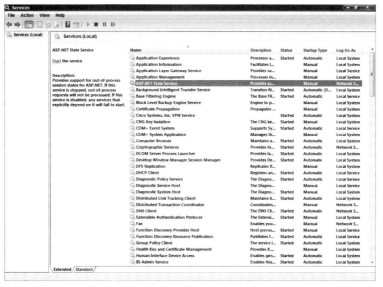

Figure 33-1

The Status column indicates the current state of the service. If this column is blank, then the service has not been started since the last time the computer was booted. Other possible values for Status are Started, Stopped, and Paused. You can access additional settings and details concerning a service by double-clicking it.

When a service is started, it automatically logs into the system using either a user or a system account:

❑ The user account is a regular NT account that allows the program to interact with the system — in essence, the service impersonates a user.

❑ The system account is not associated with a particular user.

The Service Control Manager shown in Figure 33-1 is part of the operating system (OS), which is what supports Windows Services; it is not a part of the .NET Framework. Any service run by the OS is exposed through the Service Control Manager, regardless of how the service was created or installed. You can also interact with Windows Services via the Server Explorer in Visual Studio 2008. You will see this technique later.

Creating a Windows Service

Prior to the release of the .NET Framework, most Windows Services were created with C++. Third-party toolkits were available to enable Windows Services to be created in VB6 and earlier, but deployment problems and threading issues meant that few developers took this route.

In .NET, the functionality needed to interface to the operating system is wrapped up in the .NET Framework classes, so any .NET-compliant language can now be used to create a Windows Service.

The .NET Framework classes for Windows Services

Several base classes are needed to create a Windows Service:

❑ **System.ServiceProcess.ServiceBase** — Provides the base class for the Windows Service. The class containing the logic that will run in the service inherits from ServiceBase. A single executable can contain more than one service, but each service in the executable is a separate class that inherits from ServiceBase.

❑ **System.Configuration.Install.Installer** — This is a generic class that performs the installation chores for a variety of components. One class in a Windows Service process must inherit and extend Installer in order to provide the interface necessary to install the service under the various Windows operating systems.

Each class that inherits from Installer needs to contain an instance of each of the following classes:

❑ **System.ServiceProcess.ServiceProcessInstaller** — This class contains the information needed to install a .NET executable that contains Windows Services (that is, an executable that contains classes that inherit from ServiceBase). The .NET installation utility for Windows Services (InstallUtil.exe, discussed later) calls this class to get the information it needs to perform the installation.

❑ **System.ServiceProcess.ServiceInstaller** — This class also interacts with the InstallUtil .exe installation program. Whereas ServiceProcessInstaller contains information needed to install the executable as a whole, ServiceInstaller contains information on a specific service in the executable. If an executable contains more than one service, then an instance of ServiceInstaller is needed for each one.

For most Windows Services you develop, you can let Visual Studio 2008 take care of Installer, ServiceProcessInstaller, and ServiceInstaller. You just need to set a few properties. The class you should thoroughly understand is ServiceBase, as this is the class that contains the functionality of a Windows Service and therefore must inherit from it.

The ServiceBase Class

ServiceBase contains several useful properties and methods, but initially it is more important to understand the events of ServiceBase. Most of these events are fired by the Service Control Manager when the state of the service is changed. The most important events are as follows:

Event	How and When the Event Is Used
OnStart	Occurs when the service is started. This is where the initialization logic for a service is usually placed.
OnStop	Occurs when the service is stopped. Cleanup and shutdown logic are generally placed here.

Event	How and When the Event Is Used
OnPause	Occurs when the service is paused. Any logic required to suspend operations during a pause goes here.
OnContinue	Occurs when a service continues after being paused
OnShutdown	Occurs when the operating system is being shut down
OnSessionChange	Occurs when a change event is received from a Terminal Session service. This method was new in .NET Framework 2.0.
OnPowerEvent	Occurs when the system's power management software causes a change in the power status of the system. This is typically used to change the behavior of a service when a system is going in or out of a "suspended" power mode. This is more frequent with end users who are working on laptops.
OnCustomCommand	Occurs when an external program has told the Service Control Manager that it wants to send a command to the service. The operation of this event is covered in "Communicating with the Service."

The events used most frequently are OnStart, OnStop, and OnCustomCommand. The OnStart and OnStop events are used in almost every Windows Service written in Visual Basic, and the OnCustomCommand is used when any special configuration of the service needs to be done while the service is running.

All of these are Protected events, so they are only available to classes that inherit from ServiceBase. Because of the restricted context in which it runs, a Windows Service component that inherits from ServiceBase often lacks a public interface. While you can add public properties and methods to such a component, they are of limited use, because outside programs cannot obtain an object reference to running a Windows Service component.

To be active as a Windows Service, an instance of ServiceBase must be started via the shared Run method of the ServiceBase class. However, normally you don't have to write code to do this because the template code generated by Visual Studio 2008 places the correct code in the Main subroutine of the project for you.

The most commonly used property of ServiceBase is the AutoLog property. This Boolean property is set to True by default. If True, then the Windows Service automatically logs the Start, Stop, Pause, and Continue events to an Event Log. The Event Log used is the Application Event Log and the Source in the log entries is taken from the name of the Windows Service. This automatic event logging is stopped by setting the AutoLog property to False.

The following File Watcher example goes into more detail about the automatic logging capabilities in a Windows Service, and about Event Logs in general.

Installation-Oriented Classes

The Installer, ServiceProcessInstaller, and ServiceInstaller classes are quite simple to build and use if you are employing Visual Studio 2008. After you create your Windows Service project, Visual Studio 2008 will create a class file called Service1.vb for you. To add the Installer, ServiceProcessInstaller, and ServiceInstaller classes to your project, simply right-click the design surface of this `ServiceBase` class, `Service1.vb`, and select Add Installer. This creates the code framework necessary to use them.

The `Installer` class (named `ProjectInstaller.vb` by default in a Windows Service project) generally needs no interaction at all — it is ready to use when created by Visual Studio 2008. However, it may be appropriate to change some properties of the `ServiceProcessInstaller` and `ServiceInstaller` classes. You can do this by simply highlighting these objects on the design surface and changing their properties directly in the Properties window of Visual Studio 2008. The properties that are typically modified for `ServiceProcessInstaller` include the following:

❑ **Account** — This specifies the type of account under which the entire service application will run. Different settings give the services in the application different levels of privilege on the local system. For simplicity, this chapter uses the highest level of privilege, `LocalSystem`, for most of the examples. If this property is set to `User` (which is the default), then you must supply a username and password, and that user's account is used to determine privileges for the service. If there is any possibility that a service could access system resources that should be "out of bounds," then using the `User` setting to restrict privileges is a good idea. Besides `LocalSystem` and `User`, other possible settings for the `Account` property include `NetworkService` and `LocalService`.

❑ **Username** — If `Account` is set to `User`, then this property specifies the user account to use in determining the privileges the system will have and how it interacts with other computers on the network. If this property is left blank, then it is requested when the service is installed.

❑ **Password** — This property indicates the password to access the user account specified in the `Username` property. If the password is left blank, then it is requested when the service is installed.

❑ **HelpText** — This specifies information about the service that will be displayed in certain installation options.

If the `Account` property is set to `User`, then it is good practice to set up a special user account for the service, rather than rely on some existing account intended for a live user. The special account can be set up with exactly the appropriate privileges for the service. This way, it is not as vulnerable to having its password or its privileges inadvertently changed in a way that would cause problems in running the service.

For the `ServiceInstaller` class, the properties you might change include the following:

❑ **DisplayName** — The name of the service displayed in the Service Manager or the Server Explorer can be different from the class name and the executable name if desired, though it is better to make this name the same as the class name for the service.

❑ **StartType** — This specifies how the service is started. The default is `Manual`, which means you must start the service yourself, as it will not start automatically after the system boots. If you want the service to always start when the system starts, then change this property to `Automatic`. The Service Manager can be used to override the `StartType` setting.

❑ **ServiceName** — The name of the service that this `ServiceInstaller` handles during installation. If you changed the class name of the service after using the Add Installer option, then you would need to change this property to correspond to the new name for the service.

`ServiceProcessInstaller` and `ServiceInstaller` are used as necessary during the installation process, so there is no need to understand or manipulate the methods of these.

Multiple Services within One Executable

It is possible to place more than one class that inherits from `ServiceBase` in a single Windows Service executable. Each such class then allows for a separate service that can be started, stopped, and so on, independently of the other services in the executable.

If a Windows Service executable contains more than one service, then it must contain one `ServiceInstaller` for each service. Each `ServiceInstaller` is configured with the information used for its associated service, such as the displayed name and the start type (automatic or manual). However, the executable still needs only one `ServiceProcessInstaller`, which works for all the services in the executable. It is configured with the account information that is used for all the services in the executable.

The ServiceController Class

Another important .NET Framework class used with Windows Services is `System.ServiceProcess .ServiceController`. This class is not used when constructing a service. It is used by external applications to communicate with a running service, enabling operations such as starting and stopping the service. The `ServiceController` class is described in detail in "Communicating with the Service."

Other types of Windows Services

The `ServiceBase` and `ServiceController` classes can be used to create typical Windows Services that work with high-level system resources such as the file system or performance counters. However, some Windows Services need to interact at a deeper level. For example, a service may work at the kernel level, fulfilling functions such as that of a device driver.

Presently, the .NET Framework classes for Windows Services cannot be used to create such lower-level services, which rules out both VB and C# as tools to create them. C++ is typically the tool of choice for these types of services. If the .NET version of C++ is used, the code for such services would typically run in unmanaged mode.

Another type of service that cannot be created with the .NET Framework classes is one that interacts with the Windows desktop. Again, C++ is the preferred tool for such services.

You'll look at the types of services that *are* possible during the discussion of the `ServiceType` property of the `ServiceController` class, in "Communicating with the Service."

Creating a Windows Service in Visual Basic

Now it is time to create and use a Windows Service with Visual Basic, using the previously discussed .NET Framework classes. These tasks are demonstrated later in a detailed example. Here is a high-level description of the necessary tasks:

1. Create a new project of the type Windows Service. By default, the service will be in a module named `Service1.vb`, but it can be renamed, like any other .NET module. (The class automatically placed in `Service1.vb` is named `Service1` by default, and it inherits from `ServiceBase`.)

2. Place any logic needed to run when the service is started in the `OnStart` event of the service class. You can find the code listing for the `Service1.vb` file by double-clicking this file's design surface.

3. Add any additional logic that the service needs to carry out its operation. Logic can be placed in the class for the service, or in any other class module in the project. Such logic is typically called via some event that is generated by the operating system and passed to the service, such as a file changing in a directory, or a timer tick.

4. Add an installer to the project. This module provides the interface to the Windows operating system to install the module as a Windows Service. The installer is a class that inherits from `System.Configuration.Install.Installer`, and it contains instances of the `ServiceProcessInstaller` and `ServiceInstaller` classes.

5. Set the properties of the installer modules as necessary. The most common settings needed are the account under which the service will run and the name the service will display in the Service Control Manager.

6. Build the project. This results in an EXE file. For example, if the service were named `WindowsService1`, then the executable file would be named `WindowsService1.exe`.

7. Install the Windows Service with a command-line utility named `InstallUtil.exe`. (As previously mentioned, a service cannot be started by just running the EXE file.)

8. Start the Windows Service with the Service Control Manager (available via the Control Panel ➪ Administrative Tools folder in Windows 2000; the Start ➪ All Programs ➪ Administrative Tools folder in Windows XP; or the Start ➪ Control Panel ➪ System and Maintenance ➪ Administrative Tools folder in Windows Vista) or with the Server Explorer in Visual Studio 2008.

You can also start a service from the command console if the proper paths to .NET are set. The command is NET START <servicename>. Note that the <servicename> used in this command is the name of the service, not the name of the executable in which the service resides. Depending on the configuration of your system, a service started with any of the aforementioned methods will sometimes fail, resulting in an error message indicating that the service did not start in a timely fashion. This may be because the .NET libraries and other initialization tasks did not finish fast enough to suit the Service Control Manager. If this happens, attempt to start the service again; it usually succeeds the second time.

Steps 2 through 5 can be done in a different order. It doesn't matter whether the installer is added and configured before or after the logic that does the processing for the service is added.

At this point, a service is installed and running. The Service Manager or the Server Explorer can stop the service, or it will be automatically stopped when the system is shut down. The command to stop the service in a command console is NET STOP <servicename>.

The service does not automatically start the next time the system is booted unless it is configured for that. This can be done by setting the `StartType` property for the service to `Automatic` when developing the service, or it can be done in the Service Manager. Right-clicking the service in the Service Manager provides access to this capability.

This process is superficially similar to doing most other Visual Basic projects. There are a few important differences, however:

❑ You cannot debug the project in the environment as you normally would any other Visual Basic program. The service must be installed and started before it can be debugged. It is also necessary to attach to the process for the service to do debugging. Details about this are included in "Debugging the Service."

❑ Even though the result of the development is an EXE, you should not include any message boxes or other visual elements in the code. The Windows Service executable is more like a component library in that sense, and should not have a visual interface. If you include visual elements such as message boxes, the results can vary. In some cases, the UI code will have no effect. In other cases, the service may hang when attempting to write to the user interface.

❑ Finally, be especially careful to handle all errors within the program. The program is not running in a user context, so a runtime error has no place to report itself visually. Handle all errors with structured exception handling, and use an Event Log or other offline means to record and communicate runtime errors.

Creating a Counter Monitor Service

To illustrate the outlined steps, the following example creates a simple service that checks the value of a performance counter, and when the value of the counter exceeds a certain value, the service beeps every three seconds. This is a good example for stepping through the process of creating, installing, and starting a Windows Service. It contains very little logic, and you can easily tell when it is working.

In the first phase of the example, you create a service that always beeps. Then, in the second phase, you add logic to monitor the performance counter and only beep when the counter exceeds a specific value:

1.   Start a new Windows Service project using Visual Studio 2008. Name the project `CounterMonitor`.

2.   In the Solution Explorer, rename `Service1.vb` to `CounterMonitor.vb`.

3.   Click the design surface for `CounterMonitor.vb`. In the Properties window, change the `ServiceName` property from `Service1` to `CounterMonitor` (the `Name` property changes the name of the class on which the service is based, while the `ServiceName` property changes the name of the service as known to the Service Control Manager).

4.   Right-click the project for the service and select Properties. You will then be presented with the CounterMonitor Property Pages as one of the paged tabs directly in Visual Studio. From the Application tab, set the Application Type drop-down list to Windows Service if necessary (it should already be set to this), and from the drop-down list named Startup Object, make sure `CounterMonitor` is selected (see Figure 33-2).

5.   Go back to the `CounterMonitor.vb` file's Design view and open the Visual Studio 2008 Toolbox. Open the Components (not the Windows Forms) node in the Toolbox. Drag a `Timer` control from the Toolbox onto the `CounterMonitor` design surface. It will appear on the design surface with the name `Timer1`. It is very important that you grab the correct `Timer`

object from the Toolbox. Visual Studio 2008 does not have the `Timer` object for this example in the Toolbox, whereas earlier versions of Visual Studio before VS 2005 did. To ensure that you have the correct `Timer` object, right-click on the Toolbox and select Choose Items from the menu. In the .NET Framework Components tab of the Choose Toolbox Items dialog, scroll down until you see a couple of `Timer` objects. In the list are a couple of `Timer` objects from the `System.Windows.Forms` namespace, but you want to instead choose the `Timer` object that is part of the `System.Timers` namespace. This is the `Timer` object that you work with for the rest of this example.

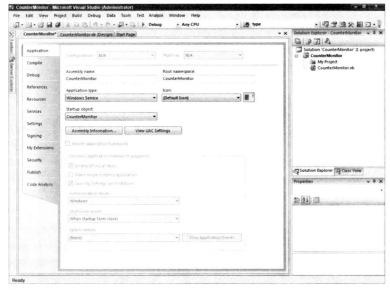

Figure 33-2

6. In the Properties window for `Timer1`, change the `Interval` property to a value of `3000` (that's 3,000 milliseconds, which causes the timer to fire every three seconds).

7. Go to the code for `CounterMonitor.vb`. Inside the `OnStart` event handler (which is already created for you in the code), enter the following:

```
Timer1.Enabled = True
```

8. In the `OnStop` event for the class, enter the following:

```
Timer1.Enabled = False
```

9. Create an `Elapsed` event for the timer by highlighting `Timer1` in the left-hand drop-down box at the top of the code editor window. Select the `Elapsed` event in the right-hand drop-down box from the Code view of the file.

10. In the `Elapsed` event, place the following line:

```
Beep()
```

11. Now add an installer to the project. Go back to the design surface for `CounterMonitor` and right-click it. Select Add Installer. A new file called `ProjectInstaller1.vb` is created and added to the project. The `ProjectInstaller1.vb` file has two components added to its design surface: `ServiceProcessInstaller1` and `ServiceInstaller1`, as shown in Figure 33-3.

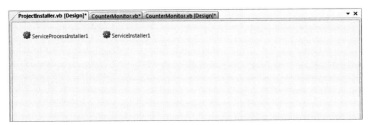

Figure 33-3

12. On the `ProjectInstaller.vb` design surface, highlight the `ServiceProcessInstaller1` control. In its Properties window, change the `Account` property to `LocalSystem`.

13. Highlight the `ServiceInstaller1` control. In its Properties window, type in **CounterMonitor** as the value of the `DisplayName` property.

14. Now build the project by right-clicking on the solution and selecting Build from the menu. An EXE named `CounterMonitor.exe` will be created for the service.

Installing the service

Now you are ready to install the service. The utility for doing this, `InstallUtil.exe`, must be run from a command line. It is located in the .NET utilities directory, found at `C:\WINNT\Microsoft .NET\Framework\v2.0.50727` on Windows 2000 and NT systems, or `C:\Windows\Microsoft.NET\ Framework\v2.0.50727` on Windows XP, Windows Vista, Windows Server 2003, and Windows Server 2008.

You can easily access this utility (and all the other .NET utilities in that directory) using an option from the Programs menu that is installed with Visual Studio 2008. Choose Microsoft Visual Studio 2008 ⇨ Visual Studio Tools ⇨ Visual Studio 2008 Command Prompt. In the command window that appears, change to the directory that contains `CounterMonitor.exe`. By default, when using Visual Studio 2008, you'll find this executable at `C:\Users\[ user ]\ Documents\Visual Studio 2008\Projects\ CounterMonitor\Projects\CounterMonitor\CounterMonitor\obj\Debug`. Once found, run the following command:

```
InstallUtil CounterMonitor.exe
```

Check the messages generated by `InstallUtil.exe` to ensure that the installation of the service was successful. The utility generates several lines of information; if successful, the last two lines are as follows:

```
The Commit phase completed successfully.

The transacted install has completed.
```

If these two lines do not appear, then you need to read all the information generated by the utility to find out why the install didn't work. Reasons might include a bad pathname for the executable, or trying to install the service when it is already installed (it must be uninstalled before it can be reinstalled), as described later.

Starting the service

Later in this chapter, you will create your own "control panel" screen to start and stop the service. For now, to test the new Windows Service, you will use the Server Explorer in Visual Studio 2008. Open the Server Explorer in Visual Studio 2008 and expand the Services node. The resulting screen is shown in Figure 33-4.

Figure 33-4

If the CounterMonitor service does not appear in the list, then the installation failed. Try the installation again and check the error messages. Right-click the CounterMonitor service and select the Start menu option. You will hear the service beep every three seconds. You can stop the service by right-clicking it again and selecting the Stop menu option.

You can also use the Service Control Manager built into Windows to start the `CounterMonitor` service, shown in Figure 33-5.

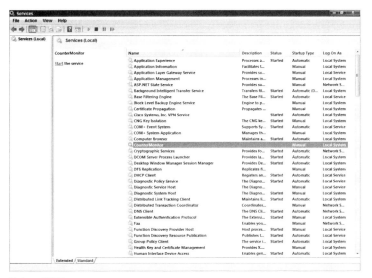

Figure 33-5

Start `CounterMonitor` by right-clicking it and selecting Start or by clicking the Start link. As before, you will hear your computer beep every three seconds. Stop the service by right-clicking `CounterMonitor` and selecting Stop or by clicking the Stop link. Note that if you already started the service via the Server Explorer (as described earlier), then it will be in a started state when you access the Service Control Manager program.

Uninstalling the service

Uninstalling the service is very similar to installing it. The service must be in a stopped state before it can be uninstalled, but the uninstall operation will attempt to stop the service if it is running. The uninstall operation is done in the same command window (with the Visual Studio 2008 Command Prompt) as the install operation, and the command used is the same as the one for installation, except that the option `/u` is included just before the name of the service. Remember that you need to navigate to `C:\Users\`
`[ user ]\Documents\Visual Studio 2008\Projects\CounterMonitor\Projects\CounterMonitor\`
`CounterMonitor\obj\Debug` to run this command:

```
InstallUtil.exe /u CounterMonitor.exe
```

You can tell that the uninstall was successful if the information displayed by the utility contains the following line:

```
Service CounterMonitor was successfully removed from the system.
```

If the uninstall is not successful, read the rest of the information to determine why. Besides typing in the wrong pathname, another common reason for failure is trying to uninstall a service that is in a running state and could not be stopped in a timely fashion.

Once you have uninstalled `CounterMonitor`, it will no longer show up in the list of available services to start and stop (at least, after a refresh it will not).

> **A Windows Service must be uninstalled and reinstalled every time you make changes to it. You should uninstall `CounterMonitor` now because you are about to add new capabilities to it.**

Monitoring a Performance Counter

Performance counters are a system-level function of Windows. They are used to track usage of system resources. Performance counters can be expressed as counts (number of times a Web page was hit), percentages (how much disk space is left), or other types of information. Many counters are automatically maintained by the operating system, but applications can create and manage their own performance counters.

To demonstrate how services can interact with system-level functionality, you will add to the `CounterMonitor` the capability to monitor a particular performance counter, and only beep when the performance counter exceeds a certain value.

Performance counters can be monitored by a user with the Performance Monitor. A variety of performance counters are built into the operating system, providing access to information such as the number of threads currently active on the system, or the number of documents in a print queue. Any of these, and any custom performance counters, can be graphed in the Performance Monitor.

Creating a performance counter

This example creates a performance counter named `ServiceCounter`. Then you will change `CounterMonitor` to check that counter and only beep when its value is over 5. To test it, you will also create a small Windows Forms application that increments and decrements the counter.

Performance counters are typically accessed in Visual Studio 2008 through the Server Explorer tab. To see the available performance counters, open the Server Explorer, shown in Figure 33-6.

To see the categories of performance counters, click the plus sign next to the Performance Counters option in the Server Explorer. Several dozen categories will be shown. You can look at the counters in any particular category by clicking the plus sign next to the category.

You can also create new categories and new counters. For this example, you need to create a new category for the counter called `Service Counters`. To do that, right-click the Performance Counters option in the Server Explorer and select the Create New Category option. In the resulting Performance Counter Builder dialog box (shown in Figure 33-7), enter the name of the category as `Service Counters`, and create a new counter by clicking the New button and entering **TestCounter** for the name. Once that is complete, click the OK button. Visual Studio 2008 will then create a new category called `Service Counters` that contains a single performance counter called `TestCounter`.

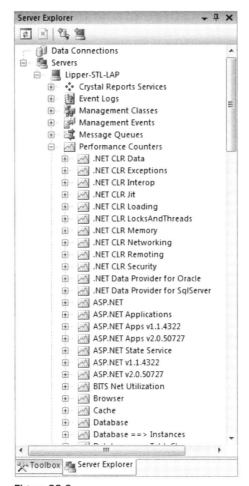

Figure 33-6

Integrating the counter into the service

Using a performance counter in the CounterMonitor service you created earlier is straightforward. Open the CounterMonitor project and go to the design surface for CounterMonitor. Then open the Server Explorer so that it shows the TestCounter performance counter you created. Click TestCounter from within the Server Explorer and drag it onto the CounterMonitor.vb design surface.

A new visual control named PerformanceCounter1 will appear on the page's design surface, ready for use. Change the logic in the Elapsed event for Timer1 as shown here:

```
If PerformanceCounter1.RawValue > mnMaxValue Then
    Beep()
End If
```

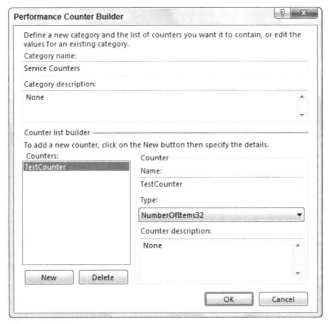

Figure 33-7

The RawValue property being used in this code fetches the unformatted value of the counter. For counters that track whole numbers (such as the number of times a Web page is hit), the RawValue property is normally used to get the value of the counter for testing or display. Some other types of counters use a NextValue method to get a formatted value. See the CounterType property of the PerformanceCounter class for more information on the types of performance counters available.

Next, put this statement in the code module just under the first line of the CounterMonitor class:

```
Dim mnMaxValue As Integer = 5
```

This creates the mnMaxValue as a Private variable. Now build the service again, install it as before, and start the service. It should not beep at this point because the value in the performance counter is zero. You can leave the counter running, because you will now create a program to change the value in the performance counter, thereby making the service begin beeping.

Changing the value in the performance counter

To manipulate the performance counter, you will build a small forms-based application. Close the CounterMonitor solution in Visual Studio and start a new Windows Application Project named CounterTest. Place two buttons on Form1 and change their properties as shown in the following table:

Name	Text
BtnIncrement	Increment Counter
BtnDecrement	Decrement Counter

Then, open the Server Explorer and drag the `TestCounter` performance counter onto the form itself, just as you did earlier with the `CounterMonitor` project. As with all nonvisible components from the Toolbox, the counter will appear in the component tray (just under the form), rather than on the form's design surface.

The `PerformanceCounter1` control for `CounterTest` needs one property change. Set the `ReadOnly` property of the control to `False`. This enables the application to manipulate the counter. (This change was unnecessary for the `CounterMonitor` Windows Service project because that project only reads the value of the performance counter and does not change it.)

Now double-click `btnIncrement` to get to its click event. Place the following code in the event:

```
PerformanceCounter1.Increment()
```

Double-click the `btnDecrement` to get to its click event. Place the following code in the event:

```
PerformanceCounter1.Decrement()
```

Build and run the program and click the Increment button six times. If the `CounterMonitor` service is running, then on the sixth click it will begin beeping because the value in the counter has exceeded five. Then click the Decrement button a couple of times, and the beeping will stop.

If you want to monitor the current value of the counter, select Start ➪ Control Panel ➪ System and Maintenance ➪ Administrative Tools ➪ Reliability and Performance Monitor. From here, select Performance Monitor from the Monitor Tools section. This program, the Performance Monitor, enables the value of counters to be graphed. To add a counter for display, click the green plus button in the tool's toolbar. Change the Performance Object drop-down list to `Service Counters` and add the `TestCounter` performance counter to the list. When completed, select the Close button. The counter that you created will be monitored by the dialog box. You can use the help for this program for more details on displaying counters in the Performance Monitor.

Communicating with the Service

Up to this point, you have learned how to do the following:

❑　Create a Windows Service using Visual Basic

❑　Start and stop a service with the Server Explorer in Visual Studio 2008 or the Service Control Manager from the Control Panel

❑　Make a service work with a system-level function such as a performance counter

If these procedures are sufficient to start, stop, and check on the service through the Server Explorer or the Service Control Manager, and there is no need for any other communication with the service, then this is all you have to do. However, it is often helpful to create a specialized application to manipulate your service. This application will typically be able to start and stop a service, and check on its status. The application may also need to communicate with the service to change its configuration. Such an application is often referred to as a *control panel* for the service, even though it does not necessarily reside in the operating system's Control Panel. A commonly used example of such an application is the SQL Server Service Manager, whose icon appears in the tray on the taskbar (normally in the lower-right section of the screen) if you have SQL Server installed.

Such an application needs a way to communicate with the service. The .NET Framework base class that is used for such communication is `ServiceController`. It is in the `System.ServiceProcess` namespace. You need to add a reference to `System.ServiceProcess.dll` (which contains this namespace) before a project can use the `ServiceController` class.

The `ServiceController` class provides an interface to the Service Control Manager, which coordinates all communication with Windows Services. However, you do not have to know anything about the Service Control Manager to use the `ServiceController` class. You just manipulate the properties and methods of the `ServiceController` class, and any necessary communication with the Service Control Manager is accomplished on your behalf behind the scenes.

It is a good idea to use exactly *one* instance of the `ServiceController` class for each service you are controlling. Multiple instances of `ServiceController` that are communicating with the same service can have timing conflicts. Typically, that means using a module-level object variable to hold the reference to the active `ServiceController`, and instantiating the `ServiceController` during the initialization logic for the application. The following example uses this technique.

The ServiceController class

The constructor for the `ServiceController` requires the name of the Windows Service with which it will be communicating. This is the same name that was placed in the `ServiceName` property of the class that defined the service. You will see how to instantiate the `ServiceController` class shortly.

The `ServiceController` class has several members that are useful in manipulating services. Here are the most important methods, followed by another table of the most important properties:

Method	Purpose
Start	A method to start the service
Stop	A method to stop the service
Refresh	A method to ensure that the `ServiceController` object contains the latest state of the service (needed because the service might be manipulated from another program)
ExecuteCommand	A method used to send a custom command to the service. This method is covered later in the section "Custom Commands."

Here are the most important properties:

Property	Purpose
CanStop	A property indicating whether the service can be stopped
ServiceName	A property containing the name of the associated service

Property	Purpose
Status	An enumerated property that indicates whether a service is stopped, started, in the process of being started, and so on. The `ToString` method on this property is useful for getting the status in a string form for text messages. The possible values of the enumeration are as follows:
	`ContinuePending` — The service is attempting to continue.
	`Paused` — The service is paused.
	`PausePending` — The service is attempting to go into a paused state.
	`Running` — The service is running.
	`StartPending` — The service is starting.
	`Stopped` — The service is not running.
	`StopPending` — The service is stopping.
ServiceType	A property that indicates the type of service. The result is an enumerated value. The enumerations are as follows:
	`Win32OwnProcess` — The service uses its own process (this is the default for a service created in .NET).
	`Win32ShareProcess` — The service shares a process with another service (this advanced capability is not covered here).
	`Adapter, FileSystemDriver, InteractiveProcess, KernelDriver, RecognizerDriver` — These are low-level service types that cannot be created with Visual Basic because the `ServiceBase` class does not support them. However, the value of the `ServiceType` property may still have these values for services created with other tools.

Integrating a ServiceController into the example

To manipulate the service, you will enhance the `CounterTest` program created earlier. Here are step-by-step instructions to do that:

1. Add three new buttons to the `CounterTest` form, with the following names and text labels:

Name	Text
BtnCheckStatus	Check Status
BtnStartService	Start Service
BtnStopService	Stop Service

2. Add a reference to the DLL that contains the `ServiceController` class: Select Project ⇨ Add Reference. On the .NET tab, highlight the `System.ServiceProcess.dll` option and click OK.

3. Add this line at the top of the code for `Form1`:

```
Imports System.ServiceProcess
```

4. As discussed, the project needs only one instance of the `ServiceController` class. Create a module-level object reference to a `ServiceController` class by adding the following line of code within the `Form1` class:

```
Dim myController As ServiceController
```

5. Create a Form Load event in `Form1`, and place the following line of code in it to instantiate the `ServiceController` class:

```
myController = New ServiceController("CounterMonitor")
```

You now have a `ServiceController` class named `myController` that you can use to manipulate the `CounterMonitor` Windows Service. In the click event for `btnCheckStatus`, place the following code:

```
Dim sStatus As String
myController.Refresh()
sStatus = myController.Status.ToString

MsgBox(myController.ServiceName & " is in state: " & sStatus)
```

In the click event for `btnStartService`, place this code:

```
Try
    myController.Start()
Catch exp As Exception
    MsgBox("Could not start service or the service is already running")
End Try
```

In the click event for `btnStopService`, place this code:

```
If myController.CanStop Then
    myController.Stop()
Else
    MsgBox("Service cannot be stopped or the service is already stopped")
End If
```

Run and test the program. The service may already be running because of one of your previous tests. Make sure the performance counter is high enough to make the service beep, and then test starting and stopping the service.

More about ServiceController

`ServiceController` classes can be created for *any* Windows Service, not just those created in .NET. For example, you could instantiate a `ServiceController` class that was associated with the Windows

Service for Internet Information Server (IIS) and use it to start, pause, and stop IIS. The code would look just like the code used earlier for the application that controlled the CounterMonitor service. The only difference is that the name of the service would need to be changed in the line that instantiates the ServiceController (step 5).

Keep in mind that the ServiceController is not communicating directly with the service. It is working through the Service Control Manager. That means the requests from the Service Controller to start, stop, or pause a service do not behave synchronously. As soon as the ServiceController has passed the request to the ServicesControlManager, it continues to execute its own code without waiting for the Service Control Manager to pass on the request, or for the service to act on the request.

Custom Commands

Some services need additional operations besides starting and stopping. For example, for the CounterMonitor Windows Service, you might want to set the threshold value of the performance counter that causes the service to begin beeping, or you might want to change the interval between beeps.

With most components, you would implement such functionality through a public interface. That is, you would put public properties and methods on the component. However, you cannot do this with a Windows Service because it has no public interface that you can access from outside the service.

To deal with this need, the interface for a Windows Service contains a special event called OnCustomCommand. The event arguments include a numeric code that can serve as a command sent to the Windows Service. The code can be any number in the range 128 to 255. (The numbers under 128 are reserved for use by the operating system.)

To fire the event and send a custom command to a service, the ExecuteCommand method of the ServiceController is used. The ExecuteCommand method takes the numeric code that needs to be sent to the service as a parameter. When this method is accessed, the ServiceController class tells the Service Control Manager to fire the OnCustomCommand event in the service, and to pass it the numeric code.

The next example demonstrates this process in action. Suppose you want to be able to change the interval between beeps for the CounterMonitor service. You cannot directly send the beep interval that you want, but you can pick various values of the interval, and associate a custom command numeric code with each.

For example, assume you want to be able to set intervals of 1 second, 3 seconds (the default), or 10 seconds. You could set up the following correspondence:

Custom Command Numeric Code	Beep Interval
201	One second (1,000 milliseconds)
203	Three seconds (3,000 milliseconds)
210	Ten seconds (10,000 milliseconds)

The correspondences in the table are completely arbitrary. You could use any codes between 128 and 255 to associate with the beep intervals. These were chosen because they are easy to remember.

First, you need to change the `CounterMonitor` service so that it is able to accept the custom commands for the beep interval. To do that, first make sure the `CounterMonitor` service is uninstalled from any previous installs. Then open the Visual Studio 2008 project for the `CounterMonitor` service.

Create an `OnCustomCommand` event in the service: Open the code window for `CounterMonitor.vb` and type **Protected Overrides OnCustomCommand**. By this point, IntelliSense will kick in and you can press the Tab key to autocomplete the shell event. Notice how it only accepts a single `Integer` as a parameter:

```
Protected Overrides Sub OnCustomCommand(ByVal command As Integer)

End Sub
```

In the `OnCustomCommand` event, place the following code:

```
Timer1.Enabled = False
Select Case command
    Case 201
        Timer1.Interval = 1000
    Case 203
        Timer1.Interval = 3000
    Case 210
        Timer1.Interval = 10000
End Select
Timer1.Enabled = True
```

Build the `countermonitor` service, reinstall it, and start it.

Now you can enhance the `CounterTest` application created earlier to set the interval. To enable users to pick the interval, you will use radio buttons. On the `CounterTest` program `Form1` (which currently contains five buttons), place three radio buttons. Set their text labels as follows:

```
RadioButton1 -  1 second
RadioButton2 -  3 seconds
RadioButton3 -  10 seconds
```

Place a button directly under these option buttons. Name it `btnSetInterval` and set its text to `Set Interval`. In the `click` event for this button, place the following code:

```
Dim nIntervalCommand As Integer = 203
If RadioButton1.Checked Then
    nIntervalCommand = 201
End If
If RadioButton2.Checked Then
    nIntervalCommand = 203
End If
If RadioButton3.Checked Then
    nIntervalCommand = 210
End If
myController.ExecuteCommand(nIntervalCommand)
```

At this point, `Form1` should look something like the screen shown in Figure 33-8.

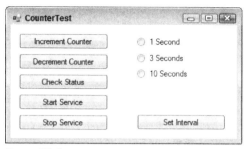

Figure 33-8

Start the `CounterTest` control program and test the capability to change the beep interval. Make sure the performance counter is high enough that the `CounterMonitor` service beeps, and remember that every time you stop and restart the service, it resets the beep interval to three seconds.

Passing Strings to a Service

Because the `OnCustomCommand` event only takes numeric codes as input parameters, you cannot directly pass strings to the service. For example, if you wanted to reconfigure a directory name for a service, you could not just send the directory name over. Instead, it would be necessary to place the information to be passed to the service in a file in some known location on disk. Then a custom command for the service could instruct it to look at the standard file location and read the information in the file. What the service did with the contents of the file would, of course, be customized for the service.

Creating a File Watcher

Now let's step through another example to illustrate what a Windows Service can do and how to construct one. You will build a service that monitors a particular directory and reacts when a new or changed file is placed in the directory. The example Windows Service application waits for those files, extracts information from them, and then logs an event to a system log to record the file change.

As before, create a Windows Service from the built-in template named Windows Service in the New Project screen. Name the new project `FileWatcherService` and click OK. This creates a new service class called `Service1.vb`. Rename this to `FileWatcherService.vb`. Right-click the design surface, select Properties, and set the `ServiceName` property to `FileWatcherService`.

As in the first example, set the application type to Windows Service and reset the project's start object to `FileWatcherService`. All of this is illustrated earlier in this chapter.

Writing events using an Event Log

The way to ensure that the service is doing its job is by having it write events to a system Event Log. Event Logs are available under the Windows operating system. As with many other system-level features, the use of Event Logs is simplified in .NET because a .NET Framework base class does most of the work for you.

There are three Event Logs on the system: Application, Security, and System. Normally, your applications should only write to the Application log. A property of a log entry called Source identifies the application writing the message. This property does not have to be the same as the executable name of the application, but it is often given that name to make it easy to identify the source of the message.

You can look at the events in the Event Log by using the Event Viewer. Select Control Panel ⇨ Administrative Tools ⇨ Event Viewer on Windows 2000; Start ⇨ All Programs ⇨ Administrative Tools ⇨ Event Viewer on Windows XP; and Start ⇨ Control Panel ⇨ System and Maintenance ⇨ Administrative Tools ⇨ Event Viewer on Windows Vista. The following example uses the Event Viewer to ensure that the service is generating events.

It was mentioned earlier in the chapter that the AutoLog property of the ServiceBase class determines whether the service automatically writes events to the Application log. The AutoLog property instructs the service to use the Application Event Log to report command failures, as well as information for OnStart, OnStop, OnPause, and OnContinue events on the service. What is actually logged to the Event Log is an entry indicating whether the service started successfully and stopped successfully, and any errors that might have occurred. If you look in the Application Event Log now, these events are logged for the CounterMonitor Windows Service that you created and ran earlier in the chapter.

You can turn off Event Log reporting by setting the AutoLog property to False in the Properties window for the service, but leave it set to True for this example. That means some events will be logged automatically (without you including any code for them). Then, you add some code to the service to log additional events not covered by the AutoLog property. First, though, you need to implement a file monitoring control in the project.

Creating a FileSystemWatcher

For performance reasons, you should do all of your work on a separate thread to your main application thread. You want to leave your main application free to accept any requests from the user or the operating system. You can do this by using some of the different components that create their own threads when they are launched. The Timer component and the FileSystemWatcher component are two examples. When the Timer component fires its Elapsed event, a thread is spawned and any code placed within that event will work on that newly created thread. The same thing happens when the events for the FileSystemWatcher component fire.

You can learn more about threading in .NET in Chapter 26.

The FileSystemWatcher Component

The FileSystemWatcher component is used to monitor a particular directory. The component implements Created, Changed, Deleted, and Renamed events, which are fired when files are placed in the directory, changed, deleted, or renamed, respectively.

The operation that takes place when one of these events is fired is determined by the application developer. Most often, logic is included to read and process the new or changed files. However, you are just going to write a message to a log file.

To implement the component in the project, drag and drop a FileSystemWatcher control from the Components tab of the Toolbox onto the designer surface of FileWatcherService.vb. This control is automatically called FileSystemWatcher1.

The EnableRaisingEvents Property

The `FileSystemWatcher` control should not generate any events until the service is initialized and ready to handle them. To prevent this, set the `EnableRaisingEvents` property to `False`. This prevents the control from firing any events. You will enable it during the `OnStart` event in the service. These events fired by the `FileSystemWatcher` are controlled using the `NotifyFilter` property, discussed later.

The Path Property

The path that you want to monitor is the `TEMP` directory on the `C:` drive, so set the `Path` property to `C:\TEMP` (be sure to confirm that there is a `TEMP` directory on your `C:` drive). Of course, this path can be changed to monitor any directory depending on your system, including any network or removable drives.

The NotifyFilter Property

You only want to monitor when a file is freshly created or the last modified value of a file has changed. To do this, set the `NotifyFilter` property to `FileName, LastWrite`. You could also watch for other changes such as attributes, security, size, and directory name changes as well, just by changing the `NotifyFilter` property. Note that you can specify multiple changes to monitor by including a comma-separated list.

The Filter Property

The types of files that you will look for are text files, so set the `Filter` property to `.txt`. Note that if you were going to watch for all file types, then the value of the `Filter` property would be set to `*.*`.

The IncludeSubdirectories Property

If you wanted to watch subdirectories, you would set the `IncludeSubdirectories` property to `True`. This example leaves it as `False`, which is the default value. Figure 33-9 shows how the properties should be set.

Figure 33-9

Adding FileSystemWatcher Code to OnStart and OnStop

Now that some properties are set, let's add some code to the OnStart event. You want to start the FileSystemWatcher1 component so it will start triggering events when files are created or copied into the directory you are monitoring, so set the EnableRaisingEvents property to True:

```
Protected Overrides Sub OnStart(ByVal args() As String)
    ' Start monitoring for files
    FileSystemWatcher1.EnableRaisingEvents = True
End Sub
```

After the file monitoring properties are initialized, you are ready to start the monitoring. When the service stops, you need to stop the file monitoring process. Add the following code to the OnStop event:

```
Protected Overrides Sub OnStop()
    ' Stop monitoring for files
    FileSystemWatcher1.EnableRaisingEvents = False
End Sub
```

The EventLog Component

Now you are ready to place an EventLog component in the service to facilitate logging of events. Drag and drop an EventLog control from the Components tab of the Toolbox onto the designer surface of FileWatcherService.vb. This control is automatically called EventLog1.

Set the Log property for Eventlog1 to Application, and set the Source property to FileWatcherService.

The Created Event

Next, you will place some logic in the Created event of the FileSystemWatcher component to log when a file has been created. This event fires when a file has been placed or created in the directory that you are monitoring. It fires because the information last modified on the file has changed.

Select FileSystemWatcher1 from the Class Name drop-down list and select Created from the Method Name drop-down list. The Created event will be added to your code. Add code to the Created event as follows:

```
Public Sub FileSystemWatcher1_Created(ByVal sender As Object, _
            ByVal e As System.IO.FileSystemEventArgs) _
            Handles FileSystemWatcher1.Created

    Dim sMessage As String
    sMessage = "File created in directory - file name is " + e.Name
    EventLog1.WriteEntry(sMessage)
End Sub
```

Notice that the event argument's object (the object named "e" in the event parameters) includes a property called Name. This property holds the name of the file that generated the event.

At this point, you could add the other events for FileSystemWatcher (Changed, Deleted, Renamed) in a similar way and create corresponding log messages for those events. To keep the example simple, you will just use the Created event in this service.

You need to add an `Installer` class to this project to install the application. This is done as it was in the `CounterMonitor` example, by right-clicking the design surface for the service and selecting Add Installer or by clicking the Add Installer link in the Properties window of Visual Studio 2008. Don't forget to change the `Account` property to `LocalSystem`, or set it to `User` and fill in the `Username` and `Password` properties.

As before, you must install the service using `InstallUtil.exe`. Then, start it with the Server Explorer or the Service Manager. Upon successful compilation of these steps, you will get a message logged for any file with a `.txt` extension that you copy or create in the monitored directory. After dropping some sample text files into the monitored directory, you can use the Event Viewer to ensure that the events are present.

Figure 33-10 shows the Event Viewer with several example messages created by the service. If you right-click one of the events for `FileWatcherService`, you will see a detail screen. Notice that the message corresponds to the Event Log message you constructed in the `Created` event of the `FileSystemWatcher` control in the service, as shown in Figure 33-11.

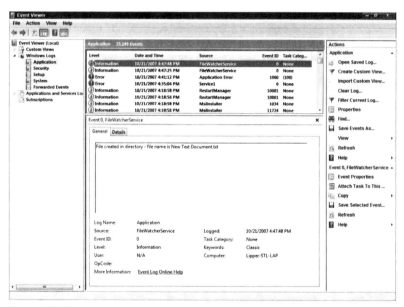

Figure 33-10

Debugging the Service

Because a service must be run from within the context of the Service Control Manager, rather than from within Visual Studio 2008, debugging a service is not as straightforward as debugging other Visual Studio 2008 application types. To debug a service, you must start the service and then attach a debugger to the process in which it is running. You can then debug the application using all of the standard debugging functionality of Visual Studio 2008.

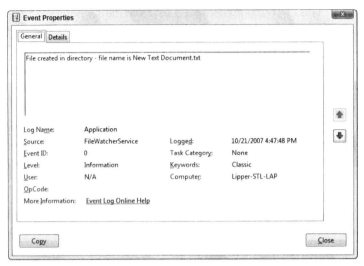

Figure 33-11

> **Don't attach to a process unless you know what the process is and understand the consequences of attaching to and possibly killing that process.**

To avoid going through this extra effort, you may want to test most of the code in your service in a standard Windows Forms application. This test-bed application can have the same components (FileSystemWatchers, EventLogs, Timers, and so on) as the Windows Service, and thus will be able to run the same logic in events. Once you have checked out the logic in this context, you can just copy and paste it into a Windows Service application.

However, sometimes the service itself needs to be debugged directly, so it is important to understand how to attach to the service's process and do direct debugging. You can only debug a service when it is running. When you attach the debugger to the service, you are interrupting it. The service is suspended for a short period while you attach to it. It is also interrupted when you place breakpoints and step through your code.

Attaching to the service's process enables you to debug most, but not all, of the service's code. For instance, because the service has already been started, you cannot debug the code in the service's OnStart method this way, or the code in the Main method that is used to load the service. To debug the OnStart event or any of the Visual Studio 2008 designer code, you have to add a dummy service and start that service first. In the dummy service, you would create an instance of the service that you want to debug. You can place some code in a Timer object and create the new instance of the object that you want to debug after 30 seconds or so. Allow enough time to attach to the debugger before the new instance is created. Meanwhile, place breakpoints in your startup code to debug those events, if desired.

Follow these steps to debug a service:

1. Install the service.

2. Start the service, either from the Service Control Manager, from Server Explorer, or from code.

3. In Visual Studio 2008, load the solution for the service. Then select Attach to Process from the Debug menu. The Attach to Process dialog box appears (see Figure 33-12).

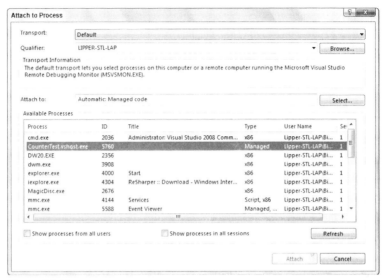

Figure 33-12

4. For a Windows Service, the desired process to attach to is not a foreground process; be sure to check the check box next to the "Show processes from all users" option.

5. In the Available Processes section, click the process indicated by the executable name for the service, and then click Attach.

6. You can now debug your process. Place a breakpoint in the code for the service at the place you want to debug. Cause the code in the service to execute (by placing a file in a monitored directory, for example).

7. When finished, select Stop Debugging from the Debug menu.

Let's go through an actual scenario, using your earlier CounterMonitor example. Bring up both the CounterMonitor project and the CounterTest project in separate instances of the Visual Studio 2008 IDE. Make sure that the CounterMonitor service has been started. It is best if you hear it beeping — that way you know it is working. If necessary, increment the performance counter to make it beep.

In the CounterMonitor project, select Debug ➪ Processes; you will get a dialog box that shows a list of the foreground processes on the system. Check the box next to Show System Processes. This will expand the list of processes, and one of the processes in the list will be CounterMonitor.exe. Highlight it and click Attach.

You will then get a dialog box asking you what program types you are interested in debugging. Because you are working solely within .NET, check the box next to Common Language Runtime and leave the rest unchecked. Click the OK button, and then click the Close button on the Processes dialog box. You are now attached to the process running CounterMonitor in the background.

Place a breakpoint on the first line of the `OnCustomCommand` event:

```
Timer1.Enabled = False
```

Now you are ready to check debugging. Bring up the `CounterTest` program and start it. Press one of the radio buttons to change the beep interval. You will hear the beeping stop because `CounterMonitor.exe` has entered debugging mode. Switch back to the `CounterMonitor` project. The cursor will be on the breakpoint line in `OnCustomCommand`. You can use the normal commands at this point to step through the code.

Summary

This chapter presented a general overview of what a Windows Service is and how to create one with Visual Basic. The techniques in this chapter can be used for many different types of background service, including the following:

- ❑ Automatically moving statistical files from a database server to a web server
- ❑ Pushing general files across computers and platforms
- ❑ A watchdog timer to ensure that a connection is always available
- ❑ An application to move and process FTP files, or indeed files received from any source

While Visual Basic cannot be used to create every type of Windows Service, it is effective at creating many of the most useful ones. The .NET Framework classes for Windows Services make this creation relatively straightforward. The designers generate much of the routine code needed, enabling you, as a developer, to concentrate on the code that is specific to your particular Windows Service.

34

Visual Basic and the Internet

In today's network-centric world, it is very likely that applications will need to work with other computers over a private network, the Internet, or both. This chapter details how to do the following:

- ❏ Download resources from the Web

- ❏ Design your own communication protocols

- ❏ Reuse Internet Explorer in your applications

Downloading Internet Resources

Downloading content from the Web is very easy, and in this chapter you will throw together a basic application before getting into some meatier topics. This application downloads HTML from a Web page and displays it in a text box. Later, you will learn how you can display HTML properly by hosting Internet Explorer (IE) directly using the `WebBrowser` control in Windows Forms applications, but for now, you will just use plain text.

In order to download a Web page, you need to be able to identify the remote page that you wish to download, make a request of the web server that can provide that page, listen for the response, and download the data for the resource.

The relevant classes for this example are `System.Uri`, `System.Net.WebRequest`, `System.Net .HttpWebRequest`, and `System.Net.HttpWebResponse`:

- ❏ `System.Uri` is a useful general-purpose class for expressing a Uniform Resource Identifier (URI). A Uniform Resource Locator (URL) is a type of URI (although, in reality, the terms are so confused that they are often used interchangeably). A URI, however, is "more than" a URL, which is why this .NET class is `Uri` and not `Url`. `System.` You will find that `Uri` has many properties for decoding a URI. For example, if you had a string such as `www.lipperweb.com:8080/myservices/myservice.asmx?WSDL`, you could use the `Port` property to extract the port number, the `Query` property to extract the query string, and so on.

❑ A `WebRequest` expresses some kind of Internet resource, whether it is located on the LAN or WAN. (A better name for this class would be `NetRequest`, as the classes are not specifically related to the Web protocol.)

❑ Protocol-specific descendants of `WebRequest` carry out the actual request: `HttpWebRequest` expresses an HTTP download and `FileWebRequest` expresses a file download — for example, `//c:/MyFile.txt`.

❑ An `HttpWebResponse` is returned once a connection to the web server has been made and the resource is available to download.

There are another two major classes related to working with the Internet in the .NET Framework: `System.Net.WebClient` and `System.Net.WebProxy`. `WebClient`, the latter being a helper class that wraps the request and response classes previously mentioned.

Because this is a professional-level book, this example shows you what to do behind the scenes — in effect, re-engineer what `WebClient` can do. You will look at `WebProxy` later, which enables you to explicitly define a proxy server to use for Internet communications.

Let's use these classes to build an application. Create a new Windows application, create a new form, and add controls to it as shown in Figure 34-1.

Figure 34-1

The control names are `textUrl`, `buttonGo`, and `textData`. The `Anchor` properties of the controls are set so that the form resizes properly. The `textUrl` should be set to `Top, Left, Right`. Set `buttonGo` to `Top, Right`, and set `textData` to `Top, Left, Bottom, Right`.

Add the following namespace import declarations to the form's code:

```
Imports System.IO
Imports System.Net
Imports System.Text
```

To keep the code simple, you will include all the functionality in the `Click` handler of `buttonGo`. Ideally, you want to break the code in the handler out to a separate method. This enriches the interface of the object and promotes good reuse.

The first thing you do here is create a new `System.Uri` based on the URL that the user enters into the text box:

```
Private Sub buttonGo_Click(ByVal sender As System.Object, _
  ByVal e As System.EventArgs) Handles buttonGo.Click

    Dim uri As New Uri(textUrl.Text)
```

Then, illustrate some of the useful properties of `System.Uri`:

```
Dim builder As New StringBuilder()
builder.Append("AbsolutePath: " & uri.AbsolutePath & VbCrLf)
builder.Append("AbsoluteUri: " & uri.AbsoluteUri & VbCrLf)
builder.Append("Host: " & uri.Host & VbCrLf)
builder.Append("HostNameType: " & uri.HostNameType.ToString() & _
            VbCrLf)
builder.Append("LocalPath: " & uri.LocalPath & VbCrLf)
builder.Append("PathAndQuery: " & uri.PathAndQuery & VbCrLf)
builder.Append("Port: " & uri.Port & VbCrLf)
builder.Append("Query: " & uri.Query & VbCrLf)
builder.Append("Scheme: " & uri.Scheme)

MessageBox.Show(builder.ToString())
```

The shared `Create` method of `System.Net.WebRequest` is used to create the actual object that you can use to download the Web resource. Note that you do not create an instance of `HttpWebRequest`; you are working with a return object of type `WebRequest`. However, you will actually be given an `HttpWebRequest` object, and `WebRequest` chooses the most appropriate class to return based on the URI. This enables you to build your own handlers for different network resources that can be used by consumers who simply supply an appropriate URL.

To make the request and get the response back from the server (so that ultimately you can access the data), you call the `GetResponse` method of `WebRequest`. In this case, you get an `HttpWebResponse` object — again, it is up to the implementation of the `WebRequest`-derived object, in this case `HttpWebRequest`, to return an object of the most suitable type.

If the request is not OK, then you will get an exception (which, for the sake of simplicity, you won't bother processing). If the request is OK, then you can get the length and type of the response using properties of the `WebResponse` object:

```
Dim request As WebRequest = WebRequest.Create(uri)
Dim response As WebResponse = request.GetResponse()
builder = New StringBuilder()
builder.Append("Request type: " & request.GetType().ToString() & VbCrLf)
builder.Append("Response type: " & response.GetType().ToString() & VbCrLf)
builder.Append("Content length: " & response.ContentLength & _
        " bytes" & VbCrLf)
builder.Append("Content type: " & response.ContentType & VbCrLf)

MessageBox.Show(builder.ToString())
```

It just remains for you to download the information. You can do this through a stream (`WebResponse` objects return a stream by overriding `GetResponseStream`); moreover, you can use a `System.IO` `.StreamReader` to download the whole lot in a single call by calling the `ReadToEnd` method. This method

1299

only downloads text, so if you want to download binary data, then you have to use the methods on the `Stream` object directly, or use a `System.IO.BinaryReader`:

```
Dim stream As Stream = response.GetResponseStream()
Dim reader As New StreamReader(stream)
Dim data As String = reader.ReadToEnd()

reader.Close()
stream.Close()

textData.Text = data
End Sub
```

If you run the application, enter a URL of www.reuters.com, and click Go, you will see debugging information about the URL, as shown in Figure 34-2.

Figure 34-2

This is a simple URL. The application tells you that the scheme is `http` and the host name type is `Dns`. If you enter an IP into the URL to be requested, rather than a host name, then this type will come back as `IPv4`. This tells you where the host name came from; in this case, it is a general Internet host name. Next, the application provides information about the response (see Figure 34-3).

Figure 34-3

The response data itself is shown in Figure 34-4.

Perhaps the most important exception to be aware of when using these classes is the `System.Net`
`.WebException` exception. If anything goes wrong on the `WebRequest.GetResponse` call, then this exception is thrown. Among other things, this exception provides access to the `WebResponse` object through the `Response` property. The `StatusCode` property of `WebResponse` tells you what actually happened through the `HttpStatusCode` enumeration. For example, `HttpStatusCode.NotFound` is the equivalent of the HTTP 404 status code.

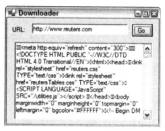

Figure 34-4

Sockets

There may be times when you need to transfer data across a network (either a private network or the Internet) but the existing techniques and protocols do not exactly suit your needs. For example, you cannot download resources using the techniques discussed at the start of this chapter, and you cannot use Web services (as described in Chapter 28) or remoting (as described in Chapter 29). When this happens, the best course of action is to roll your own protocol using *sockets*.

TCP/IP and, therefore, the Internet itself are based on sockets. The principle is simple: establish a port at one end and allow clients to "plug in" to that port from the other end. Once the connection is made, applications can send and receive data through a stream. For example, HTTP nearly always operates on port 80, so a web server opens a socket on port 80 and waits for incoming connections (Web browsers, unless told otherwise, attempt to connect to port 80 in order to make a request of that web server).

In .NET, sockets are implemented in the `System.Net.Sockets` namespace and use classes from `System.Net` and `System.IO` to get the stream classes. Although working with sockets can be a little tricky outside of .NET, the framework includes some superb classes that enable you to open a socket for inbound connections (`System.Net.TcpListener`) and for communication between two open sockets (`System.Net.TcpClient`). These two classes, in combination with some threading shenanigans, enable you to build your own protocol through which you can send any data you like. With your own protocol, you have ultimate control over the communication.

To demonstrate these techniques, you are going to build Wrox Messenger, a very basic instant messenger application similar to MSN Messenger.

Building the Application

You will wrap all the functionality of your application into a single Windows application, which will act as both a server that waits for inbound connections and a client that has established outbound connections.

Create a new project called WroxMessenger. Change the title of `Form1` to `Wrox Messenger` and add a `TextBox` control called `textConnectTo` and a `Button` control called `buttonConnect`. The form should appear as shown in Figure 34-5.

You will learn more about this in greater detail later, but for now, it is very important that all of your UI code runs in the same thread, and that the thread is actually the main application that creates and runs `Form1`.

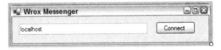

Figure 34-5

To keep track of what is happening, you will add a field to `Form1` that enables you to store the ID of the startup thread and report that ID on the caption. This helps provide a context for the thread/UI issues discussed later. You also need some namespace imports and a constant specifying the ID of the default port. Add the following code to `Form1`:

```
Imports System.Net
Imports System.Net.Sockets
Imports System.Threading

Public Class Form1

    Private Shared _mainThreadId As Integer
    Public Const ServicePort As Integer = 10101
```

Next, create a `New` method for Form1 (`Form1.vb`) and add this code to the constructor that populates the field and changes the caption:

```
Public Sub New()

    ' This call is required by the Windows Form Designer.
    InitializeComponent()

    ' Add any initialization after the InitializeComponent() call.
    _mainThreadId = System.Threading.Thread.CurrentThread.GetHashCode()

    Text &= "-" & _mainThreadId.ToString()
End Sub
```

Note that you can get to the `Form1.vb` file's `New` method by using Visual Studio and selecting `Form1` and `New` in the uppermost drop-downs in the document window. This causes the `Form1.vb` file's `New` method to be created on your behalf.

To listen for incoming connections, you will create a separate class called `Listener`. This class uses an instance of `System.Net.Sockets.TcpListener` to wait for incoming connections. Specifically, it opens a TCP port that *any* client can connect to — sockets are not platform-specific. Although connections are always made on a specific, known port, the actual communication takes place on a port of the TCP/IP subsystem's choosing, which means you can support many inbound connections at once, despite the fact that each of them connects to the same port. Sockets are an open standard available on pretty much any platform. For example, if you publish the specification for your protocol, then developers working on Linux can connect to your Wrox Messenger service.

When you detect an inbound connection, you are given a `System.Net.Sockets.TcpClient` object. This is your gateway to the remote client. To send and receive data, you need to obtain a `System.Net` `.NetworkStream` object (returned through a call to `GetStream` on `TcpClient`), which returns a stream that you can use.

Create a new class called `Listener`. This thread needs members to hold an instance of a `System` `.Threading.Thread` object, and a reference back to the `Form1` class that is the main form in the application. Not covered here is how to spin up and down threads, or synchronization. (Refer to Chapter 26 if you need more information about that.)

Here is the basic code for the `Listener` class:

```
Imports System.Net.Sockets
Imports System.Threading

Public Class Listener

  Private _main As Form1
  Private _listener As TcpListener
  Private _thread As Thread

  Public Sub New(ByVal main As Form1)
    _main = main
  End Sub

  Public Sub SpinUp()

    ' create and start the new thread...
    _thread = New Thread(AddressOf ThreadEntryPoint)
    _thread.Start()
  End Sub
End Class
```

The obvious missing method here is `ThreadEntryPoint`. This is where you need to create the socket and wait for inbound connections. When you get them, you are given a `TcpClient` object, which you pass back to `Form1`, where the conversation window can be created. You create this method in the `Listener.vb` class file.

To create the socket, create an instance of `TcpListener` and give it a port. In your application, the port you are going to use is `10101`. This port should be free on your computer, but if the debugger breaks on an exception when you instantiate `TcpListener` or call `Start`, then try another port. Once you have done that and called `Start` to configure the object to listen for connections, you drop into an infinite loop and call `AcceptTcpClient`. This method blocks until the socket is closed or a connection becomes available. If you get `Nothing` back, then either the socket is closed or there is a problem, so you drop out of the thread. If you get something back, then you pass the `TcpClient` over to `Form1` through a call to the (not yet built) `ReceiveInboundConnection` method:

```
' ThreadEntryPoint...
Protected Sub ThreadEntryPoint()

  ' Create a socket...
  _listener = New TcpListener(Form1.ServicePort)
  _listener.Start()

  ' Loop infinitely, waiting for connections.
  Do While True

    ' Get a connection...
```

```
        Dim client As TcpClient = _listener.AcceptTcpClient()
        If client Is Nothing Then
         Exit Do
        End If
        ' Process it...
        _main.ReceiveInboundConnection(client)
        Loop
    End Sub
```

It is in the ReceiveInboundConnection method that you create the Conversation form that the user can use to send messages.

Creating conversation windows

When building Windows Forms applications that support threading, there is always the possibility of running into a problem with the Windows messaging subsystem. This is a very old part of Windows that powers the Windows user interface (the idea has been around since version 1.0 of the platform, although the implementation on modern Windows versions is far removed from the original).

Even those who are not familiar with old-school Windows programming, such as MFC, Win32, or even Win16 development, should be familiar with events. When you move a mouse over a form, you get MouseMove events. When you close a form, you get a Closed event. There is a mapping between these events and the messages that Windows passes around to support the actual display of the windows. For example, whenever you receive a MouseMove event, a message called WM_MOUSEMOVE is sent to the window by Windows, in response to the mouse driver. In .NET and other rapid application development (RAD) environments such as VB and Delphi, this message is converted into an event that you can write code against.

Although this is getting way off the topic — you know how to build Windows Forms applications by now and don't need the details of messages such as WM_NCHITTEST or WM_PAINT — it has an important implication. In effect, Windows creates a message queue for each thread into which it posts the messages that the thread's windows have to work with. This queue is looped on a virtually constant basis, and the messages are distributed to the appropriate window (remember that small controls such as buttons and text boxes are also windows). In .NET, these messages are turned into events, but unless the message queue is looped, the messages do not get through.

Suppose Windows needs to paint a window. It posts a WM_PAINT message to the queue. A message loop implemented on the main thread of the process containing the window detects the message and dispatches it on to the appropriate window, where it is processed. Now suppose that the queue is not looped. The message is never picked up and the window is never painted.

In a Windows application, a single thread is usually responsible for message dispatch. This thread is typically (but not necessarily) the main application thread — the one that is created when the process is first created. If you create windows in a different thread, then that new thread has to support the message dispatch loop so that messages destined for the windows get through. However, with Listener, you have no code for processing the message loop, and there is little point in writing any because the next time you call AcceptTcpClient, you are going to block, and everything will stop working.

The trick, therefore, is to create the windows only in the main application thread, which is the thread that created Form1 and is processing the messages for all the windows created in this thread. You can pass calls from one thread to the other by calling the Invoke method of Form1.

This is where things start to get complicated. There is a very lot of code to write to get to a point where you can see that the socket connection has been established and get conversation windows to appear. Here is what you need to do:

- ❏ Create a new Conversation form. This form needs controls for displaying the total content of the conversation, plus a TextBox control for adding new messages.

- ❏ The Conversation window needs to be able to send and receive messages through its own thread.

- ❏ Form1 needs to be able to initiate new connections. This will be done in a separate thread that is managed by the thread pool. When the connection has been established, a new Conversation window needs to be created and configured.

- ❏ Form1 also needs to receive inbound connections. When it gets one of these, a new Conversation must be created and configured.

Let's look at each of these challenges.

Creating the Conversation Form

The simplest place to start is to build the new Conversation form, which needs three TextBox controls (textUsername, textMessages, and textMessage) and a Button control (buttonSend), as shown in Figure 34-6.

Figure 34-6

This class requires a number of fields and an enumeration. It needs fields to hold the username of the user (which you will default to Evjen), the underlying TcpClient, and the NetworkStream returned by that client. The enumeration indicates the direction of the connection (which will help you when debugging):

```
Imports System.Net
Imports System.Net.Sockets
Imports System.Text
Imports System.Threading
Imports System.Runtime.Serialization.Formatters.Binary

Public Class Conversation

    Private _username As String = "Evjen"
    Private _client As TcpClient
    Private _stream As NetworkStream
```

```
    Private _direction As ConversationDirection

    Public Enum ConversationDirection As Integer
        Inbound = 0
        Outbound = 1
    End Enum
```

At this point, we won't look into the issues surrounding establishing a thread for exchanging messages, but we will look at implementing the `ConfigureClient` method. This method eventually does more work than this, but for now it sets a couple of fields and calls `UpdateCaption`:

```
Public Sub ConfigureClient(ByVal client As TcpClient, _
              ByVal direction As ConversationDirection)
    ' Set it up...
    _client = client
    _direction = direction

    ' Update the window...
    UpdateCaption()
End Sub

Protected Sub UpdateCaption()

    ' Set the text.
    Dim builder As New StringBuilder(_username)
    builder.Append(" - ")
    builder.Append(_direction.ToString())
    builder.Append(" - ")
    builder.Append(Thread.CurrentThread.GetHashCode())
    builder.Append(" - ")

    If Not _client Is Nothing Then
        builder.Append("Connected")
    Else
        builder.Append("Not connected")
    End If

    Text = builder.ToString()
End Sub
```

Note a debugging issue to deal with: if you are connecting to a conversation on the same machine, then you need a way to change the name of the user sending each message; otherwise, things get confusing. That is what the topmost `TextBox` control is for. In the constructor, set the text for the `textUsername.Text` property:

```
Public Sub New()

    ' This call is required by the Windows Form Designer.
    InitializeComponent()

    ' Add any initialization after the InitializeComponent() call.
    textUsername.Text = _username
End Sub
```

On the `TextChanged` event for this control, update the caption and the internal _username field:

```
Private Sub textUsername_TextChanged(ByVal sender As System.Object, _
              ByVal e As System.EventArgs) _
              Handles textUsername.TextChanged

    _username = textUsername.Text
    UpdateCaption()
End Sub
```

Initiating Connections

`Form1` needs to be able to both initiate connections and receive inbound connections — the application is both a client and a server. You have already created some of the server portion by creating `Listener`; now you will look at the client side.

The general rule when working with sockets is that any time you send anything over the wire, you must perform the actual communication in a separate thread. Virtually all calls to send and receive do so in a blocking manner; that is, they block until data is received, block until all data is sent, and so on.

If threads are used well, then the UI will keep running as normal, irrespective of the problems that may occur during transmitting and receiving. This is why in the `InitiateConnection` method on `Form1`, you defer processing to another method called `InitiateConnectionThreadEntryPoint`, which is called from a new thread:

```
Public Sub InitiateConnection()
    InitiateConnection(textConnectTo.Text)
End Sub

Public Sub InitiateConnection(ByVal hostName As String)

    ' Give it to the threadpool to do...
    ThreadPool.QueueUserWorkItem(AddressOf _
    Me.InitiateConnectionThreadEntryPoint, hostName)
End Sub

Private Sub buttonConnect_Click(ByVal sender As System.Object, _
              ByVal e As System.EventArgs) _
              Handles buttonConnect.Click

    InitiateConnection()
End Sub
```

Inside the thread, you try to convert the host name that you are given into an IP address (`localhost` is used as the host name in the demonstration, but it could be the name of a machine on the local network or a host name on the Internet). This is done through the shared `GetHostEntry` method on `System.Net.Dns`, and returns a `System.Net.IPHostEntry` object. Because a host name can point to multiple IP addresses, you will just use the first one that you are given. You take this address expressed as an IP (for example, `192.168.0.4`) and combine it with the port number to get a new `System.Net.IPEndPoint`. Then, you create a new `TcpClient` from this `IPEndPoint` and try to connect.

If at any time an exception is thrown (which can happen because the name could not be resolved or the connection could not be established), you pass the exception to `HandleInitiateConnectionException`. If it succeeds, then you pass it to `ProcessOutboundConnection`. Both of these methods will be implemented shortly:

```vb
Private Sub InitiateConnectionThreadEntryPoint(ByVal state As Object)

    Try
        ' Get the host name...
        Dim hostName As String = CStr(state)

        ' Resolve...
        Dim hostEntry As IPHostEntry = Dns.GetHostEntry(hostName)
        If Not hostEntry Is Nothing Then

            ' Create an end point for the first address.
            Dim endPoint As New IPEndPoint(hostEntry.AddressList(0), ServicePort)

            ' Create a TCP client...
            Dim client As New TcpClient()
            client.Connect(endPoint)

            ' Create the connection window...
            ProcessOutboundConnection(client)
        Else
            Throw New ApplicationException("Host '" & hostName & _
                "' could not be resolved.")
        End If
    Catch ex As Exception
        HandleInitiateConnectionException(ex)
    End Try
End Sub
```

When it comes to `HandleInitiateConnectionException`, you start to see the inter-thread UI problems that were mentioned earlier. When there is a problem with the exception, you need to tell the user, which means you need to move the exception from the thread-pool-managed thread into the main application thread. The principle for this is the same; you need to create a delegate and call that delegate through the form's `Invoke` method. This method does all the hard work in marshaling the call across to the other thread.

Here is what the delegates look like. They have the same parameters of the calls themselves. As a naming convention, it is a good idea to use the same name as the method and tack the word `Delegate` on the end:

```vb
Public Class Form1

    Private Shared _mainThreadId As Integer
    ' delegates...
    Protected Delegate Sub HandleInitiateConnectionExceptionDelegate( _
                                    ByVal ex As Exception)
```

In the constructor for `Form1`, you capture the thread caller's thread ID and store it in `_mainThreadId`. Here is a method that compares the captured ID with the ID of the current thread:

```vb
Public Shared Function IsMainThread() As Boolean
    If Thread.CurrentThread.GetHashCode() = _mainThreadId Then
```

```
        Return True
    Else
        Return False
    End If
End Function
```

The first thing you do at the top of `HandleInitiateConnectionException` is check the thread ID. If it does not match, then you create the delegate and call it. Notice that you set the delegate to call back into the same method because the second time it is called, you would have moved to the main thread; therefore, `IsMainThread` returns `True`, and you can process the exception properly:

```
Protected Sub HandleInitiateConnectionException(ByVal ex As Exception)

    ' main thread?
    If IsMainThread() = False Then

        ' Create and call...
        Dim args(0) As Object
        args(0) = ex
        Invoke(New HandleInitiateConnectionExceptionDelegate(AddressOf _
            HandleInitiateConnectionException), args)

        ' return
        Return
    End If

    ' Show it.
    MessageBox.Show(ex.GetType().ToString() & ":" & ex.Message)
End Sub
```

The result is that when the call comes in from the thread-pool-managed thread, `IsMainThread` returns `False`, and the delegate is created and called. When the method is entered again as a result of the delegate call, `IsMainThread` returns `True`, and you see the message box.

When it comes to `ProcessOutboundConnection`, you have to again jump into the main UI thread. However, the magic behind this method is implemented in a separate method called `Process-Connection`, which can handle either inbound or outbound connections. Here is the delegate:

```
Public Class Form1

    Private Shared _mainThreadId As Integer
    Private _listener As Listener

    Protected Delegate Sub ProcessConnectionDelegate(ByVal client As _
        TcpClient, ByVal direction As Conversation.ConversationDirection)
    Protected Delegate Sub HandleInitiateConnectionExceptionDelegate(ByVal _
        ex As Exception)
```

Here is the method itself, which creates the new Conversation form and calls the `ConfigureClient` method:

```
Protected Sub ProcessConnection(ByVal client As TcpClient, _
    ByVal direction As Conversation.ConversationDirection)
```

```
' Do you have to move to another thread?
If IsMainThread() = False Then

    ' Create and call...
    Dim args(1) As Object
    args(0) = client
    args(1) = direction
    Invoke(New ProcessConnectionDelegate(AddressOf ProcessConnection), args)

    Return
End If

' Create the conversation window...
Dim conversation As New Conversation()
conversation.Show()
conversation.ConfigureClient(client, direction)
End Sub
```

Of course, `ProcessOutboundConnection` needs to defer to `ProcessConnection`:

```
Public Sub ProcessOutboundConnection(ByVal client As TcpClient)
    ProcessConnection(client, Conversation.ConversationDirection.Outbound)
End Sub
```

Now that you can connect to something on the client side, let's look at how to receive connections (on the server side).

Receiving Inbound Connections

You have already built `Listener`, but you have not created an instance of it or spun up its thread to wait for incoming connections. To do that, you need a field in `Form1` to hold an instance of the object. You also need to tweak the constructor. Here is the field:

```
Public Class Form1

    Private _mainThreadId As Integer
    Private _listener As Listener
```

Here is the new code that needs to be added to the constructor:

```
Public Sub New()

    ' This call is required by the Windows Form Designer.
    InitializeComponent()

    ' Add any initialization after the InitializeComponent() call.
    _mainThreadId = System.Threading.Thread.CurrentThread.GetHashCode()

    Text &= "-" & _mainThreadId.ToString()

    ' listener...
    _listener = New Listener(Me)
    _listener.SpinUp()
End Sub
```

1310

When inbound connections are received, you get a new `TcpClient` object. This is passed back to `Form1` through the `ReceiveInboundConnection` method. This method, like `ProcessOutboundConnection`, defers to `ProcessConnection`. Because `ProcessConnection` already handles the issue of moving the call to the main application thread, `ReceiveInboundConnection` looks like this:

```
Public Sub ReceiveInboundConnection(ByVal client As TcpClient)
    ProcessConnection(client, Conversation.ConversationDirection.Inbound)
End Sub
```

If you run the project now, you should be able to click the Connect button and see two windows — Inbound and Outbound (see Figure 34-7).

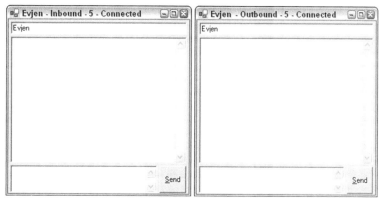

Figure 34-7

If you close all three windows, the application keeps running because you have not written code to close down the listener thread, and having an open thread like this keeps the application open. Select Debug ⇨ Stop Debugging in Visual Studio to close the application down by killing all running threads.

By clicking the Connect button, you are calling `InitiateConnection`. This spins up a new thread in the pool that resolves the given host name (`localhost`) into an IP address. This IP address, in combination with a port number, is then used in the creation of a `TcpClient` object. If the connection can be made, then `ProcessOutboundConnection` is called, which results in the first of the conversation windows being created and marked as "outbound."

This example is somewhat artificial, as the two instances of Wrox Messenger should be running on separate computers. On the remote computer (if you are connecting to `localhost`, this will be the same computer), a connection is received through the `AcceptTcpClient` method of `TcpListener`. This results in a call to `ReceiveInboundConnection`, which in turn results in the creation of the second conversation window, this time marked as "inbound."

Sending messages

The next step is to determine how to exchange messages between the two conversation windows. You already have a `TcpClient` in each case, so all you have to do is send binary data down the wire on one side and pick it up at the other end. The two conversation windows act as both client and server, so both need to be able to send and receive.

You have three challenges to meet:

❑   You need to establish one thread to send data and another thread to receive data.

❑   Data sent and received needs to be reported back to the user so that he or she can follow the conversation.

❑   The data that you want to send has to be converted into a wire-ready format, which in .NET terms usually means serialization.

The power of sockets enables you to define whatever protocol you like for data transmission. If you wanted to build your own SMTP server, you could implement the (publicly available) specifications, set up a listener to wait for connections on port 25 (the standard port for SMTP), wait for data to come in, process it, and return responses as appropriate.

It is best to work in this way when building protocols. Unless there are very strong reasons for not doing so, make your server as open as possible: don't tie it to a specific platform. This is how things are done on the Internet. To an extent, things like Web Services should negate the need to build your own protocols; as you go forward, you will rely instead on the "remote object available to local client" paradigm.

Now it is time to consider the idea of using the serialization features of .NET to transmit data across the network. After all, you have already seen this in action with Web Services and remoting. You can take an object in .NET, use serialization to convert it to a string of bytes, and expose that string to a Web Service consumer, to a remoting client, or even to a file.

Chapter 29 discussed the `BinaryFormatter` and `SoapFormatter` classes. You could use either of those classes, or create your own custom formatter, to convert data for transmission and reception. In this case, you are going to create a new class called `Message` and use `BinaryFormatter` to crunch it down into a wire-ready format and convert it back again for processing.

This approach is not ideal from the perspective of interoperability, because the actual protocol used is lost in the implementation of the .NET Framework, rather than being under your absolute control.

If you want to build an open protocol, this is *not* the best way to do it. Unfortunately, the best way is beyond the scope of this book, but a good place to start is to look at existing protocols and standards and model any protocol on their approach. `BinaryFormatter` provides a quick-and-dirty approach, which is why you are going to use it here.

The Message Class

The `Message` class contains two fields, `_username` and `_message`, which form the entirety of the data that you want to transmit. The code for this class follows; note how the `Serializable` attribute is applied to it so that `BinaryFormatter` can change it into a wire-ready form. You are also providing a new implementation of `ToString`:

```
Imports System.Text

<Serializable()> Public Class Message
```

```vb
Private _username As String
Private _message As String

Public Sub New(ByVal name As String)
   _username = name
End Sub

Public Sub New(ByVal name As String, ByVal message As String)
   _username = name
   _message = message
End Sub

Public Overrides Function ToString() As String
   Dim builder As New StringBuilder(_username)
   builder.Append(" says:")
   builder.Append(ControlChars.CrLf)
   builder.Append(_message)
   builder.Append(ControlChars.CrLf)

   Return builder.ToString()
End Function

End Class
```

Now all you have to do is spin up two threads, one for transmission and one for reception, updating the display. You need two threads *per conversation*, so if you have 10 conversations open, you need 20 threads plus the main UI thread, plus the thread running `TcpListener`.

Receiving messages is easy. When calling `Deserialize` on `BinaryFormatter`, you give it the stream returned to you from `TcpClient`. If there is no data, then this blocks. If there is data, then it is decoded into a `Message` object that you can display. If you have multiple messages coming down the pipe, then `BinaryFormatter` keeps processing them until the pipe is empty. Here is the method for this, which should be added to `Conversation`. Remember that you haven't implemented `ShowMessage` yet:

```vb
Protected Sub ReceiveThreadEntryPoint()

   ' Create a formatter...
   Dim formatter As New BinaryFormatter()

   ' Loop
   Do While True
      ' Receive...
      Dim message As Message = formatter.Deserialize(_stream)

      If message Is Nothing Then
         Exit Do
      End If

      ' Show it...
      ShowMessage(message)
   Loop
End Sub
```

Transmitting messages is a bit more complex. You want a queue (managed by a System.Collections .Queue) of outgoing messages. Every second, you will examine the state of the queue. If you find any messages, then you use BinaryFormatter to transmit them. Because you will be accessing this queue from multiple threads, you use a System.Threading.ReaderWriterLock to control access. To minimize the amount of time you spend inside locked code, you quickly transfer the contents of the shared queue into a private queue that you can process at your leisure. This enables the client to continue to add messages to the queue through the UI, even though existing messages are being sent by the transmit thread.

First, add the following members to Conversation:

```
Public Class Conversation

    Private _username As String = "Evjen"
    Private _client As TcpClient
    Private _stream As NetworkStream
    Private _direction As ConversationDirection
    Private _receiveThread As Thread
    Private _transmitThread As Thread
    Private _transmitQueue As New Queue()
    Private _transmitLock As New ReaderWriterLock()
```

Now, add this method again to Conversation:

```
Protected Sub TransmitThreadEntryPoint()

    ' Create a formatter...
    Dim formatter As New BinaryFormatter()
    Dim workQueue As New Queue()

    ' Loop
    Do While True

        ' Wait for the signal...
        Thread.Sleep(1000)

        ' Go through the queue...
        _transmitLock.AcquireWriterLock(-1)
        Dim message As Message
        workQueue.Clear()

        For Each message In _transmitQueue
            workQueue.Enqueue(message)
        Next

        _transmitQueue.Clear()
        _transmitLock.ReleaseWriterLock()

        ' Loop the outbound messages...
        For Each message In workQueue

            ' Send it...
            formatter.Serialize(_stream, message)
```

```
        Next

    Loop

End Sub
```

When you want to send a message, you call one version of the `SendMessage` method. Here are all of the implementations, and the `Click` handler for `buttonSend`:

```
Private Sub buttonSend_Click(ByVal sender As System.Object, _
    ByVal e As System.EventArgs) Handles buttonSend.Click

    SendMessage(textMessage.Text)
End Sub

Public Sub SendMessage(ByVal message As String)
    SendMessage(_username, message)
End Sub

Public Sub SendMessage(ByVal username As String, ByVal message As String)
    SendMessage(New Message(username, message))
End Sub

Public Sub SendMessage(ByVal message As Message)
    ' Queue it
    _transmitLock.AcquireWriterLock(-1)
    _transmitQueue.Enqueue(message)
    _transmitLock.ReleaseWriterLock()

    ' Show it...
    ShowMessage(message)
End Sub
```

`ShowMessage` is responsible for updating `textMessages` so that the conversation remains up to date (notice how you add the message both when you send it and when you receive it so that both parties have an up-to-date thread). This is a UI feature, so it is good practice to pass it over to the main application thread for processing. Although the call in response to the button click comes off the main application thread, the one from inside `ReceiveThreadEntryPoint` does not. Here is what the delegate looks like:

```
Public Class Conversation

    ' members...
    Private _username As String = "Evjen"
    Private _client As TcpClient
    Private _stream As NetworkStream
    Private _direction As ConversationDirection
    Private _receiveThread As Thread
    Private _transmitThread As Thread
    Private _transmitQueue As New Queue()
    Private _transmitLock As New ReaderWriterLock()

    Public Delegate Sub ShowMessageDelegate(ByVal message As Message)
```

Here is the method implementation:

```
Public Sub ShowMessage(ByVal message As Message)
    ' Thread?
    If Form1.IsMainThread() = False Then

        ' Run...
        Dim args(0) As Object
        args(0) = message
        Invoke(New ShowMessageDelegate(AddressOf ShowMessage), args)

        ' Return...
        Return
    End If

    ' Show it...
    textMessages.Text &= message.ToString()
End Sub
```

All that remains now is to spin up the threads. This should be done from within `ConfigureClient`. Before the threads are spun up, you need to obtain the stream and store it in the private _stream field. After that, you create new `Thread` objects as normal:

```
Public Sub ConfigureClient(ByVal client As TcpClient, _
        ByVal direction As ConversationDirection)

    ' Set it up...
    _client = client
    _direction = direction

    ' Update the window...
    UpdateCaption()
    ' Get the stream...
    _stream = _client.GetStream()

    ' Spin up the threads...
    _transmitThread = New Thread(AddressOf TransmitThreadEntryPoint)
    _transmitThread.Start()
    _receiveThread = New Thread(AddressOf ReceiveThreadEntryPoint)
    _receiveThread.Start()
End Sub
```

At this point, you should be able to connect and exchange messages, as shown in Figure 34-8.

Note that the screenshots show the username of the inbound connection as Tuija. This was done with the textUsername text box so that you can follow which half of the conversation comes from where.

Shutting down the application

You have yet to solve the problem of neatly closing the application, or, in fact, dealing with one person in the conversation closing down his or her window, indicating a wish to end the conversation. When the process ends (whether neatly or forcefully), Windows automatically mops up any open connections and frees up the port for other processes.

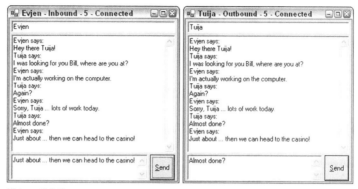

Figure 34-8

Suppose you have two computers, one window per computer, as you would in a production environment. When you close your window, you are indicating that you want to end the conversation. You need to close the socket and spin down the transmission and reception threads. At the other end, you should be able to detect that the socket has been closed, spin down the threads, and tell the user that the other user has terminated the conversation.

This all hinges on being able to detect when the socket has been closed. Unfortunately, Microsoft has made this very hard due to the design of the `TcpClient` class. `TcpClient` effectively encapsulates a `System.Net.Sockets.Socket` class, providing methods for helping to manage the connection lifetime and communication streams. However, `TcpClient` does not have a method or property that answers the question, "Am I still connected?" Therefore, you need get hold of the `Socket` object that `TcpClient` is wrapping, and then you can use its `Connected` property to determine whether the connection has been closed.

`TcpClient` does support a property called `Client` that returns a `Socket`, but this property is protected, meaning you can only access it by inheriting a new class from `TcpClient`. There is another way, though: You can use *reflection* to get at the property and call it without having to inherit a new class.

Microsoft claims that this is a legitimate technique, even though it appears to violate every rule in the book about encapsulation. Reflection is designed not only for finding out which types are available, and learning which methods and properties each type supports, but also for invoking those methods and properties whether they're protected or public. Therefore, in `Conversation`, you need to store the socket:

```
Public Class Conversation

    Private _username As String = "Evjen"
    Private _client As TcpClient
    Private _socket As Socket
```

In `ConfigureClient`, you use `Reflection` to peek into the `Type` object for `TcpClient` and dig out the `Client` property. Once you have a `System.Reflection.PropertyInfo` for this property, you can retrieve its value by using the `GetValue` method. Don't forget to import the `System.Reflection` namespace:

```
Public Sub ConfigureClient(ByVal client As TcpClient, _
            ByVal direction As ConversationDirection)
```

1317

```
    ' Set it up...
    _client = client
    _direction = direction

    ' Update the window...
    UpdateCaption()

    ' Get the stream...
    _stream = _client.GetStream()
    ' Get the socket through reflection...
    Dim propertyInfo As PropertyInfo = _
        _client.GetType().GetProperty("Client", _
        BindingFlags.Instance Or BindingFlags.Public)

    If Not propertyInfo Is Nothing Then
        _socket = propertyInfo.GetValue(_client, Nothing)
    Else
        Throw New Exception("Could not retrieve Client property from TcpClient")
    End If
    ' Spin up the threads...
    _transmitThread = New Thread(AddressOf TransmitThreadEntryPoint)
    _transmitThread.Start()
    _receiveThread = New Thread(AddressOf ReceiveThreadEntryPoint)
    _receiveThread.Start()
End Sub
```

Applications are able to check the state of the socket either by detecting when an error occurs because you have tried to send data over a closed socket or by actually checking whether the socket is connected. If you either do not have a Socket available in socket (that is, it is Nothing) or you have one and it tells you that you are disconnected, then you give the user some feedback and exit the loop. By exiting the loop, you effectively exit the thread, which is a neat way of quitting the thread. Notice as well that you might not have a window at this point (you might be the one who closed the conversation by closing the window), so you wrap the UI call in a Try Catch (the other side will see a <disconnect> message):

```
Protected Sub TransmitThreadEntryPoint()
    ' Create a formatter...
    Dim formatter As New BinaryFormatter()
    Dim workQueue As New Queue()
    ' name...
    Thread.CurrentThread.Name = "Tx-" & _direction.ToString()
    ' Loop...
    Do While True
        ' Wait for the signal...
        Thread.Sleep(1000)
        ' Disconnected?
        If _socket Is Nothing OrElse _socket.Connected = False Then
            Try
                ShowMessage(New Message("Debug", "<disconnect>"))
            Catch
            End Try
```

```
Exit Do
    End If
    ' Go through the queue...
```

ReceiveThreadEntryPoint also needs some massaging. When the socket is closed, the stream is no longer valid and so BinaryFormatter.Deserialize throws an exception. Likewise, you quit the loop and therefore neatly quit the thread:

```
Protected Sub ReceiveThreadEntryPoint()
    ' Create a formatter...
    Dim formatter As New BinaryFormatter()

    ' Loop...
    Do While True

        ' Receive...
        Dim message As Message = Nothing
        Try
            message = formatter.Deserialize(_stream)
        Catch
        End Try

        If message Is Nothing Then
            Exit Do
        End If
        ' Show it...
        ShowMessage(message)
    Loop
End Sub
```

How do you deal with actually closing the socket? You tweak the Dispose method of the form itself (you can find this method in the Windows-generated code section of the file), and if you have a _socket object, you close it:

```
Protected Overloads Overrides Sub Dispose(ByVal disposing As Boolean)
    If disposing Then
        If Not (components Is Nothing) Then
            components.Dispose()
        End If
    End If

    ' Close the socket...
    If Not _socket Is Nothing Then
        _socket.Close()
        _socket = Nothing
    End If

    MyBase.Dispose(disposing)
End Sub
```

Figure 34-9

Now you will be able to start a conversation; and if one of the windows is closed, then `<disconnect>` will appear in the other, as shown in Figure 34-9. In the background, the four threads (one transmit and one receive per window) will spin down properly.

The application itself still will not close properly, even if you close all the windows, because you need to stop the `Listener` when `Form1` closes. To do so, make `Listener` implement `IDisposable`:

```
Public Class Listener
   Implements IDisposable

   Public Sub Dispose() Implements System.IDisposable.Dispose

      ' Stop it...
      Finalize()
      GC.SuppressFinalize(Me)

   End Sub

   Protected Overrides Sub Finalize()

      ' Stop the listener...
      If Not _listener Is Nothing Then
         _listener.Stop()
         _listener = Nothing
      End If

      ' Stop the thread...
      If Not _thread Is Nothing Then
         _thread.Join()
         _thread = Nothing
      End If

      ' Call up...
      MyBase.Finalize()

   End Sub
```

Now all that remains is to call `Dispose` from within `Form1`. A good place to do this is in the `Closed` event handler:

```
Protected Overrides Sub OnClosed(ByVal e As System.EventArgs)
    If Not _listener Is Nothing Then
        _listener.Dispose()
        _listener = Nothing
    End If
End Sub
```

After the code is compiled again, the application can be closed.

Using Internet Explorer in Your Applications

A common requirement of modern applications is to display HTML files and other files commonly used with Internet applications. Although the .NET Framework has considerable support for common image formats (such as GIF, JPEG, and PNG), working with HTML used to be a touch trickier in versions 1.0 and 1.1 of the .NET Framework. Life was made considerably easier with the inclusion of the `WebBrowser` control in the .NET Framework 2.0.

> **For information on how to accomplish this task using the .NET Framework 1.0 or 1.1, please review the second and third editions of this book.**

You don't want to have to write your own HTML parser, so using this control to display HTML pages is, in most cases, your only option. Microsoft's Internet Explorer was implemented as a standalone component comprising a parser and a renderer, all packaged up in a neat COM object. The `WebBrowser` control "simply" utilizes this COM object. There is nothing to stop you from using this COM object directly in your own applications, but it is considerably easier to use the newer control for hosting Web pages in your applications.

Yes, a COM object. There is no managed version of Internet Explorer for use with .NET. Considering that writing an HTML parser is extremely hard, and writing a renderer is extremely hard, it is easy to conclude that it's much easier to use interop to get to Internet Explorer in .NET applications than to have Microsoft try to rewrite a managed version of it just for .NET. Maybe we will see "Internet Explorer .NET" within the next year or two, but for now you have to use interop.

Windows Forms and HTML — no problem!

These sections demonstrate how to build a mini-browser application. Sometimes you might want to display HTML pages without giving users UI widgets such as a toolbar or the capability to enter their own URLs. You might also want to use the control in a nonvisual manner. For example, using the `WebBrowser` control, you can retrieve Web pages and then print the results without ever needing to display the contents. Let's start, though, by first creating a simple form that contains only a `TextBox` control and a `WebBrowser` control.

Allowing Simple Web Browsing in Your Windows Application

The first step is to create a new Windows Forms application called MiniBrowser. On the default form, place a single `TextBox` control and the `WebBrowser` control, as shown in Figure 34-10.

Figure 34-10

The idea is that when the end user presses the Enter key (Return key), the URL entered in the text box will be the HTML page that is retrieved and displayed in the `WebBrowser` control. To accomplish this task, use the following code for your form:

```
Public Class Form1

    Private Sub TextBox1_KeyPress(ByVal sender As Object, _
        ByVal e As System.Windows.Forms.KeyPressEventArgs) Handles TextBox1.KeyPress

        If e.KeyChar = Chr(13) Then
            WebBrowser1.Navigate(TextBox1.Text)
        End If

    End Sub

End Class
```

For this simple example, you check the key presses that are made in the `TextBox1` control, and if the key press is a specific one — the Enter key — then you use the `WebBrowser` control's `Navigate` method to navigate to the requested page. The `Navigate` method can take a single `String` value, which represents the location of the Web page to retrieve. The example shown in Figure 34-11 shows the Wrox website.

Launching Internet Explorer from Your Windows Application

Sometimes, the goal is not to host a browser inside the application but instead to allow the user to find the website in a typical Web browser. For an example of this task, create a Windows Form that has a `LinkLabel` control on it. For instance, you can have a form that has a `LinkLabel` control on it that simply states "Visit your company website!"

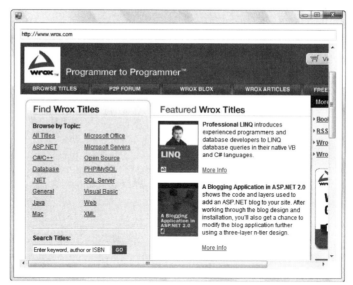

Figure 34-11

Once this control is in place, use the following code to launch the company's website in an independent browser, as opposed to directly in the form of your application:

```
Public Class Form1

    Private Sub LinkLabel1_LinkClicked(ByVal sender As System.Object, _
        ByVal e As System.Windows.Forms.LinkLabelLinkClickedEventArgs) Handles _
        LinkLabel1.LinkClicked

        Dim wb As New WebBrowser
        wb.Navigate("http://www.wrox.com", True)

    End Sub

End Class
```

In this example, when the LinkLabel control is clicked by the user, a new instance of the WebBrowser class is created. Then, using the WebBrowser's Navigate method, the code specifies the location of the Web page as well as a Boolean value that specifies whether this endpoint should be opened within the Windows Form application (a False value) or from within an independent browser (a True value). By default, this is set to False. With the preceding construct, when the end user clicks the link found in the Windows application, a browser instance is instantiated and the Wrox website is immediately launched.

Updating URLs and Page Titles

Note that when working with the MiniBrowser example in which the WebBrowser control is directly in the form, when you click the links, the text in the TextBox1 control is not updated. You can fix this by listening for events coming off the WebBrowser control and adding handlers to the control.

It is easy to update the form's title with the HTML page's title. Create a `DocumentTitleChanged` event and update the form's `Text` property:

```
Private Sub WebBrowser1_DocumentTitleChanged(ByVal sender As Object, _
    ByVal e As System.EventArgs) Handles WebBrowser1.DocumentTitleChanged

    Me.Text = WebBrowser1.DocumentTitle.ToString()

End Sub
```

In this case, when the `WebBrowser` control notices that the page title has changed (due to changing the page viewed), the `DocumentTitleChanged` event will fire. In this case, you change the form's `Text` property (its title) to the title of the page being viewed using the `DocumentTitle` property of the `WebBrowser` control.

Next, update the text string that appears in the form's text box, based on the complete URL of the page being viewed. To do this, you can use the `WebBrowser` control's `Navigated` event:

```
Private Sub WebBrowser1_Navigated(ByVal sender As Object, _
    ByVal e As System.Windows.Forms.WebBrowserNavigatedEventArgs) Handles _
    WebBrowser1.Navigated

    TextBox1.Text = WebBrowser1.Url.ToString()

End Sub
```

In this case, when the requested page is finished being downloaded in the `WebBrowser` control, the `Navigated` event is fired. You simply update the `Text` value of the `TextBox1` control to be the URL of the page. This means that once a page is loaded in the `WebBrowser` control's HTML container, if the URL changes in this process, then the new URL will be shown in the text box. For example, if you employ these steps and navigate to the Wrox website (`www.wrox.com`), the page's URL will immediately change to `http://www.wrox.com/WileyCDA/`. This process also means that if the end user clicks one of the links contained within the HTML view, then the URL of the newly requested page will also be shown in the text box.

Now if you run the application with the preceding changes put into place, the form's title and address bar will work as they do in Microsoft's Internet Explorer, as demonstrated in Figure 34-12.

Creating a Toolbar

For this exercise, you will add to the top of the control a simple toolbar that gives you the usual features you would expect from a Web browser — that is, Back, Forward, Stop, Refresh, and Home.

Rather than use the `ToolBar` control, you will add a set of button controls at the top of the control where you currently have the address bar. Add five buttons to the top of the control, as illustrated in Figure 34-13.

I have changed the text on the buttons to indicate their function. Of course, you can use a screen capture utility to "borrow" button images from IE and use those. The buttons should be named `buttonBack`, `buttonForward`, `buttonStop`, `buttonRefresh`, and `buttonHome`. To get the resizing to work properly, make sure that you set the `Anchor` property of the three buttons on the right to `Top`, `Right`.

Figure 34-12

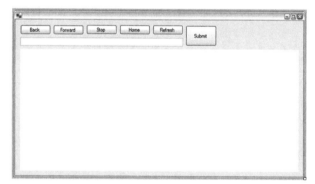

Figure 34-13

On startup, `buttonBack`, `buttonForward`, and `buttonStop` should be disabled because there is no point to the buttons if there is no initial page loaded. You will later tell the `WebBrowser` control when to enable and disable the Back and Forward buttons, depending on where the user is in the page stack. In addition, when a page is being loaded, you need to enable the Stop button, but you also need to disable the Stop button once the page has finished being loaded.

First, though, you will add the functionality behind the buttons. The `WebBrowser` class itself has all the methods you need, so this is all very straightforward:

```
Public Class Form1
    Private Sub Form1_Load(ByVal sender As System.Object, _
    ByVal e As System.EventArgs) Handles MyBase.Load
        buttonBack.Enabled = False
        buttonForward.Enabled = False
```

```
        buttonStop.Enabled = False
    End Sub

    Private Sub buttonBack_Click(ByVal sender As System.Object, _
     ByVal e As System.EventArgs) Handles buttonBack.Click
        WebBrowser1.GoBack()
        TextBox1.Text = WebBrowser1.Url.ToString()
    End Sub

    Private Sub buttonForward_Click(ByVal sender As System.Object, _
     ByVal e As System.EventArgs) Handles buttonForward.Click
        WebBrowser1.GoForward()
        TextBox1.Text = WebBrowser1.Url.ToString()
    End Sub

    Private Sub buttonStop_Click(ByVal sender As System.Object, _
     ByVal e As System.EventArgs) Handles buttonStop.Click
        WebBrowser1.Stop()
    End Sub

    Private Sub buttonRefresh_Click(ByVal sender As System.Object, _
     ByVal e As System.EventArgs) Handles buttonRefresh.Click
        WebBrowser1.Refresh()
    End Sub

    Private Sub buttonHome_Click(ByVal sender As System.Object, _
     ByVal e As System.EventArgs) Handles buttonHome.Click
        WebBrowser1.GoHome()
        TextBox1.Text = WebBrowser1.Url.ToString()
    End Sub

    Private Sub buttonSubmit_Click(ByVal sender As System.Object, _
     ByVal e As System.EventArgs) Handles buttonSubmit.Click
        WebBrowser1.Navigate(TextBox1.Text)
    End Sub

    Private Sub WebBrowser1_CanGoBackChanged(ByVal sender As Object, _
     ByVal e As System.EventArgs) Handles WebBrowser1.CanGoBackChanged
        If WebBrowser1.CanGoBack = True Then
            buttonBack.Enabled = True
        Else
            buttonBack.Enabled = False
        End If
    End Sub

    Private Sub WebBrowser1_CanGoForwardChanged(ByVal sender As Object, _
     ByVal e As System.EventArgs) Handles WebBrowser1.CanGoForwardChanged
        If WebBrowser1.CanGoForward = True Then
            buttonForward.Enabled = True
        Else
            buttonForward.Enabled = False
        End If
    End Sub
```

```
Private Sub WebBrowser1_Navigated(ByVal sender As Object, _
 ByVal e As System.Windows.Forms.WebBrowserNavigatedEventArgs) Handles _
 WebBrowser1.Navigated
     TextBox1.Text = WebBrowser1.Url.ToString()
     Me.Text = WebBrowser1.DocumentTitle.ToString()
End Sub

Private Sub WebBrowser1_Navigating(ByVal sender As Object, _
 ByVal e As System.Windows.Forms.WebBrowserNavigatingEventArgs) Handles _
 WebBrowser1.Navigating
     buttonStop.Enabled = True
End Sub

Private Sub WebBrowser1_DocumentCompleted(ByVal sender As Object, _
 ByVal e As System.Windows.Forms.WebBrowserDocumentCompletedEventArgs) _
 Handles WebBrowser1.DocumentCompleted
     buttonStop.Enabled = False
End Sub

End Class
```

Several different activities are occurring in this example, as there are many options for the end user when using this MiniBrowser application. First, for each of the button Click events, there is a specific WebBrowser class method assigned as the action to initiate. For instance, for the Back button on the form, you simply use the Web Browser control's GoBack method. The same is true for the other buttons — for the Forward button you have the GoForward method, and for the other buttons you have methods such as Stop, Refresh, and GoHome. This makes it simple and straightforward to create a toolbar that provides actions similar to those of Microsoft's Internet Explorer.

When the form is first loaded, the Form1_Load event disables the appropriate buttons. From there, users can enter a URL in the text box and click the Submit button to have the application retrieve the desired page.

To manage the enabling and disabling of the buttons, you have to key in a couple of events. As mentioned before, whenever downloading begins you need to enable Stop. For this, you simply add an event handler for the Navigating event to enable the Stop button:

```
Private Sub WebBrowser1_Navigating(ByVal sender As Object, _
 ByVal e As System.Windows.Forms.WebBrowserNavigatingEventArgs) Handles _
 WebBrowser1.Navigating
     buttonStop.Enabled = True
End Sub
```

Next, the Stop button is again disabled when the document has finished loading:

```
Private Sub WebBrowser1_DocumentCompleted(ByVal sender As Object, _
 ByVal e As System.Windows.Forms.WebBrowserDocumentCompletedEventArgs) _
 Handles WebBrowser1.DocumentCompleted
     buttonStop.Enabled = False
End Sub
```

Enabling and disabling the appropriate Back and Forward buttons depends on the ability to go backward or forward in the page stack. This is achieved by using both the `CanGoForwardChanged` and the `CanGoBackChanged` events:

```
Private Sub WebBrowser1_CanGoBackChanged(ByVal sender As Object, _
  ByVal e As System.EventArgs) Handles WebBrowser1.CanGoBackChanged
    If WebBrowser1.CanGoBack = True Then
        buttonBack.Enabled = True
    Else
        buttonBack.Enabled = False
    End If
End Sub

Private Sub WebBrowser1_CanGoForwardChanged(ByVal sender As Object, _
  ByVal e As System.EventArgs) Handles WebBrowser1.CanGoForwardChanged
    If WebBrowser1.CanGoForward = True Then
        buttonForward.Enabled = True
    Else
        buttonForward.Enabled = False
    End If
End Sub
```

Run the project now, visit a Web page, and click through a few links. You should also be able to use the toolbar to enhance your browsing experience. The end product is shown in Figure 34-14.

Figure 34-14

Showing Documents Using the WebBrowser Control

You are not limited to using just Web pages within the `WebBrowser` control. In fact, you can enable end users to view many different types of documents. So far, you have seen how to use the `WebBrowser` control to access documents that have been purely accessible by defining a URL, but the WebBrowser control also enables you to use an absolute path and define endpoints to files such as Word documents, Excel documents, PDFs, and more.

For instance, suppose you are using the following code snippet:

```
WebBrowser1.Navigate("C:\Financial Report.doc")
```

This would open the Word document in your application. Not only would the document appear in the WebBrowser control, but the Word toolbar would also be present, as shown in Figure 34-15.

In Figure 34-16, the WebBrowser control shows an Adobe PDF file.

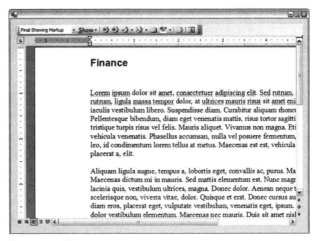

Figure 34-15

Figure 34-16

In addition to simply opening specific documents in the control, users can also drag and drop documents onto the `WebBrowser` control's surface, and the document dropped will automatically be opened within the control. To turn off this capability (which is enabled by default), set the `WebBrowser` control's `AllowWebBrowserDrop` property to `False`.

Printing Using the WebBrowser Control

Not only can users use the `WebBrowser` control to view pages and documents, they can also use the control to send these pages and documents to the printer for printing. To print the page or document being viewed in the control, simply use the following construct:

```
WebBrowser1.Print()
```

As before, it is possible to print the page or document without viewing it by using the `WebBrowser` class to load an HTML document and print it without even displaying the loaded document, as shown here:

```
Dim wb As new WebBrowser
wb.Navigate("http://www.wrox.com")
wb.Print()
```

Summary

This chapter began by examining just how easy it is to download resources from a web server using classes built into the .NET Framework. `System.Uri` enables you to express a URI, and `System.Net.WebRequest`, in combination with `System.Net.HttpWebRequest` and `System.Net. HttpWebResponse`, enables you to physically obtain the data.

This chapter also described how you can build your own network protocol by using sockets, implemented in the `System.Net.Sockets` namespace. You learned how `TcpListener` and `TcpClient` make it relatively easy to work with sockets, and you spent a lot of time working with threads and the various UI challenges that such work poses in order to make the application as usable as possible.

Finally, you learned how you can use the `WebBrowser` control in your own Windows Form application to work with HTML and other documents.

The Visual Basic Compiler

When the .NET Framework was first introduced, one nice addition for the Visual Basic developer was the inclusion of a standalone language compiler. This meant you were not required to have the Visual Studio .NET 2002 IDE in order to build Visual Basic applications. In fact, you could take the .NET Framework from the Microsoft website (free of charge), and build Web applications, classes, modules, and more simply, using a text editor such as Notepad. You could then take the completed files and compile them using the Visual Basic compiler.

The Visual Basic compiler is included along with the default .NET Framework install. Each version of the framework has a new compiler. In fact, note that while the core of the .NET 3.5 release is still running on the .NET Framework 2.0, the .NET Framework 3.5 release includes new compilers for both the Visual Basic and C# languages. The compiler for the .NET Framework 2.0 is vbc.exe, and it can be found at

```
C:\WINDOWS\Microsoft.NET\Framework\v2.0.50727\vbc.exe
```

The compiler for the .NET Framework 3.5 is also called vbc.exe, and it can be found at

```
C:\WINDOWS\Microsoft.NET\Framework\v3.5\vbc.exe
```

The vbc.exe.config File

In addition to the vbc.exe file, there is a vbc.exe.config file in the directory as well. This XML file is used to specify the versions of the .NET Framework for which the compiler should build applications. Now that there are three versions of the .NET Framework available for our applications to work with, it is important to understand how this configuration file actually works.

With the .NET Framework 3.5 installed, you will find the vbc.exe.config file with the following construction:

```
<?xml version ="1.0"?>
```

```
<configuration>
    <startup>
        <supportedRuntime version="v2.0.50727" safemode="true"/>
        <requiredRuntime version="v2.0.50727" safemode="true"/>
    </startup>
</configuration>
```

Even though you are dealing with the .NET Framework 3.5, you can see that the compiler compiles the code to run off of the 2.0 version of the framework.

This .config file, vbc.exe.config, is basically a typical .NET Framework configuration file with the default <configuration> root element included. Nested within the <configuration> element, you need to place a <startup> element. This is the only child element that is possible in the vbc.exe's configuration file.

Nested within the <startup> element, you can use two possible elements: <supportedRuntime> and <requiredRuntime>.

The <requiredRuntime> element really is only needed if your application is going to run on the .NET Framework 1.0 (the very first iteration of the .NET Framework). If your application is going to run from this version, then you build the vbc.exe.config file as follows:

```
<?xml version ="1.0"?>
<configuration>
    <startup>
        <requiredRuntime version="v1.0.3705" safemode="true"/>
    </startup>
</configuration>
```

Currently, working with three different versions of the .NET Framework, you may wish to compile your applications using the Visual Basic compiler so that they work with multiple versions of the framework. To do this, you could use the <supportedRuntime> element:

```
<?xml version ="1.0"?>
<configuration>
    <startup>
        <supportedRuntime version="v2.0.50727" safemode="true"/>
        <supportedRuntime version="v1.1.4322" safemode="true"/>
    </startup>
</configuration>
```

This construction states that the application should first try to run on version 2.0.50727 of the .NET Framework, and if this version of the .NET Framework is not found, then the next preferred version of the framework that the compiled object should work with is version 1.1.4322. When working in this kind of construction, you need to order the framework versions in the XML file so that the most preferred version of the framework you want to utilize is the uppermost element, and the least preferred version of the framework appears last in the node list.

The <supportedRuntime> element is meant for .NET Framework versions 1.1 and later. If you are going to utilize the .NET Framework version 1.0, then you should use the <requiredRuntime> element.

The `<supportedRuntime>` element contains two possible attributes: `version` and `safemode`. Both attributes are optional. The attribute `version` enables you to specify the specific version you want your application to run against, while `safemode` specifies whether the registry should be searched for the particular framework version. The `safemode` attribute takes a `Boolean` value, and the default value is `false`, meaning the framework version is not checked.

Simple Steps to Compilation

To show how the Visual Basic compiler works in the simplest manner, we can begin by looking at how to compile a single-class file:

1. Create a module called `MyModule.vb`. We will keep the module simple, as this example is meant to show you how to compile the items using the `vbc.exe` compiler:

```
Module Module1

    Sub Main()
        Console.WriteLine("Howdy there")
        Console.ReadLine()
    End Sub

End Module
```

2. Once your file is in place, it is time to use the Visual Basic compiler. If you have Visual Studio 2008 on the computer, then you can open the Visual Studio command prompt (found at Start ⇨ All Programs ⇨ Microsoft Visual Studio 2008 ⇨ Visual Studio Tools ⇨ Visual Studio 2008 Command Prompt). Once open, just navigate to the location of the file and then run the compiler against the file (shown shortly).

3. In most cases, you are probably going to be using the Visual Basic compiler on computers that do not have Visual Studio on them. In those cases, copy and paste the `vbc.exe`, `vbc.exe.config`, and `vbc.rsp` files to the folder where the class file you wish to compile is located. Then you can open a command prompt by selecting Run from the Start menu and typing **cmd** in the text box.

Another option is to add the compiler to the path itself. This is done by typing the following at the command prompt:

```
path %path%;C:\WINDOWS\Microsoft.NET\Framework\v3.5
```

Now you can work with the compilation normally, and the `vbc.exe` compiler will be found upon compilation.

4. Once the command prompt is open, navigate to the folder that contains both the Visual Basic compiler and the class file that needs compiling. From this location, type the following command at the command prompt:

```
vbc.exe MyModule.vb
```

Items can be compiled in many ways using the Visual Basic compiler, but this is the simplest way to compile this module. This command compiles the .vb file so that it can be utilized by your applications. Running the preceding command produces the following:

```
C:\CoolStuff>vbc.exe MyModule.vb
Microsoft (R) Visual Basic Compiler version 9.0.20706.1
Copyright (c) Microsoft Corporation.  All rights reserved.
```

What does this operation actually do? Well, in this case, it has created an .exe file for you in the same directory as the MyModule.vb file. Looking there, you will find MyModule.exe ready to run.

The Visual Basic compiler has a number of options that enable you to dictate what sorts of actions the compiler will take with the compilation process. These flags will be defined soon, but you can specify additional settings by using a forward slash followed by the name of the option and the setting assigned to the option. For instance, if you were going to add a reference to Microsoft.VisualBasic.dll along with the compilation, you would construct your compiler command as follows:

```
vbc.exe MyModule.vb /reference:Microsoft.VisualBasic.dll
```

Some of the options listed in this appendix have a plus sign (+) or a minus sign (-) next to them. A plus sign signifies that the option should be enabled, whereas the minus sign signifies that the option should not be enabled. For instance, the following signifies that documentation should be enabled:

```
vbc.exe MyModule.vb /reference:Microsoft.VisualBasic.dll /doc+
```

The following, however, signifies that documentation should not be enabled:

```
vbc.exe MyModule.vb /reference:Microsoft.VisualBasic.dll /doc-
```

Compiler Output

This section takes a comprehensive look at all the options available for the Visual Basic compiler. To see the full list, type the following command:

```
vbc.exe /?
```

/nologo

This option causes the compiler to perform its compilation without producing the compiler information set shown in previous examples. This is really only useful if you are invoking the compiler in your application, showing the results coming from the compiler to the end user of your application, and if you have no desire to show this information to the user in the result set.

/utf8output[+:−]

By default, when you use the Visual Basic command-line compiler, it will not do the compilation using UTF-8 encoding. In fact, the Visual Studio 2008 IDE will not even allow this to occur, but using /utf8output in the command-line compiler overrides this behavior.

/verbose

Adding this command causes the compiler to output a complete list of what it is doing, including the assemblies that are being loaded and the errors that it receives in the compilation process. Use it as follows:

```
vbc.exe MyModule.vb /reference:Microsoft.VisualBasic.dll /verbose
```

This would produce results such as the following (abbreviated because the result output is rather lengthy):

```
Adding assembly reference 'C:\WINDOWS\Microsoft.NET\Framework\v2.0.50727\System.
Data.dll'
```

In addition:

```
Adding import 'System'
Adding import 'Microsoft.VisualBasic'
Adding file 'C:\MyModule.vb'
Adding assembly reference 'C:\WINDOWS\Microsoft.NET\Framework\v2.0.50727\Microso
ft.VisualBasic.dll'
Compiling...
```

Then the compiler starts loading assemblies:

```
Loading C:\WINDOWS\Microsoft.NET\Framework\v2.0.50727\mscorlib.dll.

Loading C:\WINDOWS\Microsoft.NET\Framework\v2.0.50727\Microsoft.VisualBasic.dll.
```

Until it finishes:

```
Building 17d14f5c-a337-4978-8281-53493378c1071.vb.
Building C:\CoolStuff\MyModule.vb.
Compilation successful
```

Optimization

The following sections discuss the optimization features available.

/filealign

Not typically used by most developers, the /filealign setting enables you to specify the alignment of sections, or blocks of contiguous memory, in your output file. It uses the following construction:

```
vbc.exe MyModule.vb /filealign:2048
```

The number assigned is the byte size of the file produced, and valid values include 512, 1024, 2048, 4096, 8192, and 16384.

/optimize[+:—]

If you go to your project's property page (found by right-clicking on the project in the Visual Studio Solution Explorer), you will see a page for compilation settings. From this page, you can make all sorts of compilation optimizations. To keep your command-line compiler from ignoring these instructions, set the `/optimize` flag in your compilation instructions:

```
vbc.exe MyModule.vb /optimize
```

By default, optimizations are turned off.

Output files

The following sections explain the output files.

/doc[+:-]

By default, the compiler does not produce the XML documentation file upon compilation. This feature of Visual Basic enables developers to put structured comments in their code that can then be turned into an XML document for easy viewing (along with a style sheet). Including the `/doc` option causes the compiler to create this documentation. Structure your command as follows if you want to produce this XML documentation file:

```
vbc.exe MyModule.vb /doc
```

You can also specify the name of the XML file as follows:

```
vbc.exe MyModule.vb /doc:MyModuleXmlFile.xml
```

/netcf

This option cannot be executed from Visual Studio 2008 itself, but you can use this flag from the Visual Basic command-line compiler. Using `/netcf` causes the compiler to build your application so that the result is targeted for the .NET Compact Framework, not the full .NET Framework itself. To accomplish this, use the following construct:

```
vbc.exe MyModule.vb /netcf
```

/out

Using the `/out` option enables you to change the name and extension of the file that was produced from the compilation. By default, it is the name of the file that contains the `Main` procedure or the first source code file in a DLL. To modify this yourself instead of using the defaults, you could use something similar to the following:

```
vbc.exe MyModule.vb /out:MyReallyCoolModule.exe
```

/target

This setting enables you to specify what exactly is output from the compilation process. There are four options: an EXE, a DLL, a module, or a Windows program:

❑ **/target:exe** — Produces an executable console application. This is the default if no `/target` option is specified.

- ❏ **/target:library** — Produces a dynamic link library (also known as a DLL)
- ❏ **/target:module** — Produces a module
- ❏ **/target:winexe** — Produces a Windows program

You can also use a short form of this by just using /t:exe, /t:library, /t:module, or /t:winexe.

.NET assemblies

The following sections detail the .NET assemblies available.

/addmodule

This option is not available to Visual Studio 2008, but is possible when using the Visual Basic compiler. Using /addmodule enables you to add a .netmodule file to the resulting output of the compiler. For this, you would use something similar to the following construction:

```
vbc.exe MyModule.vb /addmodule:MyOtherModule.netmodule
```

/delaysign[+:-]

This compiler option needs to be used in conjunction with the /key or /keycontainer option, which deals with the signing of your assembly. When used with the /delaysign option, the compiler will create a space for the digital signature that is later used to sign the assembly, rather than actually signing the assembly at that point. You would use this option in the following manner:

```
vbc.exe MyModule.vb /key:myKey1.sn /delaysign
```

/imports

A commonly used compiler option, the /imports option enables you to import namespaces into the compilation process:

```
vbc.exe MyModule.vb /imports:System
```

Add multiple namespaces by separating them with a comma:

```
vbc.exe MyModule.vb /imports:System, System.Data
```

/keycontainer

This command causes the compiler to create a sharable component and places a public key into the component's assembly manifest while signing the assembly with a private key. Use this option as follows:

```
vbc.exe MyModule.vb /keycontainer:myKey1
```

If your key container has a name that includes a space, then you have to place quotes around the value as shown here:

```
vbc.exe MyModule.vb /keycontainer:"my Key1"
```

/keyfile

Similar to the /keycontainer option, the /key option causes the compiler to place a public key into the component's assembly manifest while signing the assembly with a private key. Use this as follows:

```
vbc.exe MyModule.vb /key:myKey1.sn
```

If your key has a name that includes a space, then you must place quotes around the value as shown here:

```
vbc.exe MyModule.vb /key:"my Key1.sn"
```

/libpath

When making references to other assemblies while using the /reference compiler option (described later), you will not always have these referenced assemblies in the same location as the object being compiled. You can use the /libpath option to specify the location of the referenced assemblies, as illustrated here:

```
vbc.exe MyModule.vb /reference:MyAssembly.dll /libpath:c:\Reuters\bin
```

If you want the compiler to search for the referenced DLLs in more than one location, then specify multiple locations using the /libpath option by separating the locations with a comma:

```
vbc.exe MyModule.vb /reference:MyAssembly.dll /libpath:c:\Reuters\bin, c:\
```

This command means that the compiler will look for the MyAssembly.dll in both the C:\Reuters\bin directory and the root directory found at C:\.

/platform

The /platform option enables you to specify the platform the compilation should be geared for. Possible options include the following:

- ❏ **/platform:x86** — Compiles the program for an x86 system
- ❏ **/platform:x64** — Compiles the program for a 64-bit system
- ❏ **/platform:Itanium** — Compiles the program for an Itanium system
- ❏ **/platform:anycpu** — Compiles the program so that it can be run on any CPU system. This is the default setting.

/reference

The /reference option enables you to make references to other assemblies in the compilation process. Use it as follows:

```
vbc.exe MyModule.vb /reference:MyAssembly.dll
```

You can also shorten the command option by using just /r:

```
vbc.exe MyModule.vb /r:MyAssembly.dll
```

You can make a reference to multiple assemblies by separating them with a comma:

```
vbc.exe MyModule.vb /reference:MyAssembly.dll, MyOtherAssembly.dll
```

/vbruntime[+:-]

The /vbruntime option enables you compile the program with the Visual Basic runtime. Use it as follows:

```
vbc.exe MyModule.vb /vbruntime
```

You can also specify which runtime to use, as shown here:

```
vbc.exe MyModule.vb /vbruntime:Microsoft.VisualBasic.dll
```

Debugging and error-checking

The following sections address the many features available for error-checking and debugging.

/bugreport

This option creates a file that is a full report of the compilation process. The /bugreport option creates this file, which contains your code and version information on the computer's operating system, as well as the compiler itself. Use this option in the following manner:

```
vbc.exe MyModule.vb /bugreport:bugsy.txt
```

/debug[+:-]

By default, the Visual Basic compiler will not build objects with attached debugging information included in the generated object. Using the /debug option causes the compiler to place this information in the created output file. The use of this option is shown here:

```
vbc.exe MyModule.vb /debug
```

/nowarn

The /nowarn option actually suppresses the compiler from throwing any warnings. There are a couple of ways to use this option. The first option is to simply use /nowarn without any associated values:

```
vbc.exe MyModule.vb /nowarn
```

Instead of suppressing all the warnings that the compiler can issue, the other option at your disposal is to specify the exact warnings you wish the compiler to suppress, as shown here:

```
vbc.exe MyModule.vb /nowarn:42016
```

In this case, you are telling the compiler not to throw any warnings when it encounters a 42016 error (an implicit conversion warning error). To interject more than one warning code, separate the warning codes with a comma as illustrated here:

```
vbc.exe MyModule.vb /nowarn:42016, 42024
```

1339

You can find a list of available warnings by searching for "Configuring Warnings in Visual Basic" in the MSDN documentation.

/quiet

Like some of the other compiler options, the `/quiet` option is only available to the command-line compiler and is not available when compiling your applications using Visual Studio. The `/quiet` option removes some of the error notifications from the error text output that is typically generated. Normally, when the compiler encounters an error that disallows further compilation, the error notification includes the line of code in the file where the error occurred. The line that is presented has a squiggly line underneath the exact bit of code where the error occurred. Using the `/quiet` option causes the compiler to show only the notification line, leaving the code line out of the output. This might be desirable in some situations.

/removeintchecks[+:-]

By default, the Visual Basic compiler checks all your integer calculations for any possible errors. Possible errors include division by zero or overflow situations. Using the `/removeintchecks` option causes the compiler to not look for these kinds of errors in the code of the files being compiled. You would use this option as follows:

```
vbc.exe MyModule.vb /removeintchecks
```

/warnaserror[+:-]

In addition to finding and reporting errors, the compiler can also encounter situations that are only considered warnings. Even though warnings are encountered, the compilation process continues. Using the `/warnaserror` option in the compilation process causes the compiler to treat all warnings as errors. Use this option as shown here:

```
vbc.exe MyModule.vb /warnaserror
```

You might not want each warning to cause an error to be thrown, but instead only specific warnings. For these occasions, you can state the warning ID number that you want to look out for, as shown here:

```
vbc.exe MyModule.vb /warnaserror:42016
```

You can also check for multiple warnings by separating the warning ID numbers with commas:

```
vbc.exe MyModule.vb /warnaserror:42016, 42024
```

Help

The following sections address the compiler's help features.

/?

When you don't have this book for reference, you can use the Visual Basic compiler for a list of options by using the `/?` option, as shown here:

```
vbc.exe /?
```

This causes the entire list of options and their definitions to be displayed in the command window.

/help

The /help option is the same as the /? option. Both of these options produce the same result. The /help option produces a list of options that can be used with the compiler.

Language

The following sections detail the language options.

/optionexplicit[+:-]

Always a good idea, using /optionexplicit causes the compiler to check whether any variables in the code are used before they are even declared (yes, this is possible and very bad practice). When variables are found before they are even declared, the compiler throws an error. By default, the compiler does not check the code using the option explicit option. Use this option as shown in the following example:

```
vbc.exe MyModule.vb /optionexplicit
```

/optionstrict[+:-]

It's also a good idea to use the /optionstrict option in the compilation process. Using this option causes the compiler to check whether you are making any improper type conversions in your code. Widening type conversions are allowed, but when you start performing narrowing type conversions, using this option will cause an error to be thrown by the compiler. By default, the compiler does not look for these types of errors with your type conversions. Use this option as follows:

```
vbc.exe MyModule.vb /optionstrict
```

/optioncompare

By default, the Visual Basic compiler compares strings using a binary comparison. If you want the string comparisons to use a text comparison, then use the following construction:

```
vbc.exe MyModule.vb /optioncompare:text
```

/optioninfer[+:-]

This is a new option found in the .NET Framework 3.5 version of the compiler. This option specifies that you want to allow type inference of variables. Use this option as illustrated in the following example:

```
vbc.exe MyModule.vb /optioninfer
```

Preprocessor: /define

The /define option enables you to define conditional compiler constants for the compilation process. This is quite similar to using the #Const directive in your code. Here is an example:

```
vbc.exe MyModule.vb /define:Version="4.11"
```

You can also place definitions for multiple constants, as shown here:

```
vbc.exe MyModule.vb /define:Version="4.11",DebugMode=False
```

For multiple constants, just separate the constants with commas.

Resources

The following sections elaborate on the resources in the compiler.

/linkresource

Instead of embedding resources directly in the generated output file (such as with the /resource option), the /linkresource option enables you to create the connection between your resulted objects and the resources that they require. You would use this option in the following manner:

```
vbc.exe MyModule.vb /linkresource:MyResourceFile.res
```

You can then specify whether the resource file is supposed to be public or private in the assembly manifest. By default, the resource file is referenced as public. Here is an example of its use:

```
vbc.exe MyModule.vb /linkresource:MyResourceFile.res,private
```

You can shorten the /linkresource option to just /linkres.

/resource

The /resource option enables you to reference managed resource objects. The referenced resource is then embedded in the assembly. You would do this in the following manner:

```
vbc.exe MyModule.vb /resource:MyResourceFile.res
```

Like the /linkresource option, you can specify whether the reference to the resource should be made either public or private. This is done as follows (the default is public):

```
vbc.exe MyModule.vb /resource:MyResourceFile.res,private
```

You can shorten the /resource option to just /res.

/win32icon

Use this option to embed an .ico file (an image that is actually the application's icon) in the produced file, as shown in the following example:

```
vbc.exe MyModule.vb /win32icon:MyIcon.ico
```

/win32resource

This option enables you to embed a Win32 resource file into the produced file. Use as shown in the following example:

```
vbc.exe MyModule.vb /win32resource:MyResourceFile.res
```

Miscellaneous features

The rest of this appendix covers some of the more random but very useful features in the compiler. For example, one great feature of the Visual Basic compiler is the use of *response files*. If you have a compilation that you frequently perform, or one that is rather lengthy, you can instead create an .rsp file (the response file), a simple text file containing all the compilation instructions needed for the compilation process. Here is an example .rsp file:

```
# This is a comment
/target:exe
/out:MyCoolModule.exe
/linkresource=MyResourceFile.res
MyModule.vb
SomeOtherClassFile.vb
```

If you save this as MyResponseFile.res, then you can use it as shown in the following example:

```
vbc.exe @MyResponseFile.rsp
```

You can also specify multiple response files:

```
vbc.exe @MyResponseFile.rsp @MyOtherResponseFile.rsp
```

/baseaddress

When creating a DLL using the /target:library option, you can assign the base address of the DLL. By default, this is done for you by the compiler, but if you wish to make this assignment yourself, you can. To accomplish this, you would use something similar to the following:

```
vbc.exe MyClass.vb /target:library /baseaddress:0x11110000
```

All base addresses are specified as hexadecimal numbers.

/codepage

By default, the compiler expects all files to be using an ANSI, Unicode, or UTF-8 code page. Using the compiler's /codepage option, you can specify the code page that the compiler should actually be using. Setting it to one of the defaults is shown here:

```
vbc.exe MyClass.vb /codepage:1252
```

1252 is used for American English and most European languages, although setting it to Japanese Kanji would be just as simple:

```
vbc.exe MyClass.vb /codepage:932
```

/main

Using the /main option, you can point the compiler to the class or module that contains the SubMain procedure. Use it as follows:

```
vbc.exe MyClass.vb /main:MyClass.vb
```

/noconfig

By default, the Visual Basic compiler uses the vbc.rsp resource file in the compilation process. Using the /noconfig option tells the compiler to avoid using this file in the compilation process, as shown here:

```
vbc.exe MyClass.vb /noconfig
```

/nostdlib

By default, the Visual Basic compiler uses standard libraries (System.dll) and the vbc.rsp resource file in the compilation process. Using the /nostdlib option tells the compiler to avoid using this file in the compilation process, as shown here:

```
vbc.exe MyClass.vb /nostdlib
```

/recurse

The /recurse option tells the compiler to compile all the specified files within a specified directory. Also included will be all child directories of the directory specified. Here is one example of using /recurse:

```
vbc.exe /target:library /out:MyComponent.dll /recurse:MyApplication\Classes\*.vb
```

This command takes all of the .vb files from the MyApplication/Classes directory and creates a DLL called MyComponent.dll.

/rootnamespace

Use this option to specify the namespace to use for compilation:

```
vbc.exe MyClass.vb /rootnamespace:Reuters
```

/sdkpath

This option enables you to specify the location of mscorlib.dll and Microsoft.VisualBasic.dll if they are located somewhere other than the default location. This setting is really meant to be used with the /netcf option, described earlier, and is used as follows:

```
vbc.exe /sdkpath:"C:\Program Files\Microsoft Visual Studio 8
    \CompactFrameworkSDK\v1.0.5000\Windows CE" MyModule.vb
```

Looking at the vbc.rsp File

As stated earlier, the vbc.rsp file is there for the compiler's sake. When a compilation is being done, the Visual Basic compiler uses the vbc.rsp file for each compilation (unless you specify the /noconfig option). Inside this .rsp file is a list of compiler commands:

```
# This file contains command-line options that the VB
# command-line compiler (VBC) will process as part
# of every compilation, unless the "/noconfig" option
# is specified.
```

```
# Reference the common Framework libraries
/r:Accessibility.dll
/r:Microsoft.Vsa.dll
/r:System.Configuration.Install.dll
/r:System.Data.dll
/r:System.Design.dll
/r:System.DirectoryServices.dll
/r:System.dll
/r:System.Drawing.Design.dll
/r:System.Drawing.dll
/r:System.EnterpriseServices.dll
/r:System.Management.dll
/r:System.Messaging.dll
/r:System.Runtime.Remoting.dll
/r:System.Runtime.Serialization.Formatters.Soap.dll
/r:System.Security.dll
/r:System.ServiceProcess.dll
/r:System.Web.dll
/r:System.Web.Mobile.dll
/r:System.Web.RegularExpressions.dll
/r:System.Web.Services.dll
/r:System.Windows.Forms.Dll
/r:System.XML.dll

# Import System and Microsoft.VisualBasic
/imports:System
/imports:Microsoft.VisualBasic
```

These commands reflect the references and imports that are done for each item that you compile using this command-line compiler. Feel free to play with this file as you choose. If you want to add your own references, then add them to the list and save the file. From then on, every compilation that you make will include the new reference(s). As you become more familiar with using the Visual Basic command-line compiler, you will see a lot of power in using .rsp files — even the default Visual Basic one.

B

Visual Basic Power Packs Tools

This appendix takes a look at the Visual Basic Power Packs Tools. These tools are a set of off-cycle release packages that focus on helping developers who are maintaining traditional Visual Basic 6.0 applications begin the process of transitioning to Visual Basic .NET. Additionally, they contain a set of features intended for developers with years of Visual Basic experience to replicate tasks and behaviors that were easy in Visual Basic 6.0 in Visual Basic .NET.

This appendix briefly examines the two installation packages that are currently available. These packages were released targeting Visual Studio 2005, but they are fully compatible with Visual Studio 2008. Moreover, elements of the Visual Basic Power Packs 2.0 package for printing have been fully integrated with, and ship as part of, Visual Studio 2008. It is hoped that additional portions of this package will be included in Visual Studio 2008 as part of a future update such as a service pack.

This appendix focuses on three areas:

❑ Power Packs background, including goals and installation

❑ The Interop Forms Toolkit 2.0

❑ The Visual Basic Power Packs 2.0

These tools are available as free downloads; however, due to licensing restrictions on the Express Editions, Visual Basic Express and the other Express Editions do not support any add-ins. Thus, to leverage the Power Packs, you need a licensed version of Visual Studio Standard or above. Why you would want to leverage the Power Packs is a question best answered by understanding the issues that the Power Packs address. These aren't just technology for technology's sake: they address very real issues that traditional VB developers are facing today.

Visual Basic Power Packs

The Visual Basic Power Packs were introduced by Microsoft's Visual Basic Development team to introduce new features and capabilities needed by Visual Basic developers between major releases of Visual Studio. The main focus has been on helping Visual Basic 6.0 developers who have implemented solutions that aren't easily migrated in one fell swoop to .NET. There are two problems:

❑ Like it or not, the migration wizard that originally shipped with .NET 1.0 doesn't meet the requirements of a developer migrating a real-world application.

❑ Once they are working in .NET, typical developers face challenges with certain tasks that under Visual Basic 6.0 were easy but in Visual Basic .NET are not.

Each of these two issues is currently addressed by a different package.

In a perfect world, when Visual Basic .NET 1.0 came out, the transition from Visual Basic 6.0 to .NET would have felt seamless. The migration wizard that was introduced would have looked through your project files, found all of the custom COM components for which you had source available, and then been able without any problem to convert every line of VB 6.0 source code to VB.NET. Unfortunately, we don't live in that world, and, in fact, the migration wizard left several gaps in coverage. These gaps in code migration didn't affect a demonstration, but were of significant concern if you were trying to update an application to .NET. This meant that your primary tool for migration forced you into an all-or-nothing decision with regard to moving your application, but at the same time couldn't fully complete the process. As a result, you faced a scenario in which you couldn't really add new capabilities to your application without converting it, and converting a decent-sized application with all of the associated manual migration elements could take months — time you didn't have.

Recently, the same scenario again appeared with the anticipated end of the Windows Forms user interface. However, in this case, as discussed in Chapter 18, Microsoft found a better way to handle the migration. Instead of including a wizard that tried to manage the entire application at once, they created a set of components that enabled you to interoperate between your existing code and the new feature set. The most exciting part about this is that when .NET 1.0 shipped, it actually included this same capability for COM. In theory, there was also support for calling .NET components from COM, but, in reality, that interface was difficult, so the Visual Basic team stepped up to the plate and created a package that would solve that problem.

The Visual Basic Interop Forms Toolkit 2.0 does this. It was designed to enable you to create and implement a form in .NET, after which the toolkit makes it easy for you to wrapper this form so that it can function as a working component within your existing VB6 application. The wrapper handles integrating the .NET form with your application, enabling you to maintain a common environment for the data and context and even messaging. Events can be passed between your new .NET form and your existing Visual Basic application. The result is that now you can extend your existing VB6 application with new .NET features without the cost and risk associated with attempting to migrate your entire application in one fell swoop.

Of course, this was only one aspect of the migration challenge for VB6 developers. The second key aspect was that under Visual Basic 6.0, it was easy for developers to carry out tasks such as printing. .NET follows a paradigm that is much closer to the C++ model. It provides a great deal of control and is fully customizable. However, the ability to control and customize your output also introduces a layer of complexity for managing those capabilities. VB6 developers often just wanted to output a display or add a geometric shape to the display. As a result of the added complexity of these tasks, VB6 developers were often unsure how to implement the same capabilities they had under VB6.

Again the Visual Basic team stepped up and created the Visual Basic Power Packs 2.0. This is a separate installation package from the Interop Forms Toolkit, and instead of targeting code that can be integrated with traditional COM applications, it focuses on making it just as easy to do things like printing as they were in Visual Basic 6.0.

In addition, instead of waiting for the next release of Visual Studio, the Visual Basic team scheduled these Power Packs as standalone deliverables so that users could take advantage of them much sooner.

> *Don't assume that these packages are of lower quality. In fact, to highlight how valuable the Power Packs 2.0 tools are, the printing capabilities introduced in this Power Pack are included within Visual Studio 2008, and there are plans to include many of the line and shape capabilities in a future update to Visual Studio 2008.*

Getting the Visual Basic Power Packs

The Power Packs are available as free downloads. In addition to the downloads page, the Visual Basic team also maintains a suggestion page directly related to features that you, as a Visual Basic developer, would like to see. This page also includes links to the existing Power Packs and is a great place to start when looking for more information on the Power Packs: `https://connect.microsoft.com/vbasic`.

The current download for the Interop Forms Toolkit 2.0 can be found at `www.microsoft.com/downloads/details.aspx?familyid=934de3c5-dc85-4065-9327-96801e57b81d&displaylang=en`.

The current download for the Visual Basic 2005 Power Packs 2.0 can be found at `www.microsoft.com/downloads/details.aspx?familyid=92faa81e-e9c1-432c-8c29-813493a04ecd&displaylang=en`.

Keep in mind that two separate download packages are needed to collect all of the assorted tools available to Visual Basic developers, and that both packages are currently on version 2.0.

Additional forums are available to discuss issues or ask questions regarding use of the tools. The Interop Forms Toolkit forum is at `http://forums.microsoft.com/MSDN/ShowForum.aspx?ForumID=879&SiteID=1`

The forum for the Power Packs 2.0 package is at: `http://forums.microsoft.com/MSDN/ShowForum.aspx?ForumID=903&SiteID=1`.

Using the Interop Forms Toolkit 2.0

To begin working with the Interop Forms Toolkit, download the packages. The default download page includes three files for download, shown in Figure B-1.

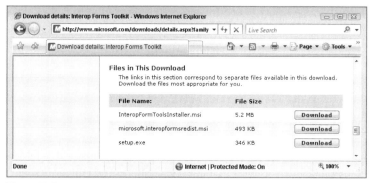

Figure B-1

Download all three of these files to a local directory of your choosing.

❑   The first file, which is also the largest, InteropFormToolsInstaller.msi, contains the actual application files that need to be installed.

❑   The second file is the microsoft.interopformsredist.msi file. As its name implies, this is a redistributable version of the Interop Forms Toolkit of tools.

❑   The third file is setup.exe. As you can tell by its size, it relies on the installation.msi file, but if you are running on Vista then you'll need this file.

Once you have downloaded all three files, run the setup file to install the tool. Aside from selecting the installation directory and similar standard setup screens, there are no special steps related to installing this package. One thing to note, regardless of whether you are running Visual Studio 2005, Visual Studio 2008, or both, is that the installation package updates your Visual Studio environments.

Because Visual Basic Express Edition does not support add-ins, this application will not be updated when you install the software.

To validate your installation, there are three easy items you can check. First, once the installation is complete, the help topic associated with the Interop Forms Toolkit 2.0 should open. Second, when you access the Tools menu, the first item in the menu should be the option to Generate Interop Form Wrapper Classes. This menu item should be located above the standard option to Attach Process. Third, and probably most important, when you access the File menu and select the New Project dialog, you should see two new project types under the My Templates section within Visual Basic Windows, as shown in Figure B-2.

The first custom project type is the VB6 Interop User Control project type. This type of project enables you to create user controls that can then be used to populate the body of an MDI window. This project type was introduced with version 2.0 of the Interop Forms Toolkit and is the solution the Visual Basic team developed to support interoperation within an MDI environment.

The second project type is the VB6 InteropForm Library project. The original project type, it was designed to enable you to create a DLL that defines a .NET form.

After you have validated that your installation is working, the next step is to create a simple Interop Form.

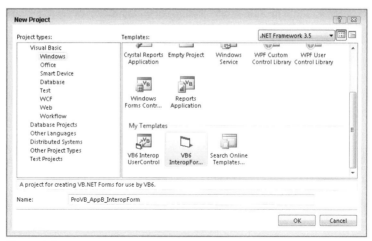

Figure B-2

Creating a simple Interop Form

Select the project type shown in Figure B-2 and rename the solution ProVB_AppB_InteropForm. Click OK to generate your source project files. The resulting project opens, and you can open and edit your new Windows Form. However, note that what you are creating, while it supports the Form Designer, isn't a standalone executable. If you open your project properties, you'll find that your project will build as a DLL, not a standalone executable.

Another thing to note is that as part of the generation of your project, a file named InteropInfo.vb is created. This file takes settings that might otherwise exist in your AssemblyInfo.vb file and places them here so they are a bit more apparent. The first line references the standard COM Interop classes and turns these settings off. This is important because you won't be using traditional COM Interop; you've added a new Interop class specifically for this purpose. By moving this setting into a separate file, if you do accidentally cause the AssemblyInfo.vb file to be regenerated by Visual Studio, you'll get a compile error. This is good because you can quickly and easily delete the newly duplicated line from AssemblyInfo.vb and not wonder why your project suddenly isn't working correctly. Compile errors are always better then runtime errors. The other item in this file is a declaration that extends the My namespace to include the Interop toolbox. In general, you shouldn't make any changes to this file, but now you know what it's doing.

Opening the InteropForm1.vb, you have a typical design surface for a form, on which you can add controls. Behind the scenes is an InteropForm1.vb that contains the following default code:

```
Imports Microsoft.InteropFormTools

<InteropForm()> _
Public Class InteropForm1

End Class
```

As you can see, the default class definition has been decorated with an attribute indicating that this class should be considered an `InteropForm`. This enables the postprocessor that is used to generate your COM wrappings to recognize which type of wrapping should be applied to this class.

1351

For now, however, go to the Form Designer, and because this is a truly simple demo, drag a `label` and a `TextBox` control onto the display. Within the code, create the four other types of interface members you'll want in your production code: an initializer, a property, a method, and an event (in that order). The following code is placed within your class definition:

```
Public Sub New()
    ' This call is required by the Windows Form Designer.
    InitializeComponent()

    ' Add any initialization after the InitializeComponent() call.
End Sub

<InteropFormInitializer()> _
Public Sub New(ByVal label As String)
    Me.New()
    Label1.Text = label

End Sub

<InteropFormProperty()> _
Public Property TextBoxText() As String
    Get
        Return TextBox1.Text
    End Get
    Set(ByVal value As String)
        TextBox1.Text = value
    End Set
End Property

<InteropFormMethod()> _
Public Sub ChangeLabel(ByVal lbl As String)
    Label1.Text = lbl
    RaiseEvent CustomEvent(lbl)
End Sub

<InteropFormEvent()> _
Public Event CustomEvent As CustomEventSig

'Declare handler signature...
Public Delegate Sub CustomEventSig(ByVal lblText As String)
```

For the initialization code you'll note that first a default `New` constructor, is created. When you define the default `New` constructor, it adds the call to `InitializeComponent`, which handles the creation of your controls within the form. Thus, when the object is initialized, you will be able to reference the controls you have placed on the form.

The next step is to create a parameterized constructor so that you can quite literally pass a parameter as part of the initialization process. Note that similar to the class itself, the exposed initialization method has an attribute on the method. Each type of class member that is to be exposed gets an attribute matching the type of that method. Thus, for the `New` method, the type of the attribute is `InteropFormInitializer`. For this simple example, the parameterized `New(ByVal label As String)` simply changes the text associated with the label. Finally, although this class is defined in .NET syntax, COM and VB6 don't allow parameterized New statements. Thus, when you go to reference this parameterized initializer, you'll find that the method name is in fact Initialize.

Next, the code defines and exposes a public property. In this case, to help simplify the code, there isn't a private member variable to hold the value; this provides an easy way for the code that creates this form to set and retrieve the value of the text box. Similarly, there is a method to allow the calling code to update the label shown on the form. Note that it has also been attributed, and after you update the label for demonstration purposes, it raises the custom event that is defined next.

That event, called CustomEvent, is defined with an attribute, but the event that is defined must also define the signature or definition of its handlers. In this case, the Delegate CustomEventSig handles a single parameter. This .NET code, as noted, provides a basic example of each of the primary types of Interop you'll want to carry out. The next step is to generate your Interop methods.

One of the key differences between an InteropForms project and an Interop User Control project is this step. Only the InteropForms project requires the generation of custom COM wrappers. To do this, access the Tools menu and select Generate InteropForm Wrapper Classes. There is no user interface; instead, the generation process will create a new directory in your project containing the InteropForm1.wrapper.vb class, as shown in Figure B-3.

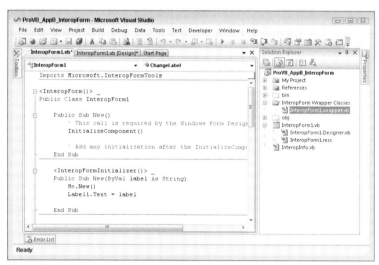

Figure B-3

For readers developing on Vista: keep in mind that registry access requires elevated permissions. You need to start Visual Studio 2008 with the Run as Administrator option on your right-click context menu. If you don't, then when you attempt to automatically register your newly built DLL as a COM component, you'll get an error, which Visual Studio 2008 reflects as a Build Error.

At this point, your application is ready to be called from VB6. If you follow best practices, you'll have the VB6 integrated development environment (IDE) installed on the machine with Visual Studio 2008. In that scenario, you can immediately go to your VB6 project and reference the necessary DLLs, both the

Interop Forms Toolkit DLL and your custom DLL. Otherwise, you'll need to get ready for deployment now instead of later.

Deployment

To deploy your Interop Forms project, you need a traditional MSI installation. Creating a setup project is covered in Chapter 24, so the details of creating your setup project aren't repeated here. However, note a couple of special steps. In order for your new Interop Forms project to work on the client, the client needs both the .NET Framework 2.0 redistributable and the second MSI you downloaded earlier in this chapter (shown in Figure B-1), the microsoft.interopformsredist.msi. If you are using Visual Studio 2005 to create your installation package, then you can add these items as prerequisites for installing your DLL via the user interface.

The recommendation is to create a simple setup project in Visual Studio 2005 for installing your Interop Forms project and the associated prerequisites and have this run in advance of whatever legacy installation project you have. To extend an existing MSI, you need to carry out the appropriate steps for the tool generating your MSI, a subject beyond the scope of this appendix.

Debugging

When you first start planning to work with the toolkit, you might try to keep the VB6 IDE on a separate machine from your primary development machine. However, this leads to two issues. First, in order to work with the Interop Forms tools on your VB6 machine, you need to install the tools package a second time. That's a minor issue. Second, because Visual Basic 6.0 doesn't know how to step into .NET applications, if you want to debug the Interop Form you created in .NET, you have a problem. The solution to this, of course, is to run both development environments on the same machine.

Alternatively, you can try to create a simple Windows Forms EXE that will call and initiate your Interop Forms project from within .NET. The debugging isn't perfect because, of course, you aren't actually calling your code across the correct interface, but it should enable you to find most pure .NET coding issues. You can also leverage the Debug and Trace classes, but you won't have any interactive breakpoints in that scenario.

This still leaves unresolved the issue that you can't just open Visual Studio 2008 and expect the VB6 IDE to call it when you are in debug mode. Therefore, this section briefly discusses debugging Interop Forms Toolkit projects when you are running your VB6 application.

Once you have compiled your .NET application, you have a DLL. This DLL is then exposed to your VB6 development environment and added as another COM component in your VB6 application. However, when you debug, you can't step into this DLL from Visual Basic. Presuming you have started your Visual Basic 6.0 project so that its process is now running, your next step is to open Visual Studio 2008 and open your Interop Forms project. It is hoped that you have set typical breakpoints in your source code and might even add new breakpoints.

Next, go to the Tools menu and select the Attach to Process menu item. At this point, you get a dialog containing a list of running processes. Locate the "Visual Basic 6.0.exe" process. Once you have found this process, which represents the running application in VB6, attach to this process.

At this point, you can work with your running application, and when the call is made into your .NET code, Visual Studio 2008 detects the call into the DLL and stops you on your breakpoint. In order for Visual Studio 2008 to detect the DLL call, you must be calling the same copy of your DLL that your Interop Forms project references. In other words, you can't just copy it off to some other location on your local machine for installation.

> *If you stop and restart your VB6 application, Visual Studio 2008 will maintain the attachment, but if you close the VB6 IDE, then you'll need to reattach the debugger in Visual Studio 2008.*

VB6 development

Overall, the development process in VB6 is simple. Once you have either built your project or deployed it to the machine on which you have the VB IDE, you'll need to add references to both the Microsoft Interop Form Toolkit library and your custom DLL. Keep in mind that both of the DLLs must be registered on your VB6 IDE machine for them to be visible. If you are building on the same machine, they are automatically visible. Once you have added references for these libraries, you can create a new instance of your Interop Form's Form class and call the standard methods and any custom methods you've exposed on that form.

The one key point to remember, which was mentioned earlier but bears repeating, is that if you have created a custom constructor, in order to use it, you will call an Initialize method on your Interop Form class.

Final Interop Tips

As noted earlier in the book during the discussion of the WPF Interop controls, the Interop control packages aren't perfect. Each has certain limitations that reduce their desirability for the long term. To resolve this, keep track of how much of various branches you have already converted. There will be a point where it is time to convert a larger section so that you can reduce the number of different Interop DLLs that you are using.

Along these lines, note that you can't put an Interop Form and an Interop User Control into the same project. Each of these items needs its own DLL, and, in fact, you should consider it best practice to only expose the DLL for a single form or control. Similarly, don't plan on calling a VB6 form from within your Interop Form. The Interop logic was written to enable you to call .NET from VB6.

In terms of interfaces, the Interop layer was designed to support only a minimum number of interface types. In particular, the String, Integer, and Boolean types should be at the core of what you expect to pass in terms of data. In theory, the Object type is supported, which enables you to pass custom data, so you could pass a Recordset from .NET to VB6 or vice versa; of course, VB6 doesn't know about a Dataset object, so you need to reference VB6 types as the generic object. In general, the best practice is to keep your interfaces as simple as possible.

When you start the VB6 IDE with your project, it attaches to your DLL. Normally this isn't an issue until you first run your VB6 application. At this point, you can't rebuild your Interop project. The Interop project is, in fact, referenced and therefore locked by VB6. If you need to rebuild your Interop project, you need to first shut down the VB6 development environment so that your code will correctly reference your latest build. As noted previously, debugging your Interop project from VB6 isn't the most productive set of steps.

If you change any of the method attributes, you need to regenerate the Interop wrapper classes that you generated in the last step of creating your Interop Forms project. Moreover, although it wasn't covered, you can raise errors from .NET into VB6. To do this, you want to leverage the following method call on the custom My namespace that was defined as part of your Interop Form:

```
My.InteropToolbox.EventMessenger.RaiseApplicationEvent("CRITICAL_ERROR", _ "Error
Detail.")
```

The other runtime issue that you may encounter is that certain internal events to your .NET application will not be triggered in the same fashion that they were in VB6. Under VB6, for example, when you referenced a property on a Form class, this triggered the Load event on that class. Under .NET, the Load event is not fired until the form is being displayed, so you need to recognize the impact on any code that you previously set to run on the Load event.

The remaining issue is related to the VB6 IDE. The IDE and VB6 don't really recognize that if you have started a .NET DLL, there are other in-memory classes to release. For a deployed application, this isn't an issue because when the application is closed, all of the memory associated with the process is automatically released. When you are debugging in VB6, however, the core process is associated with the IDE, not your application. As a result, the resources are not released between debugging cycles. To ensure that they are released, you can explicitly instantiate a series of code modifications contained in the Interop help files and release the .NET resources associated with your application. The recommendation is to implement these calls only after your references with the Interop tools are functioning correctly.

Using the Power Packs 2.0 Tools

Unlike the Interop Forms Toolkit, the Power Packs extensions are intended to facilitate some of the same development simplicity that existed in VB6 for tasks such as printing. These classes aren't meant to support Interop, they are meant to support migration in the sense that the code for creating simple geometric shapes or using the VB style of form printing could be implemented using syntax similar to that of VB6. Since these Power Packs were released, the printing syntax has proven so popular that the Visual Basic team migrated those classes into the core features of Visual Studio 2008.

Similar to the Interop Forms Toolkit, the Power Pack Tools are installed from the Microsoft downloads. However, unlike the Interop Forms Toolkit, only a single MSI is available, which you run when the tools are installed. Prior to installing the tools, Visual Studio 2008 already has the printing control installed as such. If you review a typical Windows Forms project, you'll see the display shown in Figure B-4, which already includes the PrintForm control as part of your default Toolbox.

Unlike the Interop Forms toolkit, there is no need to begin with a special project template. There is no COM Interop involved because the Power Packs don't target VB6. They target experienced VB developers who want to be able to continue to implement certain tasks in the same way they could in VB6.

When your application ships, you still need to ensure that you create a dependency for the Power Packs library if you aren't using the DLLs that are included with Visual Studio 2008, but that's it. Additionally, because the Power Packs are just another set of .NET libraries, there aren't any issues related to debugging.

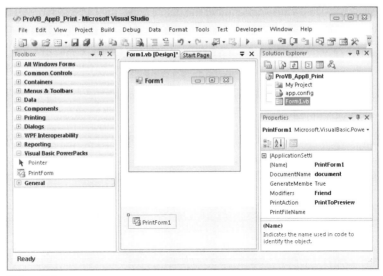

Figure B-4

For the sample project shown in Figure B-4, you can create a new Windows Forms application and add the Print control to it. At this point, close Visual Studio and install the Power Packs 2.0 installation package. After installation, when you reopen your project within the Toolbox window, Visual Studio 2008 has a new section for the Power Packs 2.0, showing the Oval and Rectangle shape controls along with the Line and Print controls, as shown in Figure B-5.

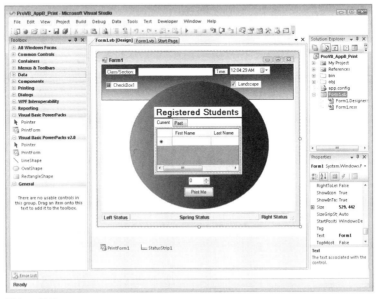

Figure B-5

Add a `Rectangle` shape to the upper section of the display and an `Oval` to the center of the display. Without getting into pages of details here, using the Visual Studio 2008 designer, you should customize the look and feel of the display by adding a variety of controls. Take some time to color and fill the shape controls with a solid color. The gradient colors are defined by selecting a fill color (Coral), a FillGradient-Color (Navy), a FillGradientStyle (Horizontal), and a FillStyle (Solid). All of this can and should be done within the Visual Studio 2008 designer to achieve a display similar to what is shown in Figure B-5.

Now try to build your project. This will probably result in an error because of an ambiguous class reference with regard to the `Print` control. In the steps just discussed, Visual Studio 2008 includes references to both versions of the Power Packs library DLL. The 9.0.0.0 version is the one that ships with Visual Studio 2008, whereas the version from the Web is labeled 8.0.0.0.

If you install the Visual Basic Power Packs 2.0 on Visual Studio 2008 and you use the graphical elements, you may need to remove the Power Packs reference that ships with Visual Studio 2008 for the Printing controls as a reference in your project. Because the Power Packs include the most recent version of this DLL for the graphics, it is recommended that you remove the version that ships with Visual Studio 2008.

Once the duplicate reference is removed, the application should build. The next step is to ensure that the check box in the upper-right corner, labeled "Landscape" in the figure, is checked. Having done this, label the button in the bottom center of the display "Print" and double-click it in the Design view to trigger the automatic event handler generation.

The only code needed for this printing demonstration is placed within the handler for this button. The code hides the button, determines whether or not the Landscape check box is checked, and uses the Power Packs Print control to Print Preview the document. Once this is completed, the Print Me button is made visible again:

```
Private Sub ButtonPrintForm_Click(ByVal sender As System.Object, _
                                  ByVal e As System.EventArgs) _
                                  Handles ButtonPrintForm.Click
    ButtonPrintForm.Visible = False
    PrintForm1.PrinterSettings.DefaultPageSettings.Landscape = _
                                  CheckBox2.Checked
    PrintForm1.PrintAction = Printing.PrintAction.PrintToPreview
    PrintForm1.Print()
    'PrintForm1.Print(Me, _
PowerPacks.Printing.PrintForm.PrintOption.CompatibleModeFullWindow)
    ButtonPrintForm.Visible = True

End Sub
```

The code shows how you can reference the `PrinterSettings` property, and within that are the page settings to change details regarding how the page is printed. The `PrintAction` defines what the control should do. There are three options: print to the default/selected printer, print to a file, or use the Print Preview window. In this case, displaying the results is the most useful option.

The next line is all you need by default to print the current window. Note that this control doesn't call the form to determine what is visible on the form. Instead, it essentially captures the current screenshot of the form for printing. This is the default behavior, but not the only option available. If you open and resize this project so that it is fairly wide and print in profile mode, you'll see how the control truncates the printed image (see Figure B-6).

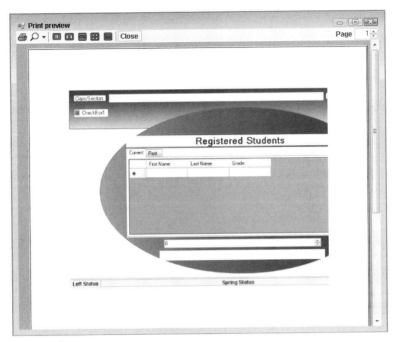

Figure B-6

As shown in Figure B-6, the default behavior is to show the contents of the screen without the border displayed. Unfortunately, in this case the printout shows less than the full window contents. Before you print again, go to the print event handler and comment out the default print line and uncomment the parameterized print line. In this case, specify the window, which is Me, and then add one of the print options.

The current code uses the CompatibleModeFullWindow option, which you are encouraged to test. The results in this case are shown in Figure B-7, and the Print Preview shows the full window with the border in place. However, don't stop at this option; try out other options. The Compatible Mode option uses a display-based logic that properly captures the screen. Other display options do not capture the screen accurately, so in some cases the only things visible in the Print Preview window are the shape controls.

Overall, the Power Packs 2.0 shape controls enable you to easily add a custom look to your otherwise gray forms. The controls are somewhat limited, but if you want a quick and easy way to add some graphics, they do the trick. Similarly, the Print control is a quick and easy way to create a hard copy of what your application is displaying. However, keep in mind that the Print control sacrifices capabilities and customizations in order to provide a simple interface.

The Power Packs 2.0 provide tools that VB6 developers can leverage for migrating an application, and for a rapid application design (RAD) prototype, they provide a dynamic and visually interesting display.

Just keep in mind that when it comes to the shape controls, if you need any sort of fancy graphics, then it is recommended that you leverage WPF and the new graphical capabilities provided as part of .NET 3.0.

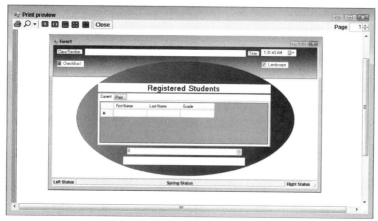

Figure B-7

Summary

This appendix covered the Visual Basic Power Packs. This set of off-cycle release tools enables experienced Visual Basic developers to leverage their knowledge and existing code with the new capabilities of .NET. The Visual Basic team has created two downloadable packages that improve your ability to manage COM to .NET Interop migration and to continue to print and create graphics the same way you did before. As with all Interop-focused solutions, there are key limitations in working with the Interop Forms toolkit, but in general it provides classes that will help you if you need to migrate an existing application in a controlled and cost-effective manner. In particular, this appendix highlighted the following:

❑ The focus of the Visual Basic Power Packs

❑ How to integrate Visual Basic 2008 forms with Visual Basic 6.0 applications

❑ Leveraging printing and drawing controls that behave similarly to those in Visual Basic 6.0.

Although there are currently only two Power Packs, you can keep track of what is occurring in the Visual Basic Development center at http://msdn2.microsoft.com/en-us/vbasic/default.aspx. There is talk of adding more Power Packs in the future, which would add still more features to increase the productivity of Visual Basic developers.

Visual Basic Resources

On the Web

The MSDN Visual Basic Developer Center `msdn.microsoft.com/vbasic`

Blogs of the Microsoft VB team `blogs.msdn.com/vbteam`

Visual Basic FAQs `blogs.msdn.com/vbfaq`

The Microsoft Windows Forms site `www.windowsforms.net`

The Microsoft ASP.NET site `www.asp.net`

CodePlex `www.codeplex.com`

VB City `www.vbcity.com`

VB.NET Forums `www.vbdotnetforums.com`

vbAccelerator.com `www.vbaccelerator.com`

DotNetJunkies `www.dotnetjunkies.com`

4 Guys from Rolla `www.4guysfromrolla.com`

123ASPX `www.123aspx.com`

Microsoft Newsgroups `msdn.microsoft.com/newsgroups`

Microsoft Developer Centers `msdn.microsoft.com/developercenters`

VBRun: Microsoft's Visual Basic 6.0 site `msdn.microsoft.com/VBRun`

.NET Framework 3.0 community site `www.netfx3.com`

MSDN Forums on VB `forums.microsoft.com/MSDN/default.aspx?ForumGroupID=10&SiteID=1`

Silverlight `www.silverlight.net`

Books

Professional ASP.NET 3.5 (ISBN: 9780470187579)

Beginning ASP.NET 3.5 (ISBN: 9780470187593)

Author Blogs

Bill Evjen www.geekswithblogs.net/evjen

Bill Sheldon blogs.interknowlogy.com/billsheldon

Kent Sharkey www.acmebinary.com/blog

Index

<runtime>